AF820278

STANDARD DEDUCTION

Filing Status	1997 Amount
Married individuals filing joint returns and surviving spouses	$6,900
Heads of households	6,050
Unmarried individuals (other than surviving spouses and heads of households)	4,150
Married individuals filing separate return	3,450
Additional standard deductions for the aged and the blind	
Individual who is married and surviving spouses	800*
Individual who is unmarried and not a surviving spouse	1,000*
Taxpayer claimed as dependent on another taxpayer's return	650

*These amounts are $1,600 and $2,000, respectively, for a taxpayer who is both aged and blind.

Personal Exemption: 1997 $2,650 *Reduction in personal and dependency exemptions:* The personal and dependency exemption deductions are reduced or eliminated for certain high-income taxpayers. When a taxpayer's AGI exceeds the "phaseout begins after" amount described below, the deduction is reduced by 2% for each $2,500 (or fraction thereof) by which AGI exceeds such amount. For married persons filing separately, the exemption deduction is reduced by 2% for each $1,250 (or fraction thereof) by which AGI exceeds the "phaseout begins after" amount. The personal exemption deduction amount cannot be reduced below zero. The phaseout ranges are:

Filing Status	*Phaseout Begins After*	*Phaseout Completed After*
Married individuals filing joint return and surviving spouses	$181,800	$304,300
Heads of households	151,500	274,000
Unmarried taxpayers (other than surviving spouses and heads of households)	121,200	243,700
Married individuals filing separate returns	90,900	152,150

Itemized Deductions

The itemized deductions that are otherwise deductible for the tax year are reduced by the lesser of (1) 3% of the excess of AGI over a threshold amount, or (2) 80% of the amount of itemized deductions otherwise deductible for the tax year excluding medical expenses, investment interest expense, casualty losses, and wagering losses to the extent of wagering gains. The threshold amount for the 1997 tax year is $121,200 (except for married individuals filing separate returns for which it is $60,600).

OVERVIEW

Overview

CONTENTS

CHAPTER 14

About the Editors

JOHN L. KRAMER

THOMAS R. POPE

John L. Kramer is the Arthur Andersen Professor of Accounting at the Fisher School of Accounting at the University of Florida. He is a recipient of a Teaching Improvement Program award given by the University of Florida in 1994. He holds a Ph.D. in Business Administration, an M.B.A. from the University of Michigan (Ann Arbor), and a B.B.A. from the University of Michigan (Dearborn). He is a past-president of the American Taxation Association and the Florida Association of Accounting Educators, as well as a past editor of *The Journal of the American Taxation Association.*

Kramer has taught for the American Institute of CPAs, American Tax Institute of Europe, and a number of national and regional accounting firms. He is a frequent speaker at academic and professional conferences, as well as having served as an expert witness in a number of court cases. He has published more than fifty articles in *The Accounting Review, The Journal of the American Taxation Association, The Tax Adviser, The Journal of Taxation* and other academic and professional journals.

Thomas R. Pope is an Associate Professor of Accounting at the University of Kentucky. He received a B.S. from the University of Louisville and an M.S. and doctorate in business administration from the University of Kentucky where he now serves as Director of Graduate Studies for the Masters of Accountancy program. He teaches partnership and S corporation taxation, tax research and policy, and introductory taxation and has won outstanding teaching awards at the university, college, and school of accountancy levels. He has published articles in *The Accounting Review, The Tax Adviser, Taxes,* and a number of other journals.

Pope's extensive professional experience includes eight years with Big Six accounting firms. Five of those years were with Ernst & Young, where he earned a position with their National Tax Department in Washington, D.C. He subsequently attained the position of Senior Manager in charge of the Tax Department in Lexington, Kentucky. He has also been a leader and speaker at professional tax conferences all over the United States and is active as a tax consultant.

About the Authors

ANNA C. FOWLER

SANDRA S. KRAMER

SUSAN L. NORDHAUSER

Anna C. Fowler is the John Arch White Professor in the Department of Accounting at the University of Texas at Austin and Director of its Masters in Professional Accounting Program. She received her B.S. in accounting from the University of Alabama and her M.B.A. and Ph.D. from the University of Texas at Austin. Active in the American Taxation Association, she has served on the editorial board of its journal and has held many positions, including president, within the organization. She is also active with the American Institute of CPAs and has served on its Tax Education and Estate and Gift Tax Subcommittees; recently she was chosen as a member of the Tax, Managerial, and Governmental Accounting Reporting Subcommittee of its Board of Examiners.

Currently, Fowler is a member of the Board of Trustees of the Educational Foundation of the Texas Society of CPAs. She has published a number of articles, most of which have dealt with estate planning or real estate transaction issues. She also is a frequent speaker before professional organizations on estate planning topics.

Sandra S. Kramer is a faculty member in the Fisher School of Accounting at the University of Florida. She is a recipient of a Teaching Improvement Program award made by the University of Florida in 1994. She holds a Ph.D. in Accounting from the University of Texas at Austin, an M.B.A. degree from the University of Michigan, and an A.B. degree from the University of Georgia. She is a former vice-president of the American Taxation Association, a past editor of *The Journal of the American Taxation Association,* and the current President-Elect of the American Taxation Association. Kramer has taught for a number of national, regional, and local accounting firms and is a frequent speaker at academic and professional tax conferences. She has published more than thirty articles and books. Her articles have appeared in *The Accounting Review, The Journal of Accounting Research, The Journal of the American Taxation Association, The Tax Adviser,* and other academic and professional journals.

Susan L. Nordhauser is a professor at the University of Texas at San Antonio. She received her B.A. from Cornell University, her M.S. from Purdue University, and her Ph.D. from the University of Texas at Austin. She has published many articles on taxation in journals including *The Journal of the American Taxation Association, The Accounting Review, The Tax Adviser,* and *The National Tax Journal.* Nordhauser is the recipient of the 1992 Ernst & Young Tax Literature Award. She has served on the editorial board of several academic tax journals.

PREFACE

OBJECTIVES AND USE

This text is designed principally for use in a second course in federal taxation for undergraduate accounting and business students. The text materials have been updated to reflect recent legislative (through January 1, 1997), judicial, and administrative changes in the tax law.

A companion volume, *Prentice Hall's Federal Taxation, 1998: Individuals,* is published for use in the first course in federal taxation. A combined two-semester volume, *Prentice Hall's Federal Taxation, 1998: Comprehensive* joins 14 chapters of the *Individuals* volume with 13 chapters of the *Corporations, Partnerships, Estates, and Trusts* volume. Either the *Individuals* text or the *Comprehensive* volume may be used with a one-term survey course for undergraduate or graduate students.

The *Corporations, Partnerships, Estates, and Trusts* volume is presented in the format of a mini-Masters of Taxation program. This book includes coverage of all of the major areas that are normally included in a Masters of Taxation program.

The primary objective has been to provide a readable format with a high level of technical content. We have accomplished this through a process of continuous review, improvement, and clarification of the text, examples, and problem material. If you find what you believe is an error, please provide the item to one of the editors along with your comments. We have been able to maintain this level of content by focusing on primary topics and by relegating minor exceptions to footnotes.

NEW TO THE 1998 EDITION

▶ Expanded coverage of ethics. Seven new and two revised boxes (labeled "What Would You Do in This Situation?) and a reprinting of the AICPA's Statements on Responsibilities in Tax Practice in an appendix expand our coverage of ethics. Based on timely topics, the new boxes include many controversies that are as yet unresolved or currently being considered by the courts. They represent choices that may put the practitioner at odds with the client, and are grounded on ethical parameters discussed in various standards, codes of conduct, or Treasury Department circulars. Students are asked, after analyzing the details of a situation, to indicate what they would do if they found themselves in the same situation as well as the ethical implications of their actions. The new boxes and the Statements on Responsibilities enhance the Ethical Point margin notes and the ethical issues that are found in the Case Study Problems already presented in the text.

▶ Stop & Think feature. These "speedbumps" ask students to stop and think about a business application of tax, or an extension of the basic material, at various points in the chapter. These are not "boxes," which typically fall outside the running text and can be bypassed. They are part of the text, complete with solutions to show students "how to do it," and identified by the icon you see here in the margin.

▶ Issue identification questions. Part of the process of learning involves sorting out important information from unimportant details. In an area as detail-oriented as taxation, developing the ability to identify key issues is of paramount importance. We include questions at the end of each chapter that call on students to focus on the important questions that a practitioner faces on a daily basis.

▶ Improvements in the Test Bank. Aside from the Solutions Manual, no other supplement is as important to educators as the Test Bank. This year the test bank author has placed special emphasis on refining and polishing the test questions.

▶ OneDisc CD-ROM. This CD provides all the basic information tools that tax professionals use: Code, regulations, revenue rulings, revenue procedures, IRS technical advice memoranda, letter rulings, court decisions, directories, U.S. tax treaties, and more! Tax Analysts sell the OneDisc to Prentice Hall customers for just $19.99 and has the software available in DOS, Windows, and Macintosh. Students may order their copy of the CD-ROM by using the order form in their textbook.

FEATURES RETAINED FROM PREVIOUS EDITIONS

▶ A careful choice of topics. Since the introduction of this series, users have found favor with the choice of topics and the extent of detail presented throughout the text. Areas where users have been particularly pleased with our balance between exhaustive detail and too little detail include: tax research, the corporate alternative minimum tax, and partnership taxation.

▶ Unique chapter organization. The *CPET* volume differs from other texts on the market with its life cycle approach to the taxation of the corporation, and the way that the partnership and S corporation materials are tied together.

▶ Clear examples. Users regularly praise the clarity and number of examples in this text.

▶ Margin notes. Tax students appreciate learning about more than just tax rules, so we have developed a series of comments in the margins to enrich their learning experience.

Key Points emphasize those areas where students require repetition and reinforcement.

Typical Misconceptions identify those concepts that students are likely to misunderstand, and help them to correct their thinking before they take a wrong approach.

Real World Examples provide facts and anecdotes about actual companies and real-life strategies.

Additional Comments elaborate on the material presented in the text.

Self-Study Questions provide an in-text study guide. Each question is accompanied by a full solution.

Historical Notes offer a more comprehensive understanding of concepts by examining them in their historical context.

Ethical Points focus on ethical questions that confront the tax practitioner, and are designated with an ethics icon.

▶ Topic reviews. Each chapter contains several topic reviews, presented when a topic has been completed. Topic reviews help students organize their understanding of the material and aid in preparing for exams. Many of these reviews are in tabular form for easy reference.

▶ Tax Planning Considerations. For the forward-looking part of the tax profession, students need to learn how to offer tax-saving advice for their clients. Our Tax Planning Considerations offer this insight once the basics of the rules have been established.

▶ Compliance and Procedural Considerations. Forms, procedures, and timing are addressed in the Compliance and Procedural Consideration sections at the end of each chapter.

▶ Footnotes. An important component of "learning to learn" is knowing where to turn for authoritative information. We have collected important references to the tax authorities in the footnotes for students to use as sources.

▶ A full complement of assignment material. The typical format for each chapter includes: Discussion Questions, Issue Identification Questions, Problems, Comprehensive Problems, Tax Form/Return Preparation Problems, Case Study Problems, and Tax Research Problems.

▶ Oral and written communications. More emphasis is being placed on oral and written communication skills by the various accounting professional organizations (e.g., the American Institute of CPAs and the Accounting Education Change Commission). The case study problems at the end of each chapter are designed to meet this need, by requiring students to consider a number of alternatives and present a written or oral solution to the problem. None of these case studies require the student to research the tax law.

SUPPLEMENTAL MATERIALS

The text includes a full complement of supplementary and ancillary materials. Adopters are encouraged to use these materials to enhance their teaching effectiveness and the students' learning experience. The following aids are available for instructor and student use:

INSTRUCTION AIDS

- Prentice Hall Course Manager, free upon adoption—This three-ring binder of the textbook allows the professor complete flexibility in course customization and is available on demand from Prentice Hall.
- Instructor's Guide—This specially crafted Instructor's Guide includes: a sample syllabus for semester- and quarter-length courses, instructor outlines, and solutions to the tax return/tax form problems, case study problems, and tax research problems. The instructor outlines are available in WordPerfect computer files to enable faculty members to make their own modifications to the master outlines prior to using them in class without having to retype the entire outline. The outlines highlight tax law changes affecting the 1998 Edition. Also there is a cross-reference table which cross-references problems in the 1997 and 1998 Editions as well as indicates any new problems and the nature of the change (if any) to the problems from the 1997 Edition. Additional written assignments involving deferred compensation, publicly-traded partnerships, mergers and acquisitions, and the Scholes and Wolfson paradigm are provided for faculty use in the 1998 Edition. NEW to this edition of the Instructor's Guide is a set of chapter-by-chapter transition notes to help you adapt your lecture notes from West's Federal Taxation to Prentice Hall's Federal Taxation.
- Test Bank—Carefully edited, this bank of test questions now includes fully worked-out solutions to many of the more complex problems.
- Solutions Manual—Prepared by the authors and thoroughly reviewed by the editors and a pool of graduate tax students, this volume includes solutions to the discussion questions, problems, and comprehensive problems. Solutions to all problems are available in WordPerfect computer files to facilitate the preparation of transparencies. The solutions to the tax form/return preparation problems, the case studies, and tax research problems are included in the *Instructor's Guide.*
- Solutions to Prentice Hall's Tax Practice Problems for Individuals, Corporations and Partnerships, 1998 Edition—Contains completed forms and computations to be used to solve the Tax Practice Problems for both volumes.
- PowerPoint Transparencies—Approximately 300 full color electronic transparencies have been created for each individual chapter to enrich the teaching experience. Instructors can make additions or modifications to the files prior to using them in class.
- Prentice Hall Custom Test, DOS and Windows Versions—Unmatched by other computerized testing software, Prentice Hall Custom Test is a state-of-the-art classroom management system designed to take the tedium out of creating exams.
- Supplemental Tax Law Update—Whenever major tax legislation is passed, we immediately provide an updating supplement. A mid-year update is provided for the inflation-adjusted numbers each year.
- Registered Adopter Service—Every year tax instructors have to keep up to date on the changes in the tax law. Now Prentice Hall has a service to help. It's our Registered Adopter Service.

By returning the registration card provided in the Instructor's Edition of *Prentice Hall's Federal Taxation: Corporations, Partnerships, Estates, and Trusts* text you can add your name to the list of adopters who receive regular tax law updates, product information on books and supplements, and information on Prentice Hall's tax seminars for educators. Additionally, we will plant a tree in your school's name through the National Arbor Day Foundation to help reforest an area devastated by a natural disaster once we receive your Registered Adopter card.

STUDENT AIDS

Our foremost goal has been to provide students with a perspective that stresses readability, accuracy, and familiarity with technical aids to tax practice. The following student aids are currently available:

▶ Study Guide—This study guide is designed to give students a better understanding of the laws and concepts presented in the textbook through use of extensive cross-referencing to tables and figures in the textbook.

▶ Loose-Leaf Edition—The text is now available for students in a 3-hole punched, shrinkwrapped format, which allows them to carry only the sections of the text they need as well as add-in handouts from class. Binder is NOT included.

▶ Prentice Hall's Tax Practice Problems for Corporations and Partnerships, 1997 Edition—This practice set includes three comprehensive problems with all supporting IRS forms and instructions needed to file returns for a C corporation, S corporation, and partnership.

Acknowledgments

Our policy is to provide annual editions and to prepare timely updated supplements when major tax revisions occur. We are most appreciative of the suggestions made by outside reviewers for the 1998 Edition because these extensive review procedures have been valuable to the authors and editors during the revision process.

We wish to acknowledge the following reviewers, whose contributions over the past several years have helped shape the 1998 Edition:

Becky Andrews	Roane State Community College
Kathleen E. Bauer	Midwestern State University
John Beehler	University of Texas at Arlington
Ron Blasi	SUNY at Buffalo
Rodger Bolling	Northern Illinois University
Alexandra Bolton	University of South Florida
Faye Bradwick	Indiana University of Pennsylvania
George Britton	Florida Southern College
Hughlene Burton	University of North Carolina at Charlotte
M. Robert Carver, Jr.	Southern Illinois University at Edwardsville
Arthur D. Cassill	University of North Carolina at Greensboro
Ann Burstein Cohen	SUNY at Buffalo
Julie Collins	University of North Carolina at Chapel Hill
Meg Costello	Oakland Community College
Larry Cozort	Georgia College
Terry L. Crain	University of Oklahoma
Nina Crimm	George Washington University
Philip Fink	University of Toledo
Nancy Foran	Wichita State University
George Frankel	San Francisco State University
Edward C. Foth	DePaul University
Michael Gallagher	George Washington University
John Gardner	University of Wisconsin at LaCrosse
Larry Garrison	University of Missouri at Kansas City
Deborah Garvin	University of Florida
L. Howard Godfrey	University of North Carolina at Charlotte
Harold Goedde	Woomer & Associates
Raymond L. Gonzalez	Los Angeles Trade-Tech College
E. Vance Grange	Utah State University
Ira S. Greenberg	University of Detroit-Mercy
James M. Hopkins	Morningside College
Patricia Janes	San Jose State University
John Karayan	California State University at Pomona
Ernest Larkins	Georgia State University
Joseph E. Latoof	Georgian Court College
Andrew Laviano	University of Rhode Island
Brian Levinson	SUNY at Binghamton
Richard Malamud	California State University—Dominguez Hills
Zack D. Mason	The University of Texas at San Antonio

David Mayer	City University of New York
John McGowan	Saint Louis University
David Medved	Detroit College of Business
Ken Milani	University of Notre Dame
Jon Nitschke	Montana State University
Charles J. Reichert	University of Wisconsin-Superior
Steven Rice	University of Washington
Gerald Rosson	Lynchburg College
David Ryan	Temple University
Kathleen Sinning	Western Michigan University
Dave N. Stewart	Brigham Young University
Paul Streer	University of Georgia
L. Roland Sturm	Carroll Community College
Charles Swenson	University of Southern California
Ronald Tidd	Syracuse University
Ella Ann Topham	University of Iowa
James Trebby	Marquette University
Joanne Turner	
Mark Vogel	University of Denver
William Wallace	University of Mississippi (Retired)
Richard White	University of South Carolina
Michael Whiteman	University of Massachusetts
Earl Zachry	University of Houston—Clear Lake

We are also grateful to the various graduate assistants, doctoral students, and colleagues who have reviewed the text and supplementary materials and checked solutions in order to maintain a high level of technical accuracy. In particular, we would like to acknowledge the following colleagues who assisted in the preparation of supplemental materials for this text:

Priscilla Kenney (Supplements Coordinator)	University of Florida
William Cargill	Texas A&M International University
Arthur D. Cassill	University of North Carolina at Greensboro
Edmund D. Fenton, Jr.	Belmont University
Deborah R. Garvin	University of Florida
Bobbie Martindale	Dallas Baptist University
Caroline D. Strobel	University of South Carolina

John L. Kramer
Thomas R. Pope

PRENTICE HALL'S
FEDERAL TAXATION

1998

Corporations, Partnerships, Estates, and Trusts

CHAPTER 1

TAX RESEARCH

LEARNING OBJECTIVES

After studying this chapter, you should be able to

1. Describe the steps in the tax research process
2. Explain how the facts affect the tax consequences
3. Enumerate the sources of tax law and understand the authoritative value of each
4. Use the tax services and/or electronic resources to research an issue
5. Use the citator to assess authorities
6. Understand the guidelines to which CPAs in tax practice should adhere
7. Prepare work papers and communications to clients

CHAPTER OUTLINE

This chapter introduces the reader to the tax research process. Its major focus is the sources of the tax law (i.e., the statutory and other authorities that constitute the federal tax laws) and the relative weights that are given to these sources. The steps in the tax research process are described, and particular emphasis is placed on the importance of the facts to the tax consequences. The chapter also describes how to use the citator and the most frequently used tax services and computer resources.

The end product of the tax research process—written communication of the results to an interested party in the form of a client letter—is also discussed. This text uses a hypothetical set of facts to provide a comprehensive illustration of the research process. Sample work papers demonstrating how to document the results of the research efforts are included in Appendix A. In addition, the text discusses the American Institute of Certified Public Accountants' (AICPA's) guidelines for CPAs in tax practice, its *Statements on Responsibilities in Tax Practice.* These statements are included in Appendix E.

OVERVIEW OF TAX RESEARCH

Tax research is the process of solving a specific tax-related question on the basis of both tax law sources and the specific circumstances surrounding the particular situation. Sometimes this activity involves researching several issues.Tax research can also be aimed at determining tax policy. For example, policy-oriented research would determine the extent (if any) to which the amount contributed to charitable organizations would be likely to change if such contributions were no longer deductible. This type of tax research is usually done by economists in order to assess the effect of actions by the government.

Tax research can also be conducted to determine the tax consequences to a particular taxpayer of a certain transaction. For example, client-oriented research would determine whether Smith Corporation could deduct a particular expenditure as a trade or business expense. This type of research is generally conducted by accounting and law firms for the benefit of their clients. This book considers only this type of tax research.

Client-oriented tax research is performed in one of two contexts:

KEY POINT

Closed-fact situations allow the tax advisor the least amount of flexibility. Because the facts are already established, the tax advisor must develop the best solution possible within certain predetermined constraints.

1. **Closed-fact or tax compliance situations:** The client contacts the tax advisor after a transaction has occurred or a question arises while the tax return preparer is preparing the client's tax return. Unfortunately, in such situations, the tax consequences can be costly because the facts cannot be restructured to obtain more favorable tax results.

EXAMPLE C1-1 ▶

Tom advises Carol, his tax advisor, that on November 4 of the current year, he sold land held as an investment for $500,000 cash. His basis in the land was $50,000. On November 9, Tom reinvested the sales proceeds in another plot of investment land costing $500,000. This is a closed-fact situation. Tom wants to know the amount and the character of the gain (if any) he must recognize. Because the tax advisor's advice is solicited after the sale and reinvestment occur, the opportunity for tax planning is limited. The opportunity to defer taxes by using a like-kind exchange or an installment sale has been lost. ◀

KEY POINT

Open-fact or tax-planning situations allow a tax advisor the flexibility to help structure the transaction to accomplish the client's objectives. In this type of situation, a creative tax advisor can often save taxpayers considerable tax dollars through effective tax planning.

2. **Open-fact or tax-planning situations:** The client contacts the tax advisor before the transaction has been finalized. Sometimes, the tax advisor is even approached to discuss the available tax strategies before any particular transaction is decided upon. Tax-planning situations are generally more difficult and challenging because the tax advisor must keep in mind both the client's tax and nontax objectives. Most clients will not be interested in a transaction that minimizes their taxes if it is inconsistent with their nontax objectives.

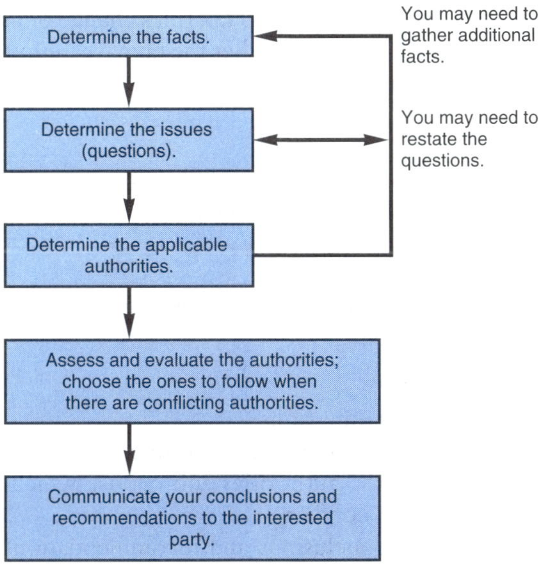

FIGURE C1-1 ▶ STEPS IN THE TAX RESEARCH PROCESS

EXAMPLE C1-2 ▶ Diane seeks advice from Carol, her tax advisor, about how to minimize her estate taxes and pass the most property to her descendants. Diane is a widow with three children and five grandchildren and at present has property valued at $10,000,000. This is an open-fact situation. Carol could advise Diane to leave all but a few hundred thousand dollars of her property to a charitable organization so that her estate would owe no estate taxes. Although this recommendation would minimize Diane's estate taxes, Diane would reject it because she wants her children or grandchildren to be her primary beneficiaries. Thus, reducing estate taxes to zero is inconsistent with her objective of allowing her descendants to receive as much after-tax wealth as possible. ◀

ADDITIONAL COMMENT

It is important to consider nontax objectives as well as tax objectives. In many situations, the nontax considerations outweigh the tax considerations. Thus, the plan that is eventually adopted by a taxpayer may not always be the best when viewed strictly from a tax perspective.

When doing tax research in the context of tax planning, the tax professional needs to keep a number of points in mind. First, the objective is not to minimize taxes per se but rather to maximize the after-tax return. For example, if the federal income tax rate is a constant 40%, an investor should not buy a tax-exempt bond yielding 5% when he could buy a corporate bond of equal risk that yields 9% before tax and 5.4% after tax, even though his explicit taxes (his actual tax liability) would be minimized with the investment in the tax-exempt bond.[1] Second, one does not engage in unilateral transactions; thus, the tax ramifications to all parties to a contract are relevant. For example, in the executive compensation context, employees may prefer to receive incentive stock options (because income recognition is postponed until the stock is sold), but the employer receives no tax deduction with respect to incentive stock options. Thus, the employer might grant a different number of options if it uses one type of stock option versus another as compensation. Third, taxes are but one cost of doing business. In deciding where to locate a manufacturing plant, for example, factors more important to some businesses than the amount of state and local taxes might be the proximity to raw materials and good transportation systems, the cost of labor, the quantity of skilled labor available, and the quality of life in the area. Fourth, the time for tax planning is not restricted to when one enters into an investment, contract, or other arrangement; the time extends

---

[1] For an excellent discussion of explicit and implicit taxes and tax planning see Myron S. Scholes and Mark A. Wolfson, *Taxes and Business Strategy: A Planning Approach* (Englewood Cliffs, NJ: Prentice Hall, 1992), Chs. 1, 2, 5,and 7. See also Chapter C18 of the the Individuals book. An example of an implicit tax is the excess of the before-tax earnings on a taxable bond over the risk-adjusted before-tax earnings on a tax-favored investment (e.g., a municipal bond).

throughout the life of the activity. As tax rules change or as the environment changes, the tax advisor needs to reevaluate whether the taxpayer should continue with an investment and determine the transaction costs of making changes.

STEPS IN THE TAX RESEARCH PROCESS

OBJECTIVE 1

Describe the steps in the tax research process

ADDITIONAL COMMENT

The steps of tax research, as outlined on this page, also provide an excellent format for a written tax communication. For example, a good format for a client memo includes (1) statement of facts, (2) list of issues, (3) discussion of relevant authority, and (4) recommendations to the client of appropriate actions that are based on the results of the research.

TYPICAL MISCONCEPTION

Many taxpayers think that the tax law is all black and white. However, most tax research deals with gray areas. Ultimately, the ability, when confronted with tough issues, to develop strategies that favor the taxpayer and then to find relevant authority to support those strategies will make a successful tax advisor.

In both the open-fact and closed-fact situations, the tax research process consists of the following five basic steps:

1. Determine the facts.
2. Determine the issues (questions).
3. Determine which authorities are applicable.
4. Assess and evaluate the authorities and choose which to follow in situations where the authorities are in conflict.
5. Communicate your conclusions and recommendations to the client.

Although the listing of the steps suggests that you proceed from one step to the next and then the next, the tax research process is often circular. That is, it does not always proceed step-by-step from the first through the fifth step. Figure C1-1 illustrates the steps in the process.

In a closed-fact situation, the facts are often self-evident. But if one is researching the tax consequences in an open-fact context, a number of the facts have not yet occurred, and the tax advisor's task is to determine which facts are likely to result in a particular tax outcome. This goal is accomplished by reviewing the authorities, especially court cases, and denoting which facts accompanied a favorable outcome and which produced an unfavorable result. For example, if a client hopes to achieve ordinary loss treatment from the anticipated sale of several plots of land in the current year, the advisor might compare and contrast the facts that were present in cases addressing this type of situation. The advisor should consider cases won and lost by the taxpayer.

Often, the research deals with a gray area (i.e., an issue for which no clear-cut, unequivocally correct solution exists). In such situations, it is best to pursue the issue through a specifically tailored set of detailed questions. For example, in researching whether the taxpayer may deduct a loss as an ordinary loss instead of a capital loss, the tax advisor may need to investigate whether the presence of any investment motive precludes classifying a loss as ordinary.

Deciding on the particular issues that must be researched is one of the most challenging aspects of the research process. At times, the client may raise an explicit question, such as "May I deduct the costs of a winter trip to Florida recommended by my physician?" Often, however, the tax advisor must read the pertinent documents and other papers submitted by the taxpayer to formulate the issues for which an investigation is appropriate. Thus, one needs a fairly extensive knowledge of tax law in order to be able to determine which issues must be researched.[2]

The following example illustrates that frequently the tax advisor, once he or she becomes more familiar with tax law, must request additional information from the client. Example C1-3 assumes that all of the tax authorities are in agreement.

EXAMPLE C1-3 ▶ Mark calls his tax advisor, Al, and states that (1) he incurred a loss on renting his beach cottage during the current year and (2) he wonders whether he may deduct the loss. He also states

[2] Often supervisors will explain to a relatively new staff person the questions they think are appropriate issues to be researched. Based on the supervisor's past experience and knowledge, he or she will indicate the specific authorities he or she thinks will offer insight with respect to the tax consequences.

that he, his wife, and their minor child occupied the cottage only eight days during the current year.

Assume that this is the first time that Al has worked with the Sec. 280A vacation home rules. On reading Sec. 280A, Al learned that a loss is *not* deductible if Mark used the cottage as a residence for personal purposes for longer than the greater of (1) 14 days or (2) 10% of the number of days the unit was rented at a fair rental value. He also learned that the property is *deemed* to be used by the taxpayer for personal purposes on any days on which it is used by any member of his or her family (as defined in Sec. 267(c)(4)). The Sec. 267(c)(4) definition of family members includes brothers, sisters, spouse, ancestors, or lineal descendants (i.e., children and grandchildren).

Mark's eight-day use is not long enough to make the rental loss nondeductible. However, Al must inquire about the number of days, if any, Mark's brothers, sisters, or parents used the property. (He already has information about use by Mark, his spouse, and his lineal descendants.) In addition, Al must find out how many days the cottage was rented to other persons at a fair rental value. On obtaining such additional facts, Al proceeds to determine how to calculate the deductible expenses. Al then reaches his conclusion concerning the deductible loss, if any, and communicates it to Mark. Assume that the passive activity and at-risk rules restricting a taxpayer's ability to deduct losses from real estate activities will not pose a problem for Mark. (See Chapter I8 of *Prentice Hall's Federal Taxation: Individuals* for a comprehensive discussion of these topics.) ◀

Many firms require that a researcher's conclusions be communicated to the client in writing. Members or employees of such firms can answer questions orally, but their oral conclusions must be followed up with a written communication. According to the AICPA's *Statements on Responsibilities in Tax Practice* (reproduced in Appendix E).

> Although oral advice may serve a client's needs appropriately in routine matters or in well-defined areas, written communications are recommended in important, unusual, or complicated transactions. In the judgment of the CPA, oral advice may be followed by a written confirmation to the client.[3]

IMPORTANCE OF THE FACTS TO THE TAX CONSEQUENCES

OBJECTIVE 2

Explain how the facts affect the tax consequences

At times, the statute is difficult to interpret, and a dilemma arises concerning the tax results. For example, one of the requirements a taxpayer must meet to claim a personal exemption for another person is to provide more than half of such person's support.[4] Neither the Code nor the Regulations define support. Consequently, if a taxpayer purchased a used automobile costing $5,000 for an elderly parent whose only source of income was $4,800 of social security, a question would arise concerning whether the expenditure for the car constitutes support. The tax advisor would need to consult court cases and revenue rulings to find an interpretation of the word support.

In other situations, the statutory language may be quite clear, but there might be a question as to whether the taxpayer's transaction falls within the realm of the facts necessary to obtain the favorable tax consequences. The following discussion of two actual cases focuses on the importance of facts in determining the tax results. In each case the taxpayer was arguing about the proper deduction for salary expense for payments made to the shareholder's spouse. Any amounts deemed "unreasonable" would not be deductible.

---

[3] AICPA, *Statements on Responsibilities in Tax Practice*, No. 8, "Form and Content of Advice to Clients," 1991, Sec. .06.

[4] Sec. 152(a).

FACTS OF CASE WHERE TAXPAYER PARTIALLY WON

ADDITIONAL COMMENT

The *Summit Publishing Company* and *J.B.S. Enterprises* cases are used to illustrate how slightly different facts can cause entirely different tax consequences.

Excerpts of the *Summit Publishing Company, Inc.* case appear below.[5] The Tax Court concluded that the corporation was entitled to a deduction for a portion of the purported salary payments to the shareholder's spouse. The taxpayer is referred to as the "petitioner" and the government as the "respondent."

FINDINGS OF FACT

At all times pertinent to this case, petitioner, Summit Publishing Company, Inc. (Summit) was a Texas corporation with its primary place of business in San Antonio, Texas. During the taxable years ended October 31, 1982, and October 31, 1983, Summit paid corporate officer and employee Marcia J. Mogavero (Mrs. Mogavero) compensation in the amounts of $72,780 and $183,910, respectively. These amounts were deducted in arriving at Summit's taxable income for the years in issue. Respondent determined that reasonable compensation for Mrs. Mogavero for the taxable years ended October 31, 1982 and 1983, was $41,050 and $50,083, respectively, and disallowed the difference between the amount claimed and the amount determined.

Summit was incorporated during 1977 by Alfred G. Mogavero, Sr. (Mr. Mogavero) who, at all pertinent times, was Summit's sole shareholder and president. Mr. and Mrs. Mogavero were married around the time of petitioner's incorporation and continued to be married throughout the taxable years in issue.

Summit's business activity involved the publishing of an in-flight magazine for Southwest Airlines (Southwest). Summit also did a limited amount of typesetting, production, layout, and art work for other companies. . . . Kenneth E. Lively (Lively) worked for Mr. Mogavero nearly from the beginning and his expertise related to the editing-publishing or creative side of the business activity. Mr. Mogavero's expertise related to sales and management.

During 1977, . . . Mrs. Mogavero began to work at Summit. Prior to that time she had no job experience, no formal education beyond high school, or any special skills, other than typing. Initially, Mrs. Mogavero performed routine clerical tasks. In time, and during the years in issue, she performed the role of an office manager. Lively and Mr. Mogavero were principally responsible for publishing and sales. . . .

Mrs. Mogavero supervised the clerical and support personnel, oversaw accounts receivable and payable, and reviewed the credit worthiness of advertisers. Although Summit had an accountant, Mrs. Mogavero did some of the bookkeeping and assisted in the compilation of certain of the financial information necessary for top management. She also assisted in the approval and location or layout of advertisements. . . .

During the years in issue, Summit generally employed between 16 and 25 employees. . . .

Mr. Mogavero, as owner-operator of Summit, decided to increase Mrs. Mogavero's salary because the business was doing well. . . . [Between the taxable years ended October 31, 1978 through October 31, 1983 the firm's gross profit rose from $484,680 to $3,409,438. Mr. Mogavero's compensation was $52,900 and $927,530 for the taxable years ended October 31, 1978 and October 31, 1983, respectively. Mrs. Mogavero's compensation increased from $16,715 for the fiscal year ended October 31, 1978 to $183,910 for the fiscal year ended October 31, 1983.]

During the taxable years ended October 31, 1982 and 1983, Summit paid cash dividends to its sole shareholder in the amounts of $232,690 and $382,359, respectively.

OPINION

. . . Many factors are relevant in determining whether compensation is reasonable, and no single factor is decisive; the totality of the facts and circumstances must be weighed. . . .

[5] 1990 PH T.C. Memo ¶90,288, 59 TCM 833. In this and all other Tax Court cases, the *petitioner* is the person who originates the case—the taxpayer—and the government is the *respondent.* For an excellent discussion of how critical facts are for the outcome, see Robert L. Gardner and Dave N. Stewart, *Tax Research Techniques,* 4th. Ed., Rev. (New York: AICPA, 1993), pp. 11–53.

The parties in this case have focused on about six of the factors enumerated in *Foos v. Commissioner*, TC Memo 1981-61 [Para. 81,061 PH Memo TC]. In *Foos v. Commissioner*, supra, the following factors were referenced:

1. Employee's qualifications and training.
2. Nature, extent, and scope of his duties.
3. Responsibilities and hours involved.
4. Size and complexity of business.
5. Results of the employee's efforts.
6. Prevailing rates for comparable employees in comparable business.
7. Scarcity of other qualified employees.
8. Ratio of compensation to gross and net income (before salaries and Federal income tax) of the business.
9. Salary policy of the employer to its other employees.
10. Amount of compensation paid to the employee in prior years.
11. Employee's responsibility for employer's inception and/or success.

. . . .

14. Correlation between the stockholder-employees' compensation and his stockholdings.
15. Corporate dividend history.

. . . .

Employee's Qualifications and Training

Respondent argues that Mrs. Mogavero's educational background and training were insufficient to justify the level of compensation claimed by Summit. Petitioner agrees that Mrs. Mogavero "had limited qualifications" when she began working for Summit in 1977, but that she acquired "extensive on-the-job training" qualifying her for the position held.

We agree with petitioner's analysis on this point. . . . [I]t is likely that actual experience is more significant than academic achievement in the operation and success of a particular business, especially one which is relatively small and unique requiring the personal service of the particular employee. Moreover, when measuring the value of education as opposed to actual experience, greater weight should usually be afforded to actual and successful experience in a particular position or discipline.

Nature, Extent, and Scope of Employee's Work

Petitioner contends that Mrs. Mogavero should be characterized as second-in-command of Summit. Respondent counters that Mrs. Mogavero was relegated to the more menial tasks and the major contributions that resulted in Summit's success were made by Mr. Mogavero and Lively. Respondent also argues that Mrs. Mogavero's position (second-in-command) with Summit is "primarily a function of her marriage to [Mr. Mogavero]."

To the extent that the subject employee has an ownership interest or is related to the owner, we should carefully scrutinize the question of the reasonableness of compensation. . . . In so doing we find that Mrs. Mogavero did not receive, relative to her experience, a large beginning salary when she began working at Summit at a time when all agree that her experience and skill levels were not great. . . .

Mrs. Mogavero was responsible for the day to day administrative and financial operations of Summit. In addition to playing a significant role in the business relationship with Southwest, she was also primarily responsible for matters which had a direct effect on Summit's success. . . .

Most importantly, Mrs. Mogavero acted on Mr. Mogavero's behalf while he was away on the business of Summit. . . .

In summary, we have found that Mrs. Mogavero's importance and contribution to the success and operation of Summit are somewhere between Lively's and Mr. Mogavero's.

Summit's Salary Scale and Policy

Here, respondent points to the wide disparity between owner, family members and other nonowner, nonfamily employees. . . .

During the 2 years in issue, total officers' compensation increased 15 and 74 percent and total employees' compensation increased 41 and 28 percent. . . . [W]e find that petitioner appears to have had a relatively generous policy regarding the increases of officer and employee compensation. We also note that, in a relative sense, it may be appropriate to give larger raises to the officers, as opposed to other employees, if the officers' efforts were more instrumental to the success of the business. . . .

Compensation in Prior Years Size and Complexity of the Business

Regarding this aspect, respondent argues that Mrs. Mogavero's "salary increased from $16,715.53 per year to $183,910.00 per year over a period of only five years." Respondent cites several cases for the proposition that increases in salary should be a result of increases in responsibility. . . . Petitioner agrees that Mrs. Mogavero's salary was low and her experience was limited when she started with petitioner. Petitioner, however, argues that Mrs. Mogavero's salary increased in accord with her increased responsibilities in subsequent years.

. . . Considering that Summit's business was so successful, the number of employees supervised increased, inflationary indexing may have played a role, and Mrs. Mogavero played a significant role in some areas of the business which helped the business success, we believe that respondent has not determined sufficient compensation to Mrs. Mogavero for the years before the Court.

Prevailing Rates of Compensation in the Industry

. . . Accordingly, neither petitioner nor respondent has established, by expert testimony, or otherwise, the prevailing rates of compensation in this industry. We are herein limited to considering whether Mrs. Mogavero's salary is reasonable based upon the facts in the record.

Comparison of Salaries Paid with Summit's Gross and Net Income

. . . Petitioner argues that Mrs. Mogavero's salary was 2.71 and 15.34 percent of gross income and 7.55 and 13.42 percent of net income for the taxable years in issue. For the same 2 years Summit paid dividends to Mr. Mogavero (its sole shareholder) in the amounts of $232,690 and $382,359, which represented 24.14 and 27.89 percent of net income in those same 2 taxable years.

The relatively sizable dividends paid by petitioner (in addition to a relatively large salary to its president and sole shareholder) substantially diminish respondent's argument that there was a motive of tax avoidance in this case.

Summary

Our view of the record in this case results in our conclusion that Mrs. Mogavero's responsibilities and contribution to the success of Summit fell somewhere between those of Lively and Mr. Mogavero. . . . Additionally, Mrs. Mogavero did have certain responsibilities that directly contributed to the success of the business. . . .

[The court decided that a reasonable salary for Mrs. Mogavero for the taxable years ended October 31, 1982 and October 31, 1983 was $70,000 and $85,000, respectively (compared with $72,780 and $183,910 deducted on Summit's tax return).]

FACTS OF CASE WHERE TAXPAYER LOST

J.B.S. Enterprises, Inc. lost its case dealing with the deductibility of payments made to the sole shareholder's former wife.[6] The Tax Court held that the payments could not be characterized as salary.

FINDINGS OF FACT

Petitioner was a Texas corporation with its principal place of business in Fort Worth, Texas. . . . Petitioner owned three bars and restaurants in Fort Worth during the years at issue. Among the three bars was the Blues Bar, which opened for business during 1982. James B. Schusler, Mary Schusler's ex-husband, is petitioner's president and sole stockhold-

[6] 1991 PH T.C. Memo ¶91,254, 61 TCM 2,829.

er. James . . . and Mary . . . were separated during the years at issue. During this period Mary had only two sources of income, part-time secretarial work . . . and payments from petitioner. She had two minor children to support, as well as a child in college and a grown child. . . . Mary received the payments [in question] from petitioner, at James' direction. . . .

Schedule E (Compensation of Officers) of petitioner's Federal income tax returns (Form 1120) for the years at issue reported that Mary devoted "0%" of her time to business. Nevertheless, the return for the fiscal year ending April 30, 1986, reported that petitioner paid Mary compensation of $26,600 during the year, and claimed a business expense deduction for that amount. . . .

On its Federal income tax return for the year ending April 30, 1987, petitioner stated that it paid Mary a salary of $35,910 and claimed a business expense deduction in that amount. . . .

[The IRS agent disallowed the deduction for the payments to Mary. In its initial petition to the Tax Court the petitioner stated that an error was made in showing that the payments were made to Mary and that such payments should have been shown as made to James. Several months later, however, the petitioner amended its petition to the court and stated that Mary was Vice President and did in fact perform valuable services for the Corporation. It stated, further, that the amounts Mary received were reasonable in light of the services Mary performed and her experience and expertise.]

OPINION

. . . As a preliminary matter, we note that we attach little weight to the testimony of James, Mary, and Sue Ratcliff [the tax advisor]. The testimony, and documents which they signed under oath, are replete with inconsistencies.

. . . The statements made to Gerald Yentes [the IRS agent] and the [first] protest letter . . . indicate that Mary performed no services for petitioner. The only explanation petitioner offered for the inconsistency in its current position is Sue Ratcliff's testimony that she thought it would be advantageous, with respect to taxes, to initially declare that Mary performed no services. It is clear to us that petitioner's position in the instant case has been motivated throughout by tax considerations. Because of inconsistencies in testimony and sworn documents, we do not accept petitioner's recantation of its original position. . . .

While petitioner did introduce documents showing that Mary reviewed petitioner's monthly profit and loss statement, given her marital status, her dependence on petitioner for support, and comments made to Revenue Agent Gerald Yentes, we conclude her review

▼ TABLE C1-1
Summary Comparison of Facts in *Summit* and *J.B.S.*

	Decision	
Situation	*Summit*	*J.B.S.*
Type of taxpayer	Corporation	Corporation
Person to whom "salary" was paid	Spouse of sole shareholder	Former spouse of sole shareholder
Dividend history of corporation	Substantial dividends had been paid	Not disclosed
Profit history of corporation	Substantial increase over the years	Not disclosed
Services performed by recipient of salary	Extensive, valuable services	None

of the statements was for her own benefit, rather than for petitioner's. Petitioner introduced no other relevant documentary evidence. We find that petitioner has failed to carry its burden of proof, and that respondent has established that the payments at issue were a personal expense intended to provide support for Mary and her children.

COMPARISON OF THE FACTS OF THE TWO CASES

Table C1-1 provides a summary comparison of the two cases. Both taxpayers were corporations that claimed a salary deduction for payments they made to the spouse or former spouse of the sole shareholder. In *Summit* the IRS contended that only a portion of the amount claimed as a salary expense was nondeductible whereas in the *J.B.S.* case the IRS argued that none of the purported salary payments should be deductible. In *Summit* the spouse performed extensive, valuable services for the firm. In *J.B.S.*, however, the former spouse appears to have performed no services for the corporation. In *Summit* the corporation's gross profit and net income increased substantially between the date the firm was founded and the years for which the salary deduction was in question. The court record for *J.B.S.* does not discuss the firm's profitability. In *Summit,* because rather large dividends were paid to the sole shareholder, it did not appear that the objective for the payments to the shareholder's spouse was to have dividends masquerade as salary. In *J.B.S.* the taxpayer did not present any documentation to prove that the ex-wife of the sole shareholder actually performed services for *J.B.S.* Moreover, some of the testimony presented indicated that positions were being taken on the tax return to achieve the lowest tax liability for the corporation.

The court allowed expense deductions in *Summit* for a portion of the payments that the IRS argued constituted unreasonable compensation. The court was impressed with how valuable the services of the shareholder-spouse were to the firm; it also noted that dividends had been paid to the shareholder. The *J.B.S.* case is a primer in how not to structure a transaction. The sole shareholder seemed to be attempting to disguise support payments made to his former wife as salary expense. However, the recipient performed no services for which she should receive compensation.

ABILITY TO DESIGN A FACTUAL SITUATION FAVORING THE TAXPAYER

TYPICAL MISCONCEPTION

Many taxpayers believe tax practitioners spend most of their time preparing tax returns. In reality, providing tax advice that accomplishes the taxpayer's objectives is one of the most important responsibilities of a tax advisor.

By using tax research, a tax advisor can recommend to a taxpayer who is about to enter into a transaction a way to structure the facts that should increase the likelihood that his travel expenses will be deductible. For example, suppose a taxpayer is assigned to work in a different location from the city (City X) where he is currently employed. The taxpayer would like to deduct the meals and lodging expenses incurred at the new location and the cost of travel thereto. To do so, he must establish that City X is his tax home and that he is away from City X only temporarily. Incidentally, Sec. 162 precludes a taxpayer from being classified as away from home if the employment period at the new location exceeds one year. The taxpayer wonders what would happen if he was originally assigned away from City X for ten months and eventually accepted permanent employment in the new location. Tax research reveals an IRS ruling that states that in these circumstances the employment will be treated as temporary *until* the date that the realistic expectation about the temporary nature of the assignment changes.[7] Thus, if the taxpayer is offered a permanent job in the new location, it will be to his tax advantage to postpone making a decision to accept the job so that the expectation about the temporary nature of the employment will not change until near the end of the initial ten-month period. As a result, a greater amount will qualify for deduction as travel-away-from-home expenses.

[7] Rev. Rul. 93-86, 1993-2 C.B. 71.

THE SOURCES OF TAX LAW

OBJECTIVE 3

Enumerate the sources of tax law and understand the authoritative value of each

KEY POINT

One of the reasons the tax law is so complex is that it comes from a variety of sources. This chapter highlights the three principal sources of the tax law: statutory, judicial, and administrative.

When tax advisors speak of tax law, they generally refer to more than simply the tax statutes that are passed by Congress. For the most part, tax statutes (legislation) contain very general language. Congress is not capable of anticipating every type of transaction in which taxpayers might engage. Moreover, even if Congress could do so, it would not be feasible for the statute (known as the *Internal Revenue Code*) to contain details addressing the tax consequences of all such transactions.

Because the language contained in the statute generally does not provide detailed guidance about the tax treatment of a particular transaction, interpretations—both administrative and judicial—are necessary. Administrative interpretations include, for example, Treasury regulations, revenue rulings, and revenue procedures. Judicial interpretations consist of court decisions. The term *tax law* as used by most tax advisors encompasses administrative and judicial interpretations in addition to the statute. It also includes committee reports issued by the Congressional committees involved in the legislative process.

THE LEGISLATIVE PROCESS

Chapter I1 of *Prentice Hall's Federal Taxation: Individuals* describes the legislative process. That process is summarized here as well. All tax legislation must begin in the House of Representatives. The committee responsible for initiating statutory changes dealing with taxation is the Ways and Means Committee. Once proposed legislation is approved by the Ways and Means Committee, it goes to the floor of the House for consideration by the full membership. Legislation approved by a majority vote in the House then goes to the Senate, where it is considered by the Senate Finance Committee. The bill moves from the Finance Committee to the full Senate. Upon being approved by the Senate, the bill goes to the President for approval or veto, provided the House and Senate versions of the bill are in complete agreement. If the President signs the bill, it becomes law. If the President vetoes the bill, Congress can override the veto by a vote of at least two-thirds of the members of each house.

Often, the House and Senate versions are not in complete agreement. Whenever the two versions of a bill are not identical, the bill goes to a Conference Committee,[8] consisting of members of each house, and the revised bill goes back to the House and Senate for approval. For example, in 1990 the House and Senate disagreed about the earned income credit. The House approved a higher increase in the credit percentage than did the Senate. The Senate's provision provided one credit percentage for taxpayers with one qualifying child and a higher percentage for taxpayers with two or more children. The Conference Committee compromised by choosing a different rate from either of the two houses and approving different rates, depending on whether there was one child or two or more children. The House and Senate approved the Conference version.

KEY POINT

Committee Reports can be very helpful in interpreting new legislation because these reports indicate the intent of Congress. Due to the proliferation of tax legislation, Committee Reports are especially important because the Treasury is often unable to draft the needed regulations in a timely manner.

Before embarking on drafting statutory changes, both the House of Representatives and the Senate often hold hearings at which various persons testify. Often the Secretary of the Treasury or another member of the Treasury Department offers extensive testimony. Generally, persons testifying express their opinions concerning provisions that should or should not be enacted. The U.S. Government Printing Office publishes the statements made at the hearings.

Most major legislation is also accompanied by Committee Reports. These reports, published by the U.S. Government Printing Office as separate publications and as part of the *Cumulative Bulletin*, explain Congress's purpose in drafting legislation.[9] Because

[8] The size of the Conference Committee can vary. It is made up of an equal number of members from the House and the Senate.

[9] The *Cumulative Bulletin* is described in the discussion of revenue rulings on page C1-16.

Committee Reports give clues to Congressional intent, they can be invaluable aids in interpreting the statute, especially in situations where there are no regulations concerning the statutory language in question.

EXAMPLE C1-4 ▶ In 1984 Congress enacted Sec. 7872 of the Internal Revenue Code concerning the tax treatment of below-market-interest-rate loans. One subset of the rules applies to "gift loans," defined in Sec. 7872(f)(3) as "any below-market loan where the forgoing of interest is in the nature of a gift." The Conference Report elaborates on the transactions classified as gift loans as follows: "In general, there is a gift if property (including forgone interest) is transferred for less than full and adequate consideration under circumstances where the transfer is a gift for gift tax purposes. A sale, exchange, or other transfer made in the ordinary course of business . . . generally is considered as made for full and adequate consideration. A loan between unrelated persons can qualify as a gift loan."[10] This definition was quite important to a tax advisor because the Treasury did not issue proposed regulations on the Sec. 7872(f)(3) definition until ten months after the statute was enacted. Until such regulations were issued, this definition may have been the only "authoritative" interpretation available concerning the term "gift loans". ◀

THE INTERNAL REVENUE CODE

The Internal Revenue Code (the Code), which constitutes Title 26 of the federal statutes, is the foundation of all tax law. First codified (i.e., organized into a single compilation of the internal revenue statutes) in 1939, the law was recodified in 1954. The Code was known as the Internal Revenue Code of 1954 until 1986, when its name was changed to the Internal Revenue Code of 1986. Whenever changes to the statute are approved, the old language is deleted and the new language added. Thus, the statutes are organized as a single document, and a researcher does not have to read through the applicable parts of all previous tax bills to find the current version of the law.

The Code contains provisions addressing income taxes, estate and gift taxes, employment taxes, alcohol and tobacco taxes, and other excise taxes. For purposes of organization, the Code (Title 26) is subdivided into subtitles, chapters, subchapters, parts,

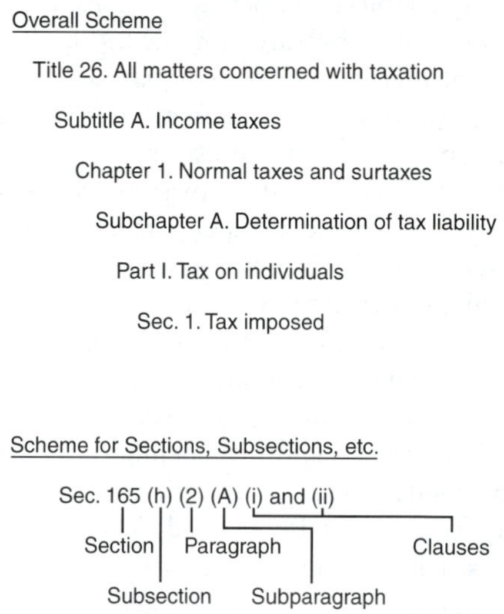

FIGURE C1-2 ▶ ORGANIZATIONAL SCHEME OF THE INTERNAL REVENUE CODE

[10] H. Rept. No. 98-861, 98th Cong., 2d Sess., p. 1,018 (1984).

subparts, sections, subsections, paragraphs, subparagraphs, and clauses. Subtitle A contains the rules concerning income taxes, and Subtitle B focuses on estate and gift taxes. A set of provisions concerned with one general area generally constitutes a subchapter. For example, the topics of corporate distributions and adjustments and partners and partnerships appear in Subchapters C and K, respectively. Figure C1-2 presents the organizational scheme of the Code.

A section is the organizational category that tax advisors refer to most often. For example, they speak of "Sec. 351 transactions," "Sec. 306 stock," and "Sec. 1231 gains and losses." Although it is generally not important to differentiate between a section and a paragraph or a part, one must be familiar with the Code's organizational scheme in order to read and interpret it correctly. The language of the Code is replete with cross-references to titles, paragraphs, subparagraphs, and so on.

EXAMPLE C1-5 ▶ Section 7701, a definitional section, begins by stating, "When used in this title . . ." and then lists a series of definitions. Thus, a definition in Sec. 7701 applies for all of Title 26; that is, it applies for purposes of the income tax, estate and gift tax, excise tax, and so on. ◀

EXAMPLE C1-6 ▶ Section 302(b)(3) allows taxpayers whose stock holdings are completely terminated in a redemption (a corporation's purchase of its stock from one of its shareholders) to receive capital gain treatment on the excess of the redemption proceeds over the stock's basis instead of ordinary income treatment on the entire proceeds. Section 302(c)(2)(A) states, "In the case of a distribution described in subsection (b)(3), section 318(a)(1) shall not apply if. . . ." Further, Sec. 302(c)(2)(C)(i) indicates "Subparagraph (A) shall not apply to a distribution to any entity unless. . . ." Thus, in determining whether a taxpayer will receive capital gain treatment for a stock redemption transaction, a tax advisor must be able to locate and interpret various Code sections, subsections, paragraphs, subparagraphs, and clauses. ◀

KEY POINT

When attempting to read a provision in the Code, the tax advisor must understand the organization of a Code section. Example C1-6 shows that in order to properly understand Sec. 302, the tax advisor must understand how references to terms such as subsections and subparagraphs can limit the application of the particular phrase being examined.

REGULATIONS

The Treasury Department (the Treasury) issues regulations as interpretations of the statute. The Regulations often give extensive examples, complete with computations providing invaluable assistance in understanding the statutory language.

Because of the frequency of statutory changes, the Treasury Department is not always able to update the regulations in a timely manner. Consequently, when referring to a regulation, a tax advisor should consult its introductory note to determine when the regulation was adopted. If the regulation was adopted before the most recent revision of this Code section, the regulation should be applied with the understanding that it does not reflect the most recent version of the statute. For example, a revised dollar amount stated in the Code would need to be substituted for an out-of-date amount in the regulation.

PROPOSED, TEMPORARY, AND FINAL REGULATIONS. Generally, regulations are first issued to the public in proposed form. The public is given the opportunity to comment on them and suggest changes. The individuals most likely to issue comments are tax accountants and tax attorneys. Organizations such as the American Bar Association, the Tax Division of the AICPA, and the American Taxation Association also regularly comment on proposed regulations. In general, such comments suggest that the proposed treatment affects the taxpayer more adversely than warranted by Congressional intent. In drafting final regulations, the Treasury usually takes the remarks into consideration and modifies the proposed regulations somewhat.

Proposed regulations are just that—proposed—and, consequently, have no more weight than the position the IRS argues for in a court brief. However, they do provide guidance concerning the Treasury's interpretation of the statute. Thus, if the proposed regulations take a fairly pro-taxpayer approach, one can be sure that tax advisors will not attack them as being too lenient. Therefore, the final regulations will probably take the same approach as the proposed regulations. On the other hand, if the Treasury receives considerable criticism about proposed regulations, it will probably adopt a more moderate approach in drafting the final regulations.

KEY POINT

Temporary regulations have the force and effect of final regulations. However, they cannot remain effective for more than three years.

Often the Treasury issues **temporary regulations** (which generally are effective on publication) soon after a major statutory change in order to give taxpayers and their advisors guidance about procedural or computational matters. For example, in 1980 Congress essentially rewrote the law concerning the qualification for, and the tax results of, installment sales. In January 1981, the Treasury issued temporary regulations interpreting the amended statute. Temporary regulations have the same authoritative value as final regulations. According to the Technical Amendments and Miscellaneous Revenue Act of 1988, temporary regulations may remain effective for up to three years. Also, a temporary regulation must be issued concurrently as a proposed regulation.

The Treasury drafts final regulations after the public has had time to comment on the proposed regulations. Most of the time, the final regulations differ at least slightly from the proposed version. As discussed under the next heading, final regulations have the same authoritative weight as the statute. Final regulations generally are retroactive to the effective date of the statutory language they interpret.

For changes to the Code enacted after July 29, 1996, the Treasury is generally precluded from issuing regulations with retroactive effect. In the case of final regulations, however, a regulation can be effective on the date proposed or temporary regulations are filed with the *Federal Register*. Regulations issued within 18 months of the date of a change to the statute can be issued with retroactive effect, however.

INTERPRETATIVE AND STATUTORY REGULATIONS. In addition to being classified as proposed, temporary, or final, regulations are categorized as interpretative or statutory. **Interpretative regulations** are issued under the general authority of Sec. 7805 and, as the name implies, merely make the statutory language easier to understand and apply. In addition, they may provide illustrations about how to perform certain computations. **Statutory (or legislative) regulations**, in comparison with interpretative regulations, are written in situations where Congress delegated its rule-making duties to the Treasury. Because Congress feels it lacks the expertise necessary to deal with a highly technical matter, it instructs the Treasury to write the rules in the form of statutory regulations.

KEY POINT

Regulations may be interpretative or legislative. Occasionally, Congress delegates its law-making responsibility to the Treasury. In such cases, the regulations are elevated from being an interpretation of the statute to being treated as the statute.

Whenever the statute contains language such as "The Secretary shall prescribe such regulations as he may deem necessary" or "under regulations prescribed by the Secretary," the regulations interpreting such a statute are legislative regulations. Perhaps the consolidated tax return regulations are the most dramatic example of statutory regulations. In Sec. 1502 Congress delegated to Treasury the responsibility for writing regulations that would enable the tax liability of a group of affiliated corporations filing a consolidated tax return to be determined. As a requirement of electing the privilege of filing a consolidated tax return, the corporations must consent to following the consolidated return regulations.[11] By consenting to follow the regulations, a taxpayer generally gives up the chance to argue that provisions in the regulations should be overturned by the courts.

AUTHORITATIVE WEIGHT. The presumption is that final regulations have the same authoritative weight as the statute. Section 7805 expressly grants to the Secretary of the Treasury the right to prescribe regulations for enforcing the tax laws and to prescribe the extent, if any, to which the regulations are to be applied without retroactive effect. Despite the presumption concerning the validity of final regulations, occasionally

[11] Sec. 1501.

taxpayers can successfully argue that a regulation is invalid and, consequently, should not be followed.

A court will not conclude that an interpretative regulation is invalid unless, in its opinion, such regulation is "unreasonable and plainly inconsistent with the revenue statutes."[12] The courts are less likely to conclude that a legislative regulation is invalid because Congress has abdicated its rule-making authority with respect to such regulations to the Treasury. However, the courts have held that legislative regulations were invalid in situations where the courts concluded the regulations exceeded the scope of the power delegated to the Treasury,[13] were contrary to the statute,[14] or were unreasonable.[15]

KEY POINT

The older a regulation becomes, the less likely a court is to invalidate the regulation. The legislative reenactment doctrine holds that if a regulation did not reflect the intent of Congress, lawmakers would have changed the statute in subsequent legislation to obtain their desired objectives.

In assessing the validity of regulations, courts often apply the **legislative reenactment doctrine**. Under this doctrine, a regulation is deemed to have received Congressional approval if such regulation was finalized many years earlier and during the interim period Congress did not amend the statutory language that the regulation addresses. In other words, if Congress had deemed the regulatory language to be an inappropriate interpretation, it could have changed the words of the statute to achieve a different result. Congress's failure to change the wording in the Code signifies its approval of the regulatory provisions.

STOP & THINK

Question: You are doing research about a certain calculation that affects a client's deductions. You consult the Regulations for guidance because the Code states that the calculation is to be done "in a manner prescribed by the Secretary." After studying the Code and the Regulations, you conclude that another way of doing the calculations is arguably correct under an intuitive approach. This intuitive approach would result in a lower tax liability for the client. Should you follow the Regulations or use the intuitive approach and argue that the Regulations are not valid?

Solution: Because of the language "in a manner prescribed by the Secretary," any Regulations dealing with the calculations are legislative (statutory) regulations. Because Congress explicitly asks the Treasury to write the "rules" whenever it calls for legislative Regulations, such regulations are more difficult than interpretative Regulations to get overturned by the courts as being invalid. Grounds for overruling legislative Regulations include exceeding the scope of the power that Congress delegated, being contrary to the statute, and being unreasonable. If based on your research you do not believe that the Regulations would be overturned by a court, you should follow them.

CITATIONS. Citations to regulations are relatively easy to understand. One or more numbers appear before a decimal place, and several numbers follow the decimal place. The numbers immediately following the decimal place indicate the Code section being interpreted. The numbers preceding the decimal place indicate the general subject matter of the regulation. Numbers that often appear before the decimal place and their general subject matter are as follows:

Number	*General Subject Matter*
1	Income tax
20	Estate tax
25	Gift tax
301	Administrative and procedural matters
601	Procedural rules

[12] *CIR v. South Texas Lumber Co.*, 36 AFTR 604, 48-1 USTC ¶5922 (USSC, 1948). In *U.S. v. Douglas B. Cartwright, Executor*, 31 AFTR 2d 73-1461, 73-1 USTC ¶12,926 (USSC, 1973), the Supreme Court concluded that a regulation dealing with the valuation of mutual fund shares for estate and gift tax purposes was invalid.

[13] *Panama Refining Co. v. U.S.*, 293 U.S. 388 (USSC, 1935).

[14] *M. E. Blatt Co. v. U.S.*, 21 AFTR 1007, 38-2 USTC ¶9599 (USSC, 1938).

[15] *Joseph Weidenhoff, Inc.*, 32 T.C. 1222 (1959).

The number following the Code section number indicates the number of the regulation, such as the fifth regulation. There is no relationship between this number and the subsection of the Code being interpreted. An example of a citation to a final regulation is

Reg. Sec. 1.165 – 5

Income tax — Code section — Fifth regulation

Citations to proposed or temporary regulations are in the same format. They are referenced as Prop. Reg. Sec. or Temp. Reg. Sec. For temporary regulations the numbering system following the Code section number always begins with the number of the regulation and an upper case T (e.g., -1T).

Section 165 itself addresses the broad topic of losses and is accompanied by several regulations. According to its caption, the topic of Reg. Sec. 1.165-5 is worthless securities, a topic addressed in subsection (g) of Code Sec. 165. Parenthetical information following the caption to this regulation indicates that this regulation was last amended December 5, 1972 by Treasury Decision (T.D.) 7224. Section 165(g) was last revised in 1971.

When referencing a regulation, the researcher should fine tune the citation as much as possible to indicate the precise wording that provides the basis for his or her conclusion. An example of such a detailed citation is Reg. Sec. 1.165-5(i), Ex. 2(i), which refers to the first portion of Example 2, an example contained in the ith portion of the fifth regulation interpreting Sec. 165.

ADMINISTRATIVE INTERPRETATIONS

The IRS uses several forums as means of interpreting the statute. The IRS's interpretations are referred to generically as **administrative interpretations**. After referring to the Code and the Regulations, tax advisors are likely to refer next to IRS interpretations for further authority for answering a tax question. Some of the most important categories of interpretations are discussed below.

TYPICAL MISCONCEPTION

Even though revenue rulings do not have the same weight as regulations or court cases, one should not underestimate their importance. Because a revenue ruling is the official published position of the IRS, in audits the revenue agent will place considerable weight on any applicable revenue rulings.

REVENUE RULINGS. In **revenue rulings**, the IRS indicates the tax consequences of a particular transaction in which a number of taxpayers might be interested. For example, a revenue ruling might indicate whether certain expenditures constitute support for purposes of claiming a dependency exemption for another individual.

The IRS frequently issues more than one hundred revenue rulings a year. Revenue rulings do not rank as high as regulations and court cases in the hierarchy of authorities. They simply represent the viewpoint of the IRS. Taxpayers do not have to follow revenue rulings if they have sufficient authority for different treatment.[16] However, the IRS presumes that the tax treatment specified in a revenue ruling is correct. Consequently, if an examining agent discovers in an audit that a taxpayer did not adopt the position espoused in a revenue ruling, the agent will contend that the taxpayer's tax liability should be adjusted to reflect the tax results prescribed in the ruling.

Soon after the IRS issues a revenue ruling, it appears in the weekly *Internal Revenue Bulletin* (cited as I.R.B.), published by the U.S. Government Printing Office. Revenue rulings are also published in the *Cumulative Bulletin* (cited as C.B.), a bound publication issued semiannually by the U.S. Government Printing Office. An example of a citation to a revenue ruling appearing in the *Cumulative Bulletin* is as follows:

[16] Chapter C15 discusses in depth the authoritative support taxpayers and tax advisors should have for positions they adopt on a tax return.

Rev. Rul. 80-265, 1980-2 C.B. 378.

This is the 265th ruling issued during 1980, and it appears on page 378 of Volume 2 of the 1980 *Cumulative Bulletin.* Before the issuance of the appropriate volume of the *Cumulative Bulletin,* citations are given to the *Internal Revenue Bulletin.* An example of such a citation follows:

Rev. Rul. 97-1, I.R.B. 1997-2, 1.

The ruling is the first issued during 1997. It was published on page 1 of the *Internal Revenue Bulletin* for the second week of 1997. Once a revenue ruling is published in the *Cumulative Bulletin,* the citation to the *Cumulative Bulletin* should be used.

REVENUE PROCEDURES. As the name suggests, **revenue procedures** are pronouncements by the IRS that generally deal with the procedural aspects of tax practice. For example, in a revenue procedure the IRS provides guidance concerning the reporting of tip income. Another revenue procedure describes the requirements for reproducing paper substitutes for informational returns such as Form 1099.

Revenue procedures are published first in the *Internal Revenue Bulletin* and later in the *Cumulative Bulletin.* An example of a citation to a revenue procedure appearing in a *Cumulative Bulletin* is as follows:

Rev. Proc. 65-19, 1965-2 C.B. 1002.

This item was published in Volume 2 of the 1965 *Cumulative Bulletin* on page 1002; it was the nineteenth revenue procedure issued during 1965.

In addition to revenue rulings and revenue procedures, the *Cumulative Bulletin* includes IRS notices, as well as texts of proposed regulations, treaties and tax conventions, committee reports, and Supreme Court decisions.

SELF-STUDY QUESTION

Do letter rulings provide precedential value for clients?

ANSWER

Not really. A letter ruling is binding only on the taxpayer to whom the ruling was issued. However, letter rulings can be very beneficial in tax research because they provide insight as to the IRS's opinion about the tax consequences of various transactions.

LETTER RULINGS. **Letter rulings** are initiated by taxpayers who write and ask the IRS to explain the tax consequences of a particular transaction.[17] The IRS provides its explanation in the form of a letter ruling, that is, a personal response to the individual or corporation requesting an answer. Only the taxpayer to whom the ruling is addressed may rely on it as an authority. Nevertheless, letter rulings can furnish significant information to other taxpayers and to tax advisors because the rulings lend insight into the IRS's opinion about the tax consequences of particular transactions.

Originally the public did not have access to letter rulings issued to other taxpayers. As a result of Code Sec. 6110, enacted in 1976, letter rulings (with any confidential information deleted) are accessible to the general public. Commerce Clearing House publishes letter rulings in a letter rulings service titled *IRS Letter Rulings.* An example of a citation to a letter ruling appears below.

Ltr. Rul. 8511075.

The numbering system for all letter rulings consists of seven digits.[18] The first two digits indicate that this ruling was made public during 1985. The next two digits denote the week it was made public, here the eleventh. The last three numbers reflect that it was the seventy-fifth ruling that week.

[17] Chapter C15 provides a more in-depth discussion of letter rulings.

[18] Sometimes letter rulings are cited as PLR (private letter ruling) instead of Ltr. Rul.

KEY POINT

A technical advice memorandum is published as a letter ruling. Whereas a taxpayer-requested letter ruling deals with prospective transactions, a technical advice memorandum is obtained after a transaction has occurred.

OTHER INTERPRETATIONS

Technical Advice Memoranda. When a taxpayer's return is being audited about a complicated, technical matter, the IRS district or appeals office may refer the matter to the IRS National Office in Washington, D.C., for technical advice concerning the appropriate tax treatment. The answer from the National Office, in the form of a **technical advice memorandum,**[19] is made available to the public as a letter ruling. Researchers are able to recognize which letter rulings are technical advice memos because they generally begin with language such as, "In response to a request for technical advice. . . ."

Information Releases. If the IRS thinks that vast numbers of the general public will be interested in a particular interpretation, it may issue an **information release**. Information releases are written in lay terms and are dispatched to thousands of newspapers throughout the United States for publication therein. The IRS may, for example, write an information release to announce the amount of the standard mileage rate applicable to taxpayers who deduct this standard allowance per mile instead of deducting their actual automobile expenses for business travel. An example of a citation to an information release is

I.R. 86-70.

This is the seventieth information release issued in 1986.

ADDITIONAL COMMENT

Announcements are used to summarize new tax law or publicize procedural matters. Announcements are generally aimed at tax practitioners and are "the equivalent of revenue rulings and revenue procedures" [Rev. Rul. 87-138, 1987-2 C.B. 287].

Announcements and Notices. The IRS also issues documents that are more technical in nature and generally aimed at tax practitioners. These documents are called **announcements** and **notices** and provide technical explanations of a tax issue that is of current importance. The IRS is bound to follow the guidance contained in announcements and notices in the same way as if contained in a revenue procedure or a revenue ruling. The IRS used a number of announcements to provide technical interpretations of the Tax Reform Act of 1986 before the Treasury was able to issue either proposed or temporary regulations. Examples of citations for announcements and notices are presented below.

Ann. 96-119, I.R.B. 1996-46, 13.
Notice 96-54, I.R.B. 1996-44, 13.

The first citation is for the 119th announcement issued in 1996. It can be found on page 13 of the forty-sixth *Internal Revenue Bulletin* of 1996. The second citation is for the 54th notice issued in 1996. It can be found on page 13 of the forty-fourth *Internal Revenue Bulletin* of 1996.

JUDICIAL DECISIONS

Judicial decisions constitute important sources of tax law. Judges are unbiased persons who decide questions of fact (the appropriate tax result for a given set of facts) or questions of law (the proper interpretation of ambiguous language in the statute). Judges, like other persons, do not always agree on the tax consequences; therefore, tax advisors must often reach their conclusions against the background of conflicting judicial authorities. For example, a district court decision may differ from a Tax Court decision, or different circuit courts may have disagreed on an issue.

OVERVIEW OF THE COURT SYSTEM. With respect to tax matters, there are three trial courts: the U.S. Tax Court, the U.S. Court of Federal Claims (formerly the U.S. Claims Court), and U.S. District Courts. The taxpayer may begin litigation in any of the

[19] Technical advice memoranda are discussed in more depth in Chapter C15.

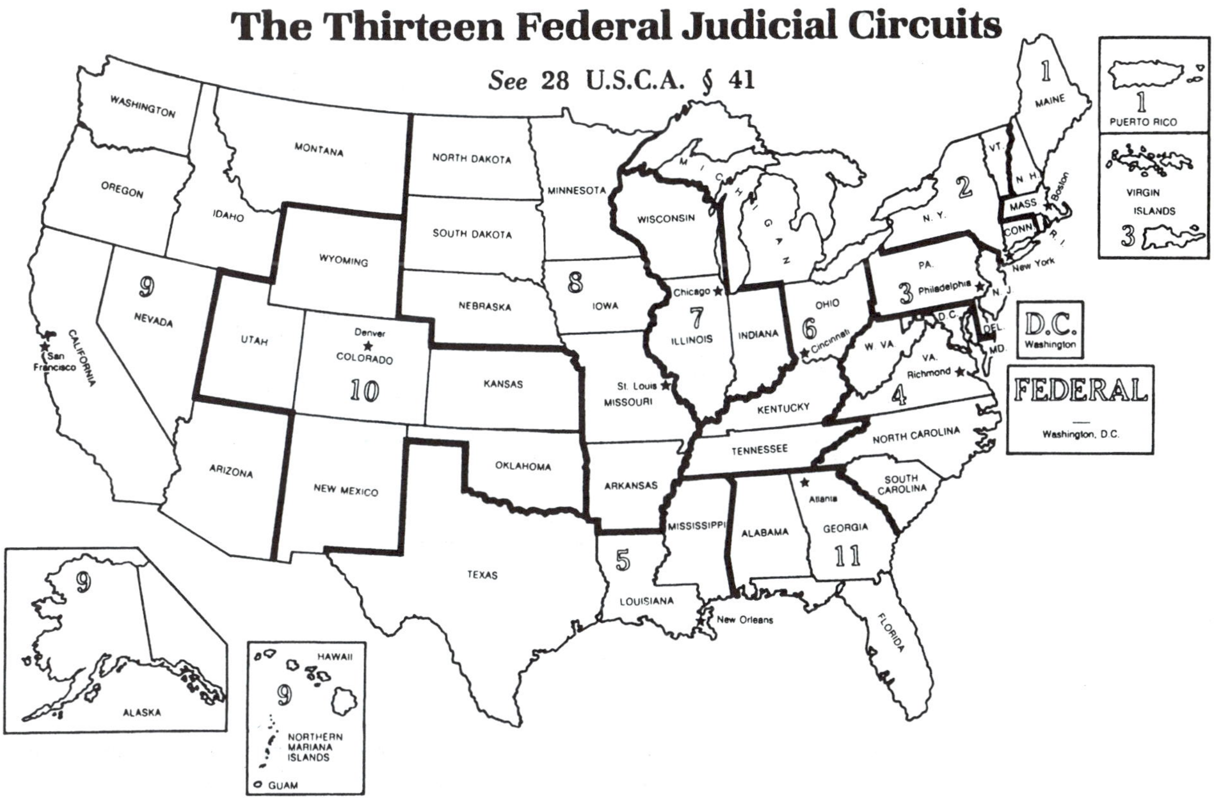

FIGURE C1-3 ▶ MAP OF THE GEOGRAPHICAL BOUNDARIES OF THE CIRCUIT COURTS OF APPEALS

Source: Reprinted with permission from *West's Federal Reporter,* Third Series, Copyright © by West Publishing Company.

three. Precedents of the various courts are an important factor in a taxpayer's decision process of where to begin litigation (see page C1-26 for a discussion of precedent). Another important influence is the timing of the cash flow to pay the deficiency. A taxpayer who wants to litigate either in a U.S. District Court or in the U.S. Court of Federal Claims must first pay the additional tax that the IRS contends is due. The taxpayer then files a claim for refund, which the IRS will deny. This denial must be followed by a suit for obtaining a refund of the taxes. If the taxpayer wins the refund suit, he or she receives a refund of the taxes in question plus interest thereon. If the taxpayer begins litigation in the Tax Court, however, payment of the deficiency need not occur until the case has been decided. If the taxpayer loses in the Tax Court, he or she must pay the deficiency plus any interest and penalties.[20] A taxpayer who thinks that a jury trial would be especially favorable should litigate in a U.S. District Court, the only place where a jury trial is possible.

SELF-STUDY QUESTION

What are some of the factors that should be considered when deciding in which court to initiate the litigation of a tax case?

ANSWER

(1) Each court's published precedent pertaining to the issue, (2) desirability of a jury trial, (3) tax expertise of each court, and (4) effect on cash flow.

Regardless of which party loses at the trial court level, such party can appeal the decision. Appeals from Tax Court and U.S. District Court decisions are made to the Court of Appeals for the taxpayer's circuit (i.e., geographical area). There are eleven numbered circuits plus the circuit for the District of Columbia. The map in Figure C1-3 shows which states lie in the various circuits. California, for example, is in the Ninth Circuit. Instead of saying "the Court of Appeals for the Ninth Circuit," one generally says "the Ninth Circuit." All decisions of the U.S. Court of Federal Claims are appealable

[20] Revenue Procedure 84-58, 1984-2 C.B. 501, provides procedures for taxpayers to make remittances in order to stop the running of interest on deficiencies. This action is more important now that the deduction for personal interest has been eliminated.

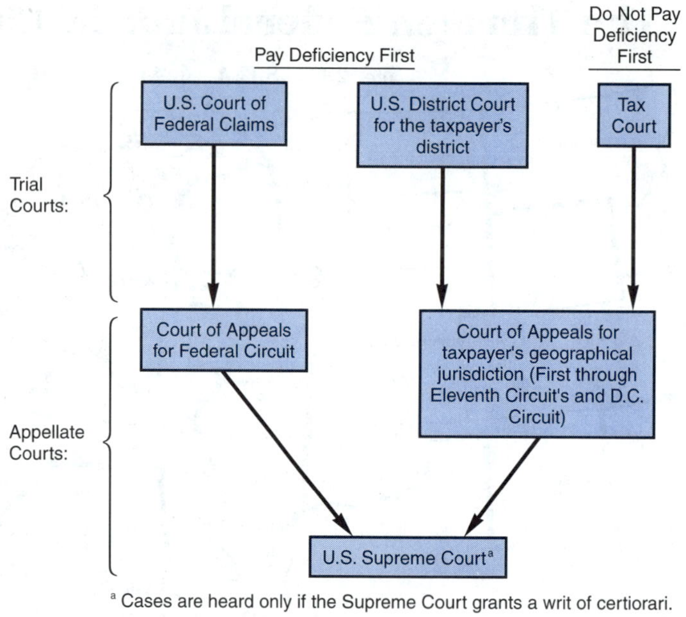

FIGURE C1-4 ▶ OVERVIEW OF COURT SYSTEM—TAX MATTERS

to one court—the Court of Appeals for the Federal Circuit—irrespective of the taxpayer's geographical location.[21] The only cases that the Federal Circuit hears are those that originate in the U.S. Court of Federal Claims.

The party losing at the Court of Appeals level can petition by a **writ of certiorari** that the Supreme Court hear the case. If the Supreme Court agrees to consider the issue, it grants certiorari.[22] In recent years, the Court has heard only about six to ten tax cases per year. Figure C1-4 provides an overview of the court system with respect to tax matters.

KEY POINT

Because the Tax Court deals only with tax cases, the Tax Court presumably has a higher level of tax expertise than do other courts. Tax Court judges are appointed by the President, in part, due to their considerable tax experience. In July, 1996, the Tax Court judges faced a backlog of just under 28,000 cases. This is a marked improvement over its record 84,000 cases in 1986.

THE U.S. TAX COURT. The U.S. Tax Court originated in 1942 as a successor to the Board of Tax Appeals. It is a court of national jurisdiction that hears cases dealing only with tax matters. Regardless of a taxpayer's state of residence, all litigated Tax Court cases end up in the same court. There are nineteen Tax Court judges, including one chief judge. The President, with the consent of the Senate, appoints the judges for fifteen years and may reappoint them for an additional term. The judges, specialists in issues concerning taxation, periodically travel to various major cities to hear cases. At present, the Tax Court hears cases in approximately 100 cities. In most instances, only one judge hears a particular case.

The Tax Court issues both regular and memorandum (memo) decisions. The chief judge decides whether to publish each opinion as a memo or regular decision. Generally, the first time the Tax Court decides a particular legal issue, its decision appears as a **regular decision**. **Memo decisions** usually deal with some factual variation on a matter for which an earlier case decided the interpretation of the law. Regular and memo decisions have the same precedential value.

---

[21] The creation of the U.S. Court of Federal Claims in 1992 is the result of a name change. There is no change in the court's operations from its predecessor, the U.S. Claims Court, which operated from 1982 to 1992. Before the 1982 restructuring, this court was known as the U.S. Court of Claims; its decisions were appealable only to the U.S. Supreme Court.

[22] In granting certiorari, the Supreme Court denotes its granting of an appellate review. The denial of certiorari does not necessarily mean that the Supreme Court agrees with the lower court's decision. It simply decides not to hear the case.

KEY POINT

If a particular case is considered important enough, the chief judge will instruct the other judges to review the case. If a case is considered by the entire court, the phrase *reviewed by the court* is inserted immediately following the text of the majority opinion. A reviewed decision provides an opportunity for Tax Court judges to express their dissenting opinions.

At times the chief judge determines that a particular decision deals with a very important matter that the entire Tax Court should have a chance to consider. In such a situation, the words *reviewed by the court* will appear at the end of the majority decision. If there are any concurring or dissenting opinions, they will appear after the opinion of the majority.[23]

Other language sometimes appearing at the end of a Tax Court decision is *Entered under Rule 155*. These words signify that the court has reached a decision concerning the appropriate tax treatment of an issue but it has left the computation of the exact amount of the deficiency to the two litigating parties.

SELF-STUDY QUESTION

What are some of the consequences of the small cases procedure of the Tax Court?

ANSWER

The small cases procedure allows a taxpayer the advantage of having his or her "day in court" without the expense of an attorney. But if the taxpayer loses, the decision cannot be appealed.

Small Cases Procedure. The Tax Court has a special policy concerning small cases. Taxpayers have the option of having their cases heard under the **small cases procedure** if the amount in question for a particular year does not exceed $10,000.[24] Such procedures are less formal than the regular Tax Court procedures, and taxpayers can appear without an attorney.[25] The cases are heard by special commissioners instead of by one of the nineteen Tax Court judges. For the losing party, a disadvantage of the small case procedure is that the decision cannot be appealed. The opinions in the small cases are not published and have no precedential value.

Acquiescence Policy. Years ago the IRS adopted the policy of announcing whether it agreed or disagreed with Tax Court cases decided in favor of the taxpayer. This policy is known as the **acquiescence policy**. If the IRS wants to announce that it agrees with a Tax Court decision, it acquiesces to the decision. If it wishes to go on record as disagreeing with a decision, it issues a nonacquiescence to such decision. The acquiescence policy extends only to regular Board of Tax Appeals and Tax Court decisions.[26] The IRS does not, however, make a formal statement, an acquiescence or nonacquiescence, to every regular decision decided in a taxpayer's favor.

KEY POINT

The only cases to which the IRS will consider publishing an acquiescence or nonacquiescence are those "regular" Tax Court decisions that the government loses. Because the vast majority of Tax Court cases are won by the government, the IRS will potentially acquiescence to only a small number of cases.

The IRS's decision to acquiesce or nonacquiesce has important implications for taxpayers. For example, suppose the IRS has nonacquiesced to a particular decision, and another taxpayer in similar circumstances files a return that adopts the Tax Court position. If the taxpayer's return is audited and the examining agent discovers that the taxpayer's return was prepared on the basis of the Tax Court holding rather than the nonacquiescence statement, the agent must argue that the taxpayer owes more tax. Because an acquiescence or nonacquiescence statement is binding on the agent, about the only way the taxpayer can prevail is by litigation. If the IRS acquiesces to a decision, however, the implication is that the IRS will no longer oppose a pro-taxpayer position on this issue.

When the IRS issues an acquiescence or nonacquiescence, information to this effect appears in the weekly *Internal Revenue Bulletin*. Such information is also published near the front of the *Cumulative Bulletin* for the period in which the announcement was made. If the case dealt with more than one issue, the acquiescence or nonacquiescence may extend to only one issue. Sometimes the IRS acquiesces "in result only," meaning that it agrees with the ultimate outcome (for example, an expenditure is deductible) but not with the court's rationale. The *Cumulative Bulletin*, by way of footnotes, contains details about whether the IRS's acquiescence is complete, partial, or in result only.

---

[23] A judge who issues a concurring opinion agrees with the basic outcome of the majority's decision but not with its rationale. A judge who issues a dissenting opinion believes that the majority decided on an inappropriate outcome.

[24] Sec. 7463. The $10,000 limitation on the amount in dispute includes penalties but excludes interest.

[25] Taxpayers can represent themselves in regular Tax Court proceedings also, even though they are not attorneys. In situations where taxpayers represent themselves, the words *pro se* appear after the taxpayer's name.

[26] Board of Tax Appeals decisions can serve as precedent for current Tax Court decisions, although it is less likely now that the cases are so old. It is also less likely that the IRS will acquiesce or nonacquiesce to a Board of Tax Appeals decision today.

Published Opinions and Citations. Regular decisions of the Tax Court are published by the U.S. Government Printing Office in a bound volume known as the *Tax Court of the United States Reports.* Soon after a decision is made public, it is also published by Research Institute of America and Commerce Clearing House in their looseleaf reporters of Tax Court decisions. An official citation to a Tax Court decision is as follows:[27]

J. Simpson Dean, 35 T.C. 1083 (1961).

The information in the citation indicates that this case appears on page 1083 in Volume 35 of the official *Tax Court of the United States Reports* and that the case was decided in 1961.

Regular decisions of the Board of Tax Appeals were published by the U.S. Government Printing Office in the *United States Board of Tax Appeals Reports* from 1924 to 1942. A reference to a Board of Tax Appeals case can be cited as follows:

KEY POINT

Once the IRS has acquiesced to a Tax Court position, other taxpayers generally will not need to litigate the same issue. However, the IRS can change its mind and revoke a previous acquiescence or nonacquiescence. References regarding acquiescences or nonacquiescences to Tax Court decisions can be found in the citators.

J. W. Wells Lumber Co. Trust A., 44 B.T.A. 551 (1941).

This case is printed in Volume 44 of the *United States Board of Tax Appeals Reports* on page 551. It is a 1941 decision.

If the IRS has acquiesced or nonacquiesced to a regular Tax Court or Board of Tax Appeals decision, information concerning the IRS's action should appear as part of the citation. At times the IRS's announcement may not occur until several years after the date of the court decision. An example of a citation involving an acquiescence is as follows:

Estate of John A. Moss, 74 T.C. 1239 (1980), *acq.* 1981-1 C.B. 2.

The case appears on page 1239 of Volume 74 of the *Tax Court of the United States Reports* and the acquiescence is reported on page 2 of Volume 1 of the 1981 *Cumulative Bulletin.* The IRS acquiesced to this 1980 decision in 1981.

A citation to a decision to which the IRS has nonacquiesced is as follows:

Warren Jones Co., 60 T.C. 663 (1973), *nonacq.* 1980-1 C.B. 2.

The case appears in Volume 60 of the *Tax Court of the United States Reports* on page 663. The nonacquiescence is reported on page 2 of Volume 1 of the 1980 *Cumulative Bulletin.* The IRS nonacquiesced to this 1973 decision in 1980.

Tax Court memorandum decisions are not published by the U.S. Government Printing Office. The decisions are available in bound form from Research Institute of America in *RIA T.C. Memorandum Decisions* and from Commerce Clearing House in *CCH Tax Court Memorandum Decisions.* In addition, soon after an opinion is completed, it is published in loose-leaf form by the two publishers. Following are the citations to a Tax Court memorandum decision.

Edith G. McKinney, 1981 PH T.C. Memo ¶81,181, 41 *TCM* 1272.

---

[27] In a Tax Court case only the plaintiff (taxpayer) is listed. The defendant is understood to be the Commissioner of Internal Revenue and sometimes is not shown in the citation. In cases litigated outside the Tax Court, the plaintiff is listed first and the defendant second. The Commissioner of Internal Revenue is listed as *CIR* in our footnotes and text for cases outside of the Tax Court.

McKinney is reproduced in Prentice Hall's (now Research Institute of America's)[28] 1981 *PH T.C. Memorandum Decisions* reporter in paragraph 81,181, and in Volume 41, page 1272, of Commerce Clearing House's *Tax Court Memorandum Decisions.* The 181 in the PH citation denotes that the case is the Tax Court's 181st memorandum decision of the year. A more recent citation continues the same basic format to refer to Research Institute of America's (RIA) memorandum decisions.

KEY POINT

To have access to all Tax Court cases, a tax advisor must refer to two different publications. The regular opinions are found in the *Tax Court of the United States Reports*, published by the U.S. Government Printing Office, and the memorandum decisions are published by both RIA (formerly PH) and CCH.

Paul F. Belloff, 1992 RIA T.C. Memo ¶92,346, 63 *TCM* 3150.

U.S. DISTRICT COURTS. Each state has at least one U.S. district court, and more populous states have more than one. Each district court is a separate entity and is free to reach its own decision, subject to the precedential constraints discussed later (see page C1-26). Many different types of cases—not just tax cases—are heard in this forum. A district court is the only forum in which the taxpayer has an opportunity for a jury trial for questions of fact. Depending on the particular taxpayer and the circumstances involved, a jury trial might or might not be perceived as beneficial.[29]

District court decisions are officially reported in the *Federal Supplement* (cited as F. Supp.) published by West Publishing Co. However, some decisions are not officially reported and are referred to as **unreported decisions.** Decisions by U.S. district courts on the topic of taxation are also published by Research Institute of America and Commerce Clearing House in secondary reporters that include only tax-related cases. The Research Institute of America's reporter is called *American Federal Tax Reports* (cited as AFTR),[30] and the Commerce Clearing House reporter is known as *U.S. Tax Cases* (cited as USTC). Even though a case is not officially reported, it may nevertheless be published in the AFTR and USTC. An example of a citation to a U.S. district court decision is as follows:

Margie J. Thompson v. U.S., 429 F. Supp. 13, 39 AFTR 2d 77-1485, 77-1 USTC ¶9343 (D.C. PA., 1977).

KEY POINT

A cite, at a minimum, should contain the following information: (1) the name of the case, (2) the reporter that contains the case along with both a volume and page (or paragraph) number, (3) the year the case was decided, and (4) the court that decided the case.

In the example above, the citation to the *Federal Supplement* is referred to as the **primary cite**. The case appears on page 13 of Volume 429 of the *Federal Supplement.* **Secondary cites** are to Volume 39 of the second series of the AFTR, page 77-1485 (meaning page 1485 in the volume containing 1977 cases) and to Volume 1 of the 1977 USTC in paragraph 9343. The parenthetical information denotes that the case was decided by a district court in Pennsylvania in 1977. Because some judicial decisions have greater value as precedents (i.e., a Supreme Court decision versus a District Court decision), the reader finds it useful to know which court decided the case.

U.S. COURT OF FEDERAL CLAIMS. The U.S. Court of Federal Claims, another trial court that addresses tax matter, has nationwide jurisdiction. Originally this court was named the U.S. Court of Claims (cited as Ct. Cl.), and its decisions were appealable to the Supreme Court only. In a restructuring, effective as of October 1, 1982, the court was

[28] For a number of years the Prentice Hall Information Services division published its *Federal Taxes 2nd* tax service and a number of related publications such as the *PH T.C. Memorandum Decisions.* Changes in ownership occurred, and in late 1991 Thomson Professional Publishing added the former Prentice Hall tax materials to the product line of its Research Institute of America tax publishing division. Some products such as the *PH T.C. Memorandum Decisions* still have the Prentice Hall name on the spine of older editions.

[29] Taxpayers usually prefer to have a jury trial if they think that a jury will be sympathetic to their circumstances.

[30] The *American Federal Tax Reports* (AFTR) comes in two series. The first series is cited as AFTR. The second series, which includes decisions published after 1957, is cited as AFTR 2d. The *Margie Thompson* decision cited as an illustration of a District Court decision is from the second *American Federal Tax Reports* series.

KEY POINT

The U.S. Court of Federal Claims handles any claims (including suits to recover federal income taxes) against the U.S. government. Unlike the Tax Court, which regularly travels to various cities, the U.S. Court of Federal Claims usually hears cases only in Washington, D.C., but will hold sessions in other locations as the court deems necessary.

renamed the U.S. Claims Court (cited as Cl. Ct.), and its decisions became appealable to the Circuit Court of Appeals for the Federal Circuit. In October 1992, the court's name was changed to the U.S. Court of Federal Claims (cited as Fed. Cl.).

Beginning in 1982, U.S. Claims Court decisions were reported officially in the *Claims Court Reporter*, a reporter published by West Publishing Co. from 1982 to 1992.[31] An example of a citation for a U.S. Claims Court decision appears below.

> *Benjamin Raphan v. U.S.*, 3 Cl. Ct. 457, 52 AFTR 2d 83-5987, 83-2 USTC ¶9613 (1983).

The *Raphan* case appears in Volume 3 of the *Claims Court Reporter* on page 457. Secondary cites are to Volume 52, page 83-5987 of the AFTR, second series, and to Volume 2 of the 1983 USTC in paragraph 9613.

Effective with the 1992 name change, decisions of the U.S. Court of Federal Claims are now reported in the *Federal Claims Reporter*. An example of the citation appears below.

> *Jeffrey G. Sharp v. U.S.*, 27 Fed. Cl. 52, 70 AFTR 2d 92-6040, 92-2 USTC ¶50,561 (1992).

The *Sharp* case appears in Volume 27 of the *Federal Claims Reporter* on page 52, on page 6040 of the 70th volume of the AFTR, second series, and in Volume 2 of the 1992 USTC reporter in paragraph 50,561. Note that even though the name of the reporter published by West Publishing Co. has changed, the volume numbers continue as if there were no name change.

CIRCUIT COURTS OF APPEALS. Trial court decisions are appealable by the losing party to a circuit court of appeals. The applicable circuit is a function of where the litigation originated. Generally, if the case began in the Tax Court or a U.S. district court, the case is appealable to the circuit for the taxpayer's residence as of the date of the appeal. In the case of a corporation, the case is appealable to the circuit where the corporation's principal place of business is located. As mentioned above, the Federal Circuit handles all appeals of cases originating in the U.S. Court of Federal Claims.

There are eleven geographical circuits designated by numbers, the circuit for the District of Columbia, and the Federal Circuit. A map of the circuits and their jurisdictions appears on page C1-19. The eleven numbered circuits and the D.C. circuit hear appeals of persons or firms from their locality. In October 1981, the Eleventh Circuit was created by moving Alabama, Georgia, and Florida from the Fifth to the new Eleventh Circuit. The Eleventh Circuit voluntarily adopted the policy that it will follow as precedent all decisions made by the Fifth Circuit during the time the states currently constituting the Eleventh Circuit were part of the Fifth Circuit.[32]

EXAMPLE C1-7 ▶ The Eleventh Circuit first faced a particular issue in 1997; the case concerns a Florida taxpayer. In 1980 the Fifth Circuit had ruled on this issue in a case involving a Louisiana taxpayer. Because Florida was part of the Fifth Circuit in 1980, under the policy adopted by the Eleventh Circuit, it will follow the Fifth Circuit's earlier decision. If the Fifth Circuit's decision had been

---

[31] Before the creation in 1982 of the U.S. Claims Court (and the *Claims Court Reporter*), the decisions of the U.S. Court of Claims were reported in either the *Federal Supplement* (F. Supp.) or the *Federal Reporter, Second Series* (F.2d). The *Federal Supplement* was used as the primary reference for the U.S. Court of Claims from 1932 through January 19, 1960. From January 20, 1960, to October 1982, these decisions were reported in the *Federal Reporter, Second Series.*

[32] *Bonner v. City of Prichard*, 661 F.2d 1206 (11th Cir., 1981).

rendered in 1982—after the creation of the Eleventh Circuit—the Eleventh Circuit would not have been bound by the Fifth Circuit's decision.

As the later discussion of precedential value points out, different circuits may reach different conclusions concerning the same issue.

Circuit courts of appeals decisions—regardless of the topic (e.g., civil rights, securities law, taxation, etc.)—are now reported officially in the *Federal Reporter, Third Series* (cited as F.3d), published by West Publishing Co. The third series began in October 1993 after the volume number for the second series reached 999. The *Federal Reporter, Third Series* is the primary citation. In addition, tax decisions of the circuit courts appear in the *American Federal Tax Reports* and *U.S. Tax Cases.* Below is an example of a citation to a 1994 decision by a circuit court.

> *Leonard Greene v. U.S.,* 13 F.3d 577, 73 AFTR 2d 94-746, 94-1 USTC ¶50,022 (2nd Cir., 1994).

The *Greene* case appears on page 577 of Volume 13 of the *Federal Reporter, Third Series.* It is also reported in Volume 73, page 94-746 of the AFTR, second series, and in Volume 1, paragraph 50,022, of the 1994 USTC. Parenthetical information indicates that the Second Circuit decided the case in 1994. (A reference to a *Federal Reporter, Second Series* citation can be found in footnote 32 of this chapter.)

KEY POINT

Supreme Court decisions are binding on all courts in all jurisdictions; however, the Supreme Court hears only a few tax cases each year. The Supreme Court generally will not hear a tax case unless there is a split among the circuit courts or the issue is of considerable importance.

KEY POINT

A judge is required to follow prior court precedent only to the extent that the judge's decision is appealable to that court. Also, a court usually follows its own prior precedent except for situations in which the *Golsen* rule requires the Tax Court to issue inconsistent opinions. Thus, the Tax Court, the U.S. district courts, and the U.S. Court of Federal Claims are not required to follow each other's decisions, nor is a circuit court required to follow the decision of a different circuit court.

SUPREME COURT. Whichever party loses at the appellate court level can request that the Supreme Court hear the case. The Supreme Court, however, hears very few tax cases. Unless the circuits are divided on the proper treatment, or the issue is deemed to be of great significance, the Supreme Court probably will not hear the case.[33] Supreme Court decisions are the law of the land and supersede earlier cases. As a practical matter, a Supreme Court ruling on an interpretation of the Code has the same effect as if its interpretative language was added to the Code. If Congress does not approve of the Court's interpretation, it can amend the statutory language to achieve a result to the contrary. From time to time Congress has reacted to Supreme Court decisions by amending the Code.[34] If a Supreme Court decision concludes that a particular statute is unconstitutional, the provision is ineffective and must be revised.

All Supreme Court decisions, regardless of the subject matter, are published in the *United States Supreme Court Reports* (cited as U.S.), by the U.S. Government Printing Office, the *Supreme Court Reporter* (cited as S.Ct.), by West Publishing Co., and the *United States Reports, Lawyers' Edition* (cited as L. Ed.) by Lawyer's Co-Operative Publishing Co. In addition, the AFTR and USTC reporters published by Research Institute of America and Commerce Clearing House, respectively, contain Supreme Court decisions concerned with taxation. An example of a citation to a Supreme Court case appears below.

> *U.S. v. Maclin P. Davis,* 397 U.S. 301, 25 AFTR 2d 70-827, 70-1 USTC ¶9289 (1970).

According to the primary cite, this case appears in Volume 397, page 301, of the *United States Supreme Court Reports.* It is also reported in Volume 25, page 70-827, of the AFTR, second series, and in Volume 1, paragraph 9289, of the 1970 USTC.

---

[33] *Vogel Fertilizer Co. v. U.S.*, 49 AFTR 2d 82-491, 82-1 USTC ¶9134 (USSC, 1982), is an example of a case the Supreme Court decided to hear to settle the controversy existing in the courts. The Fifth Circuit, the Tax Court, and the Court of Claims had reached one interpretation, whereas the Second, Fourth, and Eighth Circuits had ruled to the contrary.

[34] For an example of a situation where Congress enacted legislation to achieve a result contrary to that of a Supreme Court decision, see *U.S. v. Marian A. Byrum*, 30 AFTR 2d 72-5811, 72-2 USTC ¶12,859 (USSC, 1972).

▼ TABLE C1-2
Summary of Format for Citations

Court	Citation
	Court Cases
Tax Court—regular decisions	*J. Simpson Dean,* 35 T.C. 1083 (1961)
Tax Court—memo decisions	*Paul F. Belloff,* 1992 RIA T.C. Memo ¶92,346, 63 TCM 3150
Board of Tax Appeals—regular decisions	*J. W. Wells Lumber Co. Trust A.,* 44 B.T.A. 551 (1941)
U.S. District Court	*Margie J. Thompson v. U.S.,* 429 F. Supp. 13, 39 AFTR 2d 77-1485, 77-1 USTC ¶9343 (DC PA, 1977)
U.S. Court of Federal Claims	*Jeffrey G. Sharp v. U.S.,* 27 Fed. Cl. 52, 70 AFTR 2d 92-6040, 92-2 USTC ¶50,561 (1992)
U.S. Claims Court	*Benjamin Raphan v. U.S.,* 3 Cl. Ct. 457, 52 AFTR 2d 83-5987, 83-2 USTC ¶9613 (1983)
Circuit Court of Appeals	*Leonard Greene v. U.S.,* 13 F.3d 577, 73 AFTR 2d 94-746, 94-1 USTC ¶50,022 (2nd Cir., 1994)
Supreme Court	*U.S. v. Maclin P. Davis,* 397 U.S. 301, 25 AFTR 2d 70-827, 70-1 USTC ¶9289 (1970)
ADMINISTRATIVE INTERPRETATIONS	
Revenue Rulings—prior to publication in *Cumulative Bulletin*	Rev. Rul. 97-1, I.R.B. 1997-2, 1
Revenue Rulings—after publication in *Cumulative Bulletin*	Rev. Rul. 80-265, 1980-2 C.B. 378
Revenue Procedures	Rev. Proc. 65-19, 1965-2 C.B. 1002
Letter Rulings	Ltr. Rul. 8511075
Information Release	I.R. 86-70
Announcement	Ann. 96-119, I.R.B. 1996-46, 13
Notice	Notice 96-54, I.R.B. 1996-44, 13

SELF-STUDY QUESTION

Is it possible for the Tax Court to intentionally issue conflicting decisions?

ANSWERS

Yes. If the Tax Court is issuing two decisions that are appealable to different circuit courts and these circuit courts have previously reached different conclusions on the issue, the Tax Court follows the respective precedent in each circuit and issues conflicting decisions. This is a result of following the *Golsen* rule.

Table C1-2 provides a summary of how court decisions, revenue rulings, revenue procedures, and other administrative interpretations should be cited. Primary citations are to the reporters published by West Publishing Co. or the U.S. Government Printing Office, and secondary citations are to the AFTR and USTC reporters.

PRECEDENTIAL VALUE OF VARIOUS DECISIONS.

Tax Court. The Tax Court is a court of national jurisdiction. Consequently, in general it rules uniformly for all taxpayers, regardless of their geographical location. It follows Supreme Court decisions and its own earlier decisions. It is not bound by cases decided by the U.S. Court of Federal Claims or a U.S. district court, even if the district court is the court for the taxpayer's jurisdiction.

In 1970 the Tax Court voluntarily adopted what has become known as the *Golsen* rule.[35] Under the *Golsen* rule, the Tax Court departs from its general policy of ruling uniformly for all taxpayers and instead follows decisions to the contrary made by the court of appeals to which the case in question is appealable. Stated differently, the *Golsen* rule provides that the Tax Court rules consistently with decisions of the circuit court for the taxpayer's jurisdiction.

EXAMPLE C1-8 ▶ In 1991, the first time the issue was litigated, the Tax Court decided that an expenditure was deductible. The government appealed the case to the Tenth Circuit and won a reversal. This is the only appellate case that has been decided regarding this issue. If and when the Tax Court faces this issue again, it will hold, with one exception, that the expenditure is deductible. The sole exception involves taxpayers of the Tenth Circuit; for them the Tax Court applies the *Golsen* rule and denies the deduction. ◀

U.S. District Court. Because each U.S. district court is a separate court, district court decisions have precedential value only for subsequent cases before that same U.S. district court. District courts must follow decisions of the Supreme Court and the circuit court to which the case is appealable.

EXAMPLE C1-9 ▶ The U.S. District Court for Rhode Island, the Tax Court, and the Eleventh Circuit have ruled on a particular issue. Any U.S. district court within the Eleventh Circuit must follow that circuit's decision. Similarly, the U.S. District Court for Rhode Island must rule consistently with the way it ruled earlier. Tax Court decisions are not binding precedents for district courts. Thus, all district courts other than the one for Rhode Island and those within the Eleventh Circuit are free to reach their own independent decisions. ◀

U.S. Court of Federal Claims. In reaching decisions today, the U.S. Court of Federal Claims must rule consistently with Supreme Court cases, cases decided by the Circuit Court of Appeals for the Federal Circuit, and its own earlier decisions, including decisions rendered when the court had a different name. It need not follow decisions of other circuit courts, the Tax Court, or district courts.

EXAMPLE C1-10 ▶ Assume the same facts as in Example C1-9. In a later year the same issue is litigated in the U.S. Court of Federal Claims. This court is not bound by any of the authorities that have addressed the issue. Thus, it has complete flexibility to reach its own answer. ◀

Circuit Courts of Appeals. A circuit court is bound by Supreme Court cases and earlier cases decided by that particular circuit. If neither the Supreme Court nor the circuit in question has already faced the issue, there is no precedent that the circuit court must follow, regardless of whether other circuits have ruled on this point. In such a situation, the circuit court is said to be writing on a clean slate. In reaching a decision, the judges may adopt the viewpoint articulated in another circuit's opinion if they deem it appropriate.

EXAMPLE C1-11 ▶ Assume the same facts as in Example C1-9. Any circuit other than the Eleventh would be writing on a clean slate if it faced the same issue. After reviewing the Eleventh Circuit's decision, another circuit court might or might not decide to rule the same way. ◀

Forum Shopping. Not surprisingly, courts are not always unanimous in their conclusions concerning the appropriate tax treatment. Consequently, conflicts sometimes exist

---

[35] The *Golsen* rule is based on the decision in *Jack E. Golsen*, 54 T.C. 742 (1970).

among the courts—trial courts and appellate courts. Because taxpayers have the flexibility of choosing where to begin their litigation, part of their decision-making process should involve considering the precedents applicable in the various courts. The ability to consider differing precedents in choosing the forum for litigation is sometimes called **forum shopping**.

An example of a situation where until recently a conflict in the circuits existed was the issue of when it became too late for the IRS to question the proper treatment of items that flowed through from an S corporation's tax return to a shareholder's tax return. For example, if the time (statute of limitations) had already expired for the corporation's but not the shareholder's tax return, was the IRS precluded from collecting additional taxes from the shareholder? The Ninth Circuit in *Kelley*[36] held that the IRS would be barred from collecting from the shareholder if the statute of limitations was already up for the S corporation's information return. On the other hand, three other circuits held in *Bufferd,*[37] *Fehlhaber,*[38] and *Green*[39] that the statute of limitations for flow-through items did not expire until the statute of limitations for flow-through items was up for the shareholder. The Supreme Court affirmed the *Bufferd*[40] case and created certainty and uniformity for the interpretation of this important issue.

STOP & THINK

Question: You have been researching whether a certain amount received by your new client can be excluded from her gross income. The client's tax return for two years ago is being audited; another firm prepared the return. In a similar case decided a few years ago the Tax Court allowed an exclusion, but the IRS nonacquiesced to the case. The case involved a taxpayer from the Fourth Circuit. Your client is a resident of Maine, which is in the First Circuit. Twelve years ago in a case involving another taxpayer, the district court for the client's district ruled that this type of receipt was not excludable. There has been no other litigation. To sustain a deduction, will your client likely need to litigate? Explain. If your client litigates, in which trial court should she begin her litigation?

Solution: Because of the IRS's nonacquiescence, your client's exclusion is not likely to be sustained unless she litigates. She would not want to begin litigation in her district court because it would need to follow its earlier decision, which is unfavorable to taxpayers. A good place to begin would be the Tax Court because of its earlier pro-taxpayer position. There is no way to predict how the U.S. Court of Federal Claims would rule because there is no precedent it must follow.

Dictum. At times a court may comment on an issue or a set of facts that it did not face in the case being tried. Comments by a court on facts or an issue on which it does not have to rule are called *dictum*. In building an argument in favor of a particular tax result, a party may reference *dictum* as support for the argument. The *Central Illinois Public Service Co.*[41] case addressed whether lunch reimbursements received by employees constituted wages subject to withholding. In this case, Justice Blackman remarked that income in such forms as interest, rent, and dividends is not wages. This remark by Justice Blackman is *dictum* because the case concerned only reimbursements for expenditures for lunches.

---

[36] *Daniel M. Kelley v. CIR,* 64 AFTR 2d 89-5025, 89-1 USTC ¶9360 (9th Cir., 1989).

[37] *Sheldon B. Bufferd v. CIR,* 69 AFTR 2d 92-465, 92-1 USTC ¶50,031 (2nd Cir., 1992).

[38] *Robert Fehlhaber v. CIR,* 69 AFTR 2d 92-850, 92-1 USTC ¶50,131 (11th Cir., 1992).

[39] *Charles T. Green v. CIR,* 70 AFTR 2d 92-5077, 92-2 USTC ¶50,340 (5th Cir., 1992).

[40] *Sheldon B. Bufferd v. CIR,* 71 AFTR 2d 93-573, 93-1 USTC ¶50,038 (USSC, 1993).

[41] *Central Illinois Public Service Co. v. CIR,* 41 AFTR 2d 78-718, 78-1 USTC ¶9254 (USSC, 1978).

TAX TREATIES

KEY POINT

A tax treaty is the equivalent of a statute. A tax advisor needs to be aware of provisions in tax treaties that will affect a taxpayer's worldwide tax liability.

The United States has reached treaty agreements with numerous foreign countries. These treaties address tax and other matters. As a result, a tax advisor addressing the U.S. tax results of a U.S. corporation's business operations in another country, for example, Sweden, should determine whether there is a treaty between Sweden and the United States and, if there is, the applicable provisions of the treaty. (See Chapter C16 for a more extensive discussion of treaties.)

TAX PERIODICALS

KEY POINT

Tax articles can be used to help *find* answers to tax questions. Where possible the underlying statutory, administrative, or judicial authority used in the tax article should be cited as the authority and not the author of the article. The Courts and the IRS will place little, if any, reliance on mere editorial opinion.

Writings of experts in tax periodicals can lend informative assistance for interpreting the tax law. For example, such writings can be especially helpful if they address a recently enacted statutory provision and it is too early for there to be any regulations, cases, or rulings on point.

Tax experts also often write articles in which they discuss the judicial authorities—often conflicting ones—with respect to a particular issue. The experts who most frequently write articles concerning technical tax matters are attorneys, accountants, and professors. Some periodicals that are devoted to providing in-depth discussions of tax matters are listed below.

The Journal of Taxation
The Tax Adviser
Taxation for Accountants
Taxes—the Tax Magazine
Tax Law Review
The Journal of Corporate Taxation
The Journal of Partnership Taxation
The Journal of Real Estate Taxation
The Review of Taxation of Individuals
Estate Planning
Tax Notes

The first five journals listed above contain articles dealing with a variety of topical areas. As the titles of the next five suggest, these publications deal with specialized areas. All of these publications (other than *Tax Notes*, which is published weekly) are monthly or quarterly publications. Daily reports, such as the *Daily Tax Report*, published by the Bureau of National Affairs, are used by tax professionals when more timely updates on tax matters are needed than can be provided by monthly and quarterly publications.

Published articles and tax services are examples of secondary sources of authority. The Code and administrative and judicial interpretations are primary sources of authority. Your research efforts should always involve citing primary authorities.

TAX SERVICES

OBJECTIVE 4

Use the tax services and/or electronic resources to research an issue

Multivolume commentaries on the tax law are published by several publishers. These commentaries are known generically as **tax services**. Each of these tax services is encyclopedic in scope and most come in looseleaf form so that information concerning current developments can be easily added. The organizational scheme differs from one service to another; some are updated more frequently than others. Each has its own special features and unique way of presenting certain material. The only way to become familiar with the various tax services is to use them in researching hypothetical or actual problems.

KEY POINT

Tax services are often where the research process begins. A tax service helps identify the tax authorities pertaining to a particular tax issue. The actual tax authorities, and not the tax service, are generally cited as support for a particular tax position.

As with almost any other activity, the more familiar one becomes with the organizational scheme with which one is working, the more comfortable one feels. Knowledge of the organization is relevant even if the researcher is using the CD-ROM or the on-line version of a tax service. The following discussion provides an overview of the most commonly used tax services.

UNITED STATES TAX REPORTER

United States Tax Reporter, the tax reporter service published by Research Institute of America, consists of an eighteen-volume series devoted to income taxes, a two-volume series covering estate and gift taxes, and a single volume dealing with excise taxes. This service also contains two volumes that reproduce the Internal Revenue Code.

KEY POINT

Both the *United States Tax Reporter* and the *Standard Federal Tax Reporter* services are organized by Code section. Accordingly, many tax advisors find both of these services easy to use. The other major tax services are organized by topic and offer more of a commentary style.

The *United States Tax Reporter* service is organized by Code section (i.e., its commentary begins with Sec. 1 of the Code and proceeds in numerical order through the last section of the Code). Researchers familiar with the Code section applicable to their problem can begin their research process by turning directly to the paragraphs discussing this section. For each Code section, a code-based paragraph sequencing is used for the Code text, the Regulations text, committee reports, editorial explanations, and digests of cases and rulings so that the researcher does not have to learn a different numbering system. Another technique for beginning the research process is to think of key words that capture the flavor of the problem and consult the index. The topical index appears in a separate volume. It refers the researcher to the paragraph number(s) of the service where the topics of interest are discussed. A researcher who knows which Code section addresses the issue (e.g., Sec. 280A) can go immediately to whichever volume provides commentary on that section.

For each Code section, the *United States Tax Reporter* service reproduces verbatim the statutory language and the regulations, provides an editorial explanation of the provisions, and furnishes brief summaries of cases and rulings interpreting the Code section. It provides citations to the full text of each case or ruling. The summaries are categorized into fairly explicit topical areas, such as the deductibility as a medical expense of the cost of special food and beverages and food supplements.

The *United States Tax Reporter* service is updated weekly; the most recent developments are highlighted in Volume 16 in a cross-reference table and regularly moved into the body of the text. The cross-reference table is organized by paragraph number. To determine whether any recent developments affect your question, look in the table for entries for the paragraph number where you found helpful information in the main body of the service. Because of the need to consult the cross-reference table, it is helpful to take note as you go along of the paragraph numbers that proved fruitful in your research process. The supplementary index in the Index Volume (Volume 1) of the service is updated monthly to reflect recent developments. Supplementary tables of cases and rulings in the Tables Volume (Volume 2) provide information on new authorities that have been incorporated into the main body of the service.

REAL WORLD EXAMPLE

The 1913 CCH explanation of the federal tax law was a single 400 page volume. The 1997 *Standard Federal Tax Reporter* is 22 volumes and 40,800 pages in length.

STANDARD FEDERAL TAX REPORTER

Commerce Clearing House (CCH) publishes the *Standard Federal Tax Reporter* (referred to in this text as the CCH service). This service is also organized by Code section. Separate services devoted to excise taxes and estate and gift taxes are available, as well as the multivolume income tax service. The CCH service reproduces the statute and the regulations for each Code section and summarizes and provides citations to other authorities in much the same way as the *United States Tax Reporter* service does.[42]

[42] Citations for the two primary tax services are not often used. If one wanted to cite these services, it might be as follows: (1997) 6 *United States Tax Reporter* (RIA) ¶3,025 and (1997) 8 *Std. Fed. Tax Rep.* (CCH) ¶22,609.01, where 6 and 8 are the volume numbers and the paragraph numbers refer to the cited portion of the volume.

An index volume contains a topical index that lists references by paragraph number. Because the volumes are organized by Code section number, a researcher who knows the number of the relevant Code section can bypass the index.

The approach for looking for any recent authorities on an issue is similar to the *United States Tax Reporter* service. Consult the Cumulative Index table in Volume 16 and search for entries applicable to the paragraph numbers in the main body of the service where you found relevant authorities. The CCH service publishes supplements with current developments weekly. Updates for court cases and revenue rulings are retained in Volume 16 until the end of the calendar year, when an entire new service is published. Major events such as new legislation and Supreme Court decisions are integrated into the service text throughout the year.

FEDERAL TAX COORDINATOR 2d

The *Federal Tax Coordinator 2d* is published by the Research Institute of America (RIA) and is referred to here as the *RIA* service. It covers all three areas of tax law: income tax analysis, estate and gift tax analysis, and excise tax analysis. The RIA income tax service is a multi-volume looseleaf publication organized by fairly broad topics. For example, Volume K explores the tax law with respect to the following deductions: taxes, interest, charitable contributions, medical, and other. The topical index, contained in a separate volume, refers to the chapter and paragraph numbers where the matters of interest are discussed. Another volume furnishes a finding table of where the various Code sections and regulations are discussed and where they are reproduced in the commentary volumes.

ADDITIONAL COMMENT

The RIA *Federal Tax Coordinator 2d* service is a larger service than either the *United States Tax Reporter* or *Standard Federal Tax Reporter* services because it has more editorial commentary. The *Federal Tax Coordinator 2d* updates are integrated into the main body of the text. The service is not replaced each year. In contrast, both the *United States Tax Reporter* and *Standard Federal Tax Reporter* services put their updates in one volume. CCH issues a new *Standard Federal Tax Reporter* service each year. The other services integrate the updates into the body of the existing service at the beginning of each year.

The RIA service reproduces all of the Code sections and regulations applicable to a particular volume behind a tab marker titled "Code & Regs." Using detailed captions, the various volumes provide an editorial-type commentary about the tax results. References to cases, including citations, appear in footnote form. The RIA service does not compile in a single volume information about new developments for all topics. Although, each volume has a tab marker titled "Developments," current developments for that volume are now included in the main body of the service. Originally, however, they appeared behind the "Developments" tab. Separate volumes are devoted to proposed regulations and revenue rulings and procedures. The RIA service publishes current developments weekly.

LAW OF FEDERAL INCOME TAXATION (MERTENS)

The *Law of Federal Income Taxation,* published by Clark Boardman & Callaghan, was originally edited by Jacob Mertens and is usually called Mertens by tax practitioners. Mertens is generally deemed to be the most authoritative tax service. It is the service most frequently cited by the courts and, in fact, the only service cited by the judiciary with any regularity. Like the RIA *Federal Tax Coordinator 2d* service, Mertens is organized by general topical area. Volume 7, for example, provides a comprehensive discussion of wages, travel, interest, taxes, and net operating losses. The commentary is in narrative form and reads like an article. References to the authorities appear in footnotes.

ADDITIONAL COMMENT

Mertens is reputed to be the most scholarly tax service. For this reason, it is the only service cited by the judiciary with any regularity.

One volume is devoted to a topical index. References are to section numbers (assigned by Mertens) instead of to paragraph numbers. Another volume, titled *Tables,* discloses where Code sections, regulations, and rulings are discussed in the commentary volumes. The *Table of Cases* volume does the same with respect to cases.

Mertens is updated monthly to reflect current developments. Like the RIA *Federal Tax Coordinator 2d* service, the supplementary material for a particular volume is filed in that volume. The new material is organized by Mertens' section numbers and is reported under the section number assigned to the topic in question in the main body of the service. The volume titled *Highlights* contains in-depth articles on current developments as well as monthly updates that complement the supplementary material included in the treatise volumes.

Mertens devotes separate volumes to reproducing the Code and the regulations, and these items do not appear in the commentary volumes. A special feature of Mertens is its *Rulings Volume,* which contains a Code-Rulings Table organized by Code section number. The table lists the numbers of all of the revenue rulings that have been issued after 1953 with respect to a particular Code section. For example, for the period 1954 through 1994, the table lists one ruling interpreting Sec. 1034(b)(1). The post-1994 table lists no further rulings interpreting Sec. 1034(b)(1).

Another part of the rulings volume consists of a Rulings Status Table. For all post-1953 revenue rulings, this table denotes any subsequent action taken concerning each ruling. Examples of actions the IRS could have taken include revoking, modifying, and superseding a ruling. The Research Institute of America and Commerce Clearing House citator volumes contain the same information, but in a different format.[43]

TAX MANAGEMENT PORTFOLIOS

KEY POINT

The *Tax Management Portfolios* are popular with many tax advisors because they are very readable yet still provide a comprehensive discussion of the pertinent tax issues. However, because the published portfolios do not cover all areas of the tax law, another service is necessary to supplement the gaps in the portfolio coverage.

The Bureau of National Affairs (BNA) publishes booklets of approximately 100 pages each called *Tax Management Portfolios* (referred to as BNA portfolios by many practitioners and in this text). Each portfolio provides an in-depth discussion of a relatively narrow issue, such as involuntary conversions or the estate tax marital deduction. Thus, when the research question has been narrowed down to a very precise issue, consultation of a BNA portfolio can be quite helpful.

BNA provides a notebook that contains a Code section index and a key words list or topical index. Each index references appropriate page numbers.

Each portfolio contains a narrative discussion called *Detailed Analysis* and a section called *Working Papers.* In the Detailed Analysis portion, citations to authorities appear in the footnotes. The Working Papers section often contains items such as excerpts from committee reports, copies of tax forms applicable to the matter under discussion, and sample language for making a particular election. Each portfolio also has a bibliography and a list of references where relevant articles are listed and revenue rulings and letter rulings on the topic are summarized.

BNA portfolios are updated a few times a year with sheets filed in the front of the applicable booklet. The current developments material is organized according to the page number of the Detailed Analysis that it supplements. From time to time, a portfolio may be revised or a new portfolio published to reflect major changes in the law.

CCH FEDERAL TAX SERVICE

ADDITIONAL COMMENT

The *CCH Federal Tax Service* is the newest of the major tax services.

The newest of the major tax services is the *CCH Federal Tax Service,* which is published by Commerce Clearing House and was formerly published by Matthew Bender & Company. This service is a multi-volume looseleaf publication that, like the RIA *Federal Tax Coordinator 2d* and Mertens services, is organized by fairly broad topics. An analysis is provided of broad topical areas such as individuals, partnerships, sales and exchanges, and farming and natural resources.

The *CCH Federal Tax Service* does not reproduce the Code and Treasury Regulations in the volumes with the topical commentary or analysis. Instead, it devotes separate volumes to the Internal Revenue Code and proposed, temporary, and final Treasury Regulations. A Code section and the related Treasury Regulations appear together in the same volume.

The *CCH Federal Tax Service* is updated twice a month to reflect current develop-

[43] Citators are described elsewhere in this chapter.

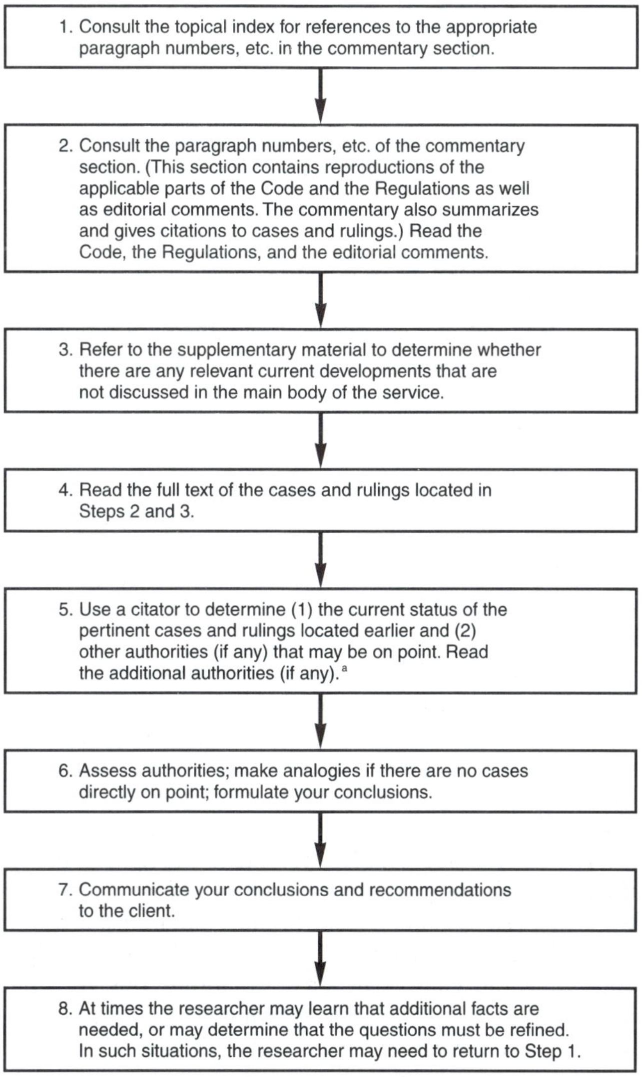

[a] Citators are described and discussed elsewhere in this chapter.

FIGURE C1-5 ▶ USE OF TAX SERVICES TO RESEARCH A TAX QUESTION

ments. In addition, a weekly newsletter is sent to subscribers. The current developments material is combined with the analysis to which it relates.

Figure C1-5 provides an overview of one approach for using the tax services to research a tax question.

CITATORS

OBJECTIVE 5

Use the citator to assess authorities

Citators serve two functions: they give a history of the case (i.e., if the case in question is an appeals court decision, the citator lists the trial court decision and the Supreme Court decision, if any, for the case); and they list the other authorities (i.e., cases and revenue rulings) that have cited the case in question. A citator of judicial decisions is included with the Commerce Clearing House tax service at no additional charge. The RIA citator is available separately from either of its basic tax services.

COMMERCE CLEARING HOUSE CITATOR

The Commerce Clearing House Citator (herein referred to as the CCH citator) consists of two loose-leaf volumes, one for cases with names beginning with the letters A through L and the other for cases with names starting with the letters M through Z, revenue rulings, and other government promulgations. This citator lists all cases reported in CCH's *Standard Federal Tax Reporter;* citations are also provided for cases in its *Excise Tax Reporter* and its *Federal Estate and Gift Tax Reporter.* Citing cases that comment on or add information relevant to a reported decision are determined by CCH editors and therefore reported on a selective basis. In the case of rulings and other government promulgations, the Finding Lists section provides full histories of all actions affected by or affecting each ruling. For example, the publication notes that a certain 1993 revenue ruling revokes a certain 1989 revenue ruling. A sample page from the CCH citator appears in Figure C1-6.

KEY POINT

Citators are useful in obtaining the history of a tax case and finding additional cases and rulings that have cited the particular case in question.

Refer to Figure C1-6 and find the *Leonarda C. Diaz* case. The information in bold print with bullets to the left denotes that *Diaz* was a decision of the Second Circuit and the Tax Court and that the Second Circuit affirmed (upheld) the Tax Court's decision. The two cases listed beneath the Second Circuit decision (i.e., *Kuh* and *Damm*) cited the *Diaz* decision. The six cases listed beneath the Tax Court decision (i.e., *German, Jr., Orr, Zeidler, Schwerm, Wassenaar,* and *Toner*) cited the Tax Court's opinion in *Diaz.* The abbreviation *Dec.* appearing in some of the citations stands for *decision.* CCH lists the decision numbers of the Tax Court cases.

The basic CCH citator is published once a year. The first volume contains an update section, titled "Current Citator Table," which shows listings for new court decisions and additional citations of earlier court decisions; updates supplement the Citator on a quarterly basis. The *Diaz* decision has not been cited by any additional decisions since the CCH citator was last published in late 1996. The appropriate page for *Diaz* in the Current Citator Table is not reproduced here.

The entry "¶5504.195" appearing to the right of the Alfonso Diaz case name denotes the paragraph number of the *Standard Federal Tax Reporter* (the CCH service) at which the *Diaz* case is summarized. In most situations, a researcher would have already read about this case in the tax service and decided it was helpful for the research issue before consulting the citator. In such situations, this paragraph reference is not necessary because the citator is used to determine whether there are other relevant cases. At other times, the reference to the paragraph in the CCH tax service summarizing the case in question can be helpful. For example, if a researcher learned about the case from a colleague and wants to read in the tax service about the general topical area of the case, the discussion of the case can be easily located.

Cases are included in the CCH citator even though they have not been cited by a later case. This point is illustrated by the entry for *Frank Diaz,* a Tax Court memo decision for which no subsequent case citations are listed. The citator also indicates whether the Commissioner has acquiesced or nonacquiesced to Tax Court decisions. For example, if you refer to the entry for *Alfonso Diaz* in Figure C1-6, you will note that the capital "A" following the Tax Court citation shows that the Commissioner's acquiescence is reported on page 2 of Volume 2 of the 1972 *Cumulative Bulletin.*

RESEARCH INSTITUTE OF AMERICA CITATOR 2ND SERIES

Like the CCH citator, the *Research Institute of America Citator 2nd Series*[44] (referred to here as the RIA citator) gives the history of each case and ruling and lists the cases and

[44] The *Research Institute of America Citator 2nd Series* is published currently by Research Institute of America, Inc. It was originally published by Prentice Hall's Information Services Division, which was acquired in 1990 by Maxwell Macmillan. *Prentice Hall* and/or *Maxwell Macmillan* appears on the spines and title pages of the older citators and will remain there because, unlike the CCH citator, the RIA citator is not republished each year.

———CCH——— **93,223** **DIB**

Diamond Red Paint Co.—continued
Halters Co., BTA, Dec. 5124, 16 BTA 325
Fidelity Trust Co., BTA, Dec. 4285, 13 BTA 109
Diamond Shoe Co. ..... (Expired Excess Profits Tax)
● **SCt**—Cert. denied, 282 US 859; 51 SCt 34
● **CA-2**—(aff'g BTA), 5 USTC ¶ 1392; 42 F2d 144
● **BTA**—Dec. 5272; 16 BTA 1069
● **BTA**—Dec. 4939; 15 BTA 826
Diamond, Sol . ¶ 5508.085, 8470.517, 25,383.2683, 25,543.016, 25,543.08, 25,742.023
● **CA-7**—(aff'g TC), 74-1 USTC ¶ 9306; 492 F2d 286
Campbell, CA-8, 91-2 USTC ¶ 50,420
Rev. Proc. 93-27
Anderson, TC, Dec. 50,410(M), 69 TCM 1609, TC Memo. 1995-8
Banks, TC, Dec. 47,832(M), 62 TCM 1611, TC Memo. 1991-641
Pacheco, CA-9, 90-2 USTC ¶ 50,458
Vestal, CA-8, 74-2 USTC ¶ 9501, 498 F2d 487
St. John, DC-Ill, 84-1 USTC ¶ 9158
Campbell, TC, Dec. 46,493(M), 59 TCM 236, TC Memo. 1990-162
McNulty, TC, Dec. 44,857(M), 55 TCM 1138, TC Memo. 1988-274
Greater Display & Wire Forming, Inc., TC, Dec. 44,802(M), 55 TCM 922, TC Memo. 1988-231
National Oil Co., TC, Dec. 43,557(M), 52 TCM 1223, TC Memo. 1986-596
Hirst, TC, Dec. 43,215(M), 51 TCM 1597, TC Memo. 1986-321
Mouriz, TC, Dec. 42,851(M), 51 TCM 392, TC Memo. 1986-43
Parker, TC, Dec. 42,129(M), 50 TCM 14, TC Memo. 1985-263
Kenroy, Inc., TC, Dec. 41,186(M), 47 TCM 1749, TC Memo. 1984-232
Bertolini Trucking Co., TC, Dec. 39,474(M), 45 TCM 44, TC Memo. 1982-643
Kessler, TC, Dec. 39,226(M), 44 TCM 624, TC Memo. 1982-432
Tooke, TC, Dec. 34,336(M), 36 TCM 396, TC Memo. 1977-91
Pierson, TC, Dec. 34,009(M), 35 TCM 1256, TC Memo. 1976-281
● **TC**—Dec. 30,838; 56 TC 530
Manchester Music Co., Inc., DC-NH, 90-1 USTC ¶ 50,168, 733 FSupp 473
Miller, Jr., TC, Dec. 45,977(M), 57 TCM 1419, TC Memo. 1989-461
McNulty, TC, Dec. 44,857(M), 55 TCM 1138, TC Memo. 1988-274
Greater Display & Wire Forming, Inc., TC, Dec. 44,802(M), 55 TCM 922, TC Memo. 1988-231
National Oil Co., TC, Dec. 43,557(M), 52 TCM 1223, TC Memo. 1986-596
Goodwin, David C., TC, Dec. 36,413, 73 TC 215
Schaevitz, TC, Dec. 30,925(M), 30 TCM 823, TC Memo. 1971-197
Diamond, Solomon
● **TC**—Dec. 25,981(M); 22 TCM 229; TC Memo. 1963-57
Diamond T Motor Car Co.: Allen v. ..... ¶ 39,060.82
● **CA-10**—(rev'g DC), 61-1 USTC ¶ 9484; 291 F2d 115
Randall, CA-5, 76-2 USTC ¶ 9770, 542 F2d 270
Jefferson Bank and Trust, DC-Colo, 89-1 USTC ¶ 9221
Rodkey, DC-Okla, 87-1 USTC ¶ 9218
Nevada Rock & Sand Co., DC-Nev, 74-2 USTC ¶ 9617, 376 FSupp 161
Nomellini Construction Co., DC-Calif, 71-2 USTC ¶ 9510, 328 FSupp 1281
● **DC-Colo**—60-2 USTC ¶ 9557
Diamondhead Corp. v. Fort Hope Development, Inc. .... ¶ 41,520.1945
● **DC-Ga**—78-2 USTC ¶ 9718
Diamondstone, I. A. (See Kann, William L.)
DiAndre, Anthony F. ...... ¶ 37,894.7255, 42,358.30
● **SCt**—Cert. denied, 3/19/93
● **CA-10**—(rev'g and rem'g unreported DC), 92-2 USTC ¶ 50,373; 968 F2d 1049
Stewart, DC-Ohio, 95-1 USTC ¶ 50,249
Russell, DC-Mich, 95-1 USTC ¶ 50,029
Jones, DC-Neb, 94-2 USTC ¶ 50,562, 869 FSupp 747
Schachter, DC-Calif, 94-1 USTC ¶ 50,242
Fostvedt, DC-Colo, 93-1 USTC ¶ 50,299, 824 FSupp 978
Jones, DC-Neb, 95-2 USTC ¶ 50,567, 898 FSupp 1360
May, DC-Mo, 95-2 USTC ¶ 50,605
DiAndrea, Inc. .. ¶ 16,233.25, 21,817.108, 45,257.09
● **TC**—Dec. 40,697(M); 47 TCM 731; TC Memo. 1983-768

DiAndrea, Inc.—continued
Johnson, TC, Dec. 47,836(M), 62 TCM 1629, TC Memo. 1991-645
Diaz, Alfonso .... ¶ 5504.195
● **TC**—Dec. 31,442; 58 TC 560; A. 1972-2 CB 2
Marrone, TC, Dec. 50,424(M), 69 TCM 1684, TC Memo. 1995-22
Sloan, TC, Dec. 50,305(M), 68 TCM 1489, TC Memo. 1994-628
Muniz, TC, Dec. 49,775(M), 67 TCM 2625, TC Memo. 1994-151
Drabiuk, TC, Dec. 50,692(M), 69 TCM 2890, TC Memo. 1995-260
Jackson, TC, Dec. 50,736(M), TC Memo. 1995-300, 70 TCM 12
Levin, TC, Dec. 51,326(M), 71 TCM 2938, TC Memo. 1996-211
Kong, TC, Dec. 46,090(M), 58 TCM 378, TC Memo. 1989-560
Caglia, E. Bonnie, TC, Dec. 45,585(M), 57 TCM 1, TC Memo. 1989-143
Ettig, TC, Dec. 44,736(M), 55 TCM 720, TC Memo. 1988-182
Heller, TC, Dec. 44,083(M), 53 TCM 1486, TC Memo. 1987-376
Anastasato, TC, Dec. 43,309(M), 52 TCM 293, TC Memo. 1986-400
Stevenson, TC, Dec. 43,068(M), 51 TCM 1050, TC Memo. 1986-207
Wilhelm, TC, Dec. 42,813(M), 51 TCM 261, TC Memo. 1986-12
Branson, TC, Dec. 38,026(M), 42 TCM 281, TC Memo. 1981-338
Calloway, TC, Dec. 37,019(M), 40 TCM 495, TC Memo. 1980-211
Greenfield, TC, Dec. 35,253(M), 37 TCM 1082, TC Memo. 1978-251
Leong, TC, Dec. 34,232(M), 36 TCM 89, TC Memo. 1977-19
Dougherty, TC, Dec. 32,138, 60 TC 917
Diaz, Antonio A. v. Southern Drilling Corp. .... ¶ 42,299.45
● **CA-5**—(aff'g unreported DC), 71-1 USTC ¶ 9236
Diaz, Enrique .. ¶ 35,038.43, 40,375.65, 40,485.63, 42,288.377
● **DC-Calif**—90-1 USTC ¶ 50,209
Van Camp & Bennion, P.S., DC-Wash, 96-2 USTC ¶ 50,438
Diaz, Frank .... ¶ 29,762.9911
● **TC**—Dec. 42,922(M); 51 TCM 594; TC Memo. 1986-98
Diaz, Humberto (See Flicker, Marvin)
Diaz, Juan (See Setal, Manuel G.)
Diaz, Leonarda C.
● **CA-2**—(aff'g TC), 79-2 USTC ¶ 9473; 607 F2d 995
Kuh, TC, Dec. 40,461(M), 46 TCM 1405, TC Memo. 1983-572
Damm, TC, Dec. 37,861(M), 41 TCM 1359, TC Memo. 1981-203
● **TC**—Dec. 35,436; 70 TC 1067
German, Jr., TC, Dec. 48,867(M), 65 TCM 1931, TC Memo. 1993-59
Orr, TC, Dec. 48,532(M), 64 TCM 882, TC Memo. 1992-566
Zeidler, TC, Dec. 51,264(M), 71 TCM 2603, TC Memo. 1996-157
Schwerm, TC, Dec. 42,817(M), 51 TCM 270, TC Memo. 1986-16
Wassenaar, TC, Dec. 36,359, 72 TC 1195
Toner, TC, Dec. 35,877, 71 TC 772
Diaz, Miguel A. (See Powers (Belcher), Sandra L.)
Dibble, Leon N., Exr. .... ¶ 29,625.442
● **BTA**—Dec. 2320; 6 BTA 732; A. VI-2 CB 2
Dibble, Phillip A. .... ¶ 25,424.415
● **TC**—Dec. 41,602(M); 49 TCM 32; TC Memo. 1984-589
Ogden, CA-5, 86-1 USTC ¶ 9368, 788 F2d 252
Elrod, TC, Dec. 43,486, 87 TC 1046
Dibblee, Isabel K. .... ¶ 32,263.381, 44,840.04
● **SCt**—(rev'g CA-9), 36-1 USTC ¶ 9008; 296 US 102; 56 SCt 54
● **CA-9**—(aff'g BTA), 35-1 USTC ¶ 9128; 75 F2d 617
● **BTA**—Dec. 8415; 29 BTA 1070
Di Benedetto, Frank R. .... ¶ 40,580.43
● **DC-RI**—75-1 USTC ¶ 9503
Carlucci, DC-NY, 93-1 USTC ¶ 50,211, 793 FSupp 482
Cook, DC-Pa, 91-1 USTC ¶ 50,284, 765 FSupp 217
Seachrist v. Riggs, DC-Va, 91-1 USTC ¶ 50,019
Continental Illinois Nat'l Bk. and Trust Co., Chicago, DC-Ill, 87-2 USTC ¶ 9442
Swift, DC-Conn, 86-1 USTC ¶ 9109, 614 FSupp 172
Rebelle, DC-La, 85-2 USTC ¶ 9493
Rebelle, III, DC-La, 84-2 USTC ¶ 9717, 588 FSupp 49

FIGURE C1-6 ▶ EXCERPT FROM COMMERCE CLEARING HOUSE CITATOR

rulings that have cited the authority in question. The RIA citator, however, conveys more extensive information than the CCH citator. Specifically, the citator includes information about the following:

1. Cases that have referenced the case in question, including whether the citing cases commented in a favorable or unfavorable manner or distinguished the cited cases.[45]
2. The specific issue in the case in question (the cited case) for which the citing authorities have referenced the case.

KEY POINT

The history of a case may be easier to find in CCH because each of the courts that tried the case is listed in a single volume in **boldface print**. For example, see the *Isabel K. Dibblee* case from the CCH citator reproduced here.

The RIA (formerly Prentice Hall) Citator consists of five hard-bound volumes plus softback cumulative supplements. The first hard-bound volume denotes citations made to cases during the period 1863 through 1941; the second volume contains citations made from 1942 through September 30, 1948; the third volume gives citations made from October 1, 1948 through July 29, 1954; the fourth volume contains citations made from July 30, 1954 through December 15, 1977; the fifth volume lists citations made from December 15, 1977 through December 20, 1989. The softback cumulative supplements contain citations made after December 20, 1989. Each year a revised cumulative supplement is prepared. In addition, monthly supplements are issued. A researcher interested in determining how the courts have subsequently evaluated a 1945 case should consult all volumes of the citator except the first. If the case in question is a 1980 case, the researcher need consult only the most recent bound volume plus the supplements.

As mentioned, the RIA citator discloses how the citing cases commented on the case in question. The nature of the comment is denoted by letters that appear to the left of the name of the citing case. Letters are also used to denote the history of the cited case (i.e., whether it was affirmed, etc.).[46] Figure C1-7 indicates what the various abbreviations symbolize.

The RIA citator is especially helpful if the cited case deals with more than one issue. As mentioned, the citator reports the issue(s) for which the case was cited. The numbers to the left of the citing authority denote the issue number of the cited case for which the citation is made. The number designation is not universally associated with a particular topic. Instead, the issue number refers to the number used to designate a particular issue in the cited case. Issue numbers appear in the headnotes to the case (at the top of the first page of the case). To save time, researchers should take note of the applicable issue number when reading cases.

Part of a sample page from the 1977–1989 citator appears in Figure C1-8. Refer to Figure C1-8 and locate the Tax Court decision for *Leonarda C. Diaz*. All of the cases citing the Tax Court's *Diaz* decision after 1977 and through 1989 are listed. (*Diaz* was decided by the Tax Court in 1978, so no earlier references will be found.) *Diaz* has been cited with respect to both the first and second issues in the case. If the case was concerned with additional issues, it has not been cited for them.

The "a" on the first line beneath the name of the case indicates that the Tax Court's decision was affirmed by the Second Circuit. The Tax Court's opinion has been explained and followed in various cases, but it has not been cited in an unfavorable manner. Thus, its authoritative value is strong.

The Second Circuit's decision appears as a separate entry. The letters "sa" signify that the circuit court affirmed the Tax Court decision in the *Diaz* case. The cases that have

[45] When a court distinguishes its conclusion in one case from an earlier decision, it points out that the two different outcomes are justifiable because the facts in the two cases are not the same.

[46] If a case is *affirmed*, the decision of the lower court is upheld. *Reversed* means that the higher court arrived at the opposite decision of the court from which the case was appealed. *Remanded* signifies that the higher court sent the case back to the lower court with instructions to address certain matters not earlier addressed.

a	affirmed by a higher court (Note: When available, the official cite to the affirmance is provided; if the affirmance is by unpublished order or opinion, the date of the decision and the court deciding the case are provided.)
App auth	appeal authorized by the Treasury
App	appeal pending (Note: Later volumes may have to be consulted to determine if the appellate case was decided.)
cert gr	petition for certiorari was granted by the U.S. Supreme Court
d	appeal dismissed by the court or withdrawn by the party filing the appeal
(G)	following an appeal notation, this symbol indicates that it was the government filing an appeal.
m	the earlier decision has been modified by the higher court, or by a later decision.
r	the decision of the lower court has been reversed on appeal
rc	related case arising out of the same taxable event or concerning the same taxpayer.
reh den	rehearing has been denied by the same court in which the original case was heard.
reinst	a dismissed appeal has been reinstated by the appellate court and is under consideration again.
remd	the case has been remanded for proceedings consistent with the higher court decision.
remg	the cited case is remanding the earlier case
revg & remg	the decision of the lower court has been reversed and remanded by a higher court on appeal
s	same case or ruling
sa	the cited case is affirming the earlier case
sm	the cited case is modifying the earlier case
sr	the cited case is reversing the earlier case
sx	the cited case is an earlier proceeding in a case for which a petition for certiorari was denied
(T)	an appeal was filed from the lower court decision by the taxpayer
vacd	the lower court decision was vacated on appeal or by the original court on remand.
vacg	a higher court or the original court on remand has vacated the lower court decision
widrn	the original opinion was withdrawn by the court
x	petition for certiorari was denied by the U.S. Supreme Court
●	Supreme Court cases are designated by a bold-faced bullet (●) before the case line for easy location.

Certain notations appear at the end of the cited case line. These notations include:

Notation	Meaning
(A)	the government has acquiesced in the reasoning or the result of the cited case
(NA)	the government has refused to acquiesce or to adopt the reasoning or the result of the cited case, and will challenge the position adopted if future proceedings arise on the same issue
on rem	the case has been remanded by a higher court and the case cited is the resulting decision

Evaluation of Cited Cases

c	the citing case court has adversely commented on the reasoning of the cited case, and has criticized the earlier decision.
e	the cited case is used favorably by the citing case court
f	the reasoning of the court in the cited case is followed by the later decision
g	the cited and citing cases are distinguished from each other on either facts or law
inap	the citing case court has specifically indicated that the cited case does not apply to the situation stated in the citing case.
iv	on all fours (both the cited and citing cases are virtually identical)
k	the cited and citing case principles are reconciled
l	the rationale of the cited case is limited to the facts or circumstances surrounding that case (this can occur frequently in situations in which there has been an intervening higher court decision or law change)
n	the cited case was noted in a dissenting opinion
o	the later case directly overrules the cited case (use of the evaluation is generally limited to situations in which the court notes that it is specifically overturning the cited case, and that the case will no longer be of any value)
q	the decision of the cited case is questioned and its validity debated in relation to the citing case at issue

The evaluations used for the court decisions generally are followed by a number. That number refers to the headnoted issue in the American Federal Tax Reports (AFTR) or Tax Court decision to which the citing case relates. If the case is not directly on point with any headnote, a bracketed notation at the end of the citing case line directs the researcher to the page in the cited case on which the issue appears.

FIGURE C1-7 ▶ ABBREVIATIONS USED IN RIA CITATOR 2ND SERIES

Source: Reproduced with permission from Research Institute of America, Inc.

cited the circuit court's opinion are listed under the entry for such opinion. The appellate decision has not been questioned or criticized; thus, it is a relatively strong decision.

Recall that for the *Alfonso Diaz* case, the CCH Citator reported that in 1972 the Commissioner acquiesced to the decision. Because the page from the 1978–1989 PH *Federal Taxes 2nd* Citator reproduced in Figure C1-8 includes developments from December 15, 1977 through December 20, 1989, it does not report the 1972 acquiescence. The bound citator for 1954–1977 reports the 1972 acquiescence. In order to locate the most recent references to the *Leonarda C. Diaz* case, one would need to refer to the cumulative supplements. The appropriate excerpts from the 1990–1995 cumulative supplement is illustrated here and indicates one subsequent case that cites the Second Circuit's *Leonarda C. Diaz* decision and seven that cite the Tax Court decision.[47]

1990–1995 Cumulative Supplement	*January–November 1996 Cumulative Supplement*

DIAZ, LEONARDA C., 70 TC 1067, ¶ 70.95 PH TC
a—Diaz, Leonarda C. V Comm., 44 AFTR 2d 79-6027, (CA2)
f—Wiertzema, Vance v U.S., 66 AFTR 2d 90-5371, 747 F Supp 1365, (DC ND), [See 70 TC 1074-1075]
e—Barboza, David, 1991 TC Memo 91-1905, [See 70 TC 1074]
e—Orr, J. Thomas, 1992 RIA TC Memo 92-2912, [See 70 TC 1073]
e—German, Harry, Jr. & Carol, 1993 RIA TC Memo 93-261-93-262, [See 70 TC 1074-1075]
e—Meredith, Judith R., 1993 RIA TC Memo 93-1247, [See 70 TC 1074, cited at 73 TC 726]
e—Holmes, Lynn J., 1993 RIA TC Memo 93-1978, [See 70 TC 1072-1073]
e—Kersey, Robert C., 1993 RIA TC Memo 93-3396, [See 70 TC 1072-1073]
DIAZ, LEONARDA C. v COMM., 44 AFTR 2d 79-6027, 607 F2d 995, (CA2, 6-25-79)
e—Wiertzema, Vance v U.S., 66 AFTR 2d 90-5371, 747 F Supp 1363, (DC ND)

One additional case is shown in the January 1996–November 1996 Cumulative Supplement volumes as citing each of the *Leonarda C. Diaz* decisions.

COMPUTERS AS A RESEARCH TOOL

KEY POINT

The use of computers in tax research is clearly increasing. With the technological advances in computer hardware and software, large data bases are becoming more accessible and less costly. In the coming years, computer-assisted tax research will become an even more important tool for the tax advisor.

CD-ROM AND ONLINE RESEARCH

Computers are now being used by most tax professionals as a tax research tool. Three computer-based legal data bases for taxation are now available. These data bases cover federal and state tax matters as well as other federal and state legal matters. The names of the services and their providers are indicated below.

Name of Data Base	*Provider*
ACCESS	Commerce Clearing House
LEXIS	Mead Data Central
WESTLAW	West Publishing

Each of the above tax data bases includes the basic tax research sources: Code, regulations, government promulgations, private letter rulings, legislative histories, committee reports, treaties, and judicial decisions. In addition, the computerized tax data bases contain a number of tax services. For example, WESTLAW contains the index and

[47] No additional references have been reported as of January 17, 1997.

ADDITIONAL COMMENT

The RIA citator has the advantage of providing the most citations for a given case. This is obvious when one compares RIA's five volumes plus supplements with CCH's two volumes. Also, RIA numbers each tax issue litigated in a court case. This coding allows the tax advisor to identify cases dealing specifically with the issue being researched. For example, if one is interested in the 2nd issue in the *Leonarda Diaz* Tax Court decision, the citator reproduced in Figure C1-8 denotes five cases that deal specifically with issue 1 of which three follow the *Diaz* reasoning.

DIAZ, LEONARDA C. v COMM., 44 AFTR 2d 79-6027, 607 F2d 995, (CA2, 6-25-79)
e—Zeidler, Gerald L. & Joy M., 1996 RIA TC Memo 96-1151
DiBENEDETTO, FRANK R. v U.S., 35 AFTR 2d 75-1502, 75-1 USTC ¶ 9503, (DC RI, 11-7-74)
e-1—Padalino, Vincent v. U.S., 71A AFTR 2d 93-3016, (DC NJ)
DIBERT, BANCROFT & ROSS CO, LTD, IN RE, 77 AFTR 2d 96-1152, (DC LA, 2/12/96)
sa—Marrero, Robert L., Trustee v. Central Progressive Bank, et al, 74 AFTR 2d 94-6470, (Bktcy Ct LA)
DICARLO, STEPHEN ALAN, 1992 RIA TC Memo ¶ 92,280
e—Lisle, Helen v. U.S., 76 AFTR 2d 95-7886, (DC CA), [See 1992 RIA TC Memo 92-1385]
e—Talmage, Stephen V., 1996 RIA TC Memo 96-875, [See 1992 RIA TC Memo 92-1387]
DICKENS, JACK v U.S., 49 AFTR 2d 82-1238, 671 F2d 969, 82-1 USTC ¶ 16,377, (CA6, 3-1-82)
e—Houch, Buford F. v. U.S., 77 AFTR 2d 96-1947, (DC OH), [See 49 AFTR2d 82-1239, 671 F2d 971]
e—Kruzel, Dennis A. v. I.R.S., et al, 77 AFTR 2d 96-1978, (DC MI), [See 49 AFTR2d 82-1239, 671 F2d 971-972]
DICKERSON, M. ASHLEY, 1990 PH TC Memo ¶ 90,577
e-1—Bauman, Carl J. D. & Margaret A., 1996 RIA TC Memo 96-1595
DICKEY, RAYMOND L., 1985 PH TC Memo ¶ 85,478
e—Barnhill, Joseph L., Jr. & Cynthia A., 1996 RIA TC Memo 96-778, [See 1985 PH TC Memo 85-2145]
DICKEY, WILLIAM L., IN RE, 57 AFTR 2d 86-1101, 86-1 USTC ¶ 9424, (Bktcy Ct VA, 4-30-85)
k-1—Curasi, James B. v. U.S., 76 AFTR 2d 95-6407, 907 F Supp 378, (DC FL)
•DICKMAN, ESTHER C. v COMM., 53 AFTR 2d 84-1608, 465 US 330, 104 S Ct 1086, 79 L Ed 343, 84-1 USTC ¶ 9240, (2-22-84), [re]reh den, 466 US 945, 104 S Ct 1932, 80 LEd2d 477, 4-16-84
e—White, Clayton S. v. U.S., 71A AFTR 2d 93-3123, 93-3124, (DC NM), [See 53 AFTR2d 84-1612, 465 US 343]
e—Indianapolis Life Insurance Co v. U.S., 78 AFTR 2d 96-6150, (DC IN), [See 53 AFTR2d 84-1613—84-1614, 465 US 343]
f—Bankers Trust New York Corp & Consolidated Subsidi aries v. U.S., 78 AFTR 2d 95-5104, 36 Fed Cl 36, (Ct Fed Cl), [See 53 AFTR2d 84-1612, 465 US 343]
e—McLendon, Gordon B., Est of, 1996 RIA TC Memo 96-2223, [See 53 AFTR2d 84-1612, 465 US 343]
g-1—Miller, Elizabeth B., 1996 RIA TC Memo 96-19
DICKSON, ROBERT W. & JEANNE K., 1983 PH TC Memo ¶ 83,723
g-1—Ballard, Charles A., 1996 RIA TC Memo 96-571
DIEBOLD, INC. v U.S., 65 AFTR 2d 90-648, 891 F2d 1579, 90-1 USTC ¶ 50,003, (CA Fed Cir, 12-19-89)
e—Piccadilly Cafeterias Inc v. U.S., 78 AFTR 2d 96-6189, 96-6190, 36 Fed Cl 335, 336, (Ct Fed Cl), [See 65 AFTR2d 90-651, 891 F2d 1583]
e-1—Girling Health Systems, Inc v. U.S., 71A AFTR 2d 93-3308, (Cl Ct)
DIECKMANN, RICHARD R. v U.S., 39 AFTR 2d 77-845, 550 F2d 622, 77-1 USTC ¶ 9224, (CA10, 2-18-77)
e—Berlanga, Cristofora v. U.S., 71A AFTR 2d 93-3202, (DC MI), [See 39 AFTR2d 77-846, 550 F2d 624]
e—Southtrust Bank of Etowah County, N.P. v. Cheerzportz, Inc, et al, 71A AFTR 2d 93-3291, (DC AL), [See 39 AFTR2d 77-846, 550 F2d 624]
e—Pederson, Roland v. U.S., 71A AFTR 2d 93-3503, (DC MT), [See 39 AFTR2d 77-846, 550 F2d 624]
e-1—Sanders, Marjorie v. U.S., 77 AFTR 2d 96-1842, (DC CO)
e-1—Compagnoni, Jacqueline M. v. U.S., 78 AFTR 2d 96-6503, (DC FL)
DIEGO INVESTORS-IV, 1989 PH TC Memo ¶ 89,630
rc—Fox, Johana C. v. U.S., 78 AFTR 2d 96-5725, (DC CA)
e—Bealor, Barry B. & Nancy L., 1996 RIA TC Memo 96-3101
DIEHL, THOMAS C., 1990 PH TC Memo ¶ 90,048
e-1—McKee, Wayne Curtis, 1996 RIA TC Memo 96-1061
e-1—Cowan, Ted, 1996 RIA TC Memo 96-1206
DIELECTRIC MATERIALS CO., 57 TC 587, ¶ 57.61 PH TC, (A), 1972-1 CB 2
e—Wy'East Color Inc, 1996 RIA TC Memo 96-1031, [See 57 TC 591]
DIEMER, JAMES D.; U.S. v., 76 AFTR 2d 95-7587, 859 F Supp 126, 94-2 USTC ¶ 50420, (DC NJ, 8/1/94)
revg & remg—Avila, Fred A., et al; U.S. v., 78 AFTR 2d 96-5189, 88 F3d 229, (CA3)
DIERCKS, KENNETH W., 1996 RIA TC Memo ¶ 96,345
DIESCHER, ALFRED J., 18 BTA 353
e—Mullings, Manley v. Com., 78 AFTR 2d 96-6111, (DC NY), [See 18 BTA 358]
DIETRICH INDUSTRIES, INC. v U.S., 71 AFTR 2d 93-1623, 988 F2d 568, (CA5, 4-16-93)
e-1—Progressive Consumers Federal Credit Union v. U.S., 77 AFTR 2d 96-1427, 79 F3d 1237, (CA1)
g-1—First Federal Savings Bank of Wabash v. U.S., 78 AFTR 2d 96-6064, (DC IN)
DIETRICK, GERALD PATRICK & ANITA LEA, 1988 PH TC Memo ¶ 88,180
e-1—Zand, J.J., 1996 RIA TC Memo 96-201
DIETRICK, GERALD PATRICK v COMM., 64 AFTR 2d 89-5353, 881 F2d 336, 89-2 USTC ¶ 9469, (CA6, 8-10-89)
e-1—Zand, J.J., 1996 RIA TC Memo 96-201
DIETZ, C. RAYMOND, SR.; U.S. v, 75 AFTR 2d 95-1613, (CA4, 3/28/95)
rc—Dietz, C. Raymond, Sr. v. U.S., 78 AFTR 2d 96-5500, (DC MD)
DIETZ, C. RAYMOND, SR. v. U.S., 78 AFTR 2d 96-5500, (DC MD, 6/7/96)
rc—Dietz, C. Raymond, Sr.; U.S. v., 75 AFTR 2d 95-1613, (CA4)
DIETZ, MYRTLE V., ESTATE OF, 1996 RIA TC Memo ¶ 96,471
DIETZ, R.E., CORP. v U.S., 68 AFTR 2d 91-5238, 939 F2d 1, 91-2 USTC ¶ 50,375, (CA2, 7-22-91)
e—Bausch & Lomb Inc & Consol. Subs., 1996 RIA TC Memo 96-487, [See 68 AFTR 2d 91-5241-91-5242, 939 F2d 5]
DIFFERENTIAL STEEL CAR CO., 16 TC 413, ¶ 16.52 PH TC 1951
e—Medieval Attractions N.V., 1996 RIA TC Memo 96-3318, [See 16 TC 423-425]
DIGBY, DONALD R. & LYDIA, 103 TC 441, ¶ 103.24 TCR
e—Ackerman, Robert W. & Patricia A., 1996 RIA TC Memo 96-2267, [See 103 TC 447]
DiLEO, JOSEPH R. & MARY A., 96 TC 858, ¶ 96.42 PH TC
e—Lee, Chong-Kak & Sang-Ok, 1995 RIA TC Memo 95-3814, 95-3815, [See 96 TC 874]
e—Wynn, Eric, 1995 RIA TC Memo 95-3883, 95-3884, [See 96 TC 873]
e—Marason, Keith F., 1996 RIA TC Memo 96-34, [See 96 TC 867]
e—Rouzmehr, Yousef, 1996 RIA TC Memo 96-217, [See 96 TC 867]
e—Sharer, Mary Lee, 1996 RIA TC Memo 96-747, [See 96 TC 867]
e—Eresian, Ara & Evelyn, 1996 RIA TC Memo 96-1371, [See 96 TC 867]
e—Kale, William, 1996 RIA TC Memo 96-1459, [See 96 TC 873]
e—M.S. Food Stores, Inc., 1996 RIA TC Memo 96-1612, [See 96 TC 867, 868]
e—Sparrow, Robert D., 1996 RIA TC Memo 96-1927, [See 96 TC 874]
e—Van Heemst, John, 1996 RIA TC Memo 96-2206, 96-2210, 96-2211, [See 96 TC 871, 873-874]
e—McGirl, Richard K. & Christine M., 1996 RIA TC Memo 96-2256, [See 96 TC 867, 868]
e—Katerelos, Haralampos & Irene, 1996 RIA TC Memo 96-2428, [See 96 TC 872]
e—Wagner, Edward A. & Barbara, 1996 RIA TC Memo 96-2542, [See 96 TC 873]
e—DeCaprio, Ferdinand & Claire, 1996 RIA TC Memo 96-2584, [See 96 TC 880]
e—Harp, Charles R. & April B., 1996 RIA TC Memo 96-2657, 96-2659, 96-2664, [See 96 TC 868, 869]
e—Meilak, Inez, 1996 RIA TC Memo 96-2672, [See 96 TC 874]

FIGURE C1-8 ▶ EXCERPT FROM PRENTICE HALL FEDERAL TAXES 2ND CITATOR, 1978–1989

Reproduced with permission from Research Institute of America, Inc.

text for BNA's *Tax Management Portfolios*. LEXIS includes the TAXRIA data base, which has the index and text for RIA's *United States Tax Reporter* service and the RIA citator along with many other materials including state and international tax services. LEXIS also includes the *RIA Federal Tax Coordinator 2d* and BNA's *Tax Management Portfolios*. The ACCESS data base includes the CCH service and citator, as well as the *U.S. Master Tax Guide*. ACCESS also includes court cases, letter rulings, state tax reports, and BNA's *Tax Management Portfolios*, among other items. Each of these data bases also contains the text for a number of tax newsletters and some data bases include the text of tax journals and law reviews.

Unlike the tax services, some computerized data bases do not contain an index. Rather, the researcher locates applicable authorities by using key-word search requests. That is, he or she instructs the computer to locate all of the authorities containing certain words or phrases. Researchers need to be imaginative in thinking of search requests; under the key-word approach the computer will not locate an authority on point unless it contains the exact wording the researcher specifies, even though it contains synonymous terms.

EXAMPLE C1-12 ▶ A researcher is interested in whether a certain expenditure for clothing is deductible under Sec. 162 as a uniform expense. The researcher might instruct the computer to retrieve all cases containing the words *uniform* and *Sec. 162* in close proximity to each other. This search will turn up only cases containing those words if the system uses the key-word approach. Cases using the words *work clothing* will not be retrieved. A more comprehensive search will take place if the researcher instructs the computer to look for either *uniform* or *work clothing* in close proximity of *Sec. 162.* ◀

Use of these data bases can be especially valuable as a supplement to the research conducted manually through the tax services. After researchers have located some authorities through the tax services, they can use the computerized data base to

WHAT WOULD YOU DO IN THIS SITUATION?

You are a new associate of the accounting firm of Smith, Wesson, and Swilley, P.C., of Yuma, Arizona. Your undergraduate specialty was behavioral accounting, where you were constantly on the lookout for misbehaving accountants. But as you enter the real world, the specter of taxation over your practice and your clients' business and personal decisions has become a much more consuming passion. As a matter of fact, you have found that doing tax research gives you the opportunity to grow in the area of your first real intellectual love, the computer. You simply love to sit at the controls of your Super-duper Model XYZ, 1.3 giga-byte personal computer all day. Your colleagues have come to nickname you the "ROM-Roamer" because of your uncanny ability to locate the most insignificant minutiae at the push of a button.

Your managing partner, Ms. Sandra Smith, sees a wonderful potential in your computing research skills and assigns you to the firm's tax section. In a short time, you have mastered the intricacies of all the major computer databases that provide tax research tools, including but not limited to ACCESS, LEXIS, and Westlaw, copyrighted by Commerce Clearing House, Mead Data Central, and West Publishing Company, respectively.

Assume that your firm's on-line cost for these research services is approximately $5 per minute. Because of your demonstrated expertise in the use of these research tools, in 15 minutes you are able to do tax research for a client that has historically taken and was billed for six hours. Given the fact that the end product to the client is the same in both cases, can you or your firm ethically continue to bill the client for six hours of research time? What other ethical issues are raised by this scenario? What guidelines are provided on this issue in the AICPA Code of Professional Conduct or the AICPA's Statements on Responsibilities in Tax Practice?

determine whether there are additional authorities on point. The data bases are updated for new developments on a very timely basis; for example, some court cases may appear within a few days of the decision.

A number of tax services, including CCH's *Federal Tax Service,* RIA's *Federal Tax Coordinator 2d (RIA On Point),* CCH's *Standard Federal Tax Reporter (CCH Access),* BNA's *Tax Management Portfolios,* RIA's *United States Tax Reporter,* and West's *Federal Taxation,* are available on CD-ROM (compact disc read-only memory). The material is organized the same as in the loose-leaf services. The compact discs allow pages and pages of information to be stored in practically no space. The compact discs generally are updated monthly, and the filing of supplementary pages is avoided. One way to retrieve information from the compact discs is to type key words into the computer. Alternatively, you could locate the index on the disk, consult the index, and then refer to the portion of the disk discussing your topic, for example, the deductibility of the cost of uniforms. Extensive material is available on the CCH ACCESS CD-ROM, including *Standard Federal Tax Reports, State Tax Reports,* Letter Rulings and IRS Positions, Revenue Rulings and Revenue Procedures, IRS Publications, Tax Forms and Instructions, and court cases dating back to 1913. Tax-oriented periodicals often provide listings and reviews of computer-based or CD-ROM research products.[48]

STATEMENTS ON RESPONSIBILITIES IN TAX PRACTICE

OBJECTIVE 6

Understand the guidelines to which CPAs in tax practice should adhere

Tax advisors often wonder what they should do in certain circumstances and may turn to a professional organization for guidance. The standards set by professional organizations are not legally enforceable, although they have a great deal of moral clout. The most comprehensive guidelines for CPAs in tax practice were set forth by the Tax Division of the American Institute of Certified Public Accountants (AICPA) in their advisory ***Statements on Responsibilities in Tax Practice*** (**SRTP**) (reproduced in Appendix E).[49] The Tax Division articulated the following objectives for the SRTPs:

- To recommend appropriate standards of responsibilities . . . and to promote their uniform application by CPAs
- To encourage the development of increased understanding of the responsibilities of CPAs by the Treasury Department and Internal Revenue Service . . .
- To foster increased public understanding of, compliance with, and confidence in our tax system through awareness of the recommended standards of responsibilities of CPAs . . . [50]

KEY POINT

According to the AICPA's SRTP, a CPA should (1) use client's estimates, when reasonable; (2) inform the client of errors; and (3) except where required by law, not inform the IRS of errors without the permission of the client.

The SRTPs are not enforceable standards, but rather are advisory guidelines. Some of the more important guidelines contained in the SRTP are highlighted below.

At times, a CPA may wonder whether it is appropriate to use an estimated amount on a tax return. *Statement No. 4* discusses the use of estimates in the following manner:

[48] For a discussion of the benefits of CD-ROM vs. hard copy research, the alternative CD-ROM products, and the structure of CD-ROM searches, see: Robert L. Black, "CD-ROM Tax Research: Tips, Tricks, and Traps," *The Tax Adviser,* Parts 1 (October, 1995, pp. 583-589) and 2 (January, 1996, pp. 23-27). Also, for a more detailed discussion of computerized tax research, see William A. Raabe, Gerald E. Whittenburg, and John C. Bost, *West's Federal Tax Research,* 3rd Edition (Minneapolis/St. Paul, MN: West Publishing Co., 1994), Chapters 13 and 14.

[49] AICPA, *Statements on Responsibilities in Tax Practice, 1991 Revision,* Introduction, ¶.03. For a thorough discussion of ethical responsibilities in the tax context, see Bernard Wolfman, James P. Holden, and Kenneth Harris, *Standards of Tax Practice* (Boston, MA: Little, Brown and Company, 1995).

[50] Ibid.

- A CPA may prepare tax returns involving the use of the taxpayer's estimates if it is impracticable to obtain exact data, and the estimated amounts are reasonable under the facts and circumstances known to the CPA. When the taxpayer's estimates are used, they should be presented in such a manner as to avoid the implication of greater accuracy than exists.

Keep in mind, however, that certain expenses are not deductible unless the taxpayer has the proper documentation.[51] Thus, a CPA cannot use estimates for such amounts.

It is not unusual for a CPA to discover that a client's tax return for an earlier year contains one or more errors. *Statement No. 6* contains guidelines concerning what CPAs should do when they know about errors their clients, or prior return preparers, made. The recommendations are as follows:

- The CPA should inform the client promptly upon becoming aware of an error in a previously filed return or . . . a client's failure to file a required return. The CPA should recommend the measures to be taken. Such recommendation may be given orally. The CPA is not obligated to inform the Internal Revenue Service, and the CPA may not do so without the client's permission, except where required by law.

Statement No. 7 describes the CPA's responsibilities in an administrative proceeding (e.g., an audit) if the CPA is aware of an error on the return.

- [T]he CPA should inform the client promptly upon becoming aware of the error. The CPA should recommend the measures to be taken. Such recommendation may be given orally. The CPA is neither obligated to inform the Internal Revenue Service nor may the CPA do so without the client's permission, except where required by law.
- The CPA should request the client's agreement to disclose the error to the Internal Revenue Service.

Some CPAs, especially newer ones, may wonder about the advisability of giving advice orally. *Statement No. 8* makes the following comments about the form—oral or written—of the advice given by CPAs.

- Although oral advice may serve a client's needs appropriately in routine matters or in well-defined areas, written communications are recommended in important, unusual, or complicated transactions.

With respect to the procedural aspects of return preparation, including relying on the client's "numbers," *Statement No. 3* furnishes the guidance shown below.

- In preparing or signing a return, the CPA may in good faith rely without verification upon information furnished by the client or by third parties. Yet, the CPA should not ignore the implications of information furnished and should make reasonable inquiries if the information furnished appears to be incorrect, incomplete, or inconsistent either on its face or on the basis of other facts known to the CPA. In this connection, the CPA should refer to the client's returns for prior years whenever feasible.
- Where the Internal Revenue Code or income tax regulations impose a condition with respect to deductibility or other tax treatment of an item (such as taxpayer maintenance of books and records or substantiating documentation to support the reported deduction or tax treatment), the CPA should make appropriate inquiries to determine to his or her satisfaction whether such condition has been met.

---

[51] Section 274(d) precludes deductions for certain expenditures (e.g., travel expenses including meals and lodging) unless the taxpayer can substantiate them by "adequate records or sufficient" corroborating evidence.

- The individual CPA who is required to sign the return should consider information actually known to that CPA from the tax return of another client when preparing a tax return if the information is relevant to that tax return, its consideration is necessary to properly prepare that tax return, and use of such information does not violate any law or rule relating to confidentiality.

One should keep in mind that unlike an auditor, a tax practitioner should serve as an advocate for the client. Nevertheless, tax professionals should not adopt or recommend pro-taxpayer positions that lack sufficient support. *Statement No. 1* provides standards for taking pro-taxpayer positions on a tax return or in recommending such positions. The following guidance is given.

KEY POINT

According to the SRTPs, a CPA should (1) rely on reasonable information from the client without verification; (2) not recommend a position that would not have a realistic possibility of being sustained administratively or judicially, nor sign a return that takes such a position; and (3) advise a client of potential penalties for any recommended tax positions.

- A CPA should not recommend to a client that a position be taken . . . on a return unless the CPA has a good faith belief that the position has a realistic possibility of being sustained administratively or judicially on its merits if challenged.
- A CPA should not prepare or sign a return as an income tax return preparer if the CPA knows that the return takes a position that the CPA could not recommend under the standard expressed [above].
- Notwithstanding [the above], a CPA may recommend a position that the CPA concludes is not frivolous as long as the position is adequately disclosed on the return or claim for refund.
- In recommending certain tax return positions and in signing a return . . . a CPA should, where relevant, advise the client as to the potential penalty consequences of the recommended tax return position and the opportunity, if any, to avoid such penalties through disclosure.

Statement No. 1 elaborates on the "good faith" belief requirement for a pro-taxpayer position as follows:

- The standards suggested herein require that a CPA in good faith believe that the position is warranted in existing law or can be supported by a good faith argument for an extension, modification, or reversal of existing law. For example, the CPA may reach such a conclusion on the basis of well-reasoned articles, treatises, IRS General Counsel Memoranda, a General Explanation of a Revenue Act prepared by the staff of the Joint Committee on Taxation, and Internal Revenue Service written determinations (such as private letter rulings), whether or not such sources are treated as "authority" under Sec. 6661.[52]

STOP & THINK

Question: As described on page C1-15, you are researching a certain calculation that affects a client's deductions. The Code states that the calculation is to be done "in a manner prescribed by the Secretary." After studying the Code and the Regulations and the Committee Reports, you conclude that another way of doing the calculations is arguably correct under an intuitive approach. This intuitive approach would result in a lower tax liability for the client. According to the *Statements on Responsibilities in Tax Practice,* may you take a position contrary to the Regulations (which are final Regulations) on the basis that the Regulations are not valid?

Solution: You should not take a position that goes against the Regulations unless you have a "good faith belief that the position has a realistic possibility of being sustained administratively or judicially." However, you can take a position that does not meet the above standard, provided you adequately disclose the position and the position is not

[52] Chapter C15 provides a discussion of Sec. 6661, which has been renumbered as Sec. 6662. In the context of Sec. 6662 the taxpayer can potentially incur a penalty even if a position is disclosed on a tax return unless there is a reasonable basis (i.e., a higher standard than non-frivolous) for the position.

frivolous. We need more detailed information about the situation before we can definitively assess whether we meet the "good faith belief" test. Chapter 15 also discusses tax-return preparers taking positions contrary to the Regulations.

SAMPLE WORK PAPERS AND CLIENT LETTER

OBJECTIVE 7

Prepare work papers and communications to clients

A sample set of work papers, including a draft of a client letter and a memo to the file describing the facts on which the research is based, is presented in Appendix A. The purpose of the work papers is to denote the issues to be researched, the authorities addressing the issues, and the researcher's conclusions concerning the appropriate tax treatment, with rationale therefor.

The format and other details of a set of work papers differ from firm to firm. The sample in this text is designed to give general guidance concerning the content of work papers. In practice, work papers may include less detail.

PROBLEM MATERIALS

DISCUSSION QUESTIONS

C1-1 Explain the difference between closed-fact and open-fact situations.

C1-2 List the steps of the tax research process.

C1-3 Explain why the steps in the tax research process are sometimes circular.

C1-4 In what circumstances do the AICPA's *Statements on Responsibilities in Tax Practice* recommend that tax advisors communicate with their clients in writing instead of orally?

C1-5 Refer to the *Summit Publishing Company, Inc.* case reproduced in part on pages C1-6 to C1-8 and indicate whether the taxpayer had to pay any additional taxes.

C1-6 Refer to the *J.B.S. Enterprises, Inc.* case reproduced in part on pages C1-8 and C1-10 and indicate what information reported on the tax return probably triggered the audit.

C1-7 Explain what is encompassed by the term *tax law* when tax advisors use this phrase.

C1-8 The U.S. Government Printing Office publishes both hearings on proposed legislation and committee reports. Distinguish between these two publications.

C1-9 Explain why committee reports can be valuable research aids.

C1-10 Why has the tax researcher's job been simplified as a result of the codification of the tax statutes?

C1-11 A friend notices that you are reading from the *Internal Revenue Code of 1986*. Your friend inquires why you are consulting a 1986 publication, especially given that tax laws change so frequently. What is your response?

C1-12 Does Title 26 contain statutory provisions dealing only with income taxation? Explain.

C1-13 Refer to Sec. 301 of the Code.

a. Which subsection discusses the general rule for the tax treatment of a distribution of property?

b. Where should one look for exceptions to the general rule?

c. What type of Regulations would relate to subsection (e)?

C1-14 Why should tax researchers take note of the date on which a regulation was adopted?

C1-15 a. Distinguish between proposed, temporary, and final regulations.

b. Distinguish between interpretative and statutory regulations.

C1-16 Which type of regulation is more difficult for a taxpayer to successfully challenge, and why?

C1-17 Explain the legislative reenactment doctrine.

C1-18 a. Discuss the authoritative weight of revenue rulings.
b. As a practical matter, what will happen if a taxpayer does not follow a revenue ruling and his or her return is audited?

C1-19 a. In which courts may litigation dealing with tax matters begin?
b. Discuss the factors that would probably be important to a taxpayer who is deciding in which trial court to begin litigation.
c. Describe the appeals court structure that exists for the various trial courts.

C1-20 May a taxpayer appeal a case litigated under the Small Cases Procedures of the Tax Court?

C1-21 Explain whether the following decisions have the same precedential value: (1) Tax Court regular decisions, (2) Tax Court memorandum decisions, (3) decisions under the Small Cases Procedures of the Tax Court.

C1-22 Does the IRS potentially issue acquiescences to decisions of a U.S. district court?

C1-23 Which courts' decisions are reported in the AFTR 2d? In the USTC?

C1-24 Who publishes regular decisions of the Tax Court? Memorandum decisions?

C1-25 Explain the *Golsen* rule. Design an example to illustrate its application.

C1-26 Assume that the only litigation to date on a particular issue is as follows:
Tax Court—decided for the taxpayer
Eighth Circuit Court of Appeals—decided for the taxpayer (affirming the Tax Court)
District Court of Louisiana—decided for the taxpayer
Fifth Circuit Court of Appeals—decided for the government (reversing the District Court of Louisiana)
a. Discuss the precedential value of the cases listed above for your client, who is a California resident.
b. If your client, a Texas resident instead, litigates in the Tax Court, how will the court rule? Explain.

C1-27 When might a tax advisor need to consult the provisions contained in a tax treaty?

C1-28 Compare the tax services listed below that are found in your tax library with respect to (a) how they are organized and (b) where current developments appear.
a. *United States Tax Reporter*
b. *Standard Federal Tax Reporter*
c. *Federal Tax Coordinator 2d*
d. *Law of Federal Income Taxation* (Mertens)
e. BNA's *Tax Management Portfolios*
f. CCH's *Federal Tax Service*

C1-29 What two functions does a citator serve?

C1-30 Describe two types of information reported in the *Research Institute of America Citator 2nd Series* but not in the Commerce Clearing House citator.

C1-31 Explain how your research approach might differ if you were using a computerized data base instead of a looseleaf tax service (e.g., the *Standard Federal Tax Reporter* service) at the beginning of your research.

C1-32 According to the *Statements on Responsibilities in Tax Practice,* how much support should exist before a CPA should take a pro-taxpayer position on a tax return?

PROBLEMS

C1-33 ***Interpretation of the Code.*** Under a divorce instrument executed in 1996, an ex-wife receives cash of $25,000 per year for eight years from her former husband. The instrument does not explicitly state that the payment is not includable in income.
a. Does the ex-wife have gross income? If so, how much?
b. Does the former husband receive a tax deduction? If so, is it for or from AGI?
Refer only to the Internal Revenue Code in answering this problem. Start with Sec. 71.

C1-34 ***Interpretation of the Code.*** Refer to Code Sec. 385 and answer the questions below.
a. Whenever regulations are adopted, what type will they be: statutory or interpretative? Explain.
b. Assume regulations have been finalized for Sec. 385. Will they have any relevance to estate tax matters? Explain.

C1-35 ***Using the Cumulative Bulletin.*** Consult any *Cumulative Bulletin.* In what order are revenue rulings arranged?

C1-36 ***Using the Cumulative Bulletin.*** Which Code section does Rev. Rul. 85-44 interpret? (Hint: Consult the 1985-1 *Cumulative Bulletin.*)

C1-37 ***Using the Cumulative Bulletin.*** Refer to the 1989-1 *Cumulative Bulletin.*

a. What time period is covered by this bulletin?
b. What appears on page 1?
c. What items are printed in Part I of the bulletin?
d. In what order are the items presented in Part I?
e. What items are printed in Part II?
f. What items are printed in Part III?

C1-38 ***Using the Cumulative Bulletin.*** Refer to the 1990-1 *Cumulative Bulletin.*

a. For the time period covered by the bulletin, to which cases did the IRS issue a nonacquiescence?
b. What is the topical area of Rev. Rul. 90-10?
c. Does this bulletin contain any revenue ruling that interprets Sec. 162? If so, list it.

C1-39 ***Determination of Acquiescence.***

a. What official action did the Commissioner take in 1986 concerning the Tax Court case of *John McIntosh*? (Hint: Consult the 1986-1 *Cumulative Bulletin.*)
b. Did such action concern *all* the issues in the case? If not, explain. (Consult the headnote to the case before answering this part of the question.)

C1-40 ***Determination of Acquiescence.***

a. What original action (acquiescence or nonacquiescence) did the Commissioner take concerning *Streckfus Steamers, Inc.*, 19 T.C. 1 (1952)?
b. Was the action complete or partial?
c. Did the Commissioner subsequently change his mind? If so, when?

C1-41 ***Determination of Acquiescence.***

a. What original action (acquiescence or nonacquiescence) did the Commissioner take concerning *Pittsburgh Milk Co.*, 26 T.C. 707 (1956)?
b. Did the Commissioner subsequently change his mind? If so, when?

C1-42 ***Assessing a Case.*** Look up the decision for *Everett J. Gordon*, 85 T.C. 309 (1985), and answer the questions below.

a. Was the decision reviewed by the court? If so, was it a unanimous decision? Explain.
b. Was the decision entered under Rule 155?
c. Consult a citator. Was the case heard by an appellate court? If so, which court?

C1-43 ***Assessing a Case.*** Look up the decision for *Bush Brothers & Co.*, 73 T.C. 424 (1979), and answer the questions below.

a. Was the decision reviewed by the court? If so, was it a unanimous decision? Explain.
b. Was the decision entered under Rule 155?
c. Consult a citator. Was the case heard by an appellate court? If so, which court?

C1-44 ***Writing Citations.*** Provide the proper citations (including both primary and secondary cites where applicable) for the authorities listed below. (For secondary cites, give both the AFTR and USTC cites.)

a. *Ruth K. Dowell v. U.S.*, a 10th Circuit decision
b. *Thomas M. Dragoun v. CIR*, a Tax Court memo decision
c. *John M. Grabinski v. U.S.*, a District Court of Minnesota decision
d. *John M. Grabinski v. U.S.*, an Eighth Circuit decision
e. *Rebekah Harkness*, a 1972 Court of Claims decision

f. *Hillsboro National Bank v. CIR,* a Supreme Court decision
g. Rev. Rul. 78-129

C1-45 ***Writing Citations.*** Provide the proper citations (including both primary and secondary cites where applicable) for the authorities listed below. (For secondary cites, give both the AFTR and USTC cites.)
a. Rev. Rul. 69-125
b. *Frank H. Sullivan,* a Board of Tax Appeals decision
c. *Lloyd Weaver,* a Tax Court decision
d. *Ralph L. Rogers v. U.S.,* an Ohio District Court decision
e. *Norman Rodman v. CIR,* a Second Circuit Court decision

C1-46 ***Interpreting Citations.*** Following are some actual citations. For each case, indicate which court decided the case. In addition, for each authority, indicate on which pages and in which publications the authority was reported.
a. *Lloyd M. Shumaker v. CIR,* 648 F.2d 1198, 48 AFTR 2d 81-5353 (9th Cir., 1981)
b. *Dean R. Shore,* 69 T.C. 689 (1978)
c. *Real Estate Land Title & Trust Co. v. U.S.,* 309 U.S. 13, 23 AFTR 816 (USSC, 1940)
d. *J. B. Morris v. U.S.,* 441 F. Supp. 76, 41 AFTR 2d 78-335 (D.C. TX, 1977)
e. Rev. Rul. 83-3, 1983-1 C.B. 72
f. *Malone & Hyde, Inc. v. U.S.,* 568 F.2d 474, 78-1 USTC ¶9199 (6th Cir., 1978)

C1-47 ***Using a Tax Service.*** Use the topical index of the *United States Tax Reporter* tax service to locate authorities dealing with the deductibility of the cost of a facelift.
a. In which paragraph(s) does the *United States Tax Reporter* service give a synopsis of these authorities and citations to them?
b. List the authorities.
c. Have there been any recent non-statutory developments concerning the tax consequences of facelifts? (*Recent* means authorities appearing in the cross-reference section.)
d. May a taxpayer deduct the cost of a facelift paid for in 1996? Explain.

C1-48 ***Using a Tax Service.*** Refer to Reg. Sec. 1.302-1 at ¶3022 of the *United States Tax Reporter* service. Does the regulation interpret today's version of the Code? Explain.

C1-49 ***Using a Tax Service.*** Use the topical index of the *Standard Federal Tax Reporter* to locate authorities dealing with whether termite damage qualifies for a casualty loss deduction.
a. In which paragraph(s) does the *Standard Federal Tax Reporter* service give a synopsis of these authorities and citations to them?
b. List the authorities.
c. Have there been any recent developments concerning the tax consequences of termite damage? (*Recent* means authorities appearing in the cumulative index section.)

C1-50 ***Using a Tax Service.***
a. Locate in the *Standard Federal Tax Reporter* service the place where Sec. 303(b)(2)(A) is reproduced. This provision states that Sec. 303(a) applies only if the stock meets a certain percentage test. What is the applicable percentage?
b. Locate Reg. Sec. 1.303-2(a) in the same tax service as in Part a. Does this regulation interpret today's version of the Code with respect to the percentage test addressed in Part a? Explain.

C1-51 ***Using a Tax Service.*** The questions below deal with the *Tax Management Portfolios* published by the Bureau of National Affairs.
a. What is the portfolio number of the volume that provides a detailed examination of only the topic of tax-free exchanges under Sec. 1031?

b. On which page does a discussion of "boot" begin?
c. What are the purposes of Worksheets 1 and 5 of this portfolio?
d. Refer to the bibliography and references at the back of the portfolio. List the numbers (e.g., 90-5) of the 1990 revenue rulings that, according to the portfolio, dealt with the sale or exchange of a personal residence.

C1-52 ***Using a Tax Service.*** This problem deals with the Mertens' *Law of Federal Income Taxation* tax service.
a. Refer to Volume 5. What broad, general topics does it discuss?
b. Which section of Volume 5 is devoted to a discussion of the principal methods of determining depreciation?
c. In Volume 5, what is the purpose of the yellow and white sheets appearing before the tab labeled "Text"?
d. Refer to the Ruling Status Table in the Rulings volume. What is the current status of Rev. Ruls. 79-433 and 75-335?
e. Refer to the Code-Rulings Tables in the Rulings volume. List the numbers (e.g., Rev. Rul. 84-88) of all 1984 revenue rulings and revenue procedures interpreting Sec. 121.

C1-53 ***Using a Tax Service.*** The questions below deal with the *Federal Tax Coordinator 2d* published by the Research Institute of America.
a. Use the topical index to locate authorities dealing with the deductibility of the cost of work clothing by ministers (clergymen). List the authorities.
b. Where does this tax service report new developments?

C1-54 ***Using a Tax Service.*** Refer to the *United States Tax Reporter* and *Standard Federal Tax Reporter* services. Then for each tax service, answer the following questions.
a. In which volume is the index located?
b. Is the index arranged by topic or by Code section?
c. If all you know is a Code section number, how do you locate additional materials?
d. If all you know is the name of a court decision, how do you locate additional materials?

C1-55 ***Using a Citator.*** Trace *Biltmore Homes, Inc.*, a 1960 Tax Court memorandum decision, through both citators described in the text.
a. According to the *RIA Citator 2nd Series*, how many times has the Tax Court decision been cited by other courts on Issue Number 5?
b. How many issues were involved in the trial court litigation? (Hint: Refer to the headnote of the case.)
c. Did an appellate court hear the case? If so, which court?
d. According to the CCH citator, how many times has the Tax Court decision been cited by other courts?
e. According to the CCH citator, how many times has the Circuit Court decision been cited by other courts on Issue Number 5?

C1-56 ***Using a Citator.*** Trace *Stephen Bolaris*, 776 F.2d 1428, through both citators described in the text.
a. According to the *RIA Citator 2nd Series*, how many times has the Ninth Circuit's decision been cited?
b. Did the case address more than one issue? Explain.
c. Was the case ever commented on in an unfavorable manner? Explain.
d. According to the CCH citator, how many times has the Ninth Circuit's decision been cited?
e. According to the CCH citator, how many times has the Tax Court's decision been cited for Issue Number 1?

C1-57 ***Interpreting a Case.*** Refer to the *Levin Metals Corporation* case (92 T.C. 307).

a. In which year was the case decided?
b. What controversy was litigated?
c. Who won the case?
d. Was the decision reviewed?
e. Is there an appellate decision?
f. Has the case been cited in other cases?

CASE STUDY PROBLEM

C1-58 A client, Mal Manley, fills out his client questionnaire for the year just past, and on it he provides you with information to be used in the preparation of his individual income tax return. Mal's returns have never been audited by the IRS. Mal reports that he made over a hundred relatively small cash contributions in the total amount of $24,785 to charitable organizations. In the last few years, Mal's charitable contributions have averaged about $15,000 per year. For the year just past, Mal's adjusted gross income is about $350,000, about a 10% increase from the preceding year.

Required: According to the *Statements on Responsibilities in Tax Practice,* may you accept Mal's information concerning his charitable contributions at face value? Now assume, instead, that Mal's tax return for two years ago was audited recently and that 75% of the charitable contribution deduction claimed thereon were denied because of a lack of substantiation. Assume also that for the year just past Mal indicates he contributed $25,000 (instead of $24,785). How does this change in the information affect your earlier answer?

TAX RESEARCH PROBLEMS

C1-59 In answering these questions, refer only to *Thomas A. Curtis, M.D., Inc.,* 1994 RIA TC Memo ¶94,015. The purpose of this question is to enhance your skills in interpreting authorities that you locate while doing research.

a. What is the general controversy being litigated in this case?
b. Which party—the taxpayer or the goverment—won the case?
c. Why is the plaintiff the corporation instead of Dr. and/or Ms. Curtis?
d. What is the relationship between Ellen Barnert Curtis and Dr. Thomas A. Curtis?
e. Approximately how many hours a week did Ms. Curtis work, and what are her credentials?
f. For the fiscal year ended in 1989 how much salary did Ms. Curtis receive from the corporation? What amount did the court decide was a reasonable amount of compensation for her for that year?
g. What dividends did the corporation pay for its fiscal years ended in 1988 and 1989?
h. To which circuit would this case be appealable?
i. According to the *Curtis* case, what five factors did the Ninth Circuit enumerate in *Elliotts, Inc.* as having relevance in determining reasonable compensation?

C1-60 Josh contributes $5,000 toward the support of his widowed mother, aged 69. His mother, a U.S. citizen and resident, has $2,000 of gross income and spends it all on her own support. In addition, $3,200 of her medical expenses are paid for by Medicare. She does not receive any support from sources other than those described above. Must the Medicare payments be counted as support that Josh's mother provides for herself?

Prepare work papers and a client letter (to Josh) dealing with the question about the Medicare payments.

C1-61 Amy owns a vacation cottage in Maine. She estimates that use of the cottage during the current year will be as follows:

By Amy, solely for vacation	12 days
By Amy, making repairs ten hours per day and vacationing the rest of the day	2 days
By her sister, who paid fair rental value	8 days
By her cousin, who paid fair rental value	4 days
By her friend, who paid a token amount of rent	2 days
By three families from the Northeast, who paid fair rental value for forty days each	120 days
Not used	217 days

Determine the ratio to be used for allocating the following expenses against the rental income received from the cottage: interest, taxes, repairs, insurance, and depreciation. The ratio will affect the deductible expenses and, thus, Amy's taxable income for the year.

Prepare for the tax manager to whom you are regularly assigned work papers in which you address the ratios to be used in making the allocations. Also, draft a memorandum to the client's file dealing with the results of your tax research.

CHAPTER 2

CORPORATE FORMATIONS AND CAPITAL STRUCTURE

LEARNING OBJECTIVES

After studying this chapter, you should be able to

1. Explain the tax advantages and disadvantages of using each of the alternative business forms
2. Determine the tax rules that distinguish partnerships, corporations, and trusts
3. Determine the legal requirements for forming a corporation
4. Explain the requirements for deferring gain or loss upon incorporation
5. Determine the tax consequences of alternative capital structures
6. Determine the tax consequences of worthless stock or debt obligations

CHAPTER OUTLINE

When a business is started, its owners must decide whether to operate it as a sole proprietorship, a partnership, or a corporation. This chapter discusses the advantages and disadvantages of each of these business entities. Because many businesses find it advantageous to operate as a corporation, this chapter looks at the definition of a corporation for federal income tax purposes. It also discusses the tax consequences of incorporating a business. The chapter closes by looking at the selection of the corporation's capital structure and the tax advantages and disadvantages of alternative capital forms.

The corporate taxation discussion takes a life-cycle approach. The corporate life cycle starts in this chapter with its formation. Once it is formed, the corporation is in operation and its taxable income (or loss), its federal income tax and other liabilities, and the tax consequences of any distributions to its shareholders must be determined. Finally, at some point the corporation may outlive its usefulness and be liquidated, thus ending the life of the corporation. The corporate life cycle is too complex to discuss in one chapter, however, so more detailed coverage follows in Chapters C3 through C8.

ORGANIZATION FORMS AVAILABLE

OBJECTIVE 1

Explain the tax advantages and disadvantages of using each of the alternative business forms

Business can be conducted in several entities or forms, the most common of which are

- Sole proprietorships
- Partnerships
- Corporations

An overview of each entity form is presented below.

SOLE PROPRIETORSHIPS

SELF-STUDY QUESTION

What is involved in reporting the activities of a sole proprietorship?

ANSWER

The income/loss of a sole proprietorship is reported on Schedule C. This schedule is simply a summary of the operating income and expense items of the sole proprietorship. The net income/loss is then carried to Form 1040 and included in the computation of the individual's taxable income.

A **sole proprietorship** is a business that is owned by a single individual. The sole proprietorship form of business is often selected by individuals who are beginning a new business. It is not a separate entity. The income or loss from a sole proprietorship is reported directly on the proprietor's individual tax return. The proprietor (owner) must report all of the business's income and expenses for the year on Schedule C (Profit or Loss from Business) or Schedule C-EZ (Net Profit from Business) of Form 1040. If the business is profitable, the profit is added to the proprietor's other income and is taxed at his or her marginal tax rate. A completed Schedule C is included in Appendix B. A common set of facts (with minor modifications) is used to illustrate the similarities and differences in the tax reporting process for a sole proprietorship, C corporation, partnership, and S corporation.

EXAMPLE C2-1 ▶ John is single and owns a computer store, which he operates as a sole proprietorship. John reports a $15,000 profit from the store for the year. Assuming he has enough income from other sources to be taxed at a 36% marginal tax rate, his tax on the $15,000 of profit from the store is $5,400 (0.36 × $15,000). ◀

If the business operates at a loss, the loss reduces the proprietor's taxable income and provides a tax savings based on the proprietor's marginal tax rate.

EXAMPLE C2-2 ▶ Assume the same facts as in Example C2-1, except that John reports a $15,000 loss on his computer business instead of a $15,000 profit. Assuming he is still taxed at a 36% marginal tax rate, the $15,000 loss produces a $5,400 (0.36 × $15,000) tax savings. ◀

TYPICAL MISCONCEPTION

Although this chapter emphasizes the tax consequences of selecting the entity in which a business will be conducted, other issues are often more important in making such a decision. For example, the amount of legal liability assumed by an owner is very important and can vary substantially between the different business entities.

TAX ADVANTAGES. The tax advantages of doing business as a sole proprietorship include

- The entity itself is not subject to taxation. Any income is taxed to the sole proprietor at his or her marginal tax rate. The proprietor's marginal tax rate may be lower than the corporation's marginal tax rate that would be imposed on the same amount of income.
- The owner can contribute money to, or withdraw money from, the business without any tax consequences. Although the owner usually maintains separate books and records and a separate bank account for his or her business, the money in that bank account is still the owner's. The owner may withdraw money from or put money into the business bank account without any tax consequences. He or she can also contribute property to or withdraw property from the business without any tax consequences. However, the owner is taxed on the profits of the business whether those profits are retained in the business or distributed for the owner's use.
- Losses can be used to offset income from other sources such as interest, dividends, and the salary of the taxpayer's spouse, subject to the passive loss limitations.

TAX DISADVANTAGES. The tax disadvantages of doing business as a sole proprietorship include

- All of the profits are taxed to the proprietor when they are earned, even if they are not distributed to him or her but are reinvested in the business. A corporation's earnings, however, are taxed to its shareholders only when they are distributed. Corporate tax rates may be lower than those imposed on a sole proprietor.
- A sole proprietor is not considered an employee of the business. Therefore, the proprietor must pay self-employment taxes on the self-employment income derived from the business. This can be a disadvantage where the business profit is more than would be withdrawn as salary (and subject to the FICA taxes) if incorporated. In addition, tax-exempt fringe benefits (e.g., premiums paid on accident and health insurance and group term life insurance) generally are not available to a sole proprietor.[1]
- A sole proprietor must use the same reporting period for both business and individual tax returns. Income cannot be deferred by choosing a fiscal year for the business that is different from the proprietor's own tax year.

PARTNERSHIPS

KEY POINT

A partnership is not a taxpaying entity, but rather a tax-reporting entity. The income, gain, loss, deductions, and tax credits of the partnership flow through to the partners, and the partners determine the tax implications of these particular items.

A **partnership** is a business carried on by two or more individuals or other entities. The partnership form is often used by friends or relatives who decide to go into business together and by groups of investors who want to share the profits and expenses of some type of business or investment such as a real estate project.

A partnership is a tax reporting, but not generally a taxpaying entity. The partnership acts as a conduit. Its income, expenses, losses, credits, and so on flow through to the partners, who report those items on their own tax returns. Tax payments are required only of partnerships that elect a fiscal year reporting period. These payments are based on the amount of the income deferral that is claimed by the partnership.

A partnership must file a tax return every year (Form 1065—U.S. Partnership Return of Income) to report the results of its operations. When the partnership return is filed, the

[1] IRC Sec. 162(l) permits self-employed individuals to deduct a percentage of the health insurance costs incurred on behalf of themselves, their spouses, and their dependents as a trade or business expense. Excess health insurance costs may be deducted as an itemized deduction subject to the 7.5% of AGI limitation. The percentage allowed is 30% in 1996, 40% in 1997, 45% in 1998–2002, 50% in 2003, 60% in 2004, 70% in 2005, and 80% in 2006 and thereafter.

preparer must send each partner a statement (Schedule K-1, Form 1065) that reports the partner's share of the partnership's income, expenses, losses, credits, and so on. The partners must then report these items on their individual tax returns. A completed Form 1065 is included in Appendix B.

Just as with a sole proprietorship, if the business is profitable, the partners' allocable shares of the profit are added to the partners' other income and taxed at the partners' marginal tax rates.

EXAMPLE C2-3 ▶ Bob is single and owns a 50% interest in the BT Partnership, a calendar year taxpayer. The BT Partnership reports $30,000 of profits for the year, of which $15,000 is Bob's share. Assuming Bob is taxed at a 36% marginal tax rate, his tax on his $15,000 share of partnership profits is $5,400 (0.36 × $15,000). Bob owes the $5,400 in taxes whether the BT Partnership distributes any of its profits to him or not. ◀

If a partnership reports a loss, the partners' allocable shares of the loss reduce the partners' other income and provide a tax savings based on the partners' marginal tax rates.

EXAMPLE C2-4 ▶ Assume the same facts as in Example C2-3, except that the BT Partnership reports a $30,000 loss for the year instead of a profit. Assuming Bob is taxed at a 36% marginal tax rate, his $15,000 share of the loss produces a $5,400 (0.36 × $15,000) tax savings. ◀

The advantages and disadvantages of doing business as a partnership are similar to those of a sole proprietorship, and are presented below.

TAX ADVANTAGES. The tax advantages of doing business as a partnership are

- The partnership itself is exempt from taxation. The income of the partnership is taxed directly to the partners. Their individual tax rates may be lower than the corporate marginal tax rate on the same amount of taxable income.
- Profits are taxed only when they are earned. Additional taxes generally are not imposed on withdrawals made by the partners. Although the partners usually maintain a separate bank account for the partnership, the money in that account belongs to them. They can withdraw money from or put money into the partnership account without any tax consequences. With limited exceptions, they can also contribute property to or withdraw property from the partnership without any tax consequences.
- Losses can be used by partners to offset income from other sources.
- A partner's basis in a partnership interest is increased by his or her share of partnership income. This reduces the amount of gain recognized when the partnership interest is sold.

ADDITIONAL COMMENT

If two or more owners exist, a business cannot be conducted as a sole proprietorship. From a tax compliance and record-keeping perspective, conducting a business as a partnership is more complicated than conducting the business as a sole proprietorship.

TAX DISADVANTAGES. The tax disadvantages of doing business as a partnership are

- All of the partnership's profits are taxed to the partners when they are earned, even if they are reinvested in the business. The partners' tax rates may be higher than the marginal tax rate that applies to a corporation.
- A partner is not considered an employee of the partnership. Therefore, partners must pay self-employment taxes on their share of the partnership's self-employment income. Tax-exempt fringe benefits (e.g., premiums paid on accident and health insurance[2] and group term life insurance) are not generally available to the partners.

[2] Partners are also eligible to deduct a percentage of their health insurance costs in the same manner as a sole proprietor. See footnote 1 for details.

When such amounts are paid by the partnership on behalf of a partner, the payment is considered to be a guaranteed payment that is taxable to the partner.

- Partners generally cannot defer income by choosing a fiscal year for the partnership that is different from the tax year of the partner(s) who own a majority interest in the capital and profits of the partnership. A fiscal year can be elected by the partnership in certain situations, which results in a limited income deferral.

Partnerships are discussed in detail in Chapters C9 and C10 of this volume.

HISTORICAL NOTE

The following business entity returns were filed for 1994:

Entity	Number
C corporation	2.53 million
S corporation	2.04 million
Partnership	1.55 million

CORPORATIONS

Corporations can be divided into two categories. A **regular corporation**, or C corporation, is taxed annually on its earnings. These earnings are taxed to the corporation's shareholders when distributed as a dividend. A special S election is also available that permits a corporation to be taxed similarly to a partnership.

KEY POINT

Unlike a sole proprietorship and a partnership, a C corporation is a separate taxpaying entity. This can be an advantage because corporate rates start at 15%, which may be much lower than an individual shareholder's rate, which might be as high as 39.6%.

C CORPORATIONS. A **C corporation** is a separate taxpaying entity that is taxed on its taxable income at rates ranging from 15% to 35%. A corporation must report all of its income and expenses and compute its tax liability on Form 1120 (U.S. Corporation Income Tax Return). A completed Form 1120 is included in Appendix B. Shareholders are not taxed on the corporation's earnings unless they are distributed as dividends. Thus, income is taxed twice: first to the corporation and then to its shareholders when it is distributed as a dividend.

EXAMPLE C2-5 ▶ Jane owns 100% of the stock of York Corporation. York reports taxable income of $50,000 for the year. The first $50,000 of taxable income is taxed at a 15% rate, so York pays a corporate income tax of $7,500 (0.15 × $50,000). If no distributions are made to Jane during the year, she pays no taxes on York's earnings. However, if York distributes its current after-tax earnings to Jane, she must pay tax on $42,500 ($50,000 − $7,500) of dividend income. Assuming she is in the 36% marginal tax bracket, the tax on the dividend income paid by Jane is $15,300 (0.36 × $42,500). The total tax on York's $50,000 of profits is $22,800 ($7,500 paid by York + $15,300 paid by Jane). A strategy for withdrawing earnings from the corporation without double taxation is by paying a salary that is deductible by the corporation. This technique is discussed in Chapter C3. ◀

Even when a corporation doesn't distribute its profits, double taxation may occur. The profits are taxed to the corporation when they are earned. Then they may be taxed a second time (as capital gains) when the shareholder sells his or her stock or the corporation is liquidated.

EXAMPLE C2-6 ▶ On January 1, 1997, Ken purchases 100% of the stock of York Corporation for $60,000. York Corporation reports taxable income of $50,000 in 1997, on which it pays tax of $7,500. None of the remaining $42,500 is distributed to Ken. However, on January 1, 1998, Ken sells his stock to Mary for $102,500 (his initial investment plus 1997's accumulated earnings). Ken must report a gain of $42,500 ($102,500 − $60,000). Thus, York's profit is taxed twice—once at the corporate level and again at the shareholder level when the stock is sold. ◀

Tax Advantages. The tax advantages of the C corporation form of doing business are

- Corporations (other than personal service corporations) are taxed at rates starting at 15%. Because a corporation is an entity independent from its owners, its marginal tax rate may be lower than the shareholder's marginal tax rate for the first $75,000 of taxable income. As long as the earnings are not distributed and taxed to both the shareholder and the corporation, considerable tax savings may result. As a result, more earnings may be available for reinvestment and the retirement of debt. This advantage is limited, however, by the accumulated earnings tax and the personal holding company tax (see Chapter C5 for a discussion of the two penalty taxes).

- Shareholders who are employed by their own corporation are treated as employees for tax purposes. As employees, they are eligible to receive deductible salary payments. This lets them adjust their compensation (within limits) to cause the income to be taxed partly on the corporate return and partly on the individual returns, to minimize their overall tax liability. In addition, they are entitled to tax-free fringe benefits (e.g., premiums paid on group term life insurance and accident and health insurance). These fringe benefits can be provided by the corporation with *before-tax* dollars (instead of after-tax dollars). Sole proprietors and partners are not considered to be employees and, therefore, generally are ineligible for such benefits. They are permitted to deduct a portion of their health insurance premiums.[3] Other benefits must be paid for with *after-tax* dollars.
- A C corporation is allowed to use a fiscal year instead of a calendar year as its reporting period. A fiscal year may enable a corporation to defer income to a later reporting period. A personal service corporation, however, generally must use a calendar year as its tax year.[4]
- There are special rules allowing the exclusion of 50% of the gain realized on the sale or exchange of stock of qualifying C corporations that has been held for at least five years.[5]

Tax Disadvantages. The tax disadvantages of the C corporation form of doing business are

SELF-STUDY QUESTION

How are corporate earnings subject to double taxation?

ANSWER

Corporate earnings are initially taxed to the corporation. In addition, once these earnings are distributed to the shareholders (dividends), they are taxed again. Because the corporation does not receive a deduction for the distribution, these earnings have been taxed twice.

- Double taxation of income occurs when corporate earnings are distributed as dividends to shareholders or the stock is sold or exchanged.
- Shareholders generally cannot withdraw money or property from the corporation without tax consequences. A distribution of profits to a shareholder is taxable to the shareholder if the corporation has sufficient earnings and profits (E&P).[6]
- Net operating losses can be carried back or carried forward only to offset the corporation's income in other years. For corporations in the start-up phase of operations, these losses cannot provide any tax benefits until a profit is earned in a subsequent year. Shareholders cannot use these losses to offset their income from other sources.
- Capital losses cannot offset any ordinary income of the corporation or of its shareholders. These losses must be carried back or carried forward to offset corporate capital gains reported in other years.

S CORPORATIONS. **S corporations** are corporations that elect to be taxed like a partnership for federal income tax purposes. A completed Form 1120S (U.S. Income Tax Return for an S Corporation) is included in Appendix B. If the shareholders elect S corporation status, the corporation generally pays no tax. Instead, the corporation acts as a conduit that passes the corporation's income, expenses, losses, and credits through to the individual shareholders just as a partnership does.

[3] See footnote 1 for details.
[4] Sec. 441. See Chapter C3 for the special tax year restrictions applying to personal service corporations.
[5] Sec. 1202 applies to stock issued after August 8, 1993.
[6] The term *earnings and profits* is a technical term that is defined generally as the corporation's after-tax earnings and represents the corporation's ability to pay a dividend. The term is discussed in Chapter C4.

EXAMPLE C2-7 ▶ Chuck owns 50% of the stock of Maine Corporation, a qualifying S corporation that is a calendar year taxpayer. For the current year, Maine reports $30,000 of taxable income, all of it ordinary income. Maine pays no corporate income taxes. Chuck must pay taxes on his share of Maine's income, $15,000 (0.50 × $30,000), whether it is distributed to him or not. If Chuck's marginal tax rate is 36%, he pays $5,400 (0.36 × $15,000) of tax on his share of Maine's income. If Maine instead reports a $30,000 loss, Chuck's $15,000 share of the loss reduces his tax liability by $5,400 (0.36 × $15,000). ◀

TYPICAL MISCONCEPTION

An S corporation is still a corporation for legal purposes, and has simply elected to be taxed under Subchapter S (instead of Subchapter C) of the IRC. One benefit of this election is that an S corporation not only enjoys the corporate attribute of limited liability but also is treated as a flow-through entity for tax purposes.

Tax Advantages. The tax advantages of doing business as an S corporation are

- S corporations are generally exempt from taxation. Income is taxed to the shareholders. The shareholders' marginal tax rates may be lower than the corporation's marginal tax rate. An S corporation pays a tax levy only if it formerly was a C corporation and has either substantial passive income or realizes a net built-in gain.
- Losses flow through to shareholders and can be used to offset income earned from other sources. This is particularly important to corporations just commencing their operations.
- Capital gains are taxed to individual shareholders as though they were earned by the individual. An individual may be able to offset those gains with capital losses from other sources or have them taxed at the 28% maximum rate applicable to individuals.
- Shareholders generally can contribute money to or withdraw money from an S corporation without any tax consequences. Shareholders are taxed only on the annual income of the S corporation.
- Profits are taxed only when they are earned. Additional taxes are generally not imposed on distributions of profits to the S corporation's shareholders.
- A shareholder's basis in S corporation stock is increased by his or her share of the corporation's income. This reduces the shareholder's gain when he or she sells the S corporation stock.

Tax Disadvantages. The tax disadvantages of doing business as an S corporation are

- All of the corporation's current year profits, whether distributed or not, are taxed to the shareholders. If the shareholders' marginal tax rates exceed those for a C corporation, the capital that is available for reinvestment and debt retirement may be reduced.
- Tax-free corporate fringe benefits generally are not available to S corporation shareholders who are employed by the business.[7] Fringe benefits provided by an S corporation are generally deductible by the corporation and taxable to the shareholder. The S corporation's shareholder-employees are treated as employees for purposes of social security tax payments on their salary income.
- S corporations generally cannot defer income by choosing a fiscal year for the S corporation that is different from the tax year of the individual shareholders. An S corporation that elects fiscal year reporting also may have to make a special payment based on the amount of the income deferral that is claimed.

S corporations are discussed in detail in Chapter C11 of this volume. In addition, a comparison of the tax rules for partnerships, C corporations, and S corporations is found in Appendix F.

---

[7] S corporation shareholders are also eligible to deduct a percentage of their health insurance costs in the same manner as a sole proprietor and partner. See footnote 1 for details.

TAX DEFINITION OF COMMON BUSINESS ENTITY FORMS

OBJECTIVE 2

Determine the tax rules that distinguish partnerships, corporations, and trusts

The Internal Revenue Code includes "associations, joint stock companies, and insurance companies" in its definition of a corporation.[8] Prior to 1997, the Treasury Regulations required unincorporated businesses (e.g., a partnership) to be taxed as corporations if they possessed at least three of the following four corporate characteristics: limited liability, centralized management, free transferability of interests, and continuity of life. Two other characteristics—associates and joint profit motive—were considered neutral factors. State law was used to determine whether businesses possessed any or all of these characteristics. Generally, if a partnership was formed under the Uniform Partnership Act or Uniform Limited Partnership Act, it was taxed as a partnership. The two "neutral" characteristics for classification of a partnership were used to classify a trust for tax purposes. If a trust had associates and a joint profit motive, it was taxed as a corporation (e.g., a business trust).

As a result of these rules, two new business entity forms were created in recent years—a **limited liability company** (LLC) and a **limited liability partnership** (LLP). LLCs combine the corporate characteristics of limited liability for the owners with the possibility of tax treatment of the entity as a partnership. The organizers of an LLC achieved this by insuring that at most two of the four corporate characteristics required under the Treasury Regulations to be taxed as a corporation were present.

A **limited liability partnership** (LLP) is similar to an LLC but is formed under a separate state statute that generally applies to service organizations. Many large accounting and law firms have become LLPs in recent years because they wanted the advantage of some limits on liability, but they still wanted to be taxed as partnerships. A further discussion of these two entity forms can be found in Chapter C10.

REAL WORLD EXAMPLE

All the Big 6 public accounting firms have converted general partnerships into LLPs.

Many state statutes provide flexibility to allow LLCs and LLPs to be formed with two or more of the four critical corporate characteristics that are important in determining whether a partnership is taxed as a corporation not being present. As a result, a knowledgeable taxpayer could determine whether a business entity would be taxed as a corporation or not. If he wanted his business to be taxed as a corporation, he would form a corporation or LLC (or LLP) with at least three of the four critical corporate characteristics present. If he wanted his business to be taxed as a partnership, he could form an LLC (or LLP) with two or more owners with no more than two of the four critical corporate characteristics present.

However, the IRS and thousands of taxpayers continued to spend considerable resources throughout the years in determining the proper classification of business entities. Many small unincorporated businesses could not afford to commit the resources necessary to acquire a private letter ruling in order to obtain certainty under the regulations. At the same time, the IRS challenged the classification of certain LLCs, LLPs, and corporations. As a result, there was substantial uncertainty as to whether the IRS would respect the tax treatment selected by the entity because there was often uncertainty as to the number of critical corporate characteristics that an entity actually possessed.

CHECK-THE-BOX REGULATIONS

In an effort to simplify the rules, the IRS finalized new regulations that became effective on January 1, 1997. The new rules, commonly known as **"check-the-box" regulations,** replace the old classification system with a simplified regime that allows most unincorporated businesses to choose whether to be taxed as a partnership or corporation. A flowchart outlining how this new system works may be found in Figure C2-1.

---

[8] Sec. 7701(a)(3).

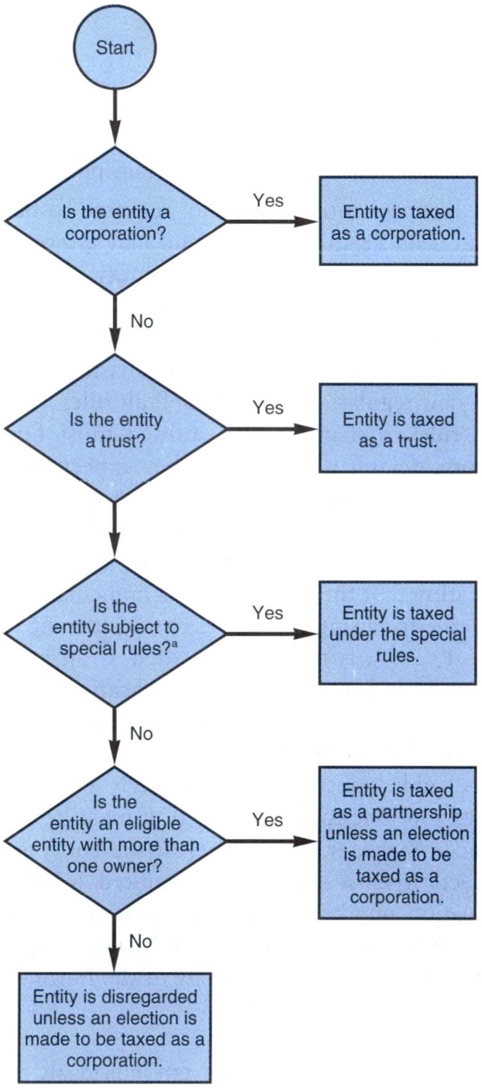

[a] **Special rules include, for example, the Real Estate Investment Trust (REIT) and Real Estate Mortgage Investment Conduit (REMIC) rules.**

FIGURE C2-1 ▶ Flowchart of Check-the-Box Entity Classification Rules

Under this new system, an unincorporated organization that is recognized as a separate entity for federal tax purposes is either a trust or an eligible entity unless a particular Code provision provides special tax treatment. For example, a trust, without associates and a joint-profit-motive, is taxed under the rules of IRC Subchapter J (Secs. 641-692). Real Estate Investment Trusts and Real Estate Mortgage Investment Conduits receive special tax treatment under IRC Secs. 856 and 860A, respectively. Certain organizations must be treated as corporations for federal income tax purposes. They are not eligible to elect partnership status. These include:[9]

- A business entity organized as a corporation under a federal or state statute;
- An association;

[9] Reg. Sec. 301.7701-2(b)(8). Publicly-traded partnerships are discussed in Chapter C10. Special check-the-box rules apply to foreign corporations. These rules are beyond the scope of an introductory text.

- A joint-stock company;
- An insurance company;
- A bank;
- A business owned by a State or any political subdivision thereof;
- A business entity that is taxable as a corporation under any special provision of the Internal Revenue Code (e.g., certain publicly traded partnerships).

Any business entity that is not required to be treated as a coporation for federal tax purposes is an "eligible entity" and may choose its classification under specified rules.[10] These rules provide that an eligible entity with at least two members can be classified as either a partnership or a corporation. An eligible entity with a single member can be classified as a corporation or disregarded as an entity separate from its owner (i.e., taxed as a sole proprietorship, branch, or division).

The new regulations provide default rules if no election is made. The rationale for the default rules is that the IRS wanted most firms not to need to make an election. Therefore, default is the choice they expect from most taxpayers.

Under these default rules, any new eligible entity having at least two members is classified as a partnership. Any new eligible entity with a single member is disregarded as an entity separate from its owner. The default classification for an existing entity is the classification that the entity claimed immediately prior to January 1, 1997. However, the default rule for a single-member entity claiming to be a partnership immediately prior to January 1, 1997, is to be disregarded as an entity separate from its owner. The basic presumption is that an entity's classification on January 1, 1997 is correct, and that an entity's default classification continues until the entity elects to change its classification by means of an affirmative election.[11]

An eligible entity may affirmatively elect its classification on Form 8832 [Entity Classification Election]. The election must be signed by each member of the entity, or any officer, manager, or member of the entity who is authorized to make the election. The election must include all required information, including the entity's taxpayer identification number. Taxpayers must specify the date on which an election will be effective. The effective date cannot be more than 75 days before or 12 months after the date the election was filed. A copy of the Form 8832 must be attached to the entity's tax return for the election year.

EXAMPLE C2-8 ▶ On January 10, 1997, a group of ten individuals organizes a LLC to conduct a bookbinding business in Texas. Prior to 1997, this entity might have been taxed as a corporation if it possessed at least three of the four corporate characteristics of limited liability, continuity of life, centralized management, and free transferability of interests. Whether it possessed these characteristics depended on the laws of the State of Texas. In 1997, the LLC is an eligible entity under federal law. Its owners may elect to have the LLC taxed as a corporation. However, if they do not make an election to be taxed as a corporation, the LLC is taxed as a partnership. ◀

EXAMPLE C2-9 ▶ Assume the same facts as in Example C2-8 except the LLC was created by a single individual. Because one individual organized the LLC and did not elect to have it taxed as a corporation, the LLC is disregarded for tax purposes. Its income is taxed to the owner under the rules for a sole proprietorship. ◀

If an entity makes an election to change its classification, it cannot again change its classification by election during the 60 months following the effective date of the election.

[10] Reg. Sec. 301.7701-2.

[11] An exception to this presumption applies if an IRS examination of the classification was in process prior to May 8, 1996.

The change made by an eligible entity from one classification to another may produce some tax consequences. The consequences of changing from a partnership to an LLC or an LLP are discussed in Chapter C10. An election by an LLC to be taxed as a corporation would cause the Sec. 351 corporate formation rules to apply. As discussed below, the corporate formation transaction generally will be tax-free. An election by an LLC to change from being taxed as a corporation to a sole proprietorship or partnership is a corporate liquidation (see Chapter C6).[12]

LEGAL REQUIREMENTS FOR FORMING A CORPORATION

OBJECTIVE 3

Determine the legal requirements for forming a corporation

The legal requirements for forming a corporation depend on state law. These requirements may include

- A minimum amount of capital
- The filing of the articles of incorporation
- The granting of a corporate charter by the state
- The issuance of stock
- The payment of incorporation fees to the state

One of the first decisions that must be made when plans are made to form a corporation is selecting the state in which the organization is to be incorporated. A particular state may provide certain advantages to the corporation and/or its shareholders because its laws provide smaller legal capital minimums, a smaller incorporation fee, a lower annual franchise tax liability, or a lower corporate income tax liability. Most corporations, however, are incorporated in the state in which they initially conduct their primary business activities.

ADDITIONAL COMMENT

States are not consistent in how they tax corporations. Certain states have no state income taxes. Other states will not recognize an S election, thereby taxing an S corporation as a C corporation.

Regardless of which state is selected for incorporation, the laws of that state must be followed in the incorporation process. Normally, articles of incorporation must be filed with the appropriate state agency. The articles must contain such information as the name of the corporation, the purpose of the corporation, the amount and types of stock the corporation is authorized to issue, and the names of the individuals on the corporation's board of directors. A fee is charged by the state at the time of the incorporation. In addition, an annual franchise tax may be imposed for the privilege of doing business as a corporation.

Even if all the state law requirements are met, an entity is not necessarily treated as a corporation for tax purposes. For example, if an entity organized as a corporation is found to be a mere agent for its shareholders that does not engage in any significant business activity of its own, its status as a separate entity may be ignored for tax purposes. Conversely, an entity may be taxed as a corporation even if it does *not* qualify as a corporation under state law. For example, if a corporation has not been properly organized and has failed one or more of the state's requirements for corporation status, but is an "association" under the Internal Revenue Code, it will be taxed as a corporation.

[12] An alternative way for a C corporation to be taxed as a flowthrough entity is by making an S election to be taxed under IRC Subchapter S. See Chapter C11.

TAX CONSIDERATIONS IN FORMING A CORPORATION

Once a decision has been reached to use the corporate form for conducting a business, the investors generally must transfer money, property (e.g., equipment, furniture, inventory, and receivables), or services (e.g., accounting, legal, or architectural services) to the corporation in exchange for a debt or equity interest in the corporation. These transfers may have tax consequences to both the transferor and the corporation. For instance, an exchange of property for stock is usually a taxable exchange to the transferors.[13] However, if Sec. 351(a) (which considers certain transferred business assets to be "changed in form" rather than "disposed of") applies, any gain or loss realized on the exchange is deferred. Thus, the answers to the following questions must be considered carefully in relation to the tax consequences of incorporation:

- What property should be transferred to the corporation?
- What services should be provided to the corporation by the transferors or by third parties?
- What liabilities should be transferred to the corporation in addition to the transferred property?
- How should the property be transferred to the corporation (e.g., sale, contribution to capital, or loan)?

The tax consequences of taxable and tax-free asset transfers are compared in Table C2-1 and in Example C2-10.

EXAMPLE C2-10 ▶ Brad has operated a successful manufacturing business as a sole proprietorship for several years. For good business reasons, he decides to incorporate his business. Immediately preceding the formation of Block Corporation, the balance sheet for his sole proprietorship, which uses the accrual method of accounting, is as follows:

		Adjusted Basis	*Fair Market Value*
Assets:			
Cash		$ 10,000	$ 10,000
Accounts receivable		15,000	15,000
Inventory		20,000	25,000
Equipment	$120,000		
Minus: Depreciation	(35,000)	85,000	100,000
Total		$130,000	$150,000
Liabilities and owner's equity:			
Accounts payable		$ 30,000	$ 30,000
Note payable on equipment		50,000	50,000
Owner's equity		50,000	70,000
Total		$130,000	$150,000

If the transfer of these assets and liabilities to Block Corporation is a taxable event, Brad must recognize a $5,000 ordinary gain on the transfer of the inventory ($25,000 FMV − $20,000 basis) and a $15,000 ordinary gain on the transfer of the equipment ($100,000 FMV − $85,000 basis). However, if the transaction meets the requirements of Sec. 351(a), the exchange is tax-free; any gain realized on the transfer of the assets and liabilities to the corporation is not recognized. ◀

[13] Sec. 1001.

▼ **TABLE C2-1**
Overview of Corporate Formation Rules

Tax Treatment for:	Taxable Transaction	Tax-Free Transaction
Transferors:		
1. Gain realized	FMV of stock received FMV of securities received Money received FMV of nonmoney boot property received Amount of liabilities assumed or acquired by transferee corporation Minus: Adjusted basis of property transferred Realized gain (Sec. 1001(a))	Same as taxable transaction
2. Gain recognized	Entire amount of realized gain is recognized (Sec. 1001(c)) Losses may be disallowed under Sec. 267(a)(1) related party rules Installment method of accounting may apply to the sale (Sec. 453) Restrictions on characterizing the recognized gain are imposed on certain sales of depreciable property	None of the realized gain is recognized unless one of the following exceptions applies (Sec. 351(a)): a. Boot property is received (Sec. 351(b)) b. Liabilities having nonbusiness or tax avoidance purpose are transferred (Sec. 357(b)) c. Liabilities in excess of basis are transferred (Sec. 357(c)) d. Services, certain corporate indebtednesses, and interest claims are transferred (Sec. 351(d)) The installment method of accounting may defer recognition of gain when boot property (e.g., corporate note) is received (Sec. 453)
3. Basis of property received	Cost/FMV (Sec. 1012)	Basis of property transferred Plus: Gain recognized Minus: Money received (including liabilities treated as money) FMV of nonmoney boot property Total basis of stock received (carryover basis property) (Sec. 358(a)) Allocation of total basis for carryover basis property is based on relative FMVs Basis of nonmoney boot property is its FMV
4. Holding period of property received	Day after the exchange date	Holding period for stock includes holding period of property transferred if received for Sec. 1231 property or capital assets (Sec. 1223); otherwise it is the day after the exchange date
Transferee Corporation:		
1. Gain recognized	No gain or loss is recognized by a corporation on the receipt of money or other property in exchange for its stock (including treasury stock) (Sec. 1012)	Same except that gain may be recognized under Sec. 311 if nonmoney boot property is given (Sec. 351(f))
2. Basis	Cost/FMV (Sec. 1012)	Same as in transferor's hands and increased by amount of gain recognized by transferor (Sec. 362)
3. Holding period	Day after the exchange date	Carryover holding period from transferor applies regardless of character of asset (Sec. 1223(2))

STOP & THINK

Question: Joyce has been operating a business as a sole proprietorship for several years. She needs additional capital and wants to incorporate her business. The assets of her business (building, land, inventory, and so on) have a $400,000 adjusted basis and a $1,500,000 FMV. Joyce is willing to exchange the assets for 1,500 shares of Ace Corporation stock each having a $1,000 fair market value. Bill and John are each willing to invest $500,000 in Joyce's business for 500 shares of stock. Why is Sec. 351 important to Joyce? Does it matter to Bill and John?

Solution: If not for Sec. 351, Joyce would have to recognize gain on the incorporation of her business. She has a $1,100,000 ($1,500,000 − $400,000) realized gain on her contribution of the proprietorship's assets to a new corporation in exchange for 60% of its outstanding shares (1,500 ÷ [1,500 + 500 + 500] = 0.60) None of this gain is recognized under Sec. 351. Section 351 does not affect Bill or John because each individual is simply purchasing 20% of the new corporation's stock for $500,000 cash. They do not realize or recognize any gain whether Sec. 351 applies or not.

TYPICAL MISCONCEPTION

Section 351 is an example of a nontaxable exchange. However, a nontaxable exchange really means that the recognition of gain/loss is merely deferred. In other words, any gain/loss realized by the transferor shareholders is deferred and will be recognized by such shareholders in subsequent taxable dispositions of the transferee corporation's stock.

If all exchanges of property for corporate stock were taxable, many business owners would find the tax cost of incorporating prohibitively expensive. In Example C2-10, for example, Brad would recognize a $20,000 gain on the exchange of his assets for the corporate stock.

A second problem is that losses also are realized in an exchange transaction. Therefore, taxpayers might be able to exchange loss properties for stock and securities and recognize the loss while maintaining an economic interest in the property through stock ownership.

Section 351 was enacted to respond to these two problems: to allow taxpayers to incorporate without incurring adverse tax consequences and to prevent taxpayers from recognizing losses while maintaining ownership of the loss assets indirectly through stock ownership.

SECTION 351: DEFERRING GAIN OR LOSS UPON INCORPORATION

OBJECTIVE 4

Explain the requirements for deferring gain or loss upon incorporation

Section 351(a) provides that no gain or loss is recognized when property is transferred to a corporation in exchange for the corporation's stock provided that, immediately after the exchange, the transferors are in control of the corporation. Section 351 does not apply to a transfer of property to an investment company, nor does it apply in certain bankruptcy cases.[14]

SELF-STUDY QUESTION

What rationale exists for treating a Sec. 351 transaction as a nontaxable exchange?

ANSWER

A Sec. 351 transaction is nontaxable because a taxpayer merely exchanges a direct ownership in some assets for an indirect ownership in those same assets through stock ownership in the transferee corporation. The wherewithal-to-pay doctrine suggests that if the transferor does not receive money or money equivalents, then the transaction is not an appropriate taxing event.

Underlying this rule is the belief that when property is transferred to a controlled corporation, the transferors have merely exchanged direct ownership for indirect ownership by means of having a stock interest in the transferee corporation. If all the shareholders receive is stock, they do not have any cash with which to pay any taxes. This scenario is an example of a case in which Congress applied the "wherewithal-to-pay doctrine." If the transferors of property receive anything in addition to stock, such as cash or debt instruments, they do have the wherewithal to pay and may be required to recognize some or all of their realized gain under the provisions of Sec. 351(b).

A transferor's gain or loss that goes unrecognized when Sec. 351 applies is not permanently exempt from taxation; it is only *deferred* until the stock received in the exchange is sold or exchanged. Shareholders who receive stock in an exchange qualifying under Sec. 351 must adjust the basis of their investment to reflect the deferred gain or loss. Thus, to obtain the adjusted basis of the stock, the deferred gain amount must be

[14] Secs. 351(e)(1) and (2).

deducted from (or the deferred loss must be added to) the FMV of the stock the shareholders.

EXAMPLE C2-11 ▶ Assume the same facts as in Example C2-10. If Sec. 351 applies, Brad does not recognize any gain or loss when the assets and liabilities of his sole proprietorship are transferred to Block Corporation. The $20,000 realized gain ($15,000 gain on equipment + $5,000 gain on inventory) is deferred until Brad sells his Block stock. Brad's basis for the Block stock is decreased to reflect the deferred gain. Thus, Brad's basis in the Block stock is $50,000 ($70,000 FMV of Block stock − $20,000 deferred gain). ◀

The specific requirements for complete deferral of gain and loss under Sec. 351(a) are

- Property must be transferred to the corporation in an exchange transaction.
- The transferors of the property must be in control of the corporation immediately after the exchange.
- The transferors must receive stock of the transferee corporation in exchange for their property.

Each of these requirements is explained below.

THE PROPERTY REQUIREMENT

Nonrecognition of gain or loss applies only to transfers of property to a corporation that are in exchange for the corporation's stock. Section 351 does not define the term *property*. However, the courts and the government have defined the term *property* to include money and almost any other kind of property, including installment obligations, accounts receivable, inventory, equipment, patents and other intangibles representing "know how," trademarks, trade names, and computer software.[15]

SELF-STUDY QUESTION

How is the contribution of services treated in a Sec. 351 transaction?

ANSWER

When a corporation is formed, it is not uncommon for some shareholders to contribute property and for other shareholders to contribute services. The contribution of services does not qualify for nonrecognition treatment under Sec. 351. Thus, the FMV of stock and other property received by shareholders who contribute their services to a corporation is treated as compensation income.

Statutorily excluded from the property definition are[16]

- Services (such as legal or accounting services) received in exchange for stock in a corporation
- Indebtedness of the transferee corporation that is not evidenced by a security
- Interest on an indebtedness of the transferee corporation that accrued on or after the beginning of the transferor's holding period for the debt

The first of these exclusions is perhaps the most important. A person receiving stock as compensation for services must recognize the stock's FMV as compensation (ordinary income) for tax purposes. In other words, an exchange of services for stock is a taxable transaction.[17] A shareholder's basis in the stock received as compensation for services is the stock's FMV.

EXAMPLE C2-12 ▶ Amy and Bill form West Corporation. Amy exchanges cash and other property for 90 shares (90% of the outstanding shares) of West stock. The exchange is tax-free because Sec. 351(a) applies. Bill performs accounting services in exchange for 10 shares of West stock worth $10,000. Bill's exchange is *not* tax-free under Sec. 351. Thus, Bill must recognize $10,000 of ordinary income—the FMV of the West stock received—as compensation for services. Bill's basis in the West stock received is $10,000, its FMV. ◀

ADDITIONAL COMMENT

The control requirement is satisfied if, immediately after the transfer, the transferor shareholders own at least 80% of the aggregate voting power and at least 80% of each class of nonvoting stock. Although this is the same control test that is used in the corporate reorganization area, it is different from the affiliated group stock ownership requirements for consolidated tax return purposes.

THE CONTROL REQUIREMENT

Section 351 requires the transferors, as a group, to be in control of the transferee corporation immediately after the exchange. A transferor can be any type of tax entity (such as an individual, a partnership, another corporation, or a trust). Under Sec. 368(c), *control* is defined as ownership of at least 80% of the total combined voting power of all

[15] For an excellent discussion of the definition of *property*, see footnote 6 of *D. N. Stafford v. U.S.*, 45 AFTR 2d 80-785, 80-1 USTC ¶9218 (5th Cir., 1980).

[16] Sec. 351(d).

[17] Sec. 61.

classes of stock entitled to vote and at least 80% of the total number of shares of all other classes of stock (e.g., nonvoting preferred stock).[18] The minimum ownership levels for nonvoting stock are applied to each class of stock rather than to the nonvoting stock in total.[19]

EXAMPLE C2-13 ▶ Dan exchanges property having a $22,000 adjusted basis and a $30,000 FMV for 60% of newly created Sun Corporation's single class of stock. Ed exchanges $20,000 cash for the remaining 40% of the Sun stock. The transaction qualifies under Sec. 351 because the transferors, Dan and Ed, together own at least 80% of the Sun stock immediately after the exchange. Therefore, Dan defers recognition of his $8,000 ($30,000 − $22,000) gain on the exchange. ◀

KEY POINT

Even though the 80% control requirement may be satisfied, Sec. 351 does not cause the transaction to be nontaxable to a transferor of services.

Because services do not qualify as property, stock received by a transferor in exchange for services does not count in determining whether the 80% control test has been met. Unless 80% of the corporation's stock is owned by the transferors who exchanged property for stock, Sec. 351 does not apply and the entire transaction is taxable.

EXAMPLE C2-14 ▶ Dana exchanges property having an $18,000 adjusted basis and a $35,000 FMV for 70 shares of newly created York Corporation stock. Ellen exchanges legal services worth $15,000 for the remaining 30 shares of York stock. Because Ellen does not transfer any property to York Corporation, her stock is not counted for purposes of the control requirement. Only Dana transfers property to York and is counted for purposes of the control test. However, Dana is not in control of York immediately after the exchange because he owns only 70% of the York stock. Therefore, Sec. 351 does not apply to the transaction. Dana must recognize $17,000 ($35,000 − $18,000) of gain on the exchange. Dana's basis in his York stock is $35,000, its FMV. Ellen must recognize $15,000 of ordinary income, the FMV of the stock received for her services. The tax consequences to Ellen are the same whether Sec. 351 applies to Dana or not. Ellen's basis in her York stock is $15,000. ◀

If the transferors of property own at least 80% of the stock after the exchange, Sec. 351 applies to them, even if it does not apply to a transferor of services.

EXAMPLE C2-15 ▶ Assume the same facts as in Example C2-14, except that a third individual, Fred, provides $35,000 of cash for 70 shares of York stock. Now Dana and Fred together own more than 80% of the York stock (140 ÷ 170 = 0.82). Therefore, Sec. 351 applies to the transaction. Neither Dana nor Fred recognizes any gain on the exchange. Ellen still must recognize $15,000 of ordinary income, the FMV of the stock she receives for her services. ◀

TRANSFERORS OF BOTH PROPERTY AND SERVICES. If a person transfers both services *and* property to a corporation in exchange for the corporation's stock, all of the stock received by that person is counted in determining whether the transferors of property have acquired control.[20]

EXAMPLE C2-16 ▶ Assume the same facts as in Example C2-14, except that in addition to legal services worth $15,000, Ellen also contributes property worth at least $1,500. In such case, all of Ellen's stock counts in determining whether the 80% minimum stock ownership requirement has been met. Because Dana and Ellen together own 100% of the York stock, the exchange meets the

[18] In determining whether the 80% requirements are satisfied, the constructive ownership rules of Sec. 318 do not apply (see Rev. Rul. 56-613, 1956-2 C.B. 212).

[19] Rev. Rul. 59-259, 1959-2 C.B. 115.

[20] Reg. Sec. 1.351-1(a)(2), Ex. (3).

TYPICAL MISCONCEPTION

If a shareholder contributes both services and more than a minimum amount of property, the stock received for the services can be counted in satisfying the 80% control requirement. However, the FMV of stock received for services is still considered compensation to the shareholder.

control requirement of Sec. 351. Therefore, Dana does not recognize any gain on the exchange. However, Ellen still must recognize $15,000 of ordinary income, the FMV of the stock received as compensation for services. ◀

When a person transfers both property and services in exchange for a corporation's stock, the property must be of more than nominal value in order for that person's stock to count toward the 80% control requirement.[21] The IRS generally requires that the FMV of the transferred property be at least 10% of the value of the services provided. If the value of the transferred property is less than 10% of the value of the services provided, the IRS will not issue an advance ruling stating that the transaction meets the requirements of Sec. 351.[22]

EXAMPLE C2-17 ▶ Assume the same facts as in Example C2-16, except that Ellen contributes only $1,000 worth of property in addition to $15,000 of legal services. In such case, the IRS will not issue an advance ruling that the transaction meets the requirements of Sec. 351 because the FMV of the property transferred ($1,000) is less than 10% of the value of the services provided ($1,500 = 0.10 × $15,000). Because the transaction does not meet the IRS requirement for an advance ruling, it is likely to be challenged by the IRS if Ellen treats the transfer as coming under Sec. 351 and her tax return for the year of transfer is audited. ◀

TRANSFERS TO EXISTING CORPORATIONS. Section 351 can apply to transfers to an existing corporation as well as transfers to a newly-created corporation. The same requirements apply in both cases. Property must be transferred in exchange for stock, and the transferors of the property must be in control of the corporation immediately after the exchange.

EXAMPLE C2-18 ▶ Jack and Karen own 75 shares and 25 shares of Texas Corporation stock, respectively. Jack transfers property with a $15,000 adjusted basis and a $25,000 FMV to Texas Corporation in exchange for an additional 25 shares of Texas stock. Section 351 applies because, after the transaction, Jack owns 80% (100 ÷ 125 = 0.80) of the Texas stock and is in control of Texas Corporation. Therefore, Jack does not recognize any gain on the exchange. ◀

TYPICAL MISCONCEPTION

Taxpayers often think that Sec. 351 applies only to contributions of property to newly formed corporations. This is not true. Section 351 can apply to contributions of property to existing corporations as long as the transferor shareholders have control of the transferee corporation immediately after the transaction.

If a shareholder transfers property to an existing corporation for additional stock but does not own at least 80% of the stock after the exchange, Sec. 351 does not apply. The 80% control requirement precludes many transfers of property to an existing corporation by a new shareholder from qualifying as tax-free. A transfer to an existing corporation is tax-free for a new shareholder only if an 80% interest in the corporation is acquired, or enough existing shareholders also transfer property to the corporation to permit the 80% requirement to be satisfied by the transferors as a group.

EXAMPLE C2-19 ▶ Alice owns all 100 shares of Local Corporation's stock, valued at $100,000. Beth owns property that has a $15,000 adjusted basis and a $100,000 FMV. Beth contributes the property to Local Corporation in exchange for 100 shares of newly-issued Local stock. Section 351 does not apply because Beth owns only 50% of the Local stock after the exchange and is not in control of Local Corporation. Beth must recognize an $85,000 ($100,000 − $15,000) gain on the exchange. ◀

If an existing shareholder exchanges property for additional stock in order to help another shareholder qualify under Sec. 351, the stock received must be of more than nominal value.[23] For advance ruling purposes, the IRS requires that the value of the

---

[21] Reg. Sec. 1.351-1(a)(1)(ii).

[22] Rev. Proc. 77-37, 1977-2 C.B. 568, Sec. 3.07.

[23] Reg. Sec. 1.351-1(a)(1)(ii).

property transferred be at least 10% of the value of the stock and securities already owned.[24]

EXAMPLE C2-20 ▶ Assume the same facts as in Example C2-19, except that Alice transfers additional property worth $10,000 for an additional 10 shares of Local stock. Now Alice and Beth are both considered to be transferors and Sec. 351 does apply. Neither Alice nor Beth recognizes any gain on the exchange. If Alice transfers property worth less than $10,000, the IRS will not issue an advance ruling that Sec. 351 applies to the exchange. ◀

STOP & THINK

Question: Matthew and Michael each own 50 shares of Main Corporation stock having a $250,000 FMV. Matthew wants to transfer property with a $40,000 adjusted basis and a $100,000 FMV to Main Corporation for an additional 20 shares of Main stock. Can Matthew avoid recognizing $60,000 ($100,000 − $40,000) of gain on the transfer?

Solution: If Matthew simply exchanges the property for additional stock, he will have to recognize the gain. IRC Section 351 will not apply because Matthew owns only 70 out of 120 outstanding shares (or 58.33%) of the Main stock immediately after the exchange.

Matthew can avoid recognizing gain in two ways:

1. Matthew can transfer sufficient property to Main Corporation to receive 150 additional shares (i.e., $750,000 worth of property) so that after the exchange he owns 80% (200 out of 250 shares) of the Main stock.
2. Alternatively, Matthew can avoid recognizing gain if Michael contributes sufficient property to be counted in the control group since, together, the two shareholders will own 100% of the Main stock. To count, Michael must contribute cash or other property worth at least $25,000, 10% of the $250,000 value of the Main stock that Michael already owns.

DISPROPORTIONATE EXCHANGES OF PROPERTY AND STOCK. Section 351 does not require that the value of the stock received by the transferors be proportional to the value of the property transferred. However, if the value of the stock received is *not* proportional to the value of the property transferred, the exchange must be treated in accordance with its true nature, that is, a proportional exchange followed by a gift, payment of compensation, or payment of a liability owed by one shareholder to another.[25] If the true nature of the transaction is a gift from one transferor to another transferor, for example, the donor is treated as though he or she received stock equal in value to the property contributed to the corporation and then gave some of the stock to the donee.

EXAMPLE C2-21 ▶ Don and his son John transfer property worth $75,000 (adjusted basis to Don of $42,000) and $25,000 (adjusted basis to John of $20,000), respectively, to newly-formed Star Corporation in exchange for all 100 shares of Star stock. Don and John receive 25 and 75 shares of Star stock, respectively. Because Don and John are in control of Star Corporation immediately after the transaction, Sec. 351 applies and no gain or loss is recognized on the exchange. However, because the stock was not received by Don and John in proportion to the FMV of their property contributions, it is likely that Don has received 75 shares of Star stock (worth $75,000) and made a gift of 50 shares of Star stock (worth $50,000) to John, thereby leaving Don with $25,000 of Star stock. If a gift has in fact been made, Don may be required to pay gift taxes on the gift to John. Don's basis in the 25 shares of Star stock is $14,000 [(25 ÷ 75) × $42,000 basis in the property transferred]. John's basis in the 75 shares is $48,000 [$20,000 basis in the property transferred by John + ($42,000 − $14,000) basis in the shares received from Don]. ◀

[24] Rev. Proc. 77-37, 1977-2 C.B. 568, Sec. 3.07.

[25] Reg. Sec. 1.351-1(b)(1).

IMMEDIATELY AFTER THE EXCHANGE. Section 351 requires that the transferors be in control of the transferee corporation "immediately after the exchange." This requirement does not mean that all transferors must exchange their property for stock simultaneously. The exchanges must all be agreed to beforehand, and the agreement must be executed in an expeditious and orderly manner.[26]

EXAMPLE C2-22 ▶ Art, Beth, and Carlos agree to form New Corporation. Art and Beth each transfer noncash property worth $25,000 for one-third of the New stock. Carlos contributes $25,000 cash for one-third of the New stock. Art and Carlos exchange their property and cash, respectively, for stock on January 10. Beth exchanges her property for stock on March 3. Since all three of the exchanges are part of the same prearranged transaction, the Sec. 351 nonrecognition rules apply to all three exchanges. ◀

ADDITIONAL COMMENT

If one shareholder has a prearranged plan to dispose of his or her stock, and the disposition drops the ownership of the transferor shareholders below the required 80% control, such disposition can disqualify the Sec. 351 transaction for all of the shareholders. As a possible protection, all shareholders could be required to provide a written representation that they do not currently have a plan to dispose of their stock.

Section 351 does not require the transferors to retain control of the transferee corporation for any specific length of time after the exchange takes place. Control is only required "immediately after the exchange." However, the transferors must not have a prearranged plan to dispose of their stock outside the group. If they have such an arrangement, they are not considered to be in control immediately after the exchange.[27]

EXAMPLE C2-23 ▶ Amir, Bill, and Carl form White Corporation. Each contributes appreciated property worth $25,000 for one-third of the White stock. Before the exchange, Amir arranges to sell his stock to Dana as soon as he receives it. This prearranged plan means that Amir, Bill, and Carl do *not* have control immediately after the exchange. Therefore, Sec. 351 does not apply to the transaction. ◀

Topic Review C2-1

Major Requirements of Sec. 351

1. Nonrecognition of gain or loss applies only to transfers of property in exchange for a corporation's stock. It does not apply to an exchange of services for stock.
2. The transferors of property must be in control of the transferee corporation immediately after the exchange. Control means ownership of at least 80% of the voting power and 80% of the total number of shares of all other classes of stock. There must not be any prearranged plan to dispose of the stock after the exchange.
3. Nonrecognition applies only to an exchange of property for stock. If anything other than stock is received, it is considered boot. Gain is recognized to the extent of the lesser of the FMV of any boot received or the realized gain.

THE STOCK REQUIREMENT

Under Sec. 351, no gain or loss is recognized by transferors who exchange property solely for transferee corporation stock. Under Sec. 351 any type of stock of the controlled corporation—voting or nonvoting stock, preferred or common stock—may be received by the transferors. However, stock does not include stock rights or stock warrants.[28]

Topic Review C2-1 presents a summary of the major requirements to achieve a tax-free transfer under Sec. 351.

---

[26] Reg. Sec. 1.351-1(a)(1).

[27] Rev. Rul. 79-70, 1979-1 C.B. 144.

[28] Reg. Sec. 1.351-1(a)(1)(ii).

EFFECT OF SEC. 351 ON THE TRANSFERORS

If all of the Sec. 351 requirements have been met, the transferors do not recognize any gain or loss on the exchange of their property for stock in the corporation to which they have contributed their property. The receipt of property other than stock does not completely disqualify the transaction from coming under Sec. 351. However, the receipt of property other than stock may require the transferors to recognize part or all of their realized gain under Sec. 351(b).

KEY POINT

If boot property is received by transferor shareholders, they must recognize gain to the extent of the lesser of (1) realized gain or (2) FMV of boot received. However, no matter how much boot is received, realized losses are not recognized in a Sec. 351 transaction.

RECEIPT OF BOOT. If a transferor receives any money or property other than stock of the transferee corporation, the additional property is considered **boot.** Boot may include cash, notes, securities, or stock in another corporation. When boot is received, gain must be recognized to the extent of the lesser of the transferor's realized gain or the FMV of the boot property received.[29] However, a loss is never recognized in an exchange qualifying under Sec. 351 whether boot is received or not.

The character of the gain recognized when boot is received in a Sec. 351 transaction depends on the type of property that is transferred. For example, if a capital asset such as stock of another corporation is transferred, the recognized gain is a capital gain. If a Sec. 1231 property such as equipment or a building is transferred, the recognized gain is Sec. 1231 gain, except for any ordinary income that is recaptured under Secs. 1245 or 1250.[30] If inventory is transferred, the recognized gain is ordinary income. Note that depreciation recapture is *not* required unless boot is received by the transferor and a gain must be recognized.[31]

EXAMPLE C2-24 ▶ Pam, Rob, and Sam form East Corporation by transferring the following properties.

		Property Transferred		
Transferor	*Asset*	*Transferor's Adj. Basis*	*FMV*	*Consideration Received*
Pam	Machinery	$10,000	$12,500	25 shares East stock
Rob	Land	18,000	25,000	40 shares East stock and $5,000 East note
Sam	Cash	17,500	17,500	35 shares East stock

The machinery and land are a Sec. 1231 property and a capital asset, respectively. The transaction meets the requirements of Sec. 351 except that, in addition to East stock, Rob receives boot of $5,000 (the FMV of the note). Rob realizes a $7,000 ($25,000 − $18,000) gain on the exchange. Rob must recognize $5,000 of gain—the lesser of the $7,000 realized gain or the $5,000 boot received. The gain is a capital gain because the property transferred was a capital asset in Rob's hands. Pam realizes a $2,500 gain on her exchange of machinery for East stock. But even though Pam might be required to recapture depreciation taken on the machinery as ordinary income if the machinery were sold or exchanged, Pam does not recognize any gain on the exchange because Sec. 351 applies to the exchange and Pam did not receive any boot. Sam does not realize or recognize any gain on his cash purchase of the East stock. ◀

KEY POINT

If multiple assets are contributed by a transferor, the gain/loss realized on the exchange must be computed on an asset-by-asset basis. If all the assets were aggregated into one computation, then any built-in losses would be netted against the gains. Such a result is inappropriate because losses cannot be recognized in a Sec. 351 transaction.

COMPUTING GAIN WHEN SEVERAL ASSETS ARE TRANSFERRED. If more than one asset is transferred, Rev. Rul. 68-55 adopts a "separate properties approach" for computing gain or loss.[32] The gain or loss realized and recognized is computed separately for each property transferred. The transferor is assumed to have received a proportionate share of the stock, securities, and boot for each property transferred based on the assets' relative FMVs.

EXAMPLE C2-25 ▶ Joan transfers two properties to newly created North Corporation in a transaction qualifying under Sec. 351. The total FMV of the assets transferred is $100,000. The consideration

[29] Sec. 351(b).

[30] Section 1239 may also require some gain to be characterized as ordinary income.

[31] Secs. 1245(b)(3) and 1250(c)(3).

[32] 1968-1 C.B. 140.

received by Joan consists of $90,000 of North stock and $10,000 of North notes. The following summary shows how Joan determines her realized and recognized gain using the procedure outlined in Rev. Rul. 68-55.

	Asset 1	*Asset 2*	*Total*
Asset's FMV	$40,000	$60,000	$100,000
Percent of total FMV	40%	60%	100%
Consideration received in exchange for asset:			
Stock (Stock × percent of total FMV)	$36,000	$54,000	$90,000
Notes (Notes × percent of total FMV)	4,000	6,000	10,000
Total proceeds	$40,000	$60,000	$100,000
Minus: Adjusted basis	(65,000)	(25,000)	(90,000)
Realized gain (loss)	($25,000)	$35,000	$10,000
Boot received	$ 4,000	$ 6,000	$10,000
Recognized gain (loss)	None	$ 6,000	$ 6,000

Under the separate properties approach, the loss realized on the transfer of asset 1 does not offset the gain realized on the transfer of asset 2. Therefore, only $6,000 of the total $10,000 realized gain is recognized, even though Joan receives $10,000 of boot. It may be advisable to sell asset 1 to North Corporation in order to recognize the loss. See, however, the possible loss limitation under Sec. 267 if Joan is a controlling shareholder (page C2-39). ◀

COMPUTING A SHAREHOLDER'S BASIS.

Boot Property. A transferor's basis for any boot property received is the property's FMV.[33]

Stock. A shareholder's adjusted basis for stock received in an exchange qualifying under Sec. 351 is computed as follows:[34]

Adjusted basis of property transferred to the corporation
Plus: Any gain recognized by the transferor
Minus: FMV of boot received from the corporation
Money received from the corporation
Amount of any liabilities assumed or acquired by the corporation

Adjusted basis of stock received

EXAMPLE C2-26 ▶

KEY POINT

Because Sec. 351 is a deferral provision, any unrecognized gain must be reflected in the basis of the stock received by the transferor shareholder. This is accomplished by substituting the transferor's basis in the property given up (plus certain adjustments) for the basis of the stock received.

SELF-STUDY QUESTION

What is the simplest method of determining the basis of the assets received by the transferor shareholder?

Bob transfers Sec. 1231 property acquired two years earlier having a $50,000 basis and an $80,000 FMV to South Corporation. Bob receives all 100 shares of South stock, having a $70,000 FMV, and a $10,000 90-day South note (boot property). Bob realizes a $30,000 gain on the exchange, computed as follows:

FMV of stock received	$70,000
Plus: FMV of 90-day note	10,000
Amount realized	$80,000
Minus: Adjusted basis of property transferred	(50,000)
Realized gain	$30,000

Bob's recognized gain is the lesser of the $30,000 realized gain or the $10,000 FMV of the boot property, resulting in $10,000 of Sec. 1231 gain. The Sec. 351 rules thus require Bob to defer $20,000 ($30,000 − $10,000) of gain. Bob's basis for the South stock is $50,000, computed as follows:

[33] Sec. 358(a)(2).

[34] Sec. 358(a)(1).

ANSWER

The basis of all boot property is its FMV, and the basis of stock received is the stock's FMV minus any deferred gain or plus any deferred loss.

Adjusted basis of property transferred	$50,000
Plus: Gain recognized by Bob	10,000
Minus: FMV of boot received	(10,000)
Adjusted basis of stock to Bob	$50,000 ◀

If a transferor receives more than one class of stock, his or her basis for the stocks received must be allocated among the classes of stock received in accordance with their relative FMVs.[35]

EXAMPLE C2-27 ▶ Assume the same facts as in Example C2-26, except that Bob receives 100 shares of South common stock with a $50,000 FMV, 50 shares of South preferred stock with a $20,000 FMV, and a 90-day South note with a $10,000 FMV. The recognized gain remains $10,000. The total adjusted basis of the stocks is $50,000 ($50,000 basis of property transferred + $10,000 gain recognized − $10,000 FMV of boot received). This basis must be allocated between the common and preferred stocks that are received in accordance with their relative FMVs, as follows:

$$\text{Basis of common stock} = \frac{\$50,000}{\$50,000 + \$20,000} \times \$50,000 = \$35,714$$

$$\text{Basis of preferred stock} = \frac{\$20,000}{\$50,000 + \$20,000} \times \$50,000 = \$14,286$$

Bob's basis for the note is $10,000, its FMV. ◀

Topic Review C2-2

Tax Consequences of a Sec. 351 Transaction

To Shareholders:

General Rules:

1. No gain or loss is recognized when property is exchanged for stock. Exception: Gain is recognized equal to the lesser of the realized gain or the sum of any money received plus the FMV of any other boot property received. The character of the gain recognized depends on the type of property given up.
2. The basis of the stock received equals the adjusted basis of the property transferred plus the gain recognized minus the FMV of the boot property received minus any money received (including liabilities assumed or acquired by the transferee corporation).
3. The holding period of stock received for capital assets or Sec. 1231 property includes the holding period for the transferred property. The holding period of stock received for other property begins on the day after the exchange.

To Transferee Corporation:

General Rules:

1. No gain or loss is recognized by a corporation when it exchanges its own stock for property or services.
2. The corporation's basis in any property received in a Sec. 351 exchange is the transferor's basis plus any gain recognized by the transferor.
3. The corporation's holding period for property received in a Sec. 351 exchange includes the transferor's holding period.

[35] Sec. 358(b)(1) and Reg. Sec. 1.358-2(b)(2).

TRANSFEROR'S HOLDING PERIOD. The transferor's holding period for any stock received in exchange for a capital asset or Sec. 1231 property is a substituted basis that includes the holding period for the property transferred.[36] If any other kind of property (i.e., inventory) is exchanged for the stock, the transferor's holding period for the stock received begins on the day after the exchange. The holding period for boot property begins on the day after the exchange.

EXAMPLE C2-28 ▶ Assume the same facts as in Example C2-26. Bob's holding period for the stock includes the time period that the Sec. 1231 property was held. His holding period for the note starts on the day after the exchange. ◀

STOP & THINK

Question: The holding period for stock received in exchange for a capital asset or Sec. 1231 asset includes the holding period for the transferred asset. The holding period for inventory or other assets begins on the day after the exchange. Why the difference?

Solution: Stock received in a Sec. 351 transaction is generally a capital asset. The holding period for the stock includes the transferred property's holding period if a sale of the asset would have meant recognizing a capital gain or loss. The holding period for the stock does not include the holding period for the asset if a sale of the transferred assets would have meant recognizing ordinary gain or loss (e.g., a sale of inventory). In the latter case, a sale of the stock within one year of the transfer date means recognizing a short-term capital gain or loss. For an individual shareholder, this outcome is not the same as recognizing an ordinary gain or loss from the inventory sale. Note that the gain is not eligible for the reduced 28% maximum tax rate for long-term capital gains until the stock has been held for at least one year.

Topic Review C2-2 presents a summary of the tax consequences of a tax-free asset transfer to the transferor and the transferee corporation.

EFFECT OF SEC. 351 ON TRANSFEREE CORPORATION

SELF-STUDY QUESTION

What gain or loss is recognized by the transferee corporation when a Sec. 351 transaction occurs?

ANSWER

A corporation does not recognize gain/loss when it acquires property in exchange for its own stock. This general rule applies not only to Sec. 351 transfers but also to other acquisitions of property when the consideration given is the corporation's own stock.

The transferee corporation must determine the amount of gain or loss (if any) it must recognize when it issues stock or debt instruments in exchange for property or services and the basis for any property or services that are acquired.

GAIN OR LOSS RECOGNIZED BY THE TRANSFEREE CORPORATION. Corporations do not recognize any gain or loss when they exchange their own stock for property or services.[37] This rule applies whether the exchange is subject to Sec. 351 or not. It is irrelevant whether the stock the corporation is exchanging is newly-issued stock or treasury stock.

EXAMPLE C2-29 ▶ West Corporation acquires 100 shares of treasury stock for $10,000. The next year West exchanges the 100 shares for land having a $15,000 FMV. West realizes a $5,000 ($15,000 − $10,000) gain on the exchange. None of this gain is recognized. ◀

Corporations do not recognize any gain or loss when they exchange their own debt instruments for property or services.

[36] Sec. 1223(1). Revenue Ruling 85-164 (1985-2 C.B. 117) holds that a single share of stock may have two holding periods: a carryover holding period for the portion of such share received in exchange for a capital asset or a Sec. 1231 property and a holding period that begins on the day after the exchange for the portion of such share received for inventory or other property. The split holding period is relevant only if stock received by the transferor is sold within one year of the transfer date.

[37] Sec. 1032.

A corporation must recognize gain (but not loss) if it transfers appreciated property to a transferor as part of a Sec. 351 exchange. The amount and character of the gain that is recognized are determined as though the property had been sold by the transferee corporation immediately before the transfer.[38]

EXAMPLE C2-30 ▶

Alice, who owns 100% of Ace Corporation, transfers land having a $100,000 FMV and a $60,000 adjusted basis to Ace. In return Alice receives 75 additional shares of Ace common stock having a $75,000 FMV and Zero Corporation common stock having a $25,000 FMV. The Zero stock, a capital asset, has a $10,000 basis on Ace's books. Alice realizes a $40,000 gain [($75,000 + $25,000) − $60,000] on the land transfer, of which $25,000 must be recognized. In addition, Ace Corporation must recognize a $15,000 capital gain ($25,000 − $10,000) when transferring the Zero stock to Alice. ◀

KEY POINT

Because Sec. 351 transfers are nontaxable exchanges, the transferee corporation takes a carryover basis (including gains recognized by the transferor shareholder) in the assets received. Thus, any of the built-in gains or losses in the contributed property may be subsequently recognized by the transferee corporation.

ADDITIONAL COMMENT

If built-in gain property is contributed in a Sec. 351 transfer, the built-in gain is actually duplicated. This duplication occurs because the transferee corporation assumes the potential gain through its carryover basis in the assets it receives and the transferor shareholder assumes the potential gain through its substituted basis in the transferee corporation stock. A similar duplication occurs for built-in loss property.

TRANSFEREE CORPORATION'S BASIS FOR PROPERTY RECEIVED. A corporation that purchases property by exchanging its stock in a transaction that is taxable to the transferor uses the property's acquisition cost (i.e., its FMV) as its basis for the property. However, if the exchange qualifies for nonrecognition treatment under Sec. 351 and is wholly or partially tax-free to the transferor, the corporation's basis for the property is computed as follows:[39]

Transferor's adjusted basis for property transferred to the corporation
Plus: Gain recognized by transferor

Transferee corporation's basis for property

The transferee corporation's holding period for property acquired in a transaction satisfying the Sec. 351 requirements includes the period of time the property was held by the transferor.[40] This general rule applies to all properties without regard to their character in the transferor's hands or the amount of gain recognized by the transferor.

EXAMPLE C2-31 ▶

Top Corporation exchanges 100 shares of its stock for land having a $15,000 FMV. The land is held by Tina, whose adjusted basis for the land is $12,000. If the exchange satisfies the Sec. 351 requirements, Tina does not recognize any gain on the exchange. Top Corporation's basis in the land is $12,000, the same basis that Tina had in the land. Top Corporation's holding period includes the period of time the land was held by Tina. However, if the exchange does *not* satisfy the Sec. 351 requirements, Tina must recognize $3,000 of gain. Top Corporation's basis in the land is its $15,000 acquisition cost. Its holding period for the land begins on the day after the acquisition date. ◀

ASSUMPTION OF THE TRANSFEROR'S LIABILITIES

SELF-STUDY QUESTION

Can the assumption of liabilities by the transferor corporation be disregarded?

ANSWER

Generally the answer is yes. However, two exceptions exist: (1) if the liabilities assumed are created for tax avoidance purposes or have no bona fide business purpose, or (2) if the liabilities assumed are in excess of the transferor's basis for the contributed property.

When property is transferred to a controlled corporation, the transferor's liabilities are often assumed (or the property is taken subject to a mortgage) by the corporation as well. The question arises as to whether the assumption of liabilities by the transferee is equivalent to a cash payment to the transferor and, therefore, is boot. In many other kinds of transactions, the assumption of a transferor's liability by the transferee is treated as a payment of cash to the transferor. For example, in a like-kind exchange, if a transferor's liability is assumed by a transferee, the transferor is treated as though he or she received a cash payment equal to the amount of the liability assumed. However, if a transaction satisfies the Sec. 351 requirements, the special rules of Sec. 357 apply and the liability transfer is not treated as a cash payment.

[38] Sec. 351(f).
[39] Sec. 362.
[40] Sec. 1223(2).

GENERAL RULE—SEC. 357(a). The assumption of liabilities by a transferee corporation in a property transfer qualifying under Sec. 351 is *not* considered to result in the receipt of money by the transferor. Therefore, the transferee corporation's assumption of liabilities does not cause the transferor to recognize part or all of his or her realized gain.

EXAMPLE C2-32 ▶ Roy and Eduardo form Palm Corporation by transferring the following assets and liabilities.

Transferor	*Asset/ Liability*	*Transferor's Adj. Basis*	*FMV*	*Consideration Received*
Roy	Machinery	$15,000	$32,000	50 shares Palm stock
	Mortgage	8,000		Assumed by Palm
Eduardo	Cash	24,000	24,000	50 shares Palm stock

The transaction meets the requirements of Sec. 351. Roy's recognized gain is determined as follows:

FMV of stock received	$24,000
Plus: Release from mortgage	8,000
Amount realized	$32,000
Minus: Basis of machinery	(15,000)
Realized gain	$17,000
Boot received	$—0—
Recognized gain	$—0—

Roy recognizes none of this gain because Sec. 351 applies and he receives no boot. The mortgage assumption is not considered to be money paid to Roy. Eduardo recognizes no gain since he did not receive boot property. ◀

ADDITIONAL COMMENT

If any of the assumed liabilities are created for tax avoidance purposes, this taints *all* of the assumed liabilities.

However, there are two exceptions to the general rule of Sec. 357(a). These exceptions, which are discussed below, are transfers that are made for the purpose of tax avoidance or that have no bona fide business purpose and transfers where the liabilities assumed or acquired by the corporation exceed the basis of the properties transferred by the transferor.

ETHICAL POINT

Information about any transferor liabilities that are assumed or acquired by the transferee corporation must be reported with the transferee and transferor's tax returns for the year of transfer (see page C2-40). Where a client asks a tax practitioner to ignore the fact that tax avoidance is the primary purpose for transferring a liability to a corporation, the tax practitioner must examine the ethical considerations of continuing to prepare returns and provide tax advice for the client.

TAX AVOIDANCE OR NO BONA FIDE BUSINESS PURPOSE—SEC. 357(b). All liabilities assumed by a controlled corporation (or taken subject to the property) *are* considered money received by the transferor (and, therefore, are considered boot) if the principal purpose of the transfer of any portion of such liabilities is to avoid tax or if there is no bona fide business purpose for the transfer.

Liabilities whose transfer might be considered to have tax avoidance as the principal purpose are those that were incurred shortly before the property and liability were transferred to the corporation. Perhaps the most important factor in determining whether a tax avoidance purpose is present when liabilities are transferred is the length of time between the incurrence of the liability and the transfer of the liability to the corporation.

The assumption of liabilities is normally considered to have a business purpose if the liabilities were incurred by the transferor in the normal course of business or in the course of acquiring business property. Examples of liabilities that have no business purpose and whose transfer would cause **all** liabilities transferred to be considered boot are personal obligations of the transferor, including a home mortgage or any other loans of a personal nature.

EXAMPLE C2-33 ▶ David owns land having a $100,000 FMV and a $60,000 adjusted basis. The land is not encumbered by any liabilities. In order to obtain cash for his personal use, David transfers the land to his wholly owned corporation in exchange for additional stock and $25,000 cash.

Because the cash received is considered boot, David must recognize $25,000 of gain. Assume instead that David mortgages the land for $25,000 to obtain the needed cash. If shortly after obtaining the mortgage, David transfers the land and the mortgage to his corporation for additional stock, it appears that there is no business purpose for the transfer of the mortgage. Therefore the $25,000 mortgage assumed by the corporation would be considered boot. David's recognized gain is the lesser of the boot received ($25,000) and his realized gain ($40,000), or $25,000. ◀

SELF-STUDY QUESTION

Is the excess liability amount treated as boot under Sec. 357(c)?

ANSWER

The amount by which the assumed liabilities exceed the basis of contributed property is not considered boot. Instead, this excess amount is a recognized gain regardless of whether any realized gain exists.

LIABILITIES IN EXCESS OF BASIS—SEC. 357(c). Under Sec. 357(c), if the total amount of liabilities transferred to a controlled corporation by a transferor exceeds the total adjusted basis of all properties transferred by such transferor, the excess liability amount is a gain that is taxable to the transferor. This rule applies regardless of whether there is any realized gain or loss. The rule recognizes the fact that the transferor has received a benefit (in the form of a release from liabilities) that is greater than his or her original investment in the transferred property. Therefore, the excess amount is taxable. The character of the recognized gain depends on the types of properties that were transferred to the transferee corporation. The transferor's basis in any stock received is zero.

EXAMPLE C2-34 ▶

Thus, this exception is more punitive to the transferor shareholder than the Sec. 357(b) tax avoidance exception.

Judy transfers land, a capital asset, having a $70,000 adjusted basis and a $125,000 FMV and $10,000 cash to Duke Corporation in exchange for all of its stock. Duke Corporation assumes the $100,000 mortgage on the land. There is no tax-avoidance purpose in the mortgage assumption, and the liability assumption does have the requisite business purpose. Although Judy does not receive any boot, Judy must recognize a $20,000 ($100,000 − $80,000) capital gain, the amount by which the liabilities assumed by Duke Corporation exceed the basis of the land and the cash transferred by Judy. Judy's basis for the Duke stock is zero, computed as follows:

Judy's basis in the land transferred		$70,000
Plus:	Cash transferred	10,000
	Gain recognized	20,000
Minus:	Boot received (i.e., liabilities assumed by Duke)	(100,000)
Judy's basis in the Duke stock		—0—

Note that if it were not for the Sec. 357(c) requirement to recognize a $20,000 gain, Judy's basis in the Duke stock would be a negative $20,000 ($80,000 − $100,000). ◀

STOP & THINK

Question: Why must a transferor recognize gain if the amount of liabilities transferred to a corporation under Sec. 351 exceed the basis of all assets transferred?

Solution: If the amount of liabilities transferred exceed the basis of all assets transferred, this means that the shareholder has borrowed more against the properties transferred than his or her investment in the properties. Thus, the shareholder must recognize the excess amount as gain. In addition, if the transferor did not recognize this amount, his or her basis in the stock would be negative. Since a shareholder cannot have a negative basis, he or she must recognize the excess amount as gain.

LIABILITIES OF A TAXPAYER USING THE CASH METHOD OF ACCOUNTING—SEC. 357(c)(3). Special problems arise when a taxpayer using the cash or hybrid method of accounting transfers the properties and liabilities of an ongoing business to a

KEY POINT

Because of the "liabilities in excess of basis" exception, many cash basis transferor shareholders might inadvertently create recognized gain in a Sec. 351 transaction. However, a special exception exists that protects cash basis taxpayers. This exception provides that liabilities that would give rise to a deduction when paid are not treated as liabilities for purposes of Sec. 357(c).

corporation in a tax-free exchange under Sec. 351.[41] Quite often, the main assets that are transferred are accounts receivable that have a zero basis. Liabilities are usually transferred as well. Consequently, the amount of liabilities transferred often exceeds the total basis (but not the FMV) of the properties transferred.

Under Sec. 357(c), gain equal to the amount by which the liabilities assumed or acquired exceed the total basis of the properties transferred would have to be recognized. However, a special exception to Sec. 357(c) provides that the term *liabilities* does *not* include any amount that (1) would give rise to a deduction when paid or (2) any amount payable under Sec. 736(a) (i.e., amounts payable to a retiring partner or to liquidate a deceased partner's interest). These amounts are also not considered liabilities for purposes of applying the Sec. 358 basis rules to determine the shareholder's basis for any stock items.[42] Therefore, they do not reduce the shareholder's basis in his or her stock.

EXAMPLE C2-35 ▶ Tracy operates an accounting practice as a sole proprietorship. She transfers the assets of her cash basis accounting practice to Prime Corporation in exchange for all of the Prime stock. The items transferred are

Assets and Liabilities	*Adjusted Basis*	*FMV*
Cash	$ 5,000	$ 5,000
Furniture	5,000	8,000
Accounts receivable	—0—	50,000
Total	$10,000	$63,000
Accounts payable (expenses)	$—0—	$25,000
Note payable (on office furniture)	2,000	2,000
Owner's equity	8,000	36,000
Total	$10,000	$63,000

If the accounts payable were considered *liabilities,* the $27,000 of liabilities transferred (i.e., the $25,000 of accounts payable and the $2,000 note payable) would exceed the $10,000 basis for the properties transferred. However, because payment of the $25,000 of accounts payable gives rise to a deduction, they are not considered liabilities for purposes of applying Sec. 357(c). The $2,000 note payable *is* considered a liability because paying it would *not* give rise to a deduction. Thus, for purposes of applying Sec. 357(c), the total liabilities transferred to Prime Corporation amount to $2,000. Because that amount does not exceed the $10,000 basis of the properties transferred, no gain is recognized. The accounts payable are not considered liabilities for purposes of computing Tracy's basis for the Prime stock. Therefore, Tracy's basis for her stock is $8,000 ($10,000 − $2,000). ◀

Topic Review C2-3 presents a summary of the liability assumption and acquisition rules of Sec. 357.

KEY POINT

Unless gain is recognized by the transferor, any potential depreciation recapture follows the contributed property into the transferee corporation. When such property is subsequently disposed of, the depreciation recapture rules must be applied at that time.

OTHER CONSIDERATIONS IN A SEC. 351 EXCHANGE

RECAPTURE OF DEPRECIATION. If a Sec. 351 exchange is completely nontaxable (i.e., no boot is received by the transferor), no depreciation recapture is required.[43] Instead, the entire amount of the transferor's recapture potential is transferred to the transferee corporation. Where part of the depreciation recapture is recognized by the transferor as ordinary income (e.g., under Sec. 351(b)), the remaining recapture potential

[41] Sec. 357(c)(3).
[42] Sec. 358(d)(2).
[43] Secs. 1245(b)(3) and 1250(d)(3).

Topic Review C2-3

Liability Assumption and Acquisition Rules of Sec. 357

1. *General Rule (Sec. 357(a)):* The assumption or acquisition of liabilities by a transferee corporation in a Sec. 351 exchange does not result in the receipt of money/boot by the shareholder for gain recognition purposes. The liabilities are treated as money for purposes of determining the basis of the stock received.
2. *Exception 1 (Sec. 357(b)):* All liabilities assumed or acquired by a transferee corporation *are* considered money/boot received by the transferor if the principal purpose of the transfer of any of the liabilities was tax avoidance or if there is no bona fide business purpose for the transfer.
3. *Exception 2 (Sec. 357(c)):* If the total amount of liabilities assumed or acquired by a transferee corporation exceeds the total basis of properties transferred by a transferor, the excess liability amount is recognized as gain by the transferor.
4. *Special Rule (Sec. 357(c)(3)):* For purposes of Exception 2, the term *liabilities* for a transferor using a cash or hybrid method of accounting does not include any amount that (a) would give rise to a deduction when paid or (b) is payable to a retiring partner or to liquidate a deceased partner's interest.

is transferred to the transferee corporation. If the transferee corporation subsequently disposes of the property, it is subject to the depreciation recapture rules on all depreciation that it has claimed plus the recapture potential transferred by the transferor.

EXAMPLE C2-36 ▶ Azeem transfers machinery having an $18,000 adjusted basis and a $35,000 FMV for all 100 shares of Wheel Corporation's stock. Before the transfer, Azeem used the machinery in his business. He originally paid $25,000 for the machinery and claimed $7,000 of depreciation before transferring the machinery. Azeem does not recapture any depreciation on the transfer. Instead, the $7,000 recapture potential is transferred to Wheel Corporation. After claiming an additional $2,000 of depreciation on the machinery, Wheel's basis in the machinery is $16,000. If Wheel Corporation now sells the machinery for $33,000, it must recognize a $17,000 ($33,000 − $16,000) gain on the sale. Of this gain, $9,000 is ordinary income recaptured under Sec. 1245. The remaining $8,000 is Sec. 1231 gain. ◀

KEY POINT

Not only does the basis of contributed property carry over to the transferee corporation, but so do the depreciation method and recovery period for such property. However, if the transferee corporation's basis is higher than the transferor's basis, such excess is treated as new property subject to the MACRS rules.

COMPUTING DEPRECIATION. When a shareholder transfers depreciable property to a corporation in a nontaxable Sec. 351 exchange, and the shareholder has been depreciating the property, the corporation must continue to use the same depreciation method and recovery period with respect to the transferor's basis in the property.[44] For the year of the transfer, the depreciation must be allocated between the transferor and the transferee corporation according to the number of months the property was held by each. The transferee corporation is assumed to have held the property for the entire month in which the property was transferred.[45]

EXAMPLE C2-37 ▶ On June 10, 1996, Carla purchases a computer (five-year property for MACRS purposes) for $6,000, which she uses in her sole proprietorship. She claims $1,200 (0.20 × $6,000) of depreciation for 1996. On February 10, 1997, she transfers the computer and other assets of her sole proprietorship to King Corporation in exchange for King stock in a tax-free transfer coming under Sec. 351 where no gain or loss is recognized. King Corporation must use the

[44] Sec. 168(i)(7).

[45] Prop. Reg. Secs. 1.168-5(b)(4)(i) and 1.168-5(b)(2)(i)(B).

same MACRS recovery period and method that Carla used. Depreciation for 1997 is $1,920 (0.32 × $6,000). That amount must be allocated between Carla and King Corporation. The computer is considered to have been held by Carla for one month and by King Corporation for 11 months (including the month of transfer). The 1997 depreciation claimed by Carla and King Corporation is calculated as follows:

Carla	$6,000 × 0.32 × 1/12	= $ 160
King Corporation	$6,000 × 0.32 × 11/12	= $1,760

King Corporation's basis in the computer is calculated as follows:

Original cost of computer	$6,000
Minus: 1996 depreciation taken by Carla	(1,200)
1997 depreciation taken by Carla	(160)
Adjusted basis on transfer date	$4,640

◀

If the transferee corporation's basis for the depreciable property exceeds the transferor's basis, the corporation treats the excess amount as a newly purchased MACRS property and may select whatever recovery period and method it desires.[46]

EXAMPLE C2-38 ▶ Assume the same facts as in Example C2-37 except that, in addition to King stock, Carla receives a King note and must recognize $1,000 of gain on the transfer of the computer. King Corporation's basis in the computer is calculated as follows:

Original cost	$6,000
Depreciation claimed by Carla	(1,360)
Adjusted basis on transfer date	$4,640
Plus: Gain recognized by Carla on transfer	1,000
Basis to King Corporation on transfer date	$5,640

The additional $1,000 of basis is depreciated as though it is a separate, newly-purchased MACRS property. Thus, King claims depreciation of $200 (0.20 × $1,000) on this portion of the basis in addition to the $1,760 of depreciation on the $4,640 of carryover basis. ◀

ASSIGNMENT OF INCOME DOCTRINE. The **assignment of income doctrine** is a judicial requirement that income be taxed to the person who earns it.[47] Income may not be assigned to another taxpayer. The question arises as to whether the assignment of income doctrine applies when a taxpayer using the cash method of accounting transfers uncollected accounts receivable to a corporation in a Sec. 351 exchange. The question is who must recognize the income when it is collected—the taxpayer who earned it and transferred the receivable to the corporation before the income was recognized or the corporation that owns the receivable and collects it. The IRS has ruled that the doctrine does *not* apply in a Sec. 351 exchange if the transferor transfers substantially all the business assets and liabilities and a business purpose exists for the transfer. Instead, the accounts receivable take a zero basis in the corporation's hands and are included in the corporation's income when collected.[48]

EXAMPLE C2-39 ▶ For good business reasons, Ruth, a lawyer who uses the cash method of accounting, transfers all of the assets and liabilities of her legal practice to Legal Services Corporation in exchange for all of Legal Services' stock. The assets include $30,000 of accounts receivable. The assignment of income doctrine does not apply to the accounts receivable. Legal Services

[46] Prop. Reg. Sec. 1.168-5(b)(7).

[47] See, for example, *Lucas v. Guy C. Earl*, 8 AFTR 10287, 2 USTC ¶496 (USSC, 1930).

[48] Rev. Rul. 80-198, 1980-2 C.B. 113.

Corporation's basis in the receivables is zero, and the corporation includes the receivables in income as they are collected. ◀

There have been many cases disputing whether a transferee corporation could deduct the accounts payable transferred to it in a nontaxable transfer.[49] Normally, expenses are deductible only by the party that incurred those liabilities in the course of its trade or business. However, the IRS has ruled that the transferee corporation is allowed deductions for the payments it makes to satisfy otherwise deductible business expenses incurred by a transferor.[50]

COMPREHENSIVE EXAMPLE. On March 3 of the current year, John, Eric, and Martha form Chip Corporation with the following investment:

Transferor	*Asset*	*Adjusted Basis to Transferor*	*FMV*	*Number of Shares of Stock Issued*
John	Land	$10,000	$10,000	
	Building	40,000	60,000	
	Mortgage on land and building	55,000	55,000	
	Equipment	—0—	25,000	40
Eric	Truck	8,000	6,000	
	Cash	34,000	34,000	30
Martha	Services	—0—	10,000	10

Eric also receives a Chip Corporation note for $10,000 due in two years. The land, building, and equipment were used in John's business for more than one year and the truck was inventory to Eric. The building was depreciated under the MACRS rules, with $12,000 of depreciation having been claimed by John. The equipment, which cost $60,000, was fully depreciated under the MACRS rules.

The transaction satisfies the Sec. 351 requirements. John and Eric transferred property in exchange for stock and they received 87.5% (70 of 80 shares) of the Chip Corporation stock. John must recognize a $5,000 gain on the transfer because the liability transferred ($55,000) exceeds the total basis of all assets transferred ($50,000) by $5,000. The amount of John's realized gain on the asset transfer is immaterial because Sec. 357(c) applies. Because the liability relates to the land and building, the gain is Sec. 1231 gain. John's basis in the stock is zero ($50,000 basis of assets transferred − $55,000 liabilities assumed by Chip + $5,000 gain). His holding period for each share of stock is divided into three parts, based on the holding period for each of the three assets contributed. Chip's basis in the building is $45,000 ($40,000 + $5,000 gain) and its basis for the equipment is zero. The holding period for the land, building, and equipment includes John's holding period for each asset.

Eric does not recognize any of the $2,000 loss ($6,000 − $8,000) on the transfer of the truck even though $10,000 in boot property is received. His basis in the Chip note received is its FMV, or $10,000. Eric's basis in the Chip stock received is $32,000 ($8,000 + $34,000 − $10,000). Eric's holding period for each share of stock begins on the day after the exchange because it is received in exchange for inventory and cash.

Martha must recognize $10,000 of ordinary income, the value of the stock received for her services. Her basis in the stock is $10,000, the amount of ordinary

[49] See, for example, *Wilford E. Thatcher* v. *CIR*, 37 AFTR 2d 76-1068, 76-1 USTC ¶9324 (9th Cir., 1976), and *John P. Bongiovanni* v. *CIR*, 31 AFTR 2d 73-409, 73-1 USTC ¶9133 (2nd Cir., 1972).

[50] Rev. Rul. 80-198, 1980-2 C.B. 113.

income recognized. Martha's holding period begins on the day after the date she received it.

CHOICE OF CAPITAL STRUCTURE

OBJECTIVE 5

Determine the tax consequences of alternative capital structures

When a corporation is formed, decisions must be made as to the capital structure of the corporation. The corporation may derive its capital from shareholders, nonshareholders, and creditors. In exchange for their capital, shareholders may receive common stock or preferred stock; nonshareholders may receive benefits such as employment for a city's residents or special rates on products produced by the corporation; creditors may receive long-term or short-term debt obligations. Each of these alternatives has tax consequences and other advantages and disadvantages for the shareholders, the creditors, and the corporation itself.

CHARACTERIZATION OF OBLIGATIONS AS DEBT OR EQUITY CAPITAL

SELF-STUDY QUESTION

From a tax perspective, why is the distinction between debt and equity important?

ANSWER

Interest paid with respect to a debt instrument is generally deductible by the payor corporation. Dividends paid with respect to an equity instrument are not deductible by the payor corporation. Thus, the determination of whether an instrument is debt or equity can provide very different results to the payor corporation.

The tax laws provide a strong incentive for many corporations to use as much debt financing as possible (because of the deduction allowed for annual interest payments). Debt financing often resembles equity obligations (i.e., preferred stock), and the IRS and the courts have refused in some cases to accept the form of the obligation as controlling.[51] In some cases, obligations labeled as debt that possessed more characteristics of equity than debt have been reclassified as common or preferred stock. No single factor has been relied on by the courts in making this determination.

In 1969 Congress enacted Sec. 385 in an attempt to establish a workable standard for determining whether an obligation is debt or equity capital. Unfortunately, regulations have still not been issued, and taxpayers are forced to rely on prior judicial decisions.

Section 385 suggests that the following factors be taken into account in determining whether an amount advanced to a corporation should be characterized as debt or equity capital:

- Whether there is a written unconditional promise to pay on demand or on a specified date a certain sum of money in return for an adequate consideration in money or money's worth, and to pay a fixed rate of interest
- Whether there is subordination to or preference over any indebtedness of the corporation
- The ratio of debt to equity of the corporation
- Whether there is convertibility into the stock of the corporation
- The relationship between holdings of stock in the corporation and holdings of the interest in question[52]

HISTORICAL NOTE

To illustrate the difficulty of distinguishing between debt and equity, note that the Treasury at one time issued proposed and final regulations covering Sec. 385. These regulations were the subject of so much criticism that the Treasury eventually withdrew them. The 1989 amendment to Sec. 385 makes it clear that Congress wants the Treasury to make another attempt at clarifying the debt-equity issue. So far no "new" proposed or final regulations have been issued.

Section 385 was amended in 1989 to give the Treasury the authority to characterize a corporate instrument that has significant debt and equity characteristics as part debt and part equity. This change may make it easier to develop a final set of Sec. 385 Regulations.

DEBT CAPITAL

Tax laws affect on the use of debt capital when the debt is issued, annually as the interest is paid on the obligation, and when the debt is satisfied, retired, or declared worthless. The tax implications for each of these three events are examined next.

---

[51] See, for example, *Aqualane Shores, Inc. v. CIR*, 4 AFTR 2d 5346, 59-2 USTC ¶9632 (5th Cir., 1959) and *Sun Properties, Inc. v. U.S.*, 47 AFTR 273, 55-1 USTC ¶9261 (5th Cir., 1955).

[52] See also the O.H. *Kruse Grain & Milling v. CIR* case (5 AFTR 2d 1544, 60-2 USTC ¶9490 (9th Cir., 1960)) which lists additional factors that the courts might consider.

ISSUANCE OF DEBT. Under Sec. 351, appreciated assets may be exchanged tax-free for stock provided the transferors have control of the transferee corporation immediately after the exchange. However, if assets are exchanged for debt instruments, whether part of the same transaction or not, the FMV of the debt received is treated as boot. Therefore, the receipt of debt by the transferor may result in the recognition of gain.

WHEN INTEREST IS PAID. Interest paid on an indebtedness is deductible by the corporation in arriving at taxable income.[53] Dividends paid on equity capital are not deductible. A corporation is not subject to the limitations on interest deductions that apply to individual taxpayers (e.g., investment interest or personal interest limitations).

If a debt instrument is issued at a discount, Sec. 163(e) requires that the original issue discount be determined and amortized by the holder under the rules of Secs. 1272 through 1275. The debtor corporation amortizes the original issue discount over the life of the obligation and treats the discount as an additional cost of borrowing.[54] If a corporate debt obligation is repurchased by the corporation for more than the issue price (plus any original issue discount deducted as interest), the excess of the purchase price over the issue price (adjusted for any amortization of original issue discount) is deductible by the corporation as interest expense.[55]

If the debt instrument is issued at a premium, Sec. 171 permits the holder to elect to amortize the premium over the life of the obligation and treat the premium as a reduction in the interest income earned from the obligation. The debtor corporation must amortize the premium over the life of the obligation and report such amount as additional interest income.[56] If a debt obligation is repurchased at a price greater than the issue price (minus any premium reported as income), the excess of the purchase price over the issue price (adjusted for any amortization of premium) is deductible by the corporation as interest expense.[57]

WHEN AN INDEBTEDNESS IS SATISFIED. Generally, the repayment of an indebtedness is not considered an exchange transaction. Thus, an obligation that is repaid by a corporation does not result in a gain or loss being recognized by the creditor. However, Sec. 1271(a) considers amounts received by the holder of a debt instrument (e.g., note, bond, or debenture) at the time of its retirement to be received in exchange for the obligation. Thus, if the obligation is a capital asset in the holder's hands, the holder will recognize a capital gain or loss if the amount received in retirement of the obligation is different from its adjusted basis, unless the difference is due to original issue discount or market discount.

EXAMPLE C2-40 ▶

Titan Corporation issues a ten-year obligation at its $1,000 face amount. The obligation is purchased by Rick for $1,000 on the issue date. Due to a decline in interest rates, Titan Corporation calls the obligation by paying $1,050 to each of the holders of the ten-year obligations. Rick will recognize a $50 capital gain on the repayment of the debt instrument. The premium paid by Titan Corporation is deductible as interest expense. ◀

ADDITIONAL COMMENT

Even though debt is often thought of as a preferred instrument because of the deductibility of the interest paid, it should be noted that the debt must be repaid at its maturity, whereas stock has no specified maturity date. Also, interest usually must be paid at regular intervals, whereas dividends do not have to be declared if sufficient funds are not available.

Table C2-2 presents a comparison of the tax advantages and disadvantages of using debt in the capital structure.

EQUITY CAPITAL

Equity capital issues come in a variety of forms. Some corporations have only a single class of stock, whereas others have a number of outstanding classes of stock. Reasons for the use of multiple classes of stock include

---

[53] Sec. 163(a).
[54] Sec. 163(e).
[55] Reg. Sec. 1.163-7(c).
[56] Reg. Sec. 1.61-12(c)(2).
[57] Reg. Sec. 1.163-7(c).

▼ TABLE C2-2
Tax Advantages and Disadvantages of Using Debt in the Capital Structure

Advantages:

1. A corporation can deduct interest payments made on debt instruments.
2. Shareholders do not have to recognize income when an amount is received in repayment of debt as they would in the case of a stock redemption.

Disadvantages:

1. If a shareholder receives a debt instrument in exchange for property at the time the corporation is formed or later when a capital contribution is made, the debt is considered boot and the realized gain must be recognized to the extent of the lesser of the boot received or the realized gain.
2. If debt becomes worthless or is sold at a loss, the loss is generally a nonbusiness bad debt (short-term capital loss) or a capital loss. Section 1244 ordinary loss treatment applies only to stock.

- Permitting the employees of family-owned corporations to obtain an equity interest in the business while keeping voting control in the hands of the family members
- Permitting a **closely held corporation** to acquire outside financing from a corporate investor or wealthy individual who acquires a preferred stock interest and to enable the existing shareholders to retain their voting control by owning the common stock.

Because of the wide variety of situations that can occur and the unlimited number of equity forms that can be issued, it is impossible to list all of the tax and nontax advantages of each type of equity form. Therefore, a list of the major tax advantages and disadvantages of common and preferred stock issues is presented in Table C2-3.

SELF-STUDY QUESTION

Does the transferee corporation recognize gain on the receipt of appreciated property from a shareholder?

ANSWER

No. A corporation does not recognize gain when it receives property from its shareholders, regardless of whether or not it exchanges its own stock. However, the transfer must qualify as a Sec. 351 exchange or the transaction will be taxable to the shareholders.

CAPITAL CONTRIBUTIONS BY SHAREHOLDERS

A corporation does not recognize any income when it receives money or property as a capital contribution from a shareholder.[58] If the shareholders make voluntary pro rata payments to a corporation but do not receive any additional stock, the payments are regarded as an additional price paid for the stock already owned.[59] The shareholders'

WHAT WOULD YOU DO IN THIS SITUATION?

You are a CPA who has a corporate client that wants to issue 100-year bonds. The corporation's CEO reads the *Wall Street Journal* regularly and has seen that similar bonds have been issued by a number of companies, including Coca-Cola and Disney. He touts the fact that the interest rate on these bonds is little more than 30-year U.S. Treasury Notes. In addition, the interest on the bonds will be deductible. Whereas dividends paid on preferred or common stock would be nondeductible. You are concerned that the bonds may be treated as equity by the IRS because of the length of time they will be outstanding. If they are, the "interest" paid will be treated as dividends and will not be deductible.

Your CPA firm is acting as an advisor to your client with regard to the new bond issue. What advice would you give your client in this situation? When preparing their tax return if the new bonds are issued?

[58] Sec. 118(a).

[59] Reg. Sec. 1.118-1.

TYPICAL MISCONCEPTION

The characteristics of preferred stock can be similar to those of a debt security. Often, a regular dividend is required at a stated rate, much like what would be required with respect to a debt obligation. The holder of preferred stock, like a debt holder, may have preferred liquidation rights over holders of common stock. Also, it is not required that preferred stock possess voting rights. Thus, where preferred stock is concerned, the differences between debt and equity can be minimal.

▼ TABLE C2-3

Tax Advantages and Disadvantages of Using Stock in the Capital Structure

Advantages:

1. A 70%, 80%, or 100% dividends-received deduction is available for a corporate shareholder receiving dividends. A special deduction is not available for interest income (see Chapter C3).
2. Common and preferred stock can be received by a shareholder participating in a tax-free corporate formation coming under Sec. 351 or a tax-free reorganization coming under Sec. 368 without any need to recognize gain (see Chapters C2 and C7, respectively). Receipt of debt obligations in each of these two types of transactions generally triggers the recognition of gain by the shareholder.
3. Common and preferred stock can be distributed tax-free to the shareholders of a corporation as a stock dividend. Some common and preferred stock distributions may be taxable as dividends under Sec. 305(b). Distributions of debt obligations of the distributing corporation are taxable as a dividend (see Chapter C4).
4. Common or preferred stock that is sold or exchanged or becomes worthless is eligible for ordinary loss treatment under the Sec. 1244 rules (see pages C2-34 and C2-35). The loss recognized on similar transactions involving debt obligations is generally a capital loss.
5. Section 1202 permits a capital gains exclusion of up to 50% on the sale or exchange of qualified small business (C) corporation stock that has been held for more than five years.

Disadvantages:

1. Dividends are not deductible in determining taxable income.
2. Redemption of common or preferred stock is generally taxable as a dividend. Under this general rule, none of the distribution offsets the shareholder's basis for the stock investment. Redemption of common and preferred stock by the issuing corporation is eligible for exchange treatment only in specific situations contained in Secs. 302 and 303 (see Chapter C4).
3. Preferred stock that is received by a shareholder as a tax-free stock dividend can be labeled Sec. 306 stock. Sale, exchange, or redemption of such stock can result in the recognition of ordinary income or dividend income instead of capital gains (see Chapter C4).

bases in their stock is increased by the amount of money contributed, plus the basis of any nonmoney property contributed, plus any gain recognized by the shareholders. The corporation's basis in any property received as a capital contribution from a shareholder equals the shareholder's basis plus any gain recognized by the shareholder.[60] Normally, the shareholders do not recognize any gain when property is contributed to a controlled corporation as a capital contribution.

EXAMPLE C2-41 ▶

Dot and Fred own equally all of Trail Corporation's stock, and each has a $50,000 basis in that stock. Later, as a voluntary contribution to capital, Dot contributes $40,000 in cash and Fred contributes property having a $25,000 basis and a $40,000 FMV. Trail Corporation recognizes no gross income because of the contributions. However, Dot's basis in her stock is increased to $90,000 ($50,000 + $40,000) and Fred's basis in his stock is increased to $75,000 ($50,000 + $25,000). Trail's basis in the property contributed by Fred is $25,000—the same as Fred's basis in the property. ◀

An involuntary contribution of property by a shareholder in satisfaction of an assessment made by the corporation is treated by the tax laws as an exchange transaction.

[60] Sec. 362(a).

Therefore, the shareholder must recognize gain or loss equal to the FMV of the property contributed minus its basis to the shareholder. The shareholder's basis for his or her stock is increased by the FMV of the transferred property. The transferee corporation's basis in the contributed property is its FMV on the exchange date.

If a shareholder gratuitously forgives an indebtedness of the corporation, the transaction generally represents a contribution to the corporation's capital equal to the principal amount of the indebtedness. The determination of whether a forgiveness is a capital contribution is based on the facts and circumstances surrounding the situation.

CAPITAL CONTRIBUTIONS BY NONSHAREHOLDERS

Nonshareholders sometimes make capital contributions in the form of money or property. For example, a city government might contribute land to a corporation to induce the corporation to locate within the city and provide jobs for its citizens. Such contributions are excluded from gross income if the money or property contributed is neither a payment for goods or services rendered nor a subsidy to induce the corporation to limit production.[61]

SELF-STUDY QUESTION

What basis does a transferee corporation take in capital contributions of property from nonshareholders?

ANSWER

Capital contributions by nonshareholders are not common. In the unusual occurrences that do qualify as nonshareholder contributions, the transferee corporation takes a zero basis in any property received.

If a nonshareholder contributes property other than money to a corporation, the basis of such property to the corporation is zero.[62] The zero basis that is assigned to the property prevents the transferee corporation from claiming either a depreciation or capital recovery deduction with respect to the contributed property.

If a nonshareholder contributes money, the basis of any property acquired with the money during a twelve-month period beginning on the day the contribution was received is reduced by the amount of the contribution. This limits the corporation's deduction to the amount of funds it invested to purchase the property. The amount of any monies received from nonshareholders that are not spent to purchase property during the twelve-month period reduces the basis of any other property held by the corporation on the last day of the twelve-month period.[63]

The basis reduction is applied to the corporation's properties in the following order:

1. Depreciable property
2. Amortizable property
3. Depletable property
4. All other property

A property's basis may not be reduced below zero as a result of these downward basis adjustments.

EXAMPLE C2-42 ▶ The City of San Antonio contributes $100,000 in cash and a tract of land having a $500,000 FMV to Circle Corporation to induce the company to locate there. Because of a downturn in Circle's business, only $70,000 of the contributed funds are spent in the next twelve months. Circle does not have any gross income on account of the contribution. Circle's basis in the land and the properties purchased with the contributed funds are zero. The basis of Circle's remaining properties must be reduced by the $30,000 ($100,000 − $70,000) that was contributed but not spent, starting with its depreciable properties. ◀

[61] Reg. Sec. 1.118-1.

[62] Sec. 362(c)(1).

[63] Sec. 362(c)(2).

Worthlessness of Stock or Debt Obligations

OBJECTIVE 6

Determine the tax consequences of worthless stock or debt obligations

Investors who invest or lend money to a corporation usually intend to earn a profit and recover their investment. Unfortunately, some investments do not provide a good return and an investor may lose part or all of the investment. This section of the chapter examines the tax consequences of stock or debt becoming worthless.

Securities

A debt or equity investment that is evidenced by a **security** and that becomes worthless results in a capital loss for the investor on the last day of the tax year in which worthlessness occurs.[64] A security includes (1) a share of stock in the corporation; (2) a right to subscribe for, or the right to receive, a share of stock in the corporation; or (3) a bond, debenture, note, or other evidence of indebtedness issued by a corporation with interest coupons or in registered form.[65]

In some situations, investors can report an ordinary loss when a security becomes worthless. Investors who advance monies to an unsuccessful corporation, either in the form of equity or debt capital, will generally find it advantageous if the loss is an ordinary deduction. Ordinary losses are not subject to the $3,000 annual limitation on capital losses. Ordinary losses are deductible against any ordinary income reported on the investor's tax return. Ordinary losses that produce an NOL on the investor's tax return can be carried back or forward under the general NOL rules. Situations permitting the deduction of an ordinary loss include

- *Securities that are noncapital assets.* Ordinary loss treatment results when a security that is a noncapital asset is sold or exchanged or becomes totally worthless. Securities fitting into this category include those held as inventory by a securities dealer. Whether stock is a capital asset depends on the investor's motive for making the investment. Generally, the courts have found that stock is a capital asset when a substantial investment motive exists for acquiring and holding the stock.[66]
- *Affiliated corporations.* A domestic corporation can claim an ordinary loss incurred in connection with any security of an affiliated corporation that becomes worthless during the tax year. The domestic corporation must own at least 80% of the total voting power of all classes of stock entitled to vote, and at least 80% of each class of nonvoting stock (other than stock that is limited and preferred as to dividends). At least 90% of the aggregate gross receipts of the loss corporation for all tax years must come from sources other than passive income.[67]
- *Section 1244 stock.* The Sec. 1244 rules permit an ordinary loss to be claimed for qualifying stock issued by small business corporations that is sold or exchanged or becomes worthless.[68] Ordinary loss treatment is available only to an individual who sustains a loss and was issued the qualifying stock by an eligible small business corporation, or to an individual who was a partner in a partnership at the time the partnership acquired the stock from the issuing corporation and whose distributive share of partnership losses includes the loss sustained by the partnership on such stock. Thus, ordinary loss treatment is not available for stock inherited, received as a gift, or purchased from another shareholder. The ordinary loss is limited to $50,000

TYPICAL MISCONCEPTION

Probably the most difficult aspect of deducting a loss on a worthless security is establishing that the security is actually worthless. A mere decline in value is not sufficient to create a loss. The burden of proof of establishing total worthlessness rests with the taxpayer.

SELF-STUDY QUESTION

Why would a shareholder want his or her stock to qualify as Sec. 1244 stock?

ANSWER

Section 1244 is a provision that may help the taxpayer but that can never hurt. If the Sec. 1244 requirements are satisfied, the individual shareholders of a small business corporation may treat losses from the sale or worthlessness of their stock as ordinary rather than capital losses. If the Sec. 1244 requirements are not satisfied, such losses are generally capital losses.

---

[64] Sec. 165(g)(1).
[65] Sec. 165(g)(2).
[66] Rev. Rul. 78-94, 1978-1 C.B. 58. See also *W. W. Windle Co.*, 65 T.C. 694 (1976) and *Bell Fibre Products Corp.*, 1977 PH T.C. Memo ¶77,042, 36 TCM 182.
[67] Sec. 165(g)(3).
[68] Sec. 1244(a).

per year (or $100,000 if the taxpayer is married and files a joint return). Losses in excess of the dollar ceiling in any given year are considered capital losses.

EXAMPLE C2-43 ▶ Tammy and her husband purchased 25% of the initial offering of Minor Corporation's single class of stock for $175,000. Minor Corporation is a qualifying small business corporation, and the Minor stock satisfies all of the Sec. 1244 requirements. On September 1, 1995, Minor Corporation filed for bankruptcy. After substantial litigation, the shareholders are notified in 1997 that the Minor stock is worthless. Tammy and her husband can deduct $100,000 of their loss as an ordinary loss. The remaining $75,000 loss is a capital loss. ◀

If the stock is issued for property whose adjusted basis exceeds its FMV immediately before the exchange, the basis of the stock is reduced to the property's FMV for purposes of determining the amount of ordinary loss claimed under Sec. 1244.

EXAMPLE C2-44 ▶ Penny exchanges property having a $40,000 adjusted basis and a $32,000 FMV for 100 shares of Bear Corporation stock in a transaction qualifying under Sec. 351. The stock qualifies as Sec. 1244 stock. Penny's basis in her Bear stock is $40,000. However, for Sec. 1244 purposes only, her basis in the stock is the transferred property's FMV, or $32,000. If the stock is sold for $10,000, Penny's recognized loss is $30,000 ($10,000 − $40,000). Her ordinary loss under Sec. 1244 is $22,000 ($10,000 − $32,000 Sec. 1244 basis). The remaining $8,000 loss is a capital loss. ◀

No special election is required to take advantage of Sec. 1244. Investors should be aware of the special requirements that must be satisfied. Failure to satisfy any of these requirements will disqualify the stock from Sec. 1244 treatment and generally cause the shareholder's loss to be a capital loss. The special requirements include

- The issuing corporation must be a small business corporation at the time the stock is issued. A small business corporation is one whose aggregate money and other property received for stock is $1 million or less.[69]
- The stock must be issued for money or property (other than stock and securities).
- The issuing corporation must have derived more than 50% of its aggregate gross receipts from "active" sources (i.e., other than royalties, rents, dividends, interest, annuities, and gains on sales of stock and securities) during the five most recent tax years ending before the date on which the stock is sold or exchanged or becomes worthless.

UNSECURED DEBT OBLIGATIONS

KEY POINT

Unsecured shareholder advances to a corporation may be treated as either additional paid-in capital or as an unsecured loan. If the advance is treated as paid-in capital and becomes worthless, this will increase the amount of the worthless security loss. If the advance is treated as an unsecured debt, it is treated as a bad debt when it becomes worthless.

Shareholders may lend money to the corporation in addition to their stock investment. The type of loss allowed if these advances are not repaid depends on the nature of the loan or advance. If the advance is treated as additional paid-in capital, the worthless security loss claimed by the shareholder for his or her stock investment is increased.

If the unpaid loan was not evidenced by a security (i.e., an unsecured debt obligation) it is either a business or nonbusiness bad debt. Under Code Sec. 166, nonbusiness bad debts receive less favorable tax treatment than business bad debts. Nonbusiness bad debts are deductible only as short-term capital losses (up to the $3,000 annual limit for all capital losses) when the debt is determined to be totally worthless. Business bad debts

[69] Special rules are provided in Reg. Sec. 1.1244(c)-2 for designating which shares of stock are eligible for Sec. 1244 treatment when more than $1 million of stock has been issued by the corporation.

are deductible without limit when they are either partially or totally worthless. The IRS generally treats a loan made by a shareholder to a corporation in connection with his or her stock investment as a nonbusiness activity.[70] It is simple to see why a shareholder might like to rebut this presumption and say that there is a business purpose behind the making of the loan.

An advance made in connection with the shareholder's trade or business, such as a loan made to protect the shareholder's employment with the corporation, may be treated as an ordinary loss under the business bad debt rules. Regulation Sec. 1.166-5(b) indicates that whether the loss is treated as a business or nonbusiness bad debt depends on the taxpayer's motive for making the advance. The debt qualifies as a business bad debt should the necessary relationship between the loss and the conduct of the taxpayer's trade or business exist at the time the debt was created or acquired, or when the debt becomes worthless.

KEY POINT

In many closely held corporations, the shareholders are also employees. Thus, when a shareholder-employee makes a loan to the corporation, a question arises whether the loan is being made in the individual's capacity as an employee or a shareholder. The distinction is important because an employee loan that is worthless is entitled to ordinary loss treatment, whereas a shareholder loan that is worthless is treated as a nonbusiness bad debt (short-term capital loss).

In *U.S. v. Edna Generes,* the Supreme Court held that when multiple motives exist for making an advance to a corporation, such as when a shareholder is also an employee of the corporation, the distinction between whether a business or nonbusiness loan exists is based on the "dominant motivation" for making the loan.[71] If only a "significant motivation" exists relating the debt and the taxpayer's trade or business, this is usually insufficient to satisfy the proximate relationship required between the bad debt and the taxpayer's trade or business under Reg. Sec. 1.166-5(b) in order to have a business bad debt.

Factors that have proven to be important in making the business bad debt determination include the relative dollar amounts of the taxpayer's stock investment in the corporation, compensation from the corporation, and other compensation. A small salary and a large stock investment would be indicative of an investment purpose for making the loan. A large salary and a small stock investment would be indicative of a business purpose for making the loan. Because these factors are subjective in nature and the dollars that are involved may be substantial, this issue still remains open to litigation.

EXAMPLE C2-45 ▶

Mary is employed by Top Corporation as its legal counsel. Her annual compensation from Top Corporation is $100,000. Top Corporation is experiencing financial problems, and Mary lends the corporation $50,000 in 1995 in an attempt to help it through its financial difficulties. Top Corporation subsequently declares bankruptcy, and in 1997 Mary and the other creditors receive 10 cents on each dollar they are owed. Mary's $45,000 ($50,000 × 0.90) loss is an ordinary loss and is fully deductible in the year the loss is incurred if Mary can prove that the dominant motivation for making the loan is in connection with her employment. If there is a significant relationship between Mary's loan and her investment in the Top stock, it is likely that the loss will be a nonbusiness bad debt, of which only $3,000 can be deducted each year. ◀

ADDITIONAL COMMENT

In order for the act of lending money to a corporation to be considered the taxpayer's trade or business, the taxpayer must show that he or she was individually in the business of seeking out, promoting, organizing, and financing business ventures. *Ronald L. Farrington v. CIR,* 65 AFTR 2d 90-617, 90-1 USTC ¶50,125 (DC, OK, 1990).

A loss sustained by a shareholder who acts as a guarantor on a loan made by a third party to the corporation is generally considered to be a nonbusiness bad debt. The loss can be claimed only to the extent that the shareholder actually makes a payment to the third party and is unable to collect any amount due from the debtor corporation.[72]

[70] The assumption is made here that the loan is not considered to be an additional capital contribution. In such a case, the Sec. 165 worthless security rules apply instead of the Sec. 166 bad debt rules.

[71] 29 AFTR 2d 72-609, 72-1 USTC ¶9259 (USSC, 1972).

[72] Reg. Sec. 1.166-8(a).

TAX PLANNING CONSIDERATIONS

AVOIDING SEC. 351

Section 351 is not an elective provision. If its provisions are met, Sec. 351 applies even if the taxpayer does not want it to apply. Most often, Sec. 351 treatment is desired by taxpayers because it enables them to defer gains when transferring property to a corporation. In some cases, however, shareholders find it disadvantageous and seek to avoid it. Sometimes shareholders have gains or losses that they want to recognize.

TYPICAL MISCONCEPTION

Section 351 is generally considered a beneficial taxpayer provision. However, it is not an elective provision. Therefore, even though a shareholder wants to recognize gain on a transfer of property to a controlled corporation, such gain must be deferred if the Sec. 351 requirements are satisfied.

SELF-STUDY QUESTION

Which tax provisions may potentially limit a transferor shareholder from recognizing a loss on the transfer of property to a corporation?

ANSWER

(1) Such transfer cannot be to a controlled corporation or Sec. 351 will defer the loss. (2) Even if Sec. 351 can be avoided, losses on sales between a corporation and a more than 50% shareholder are disallowed under Sec. 267. Thus, to recognize a loss on the sale of property, such shareholders must, directly or indirectly, own 50% or less of the stock of the transferee corporation.

AVOIDING NONRECOGNITION OF LOSSES UNDER SEC. 351. If a shareholder is transferring property on which he or she has a loss to a corporation, he or she may want to recognize the loss on that property so that income from other sources can be offset. However, the loss is not recognized if Sec. 351 applies to the transfer. The shareholder can recognize the loss only if Sec. 351 does not apply to the exchange.

To avoid Sec. 351 entirely requires that one or more of its requirements not be met. The best way to accomplish this is to make sure that the transferors of property do not receive 80% of the voting stock.

Even if a shareholder avoids Sec. 351, he or she still may not be able to recognize the losses because of the Sec. 267 related party transaction rules. Under Sec. 267(a)(1), if the shareholder owns more than 50% of the corporation's stock, directly or indirectly, he or she cannot recognize any losses on an exchange of the property for the corporation's stock or other property.

Thus, to recognize a loss when property is exchanged for stock, the shareholder must avoid both Sec. 351 and Sec. 267. If the transferors of property receive less than 80% of the voting stock of the corporation and the transferor of the loss property does not own more than 50% of the corporate stock, the transferor of the loss property may recognize the loss.

EXAMPLE C2-46 ▶

Lynn owns property that has a $100,000 basis and a $60,000 FMV. If Lynn transfers the property to White Corporation in a transaction qualifying under Sec. 351, her loss is not recognized. It is postponed until she sells her White stock. If Sec. 351 does not apply, she may be able to recognize a $40,000 loss in the year the property is transferred. If Lynn receives 50% of the White stock in exchange for her property; and Cathy, an unrelated individual, receives 25% of the stock in exchange for $30,000 cash; and John, another unrelated individual, receives the remaining 25% of stock for services performed, Sec. 351 does not apply because less than 80% of the stock was received by transferors of property. Moreover, Sec. 267 does not apply to the exchange because Lynn does not own more than 50% of the stock either directly or indirectly. Therefore, Lynn recognizes a $40,000 loss on the exchange of her property for the White stock. ◀

ADDITIONAL COMMENT

Any potential built-in gain on property transferred to the transferee corporation is duplicated because such gain may be recognized at the corporate level and at the shareholder level. This may be another reason for avoiding the nonrecognition of gain under Sec. 351.

AVOIDING NONRECOGNITION OF GAIN UNDER SEC. 351. Sometimes a transferor wants to recognize a gain when appreciated property is transferred to a corporation so that the transferee corporation has a higher basis in the transferred property. Some other possible reasons for this are as follows:

- ▶ The transferor's gain is capital gain that he or she can offset with capital losses from other sources.
- ▶ For 1991 and later years, individual long-term capital gains are taxed at a maximum 28% rate. This rate is below the 35% marginal tax rate generally applicable to corporate capital gains.

- The corporation's marginal tax rate may be higher than the marginal tax rate applicable to a noncorporate transferor. In such case, it might be beneficial for the transferor to recognize gain on the transfer so that the corporation can obtain a higher basis in the property. A higher basis would either reduce the corporation's gain when it sells the property or allow the corporation to claim higher depreciation deductions on the property while it is using it.

A transferor who cannot recognize a gain on a transfer of appreciated property because of Sec. 351 may be able to avoid Sec. 351 and recognize the gain by using one of the following methods:

- The transferor can sell the property to the controlled corporation for cash, thereby avoiding Sec. 351 altogether.
- The transferor can sell the property to the controlled corporation for cash and debt. This method requires less cash than the previous method. However, the sale may be treated as a transfer coming under Sec. 351 if the debt instruments received are considered equity.[73]
- The transferor can sell the property to a third party for cash and have the third party transfer the property to the corporation for stock.
- The transferor can arrange to receive sufficient boot property so that, even if Sec. 351 applies to the transaction, gain is recognized.
- The transferors can fail one or more of the Sec. 351 provisions. If the transferors of property do not obtain control of the corporation (i.e., 80% of the voting stock), Sec. 351 does not apply and gain is recognized.
- The transferors may transfer to the corporation either sufficient debt so that the debt exceeds the basis of all properties transferred or debt that lacks a business purpose in order to trigger the gain recognition provisions of Secs. 357(b) or (c).

EXAMPLE C2-47 ▶ Jaime owns land purchased as an investment ten years ago for $100,000. The land is now worth $500,000. Jaime plans to transfer the land to Bell Corporation in exchange for all of its stock. Bell Corporation will subdivide the land and sell individual parcels. Its gain on the land sales will be ordinary income. Jaime has a large capital loss in the current year and would like to recognize a capital gain on the transfer of the land to Bell Corporation. One way for Jaime to accomplish this is to transfer the land to Bell Corporation in exchange for all of the Bell stock plus a note for $400,000. Jaime recognizes $400,000 of gain even though Sec. 351 applies to the exchange. However, if the note is reclassified as a second class of stock, Jaime will not be allowed to recognize the gain. ◀

The transferor can postpone recognition of the gain while still allowing the transferee corporation to obtain a step-up in basis for the transferred property by having the debt made payable several years in the future. Under the installment sale rules of Sec. 453, gain generally is not recognized until the note is actually collected.

EXAMPLE C2-48 ▶ In Example C2-46, if the note is due in four years, Jaime can postpone recognition of the gain for four years until the note is collected by treating the exchange as an installment sale. ◀

---

[73] See, for example, *Aqualane Shores, Inc.* v. *CIR*, 4 AFTR 2d 5346, 59-2 USTC ¶9632 (5th Cir., 1959) and *Sun Properties, Inc.* v. *U.S.*, 47 AFTR 273, 55-1 USTC ¶9261 (5th Cir., 1955).

COMPLIANCE AND PROCEDURAL CONSIDERATIONS

REPORTING REQUIREMENTS UNDER SEC. 351

KEY POINT

The required information provided to the IRS by both the transferor-shareholders and the transferee corporation should be consistent. For example, the FMVs assigned to the stock and other properties included in the exchange should be the same for both sides of the transaction.

Every person who receives stock or other property in an exchange qualifying under Sec. 351 must attach a statement to his or her tax return for the period that includes the date of the exchange.[74] The statement must include all the facts pertinent to the exchange, including

- A description of the property transferred and its adjusted basis to the transferor
- A description of the stock received in the exchange, including its kind, number of shares, and FMV
- A description of the securities received in the exchange, including principal amount, terms, and FMV
- The amount of money received
- A description of any other property received, including its FMV
- A statement on the liabilities transferred to the corporation, including the nature of the liabilities, when and why they were created, and the corporate business reason for their transfer

The transferee corporation must attach a statement to its tax return for the year in which the exchange took place.[75] The statement must include

- A complete description of all property received from the transferors
- The adjusted basis of the property to the transferors
- A description of the stock issued to the transferors
- A description of the securities issued to the transferors
- The amount of money distributed to the transferors
- A description of any other property distributed to the transferors
- Information regarding the transferor's liabilities that are assumed by the corporation

PROBLEM MATERIALS

DISCUSSION QUESTIONS

C2-1 What entities or business forms are available for a new business? Explain the advantages and disadvantages of each.

C2-2 Alice and Bill are planning to go into business together. They anticipate losses for the first two or three years, which they would like to use to offset income from other sources. They are also concerned about exposing their personal assets to the business liabilities. Advise Alice and Bill as to what business form would best satisfy their concern.

C2-3 Bruce and Bob organize Black LLC on May 10 of the current year. What is the default rule for the entity's tax classification? Are any alternative classification(s) available? If so, (1) how do Bruce and Bob elect the alternative classification(s) (if any)? and, (2) what are the tax consequences of electing an alternative classification?

[74] Reg. Sec. 1.351-3(a).

[75] Reg. Sec. 1.351-3(b).

C2-4 John and Wilbur form White Corporation on May 3 of the current year. What is the default rule for the entity's tax classification? Are any alternative classification(s) available? If so, (1) how do John and Wilbur elect the alternative classification(s) (if any)? and, (2) what are the tax consequences of electing an alternative classification?

C2-5 Barbara organizes Blue LLC on May 17 of the current year. What is the default rule for the entity's tax classification? Are any alternative classification(s) available? If so, (1) how does Barbara elect the alternative classification(s) (if any)? and, (2) what are the tax consequences of electing an alternative classification?

C2-6 Debate the following proposition: All corporate formation transactions should be treated as taxable events.

C2-7 What are the tax consequences of Sec. 351 for the transferor and transferee when property is transferred to a newly-created corporation?

C2-8 What items are included in the property definition for purposes of Sec. 351(a)? What items are statutorily excluded from the property definition?

C2-9 How is the *control* requirement defined for purposes of Sec. 351(a)?

C2-10 Explain how the IRS has interpreted the phrase "in control immediately after the exchange" for purposes of a Sec. 351 exchange.

C2-11 John and Mary each exchange property worth \$50,000 for 100 shares of New Corporation stock. Peter exchanges services for 98 shares of stock and \$1,000 in money for two shares of stock. Does Sec. 351 apply to the exchange? Explain why or why not. What advice would you give to the shareholders?

C2-12 Does Sec. 351 require shareholders to receive stock equal in value to the property transferred? Suppose Fred and Susan each transfer property worth \$50,000 of Spade Corporation. Fred receives 25 shares of Spade stock and Susan receives 75 shares. Does Sec. 351 apply? Explain the tax consequences of the transaction.

C2-13 Can Sec. 351 apply to property transferred to an existing corporation? Suppose Ken and Lynn each own 50 shares of North Corporation stock. Ken transfers property worth \$50,000 to North for an additional 25 shares of stock. Does Sec. 351 apply? Explain why or why not. If not, what can be done to make the transaction qualify?

C2-14 How are a transferor's basis and holding period for stocks and other property (boot) received in a Sec. 351 exchange determined? How does the assumption of liabilities by the transferee corporation affect the transferor's basis for the stock?

C2-15 How are the transferee corporation's basis and holding period for property received in a Sec. 351 exchange determined?

C2-16 Under what circumstances is the assumption of liabilities by a corporation considered boot in a Sec. 351 exchange?

C2-17 What factor(s) would the IRS likely use to determine whether a liability transferred by an individual to a corporation in a Sec. 351 transaction possessed the necessary business purpose to avoid being treated as boot under Sec. 357(b)?

C2-18 Mark transfers all the properties of his sole proprietorship to newly formed Utah Corporation in exchange for all of the Utah stock. Some of the properties are depreciable properties on which Mark has claimed depreciation. Under what circumstances is Mark required to recapture previously claimed depreciation deductions? How is the depreciation deduction calculated for the year of transfer? What happens if Utah Corporation sells the depreciable properties?

C2-19 How does the assignment of income doctrine affect a Sec. 351 exchange?

C2-20 What factors did Congress mandate should be used in determining whether an indebtedness is classified as debt or equity for tax purposes?

C2-21 What are the advantages and disadvantages of using debt as part of a firm's capital structure?

C2-22 How are capital contributions by shareholders and nonshareholders treated by the recipient corporation?

C2-23 What are the advantages of qualifying for Sec. 1244 loss treatment when a stock investment becomes worthless? What requirements must be satisfied in order to be able to take advantage of the Sec. 1244 benefits?

C2-24 What are the advantages of business bad debt treatment when a shareholder's loan or advance to a corporation cannot be repaid? How can one avoid having such a loss treated as a nonbusiness bad debt?

C2-25 Why might shareholders want to avoid Sec. 351? Explain three ways that they can accomplish this.

C2-26 What are the reporting requirements under Sec. 351?

ISSUE IDENTIFICATION QUESTIONS

C2-27 Peter Jones has owned all 100 shares of Trenton Corporation's stock for the past five years. This year Mary Smith contributes property with a $50,000 basis and an $80,000 FMV for 80 newly-issued Trenton shares. At the same time Peter contributes $15,000 in cash for fifteen newly-issued Trenton shares. What tax issues should be considered by Mary and Peter with respect to the stock acquisitions?

C2-28 Carl contributes equipment with a $50,000 adjusted basis and an $80,000 FMV to Cook Corporation for 50 of its 100 shares of stock. His son, Carl Jr., contributes $20,000 cash for the remaining 50 Cook shares. What tax issues should be considered by Carl and his son with respect to the stock acquisitions?

C2-29 Several years ago, Bill acquired 100 shares of Bold Corporation stock directly from the corporation for $100,000 in cash. This year he sold the stock to Sam for $35,000. What tax issues should be considered by Bill with repsect to the stock sale?

PROBLEMS

C2-30 ***Transfer of Property and Services to a Controlled Corporation.*** In 1997, Alice, Bob, and Charles form Star Corporation. Alice contributes land (a capital asset) purchased in 1995 for $15,000 that has a $40,000 FMV in exchange for 40 shares of Star stock. Bob contributes machinery (Sec. 1231 property) purchased in 1994 that has a $45,000 adjusted basis and a $40,000 FMV in exchange for 40 shares of Star stock. Charles contributes services worth $20,000 in exchange for 20 shares of Star stock.

a. What is the amount of Alice's recognized gain or loss?
b. What is Alice's basis in her Star shares? When does her holding period begin?
c. What is the amount of Bob's recognized gain or loss?
d. What is Bob's basis in his Star shares? When does his holding period begin?
e. How much income, if any, must Charles recognize?
f. What is Charles's basis in his Star shares? When does his holding period begin?
g. What is Star Corporation's basis in the land and the machinery? When does its holding period begin? How does Star Corporation treat the amount paid to Charles for his services?

C2-31 ***Transfer of Property and Services to a Controlled Corporation.*** In 1997, Ed, Fran, and George form Jet Corporation. Ed contributes land purchased as an investment in 1993 for $15,000 that has a $35,000 FMV in exchange for 35 shares of Jet stock. Fran contributes machinery (Sec. 1231 property) purchased in 1993 and used in her business having a $45,000 adjusted basis and a $35,000 FMV in exchange for 35 shares of Jet stock. George contributes services worth $30,000 in exchange for 30 shares of Jet stock.

a. What is the amount of Ed's recognized gain or loss?
b. What is Ed's basis in his Jet shares? When does his holding period begin?
c. What is the amount of Fran's recognized gain or loss?
d. What is Fran's basis in her Jet shares? When does her holding period begin?
e. How much income, if any, must George recognize?
f. What is George's basis in his Jet shares? When does his holding period begin?
g. What is Jet Corporation's basis in the land and the machinery? When does its holding period begin? How does Jet Corporation treat the amount paid to George for his services?
h. How would your answers to Parts a through g change if George instead contributed $5,000 cash and services worth $25,000 for his 30 shares of Jet stock?

C2-32 ***Control Test.*** In which of the following independent situations is the Sec. 351 control requirement met?
a. Olive transfers property to Quick Corporation for 75% of Quick's stock, and Mary provides services to Quick Corporation for the remaining 25% of Quick's stock.
b. Pete transfers property to Target Corporation for 60% of Target's stock, and Robert transfers property worth $15,000 and performs services worth $25,000 for the remaining 40% of Target's stock.
c. Herb and his wife, Wilma, each have owned 50 of the 100 outstanding shares of Vast Corporation stock since it was formed three years ago. In the current year, their son, Sam, transfers property to Vast Corporation for 50 newly issued shares of Vast stock.
d. Charles and Ruth develop a plan to form Tiny Corporation. On June 3 of this year, Charles transfers property worth $50,000 for 50 shares of Tiny stock. On August 1, Ruth transfers $50,000 cash for 50 shares of Tiny stock.
e. Assume the same facts as in Part d, except that Charles has a prearranged plan to sell 30 of his shares to Sam on October 1.

C2-33 ***Sec. 351 Requirements.*** To which of the following exchanges does Sec. 351 apply?
a. Fred exchanges property worth $50,000 and services worth $50,000 for 100 shares of New Corporation stock. Greta exchanges $100,000 cash for the remaining 100 shares of New stock.
b. Maureen exchanges property worth $2,000 and services worth $48,000 for 100 shares of Gemini Corporation stock. Norman exchanges property worth $50,000 for the remaining 100 shares of Gemini stock.

If the transaction does not comply with the Sec. 351 requirements, suggest ways in which the transaction can be made to comply.

C2-34 ***Sec. 351 Requirements.*** Al, Bob, and Carl form West Corporation with the following assets:

		Property Transferred		
Transferor	*Asset*	*Transferor's Basis*	*FMV*	*Shares Received by Transferor*
Al	Patent	—0—	$25,000	1,000 common
Bob	Cash	$25,000	25,000	250 preferred
Carl	Services	—0—	7,500	300 common

The common stock has voting rights. The preferred stock is nonvoting stock.
a. Does the transaction qualify as tax-free under Sec. 351? Explain the tax consequences of the transaction to Al, Bob, Carl, and West Corporation.

b. How would your answer to Part a change if Bob had instead received 200 shares of common stock and 200 shares of preferred stock?

c. How would your answer to Part a change if Carl had instead contributed $800 cash as well as services worth $6,700?

C2-35 ***Incorporating a Sole Proprietorship.*** Tom incorporates his sole proprietorship by transferring all of its assets to newly-formed Total Corporation for all 100 shares of Total stock, with a $125,000 FMV, and four $10,000 interest-bearing notes that mature consecutively on the first four anniversaries of the incorporation date. The assets transferred are

Assets		*Adjusted Basis*	*FMV*
Cash		$ 5,000	$ 5,000
Equipment	$130,000		
Minus: Accumulated depreciation	(70,000)	60,000	90,000
Building	$100,000		
Minus: Accumulated depreciation	(49,000)	51,000	40,000
Land		24,000	30,000
Total		$140,000	$165,000

a. What are the amount and character of Tom's recognized gain or loss?

b. What is Tom's basis in his Total stock and notes?

c. What is Total Corporation's basis in the properties received from Tom?

C2-36 ***Transfer to an Existing Corporation.*** For the last five years, Ann and Fred have each owned 50 of the 100 outstanding shares of Zero Corporation's stock. Ann transfers land having a $10,000 basis and a $25,000 FMV to Zero Corporation for an additional 25 shares of Zero stock. Fred transfers $1,000 to Zero Corporation for one additional share of Zero stock. What is the amount of the gain or loss that Ann must recognize on the exchange? If the transaction does not comply with the Sec. 351 requirements, suggest ways in which the transaction can be made to comply.

C2-37 ***Transfer to an Existing Corporation.*** For the last three years, Lucy and Marvin have each owned 50 of the 100 outstanding shares of Lucky Corporation's stock. Lucy transfers property that has an $8,000 basis and a $12,000 FMV to Lucky Corporation for an additional ten shares of Lucky stock. How much gain or loss must Lucy recognize on the exchange? If the transaction does not comply with the Sec. 351 requirements, suggest ways in which the transaction can be made to comply.

C2-38 ***Disproportionate Receipt of Stock.*** Jerry transfers property with a $28,000 adjusted basis and a $50,000 FMV to Texas Corporation for 75 shares of Texas stock. Frank, Jerry's father, transfers property with a $32,000 adjusted basis and a $50,000 FMV to Texas Corporation for the remaining 25 shares of Texas stock.

a. What is the amount of each transferor's recognized gain or loss?

b. What is Jerry's basis for his Texas stock?

c. What is Frank's basis for his Texas stock?

C2-39 ***Sec. 351: Boot Property Received.*** Jane transfers land (a capital asset) having a $50,000 adjusted basis to Jones Corporation in a transaction qualifying under Sec. 351. In exchange, Jane receives the following consideration:

Consideration	*FMV*
100 shares of Jones Corporation common stock	$100,000
Jones Corporation bond due in ten years	30,000
Jones Corporation note due in three years	20,000
Total	$150,000

a. What are the amount and character of Jane's recognized gain or loss?
b. What is Jane's basis for her stock, bond, and note?
c. What is Jones Corporation's basis for the land?

C2-40 ***Receipt of Bonds for Property.*** Joe, Karen, and Larry form Gray Corporation. Joe contributes land (a capital asset) having an $8,000 adjusted basis and a $15,000 FMV to Gray Corporation in exchange for a similar dollar amount of its ten-year bonds. Karen contributes equipment (a Sec. 1231 asset) having an $18,000 adjusted basis and a $25,000 FMV on which $10,000 of depreciation had previously been claimed for 50 shares of Gray stock. Larry contributes $25,000 cash for 50 shares of Gray stock.
a. What are the amount and character of Joe's, Karen's, and Larry's recognized gains or losses on the transactions?
b. What basis do Joe, Karen, and Larry take in the stock or bonds they receive?
c. What basis does Gray Corporation take in the land and equipment? What happens to the $10,000 of depreciation recapture potential on the equipment?

C2-41 ***Transfer of Depreciable Property.*** Dana transfers depreciable machinery that originally cost $25,000 and has a $15,000 adjusted basis to Booth Corporation in exchange for all 100 shares of Booth's stock, having an $18,000 FMV, and a three-year Booth Corporation note having a $7,000 FMV.
a. What are the amount and character of Dana's recognized gain or loss?
b. What are Dana's bases for the stock and note she received?
c. What is Booth Corporation's basis for the depreciable machinery received from Dana?

C2-42 ***Transfer of Personal Liabilities.*** Jim owns 80% of the stock of Gold Corporation. He transfers a business automobile to Gold Corporation in exchange for additional Gold stock worth $5,000 and its assumption of his $1,000 debt on the automobile and his $2,000 education loan. The automobile originally cost Jim $12,000, has a $4,500 adjusted basis, and has an $8,000 FMV on the transfer date.
a. What are the amount and character of Jim's recognized gain or loss?
b. What is Jim's basis for his additional Gold shares?
c. When does Jim's holding period start for the additional shares?
d. What basis does Gold Corporation take in the automobile?

C2-43 ***Liabilities in Excess of Basis.*** Barbara transfers machinery that has a $15,000 basis and a $35,000 FMV and $10,000 in money to Moore Corporation in exchange for 50 shares of Moore stock. The machinery was used in Barbara's business, originally cost Barbara $50,000, and is subject to a $28,000 liability, which Moore Corporation assumes. Sam exchanges $17,000 cash for the remaining 50 shares of Moore stock.
a. What are the amount and character of Barbara's recognized gain or loss?
b. What is her basis in the Moore stock?
c. What is Moore Corporation's basis in the machinery?
d. What are the amount and character of Sam's recognized gain or loss?
e. What is Sam's basis in the Moore stock?

f. When do Barbara and Sam's holding periods for their stock begin?
g. How would your answers to Parts a through f change if Sam received $17,000 of Moore stock for legal services (instead of for money)?

C2-44 ***Transfer of Business Properties.*** Marty transfers property that has a $28,000 adjusted basis and a $45,000 FMV to Silver Corporation in exchange for all of its stock worth $30,000, and for Silver Corporation's assumption of a $15,000 mortgage on the property.
a. What is the amount of Marty's recognized gain or loss?
b. What is Marty's basis in his Silver stock?
c. What is Silver Corporation's basis in the property?
d. How would your answers to Parts a through c change if the mortgage assumed by Silver were $30,000 and the Silver stock were worth $15,000?

C2-45 ***Incorporating a Cash Basis Proprietorship.*** Ted decides to incorporate his medical practice. He uses the cash method of accounting. On the date of incorporation, the practice has the following balance sheet:

	Basis	*FMV*
Assets:		
Cash	$ 5,000	$ 5,000
Accounts receivable	—0—	65,000
Equipment (net of $15,000 depreciation)	35,000	40,000
Total	$40,000	$110,000
Liabilities and Owner's Equity:		
Current liabilities	$—0—	$ 35,000
Note payable on equipment	15,000	15,000
Owner's equity	25,000	60,000
Total	$40,000	$110,000

All of the current liabilities would be deductible by Ted if he paid them. Ted transfers all the assets and liabilities to a professional corporation in exchange for all of its stock.
a. What are the amount and character of Ted's recognized gain or loss?
b. What is Ted's basis in the shares he receives?
c. What is the corporation's basis in the properties it receives?
d. Who must recognize the income from the receivables when they are collected? Can the corporation obtain a deduction for the liabilities when they are paid?

C2-46 ***Transfer of Depreciable Property.*** On January 10, 1997, Mary transfers to Green Corporation a machine purchased on March 3, 1994, for $100,000. The machine has a $60,000 adjusted basis and a $110,000 FMV on the transfer date. Mary receives all 100 shares of Green stock, worth $100,000, and a two-year Green Corporation note worth $10,000.
a. What are the amount and character of Mary's recognized gain or loss?
b. What is Mary's basis in the stock and note? When does her holding period begin?
c. What are the amount and character of Green Corporation's gain or loss?
d. What is Green Corporation's basis for the machine? When does Green Corporation's holding period begin?

C2-47 ***Contribution to Capital by a Nonshareholder.*** The City of San Antonio donates land worth $500,000 to Ace Corporation to induce it to locate in San Antonio and provide 2,000 jobs for its citizens.

a. How much income, if any, must Ace Corporation report because of the land contribution?
b. What basis does the land have to Ace Corporation?
c. Assume the same facts except that the City of San Antonio also donated $100,000 cash to Ace Corporation, which the corporation used to pay a portion of the $250,000 cost of equipment that it purchased six months later. How much income, if any, must Ace Corporation report because of the cash contribution? What basis does the equipment that was purchased have to Ace Corporation?

C2-48 ***Choice of Capital Structure.*** Reggie transfers $500,000 in cash to newly-formed Jackson Corporation for 100% of Jackson's stock. In the first year of operations, Jackson's taxable income before any payments to Reggie is $120,000. What is the total amount of taxable income that Reggie and Jackson Corporation must each report in the following two scenarios?
a. Jackson Corporation distributes a $70,000 dividend to Reggie.
b. Assume that when Jackson Corporation was formed, Reggie transferred his $500,000 to the corporation for $250,000 of Jackson stock and $250,000 in Jackson notes that are payable in five annual installments of $50,000 plus 8% annual interest on the unpaid balance. During the current year Jackson Corporation pays Reggie $50,000 in repayment of the first note plus $20,000 interest.

C2-49 ***Worthless Stock or Securities.*** Tom and Vicki, who are husband and wife and who file a joint tax return, each purchase one-half of the stock of Guest Corporation from Al, for which they each pay $75,000. Tom is employed full-time by Guest Corporation and is paid $100,000 in salary annually. Because of Guest Corporation's financial difficulties, Tom and Vicki each lend Guest Corporation an additional $25,000. The $25,000 is secured by registered bonds and is to be repaid in five years, with interest being charged at a rate acceptable to the IRS. Guest Corporation's financial difficulties continue and bankruptcy is declared. Tom and Vicki receive nothing for their Guest stock or for their Guest Corporation bonds.
a. What are the amount and character of each shareholder's loss on the worthless stock and bonds?
b. How would your answer to Part a change if the liability were not secured by a bond?
c. How would your answer to Part a change if Tom and Vicki had each purchased their stock for $75,000 at the time Guest Corporation was formed?

C2-50 ***Worthless Stock.*** Duck Corporation is owned equally by Harry, Susan, and Big Corporation. Harry and Susan are both single. Harry, Tom, and Big Corporation, the original investors in Duck Corporation, each paid $125,000 for their Duck stock in 1989. Susan purchased her stock from Tom in 1992 for $175,000. No adjustments to basis occur after the stock acquisition date. Duck Corporation suffers some financial difficulties as the result of losing a large judgment in a lawsuit brought by a person who purchased a defective product, resulting in a serious personal injury. Duck Corporation files for bankruptcy, and all of its assets are ultimately used to pay its creditors in 1997. What are the amount and character of each shareholder's loss?

C2-51 ***Sale of Sec. 1244 Stock.*** Lois, who is single, transfers property with an $80,000 basis and a $120,000 FMV to Water Corporation in exchange for all of Water's 100 shares of stock. The Water stock qualifies as Sec. 1244 stock. Two years later, Lois sells the stock for $28,000.

a. What are the amount and character of Lois's recognized gain or loss?
b. How would your answer to Part a change if the FMV of the property transferred were $70,000?

C2-52 *Transfer of Sec. 1244 Stock.* Assume the same facts as in Problem C2-51 except that Lois gave the Water stock to her daughter, Sue, six months after she received it. The stock had a $120,000 FMV when Lois received it and when she made the gift. Sue sold the stock two years later for $28,000. How is the loss treated for tax purposes?

C2-53 *Avoiding Sec. 351 Treatment.* Donna purchased land six years ago as an investment. The land cost her $150,000 and is now worth $480,000. Donna plans to transfer the land to Development Corporation. Development Corporation will subdivide the land and sell individual parcels. Development Corporation's profit on the land sales will be ordinary income.
a. What are the tax consequences of the asset transfer and land sales if Donna contributes the land to Development Corporation in exchange for all of its stock?
b. What alternative methods can be used to structure the transaction in order to achieve better tax consequences? Assume Donna's marginal tax rate is 39.6%; Development Corporation's marginal tax rate is 34%.

COMPREHENSIVE PROBLEM

C2-54 On March 1 of the current year, Alice, Bob, Carla, and Dick form Bear Corporation with the following investments:

	Property Transferred			
Transferor	*Asset*	*Basis to Transferor*	*FMV*	*Number of Common Shares Issued*
Alice	Land	$12,000	$30,000	
	Building	38,000	70,000	400
	Mortgage on the land and building	60,000	60,000	
Bob	Equipment	25,000	40,000	300
Carla	Van	15,000	10,000	50
Dick	Accounting services	—0—	10,000	100

The land and building were purchased by Alice several years ago for $12,000 and $50,000, respectively. Alice has claimed straight-line depreciation on the building. Bob also receives a Bear Corporation note for $10,000 due in three years. The note bears interest at a rate acceptable to the IRS. The equipment was purchased by Bob three years ago for $50,000. Carla also receives $5,000 cash. The van was purchased by Carla two years ago for $20,000.
a. Does the transaction satisfy the requirements of Sec. 351?
b. What are the amount and character of the recognized gains or losses for Alice, Bob, Carla, Dick, and Bear Corporation?
c. What is each shareholder's basis for his or her Bear stock? When does the holding period for the stock begin?
d. What is Bear Corporation's basis for its properties and services? When does its holding period begin for each property?

CASE STUDY PROBLEMS

C2-55 Bob Jones has approached you for advice. He has a small repair shop that he has run for several years as a sole proprietorship. The proprietorship has used the cash method of accounting and the calendar year as its tax year. He needs additional capital for expansion and knows two people who might be interested in investing in the business. One would like to work in the business. The other would be an investor only.

Bob wants to know what the tax consequences of incorporating his business are. His business assets include a small building, equipment, accounts receivable, and cash. There is a mortgage on the building and a small amount of accounts payable, which represent deductible expenses.

Required: Write a memorandum to Bob explaining the tax consequences of the incorporation. As part of your memorandum examine the possibility of having the corporation issue common and preferred stock and debt for the shareholders' property and money.

C2-56 Eric Wright operates a dry cleaning business as a sole proprietorship. The business operates in a building that Eric owns. Last year, he borrowed $150,000 by placing a mortgage on the building and the land on which the building sits. He used the money for a down payment on his personal residence and college expenses for his two children. He now wants to incorporate his business and transfer the building and the mortgage to his new corporation, along with other assets and some accounts payable. The amount of the unpaid mortgage balance will not exceed Eric's adjusted basis for the land and building at the time it is transferred to the corporation. Eric is aware that Sec. 357(b) is likely to apply to this transaction because there is no bona fide business purpose for the transfer of the mortgage, and it is likely that the IRS will consider it to have been transferred for tax avoidance purposes. However, the client refuses to acknowledge this problem when you confront him about the situation. He maintains that many taxpayers play the audit lottery and that, in the event of an audit, this issue can be used as a bargaining ploy.

Required: What information about the transaction must accompany the transferor and transferee's tax returns for the year in which the transfer takes place? Discuss the ethical issues in the AICPA's *Statements of Responsibilities in Tax Practice No. 1* (which can be found in Appendix E) as it relates to this situation. Should the tax practitioner act as an advocate for the client's position in this situation? Should the practitioner sign the return?

C2-57 You are a tax manager with Dewey, Cheatem, and Howe, a regional accounting firm. Peter Moon has been a client of your firm for a number of years. He asked your assistance in starting his new manufacturing corporation two years ago. Peter contributed $100,000 to purchase all 100 shares of Moon Corporation stock. An additional $400,000 was borrowed from Third National Bank to purchase land, a building, and manufacturing equipment. Interest at a floating rate is being charged on the bank loan. The bank rate is currently 12%, and has been no lower than 10.25%. Peter is a guarantor on the bank loans. In addition, Peter loaned the corporation $500,000 for working capital with interest being charged at a 5% rate. The loan is not secured by a note. None of the principal or current year interest has been paid. Upon your initial review of the work papers for Moon's current year tax return you become concerned about the high debt/equity ratio and whether the interest that has been incurred is deductible. What factors will the IRS use to determine whether the loans are in fact debt or equity? Do these factors appear to favor the IRS or the taxpayer?

TAX RESEARCH PROBLEMS

C2-58 Anne and Michael own and operate a mattress business. It has been quite successful and they have now determined to take it public. They contribute all the assets of the business to newly-formed Spring Corporation in exchange for 20% of the stock for each of them. The remaining 60% of the stock is issued to an underwriting company which will sell the stock to the public and keep 10% of the sales proceeds as a commission. Prepare a memorandum for your tax manager explaining whether or not this transaction meets the nonrecognition of gain or loss requirements of Sec. 351.

C2-59 Bob and Carl transfer property to Stone Corporation for 90% and 10% of the Stone stock, respectively. Pursuant to a binding agreement entered into before the transfer, Bob sells half of his stock to Carl. Prepare a memorandum for your tax manager explaining why Sec. 351 does or does not apply to this exchange. Your manager has suggested that, as a minimum, you consult the following resources:

- Sec. 351
- Reg. Sec. 1.351-1

C2-60 In an exchange qualifying under Sec. 351, Greta receives 100 shares of White Corporation stock plus a contingent right to receive another 25 shares. The shares are contingent on the determination of the value of a patent contributed by Greta. The licensing of the patent is pending and consequently the patent cannot be valued for several months. Prepare a memorandum for your tax manager explaining whether the contingent shares are considered "stock" for purposes of Sec. 351 and what tax consequences result from Greta's receipt of the actual and contingent shares of stock.

CHAPTER 3

THE CORPORATE INCOME TAX

LEARNING OBJECTIVES

After studying this chapter, you should be able to

1. Explain the requirements for selecting tax years and accounting methods
2. Compute a corporation's taxable income
3. Compute a corporation's income tax liability
4. Explain what a controlled group is and the tax consequences of being a controlled group
5. Explain how compensation planning can reduce taxes for corporations and their shareholders
6. Determine the requirements for paying corporate income taxes and filing a corporate tax return

CHAPTER OUTLINE

A **corporation** is a separate taxpaying entity that must file a tax return every year, even if it has no income or loss for the year. This chapter covers the tax rules for **domestic corporations** (i.e., corporations incorporated in one of the fifty states or under federal law) and other entities that are taxed as domestic corporations under the check-the-box rules.[1] It explains the rules for determining a corporation's taxable income, loss, and tax liability and for filing corporate tax returns.

See Table C3-1 for the general formula for determining the corporate tax liability.

The corporations discussed in this chapter are sometimes referred to as regular or C corporations. Such corporations are taxed under the provisions of Subchapter C of the Internal Revenue Code. Corporations that have a special tax status include S corporations and affiliated groups of corporations that file consolidated returns. A comparison of the tax treatments of C corporations, S corporations, and partnerships is presented in Appendix F.

CORPORATE ELECTIONS

OBJECTIVE 1

Explain the requirements for selecting tax years and accounting methods

KEY POINT

Whereas partnerships and S corporations must generally adopt a calendar year, C corporations (other than personal service corporations) have the flexibility of adopting a fiscal year. The fiscal year must end on the last day of the month.

REAL WORLD EXAMPLE

For 1994, 2.53 million corporations filed separate C corporation returns while 2.04 million corporations filed as S corporations. Only 75,000 consolidated tax returns were filed in 1994, but these consolidated returns accounted for approximately 80% of the $154 billion of corporate tax payments in 1994.

When a corporation is formed, certain elections must be made. The corporation must select its **tax year**. It must also select its basic accounting method. These elections are made on the corporation's first tax return. They are important and should be considered carefully because, once made, they generally can be changed only with permission from the Internal Revenue Service (IRS).

CHOOSING A CALENDAR OR FISCAL YEAR

A new corporation may elect to use either a calendar year or a fiscal year as its accounting period. The corporation's tax year must be the same as its annual accounting period that is used for financial accounting purposes. The election is made by filing the corporation's first tax return for the selected period. A calendar year is a twelve-month period ending on December 31. A fiscal year is a twelve-month period ending on the last day of any month other than December.[2] Examples of acceptable fiscal years are February 1, 1997 to January 31, 1998; and October 1, 1997 to September 30, 1998. A fiscal year that runs from September 16, 1997 through September 15, 1998 is not an acceptable tax year because it does not end on the last day of the month. The IRS will require a corporation using an unacceptable tax year to change to a calendar year.[3]

SHORT TAX PERIOD. A corporation's first tax year may not cover a full twelve-month period. If, for example, a corporation begins business on March 10, 1997 and elects a fiscal year ending on September 30, its first tax year covers the period from March 10, 1997 through September 30, 1997. Its second tax year covers the period from October 1, 1997 through September 30, 1998. The corporation must file a **short-period tax return** for its first tax year.[4] From then on, its tax returns cover a full twelve-month period. The last year of a corporation's life may also be a short period covering the period of time from the beginning of the last tax year through the date that the corporation goes out of existence.

RESTRICTIONS ON ADOPTING A TAX YEAR. A corporation may be subject to restrictions in its choice of a tax year. An S corporation generally must use a calendar year (see Chapter C11). All members of an affiliated group filing a consolidated return must use the same tax year as the group's parent corporation (see Chapter C8).

[1] Sec. 7701(a)(4). Corporations that are not classified as domestic are **foreign corporations**. Foreign corporations are taxed like domestic corporations if they conduct a trade or business in the United States.

[2] Sec. 441. Accounting periods of either 52 or 53 weeks that always end on the same day of the week (such as Friday) are also permitted under Sec. 441.

[3] Sec. 441(i).

[4] Sec. 443(a)(2).

▼ **TABLE C3-1**

General Rules for Determining the Corporate Tax Liability

Income Tax	Alternative Minimum Tax (AMT)
Gross income Minus: Deductions and losses	
Taxable income before special deductions Minus: Special deductions	
Taxable income →	Taxable income before NOL deduction Plus or minus: Adjustments to taxable income Plus: Tax preference items Minus: Alternative tax NOL deduction
Times: Corporate tax rates	
Regular tax liability Minus: Foreign tax credit and possessions tax credit	Alternative minimum taxable income Minus: Statutory exemption
Regular tax (→ to Regular (income) tax in AMT column) Minus: Other tax credits Plus: Recapture of previously claimed tax credits	Tax base Times: 20%
Income tax liability	Tentative minimum tax before credits Minus: AMT foreign tax credit
	Tentative minimum tax Minus: AMT investment tax credit Regular (income) tax
	Alternative minimum tax liability (See Table C5-1) (only if greater than zero)

Income (regular) tax liability
Plus: Alternative minimum tax liability
Special taxes:
Accumulated earnings tax
Personal holding company tax
Minus: Estimated tax payments

Net tax liability (or refund due)

TYPICAL MISCONCEPTION

Taxpayers usually have a difficult time understanding the relationship between the income (regular) tax and the alternative minimum tax. Table C3-1 illustrates that, in total, a taxpayer ends up paying the higher of the income (regular) tax liability or the tentative minimum tax.

A personal service corporation generally must use a calendar year as its tax year. The reason for this restriction is to prevent a personal service corporation with, for example, a January 31 year-end from distributing a large portion of its income that was earned during the February–December portion of 1997 to its calendar-year shareholder-employees in January 1998, and thereby deferring income largely earned in 1997 to 1998. A **personal service corporation** (PSC) is defined for this purpose as a corporation whose principal activity is the performance of personal services. A corporation is not a PSC unless its employee-owners own more than 10% of the stock (by value) on any day of the year and the personal services are substantially performed by employee-owners. An employee-owner is any employee who owns any of the corporation's stock on any day of the tax year.[5]

[5] Sec. 441(i).

SELF-STUDY QUESTION

What choices does a PSC have relative to its tax year?

ANSWER

In general, a PSC is limited to a calendar year, but if it can show a business purpose, a fiscal year can be selected. Finally, like partnerships and S corporations, a PSC can elect under Sec. 444 a fiscal year that can provide as much as a three-month deferral.

A PSC is allowed to adopt or retain a fiscal tax year if it can establish a business purpose for such a year. For example, it may be able to establish a natural business year and use that year as its tax year.[6] Deferral of income by shareholders is not an acceptable business purpose.

A PSC may elect to use a fiscal year that does not satisfy the normal business purpose requirement.[7] A new PSC may elect to use a September 30, October 31, or November 30 year-end. An existing PSC that has a fiscal year may elect (1) to adopt a tax year whose deferral period is not longer than the shorter of (a) its current deferral period or (b) three months, or (2) to change to its required year (i.e., a calendar year). The deferral period is the number of months from the beginning of the corporation's fiscal year to December 31.

If a PSC elects a fiscal year, it must meet minimum distribution requirements to employee-owners during the deferral period. If these distribution requirements are not met, the PSC's deduction for amounts paid to employee-owners may have to be deferred to the corporation's next fiscal year.[8]

EXAMPLE C3-1 ▶

Cole Corporation is created by Alice and Bob, each of whom owns 50% of its stock. Alice and Bob use the calendar year as their tax year. Alice and Bob are both active in the business and, along with a professional staff of thirty, are the corporation's primary employees. The new corporation performs engineering services for the automotive industry. Cole Corporation must use a calendar year as its tax year unless it qualifies to use a fiscal year based on a business purpose exception. Alternatively, it may elect under Sec. 444 to adopt a fiscal year with a three-month or shorter deferral period. If such an election is made, the minimum distribution requirements of Sec. 280H must be complied with. ◀

CHANGING THE ANNUAL ACCOUNTING PERIOD. A corporation that desires to change its annual accounting period must secure the prior approval of the IRS unless the change is specifically authorized under the Regulations. A change in accounting period usually results in a short period running from the end of the old annual accounting period to the beginning of the new accounting period. A request for approval of an accounting period change must be filed on Form 1128 (Application for Change in Annual Accounting Period) on or before the fifteenth day of the second calendar month following the close of the short period.

In general, a request for change will be approved if there is a substantial business purpose for the change. But if the change would result in a substantial distortion of income, the taxpayer and the IRS must agree to the terms, conditions, and adjustments necessary to prevent the substantial distortion of income before the change can be effected. A substantial distortion of income includes, for example, a change that causes the "deferral of a substantial portion of the taxpayer's income or shifting of a substantial portion of deductions from one year to another so as to reduce substantially the taxpayer's tax liability."[9]

KEY POINT

Normally, a corporation must obtain permission from the IRS before changing its tax year. This usually requires that the corporation establish a substantial business purpose for the change of accounting period. However, the Regulations do allow a corporation, in limited situations, to change its accounting period without prior IRS approval.

Under the Regulations, a corporation may change its annual accounting period without prior IRS approval if all of the following conditions are met: the corporation has not changed its annual accounting period within the prior ten years; the resulting short period does not have a net operating loss (NOL); the taxable income in the resulting short period is, if annualized, at least 80% of the corporation's taxable income for the tax year preceding the short period; if the corporation has a special status (i.e., personal holding company or exempt status) for the short period or the tax year before

[6] The natural business year exception requires that the year-end used for tax purposes coincide with the end of the taxpayer's peak business period. (See the partnership and S corporation chapters and Rev. Proc. 87-32, 1987-2 C.B. 396, for a further explanation of this exception.)

[7] Sec. 444.

[8] Sec. 280H.

[9] Reg. Sec. 1.442-1(b)(1).

the short period, it has the same status for both; and the corporation does not elect S corporation status for the year following the short period.[10]

ACCOUNTING METHODS

A new corporation must select the overall **accounting method** it will use to keep its books and records. The method chosen must be indicated on the corporation's initial return. The same method must be used to compute its financial accounting income and its taxable income. The three possible accounting methods are: accrual, cash, and hybrid.[11]

ACCRUAL METHOD. Income is reported when it has been earned; expenses are reported when they have been incurred. Corporations must use this method unless they come under one of the following exceptions:

- A qualified family farming corporation.[12]
- A qualified personal service corporation: a corporation substantially all of whose activities involve the performance of services in the fields of health, law, engineering, architecture, accounting, actuarial science, performing arts, or consulting; and substantially all of whose stock is held by current (or retired) employees performing the services listed above, their estates, or (for two years only) persons who inherited their stock from such employees.[13]
- Corporations with annual gross receipts of $5 million or less for all prior tax years beginning after December 31, 1985. A corporation meets this test for any prior tax year if its average gross receipts for the three-year period ending with that prior tax year do not exceed $5,000,000. If the corporation was not in existence for the entire three-year period, the period during which the corporation *was* in existence may be used.
- S corporations.

If a corporation meets one of the exceptions listed above, it may use either the accrual method or one of the following two methods.

ADDITIONAL COMMENT

Whereas partnerships and S corporations are generally allowed to be cash method taxpayers, most C corporations must use the accrual method of accounting. This restriction can prove inconvenient for many small corporations (with more than $5 million of gross receipts) that would rather use the less complicated cash method of accounting.

CASH METHOD. Income is reported when it is received; expenses are reported when they are paid. Corporations in service industries such as engineering, medicine, law, and accounting generally use this method because they do not want to report their income until they actually receive payment. This method may not be used if inventories are a material income-producing factor. In such case, the corporation must use either the *accrual* method or the *hybrid* method of accounting.

HYBRID METHOD. Under this method, a corporation uses the accrual method of accounting for sales, cost of goods sold, inventories, accounts receivable, and accounts payable, and the cash method of accounting for all other income and expense items. Small businesses with inventories (e.g., retail stores) often use this method. Although they must use the accrual method of accounting for sales-related income and expense items, they often find the cash method less burdensome to use for other income and expense items, such as utilities, rents, salaries, and taxes.

[10] Reg. Sec. 1.442-1(c). 92-13, 1992-1 C.B. 665).
[11] Sec. 446.
[12] Sec. 448. Certain family farming corporations having gross receipts of less than $25 million may use the cash method of accounting. Section 447 requires farming corporations with gross receipts over $25 million to use the accrual method of accounting.
[13] The personal service corporation definition for the tax year election [Sec. 441(i)] is different from the personal service corporation definition for the cash accounting method election [Sec. 448].

GENERAL FORMULA FOR DETERMINING THE CORPORATE TAX LIABILITY

HISTORICAL NOTE

Fortune 500 companies spent over $1 billion in 1993 complying with the tax laws, or $2.11 million per firm. The largest share of the cost is for return filing. Federal and state tax compliance costs account for 70% and 30%, respectively, of these costs.

Each year, C corporations are responsible for determining their corporate income (or regular) tax liability. In addition to the income tax, a C corporation may owe the corporate alternative minimum tax and possibly either, the accumulated earnings tax or the personal holding company tax. A corporation's total tax liability equals the sum of its regular or income tax liability plus the amount of any additional tax levy that it owes.

This chapter explains how to compute a corporation's income (or regular) tax liability. Chapter C5 explains the computation of the corporate alternative minimum tax, personal holding company, tax and accumulated earnings tax.

COMPUTING A CORPORATION'S TAXABLE INCOME

OBJECTIVE 2

Compute a corporation's taxable income

The rules for computing a C corporation's taxable income are similar to those for computing an individual's taxable income. The differences are explained in the first part of this section. Some rules for computing a C corporation's taxable income are unique to C corporations and require a detailed explanation. The second part of this section presents detailed coverage of the C corporation rules.

DIFFERENCES BETWEEN INDIVIDUAL AND CORPORATE TAXABLE INCOME

The computation of a corporation's taxable income was outlined in Table C3-1. The primary differences between the individual and corporate tax rules for computing gross income and deductions are explained below and in Topic Review C3-1.

GROSS INCOME. Gross income is computed in much the same way for a corporation as it is for an individual. A corporation's gross income includes most of the same items that an individual's gross income includes, such as receipts for services, gross profits on sales, rents, gains on sales of property, interest, dividends, and commissions. A corporation's gross income also excludes most of the same items that are excluded from an individual's gross income, such as tax-exempt interest on state and municipal bonds and proceeds from life insurance policies.

Some exclusions available to individuals obviously do not apply to corporations; for example, corporations cannot exclude employee fringe benefits such as premiums on $50,000 of group term life insurance. Conversely, some exclusions that apply to corporations do not apply to individuals; for example, a corporation excludes from its gross income amounts contributed to its capital.

KEY POINT

Corporations do not make a distinction between "for" and "from" AGI deductions. For corporations, all ordinary and necessary business expenses are deductions from gross income.

DEDUCTIONS AND LOSSES. A corporation's deductions are similar to an individual's *for* AGI (above the line) deductions. But a corporation does not have the equivalent of an individual's itemized deductions because all of its deductions are deducted directly from gross income. All of a corporation's business deductions must be ordinary and necessary trade or business expenses under Sec. 162. The distinction between an individual's expenses deductible under Sec. 162 (trade or business expenses) and those deductible under Sec. 212 (expenses for the production of income) does not apply to corporations. A corporation is not eligible to deduct expenses incurred for the production of income

Topic Review C3-1

Differences Between Individual and Corporate Taxation

1. **Gross income:** Generally the same gross income definition applies to individuals and corporations. Certain exclusions are available to individuals but not to corporations (e.g, fringe benefits); other exclusions are available to corporations but not to individuals (e.g., capital contributions).
2. **Deduction categories:** Individuals have above-the-line (''for'' AGI) and below-the-line (''from'' AGI) deductions. Corporations also have two categories of deductions--business deductions and special deductions.
3. **Charitable contributions:** (a) Individuals are limited to 50% of AGI (30% in the case of capital gain property). Corporations are limited to 10% of taxable income without regard to any dividends-received deductions, NOL and capital loss carrybacks, and the contribution deduction itself. (b) Individuals deduct a contribution only in the year in which it is made. Accrual basis corporations may deduct contributions in the year of accrual if the contribution is authorized by the board of directors by the end of the tax year and paid by the 15th day of the third month of the next year.
4. **Depreciation recapture on Sec. 1250 property:** Individuals generally do not recapture any depreciation under the MACRS rules since straight-line depreciation is used for realty. Corporations must recapture 20% of the excess of the amount that would be recaptured under Sec. 1245 over any amount recaptured under Sec. 1250.
5. **Dividends-received deduction:** Not available for individuals. Corporations receive a 70%, 80%, or 100% special deduction depending on the percentage of stock ownership.
6. **Net capital gains:** Individuals are taxed at a maximum rate of 28%. Corporate capital gains are taxed at the regular corporate tax rates without any special rate ceiling.
7. **Capital losses:** Individuals can deduct $3,000 of net capital losses to offset ordinary income. Individual capital losses are carried over indefinitely. Corporations cannot offset any ordinary income with capital losses. However, capital losses can be carried back three years and forward five years and used to offset capital gains only in those years.
8. **NOLs:** Individuals must make many adjustments to arrive at the NOL they are allowed to carry back or forward. A corporation's NOL is simply the excess of its deductions over its income for the year. It may be carried back 3 years and forward 15 years, or a special election can be made to only carry the NOL forward.
9. **Tax rates:** Individual's tax rates are between 15% and 39.6%. Corporate tax rates are between 15% and 39%.
10. **AMT:** Individual AMT rates are 26% or 28%. The corporate AMT rate is 20%. Corporations are subject to a special AMTI adjustment called the ''Adjusted Current Earnings'' (ACE) adjustment that does not apply to individuals.
11. **Passive Losses:** Passive loss rules apply to individuals, partners, S corporation shareholders, closely held C corporations and PSCs. They do not apply to widely-held C corporations.

under Sec. 212. A corporation has no standard deduction amount and no personal or dependency exemptions. C corporations are not subject to the hobby loss limitations of Sec. 183 or the investment interest limitations of Sec. 163(d), as an individual taxpayer would be. Closely held C corporations, however, are subject to the at-risk rules of Sec. 465 and the passive activity loss and credit limitations of Sec. 469 in much the same manner as an individual taxpayer would be.

Some deductions available to individuals obviously do not apply to corporations. Among the deductions that do not apply to a corporation are those for alimony, contributions to an IRA or a Keogh plan, and moving expenses. Corporations do not have nonbusiness bad debts. All of a corporation's bad debts are considered to be business related. On the other hand, corporations are allowed some special deductions not available to individuals. These include amortization of organizational expenditures[14] and a dividends-received deduction.[15]

ADDITIONAL COMMENT

Most expenditures made by large corporations are either legitimate deductions or are capitalized. Expenditures made by closely held corporations are subject to close IRS scrutiny because the potential exists that the payments may be made for personal shareholder expenses.

Many deductions are available both to corporations and to individuals. But in some cases, the computation of the deduction is different for corporations from that for individuals (e.g., the deductions for charitable contributions and net operating losses).

Capital gains and losses are computed on sales or exchanges of capital assets in the same way they are for individuals, but capital gains and losses are treated differently on a corporate tax return when calculating the tax liability.

Casualty losses are deductible in full by a corporation. All corporate casualty losses are considered to be business related. They are not reduced by a $100 offset nor are they restricted to losses exceeding 10% of AGI, as are an individual's nonbusiness casualty losses.

SALES AND EXCHANGES OF PROPERTY

Sales and exchanges of property are generally treated the same way for corporations as they are for an individual. However, special rules apply in the case of capital gains and losses and corporations are subject to an additional 20% depreciation recapture rule under Sec. 291 on sales of Sec. 1250 property.

REAL WORLD SITUATION

C corporations generally have few capital gains or losses. Most gains or losses resulting from the sale or exchange of business assets are Sec. 1231 gains and losses. Section 1231 gains, however, can be used to offset capital losses. The remaining gains and losses are likely ordinary in nature arising from the sale of inventory or depreciable property (e.g., Sec. 1245 property).

CAPITAL GAINS AND LOSSES. Corporations compute capital gains and losses the same way that individuals do. A corporation has a capital gain or loss if it sells or exchanges a capital asset. A corporation must net all of its capital gains and losses together to obtain its net capital gain or loss position.

Net Capital Gain. All of a corporation's net capital gains (net long-term capital gains in excess of net short-term capital losses) for the tax year are included in gross income. Unlike with individuals, a corporation's capital gains receive no special tax treatment and are taxed in the same manner as any other ordinary income item.

EXAMPLE C3-2 ▶

Beta Corporation has a net capital gain of $40,000, gross profits on sales of $110,000, and deductible expenses of $28,000. Beta's gross income is $150,000 ($40,000 + $110,000). Its taxable income is $122,000 ($150,000 − $28,000). The $40,000 of net capital gain receives no special treatment and is taxed using the regular corporate tax rates of Sec. 11 described below. ◀

Net Capital Losses. If a corporation has a net capital loss, the loss may not be deducted in the current year. A corporation's capital losses may be used only to offset capital gains. They may *never* be used to offset the corporation's ordinary income.

A net capital loss must be carried back as a short-term capital loss to the three previous tax years and used to offset capital gains in the earliest year possible (i.e., the losses must be carried to the third previous year first). If the loss is not totally absorbed as a carryback, the remainder is carried forward as a short-term capital loss for five years. Any losses that remain unused at the end of the carryforward period are lost.

[14] Sec. 248.

[15] Secs. 243 through 245.

EXAMPLE C3-3

SELF-STUDY QUESTION

How does the use of a net capital loss differ for individual and corporate taxpayers?

ANSWER

Net capital losses are treated differently by individuals and corporations. Individuals may use up to $3,000 per year of net capital losses to offset ordinary income, cannot carry back net capital losses, and can carry forward net capital losses indefinitely. In contrast, corporations may not use any net capital losses to offset ordinary income, can carry back net capital losses three years, and can carry forward net capital losses for only five years.

In 1997 East Corporation reports gross profits of $150,000, deductible expenses of $28,000, and a net capital loss of $10,000. East reported the following capital gain net income (excess of gains from sales or exchanges of capital assets over losses from such sales or exchanges) during 1994–1996:

Year	*Capital Gain Net Income*
1994	$6,000
1995	—0—
1996	3,000

East has gross income of $150,000 and taxable income of $122,000 ($150,000 − $28,000) for 1997. East also has a $10,000 net capital loss that can be carried back. This loss is carried back to 1994 first and offsets the $6,000 capital gain net income reported in that year. East receives a refund for the taxes paid on the $6,000 of capital gains in 1994. The $4,000 ($10,000 − $6,000) remainder of the loss carryback is carried to 1996 and offsets East's $3,000 capital gain net income reported in that year. East still has a $1,000 net capital loss to carry forward to 1998.

SEC. 291: TAX BENEFIT RECAPTURE RULE. If Sec. 1250 property is sold at a gain, Sec. 1250 requires that the recognized gain be reported as ordinary income to the extent the depreciation taken exceeds the depreciation that would have been allowed if the straight-line method had been used. This ordinary income is known as Sec. 1250 depreciation recapture. For individuals, any remaining gain is characterized as Sec. 1231 gain. However, corporations must recapture as ordinary income an additional amount equal to 20% of the additional ordinary income that would have been recognized had the property been Sec. 1245 property instead of Sec. 1250 property.

EXAMPLE C3-4

ADDITIONAL COMMENT

Section 291 results in the recapture, as ordinary income, of an additional 20% of the gain on sales of Sec. 1250 property. This recapture requirement reduces the amount of net Sec.1231 gains that can be used to offset corporate capital losses.

Texas Corporation purchased residential real estate in January 1995 for $125,000, of which $25,000 is allocated to the land and $100,000 to the building. Texas took straight-line MACRS depreciation deductions of $10,606 on the building in the years 1995 through 1997. In December 1997, Texas sells the property for $155,000, of which $45,000 is allocated to the land and $110,000 to the building. Texas has a $20,000 ($45,000 − $25,000) gain on the land sale, all of which is Sec. 1231 gain. This gain is not affected by Sec. 291 because land is not Sec. 1250 property. Texas has a $20,606 [$110,000 sales price − ($100,000 original cost − $10,606 depreciation)] gain on the sale of the building. If Texas were an individual taxpayer, the entire $20,606 recognized gain would be Sec. 1231 gain. But as a *corporate* taxpayer, $2,121 of gain must be reported as ordinary income. These amounts are summarized below:

	Land	Building	Total
Amount of gain:			
Sales price	$45,000	$110,000	$155,000
Minus: adjusted basis	(25,000)	(89,394)	(114,394)
Recognized gain	$20,000	$ 20,606	$ 40,606
Character of gain:			
Ordinary income	$—0—	$ 2,121[a]	$ 2,121
Sec. 1231	20,000	18,485	38,485
Recognized gain	$20,000	$ 20,606	$ 40,606

[a] 20% × lesser of $10,606 depreciation claimed or $20,606 recognized gain.

WHAT WOULD YOU DO IN THIS SITUATION?

You are a CPA with a medium-size accounting firm. One of your corporate clients is an electrical contractor in New York City. The client is successful and had $10 million of sales last year. The contracts involve private and goverment electrical work. Among the corporation's expenses are $400,000 of kickbacks paid to people working for general contractors who award electrical subcontracts to the corporation, and $100,000 of payments made to individuals in the electricans' union. Technically, these payments are illegal. However your client says that everyone in this business needs to pay kickbacks to obtain contracts and to have enough electricians to finish the projects in a timely manner. He maintains that it is impossible to stay in business without making these payments. Your client wants you to deduct these expenses. What are your options and responsibilities under the AICPA's *Statements on Responsibilities in Tax Practice? Treasury Department Circular 230?*

BUSINESS EXPENSES

Corporations may deduct most of the same business expenses that a sole proprietor may deduct on Schedule C (or Schedule C-EZ) of an individual return. Deductions are allowed for ordinary and necessary business expenses, including salaries paid to officers and other employees of the corporation, rent, repairs, insurance premiums, advertising, interest, taxes, losses on sales of inventory or other property, bad debts, and depreciation.[16]

No deductions are allowed for interest on amounts borrowed to purchase tax-exempt securities, illegal bribes or kickbacks, fines or penalties imposed by a government, or insurance premiums incurred to insure the lives of officers and employees when the corporation is the beneficiary.

KEY POINT

Without the election available under Sec. 248, organizational expenditures would be capitalized and would not be recovered until the corporation is liquidated. Thus, the election to amortize organizational expenditures over a period of sixty months is certainly preferable to the alternative.

ORGANIZATIONAL EXPENDITURES. When a corporation is formed, it may incur some organizational expenditures such as legal fees and accounting fees incident to the incorporation process. These expenditures must be capitalized. Unless an election is made under Sec. 248, however, these expenditures cannot be amortized because they have an unlimited life. A Sec. 248 election allows organizational expenditures to be amortized over a period of sixty or more months beginning with the month in which the corporation begins its business. The election must be made in a statement attached to the first return filed by the corporate entity. The return and statement must be filed no later than the due date of the tax return (including any permitted extensions).[17] If an amortization election is not made, organizational expenditures cannot be deducted until the corporation is liquidated.

The election applies only to expenditures incurred before the end of the tax year in which the corporation begins business. A corporation begins business when it starts the business operations for which it was organized. In determining when an organizational expenditure has been incurred, it is irrelevant whether the corporation uses the cash or accrual method of accounting. Expenditures incurred *after* the first tax year has ended (e.g., legal expenses incurred to modify the corporate charter) must be capitalized and cannot be deducted until the corporation is liquidated.[18]

Organizational expenditures are defined by Sec. 248(b) to include any expenditure that is incident to the creation of the corporation, chargeable to the corporation's capital account, and of a character that, if expended incident to the creation of a corporation having a limited life, would be amortizable over that life.

[16] Sec. 162.
[17] Sec. 248(c).
[18] Reg. Sec. 1.248-1(a).

Organizational expenditures include

- Legal services incident to the organization of the corporation (e.g., drafting the corporate charter and bylaws, minutes of organizational meetings, and terms of original stock certificates)
- Accounting services necessary to the creation of the corporation
- Expenses of temporary directors and of organizational meetings of directors and stockholders
- Fees paid to the state of incorporation.[19]

Organizational expenditures do not include any expenditures connected with the issuing or selling of the corporation's stock or other securities (e.g., commissions, professional fees, and printing costs) and expenditures related to the transfer of assets to the corporation.

EXAMPLE C3-5 ▶ Heart Corporation is incorporated on July 1 of the current year, starts in business on August 1, and elects a tax year ending on September 30. Heart incurs the following expenses during the current year while organizing the corporation:

Date	*Type of Expenditure*	*Amount*
June 10	Legal expenses to draft charter	$ 2,000
July 17	Commission to stockbroker for issuing and selling stock	40,000
July 18	Accounting fees to set up corporate books	2,400
July 20	Temporary directors' fees	1,000
August 25	Directors' fees	1,500
October 9	Legal fees to modify corporate charter	1,000

Heart's first tax year begins July 1 and ends on September 30. Heart may amortize organizational expenditures of $5,400. The legal expenses to modify the corporate charter may not be amortized because they were not incurred during the tax year in which Heart commenced to conduct its business. The commission for selling the Heart stock is treated as a reduction in the amount of Heart's paid-in capital. The directors' fees incurred in August are deducted as a trade or business expense under Sec. 162 because Heart has commenced in business by that date. If Heart elects to amortize its organizational expenditures over 60 months, it deducts $90 ($5,400 ÷ 60) per month. A $180 deduction can be claimed in Heart's first tax year ($90 per month × 2 months).

The classification of expenses is summarized below.

			Type of Expenditure		
Date	*Expense*	*Amount*	*Organizational*	*Capital*	*Business*
6/10	Legal	$ 2,000	$2,000		
7/17	Commission	40,000		$40,000	
7/18	Accounting	2,400	2,400		
7/20	Directors' fees	1,000	1,000		
8/25	Directors' fees	1,500			$1,500
10/9	Legal	1,000		1,000	
	Total	$47,900	$5,400	$41,000	$1,500 ◀

If the business is discontinued or disposed of before the end of the amortization period, any remaining organizational expenditures may be deducted as a loss.[20]

[19] Reg. Sec. 1.248-1(b)(2).

[20] *Malta Temple Association*, 16 B.T.A. 409 (1929), acq. XIII-2 C.B. 12.

SELF-STUDY QUESTION

What are start-up expenditures?

ANSWER

Start-up expenditures usually occur before the actual operation of a trade or business and involve the costs incurred in investigating and creating an active trade or business.

START-UP EXPENDITURES. A distinction must be made between a corporation's organizational expenditures and its start-up expenditures. Start-up expenditures are ordinary and necessary business expenses that are paid or incurred by an individual or corporate taxpayer[21]

- To investigate the creation or acquisition of an active trade or business
- To create an active trade or business
- To conduct an activity engaged in for profit or the production of income before the time the activity becomes an active trade or business

Examples of start-up expenditures are the costs incurred for a survey of potential markets, an analysis of available facilities, advertisements relating to the opening of the business, the training of employees, travel and other expenses for securing prospective distributors, suppliers, or customers, and the hiring of management personnel and outside consultants.

The expenditures must be such that if they were incurred in connection with the operation of an existing active trade or business they would be allowable as a deduction for the year in which they are paid or incurred. However, under Sec. 195, they must be capitalized.

Under Sec. 195, an election may be made to amortize start-up expenditures over a period of sixty or more months starting with the month in which an active trade or business begins. If the election is not made, the expenditures are capitalized and cannot be deducted until the corporation is liquidated. If the business is discontinued or disposed of before the end of the amortization period, any remaining start-up expenditures may be deducted as a loss.[22]

STOP & THINK

Question: What is the difference between an "organizational expenditure" and a "start-up" expenditure?

Solution: Organizational expenditures are outlays made in forming a corporation, such as fees paid to the state of incorporation for the corporate chapter and fees paid to an attorney to draft the documents needed to form the corporation. Start-up expenditures are outlays that would otherwise be deductible as "ordinary and necessary" business expenses but that are capitalized because they were incurred prior to the start of the corporation's business activities.

A corporation may elect to amortize both organizational expenditures and start-up expenditures over 60 or more months. Like a corporation, a partnership can capitalize and amortize its organizational and start-up expenditures, but not its syndication costs. A sole proprietorship may incur start-up expenditures that can be capitalized and amortized. However, organizational expenditures are not incurred by sole proprietorships.

LIMITATION ON DEDUCTIONS FOR ACCRUED COMPENSATION. If a corporation accrues an obligation to pay compensation, the payment must be made within 2½ months after the close of the corporation's tax year. Otherwise, the deduction cannot be taken until the year of payment.[23] The reason is that if a payment is delayed beyond 2½ months, the IRS treats it as a deferred compensation plan. Deferred compensation cannot be deducted until the year payment is made and the recipient includes the payment in income.[24]

[21] Sec. 195(c)(1).
[22] Sec. 195(b).
[23] Temp. Reg. Sec. 1.404(b)-1T.
[24] Sec. 404(b).

EXAMPLE C3-6 ▶ On December 10, 1997, Bell Corporation (a calendar-year taxpayer) accrues an obligation for a $100,000 bonus to Marge, a sales representative who has had an outstanding year. Marge does not own any Bell stock. The payment must be made by March 15, 1998. Otherwise, Bell Corporation cannot deduct the $100,000 on its 1997 tax return but must wait until the year the payment is made. ◀

CHARITABLE CONTRIBUTIONS. The treatment of charitable contributions by individual and corporate taxpayers differs in three ways: the timing of the deduction, the amount of the deduction permitted for the contribution of certain nonmoney properties, and the maximum deduction permitted in any given year.

KEY POINT

Accrual method corporate taxpayers have some flexibility in the timing of their charitable contribution deductions. The charitable contributions are deducted in the year paid or when accrued if the board of directors authorizes the contribution and the contribution is made by the fifteenth day of the third month following the end of the accrual year.

Timing Of The Deduction. Corporations are allowed a deduction for contributions to qualified charitable organizations just as individuals are.[25] Generally, the contribution must have been *paid* during the year (not just pledged) for a deduction to be allowed for a given year. A special rule applies to corporations using the accrual method of accounting (corporations using the cash or hybrid methods of accounting are not eligible).[26] These corporations may elect to treat part or all of a charitable contribution as having been made in the year in which it was accrued (instead of being deducted in the year paid) if

- The board of directors authorizes the contribution in the year it was accrued
- The contribution is paid on or before the fifteenth day of the third month following the end of the accrual year.

The election is made by deducting the contribution on the corporation's tax return for the year it was accrued and attaching a copy of the board of director's resolution to the return. Any portion of the contribution for which the election is not made is deducted in the year that it is paid.

EXAMPLE C3-7 ▶ Echo Corporation is a calendar-year taxpayer using the accrual method of accounting. In 1997, its board of directors authorizes a $10,000 contribution to the Girl Scouts. The contribution is paid on March 10, 1998. Echo may elect to treat part or all of the contribution as having been paid in 1997. If the contribution is paid after March 15, 1998, it may not be deducted in 1997 but may be deducted in 1998. ◀

KEY POINT

Congress has provided corporations with added incentive to help support charitable organizations that care for the ill, needy, or infants. If corporations donate ordinary income property to such charities, the corporation gets to deduct not only the usual adjusted basis in the property but also an additional 50% of the appreciation in the contributed property. This incentive also applies to property contributed to educational institutions or research organizations for use in research or experimentation.

Deducting Contributions Of Nonnonetary Property. If money is donated to a qualified charitable organization, the amount of the charitable contribution deduction equals the amount of money donated. If property is donated, the amount of the charitable contribution deduction generally equals the property's fair market value (FMV). However, special rules apply to donations of appreciated nonmonetary property known as ordinary income property and capital gain property.

Ordinary income property is defined as property whose sale would have resulted in a gain other than a long-term capital gain (i.e., ordinary income or short-term capital gain).[27] Examples of ordinary income property include investment property held for one year or less, inventory property, and property subject to recapture under Secs. 1245 and 1250. The deduction allowed for a donation of such property is limited to the property's FMV minus the amount of ordinary income or short-term capital gain that would have been recognized if the property had instead been sold. For certain inventory

[25] Sec. 170(a)(1).
[26] Sec. 170(a)(2).
[27] Sec. 170(e)(1)(A).

properties, however, the corporate donor is allowed to deduct the property's adjusted basis plus one-half of the excess of the property's FMV over its adjusted basis if

1. The use of the property is related to the donee's exempt function and it is used solely for the care of the ill, the needy, or infants;
2. The property is not transferred to the donee in exchange for money, other property, or services; and
3. The donor receives a statement from the charitable organization stating that conditions (1) and (2) will be complied with.[28]

The amount of the deduction cannot exceed twice the property's adjusted basis.

A similar rule applies to contributions of scientific research property if

1. The contribution is to a college or university or tax-exempt scientific research organization;
2. The property was constructed by the taxpayer;
3. The contribution is made not later than two years after the property is substantially completed;
4. The donee is the original user of the property;
5. The property is scientific equipment or an apparatus substantially all of which is used by the donee for research or experimentation;
6. The property is not sold or exchanged by the donee for money, property, or services; and
7. The corporation receives from the donee a written statement that the property will be used in accordance with conditions 5 and 6.[29]

EXAMPLE C3-8 ▶ King Corporation donates inventory having a $26,000 adjusted basis and a $40,000 FMV to a qualified public charity. A $33,000 [$26,000 + (0.50 × $14,000)] deduction is allowed for the contribution of the inventory if the inventory is to be used by the charitable organization for the care of the ill, needy, or infants, or if the donee is an educational institution or research organization that will use the scientific research property for research or experimentation. Otherwise, the deduction is limited to the property's $26,000 adjusted basis. If the inventory's FMV is instead $100,000 and the donation meets either of the two sets of requirements outlined above, the charitable contribution deduction is limited to the lesser of the property's adjusted basis plus one-half of the appreciation [$63,000 = $26,000 + (0.50 × $74,000)] or twice the property's adjusted basis ($52,000 = $26,000 × 2), or $52,000. ◀

When a corporation donates appreciated property whose sale would result in long-term capital gain (also known as **capital gain property**) to a charitable organization, the amount of the contribution deduction generally equals the property's FMV. However, special restrictions apply if

▶ A corporation donates tangible personal property to a charitable organization and the organization's use of the property is unrelated to its tax-exempt purpose or

▶ A corporation donates appreciated property to certain private nonoperating foundations.[30]

In both cases, the amount of the corporation's contribution is limited to the property's FMV minus the long-term capital gain that would have resulted from the property's sale.[31]

[28] Sec. 170(e)(3).
[29] Sec. 170(e)(4).
[30] Sec. 170(e)(5). The restriction on contributions of appreciated property to private nonoperating foundations does not include contributions of stock for which market quotations are readily available.
[31] Sec. 170(e)(1)(B).

EXAMPLE C3-9 ▶ Fox Corporation donates an artwork to the MacNay Museum. The artwork, purchased two years earlier for $15,000, is worth $38,000 on the date of the gift. At the time of the donation, it is known that the MacNay Museum intends to sell the work to raise funds to conduct its activities. Fox's deduction for the gift is limited to $15,000. If the artwork is to be displayed by the MacNay Museum to be viewed by the public, the entire $38,000 deduction is permitted. Fox Corporation can avoid the loss of a portion of its charitable contribution deduction by placing restrictions on the sale or use of the property at the time it is donated. ◀

Maxium Deduction Permitted. There is a limit on the amount of charitable contributions a corporation can deduct in a given year. The limit is calculated differently for corporations than for individuals. Contribution deductions by corporations are limited to 10% of adjusted taxable income. Adjusted taxable income is the corporation's taxable income computed without regard to any of the following:

- The charitable contribution deduction
- An NOL carryback
- A capital loss carryback
- Any dividends-received deduction[32]

Contributions that exceed the 10% limit are not deductible in the current year. Instead, they are carried forward to the next five tax years. Any excess contributions not deducted within those five years are lost. Excess contributions may be deducted in the carryover year only after any contributions that were made in that year have been deducted. The total charitable contribution deduction (including any deduction for contribution carryovers) is limited to 10% of the corporation's adjusted taxable income in the carryover year.[33]

SELF-STUDY QUESTION

What happens to excess charitable contributions?

ANSWER

Corporations may not deduct charitable contributions in excess of 10% of adjusted taxable income. Excess charitable contributions cannot be carried back, but are eligible for a five-year carryforward. Excess charitable contributions are subject to the same 10% limitation in future years.

EXAMPLE C3-10 ▶ Golf Corporation reports the following results in 1997 and 1998:

	1997	*1998*
Adjusted taxable income	$200,000	$300,000
Charitable contributions	35,000	25,000

Golf's 1997 contribution deduction is limited to $20,000 (0.10 × $200,000). Golf has a $15,000 ($35,000 − $20,000) contribution carryover to 1998. The 1998 contribution deduction is limited to $30,000 (0.10 × $300,000). Golf's deduction for 1998 is composed of the $25,000 that is donated in 1998 and $5,000 of the 1997 carryover. A $10,000 carryover from 1997 may be carried over to 1999, 2000, 2001, and 2002. ◀

Topic Review C3-2 summarizes the basic corporate charitable contribution deduction rules.

SPECIAL DEDUCTIONS

C corporations commonly encounter two types of special deductions: dividends-received deductions and NOL deductions.

DIVIDENDS-RECEIVED DEDUCTION. Any dividend that a corporation receives because of owning stock in another corporation is included in its gross income. As was described in Chapter C2, the taxation of dividend payments to a shareholder generally

[32] Sec. 170(b)(2).

[33] Sec. 170(d)(2).

Topic Review C3-2

Corporate Charitable Contribution Rules

1. Timing of the contribution deduction
   a. General rule: A deduction is allowed for contributions paid during the year.
   b. Accrual method of accounting corporations can accrue contributions approved by their board of directors prior to the end of the accrual year and paid within 2½ months of the end of the accrual year.
2. Amount of the contribution deduction
   a. General rule: A deduction is allowed for the amount of money and the FMV of other property donated.
   b. Exceptions for ordinary income property:
      1. If property is donated that would result in ordinary income or short-term capital gain being recognized when sold, the deduction is limited to the property's FMV minus the ordinary income or short-term capital gain that would be recognized if the property were sold. This often means that the deduction equals the property's cost or adjusted basis.
      2. Special rule: For donations of inventory used for the care of the ill, needy, or infants, or scientific research property, a corporate donor is allowed to deduct the property's basis plus one-half of the excess of the property's FMV over its adjusted basis. The deduction may not exceed twice the property's adjusted basis.
   c. Exceptions for capital gain property: If tangible personal property is donated to a charitable organization for a use unrelated to its tax-exempt purpose, or appreciated property is donated to a private nonoperating foundation, the corporation's contribution is limited to the property's FMV minus the long-term capital gain that would result if the property were instead sold.
3. Limitation on contribution deduction
   a. The amount of the contribution deduction is limited to 10% of the corporation's taxable income computed without regard to the charitable contribution deduction, any NOL or capital loss carryback, and any dividends-received deduction.
   b. Excess contributions can be carried forward for a five-year period.

results in double taxation. When the dividend payment is made to a corporate shareholder and the distributee corporation subsequently pays these earnings out to its shareholders, triple taxation of the earnings can result.

EXAMPLE C3-11 ▶

Adobe Corporation owns stock in Bell Corporation. Bell Corporation reports taxable income of $100,000 and pays federal income taxes on its income. Bell distributes its after-tax income to its shareholders. The dividend Adobe Corporation receives from Bell must be included in its gross income and, to the extent that it reports a profit for the year, Adobe will pay taxes on the dividend. Adobe Corporation distributes its remaining after-tax income to its shareholders. The shareholders must include Adobe's dividends in their gross income and generally end up paying federal income taxes on the distribution. Thus, Bell's income in this example is eventually taxed three times. ◀

KEY POINT

To avoid the possibility of triple taxation, corporate shareholders are entitled to a dividends-received deduction (DRD). The amount of this deduction differs depending on the amount of stock ownership:

Stock Ownership—DRD %

Less than 20%—70% DRD

At least 20% but less than 80%—80% DRD

80% or more—100% DRD

To partially mitigate the effects of the multiple taxation, corporations are allowed a **dividends-received deduction** for dividends received from other domestic corporations and from certain foreign corporations.

General Rule for Dividends-Received Deduction. Corporations that own less than 20% of the distributing corporation's stock may deduct 70% of the dividends received. If the shareholder corporation owns 20% or more of the distributing corporation's stock (both voting power and value) but less than 80% of such stock, it may deduct 80% of the dividends received.[34]

EXAMPLE C3-12 ▶ Hale Corporation reports the following results in the current year:

Gross income from operations	$300,000
Dividends from 15%-owned domestic corporation	100,000
Expenses	280,000

Hale's dividends-received deduction is $70,000 (0.70 × $100,000). Thus, Hale's taxable income is computed as follows:

Gross income	$400,000
Minus: Expenses	(280,000)
Taxable income before special deductions	$120,000
Minus: Dividends-received deduction	(70,000)
Taxable income	$ 50,000 ◀

Limitation on Dividends-Received Deduction. In the case of dividends from corporations that are less than 20% owned, the deduction is limited to the lesser of 70% of dividends received or 70% of taxable income computed without regard to any NOL deduction, any capital loss carryback, or the dividends-received deduction itself.[35] In the case of dividends received from a 20% or more owned corporation, the dividends-received deduction is limited to the lesser of 80% of dividends received or 80% of taxable income computed without regard to any NOL deduction, any capital loss carryback, or the dividends-received deduction itself.

EXAMPLE C3-13 ▶ Assume the same facts as in Example C3-12 except that Hale Corporation's expenses for the year are $310,000. Hale's taxable income before the dividends-received deduction is $90,000 ($300,000 + $100,000 − $310,000). The dividends-received deduction is limited to the lesser of 70% of dividends received ($70,000) or 70% of taxable income before the dividends-received deduction ($63,000 = $90,000 × 0.70). Thus, the dividends-received deduction is $63,000. Hale's taxable income is $27,000 ($90,000 − $63,000). ◀

A corporation that receives dividends eligible for both the 80% dividends-received deduction and the 70% dividends-received deduction must reduce taxable income by the aggregate amount of dividends eligible for the 80% deduction before computing the 70% deduction.[36]

Exception to the Limitation. The limitation noted above does not apply if, after taking into account the full dividends-received deduction, the corporation has an NOL for the year.[37]

EXAMPLE C3-14 ▶ Assume the same facts as in Example C3-12, except that Hale Corporation's expenses for the year are $331,000. Hale's taxable income before the dividends-received deduction is $69,000 ($300,000 + $100,000 − $331,000). The tentative dividends-received deduction is $70,000 (0.70 × $100,000). Hale's dividends-received deduction is not restricted by the limitation of

[34] Secs. 243(a) and (c).
[35] Sec. 246(b)(1).
[36] Sec. 246(b)(3)(B).
[37] Sec. 246(b)(2).

70% of taxable income before the dividends-received deduction because, after taking into account the tentative $70,000 dividends-received deduction, the corporation has a $1,000 ($69,000 − $70,000) NOL for the year. ◀

The results of Examples C3-12, C3-13, and C3-14 are compared in the following table:

	Example C3-12	*Example C3-13*	*Example C3-14*
Gross income	$400,000	$400,000	$400,000
Minus: Expenses	(280,000)	(310,000)	(331,000)
Taxable income before special deductions	$120,000	$ 90,000	$ 69,000
Minus: Dividends-received deduction	(70,000)	(63,000)	(70,000)
Taxable income	$ 50,000	$ 27,000	$ (1,000)

TYPICAL MISCONCEPTION

The 70% dividends-received deduction is limited to 70% of a corporation's taxable income unless, by taking the entire dividends-received deduction, the deduction creates or adds to an NOL (a similar rule also exists for the 80% dividends-received deduction). This limitation can produce unusual results, as illustrated in Example C3-14, where $21,000 of additional deductions provides a $28,000 reduction in taxable income.

The only case where the dividends-received deduction is not equal to the full 70% of the $100,000 dividend is Example C3-13. In that case, the deduction is limited to $63,000 because taxable income before special deductions is less than the $100,000 dividend *and* the full $70,000 deduction would not create an NOL. The special exception to the dividends-received deduction can create interesting situations. For example, the additional $21,000 of deductions incurred in Example C3-14 resulted in a $28,000 reduction in taxable income. Corporate taxpayers should be cognizant of these rules and consider deferring income or recognizing expenses to ensure being able to deduct the full 70% or 80% dividends-received deduction. If the taxable income limitation applies, there is no carryover of unused dividends-received deductions.

Members of an Affilliated Group. Members of an affiliated group of corporations can claim a 100% dividends-received deduction with respect to dividends received from other group members.[38] A group of corporations is affiliated if a parent corporation owns at least 80% of the stock (both voting power and value) of at least one subsidiary corporation and at least 80% of the stock (both voting power and value) of each other corporation is owned by other group members. There is no taxable income limitation on the 100% dividends-received deduction.[39]

KEY POINT

Stock purchased on which a dividend has been declared has an increased value. This value will drop when the dividend is paid. If the dividend is eligible for a dividends-received deduction and the drop in value also creates a capital loss, corporate shareholders could use this as a tax-planning device. To avoid this result, no dividends-received deduction is available for stock held forty-five days or less.

Dividends Received from Foreign Corporations. The dividends-received deduction applies primarily to dividends received from domestic corporations. A dividends-received deduction is not allowed on dividends received from a foreign corporation because its income is not taxed by the U.S. government and, therefore, is not subject to the multiple taxation illustrated above.[40]

Stock Held Forty-Five Days or Less. A dividends-received deduction is not allowed for dividends received on any share of stock that the corporate shareholder has held for forty-five days or less.[41] This rule prevents a corporation from claiming a dividends-received deduction if it purchases stock immediately before an ex-dividend date and sells the stock immediately thereafter. (The ex-dividend date is the first day on which a

[38] Sec. 243(a)(3).
[39] Secs. 243(b)(5) and 1504.
[40] Sec. 245. A limited dividends-received deduction is allowed on dividends received from a foreign corporationthat earns income by conducting a trade or business in the United States and, therefore, is subject to U.S. taxes.
[41] Sec. 246(c)(1).

purchaser of stock is not entitled to a previously declared dividend.) Absent this rule, such a purchase and sale would allow the corporation to receive dividends at a low tax rate—a maximum of a 10.5% [(100% − 70%) × 0.35] effective tax rate—and to obtain a capital loss on the sale of stock that could offset capital gains taxed at a 35% tax rate.

EXAMPLE C3-15 ▶

Rose Corporation purchases 100 shares of Maine Corporation's stock (less than 1% of the outstanding stock) for $100,000 one day before Maine's ex-dividend date. Rose receives a $5,000 dividend on the stock. Rose sells the stock for $95,000 on the forty-fifth day *after* the dividend payment date. (Because the stock is worth $100,000 immediately before the $5,000 dividend is paid, the stock is worth $95,000 ($100,000 − $5,000) immediately after the dividend is paid.) The sale results in a $5,000 ($100,000 − $95,000) capital loss that may offset a $5,000 capital gain. The profit (loss) to Rose Corporation with and without the rule disallowing the dividends-received deduction on stock held less than forty-five days is summarized below:

	If Deduction Is Allowed	*If Deduction Is Not Allowed*
Dividends	$5,000	$ 5,000
Minus: 35% tax on dividend	(525)[a]	(1,750)
Dividend (after taxes)	$4,475	$ 3,250
Capital loss	$5,000	$ 5,000
Minus: 35% tax savings	(1,750)	(1,750)
Net loss on stock	$3,250	$ 3,250
Dividend (after taxes)	$4,475	$ 3,250
Minus: Net loss on stock	(3,250)	(3,250)
Net profit (loss)	$1,225	$—0—

[a] [$5,000 − (0.70 × $5,000)] × 0.35 = $525

KEY POINT

If money is borrowed by a corporation to acquire stock, a significant tax advantage could result. The interest on the debt would be deductible and the dividend income from the stock investment would be eligible for a dividends-received deduction. Thus, the statute does not allow a full dividends-received deduction on debt-financed stock.

The profit is not available if Rose sells the stock shortly after receiving the dividend because Rose must hold the Maine stock for at least forty-six days to obtain the dividends-received deduction. ◀

Debt-Financed Stock. The dividends-received deduction is not allowed to the extent that the stock on which a dividend is paid is debt-financed (i.e., purchased with borrowed money).[42] This rule prevents a corporation from deducting interest paid on money borrowed to purchase the stock, while paying little or no tax on the dividends received on the stock.

EXAMPLE C3-16 ▶

Peach Corporation borrows $100,000 at a 10% interest rate to purchase 30% of Sun Corporation's stock. The Sun stock pays an $8,000 annual dividend. If a dividends-received deduction were allowed for this investment, Peach would have a net profit of $940 annually on owning the Sun stock even though the dividend received is less than the interest paid. The profit (loss) to Peach Corporation with and without the rule disallowing the dividends-received deduction on debt-financed stock is summarized below:

[42] Sec. 246A.

	If Deduction Is Allowed	*If Deduction Is Not Allowed*
Dividends	$ 8,000	$ 8,000
Minus: 35% tax on dividend	(560)	(2,800)
Dividend (after taxes)	$ 7,440	$ 5,200
Interest paid	$10,000	$10,000
Minus: 35% tax savings	(3,500)	(3,500)
Net cost of borrowing	$ 6,500	$ 6,500
Dividend (after taxes)	$ 7,440	$ 5,200
Minus: net cost of borrowing	(6,500)	(6,500)
Net profit (loss)	$ 940	$ (1,300)

[a] [$8,000 − (0.80 × $8,000)] × 0.35 = $560

This example illustrates how the rule disallowing the dividends-received deduction on debt-financed stock prevents corporations from making an after-tax profit by borrowing funds to purchase stocks paying dividends that are less than the cost of the borrowing. ◀

SELF-STUDY QUESTION

How does the use of an NOL differ for individual and corporate taxpayers?

ANSWER

An individual must make many adjustments to his taxable income to calculate his NOL. A corporation's NOL is simply the excess of its deductions over its income.

NET OPERATING LOSSES (NOLs). If a corporation's deductions exceed its gross income for the year, the corporation has a **net operating loss (NOL)**. The NOL is the amount by which the corporation's deductions (including any dividends-received deduction) exceed its gross income.[43] In computing an NOL for a given year, no deduction is permitted for a carryover or carryback of an NOL from a preceding or succeeding year. However, unlike an individual's NOL, no other adjustments are required to compute a corporation's NOL.

A corporation's NOL may be carried back three years and carried forward fifteen years. It is carried to the earliest of the three preceding years first and used to offset taxable income reported in that year. If the loss cannot be used in that year it is carried to the second preceding year, then to the immediately preceding year, and then to the next fifteen years in order. The corporation may elect to forgo the carryback period entirely and instead carry the entire loss forward to the next fifteen years.

EXAMPLE C3-17 ▶

In 1997, Gray Corporation has gross income of $150,000 (including $100,000 from operations and $50,000 in dividends from a 30%-owned domestic corporation) and $180,000 of expenses. Gray has a $70,000 [$150,000 − $180,000 − (0.80 × $50,000)] NOL. The loss is carried back to 1994 unless Gray elects to relinquish the carryback period. If Gray had $20,000 of taxable income in 1994, $20,000 of Gray's 1997 NOL is used to offset that income. Gray receives a refund of all taxes paid in 1994. Gray carries the remaining $50,000 of NOL from 1994 to 1995. ◀

A corporation might elect not to carry an NOL back because its income was taxed at a low marginal tax rate in the carryback period and the corporation anticipates income being taxed at a higher marginal tax rate in later years or it used tax credit carryovers in the earlier year that were about to expire. This election must be made for the entire carryback by the due date (including any permitted extensions) for filing the return for the year in which the NOL was incurred. It is made by checking a box on the Form 1120 when it is filed. Once made for a tax year, the election is irrevocable.[44] However, if the corporation has an NOL in another year, the decision as to whether that NOL should be carried back is a separate decision. In other words, each year's NOL is treated separately and is subject to a separate election.

[43] Sec. 172(c).

[44] Sec. 172(b)(3)(C).

To obtain a refund due to carrying an NOL back to a preceding year, a corporation must file either Form 1120X (Amended U.S. Corporation Income Tax Return) or Form 1139 (Corporation Application for a Tentative Refund).

TYPICAL MISCONCEPTION

The sequencing of deductions is normally straightforward. However, if an NOL carryforward exists, the NOL deduction must be computed twice. The NOL must first be calculated in determining taxable income for the charitable contribution limitation. The NOL deduction is then added back to taxable income and recomputed after both the charitable contribution and dividends-received deductions have been computed.

THE SEQUENCING OF THE DEDUCTION CALCULATIONS. The rules for charitable contributions deductions, dividends-received deductions, and NOL deductions require that these deductions be taken in the correct sequence. Otherwise, the computation of the amount of these deductions allowed for the year may be incorrect. The correct order for taking deductions is

1. All deductions other than the charitable contributions deduction, the dividends-received deduction, and the NOL deduction
2. The charitable contributions deduction
3. The dividends-received deduction
4. The NOL deduction

As stated previously, the charitable contributions deduction is limited to 10% of taxable income before the charitable contributions deduction, any NOL or capital loss carryback, or any dividends-received deduction, but *after* any NOL carryover deduction. Once the charitable contributions deduction has been computed, any NOL carryover deduction must be added back and the charitable contributions deduction subtracted before the dividends-received deduction is computed and subtracted. Then the NOL deduction is subtracted.

EXAMPLE C3-18 ▶ East Corporation reports the following results:

Gross income from operations	$150,000
Dividends from 30%-owned domestic corporation	100,000
Operating expenses	100,000
Charitable contributions	30,000

In addition, East has a $40,000 NOL carryforward available. East's charitable contributions deduction is computed as follows:

Gross income from operations		$150,000
Plus:	Dividends	100,000
Gross income		$250,000
Minus:	Operating expenses	(100,000)
	NOL carryforward	(40,000)
Base for calculation of the charitable contributions limitation		$110,000

East's charitable contributions deduction is limited to $11,000 (0.10 × $110,000). The $11,000 limitation means that East has a $19,000 ($30,000 − $11,000) contribution carryforward that may be carried forward for five years. East Corporation computes its taxable income as follows:

Gross income		$250,000
Minus:	Operating expenses	(100,000)
	Charitable contributions deduction	(11,000)
Taxable income before special deductions		$139,000
Minus:	Dividends-received deduction	(80,000)
	NOL carryover deduction	(40,000)
Taxable income		$ 19,000

East's dividends-received deduction is $80,000 (0.80 × $100,000). The entire NOL carryforward is deductible because taxable income before the NOL deduction is $59,000 ($139,000 − $80,000). ◀

Note that if an NOL is carried *back* from a later year, it is *not* taken into account in computing a corporation's charitable contributions limitation. In other words, the contribution deduction remains the same as it was in the year the return was filed.

EXAMPLE C3-19 ▶ Assume the same facts as in Example C3-18 except that East instead has a $40,000 NOL carryback from a later year. East's base for calculation of the charitable contributions limitation was computed as follows when the return was originally filed:

Gross income from operations	$150,000
Plus: Dividends	100,000
Gross income	$250,000
Minus: Operating expenses	(100,000)
Base for calculation of the charitable contributions limitation	$150,000

East's charitable contributions deduction was limited to $15,000 (0.10 × $150,000). The $15,000 limitation means that East has a $15,000 ($30,000 − $15,000) contribution carryforward. East Corporation computes its taxable income after the NOL carryback as follows:

Gross income		$250,000
Minus:	Operating expenses	(100,000)
	Charitable contributions deduction	(15,000)
Taxable income before special deductions		$135,000
Minus:	Dividends-received deduction	(80,000)
	NOL carryback deduction	(40,000)
Taxable income as recomputed		$ 15,000

KEY POINT

NOL carrybacks do not affect either the charitable contribution or dividends-received deductions. This rule certainly simplifies the calculation of the NOL deduction created by an NOL carryback.

East's dividends-received deduction remains $80,000 as in the preceding example. The entire NOL carryback is deductible because taxable income before the NOL deduction was $55,000 ($135,000 − $80,000). ◀

STOP & THINK

Question: Why does a corporation's NOL or capital loss carryback not affect its charitable contribution deduction, but yet an NOL or capital loss carryforward must be taken into account when calculating its charitable contribution limition?

Solution: Remember that a carryback will affect a tax return for a prior year already filed. If a carryback had to be taken into account when calculating the charitable contribution deduction limitation in the prior year, it might change the amount of the allowable charitable contribution. This change in turn might affect other items such as the carryback year's dividends-received deduction and some later years' deductions as well. For example, assume Alpha Corporation has a $10,000 NOL in 1997 that it carries back to 1994. If the NOL were permitted to reduce Alpha's allowable charitable contribution for 1994 by $1,000, then Alpha's dividends-received deduction for 1994 and its charitable contribution deductions for 1995 and 1996 as well might change.

To avoid these complications, which might force Alpha to amend its tax returns from the carryback year (1994) to the current year (1997), the law states that carrybacks are not taken into account in calculating the charitable contribution deduction limitation.

EXCEPTIONS FOR CLOSELY-HELD CORPORATIONS

Congress has placed certain limits on the rules explained above to prevent abuse in situations where a corporation is closely held. Some of these rules are explained below.

TRANSACTIONS BETWEEN A CORPORATION AND ITS SHAREHOLDERS.

Special rules apply to transactions between a corporation and a controlling shareholder. Section 1239 may convert a capital gain realized on the sale of depreciable property between a corporation and a controlling shareholder into ordinary income. Section 267(a)(1) denies a deduction for losses realized on property sales between a corporation and a controlling shareholder. Section 267(a)(2) defers a deduction for accrued expenses and interest on certain transactions involving a corporation and a controlling shareholder.

In all three of the preceding situations, a controlling shareholder is defined as one who owns more than 50% (in value) of the corporation's stock.[45] In determining whether a shareholder owns more than 50% of a corporation's stock, certain constructive stock ownership rules apply.[46] Under these rules, a shareholder is considered to own not only his or her own stock, but stock owned by family members (e.g., brothers, sisters, spouse, ancestors, and lineal descendants) and entities in which the shareholder has an ownership or beneficial interest (e.g., corporations, partnerships, trusts, and estates).

Gains on Sale or Exchange Transactions. If a controlling shareholder sells depreciable property to a controlled corporation (or vice versa) and the property is depreciable in the purchaser's hands, any gain on the sale is treated as ordinary income under Sec. 1239(a).

EXAMPLE C3-20 ▶ Ann owns all of the stock of Cape Corporation. Ann sells a building to Cape Corporation and recognizes a $25,000 gain, which would ordinarily be Sec. 1231 gain. However, because Ann owns more than 50% of the Cape stock and the building is a depreciable property in Cape Corporation's hands, Sec. 1239 causes the entire $25,000 gain to be ordinary income to Ann. ◀

KEY POINT

Section 1239 states that if a sale or exchange of property is between a corporation and a more than 50% shareholder and the property is depreciable by the transferee, then the character of any gain recognized on the sale must be ordinary income.

Losses on Sale or Exchange Transactions. Section 267(a)(1) denies a deduction for losses realized on a sale of property by a corporation to a controlling shareholder or on a sale of property by the controlling shareholder to the corporation. If the purchaser later sells the property to another party at a gain, gain is recognized only to the extent that it exceeds the disallowed loss.[47] Should the purchaser instead sell the property at a loss, the disallowed loss is never recognized.

EXAMPLE C3-21 ▶ Hope Corporation sells an automobile to Juan, its sole shareholder, for $6,500. The corporation's adjusted basis for the automobile is $8,000. Hope realizes a $1,500 ($6,500 − $8,000) loss on the sale. Section 267(a)(1) disallows the loss to the corporation. If Juan later sells the auto for $8,500, he realizes a $2,000 ($8,500 − $6,500) gain. He recognizes only $500 of that gain, the amount by which his $2,000 gain exceeds the $1,500 loss that was disallowed to Hope Corporation. If Juan instead sells the auto for $4,000, he realizes and may be able to recognize a $2,500 ($4,000 − $6,500) loss. However, the $1,500 loss disallowed to Hope Corporation is permanently lost. ◀

KEY POINT

Section 267(a)(2) is primarily aimed at the situation involving an accrual method corporation that accrues compensation to a cash method shareholder-employee. This provision forces a matching of the income and expense recognition by deferring the deduction to the day the shareholder recognizes the income.

Corporation and Controlling Shareholder Using Different Accounting Methods. Section 267(a)(2) defers a deduction for accrued expenses or interest owed by a corporation to a controlling shareholder or by a controlling shareholder to a corporation when the

[45] Sec. 267(b)(2).
[46] Sec. 267(e)(3).
[47] Sec. 267(d).

two parties use different accounting methods and the payee will include the accrued expense as part of gross income at a date that is later than when it is accrued by the payer. Under this rule, accrued expenses or interest owed by a corporation to a controlling shareholder may not be deducted until the day the shareholder includes the payment in gross income.

EXAMPLE C3-22 ▶ Hill Corporation uses the accrual method of accounting. Hill's sole shareholder, Ruth, uses the cash method of accounting. Both taxpayers use the calendar year as their tax year. The corporation accrues a $25,000 interest payment to Ruth on December 20, 1997. The payment is made on March 20, 1998. Hill Corporation cannot deduct the interest in 1997 but must wait until Ruth reports the income in 1998. Thus the expense and income are matched. ◀

LOSS LIMITATION RULES

AT-RISK RULES If five or fewer shareholders own more than 50% of the value of the outstanding stock of a C corporation at any time during the last half of the corporation's tax year, it is subject to the at-risk rules.[48] In such case, the corporation's losses for any activity are deductible only to the extent that the corporation is at risk for that activity at the close of its tax year. Any losses not deductible because of the at-risk rules must be carried over and deducted in a succeeding year when the corporation's risk with respect to the activity has increased. (See Chapter C9 for additional discussion of the at-risk rules and the at-risk amount.)

TYPICAL MISCONCEPTION

Closely held corporations and PSCs are subject to the passive activity limitation rules. Certain closely held corporations (other than PSCs) can offset their net active income (but not portfolio income) for the tax year with passive losses. This offset of passive losses against net active income is unique to closely held C corporations.

Passive Activity Limitation Rules. Personal service corporations (PSCs) and **closely held C corporations** (those subject to the at-risk rules described above) may be subject to the **passive activity limitations.**[49] If a PSC does not meet the material participation requirements, its net **passive losses** and credits must be carried over to a year when it has **passive income.** In the case of closely held C corporations that do not meet material participation requirements, passive losses and credits are allowed to offset the corporation's net active income but not its portfolio income (i.e., interest, dividends, annuities, royalties, and capital gains on the sale of investment property).[50]

COMPUTING A CORPORATION'S INCOME TAX LIABILITY

OBJECTIVE 3

Compute a corporation's income tax liability

Once a corporation's taxable income has been computed, the next step is to compute the corporation's tax liability for the year. Table C3-2 outlines the steps in the computation of a corporation's regular (income) tax liability. This section explains the steps involved in arriving at a corporation's income tax liability in detail.

GENERAL RULES

All C corporations (other than members of controlled groups of corporations and personal service corporations) use the same tax rate schedule to compute their income or regular tax liability. These rates are shown below and are reproduced on the inside back cover.

[48] Sec. 465(a).

[49] Secs. 469(a)(2)(B) and (C).

[50] Sec. 469(e)(2).

▼ TABLE C3-1
Computation of the Corporate Regular (Income) Tax Liability

Taxable income	
Times:	Income tax rates
Regular tax liability	
Minus:	Foreign tax credit (Sec. 27)
	Puerto Rico and U.S. Possessions credit (Sec. 936)
Regular tax	
Minus:	General business credit (Sec. 38)
	Minimum tax credit (Sec. 53)
	Drug testing credit (Sec. 28)
	Nonconventional fuels production credit (Sec. 29)
	Credit for qualified electric vehicles (Sec. 30)
	Puerto Rican economic activity credit (Sec. 30A)
	Nonhighway use of gasoline and special fuels credit (Sec. 34)
Plus:	Recapture of previously claimed tax credits
Income tax liability	

Taxable Income Over	*But Not Over*	*The Tax Is*	*Of the Amount Over*
—0—	$50,000	15%	—0—
$50,000	75,000	$7,500 + 25%	$50,000
75,000	100,000	13,750 + 34%	75,000
100,000	335,000	22,250 + 39%	100,000
335,000	10,000,000	113,900 + 34%	335,000
10,000,000	15,000,000	3,400,000 + 35%	10,000,000
15,000,000	18,333,333	5,150,000 + 38%	15,000,000
18,333,333	—	6,416,667 + 35%	18,333,333

EXAMPLE C3-23 ▶ Copper Corporation reports taxable income of $100,000. Copper's regular tax liability is computed as follows:

Tax on first $50,000:	0.15 × $50,000 =	$7,500
Tax on second $25,000:	0.25 × 25,000 =	6,250
Tax on remaining $25,000:	0.34 × 25,000 =	8,500
Regular tax liability		$22,250

◀

If taxable income exceeds $100,000, a 5 percentage point surcharge on the corporation's taxable income in excess of $100,000 is imposed. The maximum surcharge is $11,750 (in 1997). The surcharge phases out the lower graduated tax rates that apply to the first $75,000 of taxable income for corporations earning between $100,000 and $335,000 [$11,750 = ($335,000 − $100,000) × 0.05] of taxable income. The tax rates listed above incorporate the 5 percentage point surcharge by imposing a 39% rate on taxable income from $100,000 to $335,000.

EXAMPLE C3-24 ▶ Delta Corporation has taxable income of $200,000. Delta's regular tax liability is computed as follows:

Tax on first $50,000:	0.15 × $ 50,000 =	$ 7,500
Tax on next $25,000:	0.25 × 25,000 =	6,250
Tax on remaining $125,000:	0.34 × 125,000 =	42,500
Surcharge (income over $100,000):	0.05 × 100,000 =	5,000
Regular tax liability		$61,250

◀

If taxable income is at least $335,000 but less than $10 million, the corporation pays a 34% tax rate on all of its taxable income. A corporation whose income is at least $10 million but less than $15 million pays $3,400,000 plus 35% of the income above $10 million.

EXAMPLE C3-25 ▶ Elgin Corporation has taxable income of $350,000. Elgin's regular tax liability is $119,000 (0.34 × $350,000). If Elgin's taxable income is instead $12,000,000, its tax liability is $4,100,000 [$3,400,000 + (0.35 × $2,000,000)]. ◀

If a corporation's taxable income exceeds $15 million, a 3 percentage point surcharge is imposed on the corporation's taxable income in excess of $15 million (but not in excess of $18,333,333). The maximum surcharge is $100,000. The surcharge phases out the one percentage point lower rate (34% vs. 35%) that applies to the first $10 million of taxable income. A corporation whose taxable income exceeds $18,333,333 pays a 35% tax rate on all of its taxable income.

STOP & THINK

Question: Why does the corporate tax rate increase to 39%, drop back to 34%, increase to 38%, and drop back to 35% as taxable income increases?

Solution: Actually, corporate tax rates increase progressively from 15% on the first $50,000 of taxable income to 35% on taxable income in excess of $10 million. However, there is a 5 percentage point surcharge when taxable income is between $100,000 and $335,000. This surcharge gradually eliminates the benefits of the 15% and 25% rate brackets on the first $75,000 of taxable income. Once taxable income reaches $335,000, the benefit of the lower rate brackets are completely eliminated and all taxable income is taxed at a flat 34% rate until it reaches $10 million. At this point the tax rate increases to 35% and stays there until taxable income is $15 million. A 3 percentage point surcharge applies to taxable income from $15 million to $18,333,333. This surcharge eliminates the benefit of the 34% tax rate that applies to the first $10 million of taxable income. Thus the 39% and 38% marginal tax rates simply include a 5 percentage point and a 3 percentage point surcharge, respectively. Note that once taxable income reaches $18,333,333, a flat 35% marginal rate applies.

SELF-STUDY QUESTION

Does the selection of a corporate entity ever make sense based on a desire for lower marginal tax rates?

ANSWER

Entities with projected income of $50,000 or less may be better off with the selection of the C corporation entity because the first $50,000 of corporate taxable income is taxed at a 15% rate. Once the income level increases above $75,000, the C corporation marginal rate jumps to 34% or 35%. In contrast, if the corporation made an S election, income above $75,000 would be taxed at a marginal rate of 31% to 39.6%. A 4.6 percentage point differential exists between the two top rates.

PERSONAL SERVICE CORPORATIONS

Personal service corporations are denied the benefit of the graduated corporate tax rates. All of the income of personal service corporations is taxed at a flat 35% rate.

A personal service corporation is defined in Sec. 448(d) as a corporation that meets the following two tests:

- Substantially all of its activities involve the performance of services in the fields of health, law, engineering, architecture, accounting, actuarial science, performing arts, and consulting.
- Substantially all of its stock (by value) is held directly or indirectly by employees performing the services or retired employees who performed the services in the past, their estates, or persons who hold stock in the corporation by reason of the death of an employee or retired employee within the past two years.

This rule encourages employee-owners of personal service corporations to withdraw earnings from the corporation as salary (rather than have the corporation retain them) or make an S election.

CONTROLLED GROUPS OF CORPORATIONS

OBJECTIVE 4

Explain what a controlled group is and the tax consequences of being a controlled group

Special tax rules apply to corporations that are under common control to prevent them from being used to avoid taxes that would otherwise be due. The rules apply to corporations that meet the definition of a controlled group of corporations. This section explains why special rules apply to controlled groups, how controlled groups are defined, and what special rules apply to controlled groups.

WHY SPECIAL RULES ARE NEEDED

Special controlled group rules are needed to prevent shareholders from using multiple corporations to avoid having corporate income taxed at a 35% rate. If these rules were not in effect, the owners of a corporation could allocate the corporation's income among two or more corporations and take advantage of the lower 15%, 25%, and 34% rates on the first $10,000,000 of corporate income for each corporation.

The following example demonstrates how a group of shareholders could obtain a significant tax advantage by dividing a business enterprise among several corporate entities. Each corporation then would be able to take advantage of the graduated corporate tax rates. To prevent a group of shareholders from using multiple corporations to gain such tax advantages, Congress enacted laws that limit the tax benefits of multiple corporations.[51]

EXAMPLE C3-26 ▶

Axle Corporation has taxable income of $450,000. Axle's regular tax liability on that income is $153,000 (0.34 × $450,000). If Axle's taxable income could be divided equally among six corporations ($75,000 apiece), each corporation's federal income tax liability would be $13,750 [(0.15 × $50,000) + (0.25 × $25,000)], or a total regular tax liability of $82,500 for all of the corporations. Thus, Axle could save $70,500 ($153,000 − $82,500) in federal income taxes if it could arrange to have its $450,000 of taxable income divided among itself and five other corporations. ◀

SELF-STUDY QUESTION

What are the tax consequences of being a member of a controlled group?

ANSWER

Several of the tax consequences that can result from being a member of a controlled group are mentioned in this chapter. The most important purpose of the controlled group rules is to prevent shareholders from using multiple corporations to gain the benefits of the 15% and 25% graduated rate structure for corporations. Example C3-26 illustrates what could be accomplished without the controlled group rules.

The law governing controlled corporations operates by requiring special treatment for two or more corporations controlled by the same shareholder or group of shareholders. The most important restrictions on a controlled group of corporations are that the entire group must share the tax benefits from the progressive corporate tax rate schedule and pay a 5 percentage point surcharge on the group's total taxable income that exceeds $100,000 (up to $335,000 for a maximum surcharge of $11,750). If the group's total taxable income is $335,000 or more (but not in excess of $10 million), each group member will have a regular income tax liability equal to 34% times its taxable income.

EXAMPLE C3-27 ▶

White, Blue, Yellow, and Green Corporations belong to a controlled group. Each corporation has $100,000 of taxable income (a total of $400,000). Only one $50,000 amount is taxed at 15% and only one $25,000 amount is taxed at 25%. Furthermore, the group is subject to the maximum $11,750 surcharge because its total taxable income exceeds $335,000. This surcharge is levied on the group member(s) that received the benefit of the 15 and 25% rates. Therefore, the group's total regular tax liability is $136,000 (0.34 × $400,000), the same as though the entire $400,000 were earned by one corporation. ◀

WHAT IS A CONTROLLED GROUP?

A **controlled group** is a group of two or more corporations that are owned directly or indirectly by the same shareholder or group of shareholders. There are three types of

[51] Secs. 1561 and 1563.

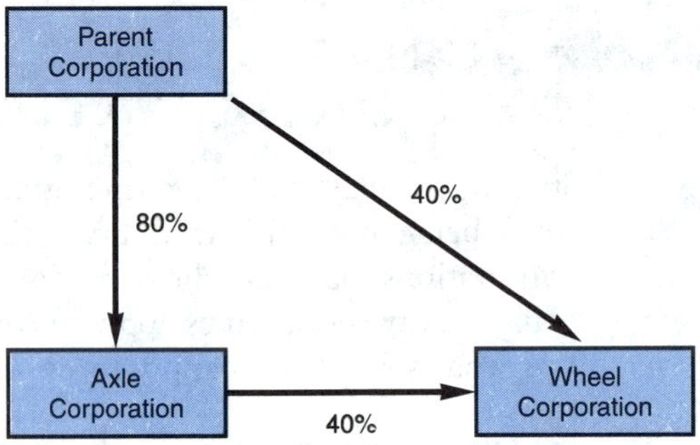

FIGURE C3-1 ▶ PARENT-SUBSIDIARY CONTROLLED GROUP (EXAMPLE C3-28)

controlled groups: a parent-subsidiary controlled group, a brother-sister controlled group, and a combined controlled group. Each of these groups is subject to the limitations described above. That is, if a group of corporations meets any of the following three definitions, the group must share the benefits of the progressive corporate tax rate schedule and pay a 5 percentage point surcharge on the group's taxable income exceeding $100,000, up to a maximum surcharge of $11,750, and also pay a 3 percentage point surcharge on the group's taxable income exceeding $15 million, up to a maximum surcharge of $100,000.

KEY POINT

The statute identifies three types of controlled groups: parent-subsidiary, brother-sister, and combined. A group of corporations that satisfy the definition of any of these three controlled groups must share one corporate graduated rate structure.

PARENT-SUBSIDIARY CONTROLLED GROUPS. A **parent-subsidiary controlled group** is a group of two or more corporations where one corporation (the parent corporation) owns directly at least 80% of the voting power of all classes of voting stock, or 80% of the total value of all classes of stock of a second corporation (the subsidiary corporation).[52] There can be more than one subsidiary corporation in the group. If the parent corporation, the subsidiary corporation, or any other members of the controlled group in total own at least 80% of the voting power of all classes of voting stock, or 80% of the total value of all classes of stock of another corporation, that other corporation is included in the parent-subsidiary controlled group.

EXAMPLE C3-28 ▶ Parent Corporation owns 80% of Axle Corporation's single class of stock and 40% of Wheel Corporation's single class of stock. Axle Corporation also owns 40% of Wheel's stock. Parent, Axle, and Wheel are members of the same parent-subsidiary controlled group because Parent directly owns 80% of Axle's stock and is therefore its parent corporation, and Wheel's stock is 80% owned by Parent (40%) and Axle (40%). (See Figure C3-1.)

If Parent and Axle together owned only 70% of Wheel's stock and the remaining 30% was owned by an unrelated shareholder, Wheel would not be included in the parent-subsidiary group. The controlled group then would consist only of Parent and Axle Corporations. ◀

To have a parent-subsidiary controlled group, there must be a direct ownership by one corporation of 80% or more of the voting power or value of a second corporation.

EXAMPLE C3-29 ▶ Beta Corporation owns 70% of Cove Corporation's single class of stock and 60% of Red Corporation's single class of stock. Blue Corporation owns the remaining stock of Cove Corporation (30%) and Red Corporation (40%). No combination of these corporations forms a parent-subsidiary group because there is no direct stock ownership by one corporation of at least 80% of any other corporation's stock. ◀

[52] Sec. 1563(a)(1). Section 1563(d)(1) requires that certain attribution rules apply to determine stock ownership for parent-subsidiary controlled groups. If any person has an option to acquire stock, such stock is considered to be owned by the person having the option. Certain types of stock are excluded by Sec. 1563(c) from the controlled group definition of stock.

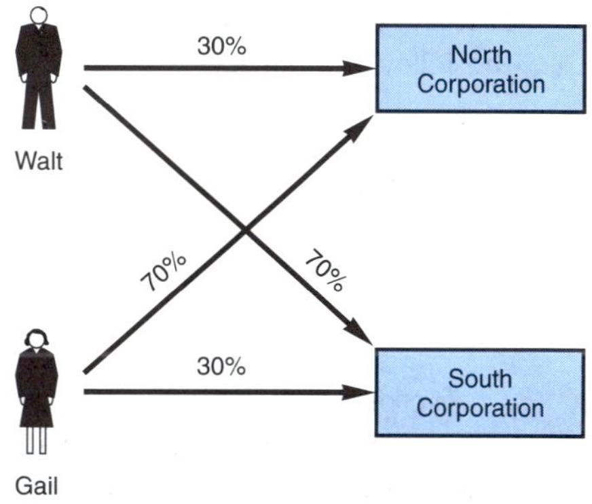

FIGURE C3-2 ▶ BROTHER-SISTER CONTROLLED GROUP (EXAMPLE C3-30)

BROTHER-SISTER CONTROLLED GROUPS. A group of two or more corporations is a **brother-sister controlled group** if five or fewer individuals, trusts, or estates own

- At least 80% of the voting power of all classes of voting stock (or at least 80% of the total value of the outstanding stock) of each corporation, and
- More than 50% of the voting power of all classes of stock (or more than 50% of the total value of the outstanding stock) of each corporation, taking into account only the stock ownership that each person has that is identical with respect to each corporation.[53] A shareholder's identical ownership is the percentage of stock the shareholder owns in common in each of the corporations. If, for example, a shareholder owns 30% of New Corporation and 70% of Old Corporation, his or her identical ownership is 30%.

EXAMPLE C3-30 ▶ North and South Corporations have only one class of stock outstanding. Their stock is owned by the following individuals:

	Stock Ownership Percentages		
Shareholder	*North Corp.*	*South Corp.*	*Identical Ownership*
Walt	30%	70%	30%
Gail	70%	30%	30%
Total	100%	100%	60%

Five or fewer individuals (Walt and Gail) own at least 80% (they own 100%) of each corporation's stock, and the same individuals own more than 50% (they own 60%) of each corporation's stock, taking into account only their identical ownership. Because both tests are satisfied, North and South Corporations are a brother-sister controlled group (see Figure C3-2). ◀

It is not sufficient for five or fewer shareholders to own 80% or more of the stock of two corporations. The shareholders also must have more than 50% identical ownership in the corporations for them to be brother-sister corporations.

[53] Sec. 1563(a)(2). Section 1563(d)(2) requires that certain attribution rules apply to determine stock ownership for brother-sister controlled groups. If any person has an option to acquire stock, such stock is considered to be owned by the person having the option. A proportionate amount of stock owned by a partnership, estate, or trust is attributed to partners having an interest of 5% or more in the capital or profits of the partnership or beneficiaries having a 5% or more actuarial interest in the estate or trust. A proportionate amount of stock owned by a corporation is attributed to shareholders owning 5% or more in value of the corporate stock. Family attribution rules can also cause an individual to be considered to own the stock of a spouse, child, grandchild, parent, or grandparent.

EXAMPLE C3-31 ▶ East and West Corporations have only one class of stock outstanding. Their stock is owned by the following individuals:

	Stock Ownership Percentages		
Shareholder	*East Corp.*	*West Corp.*	*Identical Ownership*
Javier	80%	25%	25%
Sara	20%	75%	20%
Total	100%	100%	45%

Five or fewer individuals (Javier and Sara) own at least 80% (they own 100%) of each corporation's stock. But those same individuals own only 45% of each corporation's stock, taking into account only their identical ownership. Because the more-than-50% test is not satisfied, East and West Corporations are not a controlled group. Because they are not members of a controlled group, each corporation is taxed on its own income without regard to the earnings of the other. ◀

TYPICAL MISCONCEPTION

The application of the 50% identical ownership test for purposes of the brother-sister controlled group definition is confusing. Examples C3-30 and C3-31 illustrate a case when the 50% test is satisfied and one when it is not satisfied. Also note that both the 80% *and* the 50% tests must be satisfied for a brother-sister controlled group to exist.

An individual's stock ownership can be counted for the 80% test only if that individual owns stock in each and every corporation in the controlled group.[54]

EXAMPLE C3-32 ▶ Toy and Robot Corporations each have only a single class of stock outstanding. Their stock is owned by the following individuals:

	Stock Ownership Percentages		
Shareholder	*Toy Corp.*	*Robot Corp.*	*Identical Ownership*
Ali	50%	40%	40%
Beth	20%	60%	20%
Carol	30%	—	—
Total	100%	100%	60%

Carol's stock is not counted for purposes of Toy's 80% stock ownership requirement because she does not own any stock in Robot Corporation. Only Ali and Beth's stock holdings are counted, and together they own only 70% of Toy Corporation's stock. Thus the 80% test is failed, and Toy and Robot Corporations are *not* a controlled group of corporations. ◀

COMBINED CONTROLLED GROUPS. A **combined controlled group** is a group of three or more corporations where the following criteria are met:

- Each corporation is a member of a parent-subsidiary controlled group or a brother-sister controlled group
- At least one of the corporations is both the parent corporation of a parent-subsidiary controlled group and a member of a brother-sister controlled group.[55]

EXAMPLE C3-33 ▶ Able, Best, and Coast Corporations each have a single class of stock outstanding. Their stock is owned by the following shareholders:

	Stock Ownership Percentages		
Shareholder	*Able Corp.*	*Coast Corp.*	*Best Corp.*
Art	50%	50%	—
Barbara	50%	50%	—
Able Corp.	—	—	100%

[54] Reg. Sec. 1.1563-1(a)(3).

[55] Sec. 1563(a)(3).

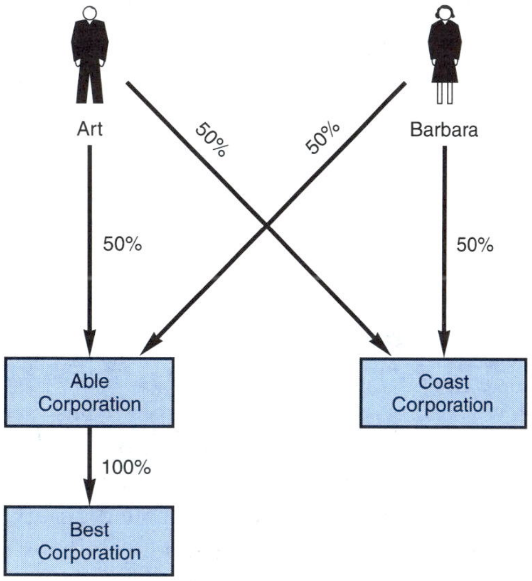

FIGURE C3-3 ▶ COMBINED CONTROLLED GROUP (EXAMPLE C3-33)

KEY POINT

The combined controlled group definition does just what its name implies: It combines a parent-subsidiary controlled group and a brother-sister controlled group. Thus, instead of trying to apply the controlled group rules to two different groups, the combined group definition eliminates the issue by combining the groups into one controlled group.

Able and Coast Corporations are a brother-sister controlled group because both the 80% and 50% tests are satisfied by Art and Barbara. Able and Best Corporations are a parent-subsidiary controlled group because Able owns all of Best's stock. Each of the three corporations is a member of either the parent-subsidiary controlled group (Able and Best) or the brother-sister controlled group (Able and Coast), and the parent corporation (Able) of the parent-subsidiary controlled group is also a member of the brother-sister controlled group. Therefore, Able, Best, and Coast Corporations are members of a combined controlled group (see Figure C3-3). ◀

APPLICATION OF THE CONTROLLED GROUP TEST

The controlled group test is generally applied on December 31. A corporation is included in a controlled group if it is a group member on December 31 and has been a group member on at least one-half of the days in its tax year that precede December 31. A corporation that is not a group member on December 31 is considered a member for the tax year if it has been a group member on at least one-half of the days in its tax year that precede December 31. Corporations are excluded if they were members for less than one-half of the days in their tax year that precede December 31 or if they retain certain special tax statuses such as being a tax-exempt corporation.

EXAMPLE C3-34 ▶ Ace and Copper Corporations are members of a parent-subsidiary controlled group of which Ace is the common parent corporation. Both corporations are calendar-year taxpayers and have been group members for the entire year. They do not file a consolidated return. Bell Corporation, which has a fiscal year ending on August 31, becomes a group member on December 1, 1997. Although Bell is a group member on December 31, 1997, it has been a group member for less than half of the days in its tax year that precede December 31—only 30 of 121 days starting on September 1. Therefore, Bell is *not* a component member of the Ace-Copper controlled group for its tax year beginning on September 1, 1997. ◀

If a corporation is a component member of the group on December 31, it must share the tax benefits of the Sec. 11(b) progressive corporate tax rate schedule. Members of a controlled group are treated as one corporation for purposes of figuring the applicability of the additional 5 percentage point surcharge that must be paid by corporations with taxable income in excess of $100,000, and the 3 percentage point surcharge that applies when taxable income is in excess of $15 million. If a corporation is *not* a component member of the group (i.e., an excluded member) on December 31, it is excluded from the controlled group for that year and can take full advantage of the reduced 15% and 25% corporate tax rates on its first $75,000 of taxable income, and the 34% rate on taxable income up to $10 million.

KEY POINT

The controlled group definition is important in a number of areas other than the corporate graduated rate structure. For example, Sec. 267 treats members of a controlled group as related parties when applying the loss disallowance and the expense deferral rules described above. Examples of other items affected by the controlled group definition are listed here.

SPECIAL RULES APPLYING TO CONTROLLED GROUPS

If two or more corporations are members of a controlled group, the member corporations are limited to a total of $50,000 being taxed at 15%, $25,000 being taxed at 25%, and $10 million being taxed at 34%—the reduced tax rates found in Sec. 11(b).

In addition, a controlled group must apportion certain other tax benefits among its group members. Among the items requiring allocation are

- The $250,000 minimum accumulated earnings tax credit
- The $25,000 amount for general business tax credit limitation purposes
- The $40,000 statutory exemption for the alternative minimum tax
- The $18,000 (in 1997) of depreciable assets that can be expensed annually
- The $100,000 exemption for the 5 percentage point surcharge on taxable income and the $15,000,000 exemption for the 3 percentage point surcharge on taxable income.

Furthermore, under Sec. 267(a)(1), no deduction is allowed for any loss on the sale or exchange of property between two members of the same controlled group. The loss realized on the sale of property between members of a controlled group receives special treatment. A loss realized on a transaction between members of a controlled group is deferred (instead of being disallowed). The deferred loss is recognized by the selling member when the property that is sold or exchanged in the intragroup transaction is sold outside the group. The entire deferred loss is recognized when the property is disposed of outside the controlled group. Under Sec. 267(a)(2), no deduction is allowed for certain accrued expenses or interest owed by one member of a controlled group to another member of the same controlled group when the two corporations use different accounting methods so that the payments would be reported in different tax years. (See page C3-23 for a detailed discussion of Sec. 267.) The Sec. 1239 rules that convert capital gain into ordinary income when (1) property is sold by a controlling shareholder to a corporation or by a corporation to a controlling shareholder and (2) such property is depreciable in the purchasing party's hands also apply to sales or exchanges involving two members of the same controlled group.

TYPICAL MISCONCEPTION

The definitions of a parent-subsidiary controlled group and an affiliated group are similar, but not identical. For example, the 80% stock ownership test for controlled group purposes is satisfied if 80% of the voting power *or* 80% of the FMV of a corporation's stock is owned. For purposes of an affiliated group, 80% of both the voting power and the FMV of a corporation's stock must be owned.

CONSOLIDATED TAX RETURNS

WHO CAN FILE A CONSOLIDATED RETURN. Some groups of related corporations (i.e., affiliated groups) may elect to file a single income tax return called a **consolidated tax return**. An **affiliated group** is one or more chains of includible corporations connected through stock ownership with a common parent,[56] but only if the following criteria are met:

- The common parent directly owns stock with at least 80% of the voting power and 80% of the value of at least one includible corporation.

[56] Includible corporations are those eligible to join in the consolidated tax return election under Sec. 1504(b).

- Stock with at least 80% of the voting power and 80% of the value of each other corporation included in the affiliated group is owned directly by one or more group members.[57]

Most parent-subsidiary controlled groups are eligible to file a single consolidated return in place of separate tax returns for each corporation. The parent-subsidiary portion of a combined group generally can also file a consolidated tax return. Brother-sister controlled groups are not eligible to file consolidated returns because the requisite parent-subsidiary relationship has not been established.

An affiliated group makes the election to file a consolidated tax return by filing Form 1120, which includes all of the income and expenses of each of its members. Each corporate member of the affiliated group must consent to the election.

SELF-STUDY QUESTION

What is probably the most common reason for making a consolidated return election?

ANSWER

Filing consolidated returns allows the group to offset losses of one corporation against the profits of other members of the group.

ADVANTAGES OF FILING A CONSOLIDATED RETURN. A consolidated return is, in effect, one tax return for the entire affiliated group of corporations. The main advantages of filing a consolidated return are

- Profits of one member of the group can be offset against losses of another member of the group.
- Capital gains of one member of the group can be offset against capital losses of another member of the group.
- Profits or gains reported on intercompany transactions are deferred generally until a sale outside the group takes place (i.e., if one member sells property to another member, the gain is postponed until the property is sold to someone outside the affiliated group).

If the group members file separate returns, members with NOLs or capital losses must either carry back these losses to earlier years or carry them forward to future years. Although the losses of one group member can be offset against the profits of another group member when a consolidated return is filed, there are some important limitations on the use of a member corporation's NOL. These limitations are designed to prevent one corporation from purchasing another corporation's NOL carryovers to offset its own taxable income or purchasing a profitable corporation to facilitate the use of its NOL carryovers.

The following example illustrates the advantage of a consolidated return election.

EXAMPLE C3-35 ▶ Parent Corporation owns 100% of the stock of Subsidiary Corporation. Parent reports $110,000 of taxable income, including a $10,000 capital gain. Subsidiary has a $100,000 NOL and a $10,000 capital loss. If Parent and Subsidiary file separate returns, Parent has a $26,150 [($50,000 × 0.15) + ($25,000 × 0.25) + ($25,000 × 0.34) + ($10,000 × 0.39)] tax liability. Subsidiary has no tax liability but may be able to use its $100,000 NOL and $10,000 capital loss to offset taxable income in other years. If Parent and Subsidiary file a consolidated return, the group's consolidated taxable income is zero and the group has no tax liability. By filing a consolidated return, the group saves $26,150 in taxes for the year. ◀

SELF-STUDY QUESTION

What are some of the disadvantages of filing consolidated returns?

ANSWER

Taxpayers may think that it would reduce administrative costs to file one consolidated return rather than a number of separate returns. This is not necessarily true because of the need to keep track of intercompany transactions and special loss limitations. Also, a consolidated return election is binding for all subsequent tax years.

DISADVANTAGES OF FILING A CONSOLIDATED RETURN. The main disadvantages of a consolidated return election are

- The election is binding on all subsequent tax years unless the IRS grants permission to discontinue filing consolidated returns or the affiliated group is terminated.
- Losses on intercompany transactions are deferred generally until a sale outside the group takes place.

[57] Sec. 1504(a).

- Sec. 1231 losses are offset by Sec. 1231 gains instead of being reported as an ordinary loss.
- Losses of an unprofitable member of the group may reduce the deduction or credit limitations of the group below what would be available if separate tax returns were filed.
- Additional administrative costs may be incurred in maintaining the records needed to file a consolidated return.

Determining whether to make a consolidated tax return election is a complex decision because of the various advantages and disadvantages and the fact that the election is so difficult to break once it is made.

TAX PLANNING CONSIDERATIONS

COMPENSATION PLANNING FOR SHAREHOLDER-EMPLOYEES

OBJECTIVE 5

Explain how compensation planning can reduce taxes for corporations and their shareholders

Compensation paid to a shareholder-employee in the form of salary carries with it the advantage of single taxation; that is, the salary is taxable to the employee and deductible by the payer corporation. A dividend payment, however, is taxed twice. The corporation is taxed on its income when it is earned, and the shareholder is taxed on the profits paid out in the form of dividends. Some owners of closely held corporations elect to be taxed under the rules of Subchapter S in order to avoid double taxation. Other owners of closely held corporations retain C corporation status to use the 15% and 25% marginal corporate tax rates and to benefit from tax-free fringe benefits such as health and accident insurance. These fringe benefits are nontaxable to the employee and deductible by the payer corporation. Closely held corporations must determine the appropriate level of earnings to be withdrawn from the business in the form of salary and fringe benefits and earnings to be retained in the business for tax and nontax reasons.

KEY POINT

The basic objective of compensation planning is to provide employees with the greatest possible benefits for the least amount of cost to the employer. If the employer is a C corporation, the compensation package of a shareholder-employee usually includes salary, fringe benefits, and some type of deferred compensation arrangement. In contrast, the least desirable method of getting money out of the corporation and into the hands of a shareholder-employee is through the payment of corporate dividends.

Advantage Of Salary Payments. If all corporate profits are paid out as salary and fringe benefit payments, double taxation is eliminated. However, the following considerations limit the tax planning that can be undertaken in the salary and fringe benefits area:

- Regulation Sec. 1.162-7(a) requires salary or fringe benefit payments to be reasonable in amount and to be paid for services rendered by the employee. Compensation deemed to be unreasonable is generally characterized as a dividend (see Chapter C4) and results in double taxation.
- A corporation may not deduct compensation paid to an executive of a publicly traded corporation in excess of $1 million during a tax year beginning after December 31, 1993. However, this limitation does not apply to compensation paid to an executive other than the corporation's top five officers, or to performance-based compensation.[58]
- A corporation is a tax-paying entity independent of its owners. The first $75,000 of a corporation's earnings is taxed at 15% and 25% corporate tax rates. These rates are lower than the marginal tax rate that may apply to an individual taxpayer and provides an incentive to retain some earnings in the corporation instead of paying them out as salaries. For large corporations, the 34% and 35% marginal tax rates for a C corporation are lower than the top individual tax rates and may permit larger accumulations of earnings for reinvestment and debt repayment if salary levels for shareholder-employees are kept low.

[58] Sec. 162(m).

- A combined employee–employer social security tax rate of 15.30% applies in 1997. Employers and employees are each liable for 6.20% of old age security and disability insurance tax, or a total of 12.40% of the first $65,400 of wages for 1997. Employers and employees also are each liable for a 1.45% Medicare hospital insurance tax, for a total of 2.90% of all wages. In addition to these taxes, state and federal unemployment taxes may be imposed on a portion of the wages paid.

The items listed above may affect the tax-planning possibilities regarding salaries or fringe benefits for the owners of a closely held corporation.

ADDITIONAL COMMENT

A fringe benefit is probably the most cost effective form of compensation because the amount of the benefit is deductible by the employer and never taxed to the employee. Thus, where possible, fringe benefits are an excellent compensation planning tool. For closely held corporations, however, the tax savings to shareholder-employees are reduced because the fringe benefit must be offered to all employees without discrimination.

Advantage Of Fringe Benefits. Fringe benefits provide two types of tax advantages: a tax deferral or an exclusion. Qualified pension, profit-sharing, and stock bonus plans generally provide a tax deferral; that is, the corporation's contribution to such a plan is not taxable to the employees when the contribution is made, but the benefits from the plan are taxed to the employees when they are received. Other fringe benefits that closely held corporations commonly provide, such as group term life insurance, accident and health insurance, and disability insurance, are exempt from tax altogether; that is, the employee is never taxed on the value of these fringe benefits.

The value of fringe benefits is excluded from an employee's gross income. The marginal individual tax rate applicable to these employee benefits is zero. The conversion of a salary payment into a fringe benefit provides a tax savings for the shareholder-employee equal to the amount paid times the marginal individual tax rate when a payment made by the shareholder-employee for the fringe benefit would not be deductible on his or her individual tax return.

Limitation On Deductible Compensation Payments For Shareholder-Employees. The amount of compensation that is reasonable for a shareholder-employee of a closely held corporation depends on the facts and circumstances of the situation. Any portion of the compensation considered to be unreasonable generally is treated as a constructive dividend and subject to double taxation. The corporation bears the burden of proof to show that the amount of cash and deferred compensation plus fringe benefits paid to a shareholder-employee is reasonable. Further discussion on the tax consequences of paying an unreasonable amount of compensation is presented in Chapter C4.

SPECIAL ELECTION TO ALLOCATE REDUCED TAX RATE BENEFITS

A controlled group may elect to apportion the tax benefits of the 15%, 25%, and 34% tax rates to the member corporations in any manner it chooses. If no special apportionment plan is elected, the $50,000, $25,000, and $10 million amounts allocated to the three reduced tax rate brackets are divided equally among all the corporations in the group.[59] If a controlled group has one or more group members that report little or no taxable income, a special apportionment of the reduced tax benefits should be elected to obtain the full tax savings resulting from the reduced rates.

EXAMPLE C3-36 ▶ North and South Corporations are members of the North-South controlled group. The corporations file separate tax returns for the current year and report the following results:

Corporation	*Taxable Income (NOL)*
North	$(25,000)
South	100,000

[59] Sec. 1561(a).

If no special apportionment plan is elected, North and South are limited to $25,000 each that is taxed at a 15% rate and $12,500 each that is taxed at a 25% rate, and their tax liability is determined as follows:

KEY POINT

A special apportionment of the 15%, 25%, and 34% tax rates can reduce a controlled group's overall tax liability. Example C3-36 illustrates how the North-South controlled group can save $5,875 of taxes through a special apportionment plan. Without the special apportionment, all of the benefits of the reduced rates are not used.

Corporation	*Calculation*	*Tax*
North		—0—
South	15% tax bracket: 0.15 × $25,000	$ 3,750
	25% tax bracket: 0.25 × $12,500	3,125
	34% tax bracket: 0.34 × $62,500	21,250
	Subtotal for South Corporation	$28,125
Total for North-South controlled group		$28,125

If a special apportionment plan is elected, the group may apportion the full $50,000 and $25,000 amounts for each of the reduced tax rate brackets to South Corporation. The tax owed by each corporation is determined as follows:

Corporation	*Calculation*	*Tax*
North		—0—
South	15% tax bracket: 0.15 × $50,000	$ 7,500
	25% tax bracket: 0.25 × $25,000	6,250
	34% tax bracket: 0.34 × $25,000	8,500
	Subtotal for South Corporation	$22,250
Total for North-South controlled group		$22,250

Use of the special apportionment election reduces the total tax liability for the North-South group by $5,875 ($28,125 − $22,250). The filing of a consolidated tax return could provide an immediate $7,500 (0.34 × $25,000) tax benefit by permitting North's NOL to offset South's taxable income in the current year. Such an election can prevent North's management from having to carry over the NOL to the next year if it could not be used as a carryback to a prior year. ◀

If a controlled group's total taxable income exceeds $100,000 ($10 million), then a 5 (3) percentage point surcharge is imposed to recapture the benefits of the reduced tax rates. This additional tax is paid by the component member (or members) that took advantage of the lower tax rates.

EXAMPLE C3-37 ▶

Hill, Jet, and King Corporations are members of the Hill-Jet-King controlled group. The corporations file separate tax returns and report the following results:

Corporation	*Taxable Income*
Hill	$200,000
Jet	100,000
King	100,000
Total	$400,000

All of the reduced tax rate benefits are allocated to Hill Corporation under a special apportionment plan. Hill's income tax is calculated as follows:

15% tax bracket: 0.15 × $50,000	$ 7,500
25% tax bracket: 0.25 × $25,000	6,250
34% tax bracket: 0.34 × $125,000	42,500
Surcharge	11,750
Hill's total tax liability	$68,000

Jet and King each have a regular tax liability of $34,000 (0.34 × $100,000). Thus the group's regular tax liability is $136,000 ($68,000 + $34,000 + $34,000). Because Hill, Jet, and King each report taxable income in excess of $75,000, the group would have the same total regular tax liability if the special apportionment plan apportioned all of the tax benefit to Jet or King Corporation or divided it equally among the three corporations.[60] ◀

TYPICAL MISCONCEPTION

A corporation may want to elect to forgo the NOL carryback when tax credit carryovers are being used in the earlier years. If the NOLs are carried back, the tax credits may expire. Thus, before deciding to carry back NOLs, the prior tax returns should be carefully examined to ensure that expiring tax credits do not exist.

USING NOL CARRYOVERS AND CARRYBACKS

When a corporation incurs an NOL for the year, it has two choices:

- Carry the NOL back to the third, second, and first preceding years in that order, and then forward to the succeeding fifteen years in order until the NOL is exhausted.
- Forgo any carryback and just carry the NOL forward to the fifteen succeeding years.

A corporation might elect to forgo an NOL carryback because it would offset income taxed at a low rate so that the tax refund obtained due to the NOL would not be as great as is anticipated if the NOL were carried forward instead.

EXAMPLE C3-38 ▶

Boyd Corporation incurs a $25,000 NOL in 1997. Boyd's 1994 taxable income was $50,000. If Boyd carries the NOL back to 1994, Boyd's tax refund is computed as follows:

Original tax on $50,000 (using 1994 rates)	$7,500
Minus: Recomputed tax on $25,000 [($50,000 − $25,000) × 0.15]	(3,750)
Tax refund	$3,750

ETHICAL POINT

When tax practitioners take on a new client, they should review the client's prior year tax returns and tax elections for accuracy and completeness. Tax matters arising in the current year, such as an NOL, can affect prior year tax returns prepared by another tax practitioner. Positions taken or errors discovered in a prior year return may have ethical consequences for a practitioner who takes on a new client.

If Boyd anticipates taxable income (before reduction for any NOL carryovers) of $75,000 or more in 1998, carrying the NOL forward will result in the entire loss offsetting taxable income that would otherwise be taxed at a 34% or higher marginal tax rate. The refund is computed as follows:

Tax on $100,000	$22,250
Minus: Tax on $75,000 ($100,000 − $25,000)	(13,750)
Tax savings in 1998	$ 8,500

Thus, if Boyd expects taxable income to be $100,000 in 1998, it might elect to forgo the NOL carryback and obtain the additional $4,750 tax benefit. Of course, by carrying the NOL over to 1998, Boyd loses the value of having the funds immediately available. However, the NOL may be used to reduce Boyd's estimated tax payments for 1998. ◀

COMPLIANCE AND PROCEDURAL CONSIDERATIONS

ESTIMATED TAXES

Every corporation that expects to owe more than $500 in tax for the current year must pay four installments of estimated tax, each equal to 25% of its required annual

[60] A 3 percentage point surcharge applies if the controlled group's total taxable income exceeds $15 million. The recapture rule applies in a fashion similar to Example C3-37.

payment. For corporations that are not large corporations (defined below), the required annual payment for tax years beginning after December 31, 1993 is the lesser of 100% of the tax shown on the return for the current year or 100% of the tax shown on the return for the preceding year.[61] The estimated tax amount is defined as the sum of the corporation's income tax and alternative minimum tax liabilities that is in excess of its tax credits.[62] The amount of estimated tax due may be computed on Schedule 1120-W (Corporation Estimated Tax).

ESTIMATED TAX PAYMENT DATES. A calendar year corporation must deposit estimated tax payments in a Federal Reserve bank or authorized commercial bank on or before April 15th, June 15th, September 15th, and December 15th.[63] This schedule differs from that of an individual taxpayer. The final estimated tax installment for a calendar-year corporation is due in December of the tax year, rather than in January of the following tax year, as is the case for individual taxpayers.

EXAMPLE C3-39 ▶ Garden Corporation uses a calendar year as its tax year. For 1997 Garden expects to report the following results:

Regular tax	$119,000
Alternative minimum tax	25,000

Garden's 1997 estimated tax liability is $144,000 ($119,000 regular tax liability + $25,000 AMT liability). Garden's tax liability for 1996 was $120,000. Assuming Garden is not a large corporation, its required annual payment for 1997 is the lesser of its 1996 liability ($120,000) or its 1997 tax return liability ($144,000), or $120,000. Garden will not incur any penalty if it deposits four equal installments of $30,000 ($120,000 ÷ 4) on or before April 15, June 15, September 15, and December 15, 1997. ◀

TYPICAL MISCONCEPTION

The easiest method of determining a corporation's estimated tax payments is to pay 100% of last year's tax liability. Unfortunately, for "large corporations," other than for its first quarterly payment, last year's tax liability is not an acceptable method of determining the required estimated tax payments. Also, last year's tax liability cannot be used if no tax liability existed in the prior year or a short-year return was filed for the prior year.

Different estimated tax payment rules are used for large corporations. A large corporation's required annual payment is 100% of the tax shown on the return for the current tax year.[64] The estimated tax payments for a large corporation cannot be based on the prior year's tax liability, although a large corporation is allowed to base its first installment payment for the year on last year's tax liability. If a large corporation elects to base its first estimated tax payment on the prior year's liability, any shortfall between the required payment based on the current year's tax liability and the actual payment must be made up when the second payment is made.[65] A large corporation is one whose taxable income was $1 million or more in any of its three immediately preceding tax years.[66] Controlled groups of corporations must allocate the $1 million amount among its group members.[67]

EXAMPLE C3-40 ▶ Assume the same facts as in Example C3-39 except that Garden is a large corporation (i.e., it had more than $1 million of taxable income in 1995). Garden can base its first estimated tax payment on either 25% of its 1997 tax liability, or 25% of its 1996 tax liability. Garden should elect to use its 1996 tax liability as the basis for its first installment because it can

[61] Under Rev. Rul. 92-54 (1992-2 C.B. 320) a corporation may not base its required estimated tax installments on the tax shown on the return for the preceding tax year if the preceding year tax return showed a zero tax liability.

[62] Secs. 6655(d)(1) and (g)(1).

[63] Sec. 6655(c)(2). Fiscal year taxpayers are required by Sec. 6655(i)(1) to deposit their taxes on or before the fifteenth day of the fourth, sixth, ninth, and twelfth month of their tax year.

[64] Sec. 6655(d)(2)(A).

[65] Sec. 6655(d)(2)(B). A revision to the required estimated tax payment amount may also be needed if the corporation is basing its quarterly payments on the current year's tax liability. Installments paid after the estimate of the current year's liability has been revised must take into account any shortage or excess in previous installment payments resulting from the change in the original estimate.

[66] Sec. 6655(g)(2)(A).

[67] Sec. 6655(g)(2)(B)(ii).

reduce the needed payment from \$36,000 (0.25 × \$144,000) to \$30,000 (0.25 × \$120,000). It must recapture the shortfall of \$6,000 (\$36,000 − \$30,000) when it pays its second installment. Therefore, the total second installment is \$42,000 (\$36,000 second installment + \$6,000 recapture from first installment). ◀

SELF-STUDY QUESTION

What is the consequence of underpaying a corporation's estimated taxes?

ANSWER

A nondeductible penalty is assessed if estimated taxes are not timely paid. The amount of the penalty is dependent on three factors: the underpayment rate in Sec. 6621, the amount of the underpayment, and the amount of time that lapses until payment is actually made.

PENALITES FOR UNDERPAYMENT OF ESTIMATED TAX. A nondeductible penalty is assessed if a corporation does not deposit its required estimated tax installment on or before the due date for that installment. The penalty is the underpayment rate found in Sec. 6621 times the amount by which the installment(s) due by a payment date exceed the payment(s) actually made.[68] The penalty is owed from the payment due date for the installment until the earlier of the date the payment is actually made or the due date for the tax return (excluding extensions).

EXAMPLE C3-41 ▶ Globe Corporation is a calendar-year taxpayer whose tax liability for 1996 is \$100,000. Globe's tax liability for 1995 was \$125,000. It should have made estimated tax payments of \$25,000 (\$100,000 ÷ 4) on or before April 15, June 15, September 15, and December 15, 1996. No penalty is assessed if Globe deposited at least \$25,000 on or before each of the four dates. If, for example, a deposit of only \$16,000 (\$9,000 less than the required \$25,000) was made on April 15, 1996, and the remaining \$9,000 was not deposited before the due date for the 1996 return, Globe must pay a penalty at the Sec. 6621 rate on the \$9,000 underpayment for the period of time from April 15, 1996 through March 15, 1997. The penalty is calculated on the completed Form 2220 in Appendix B. If Globe deposits \$34,000 on the second installment date (June 15, 1996), so that a total of \$50,000 has been paid by the due date for the second installment, the penalty runs only from April 16, 1996 through June 15, 1996. ◀

Special Computation Methods. Corporations are allowed to use two special methods for calculating estimated tax installments:

- The "annualized income" method or
- The "adjusted seasonal income" method.

THE ANNUALIZED INCOME METHOD. This method is useful if a corporation's income is likely to increase a great deal toward the end of the year. It allows a corporation to base its first and second quarterly estimated tax payments on its annualized taxable income for the first three months of the year. The corporation must then base its third payment on its annualized taxable income for the first six months of the year and its fourth payment must be based on annualized taxable income for the first nine months of the year. (Two other options for the number of months used for each installment are available.)[69]

KEY POINT

Both the "annualized income exception" and the "adjusted seasonal income exception" are complicated computations. However, due to the large amounts of money involved in making corporate estimated tax payments along with the possible underpayment penalties, the time and effort spent in determining the least amount necessary for a required estimated tax payment are often worthwhile.

Taxable income for a period of less than twelve months (short period) is placed on an annual basis by (1) multiplying the taxable income for the short period by 12 and (2) dividing the resulting amount by the number of months in the short period.

A corporation may use the annualized income method for an installment payment only if it is less than the regular required installment. It must recapture any reduction in an earlier required installment resulting from use of the annualized income method by increasing the amount of the next installment that does not qualify for the annualized income method.

[68] Sec. 6621. This interest rate is the short-term federal rate as determined by the Secretary of the Treasury plus three percentage points. It is subject to change every three months. These rates are provided for recent time periods on page C15–16. For periods after December 31, 1990, the interest rate for large corporations is the short-term federal rate plus five percentage points. This higher interest rate commences thirty days after the issuance of either a thirty-day or ninety-day deficiency notice.

[69] Sec. 6655(e)(2)(C).

For small corporations, the best way to ensure that no penalty will be imposed for the underpayment of estimated tax is to make sure that the current year's estimated tax payments are based on 100% of last year's tax. This is not possible, however, for large corporations or for corporations that did not owe any tax in the prior year or filed a short period tax return for the prior year.

EXAMPLE C3-42 ▶ Erratic Corporation, a calendar year taxpayer, reports taxable income of: $10,000 in each of January, February, and March; $20,000 in each of April, May, and June; and $50,000 in each of the last six months of 1997. Its annualized income for the first three months is calculated as follows:

Taxable income from January through March	$30,000
times: Annualization factor	× 12/3[a]
Annualized taxable income	$120,000

[a] Number of months in the tax year divided by number of months that have passed since the beginning of the tax year.

Erratic may base its first and second estimated tax payments on annualized taxable income of $120,000 (see calculation above). Its third installment is based on annualized taxable income of $180,000 ($90,000 taxable income for first six months × 12/6), and its fourth estimated tax payment is based on annualized taxable income of $320,000 ($240,000 taxable income for first nine months × 12/9). ◀

Adjusted Seasonal Income Exception. A corporation may base its installments on its adjusted seasonal income. This rule permits corporations that earn seasonal income to annualize their income by assuming income earned in the current year is earned in the same pattern as in preceding years. As in the case of the annualized income exception, the seasonal income exception may be used only if the resulting installment payment is less than the regular required installment. Once the exception no longer applies, any savings resulting from its use for prior installments must be recaptured.[70]

Reporting The Underpayment. A corporation reports its underpayment of estimated taxes and the amount of any penalty that is owed on Form 2220 (Underpayment of Estimated Tax by Corporations). A copy of a completed Form 2220 using the facts from Example C3-41 is presented in Appendix B.

PAYING THE REMAINING TAX LIABILITY. A corporation must pay all of its remaining tax liability for the year when it files its corporate tax return. An extension of time to file the tax return does *not* extend the time to pay the tax liability. If any amount of tax is not paid by the original due date for the tax return, interest at the underpayment rate prescribed by Sec. 6621 must be paid from the due date until the tax is paid. In addition to interest, a penalty is assessed if the tax is not paid on time, and the corporation cannot show reasonable cause for the failure to pay. Reasonable cause is presumed if the corporation requests an extension of time to file its tax return and the amount of tax shown on the request for extension (Form 7004) or the amount of tax paid by the original due date of the return is at least 90% of the corporation's tax shown on its Form 1120.[71] A discussion of the failure-to-pay penalty and the interest calculation can be found in Chapter C15.

[70] Sec. 6655(e)(3).

[71] Reg. Sec. 301.6651-1(c)(4).

STOP & THINK

Question: Why does the tax law permit a corporation to use special methods such as the "annualized income" method to calculate its required estimated tax installments?

Solution: A large corporation whose income varies widely may not be able to estimate its taxable income for the year until late in the year and it is not allowed to base its estimates on last year's income. If, for example, a calendar year corporation has an income of $100,000 per month during the first six months of its year, it may base its first two installments on a total taxable income of $1,200,000. But if its income unexpectedly increases to $500,000 per month in the seventh month, it would need to use the annualized method to avoid an underpayment penalty for the first two installments. If it were not for the ability to use the annualized method, the corporation would have no way to avoid an underpayment penalty even though it was impossible for the corporation to predict its taxable income for the year when it made the first two installment payments.

OBJECTIVE 6

Determine the requirements for paying corporate incomes taxes and filing a corporate tax return

HISTORICAL NOTE

A recent report by a consulting group indicated that it took 160 hours on average to complete a Form 1120. The 1994 Mobil Oil federal corporate tax return consisted of 7 volumes with 6,300 pages. The return weighed 76 pounds. It took 57 person years to complete the return at a cost of $10 million.

HISTORICAL NOTE

About 2.5% of corporate returns were audited in 1994 and $17.7 billion of additional taxes and penalties were assessed. 52% of the 6,000 or so corporations or corporate groups having assets of $250 million or more were audited.

REQUIREMENTS FOR FILING AND PAYING TAXES

A corporation must file a tax return even if it has no taxable income for the year.[72] If the corporation was not in existence for its entire annual accounting period (either calendar year or fiscal year), it must file a return for the part of the year during which it was in existence. A corporation is not in existence after it ceases business and dissolves, retaining no assets, even if, under state law, it is treated as continuing as a corporation for purposes of winding up its affairs.[73]

Corporations must use Form 1120 (U.S. Corporation Income Tax Return) or Form 1120-A (U.S. Corporation Short-Form Income Tax Return) to file their tax returns. A corporation generally is eligible to use Form 1120-A if the following requirements are satisfied:[74]

- The corporation's gross receipts must be under $500,000.
- Its total income must be under $500,000.
- Its total assets must be under $500,000.

Completed Forms 1120 corporate income tax return is reproduced in Appendix B. A spreadsheet that converts book income into taxable income for the Johns and Lawrence business enterprise (introduced in Chapter C2) is presented with the C corporation tax return.

WHEN THE RETURN MUST BE FILED

Corporate returns must be filed by the fifteenth day of the third month following the close of the corporation's tax year.[75] A corporation can obtain an automatic six-month extension of time to file its tax return by filing Form 7004 (Application for Automatic Extension of Time to File Corporation Income Tax Return) by the original due date for the return. Corporations that fail to file a timely tax return are subject to the failure-to-file penalty. A discussion of this penalty is presented in Chapter C15.

---

[72] Sec. 6012(a)(2).

[73] Reg. Sec. 1.6012-2(a)(2).

[74] See the instructions to Form 1120-A for a series of additional requirements (e.g., the corporation is not filing its final return).

[75] Sec. 6072(b).

EXAMPLE C3-43 ▶ Perry Corporation uses a fiscal year ending on September 30 as its tax year. Its corporate tax return for the year ending September 30, 1997 is due on or before December 15, 1997. If Perry files a Form 7004 by December 15, 1997, it can obtain an automatic extension of time to file until June 15, 1998. Assuming Perry expects its 1997 tax liability to be $72,000 and it has paid $68,000 in estimated tax during the year, it must pay an additional $4,000 to the IRS by December 15, 1997. A completed Form 7004 can be found in Appendix B. ◀

TYPICAL MISCONCEPTION

Corporate returns are due by the fifteenth day of the third month following a corporation's year-end. An automatic six-month extension is available. Remember that an extension merely extends the time for filing the return, not the time for payment of the corporate income tax liability.

Additional extensions beyond the automatic six-month period are not available. The IRS can rescind the extension period by mailing a ten-day notice to the corporation before the end of the six-month period.[76]

TAX RETURN SCHEDULES

SELF-STUDY QUESTION

Is the balance sheet that is required on Schedule L a tax balance sheet or a financial accounting balance sheet?

ANSWER

Schedule L requires a financial accounting balance sheet rather than a tax balance sheet. However, for many smaller corporations, the tax balance sheet is the same as the financial accounting balance sheet.

SCHEDULE L (OF FORM 1120): THE BALANCE SHEET. Form 1120 requires a balance sheet showing the financial accounting results at the beginning and end of the tax year. The balance sheets must be provided on Schedule L of Form 1120. Both forms also require the reconciliation of the corporation's financial accounting income (also known as *book income*) and its taxable income (before special deductions). The reconciliation must be provided on Schedule M-1 of Form 1120. Form 1120 also requires an analysis of the unappropriated retained earnings account on Schedule M-2.

SCHEDULE M-1 (OF FORM 1120) OR PART IV (OF FORM 1120-A): RECONCILIATION OF BOOK INCOME AND INCOME PER RETURN. A corporation's book income usually differs from the corporation's taxable income. These differences arise because

- Some book income is not taxable (e.g., tax-exempt interest)
- Some gross income is not reflected in book income for the current period (e.g., prepaid rent)
- Some financial accounting expenses are not deductible for tax purposes (e.g., federal income taxes)
- Some deductions allowed for tax purposes are not expenses in determining book income for the current period (e.g., asset costs expensed under Sec. 179)

SELF-STUDY QUESTION

Why might the IRS be interested in reviewing a corporation's Schedule M-1?

ANSWER

Because the Schedule M-1 adjustments reconcile book income to taxable income, this schedule can prove illuminating to an IRS agent who is auditing a corporate return. Because Schedule M-1 highlights each departure from the financial accounting rules, the schedule sometimes helps the IRS identify tax issues that it may want to examine further.

Some book income items that are nontaxable in the current year will never be taxed; some book expense items that are nondeductible in computing taxable income for the current year will never be deductible. These income and deduction items are called **permanent differences.** They include tax-exempt interest and IRS penalties.

Some book income items that are nontaxable in the current year will be taxed in a later year or were taxed in an earlier year. Some book expense items that are nondeductible in computing taxable income for the current year will be deductible in a later year or were deductible in an earlier year. These differences are called **temporary differences.** They include prepaid rent and charitable contributions in excess of the 10% of taxable income limitation.

The reconciliation of book income to taxable income starts with net book income. The result of the reconciliation is the corporation's taxable income before special deductions (e.g., NOL and dividends-received deductions).

The items that must be added to the book income amount in order to arrive at the reconciling figure are listed on the left side of Schedule M-1 and include

[76] Reg. Sec. 1.6081-3.

1. *Federal income tax expense.* This amount is deducted in arriving at book income but is not deductible for tax purposes.
2. *Excess of capital losses over capital gains.* This amount is deducted in arriving at book income but is not deductible for tax purposes. (The loss, however, may be carried back or forward and will "reverse" when used.)
3. *Income subject to tax but not recorded on the books this year.* This item includes prepayments received during the current year (e.g., prepaid rent or prepaid interest) that must be included in gross income during the current year but will be included in book income in a later year when earned.
4. *Expenses recorded on the books but not deductible for tax purposes this year.* Among the items included are
   a. Contributions in excess of the 10% of taxable income limitation
   b. Book depreciation expense in excess of that allowed for tax purposes
   c. Travel and entertainment costs that are disallowed (e.g., 50% nondeductible portion of meal and entertainment expenditures)
   d. Life insurance premiums on key personnel where the corporation is the beneficiary of the policy
   e. Interest payments on money borrowed to purchase tax-exempt securities
   f. Estimated costs of warranty service
   g. Political contributions

The items that must be deducted from book income in order to arrive at the reconciling figure are listed on the right side of Schedule M-1 and include

1. *Income recorded on books this year that is not taxable in the current year.* Among the items included are
   a. Prepaid rent or interest that was received and reported for tax purposes in an earlier year but earned in the current year
   b. Life insurance proceeds received on the death of key personnel
   c. Tax-exempt interest
2. *Deductions or losses claimed in the tax return that do not reduce book income in the current year.* Among the items included are
   a. Depreciation, cost recovery deductions, and asset costs expensed under Sec. 179 that are in excess of the depreciation taken for book purposes.
   b. Charitable contribution carryovers from an earlier year deducted on this year's tax return
   c. Capital losses from another year used to offset capital gains on this year's tax return
   d. Amortization of organizational expenditures in excess of the amortization allowed for book purposes

Temporary Differences. The effects of a temporary difference on the reconciliation of book income to taxable income can be illustrated by examining the adjustments required for the amortization of organizational expenditures. For book purposes, organizational expenditures generally are amortized over a period of ten years. For tax purposes, organizational expenditures generally are amortized over a five-year period. Thus, the monthly deduction claimed in determining taxable income for the first five years is twice the expense claimed in determining book income. For the next five years, no expense may be claimed for tax purposes, while the expense reported for book income purposes is the same as it was for the first five years. Therefore, to reconcile taxable income and book income, a downward adjustment must be made to book income during each of the first five years in which such expenditures are amortized. An upward adjustment must be made to book income during the sixth through tenth years to arrive at the taxable income amount.

EXAMPLE C3-44 ▶ Ace Corporation is incorporated and begins business on January 1, 1994. In 1997, Ace Corporation's book income is $25,000. For book purposes, Ace is amortizing its $7,200 of organizational expenditures over ten years. For tax purposes, the organizational expenditures are being amortized over five years. To arrive at taxable income for 1997, Ace must deduct $720—one-tenth of the total organizational expenditures—from book income. Because Ace has already deducted $720 ($7,200 ÷ 10) of amortization in arriving at book income, an additional $720 deduction is required to equal the $1,440 ($7,200 ÷ 5) of amortization allowed for tax purposes. If no other adjustments are required, Ace's taxable income for the year is $24,280 ($25,000 − $720). After its first five tax years, Ace's taxable income will be $720 *more* than its book income for five years because the amortization for book purposes is $720 each year for the first ten years, whereas the amortization for tax purposes is $1,440 for the first five years and zero from then on. ◀

The following example illustrates the reconciliation required on Schedule M-1:

1 Net income per books	121,700	7 Income recorded on books this year not included in this return (itemize):	
2 Federal income tax	27,250	a Tax-exempt interest $ 12,500	
3 Excess of capital losses over capital gains	10,750	Insurance proceeds 50,000	62,500
4 Income subject to tax not recorded on books this year (itemize): Prepaid rent	10,000	8 Deductions in this tax return not charged against book income this year (itemize):	
5 Expenses recorded on books this year not deducted in this return (itemize):		a Depreciation $ 2,000	
a Depreciation $		b Contributions carryover $	
b Contributions carryover $			
c Travel and entertainment $			
Insurance premiums 800			2,000
Interest on loan 15,000	15,800	9 Total of lines 7 and 8	64,500
6 Total of lines 1 through 5	185,500	10 Income (line 28, page 1)—line 6 less line 9	121,000

FIGURE C3-4 ▶ VALLEY CORPORATION'S FORM 1120 SCHEDULE M-1 (EXAMPLE C3-45)

EXAMPLE C3-45 ▶ Valley Corporation reports the following results:

Net income per books (after taxes)	$121,700
Federal income taxes	27,250
Prepaid rent	10,000
Net capital loss	10,750
Tax-exempt interest income	12,500
Insurance premiums on life of key employee where Valley is the beneficiary	800
Proceeds of insurance policy on life of key employee	50,000
Interest paid on loan to buy tax-exempt bonds	15,000
MACRS deductions in excess of book depreciation deduction (straight-line depreciation was used for book purposes)	2,000

Valley's Schedule M-1 reconciliation is shown in Figure C3-4.[77] ◀

KEY POINT

Turn to Figure C3-4. The Schedule M-1 can be used to summarize the adjustments needed to reconcile book and taxable income. The general adjustments on lines 4, 5, 7, and 8, along with federal income tax expense and excess capital losses, represent all of the required adjustments. A review of Schedule M-1 is an excellent way to review the financial accounting and tax accounting differences in a corporation.

SCHEDULE M-2 (OF FORM 1120). Schedule M-2 on Form 1120 requires an analysis of the changes in the unappropriated retained earnings account from the beginning of the year to the end of the year. The schedule supplies the IRS with information regarding dividends paid during the year and any special transactions that caused a change in retained earnings for the year.

[77] A worksheet for converting book income to taxable income for the sample Form 1120 return is provided in Appendix C with that return.

Schedule M-2	**Analysis of Unappropriated Retained Earnings per Books (Line 25, Schedule L)**			
1 Balance at beginning of year	400,000	5 Distributions:	a Cash	250,000
2 Net income (loss) per books	350,000		b Stock	
3 Other increases (itemize): Federal income tax refund for 1995	15,000		c Property	
		6 Other decreases (itemize):		
		7 Add lines 5 and 6		250,000
4 Add lines 1, 2, and 3	765,000	8 Balance at end of year (line 4 less line 7)		515,000

FIGURE C3-5 ▶ BETA CORPORATION'S FORM 1120 SCHEDULE M-2 (EXAMPLE C3-45)

ADDITIONAL COMMENT

Schedule M-2 requires an analysis of a corporation's retained earnings. Retained earnings is a financial accounting number that has little relevance to tax accounting. It would seem much more worthwhile for the IRS to require an analysis of a corporation's earnings and profits, which is an extremely important number in determining the taxation of a corporation and its shareholders.

Schedule M-2 starts with the balance in the unappropriated retained earnings account at the beginning of the year. The following items, which must be added to the beginning balance amount, are listed on the left side of the schedule:

- Net income per books
- Other increases (e.g., refund of federal income taxes paid in a prior year taken directly to the retained earnings account instead of used to reduce federal income tax expense)

Topic Review C3-3

Requirements for Paying Taxes Due and Filing Tax Returns

1. Estimated Tax Requirement
   a. Every corporation that expects to owe more than $500 in tax for the current year must pay four installments of estimated tax, each equal to 25% of its required annual payment.
   b. If a corporation is not a large corporation, its required annual payment for tax years beginning after December 31, 1993 is the lesser of 100% of the tax shown on the current year's return or 100% of the tax shown on the preceding year's return.
   c. Taxes for which estimated payments are required of a C corporation include regular tax and alternative minimum tax, minus any tax credits.
   d. No estimated tax payment is required if the tax due for the tax year is less than $500.
   e. If a corporation is a large corporation, its required annual payment for tax years is 100% of the tax shown on the current year's return. Its first estimated tax payment may be based on the preceding year's tax liability, but any shortfall must be made up when the second installment is due.
   f. Special rules apply if the corporation bases its estimated tax payments on the annualized income or adjusted seasonal income methods.
2. Filing Requirements
   a. The corporate tax return is due by the fifteenth day of the third month after the end of the tax year.
   b. A corporate taxpayer may request an automatic six-month extension.

The following items, which must be deducted from the beginning balance amount, are listed on the right side of the schedule:

- Dividends (e.g., cash or property)
- Other decreases (e.g., appropriation of retained earnings made during the tax year)

The result is the balance in the unappropriated retained earnings account at the end of the year.

EXAMPLE C3-46 In 1997, Beta Corporation reports net income and other capital account items as follows:

Unappropriated retained earnings, January 1, 1997	$400,000
Net income	350,000
Federal income tax refund for 1995	15,000
Cash dividends paid in 1997	250,000
Unappropriated retained earnings, December 31, 1997	515,000

Beta Corporation's Schedule M-2 is shown in Figure C3-5.

Topic Review C3-3 summarizes the requirements for paying the taxes due and filing the corporate tax return.

PROBLEM MATERIALS

DISCUSSION QUESTIONS

C3-1 High Corporation is incorporated on May 1 and commences business on May 10 of the current year. What alternative tax years can High elect to report its initial year's income?

C3-2 Port Corporation wants to change its tax year from a calendar year to a fiscal year ending June 30. Port is a C corporation owned by 100 shareholders, none of whom own more than 5% of the stock. Can Port Corporation change its tax year? If so, how can the change be accomplished?

C3-3 Stan and Susan, two calendar-year taxpayers, are starting a new business to manufacture and sell digital circuits. They intend to incorporate the business with $600,000 of their own capital and $2 million of equity capital obtained from other investors. Organizational and start-up expenditures in the amount of $100,000 are expected to be incurred in the first year. Inventories are a material income-producing factor. Losses of $500,000 are expected to be incurred in their first two years of operations. During the first three years, substantial research and development expenses will be incurred. The company expects to break even in the third year and be profitable at the end of the fourth year, even though the nature of the digital circuit business will require continual research and development activities.

a. What accounting methods and tax elections need to be considered by Stan and Susan in their first year of operation?

b. For each method/election, explain the possible alternatives and the advantages and disadvantages of each alternative.

C3-4 Compare the tax treatment of capital gains and losses by a corporation and by an individual.

C3-5 Explain the effect of the Sec. 291 recapture rule when a corporation sells depreciable real estate.

C3-6 What are organizational expenditures? How are they treated for tax purposes?

C3-7 What are start-up expenditures? How are they treated for tax purposes?

C3-8 Describe three ways in which the treatment of charitable contributions by individual and corporate taxpayers differ.

C3-9 Carver Corporation uses the accrual method of accounting and the calendar year as its tax year. Its board of directors authorizes a cash contribution on November 3, 1997 that is paid on March 10, 1998. In what year(s) is it deductible? What happens if the contribution is not paid until April 20, 1998?

C3-10 Zero Corporation contributes inventory (computers) to State University for use in its mathematics program. The computers have a $1,225 cost basis and an $2,800 FMV. How much is Zero's charitable contribution deduction for the computers? (Ignore the 10% limit.)

C3-11 Why are corporations allowed a dividends-received deduction? What dividends are eligible for this special deduction?

C3-12 Why is a dividends-received deduction disallowed if the stock on which the dividend is paid is debt-financed?

C3-13 Crane Corporation incurs a $75,000 NOL in the current year. In which years can Crane Corporation use this NOL if no special elections are made? When might a special election to forgo the carryback of the NOL be beneficial for Crane Corporation?

C3-14 What special restrictions apply to the deduction of a loss realized on the sale of property between a corporation and a shareholder who owns 60% of the corporation's stock? What restrictions apply to the deduction of expenses accrued by a corporation at year-end and owed to a cash method of accounting shareholder who owns 60% of the corporation's stock?

C3-15 Deer Corporation is a C corporation. Its taxable income for the current year is $200,000. What is Deer Corporation's income tax liability for the year?

C3-16 Budget Corporation is a personal service corporation. Its taxable income for the current year is $75,000. What is Budget Corporation's income tax liability for the year?

C3-17 Why do special restrictions on using the progressive corporate tax rates apply to controlled groups of corporations?

C3-18 Describe the three types of controlled groups.

C3-19 List five restrictions on the claiming of multiple tax benefits that apply to controlled groups of corporations.

C3-20 What are the major advantages and disadvantages of filing a consolidated tax return?

C3-21 What are the tax advantages of substituting fringe benefits for salary paid to a shareholder-employee?

C3-22 Explain the tax consequences to both the corporation and a shareholder-employee of an IRS determination that a portion of the compensation paid in a prior tax year exceeds the reasonable compensation limit.

C3-23 What is the advantage of a special apportionment plan for the benefits of the 15%, 25%, and 34% tax rates to members of a controlled group?

C3-24 Describe the circumstances when a corporation should consider electing *not* to carry a net operating loss back to its three preceding tax years.

C3-25 What corporations must pay estimated taxes? When are the estimated tax payments due?

C3-26 What penalties are assessed for the underpayment of estimated taxes? The late payment of the remaining tax liability?

C3-27 Describe the situations in which a corporation must file a tax return.

C3-28 When is a corporate tax return due for a calendar-year taxpayer? What extension(s) of time in which to file the return are available?

C3-29 List four types of differences that can cause a corporation's book income to differ from its taxable income.

ISSUE IDENTIFICATION QUESTIONS

C3-30 X-Ray Corporation received a $100,000 dividend from Yancey Corporation this year. X-Ray owns 10% of the Yancey's single class of stock. What tax issues should be considered by X-Ray with respect to its dividend income?

C3-31 Williams Corporation sold a truck with an adjusted basis of $100,000 to Barbara for $80,000. Barbara owns 25% of the Williams stock. What tax issues should be considered by Williams and Barbara with respect to the sale/purchase?

C3-32 You are the CPA who prepares the tax returns for Don, his wife, Mary, and their two corporations. Don owns 100% of Pencil Corporation's stock. Pencil's current year taxable income is $100,000. Mary owns 100% of Eraser Corporation's stock. Eraser's current year taxable income is $150,000. Don and Mary file a joint federal income tax return. What issues should be considered with respect to the calculation of the three tax return liabilities?

C3-33 Rugby Corporation has a $50,000 NOL in the current year. Rugby's taxable income in each of the previous three years was $25,000. Rugby expects its taxable income for next year to exceed $400,000. What issues should be considered with respect to the use of the NOL?

PROBLEMS

C3-34 ***Depreciation Recapture.*** Young Corporation purchased residential real estate in 1993 for $225,000, of which $25,000 was allocated to the land and $200,000 was allocated to the building. Young took straight-line MACRS deductions of $50,000 during the years 1993–1997. In 1997 Young sells the property for $275,000, of which $50,000 is allocated to the land and $225,000 is allocated to the building. What are the amount and character of Young's recognized gain or loss on the sale?

C3-35 ***Organizational and Start-up Expenditures.*** Delta Corporation is incorporated on January 1, commences business on July 1, and elects to have its initial tax year end on October 31. Delta incurs the following expenses related to its organization during the current year:

January 30	Travel to investigate potential business site	$2,000
May 15	Legal expenses to draft corporate charter	2,500
May 30	Commissions to stockbroker for issuing and selling stock	4,000
May 30	Temporary directors' fees	2,500
June 5	Accounting fees to set up corporate books	1,500
June 10	Training expenses for employees	5,000
June 15	Rent expense for June	1,000
July 15	Rent expense for July	1,000

a. What alternative treatments are available for Delta's expenditures?
b. What amount of organizational expenditures can Delta Corporation deduct on its first tax return for the fiscal year ending October 31?

C3-36 ***Charitable Contribution of Property.*** Yellow Corporation donates the following properties to the State University:

- ABC Corporation stock purchased two years ago for $18,000. The stock, which is traded on a regional stock exchange, has a $25,000 FMV on the contribution date.
- Inventory with a $17,000 adjusted basis and a $22,000 FMV. The inventory is to be used for scientific research and qualifies under the special Sec. 170(e)(4) rules.
- An antique vase purchased two years ago for $10,000 and having an $18,000 FMV. State University plans to sell the vase to obtain funds for educational purposes.

Yellow Corporation's taxable income before any charitable contributions deduction, NOL or capital loss carryback, or dividends-received deduction is $250,000.
a. What is Yellow Corporation's charitable contributions deduction for the current year?
b. What is the amount of its charitable contributions carryover (if any)?

C3-37 ***Charitable Contribution Deduction Limitation.*** Zeta Corporation reports the following results for 1997 and 1998:

	1997	*1998*
Adjusted taxable income	$180,000	$125,000
Charitable contributions (cash)	20,000	12,000

The adjusted taxable income is before any charitable contributions deduction, NOL or capital loss carryback, or dividends-received deduction is claimed.
a. How much is Zeta Corporation's charitable contributions deduction in 1997? in 1998?
b. What is Zeta Corporation's contribution carryover to 1999, if any?

C3-38 ***Taxable Income Computation.*** Old Corporation reports the following results for the current year:

Gross profits on sales	$100,000
Dividends from less-than-20%-owned domestic corporations	50,000
Operating expenses	80,000
Charitable contributions (cash)	10,000

a. What is Old Corporation's charitable contributions deduction for the current year and its charitable contributions carryover to next year, if any?
b. What is Old Corporation's taxable income for the current year?

C3-39 ***Dividends-Received Deduction.*** Theta Corporation reports the following results for the current year:

Gross profits on sales	$220,000
Dividends from less-than-20%-owned domestic corporations	100,000
Operating expenses	218,000

a. What is Theta Corporation's taxable income for the current year?
b. How would your answer to Part a change if Theta's operating expenses are instead $234,000?
c. How would your answer to Part a change if Theta's operating expenses are instead $252,000?

C3-40 ***Stock Held Forty-Five Days or Less.*** Beta Corporation purchased 100 shares of Gamma Corporation common stock (less than 5% of the outstanding stock) two days before the ex-dividend date for $200,000. Beta receives a $10,000 cash dividend from Gamma. Beta sells the Gamma stock one week after purchasing it for $190,000. What are the tax consequences of these three events?

C3-41 ***Debt-financed Stock.*** Cheers Corporation borrowed $400,000 and used $100,000 of its cash to purchase 5,000 shares of Beer Corporation common stock (less than 5% of the outstanding Beer stock) at the beginning of the current year. Cheers paid $50,000 of interest on the debt this year. Cheers received a $40,000 cash dividend on the Beer stock on September 1 of the current year.
a. What is the amount that Cheers can deduct for the interest paid on the loan?
b. What is the amount of the dividends-received deduction that Cheers can claim with respect to the dividend?

C3-42 ***Net Operating Loss Carrybacks and Carryovers.*** In 1997, Ace Corporation reports gross income of $200,000 (including $150,000 of profit from its operations and $50,000 in dividends from less-than-20%-owned domestic corporations) and $220,000 of operating expenses. Ace's 1994 taxable income (all ordinary income) was $75,000, on which taxes of $13,750 were paid.
a. What is Ace's NOL for 1997?
b. What is the amount of Ace's tax refund if the 1997 NOL is carried back to 1994?
c. Assume that Ace expects 1998's taxable income to be $400,000. What election could Ace make in order to increase the tax benefit from its NOL? What is the dollar amount of the expected benefit (if any)?

C3-43 ***Ordering of Deductions.*** Beta Corporation reports the following results for the current year:

Gross income from operations	$180,000
Dividends from less-than-20%-owned domestic corporations	100,000
Operating expenses	150,000
Charitable contributions	20,000

In addition, Beta has a $50,000 NOL carryover from the preceding tax year.

a. What is Beta's taxable income for the current year?
b. What carrybacks or carryovers are available to other tax years?

C3-44 ***Sale to a Related Party.*** Union Corporation sells a truck for $18,000 to Jane, who owns 70% of its stock. The truck has a $24,000 adjusted basis on the sale date. Jane sells the truck to an unrelated party, Mike, for $25,000 two years later after $5,000 in depreciation has been claimed.

a. What is Union Corporation's realized and recognized gain or loss on selling the truck?
b. What is Jane's realized and recognized gain or loss on selling the truck to Mike?
c. How would your answers to Part b change if Jane instead sold the truck for $8,000?

C3-45 ***Payment to a Cash Basis Employee/Shareholder.*** Value Corporation is a calendar-year taxpayer that uses the accrual method of accounting. On December 10, 1997, Value accrues a bonus payment of $100,000 to Brett, its president and sole shareholder. Brett is a calendar-year taxpayer who uses the cash method of accounting.

a. When can Value Corporation deduct the bonus if it is paid to Brett on March 13, 1998? on March 16, 1998?
b. How would your answers to Part a change if Brett were an employee of Value Corporation who owns no stock in the corporation?

C3-46 ***Capital Gains and Losses.*** North Corporation reports the following results for the current year:

Gross profits on sales	$100,000
Long-term capital gain	10,000
Long-term capital loss	5,000
Short-term capital gain	3,000
Short-term capital loss	5,000
Operating expenses	32,000

What are North's taxable income and income tax liability for the current year?

C3-47 ***Computing the Corporate Income Tax Liability.*** What is Booker Corporation's income tax liability assuming its taxable income is (a) $100,000, (b) $225,000, and (c) $500,000. How would your answers change if Booker Corporation were characterized as a personal service corporation?

C3-48 ***Computing the Corporate Income Tax Liability.*** Brodie Corporation, a C corporation, paid no dividends and had no capital gains or losses in the current year. What is its income tax liability assuming its taxable income for the year was

a. $75,000
b. $13,500,000
c. $17,500,000
d. $33,500,000

C3-49 ***Computing Taxable Income and Income Tax Liability.*** Pace Corporation reports the following results for the current year:

Gross profit on sales	$120,000
Long-term capital loss	10,000
Short-term capital loss	5,000
Dividends from 40%-owned domestic corporation	30,000
Operating expenses	65,000
Charitable contributions	10,000

a. What are Pace's taxable income and income tax liability?
b. What carrybacks and carryovers (if any) are available and to what years must they be carried?

C3-50 ***Computing Taxable Income and Income Tax Liability.*** Roper Corporation reports the following results for the current year:

Gross profits on sales	$80,000
Short-term capital gain	40,000
Long-term capital gain	25,000
Dividends from 25%-owned domestic corporation	10,000
NOL carryover from the preceding tax year	8,000
Operating expenses	45,000

What are Roper's taxable income and income tax liability?

C3-51 ***Controlled Groups.*** Which of the following groups constitute controlled groups? (Any stock not listed below is held by unrelated individuals each owning less than 1% of the outstanding stock.)
a. Judy owns 90% of the single classes of stock of Hot and Ice Corporations.
b. Jones and Kane Corporations each have only a single class of stock outstanding. The stock is owned by two controlling individual shareholders as follows:

	Stock Ownership Percentages	
Shareholder	*Jones Corp.*	*Kane Corp.*
Tom	60%	80%
Mary	30%	0%

c. Link, Model, and Name Corporations each have a single class of stock outstanding. The stock is owned as follows:

	Stock Ownership Percentages	
Shareholder	*Model Corp.*	*Name Corp.*
Link Corp.	80%	50%
Model Corp.		40%

Link Corporation's stock is widely held by over 1,000 shareholders, none of whom owns directly or indirectly more than 1% of Link's stock.
d. Oat, Peach, Rye, and Seed Corporations each have a single class of stock outstanding. The stock is owned as follows:

	Stock Ownership Percentages			
Shareholder	*Oat Corp.*	*Peach Corp.*	*Rye Corp.*	*Seed Corp.*
Bob	100%	90%		
Oat Corp.			80%	30%
Rye Corp.				60%

C3-52 ***Controlled Groups of Corporations.*** Sally owns 100% of the outstanding stock of Eta, Theta, Phi, and Gamma Corporations, each of which files a separate return for the current year. During the current year, the corporations report taxable income as follows:

Corporation	*Taxable Income*
Eta	$40,000
Theta	(25,000)
Phi	50,000
Gamma	10,000

a. What are each corporation's separate tax liabilities, assuming no special apportionment plan governing the reduced Sec. 11(b) corporate tax rates has been elected?
b. What are each corporation's separate tax liabilities, assuming a special election is made for apportioning the Sec. 11(b) reduced corporate tax rates that minimizes the group's total tax liability?

C3-53 ***Compensation Planning.*** Marilyn owns all of the stock of Bell Corporation. Bell Corporation is taxed as a C corporation and employs forty people. She is married, has two children, and files a joint tax return with her husband. In the past Marilyn has not itemized her deductions. She projects that Bell Corporation will report $400,000 of pretax profits for the current year. Five salary levels are being considered by Marilyn as follows:

			Tax Liability		
Total Income	*Salary Paid to Marilyn*	*Earnings Retained by Bell Corporation*	*Marilyn*	*Bell Corporation*	*Total*
$400,000	—0—	$400,000			
400,000	$100,000	300,000			
400,000	200,000	200,000			
400,000	300,000	100,000			
400,000	400,000	—0—			

a. Determine the total tax liability for Marilyn and Bell Corporation for each of the five proposed salary levels. (Assume no other income for Marilyn's family).
b. What recommendations can you make about a salary level for Marilyn that will minimize the total tax liability? Assume salaries paid up to $400,000 are considered reasonable compensation.
c. What possible disadvantage could accrue to Marilyn if Bell Corporation retains funds in the business and distributes some of the accumulated earnings as a dividend in a later tax year?

C3-54 ***Fringe Benefits.*** Refer to the facts in Problem C3-53. Marilyn has read an article explaining the advantages of paying tax-free fringe benefits (e.g., premiums on group term life insurance, accident and health insurance, etc.) and having deferred compensation plans (e.g., qualified pension and profit-sharing plans). Provide Marilyn with information on the tax savings associated with converting $3,000 of her salary into tax-free fringe benefits. What additional costs may be incurred by Bell Corporation if it adopts a fringe benefit plan?

C3-55 ***Converting Book Income to Taxable Income.*** The following income and expense accounts appeared in the accounting records of Rocket Corporation, an accrual basis taxpayer, for the current calendar year.

	Book Income	
Account Title	*Debit*	*Credit*
Net sales		$ 3,000,000
Dividends		8,000 (1)
Interest		18,000 (2)
Gain on sale of stock		5,000 (3)
Key-man life insurance proceeds		100,000
Cost of goods sold	$2,000,000	
Salaries and wages	500,000	
Bad debts	13,000 (4)	
Payroll taxes	62,000	
Interest expense	12,000 (5)	
Charitable contributions	50,000 (6)	
Depreciation	60,000 (7)	
Other expenses	40,000 (8)	
Federal income taxes	96,000	
Net income	298,000	
Total	$3,131,000	$3,131,000

The following additional information is provided.

1. Dividends were from Star Corporation, a 30%-owned domestic corporation.
2. Interest revenue consists of interest on corporate bonds, $15,000; and municipal bonds, $3,000.
3. The stock is a capital asset that was held for three years prior to sale.
4. Rocket Corporation uses the specific chargeoff method of accounting for bad debts.
5. Interest expense consists of $11,000 interest incurred on funds borrowed for working capital, and $1,000 interest on funds borrowed to purchase municipal bonds.
6. All contributions were paid in cash during the current year to State University.
7. Depreciation per books is calculated using the straight-line method. For income tax purposes, depreciation amounted to $85,000.
8. Other expenses include premiums of $5,000 on the key-man life insurance policy covering the Rocket Corporation's president, who died in December.

Required: Prepare a worksheet reconciling Rocket Corporation's book income with its taxable income (before special deductions). Six columns should be used—two (one debit and one credit) for each of the following three major headings: book income, Schedule M-1 adjustments, and taxable income. (See sample worksheet with Form 1120 in Appendix B if you need assistance).

C3-56 ***Reconciling Book Income and Taxable Income.*** Zero Corporation reports the following results for the current year:

Net income per books (after taxes)	$33,000
Federal income taxes	12,000
Tax-exempt interest income	6,000
Interest on loan to purchase tax-exempt bonds	8,000
MACRS depreciation in excess of book depreciation	3,000
Net capital loss	5,000
Insurance premium on life of corporate officer where Zero is the beneficiary	10,000
Excess charitable contributions carried over to next year	2,500

Prepare a reconciliation of Zero's taxable income before special deductions with its book income.

C3-57 ***Reconciling Unappropriated Retained Earnings.*** White Corporation's financial accounting records disclose the following results for the period ending December 31 of the current year:

Retained earnings balance on January 1	$246,500
Net income for year	259,574
Contingency reserve established on December 31	60,000
Cash dividend paid on July 23	23,000

What is White's unappropriated retained earnings balance on December 31 of the current year?

C3-58 ***Estimated Tax Requirement.*** Zeta Corporation's taxable income for 1996 was $1,500,000, on which federal income taxes of $510,000 were paid. Zeta estimates calendar year 1997's taxable income to be $2,000,000, on which it will owe $680,000 in federal income taxes.

a. What are Zeta's minimum quarterly estimated tax payments for 1997 in order to avoid an underpayment penalty?
b. When is Zeta's 1997 tax return due?
c. When are any remaining taxes due? What amount of taxes are due when the return is filed assuming timely estimated tax payments equal to the amount determined in Part (b) have been paid?
d. If Zeta obtains an extension, when is its tax return due? Will the extension permit Zeta to delay making its final tax payments?

C3-59 ***Filing the Tax Return and Paying the Tax Liability.*** Wright Corporation's taxable income for calendar years 1994, 1995, and 1996 was $120,000, $150,000, and $100,000, respectively. Its total tax due for 1996 is $22,250. Wright estimates that its 1997 taxable income will be $500,000, on which it will owe federal income taxes of $170,000. 1997's taxable income is assumed to be earned evenly throughout the year.

a. What are Wright's minimum quarterly estimated tax payments for 1997 in order to avoid an underpayment penalty?
b. When is Wright's 1997 tax return due?
c. When are any remaining taxes due? What amount of taxes are due when the return is filed assuming timely estimated tax payments equal to the amount determined in Part (a) have been paid?
d. How would your answer to Part (a) change if Wright's tax liability for 1996 were $200,000?

TAX FORM/RETURN PREPARATION PROBLEM

C3-60 Packer Corporation, incorporated on January 3, 1987, is a calendar-year taxpayer that uses the accrual method of accounting. Its employer identification number is 74-1234567. Its address is 1010 West Avenue, San Antonio, Texas 78213. Packer operates a bookstore. Bob Parks (social security number 000-45-3000) owns 100% of the single class of stock. Bob resides at 25 Ancient Bend, San Antonio, TX 78248. He receives $65,000 in salary from Packer in the current year. During the current year, Packer reports the following income and expense items:

Gross receipts		$595,000
Purchases		300,000
Salaries:	Officers	65,000
	Other employees	50,000
Rent payments		48,000
Taxes:		
	Payroll	9,000
	Franchise	250
Interest payments		250
Charitable contributions (cash)		8,000
Depreciation (see schedule below)		38,820
Advertising		15,000
Telephone		500
Utilities		17,080
Officer's life insurance premium (firm is the beneficiary)		1,500

Depreciation Schedule

Asset	*Cost*	*Prior Depreciation*	*Method*	*Current Year Depreciation*
Light truck	$ 20,000	$10,400	MACRS	$ 3,840
Fixtures	200,000	77,560	MACRS	34,980
Total	$220,000	$87,960		$38,820

A truck purchased seven years earlier for $8,000, which was fully depreciated using the regular MACRS tables, was sold on May 10 for $3,500. Packer uses the same depreciation method for tax and book purposes. The corporation made estimated tax payments on April 14, June 15, September 10, and December 15 of the current year of $2,000 each (total of $8,000). Its prior year tax liability was $8,000. Packer's balance sheet at the beginning and end of the current year is as follows:

Assets	*January 1*	*December 31*
Cash	$ 34,000	$ 32,420
Other current assets	—0—	48,075
Depreciable assets	228,000	220,000
Minus: Accumulated depreciation	(95,960)	(126,780)
Inventory	125,000	145,000
Total assets	$291,040	$318,715
Liabilities and Stockholders' Equity		
Accounts payable	$ 68,900	$ 39,475
Common stock	60,000	60,000
Retained earnings (unappropriated)	162,140	219,240
Total liabilities and equity	$291,040	$318,715

Packer Corporation uses the first-in, first-out inventory method. The corporation does not claim any deduction for expenses connected with entertainment facilities, living accommodations, or employees attending foreign conventions. The corporation does not own any stock in any other corporation and has no interest in or authority over any foreign bank account or other foreign assets. The corporation did not pay any dividends in the current year. The other current assets amount at year-end consists entirely of marketable securities. No NOL carryovers are available from prior tax years. Prepare

Form 1120 for Packer Corporation for the current year. *Editor's Note:* In computing the year-end retained earnings balance, Packer expensed $8,000 of federal income taxes (i.e., the amount paid in estimated taxes during the year).

CASE STUDY PROBLEMS

C3-61 Marquette Corporation, a tax client since its creation three years ago, has requested that you prepare a memorandum explaining its estimated tax requirements for 1998. The corporation is in the fabricated steel business. Its earnings have been growing each year. Marquette's taxable income for the last three tax years has been $500,000, $1,500,000, and $2,500,000, respectively. The Chief Financial Officer expects its taxable income in 1998 to be approximately $3,000,000.

Required: Prepare a one-page client memorandum explaining Marquette's estimated tax requirements for 1998 providing the necessary supporting authorities.

C3-62 Susan Smith accepted a new corporate client, Winter Park Corporation. A review was conducted by one of Susan's tax managers of Winter Park's prior year tax returns. The review reveals that an NOL for a prior tax year was incorrectly computed, resulting in an overstatement of NOL carrybacks and carryovers to prior tax years.

a. Assume the incorrect NOL calculation does not affect the current year's tax liability. What recommendations (if any) should be made to the new client?

b. Assume that a prior year is currently being audited by the IRS? What are Susan's responsibilities in this situation?

c. Assume that the NOL carryover is being carried to the current year and that Winter Park Corporation does not want to file amended tax returns to correct the error? What should Susan do in this case?

C3-63 The Chief Executive Officer of a client of your public accounting firm saw the following advertisement in the **Wall Street Journal:**

DONATIONS WANTED
The Center for Restoration of Waters
A Nonprofit Research and Educational Organization
Needs Donations—Autos, Boats, Real Estate, Etc.
ALL DONATIONS ARE TAX-DEDUCTIBLE

Prepare a memorandum to your client Phil Mickelson explaining how the federal income tax laws regarding donations of cash, automobiles, boats, and real estate apply to corporate taxpayers.

TAX RESEARCH PROBLEMS

C3-64 Wicker Corporation makes estimated tax payments of $6,000 in 1996. On March 15, 1997, it files its 1996 tax return, showing a tax liability of $20,000, and it pays the balance of $14,000. On April 15, 1997, it discovers an error and files an amended return for 1996 showing a reduced tax liability of $8,000. Prepare a memorandum for your tax manager explaining whether Wicker Corporation can base its estimated tax payments for 1997 on the $8,000 tax liability for 1996, or must it use the $20,000 tax liability reported on its original return. Your manager has suggested that, at a minimum, you consult the following resources:

- Sec. 6655(d)(1)
- Rev. Rul. 86-58, 1986-1 C.B. 365

C3-65 King Corporation is owned equally by three individuals: Alice, Bill, and Charles, who purchased King stock when King Corporation was created. King Corporation has used the cash method of accounting since its inception in 1985. Alice, Bill, and Charles operate an environmental engineering firm of sixty employees, which had gross receipts of $4,000,000 in 1996. Gross receipts have grown by about 15% in each of the last three years and were just under $5,000,000 in 1997. The 15% growth rate is expected to continue for at least five years. Outstanding accounts receivable average about $600,000 at the end of each month. Forty-four of the employees (including Alice, Bill, and Charles) are actively engaged in providing engineering services on a full-time basis. Sixteen of the employees serve in a clerical and support capacity (e.g., secretarial staff, accountants, etc.). Bill has read about special restrictions on the use of the cash method of accounting and requests information from you about the impact these rules might have on King Corporation's continued use of the cash method of accounting. Prepare a memorandum for your tax manager addressing the following issues: (1) If the corporation changes to the accrual method of accounting, what adjustments must be made? (2) Would an S election relieve King Corporation from having to make a change? (3) If the S election relieves King from having to make a change, what factors should enter into the decision about whether King should make an S election?

Your manager has suggested that, at a minimum, you should consult the following

- Secs. 446 and 448
- Temp. Reg. Secs. 1.448-1T and -2T
- H. Rept. No. 99-841, 99th Cong., 2d Sess., pp. 285-289 (1986)

CHAPTER 4

CORPORATE NONLIQUIDATING DISTRIBUTIONS

LEARNING OBJECTIVES

After studying this chapter, you should be able to

1. Explain how current E&P is calculated
2. Explain the difference between current and accumulated E&P
3. Determine the tax consequences of property distributions
4. Determine the tax consequences of stock dividends and distributions of stock rights
5. Distinguish between a stock redemption treated as a sale and one treated as a dividend
6. Explain the tax treatment for preferred stock bailouts
7. Determine when Sec. 304 applies to a stock sale and its tax consequences

CHAPTER OUTLINE

A corporation may distribute money, property, or stock to its shareholders. Shareholders who receive such distributions may have ordinary income, capital gain, or no taxable income at all. The distributing corporation may or may not be required to recognize gain or loss when the distribution is made. How distributions are treated for tax purposes by shareholders and by the distributing corporation depends not only on what is distributed but also on the circumstances surrounding the distribution. Was the corporation in the process of liquidating? Was the distribution made in exchange for some of the shareholder's stock?

This chapter discusses distributions made when a corporation is not in the process of liquidating. It discusses the tax consequences of the following types of distributions:

- Distributions of cash or other property where the shareholder does not surrender any stock
- Distributions of stock or rights to acquire stock of the distributing corporation
- Distributions of property in exchange for the corporation's own stock (i.e., stock redemptions)

Chapter C6 discusses **liquidating distributions.** Chapter C7 discusses distributions of the stock of a controlled subsidiary corporation.

DISTRIBUTIONS IN GENERAL

SELF-STUDY QUESTION

How does a shareholder classify a distribution for tax purposes?

ANSWER

Distributions are treated as follows: (1) dividends to the extent of corporate E&P, (2) return of capital to the extent of the shareholder's stock basis, and (3) gain from the sale of stock.

When a distribution is made to a shareholder, the shareholder must answer the following three questions:

- What is the amount of the distribution?
- To what extent is the amount distributing a dividend?
- What is the basis of the distributed property, and when does its holding period begin?

In addition, the distributing corporation must answer the following two questions:

- What are the amount and character of the gain or loss that must be recognized on the distribution?
- What effect does the distribution have on the distributing corporation's E&P account?

A brief summary of the rules for determining the taxability of a distribution follow, along with a simple example.

Section 301 requires a shareholder to include in gross income the amount of any distribution from a corporation to the extent that it is a dividend. A **dividend** is defined by Sec. 316(a) as a distribution of property made by a corporation out of its earnings and profits (E&P). The term *E&P* is defined in the next section of this chapter. **Property** is defined broadly by Sec. 317(a) to include money, securities, and any other property except stock or stock rights of the distributing corporation. Distributed amounts that exceed a corporation's E&P are treated as a return of capital. They reduce the shareholder's basis in his or her stock. If such distributions exceed the shareholder's basis, the remainder is treated as gain from the sale of the stock. If the stock is a capital asset in the shareholder's hands, the gain is a capital gain.

EXAMPLE C4-1 ▶ On March 1 Gamma Corporation distributes $60,000 in cash to each of its two equal shareholders, Ellen and Bob. At the time of the distribution, Gamma's E&P is $80,000. Ellen's basis in her stock is $25,000 and Bob's basis in his stock is $10,000. Ellen and Bob each must recognize $40,000 (0.50 × $80,000) of dividend income. This portion of the distribution reduces Gamma's E&P to zero. The additional $20,000 that each one receives is treated as a capital gain or a return of capital as summarized in the table below.

	Ellen	Bob	Total
Distribution	$60,000	$60,000	$120,000
Dividend income[a]	(40,000)	(40,000)	(80,000)
Remaining distribution	$20,000	$20,000	$ 40,000
Return of capital[b]	(20,000)	(10,000)	(30,000)
Capital gain[c]	$—0—	$10,000	$ 10,000

[a]Smaller of E&P allocable to the distribution or the amount of the distribution.
[b]Smaller of remaining distribution to shareholder or his or her stock basis.
[c]Any amount received in excess of the shareholder's basis in his or her stock.

EARNINGS AND PROFITS (E&P)

TYPICAL MISCONCEPTION

Because E&P is such an important concept in many corporate transactions, one would assume that corporations know exactly what their E&P is. However, many corporations do not compute their E&P on a regular basis.

The term *E&P* is not specifically defined in the Code. Its meaning must be inferred from its function in judicial decisions, Treasury Regulations, and some rules provided in the Code regarding how certain transactions affect E&P.

The function of E&P is to provide a measure of the corporation's economic ability to pay dividends to shareholders. Distributions are considered to come from the corporation's E&P unless the corporation can show that it has no E&P. A corporation at the time it is formed, for example, has no E&P. Any payments made to shareholders by such a corporation are simply a return of the capital contributed by the shareholders until it reports E&P. However, if a corporation has $10,000 of E&P, the first $10,000 of cash or property distributed to its shareholders is treated as a dividend.

CURRENT EARNINGS AND PROFITS

E&P consists of two parts: current E&P and accumulated E&P. **Current E&P** is calculated annually as explained below. **Accumulated E&P** is the sum of the undistributed current E&P balances for all previous years reduced by the sum of all previous current E&P deficits and any distributions that have been made out of accumulated E&P. Distributions come first from current E&P and then from accumulated E&P if current E&P is insufficient.

EXAMPLE C4-2 ▶

Zeta Corporation is formed in 1994. Its current E&P (or current E&P deficit) and distributions for each year through 1997 are as follows:

Year	*Current E&P (Deficit)*	*Distributions*
1994	$(10,000)	—0—
1995	15,000	—0—
1996	18,000	$9,000
1997	8,000	—0—

The $9,000 distribution is made from 1996's current E&P. At the beginning of 1997, Zeta's accumulated E&P is $14,000 (− $10,000 + $15,000 + $18,000 − $9,000). At the beginning of 1998, Zeta's accumulated E&P is $22,000 ($14,000 + $8,000). ◀

OBJECTIVE 1

Explain how current E&P is calculated

COMPUTING CURRENT E&P. Current E&P is computed on an annual basis at the end of each year. The starting point for computing current E&P is the corporation's taxable income or net operating loss (NOL) for the year. Taxable income or the NOL must be adjusted to obtain the corporation's economic income or loss (current E&P) for the year. For example, federal income taxes are deducted from taxable income when determining E&P. Because these taxes must be paid to the U.S. government, they reduce the amount available to pay dividends to shareholders. On the other hand, tax-exempt

KEY POINT

Many of the adjustments to E&P (listed in Table C4-1) are recognition of cash outflows/inflows that don't affect taxable income but do affect the ability of the corporation to pay dividends.

▼ TABLE C4-1

Computation of Current E&P

Taxable income

Plus: Income excluded from taxable income:
- Tax-exempt interest income
- Life insurance proceeds where the corporation is the beneficiary
- Recoveries of bad debts and other deductions from which the corporation received no tax benefit
- Federal income tax refunds from prior years

Plus: Income deferred to a later year when computing taxable income:
- Deferred gain on installment sales is included in E&P in the year of sale

Plus or minus: Adjustments for items that must be recomputed:
- Income on long-term contracts must be based on percentage of completion method rather than completed contract method
- Depreciation on personalty and realty must be based on:
  - The straight-line method for property other than MACRS or ACRS property
  - A straight-line ACRS calculation with an extended recovery period for ACRS property
  - The alternative depreciation system for MACRS property
- Excess of percentage depletion claimed over cost depletion

Plus: Deductions not allowed in computing E&P:
- Dividends-received deduction
- NOL carryovers, charitable contribution carryovers, and capital loss carryovers used in the current year

Minus: Expenses and losses not deductible in computing taxable income:
- Federal income taxes
- Life insurance premiums where the corporation is the beneficiary
- Excess capital losses that are not deductible
- Excess charitable contributions that are not deductible
- Expenses related to production of tax-exempt income
- Nondeductible losses on sales to related parties
- Nondeductible penalties and fines
- Nondeductible political contributions and lobbying expenses

Current E&P (or E&P deficit)

income must be added to taxable income (or the NOL) because, even though it is not taxable, it increases the corporation's ability to pay dividends.

A partial listing of the adjustments that must be made is presented in Table C4-1. Some of the adjustments that must be made to taxable income to derive current E&P are explained below.[1]

INCOME EXCLUDED FROM TAXABLE INCOME. Although certain income is specifically excluded from taxable income, any income received by the corporation must be included in its E&P if it increases the corporation's ability to pay a dividend and is not

[1] The adjustments required are based on rules found in IRC Sec. 312 and the related regulations.

a contribution to capital. Thus, a corporation's current E&P includes both tax-exempt interest income and life insurance proceeds. Current E&P also includes any recovery of an item deducted in a previous year if the deduction did not result in a tax benefit to the corporation and therefore was excluded from taxable income.

EXAMPLE C4-3 ▶ Ace Corporation deducted $10,000 of bad debts in 1996. Because Ace Corporation had an NOL in 1996 that it was unable to carry back or forward, it received no tax benefit from the deduction. Ace Corporation recovers $8,000 of the amount due in 1997. Ace excludes the $8,000 from its gross income for 1997 because it received no tax benefit from the bad debt deduction in 1996. However, Ace must add the $8,000 to its taxable income when determining current E&P for 1997 because the NOL reduced current E&P in 1996. ◀

INCOME DEFERRED TO A LATER PERIOD. Gains and losses on property transactions are generally included in E&P in the same year they are recognized for tax purposes. For example, gain deferred in a like-kind exchange is deferred for E&P purposes as well.

EXAMPLE C4-4 ▶ Stone Corporation exchanges investment property that has a $12,000 basis and an $18,000 fair market value (FMV) for investment property worth $17,000 and $1,000 cash. Stone recognizes a $1,000 gain on the like-kind exchange—the amount of boot received. $5,000 of gain is deferred. The recognized gain is included in taxable income and in current E&P. The deferred gain is not included in taxable income or in current E&P. ◀

ADDITIONAL COMMENT

Installment sales and long-term contracts are two examples of how the government attempts to maximize the E&P in order to characterize distributions as dividends.

In the case of an installment sale, the entire gain on the sale must be included in current E&P in the year of the sale.[2] This rule applies to sales made by dealers and nondealers.

EXAMPLE C4-5 ▶ In the current year, Tally Corporation sells land that has a $12,000 basis and a $20,000 FMV to Rick, an unrelated individual. Rick makes a $5,000 down payment this year and will pay Tally an additional $5,000 in each of the next three years, plus interest at a rate acceptable to the IRS on the unpaid balance. Tally's realized gain is $8,000 ($20,000 − $12,000). Using the nondealer installment sale rules, Tally recognizes its gain on the sale using the installment method of accounting. This year, Tally recognizes $2,000 of gain [($8,000 ÷ $20,000) × $5,000] in computing taxable income. All $8,000 of Tally's realized gain must be included in current E&P. In computing current E&P for this year, Tally's taxable income must be increased by $6,000. ◀

SELF-STUDY QUESTION

In computing taxable income and E&P, different depreciation methods are often used. What happens when such assets are sold?

ANSWER

The taxpayer must calculate a gain/loss for taxable income and E&P purposes separately. This difference is an added complexity in making E&P calculations.

ADJUSTMENTS FOR ITEMS THAT MUST BE RECOMPUTED. Some deductions must be computed differently for E&P purposes than they are for taxable income purposes. Therefore, an adjustment must be made for the difference between the two computations.

- E&P must be computed using the percentage of completion method even if the corporation uses the completed contract method of accounting for tax purposes.[3]
- Depreciation must be recomputed using the alternative depreciation system of Sec. 168(g). Property expensed under Sec. 179 is expensed ratably over a five-year period starting with the month in which it is deductible for Sec. 179 purposes. Other personalty must be depreciated over the property's class life and using a half-year convention. Realty must be depreciated over a forty-year period for E&P purposes using the straight-line method and mid-month convention.[4]

[2] Sec. 312(n)(5).
[3] Sec. 312(n)(6).
[4] Sec. 312(k)(3).

EXAMPLE C4-6 ▶ In January 1994, Radon Corporation purchased equipment with a ten-year class life for $5,000. Radon expensed the entire cost of the equipment in 1994 under Sec. 179. Radon's depreciation deduction for E&P purposes is $1,000 ($5,000 ÷ 5) in every year from 1994 through 1998. ◀

ADDITIONAL COMMENT

Many corporations use retained earnings to measure the taxability of their dividend payments. Because retained earnings are based on financial accounting concepts, E&P may represent a different amount and may provide a different answer.

- Cost depletion must be used for E&P purposes even if percentage depletion is used when computing taxable income.
- Intangible drilling costs must be capitalized and amortized over sixty months for E&P purposes.

DEDUCTIONS NOT ALLOWED IN COMPUTING E&P. Some deductions claimed when computing taxable income are not allowed when computing current E&P.

- The dividends-received deduction is not permitted for E&P purposes because it does not reduce the corporation's ability to pay dividends. Therefore, it must be added back to taxable income to compute E&P.[5]
- NOL carryovers, charitable contribution carryovers, and capital loss carryovers that reduce taxable income for the current year cannot be deducted when determining E&P. These losses or excess deductions reduce E&P in the year they are incurred.
- Amortization of organizational expenses is not permitted as a deduction for E&P purposes.

EXAMPLE C4-7 ▶ Thames Corporation's taxable income is $50,000 after deducting a NOL carryover from two years ago of $10,000 and a $20,000 dividends-received deduction. Thames must add $30,000 to its taxable income to compute current E&P. The $10,000 NOL reduced E&P in the year it was incurred. ◀

EXPENSES AND LOSSES NOT DEDUCTIBLE IN COMPUTING TAXABLE INCOME. Some expenses and losses that are not deductible in computing taxable income are deductible when computing current E&P.

- Federal income taxes are not deductible when taxable income is computed. For E&P purposes, federal income taxes are deductible in the year they accrue if the corporation uses the accrual method of accounting and in the year they are paid if the corporation uses the cash method of accounting.

EXAMPLE C4-8 ▶ Perch Corporation, which uses the accrual method of accounting, has taxable income of $100,000 on which it owes $22,250 of federal income taxes. In computing its current E&P, it must reduce taxable income by $22,250. ◀

- Charitable contributions are deductible in full for E&P purposes without regard to the 10% limitation on such deductions. Thus, taxable income must be reduced by any charitable contributions that were disallowed because of the 10% limitation when current E&P is computed.

EXAMPLE C4-9 ▶ Dot Corporation has $25,000 of taxable income before any charitable contribution deduction. Dot contributed $10,000 to the Red Cross. Although Dot's contribution deduction is limited to $2,500 in computing taxable income because of the 10% of taxable income limitation on charitable contribution deductions, Dot deducts the entire $10,000 in computing current E&P. Therefore, $7,500 must be deducted from taxable income of $22,500 ($25,000 − $2,500) to compute current E&P. In a later year(s), when the $7,500 carryover is deducted in determining taxable income, it must be added to taxable income in arriving at current E&P. ◀

[5] *R. M. Weyerhaeuser*, 33 B.T.A. 594 (1935).

- Life insurance premiums paid on policies to insure the lives of key corporate personnel (net of any increase in the cash surrender value of the policy) are not deductible when taxable income is computed but are deductible when E&P is computed.
- Capital losses in excess of capital gains cannot be deducted when taxable income is computed but are deductible when computing current E&P.
- Nondeductible expenses related to the production of tax-exempt income (e.g., interest charges to borrow money to purchase tax-exempt securities) are deductible when computing E&P.
- Losses on sales to related parties that are disallowed under Sec. 267 are deductible when computing E&P.
- Nondeductible fines, penalties, and political contributions are deductible for E&P purposes.

KEY POINT

After reviewing some of the complex calculations needed to compute E&P, one can appreciate why many corporations do not make annual E&P calculations.

The adjustments listed in Table C4-1 and described above are only a partial list of the adjustments that must be made to taxable income in order to compute current E&P. The basic rule is that adjustments are made so that current E&P represents the corporation's economic ability to pay dividends out of its current earnings.

DISTINCTION BETWEEN CURRENT AND ACCUMULATED E&P

OBJECTIVE 2

Explain the difference between current and accumulated E&P

A distinction must be made between current and accumulated E&P. Corporate distributions are deemed to come from current E&P first and then from accumulated E&P only if current E&P is insufficient.[6] If current E&P is sufficient to cover all distributions made during the year, each distribution is treated as a taxable dividend. This rule applies even if there is a deficit in accumulated E&P. Current E&P is computed on the last day of the tax year. No reduction is made for distributions made during the year.

EXAMPLE C4-10 ▶

At the beginning of the current year, Water Corporation has a $30,000 accumulated E&P deficit. For the year, Water reports current E&P of $15,000. Water distributes $10,000 to its shareholders during the current year. The $10,000 distribution is a taxable dividend to the shareholders because it comes from current E&P. At the beginning of the next tax year, Water has an accumulated E&P deficit of $25,000 (− $30,000 E&P deficit + $5,000 undistributed current E&P). ◀

KEY POINT

Distributions are deemed to come from current E&P first. If current E&P is not adequate, then accumulated E&P is used.

KEY POINT

If multiple distributions are made, current E&P is allocated pro rata and accumulated E&P is allocated chronologically.

If distributions made during the year exceed current E&P, current E&P is allocated to those distributions on a pro rata basis regardless of when during the year the distributions were made. Distributions in excess of current E&P come from accumulated E&P (if any) in chronological order. Distributions in excess of current and accumulated E&P are a return of capital and reduce the shareholder's basis on a dollar-for-dollar basis. However, these distributions cannot create an E&P deficit. These rules are important if the stock changes hands during the year and total E&P is insufficient to cover all distributions.

EXAMPLE C4-11 ▶

At the beginning of the current year, Cole Corporation has $20,000 of accumulated E&P. For the current year, Cole's current E&P is $30,000. On April 10, Cole distributes $20,000 to Bob, its sole shareholder. On July 15, Cole distributes an additional $24,000 to Bob. On August 1, Bob sells all of his Cole stock to Lynn. On September 15, Cole distributes $36,000 to Lynn. Cole's current and accumulated E&P must be allocated to the three distributions made during the year as follows:

[6] The distinction between current and accumulated E&P is explained in Reg. Sec. 1.316-2.

Date	Distribution Amount	Current E&P	Accumulated E&P	Dividend Income	Return of Capital
April 10	$20,000	$ 7,500	$12,500	$20,000	$—0—
July 15	24,000	9,000	7,500	16,500	7,500
September 15	36,000	13,500	—0—	13,500	22,500
Total	$80,000	$30,000	$20,000	$50,000	$30,000

The current E&P allocated to the April 10 distribution is calculated as follows:

$$\$30{,}000 \text{ (Current E\&P)} \times \frac{\$20{,}000 \text{ (April 10 distribution)}}{\$80{,}000 \text{ (Total distributions)}}$$

Note that the total amount of dividends paid by Cole equals $50,000, the sum of $30,000 of current E&P and $20,000 of accumulated E&P. Current E&P is allocated to all three distributions on a pro rata basis, whereas accumulated E&P is allocated first to the April 10 distribution ($12,500). The remaining accumulated E&P is allocated to the July 15 distribution, so that none is available to allocate to the September 15 distribution. Thus, Bob's dividend income from Cole is $36,500 ($20,000 + $16,500). He also has a $7,500 return of capital payment that reduces the basis for his stock. Lynn's dividend income from Cole is $13,500. She also has a $22,500 return of capital payment that reduces the basis for her stock. Note that Bob cannot determine his gain on the stock sale until after the end of the year. He must wait until he knows how much of the two distributions he received reduced the basis for his stock. ◀

If there is a current E&P deficit and an accumulated E&P deficit, none of the distributions are treated as dividends. Instead, all distributions are a return of capital until the basis of a shareholder's stock is reduced to zero. Any additional amounts received are taxable as a capital gain.

EXAMPLE C4-12 ▶ At the beginning of the current year, Rose Corporation has a $15,000 accumulated E&P deficit. Rose's current E&P deficit is $20,000. Rose distributes $10,000 on July 1. The distribution is not a dividend, but a return of capital and/or a capital gain for amounts in excess of the shareholder's basis in his stock. Rose's accumulated E&P deficit at January 1 of next year is $35,000 because the distribution was in excess of both current and accumulated E&P and represents a return of capital or capital gain. ◀

SELF-STUDY QUESTION

When is E&P measured for purposes of determining whether a distribution is a dividend?

ANSWER

Usually at year-end. However, if a current deficit exists, the E&P available for measuring dividend income is determined at the distribution date.

If there is a current E&P deficit and a positive accumulated E&P balance, the two accounts must be netted at the time of the distribution to determine the amount of any distribution that comes from E&P.[7] The deficit in current E&P that has been accrued up through the day before the distribution reduces the accumulated E&P balance on that date. If the balance remaining after the reduction is made is positive, the distribution is a dividend to the extent of the lesser of the distribution amount or the E&P balance. If the E&P balance is zero or negative, the distribution is a return of capital. If the actual deficit in current E&P to the date of distribution cannot be determined, the current E&P deficit is prorated on a daily basis to the day before the distribution date.

EXAMPLE C4-13 ▶ Assume the same facts as in Example C4-12 except that Rose Corporation instead has a $15,000 accumulated E&P balance. The current E&P deficit accrues on a daily basis unless information indicates otherwise. The January 1 through June 30 deficit is $9,918 [(181/365) × $20,000]. Rose Corporation has a $5,082 ($15,000 − $9,918) E&P balance, from which the $10,000 distribution is made. $5,082 of the distribution is taxable as a dividend and $4,918 is

[7] Reg. Sec. 1.316-2(b).

a return of capital and/or a capital gain for amounts in excess of the shareholder's basis in his stock.

STOP & THINK

Question: Why is it necessary to keep separate balances for current and accumulated E&P?

Solution: If the total current and accumulated E&P is less than the total distributions made to the shareholders, E&P must be allocated to all distributions made during the year to determine the amount of each distribution that is a dividend. When no change in the shareholder's stock ownership occurs during the year and all distributions are proportional to stock ownership, an E&P allocation is needed only to track each shareholder's stock basis. Tracking E&P to individual distributions is necessary to determine the taxability of a particular distribution when a change in a shareholder's stock ownership occurs, because current E&P is allocated on a pro rata basis and accumulated E&P is allocated chronologically. Therefore, distributions made early in a tax year may be more heavily taxed than distributions made later in the year. On the other hand, current E&P deficits offset accumulated E&P balances. In such a situation, distributions made later in a tax year may be less heavily taxed than are distributions made earlier in the year.

PROPERTY DISTRIBUTIONS

OBJECTIVE 3

Determine the tax consequences of property distributions

CONSEQUENCES OF PROPERTY DISTRIBUTIONS TO THE SHAREHOLDERS

The term *property* is defined by Sec. 317(a) as money, securities, and any other property except stock in the corporation making the distribution (or rights to acquire such stock). When a property distribution is made to shareholders, the following three questions must be answered:

- What is the amount of the distribution?
- To what extent is the amount distributed a dividend to the shareholder?
- What is the basis of the property to the shareholder, and when does its holding period begin?

For cash distributions, these questions are easy to answer. The distribution amount is the amount of cash distributed. This distribution is a dividend to the extent that it comes from the corporation's current and accumulated E&P, and the E&P account is reduced by the cash dividend amount. The shareholder's basis in the cash received is its face amount. The distributing corporation does not recognize any gain on the distribution of cash.

When property such as land or inventory is distributed to a shareholder, these questions are more difficult to answer. Neither the amount of the distribution nor the basis of the property to the shareholder are immediately apparent. The corporation is required to recognize gain (but not loss) on the distribution, and the impact of the distribution on the corporation's E&P and the taxability of the distribution must be determined. The following sections explain the rules that govern the answers to these questions.

KEY POINT

The amount of the distribution is measured by the FMV of the property less liabilities assumed (but not below zero) because this represents the real economic value received by the shareholder.

When property is distributed to a shareholder, the amount of the distribution is the FMV of the property distributed.[8] The value is determined on the date of the distribution. The amount of any liability assumed by the shareholder in connection with

[8] Sec. 301(b).

the distribution, or to which the distributed property is subject, reduces the distribution amount. However, the distribution amount cannot be reduced below zero. The distribution amount is a dividend to the shareholder to the extent of the distributing corporation's E&P.

The shareholder's basis in any property received is the property's FMV. The basis is not reduced by any liabilities assumed by the shareholder or to which the property is subject.[9] The holding period of the property begins on the day after the distribution date. It does not include the holding period of the distributing corporation.

EXAMPLE C4-14 ▶

Post Corporation has $100,000 of current and accumulated E&P. On March 1, Post distributes land with a $60,000 FMV and a $35,000 adjusted basis to Meg, its sole shareholder. The land is subject to a $10,000 liability, which Meg assumes. The distribution amount is $50,000 ($60,000 – $10,000), all of which is a dividend to Meg because it does not exceed Post's E&P balance. Meg's basis in the property is $60,000, its FMV, and her holding period for the property begins on March 2. ◀

STOP & THINK

Question: Why do liabilities reduce the amount of income reported when a distribution is made to a shareholder, but do not reduce the shareholder's adjusted basis for the property?

Solution: The amount of a distribution to a shareholder is the property's FMV on the distribution date. In Example C4-14, Meg receives land worth $60,000, and also acquires the $10,000 debt which she is obligated to pay. Therefore, the value of the distribution to Meg is the net amount that she receives, or $50,000 ($60,000 – $10,000). The adjusted basis of the land to Meg is $60,000, its FMV. This rule is the same as if Meg purchased the land for $60,000, but financed the purchase by borrowing $10,000. The basis of the land to Meg would still be its $60,000 FMV.

CONSEQUENCES OF PROPERTY DISTRIBUTIONS TO THE DISTRIBUTING CORPORATION

KEY POINT

Property distributions may trigger income at both the shareholder and the distributing corporation level. This is another example of the double taxation that exists in our corporate tax system.

Two questions must be answered with respect to a corporation that distributes property:

- What are the amount and character of the gain or loss that the distributing corporation must recognize on the distribution?
- What effect does the distribution have on the corporation's E&P?

CORPORATE GAIN OR LOSS ON PROPERTY DISTRIBUTIONS. A corporation must recognize gain when it distributes property that has appreciated in value, as though the corporation had sold the property for its FMV. However, a corporation does not recognize any loss when it makes a nonliquidating distribution of property even if a sale of the property would have yielded a loss.[10]

EXAMPLE C4-15 ▶

Silver Corporation distributes land (a capital asset) worth $60,000 to Mark, a shareholder. The land has a $20,000 adjusted basis to Silver. Silver must recognize a $40,000 ($60,000 – $20,000) capital gain, as though Silver had sold the property. If the land instead has a $12,000 FMV, Silver does not recognize any loss on the distribution. ◀

SELF-STUDY QUESTION

How is the corporate gain determined if the property being distributed is subject to a liability in excess of the FMV of the property?

If the distributed property is subject to a liability or the shareholder assumes a liability in connection with the distribution, the property's FMV for purposes of determining gain on the distribution is deemed to be no less than the amount of the liability.[11]

[9] Sec. 301(d).
[10] Sec. 311(a).
[11] Sec. 311(b)(2).

EXAMPLE C4-16 ▶

ANSWER

If property is subject to a liability in excess of its FMV, the property is deemed sold at the liability amount because this debt relief represents the economic benefit recognized by the corporation on the distribution.

Assume the same facts as in Example C4-15, except that the land's FMV is instead $25,000 and the land is subject to a $35,000 mortgage. The land's FMV for gain recognition purposes is $35,000 because it cannot be less than the amount of the liability. Thus, Silver Corporation's gain is $15,000 ($35,000 − $20,000), the amount by which the land's deemed FMV exceeds its basis. Mark's basis in the land is also $35,000.[12] ◀

EFFECT OF PROPERTY DISTRIBUTIONS ON THE DISTRIBUTING CORPORATION'S E&P. Distributions have two effects on E&P:

- When a corporation distributes appreciated property to its shareholders, it must recognize gain as though it had sold the property. This results in an increase in E&P equal to the appreciation in value.[13]
- A corporation's E&P is reduced by the amount of money distributed plus the greater of the FMV or the adjusted basis of any nonmoney property distributed, minus any liabilities that the property is subject to or that are assumed by a shareholder in connection with the distribution, and the income taxes incurred on the gain recognized.[14]

EXAMPLE C4-17 ▶

Brass Corporation distributes property with a $25,000 adjusted basis and a $40,000 FMV to Joan, a shareholder. The property is subject to a $12,000 mortgage, which Joan assumes. Brass must recognize a $15,000 ($40,000 − $25,000) gain on the distribution. Brass's E&P is increased by the $15,000 gain and is reduced by $28,000 ($40,000 FMV − $12,000 liability). Thus, E&P is reduced by a net of $13,000 plus the amount of income taxes paid or accrued by Brass on the $15,000 gain. ◀

A special rule applies when a corporation distributes its own obligation (e.g., its notes, bonds, or debentures) to a shareholder. In such case, the distributing corporation's E&P is reduced by the principal amount of the obligation distributed.[15]

Topic Review C4-1 presents a summary of the tax consequences of a nonliquidating distribution to the shareholders and the distributing corporation.

CONSTRUCTIVE DIVIDENDS

KEY POINT

In general, taxpayers are most vulnerable to the assertion of a constructive dividend in a closely held corporation context.

A **constructive dividend** (or undeclared distribution) is an indirect payment made to a shareholder without the benefit of a formal declaration. Ordinarily, a corporate dividend payment is formally declared by the board of directors and is paid in cash or property on a specified date. A formal declaration is not required, however. Constructive dividends may be treated as dividends for income tax purposes even though they have not been formally authorized by the corporation's board of directors. It is not even necessary that the distribution be pro rata. Any economic benefit provided by a corporation to a shareholder may be treated as a constructive dividend to the shareholder.

Constructive dividends are most likely to arise in the context of a closely held corporation where the shareholders (or relatives of shareholders) and management groups overlap. In such situations, the dealings between the corporation and its shareholders are likely to be less structured and subject to less review than they would be in a publicly held corporation. However, constructive dividends can arise in a publicly held corporation as well.

---

[12] The appropriate basis for the shareholder's land has been questioned. Some tax commentators say that the Sec. 311(b)(2) liability rule applies only for gain recognition purposes. Therefore, the basis should be the land's actual FMV, or $25,000. Some tax commentators take the position we do in the example that Sec. 311(b)(2) applies for both gain recognition and basis purposes. Therefore, the land's basis is $35,000.

[13] Sec. 312(b). The gain recognized for E&P and taxable income purposes may be markedly different. As illustrated earlier, when depreciable personalty or realty is sold, substantially different adjusted basis amounts exist for E&P and taxable income purposes due to the different depreciation methods that have been used. The gain recognized for taxable income purposes, of course, affects the amount of federal income taxes owed at year-end.

[14] Secs. 312(a) and (c).

[15] Sec. 312(a)(2).

Topic Review C4-1

Tax Consequences of a Nonliquidating Distribution

Consequences to Shareholders:

1. The amount of a distribution is the amount of money received plus the FMV of any nonmoney property received reduced by any liabilities assumed or acquired by the shareholder.
2. The distribution is a dividend to the extent of the distributing corporation's current and accumulated E&P. Any excess distribution is a return of capital or a gain from the sale or exchange of the stock.
3. The shareholder's basis in the property received is its FMV.
4. The shareholder's holding period begins on the day after the distribution date.

Consequences to Distributing Corporation:

1. A corporation must recognize gain when it distributes appreciated property as though the property had been sold for its FMV immediately before the distribution.
2. For gain recognition purposes, a property's FMV is deemed to be at least equal to any liability to which the property is subject or that the shareholder assumes in connection with the distribution.
3. A corporation does not recognize a loss when it distributes property to its shareholders.
4. A corporation's E&P is increased by any gain (net of taxes) recognized on a distribution of appreciated property.
5. A corporation's E&P is reduced by (a) the amount of money distributed plus (b) the greater of the FMV or adjusted basis of any nonmoney property distributed, minus (c) any liabilities that the property is subject to or that are assumed by the shareholder in connection with the distribution.

INTENTIONAL EFFORTS TO AVOID DIVIDEND TREATMENT. Constructive dividends may arise from intentional attempts to bail out a corporation's E&P without subjecting it to taxation at the shareholder level or to obtain a deduction at the corporate level for distributions to shareholders that should not be deductible. If a corporation has sufficient E&P, dividend distributions are fully taxable to the shareholder, but are not deductible by the distributing corporation. For example, shareholders may try to disguise a dividend as a salary payment. If successful, the payment is taxable to the shareholder-employee, and is deductible by the distributing corporation as long as the amount is reasonable. Shareholders also may try to disguise a dividend as a loan to the shareholder. If successful, the payment is neither deductible by the corporation nor taxable to the shareholder. If the IRS reclassifies either payment as a dividend, it is taxable to the shareholder and nondeductible by the distributing corporation.

ETHICAL POINT

A CPA should always be an advocate for his or her client if the question of whether a constructive dividend has been paid is in doubt (i.e., the facts and the law are sufficiently gray and the taxpayer's position has reasonable support).

UNINTENTIONAL CONSTRUCTIVE DIVIDENDS. Some constructive dividends are unintentional. Shareholders may not realize that the benefits they receive from the corporation in which they own stock are actually taxable dividends until the transactions are examined by a tax consultant or by the IRS. A transaction that is found to be a dividend rather than a salary payment, loan, and so on will be recast as a dividend. Appropriate adjustments must then be made to the corporation's and shareholder's books. This may mean an increase in the shareholder's taxable income (e.g., because the distribution is a dividend rather than a loan) or an increase in the distributing corporation's taxable income (i.e., because of reduced deductions). Transactions most likely to be recast and treated as dividends are summarized below.

ADDITIONAL COMMENT

The government requires that when loans exist between a corporation and its shareholders, the loans must bear a reasonable interest rate. If a "below-market" interest rate loan exists, the IRS will impute a reasonable rate of interest (Sec. 7872).

LOANS TO SHAREHOLDERS. Loans to shareholders may be considered disguised dividends unless they are bona fide loans. Whether a loan is considered as bona fide ordinarily depends on the shareholder's intent when the loan is made. To prove that the loan is bona fide (and to avoid having the loan treated as a dividend), the evidence must show that the shareholder intends to repay the loan. Evidence of an intent to repay includes

- Recording the loan on the corporate books
- Evidencing the loan by a written note
- Charging a reasonable rate of interest
- Scheduling regular payments of principal and interest

Evidence that the loan is *not* bona fide includes

- Maintaining a continuing "open account" loan to the shareholder (allowing the shareholder to borrow from the corporation whenever money is required and with no fixed schedule for repayment)
- Failing to charge interest on the loan
- Failing to enforce the payment of interest and principal
- Making advances in proportion to stockholdings
- Making advances to a controlling shareholder

If the corporation lends money to a shareholder and then, after a period of time, cancels the loan, the amount cancelled is treated as a dividend distribution under Sec. 301. If inadequate interest is charged, interest is imputed on the loan. The corporation will report interest income from the loan and the shareholder may have a deduction for interest deemed paid. The imputed interest is treated as a dividend paid to the shareholder, thereby resulting in no offsetting deduction for the corporation.

SELF-STUDY QUESTION

Because both compensation and dividends are taxable to a shareholder-employee, why is there such concern regarding excessive compensation?

ANSWER

The concern is not at the shareholder-employee level, but rather at the paying corporation level. Compensation is deductible to the paying corporation, whereas dividend distributions are not deductible. Excess compensation paid to an individual who does not own stock in the corporation causes a loss of the corporate deduction, but generally no dividend income is created.

EXCESSIVE COMPENSATION PAID TO SHAREHOLDER-EMPLOYEES. Shareholders may receive compensation for services in the form of salary, bonus, or fringe benefits. Such compensation payments are deductible by the distributing corporation as long as they are ordinary and necessary expenses and are reasonable in amount. However, if they are found to be excessive, the excess amounts may be considered constructive dividends to the shareholders. In such cases, the payments are not deductible by the corporation but they are still taxable to the shareholder as dividend income. There are no hard and fast rules as to when compensation is excessive. As a result, there has been much controversy and many court cases in this area.

Reasonableness of compensation paid must be determined on a case-by-case basis. Some factors considered important in determining whether compensation is reasonable were cited in *Mayson Manufacturing Co.*, a 1949 Sixth Circuit Court of Appeals case.[16] These factors include the following:

- The employee's qualifications
- The nature, extent, and scope of the employee's work
- The size of the business
- The complexities of the business
- A comparison of the salaries paid with the gross and net income of the corporation
- The prevailing general economic conditions

[16] *Mayson Manufacturing Co. v. CIR*, 38 AFTR 1028, 49-2 USTC ¶9467 (6th Cir., 1949).

- Whether the corporation has paid any dividends
- Compensation for comparable positions in comparable concerns
- The salary policy of the corporation to all of its employees
- The amount of compensation paid to the particular employee in previous years
- The amount of compensation voted by the board of directors

EXCESSIVE COMPENSATION PAID TO SHAREHOLDERS FOR THE USE OF SHAREHOLDER PROPERTY. Like salary payments, payments to shareholders for the use of property (i.e., rents, interest, and royalties) are deductible by a corporation under Sec. 162(a) if they are ordinary, necessary, and reasonable in amount. To the extent they exceed the amounts that would have been paid to an unrelated party, the excess amount may be recast as a constructive dividend to the shareholder.

CORPORATE PAYMENTS FOR THE SHAREHOLDER'S BENEFIT. If a corporation pays a personal obligation of a shareholder, the amount of the payment may be treated as a constructive dividend to the shareholder. Such payments may include payment by the corporation of the shareholder's personal debt obligations, expenses in connection with the shareholder's personal residence, expenses incurred for the improvement of the shareholder's land and property, and debt obligations personally guaranteed by the shareholder.

If a corporate expenditure is disallowed as a deduction by the corporation, it may be a constructive dividend to the shareholder if it provides the shareholder with an economic benefit. Examples of such constructive dividends are unsubstantiated travel and entertainment expenses, club dues, and automobile, airplane, and yacht expenses related to the shareholder-employee's personal use of the property.

BARGAIN PURCHASE OF CORPORATE PROPERTY. If a shareholder is allowed to purchase corporate property at a price less than the property's FMV, the discount from the FMV may be a constructive dividend to the shareholder.

SHAREHOLDER USE OF CORPORATE PROPERTY. If a shareholder is allowed to use corporate property (such as a hunting lodge, yacht, or airplane) without paying adequate compensation to the corporation, the FMV of such use (minus any amounts paid) may be a constructive dividend to the shareholder.

STOCK DIVIDENDS AND STOCK RIGHTS

OBJECTIVE 4

Determine the tax consequences of stock dividends and distributions of stock rights

In 1919, the Supreme Court ruled in *Eisner v. Macomber* that a stock dividend was not income to the shareholder because it took nothing from the property of the corporation and added nothing to the property of the shareholder.[17] Subsequently, the Revenue Act of 1921 provided that stock dividends are nontaxable. This general rule still applies today, but some exceptions have been enacted to prevent perceived abuses.

Code Sec. 305(a) provides, "Except as otherwise provided in this section, gross income does not include the amount of any distribution of the stock of a corporation made by such a corporation to its shareholders with respect to its stock." Thus, a distribution of additional common stock that is made with respect to a shareholder's common stock is a tax-free stock dividend. However, to circumvent the tax-avoidance

[17] *Eisner v. Myrtle H. Macomber*, 3 AFTR 3020, 1 USTC ¶32 (USSC, 1919).

schemes fostered by the tax-free stock dividend rule, Sec. 305(b) provides for some exceptions.

As a general rule, whenever a stock dividend changes or has the potential to change the shareholders' proportionate interests in the distributing corporation, the distribution is taxable. Taxable distributions include those where

- The shareholder can elect to receive either stock of the distributing corporation or other property (e.g., money).
- Some shareholders receive property and other shareholders receive an increase in their proportionate interests in the distributing corporation's assets or E&P.
- Some holders of common stock receive preferred stock and others receive additional common stock.
- The distribution is on preferred stock unless it is merely a change in the conversion ratio of convertible preferred stock made only to reflect a stock dividend or stock split.
- Convertible preferred stock is distributed unless it can be established that there will not be a disproportionate effect.

The following example illustrates how these exceptions work.

TYPICAL MISCONCEPTION

Stock dividends generally are nontaxable as long as a shareholder's proportionate interests in the corporation do not increase. If a shareholder's stock interest increases, Sec. 305(b) causes the dividend to be taxable.

EXAMPLE C4-18 ▶ Peach Corporation has $100,000 of current E&P. Two shareholders, Al and Beth, each own 100 of the 200 outstanding shares of Peach stock. Al has a high marginal tax rate and does not want any additional income in the current year. Beth has a low marginal tax rate and needs additional cash. Peach Corporation declares a dividend payable in stock or money. Each taxpayer can receive one share of Peach stock (valued at $100) or $100 in money for each share of Peach stock already owned. Al, who elects to receive stock, receives 100 additional shares of Peach stock. Beth, who elects to receive money, receives $10,000. Beth's distribution is taxable as a dividend. Absent any exceptions to Sec. 305, Al would have a nontaxable stock dividend because he chose to receive Peach stock. However, Al has received something of value. After the distribution, he owns two-thirds of the outstanding shares of Peach stock, whereas before the distribution he owned only one-half of the Peach stock. One of the exceptions to the general rule of Sec. 305(a) applies here, so that Al has a taxable stock dividend equal to the value of the additional shares he received. Even if both shareholders were to elect to receive stock, they have a taxable dividend because they had the option to receive cash. ◀

TAX-FREE STOCK DIVIDENDS

If a **stock dividend** is nontaxable, the basis of the stock with respect to which the distribution was made must be allocated between the old and the new shares in proportion to their relative FMVs on the distribution date.[18] The holding period of the new shares includes the holding period of the old shares.[19]

If the old shares and the new shares are identical, the basis of each share is determined by dividing the basis of the old shares by the total number of shares held by the shareholder after the distribution.

SELF-STUDY QUESTION

What (if any) tax issues exist when a stock dividend is tax free?

ANSWER

The basis of the stock received must be determined. A portion of the basis of the old stock is allocated to the new stock received in the distribution.

EXAMPLE C4-19 ▶ Barbara owns 1,000 shares of Axle Corporation common stock with a $66,000 basis, or $66 per share. Barbara receives a nontaxable 10% common stock dividend and now owns 1,100 shares of common stock. The basis for each share of common stock is now $60 ($66,000 ÷ 1,100). ◀

---

[18] Sec. 307(a) and Reg. Secs. 1.307-1 and -2.

[19] Sec. 1223(5).

If the old shares and the new shares are not identical, the allocation of the old shares' basis is based on the relative FMVs of the old and the new shares.

EXAMPLE C4-20 ▶ Mark owns 1,000 shares of Axle Corporation common stock with a $60,000 basis. Mark receives a nontaxable stock dividend payable in preferred stock. At the time of the distribution, the common stock has a $90,000 FMV ($90 × 1,000 shares) and the preferred stock has a $10,000 FMV ($200 × 50 shares). After the distribution Mark owns 50 shares of preferred stock with a basis of $6,000 [($10,000 ÷ $100,000) × $60,000]. Thus, $6,000 of the basis of the common stock is allocated to the preferred stock, and the basis of the common stock is reduced from $60,000 to $54,000. ◀

REAL WORD EXAMPLE

Tracking the effects of nontaxable dividends, stock splits, stock dividends, and stock rights distributions on the basis of a stock investment can be difficult and time consuming. A number of publishers offer reporters (such as CCH's *Capital Changes Reporter*) that provide a complete history of these four types of events for publicly-traded companies. These reporters greatly simplify the making of stock basis calculations.

TAX-FREE STOCK RIGHTS

A distribution of **stock rights** is tax-free under Sec. 305 unless it changes, or has the potential to change, the shareholders' proportionate interests in the distributing corporation. The same exceptions to tax-free treatment for stock dividends enumerated in Sec. 305(b) also apply to distributions of stock rights.

If the value of the stock rights is less than 15% of the value of the stock with respect to which the rights were distributed (i.e., the underlying stock), the basis of the rights is zero unless the shareholder elects to allocate basis to those rights.[20] If the taxpayer plans to sell the rights, it might be desirable to allocate basis to the rights so as to minimize the amount of gain recognized on the sale. The election to allocate basis to the rights must be made in the form of a statement attached to the shareholder's return for the year in which the rights are received. The allocation is based on the relative FMVs of the stock and the stock rights. The holding period for the rights includes the holding period for the underlying stock.[21]

EXAMPLE C4-21 ▶ Linda owns 100 shares of Yale Corporation common stock with a $27,000 basis and a $50,000 FMV. Linda receives 100 nontaxable stock rights with a $4,000 FMV. Because the FMV of the stock rights is less than 15% of the FMV of the stock (0.15 × $50,000 = $7,500), the basis of the stock rights is zero unless Linda elects to make an allocation. Should Linda elect to allocate the $27,000 basis of the Yale common stock between the stock and the stock rights, the basis of the rights is $2,000 [($4,000 ÷ $54,000) × $27,000] and the basis of the stock is $25,000 ($27,000 − $2,000). ◀

If the value of the stock rights is 15% or more of the value of the underlying stock, the shareholder must allocate the basis of the underlying stock between the stock and the stock rights.

EXAMPLE C4-22 ▶ Kay owns 100 shares of Minor common stock with a $14,000 basis and a $30,000 FMV. Kay receives 100 stock rights with a total FMV of $5,000. Because the FMV of the stock rights is at least 15% of the stock's FMV (0.15 × $30,000 = $4,500), the $14,000 basis must be allocated between the stock rights and the stock. The basis of the stock rights is $2,000 [($5,000 ÷ $35,000) × $14,000] and the basis of the stock is $12,000 ($14,000 − $2,000). ◀

TYPICAL MISCONCEPTION

Taxpayers often get confused about what happens to a stock right. A stock right may be sold or exercised, which means the actual stock is acquired. If the rights are not sold or exercised, they will eventually lapse.

If the stock rights are sold, gain or loss is measured by subtracting the allocated basis of the rights (if any) from the sale price. If the rights lapse, the allocated basis is added back to the basis of the underlying stock. If the rights are exercised, the basis allocated to the rights is added to the basis of the stock purchased with those rights.[22] The holding period for any stock acquired with the rights begins on the exercise date.[23]

EXAMPLE C4-23 ▶ Jeff receives 10 stock rights in a nontaxable distribution. No basis is allocated to the stock rights. With each stock right Jeff may acquire one share of Jackson stock for $20. If Jeff

[20] Sec. 307(b)(1).

[21] Sec. 1223(5).

exercises all 10 stock rights, the new Jackson stock acquired has a $200 (10 rights × $20) basis. If instead the 10 rights are sold for $30 each, Jeff has a recognized gain of $300 [($30 × 10 rights) − 0 basis] on the sale. If the rights are permitted to lapse, no loss can be claimed by Jeff. ◀

ADDITIONAL COMMENT

Note that for financial accounting purposes, stock dividends reduce retained earnings. However, for tax purposes, nontaxable stock dividends have no effect on a corporation's E&P.

EFFECT OF NONTAXABLE STOCK DIVIDENDS ON THE DISTRIBUTING CORPORATION

Nontaxable distributions of stock and stock rights have no effect on the distributing corporation. The corporation does not recognize any gain or loss on the distribution, nor does any reduction in its E&P occur.[24]

TAXABLE STOCK DIVIDENDS AND STOCK RIGHTS

If a distribution of stock or stock rights is taxable, the distribution amount equals the FMV of the stock or stock rights on the distribution date. The distribution is treated the same as any other property distribution. It is a dividend to the extent it is made out of the distributing corporation's E&P. The basis of the stock or stock rights to the recipient shareholder is its FMV.[25] The holding period of the stock or stock rights begins on the day after the distribution date. No adjustment is made to the basis of the underlying stock with respect to which the distribution was made. The distributing corporation does not recognize any gain or loss on the distribution.[26] The corporation reduces its E&P by the FMV of the stock or stock rights on the distribution date.

STOCK REDEMPTIONS

OBJECTIVE 5

Distinguish between a stock redemption treated as a sale and one treated as a dividend

A **stock redemption** is defined as the acquisition by a corporation of its own stock in exchange for property. The property exchanged may be money, securities, or any other property that the corporation wants to use in order to acquire its own stock.[27] The corporation may cancel the acquired stock, retire it, or hold it as treasury stock.

There are many reasons for a stock redemption:

- A shareholder may want to withdraw from a corporation and sell his or her stock. In such a case, the shareholder may prefer that the corporation, rather than an outsider, purchase the stock so that the remaining shareholders (who may be family members) retain complete control and ownership of the corporation after his or her withdrawal.
- A shareholder may be required to sell the stock back to the corporation by the terms of an agreement that he or she has entered into with the corporation.
- A shareholder may want to sell some stock to reduce his or her ownership in a corporation, but may be unwilling or unable to sell that stock to outsiders. There may be no market for the shares or there may be restrictions on sales to outsiders.
- A shareholder may want to withdraw some assets from a corporation before a sale of the business. A potential purchaser of the business may not be interested in acquiring all the assets of the business or able to pay the full value for the stock. A withdrawal of some assets by the seller in exchange for some of the stock allows the purchaser to acquire the remaining stock and business assets for a lower total price.

[22] Reg. Sec. 1.307-1(b).
[23] Sec. 1223(6).
[24] Secs. 311(a) and 312(d).
[25] Reg. Sec. 1.301-1(h)(2)(i).
[26] Sec. 311(a). Gain may be recognized when the shareholder can elect to receive either appreciated property or stock or stock rights of the distributing corporation.
[27] Sec. 317.

- After the death of a major shareholder, a corporation may have an agreement to purchase the decedent's stock from either the estate or a beneficiary so that they will have sufficient funds to pay estate and inheritance taxes and funeral and administrative expenses.
- Management may believe that its stock is selling at a low price and that the best use for the corporation's available cash would be to acquire the corporation's own stock on the open market.

Whatever the reason for the redemption, the shareholder must answer the following questions:

- What are the amount and character of the income, gain, or loss recognized as a result of the stock redemption?
- What basis does the shareholder take in any property received in redemption of his or her stock?
- When does the holding period for the property received begin?
- What basis does the shareholder take for any stock of the distributing corporation that he or she holds after the redemption?

The distributing corporation must answer the following questions:

- What are the amount and character of the gain or loss that the distributing corporation must recognize when property is used to redeem its stock?
- What effect does the redemption have on the corporation's E&P?[28]

EFFECT OF THE REDEMPTION ON THE SHAREHOLDER

KEY POINT

As far as a shareholder is concerned, the basic issue in a stock redemption is whether the redemption is treated as a dividend or a sale.

The general rule when a shareholder sells or exchanges stock in a corporation is that any gain or loss on the transaction is treated as a capital gain or loss. In some cases, a redemption is treated the same as any other sale or exchange of stock. In other cases, the entire amount received by a shareholder in exchange for stock is treated as a dividend. The reason for this difference is that some redemptions more closely resemble a sale of stock to a third party, whereas others are essentially equivalent to a dividend. The following two examples illustrate the difference between a redemption that is treated as a dividend distribution and a redemption that is treated as a sale or exchange.

EXAMPLE C4-24 ▶

John owns all 100 outstanding shares of Tango Corporation stock. John's basis for his stock is $50,000. Tango has E&P of $100,000. If Tango redeems 25 of John's shares for $85,000, John still owns all of the Tango stock. Because John's ownership of Tango Corporation is not affected by the redemption, the redemption is equivalent to a dividend and John is deemed to have received a $85,000 dividend. ◀

EXAMPLE C4-25 ▶

Carol has owned three of the 1,000 outstanding shares of Water Corporation's stock for two years. Her basis in the stock is $1,000. Water Corporation has E&P of $100,000. If Water redeems all three of Carol's shares for $5,000, Carol has a $4,000 ($5,000 − $1,000) capital gain. She is in essentially the same position as though she had sold the stock to a third party. She has received $5,000 for her stock and has no further ownership interest in Water Corporation. This redemption is treated the same as any other sale or exchange because it terminates her interest in the corporation. It is not equivalent to a dividend. ◀

[28] The stock redemption discussion is for C corporation stock. Different rules apply to S corporation stock that is redeemed.

Example C4-24 is an extreme case that should clearly be treated as a dividend to the shareholder. Example C4-25 is an extreme case that should clearly be treated as a sale of stock by the shareholder. There are many cases in between where it is not immediately apparent which treatment is correct. The problem for Congress and the courts has been distinguishing redemptions that should be treated as sales or exchanges from those that should be treated as dividends. Under current law, a redemption qualifies for sale or exchange treatment if it satisfies *any* of the following conditions:

- The redemption is substantially disproportionate.
- The redemption is a complete termination of the shareholder's interest.
- The redemption is not essentially equivalent to a dividend.
- The redemption is a partial liquidation of the distributing corporation in redemption of part or all of a noncorporate shareholder's stock.
- The redemption is made in order to pay death taxes.

If a redemption qualifies as a sale or exchange, the shareholder is treated as though the stock were sold to an outside party. Gain or loss is equal to the FMV of the property received less the shareholder's adjusted basis for the stock surrendered. The gain or loss is capital gain or loss if the stock is a capital asset. The shareholder's basis for any property received is its FMV. The holding period for the property begins on the day following the exchange date.

A redemption distribution that does not satisfy any of the five conditions necessary for sale or exchange treatment is treated by the shareholder as a property distribution under Sec. 301. This means that the entire amount of the distribution is a dividend to the extent of the distributing corporation's E&P.[29] The surrender of stock by the shareholder is ignored in determining the amount of the dividend. The basis of the surrendered stock is added to the basis of any remaining shares owned by the shareholder. If all of the shareholder's stock has been redeemed, the basis of the redeemed shares is added to the basis of shares owned by those individuals whose ownership is attributed to the shareholder under the constructive stock ownership rules described below.[30]

EXAMPLE C4-26 ▶ Amy and Rose each own 50 of the 100 outstanding shares of York stock. York Corporation has $100,000 of E&P. On May 10, York redeems 20 of Amy's shares with property worth $25,000. Amy's adjusted basis for those shares is $20,000. If the redemption distribution satisfies one of the conditions necessary for sale treatment, Amy has $5,000 ($25,000 − $20,000) of capital gain. Her basis for the property received is $25,000, its FMV. Its holding period begins on May 11. If the redemption does not satisfy any of the conditions necessary for sale treatment, the distribution in redemption of the stock follows the same rules as any other property distribution. Amy reports a $25,000 dividend. Her $20,000 basis for the surrendered stock is added to her basis for her remaining 30 shares of York stock. ◀

SELF-STUDY QUESTION

Why does it matter if a redemption is treated as a dividend or a sale?

ANSWER

One major difference is that the basis of the redeemed stock reduces the gain if the tax treatment is a sale. If the tax treatment is a dividend, no such reduction occurs. Capital gains also can be offset by capital losses from other transactions. In addition, the maximum tax rate on an individual taxpayer's long-term capital gains is 11.6 percentage points below the maximum rate applying to ordinary income.

Structuring a stock redemption as a sale or exchange provides several advantages. First, individuals pay a maximum tax rate of 28% on long-term capital gains. Second, capital gains may be offset by capital losses. Third, in a sale or exchange, the basis of the shares redeemed reduces the amount of gain that is recognized. If a redemption is treated as a dividend, the basis of the shares redeemed does not reduce the dividend income that is recognized, but reduces the gain (or increases the loss) recognized on a later sale or exchange of the distributing corporation stock that is held by the shareholder following the redemption.

Topic Review C4-2 presents a summary of the tax consequences of stock redemptions to both the shareholders and the distributing corporation.

[29] Sec. 302(d).

[30] Reg. Sec. 1.302-2(c).

Topic Review C4-2

Tax Consequences of Stock Redemptions

Shareholders:

General Rule: The amount received by the shareholder in exchange for his or her stock is treated as a dividend (but not in excess of the distributing corporation's E&P). The basis of the surrendered stock is added to the basis of the shareholder's remaining stock.

Exchange Exception: The amount received by the shareholder is offset by the adjusted basis of the shares surrendered. The difference is generally a capital gain or loss. No basis adjustment occurs.

Distributing Corporation:

Gain/Loss Recognition: Gain (but not loss) is recognized as though the distributed property had been sold for its FMV immediately before the redemption.

Earnings and Profits Adjustment: E&P is reduced for redemptions treated as a dividend in the same manner as for an ordinary distribution (e.g., the amount of money distributed). E&P is reduced for redemptions treated as an exchange by the portion of the current and accumulated E&P that is attributable to the redeemed stock. The remainder of the distribution reduces the capital account.

ATTRIBUTION RULES

Three of the five tests used to determine whether a redemption distribution should be treated as a dividend depend on the shareholder's stock ownership before and after the redemption. The purpose of the tests is to determine whether the shareholder's ownership of the corporation has been substantially reduced.

In general, if the shareholder's ownership is substantially reduced, the redemption is treated as a sale. If the ownership interest remains substantially the same or increases, the redemption is treated as a nonliquidating distribution.

In determining stock ownership for this purpose, the constructive ownership or attribution rules of Sec. 318 must be taken into account.[31] These rules provide that a shareholder is considered to own not only the shares he or she owns directly, but also shares owned by his or her spouse, other family members, and related entities. Furthermore, entities such as corporations, partnerships, trusts, and estates are considered to own shares that are owned by their shareholders, partners, and beneficiaries.

Stock once attributed to a person is not further reattributed from that person to another person under the same rules. Thus, stock attributed to one family member under the family attribution rules cannot be reattributed from that family member to a second family member.[32] However, stock once attributed to a person under an attribution rule may be reattributed from that person to another person under a different attribution rule. For example, stock attributed by the corporate attribution rule from a corporation to its shareholder may be reattributed from the shareholder to the shareholder's spouse under the family attribution rules.

KEY POINT

The attribution rules are designed to treat a taxpayer as owning not only the stock that is directly owned, but also all the stock owned by other related parties.

The basic purpose of the attribution rules is to prevent shareholders from either taking advantage of favorable tax rules or avoiding unfavorable rules by having family members or related entities own stock that the shareholder is not permitted to own. All stock ownership tests would be subject to potential abuse if only direct ownership of stock were considered.

[31] Sec. 302(c).

[32] Sec. 318(a)(5)(B).

Four types of attribution rules are prescribed by Sec. 318(a): family attribution, attribution from entities, attribution to entities, and option attribution. These rules are discussed below.

FAMILY ATTRIBUTION. An individual is considered to own all stock owned by or for a spouse, children, grandchildren, and parents.[33] The individual is not considered to own stock owned by brothers, sisters, or grandparents.

EXAMPLE C4-27 ▶ Harry; his wife, Wilma; their son, Steve; and Harry's father, Frank, each own 25 of the 100 outstanding shares of Strong Corporation stock. Harry is considered to own all 100 Strong shares (25 directly plus the shares owned by Wilma, Steve, and Frank). Wilma is considered to own 75 shares (25 directly plus the 50 shares owned by his parents Harry and Steve). Frank's shares are not attributed to Wilma nor are his shares that are attributed to Harry reattributed to Wilma. Steve is considered to own 75 shares (25 directly plus the 50 shares owned by his parents Harry and Wilma). Steve is not considered to own the shares owned by his grandfather (Frank), nor are the shares owned by Frank attributed to Harry and then reattributed to Steve. Frank is considered to own 75 shares (25 directly plus the shares owned by Harry and Steve (his grandson)). The shares owned by Wilma and that are attributed to Harry are not reattributed to Frank. ◀

ADDITIONAL COMMENT

The family attribution rules of Sec. 318 are not as inclusive as the family attribution rules of Sec. 267 (covered in Ch. C3). For example, siblings and grandparents are not considered family members by Sec. 318, but are included under Sec. 267.

ATTRIBUTION FROM ENTITIES. Stock owned by or for a partnership is considered to be owned proportionately by the partners, and stock owned by or for an estate is considered to be owned proportionately by the beneficiaries. Stock owned by or for a trust is considered to be owned by the beneficiaries in proportion to their actuarial interests. Stock owned by or for a C corporation is considered to be owned proportionately by any shareholders owning (directly or indirectly) 50% or more in value of the corporation's stock.[34]

EXAMPLE C4-28 ▶ Bill, who is married, has a 50% interest in a partnership. The partnership owns 40 of the 100 outstanding shares of Yellow Corporation stock. The remaining 60 shares are owned by Bill. Bill is considered to own 80 shares, 60 directly and 20 (0.50 × 40 shares) indirectly. The stock attributed to Bill under the partnership attribution rules is reattributed to Bill's spouse under the family attribution rules. ◀

KEY POINT

Stock is attributed from a shareholder to a C corporation or from a C corporation to a shareholder only if the shareholder owns at least 50% (directly or indirectly) of the corporation.

ATTRIBUTION TO ENTITIES. All stock owned by or for a partner in a partnership is considered to be owned by the partnership. All stock owned by or for a beneficiary of an estate or a trust is considered to be owned by the estate or trust. All stock owned by or for a shareholder who owns (directly or indirectly) 50% or more in value of a C corporation's stock is considered to be owned by the corporation.[35]

EXAMPLE C4-29 ▶ Assume the same facts as in Example C4-28. The partnership in which Bill is a partner is considered to own all 100 shares of Yellow stock (40 directly and 60 owned by Bill). No reattribution of the stock that is owned by Bill and attributed to the partnership can occur from the partnership to another of Bill's partners. ◀

OPTION ATTRIBUTION. A person who has an option to purchase stock is considered to own the stock.[36]

---

[33] Sec. 318(a)(1).

[34] Sec. 318(a)(2). For purposes of the attribution rules, S corporations are treated as partnerships, not as corporations. Thus, attribution occurs to and from shareholders owning less than 50% of the S corporation stock (Sec. 318(a)(5)(E). All corporations in the examples are C corporations unless otherwise stated.

[35] Sec. 318(a)(3).

[36] Sec. 318(a)(4).

EXAMPLE C4-30 ▶ John owns 25 of the 100 outstanding shares of Yard Corporation stock. He has an option to acquire an additional 50 shares. John is considered to own 75 Yard shares (25 directly plus the 50 shares he has an option to buy). ◀

SUBSTANTIALLY DISPROPORTIONATE REDEMPTIONS

If a stock redemption qualifies as substantially disproportionate under Sec. 302(b)(2), the redemption qualifies as a sale. This Code provision, then, provides a safe haven for capital gain treatment rather than dividend treatment. A redemption is substantially disproportionate with respect to a shareholder if all of the following hold true:

- After the redemption, the shareholder owns less than 50% of the total combined voting power of all classes of voting stock.
- After the redemption, the shareholder owns less than 80% of his or her percentage ownership of voting stock before the redemption.
- After the redemption the shareholder owns less than 80% of his or her percentage ownership of common stock (whether voting or nonvoting) before the redemption.[37]

KEY POINT

The mechanical (substantially disproportionate) test was added to the more subjective "not equivalent to a dividend" test in order to give taxpayers a safe harbor provision that can be used for tax planning purposes.

These tests are applied mechanically to each shareholder individually. The 50% test prevents shareholders from qualifying for capital gain treatment if they own a controlling interest in the distributing corporation after the redemption. The 80% tests indicate the degree of change in the shareholder's interest in the corporation that is required to be substantially disproportionate. A redemption may be substantially disproportionate with respect to one shareholder but not disproportionate with respect to another. If only one class of stock is outstanding, the second and third requirements are the same.

EXAMPLE C4-31 ▶ Long Corporation has 400 shares of common stock outstanding, of which Ann, Bob, Carl, and Dana (all unrelated) each own 100 shares. Long redeems 55 shares from Ann, 25 shares from Bob, and 20 shares from Carl.

KEY POINT

In calculating the percentage of stock owned *after* a redemption note that the denominator used is the number of shares outstanding *after* the redemption.

	Before Redemption			*After Redemption*	
Shareholder	*No. of Shares Owned*	*Percentage of Ownership*	*Shares Redeemed*	*No. of Shares Owned*	*Percentage of Ownership*
	(1)	(1) ÷ 400	(2)	(1) − (2)	[(1) − (2)] ÷ 300
Ann	100	25%	55	45	15.00%
Bob	100	25%	25	75	25.00%
Carl	100	25%	20	80	26.67%
Dana	100	25%	—	100	33.33%
Total	400	100%	100	300	100.00%

The redemption is substantially disproportionate with respect to Ann because after the redemption, she owns less than 50% of Long's stock, and her stock ownership percentage (15%) is less than 80% of her stock ownership percentage before the redemption (0.80 × 25% = 20%). The redemption is not substantially disproportionate with respect to Bob

[37] The formula presented below can be used to determine the number of shares of stock that must be redeemed to reduce a shareholder's stock ownership to 80% of what it was before the redemption. A redemption that is in excess of this number (X) permits a shareholder to satisfy the less-than-80% requirement.

$$X = \frac{20bt}{100t - 80b}$$

where: b = number of shares owned before the redemption
t = total number of shares outstanding
X = number of shares that must be redeemed to make post-redemption stock ownership 80% of pre-redemption stock ownership

because he does not have the necessary reduction in his stock ownership percentage. Bob owns the same percentage of stock (25%) after the redemption as he did before the redemption (25%). The redemption is not substantially disproportionate for Carl either, because his stock ownership percentage increases from 25% to 26.67%. ◀

The constructive ownership rules of Sec. 318(a) must be applied in determining whether the shareholder has met the three requirements for a substantially disproportionate redemption.[38]

EXAMPLE C4-32 ▶ Assume the same facts as in Example C4-31, except that Ann and Bob are mother and son. In this case, the redemption is not substantially disproportionate for either Ann or Bob. Ann and Bob are each considered to own 200 shares, or 50%, of the Long stock before the redemption, and each is considered to own 120 shares, or 40%, after the redemption. Although the 50% test is met, neither Ann nor Bob satisfies the requirement that after the redemption the shareholder must own *less* than 80% of the percentage of stock owned before the redemption. After the redemption each owns *exactly* 80% of the percentage owned before the redemption (0.80 × 50% = 40%). ◀

COMPLETE TERMINATION OF THE SHAREHOLDER'S INTEREST

SELF-STUDY QUESTION

Because a complete termination would always be substantially disproportionate, what possible benefit does Sec. 302(b)(3) offer to shareholders?

ANSWER

If a redemption is a complete termination of a shareholder's interest, the family attribution rules of Sec. 318 may be waived if certain requirements are satisfied.

If a stock redemption qualifies as a complete termination of the shareholder's interest in the corporation under Sec. 302(b)(3), the redemption qualifies as a sale. At first glance, this rule does not offer any additional route to sale treatment for the shareholder. If a corporation redeems all of a shareholder's stock, the requirements for a substantially disproportionate redemption under Sec. 302(b)(2) would seem to have been satisfied. However, the complete termination rule extends sale treatment to two redemptions not covered by the substantially disproportionate redemption rules of Sec. 302(b)(2):

- If a shareholder's interest in a corporation consists of nonvoting stock, a redemption of all of the stock qualifies for sale treatment under Sec. 302(b)(3).
- If a shareholder owns some voting stock and his or her entire interest in the corporation is completely terminated by a redemption, the family attribution rules of Sec. 318(a)(1) may be waived and the redemption can qualify for sale treatment even if other family members continue to own some or all of the corporation's stock.[39]

To have the family attribution rules waived, all of the following requirements must be met:[40]

- The shareholder must not retain any interest in the corporation after the redemption except as a creditor. This includes any interest as an officer, director, or employee.
- The shareholder must not acquire any such interest (other than by bequest or inheritance) for at least ten years from the date of the redemption.
- The shareholder must file a written agreement with the IRS that the Service will be notified if any prohibited interest is acquired.

The written agreement allows the IRS to assess additional taxes for the year of the distribution if the prohibited interest is acquired, even if the basic three-year statute of limitations has run.

EXAMPLE C4-33 ▶ Father and Son each own 50 of the 100 outstanding shares of Short Corporation stock. Short Corporation redeems all of Father's shares. Under the family attribution rules, Father is

[38] Reg. Sec. 1.302-3(a).
[39] Sec. 302(c)(2).
[40] Sec. 302(c)(2)(A).

considered to own 100% of the Short stock both before and after the redemption. Thus, the redemption is not substantially disproportionate. However, if Father files the necessary agreement not to retain or acquire any interest in Short Corporation for ten years (except as a creditor or an interest acquired by bequest or inheritance), the family attribution rules are waived and the redemption is treated as a stock sale. It qualifies as a complete termination of Father's interest in Short Corporation. ◀

KEY POINT

To ensure that taxpayers do not abuse this provision, the requirements for waiving the family attribution rules are rather strict.

Waiver of the family attribution rules is not permitted in the following two situations involving related parties:

- Part or all of the stock redeemed was acquired, directly or indirectly, within the ten-year period ending on the date of the distribution by the distributee from a person whose stock ownership would be attributable (at the time of the distribution) to the distributee under Sec. 318.
- Any person owns (at the time of the distribution) stock of the redeeming corporation the ownership of which is attributable to the distributee under Sec. 318 and such person acquired any stock in the redeeming corporation, directly or indirectly, from the distributee within the ten-year period ending on the distribution date.

The first situation prevents an individual from transferring stock to a related party (e.g., family member or controlled entity) and then having the related party use the complete termination exception to recognize a capital gain when the stock that was transferred is redeemed. The second situation prevents an individual from transferring a portion of his or her stock to a related party and then using the complete termination exception to recognize a capital gain when the remaining stock is redeemed. These prohibitions against waiving the family attribution rules do not apply if the transfer took place more than ten years before the redemption or the distributee can show that the acquisition or disposition of the stock of the redeeming corporation did not have as one of its purposes the avoidance of federal income taxes. The family attribution rules can also be waived in the second situation above if the stock acquired by the related party from the distributee is also redeemed in the same transaction.

Note that only the family attribution rules can be waived. However, entities are permitted to have the family attribution rules waived if both the entity and the individual whose stock is attributed to the entity agree not to have any prohibited interest in the corporation for at least ten years.[41]

EXAMPLE C4-34 ▶

The A Trust, which was created by Andrew, owns 30% of the stock of Willow Corporation. Andrew's wife, Wanda, is the sole beneficiary of the trust. The remaining 70% of the Willow stock is owned by their son Steve. Willow Corporation redeems all of its stock owned by the A Trust. The redemption is not treated as a sale because the trust is deemed to own all of the stock owned by its beneficiary (Wanda) and Wanda is deemed to own all of the stock owned by her son (Steve). However, the family attribution rules can be waived if A Trust and Wanda both agree not to have any interest in the corporation for ten years. The redemption will then be treated as a complete termination of the trust's interest in Willow Corporation and eligible for sale treatment. ◀

KEY POINT

Section 302(b)(1) has generally been interpreted to require that a shareholder incur a "meaningful reduction" of its stock interest. What constitutes a "meaningful reduction" is the subject of controversy.

REDEMPTIONS NOT ESSENTIALLY EQUIVALENT TO A DIVIDEND

Code Sec. 302(b)(1) provides that a redemption of stock is treated as a sale if the redemption is not essentially equivalent to a dividend. There is no mechanical test to determine when a redemption is not essentially equivalent to a dividend. The question depends on the facts and circumstances of each case.[42] Therefore, Sec. 302(b)(1) does not

[41] Sec. 302(c)(2)(C).

[42] Reg. Sec. 1.302-2(b).

provide the safe harbor provided by the rules for substantially disproportionate redemptions or redemptions that are a complete termination of a shareholder's interest. This exception was added to the Code in 1954 to prevent the rules on redemptions from being too restrictive, especially in the case of redemptions of preferred stock.

The Supreme Court's decision in *Maclin P. Davis* helped to define some of the criteria to be used in determining when a redemption is not essentially equivalent to a dividend.[43] The Supreme Court held that a business purpose is irrelevant in determining whether a redemption is essentially equivalent to a dividend, the Sec. 318 attribution rules must be used to determine dividend equivalency, and a redemption of part of a sole shareholder's stock is always essentially equivalent to a dividend. The court said that there had to be a "meaningful reduction" in the shareholder's proportionate interest in the corporation after taking into account the constructive ownership rules of Sec. 318(a) in order for Sec. 302(b)(1) to apply. However, the definition of "a meaningful reduction in interest" is still not clear today.

Because of the uncertainty involved in determining when Sec. 302(b)(1) applies, it generally is applied only to a redemption of nonvoting preferred stock when the shareholder does not own any common stock[44] or to redemptions resulting in a substantial reduction in the shareholder's right to vote and exercise control over the corporation, right to participate in earnings, and right to share in net assets on liquidation. Generally, the IRS allows sale treatment if a controlling shareholder reduces his or her interest to a noncontrolling position[45] or a noncontrolling shareholder reduces his or her minority interest.[46] A shareholder does not qualify for sale treatment if he or she has control both before and after the redemption,[47] or if he or she assumes a controlling position.

EXAMPLE C4-35 ▶ All of Thyme Corporation's single class of stock is owned by four unrelated individuals in the following manner: Alan, 27%; Betty, 24.33%; Clem, 24.33%, and David, 24.33%. Some of Alan's stock holdings are redeemed by Thyme, resulting in Alan's interest being reduced to 22.27%. Betty, Clem, and David own equally the remaining 77.73% of the Thyme stock. The redemption of Alan's stock does not qualify as substantially disproportionate because Alan's stock interest is not reduced below 21.6% ($0.80 \times 27\% = 21.6\%$). Nor will the redemption qualify as a complete termination of Alan's interest. The IRS has indicated in Rev. Rul. 76-364 that the redemption of Alan's stock will be treated as a sale transaction under Sec. 302(b)(1) because the transaction results in a meaningful reduction of Alan's noncontrolling interest in Thyme Corporation. ◀

SELF-STUDY QUESTION

When does a partial liquidation qualify for sale treatment?

ANSWER

A partial liquidation qualifies for sale treatment if the distribution is to a noncorporate shareholder, not essentially equivalent to a dividend, and made during the tax year (or the succeeding tax year) in which the plan of partial liquidation is adopted.

PARTIAL LIQUIDATIONS

Under Sec. 302(b)(4), a redemption is treated as a sale if the distribution qualifies as a partial liquidation and is made to a noncorporate shareholder. A **partial liquidation** occurs when a corporation discontinues one line of business, distributes the assets related to that business to its shareholders, and continues in at least one other line of business.[48] A distribution also qualifies as a partial liquidation if the distribution is not essentially equivalent to a dividend and is made within the tax year in which a plan of partial liquidation has been adopted or within the succeeding tax year.

---

[43] *U.S. v. Maclin P. Davis*, 25 AFTR 2d 70-827, 70-1 USTC ¶9289 (USSC, 1970).

[44] Reg. Sec. 1.302-2(a).

[45] A reduction in stock ownership from 57% to 50% where the shareholder no longer had control was considered a meaningful reduction in interest in Rev. Rul. 75-502 (1975-2 C.B. 111).

[46] A reduction in stock ownership from 27% to 22% was considered a meaningful reduction in interest in Rev. Rul. 76-364 (1976-2 C.B. 91).

[47] See *Jack Paparo* (71 T.C. 692 [1979]), where a reduction in stock ownership from 100% to 81.17% and from 100% to 74.15% were not considered meaningful reductions in interest.

[48] A partial liquidation also can occur when a corporation sells one line of business, distributes the sales proceeds (after paying corporate income taxes on the sale), and continues in at least one other line of business.

DETERMINATION MADE AT THE CORPORATE LEVEL. For purposes of the partial liquidation definition, whether a distribution is not essentially equivalent to a dividend is determined at the corporate level.[49] The distribution must be the result of a bona fide contraction of the corporate business. Guidance as to what constitutes a corporate contraction comes from relevant regulations and revenue rulings. Some examples of genuine corporate contractions include

- The distribution of insurance proceeds obtained as a result of a fire that destroys part of a business.[50]
- Termination of a contract representing 95% of the gross income of a domestic corporation.[51]
- Change in a corporation's business from a full-line department store to a discount apparel store resulting in the elimination of certain departments and most forms of credit and a reduction in inventory, floor space, employees, and so on.[52]

SAFE HARBOR RULE. Under Sec. 302(e)(2), a distribution satisfies the not essentially equivalent to a dividend requirement and qualifies as a partial liquidation if

- The distribution is attributable to the distributing corporation's ceasing to conduct a qualified trade or business, or consists of the assets of a qualified trade or business; and
- Immediately after the distribution, the distributing corporation is engaged in the active conduct of at least one qualified trade or business.

A qualified trade or business is any trade or business that

- Has been actively conducted throughout the five-year period ending on the date of the redemption; and
- Was not acquired by the corporation within such five-year period in a partially or wholly taxable transaction.

The definition of an active trade or business is the same as that used for Sec. 355 (corporate division) purposes and which is described in Chapter C7.

EXAMPLE C4-36 ▶ Sage Corporation has been engaged in the manufacture of hats and gloves for the past five years. In the current year, Sage discontinues the manufacture of hats, sells all of its hat-making machinery, and distributes the proceeds to its shareholders in redemption of part of their stock. The corporation continues to manufacture gloves. The distribution constitutes a partial liquidation of Sage. ◀

A partial liquidation does not have to be pro rata.

TYPICAL MISCONCEPTION

Sale treatment is not always preferable to dividend treatment. A corporate shareholder would generally prefer dividend treatment due to the availability of the dividends-received deduction.

EFFECT OF A PARTIAL LIQUIDATION ON THE SHAREHOLDERS. If a distribution qualifies as a partial liquidation, a noncorporate shareholder treats the redemption of his or her stock as a sale. However, a corporate shareholder treats the redemption distribution as a dividend unless the shareholder qualifies under one of the other tests for sale treatment (i.e., Secs. 302(b)(1)-(3) or 303). In determining whether stock is held by a corporate or noncorporate shareholder, stock held by a partnership, trust, or estate is considered to be held proportionately by its partners or beneficiaries. Dividend treatment may be more advantageous than sale treatment for a corporate shareholder because a corporation is eligible for a 70%, 80%, or 100% dividends-received deduction.

---

[49] Sec. 302(c)(1)(A).
[50] Reg. Sec. 1.346-1.
[51] Rev. Rul. 75-3, 1975-1 C.B. 108.
[52] Rev. Rul. 74-296, 1974-1 C.B. 80.

EXAMPLE C4-37 ▶ Assume the same facts as in Example C4-36, except that Sage Corporation is owned by Ted and by Jolly Corporation; each owns 50 shares of Sage stock with a $10,000 basis. Sage has $100,000 of current and accumulated E&P. Sage distributes $18,000 to each shareholder in redemption of ten shares of Sage stock worth $18,000. Because the redemption qualifies as a partial liquidation, Ted treats the transaction as a sale. He has a $16,000 ($18,000 − $2,000) capital gain. Jolly Corporation cannot treat the transaction as a sale. Therefore, Jolly must report $18,000 of dividend income. Jolly is eligible for a $14,400 (0.80 × $18,000) dividends-received deduction. Jolly's $2,000 basis in the redeemed stock is added to its basis in its remaining stock. Therefore, Jolly has a $10,000 basis in its 40 remaining Sage shares. ◀

STOP & THINK

Question: Why is a distribution in partial liquidation of a corporation treated as a sale by its noncorporate shareholders and as a dividend by its corporate shareholders?

Solution: Distributions in complete liquidation of a corporation are treated by all shareholders (corporate and noncorporate shareholders alike) as though the shareholder had sold her stock for the amount received (see Chapter C6). In a partial liquidation, a significant portion of the corporation's business is discontinued. Therefore, the shareholder is treated as though he or she sold a portion of his or her stock. On the other hand, even though there has been a partial liquidation, corporate shareholders are still allowed to treat the distribution as a dividend because it is more advantageous for them. They can receive a dividends-received deduction and, therefore, pay less tax than they would if the transaction were treated as a sale. In other words, both corporate and noncorporate shareholders participating in a partial liquidation can receive the tax treatment that is generally most favorable to them.

REDEMPTIONS TO PAY DEATH TAXES

KEY POINT

Section 303 is meant as a relief provision to lessen the tax impact of the death of a shareholder of a closely held corporation. Without this provision, an estate could find it very costly to redeem enough stock to pay the estate taxes and certain administrative expenses of the estate.

If corporate stock represents a substantial portion of a decedent's gross estate, a redemption of the stock from the estate or its beneficiaries may be eligible for sale treatment under Sec. 303. This Code section is intended to help shareholders who inherit stock in a closely held corporation and who must sell some of their stock in order to pay estate taxes, inheritance taxes, and funeral and administrative expenses. If the stock is not readily marketable, a stock redemption may be the only way to provide the estate and beneficiaries with sufficient liquidity to meet their cash needs. In most cases, the Sec. 318 attribution rules would prevent such a redemption from qualifying as substantially disproportionate or as a complete termination of the shareholder's interest. The redemption would then be treated as a dividend were it not for the special provisions of Sec. 303. However, the Sec. 318 attribution rules do not apply to the portion of a stock redemption that qualifies under Sec. 303.

Section 303 provides that a redemption of stock that was included in a decedent's gross estate is treated as a sale of stock by the shareholder (either the estate or the beneficiary of the estate) if the following conditions are met:

1. The value of the redeeming corporation's stock included in the decedent's gross estate is more than 35% of the adjusted gross estate. The adjusted gross estate is the total gross estate (i.e., the FMV of all property owned by the decedent on the date of death) less allowable deductions for funeral and administrative expenses, claims against the estate, debts, and casualty and other losses.[53]

EXAMPLE C4-38 ▶ The gross estate of a decedent is valued at $2,900,000. It includes Pepper Corporation stock worth $1,200,000 and $1,700,000 in cash. Funeral expenses, debts, and other administrative

[53] Sec. 303(b)(2)(A).

expenses allowable as estate tax deductions amount to $900,000, so that the decedent's adjusted gross estate is $2,000,000 ($2,900,000 − $900,000). Because the value of the Pepper stock included in the gross estate is more than 35% of the adjusted gross estate [$1,200,000 is more than $700,000 (0.35 × $2,000,000)], a redemption of some of Pepper's stock can qualify as a stock sale under Sec. 303. ◀

2. The maximum amount of the redemption distribution that can qualify for sale treatment under Sec. 303 is the sum of all federal and state estate and inheritance taxes, plus any interest due on those taxes, and all funeral and administrative expenses that are allowable as deductions on the federal estate tax return. The redemption must be of stock held by the estate or by heirs who are liable for the estate taxes and other administrative expenses.

3. Section 303 applies to a redemption distribution only to the extent that the recipient shareholder's interest in the estate is reduced by the payment of taxes and other expenses. The maximum distribution to any shareholder that is eligible for sale treatment under Sec. 303 is the amount of estate taxes and expenses that the shareholder is obligated to bear.[54]

EXAMPLE C4-39 ▶ Assume the same facts as in Example C4-38, except that all of the stock is bequeathed to the decedent's son, Sam. The remainder of the estate is bequeathed to the decedent's wife, Wilma, and she is liable for all taxes and expenses. In such case, Sec. 303 could not be used by Sam. He is not liable for any of the estate taxes or administrative expenses. If instead $800,000 is bequeathed to Wilma and the remainder of the estate to Sam, Sam would be liable for all estate taxes and administrative expenses. He could use Sec. 303 to receive sale treatment on a redemption of enough of his stock to pay the estate taxes and administrative expenses. ◀

4. Section 303 applies only to distributions made within certain time limits.[55]

a. In general, the redemption must take place not later than ninety days after the expiration of the period for the assessment of the federal estate tax. Because the statute of limitations for the federal estate tax expires three years after the estate tax return is due and the return is due nine months after the date of death, the redemption generally must take place within four years after the date of death.

b. If a petition for redetermination of an estate tax deficiency is filed with the Tax Court, the distribution period is extended to sixty days after the Tax Court's decision becomes final.

c. If the taxpayer made a valid election under Sec. 6166 to defer payment of federal estate taxes under an installment plan, the distribution period is extended to the time the installment payments are due.

5. The stock of two or more corporations may be aggregated in order to satisfy the 35% requirement, provided that 20% or more of the value of each corporation's outstanding stock is included in the gross estate.[56]

EXAMPLE C4-40 ▶ The gross estate of a decedent is valued at $2,900,000. It includes 80% of the stock of Curry Corporation, valued at $400,000, and 90% of the stock of Brodie Corporation, valued at $450,000. Allowable estate tax deductions for administrative expenses and debts amount to $900,000, so that the decedent's adjusted gross estate is $2,000,000. Although neither the Curry stock nor the Brodie stock has a value greater than 35% of the $2,000,000 adjusted gross estate, the value of the stock of both corporations taken together is greater than 35% of the adjusted gross estate [$850,000 ($400,000 + $450,000) is greater than $700,000 (0.35 ×

[54] Sec. 303(b)(3).
[55] Sec. 303(b)(1).
[56] Sec. 303(b)(2)(B).

$2,000,000)]. Therefore, a redemption of sufficient Curry stock and/or Brodie stock to pay estate taxes and funeral and administrative expenses is eligible for sale treatment under Sec. 303. ◀

Although the basic purpose of Sec. 303 is to provide liquidity for the payment of estate taxes when a major portion of the estate consists of stock in a closely held corporation, a redemption can qualify under Sec. 303 even when the estate has sufficient liquid assets to pay estate taxes and other expenses. The redemption proceeds do not have to be used for this purpose.

The advantage of qualifying a redemption under Sec. 303 is that, generally, the redeeming shareholder has little or no capital gain to report. This is because his or her basis in the redeemed stock is the stock's FMV on the date of death of the decedent from whom the stock was inherited (or an alternate valuation date, if applicable). On the other hand, if the redemption does *not* qualify as a sale, the redeeming shareholder may have dividend income equal to the entire distribution from the redeeming corporation.

EXAMPLE C4-41 ▶ Chili Corporation redeems 100 shares of its stock for $105,000 from Art, who inherited the stock from his father, Fred. The stock's FMV on Fred's date of death was $100,000. Chili Corporation has an E&P balance of $500,000. If the redemption qualifies as a sale under Sec. 303, Art recognizes a $5,000 capital gain ($105,000 − $100,000). However, if the redemption does not qualify as a sale under Sec. 303 or one of the other sale treatment exceptions, Art has $105,000 of dividend income. ◀

Thus, Sec. 303 can make a large difference in the amount of income a redeeming shareholder must report as well as the character of that income.

SELF-STUDY QUESTION

How much gain is the redeeming shareholder likely to recognize in a qualifying Sec. 303 redemption?

ANSWER

Probably little or none. The basis in the redeemed stock equals its FMV at the date of death of the decedent (or an alternate valuation date). The recognized gain generally is only the post-death appreciation.

EFFECT OF REDEMPTIONS ON THE DISTRIBUTING CORPORATION

As in the case of property distributions that are not in redemption of a shareholder's stock, two questions must be answered with respect to a corporation that distributes property in redemption of its stock:

- What are the amount and character of the gain or loss recognized by the distributing corporation on the distribution?
- What effect does the distribution have on the corporation's E&P?

Each of these questions is addressed below.

KEY POINT

Consistent with the distribution rules, using appreciated property in a stock redemption will create income and a corresponding increase in the E&P of the redeeming corporation.

CORPORATE GAIN OR LOSS ON PROPERTY DISTRIBUTIONS. The rules for the recognition of gain or loss by a corporation that distributes property in redemption of its stock are the same as the rules for property distributions that are not in redemption of the corporation's stock. Under Sec. 311,

- The corporation recognizes gain when it distributes appreciated property in redemption of its stock. The character of the gain depends on the character of the distributed property in the corporation's hands.
- The corporation does not recognize any loss when it distributes property that has declined in value.

EFFECT OF REDEMPTIONS ON E&P. A stock redemption affects a corporation's E&P accounts in two ways. First, if appreciated property is distributed, the gain is included in the corporation's gross income and increases the corporation's E&P account. Next, the corporation's E&P balance must be reduced because of the distribution. The amount of the reduction depends on whether the redemption distribution is treated as a sale or as a dividend by the shareholder whose stock is redeemed.

If the redemption does not qualify for sale treatment, the corporation must reduce its E&P by the amount of money, the principal amount of any obligations, and the greater of the adjusted basis or FMV of any other property distributed, the same as it does for a property distribution that is not a redemption distribution.

If the redemption qualifies for sale treatment under Secs. 302(a) or 303, E&P is reduced by only a portion of the distribution. E&P is reduced by the portion of the current and accumulated E&P that is attributable to the redeemed stock. In other words, E&P is reduced by a percentage that is equal to the percentage of the stock that was redeemed. The remainder of the distribution reduces the capital account.[57] An ordinary dividend distribution has first claim to current E&P ahead of any stock redemptions. No such priority exists for accumulated E&P. Both ordinary dividend distributions and stock redemptions reduce accumulated E&P in chronological order.

EXAMPLE C4-42 ▶ Teddy Corporation has 100 shares of stock outstanding, 30 of which are owned by Mona. All 30 of Mona's shares are redeemed by Teddy for $36,000 in a redemption qualifying as a sale under Sec. 302(b)(3). At the time of the redemption, Teddy has $60,000 in paid-in capital and $40,000 of E&P. Because 30% of the outstanding stock was redeemed, the distribution reduces Teddy's E&P by $12,000 (0.30 × $40,000). The remaining $24,000 ($36,000 − $12,000) of the distribution reduces the paid-in capital amount to $36,000 ($60,000 − $24,000). ◀

PREFERRED STOCK BAILOUTS

OBJECTIVE 6

Explain the tax treatment for preferred stock bailouts

ADDITIONAL COMMENT

When the term *bailout* is used in the corporate context, this generally refers to some scheme that allows a corporation to make a dividend distribution, but for tax purposes the transaction is treated as a sale of a capital asset.

The rules with respect to stock redemptions were added to the Code to permit sale treatment for stock redemptions under certain specific circumstances and to require dividend treatment in all other situations. In most cases, taxpayers prefer sale treatment. First, sale treatment allows taxpayers to deduct their basis in the stock redeemed. Second, the gain on the stock sale is generally long-term capital gain, which is currently taxed at a maximum rate of 28%, or may even be offset by the taxpayer's capital losses and not taxed at all. Consequently, taxpayers have devised methods to circumvent Congress's intentions.

One such method, devised by taxpayers before the enactment of the Internal Revenue Code of 1954, is known as the **preferred stock bailout**. In general, the preferred stock bailout scenario operated as follows:

1. A tax-free stock dividend of nonvoting preferred stock was issued with respect to a corporation's common stock. Under the rules for nontaxable stock dividends, a portion of the common stock's basis is allocated to the preferred stock. Its holding period includes the holding period for the common stock.
2. The preferred stock was sold to an unrelated third party at its FMV. The sale resulted in a capital gain equal to the difference between the preferred stock's sale price and its allocated basis.
3. The corporation redeemed the preferred stock from the third-party purchaser (at a small premium to reward the third party for his or her cooperation in the scheme).

The result was that the shareholder was able to receive the corporation's earnings as a long-term capital gain without changing his or her equity position in the company.

In order to prevent this tax-avoidance possibility, Congress enacted Sec. 306. Section 306 operates by "tainting" certain stock (usually preferred stock) when it is distributed. The tainted stock is not taxed at the time of its distribution, but a subsequent sale or

[57] Sec. 312(n)(7).

other disposition of the stock generally results in the recognition of ordinary or dividend income rather than capital gain. Section 306 prevents taxpayers from using a preferred stock bailout to convert dividend income into capital gain.

SEC. 306 STOCK DEFINED

Section 306 stock is defined by Sec. 306(c) as follows:

1. Stock (other than common stock issued with respect to common stock) that is received as a nontaxable stock dividend
2. Stock (other than common stock) received in a tax-free corporate reorganization or corporate division if the effect of the transaction was substantially the same as the receipt of a stock dividend, or if the stock was received in exchange for Sec. 306 stock
3. Stock that has a basis determined by reference to the basis of Sec. 306 stock (i.e., a substituted or transferred basis)
4. Stock (other than common stock) acquired in an exchange to which Sec. 351 applies if the receipt of money (in lieu of the stock) would have been treated as a dividend

Note that preferred stock issued by a corporation having no current or accumulated E&P in the year the stock is issued cannot be Sec. 306 stock.[58] Also, stock that is inherited is not Sec. 306 stock because the basis of such stock is its FMV on the date of death (or alternate valuation date) and, therefore, is not determined by reference to the basis that the stock had in the hands of the decedent.[59]

DISPOSITIONS OF SEC. 306 STOCK

TYPICAL MISCONCEPTION

Although the amount of ordinary income recognized in a sale of Sec. 306 stock is measured by the E&P existing in the year the Sec. 306 stock was distributed, the E&P of the distributing corporation is not reduced by the amount of Sec. 306 ordinary income.

If a shareholder sells or otherwise disposes of Sec. 306 stock (except in a redemption), the amount realized is treated as ordinary income to the extent that the shareholder would have had a dividend at the time of the distribution if money in an amount equal to the FMV of the stock were distributed instead of the stock itself.[61] The shareholder's ordinary income is measured by reference to the corporation's E&P in the year the Sec. 306 stock was distributed. Any additional amount received for the Sec. 306 stock generally constitutes a return of capital. If the additional amount exceeds the shareholder's basis in the Sec. 306 stock, the excess is a capital gain. If the additional amount is less than the shareholder's basis, the unrecovered basis is added back to the shareholder's basis in his or her common stock. It is not recognized as a loss.

EXAMPLE C4-43 ▶ Carlos owns all 100 outstanding shares of Adobe Corporation's stock. His basis in those shares is $100,000. Adobe Corporation, which has $150,000 of E&P, distributes 50 shares of nonvoting preferred stock to Carlos as a nontaxable stock dividend. The preferred stock has a $50,000 FMV on the distribution date and the common stock has a $200,000 FMV. Carlos must allocate his $100,000 basis for the common stock to the common and preferred stock according to relative FMVs as follows:

	FMV	Basis
Common stock	$200,000	$80,000[a]
Preferred stock	50,000	20,000[b]
Total	$250,000	$100,000

[a] $\frac{\$200,000 \times \$100,000}{\$250,000}$ [b] $\frac{\$50,000 \times \$100,000}{\$250,000}$

[58] Sec. 306(c)(2).
[59] Reg. Sec. 1.306-3(e).
[60] Sec. 306(a)(1).

Carlos subsequently sells the preferred stock to Dillon for $50,000. The $50,000 realized when the stock is sold is all ordinary income because Adobe Corporation's E&P in the year the preferred stock dividend was issued exceeds the FMV of the preferred stock. Carlos's $20,000 basis in the preferred stock is added back to his basis in his common stock so that his basis in his common stock is restored to $100,000. If instead Carlos sells the preferred stock for $100,000, he has $50,000 of ordinary income, $20,000 return of capital, and $30,000 of capital gain computed as follows:

Sales price	$100,000
Minus: Ordinary income[a]	(50,000)
	$ 50,000
Minus: Return of capital[b]	(20,000)
Capital gain[c]	$ 30,000

[a]Smaller of E&P in year stock was issued or stock's FMV on the distribution date.
[b]Smaller of remaining sales proceeds or adjusted basis of stock.
[c]Sales proceeds received in excess of adjusted basis of stock. ◀

REDEMPTIONS OF SEC. 306 STOCK

KEY POINT

The amount realized in a redemption of Sec. 306 stock is a dividend to the extent of E&P existing in the year of redemption. Unlike a sale of Sec. 306 stock, E&P is reduced as a result of a redemption.

If Sec. 306 stock is redeemed by the issuing corporation, the total amount realized by the shareholder is a distribution to which the Sec. 301 dividend distribution rules apply.[61] It is, therefore, a dividend to the extent of the redeeming corporation's E&P *in the year of the redemption.* Amounts received in excess of the corporation's E&P are treated as a recovery of the shareholder's basis in his or her Sec. 306 stock, and then as a capital gain once the basis has been recovered. If the shareholder's basis in the redeemed stock is not recovered, the unrecovered basis is added to the basis of the common stock owned by the shareholder.

EXAMPLE C4-44 ▶ Don owns all 100 shares of Brigham Corporation's common stock and has a $300,000 adjusted basis in the stock. On January 1, 1993, Brigham issues 50 shares of preferred stock to Don. The preferred stock and common stock have $100,000 and $400,000 FMVs, respectively, on the distribution date. Brigham's current and accumulated E&P for 1993 is $200,000. Don's allocated basis in the preferred stock is $60,000 {[$100,000 ÷ ($100,000 + $400,000)] × $300,000}. The basis of Don's common stock is reduced to $240,000 ($300,000 − $60,000) as a result of the basis allocation. On January 2, 1997, Brigham redeems the preferred shares for $250,000. In the year of the redemption, Brigham's current and accumulated E&P is $400,000. Don has dividend income of $250,000 (because Brigham's E&P is at least $250,000 in the year of the redemption). If Brigham's E&P is instead $200,000 in the year of the redemption, Don has $200,000 of dividend income and a $50,000 tax-free return of capital. Because Don's basis in his preferred stock is $60,000, the $10,000 unrecovered basis is added to his basis in the common stock, increasing it to $250,000 ($240,000 + $10,000). ◀

EXCEPTIONS TO SEC. 306 TREATMENT

Section 306(b) provides that Sec. 306 does not apply in the following situations.

- A shareholder sells all of his or her common and preferred stock in a corporation, thus completely terminating his or her interest in the corporation. Section 306 does not apply even if some of the stock sold is Sec. 306 stock. The sale cannot be to a related party as defined by Sec. 318(a) (i.e., a family member or related entity).
- The corporation redeems all of the shareholder's common and preferred stock, completely terminating the shareholder's interest in the corporation.

[61] Sec. 306(a)(2).

- The corporation redeems an individual shareholder's stock in a partial liquidation qualifying under Sec. 302(b)(4).
- A shareholder disposes of Sec. 306 stock in a way in which gain or loss is not recognized (e.g., a gift of Sec. 306 stock). Although no income is recognized when Sec. 306 stock is disposed of by gift, the stock retains its taint and remains Sec. 306 stock in the donee's hands.
- Section 306 does not apply if it is demonstrated to the IRS's satisfaction that the distribution and subsequent disposition of Sec. 306 stock did not have tax avoidance as one of its principal purposes.

STOCK REDEMPTIONS BY RELATED CORPORATIONS

OBJECTIVE 7

Determine when Sec. 304 applies to a stock sale and its tax consequences

If a shareholder sells stock in one corporation (the issuing corporation) to a second corporation (the acquiring corporation), the sale usually results in the recognition of a capital gain or loss by the shareholder. However, if the shareholder controls both corporations the net result may be more similar to a dividend than to a sale.

EXAMPLE C4-45 ▶ Arnie owns all 100 shares of the stock of Par and Birdie Corporations. Arnie sells 25 shares of the Par stock to Birdie Corporation for $25,000. The net result of this transaction is that Arnie has received a $25,000 cash distribution from Birdie and he still has complete control of both corporations. ◀

EXAMPLE C4-46 ▶ Bonnie owns all 100 shares of Parent Corporation stock. Parent owns all of Subsidiary Corporation's stock. Bonnie sells 25 shares of Parent stock to Subsidiary Corporation for $25,000. The net result of this transaction is that Bonnie has received a $25,000 cash distribution from Subsidiary. Bonnie still controls Parent Corporation, and Parent Corporation still owns all of the Subsidiary stock. ◀

KEY POINT

Section 304 is a backstop to Sec. 302. Section 304 prevents a shareholder from using related corporations to transfer assets out of a corporation as capital gains when they should be taxed as dividends.

As Examples C4-45 and C4-46 demonstrate, the potential exists to use two commonly controlled corporations to bail out the E&P of a corporation at capital gains rates. To prevent this kind of tax avoidance, Sec. 304 requires that a sale of stock of one controlled corporation to a second controlled corporation be treated as a stock redemption. If one of the provisions of Sec. 302(b) or Sec. 303 applies to the redemption (e.g., if the redemption is substantially disproportionate), the transaction is treated as a sale. Otherwise, the redemption is treated as a Sec. 301 distribution, which implies a dividend if there is sufficient E&P.

Section 304 applies to two types of sales. The first is a sale of stock involving two brother-sister corporations. The second is a sale of a parent corporation's stock to one of its subsidiary corporations. The following sections define brother-sister groups and parent-subsidiary groups and explain how Sec. 304 applies to each type of group.

BROTHER-SISTER CORPORATIONS

Two corporations are called brother-sister corporations when one or more shareholders are in control of each of the corporations and a parent-subsidiary relationship is not present. Control means ownership of at least 50% of the voting power or 50% of the total value of all stock of the corporation. The shareholder(s) who have such ownership are called controlling shareholders. If a controlling shareholder (or shareholders) transfers stock in one corporation to the other corporation in exchange for property, the exchange is recast as a redemption by the acquiring corporation of its own stock. In other words, the acquiring corporation is deemed to receive the issuing corporation's stock as a contribution to capital; in exchange, it is deemed to give the controlling shareholder some of its own stock; and the acquiring corporation is deemed to have redeemed its own newly issued stock from the controlling shareholder for the amount that was actually paid.

To determine whether the redemption is a sale or a dividend, reference is made to the shareholder's stock ownership in the issuing corporation. For purposes of making this test under Sec. 302(b), the attribution rules of Sec. 318(a) must be applied.[62]

REDEMPTION TREATED AS A DISTRIBUTION. If the redemption does not qualify as a sale, it is treated as a Sec. 301 distribution. The distribution is assumed to have been made first by the acquiring corporation to the extent of its E&P, and then by the issuing corporation to the extent of its E&P.[63] The shareholder's basis in the issuing corporation's stock that was sold is added to his or her basis for the acquiring corporation's stock. The acquiring corporation takes the same basis in the issuing corporation's shares that the shareholder had.

EXAMPLE C4-47 ▶ Bert owns 60 of the 100 outstanding shares of Frog Corporation stock and 60 of the 100 outstanding shares of Tree Corporation stock. Frog and Tree Corporations have $50,000 and $20,000 of E&P, respectively. Bert sells 20 shares of Frog stock (for which his adjusted basis is $10,000) to Tree Corporation for $20,000. Section 304 applies because Frog and Tree are both controlled by Bert (because of his ownership of at least 50% of each corporation's stock). The transaction is recast as a contribution by Bert of his Frog stock to Tree Corporation in exchange for Tree stock and a redemption by Tree of its newly-issued stock from Bert. To determine whether the transaction qualifies as a sale, reference is made to Bert's ownership of Frog stock. Before the redemption, Bert owned 60% of the Frog stock. After the redemption, Bert owns 52% of the Frog stock (40 shares directly and 12 [0.60 × 20] shares indirectly through Tree). The redemption is treated as a Sec. 301 distribution because it satisfies none of the tests for sale treatment. The entire distribution is a dividend because it does not exceed the $70,000 total of Frog and Tree Corporations' E&P. All $20,000 of the distribution is from Tree's E&P. Tree's basis in the Frog stock is $10,000, the same as Bert's basis in the Frog stock. Bert's basis in his Tree stock is increased by $10,000, his basis in the Frog stock that he is deemed to have contributed to Tree Corporation. ◀

REDEMPTION TREATED AS A SALE. If the redemption qualifies as a sale under Sec. 302(b) or Sec. 303(a), the shareholder's recognized gain or loss is measured by the difference between the amount received from the acquiring corporation and the shareholder's basis in the acquiring corporation's stock that was deemed to have been issued to him. The shareholder's basis in those shares is the same as his basis in the issuing corporation's shares that were contributed to the acquiring corporation. The acquiring corporation is treated as having purchased the issuing corporation's shares and takes a cost basis for such shares.

EXAMPLE C4-48 ▶ Assume the same facts as in Example C4-47, except that Bert sells 40 shares of Frog stock (for which his adjusted basis is $20,000) to Tree Corporation for $40,000. After the redemption, Bert owns 44 shares of Frog stock (20 shares directly and 24 [0.60 × 40] shares indirectly through Tree). Therefore, he meets both the 50% and the 80% tests for a substantially

---

[62] The attribution rules of Sec. 318(a) are modified for Sec. 304 purposes so that a shareholder is considered to own a proportionate amount of stock owned by any corporation of which he or she owns 5% or more (instead of 50% or more) of the value of the stock.

[63] Sec. 304(b)(2).

disproportionate redemption, and he treats the redemption as a sale. He has a $20,000 ($40,000 received from Tree − $20,000 adjusted basis in the Tree shares deemed to be redeemed) capital gain. Tree's basis in the Frog shares acquired from Bert is its $40,000 purchase price. ◀

PARENT-SUBSIDIARY CORPORATIONS

If a shareholder sells stock in a parent corporation to a subsidiary of the parent corporation, the exchange is treated as a distribution in redemption of part or all of the shareholder's stock in the parent corporation. For this purpose, a parent-subsidiary relationship exists if one corporation owns at least 50% of the voting power or 50% of the total value of all stock in the subsidiary.

To determine whether the redemption is a sale or a Sec. 301 distribution, reference is made to the shareholder's ownership of the parent corporation stock before and after the redemption. The constructive ownership rules of Sec. 318 must be taken into account in making this determination.

REDEMPTION TREATED AS A DIVIDEND. If the redemption does not qualify as a sale, the distribution is treated as having been made by the subsidiary corporation to the extent of its E&P and then from the parent corporation to the extent of its E&P. The effect of this rule is to make the E&P of both corporations available in determining the portion of the distribution that is a dividend. The shareholder's basis in his or her remaining parent corporation stock is increased by his or her basis in the stock transferred to the subsidiary. The subsidiary's basis in the parent corporation stock is the amount it paid for the stock.[64]

EXAMPLE C4-49 ▶ Brian owns 60 of the 100 shares of Parent Corporation stock and has a $15,000 basis in his shares. Parent Corporation owns 60 of the 100 shares of Subsidiary stock. Parent and Subsidiary Corporations have $10,000 and $30,000 of E&P, respectively. Brian sells 10 of his Parent shares to Subsidiary for $12,000. The sale is recast as a redemption. Parent Corporation is deemed to have redeemed its stock from Brian. Brian owned 60% of the Parent stock before the redemption. After the redemption he owns 53 shares (50 shares directly and 3 [$0.60 \times 0.50 \times 10$] shares indirectly). Because the 50% and 80% tests are not met, the redemption is not substantially disproportionate. The redemption does not qualify as a sale under Sec. 302(b)(1) because Brian remains in control of Parent after the redemption, and no other test for sale treatment is met. Therefore, Brian has a dividend. The $12,000 distribution comes from Subsidiary's E&P. Brian's $2,500 basis in the redeemed shares is added to his $12,500 basis in his remaining Parent shares, so that his total basis in those shares remains $15,000. Subsidiary's basis in the 10 Parent shares acquired from Brian is $12,000, the amount that Subsidiary paid for the shares. ◀

REDEMPTION TREATED AS A SALE. If the redemption of the parent corporation's stock qualifies as a sale, gain or loss is computed in the usual fashion. The basis of the stock transferred to the subsidiary is subtracted from the amount received in the distribution to determine the shareholder's recognized gain.

EXAMPLE C4-50 ▶ Assume the same facts as in Example C4-49, except that Brian sells 40 shares of Parent stock to Subsidiary Corporation for $48,000. Because Brian owns 60% of the Parent stock before the redemption and he owns 24.8% (20 shares directly and 4.8 [$0.60 \times 0.20 \times 40$] shares indirectly after the redemption), the redemption meets the 50% and 80% tests for a substantially disproportionate redemption. In this case, Brian has a $38,000 ($48,000 − $10,000 adjusted basis in the 40 shares sold) capital gain. Brian's adjusted basis for his

[64] Rev. Rul. 80-189, 1980-2 C.B. 106.

Topic Review C4-3

Alternative Treatments of Stock Redemptions

General Rule: A distribution in redemption of stock is a dividend (Secs. 302(d) and 301).

Exception: Redemptions Treated as Sales or Exchanges

1. Redemptions that are not essentially equivalent to a dividend (Sec. 302(b)(1))
2. Substantially disproportionate redemptions (Sec. 302(b)(2))
3. Complete terminations of a shareholder's interest (Sec. 302(b)(3))
4. Partial liquidation of a corporation in redemption of a noncorporate shareholder's stock (Sec. 302(b)(4))
5. Redemption to pay death taxes (Sec. 303)

Special Redemption Rules

1. Redemptions of Sec. 306 stock are generally treated as dividends to the shareholder (Sec. 306).
2. A sale of stock in one controlled corporation to another controlled corporation is treated as a redemption (Sec. 304).

remaining 20 shares of Parent stock is $5,000. Subsidiary Corporation's basis for the 40 Parent shares purchased from Brian is $48,000, the amount that Subsidiary paid for the shares. ◀

Topic Review C4-3 presents a summary of the methods by which a redemption transaction can be characterized as a sale or exchange as well as the special stock redemption rules.

TAX PLANNING CONSIDERATIONS

AVOIDING UNREASONABLE COMPENSATION

The advantage of using salary and fringe benefit payments to permit a shareholder of a closely held corporation to withdraw funds from the corporation and still be taxed at a single level was discussed in Chapter C3. If a corporation pays too large a salary to a shareholder-employee, some of the salary may be reclassified as a dividend. In such case, double taxation results.

Corporations can avoid the double taxation problem associated with a constructive dividend by entering into a **hedge agreement** with a shareholder-employee, which obligates the shareholder to repay any portion of the salary that is disallowed by the IRS as a deduction. The shareholder-employee deducts the amount of the repayment under Sec. 162 in the year the repayment is made, provided that a legal obligation exists under state law to make the payment.[65] If a hedge agreement is not in effect, voluntary repayment of the salary is not deductible by the shareholder-employee.[66]

EXAMPLE C4-51 ▶ Theresa owns one-half of the stock of Marine Corporation and serves as its president. The remaining Marine stock is owned by eight investors, none of whom owns more than 10% of the outstanding shares. Theresa enters into a hedge agreement with Marine Corporation in 1992 requiring all salary payments that are declared unreasonable compensation by the IRS to be repaid. Marine Corporation pays Theresa a salary and bonus of $750,000 in 1994.

[65] Rev. Rul. 69-115, 1969-1 C.B. 50, and *Vincent E. Oswald,* 49 T.C. 645 (1968), *acq.* 1968-2 C.B. 2.

[66] *Ernest H. Berger,* 37 T.C. 1026 (1962), and *John G. Pahl,* 67 T.C. 286 (1976).

The IRS subsequently holds that $300,000 of the salary is unreasonable compensation and should be taxed as a dividend. Marine Corporation and the IRS agree that $180,000 of the compensation is, in fact, unreasonable. The $180,000 is repaid in 1997. The entire $750,000 is taxable to Theresa in 1994. She can deduct the $180,000 as a trade or business expense in 1997. ◀

Hedge agreements have also been used in connection with other payments involving a corporation and its shareholders (e.g., travel and entertainment expenses). Some firms shy away from hedge agreements because the IRS is likely to consider the existence of such an agreement as evidence of unreasonable compensation.

BOOTSTRAP ACQUISITIONS

A prospective purchaser who wants to acquire the stock of a corporation may not have sufficient cash to make the purchase. Instead, corporate funds may be used to make the purchase. This can be accomplished by having the seller sell part of his or her stock to the purchaser and having the corporation redeem the remainder of the seller's stock. Such an arrangement is called a **bootstrap acquisition.**

EXAMPLE C4-52 ▶ Ted owns all 100 shares of Dragon Corporation stock. The stock has a $100,000 FMV. Vickie wants to purchase the stock from Ted but has only $60,000. Dragon Corporation has a large

WHAT WOULD YOU DO IN THIS SITUATION?

One of the most cherished traditions found in the organizational structure of many professional firms is the year-end bonus. Professionals engaged in the healing arts, law, business services, and accounting have often used the bonus pay structure to clear the books at the end of the year. In the traditional partnership format, these payments have been characterized as distributive shares or some similar form of compensation. As such, these payments are only taxed once as income paid to the professional for services rendered net of any appropriate accounting adjustments.

With the advent of the professional corporation, an entity format designed to limit personal liability exposure, many professionals have opted to do business as shareholders in C corporations. The continued use of the year-end bonus pay structure in the professional corporation context has recently come under greater IRS scrutiny. The position taken by the IRS is clear. If the payments made to the shareholder-professional are in exchange for his or her services rendered to the firm, then the corporation may deduct them as salaries (assuming they are not unreasonable). However, if they are deemed to be a payout of owners' profits, two negative consequences follow. First, the corporation cannot deduct the bonus payments, thus increasing its taxable income. Second, the payment will be treated as dividend income rather than salary to the shareholder who received the bonus.

This issue is illustrated by a case recently decided by the Second Circuit Court of Appeals (*Rapco, Inc. v. CIR,* 77 AFTR 2d 2405, 96-1 USTC ¶50,297 [CA-2, 1996]). *Rapco* is just one of a long line of cases dealing with this issue. In *Rapco,* the Second Circuit agreed with the Tax Court and denied a deduction for bonus payments to the president of the company, even though he played a significant role in the company's rapid growth and had guaranteed large loans to Rapco. Reasons for this decision were: Rapco's compensation scheme was "bonus-heavy and salary light" suggesting dividend avoidance; Rapco had ignored its own bonus structure contained in its preincorporation minutes; it had a history of never paying dividends; the shareholder who decided his own salary owned 95% of the corporation's stock; and Rapco's own expert testified that $400,000–$500,000 was fair compensation for the president's services [a salary of $405,000 was allowed by the IRS].

Assuming your CPA firm is acting as a tax advisor to several similarly situated professional C corporations, what advice would you give that is in compliance with all the rules and regulations of the Internal Revenue Code and the AICPA's *Statements on Responsibilities in Tax Practice?*

cash balance, which it does not need for its operations. Ted sells Vickie 60 shares of Dragon stock for $60,000 and then causes Dragon Corporation to redeem his remaining shares for $40,000. The redemption qualifies as a complete termination of interest for Ted under Sec. 302(b)(3) and, therefore, is eligible for capital gain treatment. ◀

Court cases have established that redemptions qualify for exchange treatment as long as the sale and redemption are all part of an integrated plan to terminate the seller's entire interest. It does not matter whether the redemption precedes the sale.[67] In such situations, however, the purchaser must be careful to avoid having dividend income. For example, a purchaser who contracts to acquire all the stock of a corporation on the installment plan and then uses corporate funds to pay the installment obligations will have dividend income. The use of corporate funds constitutes a constructive dividend to the purchaser when the corporation discharges a purchaser's legal obligation. Even if the corporation uses its own funds to redeem the seller's shares, a purchaser who was legally obligated to purchase the shares is considered to have received a constructive dividend.[68]

EXAMPLE C4-53 ▶ Assume the same facts as in Example C4-52 except that, after Vickie purchases the 60 shares from Ted, she is legally obligated to purchase the remaining 40 shares from Ted. After entering into the contract, Vickie causes Dragon Corporation to redeem Ted's 40 shares. Because Dragon Corporation has paid Vickie's legal obligation, a constructive dividend to Vickie of $40,000 results. No constructive dividend would result from the redemption if Vickie were legally obligated to purchase only 60 shares from Ted. ◀

KEY POINT

The IRS will allow a bootstrap redemption to occur without the recognition of dividend income as long as the buyer does not have an unconditional obligation to purchase the stock and the corporation redeems the stock at no more than its FMV.

Rev. Rul. 69-608 contains guidelines for the buyer of stock in a bootstrap redemption transaction to avoid the constructive dividend situation.[69] The guiding principle is that the buyer does not have a constructive dividend when the corporation redeems some of the seller's shares, as long as the buyer does not have a primary and unconditional obligation to purchase the stock, and as long as the corporation pays no more than the FMV for the stock that is redeemed. A stock purchaser who has an option—not a legal obligation—to purchase the seller's remaining stock, and who assigns the option to the corporation, is not stuck with a constructive dividend.[70]

TIMING OF DISTRIBUTIONS

Dividends can be paid only out of a corporation's E&P. Therefore, if distributions can be timed to be made when the corporation has little or no E&P, the distributions are treated as a return of capital rather than as a dividend.

If a corporation has a current E&P deficit, the deficit reduces accumulated E&P evenly throughout the year unless the corporation can demonstrate that the deficits arose at particular dates. Thus, if a distribution is made in a year in which there is a deficit in current E&P, but there is some accumulated E&P, the timing of the distribution may determine whether it is a dividend or a return of capital.

EXAMPLE C4-54 ▶ Major Corporation has a $30,000 accumulated E&P balance at the beginning of the year and incurs a $50,000 deficit during the year. Because of its poor operating performance, Major Corporation pays only two of its usual $5,000 quarterly dividend payments to its sole shareholder: those ordinarily paid on March 31 and June 30. The source of the distributions is determined as follows:

---

67 See, for example, *U.S. v. Gerald Carey*, 7 AFTR 2d 1301, 61-1 USTC ¶9428 (8th Cir., 1961).

68 *H. F. Wall v. U.S.*, 36 AFTR 423, 47-2 USTC ¶9395 (4th Cir., 1947).

69 Rev. Rul. 69-608, 1969-2 C.B. 42.

70 *Joseph R. Holsey v. CIR*, 2 AFTR 2d 5660, 58-2 USTC ¶9816 (3rd Cir., 1958).

E&P balance, January 1		$30,000
Minus:	Reduction for first quarter loss	(12,500)
	Reduction for March 31 distribution	(5,000)
E&P balance, April 1		$12,500
Minus:	Reduction for second quarter loss	(12,500)
E&P balance, June 30		—0—

The first and second quarter losses are $12,500 [($50,000) × 0.25 = ($12,500)].

TYPICAL MISCONCEPTION

The timing of distributions can affect the amount that is treated as dividend income as opposed to return of capital or capital gain. This is true in a year with deficits in current E&P because a deficit is allocated evenly throughout the year.

The operating loss reduces the accumulated E&P balance evenly throughout the year. All of the March 31 distribution is taxable because sufficient losses have not been incurred to offset the accumulated E&P amounts at the beginning of the year. The second quarter loss makes the June 30 distribution and any other distributions made before the end of the year tax-free returns of the shareholder's capital investment (assuming that the shareholder's basis in his or her stock exceeds the distribution amount). Delaying all of the distributions until late in the year could have made any cash payments to the shareholder tax-free. ◀

The timing of a distribution can also be of critical importance in determining its tax treatment if the distributing corporation has an accumulated E&P deficit and is accruing a positive current E&P balance.

EXAMPLE C4-55 ▶ Yankee Corporation has an accumulated E&P deficit of $250,000 at the beginning of 1996. During 1996 and 1997, Yankee Corporation reports the following current E&P balances and makes the following distributions to Joe, its sole shareholder:

Year	*Current E&P*	*Distributions*	*Distribution Date*
1996	$100,000	$75,000	December 31
1997	—0—	—0—	None

The $75,000 distribution made in 1996 is taxable as a dividend. The $25,000 of current E&P that is not distributed reduces Yankee's accumulated E&P deficit to $225,000. Had Yankee delayed making the $75,000 distribution until January 1, 1997 or later in 1997, the distribution would have been tax-free to the shareholder as a return of Joe's investment in Yankee Corporation. ◀

COMPLIANCE AND PROCEDURAL CONSIDERATIONS

CORPORATE REPORTING OF NONDIVIDEND DISTRIBUTIONS

PRACTICE NOTE

Information on basis adjustments for tax-free dividends, stock splits, stock dividends, etc. for individual firms can be found in special tax services. For example, CCH's *Capital Changes Reports* provides histories of these types of events for over 56,000 companies.

A corporation that makes a nondividend distribution to its shareholders must file Form 5452 (Corporate Report of Nondividend Distributions) and supporting computations with its income tax return. The basic purpose of Form 5452 is to report the E&P of the distributing corporation so that the IRS can determine whether the distributions are indeed nontaxable to shareholders.[71]

The information required on this form is the corporation's current and accumulated E&P, amounts paid to shareholders during the tax year and the percentage of each payment that is taxable and nontaxable, and a detailed computation of the corporation's E&P from the date of incorporation.

[71] Announcement 92-1, I.R.B. 1992-2, 1.

The requirement to file this report whenever a nondividend distribution is made to shareholders makes it important that corporations compute their E&P on an annual basis. In effect, this report requires a corporation to prove that distributions reported as nontaxable on Form 1099 are, in fact, nontaxable.

AGREEMENT TO TERMINATE INTEREST UNDER SEC. 302(b)(3)

KEY POINT

The statute of limitation extends to one year beyond the date a shareholder notifies the IRS that a forbidden interest has been acquired. Otherwise, it would be almost impossible for the IRS to administer this provision.

If a shareholder's interest in a corporation is completely terminated by a redemption, the family attribution rules of Sec. 318(a)(1) may be waived. In order to have the rules waived, the shareholder must file a written agreement with the Treasury that he or she will notify the IRS if any prohibited interest is acquired within the ten-year period following the redemption. A copy of this agreement (which should be in the form of a statement in duplicate signed by the distributee) must be attached to the first return filed by the shareholder for the tax year in which the redemption occurs. If the agreement is not filed on time, the District Director of the IRS is permitted to grant an extension. Regulation Sec. 1.302-4(a) provides that an extension will be granted only if there is reasonable cause for failure to file the agreement on time and if the request for such an extension is filed within such time as the District Director considers reasonable in the circumstances.

The Regulations do not indicate what constitutes a reasonable cause for failure to file or what constitutes a reasonable extension of time. In *Edward J. Fehrs* the Court of Claims held that late filing of a ten-year agreement is permissible where a taxpayer could not reasonably have expected a filing would be necessary, where the taxpayer files the agreement promptly after he or she has noticed that it is required, and where the agreement is filed before the issues in question are presented for trial.[72] However, in *Robin Haft Trust,* an agreement was filed *after* an adverse court ruling. In an appeal for a rehearing, the judge ruled that the filing of the agreement after the case came to trial was too late and the appeal for a rehearing was denied.[73]

If the shareholder *does* acquire a forbidden interest in the corporation within the ten-year period following the redemption, additional taxes may be due. Such an acquisition ordinarily results in the redemption being treated as a dividend distribution rather than a sale. The limitation period for assessing additional taxes extends to one year following the date the shareholder files notice of the acquisition of the forbidden interest with the IRS.[74]

PROBLEM MATERIALS

DISCUSSION QUESTIONS

C4-1 Explain how a corporation computes its current E&P and its accumulated E&P.

C4-2 Why is it necessary to distinguish between current and accumulated E&P?

C4-3 Describe the effect of a $100,000 cash distribution paid on January 1 to the sole shareholder of a calendar-year corporation whose stock basis is $25,000 when the corporation has

a. $100,000 of current E&P and $100,000 of accumulated E&P

b. $50,000 of accumulated E&P deficit and $60,000 of current E&P

c. $60,000 of accumulated E&P deficit and a $60,000 current E&P deficit

d. $80,000 of current E&P deficit and $100,000 of accumulated E&P

---

[72] *Edward J. Fehrs v. U.S.*, 40 AFTR 2d 77-5040, 77-1 USTC ¶9423 (Ct. Cl., 1977).

[73] *Robin Haft Trust,* 62 T.C. 145 (1974).

[74] Sec. 302(c)(2)(A).

Answer Parts a through d again, assuming that the distribution is instead made on October 1.

C4-4 Pecan Corporation distributes land to a noncorporate shareholder. Explain how the following are computed:
a. The amount of the distribution
b. The amount of the dividend
c. The basis of the land to the shareholder
d. When the holding period for the land begins
How would your answers change if the distribution were made to a corporate shareholder?

C4-5 What effect do the following transactions have on the calculation of Young Corporation's current E&P? Assume that the starting point for the calculation is Young Corporation's taxable income for the current year.
a. Tax-exempt interest income of $10,000 is earned.
b. A $10,000 dividend and a $7,000 dividends-received deduction are included in taxable income
c. A $5,000 capital loss carryover from the preceding tax year is used to offset $5,000 of capital gains.
d. Federal income taxes of $25,280 were accrued.

C4-6 Badger Corporation was incorporated in the current year. An $8,000 NOL is reported in its initial tax return. Badger distributed $2,500 to its shareholders. Is it possible for this distribution to be taxed as a dividend to Badger's shareholders? Explain.

C4-7 Does it matter when during the tax year a distribution is made as to whether it is taxed as a dividend or as a return of capital? Explain.

C4-8 Hickory Corporation owns a building with a $160,000 adjusted basis and a $120,000 FMV. Hickory's E&P is $200,000. Should the corporation sell the property and distribute the sale proceeds to its shareholders or distribute the property to its shareholders and let them sell the property? Why?

C4-9 Walnut Corporation owns a building with a $120,000 adjusted basis and a $160,000 FMV. Walnut's E&P is $200,000. Should the corporation sell the property and distribute the sale proceeds to its shareholders or distribute the property to its shareholders and let them sell the property? Why?

C4-10 What is a constructive dividend? Under what circumstances are constructive dividends most likely to arise?

C4-11 Why are stock dividends generally nontaxable? Under what circumstances are stock dividends taxable?

C4-12 How is a distribution of stock rights treated by a shareholder for tax purposes? by the distributing corporation?

C4-13 What is a stock redemption? What are some reasons for making a stock redemption? Why are some redemptions treated as sales and others as dividends?

C4-14 Field Corporation redeems 100 shares of its stock from Andrew for $10,000. Andrew's basis in those shares is $8,000. Explain the possible tax treatments of the $10,000 received by Andrew.

C4-15 What conditions are necessary for a redemption to be treated as a sale by the redeeming shareholder?

C4-16 Explain the purpose of the attribution rules in determining stock ownership in a redemption. Describe the four types of attribution rules that apply to redemptions.

C4-17 Why does a redemption that qualifies as an exchange under Sec. 303 usually result in little or no gain or loss being recognized by the shareholder?

C4-18 Under what circumstances does a corporation recognize gain or loss when it distributes noncash property in redemption of its stock? What effect does a redemption distribution have on the distributing corporation's E&P?

C4-19 What is a preferred stock bailout? How does Sec. 306 operate to prevent a shareholder from realizing the planned advantages of a preferred stock bailout?

C4-20 Define Sec. 306 stock.

C4-21 Bill owns all 100 of the outstanding shares of Plum Corporation stock and 80 of the 100 outstanding shares of Cherry Corporation stock. He sells 20 Plum shares to Cherry Corporation for $80,000. Explain why this transaction is treated as a stock redemption and how the tax consequences of the transaction are determined.

C4-22 Explain the tax consequences to both the corporation and a shareholder-employee of an IRS determination that a portion of the compensation paid in a prior tax year exceeds the reasonable compensation limit. What steps can be taken by the corporation and the shareholder-employee to avoid the double taxation usually associated with such a determination?

C4-23 What is a bootstrap acquisition? What are the tax consequences of such a transaction?

ISSUE IDENTIFICATION QUESTIONS

C4-24 Marsha receives a $10,000 cash distribution from Dye Corporation in April of the current year. Dye has $4,000 of accumulated E&P at the beginning of the year and $8,000 of current E&P. Dye also distributed $10,000 in cash to Barbara, who purchased the 200 shares of Dye stock from Marsha in June of the current year. What tax issues should be considered with respect to the distributions paid to Marsha and Barbara?

C4-25 Neil purchased land from Spring Harbor Corporation, his 100%-owned corporation, for $275,000. The corporation purchased the land three years ago for $300,000. Similar tracts of land located nearby have sold for $400,000 in recent months. What tax issues should be considered with respect to the corporation's sale of the land?

C4-26 Price Corporation has 100 shares of common stock outstanding. Price repurchased all of Penny's 30 shares for $35,000 cash during the current year. Penny received the shares as a gift from her mother three years ago. They have a basis to her of $16,000. Price Corporation has $100,000 in current and accumulated E&P. Penny's mother owns 40 of the remaining shares; the other 30 shares are owned by unrelated individuals. What tax issues should be considered with respect to the corporation's purchase of Penny's shares?

C4-27 George owns all 100 shares of Gumby's Pizza Corporation. The shares are worth $200,000, but George's basis is only $70,000. Mary and George have reached a tentative agreement for George to sell all of his shares to Mary. However, Mary is unwilling to pay more than $150,000 for the stock because the corporation currently has excess cash balances. They have agreed that George can withdraw $50,000 in cash from Gumby's before the stock sale. What tax issues should be considered with respect to George and Mary's agreement?

PROBLEMS

C4-28 ***Current E&P Calculation.*** Beach Corporation reports the following results in the current year using the accrual method of accounting:

Income:	
Gross profit from manufacturing operations	$250,000
Dividends received from 25%-owned domestic corporation	20,000
Interest income: Corporate bonds	10,000
Municipal bonds	12,000
Proceeds from life insurance policy on key employee	100,000
Section 1231 gain on sale of land	8,000
Expenses:	
Administrative expenses	110,000
Bad debt expense	5,000
Depreciation:	
Financial accounting	68,000
Taxable income	86,000
Alternative depreciation system (Sec. 168(g))	42,000

NOL carryover		40,000
Charitable contributions:	Current year	8,000
	Carryover from last year	3,500
Capital loss on sale of stock		1,200
Penalty on late payment of federal taxes		450

a. What is Beach Corporation's taxable income?
b. What is Beach Corporation's current E&P?

C4-29 ***Current E&P Computation.*** Water Corporation reports $500,000 of taxable income for the current year. The following additional information is available:

- Water Corporation reported a long-term capital loss of $80,000 for the current year. No capital gains were reported this year.
- $80,000 of dividends from a 10%-owned domestic corporation are included in taxable income.
- Water Corporation paid fines and penalties of $6,000 that were not deducted in computing taxable income.
- Water Corporation deducted a $30,000 NOL carryover from a prior tax year in computing this year's taxable income.
- Taxable income includes a deduction for $40,000 of depreciation in excess of the depreciation allowed for E&P purposes.

Assume a 34% corporate tax rate. What is Water Corporation's current E&P for this year?

C4-30 ***Calculating Accumulated E&P.*** Apple Corporation was formed in 1994. Its current E&P (or current E&P deficit) and distributions for the period 1994–1997 are as follows:

Year	*Current E&P (Deficit)*	*Distributions*
1994	$(10,000)	$2,000
1995	8,000	4,000
1996	(5,000)	—0—
1997	18,000	5,000

What is Apple's accumulated E&P at the beginning of 1995, 1996, 1997, and 1998?

C4-31 ***Consequences of a Single Cash Distribution.*** Yellow Corporation is a calendar-year taxpayer. All of the stock is owned by Edna. Her basis for the stock is $25,000. On March 1 Yellow Corporation distributes $60,000 to Edna. Determine the tax consequences of the cash distribution to Edna in each of the following independent situations:
a. Current E&P $15,000; accumulated E&P $50,000.
b. Current E&P $25,000; accumulated E&P ($25,000).
c. Current E&P ($36,500); accumulated E&P $65,000.
d. Current E&P ($10,000); accumulated E&P ($25,000).

C4-32 ***Consequences of Multiple Cash Distributions.*** At the beginning of the current year, Charles owns all of Pearl Corporation's outstanding stock. His basis in the stock is $80,000. On July 1 he sells all of his stock to Donald for $125,000. During the current year, Pearl Corporation, a calendar-year taxpayer, makes two cash distributions: $60,000 on March 1 to Charles and $90,000 on September 1 to Donald. How are these distributions treated in the following independent situations?
a. Current E&P $40,000; accumulated E&P $30,000.
b. Current E&P $100,000; accumulated E&P ($50,000).
c. Current E&P ($36,500); accumulated E&P $120,000.

C4-33 ***Distribution of Appreciated Property.*** In the current year, Ruby Corporation has $100,000 of current and accumulated E&P. On March 3, Ruby Corporation distributes a parcel of land (a capital asset) having a $60,000 FMV to Barbara, a shareholder. The land has a $30,000 adjusted basis to Ruby Corporation and is subject to an $8,000 mortgage, which Barbara assumes. Assume a 34% marginal corporate tax rate.

a. What are the amount and character of the income recognized by Barbara as a result of the distribution?

b. What is Barbara's basis for the land?

c. What are the amount and character of Ruby Corporation's gain or loss as a result of the distribution?

d. What effect does the distribution have on Ruby Corporation's E&P?

C4-34 ***Distribution of Property Subject to a Liability.*** On May 10 of the current year, Stowe Corporation distributes $20,000 in cash and land (a capital asset) having a $50,000 FMV to Arlene, a shareholder. The land has a $15,000 adjusted basis and is subject to a $60,000 mortgage, which Arlene assumes. Assume Stowe Corporation has an E&P balance in excess of the amount distributed and a 34% marginal corporate tax rate.

a. What are the amount and character of the income recognized by Arlene as a result of the distribution?

b. What is Arlene's basis for the land?

c. What are the amount and character of Stowe Corporation's gain or loss as a result of the distribution?

d. What effect does the distribution have on Stowe Corporation's E&P?

C4-35 ***Property Distribution—Comprehensive Problem.*** On May 15 of the current year, Quick Corporation distributes a building used in its business having a $250,000 FMV to Calvin, a shareholder. The building originally cost $180,000. Straight-line depreciation was taken in the amount of $30,000, so that the adjusted basis on the date of distribution for taxable income purposes is $150,000 and for E&P purposes is $160,000. The building is subject to an $80,000 mortgage, which Calvin assumes. Assume Quick Corporation has an E&P balance in excess of the amount distributed and a 34% marginal corporate tax rate.

a. What are the amount and character of the income recognized by Calvin as a result of the distribution?

b. What is Calvin's basis for the building?

c. What are the amount and character of Quick Corporation's gain or loss as a result of the distribution?

d. What effect does the distribution have on Quick Corporation's E&P?

C4-36 ***Property Distribution—Comprehensive Problem.*** During the current year, Zeta Corporation distributes the items listed below to its sole shareholder, Susan. For each item listed below, determine the gross income recognized by Susan, her basis in the item, the amount of gain or loss recognized by Zeta Corporation, and the effect of the distribution on Zeta Corporation's E&P. Assume that Zeta Corporation has an E&P balance in excess of the amount distributed and a 34% marginal corporate tax rate.

a. A parcel of land used in Zeta Corporation's business that has a $200,000 FMV and a $125,000 adjusted basis.

b. Assume the same facts as Part a, except that the land is subject to a $140,000 mortgage.

c. FIFO inventory having a $25,000 FMV and an $18,000 adjusted basis.

d. A building used in Zeta's business having an original cost of $225,000, a $450,000 FMV, and a $150,000 adjusted basis for taxable income purposes. $75,000 of depreciation has been taken for taxable income purposes using the straight-line method. $60,000 of depreciation has been taken for E&P purposes.

e. An automobile used in Zeta's business having an original cost of $12,000, an $8,000 FMV, and a $5,760 adjusted basis, on which $6,240 of MACRS depreciation was taken for taxable income purposes. For E&P purposes, depreciation was $5,200.
f. Installment obligations having a $35,000 face amount and FMV and a $24,500 adjusted basis. The obligations were created when a Sec. 1231 asset was sold.

C4-37 *Disguised Dividends.* King Corporation is a very profitable manufacturing corporation with $800,000 of E&P. It is owned equally by Harry and Wilma, who are husband and wife. Both individuals are actively involved in the business. Determine the tax consequences of the following independent events:
a. In reviewing a prior year King Corporation tax return, the IRS determines that the $500,000 of salary and bonuses paid to Wilma is unreasonable compensation. Reasonable compensation would be $280,000.
b. King has loaned Harry $400,000 over the past three years. None of the money has been repaid. Harry does not pay any interest on the loans.
c. King sells a building to Wilma for $150,000 in cash. The property has an adjusted basis of $90,000 and is subject to a $60,000 mortgage, which Wilma also assumes. The FMV of the building is $350,000.
d. Harry leases a warehouse to King for $50,000 per year. According to an IRS auditor, similar warehouses can be leased for $35,000 per year.
e. Wilma sells some land to King for $250,000 on which King intends to build a factory. According to a recent appraisal, the FMV of the land is $185,000.
f. The corporation owns an airplane that it uses to fly executives to business sites and business meetings. When it is not being used for business, Harry and Wilma use it to fly to their ranch in Texas for short vacations. The approximate cost of their trips to the ranch in the current year is $8,000.

C4-38 *Unreasonable Compensation.* Forward Corporation is owned by a group of 15 shareholders. During the current year Forward Corporation pays $450,000 in salary and bonuses to Alvin, its president and controlling shareholder. The IRS audits Forward's tax return and determines that reasonable compensation for Alvin would be $250,000. Forward Corporation agrees to the adjustment.
a. What are the effects of the disallowance of part of the deduction for Alvin's salary and bonuses to Forward Corporation and Alvin?
b. What tax savings could have been obtained by Forward Corporation and Alvin if an agreement had been in effect that required Alvin to repay Forward Corporation the monies that were determined by the IRS to be unreasonable compensation?

C4-39 *Stock Dividend Distribution.* Wilton Corporation has a single class of common stock outstanding. Robert owns 100 shares, which he purchased in 1991 for $100,000. In 1997, when the stock is worth $1,200 per share, Wilton Corporation declares a 10% stock dividend payable in common stock. Robert receives ten additional shares on December 10, 1997. On January 30, 1998, he sells five of the new shares for $7,000.
a. How much income must Robert recognize when he receives the stock dividend?
b. How much gain or loss must Robert recognize when he sells the common stock?
c. What is Robert's basis in his remaining common stock? When does his holding period in the new common stock begin?

C4-40 *Stock Dividend Distribution.* Moss Corporation has a single class of common stock outstanding. Tillie owns 1,000 shares, which she purchased in 1993 for $100,000. Moss Corporation declares a stock dividend payable in 8% preferred stock having a $100 par value. Each shareholder receives one share of preferred stock for each ten shares of common stock held. On the distribution date—November 10, 1996—the common stock was worth $180 per share and the preferred stock was worth $100 per share. On April 1, 1997, Tillie sells half of her preferred stock for $5,000.

a. How much income must Tillie recognize when she receives the stock dividend?
b. How much gain or loss must Tillie recognize when she sells the preferred stock? (Ignore the implications of Sec. 306.)
c. What is Tillie's basis in her remaining common and preferred stock? When does her holding period for the preferred stock begin?

C4-41 ***Stock Rights Distribution.*** Trusty Corporation has a single class of stock outstanding. Jim owns 200 shares of the common stock, which he purchased for $50 per share two years ago. On April 10 of the current year, Trusty Corporation distributes to its shareholders one right to purchase a share of common stock at $60 per share for each share of common stock held. At the time of the distribution, the common stock is worth $75 per share and the rights are worth $15 per right. On September 10 Jim sells 100 rights for $2,000 and exercises the remaining 100 rights. He sells 60 of the shares acquired with the rights for $80 each on November 10.
a. What are the amount and character of the income recognized when the rights are received?
b. What are the amount and character of the gain or loss recognized when the rights are sold?
c. What are the amount and character of the gain or loss recognized when the rights are exercised?
d. What are the amount and character of the gain or loss recognized when the new common stock is sold?
e. What basis does Jim have in his remaining shares?

C4-42 ***Redemption from a Sole Shareholder.*** Paul owns all 100 shares of Presto Corporation's stock. His basis in the stock is $10,000. Presto Corporation has $100,000 of E&P. Presto Corporation redeems 25 of Paul's shares for $30,000. What are the tax consequences of the redemption to Paul and to Presto Corporation?

C4-43 ***Multiple Redemptions.*** Moore Corporation has 400 shares of stock outstanding that are owned equally by four unrelated shareholders. Moore redeems 100 shares from the shareholders as shown below for $600 per share. Each shareholder has a $180 per share basis for his stock. Moore Corporation's current and accumulated E&P at the end of the tax year is $150,000.

Shareholder	*Shares Held Before the Redemption*	*Shares Redeemed*
Ann	100	70
Beth	100	20
Carol	100	10
David	100	-0-
Total	400	100

a. What are the tax consequences (e.g., amount and character of income, gain, or loss recognized and basis of remaining shares) of the redemptions to Ann, Beth, and Carol?
b. How does your answer to Part a change if Ann is Carol's mother?

C4-44 ***Attribution Rules.*** George owns 100 shares of Polar Corporation's 1,000 shares of outstanding common stock. Under the family attribution rules of Sec. 318, to which of the following individuals will George's stock be attributed?
a. George's wife
b. George's father
c. George's brother
d. George's mother-in-law
e. George's daughter
f. George's son-in law

g. George's grandfather
h. George's grandson
i. George's mother's brother (his uncle)

C4-45 ***Attribution Rules.*** Moose Corporation has 400 shares of stock outstanding that are owned as follows:

Name	*Shares*
Lara (an individual)	60
LMN Partnership (Lara is a 20% partner)	50
LST Partnership (Lara is a 70% partner)	100
Lemon Corporation (Lara is a 30% shareholder)	100
Lime Corporation (Lara is a 60% shareholder)	90
Total	400

How many shares is Lara deemed to own?

C4-46 ***Redemption—Comprehensive Illustration.*** Andrew, Bea, Carl, and Carl, Jr. (Carl's son), and Tetra Corporation own all of the single class of Excel Corporation stock as follows:

Shareholder	*Shares Held*	*Adjusted Basis*
Andrew	20	$3,000
Bea	30	6,000
Carl	25	4,000
Carl, Jr.	15	3,000
Tetra Corporation	10	2,000
Total	100	

Andrew, Bea, and Carl are unrelated. Bea owns 75% of the Tetra stock, and Andrew owns the remaining 25% of the Tetra stock. Excel Corporation's E&P is $100,000. Determine the tax consequences to the shareholders and Excel Corporation of the following independent redemptions:

a. Excel Corporation redeems 25 of Bea's shares for $30,000.
b. Excel Corporation redeems 10 of Bea's shares for $12,000.
c. Excel Corporation redeems all of Carl's shares for $30,000.
d. Assume the same facts as in Part c, except that the stock is redeemed from Carl's estate in order to pay death taxes. The entire redemption qualifies under Sec. 303. The stock has a $28,000 FMV on Carl's date of death. The alternate valuation date is not elected.
e. Excel Corporation redeems all of Andrew's shares for land having a $6,000 basis for taxable income and E&P purposes to Excel Corporation and a $24,000 FMV. Assume a 34% marginal corporate tax rate.

C4-47 ***Partial Liquidation.*** Unrelated individuals Amy, Beth, and Carla, and Delta Corporation each own 25 of the 100 outstanding shares of Axle Corporation's stock. Axle distributes $20,000 to each shareholder in exchange for five shares of Axle stock in a transaction that qualifies as a partial liquidation. Each share redeemed has a $1,000 basis to the shareholder and a $4,000 FMV. How does each shareholder treat the distribution?

C4-48 ***Effect of Redemption on E&P.*** White Corporation has 100 shares of stock outstanding, 40 of which are owned by Ann. The remaining 60 shares are owned by unrelated shareholders. White Corporation redeems 30 of Ann's shares for $30,000. In the year of the redemption, White Corporation has $30,000 of paid-in capital and $80,000 of E&P.

a. How does the redemption affect White Corporation's E&P balance if the redemption qualifies for sale treatment?

b. How does the redemption affect White Corporation's E&P balance if the redemption does *not* qualify for sale treatment?

C4-49 ***Comprehensive Redemption Problem.*** Alan, Barbara, and Dave are all unrelated. Each has owned 100 shares of Time Corporation stock for five years and each has a $60,000 basis in those 100 shares. Time's E&P is $240,000. Time redeems all 100 of Alan's shares for $100,000, their FMV.

a. What are the amount and character of Alan's recognized gain or loss? What basis do Barbara and Dave have in their remaining shares? What effect does the redemption have on Time's E&P?
b. Assuming that Alan is instead Barbara's son, answer the questions in Part a again.
c. Assume the same facts as in Part b, except that Alan signs an agreement under Sec. 302(c)(2)(A) to waive the family attribution rules. Answer the questions in Part a again.

C4-50 ***Redemption to Pay Death Taxes.*** John died on March 3. His gross estate of $2,500,000 includes First Corporation stock (400 of the 1,000 outstanding shares) worth $1,500,000. The remaining 600 shares are owned by John's wife, Myra. Funeral and administrative expenses deductible under Secs. 2053 and 2054 amount to $250,000. John, Jr. is the sole beneficiary of John's estate. Estate taxes amount to $350,000.

a. Does a redemption of First stock from John's estate, John. Jr., or John's wife qualify for sale treatment under Sec. 303?
b. On September 10 First Corporation redeems 200 shares of its stock from John's estate for $800,000. How is this redemption treated by the estate?

C4-51 ***Preferred Stock Bailout.*** In each of the following situations, does Sec. 306 apply? If so, what is its effect?

a. Beth sells her Sec. 306 stock to Marvin in a year when the issuing corporation has no E&P.
b. Zero Corporation redeems Sec. 306 stock from Jim in a year in which it has no E&P.
c. Zero Corporation redeems Sec. 306 stock from Ruth in a year in which it has a large E&P balance.
d. Joan gives 100 shares of Sec. 306 stock to her nephew, Barry.
e. Ed completely terminates his interest in Zero Corporation by having all of his common stock and preferred stock (the Sec. 306 stock in question) redeemed by Zero.
f. Carl inherits 100 shares of Sec. 306 stock from his uncle Ted.

C4-52 ***Preferred Stock Bailout.*** Fran owns all 100 shares of Star Corporation stock for which her adjusted basis is $60,000. On December 1, 1996, Star Corporation distributes 50 shares of preferred stock to Fran as a nontaxable stock dividend. In the year of the distribution, Star Corporation's E&P is $100,000, the preferred shares are worth $150,000, and the common shares are worth $300,000.

a. What are the tax consequences to Fran and to Star Corporation if Fran sells her preferred stock to Ken for $200,000 on January 10, 1997? In 1997, Star Corporation's E&P is $75,000.
b. How would your answer to Part a change if Fran sells her preferred stock to Ken for $110,000 instead of $200,000?
c. How would your answer to Part a change if Star Corporation redeems Fran's preferred stock for $200,000 on January 10, 1997?

C4-53 ***Brother-Sister Redemptions.*** Bob owns 60 of the 100 outstanding shares of Dazzle Corporation's stock and 80 of the 100 outstanding shares of Razzle Corporation's stock. Bob's basis in his Dazzle shares is $12,000, and his basis in his Razzle shares is $8,000. Bob sells 30 of his Dazzle shares to Razzle Corporation for $50,000. At the end of the year of the sale, Dazzle and Razzle Corporations have E&P of $25,000 and $40,000, respectively.

a. What are the amount and character of Bob's gain or loss on the sale?
b. What is Bob's basis in his remaining shares of the Dazzle and Razzle stock?

c. How does the sale affect the E&P of Dazzle and Razzle Corporations?
d. What basis does Razzle Corporation take in the Dazzle shares it purchases?
e. How would your answer to Part a change if Bob owns only 50 of the 100 outstanding shares of Razzle stock?

C4-54 ***Parent-Subsidiary Redemptions.*** Jane owns 150 of the 200 outstanding shares of Parent Corporation's stock. Parent owns 160 of the 200 outstanding shares of Subsidiary Corporation's stock. Jane sells 50 shares of her Parent stock to Subsidiary for $40,000. Jane's basis in her Parent shares is $15,000 ($100 per share). Subsidiary Corporation and Parent Corporation have E&P of $60,000 and $25,000, respectively, at the end of the year in which the redemption occurs.
a. What are the amount and character of Jane's gain or loss on the sale?
b. What is Jane's basis in her remaining shares of Parent stock?
c. How does the sale affect the E&P of Parent and Subsidiary Corporations?
d. What basis does Subsidiary Corporation take in the Parent shares it purchases?
e. How would your answer to Part a change if Jane instead sells 100 of her Parent shares to Subsidiary Corporation for $80,000?

C4-55 ***Bootstrap Acquisition.*** All 100 shares of Stone Corporation stock are owned by Jana Wong. Her basis for the stock is $400,000. The corporation's stock has a $1,000,000 FMV. Its E&P balance is $600,000. Michael Smith wants to purchase the Stone stock, but he does not want all of the company's assets. He wants the corporation's non-cash assets that are valued at $750,000. Michael is willing to pay $750,000 for these assets.
a. What are the tax consequences to Jana, Michael, and Stone Corporation if Michael purchases 75 shares of Stone stock for $750,000 and Stone redeems Jana's remaining 25 shares for $250,000 cash?
b. How would your answer to part *a* change (if any) should Stone first redeem 25 shares of Jana's stock for $250,000 and then Michael purchase the remaining 75 shares from Jana for $750,000?

CASE STUDY PROBLEMS

C4-56 Amy, Beth, and Meg each own 100 of the 300 outstanding shares of Theta Corporation stock. Amy wants to sell her shares which have a $40,000 basis and a $100,000 FMV. Either Beth and/or Meg can purchase her shares (50 shares each if both purchase) or Theta can redeem all of Amy's shares. Theta Corporation has a $150,000 E&P balance.

Required: Write a memorandum to the three sisters, who are active in the management of Theta, comparing the tax consequences of the two options.

C4-57 Maria Garcia is a CPA whose firm has for many years prepared the tax returns for Stanley Corporation. A review of Stanley's last three tax returns by a new staff accountant who has been assigned to the client for the first time reveals that the corporation may be paying constructive dividends to one of its key officers in the form of excessive compensation. The staff accountant feels that the firm should inform the IRS and/or report the excess amount as nondeductible dividends. The facts are sufficiently gray, i.e., there is reasonable support for the assertion that the compensation paid in the current year and prior years is reasonable in amount.

Required: Discuss Maria's role as an advocate for Stanley Corporation, and the possible consequences of a subsequent audit.

TAX RESEARCH PROBLEMS

C4-58 Hatch Corporation, a manufacturing business, was owned by Mike and his son, Steve. Hatch Corporation redeems all of Mike's stock in a transaction qualifying as a complete termination of Mike's interest in Hatch Corporation. To qualify, Mike must file an agreement not to acquire any interest in Hatch Corporation for ten years. After the redemption, Mike starts a new career as owner of a counseling firm for employees who are about to retire. Two years later, Steve wants to use Mike's firm to counsel some of his employees who are close to retirement. Mike's company charges a fixed fee for each employee counseled, and Hatch Corporation is to pay the same amount as all of Mike's other customers. Prepare a memorandum for your tax manager explaining whether Mike's counseling arrangement with Hatch Corporation violates Mike's agreement not to acquire any interest in Hatch Corporation. Your manager has suggested that, at a minimum, you consult the following resources:

- Sec. 302(c)(2).
- Reg. Sec. 1.302-4.
- Rev. Rul. 70-104, 1970-1 C.B. 66.
- *Est. of Milton S. Lennard*, 61 T.C. 554, *nonacq.* 1978-2 C.B. 3.

C4-59 When Winter Corporation is audited on its 1994 tax return, $10,000 of travel and entertainment expenses incurred by Charles, an officer-shareholder, are disallowed because of inadequate documentation. The IRS asserts that the $10,000 expenditure was a constructive dividend to Charles. Charles asserts that the expense was a business expense and that he derived no personal benefit from the expenditure and therefore should not be charged with any dividend income. Prepare a memorandum for your tax manager explaining whether the IRS's assertion or Charles's assertion is correct. Your manager has suggested that, at a minimum, you consult the following resources:

- Secs. 162 and 274.
- Reg. Secs. 1.274-1 and -2.

C4-60 Ann owns 30% of the outstanding Summer Corporation stock. The remainder is owned by unrelated individuals. Summer Corporation owns land with a $100,000 adjusted basis and a $60,000 FMV. In the current year, Summer Corporation sells the land to Ann for $50,000. Summer Corporation has E&P in excess of $200,000. Prepare a memorandum for your tax manager explaining the tax consequences of the land sale to Summer Corporation and to Ann. Assume a 34% marginal corporate tax rate. Your manager has suggested that, at a minimum, you consult the following resources:

- Secs. 301, 311, 316, and 1001.
- Reg. Secs. 1.301-1(j) and (k).
- *Jason L. Honigman v. CIR*, 30 AFTR 2d 72-5360, 72-2 USTC ¶9613 (6th Cir., 1972).

C4-61 Sara is the owner of 60% of the single class of stock of Mayfield Corporation, a calendar-year domestic corporation that uses the accrual method of accounting. The remaining 40% of Mayfield Corporation stock is owned by a group of five family members and three key employees. Sara uses the cash method of accounting. She is an officer and a member of the board of directors of Mayfield Corporation. During the period 1994-1996, Sara draws the following amounts as salary and tax-free fringe benefits from Mayfield Corporation: 1994, $160,000; 1995, $240,000; and 1996, $290,000. The amounts are earned evenly throughout the tax years in question. A revenue agent upon auditing Mayfield's tax returns for 1994-1996 determines in 1998 that reasonable compensation for Sara's services for the three years in question is $110,000, $165,000, and $175,000, respectively. The bylaws of Mayfield Corporation were amended on December 15, 1995, to provide that

> Any payments made to an officer of the corporation, including salary, commissions, bonuses, or other forms of compensation, interest, rent, or travel and entertainment expense that is incurred, and which shall be disallowed in whole or in part as a deductible expense by the Internal Revenue Service, shall be reimbursed by such officer to the corporation to the full extent of such disallowance.

Following the disallowance of the salary expense, the board of directors meets and requests payment of the aforementioned amounts from Sara. Because of the large amount of money involved, the board of directors approves an installment plan whereby the $240,000 would be repaid in five annual installments of $48,000 each over the period 1998-2002. No interest will be required to be paid on the unpaid balance of $240,000. Prepare a memorandum for your tax manager explaining what salary and fringe benefits are taxable to Sara in the period 1994-1996, and what repayments are deductible by Sara during the period 1998-2002.

CHAPTER 5

OTHER CORPORATE TAX LEVIES

LEARNING OBJECTIVES

After studying this chapter, you should be able to

1. Calculate the amount of the corporation's alternative minimum tax liability (if any)
2. Determine whether a corporation is a personal holding company (PHC)
3. Calculate the amount of the corporation's PHC tax liability
4. Evaluate whether a corporation has an accumulated earnings tax problem
5. Calculate the amount of the corporation's accumulated earnings tax liability
6. Explain how a corporation can avoid being subject to the personal holding company tax
7. Explain how a corporation can avoid being subject to the accumulated earnings tax

CHAPTER OUTLINE

Chapter C3 examined the general corporate tax liability formula and the procedures for calculating, reporting, and paying the corporate income tax liability. Chapter C5 continues this examination of the corporate tax liability formula by examining three additional tax levies that may be imposed on a C corporation. These include the corporate alternative minimum tax, personal holding company penalty tax and accumulated earnings penalty tax. Each additional tax liability may be imposed in different situations. This chapter examines when each levy is likely to be incurred, and means by which a corporate taxpayer can avoid having to pay the additional taxes.

THE CORPORATE ALTERNATIVE MINIMUM TAX

OBJECTIVE 1

Calculate the amount of the corporation's alternative minimum tax liability (if any)

THE GENERAL FORMULA

The **alternative minimum tax (AMT)** for corporations is similar to that for individuals. The objective of the tax is to ensure that every corporation with substantial economic income pays a corporate tax liability despite the use of exclusions, deductions, and credits.

The starting point for computing a corporation's AMT is its taxable income. Taxable income is increased by tax preference items, modified by adjustments, and reduced by a statutory exemption amount. The resulting tax base is multiplied by 20% to yield the **tentative minimum tax (TMT)**. If the TMT exceeds the corporation's regular (income) tax, the excess is the corporation's AMT liability. If the TMT does not exceed the corporation's regular tax, no AMT liability is owed. The computation of a corporation's AMT is outlined in Table C5-1.

ADDITIONAL COMMENT

The corporate AMT produces little tax revenue. In 1993, AMT collections were $4.9 billion compared to $149.0 billion for the corporate income tax.

▼ TABLE C5-1

Determination of the Corporate Alternative Minimum Tax Liability

Taxable income or loss before NOL deduction	
Plus:	Tax preference items
Plus or minus:	Adjustments to taxable income other than the ACE adjustment and the alternative tax NOL deduction
Pre-adjustment AMTI	
Plus or minus:	75% of the difference between pre-adjustment AMTI and adjusted current earnings (ACE)
Minus:	Alternative tax NOL deduction
Alternative minimum taxable income (AMTI)	
Minus:	Statutory exemption
Tax base	
Times:	0.20 tax rate
Tentative minimum tax before credits	
Minus:	AMT foreign tax credit (AMT FTC)
Tentative minimum tax (TMT)	
Minus:	Regular (income) tax
Alternative minimum tax (if any) owed (AMT)	

REAL WORLD EXAMPLE

The AMT is not a popular tax because it is complex and is imposed in addition to the income tax. A 1995 Mobil Oil advertisement concluded that repealing the AMT would reduce the cost of capital by 3%, which would trigger more investment, faster productivity growth, higher gross domestic product and increased employment.

ADDITIONAL COMMENT

The AMT results in an acceleration of the income recognition process as compared to the income tax. This acceleration is accomplished by adding back tax preference items and making other adjustments to taxable income in arriving at AMTI. Even though the AMT rate (20%) is lower than the top corporate income tax rate (35%), the AMT system results in a higher tax liability for some corporations because the tax base under the AMT is larger than the tax base for income tax purposes.

DEFINITIONS

This section defines the terms used in the AMT[1] computation.

ALTERNATIVE MINIMUM TAXABLE INCOME (AMTI). **Alternative minimum taxable income** is the corporation's taxable income (1) increased by tax preference items, (2) adjusted (either up or down) for income, gain, deduction, and loss items that have to be recomputed under the AMT, and (3) reduced by the alternative tax NOL deduction.

STATUTORY EXEMPTION AMOUNT. AMTI is reduced by a statutory exemption to arrive at the AMT tax base. The exemption amount is $40,000, but it is reduced by 25% of the amount by which AMTI exceeds $150,000. The statutory exemption is phased out when AMTI equals $310,000.

EXAMPLE C5-1 ▶ Yellow Corporation's AMTI is $200,000. Its exemption amount is $27,500 {$40,000 − [0.25 × ($200,000 − $150,000)]}. ◀

TENTATIVE MINIMUM TAX. The tentative minimum tax is calculated by multiplying 20% times the corporation's AMTI less a statutory exemption amount, and deducting foreign tax credits allowable under the AMT (AMT FTCs).[2]

REGULAR TAX. A corporation's **regular tax** is its tax liability for income tax purposes, as defined in Sec. 26(b), reduced by foreign tax credits and possession tax credits allowable for income tax purposes under Sec. 27 but before other tax credits.

ALTERNATIVE MINIMUM TAX. The AMT equals the amount by which a corporation's TMT exceeds its regular tax for the year.

The following example illustrates the AMT computation.

EXAMPLE C5-2 ▶ Badger Corporation has $400,000 of taxable income. It also has $350,000 of tax preferences and $250,000 of positive adjustments for AMT purposes. It has no tax credits available. Badger's regular tax liability is $136,000 (0.34 × $400,000). Badger's AMTI is $1,000,000 ($400,000 taxable income + $250,000 adjustments + $350,000 tax preferences). Its AMT exemption is zero because AMTI exceeds $310,000. Therefore, its AMT tax base (i.e., AMTI minus statutory exemption) is also $1,000,000. Its TMT is $200,000 (0.20 × $1,000,000). Badger's AMT liability is $64,000 ($200,000 − $136,000). Thus, Badger must pay a total federal tax liability of $200,000 ($136,000 + $64,000).

STOP & THINK

Question: Badger Corporation in our preceding example pays both the federal income tax and the AMT. How can this be possible if the top federal income tax rate for corporations with less than $10 million of taxable income is 34% and the AMT rate is a constant 20%?

Solution: It is possible because different tax bases are used for the two tax levies. The income tax is based on taxable income. The AMT is based on alternative minimum taxable income less a statutory exemption. The AMT is owed when the TMT amount exceeds the regular (income) tax amount. The situation where the AMT is owed can be expressed as follows:

$$[\text{Taxable Income (TI)} + \text{Preferences (P)} + \text{Adjustments (A)}] \times 0.20 > \text{TI} \times 0.34$$

Multiplying the terms on the two sides of the inequality and simplifying the terms produces the following relationship:

[1] Sec. 55.

[2] Sec. 55(b).

$$.20\ (P + A) > 0.14\ TI$$

$$(P + A) > 0.70\ TI$$

Looking back at Example C5-2 where the AMT was incurred, the preferences and adjustments were $350,000 and $250,000, respectively, or $600,000 in total. Seventy percent of taxable income is $280,000 (0.70 × $400,000). The general relationship between (P + A) and TI holds in our example.[a]

[a] The relationship between (P + A) and TI may be different if the corporation is subject to a marginal income tax rate that is lower (e.g., 15% or 25%) or higher (e.g., 35%, 38%, or 39%) than the 34% marginal income tax rate used above.

TYPICAL MISCONCEPTION

One distinction between tax preference items and adjustments is that tax preference items always increase AMTI, whereas an adjustment can result in an increase or a decrease in AMTI.

TAX PREFERENCE ITEMS

Common **tax preference items** that must be added to a corporation's taxable income to compute its AMTI include[3]

- The excess of the depletion deduction allowable for the tax year over the adjusted basis of the depletable property at the end of the tax year (excluding the current year's depletion deduction).[4]

EXAMPLE C5-3 ▶ Duffy Corporation mines iron ore in the upper peninsula of Michigan. The adjusted basis for one of its properties has been fully recovered by depletion in previous years. Current year gross income and taxable income earned from the sale of ore taken from this property are $125,000, and $45,000, respectively. The iron ore depletion percentage is 15%. Percentage depletion is $18,750 ($125,000 × 0.15) because it is less than the 50% of taxable income ceiling ($22,500 = $45,000 × 0.50). All of the percentage depletion is deductible when determining taxable income. Because the property's basis has already been reduced to zero, all of the percentage depletion is a tax preference item. The effect of the preference item is to reduce the depletion deduction to zero when determining AMTI. ◀

- The amount by which excess intangible drilling and development costs (IDCs) incurred in connection with oil, gas, and geothermal wells exceeds 65% of the net income from such properties.[5]
- Tax-exempt interest on certain private activity bonds issued after August 8, 1986. Although the interest on private activity bonds is tax-exempt for regular tax purposes it can increase the corporation's federal tax liability by being included as a preference item in determining AMTI and the AMT.

EXAMPLE C5-4 ▶ Salek Corporation reports the following interest income for the current year:

Source	*Amount*
IBM corporate bonds	$25,000
Wayne County school district bonds	30,000
City of Detroit bonds	15,000

The City of Detroit bonds were issued in 1994 to finance a parking garage, where 35% of the space is leased to a nonexempt corporation for its exclusive use, and are considered private activity bonds. The Wayne County bonds were issued to renovate existing school facilities. Only the interest from the IBM bonds is taxable for income tax purposes. Only the interest

[3] Sec. 57(a).

[4] The percentage depletion preference is repealed for oil and gas depletion claimed by independent producers and royalty owners for 1993 and later tax years. The oil and gas percentage depletion preference applies almost exclusively to integrated oil companies.

[5] The oil and gas excess IDC preference was repealed for independent producers for 1993 and later years, but continues to apply to integrated oil companies. Excess IDCs are the amount by which IDCs arising in the tax year exceed the deduction that would have been allowable if the IDCs had been capitalized and amortized using the straight-line method over a ten-year period.

from the City of Detroit bonds is a tax preference item when computing AMTI because the school district bonds were not used for a private activity. ◀

- The excess of accelerated depreciation claimed on real property for the tax year over a hypothetical straight-line depreciation allowance based on the property's useful life or a special ACRS recovery period. This preference item applies only to realty placed in service before 1987.[6]

ADJUSTMENTS TO TAXABLE INCOME

While tax preferences always *increase* taxable income, adjustments require a recomputation of certain income, gain, loss, and deduction items and may either *increase* or *decrease* taxable income. Common adjustments that must be made to taxable income to obtain AMTI are as follows:[7]

ADDITIONAL COMMENT

The accelerated depreciation on certain pre-1987 assets, which is in excess of straight-line depreciation, is a tax preference item. Because a tax preference item never decreases taxable income, no adjustment is made when the straight-line depreciation eventually exceeds the accelerated depreciation. Thus, pre-1987 assets are not fully depreciated for AMT purposes. The adjustment for post-1986 assets is more equitable because it allows both increases and decreases to taxable income. Thus, post-1986 assets can be fully depreciated for AMT purposes.

- Depreciation on property placed in service after 1986 and depreciated using the MACRS system must be recomputed using the alternative depreciation system of Sec. 168(g).[8] Taxable income is increased (or decreased) by the amount by which the total depreciation deduction for regular tax purposes exceeds (or is less than) the total depreciation allowance for AMT purposes.
- The depreciation method for personal property is generally the 150% declining balance method, switching to the straight-line method in the first year in which it results in a larger allowance. The recovery period for personal property is the property's class life determined under the asset depreciation range (ADR) system. If personal property has no class life, the recovery period is twelve years. If the straight-line depreciation method is used for regular tax purposes, no recalculation of the AMT depreciation is required.
- The depreciation method for real property is straight-line. A forty-year recovery period combined with the mid-month convention is used for commercial real property and residential rental property.

EXAMPLE C5-5 ▶ Bulldog Corporation places into service office furniture property costing $3,000 having a ten-year class life. The property's regular tax recovery period is seven years under MACRS. The property's alternative MACRS ten-year recovery period is used when computing AMTI depreciation. Regular tax depreciation is $429 [$3,000 × 0.1429 (Table 1, Appendix C)] in the first year with the half-year convention. AMTI depreciation is $225 [$3,000 × 0.075 (Table 9, Appendix C)] in the first year. The smaller AMTI depreciation results in a $204 ($429 − $225) positive adjustment to taxable income. ◀

KEY POINT

When different depreciation methods are used for regular tax and AMT purposes, the adjusted bases for the depreciable assets are affected. Thus, when these assets are disposed of, an adjustment is made to taxable income to reflect the difference in the regular tax gain or loss and the AMT gain or loss.

- Separate gain or loss calculations are made for regular tax and AMT purposes when a disposition of real or personal property occurs. A depreciable property's basis for regular tax purposes is adjusted downward by the regular tax depreciation allowance. A depreciable property's basis for AMT purposes is adjusted downward by the AMT depreciation allowance. Therefore, an asset may have different bases amounts for regular tax and AMT purposes. An adjustment is made for the difference between the amount of gain or loss that was recognized for taxable income purposes and the gain or loss that is recognized for AMTI purposes. The adjustment process is illustrated in the following example.

---

[6] Similar excess depreciation preference provisions apply to pre-1987 personal property leased by a personal holding company (see page C5-14) and pre-1987 certified pollution control facilities being amortized over a 5-year period. These preferences not often encountered.

[7] Sec. 56(a).

[8] Sec. 56(a)(1). The recovery periods and annual depreciation rates for making the regular tax and AMT depreciation calculations are contained in Appendix C of this text.

EXAMPLE C5-6 ▶ Assume the same facts as in Example C5-5 except that on April 1 of the fourth year Bulldog Corporation sells the property for $2,000. The depreciation allowances claimed for regular tax and AMT purposes, adjusted basis for the property at the beginning of the year for each tax calculation, and the positive or negative adjustment to taxable income in arriving at AMTI for each of the four years are presented below.

	Regular Tax			**AMT**			
Year	*1/1 Adj. Basis(1)*	*Depn.(2)*	*12/31 Adj. Basis(3)*[a]	*1/1 Adj. Basis(4)*	*Depn.(5)*	*12/31 Adj. Basis(6)*[b]	*Taxable Income Adjustment(7)*[c]
1	$3,000	$429	$2,571	$3,000	$225	$2,775	$224
2	2,571	735	1,836	2,775	416	2,359	319
3	1,836	525	1,311	2,359	354	2,005	171
4	1,311	187	1,124	2,005	151	1,854	36
		$1,876			$1,146		$730

[a] (3) = (1) − (2) Adjusted basis for sale date is the depreciation claimed in year 4.
[b] (6) = (4) − (5) Six months of depreciation is claimed in year 4.
[c] (7) = (2) − (5)

An $876 ($2,000 proceeds − $1,124 adjusted basis) gain is recognized in Year 4 for regular tax purposes. An $146 ($2,000 proceeds − $1,854 adjusted basis) gain is recognized for AMT purposes. This necessitates a $730 negative adjustment to taxable income when computing AMTI to take into account the different depreciation allowances in the four years. The basis adjustment amount is the net of the positive and negative depreciation adjustments for the four years. ◀

- ▶ The installment method may not be used for AMT purposes to report gains on inventory sales. The installment method may be used by nondealers to report casual sales for AMT purposes.
- ▶ Long-term contracts entered into after March 1, 1986 must be accounted for using the percentage of completion method. Corporations using the percentage of completion-capitalized cost or cash methods of accounting for regular tax purposes must make adjustments when determining AMTI.
- ▶ Closely held corporations and personal service corporations must refigure losses coming under the at-risk and passive activity limitation rules, taking into account the corporation's AMTI adjustments and tax preference items.
- ▶ The NOL deduction is replaced with the alternative tax NOL deduction. To compute the alternative tax NOL deduction, the NOL deduction is adjusted in the same way that taxable income is adjusted in arriving at AMTI. The NOL is reduced by adding back any tax preference items and any losses disallowed under the passive activity limitation and at-risk rules. Generally the alternative tax NOL is a different amount from the regular tax NOL because of these adjustments. The resulting alternative tax NOL will be carried back three years and forward fifteen years. The alternative tax NOL deduction cannot exceed 90% of AMTI before the alternative tax NOL deduction.

The following example illustrates the computation of pre-adjustment AMTI.

EXAMPLE C5-7 ▶ Marion Corporation engages in copper mining activities. In the current year it reports taxable income of $300,000, which includes deductions of $70,000 for percentage depletion and $80,000 for MACRS depreciation. $30,000 of the percentage depletion claimed was in excess of the adjusted basis of the depletable properties. The hypothetical AMT depreciation deduction under the alternative depreciation system would have been only $55,000. Pre-adjustment AMTI is determined as follows:

Taxable income		$300,000
Plus:	Percentage depletion claimed in excess of basis	30,000
	MACRS depreciation claimed	80,000
Minus:	AMTI depreciation	(55,000)
Pre-adjustment AMTI		$355,000

The depreciation adjustment results in an increase in AMTI of $25,000. ◀

ADJUSTED CURRENT EARNINGS (ACE) ADJUSTMENT

HISTORICAL NOTE

The ACE adjustment is a complex computation. It was added in an attempt to further adjust the AMT tax base towards the corporation's economic income. However, the ACE adjustment, as initially enacted by the Tax Reform Act of 1986, would have been much more complicated. The single most important simplification is that the ACE depreciation does not include the present value computations required by the 1986 Act.

For 1990 and later tax years a corporation makes a positive adjustment equal to 75% of the excess of its ACE over its AMTI (before this adjustment and the alternative tax NOL deduction).[9] **ACE** is a concept based on the earnings and profits (E&P) definition that has been used for years to determine whether a corporate distribution is a dividend or a return of capital (see Chapter C4). ACE equals pre-adjustment AMTI for the tax year plus or minus a series of special adjustments described below. However, it is emphasized that ACE is not the same as E&P, even though many items are treated in the same manner for both purposes. The ACE adjustment is not required of an S corporation since they are treated as individual taxpayers and the AMT tax preferences and adjustments flow through to their shareholders.[10] A $1 positive ACE adjustment results in a 15% (0.20 statutory rate × 0.75 inclusion ratio) effective tax rate being incurred if the corporation's TMT (before the ACE adjustment) exceeds its regular tax amount.

A negative adjustment is also permitted equal to 75% of the excess of the corporation's pre-adjustment AMTI over its ACE. The negative adjustment, however, cannot exceed the cumulative net amount of its prior year positive and negative ACE adjustments.[11] Any excess of pre-adjustment AMTI over ACE that is not allowed as a negative adjustment because of the limitation cannot be carried over to a later year to reduce a required positive ACE adjustment.

EXAMPLE C5-8 ▶ Bravo Corporation, which was organized in 1995, reports the following ACE and pre-adjustment AMTI amounts for 1995–1997.

	1995	*1996*	*1997*
ACE	$2,000	$1,500	$1,000
Pre-adjustment AMTI	1,500	1,500	1,500

A $375 [($2,000 − $1,500) × 0.75] positive ACE adjustment is made in 1995. No ACE adjustment is made in 1996 because ACE and pre-adjustment AMTI are equal. A $375 [($1,000 − $1,500) × 0.75] negative ACE adjustment is made in 1997. ◀

EXAMPLE C5-9 ▶ Assume the same facts as in Example C5-8 except that the pre-adjustment AMTI amount in 1997 is $2,000. The tentative negative ACE adjustment is $750 [($1,000 − $2,000) × 0.75]. Only a $375 negative ACE adjustment can be made because the negative ACE adjustment may not exceed the $375 ($375 + $0) total cumulative net positive ACE adjustments made in prior years. ◀

Four general rules provide a framework for the ACE calculation:

- Any amount that is permanently excluded from gross income when computing AMTI, but which is taken into account in determining E&P, is included in gross income for

[9] This amount is known as **pre-adjustment AMTI**.
[10] Sec. 56(g)(6).
[11] Sec. 56(g)(2).

ACE purposes (e.g., interest on tax-exempt bonds other than private activity bonds, and the proceeds of life insurance contracts). The adjustment is reduced by any deduction that would have been allowable in computing AMTI had the excluded income amount been included in gross income for AMTI purposes. No adjustment is made for any timing differences. Thus any item that is, has been, or will be included in pre-adjustment AMTI will not be included in this category of ACE adjustment.

- A deduction cannot be claimed when computing ACE for any item that would not be deductible in the tax year when computing E&P, even if such item would be deductible in determining pre-adjustment AMTI. These items increase ACE to the extent that they are deductible in determining pre-adjustment AMTI.[12] The 80% and 100% dividends-received deductions are claimed for ACE purposes although they cannot be deducted when computing E&P. The 70% dividends-received deduction, however, is not claimed for either ACE or E&P purposes.
- Items included in pre-adjustment AMTI are included in ACE, even if the item is not included in E&P.
- Items not deductible in determining pre-adjustment AMTI are not deducted when computing ACE, even if the item is deductible in arriving at E&P. Examples include federal income taxes and capital losses in excess of capital gains.[13]

TYPICAL MISCONCEPTION

Interest on certain state and local government obligations has traditionally not been subject to the federal income tax. However, to the extent that a corporation's tax-exempt income is not already included in AMTI as a preference item (e.g., interest income on private activity bonds), 75% of such income is subjected to the AMT through the ACE adjustment. If the corporation's TMT exceeds its regular tax before the ACE adjustment is made, a 15% effective tax rate is incurred on the bond interest income. State and local governments have expressed concern over this aspect of the ACE adjustment, which they view as an impediment to their ability to raise capital.

In addition to the four general rules, a series of specific adjustments mandated by Sec. 56(g) must be made to AMTI to arrive at ACE. The more common adjustments are presented below. As with the general AMT adjustments presented above, these items require a recomputation of certain income, gain, loss, and deduction items and may either increase or decrease AMTI. Unless otherwise indicated these changes are effective for tax years beginning after 1989.

- Depreciation on property placed in service in a tax year beginning after 1989 and before January 1, 1994 is determined using the alternative depreciation system. All property is depreciated using the straight-line method with the appropriate recovery period and averaging convention described under the alternative depreciation system rules.[14] Elimination of the ACE depreciation adjustment for property placed in service after December 31, 1993 does not keep a corporation from having to make the adjustment for property placed in service before 1994. Special transitional rules apply to property placed in service before 1990. These rules are found in Sec. 56(g)(4)(A).
- An asset's adjusted basis is determined by using the depreciation, depletion, or amortization rules appropriate for the ACE calculation. As a result, a basis adjustment similar to that described above for the AMTI calculation may be required when an asset is sold, exchanged, or otherwise disposed of.[15]
- The installment method cannot be used to compute ACE for dealer and nondealer installment sales made after 1989.[16]
- Organizational expenditures that are otherwise amortizable under Sec. 248 are not amortized for ACE purposes if incurred after December 31, 1989.[17]
- The increase or decrease in the LIFO recapture amount that takes place during the year increases or decreases ACE. The LIFO recapture amount is the amount by which the inventory amount under the first-in, first-out (FIFO) inventory method exceeds the inventory amount under the last-in, first-out (LIFO) method.[18] This adjustment

ADDITIONAL COMMENT

The ACE depreciation adjustment was the single largest ACE adjustment for tax years 1990–1993. Elimination of the need to make such an adjustment for property acquired in 1994 and later tax years reduces both the taxpayer's expense incurred in calculating the adjustment and the government's revenues from the AMT.

ADDITIONAL COMMENT

Even if a corporation is not currently subject to the AMT, both the AMT and ACE depreciation amounts should be calculated annually. A less efficient and more costly approach is to wait until the AMT applies and then try to compute the appropriate depreciation numbers for past years.

---

[12] Secs. 56(g)(4)(C)(i) and (ii). A partial list of items falling into this category is presented in Reg. Sec. 1.56(g)-1(d)(3) and (4).
[13] Reg. Sec. 1.56(g)-1(e).
[14] Sec. 56(g)(4)(A).
[15] Sec. 56(g)(4)(I).
[16] Sec. 56(g)(4)(D)(iv).
[17] Sec. 56(g)(4)(D)(ii).
[18] Secs. 56(g)(4)(D)(iii) and 312(n)(4).

converts a corporation from the LIFO method to the FIFO method for ACE purposes.

- Depletion with respect to any property placed in service after 1989 is determined by using the cost depletion method.[19] Intangible drilling costs must be amortized over 60 months commencing with the month in which they are paid or incurred.
- Charitable contribution and percentage depletion deduction limits must be recalculated to take into account AMT adjustment and preference items.[20] Taxpayers must also maintain separate carryovers for regular tax and AMT purposes. Corporations must determine separate charitable contribution limitations and carryovers for AMT and ACE purposes. For many corporations, the AMT and ACE charitable contribution limits will be larger than the regular tax limit because the ACE and AMT adjusted taxable income counterparts are usually larger.

Topic Review C5-1 summarizes the ACE calculation.

STOP & THINK

Question: Flair Corporation was considering making an investment in debt obligations issued by a state or local government. Flair's Chief Financial Officer (CFO) knew that the interest earned on these obligations was exempt from the federal income tax. In addition, the state in which Flair operates exempts interest income earned from state and local bonds issued within the state from the state income tax. The CFO was surprised to find out over a round of golf that the so-called tax-exempt interest income could be taxed at up to a 20% rate by the federal government if earned by a corporation. She called her CPA to find out more about this problem. What did the CPA say?

Solution: If the debt obligation is a private activity bond issued after 1986, the interest income is a tax preference item. Under the corporate alternative minimum tax, $1 of interest income that is a tax preference item can produce one of the following scenarios:

Excluding Interest Income	*Including Interest Income*	*Additional Tax on $1 of Interest Income*
TMT > regular tax	TMT > regular tax	$0.20
TMT < regular tax	TMT < regular tax	$0.00
TMT < regular tax	TMT > regular tax	0 to $0.20

If the interest income is not a tax preference item, then only 75% of the income is included in the ACE adjustment. The $0.20 additional tax on $1 of interest is reduced to $0.15 (0.75 × $0.20) for tax-exempt interest income earned from debt obligations other than private activity obligations.

COMPREHENSIVE EXAMPLE. Glidden Corporation reports the following taxable income and tax liability information for 1996:

Gross profit from sales	$300,000
Dividends: From 20%-owned corporation	10,000
From 10%-owned corporation	20,000
Gain on sale of depreciable property	12,778
Installment gain on sale of land	25,000
Gross income	$367,778

[19] Sec. 56(g)(4)(G).

[20] Ltr. Rul. 9320003 (February 1, 1993). Because the IRS treats the AMT as a parallel taxing system independent of the regular tax, the need to recalculate a limit apparently applies to any deduction that is restricted to a certain fraction of the firm's taxable income.

Topic Review C5-1

Summary of Common Alternative Minimum Tax Adjustments

Income/Expense Item	Most Common Adjustment to:[a] Taxable Income to Arrive at AMTI	Pre-adjustment AMTI to Arrive at ACE
Tax-exempt bond interest:		
Private activity bonds	Increase	None
Other bonds	None	Increase
Life insurance proceeds	None	Increase
Deferred gain on nondealer installment sales	None	Increase
LIFO inventory adjustment	None	Increase
"Basis adjustment" on asset sale	Decrease	Decrease
Depreciation	Increase	Increase
Excess charitable contributions	Decrease	Decrease
Excess capital losses	None	None
Dividends-received deduction:		
80% and 100% DRD	None	None
70% DRD	None	Increase
Organizational expenditure amortization	None	Increase
Federal income taxes	None	None
Penalties and fines	None	None
Disallowed travel and entertainment expenses and club dues	None	None

[a] Adjustments such as depreciation may increase or decrease taxable income to arrive at AMTI. The most common of the two possible adjustments is shown in all cases in the summary.

Operating expenses	(175,000)
Depreciation	(40,000)
Amortization of organizational expenditures	(2,500)
Dividends-received deduction	(22,000)
Total deductions	($239,500)
Taxable income	$128,278
Income (regular) tax liability	$ 33,278

The following additional information is available:

- Tax-exempt bond interest of $15,000 was earned. The income is not from private activity bonds.
- Life insurance proceeds of $100,000 were received on the death of a key executive.
- The land was sold in the current year with a total gain of $77,000, of which $25,000 was reported for regular tax purposes this year under the installment method. Glidden is not a dealer, and no interest charge is paid on the taxes owed on the deferred gain.
- The gains reported for AMTI and ACE purposes on the depreciable property sale are $5,860 and $3,750, respectively.
- Depreciation for AMTI and ACE purposes is $32,500 and $26,000, respectively. The $6,500 ACE depreciation adjustment is for property acquired before 1994.
- Organizational expenditures were incurred in 1994 and are being amortized over a sixty-month period for regular tax purposes.

Pre-adjustment AMTI is calculated as follows:

Taxable income	$128,278
Plus: Depreciation adjustment	7,500[a]
Minus: Basis adjustment on machine sale	(6,918)[b]
Pre-adjustment AMTI	$128,860

[a] $40,000 − $32,500 = $7,500.
[b] $12,778 − $5,860 = $6,918.

AMTI depreciation is smaller than taxable income depreciation because different depreciation calculations are employed. The gain on the depreciable property sale is smaller for pre-adjustment AMTI and ACE purposes (than for taxable income purposes) because smaller total depreciation was claimed before the sale under the alternative depreciation system. An installment sale adjustment for the $52,000 deferred gain is not made when calculating pre-adjustment AMTI because the land is not held as inventory.

Adjusted current earnings (ACE) is calculated as follows:

Pre-adjustment AMTI	$128,860
Plus: Tax-exempt bond interest	15,000
Life insurance proceeds	100,000
Deferred gain on land sale	52,000
Depreciation adjustment	6,500[a]
Organizational expenditures adjustment	2,500
Dividends-received deduction adjustment	14,000
Minus: Basis adjustment on machine sale	(2,110)[b]
Adjusted current earnings	$316,750

[a] $32,500 − $26,000 = $6,500.
[b] $5,860 − $3,750 = $2,110.

The life insurance policy proceeds and the tax-exempt bond interest are inclusions only for ACE. Part of the gain on the sale of the land is included in taxable income and pre-adjustment AMTI under the installment method. The entire gain is reported for ACE purposes in the year of sale because the installment method is not permitted for ACE purposes for dealers or nondealers except where interest is charged for the tax deferral privilege. No deduction is allowed for ACE purposes for the amortization of the organizational expenditures and the dividends received from the 10%-owned corporation.

The AMT liability is calculated as follows:

Pre-adjustment AMTI		$128,860
Plus: ACE	$316,750	
Minus: Pre-adjustment AMTI	(128,860)	
Difference	$187,890	
Times: 75% inclusion ratio	× 0.75	140,917
Alternative minimum taxable income		$269,777
Minus: Statutory exemption		(10,056)[a]
AMT tax base		$259,721
Times: 20% tax rate		× 0.20
Tentative minimum tax		$ 51,944
Minus: Regular tax		(33,278)
Alternative minimum tax		$ 18,666

[a] $40,000 − [0.25 × ($269,777 − $150,000)] = $10,056.

A reduced statutory exemption is available because of the phase-out that occurs when AMTI is in excess of $150,000. The AMT liability is the excess of the tentative minimum tax over the regular tax. A completed Form 4626 for this comprehensive example is presented in Appendix B.

MINIMUM TAX CREDIT

KEY POINT

Because the AMT often accelerates the recognition of income, an item of income can be taxed twice, once by the AMT and a second time by the regular tax. Thus, a minimum tax credit is necessary to ameliorate this inequity.

The AMT is simply an acceleration of the payment of a corporation's income taxes. When an AMT liability is paid, a corporation may be eligible to take a **minimum tax credit** that can be offset against its future regular tax liabilities. The minimum tax credit is necessary to prevent the same item from being taxed twice: once as part of the AMT liability and a second time as part of the regular tax liability.

For 1990 and later tax years, the entire corporate AMT liability may be claimed as a credit. This includes the portion of the AMT liability that is due to deferral adjustments and preference items that represent timing differences that will reverse in another tax year as well as the portion of the AMT liability that is due to permanent adjustments and preference items that will never reverse.[21]

The minimum tax credit that can be used by a corporation in a tax year equals the total of the net minimum taxes paid in all prior post-1986 tax years minus the amount claimed as a minimum tax credit in those years. Use of available minimum tax credits in the current year is limited to the excess of the corporation's regular tax amount (minus all credits other than refundable credits) over its tentative minimum tax.

EXAMPLE C5-10 ▶ In the current year, Seminole Corporation has $400,000 of taxable income plus $250,000 of positive adjustments plus $350,000 of tax preference items. Its regular tax liability is $136,000 (0.34 × $400,000). Its AMT liability is $64,000 [(0.20 × $1,000,000)− $136,000]. Seminole's minimum tax credit is the entire amount of its AMT liability, or $64,000. ◀

ADDITIONAL COMMENT

Use of the AMT credit is limited. 1992 corporate AMT collections were $4.86 billion. 1993 AMT credits claimed were $3.09 billion. The reason: some corporations elect to use other credits that have a limited life, or some corporations end up owing the AMT in consecutive years.

The minimum tax credit may be carried forward indefinitely and used to offset regular tax liabilities in future years, but only to the extent the regular tax amount exceeds the corporation's TMT in the carryforward year. The minimum tax credit cannot be carried back to an earlier tax year.

TAX CREDITS AND THE AMT

As illustrated in Table C3-2, a corporation is allowed to reduce its regular tax liability by any available tax credits. Special rules restrict the use of tax credits against the corporate AMT. These rules are explained below.

ADDITIONAL COMMENT

Because the general business credit limitation is tied to the TMT, ***every*** corporation with excess general business credits will have to compute its TMT, even though the corporation may not have an AMT liability.

KEY POINT

Because the purpose of the AMT is to ensure that all profitable corporations pay tax, the use of tax credits is also limited. For example, the general business credit cannot reduce the regular tax below the TMT.

AMT AND THE GENERAL BUSINESS CREDIT. Several limitations have been placed on the use of the general business credit to prevent it from offsetting all of a corporation's regular tax amount and certain other taxes. The general business credit may not be used to offset the alternative minimum tax, the accumulated earnings tax, or the personal holding company (PHC) tax.

The following rule prevents the general business credit from offsetting all of a corporation's tax, and it also prevents the credit from offsetting any of the corporation's AMT. Under Sec. 38(c), the general business credit for a tax year is limited to the excess (if any) of the corporation's net income tax over the greater of its tentative minimum tax or 25% of its net regular tax liability in excess of $25,000.

A corporation's net income tax is the sum of its regular tax and AMT liabilities reduced by any credits allowed under Secs. 21-29 (which includes nonrefundable credits such as the foreign tax credit, possessions credit, drug testing credit, and nonconventional fuel

[21] Sec. 53. Most AMT adjustments and preference items result in a deferral of the regular tax liability rather than a permanent reduction. The two permanent preferences are percentage depletion and tax-exempt private activity bond interest. Examples of permanent ACE adjustments include life insurance proceeds and tax-exempt bond interest from other than private activity bonds.

WHAT WOULD YOU DO IN THIS SITUATION?

Sheffield Corporation, a C corporation, has completed its fifth year of operation with $3.4 million in sales. The corporation had only five employees at the end of its first year of operations and has grown to over 100 employees by the end of 1996. The accounting and tax work has been done by a small accounting firm with only three accounting professionals during these first five years. Sheffield's management wants to go public in the next three years and during 1996 the firm changed to a larger accounting firm with forty professionals. Al E. Gator is the tax partner assigned to oversee the work on Sheffield's 1996 income tax return as well as the tax returns of its top executives. One of Al E. Gator's tax managers reports that Sheffield has never prepared any calculations of its alternative minimum tax position. According to Sheffield's CEO, the small accounting firm personnel always "eyeballed" the calculation and said there was no problem. The manager reminds Al that Sheffield made an installment sale of land that was adjacent to its manufacturing building this year for a $1 million profit. The Sec. 1231 gain that was realized was more than its operating profit. What can you do regarding the alternative minimum tax issue and the prior four years tax returns? Should you report your new client's problem to the IRS?

credit). A corporation's net regular tax liability is its regular tax liability reduced by any credits allowed under Secs. 21-29. Any general business credits that cannot be used in the current year may be carried back three years and forward fifteen years.[22]

The result of this limitation is that the general business credit can offset only the portion of the regular tax that exceeds the TMT, not all of a corporation's regular tax.

EXAMPLE C5-11 ▶ In the current year, Scientific Corporation's net regular tax liability before credits is $125,000. Its TMT is $50,000. Scientific's only available credit for the year is a general business credit of $140,000. Scientific's net income tax amount is $125,000 because its net regular tax liability ($125,000) is greater than its TMT ($50,000). As computed below, Scientific's general business credit is limited to the smaller of its $75,000 credit limitation or the $140,000 credit that was earned.

Net income tax amount		$125,000
Minus: Greater of:		
(1) 25% of net regular tax liability in excess of $25,000 [0.25 × ($125,000 − $25,000)]	$ 25,000	
OR		
(2) Tentative minimum tax	$ 50,000	(50,000)
General business credit limitation		$ 75,000

Scientific has an income tax liability of $50,000 ($125,000 − $75,000) and no AMT liability. Their general business credit carryback or carryover is $65,000 ($140,000 − $75,000), which can be carried back three years and forward fifteen years. ◀

AMT AND THE FOREIGN TAX CREDIT. For purposes of computing the AMT, foreign tax credits (AMT FTCs) are limited to the excess of the TMT over 10% of the TMT excluding the alternative tax NOL deduction. Credits that cannot be used in the current year may be carried back two years and forward five years and used to offset the TMT in those years.[23]

Topic Review C5-2 presents an overview of the alternative minimum tax.

[22] Sec. 39. Special rules apply to the empowerment zone employment credit, which can offset up to 25% of a taxpayer's AMT liability.

[23] Sec. 59(a)(2).

Topic Review C5-2

Alternative Minimum Tax (AMT)

1. The AMT is levied in addition to the regular (income) tax.
2. The starting point for the AMT calculation is taxable income before NOLs. Taxable income is increased by tax preference items and increased or decreased by adjustments to arrive at alternative minimum taxable income (AMTI).
3. AMTI is reduced by a $40,000 statutory exemption. The statutory exemption is phased-out between $150,000 and $310,000 of AMTI to arrive at the AMT tax base.
4. A 20% tax rate is applied to the tax base to arrive at the tentative minimum tax.
5. The tentative minimum tax amount is reduced by the AMT foreign tax credit. Other tax credits, such as the general business credit, do not reduce the tentative minimum tax amount.
6. The excess of the tentative minimum tax over the regular tax may be claimed as a minimum tax credit. This credit may be carried over to a later year to offset the excess of the regular tax over the tentative minimum tax.
7. The AMT liability, as well as the regular tax liability, are subject to the estimated tax requirements.

PERSONAL HOLDING COMPANY TAX

A corporation that satisfies both a stock ownership test and a passive income test is classified as a **personal holding company** (PHC) for the tax year. The **PHC penalty tax** was enacted to prevent taxpayers from using closely held corporations to shelter passive income from the higher individual tax rates. This penalty tax is levied at a 39.6% tax rate on the PHC's undistributed personal holding company income (UPHCI). A corporation that is classified as a PHC must pay either the corporate regular tax or the corporate alternative minimum tax and possibly the PHC penalty tax. Corporations can avoid the PHC tax by failing either the stock ownership or passive income tests or by reducing UPHCI to zero by making dividend distributions.

The PHC tax has taken on added importance following the Omnibus Budget Reconciliation Act of 1993 which increased the top marginal tax rate for individuals to 39.6%. The top marginal tax rate for individuals is now higher than the 34% or 35% C corporation tax rate that applies to most corporations. The 1993 Act reversed a situation where the top marginal tax rate for individuals was below the top marginal tax rate for corporations. The current rate advantage for corporations provides a situation where individuals may find a substantial tax savings by having their investment assets held by a corporate entity. This portion of the chapter emphasizes determining whether a corporation is a PHC and finding ways in which the PHC tax can be avoided.

HISTORICAL NOTE

The PHC penalty tax was enacted in 1934 and was aimed at the so-called incorporated pocketbook. At one time the top marginal corporate tax rate was 39 percentage points (52% vs. 91%) below that for individuals. Today, this differential is only 4.6 percentage points. However, the availability of 15% and 25% marginal corporate tax rates and/or a dividends-received deduction may produce substantially lower effective corporate tax rates for certain types of income, which necessitates retention of the PHC tax.

ADDITIONAL COMMENT

The Congressional intent behind enacting the personal holding company and accumulated earnings penalty taxes was not to produce large amounts of tax revenues (i.e., only $20.5 million in PHC taxes for 1992). However, the presence of these taxes in the IRS's arsenal prevents substantial revenue losses from certain tax-motivated transactions involving closely held corporations.

PERSONAL HOLDING COMPANY DEFINED

A personal holding company is any corporation that (1) has five or fewer shareholders who own more than 50% of the corporation's outstanding stock at any time during the last half of its tax year, and (2) has personal holding company income that is at least 60% of its adjusted ordinary gross income for the tax year.[24]

Corporations that retain special tax status generally are excluded from the PHC definition. Among those excluded are S corporations and tax-exempt organizations.

[24] Sec. 542(a).

OBJECTIVE 2

Determine whether a corporation is a personal holding company (PHC)

TYPICAL MISCONCEPTION

The PHC penalty tax applies to any corporation that meets the definition of a personal holding company. No improper intent is necessary. Thus, the PHC penalty tax truly fits into the category of "a trap for the unwary."

STOCK OWNERSHIP REQUIREMENT

Section 542(a)(2) provides that a corporation satisfies the PHC stock ownership requirement if more than 50% of the value of its outstanding stock is directly or indirectly owned by five or fewer individuals at any time during the last half of its tax year. Any corporation having fewer than ten individual shareholders at any time during the last half of its tax year, which is not an excluded corporation, will meet the stock ownership requirement.[25]

For purposes of determining whether the 50% requirement is met, stock owned directly or indirectly by or for an individual shareholder is considered to be owned by the individual. The Sec. 544 stock attribution rules are used for this purpose. The Sec. 544 attribution rules provide that

- Stock owned by a family member is considered to be owned by the other members of his or her family. Family members include brothers and sisters, spouse, ancestors, and lineal descendants.
- Stock owned directly or indirectly by or for a corporation, partnership, estate, or trust is considered to be owned proportionately by its shareholders, partners, or beneficiaries.
- A person who holds an option to acquire stock is considered to own such stock without regard to whether the individual intends to exercise the option.
- Stock owned by a partner is considered to be owned by his or her partners.
- The family, partnership, and option rules can be used only to make a corporation a PHC. They cannot be used to prevent a corporation from acquiring PHC status.[26]

KEY POINT

A corporation must satisfy two tests to be considered a PHC: a stock ownership test and a passive income test. Because most closely held corporations satisfy the stock ownership test, PHC status is usually determined by the passive income test.

PASSIVE INCOME REQUIREMENT

A corporation whose shareholders satisfy the stock ownership requirement is not a PHC unless it also earns predominantly passive income. The passive income requirement is met if at least 60% of the corporation's **adjusted ordinary gross income (AOGI)** for the tax year is personal holding company income (PHCI). The following text defines the terms AOGI and PHCI and outlines ways in which a corporation can take steps to avoid satisfying the passive income requirements.

KEY POINT

Computing AOGI is a three-step process. Gross income is determined and then adjusted to arrive at OGI. Finally, certain other adjustments are made in arriving at AOGI. In calculating OGI, both capital gains and Sec. 1231 gains are eliminated. Thus, capital gains and Sec. 1231 gains are neutral factors in determining whether a corporation is a PHC.

ADJUSTED ORDINARY GROSS INCOME DEFINED. The first step in calculating AOGI is calculating the corporation's gross income (see Figure C5-1). Gross income is determined using the same accounting methods used to compute taxable income. Any income item that is excluded in determining taxable income is also excluded in determining AOGI. Gross receipts from sales transactions are reduced by the corporation's cost of goods sold.

The next step in determining AOGI requires the calculation of the corporation's **ordinary gross income (OGI)**. To do this, the corporation's gross income is reduced by the amount of its capital gains and Sec. 1231 gains.[27] The exclusion of capital gains and Sec. 1231 gains from OGI (and, later, from AOGI) means that these items are neutral factors in determining whether a corporation is a PHC; that is, the realization and recognition of a large Sec. 1231 gain or capital gain cannot cause a corporation to be a PHC.

OGI is reduced for certain expenses. These expenses relate to the production of rental income; mineral, oil, and gas (M, O, & G) royalties; and income from working interests in oil or gas wells.[28] The rental income adjustment is described below.

---

[25] The PHC stock ownership test is also used to determine whether a closely held C corporation is subject to the at-risk rules (Sec. 465) or the passive activity loss and credit limitation rules (Sec. 469). Thus, a closely held corporation that is not a PHC may be subject to other special rules because of satisfying the PHC stock ownership requirement.

[26] Sec. 544(a)(4)(A).

[27] Sec. 543(b)(1).

[28] Sec. 543(b)(2).

▼ **FIGURE C5-1**
Determining Adjusted Ordinary Gross Income

Gross income (GI) reported for taxable income and PHC purposes
Minus: Gross gains from the sale of capital assets
Gross gains from the sale of Sec. 1231 properties

Ordinary gross income (OGI)
Minus: Certain expenses incurred in connection with gross income from rents; mineral, oil, and gas royalties; and working interests in oil or gas wells
Interest received on certain U.S. obligations held for sale to customers by dealers
Interest received due to condemnation awards, judgments, or tax refunds
Rents from tangible personal property manufactured or produced by the corporation, provided it has engaged in substantial manufacturing or production of the same type of personal property in the current tax year

Adjusted ordinary gross income (AOGI)

Reduction by Rental Income Expenses. Gross income from rents is reduced by the deductions claimed for depreciation or amortization, property taxes, interest, and rent. This net amount is known as the **adjusted income from rents (AIR)**.[29] No other Sec. 162 expenses incurred in the production of rental income reduce OGI. The expense adjustment that is made cannot exceed the total gross rental income.

EXAMPLE C5-12 ▶ All of Keno Corporation's single class of stock is owned by Ingrid. Both Ingrid and Keno Corporation use the calendar year as their tax years. Keno Corporation reports the following results for the current year:

Rental income	$100,000
Depreciation	15,000
Interest expense	9,000
Real estate taxes	4,000
Maintenance expenses	8,000
Administrative expenses	12,000

Keno Corporation's AIR is $72,000 [$100,000 − ($15,000 + $9,000 + $4,000)]. The maintenance and administrative expenses are deductible in determining taxable income and, consequently, UPHCI, but do not reduce the AIR amount. ◀

ADDITIONAL COMMENT

Income not included in AOGI cannot be PHCI. In calculating the 60% passive income test, PHCI is the numerator and AOGI is the denominator. Because the passive income test is purely objective, both the numerator and denominator can be manipulated. When the ratio is close to 60%, one planning opportunity is to accelerate the recognition of income that is AOGI but not PHCI.

PERSONAL HOLDING COMPANY INCOME DEFINED. **Personal holding company income** includes dividends, interest, annuities, adjusted income from rents, royalties, produced film rents, income from personal service contracts involving a 25% or more shareholder, rental income for corporate property used by a 25% or more shareholder, and distributions from estates or trusts.

PHCI is determined according to the following general rules:

- *Dividends:* Includes only distributions made out of E&P. Any amounts that are tax exempt (e.g., return of capital distributions) or that are eligible for capital gain treatment (e.g., liquidating distributions) are excluded from PHCI.[30]
- *Interest income:* Includes interest that is included in gross income. Any interest that is excluded from gross income is excluded from PHCI.[31]
- *Annuity proceeds:* Includes annuities that are included in gross income. Any annuity amount that is excluded from gross income is excluded from PHCI.[32]

[29] Sec. 543(b)(3).
[30] Reg. Sec. 1.543-1(b)(1).
[31] Reg. Sec. 1.543-1(b)(2).
[32] Reg. Sec. 1.543-1(b)(4).

HISTORICAL NOTE

The exception for royalties on computer software was added by the Tax Reform Act of 1986. Without this exception, most computer software companies would almost certainly be classified as PHCs.

- *Royalty income:* Includes amounts received for the use of intangible property (e.g., patents, copyrights, and trademarks). Special rules apply to copyright royalties, M, O, & G royalties, active business computer software royalties, and produced film rents. Each of these four special types of royalty income constitutes a separate PHCI category that may be excluded under one of the exceptions described below and shown in Table C5-2.[33]
- *Distributions from an estate or trust:* Included in PHCI.[34]

Special exclusions apply which could result in the exclusion of rents; M, O, & G royalties; copyright royalties; produced film rents; rental income from the use of property by a 25% or more shareholder; and active business computer software royalties from PHCI. These exclusions, which are summarized in Table C5-2, reduce the probability that a corporation will be a PHC. The two most commonly encountered exclusions, the ones for rental income and personal service contract income, are explained below.

SELF-STUDY QUESTION

What is the effect of the two-pronged test that allows the exclusion from PHCI of certain AIR?

ANSWER

The effect of this two-pronged test is to make it difficult to use rents to shelter other passive income. For example, the 50% test would require at least $100 of AIR to shelter $100 of interest income. The 10% test is even more restrictive. To satisfy this test, it would be necessary to generate $900 of OGI (AIR and other items) to shelter the same $100 of interest income.

Exclusion for Rents. Adjusted income from rents is included in PHCI unless the special exception applies for corporations earning predominantly rental income. PHCI does not include rents if (1) AIR is at least 50% of AOGI and (2) the dividends-paid deduction equals or exceeds the amount by which nonrental PHCI exceeds 10% of OGI.[35] The special exception permits corporations earning predominantly rental income and having very little nonrental PHCI to avoid PHC status. The dividends-paid deduction is

▼ TABLE C5-2

Tests to Determine Exclusions From Personal Holding Company Income

	A PHCI Category is Excluded If:		
PHCI Category	Income in the Category Is:	Other PHCI Is:	Business Expenses Are:
Rents	≥50% of AOGI[a]	≤10% of OGI (unless reduced by distributions)	—
Mineral, oil, and gas royalties	≥50% of AOGI[a]	≤10% of OGI	≥15% of AOGI
Copyright royalties	≥50% of OGI	≤10% of OGI	≥25% of OGI
Produced film rents	≥50% of OGI	—	—
Compensation for use of property by a shareholder owning at least 25% of the outstanding stock	—	≤10% of OGI	—
Active business computer software royalties	≥50% of OGI	≤10% of OGI (unless reduced by distributions)	≥25% of OGI[b]
Personal services contract income	—[c]	—	—

[a] Measured in terms of adjusted income from rents or mineral, oil, and gas royalties, respectively.
[b] The deduction test can be applied to either the single tax year in question or the five-year period ending with the tax year in question.
[c] Personal services income is excluded from PHCI if the corporation has the right to designate the person who is to perform the services or the person performing the services owns less than 25% of the corporation's outstanding stock.

[33] Reg. Sec. 1.543-1(b)(3). Royalties include M, O, & G royalties, working interests in oil or gas wells, computer software royalties, copyright royalties, and all other royalties.

[34] Sec. 543(a)(8).

[35] Sec. 543(a)(2). The AIR term excludes rental income earned from leasing property to a shareholder owning 25% or more of the stock, which is included in PHCI under its own separate category.

available for dividends paid during the tax year, dividends paid within 2½ months of the end of the tax year for which a special throwback election is made to treat the distribution as having been paid on the last day of the preceding tax year, and consent dividends (see page C5-20). Nonrental PHCI includes all PHCI (determined without regard to the exclusions for copyright royalties and M, O, & G royalties) *other than* adjusted income from rents and rental income earned from leasing property to a shareholder owning 25% or more of the stock.

EXAMPLE C5-13 ▶ All of Texas Corporation's single class of stock is owned by Kwame. Both Kwame and Texas use the calendar year as their tax years. Texas reports the following results for the current year:

Rental income	$100,000
Operating profit from sales	40,000
Dividend income	15,000
Interest income from corporate bonds	10,000
Rental expenses:	
Depreciation	15,000
Interest	9,000
Real estate taxes	4,000
Other expenses	20,000

No dividends are paid by Texas during the current year or during the 2½ month throwback period following year-end. Because all of the Texas stock is owned by a single shareholder, Texas satisfies the stock ownership requirement. Texas's AOGI is calculated as follows:

Rental income		$100,000
Operating profit from sales		40,000
Dividends		15,000
Interest		10,000
Gross income and OGI		$165,000
Minus: Depreciation	$15,000	
Interest	9,000	
Real estate taxes	4,000	(28,000)
AOGI		$137,000

The two AIR tests are performed as follows:

Test 1: Rental income	$100,000
Minus: Depreciation	(15,000)
Interest	(9,000)
Real estate taxes	(4,000)
AIR	$ 72,000
50% of AOGI (0.50 × $137,000 AOGI)	$ 68,500
Test 2: Dividends	$ 15,000
Interest	10,000
Nonrental income	$ 25,000
Minus: 10% of OGI (0.10 × $165,000)	(16,500)
Minimum amount of distributions	$ 8,500
Actual dividends paid	$ —0—

AIR exceeds the 50% threshold so Test 1 is satisfied. Because no dividends were paid, the nonrental income ceiling is exceeded and Test 2 is failed. AIR is included in PHCI since only one of the two tests was satisfied. The PHC income test is performed as follows:

AIR	$ 72,000
Dividends	15,000
Interest	10,000
PHCI	$ 97,000
AOGI	$137,000
Times: AOGI threshold	× 0.60
AOGI ceiling	$ 82,200

Texas is a PHC because PHCI exceeds 60% of AOGI.

Texas could avoid PHC status by paying a sufficient amount of cash dividends during the current year or a consent dividend following year-end for the AIR exclusion to be satisfied. The necessary amount of dividend payments is the amount by which nonrental PHCI ($25,000) exceeds 10% of OGI ($16,500), or $8,500. An $8,500 cash dividend paid during the current year or a consent dividend paid after the year-end would permit Texas to exclude the $72,000 of AIR from PHCI. PHCI would then be $25,000 ($15,000 + $10,000), which is less than 60% of AOGI ($82,200). (Consent dividends are described on page C5-21.) ◀

ADDITIONAL COMMENT

The provision for personal service contracts was enacted to prevent entertainers, athletes, and other highly compensated professionals from incorporating their activities and, after taking a below-normal salary, having the rest of the income taxed at the corporate rates. Even if it is apparent that a 25%-shareholder will perform the services, as long as no one other than the corporation has the right to designate who performs the services, the income is not PHCI. Thus, the careful drafting of contracts is important in this area.

Exclusion for Personal Service Contracts. Income earned from contracts under which the corporation is to perform personal services and income earned from the sale of such contracts is included in PHCI if the following two conditions are met:

- (a) Some person other than the corporation has the right to designate (by name or by description) the individual who is to perform the services or (b) the individual who is to perform the services is designated (by name or by description) in the contract.
- 25% or more of the value of the corporation's outstanding stock is directly or indirectly owned by the person who has performed, is to perform, or is designated as the person to perform the services.[36]

The 25% or more requirement only needs to be satisfied at some point during the tax year and is determined by using the Sec. 544 constructive stock ownership rules. This provision was enacted to prevent professionals, entertainers, and sports figures from incorporating their activities, paying themselves a below-normal salary, and sheltering at the lower corporate tax rates the difference between their actual earnings and their below-normal salary.

EXAMPLE C5-14 ▶

Dr. Kellner owns all of the stock of a professional corporation that provides medical services. The professional corporation has an employment contract with Dr. Kellner that specifies the terms of his employment and his salary. Dr. Kellner is the only doctor under contract with the professional corporation. The corporation provides office space for Dr. Kellner and employs the necessary office staff to enable Dr. Kellner to perform the medical services. The income earned by Dr. Kellner does not constitute PHCI because (1) the normal patient–physician relationship does not generally involve a contract that includes a designation of the doctor who will perform the services, nor will the patient generally be permitted to designate the doctor who will perform the services, and (2) the professional corporation will be able to substitute a qualified replacement when Dr. Kellner is not on duty (i.e., when he is on vacation or not on call).[37]

The compensation received by the corporation for Dr. Kellner's services would constitute PHCI if the contract with the patient specified that only Dr. Kellner would provide the services, or if the services provided by Dr. Kellner were so unique that only he could provide them. Any portion of the corporation's income from the personal service contract that is attributable to

[36] Sec. 543(a)(7).

[37] Rev. Rul. 75-67, 1975-1 C.B. 169. See also Rev. Ruls. 75-249, 1975-1 C.B. 171 (relating to a composer), and 75-250, 1975-1 C.B. 172 (relating to an accountant).

"important and essential" services provided by persons other than Dr. Kellner is not included in PHCI.[38] ◀

OBJECTIVE 3

Calculate the amount of the corporation's PHC tax liability

DETERMINING THE PHC PENALTY TAX

Determination of the PHC penalty tax is illustrated in Figure C5-2. First, the amount of undistributed personal holding company income (UPHCI) must be determined. Then the 39.6% PHC tax rate is applied to the UPHCI. If the PHC tax is owed, a corporation can avoid paying the tax if it makes a timely deficiency dividend distribution.

KEY POINT

The PHC penalty tax is assessed at a 39.6% rate. This tax is in addition to the corporate income tax. Thus, the existence of both taxes eliminates any advantage obtained by interposing a corporation between the taxpayer and his or her income-producing assets.

CALCULATING UPHCI.

The starting point for the UPHCI calculation is the corporation's taxable income. A series of adjustments must be made to taxable income to arrive at UPHCI. The most important of these adjustments are described below.

Positive Adjustments to Taxable Income. A PHC may not claim a dividends-received deduction. Thus, its taxable income must be increased by the amount of any dividends-received deductions claimed.[39]

Because PHCs are restricted to deducting only the NOL for the immediately preceding tax year, two compensating adjustments must be made for NOLs. First, the amount of the NOL deduction claimed in determining taxable income must be added back to taxable income. Second, the entire amount of the corporation's NOL (computed without regard to the dividends-received deduction) for the immediately preceding tax year is deducted as a negative adjustment.[40]

Negative Adjustments to Taxable Income. Charitable contributions are deductible up to the 20% and 50% of adjusted gross income limitations for individuals. Thus, two adjustments may be required: the deduction of charitable contributions in excess of the 10% corporate limitation (but not in excess of the individual limitations); and the addition of charitable contribution carryovers deducted for regular tax purposes in the current year, but deducted for PHC tax purposes in an earlier year.[41]

KEY POINT

The negative adjustments made to taxable income in arriving at UPHCI (e.g., federal income taxes) represent items that do not reduce taxable income but reduce the earnings available for distribution to the shareholders. In contrast, positive adjustments made to taxable income (e.g., the dividends-received deduction) are not allowed in arriving at UPHCI because they do not represent a reduction in earnings that are available for distribution to shareholders.

Income taxes (i.e., federal income taxes [including the AMT], foreign income taxes, and U.S. possessions' income taxes) accrued by the corporation reduce UPHCI.[42]

Capital gains and losses reduce UPHCI. A PHC is permitted a deduction for the amount of its net capital gain (i.e., net long-term capital gain over net short-term capital loss) minus the amount of income taxes attributable to the net capital gain.[43] The federal income taxes that are attributable to the net capital gain equal the taxes imposed on the corporation's taxable income minus the taxes imposed on the corporation's taxable income as computed by excluding the net capital gain.

The capital gains adjustment that is made when determining AOGI prevents a large capital gain from causing a corporation to be taxed as a PHC. Even if the corporation is a PHC, the capital gains adjustment made in determining UPHCI prevents the corporation from paying the PHC tax on the amount of its long-term (but not its short-term) capital gains.

AVOIDING THE PHC DESIGNATION AND TAX LIABILITY BY MAKING DIVIDEND DISTRIBUTIONS

The PHC can claim a **dividends-paid deduction** for distributions made during the current year if they are made out of the corporation's current or accumulated E&P.[44] A

[38] Reg. Sec. 1.543-1(b)(8)(B)(ii).
[39] Sec. 545(b)(3).
[40] Sec. 545(b)(4) and Rev. Rul. 79-59, 1979-1 C.B. 209.
[41] Sec. 545(b)(2).
[42] Sec. 545(b)(1).
[43] Sec. 545(b)(5).
[44] Secs. 561(a) and 562(a).

▼ **FIGURE C5-2**
Determination of the Personal Holding Company Tax

Taxable income
Plus: Positive adjustments
1. Dividends-received deduction claimed
2. NOL deduction claimed
3. Excess charitable contributions carried over from a preceding tax year and deducted in determining taxable income
4. Net loss attributable to the operation or maintenance of property leased by the corporation

Minus: Negative adjustments
1. Accrued U.S. and foreign income taxes
2. Charitable contributions in excess of the 10% corporate limitation
3. NOL (computed without regard to the dividends-received deduction) incurred in the immediately preceding tax year
4. Net capital gain minus the amount of any income taxes attributed to it

Minus: Dividends-paid deduction claimed

Undistributed personal holding company income (UPHCI)
Times: 0.396

Personal holding company tax

ADDITIONAL COMMENT

The intent of the PHC rules is not to collect taxes from a corporation. Instead, the rules are meant to compel the distribution of income by a closely held corporation so that such income will be taxed at the shareholders' individual tax rates. This purpose is evidenced by the flexibility of the dividends-paid deduction.

dividends-paid deduction is not available for **preferential dividends**. A dividend payment is preferential when (1) the amount distributed to a shareholder exceeds his or her ratable share of the distribution as determined by the number of shares of stock that are owned or (2) the amount received by a class of stock is more or less than its rightful amount.[45] In either case, the entire distribution (and not just any excess distributions) is a preferential dividend.

Throwback dividends are distributions paid in the first 2½ months after the close of the tax year. A dividend distribution made in the first 2½ months of the next tax year is treated as a throwback distribution of the preceding tax year for PHC tax purposes only if the PHC makes the appropriate election.[46] Otherwise, the dividends-paid deduction is claimed in the tax year in which the distribution is made. Throwback dividends made by a PHC are limited to the lesser of the PHC's UPHCI or 20% of the amount of any dividends (other than consent dividends) paid during the tax year. Thus, a PHC that fails to make any dividend distributions during its tax year is prevented from paying a throwback dividend.

Consent dividends are hypothetical dividends deemed paid to shareholders on the last day of the corporation's tax year. Consent dividends permit a corporation to reduce its PHC tax liability when it is prevented from making an actual dividend distribution because of a lack of available money, a restrictive loan covenant, and so on. A consent dividend election can be made by any shareholder who owns stock on the last day of the corporation's tax year.[47] For tax purposes, the making of the election results in a hypothetical money dividend being paid on the last day of the PHC's tax year for which the dividends-paid deduction is claimed. The consent dividend is treated by the

[45] Sec. 562(c).
[46] Sec. 563(b).
[47] Sec. 565.

shareholder as being received on the distribution date and immediately contributed by the shareholder to the distributing corporation's capital account. The contribution increases the basis for the shareholder's stock investment. The consent dividend election can be made through the due date for the corporation's income tax return (including any permitted extensions).

Dividend Carryovers. Dividends that are paid in the preceding two tax years can be used as a dividend carryover to reduce the amount of the current year's PHC tax liability.[48] Section 564 permits a PHC to deduct the amount by which its dividend distributions that were eligible for a dividends-paid deduction in each of the two preceding tax years exceed the corporation's UPHCI for such a year.

Liquidating Dividends. A dividends-paid deduction is available for liquidating distributions that are made by a PHC within twenty-four months of the adoption of a plan of liquidation.[49]

SELF-STUDY QUESTION

When would a deficiency dividend be beneficial to a corporation?

ANSWER

A deficiency dividend can be very beneficial if a corporation fails to eliminate its UPHCI, either under the erroneous assumption that it was not a PHC or due to a miscalculation of its UPHCI. If certain requirements are satisfied, a deficiency dividend can be distributed and designated as a retroactive dividend deductible against UPHCI earned in a previous year.

Deficiency Dividends. A corporation that is determined to owe the PHC penalty tax can avoid paying the tax by electing to pay a **deficiency dividend** under Sec. 547. The deficiency dividend procedures substitute an income tax levy on the dividend payment at the shareholder level for the payment of the PHC tax. The distributing corporation's shareholders include the deficiency dividend in their gross income for the tax year in which it is received, not the tax year for which the PHC claims a dividends-paid deduction. Payment of a deficiency dividend does not relieve the PHC from any interest and penalties owed with respect to the PHC tax.

The following requirements must be satisfied in order to claim a dividends-paid deduction for a deficiency dividend:

- A determination (e.g., judicial decision or agreement entered into by the taxpayer with the IRS) must be made that establishes the amount of the PHC tax liability.
- A dividend must be paid within ninety days after establishing the PHC tax liability.
- A claim for a dividends-paid deduction based on the payment of the deficiency dividend must be filed within 120 days of the determination date.[50]

EXAMPLE C5-15 ▶

Boston Corporation files its current year tax return reporting a $200,000 distribution received pursuant to a stock redemption as a capital gain. Upon an IRS audit of Boston's return, both parties agree that the capital gain classification is erroneous and that dividend treatment for the distribution is indeed correct. This change causes Boston to be classified as a PHC. The liability for the payment of the PHC tax is eliminated if Boston pays a deficiency dividend within ninety days after signing the agreement with the IRS establishing the existence of the PHC tax liability and a timely claim is filed. ◀

PHC TAX CALCULATION

The following example illustrates the calculation of the PHC's UPHCI and the determination of the PHC's income tax and penalty tax liabilities.

EXAMPLE C5-16 ▶

Marlo Corporation is classified as a PHC for the current year, reporting $227,000 of taxable income on its federal income tax return:

48 Sec. 561(a)(3).
49 Sec. 562(b).
50 Secs. 547(c) through (e).

Operating profit	$100,000
Long-term capital gain	60,000
Short-term capital gain	30,000
Dividends (20%-owned corporation)	200,000
Interest	100,000
Gross income	$490,000
Salaries	(40,000)
General and administrative expenses	(20,000)
Charitable contributions	(43,000)[a]
Dividends-received deduction	(160,000)
Taxable income	$227,000

[a] $43,000 = 0.10 × ($490,000 − $40,000 − $20,000).

Federal income taxes (using 1997 rates and ignoring any alternative minimum tax liability) accrued by Marlo are $71,780 [$22,250 tax on first $100,000 + (0.39 × $127,000)]. Actual charitable contributions made by Marlo are $60,000 in the current year. $50,000 in dividends were paid by Marlo in August.

Calculation of the PHC tax liability is as follows:

Taxable income			$227,000
Plus:	Dividends-received deduction		160,000
Minus:	Excess charitable contributions		(17,000)[b]
	Federal income taxes		(71,780)
	Dividends-paid deduction		(50,000)
	Long-term capital gain	$60,000	
	Minus: Federal income taxes	(23,400)	
	LTCG adjustment		(36,600)
Undistributed personal holding company income			$211,620
Times:	Tax rate		× 0.396
Personal holding company tax			$ 83,802

[b] $60,000 total contributions − $43,000 limitation = $17,000 excess contributions.

Marlo's total federal tax liability is $155,582 ($71,780 + $83,802). Payment of the PHC tax ($83,802) can be avoided by paying a timely deficiency dividend in the amount of $211,620. ◀

Topic Review C5-3 presents an overview of the personal holding company penalty tax.

ACCUMULATED EARNINGS TAX

ADDITIONAL COMMENT

The accumulated earnings tax is a penalty tax imposed on corporations that accumulate unreasonable amounts of earnings for the purpose of avoiding shareholder taxes. With corporate tax rates again lower than individual rates, greater tax incentives exist for accumulating earnings inside a corporation. These opportunities should lead to the IRS applying the accumulated earnings tax more often.

Corporations that are not subject to the personal holding company tax may be subject to the accumulated earnings tax. The **accumulated earnings tax** attempts "to compel the company to distribute any profits not needed for the conduct of its business so that, when so distributed, individual stockholders will become liable" for taxes on the dividends received.[51] Unlike its name, the tax is not levied on the corporation's total accumulated earnings balance, but only on its current year addition to the balance. In other words, the tax is levied on accumulated earnings earned currently that are not needed for a reasonable business purpose.

---

[51] *Helvering v. Chicago Stock Yards Co.*, 30 AFTR 1091, 43-1 USTC ¶9379 (USSC, 1943).

Topic Review C5-3

Personal Holding Company (PHC) Tax

1. The PHC tax only applies to corporations qualifying as PHCs. A PHC has (1) five or fewer shareholders owning more than 50% in value of the corporation's stock at any time during the last half of the tax year and (2) PHCI that is at least 60% of its adjusted ordinary gross income for the tax year.
2. Two special exemptions exist for the PHC test. First, certain special corporate forms are excluded from the penalty tax (e.g., S corporations). Second, certain income forms (e.g., rents and active business computer software royalties) are excluded if the percentage of income, maximum level of other PHC income, and minimum level of business expense requirements are met. The excludable income forms are summarized in Table C5-2.
3. The PHC tax equals 39.6% of the UPHCI. UPHCI equals taxable income plus certain positive adjustments (e.g., dividends-received deduction) and minus certain negative adjustments (e.g., federal income taxes, excess charitable contributions, and net capital gain reduced by federal income taxes attributable to the gain).
4. UPHCI can be reduced by a dividends-paid deduction claimed for cash and property dividends paid during the tax year and consent and throwback dividends distributed after year-end.
5. A PHC tax liability (but not interest and penalties) can be eliminated by the payment of a deficiency dividend. This distribution substitutes an income tax levy at the shareholder level for the PHC tax.

CORPORATIONS SUBJECT TO THE PENALTY TAX

Section 532(a) states that the accumulated earnings tax applies "to every corporation . . . formed or availed of for the purpose of avoiding the income tax with respect to its shareholders . . . by permitting earnings and profits to accumulate instead of being divided or distributed." Three special corporate forms are statutorily excluded from the accumulated earnings tax:

- Personal holding companies
- Corporations that are exempt from tax under Secs. 501-504
- S corporations[52]

Theoretically, the accumulated earnings tax applies to both large and small corporations.[53] In practice, however, the accumulated earnings tax only applies to closely held corporations where management can use the corporate dividend policy to reduce the tax liability of the shareholder group.

OBJECTIVE 4

Evaluate whether a corporation has an accumulated earnings tax problem

PROVING A TAX-AVOIDANCE PURPOSE

Section 533(a) provides that the accumulation of E&P by a corporation beyond the reasonable needs of the business indicates a tax-avoidance purpose unless the corporation can prove that the earnings are not being accumulated merely to avoid taxes. This burden of proof may be shifted to the IRS under the rules outlined in Sec. 534.

The existence of a tax-avoidance purpose is based on the facts and circumstances of each situation. Under Reg. Sec. 1.533-1(a)(2), the following circumstances indicate a tax-avoidance purpose:

---

52 Secs. 532(b) and 1363(a).

53 Sec. 532(c). See, however, *Technalysis Corporation v. CIR* [101 T.C. 397 (1993)] where the Tax Court held that the accumulated earnings tax can apply to a publicly held corporation regardless of the concentration of ownership or whether the shareholders are actively involved in the operation of the corporation.

ADDITIONAL COMMENT

If the IRS determines that the accumulation of earnings is unreasonable, the presumption is that the IRS determination is correct. To rebut this presumption, the taxpayer must be able to show that the IRS's determination is improper by a preponderance of the evidence.

- Dealings between the corporation and its shareholders (e.g., loans made by the corporation to its shareholders or funds expended by the corporation for the shareholders' benefit).
- Investments made by the corporation of undistributed earnings in assets having no reasonable connection to the corporation's business.
- The extent to which the corporation has distributed its E & P (e.g., a low dividend payout rate, low salaries, and a large earnings accumulation may indicate a tax-avoidance purpose).

Holding or investment companies are held to a different standard than operating companies. Section 533(b) provides that the fact that a corporation is a holding or investment company is prima facie evidence of the requisite tax-avoidance purpose.[54] Holding companies, like operating companies, can rebut this presumption by showing that it was neither formed or availed of for the purpose of avoiding shareholder income taxes.

The presence or absence of a tax-avoidance purpose may be only one of several motives for the corporation's accumulation of corporate earnings. In *U.S. v. The Donruss Company*, the Supreme Court held that tax avoidance does not have to be the dominant motive for the accumulation of earnings in order for the accumulated earnings tax to be imposed. According to the court, the corporation must know about the tax consequences of accumulating corporate earnings in order for a tax avoidance purpose to be present.[55] Such knowledge does not need to be the dominant motive or purpose for the accumulation of the earnings.

EVIDENCE CONCERNING THE REASONABLENESS OF AN EARNINGS ACCUMULATION

The courts have not held a single factor to be indicative of an unreasonable amount of accumulated earnings. Instead, some factors have been found to exhibit evidence of a tax-avoidance motive. Other factors have gained acceptance from the IRS and the courts as reasonable needs of the business for an accumulation of earnings and profits.

TYPICAL MISCONCEPTION

The statute refers to the existence of a tax-avoidance purpose, which would appear to be a subjective test. However, the existence of the tax-avoidance purpose really hinges on the more-objective determination of whether a corporation has accumulated earnings beyond the reasonable needs of the business.

EVIDENCE OF A TAX-AVOIDANCE MOTIVE. A corporation that wants to avoid problems concerning the accumulated earnings tax should be careful to act defensively. Exposure to the accumulated earnings tax can be avoided by minimizing the presence of the following factors:

- Loans to shareholders
- Expenditure of corporate funds for the personal benefit of the shareholders
- Loans having no reasonable relation to the conduct of business (e.g., loans made to relatives or friends of shareholders)
- Loans to a corporation controlled by the same shareholders that control the taxpayer corporation
- Investments in properties or securities unrelated to the activities of the taxpayer corporation
- Protection against unrealistic hazards[56]

Loans to shareholders or the expenditure of corporate funds for the personal benefit of shareholders act as substitutes for dividend payments to the shareholders. Similarly, loans made to relatives or friends of shareholders by the taxpayer corporation are

[54] Regulation Sec. 1.533-1(c) defines a holding or investment company as "a corporation having no activities except holding property and collecting income therefrom or investing therein."

[55] *U.S. v. The Donruss Company*, 23 AFTR 2d 69-418, 69-1 USTC ¶9167 (USSC, 1969).

[56] Reg. Sec. 1.537-2(c).

substitutes for paying dividends to shareholders, who then make personal loans to their friends and relatives. All three actions may indicate an unreasonable accumulation of corporate earnings, which should instead be distributed as dividends.

Loans or corporate expenditures made for the benefit of a corporation controlled by the shareholder (or the shareholder group) who controls the payor corporation may be considered to have a tax-avoidance purpose. The taxpayer corporation could instead make a dividend payment to the shareholder and then have the shareholder make a capital contribution of the funds to the related corporation.

Other factors not mentioned in the Regulations that are indicative of a tax-avoidance motive include corporations that are run as holding or investment companies and that have a poor dividend payment record.

STOP & THINK

Question: An IRS auditor is auditing Baylor Corporation's 1995 C corporation tax return. What information would the auditor use from the tax return to see if a potential excess earnings accumulation existed which might trigger the imposition of the accumulated earnings tax?

Solution: The auditor would look first at the beginning and year-end balance sheets (Schedule L, Page 4 of Form 1120) to see the retained earnings balances. Next the auditor would review Schedule M-2 (Analysis of Unappropriated Retained Earnings per Books) to see the current year's earnings, the amount of earnings distributed as dividends, and any appropriations of retained earnings that might have occurred during the year. Next, the auditor would return to the beginning and year-end balance sheets looking for transactions evidencing a tax-avoidance motive. These might include loans to stockholders (Schedule L, Line 7), loans to persons other than stockholders (Schedule L, Line 6), and portfolio investments (Schedule L, Lines 4, 5, 6, and 9), Information about expenditures of corporate funds made for personal benefit of shareholders might be found in the noncurrent asset section of the balance sheets (e.g., corporate ownership of a boat, airplane, or second home of a major stockholder).

KEY POINT

In determining whether an accumulation of earnings is reasonable, the regulations specify the adoption of a "prudent businessman" standard. In applying this standard, the courts are reluctant to substitute their judgment for that of corporate management unless the facts and circumstances clearly suggest that the accumulations of earnings are not for reasonable business needs.

EVIDENCE OF REASONABLE BUSINESS NEEDS. Code Sec. 537 defines **reasonable business needs** as

- Reasonably anticipated needs of the business
- Section 303 (death tax) redemption needs
- Excess business holdings redemption needs

Regulation Sec. 1.537-1(a) elaborates on this standard by indicating

> An accumulation of the earnings and profits . . . is in excess of reasonable needs of the business if it exceeds the amount that a prudent businessman would consider appropriate for the present business purposes and for the reasonably anticipated future needs of the business. The need to retain earnings and profits must be directly connected with the needs of the corporation itself and must be for bona fide business purposes.

Specific, Definite, and Feasible Plans. A corporation can justify an accumulation of earnings as being for reasonably anticipated future needs only if there is an indication that the future needs of the business require such an accumulation. The corporation must usually have specific, definite, and feasible plans for the use of such accumulations.

No Specific Time Limitations. The earnings accumulation does not need to be used within a short period of time after the close of the tax year, but the plans must provide that the accumulation will be used within a reasonable period of time after the close of the tax year, based on all the facts and circumstances associated with the future needs of the business.

Impact of Subsequent Events. Determination of the reasonably anticipated needs of the business is based on the facts and circumstances that exist at the end of the tax year. Regulation Sec. 1.537-1(b)(2) indicates that subsequent events cannot be used to show that an earnings accumulation is unreasonable if all the elements of reasonable anticipation are present at the close of the tax year. However, subsequent events can be used to determine whether the taxpayer actually intended to consummate the plans for which the earnings are accumulated.

A number of reasons are mentioned in the Regulations, or have been accepted by the courts, as representing reasonable needs of the business for accumulating earnings.

- Expansion of a business or replacement of plant
- Acquisition of a business enterprise
- Debt retirement
- Working capital
- Loans to suppliers or customers
- Product liability losses
- Stock redemptions
- Business contingencies

Some of the more important reasons are now examined.

ADDITIONAL COMMENT

The courts have allowed accumulations for the acquisition or expansion of property, plant, or equipment if the taxpayer establishes specific, definite, and feasible plans for the proposed outlay. If the expansion is into a new business, taxpayers should be careful to make the investment substantial enough that it will not be considered a passive investment.

Expansion of a Business or Replacement of Plant. The expansion of a corporation's present business facilities or the replacement of existing plant and equipment have always been accepted by the IRS and the courts as reasonable needs of a business. Taxpayers have encountered problems only when the plans are undocumented, indefinite, vague, or infeasible.[57] Although the plans do not need to be reduced to writing, it is probably best to provide sufficient written documentation.

Acquisition of a Business Enterprise. The acquisition of a business enterprise can involve either the same business or expansion into a new business. It can involve the purchase of either the stock or the assets of the new business. Taxpayers should be careful to acquire a sufficient interest in the new business so that it will not be considered a passive investment.

Working Capital: The Bardahl Formula. Working capital is generally defined as the excess of current assets over current liabilities.The *Bardahl* formula attempts to measure the amount of working capital necessary for an operating cycle. The operating cycle usually includes the period of time needed for acquisition of the inventory, sale of the inventory, and collection of the resulting accounts receivable. Thus, the amount of earnings accumulated to cover one full operating cycle is considered a reasonable business need.

Providing for the needed amount of working capital is considered a reasonable need of a business. The needs of a manufacturing business for working capital differ from those of a service business. At one time, the courts used certain rules of thumb (e.g., a

[57] See, for example, *Myron's Enterprises v. U.S.*, 39 AFTR 2d 77-693, 77-1 USTC ¶9253 (9th Cir., 1977) and *Atlas Tool Co., Inc. v. CIR*, 45 AFTR 2d 80-645, 80-1 USTC ¶9177 (3rd Cir., 1980).

current ratio of 2 to 1 or 3 to 1 or the accumulation of funds to cover a single year's operating expenses) to determine an adequate amount of working capital. However, in the first of two *Bardahl* cases, the Tax Court established a mathematical formula for determining an operating cycle. This formula is now used to ascertain the appropriate amount of working capital in many situations.

For purposes of a manufacturing business, an operating cycle is defined as the "period of time required to convert cash into raw materials, raw materials into an inventory of marketable Bardahl products, the inventory into sales and accounts receivable, and the period of time to collect its outstanding accounts."[58]

In the second *Bardahl* case, the Tax Court determined that monies advanced to a corporation by its suppliers in the form of short-term credit (e.g., trade payables) reduce the required amount of working capital.[59] The ***Bardahl* formula** for determining the required amount of working capital is as follows:

$$\text{Average operating cycle} = \text{Inventory period} + \text{Accounts receivable period} - \text{Credit period}$$

The *inventory period* in the formula is the time (as a percentage of a year) from the acquisition of the raw materials inventory to the sale of the finished goods inventory. The *accounts receivable period* is the time (as a percentage of a year) from the sale date to the collection of the accounts receivable. The *credit period* is the time (as a percentage of a year) from when an expense is incurred or inventory is purchased to the payment of the liability.

The average operating cycle can be expressed with the following equation:

$$\left[\frac{\text{Inventory amount}}{\text{Annual cost of goods sold}} + \frac{\text{Accounts receivable amount}}{\text{Annual sales}} - \frac{\text{Accounts payable amount}}{\text{Annual operating expenses and purchases (less noncash expenses)}}\right] \times 100$$
$$= \text{Average operating cycle (as a percentage of a year)}$$

The average operating cycle and the cash needs of the business for the year are combined to determine the working capital requirements, as follows:

$$\text{Average operating cycle (as a percentage of a year)} \times \left[\text{Cost of goods sold} + \text{Operating expenses}\right] = \text{Working capital requirements}$$

The cost of goods sold amount is determined on a full-cost basis (i.e., including both direct and indirect expenses). Operating expenses exclude noncash expenses such as depreciation, amortization, and depletion, as well as capital expenditures and charitable contributions. The Tax Court has allowed federal income taxes (e.g., quarterly estimated tax payments) to be included as operating expenses as well as permitting an adjustment to the operating cycle calculation for an inflation factor.[60]

The working capital requirements for one operating cycle of the business are compared with the actual working capital available at year-end. If the working capital requirements exceed the corporation's actual working capital, this need for additional working capital can be used, along with any specific needs of the business, to justify accumulating a portion of the corporation's earnings. If the working capital requirements

[58] *Bardahl Manufacturing Corp.*, 1965 PH T.C. Memo ¶65,200, 24 TCM 1030, at 1044.

[59] *Bardahl International Corp.*, 1966 PH T.C. Memo ¶66,182, 25 TCM 935.

[60] *Doug-Long, Inc.*, 72 T.C. 158 (1979).

are less than the corporation's actual working capital, the excess working capital is treated as an unreasonable accumulation and available for distribution to the shareholders unless some other justification for its accumulation can be determined (e.g., plant replacement).

TYPICAL MISCONCEPTION

There is no exact method for determining the working capital needs of a corporation. The *Bardahl* formula is merely a rule of thumb adopted by the Tax Court. Even the correct measurement of the components (peak cycle approach versus the average cycle approach) of the *Bardahl* formula is subject to dispute among the courts.

The *Bardahl* formula may provide a false sense of mathematical exactness in calculating working capital because the IRS and the courts have interpreted it differently. Some courts have used the peak month inventory, accounts receivable, and trade payables turnover amounts (instead of an annual average) to determine the length of an operating cycle.[61] The peak month method generally lengthens the corporation's operating cycle. Use of these two different methods can lead to very different estimates of working capital needs. As a result, significant disputes have arisen between the IRS and taxpayers over what constitutes an appropriate working capital amount.

EXAMPLE C5-17 ▶ The Austin Corporation management feels that it may have an accumulated earnings tax problem and asks that its working capital requirements on December 31 of the current year be determined using the *Bardahl* formula. The following information is available from Austin's records for the current year.

Cost of goods sold	$2,700,000
Average inventory	675,000
Purchases	3,000,000
Sales (all on account)	6,000,000
Average accounts receivable	750,000
Operating expenses (including depreciation and other noncash expenditures)	875,000
Depreciation and other noncash expenditures	75,000
Average trade payables	350,000
Federal income taxes	100,000
Working capital on December 31	825,000

Calculation of the operating cycle takes place as follows:

$$\text{Inventory turnover} = (\$675,000 \div \$2,700,000) \times 365 = 91.25 \text{ days}$$

$$\text{Receivables turnover} = (\$750,000 \div \$6,000,000) \times 365 = 45.625 \text{ days}$$

$$\text{Payables turnover} = \left[\frac{\$350,000}{\$3,000,000 + \$800,000}\right] \times 365 = 33.62 \text{ days}$$

$$\text{Operating cycle} = \left[\frac{91.25 + 45.625 - 33.62}{365}\right] \times 100 = 28.3\% \text{ of a year}$$

$$\text{Annual operating expenses} = \$2,700,000 + \$875,000 - \$75,000 + \$100,000 = \$3,600,000$$

$$\text{Working capital requirement} = \$3,600,000 \times 0.283 = \$1,018,800^{a}$$

[a] Removal of the estimated federal income tax payments from the annual operating expenses would reduce the working capital requirement that has been calculated.

The working capital requirement is $193,800 ($1,018,800 − $825,000) in excess of the actual working capital available on December 31. This calculation apparently permits Austin to justify the accumulation of additional current year earnings by needing to expand its working capital. ◀

The *Bardahl* formula is also used to estimate the working capital needs of service companies. A different calculation is used because service companies do not have the same inventory needs. For service companies, one looks primarily to the company's need to finance its accounts receivables. Because the maintenance of an adequate labor supply is important, service companies also need to maintain adequate working capital to be

[61] *State Office Supply, Inc.*, 1982 PH T.C. Memo ¶82,292, 43 TCM 1481.

able to retain key personnel when a below-normal level of business is expected. Therefore, some amount may be added to the basic working capital needs to cover the cost of retaining this part of the labor force for a period of time.[62]

REAL-WORLD EXAMPLE

Apparently, an accumulation of funds to redeem stock where a buy–sell agreement exists is not an acceptable business need. Even though a 50% shareholder was killed in a plane crash shortly after the year-end, the Tax Court refused to recognize the validity of an accumulation to redeem such shareholder's stock (*Technalysis Corp.*, 101 T.C. 397 (1993)).

Stock Redemptions. Section 537(a) permits corporations to accumulate earnings for two types of stock redemptions: Sec. 303 (death tax) redemptions and excess business holdings redemptions. In the first situation, monies can be accumulated after the death of the shareholder to redeem stock from the shareholder's estate or a beneficiary of the estate. These monies cannot exceed the amount that can be redeemed under the Sec. 303 rules. In the second situation, monies can be accumulated by a corporation to redeem stock held by a private foundation in excess of the business holdings limit of Sec. 4943.

Business Contingencies. The courts have permitted earnings to be accumulated for a number of business contingencies that were not specifically sanctioned in the Sec. 537 Regulations. Among the events recognized by the IRS audit guidelines and the courts as business contingencies for which earnings can properly be accumulated are actual or potential litigation, a decline in business activities following the loss of a major customer, a reserve for self-insurance against a particular loss, a threatened strike, and an employee retirement plan.

OBJECTIVE 5

Calculate the amount of the corporation's accumulated earnings tax liability

DETERMINING THE ACCUMULATED EARNINGS TAX LIABILITY

Determination of the accumulated earnings tax liability is illustrated in Figure C5-3. The accumulated earnings tax is levied at a 39.6% rate. As with the PHC penalty tax, a corporation can reduce its tax base by making dividend distributions. However, corporations generally do not avail themselves of this tax planning strategy because they often pay only a nominal dividend or no dividend, and because the accumulated earnings tax issue usually is not raised by the IRS auditors until one or more years after the tax return is filed. Unlike the PHC penalty tax, once the IRS or the courts have determined that the accumulated earnings tax is owed, its payment cannot be avoided by paying deficiency dividends.

KEY POINT

Accumulated taxable income should not be confused with current E&P. In fact, the accumulated earnings tax has been assessed in years where there was no increase in the E&P of a corporation.

ACCUMULATED TAXABLE INCOME.

The starting point for the **accumulated taxable income** calculation is the corporation's taxable income. A series of positive and negative adjustments to taxable income are needed to arrive at the accumulated taxable income.

KEY POINT

Accumulated taxable income equals taxable income (with certain adjustments) minus both the dividends-paid deduction and the accumulated earnings credit. These adjustments are primarily for the purpose of deriving an amount that more closely corresponds to the corporation's economic income and thus better measures the dividend-paying capability of the corporation.

Positive Adjustments to Taxable Income. As with the PHC penalty tax, a corporation is prohibited from claiming a dividends-received deduction. Taxable income must be increased by the amount of the dividends-received deduction that was claimed when determining the regular tax liability.[63]

The amount of any NOL deduction claimed when determining taxable income must be added back to determine accumulated taxable income. Unlike with the PHC tax, no special deduction is provided for an NOL incurred in the immediately preceding year.[64]

Negative Adjustments to Taxable Income. Charitable contributions are deductible without regard to either the 10% corporate limitation or the individual charitable contribution limitations. The same adjustments required for PHC tax purposes are required here.[65]

---

[62] See, for example, *Simons-Eastern Co. v. U.S.*, 31 AFTR 2d 73-640, 73-1 USTC ¶9279 (D.C. GA, 1972).
[63] Sec. 535(b)(3).
[64] Sec. 535(b)(4).
[65] Sec. 535(b)(2).

▼ **FIGURE C5-3**
Determining the Accumulated Earnings Tax Liability

Taxable income
Plus: Positive adjustments
1. Dividends-received deduction claimed
2. NOL deduction claimed
3. Excess charitable contributions carried over from a preceding tax year and deducted in determining taxable income
4. Capital loss carryover deduction
Minus: Negative adjustments
1. Accrued U.S. and foreign income taxes
2. Charitable contributions made in excess of the 10% corporate limitation
3. Nondeductible capital losses
4. Net capital gain minus the amount of any income taxes attributed to it
Minus: Dividends-paid deduction claimed
Minus: Accumulated earnings credit

Accumulated taxable income
Times: 0.396

Accumulated earnings tax

U.S. and foreign income taxes accrued by the corporation reduce accumulated taxable income, whether the corporation uses the accrual or cash method of accounting.[66]

A corporation is permitted a deduction for the amount of its net capital gain, minus the income taxes attributable to the net capital gain.[67] The capital gains adjustment prevents a corporation having large capital gains from paying the accumulated earnings tax on the portion of the gains that were retained in the business. Net capital losses in excess of net capital gains for the tax year are a negative adjustment to taxable income.[68]

Dividends-Paid Deduction. The dividends-paid deduction is available for four types of dividends:

- Dividends paid during the tax year
- Throwback dividends
- Consent dividends
- Liquidating distributions

ADDITIONAL COMMENT

The dividends-paid deduction can be helpful in avoiding the accumulated earnings penalty tax. However, deficiency dividends cannot be paid to reduce accumulated taxable income. In addition, because the accumulated earnings tax is usually asserted during an IRS audit, throwback and consent dividends are of limited benefit.

With some minor exceptions, the rules for the dividends-paid deduction are the same as for the PHC tax. Nonliquidating distributions paid during the tax year are eligible for the dividends-paid deduction only if they are paid from the corporation's E&P. A dividends-paid deduction is not available for preferential dividends.[69]

Throwback dividends are distributions made out of E&P in the first 2½ months following the close of the tax year. The accumulated earnings tax rules mandate that any distribution made in the first 2½ months following the close of the tax year must be treated as if it were paid on the last day of the preceding tax year without regard to the amount of actual dividends that were paid during the preceding tax year.[70] Because the

[66] Sec. 535(b)(1).
[67] Sec. 535(b)(6).
[68] Secs. 535(b)(5) and (7).
[69] Sec. 562(c). See page C5-21 for a more detailed discussion.
[70] Sec. 563(a).

ADDITIONAL COMMENT

The minimum accumulated earnings credit is $250,000 ($150,000 for certain personal service corporations) reduced by the accumulated E&P at the close of the preceding year. In many situations, however, corporations that have been in existence for some time have accumulated E&P in excess of $250,000. Thus, the minimum credit is often of little practical significance.

TYPICAL MISCONCEPTION

The maximum accumulated earnings credit is the amount of current E&P retained to meet the reasonable needs of the business minus an adjustment for net capital gains. This amount does not include the entire accumulation needed for business needs, but only the accumulation in the current tax year. Thus, to calculate the maximum credit, it is necessary to determine how much of the prior accumulations are retained for reasonable business needs.

accumulated earnings tax issue is not usually raised until the IRS audits the corporation's tax return, throwback dividends and consent dividends have limited value in avoiding the accumulated earnings tax.

Liquidating distributions made by corporations are eligible for the dividends-paid deduction. Eligible distributions include those made in connection with a complete liquidation, a partial liquidation, or a stock redemption.[71]

Accumulated Earnings Credit. Unlike other credits, the **accumulated earnings credit** does not offset the accumulated earnings tax liability on a dollar-for-dollar basis. Instead, it serves to reduce the accumulated taxable income amount. Different rules for the accumulated earnings credit exist for operating companies, service companies, and holding or investment companies.[72]

- Operating companies can claim a credit equal to the greater of (1) $250,000 minus the accumulated E&P at the end of the preceding tax year,[73] or (2) the current E&P retained to meet the reasonable needs of the business.
- The accumulated E&P balance used in (1) to compute the accumulated earnings credit is reduced by the amount of any throwback distributions paid during the current year that are treated as having been paid out of the preceding year's E&P.
- Current E&P is reduced by any dividends-paid deduction claimed and net capital gains (reduced by federal taxes attributable to the gain).
- Special rules apply to personal service companies providing their principal services in the fields of health, law, engineering, architecture, accounting, actuarial science, performing arts, and consulting. The basic calculation described above still applies, but the $250,000 minimum credit is reduced to $150,000 for these companies.
- Holding and investment companies can claim a credit equal to $250,000 minus the accumulated E&P at the end of the preceding tax year. An increased credit is not available to a holding or investment company based on the reasonable needs of the business.

EXAMPLE C5-18 ▶

Midway Corporation, a C corporation that is not a personal service or investment company, reports accumulated E&P, current E&P, and current E&P retained for business needs as shown in the table below. Its lifetime minimum credit is $250,000. No dividends were paid during the current year.

Tax Characteristics	*Situation No. One*	*Situation No. Two*
1. Accumulated E&P	$ 75,000	$ 75,000
2. Lifetime minimum credit	250,000	250,000
2a. Current year minimum credit (2a = 2 − 1)	175,000	175,000
3. Current E&P	400,000	400,000
3a. Current E&P retained for business needs	300,000	50,000
3b. Current E&P greater than business needs (3b = 3 − 3a)	100,000	350,000
4. Accumulated earnings credit (Greater of 2a or 3a)	300,000	175,000

In both situations $175,000 of the lifetime minimum credit remains. In Situation One, the $175,000 lifetime credit that remains is less than the $300,000 of E&P retained for business needs, so the accumulated earnings credit is the $300,000 business needs amount. In

[71] Sec. 562(b)(1)(B).
[72] Sec. 535(c).
[73] Section 1561(a)(2) limits controlled groups to a single statutory exemption.

Situation Two, the $175,000 lifetime minimum credit that remains is greater than the $50,000 of E&P retained for business needs, so the accumulated earnings credit is the $175,000 remaining lifetime minimum credit. In both situations, no lifetime minimum credit remains to be used in future years. All future accumulated earnings credits are based on E&P retained for business needs. ◀

ACCUMULATED EARNINGS TAX CALCULATION

The following example illustrates the calculation of accumulated taxable income and the determination of the accumulated earnings tax liability.

EXAMPLE C5-19 ▶ Pasadena Corporation is a closely held family corporation that has conducted a highly successful manufacturing operation for a number of years. On January 1 of the current year, Pasadena Corporation has a $750,000 accumulated E&P balance. The following information is available about the current year's operations:

Operating profit	$650,000
Long-term capital gain	30,000
Dividends (20%-owned corporation)	150,000
Interest	70,000
Gross income	$900,000
Dividends-received deduction	(120,000)
Salaries	(100,000)
General and administrative expenses	(200,000)
Charitable contributions	(60,000)[a]
Taxable income	$420,000

[a] $60,000 = 0.10 × [$900,000 − ($100,000 + $200,000)].

Federal income taxes (using 1997 rates and assuming no alternative minimum tax liability) accrued by Pasadena Corporation are $142,800. Actual charitable contributions are $70,000. Cash dividends of $20,000 were paid on June 30. Pasadena's current E&P retained for the reasonable needs of the business (after reduction for the dividends-paid deduction) is $160,000.

If an IRS agent challenges Pasadena in a later year on the accumulated earnings tax issue, and the facts as noted above are held to be correct, the accumulated earnings tax liability would be calculated as follows:

Taxable income			$420,000
Plus:	Dividends-received deduction		120,000
Minus:	Excess charitable contributions		(10,000)[a]
	Federal income taxes		(142,800)
	Long-term capital gain	$ 30,000	
	Minus: Federal income taxes	(10,200)[b]	(19,800)
	Dividends-paid deduction		(20,000)
	Accumulated earnings credit:		
	Increase in current year reasonable needs	$160,000	
	Minus: Long-term capital gain (net of taxes)	(19,800)	(140,200)
Accumulated taxable income			$207,200
Times:	Tax rate		× 0.396
Accumulated earnings tax liability			$ 82,051

[a] $70,000 total contributions − $60,000 limitation = $10,000 excess contributions.
[b] $10,200 = $30,000 × 0.34

Pasadena's total federal tax liability for the current year is $224,851 ($142,800 + $82,051). ◀

Topic Review C5-4

Accumulated Earnings Tax

1. The accumulated earnings tax applies to all corporations except ones that are specially excluded (e.g., S corporations). In practice, the accumulated earnings tax applies only to closely held corporations.
2. Transactions that provide evidence of a tax avoidance motive generally lead IRS auditors to conclude that an accumulated earnings tax problem exists. These transactions include loans made by the corporation to shareholders, expenditures of corporate funds for the personal benefit of the shareholders, and investments in properties or securities unrelated to the corporation's activities.
3. Earnings accumulated for the reasonable needs of the business are exempt from the accumulated earnings tax. Business needs for retention of earnings include acquisition of a business enterprise, debt retirement, and working capital. A $250,000 lifetime minimum credit is available. This amount is reduced to $150,000 for certain personal service corporations.
4. The accumulated earnings tax equals 39.6% of accumulated taxable income. Accumulated taxable income equals taxable income plus certain positive adjustments (e.g., dividends-received deduction) and minus certain negative adjustments (e.g., federal income taxes, excess charitable contributions, and net capital gain reduced by federal income taxes attributable to the gain). A deduction for the accumulated earnings credit is also available equal to the greater of the unused lifetime earnings exemption or the earnings accumulated during the year for the reasonable needs of the business.
5. Accumulated taxable income can be reduced by a dividends-paid deduction for cash and property dividends paid during the year and consent and throwback dividends paid after the year-end. The deficiency dividend opportunity available to PHCs is not available for accumulated earnings tax purposes.

Topic Review C5-4 presents an overview of the accumulated earnings penalty tax.

TAX PLANNING CONSIDERATIONS

This section examines three areas of tax planning: making special accounting method elections for AMT purposes, avoiding the personal holding company (PHC) tax, and avoiding the accumulated earnings tax.

SPECIAL AMT ELECTIONS

KEY POINT

Not only can these special AMT elections reduce a taxpayer's AMT liability, but these elections should also reduce compliance costs by eliminating the need to keep an additional set of depreciation or amortization records.

Two special elections are available under the AMT rules that permit taxpayers to defer the claiming of certain deductions for income tax purposes. The deferral of these deductions will increase the taxpayer's regular tax liability, but can provide an overall savings by reducing the taxpayer's AMT liability.

Code Sec. 59(e) permits an extended writeoff period to apply to certain expenditures that would otherwise be tax preference items or adjustments. If the extended writeoff period is elected, Code Sec. 59(e)(6) exempts each expenditure from being a tax preference item under Sec. 57, or prevents an adjustment from having to be made for the expenditure under Sec. 56. The expenditures for which the special election can be made and the writeoff periods that apply are as follows:

Code Section	*Type of Expenditure*	*Writeoff Period*
173	Circulation	3 yrs.
174	Research and experimental	10 yrs.
263	Intangible drilling and development	5 yrs.
616	Mining and natural resource development	10 yrs.
617	Mining exploration	10 yrs.

The special election can be made with respect to any portion of a qualified expenditure, and can be revoked only with IRS consent.[74]

The second election permits a taxpayer to elect to use the depreciation method generally required for AMT purposes—the 150% declining balance method over the property's class life for personalty—in computing their regular tax liability. Such an election permits the taxpayer to change the depreciation method for personalty from the 200% declining balance method to the 150% declining balance method, and the depreciation period from the property's recovery period specified in the MACRS rules to its class life. The election cannot be made with respect to nonresidential real property or residential rental property. By making this election one reduces the amount of the annual depreciation adjustments and basis adjustments. This election may be made with respect to one or more classes of property for any tax year and, once made with respect to a class of property, shall apply to all property in such class placed in service during the tax year. The election must be made by the due date for the taxpayer's return (including any extensions that are permitted).[75]

ELIMINATING THE ACE ADJUSTMENT

C corporations must increase their AMTI by the amount of the ACE adjustment. This adjustment can be significant for some C corporations. If the C corporation is closely held, it can elect to be taxed as an S corporation and this adjustment can be avoided.[76]

OBJECTIVE 6

Explain how a corporation can avoid being subject to the personal holding company tax

AVOIDING THE PERSONAL HOLDING COMPANY TAX

Five types of tax planning can be used to avoid the PHC tax, as discussed in the following sections.

MAKING CHANGES IN THE CORPORATION'S STOCK OWNERSHIP. Additional stock can be sold to unrelated parties in order to avoid having five or fewer shareholders owning more than 50% (in value) of the stock at any time during the last half of the tax year. Sales of either common or preferred stock can be made. The sale of nonvoting preferred stock to unrelated parties permits the corporation's stock ownership to be spread among a larger number of individuals without diluting the voting power of the current shareholder group.

CHANGING THE AMOUNT AND TYPE OF INCOME EARNED BY THE CORPORATION. Several tax planning options are available to change the amount and type of corporate income. These include

- Adding additional "operating" activities to the corporation's line of business. Passive income will become a smaller portion of the corporation's total income.

[74] Secs. 59(e)(4)(A) and (B).
[75] Secs. 168(b)(2) and (5).
[76] Sec. 56(g)(6).

- Converting taxable interest or dividend income earned on an investment portfolio into nontaxable interest income or long-term capital gains. Nontaxable interest income and long-term capital gains are not included in the PHCI definition and, therefore, cannot cause a corporation to be a PHC.
- Adding additional passive income of a type that either is eligible to be excluded from PHCI or reduces the amount of other PHCI that is earned. For example, a corporation might increase the proportion of its income that is earned from rents in order to exceed the 50% of AOGI requirement to exclude adjusted income from rents from PHCI.

KEY POINT

One of the easiest methods of avoiding the PHC penalty tax is through a dividend distribution. If a corporation lacks the funds to pay a dividend, a consent dividend (which is a hypothetical dividend) may be useful. In addition, certain dividends can be declared after year-end to help in after-the-fact tax planning.

MAKING DIVIDEND DISTRIBUTIONS. Dividends reduce the tax base used to levy the PHC tax. The inclusion in PHCI of certain income forms (e.g., adjusted income from rents) can be avoided by paying enough dividends to reduce the amount of other PHCI to 10% of OGI or less. Some of these dividends (e.g., throwback dividends, consent dividends, and deficiency dividends) can be paid after year-end in order to engage in last-minute tax planning.

MAKING AN S ELECTION. An S election prevents the imposition of the PHC tax because S corporations are statutorily exempt from the penalty tax. Such an election is less attractive because the individual tax rates are now generally above the corporate tax rates, but may avoid double taxation of corporate earnings that are distributed as dividends (see Chapter C11).

LIQUIDATING THE CORPORATION. A PHC could be liquidated and have the assets held by the shareholders instead. The liquidating distributions are eligible for the dividends-paid deduction and can reduce the UPHCI amount. This alternative is less attractive because the individual tax rates are now generally above the corporate tax rates, but may avoid double taxation of corporate earnings that are distributed as dividends.

OBJECTIVE 7

Explain how a corporation can avoid being subject to the accumulated earnings tax

KEY POINT

An S election can be useful in avoiding both the PHC penalty tax and the accumulated earnings tax because an S corporation is statutorily exempt from both taxes. However, the S election cannot eliminate potential accumulated earnings tax problems arising in prior C corporation tax years.

AVOIDING THE ACCUMULATED EARNINGS TAX

The primary defense against an IRS position that the corporation has accumulated an unreasonable amount of earnings is to document that the earnings accumulations are necessary to meet the future capital needs of the business. The existence of these business plans must be documented each year. The plans, which should be as specific as possible, should be revised periodically. Completed projects should be documented. Abandoned projects should be eliminated from the plan. A tentative timetable for the current set of projects is a positive factor for the corporation should an IRS challenge be encountered. Such plans might be incorporated into the minutes of one or more board of directors meetings.

Transactions that are indicative of an unreasonable earnings accumulation (e.g., loans to shareholders or large investment portfolios) should be avoided. The business purpose for engaging in any transaction that appears to indicate an unreasonable earnings accumulation should be thoroughly documented.

Corporations that have a potential accumulated earnings tax problem should consider making an S election. S corporations are able to avoid accumulated earnings tax problems only on a prospective basis. The making of the election does not eliminate the possibility that the penalty tax might be imposed for a tax year prior to the election year in which a determination is made that an unreasonable earnings accumulation exists.

COMPLIANCE AND PROCEDURAL CONSIDERATIONS

ALTERNATIVE MINIMUM TAX

The corporate AMT liability is reported on Form 4626 (Alternative Minimum Tax—Corporations). A completed Form 4626 is included in Appendix B that uses the facts in the comprehensive example on pages C5-9 thru C5-12.

Chapter C3 discussed the corporate estimated tax payment requirements. Section 6655(g) includes the corporate AMT liability as part of the required annual payment. Therefore, corporations must estimate their AMT liability properly when making their quarterly payments or possibly be subject to the underpayment penalties described in Sec. 6655.

ETHICAL POINT

A tax practitioner has a responsibility to advise his or her client early in the year about potential PHC problems and steps that can be taken to avoid the penalty tax. Because the PHC tax is self-assessed, a Schedule PH must be filed with the Form 1120 even if no PHC tax is owed.

PERSONAL HOLDING COMPANY TAX

FILING REQUIREMENTS FOR TAX RETURNS. A PHC must file a corporate income tax return (Form 1120). Schedule PH must accompany the return. Schedule PH includes the steps necessary to determine whether the corporation is a PHC and to calculate the UPHCI and PHC tax amounts. Regulation Sec. 301.6501(f)-1 extends the statute of limitations for the PHC penalty tax from three to six years if a PHC fails to file the Schedule PH, even if no additional tax is owed.

PAYMENT OF THE TAX, INTEREST, AND PENALTIES. Corporations ordinarily pay the PHC tax when they file their Form 1120 and Schedule PH or when a determination is made by the IRS or the courts that the tax is owed. The penalty tax is not part of the corporation's required estimated tax payments. Corporations that pay the PHC penalty tax after the due date for filing their return (without regard to any extensions) will generally also owe interest and penalties on the unpaid PHC tax from the date that the return is originally due (without regard to any extensions) until the tax is paid.[77]

ETHICAL POINT

A tax practitioner has a responsibility to advise his or her client during the year about potential accumulated earnings tax problems and steps to be taken to avoid the penalty tax. Because the accumulated earnings tax is not self-assessed, there is no requirement that the CPA or the client notify the IRS of any potential accumulated earnings tax problem.

ACCUMULATED EARNINGS TAX

No formal schedule or return is required of a corporation that owes the accumulated earnings tax. Because of the subjective nature of this tax, a firm generally will not pay the penalty tax until some time after the IRS has audited their income tax return. Because the tax is not paid when the return is filed, Sec. 6601(b) requires interest to be charged on the accumulated earnings tax from the date the return is originally due (without regard to any extensions) until the date the tax payment is received.[78] The penalty for negligent underpayment of taxes imposed by Sec. 6653 may be assessed in accumulated earnings tax situations.[79]

PROBLEM MATERIALS

DISCUSSION QUESTIONS

C5-1 Explain the legislative intent behind enacting the alternative minimum tax.

C5-2 Define the following terms:

a. Tax preference item

[77] *Hart Metal Products Corp. v. U.S.*, 38 AFTR 2d 76-6118, 76-2 USTC ¶9781 (Ct. Cls., 1976).

[78] Rev. Rul. 87-54, 1987-1 C.B. 349.

[79] Rev. Rul. 75-330, 1975-2 C.B. 496.

b. Adjustment item
c. Alternative minimum taxable income
d. Statutory exemption amount
e. Tentative minimum tax

C5-3 Dunn Corporation has taxable income of less than $40,000. The CPA preparing the corporate tax return does not calculate the AMT liability because he knows that taxable income is less than the AMT statutory exemption. Is he correct in his action? Explain.

C5-4 Identify the following items as adjustments to taxable income (A) or as tax preference items (P):

a. Percentage depletion claimed in excess of a property's adjusted basis at the end of the tax year.
b. MACRS depreciation claimed on tangible personal property placed in service after 1986 in excess of the depreciation claimed under the alternative depreciation system.
c. ACRS cost recovery deduction claimed on real estate placed in service before 1987 in excess of hypothetical straight-line depreciation allowance.
d. Tax-exempt interest on private activity bonds.
e. Difference between gain reported on the sale of the asset in Part b when determining taxable income and alternative minimum taxable income.
f. 75% of the excess of adjusted current earnings (ACE) over pre-adjustment AMTI.

C5-5 Determine whether the following statements are true or false for the corporate AMT. If false, explain why the statement is false.

a. Tax preference items may either increase or decrease AMTI.
b. The same NOL carryover amount is used for regular tax and AMT purposes.
c. The minimum tax credit is the entire amount by which the tentative minimum tax exceeds the regular tax.
d. A corporate taxpayer's general business credit can offset not only its regular tax liability but also its AMT liability.
e. The ACE adjustment can increase or decrease pre-adjustment AMTI.

C5-6 Florida Corporation encounters a problem with the AMT for the first time in the current year. The problem is due to a $2 million gain on a nondealer installment sale that is being reported over ten years for financial accounting and taxable income purposes and is included in full in the current year ACE. Explain the ACE adjustment to Florida Corporation's president, how the adjustment is similar to and different from the E&P concept with which he is familiar, and whether the adjustment will turn around in future years.

C5-7 What adjustment must be made if ACE exceeds pre-adjustment AMTI? is less than pre-adjustment AMTI? What restrictions are placed on negative ACE adjustments?

C5-8 Some tax authorities say a positive ACE adjustment can produce three different effective tax rates depending on the corporation's tax situation: (1) a 0% effective tax rate, (2) a 15% effective tax rate, and (3) between a 0% and 15% effective tax rate. Explain what the tax authorities are talking about.

C5-9 Indicate whether the following items are included in taxable income, pre-adjustment AMTI, and ACE.

a. Tax-exempt interest on private activity bonds
b. Proceeds of a life insurance policy on a corporate officer that has no cash surrender value
c. Profit on current year sale of inventory that a dealer reports using the installment method of accounting for book purposes
d. Gain on current year sale of Sec. 1231 property that a nondealer reports using the installment method of accounting
e. Intangible drilling costs that were incurred and deducted in the current year
f. Amortization of organizational expenditures incurred last year
g. Dividends-received deduction claimed with respect to a dividend received from a 10%-owned domestic corporation.

C5-10 Burbank Corporation incurs an AMT liability for the first time in the current year. The liability is due entirely to an ACE adjustment resulting from the receipt of $4 million of life insurance proceeds that were received on the death of the firm's Chief Executive Officer in a plane crash. Explain to Burbank's director of taxes whether it is possible to reduce future regular tax liabilities by the AMT liability paid in the current year.

C5-11 Which of the following special corporate forms are exempt from the PHC tax? the accumulated earnings tax?

a. Closely held corporations
b. S corporations
c. Professional corporations
d. Tax-exempt organizations
e. Publicly held corporations

C5-12 Carolina Corporation has always earned 30% to 40% of its gross income from passive sources due to the outstanding performance of its investments. For a number of years, the corporation has held a block of stock in a corporation that was recently acquired in a takeover. A substantial long-term capital gain has been recognized that will increase this year's passive income to 70% of gross income. Explain to the Carolina's president why she should or should not be worried about the personal holding company penalty tax in the current year.

C5-13 Which of the following types of income are included in the definition of personal holding company income (PHCI) when received by a corporation? Indicate whether any special circumstances would exclude a type of income that is generally included in PHCI.
a. Dividends
b. Interest from a corporate bond
c. Interest from a bond issued by a state government
d. Rental income from a warehouse leased to a third party
e. Rental income from a warehouse leased to the corporation's sole shareholder
f. Royalty income from a book whose copyright is owned by the corporation
g. Royalty income from a computer software copyright developed by the corporation and leased to a software marketing firm
h. Accounting fees earned by a professional corporation offering public accounting services that has three equal shareholders
i. Long-term capital gain earned on the sale of a stock investment

C5-14 Which of the following dividend payments are eligible for a dividends-paid deduction when computing the PHC tax? The accumulated earnings tax?
a. Cash dividend paid on common stock during the tax year
b. Annual cash dividend paid on preferred stock where no dividend is paid to the common stock shareholders
c. Dividend payable in the stock of an unrelated corporation
d. Stock dividend payable in the single class of stock of the distributing corporation
e. Cash dividend paid two months after the close of the tax year

C5-15 Define the term *consent dividend*. What requirements must be satisfied by the PHC or its shareholders before a consent dividend is eligible for a dividends-paid deduction? What are the tax consequences of a consent dividend to the shareholders and the distributing corporation?

C5-16 Explain the advantages of paying a deficiency dividend. What requirements must be satisfied by the PHC and its shareholders before a deficiency dividend can be used to reduce or eliminate the PHC tax liability? Can a deficiency dividend eliminate the interest and penalties imposed in addition to the PHC penalty tax?

C5-17 Determine whether the following statements about the PHC tax are true or false:
a. A corporation may not owe any PHC tax liability for a tax year even though it is classified as a PHC.
b. A sale of a large tract of land that is held for investment purposes can cause a corporation to be classified as a PHC.
c. Federal income taxes (including the alternative minimum tax) accrued by the PHC reduce the UPHCI amount for the tax year.
d. Consent dividends can be paid any time from the first day of the tax year through the due date for the corporation's tax return (including any extensions permitted) and reduce the UPHCI amount.
e. The payment of a deficiency dividend permits a PHC to eliminate its PHC tax liability as well as any interest and penalties that are imposed in addition to the liability.
f. A corporation that is classified as a PHC for a tax year can also be liable for the accumulated earnings tax for that year.

C5-18 Explain the following statement: Although the accumulated earnings tax can be imposed on both publicly held and closely held corporations, it is likely to be imposed only on closely held corporations.

C5-19 The accumulated earnings tax is imposed only when the corporation is "formed or availed of for the purpose of avoiding the income tax."

Does tax avoidance have to occur at the corporate or the shareholder level in order for the penalty tax to be imposed? Does tax avoidance have to be the sole motivation for the earnings accumulation before the penalty tax is imposed?

C5-20 Charles Corporation has substantial cash flows from its manufacturing activities. There is only a moderate need to reinvest its earnings in replacement of existing facilities or expansion. In recent years a large investment portfolio has been accumulated because management has been unwilling to pay dividends due to the possibility of double taxation of the corporate profits. The corporation is in no danger of being classified as a PHC, but is concerned about its exposure to the accumulated earnings tax. Explain to Charles's president what actions can be taken to avoid the possibility of having an accumulated earnings tax penalty imposed.

C5-21 Explain the operation of the *Bardahl* formula. Why have some tax authorities said that this formula implies a greater amount of mathematical accuracy than, in fact, actually may be present when determining working capital needs?

C5-22 Different rules apply to operating companies, holding and investment companies, and service companies when determining the accumulated earnings credit. Explain these differences.

C5-23 Determine whether the following statements about the accumulated earnings tax are true or false:

a. Before the IRS can impose the accumulated earnings tax, it only needs to show that tax avoidance was one of the motives for the corporation's unreasonable accumulation of earnings.

b. Long-term capital gains are included in the tax base for the accumulated earnings tax.

c. Each corporation that is a member of a controlled group can claim a separate $150,000 or $250,000 accumulated earnings credit.

d. A dividends-paid deduction can be claimed for both cash and property distributions (other than nontaxable stock dividends) paid by a corporation.

e. The accumulated earnings tax liability cannot be eliminated by paying a deficiency dividend.

f. Interest and penalties on the accumulated earnings tax deficiency are imposed only from the date that a determination is made by the IRS or the courts that the liability is owed.

C5-24 For each of the following statements, indicate whether the statement is correct for the PHC tax only (P), the accumulated earnings tax only (A), both penalty taxes (B), or neither penalty tax (N).

a. The penalty tax is imposed only if the corporation satisfies certain stock ownership and income requirements.

b. The penalty tax applies to both closely held and publicly held corporations.

c. The penalty tax is subjective in nature.

d. Long-term capital gains are a neutral factor in determining the amount of the penalty tax levy.

e. Tax-exempt interest income is excluded in determining the tax base used to levy the penalty tax.

f. A credit is available that reduces the penalty tax liability on a dollar-for-dollar basis.

g. Throwback dividends are permitted to be paid without limit.

h. Consent dividends are eligible for a dividends-paid deduction.

i. Throwback and consent dividends are effective tools for reducing or eliminating the penalty tax liability.

j. The penalty tax can be avoided by making a deficiency dividend distribution.

ISSUE IDENTIFICATION QUESTIONS

C5-25 Bird Corporation purchases a new precision casting machine for its manufacturing facility costing $1 million. Installation costs are $75,000. The machine is placed in service in June 1997. The old casting machine, which was placed in service in 1988, was sold to an unrelated party at a $125,000 book income profit. What asset disposition and capital recovery issues do you, as Bird's director of federal taxes, need to address when removing the old machine from, and placing the new machine on, the tax books and in calculating the 1997 tax depreciation?

C5-26 Parrish Corporation is a closely held corporation with all of the stock owned by Robert and Kim Parrish. The corporation, in its second month of operation in its initial tax year, anticipates earning $200,000 of gross income in the current year. Gross income is expected to be approximately 40% dividends, 30% corporate bond interest, and 30% net real estate rentals (after interest, property taxes, and depreciation). Administrative expenses are expected to be $10,000. What special problems does the large amount of passive income that Parrish Corporation expects to earn present to you as their CPA?

C5-27 McHale Corporation is owned by eight individuals. Three shareholders own 51% of the stock and made up the board of directors. The corporation has a successful automobile repair parts manufacturing business. It has accumulated $2,000,000 of E&P and expects to accumulate another $300,000 of E&P annually. Annual dividend payments are $30,000. Because Americans own their vehicles longer than they did twenty years ago, demand for McHale's repair parts has been strong for the past five years. However, little expansion of the current plant is projected for three to five years. Management has invested $200,000 annually in growth stocks. Its current investment portfolio is $1,200,000, which is being held primarily as protection against a business downturn. Loans to shareholder-employees are currently $400,000. As McHale's tax return preparer, what tax issues should be considered by your client?

PROBLEMS

C5-28 ***Alternative Minimum Tax Calculation.*** Whitaker Corporation reports taxable income of $700,000 for the current year. It had positive AMTI adjustments of $600,000 and tax preference items of $300,000.

a. What is Whitaker's AMTI?
b. What is Whitaker's tentative minimum tax?
c. What is Whitaker's regular tax liability?
d. What is Whitaker's AMT liability?

C5-29 ***Depreciation Calculations.*** Water Corporation placed a machine costing $10,000 in service on June 1, 1993. The machine is seven-year property under the MACRS rules. The machine has a twelve-year class life. Calculate using the half-year convention the annual depreciation deductions for purposes of determining

a. Taxable income
b. Alternative minimum taxable income
c. Adjusted current earnings

How would your answers to parts a–c change if the machine were instead purchased and placed in service on June 1, 1996?

C5-30 ***Basis Adjustment.*** Assume the same basic facts as in Problem C5-29. Water Corporation sells the machine for $5,000 on August 31, 1998.

a. What gain is reported for purposes of determining taxable income, AMTI, and adjusted current earnings?
b. If you were using taxable income as the starting point for calculating AMTI, what type of adjustment is needed to properly report the transaction for AMTI purposes?

C5-31 ***ACE Adjustment.*** Calculate the ACE adjustment for Towne Corporation for each year since its incorporation in 1993.

	1993	*1994*	*1995*	*1996*	*1997*
ACE	500	500	500	500	(500)
Pre-adjustment AMTI	(100)	600	900	—0—	(300)
ACE adjustment	?	?	?	?	?

C5-32 ***ACE Adjustment.*** Bronze Corporation reports the following information about its current year operations:

Taxable income	$600,000
Dividend from 10%-owned corporation	40,000
Life insurance proceeds received on the death of a corporate officer	200,000
Tax-exempt bond interest (not from private activity bonds)	50,000
Installment sale of land (a capital asset) made in current year:	
Total realized gain	400,000
Gain included in taxable income	32,000
Depreciation:	
For regular tax purposes	120,000
For AMTI purposes	85,000
For ACE purposes	60,000
Sec. 1245 property sold in current year:	
Recognized gain for regular tax purposes	30,000
Basis for regular tax purposes	24,000
Basis for AMTI purposes	30,000
Basis for ACE purposes	34,000

a. What is Bronze Corporation's ACE adjustment?
b. What is Bronze Corporation's AMTI?
c. What is Bronze Corporation's AMT liability?

C5-33 ***Regular Tax and AMT Calculations.*** Campbell Corporation has taxable income of $210,000 for 1997. The following items were taken into consideration in arriving at this number.

1. Equipment acquired in 1992–1997 was depreciated using the MACRS rules. MACRS depreciation on this equipment for 1997 was $100,000. Depreciation under the alternative depreciation system for AMT purposes would have been $75,000.
2. $12,000 of Sec. 1245 gain is recognized for income tax purposes on the sale of an asset. The asset's income tax basis is $9,000 less than its AMT basis.
3. Campbell's adjusted current earnings for 1997 are $480,000.

a. What is Campbell Corporation's AMTI?
b. What is Campbell Corporation's AMT liability?
c. What is the amount (if any) of Campbell Corporation's minimum tax credit? To what years can it be carried?

C5-34 ***AMTI Calculation.*** Alabama Corporation conducts copper mining activities. During the current year it reported taxable income of $400,000, which included a $100,000 deduction for percentage depletion. The depletable property's adjusted basis at year-end (before reduction for the current year's depletion) was $40,000. Cost depletion, had it been taken, would have been $30,000. Depreciation on post-1986 property acquisitions under the MACRS rules was $140,000. Under the alternative depreciation system, only $90,000 could have been claimed for AMTI purposes. In addition, $12,000 of accelerated depreciation was claimed on real property placed in service in 1985. Straight-line depreciation would have been $7,000. Alabama Corporation sold an asset for a $12,000 gain that was included in taxable income. The asset's adjusted basis was $5,000 higher for AMT purposes than it was for regular tax purposes. Alabama Corporation's adjusted current earnings are $800,000.

a. What is Alabama Corporation's AMTI?
b. What is Alabama Corporation's AMT liability?
c. What is the amount (if any) of Alabama Corporation's minimum tax credit? To what years can it be carried?

C5-35 ***Regular Tax and AMT Calculations.*** What is Middle Corporation's regular tax liability, AMT liability, and minimum tax credit (if any) in the following three independent situations? Assume that Middle Corporation has made $120,000 of positive ACE adjustments in prior years.

		Situation	
	No. 1	*No. 2*	*No. 3*
Taxable income	$200,000	$ 50,000	$300,000
Tax preference items and positive AMTI adjustments (other than the ACE adjustment)	100,000	25,000	160,000
Adjusted current earnings	500,000	150,000	400,000

C5-36 ***Regular Tax and AMT Calculations.*** Delta Corporation reports taxable income of $2,000,000, tax preference items of $100,000, and net positive AMTI adjustments of $600,000 before the ACE adjustment. Its adjusted current earnings are $4,000,000.

a. What is Delta Corporation's regular tax liability?

b. What is Delta Corporation's AMT liability?

c. What is the amount (if any) of Delta Corporation's minimum tax credit? To what years can it be carried?

C5-37 ***Minimum Tax Credit.*** Jones Corporation has $600,000 of taxable income plus $400,000 of positive AMTI adjustments and $200,000 of tax preference items.

a. What is Jones Corporation's regular tax liability and AMT liability?

b. What is Jones Corporation's minimum tax credit (if any)? To what years can it be carried back or carried over?

C5-38 ***Minimum Tax Credit.*** Gulf Corporation reports the following tax amounts for the period 1995–1997:

Tax Amounts	*1995*	*1996*	*1997*
Regular tax	$75,000	$100,000	$210,000
Tentative minimum tax	40,000	150,000	170,000

In what years does a minimum tax credit originate? To what years can the credit be carried? Do any credit carryovers remain to 1998?

C5-39 ***General Business Credit.*** Edge Corporation's regular tax amount before credits is $180,000 in the current year. Its tentative minimum tax is $100,000. The only credit Edge Corporation earns in the current year is a $200,000 general business credit relating to research expenditures.

a. What amount of this credit may Edge Corporation use to reduce its current year liability?

b. What carryovers and carrybacks are available, and to what years may they be carried?

C5-40 ***Estimated Tax Requirement.*** Ajax Corporation anticipates owing a $120,000 regular tax liability and a $60,000 AMT liability for the current year. Last year it owed a $200,000 regular tax liability and no AMT liability. What is its minimum estimated tax payment for the current year?

C5-41 ***Estimated Tax Payments.*** Dallas Corporation reports the following information with respect to its 1996 and 1997 tax liabilities:

Type of Liability	*1996*	*1997*
Regular tax	$100,000	$120,000
AMT	—0—	25,000

Both tax years cover twelve-month periods. Dallas Corporation is not a large corporation and it made $23,000 of estimated tax payments for each quarter of 1997.

a. What is the amount of tax owed when Dallas files its 1997 tax return?
b. Is Dallas potentially liable for any estimated tax underpayment penalties? If so, how much is underpaid for each quarter?

C5-42 *PHC Definition.* In which of the following situations will Small Corporation be a PHC? Assume that personal holding company income constitutes more than 60% of Small's adjusted ordinary gross income.

a. Art owns all of Parent Corporation's stock. Parent Corporation owns all of the Small stock. Parent and Small Corporations file separate tax returns.
b. Art owns one-third of the Small stock. The PRS Partnership, of which Phil, Robert, and Sue each have a one-third interest in both capital and profits, also owns one-third of the Small stock. The remaining Small stock is owned by 50 individuals unrelated to Art, Phil, Robert, and Sue.
c. Art and his wife, Becky, each own 20% of the Small stock. The remaining Small stock is owned by the Whitaker Family Trust. Becky and her three sisters each have a one-fourth beneficial interest in the trust.

C5-43 *PHC Definition.* In which of the following situations will Total Corporation, a corporation that is owned equally by Phong, Len, and Milt at all times during the tax year, be a PHC?

a. Total Corporation reports $75,000 of gross profit from manufacturing activities, $40,000 of interest income, $60,000 of dividend income, and $25,000 of long-term capital gains.
b. Total Corporation reports $100,000 of rental income, $14,000 of interest income, and $6,000 of dividend income. Depreciation, interest, and property taxes on the rental properties are $40,000. No dividends are paid by Total during the tax year.
c. Assume the same facts as in Part b, except that Total Corporation instead pays $9,000 of dividends during the year.

C5-44 *PHC Definition.* Random Corporation is owned equally by two individual shareholders. During the current year Random reports the following results:

Income:	Rentals	$200,000
	Dividend (from a 25%-owned domestic corporation)	30,000
	Interest	15,000
	Long-term capital gains	20,000
Expenses related to rental income:		
	Interest	30,000
	Depreciation	27,000
	Property taxes	8,000
	Other Sec. 162 expenses	50,000
General and administrative expenses		10,000
Dividend paid on June 30		15,000

a. What is Random's gross income?
b. What is Random's ordinary gross income?
c. What is Random's adjusted income from rents?
d. What is Random's adjusted ordinary gross income?
e. What is Random's personal holding company income?
f. Is Random Corporation a PHC?

C5-45 *PHC Tax Liability.* Mouse Corporation is a PHC for the current year. The following results are reported by Mouse for the current year:

Taxable income	$200,000
Dividend received by Mouse from a 25%-owned domestic corporation	50,000
Dividends paid by Mouse during the current year	75,000

a. What is Mouse's federal income tax liability (ignoring any AMT implications)?
b. What is Mouse's PHC tax liability?
c. What actions can be taken by Mouse to eliminate its PHC tax liability after the year-end and before its tax return is filed? After its tax return is filed?

C5-46 ***PHC Tax Liability.*** Kennedy Corporation is a PHC for the current year. The following results are reported for the current year:

Taxable income	$400,000
Federal income taxes	136,000
Dividends paid to Marlene, Kennedy's sole shareholder, during the current year	75,000

The following information is available about the federal income tax calculation:

- $100,000 of dividends were received from a 25%-owned domestic corporation.
- $30,000 of tax-exempt interest income was received.
- $175,000 of long-term capital gains were recognized on the sale of land (a Sec. 1231 asset).

a. What is Kennedy Corporation's PHC tax liability?
b. What can be done after the year-end and before the tax return is filed to eliminate the PHC tax liability? After the tax return is filed?

C5-47 ***PHC Tax Liability.*** Victor Corporation is classified as a PHC for the current year. The following results are reported by Victor for the current year:

Taxable income	$250,000
Federal income taxes	80,750
Dividends paid during the current year	40,000

The following information is available about Victor's taxable income calculation:

- Taxable income includes $50,000 of net capital gain.
- A charitable contributions carryover of $5,000 from the preceding year was deducted.
- A dividends-received deduction of $30,000 is claimed by Victor for dividends received from a 30%-owned domestic corporation.

a. What is Victor's PHC tax liability?
b. What action can be taken by Victor to eliminate the PHC tax liability after the year-end and before the tax return is filed? After the tax return is filed?

C5-48 ***Unreasonable Accumulation of Earnings.*** Indicate for each of the following independent situations why the IRS might find that an unreasonable accumulation of earnings by Adobe Corporation may exist. Provide one or more arguments that the corporation might offer to show that no unreasonable accumulation exists. Assume that all of the Adobe stock is owned by Tess.

a. Adobe Corporation established a sinking fund ten years ago in order to retire its ten-year notes. Monies have been added to the fund annually. Six months ago a decision was made to refinance the notes when they come due with a new series of notes that have been sold to an insurance company. The monies in the sinking fund remain invested in stocks and bonds. A general plan exists to use the monies currently invested in stocks and bonds to purchase operating assets. No definite plans have been established by year-end.

b. Adobe Corporation regularly lends monies to Tess at a rate slightly below the rate charged by a commercial bank. About 20% of these monies have been repaid. The current balance on the loans is $500,000, which approximates one year's net income for Adobe Corporation.
c. Adobe Corporation has made substantial investments in stocks and bonds. The current market value of its investments is $2,000,000. The investment portfolio constitutes approximately one-half of Adobe Corporation's assets.
d. Tess owns three corporations other than Adobe Corporation, which, together with Adobe Corporation, form a brother-sister controlled group. Adobe Corporation regularly lends monies to Tess's three other corporations. The current loans amount to $500,000. The interest rate that is charged approximates the commercial interest rate for similar loans.

C5-49 ***Bardahl* Formula.** Lion Corporation is concerned about a possible accumulated earnings tax problem. It accumulates E&P to maintain the working capital necessary to conduct its manufacturing activities. The following information about Lion Corporation's financial position is taken from its current year balance sheets.

Account	*Beginning Balance*	*Ending Balance*	*Peak Balance for the Year*
Accounts receivable	$300,000	$400,000	$400,000
Inventory	240,000	300,000	375,000
Accounts payable	150,000	200,000	220,000

The following information about operations is taken from Lion Corporation's current year income statement:

Sales	$3,200,000
Cost of goods sold	1,500,000
Purchases	1,200,000
Operating expenses (other than cost of goods sold)	1,000,000

Included in operating expenses are depreciation of $150,000 and federal income taxes of $100,000.

a. What is Lion's operating cycle in days? As a decimal percentage?
b. What is Lion's working capital needs as determined with the *Bardahl* formula?
c. What steps must Lion take in order to justify a larger accumulation than is indicated by the *Bardahl* formula?

C5-50 ***Accumulated Earnings Credit.*** For each of the following independent situations, calculate the amount of the available accumulated earnings credit. Assume that the corporation in question is a manufacturing company that uses a calendar year as its tax year unless otherwise stated and that it has no current year capital gains.

a. Frank Corporation, a manufacturer of plastic toys, was started last year when it reported E&P of $50,000. E&P reported in the current year totals $150,000. No dividends were paid in the current year. The current E&P retained to meet the business needs is $130,000.
b. How would your answer to Part a change if Frank Corporation were a service company that provides accounting services?
c. Hall Corporation's accumulated E&P balance at January 1 of the current year is $200,000. During the current year Hall reports $100,000 of current E&P, all of which is retained to meet the reasonable needs of the business. No dividends were paid in the current year.

C5-51 ***Accumulated Earnings Tax Liability.*** Tara Corporation has conducted manufacturing operations for a number of years. It has an accumulated E&P balance of $150,000 on January 1 of the current year. The following results of operations are presented for the current year:

Taxable income	$450,000
Federal income taxes	153,000
Dividends paid on June 1	10,000

Current year E&P is $300,000 before dividend payments. Tara can justify the retention of $175,000 of current E&P to meet the reasonable needs of the business.

a. What is Tara's accumulated taxable income?

b. What is Tara's accumulated earnings tax liability?

C5-52 ***Accumulated Earnings Tax Liability.*** Howard Corporation conducts manufacturing activities and has a substantial need to accumulate earnings. Its January 1, 1997 E&P balance is $600,000. The following results of operations are presented for 1997:

Taxable income		$600,000
Federal income taxes		204,000
Dividends paid:	July 15, 1997	50,000
	February 10, 1998	100,000

Other information about Howard's operations for 1997 is as follows:

NOL carryover from 1996 deducted in 1997	$100,000
Net capital gain	80,000
Dividends received from 10%-owned domestic corporation	75,000

Current year E&P is $400,000 before dividend payments. Howard can justify the retention of $120,000 of current E&P to meet the reasonable needs of the business.

a. What is Howard's accumulated taxable income?

b. What is Howard's accumulated earnings tax liability?

TAX FORM/RETURN PREPARATION PROBLEM

C5-53 King Corporation, I.D. No. 38-1534789, reports the following results for the current year:

Taxable income	$800,000
Regular tax liability (before credits)	272,000
Accelerated depreciation on real property placed in service in 1985	40,000
Depreciation adjustment for personal property placed in service after 1986	147,000
Personal property acquired in 1991 sold this year:	
Acquisition cost	50,000
Regular tax depreciation	38,845
AMT depreciation	26,845
Increase in LIFO recapture amount	75,000
Tax-exempt interest income:	
Private activity bonds	15,000
Other bonds	5,000
Adjusted current earnings	1,800,000
General business credit (targeted jobs credit)	10,000

Taxable income includes a land sale that resulted in $95,000 of Sec. 1231 gain being reported on the installment method. King's realized gain on the current year sale was $950,000. Prepare Form 4626 for King Corporation to report its AMT liability (if any) for the current year.

CASE STUDY PROBLEMS

C5-54 Eagle Corporation is a family corporation created by Edward Eagle, Sr. ten years ago. Edward Eagle, Sr. dies, and the Eagle stock passes to his children and grandchildren. The corporation is primarily an investment company with its assets consisting of rental property, highly appreciated stocks, and corporate bonds. The profit or loss projection for the current year that was made by the tax advisor who regularly handles Eagle Corporation's tax matters is as follows:

Rentals	$260,000
Dividend income (from a 40%-owned domestic corporation)	80,000
Interest income	20,000
Gross income	$360,000
Rental expenses:	
Depreciation expense	$ 70,000
Interest expense	100,000
Property taxes	10,000
Other Sec. 162 expenses	20,000
General and administrative expenses	15,000
Total expenses	$215,000
Net profit	$145,000

Dividends of $40,000 have been paid in each of the past three years. The stock investment has appreciated substantially in value in the past six months. As a result, dividend income is expected to increase from last year's $10,000 amount to $80,000 this year. Assume that Eagle Corporation has not been a PHC in prior years.

Required: Prepare a memorandum to Edward Eagle, Jr. regarding the possible PHC problem. As part of your discussion, make sure you discuss the following two questions.

a. Is Eagle Corporation projected to be a PHC for the current year?

b. If Eagle Corporation is projected to be a PHC for the current year, what actions (if any) should be taken before year-end to eliminate the PHC problem? after year-end?

C5-55 Goss Corporation is a leading manufacturer of hangers for the laundry and dry cleaning industry. The family-owned business has prospered for many years and has approximately $100 million of sales and $8 million in after-tax profits. Your accounting firm has done the audit and tax work for Goss Corporation and its executives since the company was created in 1948. Little technological change has occurred in the manufacturing of hangers and much of the equipment that is currently being used dates from the 1950s and 1960s. The advent of plastic hangers and improved fabrics has kept the overall market size constant, and no major plant expansions or additions are planned. Salaries paid to corporate executives, most of whom are family members, are above the national averages for similar positions. Dividend payments in recent years have not exceeded 10% of the after-tax profits. You are a recently hired tax manager who has been assigned on December 1, 1997 to oversee the preparation of the 1997 Goss Corporation tax return. Shortly after being assigned to the project you review the 1994–1996 Goss tax returns. You note from Schedule L (the balance sheet) that the corporation has made about $1.5

million in loans to three executives and regularly increased the size of its stock portfolio between 1994 and 1996. These signals lead you to believe that there may be an accumulated earnings tax problem in the current year as well as for a number of prior years.

Required:

a. What is your responsibility to make the partner in charge of the Goss account or the client aware of the potential accumulated earnings tax problem?
b. Should you advise the IRS of the potential problem with prior year returns? Should you disclose the potential problem on the current year return?
c. Prepare a list of actions that can be taken to reduce or eliminate the client's exposure to the accumulated earnings tax problem.

TAX RESEARCH PROBLEMS

C5-56 Brown Corporation purchased two assets in January 1994, its initial year of operation. The first asset, a commercial factory building, cost $200,000 with $40,000 of the acquisition price being allocated to the land. The second, a machine that is a seven-year MACRS property, cost $80,000. The class life for the machine under the Asset Depreciation Range system is ten years. Both assets were sold in March 1997 in connection with a relocation of their manufacturing activities. The sale price for the factory building was $225,000, with $45,000 of the sale price being allocated to the land. The sale price for the machine was $70,000. The maximum amount of depreciation was claimed on both assets for regular tax purposes. Assume that the half-year convention was used with respect to the machine and the mid-month convention with respect to the building. What are the amount and character of the gains reported by Brown Corporation for regular tax and alternative minimum tax purposes?

C5-57 Camp Corporation is owned by Hal and Ruthie, who have owned their stock since the corporation was formed in 1986. The corporation has filed each of its prior tax returns using the calendar year as its tax year and the accrual method of accounting. In 1996 Camp Corporation borrows $4,000,000 from a local bank. The loan is secured by a lien against some of its machinery. Ninety percent of the borrowings are lent by Camp Corporation to Vickers Corporation at the same annual rate at which the borrowing took place. Vickers Corporation is also owned equally by Hal and Ruthie. Vickers Corporation sells parts to the automobile industry that are manufactured by Camp Corporation and other unrelated manufacturers. A downturn is experienced by Camp Corporation due to a slowdown in the automobile industry, and the gross margin from its sales activities declines from $1,000,000 in 1996 to $200,000 in 1997. Interest income accrued by Camp on the loan to Vickers Corporation is $432,000 in 1997. Other passive income earned by Camp Corporation is $40,000. Camp Corporation's accountant feels that the corporation is not a personal holding company because the interest income Camp Corporation earns can be netted against the $432,000 interest expense paid to the bank for the monies lent to Vickers Corporation. Is he correct in his assumption?

A partial list of research sources is

- Secs. 542(a) and 543(a)(1)
- Reg. Sec. 1.543-1(b)(2)
- *Bell Realty Trust*, 65 T.C. 766 (1976)
- *Blair Holding Co., Inc.*, 1980 PH T.C. Memo ¶80,079, 39 TCM 1255

C5-58 William Queen owns all of the stock of Able and Baker Corporations. Able Corporation has been quite successful and has excess working capital in the amount of $3 million.

Baker Corporation is still in its developmental stages and has had tremendous needs for capital. To help provide for Baker Corporation's capital needs, William Queen has had Able Corporation lend Baker Corporation $2 million during 1995 and 1996. These loans are secured by Baker Corporation notes, but not by any Baker Corporation properties. Able Corporation has charged Baker Corporation interest at a rate acceptable to the IRS. Upon reviewing Able Corporation's books in 1997 as part of an audit of its 1995 income tax return, an IRS agent indicates that Able Corporation has an accumulated earnings tax problem because of its accumulation of excess working capital and its loans to Baker Corporation. Later this week you are to meet with the agent for a third time. Prior to this meeting you need to research whether loans to a related corporation in order to provide needed working capital are a reasonable need of the business for retaining its earnings.

A partial list of research sources is

- Secs. 532 and 537
- Reg. Secs. 1.537-2(c) and -3(b)
- *Latchis Theatres of Keene, Inc. v. CIR,* 45 AFTR 1836, 54-2 USTC ¶9544 (1st Cir., 1954)
- *Bremerton Sun Publishing Co.,* 44 T.C. 566 (1965)

CHAPTER 6

CORPORATE LIQUIDATING DISTRIBUTIONS

LEARNING OBJECTIVES

After studying this chapter, you should be able to

1. Explain the difference between a complete liquidation and a dissolution
2. Explain the general shareholder gain and loss recognition rules for a corporate liquidation
3. Determine when gains and losses are recognized by the liquidating corporation on making a liquidating distribution
4. Determine when the Sec. 332 and Sec. 337 nonrecognition rules apply to the liquidation of a subsidiary corporation
5. Determine the effect of a liquidation on the liquidating corporation's tax attributes
6. Explain the different tax treatments for open and closed liquidation transactions
7. Determine when gains and losses are recognized on the retirement of debt by a liquidating corporation

CHAPTER OUTLINE

ADDITIONAL COMMENT

Under Sec. 351, usually no tax cost is involved in forming a corporation. However, as this chapter will illustrate, the tax costs of liquidating a corporation may be substantial. The tax consequences of liquidating a corporation should be a consideration in the initial decision to use the corporate form to conduct a business.

REAL-WORLD EXAMPLE:

Many corporations may not want to incur the cost of liquidating to avoid the corporate income tax. An S election, however, provides many of the same advantages of being taxed as an unincorporated entity (see Chapters C10 and C11). The built-in gains tax incurred by a former C corporation, that operates as an S corporation, is usually less costly than liquidating (see Chapter C11).

As part of the corporate life cycle, management may decide to discontinue the operations of a profitable or unprofitable corporation by liquidating it. As a result of this decision, the shareholders may receive liquidating distributions of the corporation's assets. Preceding the formal liquidation of the corporation, management may sell part or all of the corporation's assets. The sale may be undertaken to dispose of assets that the shareholders may not want to receive in a liquidating distribution or to obtain cash that can be used to pay the corporation's liabilities (including federal income taxes incurred on the liquidation).

Ordinarily the liquidation transaction is motivated by a combination of tax and business reasons. However, sometimes it is undertaken principally for tax reasons.

- If the corporation is liquidated and its shareholders hold the assets in an unincorporated form (e.g., sole proprietorship or partnership), the marginal tax rate may be reduced from the 35% corporate rate to a lower 15%, 28%, or 31% individual rate.
- If the assets are producing losses, it may be advantageous for the shareholders to hold the assets in an unincorporated form and deduct the losses on their personal tax returns.
- Corporate earnings are taxed once under the corporate income tax rules and a second time when distributed as dividends or realized by selling or exchanging the corporate stock. Liquidation of the corporation permits the assets to be held in an unincorporated form, thereby avoiding the double taxation.

Under the new check-the-box rules, a C corporation cannot elect to be taxed as an unincorporated entity and avoid the double taxation of corporate earnings. The corporate liquidation rules impose a "toll charge" on such a conversion by imposing a tax at the corporate and shareholder levels upon existing C corporations who want to convert to proprietorship, partnership, limited liability company, or limited liability partnership status.

This chapter explains the tax consequences of liquidating distributions to both the shareholders and the distributing corporation and the special provisions that can eliminate the recognition of gain for both a corporate shareholder and the distributing subsidiary corporation. A special "deemed liquidation" election permits a corporation to acquire the stock of a target corporation, make a special tax election, and step-up the basis of the target corporation's assets to the amount paid for the stock. This topic is deferred until corporate acquisitions, divestitures, and reorganizations are covered in Chapter C7.

OVERVIEW OF CORPORATE LIQUIDATIONS

This chapter initially presents an overview of the tax and nontax consequences of a corporate liquidation to both the shareholders and the distributing corporation.

THE SHAREHOLDER

Three questions must be answered to determine the tax consequences of the liquidation transaction to each of the liquidating corporation's shareholders:

- What are the amount and character of the shareholder's recognized gain or loss?
- What is the adjusted basis of each property that is received by the shareholder?
- When does the holding period commence for each property that is received by the shareholder?

When a corporation is liquidated under the general rule, the liquidating distribution is treated as an amount received in exchange for the shareholder's stock. The shareholder recognizes the excess of any money received plus the FMV of any nonmoney property received over the adjusted basis of his or her stock as a capital gain or loss. The basis of each property that is received is stepped-up or stepped-down to the property's FMV on the liquidation date. The holding period for the asset commences on the day after the liquidation date. Special rules apply to liquidations of subsidiary corporations that permit part or all of the parent corporation's realized gain or loss to go unrecognized. Special carryover basis and holding period rules apply to liquidations of subsidiary corporations.[1]

THE CORPORATION

Two questions must be answered to determine the tax consequences of the liquidation transaction for the corporation being liquidated:

- What are the amount and character of the corporation's recognized gain or loss?
- What happens to the corporation's tax attributes upon liquidation?

TYPICAL MISCONCEPTION

In a complete liquidation other than a liquidation of a controlled subsidiary, there is a potential tax at both the shareholder and corporate levels. Assuming a 34% corporate tax rate and a 28% capital gains rate at the shareholder level, the effective tax cost of a complete liquidation would be approximately 52.5%. Clearly, a decision to liquidate should be carefully considered.

When a liquidation occurs under the general rule, the liquidating corporation must recognize gain or loss on the distribution of property to its shareholders. The amount of gain or loss recognized is the same as what would be recognized if the property were sold to the distributee. An exception to the general gain or loss recognition rule is provided when an 80%-controlled subsidiary corporation is liquidated into its parent corporation. Three exceptions to the general rule, that are intended to prevent tax avoidance, restrict the recognition of losses in specialized situations. These rules are described below.

The tax attributes (e.g., net operating loss [NOL] carryovers) of the liquidating corporation disappear when the liquidation takes place under the general liquidation rule. As a result, any loss carryovers that have not been used by the liquidation date are lost. On the other hand, the tax attributes of a liquidating subsidiary corporation generally carry over to its parent corporation.

OBJECTIVE 1

Explain the difference between a complete liquidation and a dissolution

DEFINITION OF A COMPLETE LIQUIDATION

The term *complete liquidation* is not defined in the Code, but Reg. Sec. 1.332-2(c) indicates that distributions made by a liquidating corporation must either completely cancel or redeem all of its stock in accordance with a plan of liquidation or be one of a series of distributions that completely cancels or redeems all of its stock in accordance with a plan of liquidation (see page C6-24 for a discussion of plans of liquidation). When there is more than one distribution, the corporation must be in a liquidation status at the time that the first liquidating distribution is made under the plan, and such status must continue until the liquidation is completed. A distribution that is made before a plan of liquidation is adopted will generally be taxed under the dividend distribution or stock redemption rules.

A liquidation status exists when the corporation ceases to be a going concern and its activities are merely for the purpose of winding up its affairs, paying its debts, and distributing any remaining properties to its shareholders. A liquidation is completed when the liquidating corporation has divested itself of substantially all properties. The retention of a nominal amount of assets (e.g., to retain the corporation's name) does not prevent a liquidation from occurring under the tax rules.

---

[1] The liquidation rules generally are applied the same to C and S corporations. Even though S corporations are thought of as individual taxpayers for most tax purposes, the Subchapter C rules of Secs. 331 and 332, as well as Secs. 336 and 337, govern the liquidation of a C corporation into an S corporation. An S corporation is also eligible to make a deemed liquidation election under Sec. 338 (see Chapter C7).

EXAMPLE C6-1 ▶ Able Corporation is owned by Randy Jones. In step 1, Able sells some of its assets to an unrelated purchaser for $200,000 cash. Gain or loss is recognized by Able on each asset sold. In step 2, part of the remaining assets are used to pay Able's federal income taxes and all other liabilities. In step 3, the remaining assets are distributed to Randy Jones. Gain or loss is also recognized by Able on each asset it distributes to its creditors or to Randy Jones. Randy Jones recognizes gain or loss on the exchange of his stock for the distributed property. (See Figure C6-1 for an illustration of the corporate liquidation.) ◀

KEY POINT

A corporation can go through a complete liquidation without undergoing dissolution. If it is desirable to keep the corporate charter alive, this is possible as long as certain state requirements are satisfied.

The liquidation of a corporation does not mean that a corporation has undergone dissolution. **Dissolution** is a legal term that implies that the corporation has surrendered the charter that it originally received from the state. A corporation may complete its liquidation before surrendering its charter to the state and undergoing dissolution. Dissolution may never occur if the corporation retains its charter in order to protect the corporate name from being acquired by another party.

EXAMPLE C6-2 ▶ Thomas Corporation adopts a plan of liquidation in December 1996. All but a nominal amount of Thomas's assets are distributed to its shareholders in January 1997. The nominal assets retained are the minimum amount needed to preserve the corporation's existence under state law and to prevent others from acquiring its name. The retention of a nominal amount of assets does not prevent Thomas Corporation from having been liquidated for tax purposes. ◀

STOP & THINK

Question: Peter Jennings, age 58, is considering forming a new business entity to operate the rental real estate activities that he and his wife have owned personally for a number of years. He has heard about corporations and limited liability companies from reading various real estate journals. Because of their level of personal wealth and the liability protection afforded by the corporate form of doing business, Peter wants to use a corporation to own and operate their real estate. The assets that Peter and his wife plan to transfer to the corporation have a $600,000 FMV and a $420,000 adjusted basis. As Peter's CPA, why should you consider the tax cost of liquidating the corporation as part of overall analysis of the business entity selection decision?

Solution: A transfer of real estate by Peter and his wife to a corporation is tax-free. A subsequent liquidation of the corporation is not tax-free since both the corporation and the shareholder may need to recognize gain or loss. Peter and his wife have $180,000 ($600,000 − $420,000) of appreciation on their real estate. Even if there is no change in value, liquidation of the real estate corporation at a later date will cause $180,000 to be taxed twice. One date on which a liquidation might occur is seven years from now when Peter turns 65. Liquidation of a limited liability company is not a taxable event to the entity or its owners. The difference in liquidation treatment is one of many differences that must be considered. More information on liquidation of a limited liability company can be found in Chapter C10.

GENERAL LIQUIDATION RULES

The liquidation rules are presented in two parts—the general liquidation rules, and the special rules applying to liquidations of 80%-or-more-owned subsidiary corporations. The general liquidation rules are divided into two parts—the effects of liquidating on the shareholders, and the effects of liquidating on the corporation.

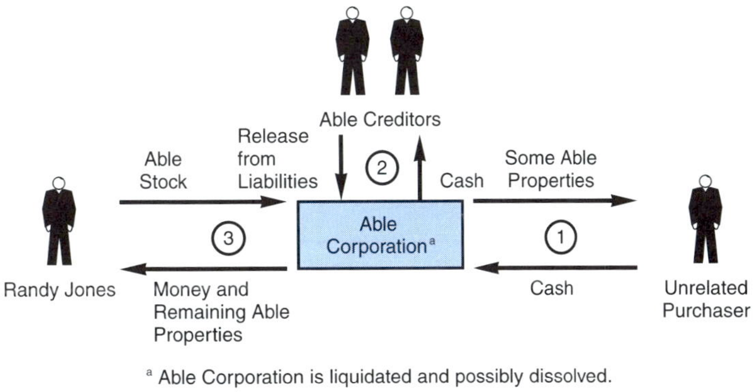

FIGURE C6-1 ▶ ILLUSTRATION OF CORPORATE LIQUIDATION (EXAMPLE C6-1)

OBJECTIVE 2

Explain the general shareholder gain and loss recognition rules for a corporate liquidation

EFFECTS OF LIQUIDATING ON THE SHAREHOLDERS

The coverage of the general liquidation rules is divided into three parts: amount and timing of gain or loss recognition, character of the recognized gain or loss, and basis of property received in the liquidation. Each of these points is discussed below. An overview of the liquidation rules applying to shareholders under both the general liquidation rules and controlled subsidiary corporation exception is presented in Table C6-1.

KEY POINT

As illustrated in Table C6-1, there are two different possibilities with respect to a shareholder in a corporate liquidation. Either the shareholder is considered to be involved in a taxable exchange with a corresponding FMV basis for the liquidated assets or the transaction is nontaxable (parent-subsidiary liquidation) with a carryover basis for the liquidated assets.

AMOUNT OF RECOGNIZED GAIN OR LOSS. Section 331(a) requires that amounts received by a shareholder as a distribution in complete liquidation of a corporation be treated as full payment in exchange for the stock. The amount of the shareholder's recognized gain or loss equals the difference between the amount realized (the FMV of the assets received from the corporation plus any monies) and his or her basis for the stock. If a shareholder assumes or acquires liabilities of the liquidating corporation, the amount of these liabilities reduces the amount realized by the shareholder.

EXAMPLE C6-3 ▶ Red Corporation is liquidated, with Rajiv receiving $10,000 in money and other property having a $12,000 FMV. Rajiv's basis in his Red stock is $16,000. Rajiv's amount realized is $22,000 ($12,000 + $10,000). He must recognize a $6,000 ($22,000 − $16,000) gain on the liquidation. ◀

EXAMPLE C6-4 ▶ Assume the same facts as in Example C6-3, except that Rajiv also assumes a $2,000 mortgage attaching to the other property. Rajiv's amount realized is reduced by the $2,000 liability assumed and is $20,000 ($22,000 − $2,000). The recognized gain on the liquidation is $4,000 ($20,000 − $16,000). ◀

Impact of Accounting Method. A shareholder who uses the accrual method of accounting reports the gain or loss using the accrual concept (i.e., the gain or loss is recognized when all the events have occurred that fix the amount of the liquidating distribution and when the shareholders are entitled to receive the distribution upon surrender of their shares). A shareholder who uses the cash method of accounting reports

▼ **TABLE C6-1**
Tax Consequences of a Liquidation to the Shareholders

	Amount of Gain or Loss Recognized	Character of Gain or Loss Recognized	Adjusted Basis of Property Received	Holding Period of Property Received
General rule	Shareholder's realized gain or loss (money + FMV of nonmoney property received − adjusted basis of stock) is recognized (Sec. 331).	Long-term or short-term capital gain or loss (Sec. 1222). Ordinary loss available (Sec. 1244).	FMV of the property (Sec. 334(a)).	Commences on the day after the liquidation date (Sec. 1223(1)).
Controlled subsidiary corporation rule	No gain or loss is recognized when an 80% controlled subsidiary corporation is liquidated into its parent corporation (Sec. 332).[a]	Not applicable.[a]	Carryover basis for property from subsidiary corporation's books (Sec. 334(b)).[a]	Includes asset's holding period for the subsidiary corporation (Sec. 1223(2)).[a]

[a] Minority shareholders use the general rule.

SELF-STUDY QUESTION

How is the gain/loss calculated if a shareholder has acquired stock at different times and at varying prices?

ANSWER

A shareholder who has purchased blocks of stock at different times and at varying prices must calculate the gain/loss on each block separately. Calculating the gain/loss separately on each block may result in (1) both gains and losses existing in the same liquidating distribution and (2) the character of the various gains/losses being different.

KEY POINT

As in other taxable exchanges, the basis of property received by a shareholder in a corporate liquidation is its FMV. Likewise, because the assets have in effect been purchased in the transaction, the holding period of such assets begins on the day after the distribution.

the gain or loss when there has been actual or constructive receipt of the liquidating distribution(s).[2]

When Stock Is Acquired. The shareholder's stockholdings may have been acquired at different times or for different per-share amounts. If this occurs, the shareholder must compute the gain or loss separately for each share or block of stock that is owned.[3]

CHARACTER OF THE RECOGNIZED GAIN OR LOSS. Generally, the liquidating corporation's stock is a capital asset in the shareholder's hands. The gain or loss that is recognized is, therefore, a capital gain or loss for most shareholders. Two exceptions to these rules are indicated below.

- Loss recognized by an individual shareholder on Sec. 1244 stock is ordinary loss (see Chapter C2).
- Loss recognized by a corporate shareholder on the worthlessness of the stock of a controlled subsidiary (as defined in Sec. 165(g)(3)) is ordinary loss (see Chapter C2).

BASIS OF PROPERTY RECEIVED IN THE LIQUIDATION. Section 334(a) provides that the basis of any property received under the general liquidation rules is its FMV on the distribution date. The holding period for the asset starts on the day after the distribution date.

[2] Rev. Rul. 80-177, 1980-2 C.B. 109.

[3] Reg. Sec. 1.331-1(e).

OBJECTIVE 3

Determine when gains and losses are recognized by the liquidating corporation on making a liquidating distribution

EFFECTS OF LIQUIDATING ON THE LIQUIDATING CORPORATION

This portion of the chapter is divided into two parts: (1) the recognition of gain or loss by the liquidating corporation when it distributes property in redemption of stock; (2) the special valuation rules used when the amount of liabilities assumed or acquired by the shareholder exceeds the property's adjusted basis in the liquidating corporation's hands. An overview of the liquidation rules applying to the liquidating corporation is presented in Table C6-2.

RECOGNITION OF GAIN OR LOSS WHEN PROPERTY IS DISTRIBUTED IN REDEMPTION OF STOCK

Section 336(a) provides that gain or loss must be recognized by the liquidating corporation when property is distributed in a complete liquidation. The amount and character of the gain or loss are determined as if the property were sold to the distributee at its FMV.

EXAMPLE C6-5 ▶ Under West Corporation's plan of liquidation, land is distributed to one of its shareholders, Arnie. The land, which is used in West's trade or business, has a $40,000 adjusted basis and a

▼ **TABLE C6-2**

Tax Consequences of a Liquidation to the Corporation

	Amount and Character of Gain, Loss, or Income Recognized	Treatment of the Liquidating Corporation's Tax Attributes
General rule	Gain or loss is recognized when a corporation distributes property as part of a complete liquidation (Sec. 336(a)).	Tax attributes disappear when the liquidation is completed.
Controlled subsidiary corporation rules	1. No gain or loss is recognized when property of a subsidiary corporation is distributed to its parent corporation when the Sec. 332 nonrecognition of gain or loss rules apply (Sec. 337(a)). 2. No loss is recognized when a distribution of property is made to minority shareholders when the Sec. 332 nonrecognition of gain or loss rules apply to the parent corporation (Sec. 336(d)(3)).	Tax attributes of a subsidiary corporation are assumed by its parent corporation when the Sec. 332 rules apply (Sec. 381(a)).
Related party rule	No loss is recognized when a distribution of property is made to a related person, unless such property is distributed ratably to all shareholders *and* the property was not acquired by the liquidating corporation in a Sec. 351 transaction or as a capital contribution during the five years preceding the distribution (Sec. 336(d)(1)).	
Tax avoidance rule	No loss is recognized when a sale, exchange, or distribution of property occurs and such property was acquired by the liquidating corporation in a Sec. 351 transaction or as a capital contribution having as a principal purpose the recognition of loss (Sec. 336(d)(2)).	

$120,000 FMV on the distribution date. West recognizes an $80,000 Sec. 1231 gain ($120,000 − $40,000) when it makes the liquidating distribution. Arnie recognizes a gain to the extent that the land's FMV exceeds his basis in the West stock. Arnie's basis for the land is its $120,000 FMV. The distribution of the land to Arnie produces double taxation as if West had sold the land and distributed the cash proceeds. The only difference is that the liquidating distribution is taxed to the shareholder at capital gains rates while a cash dividend is taxed as ordinary income. ◀

With limited exceptions, the liquidating corporation can recognize a loss when property that has declined in value is distributed to its shareholders. This rule eliminates the need for a liquidating corporation to sell properties that have declined in value in order to recognize its losses.

EXAMPLE C6-6 ▶ Assume the same facts as in Example C6-5, except that the land's FMV is instead $10,000. West is permitted to recognize a $30,000 Sec. 1231 loss ($10,000 − $40,000 adjusted basis) when the land is distributed to Arnie. Arnie's basis for the land is $10,000. ◀

The Sec. 336 rules apply only to property that is distributed in exchange for the liquidating corporation's stock as part of a complete liquidation. These rules do not apply to distributions of appreciated property as part of a partial liquidation, or when a debt of the liquidating corporation is retired in exchange for appreciated property.

KEY POINT

If the distributed property is subject to a liability, for purposes of determining the amount of gain or loss, the value of the property is treated as being not less than the amount of the liability. This is consistent with Sec. 311(b) for nonliquidating distributions and Sec. 357(c) for corporate formations.

LIABILITIES ASSUMED OR ACQUIRED BY THE SHAREHOLDERS. Property that is distributed by the liquidating corporation is treated for purposes of determining the amount of the gain or loss recognized under Sec. 336 as having been sold to the distributee for its FMV on the distribution date. Section 336(b) contains a special restriction on valuing a liquidating property distribution when liabilities are assumed or acquired by the shareholders. According to this rule, the FMV of the distributed property cannot be less than the amount of the liability assumed or acquired. Section 336(b) was enacted because the corporation has an economic gain or benefit equal to the amount of the liability assumed or acquired by the shareholder (and not just the lower FMV of the property distributed) as part of the liquidation. The shareholders of the liquidated corporation presumably will be permitted to take a basis for the distributed property equal to the amount of the liability assumed or acquired.

EXAMPLE C6-7 ▶ Jersey Corporation owns an apartment complex costing $3,000,000 that has been depreciated so that its adjusted basis is $2,400,000. The property is secured by a $2,700,000 mortgage. A plan of liquidation is adopted, and the property and the mortgage are distributed to Rex, Jersey's sole shareholder, at a time when the property's FMV is $2,200,000. Jersey must recognize a $300,000 gain ($2,700,000 − $2,400,000) on distributing the property because its FMV cannot be less than the $2,700,000 mortgage. The property's basis is $2,700,000 in Rex's hands. ◀

SELF-STUDY QUESTION

Can a subsidiary corporation recognize losses on distributions to either the parent corporation or minority shareholders in a Sec. 332 liquidation?

ANSWER

No. Section 332 liquidations are an exception to the general rule that losses can be recognized by the liquidating corporation. Losses are not recognized on distributions to either the parent corporation or the minority shareholders.

EXCEPTIONS TO THE GENERAL GAIN OR LOSS RECOGNITION RULE. Four exceptions to the general rule of Sec. 336(a) have been enacted. The first two exceptions apply to liquidations of controlled subsidiary corporations and will be covered later. The last two exceptions prevent certain abusive practices (e.g., the manufacturing of losses) from being accomplished. Both exceptions are examined below.

KEY POINT

Another exception to the general rule is that losses cannot be recognized by the liquidating corporation if property is distributed to a related party and the distribution is non–pro rata or the distribution consists of a disqualified property. The disqualified property rule prohibits a shareholder from infusing loss property into the liquidating corporation and generating losses at both the corporate and shareholder levels.

Distributions to Related Persons. Section 336(d)(1)(A) prevents the recognition of loss in connection with distributions of property to a related person if the distribution of a loss property to the related person is other than pro rata based on stock ownership or the property being distributed is a disqualified property. A related person is defined under Sec. 267(b) as including, for example, an individual and a corporation whose stock is more than 50% owned (in terms of value) by such individual, as well as two corporations that are members of the same controlled group. Disqualified property is defined by Sec. 336(d)(1)(B) as (1) any property that is acquired by the liquidating corporation in a transaction to which Sec. 351 applies, or as a contribution to capital, during the five-year period ending on the distribution date, or (2) any property having an adjusted basis that carries over from a disqualified property.

Thus, a non–pro rata distribution of any property or a pro rata distribution of a disqualified property that have declined in value to a related party among others prevents the liquidating corporation from recognizing part or all of its loss for tax purposes.

EXAMPLE C6-8 ▶ Mesa Corporation is 60% owned by Tien and 40% owned by Betty. A plan of liquidation is adopted by Mesa. Pursuant to the plan, Mesa distributes Beta stock purchased three years ago to Tien. The Beta stock, which is not a disqualified property, has a $40,000 FMV and a $100,000 adjusted basis. Betty receives only cash in the liquidation. The non–pro rata distribution of the Beta stock (the loss property), however, prevents Mesa from claiming a $60,000 capital loss when the distribution is made. If the Beta stock is instead distributed 60% to Tien and 40% to Betty, the entire capital loss is deductible by Mesa. ◀

EXAMPLE C6-9 ▶ Assume the same facts as in Example C6-8, except that the Beta stock was acquired three years ago as a capital contribution from Tien and is distributed 60% to Tien and 40% to Betty. The Beta stock is now a disqualified property. Mesa cannot deduct the portion of the $60,000 capital loss attributable to the stock distributed to the related party even though it is distributed ratably to Tien and Betty. Mesa can deduct only the $24,000 ($60,000 × 0.40) capital loss attributable to the Beta stock that was distributed to Betty because she is not a related party. A sale of the disqualified property to an unrelated purchaser permits Mesa to recognize the entire $60,000 loss. ◀

KEY POINT

Certain built-in loss property acquired by the liquidating corporation within two years of the liquidation (either as a contribution to capital or in a Sec. 351 transaction) is deemed to have been acquired for tax avoidance purposes. Consequently, such built-in losses cannot be recognized by the liquidating corporation.

Sales Having a Tax-Avoidance Purpose. Section 336(d)(2) restricts the claiming of a loss with respect to the sale, exchange, or distribution of property acquired in a Sec. 351 transaction, or as a contribution to capital, where the acquisition of the property by the liquidating corporation is part of a plan that has as its principal purpose the recognition of a loss by such corporation in connection with its liquidation. The limiting of the loss that can be claimed prevents a taxpayer from transferring loss properties into a corporation in order to reduce or eliminate the amount of gain that would otherwise have to be recognized by the liquidating corporation from the distribution of other appreciated properties.

Properties acquired by the liquidating corporation in any Sec. 351 transaction or as a contribution to capital within two years of the date on which a plan of complete liquidation is adopted are treated as part of a plan having a tax-avoidance purpose unless exempted by forthcoming regulations.[4] According to the Conference Committee Report,

[4] H. Rept. No. 99-841, 99th Cong., 2d Sess., p. II-201 (1986). The Conference Committee Report for the 1986 Tax Act indicates that property transactions occurring more than two years in advance of the adoption of the plan of liquidation will be disregarded unless there is no clear and substantial relationship between the contributed property and the conduct of the corporation's current or future business enterprises.

the Sec. 336(d)(2) regulations should not prevent corporations from deducting losses associated with dispositions of assets that are contributed to the corporation and used in a trade or business (or a line of business), or dispositions occurring during the first two years of a corporation's existence.[5]

The basis of the contributed property for loss purposes equals its adjusted basis on the liquidating corporation's books reduced (but not below zero) by the excess (if any) of the property's adjusted basis over its FMV immediately after its acquisition. No adjustment occurs to the contributed property's adjusted basis when determining the corporation's recognized gain.

EXAMPLE C6-10 ▶ Terry makes a capital contribution of a widget maker having a $1,000 adjusted basis and a $100 FMV to Pirate Corporation in exchange for additional stock on January 10, 1996. On April 1, 1997, Pirate adopts a plan of liquidation. During the time period between January 10, 1996 and the date the plan of liquidation is adopted, the widget maker is not used in connection with the conduct of Pirate's trade or business. A liquidating distribution is made on July 1, 1997 and Pirate distributes the widget maker and a second property that has a $2,500 FMV and a $900 adjusted basis. Because the widget maker is contributed to Pirate after April 1, 1995 (two years before Pirate adopted its plan of liquidation) and the widget maker is not used in the conduct of Pirate's trade or business, the presumption is that its acquisition and distribution were motivated by a desire to recognize the $900 loss. Unless Pirate can prove otherwise, Sec. 336(d)(2) will apply to the distribution of the widget maker. Pirate's basis for purposes of determining its loss will be $100 [$1,000 − ($1,000 − $100)]. Thus, Pirate cannot claim a loss on distributing the widget maker. Pirate is prevented from offsetting the $1,600 ($2,500 − $900) gain recognized on distributing the second property by the $900 loss realized on distributing the widget maker. ◀

The basis adjustment also affects sales, exchanges, or distributions of property made before the adoption of the plan of liquidation or in connection with the liquidation. Thus, losses that are claimed in a tax return filed before the adoption of the plan of liquidation may be restricted by Sec. 336(d)(2). The liquidating corporation may recapture these losses in the tax return for the tax year in which the plan of liquidation is adopted, or it can file an amended tax return for the tax year in which the loss was originally claimed.

EXAMPLE C6-11 ▶ Assume the same facts as in Example C6-10, except that Pirate sells the widget maker for $200 on July 10, 1996. An $800 loss ($200 − $1,000) is reported on Pirate's 1996 tax return. The adoption of the plan of liquidation on July 1, 1997, causes the loss on the sale of the widget maker to be covered by the Sec. 336(d)(2) rules. Pirate can file an amended 1996 tax return showing the $800 loss being disallowed, or it can file its 1997 tax return reporting $800 of income under the loss recapture rules.[6] ◀

---

[5] Ibid.

[6] The property has a $1,000 basis when determining Pirate's gain on the sale and a $100 ($1,000 − $900) basis when determining its loss on the sale. Therefore, no gain or loss is recognized because the $200 sale price lies between the gain and loss basis amounts.

OBJECTIVE 4

Determine when the Sec. 332 and Sec. 337 nonrecognition rules apply to the liquidation of a subsidiary corporation

LIQUIDATION OF A CONTROLLED SUBISDIARY CORPORATION

The discussion of the controlled subsidiary exception is divided into three parts—the requirements for using the exception, the effects of liquidating on the parent corporation, and the effects of liquidating on the subsidiary corporation. Each of these parts is presented below.

Section 332(a) provides that no gain or loss is recognized when a controlled subsidiary corporation is liquidated into its parent corporation. This liquidation rule permits a corporation to modify its corporate structure without incurring any adverse tax consequences. Section 332 applies only to the parent corporation. Shareholders owning a minority interest are taxed under the general liquidation rules of Sec. 331. The nonrecognition of gain or loss rule is logical for the distribution to the parent corporation because the assets remain within the corporate group following the distribution.

Under this exception, a corporation can take one of its operating divisions and transfer it tax-free in a Sec. 351 transaction to a new subsidiary corporation. At a later date, the subsidiary corporation can be liquidated and operated as a division of its parent corporation. Gain or loss realized from the transaction is not recognized.

ADDITIONAL COMMENT

The liquidation of a subsidiary into its parent is an exception to the general gain/loss recognition treatment of liquidating distributions. The nonrecognition rule of Sec. 332 applies because the transaction is a mere change in form and the assets remain in the corporate group.

EXAMPLE C6-12 ▶ Parent Corporation owns all of the stock of Subsidiary Corporation. Subsidiary Corporation's assets have a $1,000,000 FMV. Parent Corporation's basis for its Subsidiary stock is $250,000. The liquidation of Subsidiary Corporation results in a $750,000 ($1,000,000 − $250,000) realized gain for Parent Corporation, none of which is recognized. If Sec. 332 were not available, Parent Corporation would recognize a $750,000 capital gain on the liquidation. ◀

REQUIREMENTS

The following requirements must all be met for a liquidation transaction to come under the Sec. 332 nonrecognition rules:

- The parent corporation must own at least 80% of the total combined voting power of all classes of stock entitled to vote and 80% of the total value of all classes of stock (other than certain nonvoting preferred stock issues) from the date on which the plan of liquidation is adopted until receipt of the property of the subsidiary corporation.[7]
- The distribution of the property must be in complete cancellation or redemption of all of the subsidiary corporation's stock.
- Distribution of the property must occur within a single tax year or be one of a series of distributions that are completed within three years of the close of the tax year during which the first of the series of liquidating distributions is made.

If all of these requirements are met, the nonrecognition of gain or loss rules contained in Sec. 332 are mandatory. If one or more of the conditions listed above are not met, the parent corporation is taxed under the previously discussed general liquidation rules.

STOCK OWNERSHIP. For Sec. 332 to apply, the parent corporation must own the requisite amount of voting and nonvoting stock. In applying this requirement, the Sec.

[7] The stock definition used for Sec. 332 purposes excludes any stock that is not entitled to vote, is limited and preferred as to dividends and does not participate in corporate growth to any significant extent, has redemption and liquidation rights that do not exceed its issue price (except for a reasonable redemption or liquidation premium), and is not convertible into another class of stock.

TYPICAL MISCONCEPTION

The 80% stock ownership requirement of Sec. 332 is not the same stock ownership requirement for corporate formations in Chapter C2. Instead, the Sec. 332 ownership requirement is the same one that is used for affiliated groups filing consolidated tax returns.

318 attribution rules for stock ownership are not applied (see Chapter C4).[8] The requisite 80% ownership of the voting and nonvoting stock must be owned from the date on which the plan of liquidation is adopted until the liquidation is completed. Failure to satisfy this requirement denies the transaction the benefits of Sec. 332. (See pages C6-22 through C6-23 for further discussion of the stock ownership question.)

CANCELLATION OF THE STOCK. The subsidiary corporation must distribute its properties in complete cancellation or redemption of all of its stock in accordance with a plan of liquidation. There may be more than one liquidating distribution. When more than one liquidating distribution occurs, the subsidiary corporation must have adopted a plan of liquidation and be in a status of liquidation when the first distribution is made. This status must continue until the liquidation is completed. Regulation Sec. 1.332-2(c) indicates that a liquidation is completed when the liquidating corporation has divested itself of all its properties. Retention of a nominal amount of properties to permit retention or sale of the corporate name is permitted.

KEY POINT

If the liquidating distributions are completed within one tax year, a formal plan is not required. Otherwise, a formal plan is required and the liquidating distributions must be completed within three years. If these and the other Sec. 332 requirements are satisfied, the application of Sec. 332 is mandatory.

TIMING OF THE DISTRIBUTIONS. The distribution of all the subsidiary corporation's assets within one tax year of the liquidating corporation in complete cancellation or redemption of all its stock is considered a complete liquidation.[9] Although a formal plan of liquidation can be adopted, the shareholders' adoption of a resolution authorizing the distribution of the corporation's assets in complete cancellation or redemption of its stock is considered to be the adoption of a plan of liquidation when the distribution occurs within a single tax year. The tax year in which the liquidating distribution occurs does not have to be the same as the one in which the plan of liquidation is adopted.[10]

The subsidiary corporation can carry out the plan of liquidation by making a series of distributions that extend over a period of more than one tax year to cancel or redeem its stock. A formal plan of liquidation must be adopted when the liquidating distributions extend beyond a single tax year of the liquidating corporation. The liquidating distributions must include all of the corporation's properties and must be completed within three years of the close of the tax year during which the first distribution is made under the plan.[11]

EFFECTS OF LIQUIDATING ON THE SHAREHOLDERS

RECOGNITION OF GAIN OR LOSS.

Parent Corporation. The Sec. 332(a) nonrecognition rules apply only to a parent corporation that receives a liquidating distribution from a solvent subsidiary. Section 332(a) does not apply to a parent corporation that receives a liquidating distribution from an insolvent subsidiary, to minority shareholders who receive liquidating distributions, or to a parent corporation that receives a payment to satisfy the subsidiary's indebtedness to the parent. All of these exceptions are discussed below.

SELF-STUDY QUESTION

What are the tax consequences if the liquidating subsidiary is insolvent?

Section 332 does not apply if the subsidiary corporation is insolvent at the time of the liquidation because the distributions that are made are not received by the parent corporation in exchange for its stock investment. An insolvent subsidiary is one that has

[8] Sec. 332(b)(1).

[9] Sec. 332(b)(2) and Reg. Sec. 1.332-3.

[10] Rev. Rul. 76-317, 1976-2 C.B. 98.

[11] Sec. 332(b)(3) and Reg. Sec. 1.332-4.

ANSWER

The parent is generally entitled to an ordinary loss deduction under Sec. 165(g)(3) when it fails to receive any liquidation proceeds because the subsidiary is insolvent.

liabilities in excess of the FMV of its assets. Regulation Sec. 1.332-2(b) requires the parent corporation to receive at least partial payment for the stock it owns in the subsidiary corporation in order to qualify for nonrecognition under Sec. 332. If the subsidiary is insolvent, the special worthless security rules of Sec. 165(g)(3) for affiliated corporations will generally apply and permit the parent corporation to recognize an ordinary loss with respect to its investment in the subsidiary's stock or debt obligations (see Chapter C2).

EXAMPLE C6-13 ▶

Parent Corporation owns all of the stock of Subsidiary Corporation, which it established to produce and market a product that proved unsuccessful. Parent Corporation has a $1,500,000 basis in its Subsidiary stock. In addition, it made a $1,000,000 advance to Subsidiary that is not secured by a note. Under a plan of liquidation, Subsidiary distributes all of its assets, having a $750,000 FMV, to Parent in partial satisfaction of the advance after having paid all third-party creditors. No assets remain to pay the remainder of the advance or to redeem the outstanding stock. What loss can Parent claim for the worthless debt and stock? Because Subsidiary is insolvent immediately before the liquidating distribution is made, none of its assets are distributed in redemption of the Subsidiary stock. Therefore, the liquidation cannot qualify under the Sec. 332 rules. Parent Corporation can claim a $250,000 business bad debt with respect to the unpaid portion of the advance and a $1,500,000 ordinary loss for its stock investment. ◀

TYPICAL MISCONCEPTION

Section 332 is applicable only to the parent corporation. If a minority interest exists, the general liquidation rules of Sec. 331 apply to the minority shareholders.

Minority Shareholders. Liquidating distributions made to minority shareholders are taxed under the Sec. 331 general liquidation rules. These rules require the minority shareholders to recognize gain or loss—which is generally capital—upon the redemption of their stock in the subsidiary corporation.

EXAMPLE C6-14 ▶

Parent Corporation and Jane own 80% and 20%, respectively, of Subsidiary Corporation's single class of stock. Parent Corporation and Jane have adjusted bases of $100,000 and $15,000, respectively, for their stock interests. Subsidiary Corporation adopts a plan of liquidation on May 30 and makes liquidating distributions of two parcels of land having $250,000 and $62,500 FMVs to Parent Corporation and Jane, respectively, on November 1 in exchange for their stock. Parent Corporation's $150,000 gain ($250,000 − $100,000) is not recognized because of Sec. 332. Jane's $47,500 gain ($62,500 − $15,000) is recognized as a capital gain under Sec. 331. ◀

SELF-STUDY QUESTION

What bases do both the parent and minority shareholders take in the assets received in a Sec. 332 liquidation?

ANSWER

Because the parent corporation recognizes no gain/loss in the transaction, the parent corporation takes a carryover basis in its assets. However, because the minority shareholders are involved in a taxable exchange, the minority shareholders take a FMV basis in their assets.

BASIS OF PROPERTY RECEIVED. Section 334(b)(1) provides that the parent corporation's basis for the property received in the liquidating distribution is equal to its basis to the subsidiary corporation. This rule is consistent with the principle that no gain or loss is recognized by the liquidating corporation when it distributes the property and that the property's tax attributes (e.g., the depreciation recapture potential) carry over from the subsidiary corporation to the parent corporation. The parent corporation's basis for its stock investment in the subsidiary corporation is ignored in determining the basis for the distributed property and disappears once the stock is surrendered. Property received by minority shareholders takes a basis equal to its FMV.

EXAMPLE C6-15 ▶

Assume the same facts as in Example C6-14 and that the two parcels of land received by Parent Corporation and Jane have adjusted bases of $175,000 and $40,000, respectively, in the hands of the subsidiary. Parent Corporation takes a $175,000 carryover basis for its land. Jane takes a stepped-up $62,500 basis (i.e., equal to its FMV) for her land. ◀

STOP & THINK

Question: Why should a corporation that is 100%-owned by another corporation be treated differently when it liquidates than a corporation that is 100%-owned by an individual?

Solution: A corporation that is 100%-owned by another corporation can file a consolidated tax return (see Chapters C3 and C8). As a result, the parent and its subsidiary corporations are treated as a single entity. This result is the same as if the subsidiary was one of a number of divisions of a single corporation. An extension of the single-entity concept is that a subsidiary corporation can be liquidated tax-free into its parent corporation. An individual and his or her corporation are treated as two separate tax entities when calculating their annual tax liabilities. As separate entities, nonliquidating distributions (e.g., ordinary distributions and stock redemptions) from the corporation to its shareholder(s) are taxable. The same principle applies to liquidating distributions.

EFFECTS OF LIQUIDATING ON THE SUBSIDIARY CORPORATION

RECOGNITION OF GAIN OR LOSS. An exception is provided for liquidating transfers within a parent-subsidiary group because the property (together with the other attributes of the liquidated subsidiary) is retained within the economic unit of the parent-subsidiary group. Section 337(a) provides that no gain or loss is recognized by the liquidating corporation on the distribution of property to the 80% distributee in a complete liquidation to which Sec. 332 applies.[12] The term *80% distributee* is defined by Sec. 337(c) as a corporation that meets the 80% stock ownership requirement specified in Sec. 332 (see page C6-14).

EXAMPLE C6-16 ▶ Parent Corporation owns all of the stock of Subsidiary Corporation. Pursuant to a plan of complete liquidation, Subsidiary distributes land having a $200,000 FMV and a $60,000 basis to Parent. Section 337(a) prevents Subsidiary from having to recognize gain with respect to the distribution. Parent takes a $60,000 basis for the land. ◀

KEY POINT

A corporation that sells, exchanges, or distributes the stock of a subsidiary may elect to treat the sale of the stock as a sale of the subsidiary's assets. This election could prove beneficial when a sale of the subsidiary stock occurs and the assets of the subsidiary corporation are substantially less appreciated than the subsidiary stock itself.

The depreciation recapture provisions in Secs. 1245, 1250, and 291 do not override the Sec. 337(a) nonrecognition rule if a controlled subsidiary corporation is liquidated into its parent corporation. The depreciation recapture potential associated with the property distributed is assumed by the parent corporation and is recaptured when the parent corporation sells or exchanges the property.[13]

The Sec. 337(a) nonrecognition rule applies only to distributions that are made to the parent corporation. Liquidating distributions that are made to minority shareholders are not eligible for the protection of Sec. 337(a). The liquidating corporation must recognize gain under Sec. 336(a) when appreciated property is distributed to the minority shareholders. Section 336(d)(3), however, prevents the subsidiary corporation from recognizing loss on distributions made to minority shareholders. Thus, liquidating distributions made to minority shareholders are treated in the same way as nonliquidating distributions.

[12] Section 336(e) permits a corporation to sell, exchange, or distribute the stock of a subsidiary corporation and to elect to treat such a transaction as a disposition of all the subsidiary corporation's assets. No gain or loss is recognized on the sale, exchange, or distribution of the stock. The economic consequences of making this election for a stock sale are essentially the same as if the parent corporation instead liquidates the subsidiary in a transaction to which Sec. 332 applies and then immediately sells the properties to the purchaser.

[13] Secs. 1245(b)(3) and 1250(d)(3).

EXAMPLE C6-17 ▶ Assume the same facts as in Example C6-16, except that Parent Corporation owns 80% of the Subsidiary stock, Chuck owns the remaining 20% of such stock, and two parcels of land are being distributed to Parent and Chuck. The parcels have FMVs of $160,000 and $40,000, and adjusted bases of $50,000 and $10,000, respectively. The $110,000 gain ($160,000 − $50,000) realized by Subsidiary on the distribution to Parent is not recognized. The $30,000 gain ($40,000 − $10,000) realized on the distribution to Chuck is recognized because the Sec. 337(a) nonrecognition rule applies only to distributions made to the 80% distributee. Assume that the land distributed to Chuck instead had a $40,000 FMV and a $50,000 adjusted basis. None of the $10,000 loss is deductible because the parcel is distributed to a minority shareholder. ◀

OBJECTIVE 5

Determine the effect of a liquidation on the liquidating corporation's tax attributes

TAX ATTRIBUTE CARRYOVERS. The **tax attributes** of the liquidating corporation generally disappear when the liquidation is completed. They carry over only in the case of a controlled subsidiary corporation that is liquidated into its parent corporation under Sec. 332.[14] Included among the carried-over attributes are

- NOL carryovers
- Earnings and profits
- Capital loss carryovers
- General business and other tax credit carryovers

The amount of each carryover is determined as of the close of the day on which the distribution of all of the subsidiary corporation's properties is completed. Further discussion of these rules is contained in Chapter C7.

Topic Review C6-1 presents a summary of the general corporate liquidation rules and the special rules applicable to the liquidation of a controlled subsidiary corporation.

SPECIAL SHAREHOLDER REPORTING ISSUES

There are four special shareholder reporting rules that apply to liquidation transactions that are described below. These rules add different degrees of complexity to the general liquidation rules outlined above.

PARTIALLY LIQUIDATING DISTRIBUTIONS

Liquidating distributions are often received in the form of a series of partially liquidating distributions. Section 346(a) indicates that a series of partially liquidating distributions received in complete liquidation of the corporation are taxed under the Sec. 331 liquidation rules instead of under the Sec. 302 rules applying to redemptions in partial liquidation. The IRS (1) permits the shareholder's basis to be recovered first and (2) requires the recognition of gain once the basis of a particular share or block of stock has been fully recovered. A loss cannot be recognized with respect to a share or block of stock until the final liquidating distribution has been received, or until it becomes clear that there will be no more liquidating distributions.[15]

EXAMPLE C6-18 ▶ Diane owns 1,000 shares of Adobe Corporation stock purchased for $40,000 in 1992. Diane receives the following liquidating distributions: July 23, 1995, $25,000; March 12, 1996, $17,000; and April 5, 1997, $10,000. No gain is recognized in 1995 because Diane's $40,000 basis is not fully recovered by year-end. The $15,000 ($40,000 − $25,000) unrecovered basis

---

[14] Sec. 381(a).

[15] Rev. Ruls. 68-348, 1968-2 C.B. 141, 79-10, 1979-1 C.B. 140, and 85-48, 1985-1 C.B. 126.

Topic Review C6-1

Tax Consequences of a Corporate Liquidation

General Corporate Liquidation Rules

1. The shareholder's recognized gain or loss equals the amount of cash plus the FMV of the other property received minus the adjusted basis of the stock redeemed. Corporate liabilities assumed or acquired by the shareholder reduce the amount realized.
2. The gain or loss is capital in nature if the stock investment is a capital asset. If a loss is recognized on the liquidation, Sec. 1244 permits ordinary loss treatment for qualifying individual shareholders.
3. The adjusted basis of the property received is its FMV on the distribution date.
4. The shareholder's holding period for the property commences on the day after the distribution date.
5. With certain limited exceptions, the distributing corporation recognizes gain or loss when making the distribution. The amount and character of the gain or loss are determined as if the property had been sold for its FMV immediately before the distribution. Special rules apply when corporate liabilities are assumed or acquired by the shareholders and the amount of such liabilities exceeds the property's FMV.
6. The liquidated corporation's tax attributes disappear at the time of liquidation.

Liquidation of a Controlled Subsidiary Corporation

1. Specific requirements must be met with respect to (a) stock ownership, (b) distribution of the property in complete cancellation or redemption of all of its stock, and (c) distribution of all property within a single tax year or a three-year period. To satisfy the stock ownership requirement, at least 80% of the total voting power of all voting stock and at least 80% of the total value of all classes of stock must be owned by the parent corporation.
2. No gain or loss is recognized when property is distributed to an 80% distributee (i.e., parent corporation). Section 332 does not apply to liquidations of insolvent subsidiaries and distributions to minority shareholders.
3. The basis of the distributed property carries over to the parent corporation from the subsidiary corporation's books.
4. The parent corporation's holding period for the assets includes the subsidiary corporation's holding period.
5. The subsidiary corporation does not recognize gain or loss when making a distribution to an 80% distributee. Gain (but not loss) is recognized on distributions made to minority shareholders. Gain is also not recognized by the distributing corporation when appreciated property is distributed in satisfaction of certain subsidiary debts to the parent corporation.
6. The subsidiary corporation's tax attributes are acquired by the parent corporation as part of the liquidation.

that exists after the first distribution is less than the $17,000 liquidating distribution received on March 12, 1996, so a $2,000 gain is recognized at this time. An additional $10,000 gain is recognized in 1997 when the final liquidating distribution is received. ◀

EXAMPLE C6-19 ▶ Assume the same facts as in Example C6-18, except that Diane pays $60,000 for her Adobe stock. The receipt of each of the liquidating distributions is tax-free because Diane's $60,000 basis exceeds the $52,000 ($25,000 + $17,000 + $10,000) total of the distributions. An

$8,000 ($52,000 − $60,000) loss is recognized in 1997 when Diane receives the final liquidating distribution. ◀

SUBSEQUENT ASSESSMENTS AGAINST THE SHAREHOLDERS

SELF-STUDY QUESTION

If a cash-method shareholder is subsequently obligated to pay a contingent liability of the liquidated corporation, what are the tax consequences of such a payment?

ANSWER

First, the prior tax year return is not amended. The additional payment results in a loss recognized in the year of payment. The character of the loss is dependent on the nature of the gain or loss recognized by the shareholder in the year of liquidation.

The shareholders may be required at a date after the liquidation to pay a contingent liability of the corporation or a liability that is not anticipated at the time of the liquidating distribution (e.g., an income tax deficiency determined after the liquidation is completed or a judgment that is contingent at the time the final liquidating distribution is made). The additional payment does not affect the reporting of the initial liquidating transaction. The tax treatment for the additional payment depends on the nature of the gain or loss that was originally reported by the shareholder and not on the type of loss or deduction that would have been reported by the liquidating corporation if it had instead paid the liability.[16] If the liquidation results in a capital gain or loss being recognized, the additional payment is deductible as a capital loss by a shareholder who uses the cash method of accounting in the year of payment (i.e., an amended tax return is not filed for the year in which the gain or loss from the liquidation was originally reported). A shareholder using the accrual method of accounting recognizes the additional deduction when the liability is incurred.

EXAMPLE C6-20 ▶

Coastal Corporation is liquidated in 1994, with Tammy, a cash method of accounting taxpayer, reporting a $30,000 long-term capital gain on the exchange of her Coastal stock. In 1997 Tammy pays $5,000 as her part of the settlement of a lawsuit against Coastal. An additional amount is paid by all shareholders because the settlement exceeds the amount of funds that Coastal placed into an escrow account as a result of the litigation. The amount placed into the escrow account was not included in the amount that Tammy realized from the liquidating distribution in 1994. Since Tammy had not been taxed on the monies placed in the escrow account, she can not deduct the amount of the payment that is made from the escrow account in 1997. The $5,000 amount paid from Tammy's personal funds is deducted in 1997 as a long-term capital loss. ◀

OBJECTIVE 6

Explain the different tax treatments for open and closed liquidation transactions

OPEN VERSUS CLOSED TRANSACTIONS.

Sometimes the value of a property received in a corporate liquidation cannot be determined by the usual valuation techniques. Property that can be valued only on the basis of uncertain future payments falls into this category. In such a case, the shareholders may attempt to rely on the **open transaction doctrine** of *Burnet v. Logan* and treat the liquidation as an open transaction.[17] Under this doctrine, the shareholder's gain or loss from the liquidation is not determined until the assets that cannot be valued are subsequently sold, collected, or able to be valued. Any assets that cannot be valued are assigned a zero value.

ETHICAL POINT

A tax practitioner needs to be careful that appropriate appraisals are obtained to support the values assigned to properties when liquidating distributions are being made to shareholders. A 20% substantial underpayment penalty may be imposed on corporations and shareholders that substantially understate their income tax liabilities.

The shareholder's receipt of properties that have an ascertainable FMV is reported using the general liquidation rules. Thus, a shareholder must report a gain on the liquidation if the FMV of properties that have an ascertainable FMV exceeds the shareholder's basis for the stock. A loss is not recognized if the FMV of properties that have an ascertainable FMV is less than the basis of the stock. If the assets that are not able to be valued are subsequently sold, collected, or able to be valued, the additional payments or amounts received are initially treated as a return of capital on the liquidation transaction (or as additional gain if some gain was previously recognized). The character of any additional gain that is reported is the same as was originally reported when the other properties were received.

[16] *F. Donald Arrowsmith v. CIR*, 42 AFTR 649, 52-2 USTC ¶9527 (USSC, 1952).

[17] *Burnet v. Edith A. Logan*, 9 AFTR 1453, 2 USTC ¶736 (USSC, 1931).

EXAMPLE C6-21 ▶

Mesa Corporation is owned by Tarek. Mesa's properties include $10,000 of cash, $30,000 of land, and a royalty agreement with a coal company that will pay Mesa a royalty only as the coal is produced. No coal has ever been produced on the property, and there is no minimum royalty amount mentioned in the agreement. According to a qualified appraisal company, no FMV can be assigned to the royalty agreement. Tarek's basis in his Mesa stock is $50,000. Mesa Corporation liquidates in 1995, with Tarek receiving the cash, land, and royalty agreement. Relying on the open transaction doctrine, the $40,000 representing the assets that have an ascertainable FMV is reported as a recovery of Tarek's investment in the Mesa stock. Tarek has $10,000 of unrecovered basis against which subsequent royalty payments could be offset before reporting any capital gain on the receipt of such payments.

How would Tarek report the transaction if his basis for the Mesa stock were $25,000? Tarek would report a $15,000 ($40,000 − $25,000) long-term capital gain in 1995 on the liquidation and any additional amounts that were received under the royalty agreement would also be long-term capital gain. ◀

KEY POINT

The position of the IRS is that the FMV of almost any asset should be able to be determined. Thus, the IRS assumes that the open transaction method should be used only in rare and extraordinary circumstances. For example, an open transaction generally cannot be used merely because a market valuation for an investment in a closely held corporation is not readily available through market quotations for the stock.

The IRS's position is that a taxpayer may use the open transaction method to report a corporate liquidation only in unusual circumstances. Generally the IRS opts for a **closed transaction.** All of the assets in a closed transaction have a basis equal to their FMV on the distribution date. If a transaction is closed, gain or loss is determined on the liquidation date based on the FMV of all of the assets. When a liquidated property with an uncertain value is ultimately sold or collected by the former shareholder, gain or loss is determined by comparing the sale price or amount collected with respect to the property to its basis in the former shareholder's hands. This basis is typically the FMV established on the liquidation date. The character of the gain or loss depends on whether the asset is a capital asset in the hands of the former shareholder. The closing of a liquidation transaction typically accelerates the reporting of the shareholder's gain from the transaction.

EXAMPLE C6-22 ▶

Assume the same facts as in Example C6-21, except that the FMV of the royalty agreement is $12,000 and the royalty payments received under the agreement are 1996, $9,000; and 1997, $8,000. Tarek reports a $2,000 [($10,000 + $30,000 + $12,000) − $50,000] long-term capital gain on the liquidation. The basis of the royalty agreement is $12,000 to Tarek. 1996's $9,000 royalty payment is a tax-free return of capital and reduces Tarek's basis to $3,000 ($12,000 − $9,000). 1997's $8,000 royalty payment would recover his remaining basis and result in Tarek recognizing $5,000 ($8,000 − $3,000) of ordinary income.[18] The closed transaction treatment has accelerated the recognition of the capital gain on the liquidation, and converted $5,000 of long-term capital gain into ordinary income. ◀

INSTALLMENT OBLIGATIONS RECEIVED BY A SHAREHOLDER

Shareholders who receive an installment obligation as part of their liquidating distribution ordinarily report the FMV of their obligation as part of the consideration received to calculate the amount of the recognized gain or loss. Shareholders who receive an installment obligation that was acquired by the liquidating corporation in connection with a sale or exchange of property are eligible for special treatment in reporting their gain on the liquidating transaction if the sale or exchange takes place during the twelve-month period beginning on the date a plan of complete liquidation is adopted and the liquidation is completed during such twelve-month period. These shareholders may report their gain as the installment payments are received.[19]

[18] Ordinary income is reported because the liquidation transaction is closed in 1995. The coal company's payment represents a royalty, not a liquidating distribution.

[19] Sec. 453(h)(1)(A). A tax deferral is available only with respect to the gain that is realized by the shareholder. The liquidating corporation must recognize the deferred gain when it distributes the installment obligation to the shareholder as if it had sold the obligation immediately before the distribution.

SPECIAL CORPORATE REPORTING ISSUES

EXPENSES OF THE LIQUIDATION

The corporation can deduct the expenses incurred in connection with the liquidation transaction. These expenses include attorneys' and accountants' fees, costs incurred in drafting the plan of liquidation and obtaining shareholder approval, and so on.[20] Such amounts are ordinarily deductible in the liquidating corporation's final tax return.

Expenses associated with selling the corporation's properties are treated as an offset against the sales proceeds. When a corporation sells an asset pursuant to its liquidation, the selling expenses reduce the amount of gain or increase the amount of loss reported by the corporation.[21]

EXAMPLE C6-23 ▶ Madison Corporation adopts a plan of liquidation on July 15 and shortly thereafter sells a parcel of land on which it realizes a $60,000 gain (excluding the effects of a $6,000 sales commission). Madison pays its legal counsel $1,500 to draft the plan of liquidation. All of Madison's remaining properties are distributed to its shareholders on December 15. The $1,500 paid to legal counsel is deductible as a liquidation expense in Madison's current year income tax return. The sales commission reduces the $60,000 gain realized on the land sale, so that Madison's recognized gain is $54,000 ($60,000 − $6,000). ◀

Any amounts of capitalized expenditures that are unamortized at the time of liquidation should be deducted if they have no further value to the corporation (e.g., unamortized organizational costs).[22] Capitalized expenditures that have value must be allocated to the shareholders receiving the benefit of such an outlay (e.g., prepaid insurance and prepaid rent).[23] Expenses related to the issuing of the corporation's stock are nondeductible, even at the time of liquidation, because they are treated as a reduction in paid-in capital. Unamortized bond premiums are deductible, though, at the time that the corporation retires the bonds.

ADDITIONAL COMMENT

If a liquidating corporation creates a NOL in the year of liquidation or already has NOL carryovers, these losses may well disappear with the liquidated corporation. If the liquidation is a Sec. 332 liquidation, then the parent corporation acquires the NOL. If the liquidation is taxed under Sec. 331, the liquidating corporation may want to consider an S election for the liquidation year so any NOLs created in that year can flow through to the shareholders.

TREATMENT OF NET OPERATING LOSSES

If little or no income is reported in the liquidating corporation's final income tax return, the corporation may create an NOL when it deducts its expenses of liquidating and any remaining capitalized expenditures. The NOL is carried back to offset taxes paid in prior years. This federal income tax refund increases (decreases) the gain (loss) previously reported by the shareholder. Alternatively, the shareholders might consider having the corporation elect to be taxed under the S corporation provisions for the tax year of the liquidation and have the loss reported on the shareholders' tax returns. (See Chapter C11 for a discussion on the taxation of an S corporation.)

The need for a liquidating corporation to recognize gains when distributing appreciated properties can be partially or fully offset by expenses incurred in carrying out the liquidation or any available NOL carryovers. Losses that are recognized by the liquidating corporation when distributing property that has declined in value can be used to offset operating profits or capital gains earned in the year in which the liquidation occurs. Should such losses produce an NOL or net capital loss, the losses may be able to be carried back and provide a refund of taxes paid in a prior year, or passed through to the corporation's shareholders if an election to be taxed under the S corporation provisions has been made for the tax year.

---

[20] *Pridemark, Inc. v. CIR*, 15 AFTR 2d 853, 65-1 USTC ¶9388 (4th Cir., 1965).

[21] See, for example, *J. T. Stewart III Trust*, 63 T.C. 682 (1975), *acq.* 1977-1 C.B. 1.

[22] Reg. Sec. 1.248-1(b)(3).

[23] *Koppers Co., Inc. v. U.S.*, 5 AFTR 2d 1597, 60-2 USTC ¶9505 (Ct. Cls., 1960).

RECOGNITION OF GAIN OR LOSS WHEN PROPERTY IS DISTRIBUTED IN RETIREMENT OF DEBT

OBJECTIVE 7

Determine when gains and losses are recognized on the retirement of debt by a liquidating corporation

GENERAL RULE

No gain or loss is recognized when an unsecured debt obligation owed to a shareholder is paid. An exception to this rule is made when a security is retired and the amount received by the shareholder is different from the shareholder's adjusted basis for the obligation. These same rules apply whether the debt is paid or retired as part of a debtor corporation's operations or as part of its liquidation. No gain or loss is recognized when cash is used by a debtor corporation to satisfy its debt obligations. Gain is recognized when appreciated noncash property is used by a debtor corporation to satisfy its debt obligations. Similarly, a loss is recognized when noncash property that has declined in value is used by a debtor corporation to satisfy its debt obligations.

SATISFACTION OF THE SUBSIDIARY'S DEBT OBLIGATIONS

KEY POINT

No gain/loss is recognized by a liquidating subsidiary on the distribution of its assets in retirement of an indebtedness owed to its parent corporation in a Sec. 332 liquidation.

The Sec. 332(a) nonrecognition rules apply only to amounts received by the parent corporation in its role as a shareholder. Gain or loss must generally be recognized by the parent corporation upon the receipt of property in payment of a subsidiary corporation indebtedness.[24]

As mentioned above, the use of property to satisfy an indebtedness generally results in the debtor recognizing gain or loss at the time it transfers the property.[25] Section 337(b) prevents a subsidiary corporation in the midst of a complete liquidation from recognizing gain or loss when it transfers noncash property to its parent corporation in satisfaction of an indebtedness. The exception is provided because the property is retained within the economic unit of the parent-subsidiary group.

Section 337(b) applies only to an indebtedness of the subsidiary corporation that is owed to a parent corporation on the date the plan of liquidation is adopted and that is satisfied by the transfer of property pursuant to a complete liquidation of the subsidiary corporation. It does not apply to liabilities owed to other shareholders or third-party creditors, or liabilities incurred after the plan of liquidation is adopted. In addition, if the subsidiary corporation satisfies the indebtedness for less than its face amount, it may have to recognize income from the discharge of an indebtedness.

EXAMPLE C6-24 ▶

Parent Corporation owns all of Subsidiary Corporation's single class of stock. At the time of its acquisition of the Subsidiary stock, Parent purchased $1,000,000 of Subsidiary bonds at their face amount. Subsidiary adopts a plan of liquidation. Subsequently, Subsidiary distributes property having a $1,000,000 FMV and a $400,000 adjusted basis to Parent in cancellation of the bonds. Subsidiary also distributes its remaining properties to Parent in exchange for all of its outstanding stock. Subsidiary recognizes no gain on the transfer of the property in cancellation of its bonds. Parent recognizes no gain when the liability is satisfied because the property's FMV equals the adjusted basis of the bonds. Section 334(b)(1) provides that Parent takes a $400,000 carryover basis for the property it receives in cancellation of the bonds. ◀

[24] Sec. 1001(c).

[25] Ibid.

TAX PLANNING CONSIDERATIONS

ADDITIONAL COMMENT

Timing the distribution of loss property so that the losses generated may be used to offset high-bracket taxable income at the corporate level makes good tax sense if the general liquidation rules are applicable. However, this planning possibility would not exist in a Sec. 332 parent-subsidiary liquidation because losses cannot be recognized by the liquidating subsidiary.

TIMING THE LIQUIDATION TRANSACTION

Sometimes a plan of liquidation is adopted in one year, but the liquidation is not completed until a subsequent year. Corporations that are planning to distribute properties that have both increased in value and decreased in value may find it to their advantage to sell or distribute properties that have declined in value in a tax year in which they also conducted business activities. As such, the loss recognized when making the liquidating distribution can offset profits that are taxed at higher rates. Deferring the sale or distribution of properties that have appreciated in value may delay the recognition of the gain for one tax year and also place it in a year in which the marginal tax rate is lower.

EXAMPLE C6-25 ▶ Miami Corporation adopts a plan of liquidation in November 1997, a tax year in which it earns $150,000 in profits from its operating activities. Miami's operating activities are discontinued before the end of 1997. Pursuant to the liquidation, it distributes assets, which results in the recognition of $40,000 of ordinary losses. In January 1998, Miami distributes assets that have appreciated in value, which results in the recognition of $40,000 of ordinary income. Distributing the loss property in 1997 would result in a $15,600 tax savings [$40,000 × (34% + 5%)]. Only $6,000 ($40,000 × 0.15) in taxes are owed with respect to the distribution of the appreciated properties in 1998. The rate differential provides a $9,600 ($15,600 − $6,000) net savings to Miami. ◀

Timing the liquidating distributions should not proceed without also considering the tax position of the various shareholders. Taxpayers should be careful about timing the liquidating distributions to avoid placing a taxpayer in a higher marginal tax bracket, although this problem has been reduced with the enactment of the 28% maximum tax rate for long-term capital gains. If the liquidation results in a loss being recognized, shareholders should take advantage of the opportunity to offset the loss against realized and unrealized capital gains, as well as to attempt to increase the portion of the loss eligible for ordinary loss treatment under Sec. 1244.

WHAT WOULD YOU DO IN THIS SITUATION?

Andrea has operated her trendy, upscale clothing store as a C corporation for a number of years. Annually the corporation earns $200,000 in pre-tax profits. Andrea's stock is worth about $800,000. Her stock basis is $125,000. One of her good friends, Jenna, has opened a clothing store as a limited liability company and has been telling Andrea about the advantage of not having to pay the corporate income tax. While reading the *Wall Street Journal* weekly tax column, Andrea sees an article about the new check-the-box regulations which permits corporations to elect to be taxed like partnerships and limited liability companies. She calls and tells you that she wants you to file the necessary paperwork with the IRS to make the change from being taxed as a C corporation to being taxed as a flow-through entity. What advice should you provide Andrea in this situation?

RECOGNITION OF ORDINARY LOSSES WHEN A LIQUIDATION OCCURS

KEY POINT

Losses recognized on a liquidating distribution by individual shareholders may qualify for ordinary loss treatment due to Sec. 1244; corporate shareholders with at least 80% stock ownership may qualify for ordinary loss treatment due to Sec. 165(g)(3), *but* corporate shareholders with less than 80% stock ownership are probably limited to capital loss treatment.

Losses are sometimes recognized when a liquidation occurs. Individual shareholders should recognize that, because a complete liquidation is treated as an exchange transaction, Sec. 1244 ordinary loss treatment is available when a small business corporation is liquidated. This treatment permits $50,000 of ordinary loss to be claimed when the stock is surrendered, or $100,000 if the taxpayer is married and filing a joint return.

Ordinary loss treatment is also available for a domestic corporation that owns stock in a subsidiary corporation. Because the rules in Sec. 332 regarding nonrecognition of gain or loss do not apply when a subsidiary corporation is insolvent (see page C6-13), the parent corporation can recognize a loss when the subsidiary corporation's stocks and securities are determined to be worthless. This loss is an ordinary loss (instead of a capital loss) if at least 80% of the voting stock and 80% of each class of nonvoting stock are owned by the domestic corporation and more than 90% of the liquidating corporation's gross income for all tax years has been other than passive income.[26]

USING SEC. 332 TO OBTAIN A DOUBLE TAX EXEMPTION

The 80% stock ownership requirement provides the taxpayer with an opportunity to engage in tax planning when a subsidiary corporation is liquidated. A parent corporation seeking to come under the Sec. 332 nonrecognition rules may acquire additional shares of the subsidiary corporation's stock before the adoption of the plan of liquidation. This acquisition serves to help the parent corporation meet the 80% minimum and avoid having to recognize any gain on the liquidation. If these additional shares of stock are purchased from other shareholders, Sec. 332 will not apply when the 80% minimum is satisfied by acquiring these shares after the plan of liquidation is adopted.[27]

EXAMPLE C6-26 ▶

Parent Corporation owns 75% of Subsidiary Corporation's single class of stock. On March 12, Parent Corporation purchases for cash the remaining 25% of the Subsidiary stock from three individual shareholders pursuant to a tender offer. A plan of liquidation is approved by Subsidiary's shareholder on October 1. Subsidiary Corporation's assets are distributed to Parent Corporation on December 1, in exchange for all of Subsidiary's outstanding stock. Parent Corporation does not recognize any gain or loss on the redemption of its Subsidiary stock in the liquidation because all of the Sec. 332 requirements have been satisfied. ◀

Alternatively, the parent corporation might cause the subsidiary corporation to redeem some of the shares held by its minority shareholders before the plan of liquidation is adopted. The IRS originally held that the intention to liquidate is present once the subsidiary corporation agrees to redeem the shares of the minority shareholders. Thus, the redemption of a 25% minority interest did not permit Sec. 332 to be used, even though the parent corporation owned 100% of the outstanding stock after the redemption.[28]

In *George L. Riggs, Inc.*, the Tax Court held that a tender offer to minority shareholders by the parent corporation and the calling of the subsidiary's preferred stock do not invalidate the Sec. 332 liquidation because "the formation of a conditional intention to liquidate in the future is not the adoption of a plan of liquidation."[29] The IRS has acquiesced to the *Riggs* decision.

---

[26] Sec. 165(g)(3).

[27] Rev. Rul. 75-521, 1975-2 C.B. 120.

[28] Rev. Rul. 70-106, 1970-1 C.B. 70.

[29] *George L. Riggs, Inc.*, 64 T.C. 474 (1975), *acq.* 1976-2 C.B. 2.

By having the transaction qualify under Sec. 332(a), the parent corporation can receive nonmoney distributions in liquidation of the subsidiary corporation that are nontaxable to both corporations. As discussed above, Sec. 337(a) permits the liquidating subsidiary corporation to avoid recognizing gain or loss when it distributes property to its parent corporation. Because the Sec. 337(a) exemption applies only to the 80% distributee, property distributions to minority shareholders result in recognition of gain (but not loss) by the liquidating subsidiary corporation.

EXAMPLE C6-27 ▶ Parent Corporation owns 80% of the single class of stock of Subsidiary Corporation. The remaining 20% of the Subsidiary stock is owned by Mohamed. Parent and Mohamed have adjusted bases of $200,000 and $50,000, respectively, for their Subsidiary stock. Subsidiary distributes land having a $250,000 adjusted basis and a $400,000 FMV to Parent and $100,000 in cash to Mohamed. No gain or loss is recognized by Subsidiary on the distribution of the land or the cash. Parent recognizes no gain on the liquidation and takes a $250,000 basis for the land. Mohamed recognizes a $50,000 ($100,000 − $50,000) capital gain on the receipt of the money. Distribution of the land and cash ratably to Parent and Mohamed would require Subsidiary to recognize as gain the appreciation on the portion of the land distributed to Mohamed. ◀

AVOIDING SEC. 332 IN ORDER TO RECOGNIZE LOSSES

KEY POINT

If the liquidating subsidiary corporation primarily has loss property to distribute, Sec. 332 should be avoided because those losses cannot be recognized. To avoid Sec. 332 treatment, consider having the parent corporation dispose of enough of its subsidiary's stock to drop below the requisite 80% threshold. In this situation, the general liquidation rules allow recognition of the liquidating corporation's losses.

A parent corporation may want to avoid the Sec. 332 nonrecognition rules in order to recognize a loss when a solvent subsidiary corporation is liquidated. Because the stock ownership requirement must be met during the entire liquidation process, the parent corporation can apparently sell some of its stock in the subsidiary corporation to reduce its stock ownership below the 80% level at any time during the liquidation process and be able to recognize the loss.[30] Such a sale permits the parent corporation to recognize a capital loss when it surrenders its stock interest in the subsidiary corporation.

The sale of a portion of the subsidiary's stock after the plan of liquidation is adopted prevents Sec. 332 from applying to the parent corporation. The Sec. 337 rules, which prevent the subsidiary corporation from recognizing gain or loss when making a liquidating distribution to an 80% distributee, also do not apply because nonrecognition is contingent on Sec. 332 applying to the distributee. Thus, the subsidiary corporation can also recognize a loss when it distributes properties that have declined in value.

COMPLIANCE AND PROCEDURAL CONSIDERATIONS

GENERAL LIQUIDATION PROCEDURES

Section 6043(a) requires a corporation to file a Form 966 (Information Return under Sec. 6043) within thirty days after the adoption of any resolution or plan calling for the liquidation or dissolution of the corporation. This form is filed with the district director of the IRS for the district in which the liquidating corporation's income tax return is filed. Any amendment or supplement to the resolution or plan must be filed on an additional Form 966 within thirty days of making the amendment or supplement. Form 966 must be filed by the liquidating corporation whether the shareholders' realized gain is recognized

[30] *CIR v. Day & Zimmerman, Inc.*, 34 AFTR 343, 45-2 USTC ¶9403 (3rd Cir., 1945).

or not. The information that is included with the Form 966 is described in Reg. Sec. 1.6043-1(b).

Regulation Sec. 1.6043-2(a) requires every corporation that makes a distribution of $600 or more during a calendar year to any shareholder in liquidation of part or all of its capital stock to file a Form 1099-DIV (U.S. Information Return for Recipients of Dividends and Distributions). A separate Form 1099-DIV is required for each shareholder. The information that must be included with the Form 1099-DIV is described in Reg. Secs. 1.6043-2(a) and (b).

A corporation that is in existence for part of a year is required by Reg. Sec. 1.6012-2(a)(2) to file a corporate tax return for the portion of the tax year that it was in existence. A corporation that ceases business and dissolves, while retaining no assets, is not considered to be in existence for federal tax purposes, even though under state law it may be considered for certain purposes to be continuing its affairs (e.g., for purposes of suing or being sued).

SECTION 332 LIQUIDATIONS

ADDITIONAL COMMENT

As evidenced in this chapter, the compliance and procedural requirements of complete liquidations are formidable. Any taxpayer contemplating either of these types of corporate transactions should consult competent tax and legal advisors to ensure that the technical requirements of the proposed transaction are satisfied.

Regulation Sec. 1.332-6 requires every corporation receiving distributions in a complete liquidation that comes within the purview of the Sec. 332 nonrecognition rules to maintain permanent records. A complete statement of all facts pertinent to the nonrecognition of gain or loss must be included in the corporate distributee's return for the tax year in which a liquidating distribution is received. This statement includes the following: a certified copy of the plan of liquidation, a list of all the properties received upon the distribution, a statement of any indebtedness of the liquidating corporation to the recipient corporation, and a statement of stock ownership.

A special waiver of the general three-year statute of limitations is required when the liquidation covers more than one tax year.[31] The distributee corporation must file a waiver of the statute of limitations on assessment for each of its tax years that falls partially or wholly within the liquidation period. This waiver is filed at the time the distributee corporation files its income tax return. This waiver must extend the assessment period to a date not earlier than one year after the last date of the period for assessment of such taxes for the last tax year in which the liquidation may be completed under Sec. 332.

PLAN OF LIQUIDATION

A **plan of liquidation** is generally a written document detailing the steps to be undertaken while carrying out the complete liquidation of the corporation. The date of adoption of a plan of complete liquidation ordinarily is the date on which the shareholders adopt a resolution authorizing the distribution of all the corporation's assets (other than the assets retained to meet creditor claims) in redemption of all of its stock.[32] Although it is generally a written document, the IRS and the courts have accepted informal shareholder agreements and resolutions as equivalent to the adoption of a formal plan of liquidation.[33]

Although a formal plan of liquidation is not required, it may assist the corporation in determining when it enters a liquidation status and, therefore, when distributions to the shareholders qualify for exchange treatment under Sec. 331 (instead of possibly being treated as a dividend under Sec. 301). The adoption of a formal plan of liquidation can provide the liquidating corporation or its shareholders additional benefits under the tax laws. For example, the adoption of a plan of liquidation permits a parent corporation to have a three-year time period (instead of one tax year) to carry out the complete liquidation of a subsidiary corporation.

---

31 Reg. Sec. 1.332-4(a)(2).

32 Reg. Sec. 1.337-2(b).

33 Rev. Rul. 65-235, 1965-2 C.B. 88, and *Badias & Seijas, Inc.*, 1977 PH T.C. Memo ¶77,118, 36 TCM 518.

PROBLEM MATERIALS

DISCUSSION QUESTIONS

C6-1 What is a complete liquidation? A partial liquidation? Explain the difference in the tax treatment accorded these two different events.

C6-2 Knight Corporation has manufactured and distributed basketball equipment for twenty years. Its owners would like to avoid the corporate income tax and are considering becoming a limited liability company (LLC). What tax savings may result from electing to be taxed as an LLC? What federal tax costs will be incurred to make the change from a C corporation to an LLC? Would the same transaction costs be incurred if an S election were instead made by the corporation? Would the transaction costs be incurred if LLC status had been adopted when the entity were initially organized?

C6-3 Explain why tax advisors caution people who are starting a new business that the tax costs of incorporating a business may be low while the tax costs of liquidating a business may be high.

C6-4 Explain the following statement: A corporation may be liquidated for tax purposes even though dissolution has not occurred under state corporation law.

C6-5 Compare the tax consequences to the shareholder and the distributing corporation of the following three kinds of corporate distributions: ordinary dividends; stock redemptions, complete liquidation.

C6-6 What event or occurrence determines when a cash or accrual method of accounting taxpayer reports a liquidating distribution?

C6-7 Explain why a shareholder receiving a liquidating distribution would prefer to receive either capital gain treatment or ordinary loss treatment.

C6-8 What are the differences in the distributing corporation's tax treatment for nonliquidating and liquidating distributions?

C6-9 Explain the circumstances in which a liquidating corporation does not recognize gain and/or loss when making a liquidating distribution.

C6-10 Kelly Corporation makes a liquidating distribution. One of the properties distributed is land that is subject to a mortgage. The mortgage amount exceeds both the adjusted basis and FMV for the land. Explain to Kelly Corporation's president how the amount of its recognized gain or loss on the distribution and the shareholder's basis for the land are determined.

C6-11 Explain the congressional intent behind the enactment of the Sec. 332 rules regarding the liquidation of a subsidiary corporation.

C6-12 Compare the general liquidation rules with the Sec. 332 rules for liquidation of a subsidiary corporation with respect to the following items:

a. Recognition of gain or loss by the distributee corporation
b. Recognition of gain or loss by the liquidating corporation
c. Basis of assets in the distributee corporation's hands
d. Treatment of the liquidating corporation's tax attributes

C6-13 What requirements must be satisfied for the Sec. 332 rules to apply to a corporate shareholder?

C6-14 Parent Corporation owns 80% of the stock of an insolvent subsidiary corporation. The remaining 20% of the stock is owned by Tracy. Subsidiary Corporation is determined to be bankrupt by the courts. Each shareholder receives nothing for his or her investment. How do they report their loss for tax purposes?

C6-15 Parent Corporation owns all of the stock of Subsidiary Corporation and a substantial amount of Subsidiary Corporation bonds. Subsidiary Corporation proposes to transfer appreciated property to Parent Corporation in redemption of its bonds pursuant to the liquidation of

Subsidiary Corporation. Explain the tax consequences of the redemption of the stock and bonds to Parent and Subsidiary Corporations.

C6-16 Explain the differences in the tax rules applying to distributions made to the parent corporation and a minority shareholder when a controlled subsidiary corporation is liquidated.

C6-17 Parent Corporation owns 80% of the stock of Subsidiary Corporation. Sally owns the remaining 20% of the Subsidiary stock. Subsidiary is planning on distributing cash and appreciated property pursuant to its liquidation. It has more than enough cash to redeem all of Sally's stock. What strategy for distributing the cash and appreciated property would minimize the gain recognized by Subsidiary Corporation on the distribution? Does the substitution of appreciated property for cash change the tax consequences of the liquidating distribution for Sally?

C6-18 Parent Corporation owns 70% of the stock of Subsidiary Corporation. The FMV of Subsidiary's assets is significantly greater than their basis on Subsidiary's books. The FMV of Parent's interest in the assets is also substantially in excess of Parent's basis for the Subsidiary stock. On January 30 it acquired an additional 15% of the Subsidiary stock from one of Subsidiary's shareholders who owns none of the Parent stock. Subsidiary Corporation adopts a plan of liquidation on March 12. The liquidation is completed before year-end. What advantages accrue to Parent Corporation with respect to the liquidation by acquiring the additional Subsidiary stock?

C6-19 Texas Corporation is liquidated through a series of distributions to its shareholders after a plan of liquidation has been adopted. How are these distributions taxed?

C6-20 Hill Corporation's shareholders are called on to pay an assessment that was levied against them as a result of a liability not anticipated at the time of liquidation. When will the deduction for the additional payment be claimed, assuming all shareholders use the cash method of accounting? What factors determine the character of the deduction claimed?

C6-21 Able Corporation adopts a plan of liquidation. Under the plan, Robert, who owns 60% of the Able stock, is to receive 2,000 acres of land in an area where a number of producing oil wells have been drilled. No wells have been drilled on Able's land. Discussions with two appraisers have produced widely differing market values for the land, both of which are above Able's basis for the land and Robert's basis for the Able stock. Explain the alternatives available to Able Corporation and Robert for reporting the liquidating distribution.

C6-22 Explain the IRS's position regarding whether a liquidation transaction will be considered open or closed.

C6-23 Explain the tax advantages to the shareholders of a corporation that is intending to liquidate of having the corporation (1) adopt a plan of liquidation, (2) sell its assets in an installment sale, and then (3) distribute the installment obligations to their shareholders.

C6-24 Cable Corporation is 60% owned by Anna and 40% owned by Jim, who are unrelated. It has noncash assets that are sold to an unrelated purchaser for $100,000 in cash and $900,000 in installment obligations due 50% in the current year and 50% in the following year. Cable's remaining cash, after payment of the federal income taxes on the sale and other corporate obligations, will be distributed to Jim and Anna. Explain to the two shareholders the alternatives for reporting the gain realized on their receipt of the installment obligations.

C6-25 Describe the tax treatment accorded the following expenses associated with a liquidation:

a. Commissions paid on the sale of the liquidating corporation's assets
b. Accounting fees paid to prepare the corporation's final income tax return
c. Unamortized organizational expenditures
d. Prepaid rent for office space that is occupied by one of the shareholders following the liquidation. Assume the prepaid rent was deducted in the preceding year's corporate tax return.

C6-26 Andover Corporation is 70% owned by Yong. At the beginning of the current year it has $400,000 of NOLs. Yong is planning to liquidate the corporation and distribute assets having a $600,000 FMV and a $350,000 adjusted basis to its shareholders. Explain to Yong the tax consequences of the liquidation to Andover Corporation.

C6-27 Nils Corporation, a calendar-year taxpayer, adopts a plan of liquidation on April 1, 1996. The final liquidating distribution is made on January 5, 1997. Must Nils Corporation file a tax return for 1996? For 1997?

C6-28 What is a plan of liquidation? Why is it advisable for a corporation to adopt a formal plan of liquidation?

C6-29 Indicate whether each of the following statements about a liquidation is true or false. If the statement is false, explain why.

a. Liabilities assumed by a shareholder when a corporation liquidates reduce the amount realized by the shareholder on the surrender of her stock.
b. The loss recognized by a shareholder on a liquidation is generally characterized as an ordinary loss.
c. A shareholder's basis for property received in a liquidation is the same as the property's basis in the liquidating corporation's hands.
d. The holding period for the property received in a liquidation includes the period of time that it is held by the liquidating corporation.
e. The tax attributes of a liquidating corporation are assumed ratably by its shareholders.
f. A parent corporation can elect to recognize gain or loss when it liquidates a controlled subsidiary corporation.
g. No gain or loss is recognized by a liquidating subsidiary corporation when its properties are distributed to its parent corporation.
h. A parent corporation's basis for the assets received in a liquidation where gain is not recognized remains the same as it was on the books of the liquidating subsidiary corporation.

ISSUE IDENTIFICATION QUESTIONS

C6-30 Cable Corporation, which operates a fleet of motorized trolley cars in a resort city, is undergoing a complete liquidation. John, who owns 80% of the Cable stock, plans to continue the business in another city, and will receive the cable cars, two support vehicles, the repair parts inventory, and other tools and equipment. Peter, who owns the remaining 20% of the Cable stock, will receive a cash distribution. $15,000 of liquidation expenses will be incurred by the corporation to break its lease on its office and garage space and cancel other contracts. What tax issues should be considered by Cable, John, and Peter with respect to the liquidation?

C6-31 Parent Corporation, which operates an electric utility, created a 100%-owned corporation, Subsidiary, that built and managed an office building. Assume the two corporations have filed separate tax returns for a number of years. Two floors of the office building were occupied by the utility, and ten floors were offered for lease by Subsidiary. Only 25% of the total rental space was leased because of the high crime rate in the area surrounding the building. Rental income was insufficient to cover the mortgage payments and, Subsidiary filed for bankruptcy because of the poor prospects. Subsidiary's assets were taken over by the mortgage lender. Parent lost its entire $500,000 investment. Another $100,000 of debts remained unpaid for the general creditors, which included a $35,000 account payable to Parent, at the time Subsidiary was liquidated. What tax issues should be considered by Parent and Subsidiary with respect to the bankruptcy and liquidation of Subsidiary?

C6-32 Grace Corporation is a holding company owned equally by Spin and Marty. The Grace stock was acquired many years ago when the corporation was formed. Grace has its money invested almost entirely in stocks, bonds, rental real estate and land. Market quotations are available for all of its stock and bond investments except for 10,000 shares of Mayfair Manufacturing Corporation stock. Mayfair is privately held with forty individuals owning all of the 100,000 outstanding shares. Last year Mayfair reported slightly more than $3 million in net income. In a discussion with Spin and Marty, you find that they are planning on liquidating Grace Corporation in the next six months in order to avoid the personal holding company tax. What tax issues should be considered by Spin and Marty with respect to this pending liquidation?

PROBLEMS

C6-33 ***Shareholder Gain or Loss Calculation.*** For seven years, Monaco Corporation has been owned entirely by Stacy and Monique, who are husband and wife. Stacy and Monique have a $165,000 basis in their jointly owned Monaco stock. The Monaco stock is Sec. 1244 stock. They receive the following assets in liquidation of their corporation: accounts receivable, $25,000 FMV; a car, $16,000 FMV; office furniture, $6,000 FMV; and $5,000 cash.

a. What are the amount and character of their gain or loss?

b. How would your answer change if the accounts receivable instead had a $140,000 FMV?

c. What are the Monacos' bases for each property received in the liquidation in parts (a) and (b)?

C6-34 ***Shareholder Gain or Loss Calculation.*** For three years, Diamond Corporation has been owned equally by Arlene and Billy. Arlene and Billy have $40,000 and $20,000 adjusted bases, respectively, for their Diamond stock. Arlene receives a $30,000 cash liquidating distribution in exchange for her Diamond stock. Billy receives as a liquidating distribution a parcel of land having a $70,000 FMV that is subject to a $45,000 mortgage, which he assumes, and $5,000 of cash in exchange for his Diamond stock.

a. What are the amount and character of each shareholder's gain or loss?

b. What is each shareholder's basis for the property received in the liquidation?

C6-35 ***Timing of Gain/Loss Recognition.*** Peter owns 25% of the Crosstown Corporation stock in which he has a $200,000 adjusted basis. In each of the following situations, what amount of gain/loss will Peter report in 1996? in 1997?

a. Peter is a cash method of accounting taxpayer. Crosstown determines on December 24, 1996 that a $260,000 liquidating distribution will be made to Peter. The liquidating distribution is paid on January 3, 1997.

b. Assume the same facts as in part (a) except that Peter is an accrual method of accounting taxpayer.

C6-36 ***Corporate Formation/Corporate Liquidation.*** Ken Wallace contributed assets with a $100 adjusted basis and a $400 FMV to Ace Corporation in exchange for all of its single class of stock. The corporation conducted operations for five years and was liquidated. Ken Wallace received a liquidating distribution of $500 cash and the assets that he had contributed which now had a $100 adjusted basis and a $500 FMV.

a. What are the tax consequences of the corporate formation transaction?
b. What are the tax consequences of the corporate liquidation transaction?
c. Would your answers to parts (a) and (b) remain the same if the assets instead had been contributed by Wallace Corporation to Ace Corporation?

C6-37 ***Gain or Loss on Making a Liquidating Distribution.*** What are the amount and character of the gain or loss recognized by the distributing corporation when making liquidating distributions in the following situations? What is the shareholder's basis for the property that is received? In any situation where a loss is disallowed, indicate what changes would be necessary to improve the tax consequences of the transaction.

a. Best Corporation distributes land having a $200,000 FMV and a $100,000 adjusted basis to Tanya, its sole shareholder. The land, a capital asset, is subject to a $40,000 mortgage, which Tanya assumes.
b. Wilkins Corporation distributes depreciable property to its two equal shareholders. Robert receives a milling machine having a $50,000 adjusted basis and a $75,000 FMV. $30,000 depreciation had been claimed on the machine. The milling machine was purchased from an unrelated seller four years ago. Sharon receives an automobile that originally cost $40,000 two years earlier and has a $26,000 FMV. $20,000 in depreciation had been claimed on the automobile.
c. Jordan Corporation distributes marketable securities having a $100,000 FMV and a $175,000 adjusted basis to Brad, a 66.67% shareholder. The marketable securities were purchased by Jordan three years ago. A cash payment in the amount of $50,000 is made to Ann, a 33.33% shareholder.
d. Assume the same facts as in Part c, except that the securities and cash are instead each distributed two-thirds to Brad and one-third to Ann.

C6-38 ***Gain or Loss Recognition by a Distributing Corporation.*** Melon Corporation, which is owned equally by four individual shareholders, adopts a plan of liquidation in which it plans on distributing the following properties:

- Land (a capital asset) having a $30,000 FMV and a $12,000 adjusted basis.
- Depreciable personal property having a $15,000 FMV and a $9,000 adjusted basis. Depreciation in the amount of $10,000 has been claimed on the property during the three years since its acquisition.
- Installment obligations having a $30,000 FMV and face amount and a $21,000 adjusted basis, acquired when a Sec. 1231 property was sold.
- Supplies that cost $6,000 and were expensed in the preceding tax year. The supplies have a $7,500 FMV.
- Marketable securities having a $15,000 FMV and an $18,000 adjusted basis. The marketable securities were purchased from a broker twelve months ago.

a. Which of the properties, when distributed by Melon Corporation to one of its shareholders, will require the recognition of gain or loss by the distributing corporation?
b. How will your answer to Part a change if the distribution is instead made to Melon's parent corporation as part of a complete liquidation meeting the Sec. 332 requirements?
c. How will your answer to Part b change if the distribution is instead made to a minority shareholder?

C6-39 ***Distribution of Property Subject to a Mortgage.*** Titan Corporation adopts a plan of liquidation. It distributes an apartment building having a $3,000,000 FMV and a $1,800,000 adjusted basis, and land having a $1,000,000 FMV and a $600,000 adjusted basis, to the MNO Partnership in exchange for all of the outstanding Titan stock. The MNO Partnership has an $800,000 basis in its Titan stock. $600,000 of MACRS depreciation has been claimed on the building. The MNO Partnership agrees to assume the $3,000,000 mortgage on the land and building. All of Titan's assets other than the building and land are used to pay its federal income tax liability.

a. What are the amount and character of Titan's recognized gain or loss on the distribution?

b. What are the amount and character of the MNO Partnership's gain or loss on the liquidation? What is its basis for the land and building?

c. How would your answer to Parts a and b change if the apartment building and land were instead worth $2,000,000 and $700,000, respectively?

C6-40 ***Sale of Loss Property by a Liquidating Corporation.*** In March 1995, Mike contributes land having a $75,000 adjusted basis and a $50,000 FMV to Kansas Corporation in exchange for additional Kansas stock. The land is used as a parking lot by Kansas's employees for two years before it is sold in March 1997 for $45,000. One month after the sale, Kansas Corporation adopts a plan of liquidation.

a. What is Kansas's recognized gain or loss on the land sale?

b. How would your answer to Part a change if the land were not used in the conduct of Kansas's trade or business and if it were held for only one year before being sold?

c. How would your answer to Part b change if the land were instead sold for $80,000?

C6-41 ***Tax Consequences of a Corporate Liquidation.*** Pamela owns all of the Snapple Corporation stock. She purchased her stock ten years ago and her current basis for the stock is $300,000. On June 10, Pamela decided to liquidate Snapple. Snapple's balance sheet prior to the sale of the assets, payment of the liquidation expenses and federal income taxes is as follows:

	Basis	*FMV*
Cash	$240,000	$240,000
Marketable securities	90,000	80,000
Equipment	150,000	200,000
Land	320,000	680,000
Total assets	$800,000	$1,200,000
Paid-in capital	$300,000	
Retained earnings (and E&P)	500,000	$1,200,000
Total	$800,000	$1,200,000

- Depreciation in the amount of $150,000 has been taken on the equipment.
- The marketable securities were received as a capital contribution from Pamela three years earlier at a time when their adjusted basis was $90,000 and their FMV was $70,000.
- Snapple's incurred $20,000 in liquidation expenses in its final tax year.

What are the tax consequences of the liquidation to Pamela and Snapple Corporation? Assume a 34% corporate tax rate.

C6-42 *Tax Consequences of a Corporate Liquidation.* King Corporation is owned 75% by Lynn and 25% by Mark. Lynn and Mark have $135,000 and $60,000 bases in their stock, respectively. A plan of liquidation is adopted by King Corporation on February 1, and Lynn receives the following property as a liquidating distribution on March 12: money, $40,000; land, $140,000 FMV; and 300 shares of Blue stock, $30,000 FMV. The land is subject to a $15,000 mortgage. Mark receives $10,000 FMV of Blue stock (100 shares) and $55,000 in cash as a liquidating distribution.The land and stock (both capital assets) have adjusted bases of $50,000 and $70,000, respectively, in King Corporation's hands. The stock was purchased eight years ago by King.

a. What are the amount and character of King Corporation's recognized gain or loss on the liquidating distributions?
b. What are the amount and character of Lynn and Mark's recognized gains or losses?
c. What are the bases of the land and stock in Lynn's hands? The stock in Mark's hands?

C6-43 *Liquidation of a Subsidiary Corporation.* Parent Corporation owns all of the stock of Subsidiary Corporation. The adjusted basis of its stock investment is $175,000. A plan of liquidation is adopted and assets having a $400,000 FMV and a $300,000 adjusted basis (to Subsidiary), and liabilities in the amount of $60,000, are distributed to Parent Corporation. Subsidiary has a $150,000 E&P balance.

a. What are the amount and character of Subsidiary Corporation's recognized gain or loss on the distribution?
b. What are the amount and character of Parent Corporation's recognized gain or loss on the redemption of the Subsidiary stock?
c. What are the bases of the assets on Parent Corporation's books?
d. What happens to Parent Corporation's basis in the Subsidiary stock? Subsidiary's tax attributes?

C6-44 *Liquidation of a Subsidiary Corporation.* Parent Corporation owns all of Subsidiary Corporation's single class of stock. Its adjusted basis for the stock is $175,000. After adopting a plan of liquidation, Subsidiary Corporation distributes the following properties to Parent Corporation: money, $20,000; LIFO inventory, $200,000 FMV; and equipment, $150,000 FMV. The inventory has a $125,000 adjusted basis. The equipment originally cost $280,000. Depreciation in the amount of $160,000 has been claimed on the equipment. Subsidiary Corporation has a $150,000 E&P balance and a $40,000 NOL carryover on the liquidation date.

a. What are the amount and character of Subsidiary Corporation's recognized gain or loss when the liquidating distributions are made?
b. What are the amount and character of Parent Corporation's recognized gain or loss on its surrender of the Subsidiary stock?
c. What is the basis of each nonmoney property on the books of Parent Corporation?
d. What happens to Subsidiary's E&P balance and NOL carryover following the liquidation?
e. What happens to Parent's $175,000 basis in the Subsidiary stock?

C6-45 *Liquidation of a Subsidiary Corporation.* Parent Corporation owns all of Subsidiary Corporation's single class of stock and $2,000,000 of Subsidiary Corporation debentures. The debentures were purchased in small blocks from various unrelated parties at a $100,000 discount from their face amount. The Subsidiary stock has a $1,300,000 basis on Parent's books. Subsidiary Corporation adopts a plan of liquidation whereby it distributes property having a $4,000,000 FMV and a $2,400,000 adjusted basis in redemption of the Subsidiary stock. The debentures are redeemed for Subsidiary Corporation property having a $2,000,000 FMV and a $2,200,000 adjusted basis.

a. What income or gain is recognized by Subsidiary Corporation as a result of making the liquidating distributions?

b. What gain or loss is recognized by Parent Corporation on the redemption of the Subsidiary stock? The Subsidiary debentures?

c. What is Parent Corporation's basis for the property received from Subsidiary Corporation?

C6-46 ***Liquidation of a Subsidiary Corporation.*** Parent Corporation owns 80% of the single class of Subsidiary Corporation stock. The remaining 20% of the Subsidiary stock is owned by Ramon. Parent and Ramon have adjusted bases of $100,000 and $25,000, respectively, for their Subsidiary stock. After adopting a plan of liquidation, Subsidiary Corporation is left with two properties: land having a $40,000 adjusted basis and a $160,000 FMV, and $40,000 in money. Subsidiary Corporation has a $50,000 E&P balance on the liquidation date.

a. What are the tax consequences to Parent and Subsidiary Corporations and Ramon of distributing the land to Parent in redemption of its Subsidiary stock and distributing the money to Ramon in redemption of his Subsidiary stock?

b. How would your answer to Part a change if the land and the money were instead distributed ratably to Parent Corporation and Ramon in retirement of the Subsidiary stock?

C6-47 ***Tax Consequences of a Corporate Liquidation.*** Gabriel Corporation is owned 90% by Zeier Corporation and 10% by Ray Goff, a Gabriel employee. A preliquidation balance sheet for the corporation is presented below:

Assets	*Basis*	*FMV*
Cash	$ 100,000	$ 100,000
Inventory	420,000	700,000
Equipment	80,000	100,000
Land	400,000	300,000
Total	$1,000,000	$1,200,000
Equities		
Accounts payable	$ 100,000	$ 100,000
Bonds payable	500,000	500,000
Common stock	100,000	100,000
Retained earnings (and E&P)	300,000	500,000
Total	$1,000,000	$1,200,000

$150,000 in MACRS depreciation has been taken on the equipment. The land was purchased three years ago as a potential plant site. Plans to build the plant were never consummated, and the land has been held since then as an investment. Zeier Corporation and Ray Goff have $90,000 and $10,000 bases, respectively, in their Gabriel stock. Both shareholders have held their stock since the corporation's inception in 1986. The bonds were purchased by Zeier from an insurance company two years ago for $20,000 above their face amount. Gabriel Corporation adopts a plan of liquidation. $500,000 of inventory is transferred to Zeier to retire the bonds. Each shareholder receives their share of Gabriel's remaining assets and assumes its share of Gabriel's liabilities (other than federal income taxes). Federal income taxes owed on the liquidation are paid by Gabriel. Assume a 34% corporate tax rate. What are the tax consequences of the liquidation to Ray Goff, Zeier Corporation, and Gabriel Corporation?

C6-48 ***Basis of Assets Received in a Liquidation.*** Parent Corporation owns all of the Subsidiary Corporation stock. Parent has a $200,000 basis in its stock investment. What are the tax consequences to Parent of the following liquidating distributions made by Subsidiary?

a. Assets having a $250,000 FMV and a $200,000 adjusted basis (to Subsidiary) are distributed.

b. Assets having a $250,000 FMV and a $150,000 adjusted basis are distributed.

c. Assets having a $150,000 FMV and a $250,000 adjusted basis are distributed.

C6-49 ***Tax Consequences of a Corporate Liquidation.*** Pueblo Corporation is owned by Art and Peggy. Art owns 80% of the Pueblo stock and Peggy owns the remainder. Art and Peggy have $320,000 and $80,000 adjusted bases, respectively, for their Pueblo stock. Pueblo Corporation owns the following assets: money, $25,000; inventory, $150,000 FMV and $100,000 adjusted basis; marketable securities, $100,000 FMV and $125,000 adjusted basis; and equipment, $325,000 FMV and $185,000 adjusted basis. The equipment was purchased four years ago and subsequently $215,000 of MACRS depreciation was claimed. The securities are not a disqualified property. On July 1 of the current year Pueblo Corporation adopts a plan of liquidation at a time when it has $250,000 of E&P and no liabilities. The equipment, $50,000 of inventory, the marketable securities, and $5,000 of money are distributed to Art before year-end as a liquidating distribution. $20,000 of money and $100,000 of inventory are distributed to Peggy before year-end as a liquidating distribution.

a. What are the tax consequences of the liquidation to Pueblo Corporation and Art and Peggy?

b. Can you offer any suggestions to Pueblo Corporation's management that could improve the tax consequences of the liquidation? Explain.

c. How would your answers to Parts a and b change if Art and Peggy were instead domestic corporations?

C6-50 ***Tax Attribute Carryovers.*** Bell Corporation is owned by George, who has a $400,000 basis for his Bell stock. The activities of Bell Corporation have been unprofitable in recent years, small NOLs have been incurred, and its operating assets currently have a $300,000 FMV and a $500,000 adjusted basis. George is approached by Time Corporation, which wants to purchase Bell's assets for $300,000. Approximately $200,000 in money is expected to remain after the payment of Bell's liabilities.

a. What are the tax consequences of the transaction if Bell adopts a plan of liquidation, sells the assets, and distributes the money in redemption of the Bell stock within a twelve-month period?

b. What advantages (if any) would accrue to Bell Corporation and George if the corporation remains in existence and uses the $200,000 of money that remains after payment of the liabilities to conduct a new trade or business?

C6-51 ***Series of Liquidating Distributions.*** Union Corporation is owned equally by Ron and Steve. Ron and Steve purchased their stock in 1988 and 1990 and have adjusted bases for their Union stock of $15,000 and $27,500, respectively. Each shareholder receives two liquidating distributions. The first liquidating distribution made in 1997 results in each shareholder receiving a one-half interest in a parcel of land that has a $40,000 FMV and an $18,000 adjusted basis to Union Corporation. The second liquidating distribution made in 1998 results in each shareholder receiving $20,000 in money.

a. What are the amount and character of Ron and Steve's recognized gain or loss for 1997? For 1998?
b. What is the basis of the land in Ron and Steve's hands?
c. How would your answers to Parts a and b change if the land has a $12,000 FMV instead of a $40,000 FMV?

C6-52 ***Subsequent Assessment on the Shareholders.*** Meridian Corporation is owned equally by five individual shareholders. A plan of liquidation is adopted by Meridian Corporation, and each shareholder receives a liquidating distribution. Tina, a cash method of accounting taxpayer, reports a $30,000 long-term capital gain in 1993 on the redemption of her stock. Pending the outcome of a lawsuit in which Meridian Corporation is one of the defendents, $5,000 of Tina's liquidating distribution is held back and placed in escrow. Settlement of the lawsuit in 1997 requires that the escrowed funds plus the interest earned on these funds be paid out to the plaintiff and that each shareholder pay an additional $2,500. Tina pays the amount due in 1998. How does Tina report the settlement of the lawsuit and the payment of the additional amount?

C6-53 ***Open vs. Closed Transactions.*** Hilton Corporation is owned by Miguel, who has a $40,000 basis for his stock. Miguel receives a liquidating distribution in 1995 of $12,000 in money, a patent having a $15,000 FMV, and a contingent claim for $125,000 against Tide Corporation for infringement on the patent. According to Hilton's legal counsel, no reliable valuation can be placed on the $125,000 claim.

a. What are the amount and character of Miguel's gain or loss on the liquidation in 1995?
b. How would your answer to Part a change if the claim were settled by having Tide Corporation pay Miguel $50,000 in 1997?
c. How would your answers to Parts a and b change if litigation of the claim commenced in 1995 and legal counsel placed a $30,000 valuation on the contingent claim against Tide Corporation when the liquidating distribution was made?

C6-54 ***Open vs. Closed Transaction.*** Kane Corporation is owned equally by Maria and Martha. Both individuals are inventors who, through Kane Corporation, hold a number of patents on their inventions. Kane Corporation holds the patent on a special manufacturing process used in the production of plastics. This process has been the subject of litigation with a competitor about infringement of rights that Kane has under the patent. Kane Corporation is suing for $500,000 in royalties, which would have been earned had the competitor been licensed to use the patent. Because of a disagreement, Martha and Maria have adopted a plan to liquidate Kane Corporation. As part of the liquidation plan, Maria is to receive the patent that is the subject of the lawsuit (valued at $1,000,000) and any monies collected under the lawsuit. Martha is to receive other patents and money totaling $1,000,000. Kane Corporation's attorneys are unable to make a definite statement as to what Maria can expect to receive from the lawsuit. Each shareholder's basis for her Kane stock is $50,000. What is the appropriate tax treatment of the liquidating distributions by Kane Corporation, Martha, and Maria?

CASE STUDY PROBLEMS

C6-55 Paul, a long-time client of yours, has operated an automobile repair shop (as a C corporation) for most of his life. The shop has been fairly successful in recent years. His children are not interested in continuing the business. Paul is age 62 and has accumulated approximately $500,000 in assets outside of his business, most of which are in his personal residence and retirement plan. A recent balance sheet for the business shows the following:

Assets	*Adjusted Basis*	*FMV*	*Liabilities*	*Amount*
Cash	$ 25,000	$ 25,000	Accounts payable	$ 30,000
Inventory	60,000	75,000	Mortgage payable	70,000
Equipment	200,000	350,000		
Building	100,000	160,000		
Land	40,000	60,000		
Goodwill	—0—	100,000		
Total	$425,000	$770,000	Total	$100,000

The inventory is accounted for using the first-in, first-out inventory method. Depreciation in the amount of $250,000 has been claimed on the equipment. The building was acquired in 1987 and has been depreciated in the amount of $25,000 under the MACRS rules. The goodwill is an estimate that Paul feels reflects the value of his business over and above the other assets that are listed.

Paul has received an offer of $775,000 from a competing automobile repair company for the noncash assets of his business, which will be used to establish a second location for the competing company. The sale will be made in cash within 60 days. The purchaser has obtained the necessary bank financing to make the acquisition. Paul's basis in his stock is $300,000.

Required: Prepare a memorandum for Paul outlining the tax consequences of the sale transaction and liquidation of the corporation.

C6-56 Your accounting firm has done the audit and tax work for the Peerless family and their business entities for twenty years. Approximately 25% of your accounting and tax practice billings come from Peerless family work. Peerless Real Estate Corporation owns land and a building (an ACRS property) having a $4.5 million FMV and a $1.0 million adjusted basis. A $1.3 million mortgage balance is owed on the building. The corporation used substantial leverage to acquire the building so Myron Peerless and his brother Mark Peerless, who are equal shareholders in Peerless Real Estate, each have only $200,000 adjusted bases in their stock. Cash flows are good from the building, and only a small portion of the annual profits is needed for reinvestment in the building. Myron and Mark have decided to liquidate the corporation so as to avoid the federal and state corporate income taxes and continue to operate the business as a partnership. They want the MM Partnership, which has Mark and Myron equally sharing profits, losses, and liabilities, to purchase the building from the corporation for $400,000 cash plus their assumption of the $1.3 million mortgage. Mark knows a real estate appraiser who will provide a $1.7 million appraisal for the right price. Current corporate cash balances are sufficient to pay any federal and state income taxes owed on the sale of the building. Mark and Myron would each receive $200,000 from the corporation in cancellation of their stock.

Required: Prepare notes on the points you will want to cover with Myron and Mark Peerless about the corporate liquidation and the Peerless' desire to avoid federal and state corporate income taxes at your meeting tomorrow.

TAX RESEARCH PROBLEMS

C6-57 Parent Corporation owns 85% of the common stock and 100% of the preferred stock of Subsidiary Corporation. The common stock and preferred stock have adjusted bases of $500,000 and $200,000, respectively, on Parent's books. Subsidiary Corporation adopts a plan of liquidation on July 3 of the current year, when its assets have a $1,000,000 FMV. Liabilities on that date amount to $850,000. On November 9, Subsidiary Corporation pays off its creditors and distributes $150,000 to Parent Corporation with respect to its preferred stock. No monies are left to be paid to Parent with respect to the remaining $50,000 of its liquidation preference for the preferred stock, or with respect to any of the common stock. In each of Subsidiary Corporation's tax years, less than 10% of its gross income has been passive income. What are the amount and character of Parent's loss on the preferred stock? The common stock?

A partial list of research sources is

- Secs. 165(g)(3) and 332(a)
- Reg. Sec. 1.332-2(b)
- *Spaulding Bakeries, Inc.*, 27 T.C. 684 (1957)
- *H. K. Porter Co., Inc.*, 87 T.C. 689 (1986)

C6-58 Parent Corporation has owned 60% of the single class of Subsidiary Corporation stock for a number of years. The remaining 40% of the Subsidiary stock is owned by Tyrone. On August 10 of the current year, Parent Corporation purchases Tyrone's Subsidiary Corporation stock for cash. On September 15, Subsidiary Corporation adopts a plan of liquidation. Subsidiary Corporation makes a single liquidating distibution on October 1. The activities of Subsidiary Corporation are continued as a separate division of Parent Corporation. Does the liquidation of Subsidiary Corporation qualify for nonrecognition treatment under Secs. 332 and 337? Must Parent Corporation assume the Subsidiary Corporation's E&P balance?

A partial list of research sources is

- Secs. 332(b) and 381
- Reg. Sec. 1.332-2(a)

C6-59 Able Corporation, a calendar-year taxpayer, is owned by twenty-five individual shareholders. A recent balance sheet shows Able Corporation with assets having a $3,500,000 FMV and a $2,150,000 adjusted basis. Able Corporation's management is contemplating the sale of the assets followed by a complete liquidation of the corporation. Such a sale would result in $950,000 of ordinary income and $400,000 of capital gain being recognized. The unrelated purchaser has proposed to pay $350,000 the first year and to provide a note covering the balance. $350,000 would be paid by the purchaser annually on the note plus interest at a rate acceptable to the IRS.

Required: Explain the tax consequences of the following three alternative plans being considered by management.

- Sell the assets and have the corporation hold the installment obligation. Collections on the obligation would be distributed by the corporation to the shareholders. Following receipt of the last payment, the corporation would be liquidated.
- Adopt a plan of liquidation, sell the assets, and distribute the installment obligation to the shareholders as a liquidating distribution. The shareholders would collect the interest and annual payments.
- Adopt a plan of liquidation, sell the assets, transfer the installment obligation to a liquidating trust, and liquidate the corporation. The trust would collect the interest and annual payments and distribute them to the former shareholders.

CHAPTER 7

CORPORATE ACQUISITIONS AND REORGANIZATIONS

LEARNING OBJECTIVES

After studying this chapter, you should be able to

1. Explain the types of taxable acquisition transactions.
2. Explain the differences between taxable and tax-free acquisition transactions.
3. Explain the types of tax-free reorganizations and their requirements.
4. Determine the tax consequences of a tax-free reorganization to the target corporation.
5. Determine the tax consequences of a tax-free reorganization to the acquiring corporation.
6. Determine the tax consequences of a tax-free reorganization to the target corporation's shareholders and security holders.
7. Explain how judicial doctrines can restrict a taxpayer's ability to use corporate reorganizations.
8. Determine which reorganization forms permit the carryover of tax attributes.
9. Explain how NOL carryovers are restricted following an acquisition.

CHAPTER OUTLINE

The management of a corporation may decide to acquire a second corporation. Alternatively, these same individuals may decide to divest themselves of part or all of the corporate assets, such as the assets of an operating division or the stock of a subsidiary corporation. These acquisitions or divestitures can be either taxable or tax-free transactions. In a taxable transaction, the entire amount of the realized gain or loss is recognized. To qualify as a tax-free transaction, a specific set of statutory and judicial requirements must be met. If the transaction satisfies these requirements, part or all of the realized gain or loss generally goes unrecognized. The amount of unrecognized gain or loss is deferred until the assets or stock involved are sold or exchanged in a taxable transaction. The tax-free reorganization rules are another example of the wherewithal to pay concept; that is, no tax is imposed if the taxpayer retains a continuing equity interest. A tax is imposed only when property other than stock or securities (e.g., money) has been received.[1] Taxpayers, on the other hand, are likely to use a taxable transaction (instead of a tax-free transaction) to avoid having to defer recognition of a loss on an asset or stock disposition.

This chapter presents an overview of the tax consequences of taxable and tax-free acquisitions and divestitures. It also examines the statutory provisions and judicial doctrines that apply to determine the tax consequences for the tax-free acquisition and divestiture transactions.

TAXABLE ACQUISITION TRANSACTIONS

OBJECTIVE 1

Explain the types of taxable acquisition transactions

Taxable acquisition transactions can be divided into two major categories:

- Purchase of a target corporation's assets
- Purchase of a target corporation's stock

Acquiring corporations have two primary ways to acquire the assets of a **target corporation.**[2] The acquiring corporation can acquire the needed assets directly from the target corporation. Alternatively, the acquiring corporation can acquire an indirect interest in the assets by purchasing a controlling (more than 50%) interest in the target corporation's stock. Three options exist once the stock interest is acquired.

- The acquiring corporation and its new subsidiary corporation can exist as separate entities.
- The acquiring corporation can liquidate its new subsidiary corporation in a tax-free liquidation. Following the liquidation, the parent corporation retains a direct interest in the assets.
- The acquiring corporation's management can make a Sec. 338 deemed liquidation election on behalf of the subsidiary corporation. A Sec. 338 election permits the adjusted basis of the subsidiary corporation's assets to be stepped-up to the price that the acquiring corporation paid for the subsidiary corporation's stock plus the amount of any subsidiary corporation's liabilities.

The four asset and stock acquisition alternatives are examined below. A summary of the tax consequences of these alternatives is presented in Table C7-1.

[1] The tax deferral can be permanent if the stocks and securities are held until death. At death, the carryover or substituted basis is stepped up to its fair market value (FMV) without incurring any income tax liability.

[2] The terms *target* and *acquired corporations* are used interchangeably here.

▼ TABLE C7-1
Comparison of Taxable Acquisition Alternatives

	Taxable Asset Acquisition	Taxable Stock Acquisition with: No Liquidation of Target	Tax-Free Liquidation of Target	Sec. 338 Election by Target
Acquiring corporation's basis for stock	N/A	Cost basis	Cost basis	Cost basis
Parent-subsidiary relationship created	No	Yes	Yes, until liquidation	Yes
Consolidated tax return election available	No	Yes	Yes, until liquidation	Yes
Gain/loss recognized on asset sale	Yes	No	No	Yes, on deemed sale of assets from old target corporation to new target corporation.
Gain/loss recognized by target corporation when making liquidating distribution	Yes, if target elects to liquidate after asset sale.	N/A	No	No
Gain recognized by acquiring corporation when receiving liquidating distribution	N/A	N/A	No	No
Acquiring corporation's basis for assets acquired	Cost basis on acquiring corporation's books	No change for basis of assets on target corporation's books	Carryover from target corporation's books	Cost basis of target stock acquired plus amount of target's liabilities
Transfer of tax attributes to acquiring corporation	Remain with target corporation	Remain with target corporation	Carryover to acquiring corporation	Disappear with deemed liquidation of old target corporation

N/A = Not applicable.

ASSET ACQUISITIONS

The asset acquisition is not a difficult transaction for the acquiring and target corporations to accomplish. The sale transaction is reported by determining the gain or loss recognized on the sale of each individual asset. Sales of depreciable assets (e.g., Sec. 1245 and 1250 property) result in previously claimed depreciation being recaptured.

The purchaser's bases for the assets are their acquisition cost.[3] The purchaser can claim depreciation based on the property's total acquisition cost.

A taxable asset acquisition offers the purchaser two major advantages. First, a significant portion of the acquisition can be debt-financed, whereas the tax-free reorganization requirements either restrict or prohibit the use of debt. The interest expense that is incurred with respect to the debt is deductible for tax purposes. Second, only assets and liabilities that are designated in the purchase-sale agreement are acquired. The purchaser need not acquire all or substantially all of the target corporation's assets, as is the case when the target corporation's stock is acquired in either a taxable

[3] Sec. 1012.

transaction or a tax-free reorganization or when an asset-for-stock tax-free reorganization takes place. Similarly, only liabilities that are specified in the purchase-sale agreement are assumed by the purchaser. Contingent or unknown liabilities remain the responsibility of the seller.

The target corporation (i.e., acquired corporation) may be liquidated after the asset sale takes place. The target corporation recognizes gain or loss with respect to the assets that are sold. Any properties that are retained by the target corporation are distributed to the shareholders as part of the liquidation. The liquidating corporation recognizes gain or loss at the time of the distribution as if such properties were instead sold. The target corporation's shareholders report their gain or loss on the liquidation as capital gain or loss.

EXAMPLE C7-1 ▶ Target Corporation is owned by Ann, Bob, and Cathy, who have a $20,000 basis for their stock that was acquired six years ago. Acquiring Corporation purchases Target's noncash assets for $100,000 of cash and $300,000 of Acquiring debt obligations. $50,000 of cash is retained by Target. On the sale date, Target's noncash assets have a $280,000 adjusted basis and a $400,000 FMV. Its liabilities are $100,000 on the sale date. Target must recognize a $120,000 gain [($100,000 + $300,000) − $280,000]. The character of the gains and losses recognized depends on the individual properties that are sold. Assuming a 34% corporate tax rate, Target's tax liability on the sale is $40,800 ($120,000 × 0.34). Acquiring takes a $400,000 basis for the noncash assets that are acquired. After Target pays its income tax and other liabilities, Ann, Bob, and Cathy each receive a liquidating distribution on which a capital gain is reported. ◀

STOCK ACQUISITIONS

KEY POINT

In a stock acquisition, only the shareholders of Target recognize gain. In an asset acquisition, both Target and Target's shareholders may recognize gain.

STOCK ACQUISITION WITH NO LIQUIDATION. The stock acquisition is the simplest of the acquisition transactions. The gain recognized on the sale receives capital gain treatment if the stock is a capital asset in the seller's hands. If part or all of the consideration is deferred into a later tax year, the seller's gain can be reported using the installment method of accounting.[4] If part of the total consideration received by the seller of the stock represents an agreement with the purchaser not to compete for a specified time period, the consideration received for the agreement is taxed as ordinary income.[5]

The purchaser's basis for the stock is its acquisition cost.[6] The target corporation's basis for its assets does not change as a result of the stock sale. Any payment for the stock that is in excess of the book value of the net assets of the acquired company cannot be reflected in a stepped-up basis for the assets. Any potential for depreciation recapture that exists on the transaction date stays with the target corporation's assets and is, therefore, assumed by the purchaser. If the target corporation has loss or credit carryovers, these carryovers can be subject to special limitations in the post-acquisition tax years (see page C7-49).

Stock sales have proven to be popular with sellers because they may be less costly than an asset sale, since only a single level of taxation is encountered. No adjustment occurs to the basis of the target corporation's assets following a stock sale, even though the basis of the stock that was acquired may be substantially higher than the total basis of the assets that is reported for tax purposes by the target corporation. Thus, one of the tax advantages of actually purchasing the assets of the target corporation—the higher basis for the properties for tax purposes—is not available when a stock purchase occurs.

EXAMPLE C7-2 ▶ Assume the same facts as in Example C7-1 except that Acquiring extends a tender offer whereby it will purchase the Target stock at $50 per share. Ann, Bob, and Cathy tender their

---

[4] Sec. 453.

[5] The purchaser can amortize over a fifteen-year period any amounts paid to the seller with respect to the agreement not to compete (Sec. 197).

[6] Sec. 1012.

KEY POINT

In Example C7-2, the built-in gain in Target's assets is not recognized in a stock acquisition. Likewise, Target's assets are not stepped-up in basis even though Acquiring pays $350,000 for the Target stock.

7,000 Target shares in response to Acquiring's offer. Acquiring's $350,000 (7,000 shares × $50/share) purchase price equals Target's net asset amount ($450,000 − $100,000 liabilities). Ann, Bob, and Cathy each report a long-term capital gain on the disposition of their stock. Target becomes a wholly-owned subsidiary of Acquiring and does not adjust the basis of its assets as a result of the sale unless a Sec. 338 deemed liquidation election is made. ◀

If the purchasing corporation is already part of an affiliated group that is filing a consolidated tax return, then the subsidiary corporation must join in the consolidated return election if at least 80% of the subsidiary's stock is owned and the subsidiary is an includible corporation (see Chapter C3). Otherwise, the parent and subsidiary corporations can elect to make an initial consolidated return election.

TYPICAL MISCONCEPTION

Taxpayers often do not understand that the parent's basis in its subsidiary's stock in a Sec. 332 liquidation disappears. The liquidated assets take a carryover basis from the subsidiary corporation.

STOCK ACQUISITION FOLLOWED BY A LIQUIDATION. The stock acquisition described in the preceding section can be followed by a liquidation of the acquired (subsidiary) corporation into its acquiring (parent) corporation. If the parent corporation owns at least 80% of the subsidiary corporation's stock, then the liquidation is tax-free under the Sec. 332 and 337 rules outlined in Chapter C6. The subsidiary corporation's basis for the assets on its books carries over to the parent corporation. If the parent corporation paid a premium for the assets (i.e., an amount in excess of the total of the assets' adjusted bases), then this premium is lost when the liquidation occurs because the parent corporation's basis for the stock disappears when the tax-free liquidation occurs. If the parent corporation paid less than the total of the assets' adjusted bases, the parent corporation retains this "excess" basis amount as part of the assets' carryover basis, which can provide additional tax benefits.

EXAMPLE C7-3 ▶

Assume the same facts as in Example C7-2 except that Acquiring and Target Corporations continue to file separate tax returns following the stock acquisition, and Target is liquidated into Acquiring shortly after the acquisition. Target Corporation's assets have the following adjusted bases and FMVs immediately before the sale:

Asset	Adjusted Basis	FMV
Cash	$ 50,000	$ 50,000
Marketable securities	49,000	55,000
Inventory	60,000	90,000
Accounts receivable	60,000	60,000
Building	27,000	44,000
Land	10,000	26,000
Machinery and equipment[a]	74,000	125,000
Total	$330,000	$450,000

[a]The machinery and equipment are Sec. 1245 properties. Recapture potential on the machinery and equipment is $107,000.

Target and Acquiring Corporations recognize no gains or losses on the liquidation. Acquiring assumes Target's $100,000 in liabilities and takes a $330,000 basis for the assets acquired from Target, with each of the individual basis amounts carrying over. In addition, Acquiring assumes all of Target's tax attributes, including the $107,000 depreciation recapture potential on the machinery and equipment. ◀

DEEMED LIQUIDATION ELECTION. In *Kimbell-Diamond Milling Co.*[7] the courts held that the purchase of a target corporation's stock followed by a prompt liquidation

[7] *Kimbell-Diamond Milling Co. v. CIR*, 40 AFTR 328, 51-1 USTC ¶9201 (5th Cir., 1951).

that occurs in order to obtain the target corporation's assets is treated as a single transaction. The acquiring corporation was permitted to use its acquisition price for the stock to determine the basis for the acquired assets. Congress codified this decision in 1954 by requiring that the purchase and liquidation of a subsidiary corporation be treated as an asset purchase when the controlling interest in the subsidiary's stock was acquired within a twelve-month period and the subsidiary corporation was completely liquidated within two years of the date on which acquisition of the controlling stock interest was completed. These rules created a number of uncertainties for taxpayers and were difficult for the IRS to administer. In 1982 Congress enacted an elective deemed liquidation provision that permits taxpayers to elect to adjust the basis of the target corporation's assets.

ADDITIONAL COMMENT

A Sec. 338 election allows the purchase of stock to be treated as a purchase of assets. This election treats the "old" target corporation as if it sold all of its assets to a "new" target corporation. This deemed asset sale is then treated as a taxable transaction. Therefore, in most situations it makes little sense to pay an immediate tax to obtain a step-up in basis when such additional basis can be recovered only in future years.

The Sec. 338 deemed liquidation election permits the acquiring and target corporations to elect an indirect (two-step) acquisition of the target corporation's assets. First the target corporation's shareholders sell their stock to the acquiring corporation. Then the acquiring corporation makes a deemed liquidation election with respect to the acquisition of the target corporation's stock. This election results in a hypothetical sale of the "old" target corporation's assets to a "new" target corporation for their FMV in a transaction that requires the seller to recognize all gains and losses.[8] The "old" target corporation is liquidated for tax purposes only. The "new" target corporation is treated as a new entity for tax purposes (i.e., it makes new accounting method and tax year elections). The bases of the old target corporation's assets are stepped-up or stepped-down on the new target corporation's federal income tax books to the amount paid by the acquiring corporation for the target corporation's stock plus the amount of the target corporation's liabilities (including any federal income taxes owed on the deemed sale). Corporate purchasers generally are less enthusiastic about Sec. 338[9] treatment because of the significant tax cost (e.g., the tax imposed on the deemed sale) that is usually incurred by the target corporation in the year in which the Sec. 338 election is made.

Eligible Stock Acquisitions. In this type of election, Sec. 338 requires the acquiring corporation to make a qualified stock purchase (i.e., to purchase 80% or more of the target corporation's voting stock and 80% or more of the total value of all classes of stock [except certain nonvoting preferred stock issues] during a twelve-month (or shorter) acquisition period).[10] The acquisition period must be a continuous period commencing on the date on which the acquiring corporation first purchases stock in the target corporation that is counted toward a qualified stock purchase and ending on the date that the qualified stock purchase occurs. If the acquiring corporation does not acquire the necessary 80% minimum within a continuous twelve-month period, the Sec. 338 election cannot be made.

EXAMPLE C7-4 ▶ Missouri Corporation purchases a 25% block of Target Corporation's single class of stock on each of four dates: April 1, 1996; July 1, 1996; December 1, 1996; and February 1, 1997. Because at least 80% of Target's stock is acquired within a twelve-month period (April 1, 1996 through February 1, 1997), Missouri Corporation can elect to report the transaction under the Sec. 338 deemed liquidation rules. ◀

[8] Target Corporation's legal existence does not change under the state corporation laws. For federal income tax purposes, Target Corporation (commonly referred to as "old" Target) is liquidated and goes out of existence. A "new" Target Corporation is created. This new corporation acquires for tax purposes all the assets of the "old" corporation.

[9] An alternative form of Sec. 338 election is permitted under Sec. 338(h)(10) for members of an affiliated group. This election is generally used by affiliated groups that file consolidated tax returns. The Sec. 338(h)(10) election permits the target corporation (e.g., a subsidiary) to recognize gain or loss as if it had sold its assets in a single transaction. The corporation selling the stock (e.g., a parent corporation) does not recognize gain on the stock sale thereby resulting in a single level of taxation. This special form of Sec. 338 election has become more prevalent in recent years.

[10] The basic Sec. 332 liquidation of a controlled subsidiary corporation stock definition outlined in Chapter C6 is also used for Sec. 338 purposes.

EXAMPLE C7-5 ▶ Assume the same facts as in Example C7-4, except that Missouri Corporation instead makes the final 25% purchase on May 15, 1997. In this case, only 75% of the Target stock is acquired in any twelve-month period. Two possible twelve-month periods are involved—April 1, 1996 through March 31, 1997, and May 16, 1996 through May 15, 1997. The 80% stock ownership minimum is not met in either period. A Sec. 338 election is unavailable to Missouri Corporation. ◀

Stock acquisitions that are not treated as purchases for the purpose of meeting the 80% requirement include the following:

- Stock whose adjusted basis is determined in whole or in part by its basis in the hands of the person from whom it was acquired (e.g., stock acquired as a capital contribution)
- Stock whose basis is determined under Sec. 1014(a) (i.e., FMV on the date of death or an alternative valuation date) that is acquired from a decedent
- Stock acquired in a tax-free transaction where nonrecognition of gain or loss is permitted by Secs. 351, 354, 355, or 356 (e.g., corporate formations, corporate divisions, or tax-free reorganizations)
- Stock acquired from a related party where stock ownership would be attributed to the purchaser under the attribution rules in Secs. 318(a)(1) through (3)

The Election. A Sec. 338 election must be made not later than the fifteenth day of the ninth month beginning after the month in which the acquisition date occurs. The acquisition date is the first date during the twelve-month acquisition period on which the 80% stock ownership requirement is met.[11]

EXAMPLE C7-6 ▶ Arizona Corporation purchases 40% of Target Corporation's single class of stock on April 1, 1997. An additional 50% of Target's stock is purchased on October 20, 1997. The acquisition date is October 20, 1997. The Sec. 338 election must be made on or before July 15, 1998. ◀

ADDITIONAL COMMENT

Generally, because the deemed asset sale results in immediate recognition of income, a Sec. 338 election is not advisable. However, if the target corporation has sufficient NOLs, a Sec. 338 election may be less costly if the NOLs offset the gain on the deemed sale.

Deemed Sale Transaction. When a Sec. 338 election is made, the target corporation is treated as having sold all of its assets at their FMV in a single transaction at the close of the acquisition date. The asset sale is a taxable transaction with gain or loss being recognized by the target corporation.

Because the Sec. 338 election was originally designed for transactions in which the acquisition price of the target corporation's stock exceeded the adjusted basis of the target corporation's assets, it is likely that the amount of gain recognized by the target in many of these transactions may be substantial. The size of this tax cost may result in companies forgoing the Sec. 338 election when target corporation stock is purchased or lowering the price they are willing to pay for the target corporation's stock if they intend to make a Sec. 338 election. Alternatively, the company may acquire the assets in a tax-free reorganization that is not eligible for a Sec. 338 election but permits the acquiring corporation to use its stock (instead of cash) to make the acquisition. The tax-free transaction, however, requires the use of the target corporation's basis for the assets on the acquiring corporation's books.

Basis of the Assets After the Deemed Sale. Although the target corporation's assets are treated as having been sold by the old target corporation for their FMV, the basis for the assets on the new target corporation's books is based on the amount paid by the acquiring corporation for the target corporation's stock. This amount is called the

[11] Secs. 338(g) and 338(h)(2).

adjusted grossed-up basis for the target corporation's stock. The adjusted grossed-up basis amount equals the sum of the basis of the purchasing corporation's stock interest in the target corporation plus an adjustment for the target corporation's liabilities on the day following the acquisition date, and plus or minus other relevant items.[12] The adjusted grossed-up basis amount is determined at the beginning of the day following the acquisition date.

The target corporation's stock owned by the acquiring corporation is divided into two categories: recently purchased stock and nonrecently purchased stock. This division is necessary because only the recently purchased stock is treated as a deemed purchase of the target corporation's assets. Recently purchased stock is any target corporation stock that is held on the acquisition date and that was purchased by the acquiring corporation during the twelve-month (or shorter) acquisition period. Nonrecently purchased stock is all other target corporation stock that was acquired before the acquisition period and is held by the acquiring corporation on the acquisition date.[13] The basis of the purchasing corporation's stock interest equals the grossed-up basis of the recently purchased stock plus the basis of the nonrecently purchased stock.

EXAMPLE C7-7 ▶ Apple Corporation purchases all of Target Corporation's single class of stock on July 23, 1997. All of the Target stock is considered to be recently purchased stock because it is purchased in a single transaction. The acquisition date is July 23, 1997. ◀

EXAMPLE C7-8 ▶ Assume the same facts as in Example C7-7, except that Apple Corporation already owns 10% of the Target stock (purchased in 1992) and purchases only the remaining 90% of the Target stock. The original block of Target stock is nonrecently purchased stock because it is acquired more than twelve months before the acquisition date (July 23, 1997). ◀

When the acquiring corporation does not own all of the target corporation's stock, the basis of the acquiring corporation's recently purchased stock must be increased or grossed-up to a hypothetical value that reflects ownership of all the target corporation's stock.[14]

KEY POINT

The basis of the new target's assets is equal to the amount paid for the target's stock plus the target's liabilities.

The basis of the stock is increased by the face amount of any target corporation liabilities that were outstanding at the beginning of business on the day following the acquisition date plus any tax liability resulting from gain being recognized on the deemed sale.[15] This liability adjustment is necessary to reflect the fact that if the acquisition had truly been an asset purchase, the assumption of the liabilities would have been reflected in the total purchase price.

Allocation of Basis to Individual Assets. The adjusted grossed-up basis of the stock is allocated among four classes of assets by using the residual method.[16] The residual method requires that the adjusted grossed-up basis amount be allocated to the corporation's tangible and intangible properties (other than goodwill and going concern value) on a priority basis. Any amount not allocated to specific tangible and intangible properties is then allocated to the target corporation's goodwill and going concern value.

The four classes of assets used in allocating the basis are

[12] Secs. 338(b)(1) and (2). The IRS has indicated that other relevant items include only items that arise from adjustment events that occur after the close of the new target's first tax year and items discovered as a result of an IRS examination of a tax return (e.g., the payment of contingent amounts for recently or nonrecently purchased stock).

[13] Sec. 338(b)(6).

[14] Sec. 338(b)(4).

[15] Sec. 338(b)(2) and Reg. Secs. 1.338(b)-1(f)(1) and (2).

[16] Reg. Sec. 1.338(b)-2(a).

PRACTICAL APPLICATION

Because goodwill is now amortizable, the fact that the residual purchase price is allocated to Class IV assets may be a desirable tax result. The required 15-year amortization period for goodwill under Sec. 197 is longer than four- to six-year period used by many taxpayers to amortize goodwill allocated to short-lived assets such as customer lists under the pre-Sec. 197 rules.

ADDITIONAL COMMENT

The residual method is specifically aimed at making sure that any premium paid for the target stock is reflected in goodwill. Because the residual method is the only acceptable allocation method, the only uncertainty that remains is to determine the FMVs of the assets listed in classes I, II, and III.

- Class I: cash, demand deposits, and similar accounts in banks, savings and loan associations, etc.
- Class II: certificates of deposit, U.S. government securities, readily marketable stocks and securities, foreign currency, etc.
- Class III: all assets other than Class I, II, and IV assets. Included here would be tangible and intangible properties without regard to whether they are depreciable, depletable, or amortizable.
- Class IV: intangible assets in the nature of goodwill and going concern value.[17]

Class IV intangible assets acquired after August 6, 1993 are amortizable over a fifteen-year period if they are used in the active conduct of a trade or business. Among the assets included are goodwill, going concern value, and covenants not to compete.

The adjusted grossed-up basis amount is first allocated to the individual Class I assets based on their actual dollar amounts.[18] Any amount remaining after the allocation to the Class I assets is assigned to the Class II assets (but not in excess of their FMV). Any amount remaining after the allocation to the Class II assets is allocated to the Class III assets (but not in excess of their FMV). Finally, any amount remaining after the allocation to the Class III assets is allocated to the Class IV assets. The total basis amounts allocated to the Class II, III, and IV asset categories are allocated to individual assets within the class, based on relative FMVs. When making the intraclass allocations, the allocation is based on the asset's total FMV, not its net FMV (gross FMV minus specific liens attaching to the property).

EXAMPLE C7-9 ▶ Assume the same facts as in Examples C7-2 and C7-3 except that Acquiring Corporation makes a timely Sec. 338 election. Target Corporation's assets have the following adjusted bases and FMVs at the beginning of the day after the acquisition date:

Asset Class	*Asset*	*Adjusted Basis*	*FMV*
I	Cash	$ 50,000	$ 50,000
II	Marketable securities	49,000	55,000
III	Inventory	60,000	90,000
III	Accounts receivable	60,000	60,000
III	Building[a]	27,000	44,000
III	Land	10,000	26,000
III	Machinery and equipment[b]	74,000	125,000
	Total	$330,000	$450,000

[a] Straight-line depreciation of $23,000 was claimed under the MACRS rules.
[b] The machinery and equipment are Sec. 1245 properties. Recapture potential on the machinery and equipment is $107,000.

Target Corporation's secured (i.e., mortgage) and unsecured liabilities as of the beginning of the day after the acquisition date (excluding income tax liabilities arising on the deemed sale) amount to $100,000. Target's assets are considered to have been sold for their FMV. Target must recognize the following gains on the deemed sale: marketable securities, $6,000 capital gain; inventory, $30,000 ordinary income; building, $17,000 ordinary income and Sec. 1231 gain; land, $16,000 Sec. 1231 gain; and machinery and equipment, $51,000 ordinary

[17] Temp. Reg. Sec. 1.338(b)-2T(b)(2).
[18] Ibid.

income. Assuming a 34% marginal tax rate, Target's income tax liability on the sale is $40,800 ($120,000 × 0.34).

The adjusted grossed-up basis for the Target stock is determined as follows:

Adjusted basis of Target stock		$350,000
Plus:	Income tax liability	40,800
	Other liabilities	100,000
Adjusted grossed-up basis		$490,800[a]

SELF-STUDY QUESTION

What are some of the tax consequences of a Sec. 338 election?

ANSWER

The effects of a Sec. 338 election include termination of the "old" target corporation, creation of a new target corporation with the option of a new tax year and different accounting methods, new depreciation elections without regard to anti-churning rules, and elimination of tax attributes of the old target (i.e., NOL carryforwards).

Allocation of the adjusted grossed-up basis occurs in the following manner:

Step 1: Allocate $50,000 to the cash (Class I asset).

Step 2: Allocate $55,000 to the marketable securities (Class II asset).

Step 3: Allocate $345,000 to the inventory, accounts receivable, building, land, and machinery and equipment (Class III assets). Because the total basis that remains after the allocation in Step 2 ($385,800) exceeds the FMV of the Class III assets ($345,000), each asset will take a basis equal to its FMV.

Step 4: Allocate $40,800 [$490,800 − ($50,000 + $55,000 + $345,000)] to goodwill. This amount is amortizable under Sec. 197. ◀

[a] A formula approach to determining the deemed sale price, and the allocation of the aggregate deemed sales price to the target's individual assets, can be found in Reg. Sec. 1.338-3.

STOP & THINK

Question: Target Corporation in Example C7-9 is thinking about changing from the FIFO to the LIFO inventory method once the Sec. 338 adjustments have been made. How and when will the step-up made to the inventory's basis be recovered if a LIFO election is made?

Solution: The basis step-up is recovered only if the LIFO inventory layers in existence on the acquisition date are sold. In general, such sales do not occur unless inventory levels are reduced below the amount held on the acquisition date. Other reasons for possibly not making the Sec. 338 election are the lengthy capital recovery periods for the building and goodwill adjustments, and the fact that an adjustment made to the basis of the land is neither depreciable or amortizable.

Tax Accounting Elections for the New Corporation. The "new" target corporation files a tax return separate from that of the acquiring corporation (unless a consolidated return is filed) because it is a separate legal entity. In many respects, the "new" target corporation is treated as a new entity. For example, the target corporation may adopt, without obtaining prior approval from the IRS, any tax year that meets the requirements of Sec. 441 and any accounting method that meets the requirements of Sec. 446.

The new target corporation can claim depreciation deductions under the MACRS rules without regard to the elections made by the old target corporation and without regard to the anti-churning rules.[19] The holding period for the new target corporation's assets begins on the day after the acquisition date.

The new target corporation is not a continuation of the old target corporation for purposes of the tax attribute carryover rules.[20] As a result, tax attribute carryovers that exist on the acquisition date are permanently lost when a Sec. 338 deemed liquidation election is made. Gain recognized on the deemed sale transaction can reduce the amount of any target corporation loss and credit carryovers that might otherwise be lost. The

[19] Reg. Sec. 1.338-2(d)(1)(i).

[20] Sec. 381(a)(1).

acquiring corporation must carefully consider the relative benefit of obtaining a step-up in basis for the individual assets versus the value of the available tax attributes (e.g., NOL carryovers).

Topic Review C7-1 presents a summary of the requirements for, and tax consequences of, having made a Sec. 338 deemed liquidation election.

COMPARISON OF TAXABLE AND TAX-FREE ACQUISITIONS

OBJECTIVE 2

Explain the differences between taxable and tax-free acquisition transactions

KEY POINT

Determining whether a transaction is taxable or nontaxable is doubly important to Target because it is involved in two potentially taxable exchanges: the exchange between Target and Acquiring and the exchange between Target and Target's shareholders.

SELF-STUDY QUESTION

Why would Acquiring want an acquisition to be tax-free if it gets only a substituted basis rather than a step-up in basis for the acquired assets?

ANSWER

Usually the motivation for an acquisition to be tax-free comes from Target and Target's shareholders. However, two reasons that Acquiring may desire a tax-free acquisition are (1) Acquiring has no cash to acquire the assets, so it must use stock as the consideration for the purchase, and (2) Target may have favorable tax attributes (e.g., a NOL) that Acquiring would like to use.

TAXABLE AND TAX-FREE ASSET ACQUISITIONS

One way to illustrate the difference between taxable and tax-free transactions is to compare the tax consequences. For purposes of our discussion, assume that Acquiring Corporation acquires all of the assets and liabilities of Target Corporation and that immediately following the acquisition, Target is liquidated. If Acquiring uses cash and debt obligations to make the purchase, the acquisition is taxable. If Acquiring acquires all of Target's assets using primarily its voting stock and limited cash and debt to accomplish the transaction, the acquisition may qualify as a tax-free reorganization.

TAX CONSEQUENCES FOR TARGET CORPORATION. Code Sec. 1001(c) indicates that with certain exceptions the entire gain or loss realized on a sale or exchange must be recognized. All gains and losses realized by Target Corporation on selling its assets are recognized.

A tax-free reorganization is one exception to the general rule. Gains realized by Target in a tax-free disposition of its assets are generally not recognized because it is liquidated and gain is recognized only if boot property received in the reorganization is retained by the target corporation. Losses realized on asset dispositions are not recognized. When Target is liquidated, it recognizes no gain or loss when making a distribution of stock or debt received in the reorganization to its shareholders or creditors. It must recognize gain (but not loss) when other property (e.g., nonmoney boot property) is distributed to a shareholder or creditor.

TAX CONSEQUENCES FOR ACQUIRING CORPORATION. Acquiring Corporation does not recognize gain or loss when its stock is issued in exchange for property in either a taxable or tax-free transaction. Assets that are received in a taxable transaction have their tax basis adjusted upward or downward to their acquisition cost. The holding period for the acquired assets commences on the day after the transaction date. If the assets are acquired in a tax-free reorganization, their bases are generally the same as they were on Target's books because a basis step-up is permitted only when the target corporation receives boot property that it retains, and thereby recognizes a gain. Acquiring's holding period tacks on to Target's holding period.

Because a taxable acquisition is treated as a purchase transaction, all of Target's tax attributes (e.g., a net operating loss [NOL] carryover) disappear when it is liquidated. On the other hand, the tax attributes are acquired in a tax-free reorganization.

TAX CONSEQUENCES FOR TARGET CORPORATION'S SHAREHOLDERS. When Target Corporation is liquidated as part of a taxable acquisition, its shareholders recognize gain or loss on the surrender of their stock. The assets received take a basis equal to their FMV. A tax-free reorganization requires the shareholder to recognize gain

Topic Review C7-1

Section 338 Deemed Liquidation

Election Requirements

1. The acquiring corporation must have made a qualified stock purchase (i.e., a purchase of 80% or more of the target corporation's voting stock and 80% or more of the total value of all stock within a twelve-month period). Certain nonvoting preferred stock issues are excluded from the 80% requirements.
2. Stock acquisitions involving substituted basis (e.g., tax-free reorganizations, corporate formations, and gifts), transfers at death, or related parties do not count toward the 80% minimum.
3. The election must be made not later than the fifteenth day of the ninth month beginning after the month in which the acquisition date occurs. The acquisition date is the first date on which the 80% stock ownership requirement is met.

Tax Consequences of a Sec. 338 Election

1. The old target corporation is treated as having sold all of its assets to the new target corporation at their FMV in a single transaction at the close of the acquisition date. Gain or loss is recognized on the sale by the old target corporation.
2. The new target corporation takes a basis for the assets equal to the sum of the acquiring corporation's basis for its stock interest in the target corporation on the day following the acquisition date, the target corporation's liabilities on the day following the acquisition date, and other relevant items (e.g., contingent liabilities that become fixed).
3. This total basis is allocated to the individual assets using the residual method. The residual method allocates the basis first to cash and near-cash items, other tangible and intangible assets, and finally to goodwill and going concern value.
4. The tax attributes of the old target corporation disappear with the deemed liquidation.
5. The new target corporation makes new tax year and accounting method elections.

ADDITIONAL COMMENT

For publicly traded companies, the pooling method usually is more desirable because it provides a higher net income. This preference is due to the required restatement of assets to their acquisition cost, including the recording and subsequent amortization of goodwill under the purchase accounting method. Consequently, in the planning of the transaction, qualifying for a particular financial accounting treatment may be more important than the tax consequences.

only to the extent that boot is received. The gain is generally taxed as a capital gain, although dividend income may be reported in certain situations. The stocks and securities received take a substituted basis that references the basis of the Target stocks and securities surrendered. The basis of any boot property is its FMV.

ACCOUNTING FOR THE ACQUISITION. Not all of the variables used in choosing between taxable or tax-free acquisitions relate to the tax consequences. A taxable acquisition generally is reported for financial accounting purposes using purchase accounting.[21] A tax-free reorganization generally is reported for financial accounting purposes by using the pooling method. However, because of the stringent pooling requirements, some tax-free reorganizations are not eligible for pooling treatment. These two methods can result in substantial differences in the way Acquiring reports the prior and future results of the combined activities. These reporting differences can influence how the acquisition transaction is structured.

Topic Review C7-2 presents a comparison of taxable and tax-free asset acquisition transactions.

[21] For a discussion of the purchase and pooling methods of accounting, see F.A. Beams, *Advanced Accounting*, 6th ed. (Englewood Cliffs, NJ: Prentice Hall, 1996), Chap. 1.

Topic Review C7-2

Comparison of Taxable and Tax-Free Asset Acquisitions

Variable	Taxable Acquisition	Tax-Free Reorganization
1. Consideration employed to effect acquisition	Primarily cash and debt instruments; may involve some stock of the acquiring corporation or its parent corporation.	Primarily stock and limited cash or debt of the acquiring corporation or its parent corporation.
2. Target Corporation		
a. Amount of gain or loss	All gains and losses are recognized.	Gain recognized on an asset transfer only when boot property is received and retained by the target corporation. Gain (but not loss) may be recognized on the distribution of boot property or property retained by the target corporation.
b. Character of gain or loss	Depends on nature of each asset transferred or distributed.	Depends on nature of each asset transferred or distributed.
c. Recapture provisions	Sec. 1245 or 1250 gains are recaptured.	Secs. 1245 or 1250 do not apply unless boot triggers the recognition of gain.
3. Acquiring Corporation		
a. Gain or loss when stock is issued for property	None recognized.	None recognized.
b. Basis of acquired assets	Cost.	Same as on target corporation's books, increased by gain recognized.
c. Holding period of acquired assets	Commences on day after the transaction date.	Includes holding period of the target corporation.
d. Acquisition of target corporation's tax attributes	No.	Yes.
e. Accounting for the acquisition	Purchase accounting is generally used.	"Pooling" accounting is generally used; transaction may require that purchase accounting be used.
4. Target Corporation's shareholders		
a. Amount of gain or loss	Realized gain or loss is recognized.	Gain is recognized to the extent of boot received; losses are not recognized.
b. Character of gain or loss	Capital gain or loss; may be Sec. 1244 loss.	Dividend income and/or capital gain.
c. Basis of stock and securities received	Cost; generally FMV of stock, securities, or other property received.	Substituted basis from the stock and securities surrendered; FMV for boot property.
d. Holding period of stock and securities received	Commences on day after the transaction date.	Includes holding period for the stock and securities surrendered; Day after the transaction date for boot property.

COMPARISON OF TAXABLE AND TAX-FREE STOCK ACQUISITIONS

Continuing our comparison of taxable and tax-free transactions, let's look at stock acquisitions. For purposes of our discussion, assume that Acquiring Corporation acquires all of Target Corporation's stock. Target becomes a controlled subsidiary of Acquiring. If Acquiring uses cash, debt obligations, and its stock to make the purchase, the acquisition is taxable. If Acquiring acquires all of Target's stock using solely its voting stock or voting stock of its parent corporation to effect the transaction, the acquisition qualifies as a tax-free reorganization.

KEY POINT

It is important to realize that in a tax-free or taxable stock acquisition, the transaction is between the acquiring corporation and the shareholders of the target. Because the target corporation is not directly involved in the transaction, the bases of target's assets are not affected.

TAX CONSEQUENCES FOR TARGET CORPORATION. Target Corporation's basis for its assets does not change as a result of either a taxable or tax-free transaction. Any depreciation recapture potential existing on the transaction date stays with Target's assets and is, therefore, assumed by the purchaser. If Target has loss or credit carryovers, these carryovers are retained and may be subject to special limitations in its post-acquisition tax years.

If Acquiring Corporation is part of an affiliated group that is filing a consolidated tax return, then Target must join in the consolidated return election if at least 80% of its stock is owned and Target is an includible corporation. Otherwise, Acquiring and Target can elect to make an initial consolidated tax return election.

TAX CONSEQUENCES FOR ACQUIRING CORPORATION. Acquiring Corporation does not recognize gain or loss when its stock is issued in exchange for property in either a taxable or tax-free transaction. Acquiring's basis for the stock in a taxable acquisition is its acquisition cost. The taxable stock acquisition may qualify as a purchase for purposes of the Sec. 338 deemed liquidation election. In a tax-free reorganization, Acquiring's basis for the stock is the same as it was in the hands of Target's shareholders.

TAX CONSEQUENCES FOR TARGET CORPORATION'S SHAREHOLDERS. The gain recognized on a taxable sale transaction is capital gain if the stock is a capital asset in the seller's hands. The seller's gain can be reported using the installment method of accounting if part or all of the consideration is deferred into a later year and the stock is not traded on an established securities market. Consideration received by the seller that represents compensation for an agreement with the purchaser not to compete for a specified time period is taxable as ordinary income.

Because only voting stock is used in a tax-free stock acquisition, no gain or loss is recognized by Target's shareholders. The shareholders take a carryover basis for the Acquiring stock that is the same as their basis in the Target stock.

ACCOUNTING FOR THE TRANSACTION. A taxable acquisition of Target Corporation stock is reported for financial accounting purposes using purchase accounting. A tax-free stock-for-stock reorganization ordinarily satisfies the pooling method requirements. Because only 50% stock ownership by a parent corporation is needed for a subsidiary's inclusion in a set of consolidated financial statements, some parent-subsidiary relationships may permit consolidation for financial accounting purposes yet not satisfy the 80% minimums needed for consolidation for tax purposes.

A comparison of the taxable and tax-free stock acquisitions is presented in Topic Review C7-3.

Topic Review C7-3

Comparison of Taxable and Tax-Free Stock Acquisitions

Variable	Taxable Acquisition	Tax-free Reorganization
1. Consideration employed to effect acquisition	Primarily cash and debt instruments; may involve some stock of the acquiring corporation or its parent corporation.	Solely voting stock of the acquiring corporation or its parent corporation.
2. Target Corporation		
a. Parent-subsidiary relationship established	Yes.	Yes.
b. Consolidated tax return election available	Yes.	Yes.
c. Basis for assets	Unchanged by stock acquisition unless a Sec. 338 election is made.	Unchanged by stock acquisition. No Sec. 338 election available.
d. Tax attributes	Retained by Target Corporation.	Retained by Target Corporation.
3. Acquiring Corporation		
a. Basis for stock acquired	Cost basis.	Carryover basis from Target's shareholders.
4. Target Corporation's shareholders		
a. Amount of gain or loss recognized	Realized gain or loss is recognized.	No boot is received; therefore, no gain is recognized.
b. Character of gain or loss	Capital gain or loss; may be Sec. 1244 loss.	Not applicable.
c. Basis of stock	Cost; generally FMV of stock, securities, or other property received.	Substituted basis from stock surrendered.
d. Holding period of stock and securities received	Commences on day after the transaction date.	Includes holding period for the stock surrendered.

TYPES OF REORGANIZATIONS

OBJECTIVE 3

Explain the types of tax-free reorganizations and their requirements

Section 368(a)(1) authorizes seven types of reorganizations to accommodate the major forms of business acquisitions, divestitures, and restructurings. Generally, tax practitioners refer to the specific type of reorganization by the subparagraph of Sec. 368(a)(1) that contains its definition. For example, a merger transaction is referred to as a *Type A* reorganization because it is defined in Sec. 368(a)(1)(A). The seven types of reorganizations can also be classified according to the nature of the transaction, with the most common forms being acquisitive transactions and divisive transactions. An **acquisitive reorganization** is a transaction where the acquiring corporation obtains part or all of the assets or stock of a target (or transferor) corporation. Types A, B, C, D, and G reorganizations can be classified as acquisitive transactions. A **divisive reorganization** is a transaction in which part of a transferor corporation's assets are transferred to a second corporation that is controlled by either the transferor or its shareholders. The controlled (or transferee) corporation's stock or securities that are received in exchange

TYPICAL MISCONCEPTION

For an acquisition to qualify for tax-free treatment, the transaction must be a reorganization. The term *reorganization* includes only transactions specifically enumerated in Sec. 368. Other transactions that may constitute reorganizations in a more general context are not considered tax-free reorganizations.

REFERENCE POINT

A summary of the acquisitive reorganizations is presented below:

Type	*Description*
A	Merger or consolidation
B	Stock-for-stock
C	Asset-for-stock
D	Asset-for-stock
G	Bankruptcy

for the assets are distributed as part of a reorganization plan to the transferor corporation's shareholders. The transferor corporation can either remain in existence or be liquidated. If the transferor corporation remains in existence, its assets end up being divided between at least two corporations. Type D and G reorganizations can be either acquisitive or divisive transactions.

Two reorganization forms are neither acquisitive or divisive. Type E and F reorganizations involve a single corporation that does *not* acquire additional assets and does *not* transfer a portion of its assets to a transferee corporation. The Type E reorganization—a recapitalization—involves changes to a corporation's capital structure. Type F reorganizations—a change in identity, legal form, or state of incorporation—may involve the transfer of the assets of an existing corporation to a new corporation, but the shareholders of the transferor corporation generally retain the same equity interest in the transferee corporation.

Not all reorganization transactions fit neatly into one of the seven classifications. In fact, some reorganizations may satisfy the requirements for two or more of the classifications. If this occurs, the Code or the IRS generally determines which reorganization rules prevail. In other transactions, a reorganization may satisfy the literal requirements of one of the classifications, but for other reasons the courts may find that an entirely different tax treatment results (e.g., if the transaction lacks a business purpose, it may be a taxable transaction). Further discussion of these problems is presented in the next section.

TAX CONSEQUENCES OF REORGANIZATIONS

OBJECTIVE 4

Determine the tax consequences of a tax-free reorganization to the target corporation

TYPICAL MISCONCEPTION

One perplexing aspect of the tax-free reorganization provisions is the overlap between the different statutory reorganizations. One transaction can often qualify as more than one type of tax-free reorganization.

This portion of the chapter examines the tax consequences of a tax-free reorganization to the target (or transferor) corporation, the acquiring (or transferee) corporation, and the shareholders and security holders.[22]

TARGET OR TRANSFEROR CORPORATION

RECOGNITION OF GAIN OR LOSS ON ASSET TRANSFER. Section 361(a) prevents the target corporation from having to recognize gain or loss on any exchange of property that occurs as part of a tax-free reorganization where only stock of another corporation that is a party to the reorganization is received.[23] No gain is recognized under Sec. 361(b) if the target corporation also receives money or nonmoney boot property as part of the reorga-nization and it distributes such property to its shareholders or creditors. The realized gain that is recognized equals the amount of money plus the FMV of any boot property (other than money) received in the exchange that is not distributed. Because most acquisitive and divisive reorganizations require the target corporation to be liquidated, boot is not generally retained and thus no gain is recognized by the target corporation.

[22] The corporation that transfers its assets as part of a reorganization is referred to as either a **target** or **transferor corporation**. The term target corporation is generally used with an acquisitive reorganization where substantially all of a corporation's assets are acquired by the acquiring corporation. The term *transferor corporation* is used with divisive and other reorganizations where only part of a corporation's assets are transferred to a transferee corporation and the transferor corporation may remain in existence. Tax law provisions are generally applied the same to target or transferor corporations and acquiring or transferee corporations, so only a single reference to the target or acquiring corporation is generally provided in connection with an explanation.

[23] Section 361(a) permits securities (e.g., long-term debt obligations) to be received tax-free when the same face amount of securities, or a larger amount, is surrendered by the target corporation. Generally, a securities exchange does not occur in an acquisitive reorganization, so all debt obligations that are received are boot property.

EXAMPLE C7-10 ▶ Target Corporation transfers assets having a $175,000 adjusted basis to Acquiring Corporation in exchange for $400,000 of Acquiring common stock as part of a tax-free reorganization. Target realizes a $225,000 gain ($400,000 amount realized − $175,000 adjusted basis) on the asset transfer. Because no boot is received by Target, none of the gain is recognized. If Target instead receives $350,000 of Acquiring common stock and $50,000 of money, no gain is recognized by Target if the boot property is distributed to its shareholders. ◀

TYPICAL MISCONCEPTION

Often taxpayers do not realize that Sec. 361 applies to two exchanges. Section 361(a) applies to the exchange between Acquiring and Target (which has already been discussed). Section 361(c) deals with the exchange between Target and Target's shareholders. Therefore, Target is the only party to the reorganization that may recognize two separate gains.

SELF-STUDY QUESTION

How can Target distribute appreciated boot property to its shareholders if Target receives a FMV basis in all such property received from Acquiring?

ANSWER

If the property appreciates in the hands of Target before it is distributed, gain will result. In addition, Target may retain some of its own assets and distribute these assets to its shareholders. Consistent with Secs. 311(b) and 336(a), distributing appreciated property causes gain recognition by Target.

DEPRECIATION RECAPTURE. The depreciation recapture rules of Secs. 1245 and 1250 do not override the nonrecognition of gain or loss rules of Sec. 361.[24] The recapture potential that accrues before the asset transfer carries over to the acquiring corporation and is recognized when the acquiring corporation sells or exchanges the assets in a taxable transaction.

ASSUMPTION OF LIABILITIES. Neither the acquiring corporation's assumption of the target corporation's liabilities nor the acquisition of the target corporation's property subject to a liability will trigger the recognition of gain on the asset transfer. Section 357(c) requires the target corporation to recognize gain if the sum of the liabilities assumed or acquired exceeds the total adjusted bases of the properties that are transferred *and* the tax-free reorganization is either an acquisitive or a divisive Type D reorganization. An additional explanation of the Sec. 357(c) rules is presented in connection with the discussion of the acquisitive Type D reorganization.

RECOGNITION OF GAIN OR LOSS ON DISTRIBUTION OF STOCK AND SECURITIES. No gain or loss is recognized by the target corporation when it distributes either (1) its stock, stock rights, or obligations or (2) any stock, stock rights, and obligations of a party to a reorganization that are received in the reorganization to its shareholders or creditors as part of the plan of reorganization (see page C7-54 for an explanation of a plan of reorganization).[25] Distributions of nonmoney boot property (including property retained by the target corporation) made pursuant to the reorganization plan requires the recognition of gain (but not loss) in the same manner as if such property were sold by the target corporation at its FMV.[26] Normally the gain that is recognized when boot property is distributed is small because of the short amount of time that passes between when it is received from the acquiring corporation (and takes a basis equal to its FMV) and when it is distributed to a shareholder.

EXAMPLE C7-11 ▶ Target Corporation transfers all of its assets and liabilities to Acquiring Corporation as part of its being merged into Acquiring (a Type A reorganization). To effect the merger, Acquiring transfers $300,000 of its common stock and $100,000 of money to Target in exchange for Target's assets. Target's basis for the assets is $250,000. Target realizes a $150,000 gain on the asset transfer [($300,000 + $100,000) − $250,000]. None of this gain is recognized by Target, even though boot is received, because Target must be liquidated as part of the merger transaction. Target's distribution of the Acquiring stock to its shareholders as part of the reorganization does not trigger the recognition of any gain by Target. Gain may be recognized by Target shareholders who receive money. ◀

---

[24] Secs. 1245(b)(3) and 1250(d)(3). Similar provisions are found as part of the other recapture rules.

[25] Secs. 361(c)(1)–(c)(3).

[26] Sec. 361(c).

OBJECTIVE 5

Determine the tax consequences of a tax-free reorganization to the acquiring corporation

SELF-STUDY QUESTION

Because Acquiring is merely purchasing assets, can Acquiring ever recognize gain or loss on the transaction?

ANSWER

Yes. If Acquiring uses nonmoney boot property, gain or loss will be recognized to the extent of the built-in gain or loss in such property (Sec. 361(c)(2)).

ACQUIRING OR TRANSFEREE CORPORATION

AMOUNT OF GAIN OR LOSS RECOGNIZED. Section 1032 prevents the acquiring corporation from recognizing gain or loss when it receives money or other property in exchange for its stock as part of a tax-free reorganization. Similarly, no gain or loss is recognized when a corporation receives money or other property in exchange for its securities as part of a tax-free reorganization.

BASIS OF ACQUIRED PROPERTY. Section 362(b) requires property acquired in a tax-free reorganization to take a carryover basis for the property from the target corporation's books, increased by the amount of gain recognized by the target corporation on the exchange. Because no gain or loss is generally recognized by the target corporation on the asset transfer, no step up in basis is ordinarily obtained.

EXAMPLE C7-12 ▶ Assume the same facts as in Example C7-11. Acquiring's basis for the acquired properties is the same as Target Corporation's basis, or $250,000. ◀

HOLDING PERIOD OF ACQUIRED PROPERTY. The acquiring corporation's holding period for the acquired properties includes the target corporation's holding period for the properties.[27]

OBJECTIVE 6

Determine the tax consequences of a tax-free reorganization to the target corporation's shareholders and security holders

KEY POINT

As with other nonrecognition provisions, a shareholder's recognized gain is the lesser of his or her realized gain or boot (money plus the FMV of other property) received.

SHAREHOLDERS AND SECURITY HOLDERS

AMOUNT OF GAIN OR LOSS RECOGNIZED. Section 354(a) requires that no gain or loss be recognized if stock or securities in a corporation that is a party to a reorganization are, in pursuance of a plan of reorganization, exchanged solely for stock or securities in the same corporation, or for stock or securities of another corporation that is a party to the reorganization. The receipt of property other than stock or securities (nonqualifying property) does not automatically disqualify the transaction from tax-free treatment. Section 356(a) requires that the shareholder or security holder recognize gain to the extent of the lesser of the realized gain or the amount of money received plus the FMV of any other property received. Gain is thus recognized to the extent that nonqualifying property is received that does not represent a continuation of the former equity interest.

EXAMPLE C7-13 ▶ Brian exchanges 1,000 shares of Target Corporation stock having a $13,000 basis for Acquiring Corporation stock having a $28,000 FMV as part of a tax-free reorganization. Brian's realized gain is $15,000 ($28,000 − $13,000), none of which is recognized. If Brian had instead received $25,000 of Acquiring stock and $3,000 of cash, his realized gain would remain $15,000, but Brian must now recognize a $3,000 gain. ◀

ADDITIONAL COMMENT

Acquiring may increase its basis in the assets received only by the gain recognized by Target on its exchange with Acquiring. Any gain recognized by Target on its distribution to Target's shareholders is not reflected anywhere.

TYPICAL MISCONCEPTION

Section 354 is applied to each shareholder individually. Therefore, it is possible for one shareholder to recognize gain while another shareholder recognizes no gain.

With some limitations, the general rule of Sec. 354(a) permits a tax-free exchange of stocks and securities. The receipt of securities is completely tax-free only if the principal amount of the securities that are surrendered equals or exceeds the principal amount of the securities that are received. If the principal amount of the securities received exceeds the principal amount of the securities surrendered, the FMV of the "excess" principal amount of the securities that are received constitutes boot.[28] If no securities are surrendered, the FMV of the entire principal amount of the securities received constitutes boot.

[27] Sec. 1223(1).

[28] Secs. 354(a)(2) and 356(d)(2)(B). The FMV of the debt obligations that are surrendered is irrelevant when determining the amount of the recognized gain.

EXAMPLE C7-14 ▶

Assume the same facts as in Example C7-13 except that Brian instead receives Acquiring Corporation securities having a $3,000 principal amount and a $2,850 FMV. Brian's realized gain is $14,850 [($25,000 + $2,850) − $13,000], of which $2,850 is recognized. The result would be much the same if Brian had received $3,000 in Acquiring securities and surrendered $2,000 of Target securities. Then the FMV of the $1,000 "excess" principal amount, or $950 [$1,000 × ($2,850 FMV/$3,000 principal)], is treated as boot. ◀

SELF-STUDY QUESTION

In addition to receiving stock in Acquiring, shareholder Sue receives securities with a FMV of $120,000 and a principal amount of $100,000. In the exchange, Sue surrenders securities of Target with a FMV and principal amount of $80,000. Is Sue treated as having received any boot?

ANSWER

Yes. $100,000 − $80,000 = $20,000 of excess principal amount received. The boot received is $24,000. This amount represents the FMV of the excess principal amount ($20,000/$100,000 × $120,000).

TYPICAL MISCONCEPTION

Before the *Clark* decision, the IRS looked to Target's E&P to measure the amount of dividend income. The IRS has thus far declined to rule whether they have changed this position because *Clark* treats the receipt of boot as a redemption between the Target shareholder and the Acquiring corporation.

CHARACTER OF THE RECOGNIZED GAIN. Section 356(a)(2) requires that the recognized gain be characterized as dividend income if the receipt of the boot property has the same effect as the distribution of a dividend. The dividend income that is recognized equals the lesser of the shareholder's recognized gain or the shareholder's ratable share of the acquiring corporation's current and accumulated earnings and profits (E&P). Any additional gain that must be recognized generally is reported as a capital gain.

The Sec. 302(b) stock redemption rules are used to test whether the exchange has the effect of a dividend distribution.[29] (See Chapter C4 for a review of the Sec. 302(b) rules.) Tax-free reorganizations do not generally involve actual redemptions of the stock of the target corporation's shareholders. Instead, the Supreme Court in its *Donald E. Clark* decision held that a shareholder is treated as having exchanged his or her target corporation stock in a tax-free reorganization solely for stock in the acquiring corporation. After having received the acquiring corporation's stock, a hypothetical redemption (but no actual stock redemption) of a portion of the acquiring corporation's stock occurs. Capital gain treatment results only if the boot that is received causes the hypothetical redemption to qualify for exchange treatment under Sec. 302(b).

Application of the dividend equivalency test that is used when boot is received in a tax-free reorganization is illustrated in the following example.

EXAMPLE C7-15 ▶

Betty owns all 60 of the outstanding shares of Fisher Corporation stock. Fisher Corporation is merged with Gulf Corporation in a tax-free reorganization, with Betty receiving 35 shares of Gulf stock worth $350,000 and $250,000 in money. The remaining 100 shares of Gulf stock are owned by four individuals. Betty's Fisher stock has a $200,000 basis. Fisher and Gulf Corporations have E&P balances of $300,000 and $500,000, respectively. Betty's realized gain is $400,000 [($350,000 stock + $250,000 money)− $200,000 adjusted basis], of which $250,000 must be recognized because the money is treated as boot property.

The Fisher stock is initially treated as having been exchanged for only Gulf stock. Because the Fisher stock is worth $600,000 and the Gulf stock is worth $10,000 per share ($350,000 ÷ 35), Betty is initially treated as owning 60 of the 160 (100 + 60) shares of Gulf stock that are supposedly outstanding immediately after the stock-for-stock swap. The $250,000 in money that Betty receives is treated as having been exchanged for 25 ($250,000 ÷ $10,000 per share) of the 60 shares of Gulf stock that would have been received in an all-stock transaction. Because Betty owns 37.5% of the Gulf stock before the hypothetical redemption (60 shares ÷ 160 shares) and 25.93% (35 shares ÷ 135 shares) after the hypothetical redemption, the $250,000 gain is characterized as capital gain under the substantially disproportionate redemption rules (i.e., 25.93% is less than 80% × 37.5% = 30%). ◀

The Sec. 302(b) test would be applied in the same manner if securities were received in the reorganization. In such a case, the boot portion of the transaction would equal the FMV of the "excess" principal amount received by the shareholder or security holder.

Whether capital gain treatment is available for boot received in a reorganization depends on the relative sizes of the target and acquiring corporations. If the acquiring

[29] *CIR v. Donald E. Clark*, 63 AFTR 2d 89-1437, 89-1 USTC ¶9230 (USSC, 1989). The IRS has agreed to follow the *Clark* decision in Rev. Rul. 93-61, 1993-2 C.B. 118.

corporation is larger than the target corporation, then generally the Sec. 302(b)(2) (substantially disproportionate redemption) or Sec. 302(b)(1) (not essentially equivalent to a dividend) rules will provide for capital gain treatment. If the acquiring corporation is smaller than the target corporation, it is possible that the target corporation's shareholder may be considered as having received dividend income or a combination of dividend income or capital gain (e.g., if the boot received exceeds the shareholder's ratable share of E&P).

SELF-STUDY QUESTION

From the point of view of the Target shareholder, what is the preferable characterization of gain recognized in a reorganization?

ANSWER

It depends. If the Target shareholder is a corporate shareholder, the best result is generally a dividend because of the dividends-received deduction. Currently, with a rate differential for capital gains of up to 11.6 percentage points, an individual shareholder will prefer capital gain treatment.

Capital gain treatment may be preferred by individual shareholders for the recognized gain because a 28% maximum tax rate applies to long-term capital gains, which is less than the 39.6% maximum rate applicable to ordinary income. Dividend income treatment may be preferred by corporate shareholders because they can claim a 70%, 80%, or 100% dividends-received deduction to reduce their tax burden. In addition, capital gains that are recognized in the reorganization can offset capital losses recognized by corporate and noncorporate shareholders in other transactions. Finally, Sec. 453(f)(6)(C) permits a corporate or noncorporate shareholder involved in a tax-free reorganization to use the installment method of accounting to defer the reporting of the gain recognized when securities are received, provided such gain is not characterized as a dividend.[30]

STOP & THINK

Question: The character of the shareholder's recognized gain is determined by applying the Sec. 302(b) stock redemption rules. Why are the relative sizes of the acquiring and target corporations important when determining the character of the gain recognized in a tax-free reorganization?

Solution: A shareholder receives capital gain treatment for his or her recognized gain when the hypothetical redemption qualifies for exchange treatment under the Sec. 302(b) rules. If the target corporation is smaller than the acquiring corporation, the receipt of boot should almost always qualify under one of the capital gains exceptions since no shareholder(s) will generally own more than 50% of the acquiring corporation's stock before and after the hypothetical redemption. If the boot is distributed proportionate to the stock ownership, the target corporation's shareholder(s) should see a reduction in his or her pre-and post-redemption interests. However, if the target corporation is larger than the acquiring corporation, it is possible that a shareholder(s) may own more than 50% of the acquiring corporation's stock, thereby causing the boot to be characterized as a dividend. Classification of the boot as a dividend prevents the preferential capital gains rules from applying to an individual shareholder.

KEY POINT

When a reorganization is tax-free, shareholders defer their realized gain or loss. Consequently, they take a substituted basis in the new nonrecognition property received (i.e., any deferred gain or loss is reflected in the basis of the nonrecognition property received).

BASIS OF STOCKS AND SECURITIES RECEIVED. The basis of the stocks and securities (nonrecognition property) that are received by the target corporation's shareholders and security holders is determined according to the Sec. 358 rules that were introduced in Chapter C2. The basis of these properties is determined as follows:

Adjusted basis of the stocks and securities exchanged
Plus: Any gain recognized on the exchange
Minus: Money received in the exchange
FMV of any property (other than money) received in the exchange

Basis of the nonrecognition property received

[30] *King Enterprises, Inc. v. U.S.*, 24 AFTR 2d 69-5866, 69-2 USTC ¶9720 (Ct. Cls., 1969).

If no boot is received by the shareholder or security holder, the stocks and securities will take a substituted basis from the stocks and securities that are exchanged. If a gain must be recognized, the basis of the stocks and securities that are exchanged is increased by the amount of such gain and then reduced by the amount of money plus the FMV of any other boot property received in the reorganization. The basis of any other boot property received is its FMV.

EXAMPLE C7-16 ▶ Ken owns Target Corporation stock having a $10,000 adjusted basis. As part of a tax-free reorganization involving Target and Acquiring Corporations, Ken exchanges his Target stock for $12,000 of Acquiring stock and $4,000 of Acquiring securities. Ken realizes a $6,000 gain [($12,000 + $4,000) − $10,000], of which $4,000 must be recognized. The basis of the Acquiring securities is $4,000. The basis of the Acquiring stock is $10,000 ($10,000 basis of Target stock + $4,000 gain recognized − $4,000 FMV of Acquiring securities). ◀

When the target corporation's shareholders own a single class of stock (or a single class of securities) and end up owning two or more classes of stock or securities as a result of a tax-free reorganization, the total basis for the nonrecognition property determined above must be allocated between the stocks and/or the securities owned in proportion to the relative FMVs of the classes.[31]

HOLDING PERIOD. The holding period of the stocks and securities that are nonrecognition property includes the holding period for the stocks and securities that are surrendered. The holding period for boot property commences on the day following the exchange date.[32]

Topic Review C7-4 presents a summary of the tax consequences of a tax-free reorganization to the target corporation, the acquiring corporation, and the target corporation's shareholders and security holders.

ACQUISITIVE REORGANIZATIONS

This portion of the chapter is devoted to the Types A, B, C, D, and G acquisitive reorganizations. Each of these types of reorganizations is explained below. A summary of the requirements for the acquisitive reorganizations is presented in Topic Review C7-5 on page C7-25.

TYPE A REORGANIZATION

The Code permits four kinds of **Type A reorganizations**: mergers, consolidations, triangular mergers, and reverse triangular mergers. Each of these transactions is described below, although the first two are the most important.

KEY POINT

The A reorganization is unique in comparison to the other statutory reorganizations because state law, rather than federal law, is an important factor in determining whether a transaction qualifies as a tax-free merger.

MERGER OR CONSOLIDATION. A Type A reorganization is a **merger** or a **consolidation** that satisfies the corporation laws of the United States, a state, or the District of Columbia.[33] Figure C7-1 illustrates a merger. Two types of mergers have been accepted by the IRS. The first involves the acquiring corporation transferring its stock, securities, and other consideration (boot) to the target corporation in exchange for its assets and liabilities. The acquiring corporation stock, securities, and other consideration

[31] Reg. Sec. 1.358-2(a)(2)-(4).
[32] Sec. 1223(1).
[33] Sec. 368(a)(1)(A) and Reg. Sec. 1.368-2(b)(1).

Topic Review C7-4

Tax Consequences of a Tax-Free Reorganization

Target Corporation

1. No gain or loss is recognized by the target corporation on the asset transfer except to the extent that money or other boot property is received and retained by the target corporation (Secs. 361(a)–(b)). Generally boot is not retained because the target corporation is usually liquidated.
2. The character of any gain or loss that is recognized depends on the nature of the assets transferred.
3. The acquiring corporation's assumption or acquisition of target corporation liabilities does not trigger the recognition of gain on the asset transfer except to the extent that Sec. 357(c) applies to "excess" liability situations involving Type D reorganizations (Sec. 357(a)).
4. No gain or loss is recognized by the target corporation when it distributes qualified property (i.e., stock and securities) to its shareholders and security holders. Gain may be recognized when boot property or retained assets are distributed to shareholders or security holders (Sec. 361(c)).

Acquiring Corporation

1. The acquiring corporation does not recognize gain or loss when it receives money or property in exchange for its stock or debt obligations (Sec. 1032).
2. The basis of the acquired property equals its basis in the transferor's hands increased by any gain recognized by the transferor (Sec. 362(b)).
3. The acquiring corporation's holding period for the acquired properties includes the transferor's holding period (Sec. 1223(1)).

Shareholders and Security Holders

1. No gain or loss is recognized if only stock is received (Sec. 354(a)). Gain (but not loss) is recognized when money, excess securities, or other boot property is received. The amount of the recognized gain equals the lesser of the realized gain or the amount of money plus the FMV of any other boot property received (Sec. 356(b)).
2. The character of the gain recognized is determined by applying the Sec. 302(b) rules to the acquiring corporation. Dividend income recognized, however, cannot exceed the shareholder's ratable share of the acquiring corporation's E&P (Sec. 356(a)(2)).
3. The total basis of the stocks and securities received equals the adjusted basis of the stocks and securities exchanged plus any gain recognized on the exchange minus the sum of the money and the FMV of other boot property received. This basis is allocated to the stocks and securities received based on their relative FMVs. The basis of boot property is its FMV (Sec. 358(a)).
4. The holding period of stocks and securities received includes the holding period of the stocks and securities surrendered. The holding period for boot property commences on the day following the exchange date (Sec. 1223(1)).

received by the target corporation are distributed to its shareholders and security holders in exchange for their target corporation stock and securities. The target corporation then goes out of existence. This type of merger is illustrated in Figure C7-1. The second type of merger involves the acquiring corporation exchanging its stock, securities, and other

ADDITIONAL COMMENT

The actual exchange of Acquiring stock for Target stock may be different from the illustrations provided in this chapter. These illustrations represent how the Code construes the steps in each of the reorganizations. As a practical matter, the exchange of stock between Acquiring and Target is usually performed by an independent stock transfer agent rather than flowing from Acquiring to Target and finally to Target's shareholders.

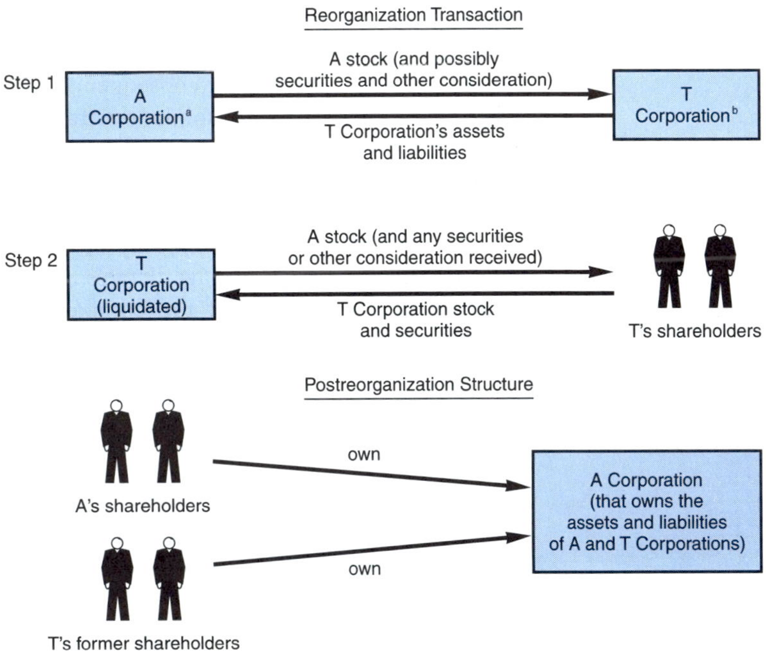

FIGURE C7-1 ▶ TYPE A REORGANIZATION—MERGER

consideration directly for the stock and securities held by the target corporation's shareholders and security holders. The acquiring corporation then liquidates the target corporation and acquires its assets and liabilities.[34]

A consolidation, illustrated in Figure C7-2, involves two or more corporations having their assets acquired by a new corporation. The stock, securities, and other consideration transferred by the acquiring corporation is distributed by each target corporation to its shareholders and security holders pursuant to its liquidation in exchange for its own stock and securities. This type of consolidation is illustrated in Figure C7-2. As with a merger, an alternative form of consolidation is permitted in which the acquiring corporation directly transfers its stock, securities, and other consideration to the target corporations' shareholders and security holders in exchange for their stock and securities. In this case, each target corporation is then liquidated, with the acquiring corporation receiving its assets and liabilities.

KEY POINT

The Type A reorganization is the most flexible reorganization with respect to the type of consideration that must be used. The only requirement that must be satisfied is the continuity of interest test, which is discussed later in the chapter.

Requirements for Mergers and Consolidations. The Type A reorganization provides the acquiring corporation with the greatest flexibility in selecting the consideration to be used to effect the reorganization. Section 368 places no restrictions on the types of consideration that can be used in a merger. The IRS interpretation of the continuity of interest judicial doctrine for a tax-free reorganization requires stock of the acquiring corporation to be at least 50% of the total consideration used.[35] The stock that is used can be voting stock, nonvoting stock, or a combination of the two. Either common or preferred stock may be used. The 50% minimum must be met only if the

[34] Rev. Rul. 69-6, 1969-1 C.B. 104.

[35] Rev. Proc. 77-37, 1977-2 C.B. 568, Sec. 3.02.

taxpayer desires to obtain a favorable advance ruling regarding the tax consequences of the transaction (see page C7-55 for a discussion of why a taxpayer might want to obtain an advance ruling and the tax consequences of proceeding without a ruling).

Because a merger or consolidation transaction must comply with state or federal corporation laws, transactions that qualify as mergers or consolidations, and the procedures that must be followed to effect them, vary according to the law of the states in which the acquiring and target corporations are incorporated. Generally, these laws require a favorable vote by a majority of the shareholders of the corporations that are involved in the merger. State law dictates the procedures that must be followed. Where the stock of one or both of the companies is publicly traded, the need to hold a shareholder's meeting, solicit proxies, and obtain the necessary approval may make the procedure both costly and time-consuming.

ADDITIONAL COMMENT

Shareholder approval is time consuming, expensive, and not always possible to obtain.

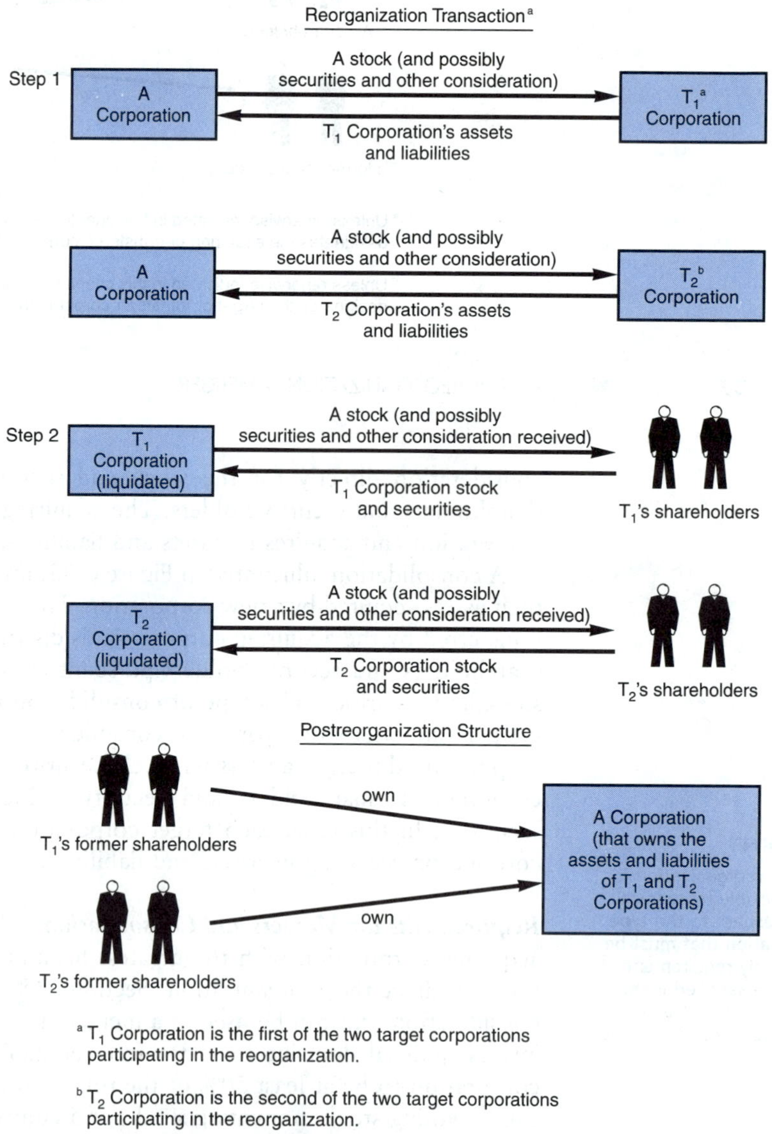

FIGURE C7-2 ▶ TYPE A REORGANIZATION: CONSOLIDATION

Topic Review C7-5

Summary of Major Acquisitive Reorganizations

Type of Reorganization	Target (T) Corporation Property Acquired	Consideration That Can Be Used	What Happens to the Target (T) Corporation?	Shareholders' Recognized Gain	Other Requirements
A—Merger or consolidation	Assets and liabilities of T Corporation.[a]	Voting and nonvoting stock, securities, and other property of A Corporation[b]	T Corporation liquidates as part of the merger.	Lesser of realized gain or boot received	For advance ruling purposes, at least 50% of the consideration employed must be A stock (continuity of interest requirement)
B—Stock for stock	At least 80% of the voting and 80% of the nonvoting T stock.	Voting stock of A Corporation	Remains in existence as a subsidiary of A Corporation.	None	Boot can be used to cause a transaction to be taxable.
C—Assets for stock	Substantially all of the assets of T Corporation (and possibly some or all of its liabilities).	Stock, securities, and other property of A Corporation, provided at least 80% of the assets are acquired for voting stock	Stock, securities, and boot received in the reorganization and all of T's remaining properties must be distributed; as a practical matter, T is usually liquidated.	Lesser of realized gain or boot received	For advance ruling purposes, ''substantially all'' is 70% of the gross assets and 90% of the net assets of T Corporation.
D—Acquisitive	Substantially all of the assets of T Corporation (and possibly some or all of its liabilities) are acquired by a ''controlled''. transferee corporation (A Corporation).	Stock, securities, and other property of A Corporation	Stocks, securities, and boot received in the reorganization and all of T's remaining properties must be distributed; as a practical matter, T is usually liquidated.	Lesser of realized gain or boot received	''Substantially all'' is defined as it was for a Type C reorganization; the continuity of interest requirement also applies here for advance ruling purposes; control is defined as 50% of the voting power or 50% of the value of A's stock.

[a] T Corporation is the target or transferor corporation.
[b] A Corporation is the acquiring or controlled transferee corporation.

The rights of any dissenting shareholders are also dictated by the state law. These shareholders may have the right under state law to dissent and have their shares independently valued and purchased for cash. A substantial number of dissenting shareholders may necessitate a large cash outlay in order to purge their interests and may make the continuity-of-interest doctrine difficult to achieve.

A transaction that fails to satisfy the state corporation laws does not qualify as a merger or consolidation.[36] Generally, this failure causes the acquisition to be a taxable transaction.

Advantages and Disadvantages of a Merger Transaction. A number of advantages and disadvantages exist with a merger transaction.

Advantages:

- A merger allows greater flexibility than other types of reorganizations because there is no restriction that the consideration be solely voting stock, as in the case of some other reorganization forms. Money, securities, assumption of liabilities, and other property can be 50% or more of the total consideration used.
- There is no requirement that substantially all of the assets of the target corporation be acquired. Dispositions of unwanted assets by the target corporation generally do not prevent a merger from being a tax-free reorganization, as in the case of a Type C reorganization.

KEY POINT

Because there is no "substantially all" requirement in a Type A reorganization, the unwanted assets of Target may be disposed of before or after the transaction without disqualifying the tax-free reorganization.

Disadvantages:

- Compliance with state corporation laws is required. In most states, the shareholders of both the acquiring and target corporations have to approve the plan. Such approvals can take time and can be costly. Dissenting shareholders of both corporations also have the right under state law to have their shares independently appraised and purchased for cash, which may require a substantial cash outlay.
- All liabilities of the target corporation must be assumed, including unknown and contingent liabilities.
- A merger requires the transfer of real estate titles, leases, and contracts. The target corporation may have contracts, rights, or other privileges that are nontransferable and may necessitate use of a reverse triangular merger or other reorganization forms that are discussed below.

Tax Consequences of a Merger Transaction. The following example illustrates the tax consequences of a merger transaction.

EXAMPLE C7-17 ▶ Acquiring Corporation acquires all of Target Corporation's assets in a merger transaction that qualifies as a Type A reorganization. Target transfers assets having a FMV and an adjusted basis of $2,000,000 and $1,300,000, respectively, and $400,000 in liabilities to Acquiring in exchange for $1,000,000 of Acquiring's common stock and $600,000 of cash. At the time of the transfer, Acquiring's E&P balance is $1,000,000. Target distributes the Acquiring stock and cash to its sole shareholder, Millie, in exchange for all of her Target stock, which has a $175,000 basis. If Millie had received only Acquiring stock in the reorganization, she would have held 6.25% of the Acquiring stock (100,000 out of 1,600,000 shares) immediately after the reorganization.

---

[36] *Edward H. Russell v. CIR*, 15 AFTR 2d 1107, 65-2 USTC ¶9448 (5th Cir., 1965).

Target realizes a $700,000 gain [($1,000,000 stock + $600,000 cash + $400,000 liabilities) − $1,300,000 adjusted basis] on the asset transfer. None of the gain is recognized by Target. Acquiring takes a $1,300,000 carryover basis for the assets it receives. No gain is recognized by Target when it distributes the stock and cash to Millie. Millie realizes a $1,425,000 gain on the liquidation of Target [($1,000,000 stock + $600,000 cash) − $175,000 adjusted basis], of which $600,000 must be recognized because of the cash that is received. Each share of Acquiring stock is worth $16 ($1,600,000 total consideration ÷ 100,000 shares that would be held if all stock was received). The hypothetical redemption of Millie's Acquiring stock required under Rev. Rul. 93-61 (see page C7-19) qualifies as an exchange under Sec. 302(b)(2) because the redemption of 37,500 ($600,000 cash ÷ $16) shares of Acquiring stock deemed to have been redeemed reduces Millie's interest from 6.25% (100,000 shares ÷ 1,600,000 shares) to 4.00% (62,500 shares ÷ 1,562,500 shares). Millie's basis for her Acquiring stock is $175,000 ($175,000 basis of Target stock + $600,000 gain recognized − $600,000 cash received). ◀

The tax-free reorganization rules permit the acquiring corporation to transfer part or all of the assets and liabilities acquired in the merger or consolidation to a controlled subsidiary corporation.[37] The asset transfer does not affect the tax-free nature of the transaction. No gain is recognized by either the parent or subsidiary corporation on the transfer. The bases of the assets to the subsidiary corporation will be their basis on the acquiring corporation's books.

HISTORICAL NOTE

Although most state laws allow triangular mergers, the IRS initially ruled that the parent corporation was not a party to the reorganization. This caused the transaction to be taxable. In response to this IRS position, in 1968 and 1971, Congress added the forward and reverse triangular mergers to Sec. 368's list of tax-free reorganizations.

TRIANGULAR MERGERS. **Triangular mergers** are authorized by Sec. 368(a)(2)(D). They are similar to the conventional Type A merger (previously discussed) except that the parent corporation uses a controlled subsidiary corporation to serve as the acquiring corporation. The target corporation is then merged into the subsidiary corporation using one of the two alternative merger forms described earlier (see Figure C7-3).

Triangular mergers must satisfy the same state law requirements as basic merger transactions. In addition, the stock used to carry out the reorganization is limited to that of the parent corporation. However, the subsidiary corporation's cash and securities can be used as part of the transaction, and the subsidiary corporation can assume the target corporation's liabilities.

The "Substantially All" Requirement. The subsidiary corporation must acquire substantially all of the target corporation's assets as part of the plan of reorganization. For advance ruling purposes, *substantially all* has been defined by the IRS to be at least 70% of the FMV of the target corporation's gross assets and 90% of the FMV of its net assets.[38]

EXAMPLE C7-18 ▶ Acquiring Corporation plans to acquire Target Corporation's assets by using a triangular merger involving its subsidiary Acquiring-Sub Corporation. Target Corporation has $2.5 million (FMV) in assets and $1 million in liabilities. To obtain an advance ruling from the IRS for the triangular merger, Acquiring must acquire at least 70% of Target's gross assets ($1.75 million = $2.5 million FMV of assets × 0.70) and 90% of its net assets [$1.35 million = ($2.5 million FMV of assets − $1.0 liabilities) × 0.90], or $1.75 million in assets. The remaining assets can be sold or otherwise disposed of by Target. ◀

[37] Sec. 368(a)(2)(C). As defined in Sec. 368(c), *control* requires the parent corporation to own at least 80% of the voting power and 80% of each class of nonvoting stock. The ability to "drop down" the assets that were acquired to a subsidiary corporation without recognizing any gain also applies to Type B, C, and G reorganizations.

[38] Rev. Proc. 77-37, 1977-2 C.B. 568, Sec. 3.01.

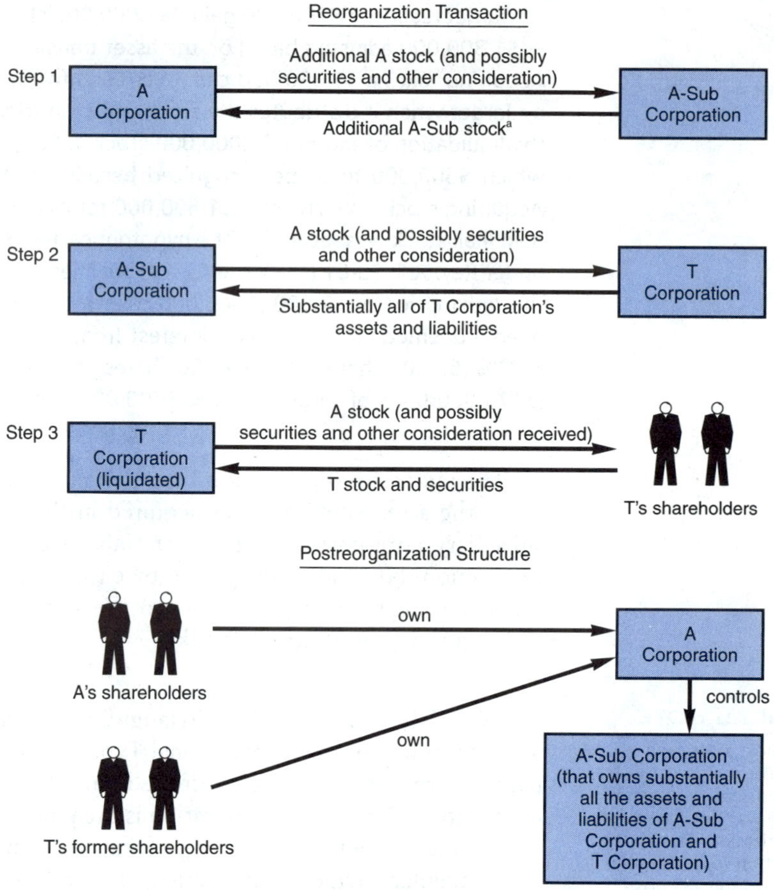

[a] A Corporation must control A-Sub Corporation. If A already owns 100% of A-Sub, the A stock may be treated as additional paid-in capital for the shares that are already owned.

FIGURE C7-3 ▶ TRIANGULAR TYPE A REORGANIZATION

PRACTICAL APPLICATION

The triangular merger is a very popular type of acquisition because the consideration that must be used is still very flexible and yet the parent corporation does not have to assume the known or unknown liabilities of Target. Rather, these liabilities are assumed by the controlled subsidiary.

Advantages of a Triangular Merger. The tax treatment accorded a triangular merger is the same as for the conventional Type A merger transaction. The triangular merger provides three additional advantages (over the conventional Type A merger):

- The target corporation's assets and liabilities become the property of the subsidiary corporation. Thus, the parent corporation generally cannot be held liable for any liabilities that are not known to the acquiring corporation at the time of the transfer or for any contingent liabilities. Creditor claims against the parent corporation's assets are thus minimized.
- Shareholder approval on behalf of the acquiring subsidiary corporation comes from its parent corporation. Thus, if the parent corporation's stock is widely held, the cost of obtaining approval of the shareholders may be reduced.
- The target corporation's shareholders may prefer to receive parent corporation stock because of its increased marketability. By receiving marketable stock, the target corporation's shareholders can sell off a portion of the parent corporation stock over an extended period of time and recognize the gain as if they were using the installment method of accounting.

REVERSE TRIANGULAR MERGERS. **Reverse triangular mergers** are similar to the triangular merger illustrated in Figure C7-3, except that the subsidiary corporation (A-

KEY POINT

In addition to the Type B reorganization, which will be discussed later, the reverse triangular merger is an acquisitive reorganization that keeps Target in existence.

Sub Corporation) is merged into the target corporation (T Corporation), and the target corporation stays alive as a subsidiary of the parent corporation (A Corporation). This type of transaction permits the target corporation to continue its corporate existence. This action may be desirable from a business standpoint (e.g., to maintain a special authorization or a special license owned by the target corporation). Technical details of this type of acquisition are beyond the scope of this text.

TYPE C REORGANIZATION

A **Type C reorganization** is an asset-for-stock or a practical merger transaction. This type of transaction, illustrated in Figure C7-4, requires the acquiring corporation to obtain substantially all of the target corporation's assets in exchange for its voting stock and a limited amount of other consideration.[39]

The "substantially all" requirement is not defined in the Code or the Regulations. For advance ruling purposes, the same standard holds here that applies to triangular Type A mergers (i.e., the 70% of the FMV of gross assets and 90% of the FMV of net assets minimums).[40]

The acquired corporation in a Type C reorganization must distribute the stock, securities, and other property it receives in the reorganization, plus any other property that it retained, to its shareholders as part of the plan of reorganization. Although the corporation does not have to formally be dissolved, as a practical matter it has been liquidated.[41] Because the Type C reorganization produces the same economic result as a merger (i.e., the acquisition of the target corporation's assets) without requiring the dissolution of the target corporation under state law, many tax practitioners call it a practical merger transaction.

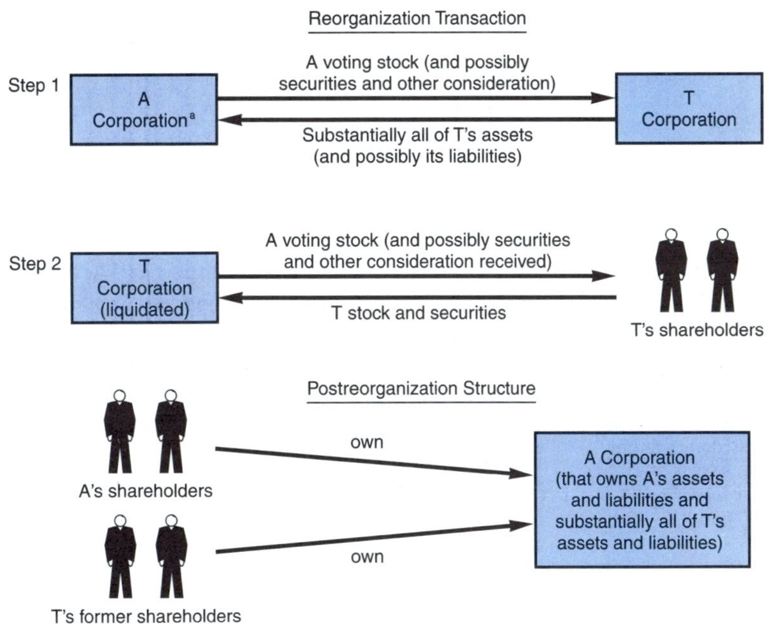

FIGURE C7-4 ▶ TYPE C (ASSET-FOR-STOCK) REORGANIZATION

[39] Sec. 368(a)(1)(C).

[40] Rev. Proc. 77-37, 1977-2 C.B. 568, Sec. 3.01.

[41] Sec. 368(a)(2)(G).

The acquired corporation may retain its corporate charter in order to prevent others from using its corporate name and obtain a special IRS waiver to the distribution requirement.[42]

KEY POINT

Because of the solely-for-voting-stock requirement, a Type C reorganization is much less flexible than a Type A reorganization in terms of the consideration that can be used.

CONSIDERATION USED TO EFFECT THE REORGANIZATION. Section 368(a)(1)(C) requires the consideration used to effect the reorganization be solely voting stock of the acquiring corporation (or its parent corporation). Both the acquiring corporation's assumption of part or all of the target corporation's liabilities and the acquisition of a property subject to a liability are disregarded for purposes of the solely-for-voting-stock requirement.

Section 368(a)(2)(B) permits other consideration to be used in the reorganization, provided the acquiring corporation obtains at least 80% of the target corporation's properties solely for its voting stock. This rule permits money, securities, nonvoting stock, or other property to be used to acquire up to 20% of the target corporation's properties. Liabilities that are assumed or acquired reduce the amount of money that can be used in the reorganization on a dollar-for-dollar basis. If the liabilities that are assumed or acquired exceed 20% of the FMV of the target corporation's assets, the transaction can take place as a Type C reorganization only if no money, securities, nonvoting stock, or other property is used.

EXAMPLE C7-19 ▶

Acquiring Corporation wants to acquire all of Target Corporation's assets and liabilities as part of a Type C reorganization. The following table illustrates the application of the solely-for-voting-stock requirement for four different situations:

	Situation 1	*Situation 2*	*Situation 3*	*Situation 4*
FMV of Target's assets	$200,000	$200,000	$200,000	$200,000
Target's liabilities assumed by Acquiring	—0—	30,000	100,000	100,000
Consideration given by Acquiring:				
FMV of Acquiring voting stock	160,000	160,000	100,000	99,900
Money	40,000	10,000	—0—	100

ADDITIONAL COMMENT

Target's liabilities assumed by Acquiring are not a problem unless boot is received by Target as part of the consideration. In this case, when applying the 20% boot relaxation rule, liabilities are treated as money. Situation 4 in Example C7-19 illustrates that if Target has liabilities in excess of 20% of the FMV of its assets, the boot relaxation rule is of no benefit.

In Situation 1, the FMV of the Acquiring stock equals 80% of the total assets, so the transaction is a Type C reorganization. The liabilities that are assumed in Situation 2 reduce the money that can be exchanged by Acquiring, but the transaction is still a Type C reorganization because the money and liabilities, in total, do not exceed 20% of the FMV of Target's total assets. In Situation 3, the high percentage of liabilities does not prevent the transaction from being a Type C reorganization because Acquiring used no money to effect the reorganization.[43] In Situation 4, the transaction is disqualified from being a Type C reorganization because some money is used along with the Acquiring stock and the total money given by Acquiring and liabilities assumed by Acquiring are more than 20% of the total FMV of Target's assets. ◀

ADVANTAGES AND DISADVANTAGES OF A TYPE C REORGANIZATION. A number of advantages and disadvantages exist when comparing a Type C reorganization and a merger.

- ▶ The acquiring corporation acquires only the assets specified in the purchase agreement in a Type C reorganization. However, it needs to acquire substantially all of the target corporation's assets. Unwanted assets that are sold or otherwise disposed of by

[42] Rev. Proc. 89-50, 1989-1 C.B.631.

[43] The IRS may attempt to treat a transaction as a purchase under the continuity of proprietary interest doctrine (see page C7-46) when the amount of liabilities assumed or acquired is high relative to the FMV of the assets acquired (see footnote 73).

the target corporation and assets that are retained by the target corporation do not count toward meeting the "substantially all" requirement. A disposition of a substantial amount of assets shortly before an asset-for-stock acquisition may prevent the transaction from being a Type C reorganization. The "substantially all" requirement does not apply to a merger, and dispositions of unwanted assets generally will not prevent an acquisition from being a merger.

- The acquiring corporation acquires only the liabilities that are specified in the purchase agreement. Unknown and contingent liabilities are not acquired, as they are in a merger.
- Shareholders of the acquiring corporation generally do not have to approve the acquisition, thus reducing the cost to accomplish the transaction.
- For many target corporations, the liabilities that are acquired or assumed are so large (i.e., in excess of 20% of total consideration) as to prevent the acquiring corporation from using any consideration other than voting stock. Merger transactions permit 50% nonstock consideration to be used, and do not require the stock to have voting rights.
- Dissenting shareholders of the target corporation may have the right under state law to have their shares independently appraised and purchased for cash.

SELF-STUDY QUESTION

Must Acquiring assume all liabilities of Target in a C reorganization?

ANSWER

No. Acquiring may leave Target's liabilities in Target. These liabilities would then have to be satisfied with assets retained by Target or with assets acquired by Target in the reorganization.

TAX CONSEQUENCES OF A TYPE C REORGANIZATION. The tax consequences of a Type C reorganization are illustrated by the following example.

EXAMPLE C7-20 ▶ Acquiring Corporation acquires all of Target Corporation's assets and liabilities in exchange for $1,200,000 of Acquiring voting stock. Target distributes the Acquiring stock to its sole shareholder, Andrew, in exchange for all of his Target stock. Target's assets have a $1,400,000 FMV and a $600,000 adjusted basis. Liabilities in the amount of $200,000 are assumed by Acquiring. Target has a $500,000 E&P balance. Andrew's basis for his Target stock is $400,000. Target realizes an $800,000 gain [($1,200,000 + $200,000) − $600,000], none of which must be recognized. Acquiring recognizes no gain when it exchanges its stock for the assets and takes a $600,000 basis in the acquired assets. Andrew realizes an $800,000 ($1,200,000 − $400,000) gain on the surrender of his shares when Target liquidates, none of which must be recognized. Andrew's basis for the Acquiring stock is $400,000. Acquiring assumes all of Target's tax attributes, including the $500,000 E&P balance. ◀

Section 368(a)(2)(B) permits the acquiring corporation in a Type C reorganization to transfer part or all of the assets and liabilities acquired in the reorganization to a controlled subsidiary corporation without destroying the tax-free nature of the transaction. Section 368(a)(2)(C) permits a triangular Type C reorganization to be used whereby voting stock of the parent corporation is used by a subsidiary corporation to acquire substantially all of the target corporation's assets. The triangular Type C reorganization requirements are the same as for the basic Type C reorganization except that the voting stock used to acquire the assets must consist solely of the stock of the acquiring corporation's parent corporation. However, the subsidiary corporation can provide additional consideration in the form of securities, money, or other property.

TYPICAL MISCONCEPTION

As with an A reorganization, a C reorganization can be structured as a triangular acquisition. Although this provides greater flexibility in tax planning, it makes the area more confusing because of the substantial overlap between the different types of reorganizations.

TYPE D REORGANIZATION

Type D reorganizations can be either acquisitive or divisive. (Divisive Type D reorganizations are discussed on pages C7-37 through C7-43.) An acquisitive Type D reorganization involves the transfer by a target corporation of substantially all of its assets to a controlled (acquiring) corporation in exchange for such corporation's stock and securities (and possibly other consideration) pursuant to a plan of reorganization. The

KEY POINT

When a Type D reorganization is used as an acquisitive reorganization, it generally involves commonly controlled corporations. However, its most common usage is as part of a divisive reorganization under Sec. 355 (discussed later in this chapter).

exchange must be followed by a distribution to the transferor's shareholders and security holders of the stock, securities, and other consideration that is received in the reorganization, plus any other properties retained by the transferor corporation, pursuant to a complete liquidation of the transferor corporation.[44] (See Figure C7-5 for an illustration of an acquisitive Type D reorganization.)

The "substantially all" requirement is based on the facts and circumstances of the situation. For advance ruling purposes, the 70% of the FMV of gross assets and 90% of the FMV of net assets standard used in the triangular Type A and Type C reorganizations is applied.[45]

SELF-STUDY QUESTION

Why does a Type D reorganization use the 50% control requirement when the rest of the Sec. 368 reorganizations use the higher 80% control requirement?

ANSWER

The use of the 50% control requirement is the result of a specific statutory change. This change was made to make the Type D reorganization a more useful tool in fighting the tax avoidance transactions.

CONTROL REQUIREMENTS. The transferor (target) corporation or one or more of its shareholders must control the transferee (acquiring) corporation immediately after the asset transfer. Control is defined as either 50% or more of the total combined voting power of all classes of voting stock, or 50% or more of the total value of all classes of stock, in Sec. 368(a)(2)(H).

Type D reorganizations are not often found because of this control requirement. One example of an acquisitive Type D reorganization is when Acquiring Corporation acquires all of the assets of a larger corporation (Target Corporation) and Target Corporation's shareholders end up controlling the Acquiring Corporation after the reorganization. Type C reorganizations (where the target does not control the acquiring corporation) and Type A reorganizations (where the transaction satisfies the state law merger requirements) are more common.

The Sec. 368(a)(1)(D) rules do not limit the consideration that may be exchanged in the transaction. The IRS and the courts require that the transferor corporation's shareholders maintain a continuing equity interest in the transferee corporation. For

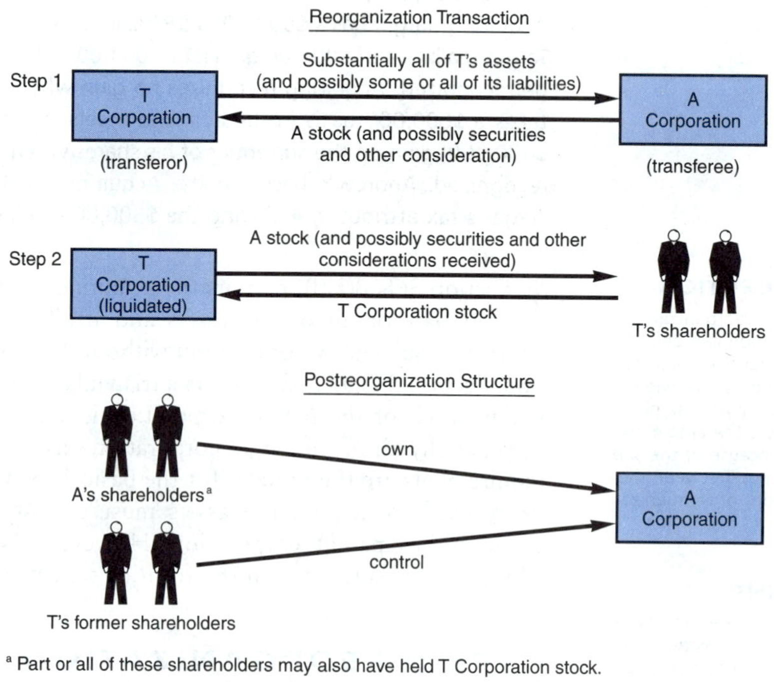

FIGURE C7-5 ▶ ACQUISITIVE TYPE D REORGANIZATION

[44] Secs. 368(a)(1)(D) and 354(b)(1).

[45] Rev. Proc. 77-37, 1977-2 C.B. 568, Sec. 3.01.

advance ruling purposes, the IRS requires that the transferor corporation's shareholders receive transferee corporation stock equal to at least 50% of the value of the transferor corporation's outstanding stock in order to satisfy this requirement.[46]

TAX CONSEQUENCES OF A TYPE D REORGANIZATION. The Type C and acquisitive Type D reorganization requirements and tax consequences are quite similar. If the reorganization satisfies both the Type C and Type D reorganization requirements, Sec. 368(a)(2)(A) requires that the transaction be treated as a Type D reorganization. The basic tax consequences of a Type D reorganization for the target corporation, the acquiring corporation, and the target corporation's shareholders are the same as for a Type C reorganization except in the application of Sec. 357(c) "excess" liability rule. Section 357(c) requires the transferor (target) corporation in a Type D reorganization to recognize gain equal to the amount by which the liabilities assumed or acquired by the transferee (acquiring) corporation exceed the total adjusted basis of the transferor corporation's assets that were transferred. Such gain does not have to be recognized if the asset acquisition qualifies only as a Type C reorganization (e.g., when the target corporation does not control the acquiring corporation).

KEY POINT

If Acquiring wants Target to remain in existence, the two choices in Sec. 368 that can accomplish this objective are a Type B reorganization or a reverse triangular merger.

TYPE B REORGANIZATION

A **Type B reorganization** is the simplest form of acquisitive reorganization. In this type of reorganization, two things happen: the target corporation's stock is exchanged for voting stock of the acquiring corporation and the target corporation remains in existence as a subsidiary of the acquiring corporation (see Figure C7-6).

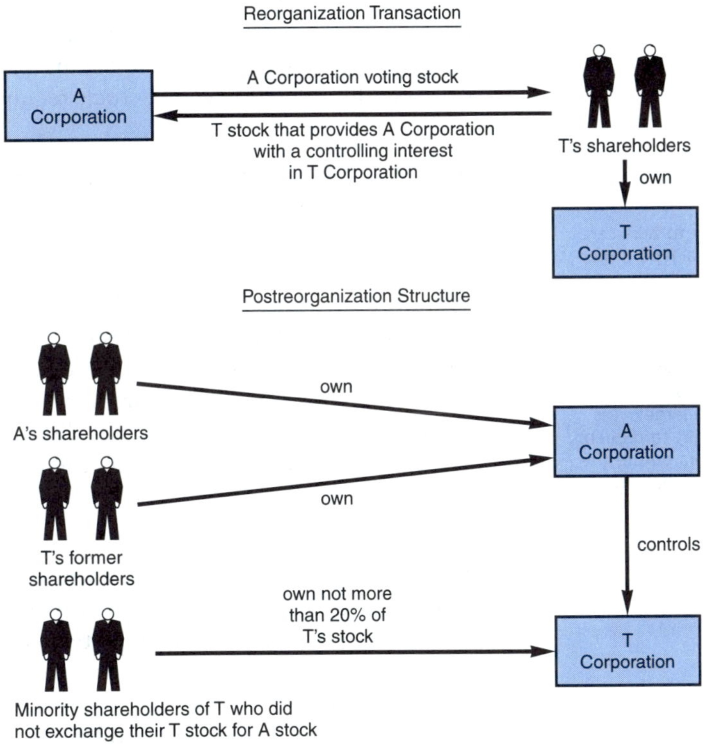

FIGURE C7-6 ▶ TYPE B (STOCK-FOR-STOCK) REORGANIZATION

[46] Rev. Proc. 77-37, 1977-2 C.B. 568, Sec. 3.02.

The Type B reorganization is generally accomplished independent of the target corporation. The basis of the target corporation's assets and the amount of its tax attributes generally remain unchanged by the reorganization. After the reorganization, the target corporation and the parent corporation may elect to file a consolidated tax return. If the target corporation is liquidated into the parent corporation shortly after the stock-for-stock exchange occurs, the IRS may attempt to collapse the two parts of the transaction into a single transaction and treat it as a Type C asset-for-stock reorganization.[47]

KEY POINT

There is no boot relaxation exception for the solely-for-voting-stock requirement for the Type B reorganization. Thus, the Type B reorganization has the least flexible consideration requirement of any of the reorganizations.

SOLELY-FOR-VOTING-STOCK REQUIREMENT. Section 368(a)(1)(B) requires the acquiring corporation to acquire the target corporation's stock in exchange solely for all or part of its voting stock. The acquiring corporation must own sufficient stock to be in control of the target corporation immediately after the exchange.

The solely-for-voting-stock requirement generally precludes the use of other property to effect the transaction. However, the voting stock used can be either common or preferred stock. If consideration other than voting stock is used to effect the reorganization (e.g., nonvoting preferred stock), the transaction does not qualify as a Type B reorganization and the transaction is taxable to the target corporation's shareholders (see page C7-53).

KEY POINT

These limited exceptions to the solely-for-voting-stock requirement apply to Type C reorganizations as well as Type B reorganizations.

Exceptions. Cash can be used in limited circumstances without violating this requirement. For example:

- The target corporation's shareholders can receive cash in exchange for their right to receive a fractional share of the acquiring corporation's stock.[48]
- Reorganization expenses of the target corporation (such as legal expenses, accounting fees, and administrative costs) can be paid by the acquiring corporation without violating the solely-for-voting-stock requirement.[49]

SELF-STUDY QUESTION

Is there any way to take care of dissenters in a Type B reorganization?

ANSWER

Yes. Even though Acquiring cannot use any boot in acquiring the stock of Target, it is possible for Target to redeem out the dissenters before the reorganization. Also, Target's nondissenting shareholders could buy out the stock of the dissenters.

Control. For Type B reorganizations, control is defined by Sec. 368(c) as 80% of the total combined voting power of all classes of voting stock and 80% of each class of nonvoting stock. Because the acquiring corporation does not have to acquire all of the target corporation's stock, it is possible that a minority interest of up to 20% may be present. Minority shareholders can have their shares independently valued and acquired for cash under state law without destroying the tax-free nature of the transaction. For example, the target corporation can use its cash to redeem the stock of the minority shareholders before or after the reorganization. A cash acquisition by the acquiring corporation of the shares of a group of dissenting minority shareholders either before or as part of the reorganization prevents the transaction from being tax-free.[50]

Timing of the Transaction. Some Type B reorganizations are accomplished by simply exchanging stock of the acquiring corporation for 100% of the target corporation's shares in a single transaction. In other cases, the reorganization is accomplished in a series of transactions taking place over an extended period of time. Regulation Sec. 1.368-2(c) states that a cash purchase of stock may be disregarded for purposes of the solely-for-voting-stock requirement if it was independent of the stock-for-stock exchange. Stock acquisitions that are made over a relatively short period of time—twelve months or

[47] Rev. Rul. 67-274, 1967-2 C.B. 141.
[48] Rev. Rul. 66-365, 1966-2 C.B. 116.
[49] Rev. Rul. 73-54, 1973-1 C.B. 187.
[50] Rev. Rul. 68-285, 1968-1 C.B. 147.

ADDITIONAL COMMENT

"Creeping acquisitions" are allowed in a Type B reorganization because the requirement is merely that 80% must be owned after the transaction. Transactions within twelve months are generally considered related transactions. This can be either an advantage or a disadvantage depending on what consideration was used in the various steps of the acquisition.

less—are, according to this regulation, to be aggregated for purposes of applying the solely-for-voting-stock requirement.

EXAMPLE C7-21 ▶ Acquiring Corporation acquires 12% of Target Corporation's single class of stock for cash in July 1997. The remaining 88% is acquired by Acquiring in January 1998 in a stock-for-stock exchange. The cash and stock-for-stock acquisitions will probably be aggregated by the IRS because they occur within a twelve-month period. Even though 80% control is acquired in a single stock-for-stock transaction, the transaction does not meet the Type B reorganization requirements because the solely-for-voting-stock requirement is not met if the two transactions are aggregated. The transaction could qualify as a Type B reorganization if Acquiring unconditionally sold its 12% interest in the Target stock and then acquired the necessary 80% interest in a single stock-for-stock exchange, or Acquiring delayed the stock-for-stock exchange until some time after July 1998, when it would probably be considered a separate transaction.[51] ◀

EXAMPLE C7-22 ▶ Acquiring Corporation acquires 85% of Target Corporation's single class of stock in April 1991 in a transaction that qualifies as a Type B reorganization. Acquiring acquires the remaining 15% of Target's stock in December 1997 in a stock-for-stock exchange. Even though Acquiring already controls Target, the second acquisition is treated as a Type B reorganization. ◀

WHAT WOULD YOU DO IN THIS SITUATION?

Tobin Rote, a wealthy investor, owns all of the single class of stock of Detroit Corporation, a calendar-year taxpayer. Mr. Rote has wanted to acquire Cleveland Corporation which produces metal and plastic parts for the automobile industry. Detroit Corporation purchases for cash 4.9% of the Cleveland voting stock on August 1, 1997. The acquisition provides Tobin Rote, as a Cleveland shareholder, access to its books and records. The 4.9% ownership position, however, is below the 5% threshold at which Detroit must make an SEC filing regarding its stock position. Based on an analysis of Cleveland's books and records made shortly after becoming a shareholder, Tobin Rote wants to make a tender offer sometime in the next two months whereby part or all of the remaining Cleveland voting and nonvoting stock would be acquired in exchange for Detroit stock. He comes to you for advice concerning the tender offer which he wants to complete by December 31, 1997. No shares would be acquired unless sufficient shares were tendered to provide Detroit Corporation with 80% of the voting stock and 80% of the nonvoting stock. The 80% minimums are higher than the 50% absolute control minimum because two individuals who own 30% of the Cleveland stock will participate in the transaction only if it qualifies as a Type B tax-free reorganization. In addition, Mr. Rote would like to use the pooling method to report the transaction for financial accounting purposes. What advice can you provide about carrying out his proposed transaction? Do you foresee any difficulties with the plan?

TAX CONSEQUENCES OF A TYPE B REORGANIZATION. The tax consequences of a Type B reorganization are straightforward.

- The target corporation's shareholders recognize no gain or loss on the exchange unless fractional shares of stock are acquired for cash or the target corporation redeems some of their stock.
- The target corporation's shareholders take a substituted basis for their acquiring corporation stock from the basis of their target corporation stock. The holding

---

[51] See, for example, *Eldon S. Chapman et al. v. CIR*, 45 AFTR 2d 80-1290, 80-1 USTC ¶9330 (1st Cir., 1980).

period for the acquiring corporation stock includes their holding period for the target corporation stock.

- The acquiring corporation recognizes no gain or loss when it issues its stock for the target corporation's stock.
- The acquiring corporation's basis for the target corporation's stock is the same as it was in the hands of the target corporation's shareholders.

EXAMPLE C7-23 ▶ Target Corporation's single class of stock is owned entirely by Mark, who has a $400,000 basis for his stock. Mark exchanges his Target stock for $700,000 of Acquiring Corporation's voting stock. Mark realizes a $300,000 gain ($700,000 − $400,000), none of which is recognized. Mark's basis for the Acquiring stock is $400,000. Acquiring Corporation recognizes no gain or loss when it issues its stock and takes a $400,000 basis for the Target stock. ◀

ADVANTAGES OF A TYPE B REORGANIZATION. The Type B reorganization has a number of advantages. First, as explained earlier, it can usually be accomplished quite simply and without formal shareholder approval. The acquiring corporation can acquire the necessary shares with a tender offer made directly to the target corporation's shareholders, even if the target corporation's management does not approve of the transaction. Second, the target corporation remains in existence and its tax attributes are not lost or subject to special limitations, as in some reorganizations (see pages C7-49 through C7-52).[52] Third, the corporate name, goodwill, licenses, and rights of the target company can continue on after the acquisition. Fourth, the acquiring corporation does not directly acquire the target corporation's liabilities, as is the case of some other reorganizations.

DISADVANTAGES OF A TYPE B REORGANIZATION. Offsetting the advantages noted above are a number of disadvantages. First, the sole consideration that may be used to effect the transaction is voting stock. The issuing of the additional voting stock can dilute the voting power of the acquiring corporation's shareholders and restrict their flexibility to structure the transaction in order to retain control of the acquiring corporation. Second, at least 80% of the target corporation's stock must be acquired, even though effective control of the acquired company might be obtained with ownership of less than 80%. Third, the acquisition of less than 100% of the target corporation's stock may lead to a vocal group of dissenting minority shareholders. These shareholders have the right under state law to have their shares appraised and purchased for cash. Fourth, the bases of the target corporation's stock and assets are not stepped up to their FMVs when the change in ownership occurs, as would be the case in a taxable asset acquisition.

TRIANGULAR TYPE B REORGANIZATIONS. As with the Type A and C reorganizations, a triangular Type B reorganization, or a drop-down of the target corporation's stock into a subsidiary corporation, can be accomplished tax-free. In a **triangular reorganization**, the stock of the acquiring corporation's parent corporation is exchanged for a controlling stock interest in the target corporation. As in the basic Type B reorganization, the target corporation remains in existence as a subsidiary of the acquiring (subsidiary) corporation.

---

[52] A Type B reorganization can result in an ownership change that restricts the ability of the target corporation's NOL carryovers to be used under Sec. 382 but does not, in total, diminish the amount of its carryovers (see page C7-48).

HISTORICAL NOTE

The Type G reorganization is the newest of the Sec. 368 reorganizations. Previously, reorganizations used in restructuring corporations involved in bankruptcy proceedings had their own statutory provisions. As part of the Bankruptcy Tax Act of 1980, the old provisions were repealed and the Type G reorganization was enacted. This change was made to allow more flexibility in restructuring bankrupt corporations.

TYPE G REORGANIZATION

Section 368(a)(1)(G) defines a **Type G reorganization** as "a transfer by a corporation of part or all of its assets to another corporation in a title 11 [bankruptcy] or similar case, but only if, in pursuance of the plan, stock or securities of the corporation to which the assets are transferred are distributed in a transaction that qualifies under sections 354, 355, or 356." Use of a Type G reorganization is quite limited because the reorganization must take place according to a court-approved plan in a bankruptcy, receivership, or other similar situation.

In an acquisitive Type G reorganization, the financially troubled corporation might transfer substantially all of its assets to an acquiring corporation according to a court-approved plan (e.g., a bankruptcy reorganization plan) and then distribute all the stock, securities, and other property received in the exchange, plus any properties it had retained, to its shareholders and creditors in exchange for their stock and debt interests.

DIVISIVE REORGANIZATIONS

A divisive reorganization involves the transfer of *part* of a transferor corporation's assets to a controlled corporation in exchange for its stock and securities (and possibly some boot property).[53] The stock and securities (and possibly some boot property) are then distributed to the transferor's shareholders. The primary divisive reorganization comes under the Type D reorganization rules, although a divisive reorganization involving a financially troubled corporation could be a Type G reorganization. A summary of the requirements for the divisive and other reorganizations is presented in Topic Review C7-6 on page C7-38.

DIVISIVE TYPE D REORGANIZATION

The Type D reorganization must take place as part of a plan of reorganization and satisfy the requirements of Secs. 368(a)(1)(D) and 355 which are explained below.[54] There are three forms of Type D divisive reorganizations: spinoffs, split-offs, and split-ups (see Figure C7-7).

A distribution of a controlled corporation's stock can be tax-free under Sec. 355, even if none of the distributing corporation's assets are transferred to the controlled corporation. For a transaction to constitute one of the three divisive Type D reorganization forms, both the asset transfer and the Sec. 355 distribution must take place as part of a single transaction that is governed by a plan of reorganization. Both divisive reorganizations and tax-free distributions of the stock of an existing controlled subsidiary are examined in this section.

TYPICAL MISCONCEPTION

The existence of a good corporate business purpose is necessary before the stock of a controlled subsidiary can be distributed to the shareholders of the distributing corporation. This requirement is much more difficult to satisfy in a Sec. 355 distribution than it is in an acquisitive reorganization.

A divisive Type D reorganization can be used to accomplish a number of types of business adjustments, including

- Dividing up a business into two corporations to separate a high-risk business from a low-risk business
- Dividing up a single business between two shareholders that have a major disagreement

[53] In a divisive Type D reorganization, control is most always defined by Sec. 368(c) because Sec. 355 (not Sec. 354) governs the distribution. Section 368(c) requires ownership of at least 80% of the voting and nonvoting stock to constitute control. An acquisitive Type D reorganization, on the other hand, requires only 50% of the voting and nonvoting stock to be owned to constitute control (see page C7-32).

[54] The requirements of the divisive Type D reorganization may be contrasted with the acquisitive Type D reorganization (previously discussed), where substantially all of the transferor's assets must be transferred to a controlled corporation.

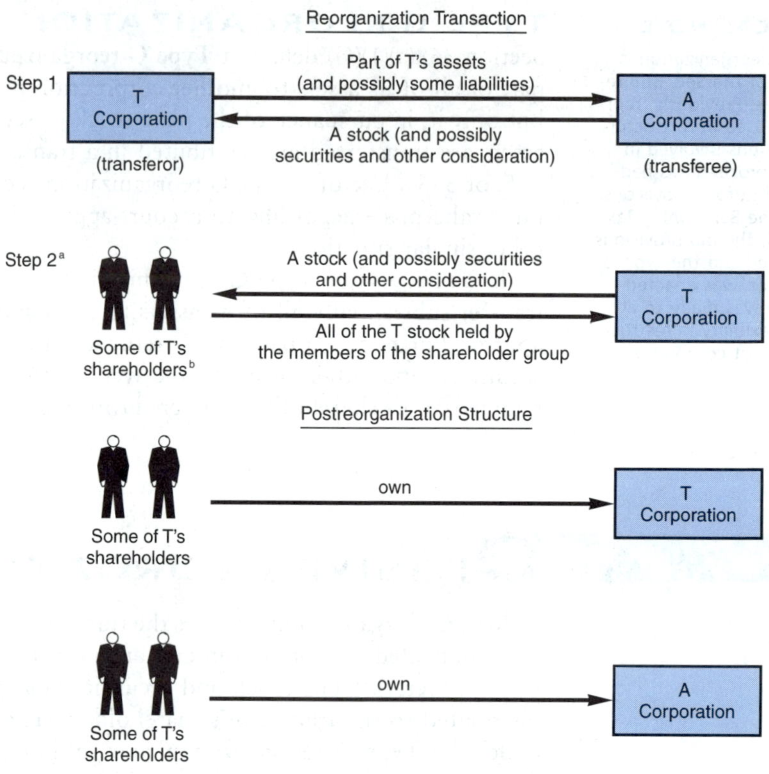

[a] Step 1 remains the same for the spinoff transaction. In a spinoff transaction. A spinoff does not require T's shareholders to surrender any of their stock. In a split-up transaction, Step 1 involves T Corporation's assets and liabilities being transferred to two controlled corporations. Step 2 involves the distribution of the stock of the two controlled corporations pursuant to the liquidation of T Corporation.
[b] This distribution could also occur on a pro rata basis to all of T's shareholders, in which case only a portion of the shares held by each shareholder is surrendered.

FIGURE C7-7 ▶ DIVISIVE TYPE D REORGANIZATION (SPLIT-OFF FORM)

- Dividing up a corporation's business activities according to its separate functions or the geographical areas in which it operates
- Dividing up a business because of antitrust law violations

FORMS OF DIVISIVE TYPE D REORGANIZATIONS. Three types of divisive transactions are tax-free if the Sec. 368(a)(1)(D) requirements are met:

- **Split-off**—a transferor corporation transfers part of its assets to a controlled corporation in exchange for stock and possibly securities, money, or other boot property. The parent corporation then distributes the stock of the subsidiary to part or all of its shareholders, receiving some of its stock in exchange. Such a transaction may occur because of a management dispute between two dissenting shareholder groups whereby the parent corporation redeems all of the stock of one of the groups (see Figure C7-7).
- **Spinoff**—a transferor corporation transfers part of its assets to a controlled corporation in exchange for stock and possibly securities, money, or other boot property. The parent corporation then distributes the stock of the subsidiary ratably to all of its shareholders, receiving nothing in exchange. Such a transaction may occur

Topic Review C7-6

Summary of Divisive and Other Reorganizations

Type of Reorganization	Transferor (T) Corporation Property Acquired	Consideration That Can Be Used	What Happens to the Transferor (T) Corporation?	Shareholders' Recognized Gain	Other Requirements
D—Divisive	Part or all of the assets of T[a] Corporation (and possibly some or all of its liabilities) are transferred to a "controlled" transferee (A[b] Corporation).	Stock, securities, and other property of A Corporation	Stock, securities, and boot received in the reorganization must be distributed; T Corporation may be liquidated, but can remain in existence.	Lesser of realized gain or boot received	Transactions can take on three forms—spinoff, split-off or split-up. Control is defined at the 80% level under Sec. 368(c).
E—Recapitalization	No increase or decrease in assets occurs. A change to the capital structure of T Corporation takes place.	Stock, securities, and other property of T Corporation	T Corporation remains in existence.	Lesser of realized gain or boot received	May involve stock-for-stock, bond-for-bond, or bond-for-stock exchanges.
F—Change in form, identity, or place of organization	Assets or stock of old T Corporation are transferred to new T Corporation.	Stock, securities, and other property of new T Corporation	Old T Corporation is liquidated.	Lesser of realized gain or boot received	Must involve only a single operating company.
G—Acquisitive or divisive	Part or all of the assets of T Corporation (and possibly some or all of its liabilities) are transferred to A Corporation in a bankruptcy case.	Stock, securities, and other property of A Corporation	T Corporation may be liquidated but can remain in existence.	Lesser of realized gain or boot received	Stock and securities of A Corporation received by T Corporation must be distributed to its shareholders, security holders, or creditors.

[a]T Corporation refers to the transferor corporation.
[b]A Corporation refers to the transferee corporation.

because of a desire to reduce the risk inherent in having two operating divisions (e.g., steel and glass manufacturing) within a single corporation.

- **Split-up**—a transferor corporation transfers all of its assets to two controlled corporations in exchange for stock and possibly securities, money, or other boot property. The parent corporation then distributes the stock of the two subsidiaries to all of its shareholders receiving in exchange all of its outstanding stock. Such a transaction may occur because of a desire to have two operating divisions transferred to new corporations, which will continue in existence as brother-sister corporations while the old corporation is liquidated.

If the Sec. 355 requirements described below are *not* met, a spinoff is taxed as a dividend to the shareholders, a split-off is taxed as a stock redemption to the shareholders, and a split-up is taxed as a liquidation of the parent corporation to the shareholders.

KEY POINT

The tax consequences of a divisive reorganization are basically the same as those of an acquisitive reorganization. The general rule is that no gain or loss is recognized by any of the parties to the reorganization and the controlled corporation takes a carryover basis in any assets it receives as part of the reorganization. In addition, the transferor's shareholders take a substituted basis in the controlled corporation stock they receive.

ASSET TRANSFER. The transferor corporation recognizes no gain or loss on the asset transfer, except when boot property is received by the transferor and retained or the transferee corporation acquires or assumes liabilities of the transferor corporation and the total of the liabilities acquired or assumed exceeds the total adjusted bases of the assets transferred.[55] No gain or loss is recognized by the controlled corporation when it exchanges its stock for the transferor corporation's property. The controlled corporation's basis for the acquired assets is the same as on the transferor corporation's books, increased for any gain recognized by the transferor corporation. Its holding period includes the transferor corporation's holding period for the assets.

TYPICAL MISCONCEPTION

Section 355 can apply to a distribution of stock of an existing subsidiary as well as the distribution of stock of a new subsidiary that is created as part of the transaction.

DISTRIBUTION OF STOCK AND SECURITIES. The same gain or loss recognition rules apply to the distributing corporation and its shareholders when a distribution of stock of an existing subsidiary is made under Sec. 355 and when it is made as part of a Type D reorganization. No gain or loss is recognized by the distributing corporation when it distributes the controlled corporation's stock (or securities) to its shareholders.[56] Gain (but not loss) is recognized when nonmoney boot property is distributed to the distributing corporation's shareholders as part of the reorganization and when a disqualified distribution of stock or securities in the controlled corporation is made.

No gain or loss is recognized by the shareholders on the receipt of the stock (and securities), except to the extent that boot property is received.[57] A shareholder's basis in the stock (or securities) held after the distribution equals his or her basis in the stock (or securities) that are held before the distribution, increased by any gain recognized and decreased by the sum of the money received and the FMV of any other boot property received. If more than one class of stock or securities is held before or after the distribution, the total basis for the nonrecognition property is allocated to each class based on their relative FMVs. The basis for any boot property (other than money) is its FMV. The holding period for the stock and nonboot securities received includes the holding period of the stock and securities surrendered. The holding period for boot property begins on the day after the distribution date.

---

[55] Secs. 361(a) and 357(c)(1)(B).

[56] Sec. 361(c)(1). A disqualifying distribution occurs if, immediately after the distribution, any person holds a 50% disqualified stock interest in either the parent corporation or the subsidiary corporation. Disqualified stock is generally defined as any stock in the parent or controlled subsidiary corporations that was purchased after October 9, 1990, and within the five-year period ending on the distribution date. The disqualifying distribution rules are intended to prevent a divisive transaction from being combined with a stock purchase, resulting in a change of ownership, to accomplish the disposition of a significant part of the historic shareholders' interests in one or more of the divided corporations.

[57] Sec. 355(a). Like with an acquisitive reorganization, Sec. 361(a) permits securities (e.g., long-term debt obligations) to be received tax-free in a divisive transaction when the same face amount of securities, or a larger amount, are surrendered by the shareholders. Excess securities that are received, of course, are boot property.

EXAMPLE C7-24 ▶

Parent Corporation transfers assets having a $600,000 FMV and a $350,000 adjusted basis to Subsidiary Corporation in exchange for all of Subsidiary's single class of stock. Parent has been owned equally by Ruth and Pat for ten years. Ruth and Pat are no longer able to agree on the management of Parent and have agreed to a division of the assets in exchange for Pat surrendering her Parent shares. Pat's basis for her Parent shares is $400,000. Parent realizes a $250,000 gain ($600,000 − $350,000) on the asset transfer, none of which is recognized. Parent also does not recognize any gain upon the distribution of the Subsidiary shares to Pat. Pat realizes a $200,000 gain ($600,000 − $400,000) on exchanging the Parent shares, none of which is recognized. Her basis in the Subsidiary stock is $400,000. Subsidiary does not recognize any gain when it issues its stock for Parent's assets and takes a $350,000 basis in the assets that were acquired. ◀

SELF-STUDY QUESTION

Does the receipt of boot make the entire Sec. 355 transaction taxable to the shareholders?

ANSWER

No. The shareholders may have a partial recognition of gain. The amount and type of gain depends on whether the shareholders surrender stock of the distributing corporation in the transaction.

TYPICAL MISCONCEPTION

In a spinoff, the FMV of the boot received is treated as a Sec. 301 distribution to the shareholder. In a split-off or split-up, the shareholders recognize gain to the extent of the lesser of boot received and gain realized.

Under Sec. 355, boot may consist of money, short-term debt, any property other than the stock or securities of a controlled corporation, any stock of the controlled corporation that was purchased within the previous five years in a taxable transaction, securities of the controlled corporation to the extent the principal amount of the securities received exceeds the principal amount of the securities surrendered by the shareholder, and stock or securities attributable to accrued interest.[58] When boot is received, the amount and character of the income or gain that must be recognized depend on whether the shareholder surrendered stock and securities in the distributing corporation (i.e., a split-off or split-up) or did not surrender any stock or securities (i.e., a spinoff).

When boot is received in a spinoff, the FMV of the boot is a dividend to the extent of the shareholder's ratable share of the distributing corporation's E&P. Any securities received by the shareholders in a spinoff are boot because the shareholders do not surrender any securities in a spinoff transaction. Thus, the FMV of the securities is a dividend to the extent of the shareholder's ratable share of the distributing corporation's E&P.

In a split-off or a split-up, in addition to the exchange of stock, a shareholder may receive some boot property. If the shareholder realizes a loss on the exchange, the loss is not recognized, whether boot is received or not.[59] If the shareholder realizes a gain on the exchange, the gain is recognized to the extent of the FMV of any boot received.

If the exchange has the effect of a dividend under the Sec. 302 stock redemption rules, the recognized gain is treated as a dividend up to the amount of the shareholder's ratable share of the distributing corporation's E&P.[60] Otherwise it is a capital gain. The Sec. 302 rules are applied by treating the shareholder as though he or she continued to own stock in the distributing corporation and surrendered only the portion of his or her shares equal in value to the amount of boot received. This hypothetical redemption is then tested under the Sec. 302(b) rules to see whether it receives exchange or dividend treatment.[61]

EXAMPLE C7-25 ▶

Parent Corporation owns assets with a $60,000 FMV plus all of the outstanding shares of Subsidiary Corporation, which was created by an asset transfer by Parent. The Subsidiary stock is worth $40,000. Parent's E&P balance is $60,000. Parent is owned by Carl and Diane, each of whom owns 100 shares of Parent stock. Parent distributes all of the Subsidiary stock to Carl in exchange for Carl's 100 shares of Parent stock in a transaction that qualifies as a split-off under the provisions of Secs. 368(a)(1)(D) and 355, except for the fact that Carl also receives $10,000 in cash. Carl's basis in the Parent shares he surrenders is $25,000. Carl has a $25,000 realized gain, determined as follows:

[58] Secs. 355(a)(3) and 356(b).
[59] Sec. 356(c).
[60] Sec. 356(a)(2).
[61] Rev. Rul. 93-62, 1993-2 C.B. 118.

FMV of Subsidiary stock	$40,000
Plus: Cash received	10,000
Amount realized	$50,000
Minus: Basis of Parent stock	(25,000)
Realized gain	$25,000

$10,000 of this gain must be recognized (i.e., the lesser of the $25,000 realized gain or the $10,000 boot received). If Carl surrenders Parent stock solely for the $10,000 boot, he would be surrendering 20 Parent shares worth $10,000 ($10,000 boot ÷ $500 FMV for each share of Parent stock). Before this hypothetical redemption, he owns 50% of the outstanding Parent shares (100 ÷ 200), and afterward he owns 44% (80 ÷ 180). Thus, the hypothetical redemption is not substantially disproportionate under Sec. 302(b)(2) because the 44% post-redemption stock ownership is more than 80% of the pre-redemption stock ownership (50% × 0.80 = 40%). If the exchange can meet one of the other tests for sale treatment (e.g., not essentially equivalent to a dividend), the $10,000 is a capital gain. Otherwise it is a dividend. ◀

TYPICAL MISCONCEPTION

Unlike Sec. 351, securities (long-term debt) can be exchanged in a Sec. 355 transaction without the recognition of gain as long as the principal amount surrendered is equal to or greater than the principal amount received.

In a split-off or a split-up, securities of the controlled corporation may be received by a shareholder tax-free but only if the shareholder surrenders securities in the distributing corporation with an equal or larger principal amount. To the extent the principal amount of the securities received by a shareholder exceeds the principal amount of the securities surrendered by that shareholder, the FMV of the excess principal amount is boot.

THE SEC. 355 REQUIREMENTS. The Sec. 355 requirements must be met in order for the distribution of a subsidiary's stock as part of a Type D reorganization or as an independent event to be tax-free.

Under Sec. 355, a parent corporation's distribution of the stock of a subsidiary corporation is tax-free to the shareholders if the following six requirements are met:[62]

KEY POINT

The control requirement for Sec. 355 is the same control requirement previously discussed relating to the formation of a corporation under Sec. 351 (Chap. C2).

TYPICAL MISCONCEPTION

The active trade or business requirement has two parts: a pre-distribution five-year history and both the distributing and controlled corporations must be actively engaged in a trade or business immediately after the distribution.

- The property distributed must consist solely of stock or securities of a corporation that was controlled by the distributing corporation immediately before the distribution. The parent corporation must own and distribute stock possessing at least 80% of the total combined voting power of all classes of stock entitled to vote and at least 80% of the total number of shares of all other classes of stock.[63]
- The distribution must not have been used principally as a device to distribute the E&P of the distributing corporation, the controlled corporation, or both. Whether a transaction has been used as a device to distribute the E&P of the distributing corporation, the controlled corporation, or both is a matter of the facts and circumstances in each case. A sale or exchange of stock of the distributing or controlled corporation after the distribution is evidence that the distribution was used as such a device, especially if the sale was prearranged.[64]
- Immediately after the distribution, the distributing corporation and the controlled corporation each must be engaged in the active conduct of a trade or business that also was actively conducted for at least five years before the distribution. The main reason for this requirement is to prevent a corporation from spinning off a newly formed subsidiary whose only assets are unneeded cash and other liquid assets. The

[62] Sec. 355(a) and Reg. Secs. 1.355-2(b) and (c). Rev. Proc. 96-30 (1996-1 C.B. 696) is a checklist questionnaire of the information that must be included in a ruling request coming under Sec. 355. Appendix A of this document contains guidelines regarding the business purpose requirement for Sec. 355 transactions including information submission requirements for nine specific situations where rulings may or may not be granted.

[63] Sec. 368(c).

[64] Reg. Sec. 1.355-2(d).

shareholders could then sell or liquidate the subsidiary and obtain the liquid assets in an exchange transaction rather than as a dividend.[65]

- The distributing corporation must distribute either all of the stock and securities in the controlled corporation held by it immediately before the distribution or an amount of stock in the controlled corporation constituting control. The distributing corporation is allowed to retain some stock if it can establish to the satisfaction of the IRS that it was not retained as part of a tax-avoidance plan.
- The distribution must have a substantial corporate business purpose. Qualifying distributions include those made to comply with antitrust litigation and those made to separate businesses where the shareholders have major disagreements.[66]
- The people who directly or indirectly owned the controlled corporation(s) before the distribution must maintain a continuing equity interest in one or more of the corporations following the division. A substantial number of the shareholders who owned the stock of the distributing corporation before the division must maintain a continuing equity interest in the parent and/or subsidiary corporations following the division.[67] The distribution of stock and securities does not have to be pro rata. Disproportionate distributions may be used to eliminate the stock ownership of a dissenting shareholder group. In a split-off transaction, some shareholders may exchange all of their parent corporation stock for all of the subsidiary's stock.

TYPE G DIVISIVE REORGANIZATION

The divisive Type G reorganization involves the transfer of *part* of the assets of a corporation to a second corporation according to a court-approved plan. The transferee corporation's stock and securities are then distributed by the transferor corporation to its shareholders, security holders, and creditors. The transferor corporation may then continue in business separate from the transferee corporation after its operations have been restructured. Alternatively, the transferor corporation may be liquidated by the courts as part of the bankruptcy proceedings.

OTHER REORGANIZATION TRANSACTIONS

Two types of transactions do not fit into the acquisitive or divisive reorganization categories. These are Type E reorganizations, a recapitalization, and Type F reorganizations, a change in identity, form, or state of incorporation. A summary of the requirements for the Type E and Type F requirements is presented in Topic Review C7-6 on page C7-38.

KEY POINT

A Type E reorganization is neither acquisitive nor divisive in nature. Instead, it simply allows a single corporation to restructure its capital without creating a taxable exchange between the corporation and its shareholders.

TYPE E REORGANIZATION

Section 368(a)(1)(E) defines a **Type E reorganization** quite simply as a "recapitalization." A 1942 Supreme Court decision defined a **recapitalization** as "the reshuffling of the corporate structure within the framework of an existing corporation."[68] A recapitalization needs to have a bona fide business purpose. One reason for engaging in

---

[65] Sec. 355(b)(2). A corporation is engaged in the active conduct of a trade or business if it actively conducts all activities needed for generating a profit and these activities encompass all steps in the process of earning income. Specifically excluded are passive investment activities such as holding stock, securities, or land.

[66] Reg. Sec. 1.355-2(b)(5), Exs. (1) and (2).

[67] Reg. Sec. 1.355-2(c).

[68] *Helvering v. Southwest Consolidated Corp.*, 28 AFTR 573, 42-1 USTC ¶9248 (USSC, 1942).

a recapitalization might be to issue additional common or preferred stock that will be exchanged for outstanding bonds in order to reduce the corporation's interest payments and its debt to equity ratio. Alternatively, a family corporation might issue preferred stock in exchange for part or all of the common stock that is held by an elderly, controlling shareholder to permit that shareholder to turn over active management of the corporation to his or her children and to engage in estate planning (see page C7-45).

Three types of adjustments to the corporate capital structure can qualify as a Type E reorganization. These are a stock-for-stock exchange, a bond-for-stock exchange, and a bond-for-bond exchange.[69] Normally, these exchanges do not result in an increase or decrease in the corporation's assets except to the extent that a distribution of money or other property is made to the shareholders as part of the transaction.

STOCK-FOR-STOCK EXCHANGE. An exchange of common stock for common stock or preferred stock for preferred stock within a single corporation can qualify as a recapitalization if it is made pursuant to a plan of reorganization. Code Sec. 1036 also permits the same types of exchanges to take place outside of the reorganization rules. In either case, shareholders recognize no gain or loss and take a substituted basis in the shares received that references the basis in the shares that are surrendered.

EXAMPLE C7-26 ▶ The shareholders of Pilot Corporation exchange all of their nonvoting Class B common stock for additional shares of Pilot's Class A common stock. The Class A stock retains voting rights. The exchange is tax-free under Sec. 1036, even if no plan of reorganization has been created. An exchange of some of Pilot's Class A preferred stock for Class B preferred stock would also be tax-free under Sec. 1036. ◀

Section 1036 does not apply to an exchange of common stock for preferred stock, or preferred stock for common stock, within the same corporation, or an exchange of stock involving two corporations. However, the recapitalization rules apply to an exchange of two different classes of stock (e.g., common for preferred) in the same corporation if the exchange is made as part of a plan of reorganization. The exchange is tax-free for the shareholders under the Sec. 354(a) nonrecognition rules, except to the extent that boot property is received. If the FMV of the stock that is received is different from that of the stock surrendered, the difference may be a gift, a contribution to capital, compensation for services, a dividend, or a payment made to satisfy a debt obligation, depending on the facts and circumstances of the situation.[70] The tax consequences of that portion of the exchange will fall outside the reorganization rules.

EXAMPLE C7-27 ▶ John owns 60% of Boise Corporation's common stock and all of its preferred stock. The remainder of Boise's common stock is held by eighty unrelated individuals. John's basis for his preferred stock is $300,000. John exchanges his preferred stock for $400,000 of additional common stock and $100,000 in money. The preferred stock is valued at $500,000. John realizes a $200,000 gain [($400,000 + $100,000) − $300,000] on the exchange. $100,000 of gain must be recognized as dividend income (assuming that Boise has sufficient E&P) because none of the Sec. 302(b) exceptions that permit capital gain treatment apply. John's basis for the additional common stock is $300,000 ($300,000 + $100,000 gain − $100,000 money). ◀

[69] An exchange of stock for bonds has been held in *J. Robert Bazely v. CIR* (35 AFTR 1190, 47-2 USTC ¶9288 [USSC, 1947]) not to be a recapitalization. Even if it were a recapitalization, it would generally be taxable because receipt of the entire principal amount of the bonds represents boot under Sec. 356. The IRS has held that if no stock is held after the exchange, the Sec. 302 stock redemption rules apply to the transaction, thereby resulting in sale or exchange treatment (Rev. Rul. 77-415, 1977-2 C.B. 311).

[70] Rev. Ruls. 74-269, 1974-2 C.B. 87 and 83-120, 1983-2 C.B. 170.

A recapitalization is often used as an estate planning device whereby a parent's controlling interest in a corporation's common stock is exchanged for both common stock and preferred stock. The common stock is often gifted to a child who, following the recapitalization, will own a controlling interest in the common stock and manage the company. The parent will receive annual income from the preferred stock's cash dividends. The preferred stock's value will not increase over time, thereby freezing the value of the parent's estate and reducing his or her estate tax liability. The capital appreciation will accrue to the child who owns the common stock.

Substantial income tax and estate and gift tax planning opportunities existed at one time when recapitalizing a closely held corporation. In order to prevent abuses in this area, Code Secs. 2701-2704 were added in 1990. These rules provide detailed procedures for more accurately valuing, for transfer tax purposes, interests that are transferred and retained in corporations and partnerships. Additional coverage of this topic is presented in the gift tax chapter.

BOND-FOR-STOCK EXCHANGE. A bond-for-stock exchange is tax-free to the shareholder except to the extent that a portion of the stock is received in satisfaction of the corporation's liability for accrued interest on the bonds.[71]

BOND-FOR-BOND EXCHANGE. These exchanges are tax-free only when the principal amount of the bonds received does not exceed the principal amount of the bonds surrendered. If the principal amount of the bonds received exceeds the principal amount of the bonds surrendered, the FMV of the "excess" principal amount received is taxed to the bondholder as boot. (See pages C7-18 and C7-19 for a discussion of the boot rules.)

TYPE F REORGANIZATION

HISTORICAL NOTE

The statute was changed in 1982 to limit a Type F reorganization to one corporation. Since that time, the importance of a Type F reorganization has greatly diminished.

A **Type F reorganization** is defined by Sec. 368(a)(1)(F) as a "mere change in identity, form, or place of organization of one corporation, however effected." Traditionally, Type F reorganizations are used to change either the state in which the business is incorporated or the name of a corporation, without requiring the old corporation or its shareholders to recognize any gain or loss. In a Type F reorganization, the assets and liabilities of the old corporation become the property of the new corporation. Thus, the shareholders and creditors of the old corporation exchange their stock and debt interests for similar interests in the new corporation.

EXAMPLE C7-28 ▶

Rider Corporation is incorporated in the State of Illinois. Its management decides to change its state of incorporation to Delaware because of the more favorable securities and corporation laws in Delaware. Old Rider Corporation exchanges its assets for all of the stock of new Rider Corporation. The shareholders of old Rider then exchange their stock for new Rider stock. Old Rider Corporation goes out of existence. Neither the shareholders nor the two corporations involved in the reorganization recognize any gain on the transaction. Each shareholder takes a substituted basis for the new Rider stock that references their basis in the old Rider stock. Their holding period for the new Rider stock includes their holding period for the old Rider stock. New Rider Corporation's assets have the same basis that they had on old Rider Corporation's books. New Rider Corporation also acquires old Rider Corporation's tax attributes. ◀

The reorganization illustrated in Example C7-28 could also take place if old Rider Corporation's shareholders exchange their stock for new Rider stock. Old Rider Corporation would then be liquidated into new Rider Corporation. The tax consequences are the same for both transaction forms.

[71] Sec. 354(a)(2)(B).

JUDICIAL RESTRICTIONS ON THE USE OF CORPORATE REORGANIZATIONS

OBJECTIVE 7

Explain how judicial doctrines can restrict a taxpayer's ability to use corporate reorganizations

The Supreme Court holds that literal compliance with the statutory requirements for a reorganization transaction is not enough for a transaction to receive tax-free treatment.[72] As a result, the courts have placed four primary restrictions on reorganization transactions:

- Continuity of the investor's proprietary interest
- Continuity of the business enterprise
- A business purpose for the transaction
- The collapsing of a series of related transactions down into a single transaction that reflects their economic substance

All four requirements relate to the overall doctrine of substance over form and are explained below.

TYPICAL MISCONCEPTION

The continuity-of-interest requirement has nothing to do with the relative sizes of Acquiring and Target. Target's shareholders may end up with a minimal amount of the total outstanding stock of Acquiring, and yet the merger will still be a good reorganization as long as 50% of the consideration received by Target's shareholders is an equity interest in Acquiring.

SELF-STUDY QUESTION

For which reorganizations is the continuity-of-interest requirement most important?

ANSWER

The only limitation on consideration used for both regular and triangular mergers is the continuity-of-interest requirement. The other reorganizations have statutory requirements more restrictive than the continuity-of-interest doctrine.

CONTINUITY OF PROPRIETARY INTEREST

The requirement for the continuity of the investor's proprietary interest is based on the principle that the tax deferral associated with a reorganization is available because the shareholder has changed his or her investment from one form to another rather than liquidating it. According to Reg. Sec. 1.368-1(b), this test is met by continuity of the business enterprise under a modified corporate form and continuity of interest on the part of the people who, directly or indirectly, own the enterprise before its reorganization. In a series of decisions, the courts have held that the continuing proprietary interest must be a common or preferred stock interest.[73] Thus, a transaction that involves the target corporation receiving only cash or short-term debt obligations does not qualify as a tax-free reorganization. The Code does not specify how much stock constitutes the required proprietary interest. For advance ruling purposes, however, the IRS requires the former shareholders of the target corporation to receive at least 50% of their total consideration in the form of acquiring corporation stock. The 50% rule applies only for advance ruling purposes, and the courts have accepted lesser percentages.[74] Despite the existence of judicial support, few taxpayers are willing to proceed with a reorganization without the receipt of an advance ruling because of the risk associated with a possible disallowance of the tax-free status and the large dollar amounts involved. Thus, the IRS exercises substantial power through its ruling position in the reorganization area.

EXAMPLE C7-29 ▶ Target Corporation transfers all of its assets to Acquiring Corporation in a Type C reorganization in exchange for $200,000 of Acquiring stock and the assumption of $800,000 of Target liabilities. The Acquiring stock is distributed by Target Corporation to its sole shareholder,

[72] *Evelyn F. Gregory v. Helvering,* 14 AFTR 1191, 35-1 USTC ¶9043 (USSC, 1935).

[73] See, for example, *V. L. LeTulle v. Scofield,* 23 AFTR 789, 40-1 USTC ¶9150 (USSC, 1940).

[74] Rev. Proc. 77-37, 1977-2 C.B. 568, Sec. 3.02. See also *John A. Nelson Co. v. Helvering,* 16 AFTR 1262, 36-1 USTC ¶9019 (USSC, 1935), where the Supreme Court permitted a tax-free reorganization to take place where the stock exchanged constituted only 38% of the total consideration.

Nancy, in exchange for all of her Target stock. Even though the transaction meets the statutory requirements for a Type C reorganization, the IRS will most likely attempt to hold that the transaction is not a reorganization because the continuity-of-proprietary-interest requirement is not met (i.e., only 20% of the total consideration received by Target represents an equity interest in Acquiring). ◀

CONTINUITY OF BUSINESS ENTERPRISE

SELF-STUDY QUESTION

Does Acquiring have to continue its own historic business?

ANSWER

No. The IRS has specifically ruled that the continuity-of-business-enterprise test requires only that the historic business of Target be continued (Rev. Rul. 81-25, 1981-1 C.B. 132).

The requirement for continuity of the business enterprise necessitates that the acquiring corporation either continue the acquired corporation's historic business or use a significant portion of the acquired corporation's historic business assets in a new business.[75] This restriction limits tax-free reorganizations to transactions involving *continuing interests* in the target corporation's business or property under a modified corporate form. The **continuity-of-interest doctrine**, however, does not require that the target corporation's historic business be continued.

Whether the requirements for continuity of the business enterprise are satisfied depends on the facts and circumstances of the particular situation. The historic business requirement can be satisfied if the acquiring corporation continues one or more of the acquired corporation's significant lines of business.

EXAMPLE C7-30 ▶ Target Corporation is merged into Acquiring Corporation. Immediately before the merger, Target is manufacturing resins and chemicals and distributing chemicals for use in making other products. All three lines of business are approximately the same size. Two months after the merger, Acquiring sells the resin manufacturing and chemicals distribution activities to an unrelated party for cash. The transaction satisfies the requirement for the continuity of the business enterprise because Acquiring is continuing at least one of Target's three significant lines of business.[76] ◀

The asset continuity requirement is satisfied if the acquiring corporation uses a significant portion of the assets that were used in the acquired corporation's historic business in its business. The significance of the assets that are used is based on the relative importance of the assets to the operation of the historic business of the acquired company.

EXAMPLE C7-31 ▶ Acquiring and Target Corporations are both computer manufacturers. Target is merged into Acquiring. Acquiring terminates Target's manufacturing activities and maintains Target's equipment as a backup source of supply for its components. Acquiring satisfies the continuity-of-business-enterprise requirement by continuing to use Target's historic business assets. If Acquiring had instead sold Target's assets for cash and invested the proceeds in an investment portfolio, the continuity-of-business-enterprise requirement would not be met. Acquiring does not need to continue Target's business in order to satisfy the continuity-of-business-enterprise requirement.[77] ◀

ADDITIONAL COMMENT

Because Target and its shareholders have the most to lose, they should protect themselves by stipulating that Acquiring retain the historic assets. If not, there is nothing to stop Acquiring from unilaterally disposing of the historic assets and busting the tax-free reorganization.

BUSINESS PURPOSE REQUIREMENT

A transaction must serve a bona fide **business purpose** to qualify as a reorganization.[78] Regulation Sec. 1.368-1(c) states that a transaction that takes "the form of a corporate reorganization as a disguise for concealing its real character, and the object and accomplishment of which is the consummation of a preconceived plan having no business or corporate purpose, is not a plan of reorganization."

---

[75] Reg. Sec. 1.368-1(d)(2).

[76] Reg. Secs. 1.368-1(d)(3) and -1(d)(5), Ex. (1).

[77] Reg. Secs. 1.368-1(d)(4) and -1(d)(5), Ex. (2).

[78] *Evelyn F. Gregory v. Helvering*, 14 AFTR 1191, 35-1 USTC ¶9043 (USSC, 1935). Other Sec. 355 requirements are probably failed, such as being a device for the distribution of E&P.

EXAMPLE C7-32 ▶

KEY POINT

Business purpose is much more difficult to establish in divisive (Sec. 355) transactions than it is in acquisitive (Sec. 354) transactions.

Parent Corporation transfers some highly appreciated stock from its investment portfolio to newly-created Subsidiary Corporation in exchange for all of its stock. The Subsidiary stock is distributed to Parent's sole shareholder, Kathy, in exchange for part of her Parent stock. Shortly after the stock transfer, Subsidiary is liquidated, with Kathy receiving the appreciated stock. Treating the liquidation of Subsidiary as a separate event, Kathy recognizes a capital gain on the liquidation, which she uses to offset capital loss carryovers from other tax years, and is able to step-up the basis of the appreciated stock to its FMV without incurring a tax liability. Even though the stock transfer to Subsidiary fits within a literal reading of the Sec. 368(a)(1)(D) definition of a divisive Type D reorganization, the IRS will probably state that the Sec. 355 trade or business requirement has not been met and also rely on *Gregory v. Helvering,* to hold that the series of transactions serves no business purpose. As a result, Kathy's receipt of the appreciated stock from Subsidiary is then a dividend. ◀

STEP TRANSACTION DOCTRINE

The **step transaction doctrine** may be used by the IRS to collapse a multistep reorganization into a single taxable transaction. Alternatively, the IRS may attempt to take a series of steps, which the taxpayer calls independent events, and collapse them into a single tax-free reorganization transaction. Both of these IRS actions are intended to prevent the taxpayer from arranging a series of business transactions in order to obtain a tax result that is not available if only a single transaction is used.

EXAMPLE C7-33 ▶

Jody transfers business properties from his sole proprietorship to his wholly owned Smith Corporation. Three days after the incorporation, Smith Corporation transfers all of its assets to Brown Corporation in a Type C reorganization in which the Brown stock is distributed to Jody pursuant to Smith Corporation's liquidation. After the liquidation, Jody owns 15% of the Brown stock. The IRS will probably attempt to collapse the two transactions (the Sec. 351 asset transfer to Smith Corporation and the Type C asset-for-stock reorganization) into a single transaction: an asset transfer by Jody to Brown Corporation. Under the IRS's position, the Sec. 351 rules do not apply because Jody does not own at least 80% of the Brown stock immediately after the transfer. Jody must recognize gain or loss on the transfer of assets from his sole proprietorship to Brown Corporation.[79] ◀

TAX ATTRIBUTES

Section 381(a) requires the acquired or transferor corporation's tax attributes (e.g., loss or tax credit carryovers) to be assumed by the acquiring or transferee corporation in certain types of reorganizations. Sections 269, 382, 383, and 384 restrict the taxpayer's ability to use certain corporate tax attributes (e.g., NOL carryovers) that are obtained through the acquisition of the loss corporation's stock or assets.

OBJECTIVE 8

Determine which reorganization forms permit the carryover of tax attributes

ASSUMPTION OF TAX ATTRIBUTES

In the Type A, C, acquisitive D, F, and acquisitive G reorganizations, the acquiring corporation obtains both the target corporation's tax attributes and assets. The tax attributes do not change hands in either the Type B or Type E reorganization because there is no transfer of assets from one corporation to another. Even though there is a division of assets between a transferor corporation and a controlled corporation in the divisive Type D and G reorganizations, the only tax attribute that is allocated between the two entities is the transferor corporation's E&P.[80]

[79] Rev. Rul. 70-140, 1970-1 C.B. 73.
[80] Reg. Sec. 1.312-10.

KEY POINT

An often-cited advantage to a tax-free asset reorganization over a taxable acquisition is that the tax attributes (e.g., NOL and NCLs) carry over to the acquiring corporation.

Some of the tax attributes that are carried over under Sec. 381(c) include

- Net operating losses
- Capital losses
- Earnings and profits
- General business credits
- Inventory methods

KEY POINT

The thrust of Sec. 381, as it relates to NOLs, is to allow Target's NOL carryforwards to offset only the post-acquisition income of the acquiring corporation.

The acquired corporation's NOL carryover is determined as of the transaction's acquisition date and is carried over to tax years ending after such date. Generally, the acquisition date for a tax-free reorganization is the date on which the assets are transferred by the transferor or target corporation. When loss carryovers from more than one tax year are present, the loss from the earliest ending tax year is used first. NOLs from the time period following the acquisition date cannot be carried back by the acquiring corporation to offset profits earned by the acquired corporation in its tax years preceding the acquisition date.[81]

EXAMPLE C7-34 ▶ Target Corporation is merged into Acquiring Corporation at the close of business on June 30, 1997. Both corporations use the calendar year as their tax year. At the beginning of 1997, Target reports a $200,000 NOL carryover from 1995. Target must file a final tax return for the period January 1, 1997 through June 30, 1997. Assume that Target reports $60,000 of taxable income (before any NOL deductions) in its tax return for the short period. Target's taxable income for the January 1 through June 30, 1997 period reduces its NOL carryover to $140,000 ($200,000 − $60,000). This carryover is assumed by Acquiring. ◀

Section 381(c) restricts the acquiring corporation's use of the NOL carryover in its first tax year that ends after the acquisition date. The NOL deduction is limited to the portion of the acquiring corporation's taxable income that is allocable on a daily basis to the post-acquisition period.

EXAMPLE C7-35 ▶ Assume the same facts as in Example C7-34, except that it is now known that Acquiring's taxable income is $146,000 in 1997. Acquiring can use Target's NOL carryover to offset its taxable income that is attributable to the 184 days in the July 1 through December 31, 1997 post-acquisition period, or $73,600 [(184 ÷ 365) × $146,000]. The remaining NOL carryover of $66,400 ($140,000 − $73,600) is carried forward to offset Acquiring's taxable income in 1998. Both the pre- and post-acquisition portions of 1997 count as full tax years for loss carryover purposes. ◀

OBJECTIVE 9

Explain how NOL carryovers are restricted following an acquisition

LIMITATION ON USE OF TAX ATTRIBUTES

Sections 382 and 269 prevent the purchasing of the assets or stock of a corporation having loss carryovers (known as the **loss corporation**) primarily to acquire the corporation's tax attributes. Similarly, Secs. 382 and 269 prevent a corporation having loss carryovers (also known as a loss corporation) from acquiring the assets or stock of a profitable corporation primarily to enable the loss corporation to use its carryovers. Section 383 provides similar restrictions for acquisitions intended to facilitate the use of capital loss and tax credit carryovers. Section 384 additionally restricts the use of pre-acquisition losses to offset built-in gains.

[81] Special rules apply to Type F reorganizations. Because only a change in form or identity involving a single corporation occurs in such a transaction, NOLs incurred following the acquisition date can be carried back to offset profits earned in pre-acquisition tax years.

SECTION 382. Section 382 restricts the use of NOLs in purchase transactions and tax-free reorganizations when a substantial change in the stock ownership of the loss corporation occurs.

TYPICAL MISCONCEPTION

To create an ownership change, the 5% shareholders must increase their stock ownership by more than 50 *percentage points.* Thus, if shareholder A increases her stock ownership from 10% to 20%, this alone is not an ownership change even though it represents a 100% increase in A's ownership.

Stock Ownership Change. The requisite stock ownership change has taken place when

- Any shift in the stock ownership involving any person(s) owning 5% or more of a corporation's stock occurs or a tax-free reorganization (other than a divisive Type D or G reorganization or a Type F reorganization) has taken place *and*
- The percentage of stock of the new loss corporation owned by one or more 5% shareholders has increased by more than 50 percentage points over the *lowest* percentage of stock in the old loss corporation owned by such shareholder(s) at *any* time during the preceding three-year (or shorter) "testing" period.[82]

The 5% shareholder test is based on the value of the loss corporation's stock. Nonvoting preferred stock is excluded from the calculation.

An **old loss corporation** is any corporation that is entitled to use a NOL carryover or has a NOL for the tax year in which the ownership change occurs, and undergoes the requisite stock ownership change. A **new loss corporation** is any corporation that is entitled to use a NOL carryover after the stock ownership change.[83] The old and new loss corporations are the same for most taxable acquisitions (e.g., the purchase of a loss corporation's stock by a new shareholder group). The old and new loss corporations are different in many acquisitive reorganizations (e.g., a merger transaction where an unprofitable target [old loss] corporation is merged into the acquiring [new loss] corporation).

KEY POINT

One of the burdensome aspects of Sec. 382 is that each time the stock ownership of a 5% shareholder is changed, all 5% shareholders must be tested at that date to see whether an ownership change has occurred.

Ownership changes are tested any time that a stock transaction occurs affecting the stock owned by a person who owns 5% or more of the stock either before or after the change. Such change may occur because of a stock transaction involving a 5% shareholder or involving a person who does not own a 5% interest in the loss corporation that affects the size of the stock interest owned by a 5% shareholder (i.e., a stock redemption). When applying the 5% rule, all people who own less than 5% of the loss corporation's stock are considered to be a single shareholder.

EXAMPLE C7-36 ▶

Spencer Corporation is a publicly traded corporation with no single individual owning more than 5% of its outstanding stock. A series of NOLs have been incurred by Spencer in recent years, substantial amounts of which are available as carryovers. On July 3, Barry acquires 80% of Spencer's single class of stock in a cash purchase. Barry had not owned any of the Spencer stock before making the acquisition. Spencer Corporation has experienced a stock ownership change because it now has a 5% shareholder (Barry), who owns 80 percentage points more stock than he owned at any time during the testing period (Barry owned 0% during the three-year testing period) because of a purchase transaction. Since Spencer Corporation both incurred the losses prior to the ownership change, and can use the NOLs after the change, it is both the old and new loss corporation. Spencer Corporation's NOLs are subject to the Sec. 382 limitations. ◀

In many acquisitive tax-free reorganizations, the Sec. 382 stock ownership test is applied against the old loss (or target) corporation and then against the new loss (or acquiring) corporation.

---

[82] Sec. 382(g). Special rules permit the use of a testing period of less than three years for applying the 50-percentage-point ownership change rule. One such situation is when a recent change in the stock ownership has occurred involving a 5% shareholder. In such case, the testing period goes back only to the date of the earlier ownership change.

[83] Secs. 382(k)(1)–(3).

EXAMPLE C7-37 ▶ Target Corporation has a single class of stock outstanding. None of its 300 shareholders owns more than 5% of the outstanding stock. Target has incurred substantial NOLs in recent years. Pursuant to a merger agreement, Target Corporation is merged into Jackson Corporation. Jackson also has a single class of stock outstanding and none of its 500 shareholders owns more than 5% of its outstanding stock. None of Target's shareholders owned any of the Jackson stock before the merger. After the merger, Target's shareholders own 40% of the Jackson stock. All of Jackson's shareholders are aggregated when applying the Sec. 382 stock ownership test. The Sec. 382 rules limit the use of Target's NOL carryovers because Jackson's shareholders owned none of the old loss corporation (Target) stock before the reorganization, and owned 60% of the new loss corporation (Jackson) stock after the reorganization. ◀

Divisive Type D and G reorganizations or Type F reorganizations may be subject to the Sec. 382 limitations if the transaction results in a more-than-50-percentage-point shift in stock ownership for the transferor corporation.

TYPICAL MISCONCEPTION

Section 382 does not disallow NOLs. Section 382 merely limits the amount of NOL carryovers that the new loss corporation can use on an annual basis.

ADDITIONAL COMMENT

The reason that the new loss corporation's use of the old loss corporation's NOLs is limited annually to the FMV of the old loss corporation multiplied by the long-term tax-exempt rate is that this limitation is supposed to approximate the rate at which the old loss corporation could have used the NOLs. Thus, the underlying theory of Sec. 382 is one of neutrality.

Loss Limitation. The Sec. 382 loss limitation for any tax year ending after the stock ownership change equals the value of the old loss corporation's stock (including nonvoting preferred stock) immediately before the ownership change multiplied by the long-term tax-exempt federal rate.[84] The long-term tax-exempt federal rate is determined by the IRS and is the highest of the adjusted federal long-term rates in effect for any month in the three-calendar-month period ending with the month in which the stock ownership change occurs.[85]

A new loss corporation can claim its current-year deductions. Then any NOLs from the old loss corporation (pre-change tax years) can be deducted. If the NOL carryovers from the old loss corporation exceed the Sec. 382 loss limitation, the unused carryovers are deferred until the following year, provided the end of the fifteen-year NOL carryforward period has not been reached. If the Sec. 382 loss limitation exceeds the new loss corporation's taxable income for the current year, the unused loss limitation is carried forward and increases the Sec. 382 loss limitation for the next year.[86] Finally any of its NOL and other deduction carryovers from post-change taxable years can be deducted. A new loss corporation that does not continue the business enterprise of the old loss corporation at all times during the two-year period beginning on the stock ownership change date must use a zero Sec. 382 limitation for any post-change year. This zero limitation, in effect, disallows the use of the NOL carryovers.[87]

EXAMPLE C7-38 ▶ Peter purchased all of the Taylor Corporation stock (the old and new loss corporation) from Karl at the close of business on December 31, 1996. Taylor is engaged in the manufacture of brooms and has a $1,000,000 NOL carryover from 1996. Taylor continues to manufacture brooms after Peter's acquisition of a controlling interest and earns $300,000 of taxable income for 1997. The value of the Taylor stock immediately before the acquisition is $3,500,000. The applicable long-term tax-exempt federal rate is 5%. The requisite stock ownership change has taken place because Peter has increased his ownership from zero during the testing period to 100% immediately after the acquisition. The Sec. 382 loss limitation for 1997 is $175,000 ($3,500,000 × 0.05). Taylor can claim a $175,000 NOL deduction in 1997, thereby reducing its taxable income to $125,000. The remaining $825,000 ($1,000,000 − $175,000) of NOL is carried over to 1998 and later years. ◀

KEY POINT

If the old loss corporation is a very large corporation relative to its NOL carryovers, Sec. 382 will not be a real obstacle in the use of the NOLs by the new loss corporation. Only when the old loss corporation has a small FMV relative to its NOL carryovers does Sec. 382 represent a major obstacle.

[84] Sec. 382(b)(1).

[85] Sec. 382(f). The long-term tax-exempt federal rate for January 1997 is 5.35% (Rev. Rul. 97-1, I.R.B. 1997-2, 1). The highest long-term tax-exempt federal rate for January 1997 and the two preceding months is 5.60%.

[86] Sec. 382(b)(2).

[87] Sec. 382(c).

ADDITIONAL COMMENT

Although the legislative intent of Sec. 382 has not been seriously opposed, the complexity of the statute with its accompanying regulations is of concern to many tax practitioners.

Special rules apply to the loss corporation for the year in which the stock ownership change occurs. Taxable income earned before the change is not subject to the Sec. 382 limitation. Taxable income earned after the change, however, is subject to the limitation. Allocation of income earned during the tax year to the time periods before and after the ownership change is based on the number of days in each of the two time periods similar to the procedures illustrated earlier for tax attributes under Sec. 381.

Old loss corporation NOLs incurred before the date of the stock ownership change are limited by Sec. 382. These include NOLs incurred in tax years ending before the date of change plus the portion of the NOL for the tax year that includes the date of change that is considered to have been incurred before the change. Allocation of an NOL for the tax year that includes the date of change is based on the number of days before and after the change.[88]

SECTION 383. Section 383 restricts the use of tax credit and capital loss carryovers when stock ownership changes occur that come under the purview of Sec. 382. The same restrictions that apply to NOLs are applied to the general business credit, the minimum tax credit, and the foreign tax credit.

SECTION 384. Section 384 prevents pre-acquisition losses of either the acquiring or target corporation (the loss corporation) from offsetting built-in gains recognized during the five-year post-acquisition recognition period by another corporation (the gain corporation). Such gains can offset pre-acquisition losses of the gain corporation. This limitation applies if a corporation acquires either a controlling stock interest or the assets of another corporation and either corporation is a gain corporation.

ADDITIONAL COMMENT

Section 269 represents the IRS's oldest and broadest weapon in dealing with trafficking in NOLs. However, because of the subjectivity of the statute, Secs. 382, 383, and 384 have turned out to be the Service's main statutory weapons in this area.

SECTION 269. Section 269 applies to transactions where control of a corporation is secured and the principal purpose of the acquisition is "the evasion or avoidance of federal income tax by securing the benefit of a deduction," or credit, that otherwise would not be available. Control is defined as 50% of the voting power or 50% of the value of the outstanding stock. The IRS can use this provision to disallow a loss or credit carryover in situations where Sec. 382 does not apply. The IRS's primary problem in applying these rules is showing that the requisite principal purpose is present.

TAX PLANNING CONSIDERATIONS

WHY USE A REORGANIZATION INSTEAD OF A TAXABLE TRANSACTION?

The choice between a taxable and tax-free transaction can be a difficult one. The advantages and disadvantages of the tax-free reorganization are important considerations for the buyer and seller. Depending on their relative importance to each party, they may serve as points for negotiation and compromise when attempting to structure the transaction.

From the point of view of the acquired company's shareholders, there are a number of considerations that must be evaluated. First, a tax-free reorganization permits a complete deferral of tax to the shareholders unless boot is received. This tax deferral may permit a shareholder to retain a higher percentage of his or her capital investment than would be possible if a taxable acquisition had been used. A second factor is that a

[88] Sec. 382(b)(3).

taxable transaction permits the shareholders of the target corporation to convert their former equity interests into liquid assets (e.g., when cash or property other than stock or securities of the acquiring corporation is received). These funds can be invested in whatever manner the shareholder chooses.

In a reorganization, the shareholder must obtain a proprietary interest in the acquiring corporation. Future success by the acquiring corporation is likely to enhance the value of this interest. If the acquiring corporation encounters financial problems, the value of the shareholder's investment may diminish. Third, losses that are realized as part of a tax-free reorganization cannot be recognized. A taxable transaction permits an immediate recognition of the loss. Fourth, gains recognized as part of a tax-free reorganization are taxed as dividend income if the boot distribution is equivalent to a dividend. Taxable transactions generally result in the shareholder recognizing only capital gains. This difference takes on increased importance now that the top ordinary income rate is 39.6%. Finally, a taxable transaction permits the shareholder to step up the basis of the stock and securities that are received to their FMV. A tax-free transaction, however, requires a substituted basis be used.

From the transferor corporation's point of view, a tax-free reorganization permits the assets to be exchanged with no gain being recognized. The depreciation recapture rules do not apply to a reorganization. In each case the recapture burden is shifted to the purchasing party.

From the purchaser's point of view, a tax-free reorganization permits an acquisition to take place without the use of substantial amounts of cash or securities. Because the target company's shareholders do not have to recognize any gain unless boot is received, they may be willing to accept a lower sales price than would be required if a taxable acquisition occurs. The purchaser must use the same basis for the properties acquired in a tax-free reorganization that they had on the transferor's books. This inability to step-up the basis of the assets to their cost or FMV reduces the attractiveness of a tax-free reorganization. This, in turn, may lower the price that the purchaser is willing to offer.

The cost of using a taxable asset or stock acquisition transaction was increased dramatically by the Tax Reform Act of 1986. Before the 1986 Tax Act, a corporation that sold its assets was able to avoid recognizing its gains on the transaction by liquidating within twelve months of adopting its plan of liquidation. Similarly, a corporation that purchased the stock of a target corporation and caused the target corporation to make a Sec. 338 election did not incur any tax costs on the deemed sale transaction. Today a target corporation that makes an actual or deemed sale of its assets ends up recognizing all of its gains and losses in a taxable transaction. These additional tax costs make the tax exemption that is available for the target corporation in a tax-free reorganization even more attractive.

A tax-free reorganization permits the purchaser to acquire the benefits of NOL, tax credit, and other carryovers from the target corporation. Such tax attributes do not carry over to the buyer in a taxable transaction.

ETHICAL POINT

The choice between making an acquisition a taxable or tax-free transaction involves a large number of considerations for both the buyer and the seller. The tax, financial, and legal considerations must be examined by all parties with the assistance of their own experts. Because what may be good for the buyer may not be good for the seller in an acquisition, it is probably not a good idea for both parties to save money by using the same experts.

SELF-STUDY QUESTION

Is a tax-free reorganization always preferable to a taxable acquisition?

ANSWER

No. The determination of what form an acquisition should take involves the resolution of a myriad of issues relating to the parties involved in the reorganization. A number of these issues are discussed in this section.

TYPICAL MISCONCEPTION

It is important to realize that when a plan for an acquisition is developed, the tax consequences are only one of many considerations that must be addressed. Often, the form of the final acquisition plan will not be optimal from a tax perspective because other factors were deemed more important.

AVOIDING THE REORGANIZATION PROVISIONS

An acquisition can be changed from a tax-free reorganization to a taxable transaction if the restrictions on the use of consideration for the particular type of reorganization are not met. This change can be advantageous for the taxpayers involved. For example, the Type B reorganization rules can be avoided if the acquiring corporation makes a tender offer to the target corporation's shareholders involving an exchange of both stock of the acquiring corporation and cash for the target corporation's stock. Because this transaction does not meet the solely-for-voting-stock requirement, it is a taxable transaction for

TYPICAL MISCONCEPTION

The tax-free reorganization provisions are not elective. If a transaction qualifies as a Sec. 368 reorganization, it must be treated as such. If the desire is for a taxable acquisition, it is usually not difficult to bust a tax-free reorganization.

the shareholders. It is also considered to be a purchase of the target corporation's stock, thereby permitting the acquiring corporation to make a Sec. 338 deemed liquidation election and step-up the basis of the target corporation's assets to the price that was paid for the stock.

EXAMPLE C7-39 ▶ Acquiring Corporation offers to exchange one share of its common stock (valued at $40) plus $20 cash for each share of Target Corporation's single class of common stock. All of Target's shareholders agree to the proposal, and exchange a total of 2,000 shares of Target stock for 2,000 shares of Acquiring common stock and $40,000 cash. At the time of the acquisition, Target's assets have a $35,000 adjusted basis and a $110,000 FMV. Target recognizes no gain or loss with respect to the exchange. The basis of its assets remains at $35,000 unless a Sec. 338 election is made. Its shareholders must recognize their gain or loss on the exchange of their Target stock, whether a Sec. 338 election is made or not. ◀

COMPLIANCE AND PROCEDURAL CONSIDERATIONS

SECTION 338 DEEMED LIQUIDATIONS

The statement of election under Sec. 338 is made by the acquiring corporation on Form 8023 (Election under Sec. 338(g)). This election is made by the fifteenth day of the ninth month beginning after the month in which the acquisition date occurs. The information about the acquiring corporation, the target corporation, and the election that is filed with Form 8023 is contained in Reg. Sec. 1.338-1(d).

PLAN OF REORGANIZATION

One requirement for nonrecognition of gain by a transferor corporation on an asset transfer (Sec. 361) or by a shareholder on a stock transfer (Sec. 354) is that there be a plan of reorganization. A written plan is not needed but it is safest for all parties involved in the reorganization when it is reduced to writing either as a communication to the shareholders, as part of the corporate records, or as part of a written agreement between the parties. If a plan of reorganization does not exist, or a transfer or distribution is not part of the plan, it is generally a taxable event.[89] A **plan of reorganization** is defined as a consummated transaction that is specifically defined as a reorganization. Nonrecognition of gain or loss is limited to exchanges or distributions that are a direct part of a reorganization and undertaken for reasons germane to the continuance of the business of a corporation that is a party to a reorganization.[90]

PARTY TO A REORGANIZATION

Sections 354 and 361 require that a shareholder or a transferor be a party to a reorganization to have the asset or stock transfer be tax-free. Section 368(b) defines a **party to a reorganization**as "including any corporation resulting from a reorganization, and both corporations involved in a reorganization where one corporation acquires the stock or assets of a second corporation." In the case of a triangular reorganization, the corporation controlling the acquiring corporation and whose stock is used to effect the reorganization is also a party to a reorganization.

[89] A. T. *Evans,* 30 B.T.A. 746 (1934), *acq.* XIII-2 C.B. 7; and *William Hewitt,* 19 B.T.A. 771 (1930).

[90] Reg. Sec. 1.368-2(g).

RULING REQUESTS

Before proceeding with a taxable or tax-free acquisition or disposition, many taxpayers request an advance ruling from the IRS on the tax consequences of the transaction. Advance rulings are generally requested because of the complexity of the tax law in the reorganization area and because these transactions involve dollar amounts that are generally quite large. A subsequent redetermination by the IRS or the courts that a completed reorganization is taxable might have substantial adverse tax consequences to the parties involved in the transaction. Note that an advance ruling is issued only for reorganizations that conform with the guidelines issued by the IRS in Rev. Proc. 77-37 and other promulgations.[91] However, these guidelines do not have the force of law, and in many cases may be stricter than the court precedents (see Chapter C15).

PROBLEM MATERIALS

DISCUSSION QUESTIONS

C7-1 Debate the following statements: All acquisition transactions should be taxable events. No acquisitions should be permitted to be tax-free reorganizations. Required: Present the arguments for and against such a tax policy change.

C7-2 What tax advantages exist for the buyer when he or she acquires the assets of a corporation in a taxable transaction? for the seller when he or she exchanges stock in a taxable transaction?

C7-3 What tax and nontax advantages accrue when an acquiring corporation purchases all of the target corporation's stock for cash and subsequently liquidates the target corporation?

C7-4 Why might a parent corporation elect to treat the acquisition of a target corporation's stock as a deemed liquidation coming under Sec. 338? When would such an election not be advisable?

C7-5 Explain the following items related to a Sec. 338 election:

a. The rule used to determine the time period within which a Sec. 338 election can be made

b. The stock acquisition transactions that are counted when determining whether a qualified stock purchase has been made

c. The method for determining the sale price for the target corporation's assets

d. The method for determining the total basis for the target corporation's assets

e. The effect of the deemed sale on the target corporation's tax attributes.

C7-6 Holt Corporation acquires all of the stock of Star Corporation and makes a timely Sec. 338 election. The adjusted grossed-up basis of the Star stock is \$2.5 million. Tangible assets on Star's balance sheet have a \$1.8 million FMV. Explain to Holt's president how the new bases for Star's individual assets are determined.

C7-7 Compare the tax consequences arising from a taxable asset acquisition transaction and an asset-for-stock tax-free reorganization, giving consideration to the following points:

a. Consideration used to effect the transaction

b. Recognition of gain or loss by the target corporation on the asset transfer

c. Basis of property to the acquiring corporation

d. Recognition of gain or loss when the target corporation is liquidated

C7-8 Which of the following events that occur as part of an acquisitive tax-free reorganization require the target corporation to recognize gain? Assume that in all cases the target corporation is liquidated as part of the reorganization.

a. Transfer of appreciated target corporation assets in exchange for stock and short-term notes

b. Transfer of appreciated target corporation assets in exchange for stock and the assumption of the target corporation's liabilities

c. Transfer of appreciated target corporation assets in exchange for stock and money. The

[91] 1977-2 C.B. 568.

money is distributed to the target corporation's shareholders.

d. Transfer of appreciated target corporation assets in exchange for stock and money. The money is used to pay off the target corporation's liabilities.

C7-9 Explain the boot rule as it applies to the shareholders in a tax-free reorganization. How is the character of the shareholders'recognized gain determined in a tax-free reorganization?

C7-10 Evaluate the following statement: Individual shareholders who must recognize gain as the result of receiving boot in a corporate reorganization generally prefer to report capital gain income, whereas corporate shareholders generally prefer to report dividend income.

C7-11 How is the basis for the stocks and securities received by a shareholder determined? How is the basis determined for boot property?

C7-12 Which tax-free reorganizations are acquisitive transactions? divisive transactions?

C7-13 Compare the type of consideration that can be used to effect Type A, B, and C reorganizations.

C7-14 How does the IRS interpret the continuity-of-interest doctrine for a Type A merger transaction?

C7-15 What are the advantages of using an asset-for-stock reorganization instead of a Type A merger transaction? the disadvantages?

C7-16 How does the IRS interpret the "substantially all" of the assets requirement for a Type C reorganization?

C7-17 Explain why an acquiring corporation is generally prohibited from using cash as part of the consideration it uses to accomplish a Type C reorganization.

C7-18 Some transactions may be characterized as either a Type C or a Type D reorganization. Which reorganization provision controls in the case of an overlap?

C7-19 Explain the circumstances in which money and other property can be used in a Type B reorganization.

C7-20 Acquiring Corporation has purchased for cash a 5% interest in Target Corporation's stock. Acquiring Corporation's management wants to make a tender offer to acquire the remaining Target stock in exchange for Acquiring stock. Can this tender offer be accomplished as a Type B reorganization? What problems may be encountered in structuring the acquisition as a tax-free reorganization?

C7-21 Acquiring Corporation wants to exchange its voting common stock for all of Target Corporation's single class of stock in a tender offer. Only 85% of Target Corporation's shareholders agree to tender their shares. Assuming the reorganization is accomplished, what options exist for Acquiring to acquire the remaining shares as part of the reorganization? at a later date?

C7-22 Compare and contrast the requirements for, and the tax treatment of, the spinoff, split-off, and split-up forms of the divisive Type D reorganization.

C7-23 Stock of a controlled subsidiary corporation can be distributed tax-free to the distributing corporation's shareholders under Sec. 355. Explain the difference between such a distribution and a divisive Type D reorganization.

C7-24 When is the distribution of a controlled corporation's stock or securities tax-free to the distributing corporation's shareholders? What events trigger the recognition of gain or loss by the shareholders?

C7-25 When does the distributing corporation recognize gain or loss on the distribution of stock or securities of a controlled corporation to its shareholders?

C7-26 What is a recapitalization?

C7-27 Explain why a transaction might satisfy a literal interpretation of the Sec. 368 requirements for a tax-free reorganization, yet fail to be treated as a reorganization.

C7-28 What restrictions are placed on the acquisition of the tax attributes of a loss corporation?

C7-29 Explain why Sec. 382 will not be an obstacle to the use of NOL carryovers following a purchase transaction taking place if the value of the old loss corporation is large relative to its NOL carryovers.

C7-30 What is a plan of reorganization?

C7-31 Why is it generally advantageous for a taxpayer to secure an advance ruling regarding a reorganization transaction?

ISSUE IDENTIFICATION QUESTIONS

C7-32 Intuit is a developer and marketer of personal finance, accounting, and tax preparation software. Its products include Quicken. ChipSoft develops and markets tax preparation software, including TurboTax. ChipSoft and Intuit entered into a merger agreement whereby ChipSoft merged with a newly formed subsidiary of Intuit. Each ChipSoft share was converted into 0.446 shares of Intuit common stock. Intuit paid cash for fractional shares. Intuit acquired all outstanding ChipSoft shares by issuing 7.26 million common shares, and assuming all outstanding ChipSoft common stock options. ChipSoft was subsequently merged into Intuit's newly formed subsidiary. The merger was treated as a triangular B reorganization. Total purchase price was $306.4 million in common stock. What tax issues should be considered by the parties to the reorganization?

C7-33 Adolph Coors Co. transferred part of its assets to ACX Technologies Corporation in exchange for all of ACX's stock. The assets transfered included its aluminum unit, which makes aluminum sheet, its paper packaging unit, which makes consumer-products packaging, and its ceramic unit, which makes high-technology ceramics used in computer boards and automotive parts. The ACX Technologies stock received for the assets was distributed to the Coors shareholders. What tax issues should be considered by the parties to the divisive reorganization?

C7-34 Sears shareholders of record on June 28, 1993 received 0.39031 shares of Dean Witter (a Sears brokerage subsidiary) common stock for each share of Sears stock owned in a spinoff transaction. The distribution qualified as tax-free under Sec. 355 and the Sears shareholders did not recognize gain on the exchange. On the distribution date, the Sears shares were selling at $40.375 and the Dean Witter shares were valued at $37.1875. What tax issues should be considered by Sears Corporation and the Sears shareholders with respect to the distribution of the Dean Witter shares?

C7-35 Rodger Powell owns all of the Fireside Bar and Grill Corporation in Pittsburgh. Rodger would like to sell his business and retire to sunny Florida now that he has turned 65. Karin, a long-time bartender at Fireside, offers to purchase all of the business's noncash assets in exchange for a 25% down payment, with the remaining 75% being paid in five equal annual installments. Interest will be charged at a 10% rate on the unpaid installments. Rodger plans to liquidate the corporation that has operated the Bar and Grill and have Fireside Bar and Grill distribute the installment notes and any remaining assets. What tax issues should be considered by Fireside Bar and Grill, Rodger, and Karin with respect to the purchase transaction?

PROBLEMS

C7-36 ***Qualified Stock Purchase.*** Acquiring Corporation purchased 20% of Target Corporation's stock on each of the following dates: January 1, 1997, April 1, 1997, June 1, 1997, October 1, 1997, and December 31, 1997.

a. Has a qualified stock purchase occurred? When must an election be made by Acquiring to have the stock purchase treated as an asset acquisition under Sec. 338?

b. How would your answer to Part a change if the purchase dates were instead January 1, 1997, April 1, 1997, September 2, 1997, January 3, 1998, and April 15, 1998?

C7-37 ***Sec. 338 Election.*** Acquiring Corporation acquires 20% of the Target Corporation stock from Milt on August 10, 1997. An additional 30% of the stock is acquired from Nick on November 15, 1997. The remaining 50% of the Target stock is acquired from Phil on

April 10, 1998. The total price paid for the stock is $1,500,000. Target Corporation's balance sheet on April 10, 1998 shows assets with a $2,500,000 FMV, a $1,800,000 adjusted basis, and $750,000 in liabilities.

a. What is the acquisition date for the Target stock for Sec. 338 purposes? By what date must the Sec. 338 election be made?
b. If a Sec. 338 election is made, what is the deemed sale price for the assets?
c. What is the total basis of the assets following the deemed sale, assuming a tax liability attributable to the deemed sale of $238,000?
d. How does the tax liability attributable to the deemed sale affect the price Acquiring Corporation should be willing to pay for the Target stock?
e. What happens to Target's tax attributes following the deemed sale?

C7-38 ***Sec. 338 Election.*** Rain Corporation is considering the purchase of Water Corporation's stock. Water Corporation's adjusted basis for its assets is $1,250,000. Sale of the Water Corporation assets at their FMV would result in $400,000 of depreciation recapture taking place under Sec. 1245, $250,000 of ordinary income being recognized on the sale of its LIFO inventory, and $1,600,000 of capital gain being recognized on the sale of its investment assets. Water Corporation's E&P balance is $750,000. No other carryovers are available to Water Corporation.

a. What advantages would accrue to Rain Corporation if a Sec. 338 election is made?
b. What tax costs would accrue to Rain and Water Corporations if the Sec. 338 election is made (assume a 34% corporate tax rate)? What effect would these tax costs have on the "new" Water's basis for its assets?
c. How would these tax costs affect the price Rain Corporation would be willing to pay for the Water stock?
d. Under what circumstances might the Sec. 338 election be ill-advised?

C7-39 ***Sec. 338 Basis Allocation.*** Apache Corporation purchases all of Target Corporation's stock for $276,000 cash. A timely Sec. 338 election is made by Apache. Target's balance sheet at the close of business on the acquisition date is as follows:

Assets	*Adjusted Basis*	*FMV*	*Liabilities*	*Amount*
Cash	$ 50,000	$ 50,000	Accounts payable	$ 40,000
Marketable securities	18,000	38,000	Note to bank	60,000
Accounts receivable	66,000	65,000	Owner's equity	300,000
Inventory (FIFO)	21,000	43,000		
Equipment[a]	95,000	144,000		
Land	6,000	12,000		
Building[b]	24,000	48,000		
Total	$280,000	$400,000	Total	$400,000

[a] The equipment cost $200,000 when purchased.
[b] The building is a MACRS property on which $10,000 of depreciation has been claimed.

a. What is the deemed sale price for Target's assets?
b. What are the amount and character of the gain or loss that Target Corporation must recognize on the deemed sale?
c. What is the adjusted grossed-up basis for the Target stock (assume a 34% corporate tax rate)? What amount is allocated to each of the individual properties?

C7-40 ***Amount of Corporate Gain or Loss.*** Thomas Corporation transfers all of its assets and $100,000 of its liabilities in exchange for Andrews Corporation voting common stock, having a $600,000 FMV, as part of a merger transaction in which Thomas is liquidated.

Thomas Corporation's basis for its assets is $475,000.

a. What is the amount of Thomas's recognized gain or loss on the asset transfer?
b. What is Andrews's basis for the assets received?
c. What is the amount of Thomas's recognized gain or loss when it distributes the stock to its shareholders?
d. How would your answers to Parts a through c change if Thomas's basis for the assets had instead been $750,000?
e. How would your answers to parts a through c change if Andrews Corporation had instead exchanged $600,000 cash for Thomas Corporation's assets and Thomas was subsequently liquidated. Assume a 34% corporate tax rate.

C7-41 ***Amount of Shareholder Gain or Loss.*** Silvia exchanges all of her Talbot Corporation stock for $300,000 of Anderson Corporation voting common stock pursuant to Talbot's merger into Anderson Corporation. Immediately after the stock-for-stock exchange Silvia owns 25% of Anderson's 2,000 outstanding shares of stock. Silvia's adjusted basis in the Talbot stock is $175,000 before the merger.

a. What are the amount and character of Silvia's recognized gain or loss?
b. What is Silvia's basis for the Anderson stock?
c. How would your answers to Parts a and b change if Silvia instead received Anderson common stock worth $250,000 and $50,000 cash?

C7-42 ***Amount and Character of Shareholder Gain or Loss.*** Yong owns 100% of the stock of Target Corporation having a $600,000 adjusted basis. As part of the merger of Target Corporation into Allied Corporation, Yong exchanges his Target stock for Allied Corporation common stock having a $3,000,000 FMV and $750,000 in cash. Yong retains a 60% interest in Allied Corporation's 100,000 shares of outstanding stock immediately after the merger.

a. What are the amount and character of Yong's recognized gain?
b. What is Yong's basis in the Allied stock?
c. How would your answer to Parts a and b change if Yong's 60,000 Allied shares were instead one-third of Allied's outstanding shares?

C7-43 ***Amount and Character of Shareholder Gain or Loss.*** Archer Corporation exchanges $375,000 of its nonvoting preferred stock for all of Town Corporation's assets pursuant to Town's merger into Archer Corporation. The assets have an adjusted basis of $225,000. Town Corporation's sole shareholder, Lois, exchanges her Town common stock having an adjusted basis of $200,000 for the preferred stock. Lois owns none of Archer's voting stock, and owns only 4% (by value) of the Archer stock immediately after the reorganization.

a. What is the amount of Town Corporation's recognized gain or loss on the asset transfer? on the distribution of the stock to Lois?
b. What is Archer Corporation's basis for the assets received?
c. What are the amount and character of Lois's recognized gain or loss?
d. What is Lois's basis for the Archer stock?

C7-44 ***Characterization of the Shareholder's Gain or Loss.*** Turbo Corporation has 1,000,000 shares of common stock and 200,000 shares of nonvoting preferred stock outstanding. Pursuant to a merger agreement, Ace Corporation exchanges its common stock worth $15,000,000 for the Turbo common stock and $10,000,000 in cash for the Turbo preferred stock. Some shareholders of Turbo Corporation received only Ace common stock for their common stock, some shareholders received only cash for their preferred stock, and some shareholders received both cash and Ace common stock for their Turbo preferred and common stock, respectively. Shareholders owning approximately 10% of the Turbo common stock also owned Turbo preferred stock. The total cash received by these shareholders amounted to $1,500,000. The Turbo Corporation common stockholders end up owning 15% of the Ace stock. What is the tax treatment of the common stock and cash received by each of the three groups of Turbo Corporation shareholders?

C7-45 ***Requirements for a Type A Reorganization.*** Anchor Corporation is planning to acquire all of the assets of Tower Corporation in a merger transaction. Tower's assets have a $5,000,000 FMV and a $2,200,000 adjusted basis. Which of the following transactions qualify as a Type A reorganization assuming that Tower Corporation is liquidated?

a. The assets are exchanged for $5,000,000 of Anchor common stock.
b. The assets are exchanged for $5,000,000 of Anchor nonvoting preferred stock.
c. The assets are exchanged for $5,000,000 of Anchor securities.
d. The assets are exchanged for $3,500,000 of Anchor nonvoting preferred stock and $1,500,000 in cash.
e. The assets are exchanged for $3,000,000 of Anchor common stock and Anchor's assumption of $2,000,000 of Tower liabilities.

C7-46 ***Tax Consequences of a Merger.*** Armor Corporation exchanges $1,000,000 of its common stock and $250,000 of Armor bonds for all of Trail Corporation's outstanding stock. Trail Corporation is then merged into Armor Corporation, with Armor receiving assets having a $1,250,000 FMV and an $875,000 adjusted basis. As part of the merger, Antonello exchanges his 15% interest (3,000 shares) in Trail Corporation's single class of stock, having an adjusted basis of $80,000, for $150,000 in Armor stock and $37,500 in Armor bonds. Following the reorganization, Antonello owns 6% (1,000 shares) of Armor's stock. Armor Corporation's E&P balance is $300,000.

a. What is the amount of Trail Corporation's recognized gain or loss on the asset transfer?
b. What is Armor Corporation's basis for the assets received in the exchange?
c. What are the amount and character of Antonello's recognized gain or loss?
d. What is Antonello's basis for the Armor stock? for the Armor bonds?

C7-47 ***Requirements for a Type C Reorganization.*** Arnold Corporation is planning to acquire all of the assets of Turner Corporation in an asset-for-stock (Type C) tax-free reorganization. Turner's assets have an adjusted basis of $600,000 and a $1,000,000 FMV. Which of the following transactions qualify as a Type C reorganization (assuming that Turner is liquidated as part of the reorganization)?

a. The assets are exchanged for $800,000 of Arnold voting common stock and $200,000 of cash.
b. The assets are exchanged for $800,000 of Arnold voting common stock and $200,000 of Arnold bonds.
c. The assets are exchanged for $1,000,000 of Arnold nonvoting preferred stock.
d. The assets are exchanged for $700,000 of Arnold voting common stock and Arnold's assumption of $300,000 of Turner's liabilities.
e. The assets are exchanged for $700,000 of Arnold voting common stock, Arnold's assumption of $200,000 of Turner's liabilities, and $100,000 in cash.

C7-48 ***Tax Consequences of a Type C Reorganization.*** Ash Corporation exchanges $250,000 of its voting common stock and $50,000 of its bonds for all of Texas Corporation's assets as part of a Type C tax-free reorganization. Texas Corporation is liquidated, with each of its two shareholders receiving equal amounts of the Ash Corporation stock and bonds. Barbara has a $50,000 basis in her stock, and George has a $200,000 basis in his stock. George and Barbara, who are unrelated, each own 8% of Ash's stock (5,000 shares) immediately after the reorganization. At the time of the reorganization, Texas Corporation's E&P balance is $75,000 and its assets have an adjusted basis of $225,000.

a. What is the amount of Texas Corporation's recognized gain or loss on the asset transfer? on the distribution of the stock and bonds?
b. What is Ash Corporation's basis in the assets it acquired?
c. What are the amount and character of each shareholder's recognized gain or loss?
d. What is the basis of each shareholder's Ash stock? Ash bonds?

C7-49 *Tax Consequences of a Type C Reorganization.* Tulsa Corporation exchanges assets having a $300,000 FMV and a $175,000 adjusted basis for $250,000 of Akron Corporation voting common stock and Akron's assumption of $50,000 of Tulsa's liabilities as part of a Type C tax-free reorganization. Tulsa is liquidated, with its sole shareholder, Michelle, receiving the Akron stock in exchange for her Tulsa stock having an adjusted basis of $100,000. Michelle owns 12% (2,500 shares) of Akron's stock immediately after the reorganization.
a. What is the amount of Tulsa's recognized gain or loss on the asset transfer? on the distribution of the stock?
b. What is Akron's basis for the assets it receives?
c. What effect would the transfer of Tulsa's assets to Subsidiary Corporation (a subsidiary controlled by Akron Corporation) have on the reorganization?
d. What are the amount and character of Michelle's recognized gain or loss?
e. What is Michelle's basis for her Akron stock?

C7-50 *Requirements for a Type B Reorganization.* Allen Corporation is planning to acquire all of the stock of Taylor Corporation in a stock-for-stock (Type B) tax-free reorganization. Which of the following transactions will qualify as a Type B reorganization?
a. All of Taylor's stock is exchanged for $1,000,000 of Allen voting preferred stock.
b. All of Taylor's stock is exchanged for $750,000 of Allen voting common stock and $250,000 of Allen bonds.
c. All of Taylor's stock is exchanged for $1,000,000 of Allen voting common stock, and the shareholders of Taylor end up owning less than 1% of Allen's stock.
d. Ninety percent of Taylor's stock is exchanged for $900,000 of Allen voting common stock. One shareholder who owns 10% of the Taylor stock exercises his right under state law to have his shares independently appraised and redeemed for cash by Taylor Corporation. He receives $100,000.

C7-51 *Tax Consequences of a Type B Reorganization.* Trent Corporation's single class of stock is owned equally by Juan and Miguel, who are unrelated. Each shareholder has a $125,000 basis for his 1,000 shares of Trent stock. Adams Corporation exchanges 2,500 shares of its voting common stock having a $100 per share FMV for each shareholder's Trent stock in a single transaction. Immediately after the reorganization each shareholder owns 15% of the Adams stock.
a. What are the amount and character of each shareholder's recognized gain or loss?
b. What is each shareholder's basis for his Adams stock?
c. What is Adams Corporation's basis for the Trent stock?
d. How would your answers to Parts a through c change if Adams Corporation instead exchanged 2,000 shares of Adams common stock and $50,000 in cash for each shareholder's Trent stock?

C7-52 *Tax Consequences of a Type B Reorganization.* Austin Corporation exchanges $1,500,000 of its voting common stock for all of Travis Corporation's single class of stock. Ingrid owns all of the Travis stock, which has a basis of $375,000. Ingrid owns 25% of the Austin stock (15,000 shares) after the reorganization.
a. What are the amount and character of Ingrid's recognized gain or loss?
b. What is Ingrid's basis for her Austin stock?
c. What is Austin Corporation's basis for the Travis stock?
d. What are the tax consequences for all parties to the acquisition if Austin Corporation subsequently liquidates Travis Corporation as part of the plan of reorganizaton?

C7-53 *Tax Consequences of a Type B Reorganization.* Ashton Corporation purchases 10% of the Todd Corporation stock from Cathy for $250,000 in cash on January 30, 1996. Andrea and Bill each exchange one-half of the remaining 90% of the Todd stock for $1,200,000 of Ashton voting common stock on May 30, 1997. Andrea and Bill each have a $200,000 basis for their Todd stock. Andrea and Bill each own 15% of the Ashton stock (12,000 shares) immediately after the reorganization.

a. What are the amount and character of each shareholder's recognized gain or loss?
b. What is each shareholder's basis for his or her Ashton stock?
c. What is Ashton Corporation's basis for the Todd stock?
d. How would your answer to Parts a through c change if Ashton Corporation had instead acquired the remaining Todd stock on May 30, 1996?

C7-54 *Tax Consequences of a Divisive Type D Reorganization.* Road Corporation is owned equally by four shareholders. Its activities are conducted in two operating divisions: the road construction division and meat packing division. In an attempt to separate the two activities into separate corporations, the assets and liabilities of the meat packing division (60% of Road's total net assets) are transferred to Food Corporation in exchange for all of Food's single class of stock. The assets of the meat packing division have a $2,750,000 FMV and a $1,100,000 adjusted basis. A total of $500,000 of liabilities are transferred to Food. The $2,250,000 of Food stock (90,000 shares) is distributed ratably to each of the four shareholders.

a. What is the amount of Road Corporation's recognized gain or loss on the asset transfer? on the distribution of the Food stock?
b. What are the amount and character of each shareholder's recognized gain or loss on the distribution? (Assume each shareholder's basis in the Road stock is $200,000.)
c. What is the basis of each shareholder's Road and Food stock after the reorganization? (Assume the Road stock is worth $1,500,000 immediately after the distribution.)

C7-55 *Tax Consequences of a Divisive Type D Reorganization.* Light Corporation is owned equally by two individual shareholders. The shareholders no longer agree on matters concerning Light's operations. Tarek agrees to a plan whereby $500,000 of Light's assets (having an adjusted basis of $350,000) and $100,000 of Light's liabilities are transferred to Dark Corporation in exchange for all of its single class of stock (5,000 shares). Tarek will exchange all of his Light common stock, having a $150,000 adjusted basis, for the $400,000 of Dark stock.

a. What is the amount of Light Corporation's recognized gain or loss on the asset transfer? on the distribution of the Dark stock?
b. What are the amount and character of Tarek's recognized gain or loss?
c. What is Tarek's basis for his Dark stock?

C7-56 *Distribution of Stock: Spinoff.* Parent Corporation has been in the business of manufacturing and selling trucks for the past eight years. Its subsidiary, Diesel Corporation, has been in the business of manufacturing and selling diesel engines for the past seven years. Parent acquired control of Diesel Corporation six years ago when it purchased 100% of its single class of stock from Large Corporation. Parent has been ordered to divest itself of Diesel Corporation by a federal court as the result of an antitrust judgment. Consequently, Parent distributes all of its Diesel Corporation stock to its shareholders. Alan owns less than 1% of Parent's outstanding stock having a $40,000 basis. He receives 25 shares of Diesel stock having a $25,000 FMV as a result of Parent's distribution. Parent's E&P at the end of the year in which the spinoff occurs is $2,500,000. The Parent stock held by Alan has a $75,000 FMV immediately after the distribution.

a. What are the amount and character of the gain, loss, or income Alan must recognize as a result of Parent's distributing the Diesel stock?
b. What basis does Alan take for the Diesel stock he receives?
c. When does Alan's holding period for the Diesel stock commence?
d. How would your answer to Part a change if Parent had been in the truck business for only three years before making the distribution and that it had acquired the Diesel stock only three years ago?

C7-57 ***Distribution of Stock: Split-Off.*** Parent Corporation has owned all 100 shares of the Subsidiary Corporation common stock since 1982. Parent Corporation has been in the business of manufacturing and selling light fixtures, and Subsidiary Corporation has been in the business of manufacturing and selling light bulbs. Amy and Bill are the two equal shareholders of the Parent stock. Amy's basis in her 50 shares of Parent stock is $80,000 and Bill's basis in his 50 shares of Parent stock is $60,000. On April 10, 1997, Parent distributes all 100 shares of Subsidiary stock to Bill in exchange for all of his Parent stock (which is cancelled). The distribution has an acceptable business purpose. The Subsidiary stock had a $30,000 basis to Parent on the distribution date. At the end of 1997, Parent has $150,000 of E&P. Immediately after the distribution, the FMVs of the Parent and Subsidiary stocks are $1,600 and $800 per share, respectively.
a. What are the amount and character of the gain, loss, or income Bill must recognize as a result of Parent's distributing the Subsidiary stock?
b. What basis does Bill take in the Subsidiary stock?
c. When does Bill's holding period for the Subsidiary stock begin?
d. Assume that Subsidiary Corporation instead was formed in 1993 by Andrew to manufacture and sell lightbulbs. Andrew sold the Subsidiary stock to Parent for cash in 1995. How would your answer to parts (a)-(c) change?

C7-58 ***Distribution of Stock and Securities: Split-Off.*** Ruby Corporation has 100 shares of common stock outstanding. Fred, a shareholder of Ruby Corporation, exchanges his 25% interest in the Ruby stock for Garnet Corporation stock and securities. Ruby purchased 80% of the Garnet stock ten years ago for $25,000. At the time of the exchange, Fred has a $50,000 basis in his Ruby stock, and the stock has an $80,000 FMV. Fred receives Garnet stock that has a $60,000 FMV and Garnet securities that have a $20,000 FMV. Ruby has $50,000 of E&P. Assume that all the requirements of Sec. 355 are met except for the receipt of boot.
a. What are the amount and character of Fred's recognized gain or loss on the exchange?
b. What is Fred's basis for the Garnet stock and the Garnet securities?
c. What are the amount and character of Ruby Corporation's recognized gain or loss on the distribution?
d. When does Fred's holding period begin for the Garnet stock and the Garnet securities?
e. How would your answer to Part a change if the exchange did not meet the requirements of Sec. 355 or Sec. 356?

C7-59 ***Requirements for a Type E Reorganization.*** Master Corporation is planning to undertake a recapitalization. Explain the tax consequences of each of the following independent transactions:
a. A class of nonvoting preferred stock is exchanged for common stock. $300,000 of dividends for the current year and prior years on the preferred stock are paid in cash.
b. Master Corporation bonds in the amount of $3,000,000 will be exchanged for a similar dollar amount of preferred stock. In addition, $180,000 of unpaid interest will be paid by issuing Master preferred stock to the former bondholders.

c. Bailey Corporation 12% bonds in the amount of $3,000,000 are exchanged before their maturity for a similar dollar amount of Bailey Corporation 8% bonds because of a decline in the prevailing market rate of interest. In addition, $180,000 of unpaid interest will be paid in cash.

C7-60 ***Tax Consequences of a Type E Reorganization.*** Milan Corporation is owned by four shareholders. Andy and Bob each own 40% of the outstanding common and preferred stock and Chris and Doug each own 10% of the two classes of stock. The shareholders want to retire the preferred stock that was issued five years ago when the corporation was in the midst of a major expansion. Retirement of the preferred stock will eliminate the need to pay annual dividends on the preferred stock. Explain the tax consequences of the following two alternatives to the shareholders:

- The $100 par preferred stock is redeemed for its $120 call price. Each shareholder purchased his preferred stock at par five years ago.
- Each share of the $100 par preferred stock is exchanged for $120 of additional common stock.

What nontax advantages might exist for selecting one alternative over the other?

C7-61 ***Reorganization Requirements.*** Discuss the tax consequences of the following corporate reorganizations to the parties to the reorganization:

a. Adobe Corporation and Tyler Corporation are merged under the laws of the State of Florida. The shareholders of Tyler Corporation receive $300,000 of Adobe common stock and $700,000 of Adobe securities for their Tyler stock.

b. Alabama Corporation exchanges $1,000,000 of its voting common stock for all of the noncash assets of Texas Corporation. The transaction meets all the requirements for a Type C reorganization. Texas Corporation is divided into two operating divisions: meat packing and meat distribution. Alabama Corporation retains the meat packing division's assets and continues to conduct its activities, but sells the assets of the meat distribution division. The meat distribution division's assets constitute 40% of Texas Corporation's noncash assets.

c. Parent Corporation transfers $500,000 of investment securities to Subsidiary Corporation in exchange for all of its single class of stock. The Subsidiary stock is exchanged for one-third of the stock held by each of Parent Corporation's shareholders. Six months after the reorganization, the investment securities are distributed to Subsidiary Corporation's shareholders pursuant to the liquidation of Subsidiary.

C7-62 ***Determining the Type of Reorganization Transaction.*** For each of the following transactions indicate its reorganization designation (e.g., Type A, Type B, etc.). Assume all common stock is voting stock.

a. Anderson and Brown Corporations exchange their assets for all of the single class of stock of newly created Computer Corporation. Following the exchange, Anderson and Brown Corporations are liquidated. The transaction satisfies the State of Michigan corporation law requirements.

b. Price Corporation (incorporated in the State of Texas) exchanges all of its assets for all of the single class of stock of Price Corporation (incorporated in the State of Delaware). Following the exchange, Price Corporation (Texas) is liquidated.

c. All of Gates Corporation's noncumulative, 10% preferred stock is exchanged for Gates Corporation common stock.

d. Hobbs Corporation exchanges its common stock for 90% of the outstanding common stock and 80% of the outstanding nonvoting preferred stock of Calvin Corporation. The remaining Calvin stock is held by about thirty individual investors.

e. Scale Corporation transfers the assets of its two operating divisions to Major and Minor Corporations in exchange for all of each corporation's single class of stock. The Major and Minor stocks are distributed pursuant to the liquidation of Scale.
f. Tobias Corporation has $3,000,000 of assets and $1,000,000 of liabilities. Andrew Corporation exchanges $2,000,000 of its voting common stock for all of Tobias Corporation's assets and liabilities. Tobias Corporation is liquidated and its shareholders end up owning 11% of the Andrew stock following the transaction.

C7-63 *Tax Attribute Carryovers.* Alaska Corporation exchanges $2,000,000 of its voting common stock for all of the noncash assets of Tennessee Corporation at the close of business on June 30, 1997. Tennessee Corporation uses its cash to pay off its liabilities and then liquidates. Tennessee and Alaska Corporations report the following taxable income amounts:

Tax Year Ending	*Alaska Corp.*	*Tennessee Corp.*
December 31, 1994	($100,000)	($75,000)
December 31, 1995	60,000	10,000
December 31, 1996	70,000	(90,000)
June 30, 1997	XXX	(40,000)
December 31, 1997	73,000	XXX

a. What tax returns must be filed by Alaska and Tennessee for 1997?
b. What is the amount of the NOL carryover acquired by Alaska?
c. Ignoring any implications of Sec. 382, what amount of Tennessee Corporation's NOL can be used by Alaska Corporation in 1997?

C7-64 *Sec. 382 Limitation: Purchase Transaction.* Murray Corporation's stock is owned by about 1,000 shareholders, none of whom own more than 1% of the stock. Pursuant to a tender offer, Said purchases all of the Murray stock for $6,000,000 cash at the close of business on December 31, 1996. Before the acquisition, Said did not own any Murray stock. Murray Corporation had incurred substantial NOLs, which at the end of 1996 totaled $1,000,000. Murray Corporation's taxable income is expected to be $200,000 and $600,000, respectively, for 1997 and 1998. Assuming that the long-term tax-exempt federal rate is 5% and Murray Corporation continues in the same trade or business, what amount of NOLs can be used by Murray Corporation in 1997 and 1998?

C7-65 *Sec. 382 Limitation: Tax-Free Reorganization.* Albert Corporation is a profitable publicly traded corporation. None of its shareholders own more than 1% of its stock. On December 31, 1996, Albert Corporation exchanges $8,000,000 of its stock for all of the stock of Turner Corporation as part of a merger transaction. Turner Corporation is owned by Tara, who receives 15% of the Albert stock as part of the reorganization. Tara owned none of the Albert stock before the merger. Turner Corporation accumulated $2,500,000 in NOL carryovers before being merged into Albert. Albert expects to earn $1,000,000 and $1,500,000 in taxable income during 1997 and 1998, respectively. Assuming that the long-term tax-exempt federal rate is 5%, what amount of NOLs can be used by Albert Corporation in 1997 and 1998?

C7-66 ***Comprehensive Problem.*** Sid Kess, a long-time tax client of yours, has decided to acquire the snow blower manufacturing firm owned by Richard Smith, one of his closest friends. Richard has a $200,000 adjusted basis for his Richard Smith Snow Blowers (RSSB) stock. Sid Kess Enterprises (SKE), a C corporation that is 100%-owned by Sid Kess, will make the acquisition. RSSB operates as a C corporation, and reports the following assets and liabilities as of November 1 of the current year.

Asset	*Adj. Basis*	*FMV*
Cash	$ 250,000	$ 250,000
Inventory (LIFO)	470,000	600,000
Equipment	150,000	250,000
Building	100,000	320,000
Land	80,000	120,000
Goodwill	—0—	200,000
Total	$1,050,000	$1,740,000

Equities	*Amount*
Accts. Payable	$ 60,000
Mortgage Payable	120,000
Paid-in Capital	220,000
Retained Earnings	650,000
Total	$1,050,000

Depreciation in the amount of $200,000 and $80,000 has been claimed on the equipment and building, respectively. No amortization has been claimed on the goodwill. Retained earnings approximate RSSB's E&P. No NOL, capital loss, or credit carryovers exist at the time of the acquisition. What are the tax consequences of each alternative acquisition methods to SKE and RSSB corporations? Assume a 34% corporate tax rate.

a. SKE acquires the all of the single class of RSSB stock for $1,560,000 in cash. RSSB is not liquidated.

b. SKE acquires all of the assets of RSSB for $1,740,000 in cash. RSSB is liquidated.

c. SKE acquires all of the RSSB stock for $1,560,000 in cash. RSSB is liquidated into SKE shortly after the acquisition.

d. SKE acquires all of the RSSB stock for $1,560,000 in cash. A timely Sec. 338 election is made.

e. SKE exchanges $1,560,000 of its common stock for all of Richard Smith's RSSB stock. Assume that RSSB is not liquidated, and that the transaction qualifies as a Type B reorganization. Each share of SKE stock has a $1,000 FMV. SKE has 10,000 shares of stock making the acquisition.

f. SKE exchanges $1,490,000 of its common stock for all of RSSB's noncash assets ($1,490,000 = $1,740,000 total assets − $250,000 cash). RSSB is liquidated as part of the transaction which qualifies as a Type A reorganization. Richard Smith uses part of the cash that has been retained to pay off the corporation's liabilities. The remaining cash is distributed with the SKE stock in liquidation of RSSB.

CASE STUDY PROBLEMS

C7-67 ***Comparative Acquisition Forms.*** Bailey Corporation owns a number of automotive parts shops. Bill Smith owns an automotive parts shop that has been in existence for forty years and has competed with one of Bailey's locations. Bill is thinking about retirement and would like to sell his business. He has his CPA prepare a balance sheet, which he takes to John Bailey, president of Bailey Corporation, who has been a long-time friend.

Assets	*Adjusted Basis*	*FMV*
Cash	$250,000	$250,000
Accounts receivable	75,000	70,000
Inventories (LIFO)	600,000	1,750,000
Equipment	200,000	250,000
Building	30,000	285,000
Land	30,000	115,000
Total	$1,185,000	$2,720,000

Should Bailey Corporation make the acquisition, it intends to operate the automotive parts shop using its own tradename in the location Bill has used for forty years. The president has asked you to prepare a summary of the tax consequences of a purchase of the noncash assets or stock of Bill's corporation using cash and Bailey Corporation notes and the consequences of an asset-for-stock tax-free reorganization using solely Bailey stock. Upon interviewing Bill, you find out the following additional information: Bill's business is operated as a C corporation, with a $160,000 adjusted basis for his stock. $200,000 of accounts payable are outstanding. Bill has depreciated the building using the straight-line method and has claimed $100,000 in depreciation. The equipment is Sec. 1245 property that has been depreciated in the amount of $150,000. The after-tax profits for each of the last three years has been in excess of $300,000, and Bill suspects that there is some goodwill value that is not shown on the balance sheet.

Required: Prepare a memorandum that outlines the tax consequences of each of the three alternative acquisition transactions assuming that $2,550,000 is the anticipated cash purchase price for the noncash assets and $2,600,000 for the stock.

C7-68 The following advertisement appeared in the *Wall Street Journal* in May 1995.

$12 MILLION CASH WITH
ADDITIONAL CASH AVAILABLE
$89 MM TAX LOSS GOOD THROUGH 2008
TIGERA GROUP, INC.
NASDAQ listed w/300 shareholders
WANTS TO ACQUIRE COMPANY
w/NBT Audited Earnings of $3MM to $7MM
Exceptional Opportunity and Participation for Sellers and
Existing Management. Contact: Albert M. Zlotnick or Ross P.
Lederer, Tel: (000)-000-0000 and Fax: (000)-000-0000.

Required: Prepare a memorandum explaining the tax advantages that would accrue to the Tigera Group if it acquired the assets of a profitable corporation in a tax-free reorganization or a taxable transaction. In addition, explain any tax law provisions that might restrict the use of these loss carryovers.

TAX RESEARCH PROBLEMS

C7-69 Austin Corporation acquires 8% of Travis Corporation's single class of stock for cash on January 10, 1997. On August 25, 1997, Austin Corporation makes a tender offer to exchange Austin common stock for the remaining Travis stock. Travis Corporation shareholders tender 85% of the outstanding Travis stock. The exchange is completed on September 25, 1997. Your tax manager has asked you to draft a memorandum explaining whether or not part or all of the two acquisition transactions qualify as a tax-free reorganization? If part or all of either transaction is taxable to Travis Corporation's shareholders, offer any suggestions for restructuring the acquisitions to improve the tax consequences of the transaction, assuming that Austin Corporation does not desire to make a Sec. 338 election?

At a minimum you should consider:

- Sec. 368(a)(1)(B)
- Reg. Sec. 1.368-2(c)
- *Eldon S. Chapman, et al. v. CIR,* 45 AFTR 2d 80-1290, 80-1 USTC ¶9330 (1st Cir., 1980)
- *Arden S. Heverly, et al. v. CIR,* 45 AFTR 2d 80-1122, 80-1 USTC ¶9322 (3rd Cir., 1980)

C7-70 Dailey Corporation has developed a new spreadsheet software package that makes all current packages obsolete. Doors '97 has been test marketed and its acceptance has been fantastic. IBN, the world's largest computer manufacturer, has offered to acquire the Dailey stock in exchange for IBN stock. The 10 million Dailey shares are trading at $45 shortly before the acquisition date. The IBN stock is trading at $30 on the same date. The tentative exchange ratio in the purchase agreement is 1.5 IBN shares for each Dailey share. If the IBN share price drops by more than 15% at any time in the twelve months following the acquisition date, then an additional $4.50 of IBN stock will be delivered for each Dailey share acquired. On July 1, 1997, the 15 million IBN shares were delivered to the Dailey shareholders. On April 12, 1998, the IBN shares closed at $22, their lowest price during the July 1, 1997–June 30, 1998 period. On August 1, 1998, IBN delivered $45 million of additional IBN stock. Your tax manager has asked you to draft a two-page memorandum dated June 1, 1997, outlining to the shareholders the tax consequences of the proposed transaction, with particular emphasis on the contingent shares issue. In addition, draft a second memorandum dated August 1, 1998, explaining the tax consequences of the delivery of the additional IBN stock to each shareholder.

At a minimum you should consider:

- Secs. 354 and 368
- Rev. Rul. 66-112, 1966-1 C.B. 68
- Rev. Proc. 77-37, 1977-2 C.B. 568

C7-71 Diversified Corporation is a successful bank with ten branches. Al, Bob, and Cathy created Diversified Corporation six years ago and own all of the Diversified stock. Diversified has constructed a new building in downtown Metropolis that houses a banking facility on the first floor, offices for its employees on the second and third floors, and office space to be leased out to third parties on the fourth through twelfth floors. Since the building was completed six months ago, approximately 20% of the floor space on the upper floors has been occupied. Pursuant to a plan of reorganization, Diversified proposes to transfer the building to Metropolis Real Estate (MRE) Corporation in exchange for all of the MRE common stock. The building will be the only property owned by MRE following the reorganization. Diversified owns no other real estate because it currently leases the locations for its ten retail banking branches. The MRE common stock will be distributed by Diversified ratably to Al, Bob, and Cathy, who will end up holding all of the Diversified and MRE common stocks. Your tax manager has asked you to draft a memorandum explaining whether or not the proposed transaction will satisfy the requirements for a tax-free reorganization?

CHAPTER 8

CONSOLIDATED TAX RETURNS

LEARNING OBJECTIVES

After studying this chapter, you should be able to

1. Determine whether a group of corporations is an affiliated group
2. Explain the advantages and disadvantages of filing a consolidated tax return
3. Calculate consolidated taxable income for an affiliated group
4. Calculate the consolidated regular tax liability for an affiliated group
5. Calculate the consolidated AMT liability for an affiliated group
6. Determine whether a transaction is an intercompany transaction
7. Explain the reporting of an intercompany transaction
8. Calculate an affiliated group's consolidated NOL
9. Calculate the carryback or carryover of a consolidated NOL
10. Determine how the special loss limitations restrict the use of separate and consolidated NOL carrybacks and carryovers
11. Explain the procedures for making an initial consolidated return election

CHAPTER OUTLINE

ADDITIONAL COMMENT

Filing a consolidated tax return does not affect the reporting of other taxes such as payroll, sales, or property taxes. Also, some states do not allow the filing of consolidated tax returns for state income tax purposes.

Affiliated corporations (i.e., a parent corporation and at least one subsidiary corporation) have two options for filing their federal income tax returns:

- Each member of the group can file separate tax returns that report its own income and expenses. No special treatment is generally provided for transactions between group members.[1] However, the group can elect to claim a 100% dividends-received deduction for intragroup dividends.
- The affiliated group can file a single tax return, called a consolidated tax return, that reports the results for all its group members. A number of special treatments are applied to transactions between group members (e.g., deferring gains and losses on intercompany transactions and eliminating intragroup dividends).

Some consolidated tax returns include as few as two corporations. Other consolidated tax returns include hundreds of corporations. The importance of the consolidated tax return election to the corporate taxing system is illustrated for 1993, when 64,080 consolidated tax returns were filed. Those consolidated tax returns represented only 0.31% of the 2.06 million C corporation federal income tax returns that were filed. These affiliated groups, which filed consolidated tax returns, reported 88.4% of total taxable income for all C corporations and paid 84.6% of total taxes paid by all C corporations even though they made up less than one-half of 1 percent of all tax returns.[2]

This chapter considers the advantages and disadvantages of filing a consolidated tax return. It also examines the basic requirements for computing the consolidated tax liability.

SOURCE OF THE CONSOLIDATED TAX RETURN RULES

REAL WORLD EXAMPLE

Mobil Oil's 1993 federal income tax return was 6,300 pages long and weighed 76 pounds. Work papers for the return constitute 146,000 documents. The return took 57 person years to prepare at a cost of $10 million. In addition, $5 million of expenses are incurred annually in connection with the IRS's audit of the return.

KEY POINT

Most of the requirements for filing consolidated tax returns are contained in the Sec. 1502 Treasury Regulations rather than in the Internal Revenue Code.

Code Secs. 1501 through 1504 are the primary statutory provisions governing the filing of a consolidated tax return. These four sections are very general and primarily define the composition of the affiliated groups that are eligible to elect to file a consolidated tax return. This topic is quite complex. The Treasury Department was given the responsibility of drafting the Regulations needed to determine (1) the consolidated tax liability and (2) the filing requirements for a consolidated tax return. Because it is unusual for the Treasury Department to have the authority to draft both statutory and interpretive regulations for a particular topical area, Sec. 1501 requires that all affiliated groups filing a consolidated tax return must consent to all of the consolidated tax return regulations in effect when the return is filed. The purpose of Sec. 1501 is to reduce or avoid conflicts in applying the statutory and interpretive regulations. The consolidated return regulations have the same authority as the Internal Revenue Code because of the consent requirement and the fact that they are legislative in nature.

[1] Some special treatments apply to related corporations filing separate returns under the controlled group rules. These include but are not limited to matching of income and deductions, Sec. 267(a)(1); deferral of loss on intragroup sales, Sec. 267(f)(2); and ordinary income recognition on intragroup sales of depreciable property, Sec. 1239.

[2] IRS, *Statistics of Income—1993 Corporation Income Tax Returns* (Washington, DC: U.S. Government Printing Office, 1997), pp. 122-123.

DEFINITION OF AN AFFILIATED GROUP

OBJECTIVE 1

Determine whether a group of corporations is an affiliated group

SELF-STUDY QUESTION

What issues determine whether an affiliated group exists?

REQUIREMENTS

STOCK OWNERSHIP REQUIREMENT. Only an affiliated group of corporations can elect to file a consolidated return. Section 1504(a) outlines the stock ownership requirements that must be satisfied, as follows:

- A parent corporation must directly own stock[3] having at least 80% of the total voting power of all classes of stock entitled to vote and at least 80% of the total value of all outstanding stock in at least one includible corporation.
- For *each* other corporation eligible to be included in the affiliated group, stock having at least 80% of the total voting power of all classes of stock entitled to vote and at least 80% of the total value of all outstanding stock must be owned directly by the parent corporation and the other group members.

EXAMPLE C8-1 ▶ P Corporation owns 90% of S_1 Corporation's single class of stock and 30% of S_2 Corporation's single class of stock.[4] S_1 Corporation owns 50% of S_2's stock. The remainder of S_1 and S_2's stock is owned by 100 individual shareholders. P, S_1, and S_2 Corporations form the P-S_1-S_2 affiliated group because P owns more than the 80% of the S_1 stock needed to satisfy the direct ownership requirement and P and S_1 together own 80% (50% + 30%) of S_2's stock. The P-S_1-S_2 group can elect to file a consolidated tax return. ◀

EXAMPLE C8-2 ▶ Ted owns all of the stock of Alpha and Beta Corporations. Alpha and Beta Corporations do not constitute an affiliated group, even though each corporation is directly owned by the same individual shareholder. Because a parent-subsidiary relationship is not present, they are ineligible to make a consolidated return election (see page C8-4). ◀

ANSWER

In determining whether an affiliated group exists, three questions must be addressed: Does a corporation (common parent) own directly 80% or more of at least one includible corporation? What are the includible corporations? What chains of includible corporations are connected by at least 80% ownership?

PRACTICAL APPLICATION

The corporations that are included in a consolidated group for financial reporting purposes may be quite different from the includible corporations for federal income tax purposes.

INCLUDIBLE CORPORATION REQUIREMENT. As few as two corporations may satisfy the affiliated group definition. In many of the nation's largest affiliated groups, however, the number of related corporations runs into the hundreds. Some of these corporate groups may have a number of subsidiary corporations that are not able to participate in the consolidated tax return election because they are not includible corporations under Sec. 1504(b). Because they are not includible corporations, their stock ownership cannot be counted toward satisfying the 80% stock ownership minimums, nor can their operating results be reported as part of the consolidated tax return. In general, each excluded corporation must file its own separate corporate tax return.

The following special tax status corporations are not includible corporations:

- Corporations exempt from tax under Sec. 501[5]
- Insurance companies subject to tax under Sec. 801[6]
- Foreign corporations

---

[3] The term *stock* does not include any nonvoting preferred stock that is limited and preferred as to its dividends (and does not participate in corporate growth to any significant extent), has redemption or liquidation rights limited to its issue price (plus a reasonable redemption or liquidation premium), and is not convertible into another class of stock (Sec. 1504(a)(4)).

[4] All corporations referred to in the examples are includible domestic corporations unless otherwise indicated. See definition of *includible corporation* later in this chapter.

[5] Two tax-exempt organizations can file a consolidated return if one is a Sec. 501(c)(2) "feeder" corporation that holds title to property, collects the income from the property, and remits such monies to the second tax-exempt organization.

[6] Two or more Sec. 801 domestic life insurance companies may join together to form an affiliated group. If an affiliated group contains one or more Sec. 801 domestic life insurance companies, Sec. 1504(c)(2)(A) permits the parent corporation to elect to treat all such companies that have met the affiliated group stock ownership test for the five immediately preceding tax years as includible corporations.

REAL WORLD EXAMPLE

The new check-the-box regulations permit partnerships and LLCs to elect C corporation tax treatment. If the election is made, an LLC or partnership can be included in a consolidated tax return.

- Corporations claiming the Puerto Rico and U.S. possessions tax credit
- Regulated investment companies
- Real estate investment trusts
- Domestic international sales corporations
- S corporations

If both the stock ownership and includible corporation requirements are satisfied, the subsidiary corporation must be included in the consolidated return election made by a parent corporation.

EXAMPLE C8-3 ▶

ADDITIONAL COMMENT

Even if S_4 were an includible corporation, S_4 would not be part of the P-S_1-S_3 affiliated group. The chain is broken because S_2 is not an includible corporation.

P Corporation owns all of the single class of stock of S_1 and S_2 Corporations. S_1 Corporation owns all of S_3 Corporation's stock. S_2 Corporation owns all of S_4 Corporation's stock. P, S_1, and S_3 are domestic corporations. S_2 and S_4 are foreign corporations. P, S_1 and S_3 Corporations constitute the P-S_1-S_3 affiliated group. S_2 and S_4 are not members of the affiliated group because as foreign corporations they are not includible corporations. ◀

COMPARISON WITH CONTROLLED GROUP DEFINITIONS

Three types of controlled groups—brother-sister groups, parent-subsidiary groups, and combined groups—were defined in Chapter C3. As illustrated in Example C8-2, the brother-sister category of controlled groups cannot elect to file a consolidated tax return because they do not satisfy the direct stock ownership requirement. However, most parent-subsidiary controlled groups and the parent-subsidiary portion of a combined controlled group can elect to file a consolidated tax return.

TYPICAL MISCONCEPTION

The terms *affiliated group, consolidated group,* and *controlled group* are sometimes used interchangeably. However, these terms have very different definitions and purposes.

Four differences between the definitions of Sec. 1504 (affiliated group) and Sec. 1563 (parent-subsidiary controlled group) do exist. These differences include:

- A parent corporation must own 80% of total voting power **and** total value (instead of voting power **or** value) of a subsidiary's stock to include the subsidiary in the affiliated group.
- The stock attribution rules are not used in determining the inclusion of a subsidiary in an affiliated group but are used in determining the existence of a controlled group.
- The types of corporations excluded from an affiliated group are different from those that are excluded from a controlled group.
- The affiliated group definition is tested on each day of the tax year (instead of only on December 31).

These differences can cause some members of a controlled group to be excluded from the affiliated group.

SHOULD A CONSOLIDATED RETURN BE FILED?

OBJECTIVE 2

Explain the advantages and disadvantages of filing a consolidated tax return

ADVANTAGES OF FILING A CONSOLIDATED TAX RETURN

Filing a consolidated tax return offers a number of advantages and disadvantages, some of the more important of which are discussed below. Some of the advantages that may be gained by filing a consolidated tax return include the following:

- The separate return losses of one affiliated group member may be offset against the taxable income of other group members in the current tax year. Such losses provide an immediate tax benefit by reducing the tax due on the other group member's income or eliminating the need to carry a loss to a subsequent tax year.

- Capital losses of one group member may be offset against the capital gains of other group members in the current tax year. Again, this avoids carrying these losses to subsequent tax years.
- Dividends paid from one group member to a second group member are "eliminated" in the consolidated tax return.
- The various credit and deduction limitations are computed on a consolidated basis. This permits group members to use "excess" credits or "excess" deductions in the current tax year and avoids carrying them to subsequent years.
- Gains on intercompany transactions are deferred until a subsequent event occurs that causes the profit or gain to be included in the consolidated return.
- Calculation of the alternative minimum tax (AMT) takes place on a consolidated basis (rather than for each group member) and may reduce the negative effects of the tax preference items and other adjustments (e.g., the ACE-AMTI adjustment) and eliminate the need for the affiliated group as a whole to pay an AMT liability.

KEY POINT

The elimination of intercompany dividends is an advantage of filing consolidated tax returns. However, even if a consolidated tax return is not filed, the owning member should be eligible for a 100% dividends-received deduction.

DISADVANTAGES OF FILING A CONSOLIDATED TAX RETURN

Some of the disadvantages of filing a consolidated tax return include the following:

- A consolidated return election is binding on all subsequent tax years unless the IRS grants the group permission to discontinue filing a consolidated return or the affiliated group is terminated.
- All group members must utilize the same taxable year.
- Losses and deductions on intercompany transactions are deferred until a subsequent event occurs that causes the loss or deduction to be included in the consolidated tax return.[7]
- Operating losses and capital losses of group members may reduce or eliminate the ability of profitable group members to take advantage of credits or deductions by lowering the applicable credit or deduction limitation for the affiliated group.
- Additional administrative costs may be incurred in maintaining the necessary records to account for deferred intercompany transactions and the special loss limitations, although some savings may occur by filing a single return and filing all tax returns at the same time.

TYPICAL MISCONCEPTION

One disadvantage of filing a consolidated tax return that should be apparent after going through this chapter is the added recordkeeping costs necessary to file a consolidated tax return.

There is no general rule that can be applied to determine whether an affiliated group should elect to file a consolidated tax return. Each group should examine the long- and short-term advantages and disadvantages of filing a consolidated tax return before making a decision.

CONSOLIDATED TAXABLE INCOME

OBJECTIVE 3

Calculate consolidated taxable income for an affiliated group

The heart of the computation of the consolidated federal income tax liability is the calculation of **consolidated taxable income**. The calculation of consolidated taxable income is divided into the following five steps. An overview of the five-step consolidated taxable income calculation is presented in Table C8-1.

[7] The deferral of losses and deductions in a consolidated return is less of a disadvantage now that loss and deduction rules also apply to controlled groups in Sec. 267.

STEP 1. The starting point is the determination of each member's taxable income. The amount of a group member's taxable income is determined as if the group member were filing a separate tax return.

STEP 2. Once each group member's taxable income has been determined, a series of adjustments (e.g., deferral of gain on certain intercompany transactions) must be made to take into account the special treatment that certain transactions receive in consolidated returns.

TYPICAL MISCONCEPTION

This table illustrates that the filing of a consolidated tax return instead of separate tax returns is clearly not easier from a compliance point of view.

▼ **TABLE C8-1**

Consolidated Taxable Income Calculation

Step 1: Compute each group member's taxable income (or loss) based on the member's own accounting methods as if the corporation were filing its own separate tax return.

Step 2: Adjust each group member's taxable income as follows:

1. Gains and losses on certain intercompany transactions are deferred. If a restoration event occurs during the year, then previously deferred gains and losses are included in the calculation.
2. An inventory adjustment may be required.
3. An adjustment for an excess loss (negative investment basis) account of an affiliate may be required.
4. Built-in deductions may be deferred.

Step 3: The following gains, losses, and deductions are removed from each member's taxable income because they must be computed on a consolidated basis:

1. Net operating loss (NOL) deductions
2. Capital gains and losses
3. Section 1231 gains and losses (including net casualty gain)
4. Charitable contribution deductions
5. Dividends-received deductions
6. Percentage depletion under Sec. 613A

The result of making the adjustments to a member's taxable income in Steps 2 and 3 is the member's separate taxable income.

Step 4: Combine the members' separate taxable income amounts. This amount is called the group's combined taxable income.

Step 5: Adjust the group's combined taxable income for the following items that are reported on a consolidated basis:

1. Deduct the consolidated Sec. 1231 net loss.
2. Deduct the consolidated net casualty loss.
3. Add the consolidated capital gain net income (taking into account capital loss carrybacks and carryovers and Sec. 1231 gains).
4. Deduct the consolidated charitable contribution deduction.
5. Deduct the consolidated percentage depletion deduction.
6. Deduct the consolidated NOL deduction (taking into account any allowable NOL carryovers and carrybacks).
7. Deduct the consolidated dividends-received deductions.

Consolidated taxable income (or consolidated NOL)

STEP 3. Any income, loss, or deduction items that must be reported on a consolidated basis are removed from the taxable income calculation. The resulting amount is the group member's **separate taxable income**.

STEP 4. The separate taxable income amounts of the individual group members are aggregated into a **combined taxable income** amount.

STEP 5. Each of the tax attributes that are stated on a consolidated basis (which were removed in Step 3) are added to or subtracted from the combined taxable income amount. The resulting amount is the affiliated group's consolidated taxable income.[8]

Consolidated taxable income is multiplied by the appropriate tax rates of Sec. 11 to determine the consolidated regular tax liability. This amount may be increased if the affiliated group is found to owe an additional amount under the corporate AMT, one of the other special tax levies, or as the result of recapturing previously claimed tax credits. Any tax credits and estimated tax payments are subtracted from the regular tax liability to determine the taxes that are owed when the return is filed. A sample consolidated tax return worksheet is included in Appendix B, which illustrates the consolidated taxable income calculation.

KEY POINT

Two basic rules exist for determining what income must be included in a consolidated tax return: common parent's income for the entire tax year and a subsidiary's income only for the period the subsidiary is a member of the consolidated group.

INCOME INCLUDED IN THE CONSOLIDATED TAX RETURN

A consolidated tax return includes the parent corporation's income for its entire tax year, except for any portion of the year that it was a member of another affiliated group that filed a consolidated tax return. A subsidiary corporation's income is included in the consolidated tax return only for the portion of the affiliated group's tax year for which it was a group member. When a corporation is a member of an affiliated group for only a portion of its tax year, the member's income for the remainder of its tax year is included in a separate tax return or the consolidated tax return of another affiliated group.[9]

A corporation that becomes or ceases to be a group member during a consolidated return year[10] changes its status at the end of the day on which such change occurs (i.e., the change date). Its tax year ends for federal income tax purposes at the end of the change date. Transactions that occur on the change date that are allocable to the portion of the day after the event resulting in the change (e.g., a stock sale or merger) are accounted for by the group member (and all related parties) as having occurred on the next day.[11]

EXAMPLE C8-4 ▶ P and S Corporations file separate tax returns for calendar year 1996. At the close of business on April 30, 1997, P Corporation acquires all of S Corporation's stock. If the P-S affiliated group files a consolidated tax return for 1997, P's income is included in the consolidated tax return for all of 1997 and S's income is included only for the period May 1 through December 31, 1997. S Corporation must file a separate tax return to report its income for the pre-affiliation period January 1 through April 30, 1997. ◀

Tax returns for the years that end and begin with a corporation becoming or ceasing to be a member of an affiliated group are separate return years. The separate returns are, in general, short period returns (i.e., for applying the MACRS rules), but do not require annualization of the tax liability or estimated tax calculations when a corporation joins

---

[8] Reg. Sec. 1.1502-12.

[9] Reg. Sec. 1.1502-76(b)(1)(i).

[10] A **consolidated return year** is defined by Reg. Sec. 1.1502-1(d) as a tax year for which a consolidated return is filed or is required to be filed by the affiliated group. A **separate return year** is defined by Reg. Sec. 1.1502-1(e) as a tax year for which a corporation files a separate return or joins in the filing of a consolidated tax return with a different affiliated group.

[11] Reg. Sec. 1.1502-76(b)(1)(ii).

an affiliated group. Allocation of income between the consolidated tax return and a member's separate return year takes place according to the accounting methods used by the individual corporation. If this allocation cannot be readily determined, allocation of items included in each tax return (other than ones considered below to be extraordinary) can be based on the relative number of days of the original tax year included in each tax year. A ratable allocation of income, expense, gain, loss, and credit items between periods is permitted if the new or departing group member is not required to change its annual accounting period or accounting method as a result of its change in status, and an irrevocable election is made by the group member and the parent corporation of the affected group. Extraordinary items are allocated to the day that they are reported using the group member's accounting methods. Extraordinary items include but are not limited to gains or losses arising from the disposition or abandonment of capital assets, Sec. 1231 property, or inventory; NOL carrybacks or carryovers; settlements of a tort or third-party liability; compensation-related deductions arising from the group member's change in status (e.g., bonuses, severance pay, and option cancellation payments).[12]

AFFILIATED GROUP ELECTIONS

TAX YEARS. An affiliated group's consolidated tax return must be filed using the parent corporation's tax year. Beginning with the initial consolidated return year for which it is includible in the consolidated tax return, each subsidiary corporation must adopt the parent corporation's tax year. The requirement for a common tax year applies to affiliated group members both when an initial consolidated tax return is being filed and when the stock of a new member is acquired.[13]

EXAMPLE C8-5 ▶ P and S Corporations file separate tax returns for 1996. P Corporation uses a calendar year as its tax year. S Corporation uses a fiscal year ending June 30 as its tax year. At the close of business on April 30, 1997, P Corporation acquires all of S Corporation's stock. If the P-S affiliated group files a consolidated tax return for 1997, S must change its tax year so that it ends on December 31. S must file a short-period tax return for the period July 1, 1996 through April 30, 1997. P's income for all of 1997 and S's income for the period May 1, 1997 through December 31, 1997 are included in the initial consolidated tax return. ◀

SELF-STUDY QUESTION

When a subsidiary leaves a consolidated group, may it select any year-end it wishes?

ANSWER

Without permission from the IRS to do otherwise, a subsidiary must retain the group's year-end (if filing a separate tax return) or adopt the year-end of the acquiring consolidated group, if applicable.

KEY POINT

Even though members of a consolidated group must use the same year-end, members are not required to use the same accounting methods. It is not uncommon to find different inventory methods (e.g., LIFO and FIFO) within the same affiliated group.

METHODS OF ACCOUNTING. Unless the IRS grants permission for a change in accounting method, the accounting methods used by each group member are determined by using the same rules as if the member were filing a separate tax return.[14] This holds true when a consolidated tax return election is made or a new corporation joins an existing affiliated group. Thus, one group member may use the cash method of accounting and another group member may use the accrual method of accounting during a consolidated return year. The possibility of finding a mixture of cash and accrual method corporations in an affiliated group is restricted because of the Sec. 448 restrictions on the use of the cash method of accounting by C corporations that were described in Chapter C3.

TERMINATION OF THE AFFILIATED GROUP

An affiliated group that elects to file a consolidated tax return must continue to file on a consolidated basis as long as the affiliated group exists unless the IRS grants permission for it to do otherwise. An affiliated group exists as long as the parent corporation and at

[12] Reg. Sec. 1.1502-76(b)(2)
[13] Reg. Sec. 1.1502-76(a).
[14] Reg. Sec. 1.1502-17(a).

least one subsidiary corporation remain affiliated. It does not matter whether the parent corporation owns the *same* subsidiary throughout the entire tax year or even whether the continuing subsidiary exists at the beginning of the year.

EXAMPLE C8-6 ▶ P and S_1 Corporations have filed a consolidated tax return for several calendar years. At the close of business on August 31, 1997, P purchases all of S_2 Corporation's stock. S_2 Corporation uses the calendar year as its tax year. At the close of business on September 30, 1997, P sells its entire holding of S_1 stock. The affiliated group, with P as the parent corporation, must file a consolidated tax return for 1997 because P remained the parent corporation of at least one subsidiary corporation (first S_1, later S_2) at all times during the year.

If the order of the purchase and sale transactions were reversed, the affiliated group would have been terminated following the sale of the S_1 stock (on August 31, 1997). A new affiliated group would have been created with the purchase of the S_2 stock (on October 1, 1997). The creation of the new affiliated group would require a new consolidated return election. If such an election were made, the consolidated return for the P-S_2 affiliated group would contain the income of P and S_2 Corporations from October 1, 1997 through December 31, 1997. ◀

SELF-STUDY QUESTION

In the second half of Example C8-6, the order of the transactions is reversed. In this case, what tax returns are required, and what income is included in these returns?

ANSWER

(1) Final P-S_1 consolidated return that includes P's income from 1/1 to 9/30 and S_1's income from 1/1 to 8/31. (2) New P-S_2 consolidated return with P and S_2's income from 10/1–12/31. (3) Short-period separate return for S_1 from 9/1–12/31. (4) Short-period separate return for S_2 from 1/1–9/30.

EXAMPLE C8-7 ▶ P and S Corporations have filed a consolidated tax return for several calendar years. At the close of business on August 31, 1997, P Corporation sells its entire holding of S stock to Artie. P's income is included in the 1997 consolidated tax return for the entire calendar year. S's income is included only for the period January 1 through August 31, 1997. S must also file a separate tax return to report its income for the period September 1 through December 31, 1997. ◀

ADDITIONAL COMMENT

Permission to discontinue the filing of consolidated tax returns is seldom granted by the IRS when the request relates to a change in the tax situation of the affiliated group that is not related to a law change.

GOOD CAUSE REQUEST TO DISCONTINUE STATUS. Permission to discontinue filing a consolidated tax return is sometimes granted by the IRS in response to a "good cause" request initiated by the taxpayer. A good cause reason for discontinuing the consolidated tax return election includes a substantial adverse effect on the consolidated tax liability for the tax year (relative to what the aggregate tax liability would be if the group members filed separate tax returns) originating from amendments to the Code or Regulations having effective dates in the tax year in question.[15]

EFFECTS ON FORMER MEMBERS. The termination of an affiliated group affects its former members in several ways, two of which are examined in subsequent sections of this chapter.

- Any gains and losses that have been deferred on intercompany transactions (e.g., intercompany profits on sales of inventory between group members) may have to be recognized.
- Consolidated tax attributes (such as NOL, capital loss, tax credit, and charitable contribution carryovers) must be allocated among the former group members.

In addition, disaffiliation of a corporation from an affiliated group prevents the corporation from being included in a consolidated return with the same affiliated group until five years after the beginning of its first tax year in which it ceased to be a group member. The IRS can waive the five-year requirement and permit the departing group member to join in a consolidated return at an earlier date.

---

[15] See Rev. Proc. 95-39, 1995-2 C.B. 399 where the IRS determined that changes to its rules regarding intercompany transactions may have adverse effects on the filing of consolidated tax returns. It granted all affiliated groups blanket permission to discontinue filing consolidated returns for its first tax year beginning after July 12, 1995, provided the election was made before June 30, 1996.

INTERCOMPANY TRANSACTIONS

OBJECTIVE 6

Determine whether a transaction is an intercompany transaction

ADDITIONAL COMMENT

The rules that apply to intercompany transactions are an excellent example of the additional recordkeeping necessary to file consolidated tax returns.

An **intercompany transaction** is defined as a transaction between corporations that are members of the same affiliated group immediately after the transaction.[21] Intercompany transactions include:

- Sales, exchanges, contributions, or other transfers of property from one group member to a second group member whether or not the gain or loss is recognized.
- The performance of services by one group member for a second group member, and the second member's payment or accrual of its expenditure.
- The licensing of technology, renting of property, or lending of money by one group member, and the second member's payment or accrual of its expenditure.
- Payment of a dividend distribution by a subsidiary corporation to its parent corporation in connection with the parent's investment in the subsidiary's stock.

For purposes of our discussion, we will divide our coverage into two categories (1) property acquired in intercompany transactions, and (2) other intercompany transactions.

OBJECTIVE 7

Explain the reporting of an intercompany transaction

PROPERTY TRANSACTIONS

GENERAL RULE. Gains and losses on intercompany transactions receive special treatment under the consolidated return regulations. In general, gains and losses on intercompany transactions involving the sale or exchange of property between two group members (also known as an intercompany item) are recognized in calculating the group member's separate taxable income. Exceptions to this general rule include intercompany transactions that qualify for nonrecognition treatment under Secs. 351 (corporate formation transaction) and 1031 (like-kind exchanges). The recognized gain/loss is deferred under the consolidated tax return regulations and therefore not included in determining consolidated taxable income until a subsequent event occurs that requires the recognition or income, gain, deduction or loss (also known as a corresponding item) by the buyer. Events that can trigger the recognition of an intercompany item include:

- The claiming of a depletion, depreciation, or amortization deduction with respect to a property acquired in an intercompany transaction.
- Amortization of services, or any other nonproperty asset, acquired by a group member in an intercompany transaction that has previously been capitalized.
- The disposition outside the affiliated group of a property acquired in an intercompany transaction.
- The departure from an affiliated group of the group member that either sells or owns a property that is acquired in an intercompany transaction.
- The first day of a separate return year for the parent corporation.

In general, buyers and sellers engaging in an intercompany transaction are treated as separate entities.[22] A sale of property by one group member to a second group member is reported on the selling and buying corporations' books using the same basic rules that would apply if the sale involved two unrelated parties. Of course, different rules would be used if the property were acquired in a like-kind exchange, or corporate formation transaction where part or all of the realized gain or loss is not recognized. The basic rules for reporting an intercompany property transaction are presented below.

---

[21] Reg. Sec. 1.1502-13(b)(1)(i).

[22] Reg. Sec. 1.1502-13(a)(2).

SELF-STUDY QUESTION

What is the basis of property purchased by the buying member in an intercompany transaction?

ANSWER

The purchasing member takes a cost basis in any assets purchased in an intercompany transaction.

AMOUNT AND CHARACTER OF THE INTERCOMPANY GAIN OR LOSS. At the time of the transaction, the amount and character of the intercompany gain or loss are determined as if the transaction had occurred in a separate return year.

BASIS AND HOLDING PERIOD. The basis and holding period for a property acquired in a intercompany transaction are determined as if the acquisition occurred in a separate return year. Thus, the adjusted basis for an asset is the property's acquisition cost if the property is purchased by the buying member for cash from the selling member. The holding period for such property begins on the day after the acquisition date.

EXAMPLE C8-9 ▶ S (Seller) and B (Buyer) Corporations have filed consolidated tax returns for several years, with S being the common parent corporation of the affiliated group.[23] S acquired a block of marketable securities in 1987 which have been held as a capital asset since that date. The adjusted basis for the securities is $120,000. S sells the marketable securities to B for $200,000 cash on August 8, 1997. This gain is reported in S's separate tax return calculation. S's deferred capital gain is $80,000 ($200,000 − $120,000). The $80,000 deferred gain is not reported in the consolidated tax return. An adjustment is made to remove it from consolidated taxable income. B's basis for the securities is $200,000. Its holding period for determining the character of the gain or loss on a subsequent sale of the securities commences with August 9, 1997. No gain is recognized by S until one of the events described above that produces a corresponding item for B occurs. At that time, part or all of the deferred gain will be included in the consolidated return (but not S's separate tax return calculation). ◀

The intercompany transaction rules are based on two concepts—intercompany items and corresponding items. **Intercompany items** are the Seller's income, gain, deduction, or loss from an intercompany transaction.[24] **Corresponding items** are the Buyer's income, gain, deduction, or loss from an intercompany transaction, or from property acquired in an intercompany transaction.[25]

EXAMPLE C8-10 ▶ Assume the same facts as in Example C8-9. S determines its gain or loss on the sale of the securities to B on a separate entity basis. Its intercompany gain is $80,000 ($200,000 − $120,000). B takes a $200,000 basis for the securities. In 2000, B sells the securities, which are still a capital asset, to Tom for $250,000 cash. B recognizes a $50,000 ($250,000 − $200,000) capital gain on the sale. This gain is reported in B's separate tax return calculation. The $50,000 gain is B's corresponding item which triggers the recognition of S's intercompany item. The rules presented below will explain the reporting of S and B's gains as part of consolidated taxable income. ◀

MATCHING AND ACCELERATION RULES. Two principles are used to implement the single entity approach to reporting intercompany transactions. They are the matching rule and the acceleration rule. The matching rule generally treats the Seller and Buyer as divisions of a single corporation for purposes taking into account the intercompany items. In general, a transfer of an asset between two divisions is not considered a taxable event. A taxable event can occur when, for example, a division sells an asset to a third party. The acceleration rule provides a series of exceptions to the general rule for taking items into account if the treatment of the Seller and Buyer as divisions within a single

---

[23] S and B Corporations are used for the two members of the consolidated group, instead of our usual P and S Corporations, to make it easier to remember which group member is the seller and which group member is the buyer.

[24] Reg. Sec. 1.1502-13(b)(2)(i).

[25] Reg. Sec. 1.1502-13(b)(3)(i).

entity cannot be achieved (e.g., if either S or B leaves the group and becomes a nonmember).

The intercompany transaction rules override the basic accounting method elections that are used by the seller. Assume that S's sale to B in Example C8-10 was instead made for a series of notes payable in equal amounts over a five-year period. Normally, the Sec. 453 installment sale rules would require the $80,000 gain to be reported as the collections were made over the five-year period. Instead, the $80,000 gain is an intercompany item which, in general, is not reported until a corresponding item is reported by the Buyer.[26]

INTERCOMPANY ITEM AMOUNT. When determining the intercompany item amount, all of the Seller's direct and indirect costs related to the sale or the providing of services are included. As a result, the Uniform Capitalization rules of Sec. 263A apply in determining the basis of inventory that is sold, an employee's wages and other related costs are included in determining the intercompany item when services are performed, and depreciation and other direct expenses are included in determining the intercompany item when property is rented.[27]

CORRESPONDING ITEM AMOUNT. Corresponding items are the Buyer's income, gain, deduction, and loss from an intercompany transaction, or from property acquired in an intercompany transaction.[28] Three corresponding items are illustrated in the text that follows:

- When a Buyer acquires property from a Seller and sells it to a nonmember of the affiliated group, the Buyer's gain or loss from the sale to the nonmember is a corresponding gain or loss.
- When a Buyer acquires property from a Seller and makes an installment sale of the property to a nonmember of the affiliated group, the Buyer's gain from the installment sale is a corresponding gain or loss.
- When a Buyer acquires depreciable property from a Seller, the Buyer's depreciation deductions are corresponding deductions.

Buyer's corresponding items also include disallowed losses and expenses or excluded income. Examples of such items include tax-exempt income, expenses related to the production of tax-exempt income and disallowed under Sec. 265, and losses disallowed on the distribution of appreciated property as a dividend under Sec. 311(a).[29]

In Example C8-10, the corresponding item is B's $50,000 gain reported on its sale of the securities. The Buyer (B) reports its corresponding item using its regular accounting method. The Seller (S) reports its intercompany item (i.e., the deferred gain) at the same time. In our example, the Regulations have matched the intercompany item and the corresponding item to affect consolidated taxable income simultaneously as if the two corporations were divisions of one corporation. Although the regulations contain an acceleration rule, which requires the intercompany item and the corresponding item to be taken into account when matching can no longer produce a single entity effect, this exception to the matching rule is not needed since the Seller and Buyer remained members of the affiliated group at the time of the Buyer's sale to the unrelated party.

The Seller and Buyer report their individual parts of an intercompany transaction as if they were separate entities when calculating their separate return taxable income. For this purpose, the Seller and Buyer are treated as engaging in their actual transaction and owning any actual property involved in the transaction. The intercompany transaction

[26] Reg. Sec. 1.1502-13(a)(3)(i).
[27] Reg. Sec. 1.1502-13(b)(2)(ii).
[28] Reg. Sec. 1.1502-13(b)(3)(i).
[29] Reg. Sec. 1.1502-13(b)(3)(ii).

rules require a recomputation of the affiliated group's gain or loss at the time a corresponding item is reported. When making the recomputation of the affiliated group's gain or loss, the Buyer takes the Seller's basis for the securities instead of the step-up in basis that normally occurs with cash sales between two related or unrelated corporations.[30]

REPORTING SELECTED INTERCOMPANY TRANSACTIONS. The reporting of the intercompany securities transaction originally illustrated in Example C8-10 is presented below in four different situations.

EXAMPLE C8-11 ▶ **Buyer sells to third party at a profit.** Assume the same facts as in Example C8-10. If S and B are divisions of a single corporation and the sale was a transfer between the divisions, B would assume S's $120,000 basis for the securities, and the affiliated group will report a $130,000 ($250,000 proceeds − $120,000 basis) recomputed capital gain in 2000. B reports $50,000 of this gain. B's $50,000 gain is reported in its separate taxable income calculation. Since the affiliated group reported none of the $80,000 deferred gain in prior years, all of the $80,000 ($130,000 − $50,000) difference between the affiliated group's total gain and B's separate taxable income gain is reported as an adjustment on the consolidated return worksheet. ◀

EXAMPLE C8-12 ▶ **Buyer sells to third party at a loss.**[31] Assume the same facts as in Example C8-10, except the securities were instead sold by B to a third party for $190,000. The recomputed gain is $70,000 ($190,000 − $120,000). B reports a $10,000 ($190,000 − $200,000 adjusted basis) capital loss in 2000. B's $10,000 capital loss is reported in its separate taxable income calculation. Since the affiliated group reported none of the $80,000 deferred gain in prior years, all of the $80,000 ($70,000 + $10,000) difference between the affiliated group's total gain and B's separate taxable income loss is reported as an adjustment on the consolidated return worksheet. ◀

EXAMPLE C8-13 ▶ **Buyer sells inventory to third party at a profit.** Assume the same facts as in Example C8-10, except that the securities were instead inventory in B's hands prior to their sale for $250,000. Although S held the securities as a capital asset, the character of the reported gain is based on the character of the asset at the time it was sold by B. Both B's $80,000 gain and S's $50,000 gain are ordinary income. ◀

EXAMPLE C8-14 ▶ Assume the same facts as in Example C8-10, except that B's $250,000 sale proceeds are to be collected in two equal, annual installments starting in 2000. Interest at a rate acceptable to the IRS is charged on the unpaid balance. The recomputed gain and the individual group member's gains are the same as in Example C8-11. After selling the securities, B reports the transaction in its separate taxable income using the installment sale provisions of Sec. 453 applicable to nondealers. The affiliated group does not report the entire amount of the deferred gain in the year 2000. Instead, the installment sale rules apply and the affiliated group reports the deferred gain as B collects the amounts due under the installment contract.

TYPICAL MISCONCEPTION

Even though the restoration event illustrated in Example C8-14 is based on the receipt of installment obligations, remember that intercompany sales cannot be reported on the installment method.

The following formula is used to determine the affiliated group's reported gain:

$$\frac{\text{Amount of the installment payment received}}{\text{Total contract price}} \times \text{Deferred intercompany gain} = \text{Affiliated group's restored gain or loss}$$

[30] Reg. Sec. 1.1502-13(c)(3).

[31] Section 267(f)(2) requires a realized loss to be deferred when a sale of property occurs between members of a controlled group. Regulation 1.267(f)-1 provides special rules for property sales involving members of a controlled group that parallel the intercompany transaction rules for consolidated groups. These rules apply to the members of an affiliated group who sells property to a member of its controlled group that is unable to join in the consolidated return election. A discussion of these rules is beyond the scope of this introductory text.

The affiliated group reports $40,000 of the deferred gain [($125,000 ÷ $250,000) × $80,000] in each 2000 and 2001 as an adjustment to determine consolidated taxable income. B reports its $50,000 gain in two installments of $25,000 each ($50,000 ÷ 2) in 2000 and 2001 plus reporting any interest income earned on the unpaid balance. ◀

Recovery property that is sold between two group members in an intercompany transaction results in a continuation of the selling group member's recovery period and recovery method under the Sec. 168(i)(7) anti-churning rules to the extent that the purchasing group member's basis equals or is less than the selling group member's adjusted basis. To the extent that the purchasing group member's basis for the property exceeds the selling group member's adjusted basis, the amount is treated under Reg. Sec. 1.1502-13(c)(7) as a separate property that was acquired from an unrelated party.

If a transaction takes place and a gain is recognized by the selling party, the anti-churning rules of Sec. 168(i)(7) would treat the purchasing party as continuing the depreciation on the portion of the asset's cost basis equal to the seller's adjusted basis. The purchasing party would treat the step-up in basis (i.e., excess of the purchase price minus seller's adjusted basis for the property) as a new property and use the appropriate MACRS depreciation method and recovery period. The purchaser's depreciation for the carryover portion of the basis is the same each year as the seller's depreciation would have been if the seller had not sold the property. The amount of the intercompany gain attributable to the sale that the seller must report in any year (that is, the amount of the increased depreciation deduction to the group) is the amount of the depreciation deduction attributable to the portion of the purchaser's basis that exceeds the carryover portion. This scenario is illustrated in the following example.

EXAMPLE C8-15 ▶ S and B Corporations form the S-B affiliated group. On January 1, 1995, S pays $10,000 to a nonmember of the group for machinery that under the MACRS rules is five-year property. S claims the following depreciation deductions:

Year	*Deduction*
1995	$2,000 ($10,000 × 0.20)
1996	$3,200 ($10,000 × 0.32)

On January 3, 1997, S sells the machinery to B for $9,000. All of the depreciation for 1997 is allocated to B. Under the MACRS rules the purchaser is allocated the depreciation for the month of transfer when depreciable property is transferred between related parties.[32] S's $4,200 Sec. 1245 gain ($9,000 proceeds − $4,800 adjusted basis) is deferred until B depreciates the asset.

B is treated as continuing the MACRS depreciation on the $4,800 portion of the acquisition price that equals the carryover portion of S's adjusted basis for the machinery. The MACRS provisions would also apply to the $4,200 portion of the acquisition price that represents a step-up in basis (or gain portion of the basis) on B's books. B recovers the asset's $4,200 step-up in basis over five years under the MACRS rules. The amount of the capital-recovery deductions claimed by B in its separate taxable income calculation and the intercompany gain or loss reported by the affiliated group as an adjustment to determine consolidated taxable income during B's holding period for the asset are as follows:[33]

KEY POINT

Depending on when an asset is placed in service and then sold in a deferred intercompany transaction, an asset can be divided into two pieces for depreciation purposes. These situations are covered by special anti-churning rules.

[32] Prop. Reg. Secs. 1.168-5(b)(4)(i) and 1.168-5(b)(2)(i)(B).

[33] Intercompany sales of property that will be depreciated in the purchasing group member's hands usually result in the recognition of ordinary income under Sec. 1239 because the selling and purchasing group members are usually also members of a controlled group and, therefore, are related parties under Sec. 1239(b).

ADDITIONAL COMMENT

The result of the depreciation restoration event is to synchronize the additional depreciation deductions with the restoration of the intercompany gain. Notice that the net depreciation reported in the 1999 consolidated return of $1,152 ($1,152 + $806 − $806 restored gain) is the same amount that would have been reported if S had never transferred the property.

		Depreciation on			
Year		Carryover Basis	Step-Up in Basis	Total Depreciation	Restoration of Deferred Gain
1997	$10,000 × 0.1920	$1,920		$1,920	
	$ 4,200 × 0.2000		$ 840	840	$ 840
				$2,760	
1998	$10,000 × 0.1152	1,152		$1,152	
	$ 4,200 × 0.3200		1,344	1,344	1,344
				$2,496	
1999	$10,000 × 0.1152	1,152		$1,152	
	$ 4,200 × 0.1920		806	806	806
				$1,958	
2000	$10,000 × 0.0576	576		$576	
	$ 4,200 × 0.1152		484	484	484
				$1,060	
2001	$ 4,200 × 0.1152		484	484	484
2002	$ 4,200 × 0.0576		242	242	242
Total depreciation and restoration		$4,800	$4,200	$9,000	$4,200

PRACTICE NOTE

Some firms that make infrequent intercompany sales will follow the practice of making the sale at the asset's tax book value to avoid having to defer and restore a gain or loss.

The $4,200 intercompany gain is recognized by S as ordinary income under Sec. 1245. A sample consolidated tax return is included in Appendix B, which includes the restoration of an intercompany gain via depreciation. ◀

DEPARTING GROUP MEMBER. The Seller's intercompany items and Buyer's corresponding items are taken into account under the acceleration rule when they no longer can be taken into account to produce the effect of treating the two entities as divisions of a single corporation.

If the Seller leaves the affiliated group and the intercompany item originated from a sale, exchange, or distribution, the acceleration rule treats the item as having been sold by the Buyer for a cash payment equal to the Buyer's adjusted basis in the property.

EXAMPLE C8-16 ▶

Assume the same facts as in Example C8-10, except that S's stock is sold by its parent corporation on the last day of 2000, and S immediately leaves the affiliated group. B continues to be owned by its parent corporation (and S's former parent corporation). No portion of S's intercompany item has been reported in 1997-2000 prior to S's leaving the affiliated group. The affiliated group must report the $80,000 ($200,000 deemed sale price − $120,000 S's adjusted basis) intercompany gain immediately before S becomes a nonmember. B continues to report its corresponding items using its regular accounting methods. Thus, it does not recognize any gain until it sells the securities. ◀

If the S and B stock had been sold together by their parent company, the two corporations would continue to be treated as divisions of a single corporation for as long as S and B continued to file a consolidated tax return. Therefore, a deemed sale of the securities would not occur and none of S's intercompany profit would be reported.

OTHER INTERCOMPANY TRANSACTIONS

Any income, gain, deduction, or loss realized or incurred on other intercompany transactions is included in the income and expense classifications for the tax year in which the transaction is ordinarily reported. Both parties report their sides of the

SELF-STUDY QUESTION

Why are the other intercompany transactions not given any special treatment?

ANSWER

Because both sides of the transaction are reported in the same consolidated return, they simply net each other out. If, due to accounting methods, the items would be reported in different tax periods, both the income and deduction must be reported in the later of the two tax years.

transaction in determining separate taxable income.[34] When both parties use the same accounting method, these amounts net to zero because the income and expense are included in consolidated taxable income.

Code Sec. 267(a)(2) imposes a special rule on related party transactions requiring the matching of the recognition of the payer's deduction item and the payee's income item. Thus, when two group members would ordinarily report the income and deduction items in different consolidated return years under their regular accounting methods, the payer must defer the reporting of the deduction until the tax year in which the payee member reports the income.

Section 267(b)(3) includes two corporations that are members of the same controlled group as related parties. This definition includes most members of affiliated groups, whether separate returns or consolidated returns are filed. It may also include certain corporations that are not included in the affiliated group because they are not includible corporations.

Regulation Sec. 1.1502-2(b)(1) requires the two group members to match the income and expense items as if they were incurred by two divisions of a single corporation. As two divisions, S and B would report a recomputed expense amount of zero (i.e., the income of one division would exactly offset the expense of the other division, so that neither income or loss would be reported to external parties). Because S's intercompany items are recognized when B's corresponding item is incurred, amounts earned by S from an intercompany transaction can be included in the consolidated tax return before they are taken into account under its separate entity method of accounting.

EXAMPLE C8-17 ▶ S and B Corporations have filed calendar-year consolidated tax returns for several years. S Corporation uses the cash method of accounting, and B Corporation uses the accrual method of accounting. S lends B $100,000 on March 1, 1997; this debt and the related interest are unpaid at the end of 1997. Interest is charged by S at an annual rate of 12%. The $10,000 interest charge owed at year-end is paid by B on March 1, 1998. Ordinarily, S, a cash-basis corporation, would report no interest income and B, an accrual-basis corporation, would report $10,000 of interest expense in the computation of their separate taxable incomes for 1997's consolidated tax return. Because B has reported $10,000 of interest expense in its separate return and the recomputed expense amount is zero, an adjustment must be made to report $10,000 of interest income in the 1997 consolidated tax return even though S has yet to receive a payment from B. After the adjustment, the income and expense items are matched within the 1997 consolidated tax return, and no "net" interest income or expense is reported. ◀

A Seller's profit or loss from the sale of the capitalized services to another group member is an intercompany item. When a Buyer capitalizes the acquisition cost of the services, the Buyer's amortization deduction becomes the corresponding item. Thus, Buyer's capitalization of the purchase under its separate method of accounting permits the Seller to spread the recognition of its profit, that otherwise would be recognized under its separate method of accounting, over the amortization time period.

EXAMPLE C8-18 ▶ S and B Corporations have filed consolidated tax returns for a number of years. S Corporation, an accrual method of accounting taxpayer, drills wells. B Corporation, operates a farm, and uses the cash method of accounting. S drills a well for B for $10,000 which creates a $2,000 profit. B pays S the cost of the well, capitalizes the well cost, and commences to amortize it

[34] Reg. Sec. 1.1502-13(b)(1) and (2). This procedure may be contrasted with financial accounting, in which both sides of the transaction are eliminated in preparing the consolidated financial statements.

Topic Review C8-1

Reporting Intercompany Transactions

Intercompany Transactions

1. Intercompany transaction definition: a transaction taking place during a consolidated return year between corporations that are members of the same affiliated group immediately after the transaction.
2. There are two types of intercompany transactions: property transactions and other intercompany transactions.
3. The selling and buying members of the affiliated group are generally treated as separate entities when reporting the intercompany transaction.
   a. **Exception:** the selling and buying members are treated as two divisions of the same entity when determining the recomputed corresponding gain, income, loss, or deduction item.
4. The reporting of intercompany transactions are based on two concepts.
   a. **Intercompany items** are the Seller's income, gain, deduction, or loss from an intercompany transaction.
   b. **Corresponding items** are the Buyer's income, gain, deduction or loss from an intercompany transaction, or from property acquired in an intercompany transaction.
5. The following are some of the corresponding items that can trigger the recognition of an intercompany item (e.g., gain, loss, income, or deduction amount).
   a. Property is sold by the Buyer to a nonmember of the group.
   b. Property acquired by the Buyer is depreciated, depleted, or amortized.
   c. The corporation which sold a property or owns a property leaves the affiliated group.
   d. The affiliated group discontinues filing consolidated tax returns.

over a 10-year period. Under the accrual method of accounting, S would report its income and expenses when the drilling occurred. Because it is an intercompany transaction, S reports its profit over the 10-year amortization period used by B. ◀

Topic Review C8-1 presents a summary of the intercompany transaction rules.

Dividends Received by Group Members

SELF-STUDY QUESTION

Are dividends received from members of the same affiliated group entitled to a dividends-received deduction?

ANSWER

Not if the affiliated group is filing consolidated tax returns because intercompany dividends are excluded, hence no dividends-received deduction is necessary.

Dividends received by group members are treated differently depending on whether they come from corporations within the affiliated group or from firms outside it. In determining consolidated taxable income, the dividends received from other group members are excluded, while those received from nonmembers of the group are eligible for a 70%, 80%, or 100% dividends-received deduction.

Exclusion Procedure

A dividend distribution from one group member to a second group member during a consolidated return year is an intercompany transaction. An intercompany distribution is not included in the gross income of the distributee member (Buyer). The exclusion applies only to distributions that otherwise would be taxable if paid to a non-affiliated

TYPICAL MISCONCEPTION

One difference between consolidated tax returns and separate tax returns is that in a consolidated setting, intercompany distributions in excess of both E&P and basis in the shareholder member's stock investment do not create a capital gain, but rather create an excess loss account (i.e., a negative basis account for the distributee's investment in the distributing corporation).

REAL WORLD EXAMPLE

When each corporation within an affiliated group prepares its own separate tax return, dividends received from related corporations may be included in gross income. In such a situation, a worksheet adjustment is then needed during the consolidation process to remove the dividend from consolidated taxable income.

corporation and which produce a corresponding negative adjustment to the basis of the distributing corporation's stock.[35]

Within an affiliated group, nondividend distributions (e.g., a distribution made when there is no earnings and profits balance) reduce the shareholder corporation's basis in the distributing corporation's stock.[36] If the amount of the distribution exceeds the distributee's adjusted basis in the stock, the excess either creates a new, or increases an existing, **excess loss account** (i.e., a negative investment account). However, the distributee does not recognize any gain from the portion of the distribution that exceeds its basis in the distributing corporation's stock (as it would with nonaffiliated corporations).[37] The creation of an excess loss account is discussed in the basis adjustment section of this chapter.

The amount of any distribution received by one group member from another equals the money distributed plus the sum of the adjusted basis of any property distributed and the gain recognized by the distributing corporation. Because under Sec. 311(b) gain is recognized on most distributions of appreciated property, the gain recognized plus the adjusted basis of the distributed property will generally equal its FMV where a distribution of appreciated property takes place between group members. Gain recognized by the distributing corporation under Sec. 311 due to the distribution of property to another group member is treated as an intercompany item. The deferred gain is included in consolidated taxable income by the distributing corporation when a corresponding item is reported by the distributee (e.g., the shareholder corporation begins to depreciate the property).[38]

CONSOLIDATED DIVIDENDS-RECEIVED DEDUCTION

The dividends-received deduction for dividends received from nonmembers is computed on a consolidated basis. It is not applied to the separate taxable income of each group member. The consolidated dividends-received deduction equals the sum of 70% of dividends received from unaffiliated domestic corporations in which a less than 20% interest is held, 80% of dividends received from unaffiliated domestic corporations in which a 20% or more interest is held, and 100% of dividends received from an 80% or more owned domestic corporation that is not included in the consolidated return election (e.g., a 100%-owned life insurance company that is prohibited from being part of a consolidated tax return). The 70% and 80% dividends-received deductions are separately limited by consolidated taxable income. The 80% dividends-received deduction limitation is calculated first, and the deduction cannot exceed 80% of consolidated taxable income excluding the consolidated dividends-received deduction, any consolidated NOL, or capital loss carryback. The 70% dividends-received deduction limitation is then calculated and the deduction cannot exceed 70% of consolidated taxable income reduced by the amount of the dividends eligible for the 80% dividends-received deduction and excluding the consolidated dividends-received deduction, any consolidated NOL, or capital loss carryback. The limitations do not apply if the full amount of the deduction creates or increases a consolidated NOL.[39]

EXAMPLE C8-19 ▶ P, S_1, and S_2 Corporations create the P-S_1-S_2 affiliated group. Consolidated taxable income (without considering any dividends-received exclusions or deductions, NOLs, and capital losses) is $200,000. The following dividend income is received by the group from unaffiliated

---

35 Reg. Sec. 1.1502-13(f)(2).

36 Reg. Sec. 1.1502-13(f)(7).

37 Reg. Sec. 1.1502-14(a)(2). The amount of the excess loss account's negative balance is reported as either ordinary income or capital gain when a disposition of the subsidiary corporation's stock occurs.

38 Reg. Secs. 1.1502-13(f).

39 Reg. Sec. 1.1502-26(a)(1).

corporations that are less than 20%-owned: P, \$6,000; S_1, \$10,000; and S_2, \$34,000. In addition, P receives a \$40,000 dividend from S_1, and S_1 receives a \$60,000 dividend from a 100%-owned life insurance company that cannot join in the consolidated return election. S_1's distribution reduces P's basis for its investment in S_1.

The \$40,000 dividend that P receives from S_1 is excluded from P's gross income since it results in a basis reduction for P's investment in S_1. S_1's \$60,000 dividend from the 100%-owned life insurance company is eligible for a 100% dividends-received deduction. This \$60,000 deduction is not subject to any limitation and reduces consolidated taxable income before applying the 70% limitation. The 70% dividends-received deductions included in the separate taxable income calculations are P, \$4,200 (0.70 × \$6,000); S_1, \$7,000 (0.70 × \$10,000); and S_2, \$23,800 (0.70 × \$34,000), or a total \$35,000 reduction in consolidated taxable income. The 70% dividends-received deduction (\$35,000) is not restricted by the dividends-received deduction limitation [(\$200,000 consolidated taxable income given in the facts − \$60,000) × 0.70 = \$98,000]. The consolidated dividends-received deduction is \$95,000 (\$35,000 + 60,000). ◀

SELF-STUDY QUESTION

What is the dividends-received deduction in Example C8-19, if the group has consolidated taxable income before special deductions of (a) \$95,000? (b) \$94,999?

ANSWER

(a) \$84,500 [\$60,000 + (0.70 × \$35,000)] due to the consolidated taxable income limitation.
(b) All \$95,000 (\$60,000 + \$35,000) is allowed because the full dividends-received deduction creates an NOL. Should a \$1 difference in consolidated taxable income make a \$10,500 difference in the dividends-received deduction?

STOP & THINK

Question: Alpha Corporation has owned the stock of a subsidiary for a number of years. Peter Gray, the CPA, who has prepared both corporations' tax returns since their creation has been trying to sell Alpha's Director of Federal Taxes on commencing to file a consolidated tax return based on the tax exemption for intragroup dividends. Is he right or wrong in his approach?

Solution: He is wrong. If the two companies file separate tax returns, a 100% dividends-received deduction is available for intragroup dividends. If a consolidated return were filed, the dividend can be excluded from Alpha's gross income. Typically, these two alternatives provide the same outcome. A difference between these two alternatives may be found when preparing state tax returns (see page C8-34). Peter should be concentrating on advantages such as offsetting profits and losses between the two companies should one company incur a loss, deferring intercompany profits, etc. (see pages C8-4 and C8-5).

CONSOLIDATED CHARITABLE CONTRIBUTIONS DEDUCTION

KEY POINT

Determining the charitable contribution deduction on a consolidated basis rather than for each corporation separately may or may not be beneficial. The outcome depends on the actual numbers in each individual situation.

The affiliated group's charitable contributions deduction is computed on a consolidated basis. The consolidated charitable contributions deduction equals the sum of the charitable contributions deductions of the individual group members for the consolidated return year (computed without regard to any individual group member's limitation) plus any charitable contribution carryovers from earlier consolidated or separate return years. The charitable contributions deduction is limited to 10% of adjusted consolidated taxable income. Adjusted consolidated taxable income is computed without regard to the consolidated dividends-received deduction, any consolidated NOL or capital loss carrybacks, and the consolidated charitable contributions deduction. Any charitable contributions made by the group in excess of the 10% limitation are carried over to the five succeeding tax years.[40] Any unused contribution amounts remaining at the end of the carryover period are lost.

[40] Reg. Sec. 1.1502-24(a).

EXAMPLE C8-20 ▶ P, S_1, and S_2 Corporations form the P-S_1-S_2 affiliated group. The group members report the following charitable contributions and "adjusted" consolidated taxable income for 1997:

Group Member	*Charitable Contributions*	*Adjusted Consolidated Taxable Income*
P	$12,500	$150,000
S_1	5,000	(40,000)
S_2	2,000	10,000
Total	$19,500	$120,000

The P-S_1-S_2 affiliated group's charitable contributions deduction is the lesser of its actual charitable contributions ($19,500) or 10% of its adjusted consolidated taxable income ($12,000). The $7,500 ($19,500 − $12,000) of excess charitable contributions can be carried over to tax years 1998 through 2002. ◀

A member leaving the affiliated group takes with it any excess contributions arising in a prior separate return year plus its allocable share of any excess consolidated charitable contributions for a consolidated return year. The excess consolidated charitable contributions are allocated to each group member based on the relative amount of their contributions (when compared to the total contributions of all group members) for the consolidated return year.

NET OPERATING LOSSES (NOLs)

OBJECTIVE 8

Calculate an affiliated group's consolidated NOL

One advantage of filing a consolidated tax return is the ability of an affiliated group to offset one member's current NOLs against the taxable income of other group members. If these losses cause the affiliated group to report a consolidated NOL, the NOL may be carried back or carried forward to other consolidated return years of the affiliated group. In some cases part or all of the consolidated NOL can be carried back or carried over to separate return years of the individual group members. NOLs of group members arising in separate return years may also be carried back or carried over to consolidated return years, subject to the separate return limitation year (SRLY) limit. In addition, NOLs, capital losses, and excess credits of a loss corporation that is a member of an affiliated group can be subject to the special consolidated return change of ownership (CRCO) and consolidated Sec. 382-384 limitations. The rules that apply to carrybacks and carryovers are examined below.

CURRENT YEAR NOLs

KEY POINT

Generally, the most significant benefit to filing consolidated tax returns is the ability to offset losses of one member against the income of other members.

Each member's separate taxable income is combined to determine combined taxable income before any adjustment is made for NOL carryovers (see Table C8-1).[41] The combining process allows the losses of one group member to offset the taxable income of other group members. A group member cannot elect separately to carry back its own losses from a consolidated return year to one of its earlier profitable separate return years. Only the consolidated NOL of the group (if any) may be carried back or over.

[41] Reg. Sec. 1.1502-12(h).

EXAMPLE C8-21 ▶ P and S Corporations form the P-S affiliated group. During 1996, the initial year of operation, P and S file separate tax returns. Beginning in 1997, the P-S group elects to file a consolidated tax return. P and S report the following results for 1996 and 1997:

Group Member	Taxable Income 1996	Taxable Income 1997
P	($15,000)	$40,000
S	250,000	(27,000)
Consolidated taxable income	N/A	$13,000

N/A = Not applicable

P's 1996 NOL may not be used to offset S's 1996 profits because separate returns were filed. This NOL carryover may be used only to reduce the $13,000 of 1997 consolidated taxable income that is reported after S's 1997 loss is offset against P's 1997 separate taxable income. Because S's 1997 loss must be offset against P's 1997 taxable income, S cannot carry its 1997 NOL back against its 1996 taxable income to increase the value of the tax savings obtained from the loss. The remaining NOL carryover of $2,000 ($15,000 loss from 1996 − $13,000 1997 consolidated taxable income) is carried over to 1998. ◀

OBJECTIVE 9

Calculate the carryback or carryover of a consolidated NOL

CARRYBACKS AND CARRYFORWARDS OF CONSOLIDATED NOLs

The consolidated NOL rules are similar to the NOL rules applying to a corporation filing a separate tax return. A consolidated NOL is determined after the following computation:[42]

Separate taxable income of each group member	
Plus:	Consolidated capital gain net income
Minus:	Consolidated Sec. 1231 net loss
	Consolidated charitable contributions deduction
	Consolidated dividends-received deduction
Consolidated NOL	

The consolidated NOL may be carried back to the three preceding consolidated return years or carried over to the fifteen succeeding consolidated return years. The parent corporation may also elect for the affiliated group to relinquish the entire carryback period for a consolidated NOL and use it only as a carryforward to succeeding years.[43] (See Chapter C3 for a discussion of the reasons for making this election and how this election is made.)

TYPICAL MISCONCEPTION

A consolidated NOL may be carried back three years and carried forward fifteen years. This is not complicated unless the members of the group change before the loss is fully used.

A carryback or carryforward of the consolidated NOL to a tax year in which the members of the affiliated group have not changed poses no real problem. The amount of the consolidated NOL that is absorbed is determined according to the basic Sec. 172 rules for NOLs outlined in Chapter C3.

Determining the amount of the consolidated NOL that may be absorbed in a tax year is more difficult when the group members are not the same in the carryback or carryforward year. In such a case, the consolidated NOL is apportioned to each corporation that was both a member of the affiliated group and incurred a separate NOL during the loss year. When a loss corporation is not also a group member in the

[42] Temp. Reg. Sec. 1.1502-21T(e).

[43] Temp. Reg. Sec. 1.1502-21T(b)(3)(i).

carryback or carryforward year, the rules relating to carrybacks and carryforwards to separate return years (discussed below) must be applied.

CARRYBACK OF CONSOLIDATED NOL TO SEPARATE RETURN YEAR

GENERAL RULE. A consolidated NOL may be carried back and absorbed against a member's taxable income from a preceding separate return year. To effect a carryback, part or all of the consolidated NOL must be apportioned to the member. To the extent that a member uses its allocable share of the consolidated NOL, such an amount is not available to the remaining members as a carryback or carryforward to a consolidated return year. The consolidated NOL is apportioned to a loss member in the following manner:[44]

$$\frac{\text{Separate NOL of the individual member}}{\text{Sum of the separate NOLs incurred by all members having such losses}} \times \text{Consolidated NOL} = \text{Portion of consolidated NOL attributable to member}$$

EXAMPLE C8-22 ▶

KEY POINT

In Example C8-22, because P-S did not file a consolidated tax return in 1994, P must either forgo the three-year carryback or allow all of the consolidated NOL to be carried back to S's 1994 separate tax return year.

P and S Corporations form the P-S affiliated group. The P-S group files separate tax returns in 1994. S reports taxable income of $275,000 in 1994. The group elects to file consolidated tax returns for 1995 through 1997. The P-S group reports a $150,000 consolidated NOL for 1997, all of which is attributable to S. S carries the $150,000 NOL back to 1994 and uses the loss to partially offset the taxable income it reported in 1994. The loss is used up in 1994 and therefore cannot be used by the P-S group in any consolidated return year. Alternatively, an election by P to forgo the carryback permits the loss to be used in 1998 and subsequent consolidated return years. ◀

SPECIAL CARRYBACK RULE FOR NEW MEMBERS. When the consolidated NOL is apportioned to a member, it is normally carried back to the third preceding consolidated or separate return year. A special rule permits an affiliated group member to carry an NOL back to a separate return year of its common parent corporation or a consolidated return year of the affiliated group if

- The member corporation with the loss carryback did not exist in the carryback year, and
- The loss corporation has been a member of the affiliated group continually since its organization.

If these two requirements are met, the portion of the consolidated NOL attributable to the loss member is carried back to a preceding consolidated return year of the affiliated group (or separate return year of the common parent corporation) only if the common parent was not a member of a different consolidated group or affiliated group filing separate returns for the year to which the loss is carried or a subsequent year in the carryback period.[45]

---

[44] Temp. Reg. Sec. 1.1502-21T(b)(iv). The member's separate NOL is determined in a manner similar to the calculation of separate taxable income except for a series of adjustments to account for the member's share of the consolidated charitable contributions and dividends-received deductions, the member's capital gain net income, and the member's net capital loss or Sec. 1231 net loss minus any portion of the consolidated amounts attributable to the member that was absorbed currently.

[45] Temp. Reg. Sec. 1.1502-21T(b)(2)(ii)(B). A consolidated group is an affiliated group that has elected to file a consolidated tax return. The carryback rules mentioned in the text apply to tax years beginning on or after January 1, 1997.

EXAMPLE C8-23 ▶

SELF-STUDY QUESTION

What is the reason for allowing S_2's portion of the consolidated NOL to be carried back to 1994?

ANSWER

Because the assets that make up S_2 Corporation in 1997 were really P's assets in 1994, it only makes sense to allow the NOLs to be carried back against whatever tax return P filed in 1994.

P, S_1, and S_2 Corporations form the P-S_1-S_2 affiliated group. P and S_1 are affiliated for 1994 and 1995 and file consolidated tax returns. P acquires all of S_2 Corporation's stock on January 1, 1996, the date on which S_2 is created. P, S_1, and S_2 report the following results (excluding NOL deductions) for 1994 through 1997:

Group Member	Taxable Income			
	1994	*1995*	*1996*	*1997*
P	$10,000	$12,000	$14,000	$16,000
S_1	7,000	8,000	10,000	4,000
S_2	XXX	XXX	(20,000)	(30,000)
Consolidated taxable income	$17,000	$20,000	$4,000	($10,000)

None of S_2's 1996 NOL can be carried back to 1994 because the affiliated group did not report a consolidated NOL. The loss is used to offset P and S_1's 1996 taxable income. All of the $10,000 consolidated NOL of 1997 is attributable to S_2. Two options are available with respect to this NOL: the NOL may be carried over to subsequent tax years, or the NOL may be carried back to the period 1994 through 1996. If the first alternative is elected, the NOL offsets consolidated taxable income amounts reported in 1998 and subsequent years. If the second alternative is selected, the $10,000 NOL is carried back to offset part of the 1994 consolidated taxable income. This result is possible because S_2 did not exist in 1994 and it joined the affiliated group immediately after it was created on January 1, 1996 and has been a group member continually since its organization. ◀

If the loss corporation is not a member of the affiliated group immediately after its organization, that member's portion of the consolidated NOL is carried back only to its prior separate return years.

EXAMPLE C8-24 ▶

SELF-STUDY QUESTION

Is there any reason for P to elect not to carry back the NOL to S_2's separate tax return years?

ANSWER

Probably not. But if S_2 has minority shareholders, because the refund is issued to S_2, the minority stock interest will share in the increase in FMV of S_2's stock. Don't overlook minority shareholders!

Assume the same facts as in Example C8-23, except that S_2 Corporation files separate tax returns for 1994 and 1995 prior to its stock being acquired by P on January 1, 1996. P, S_1, and S_2 report the following results (excluding NOL deductions) for 1994 through 1997:

Group Member	Taxable Income			
	1994	*1995*	*1996*	*1997*
P	$10,000	$12,000	$14,000	$16,000
S_1	7,000	8,000	10,000	4,000
S_2	8,000	3,000	(20,000)	(30,000)
Consolidated taxable income	$17,000[a]	$20,000[a]	$ 4,000	($10,000)

[a] Including only the results of P and S_1.

All of the 1997 consolidated NOL can be carried back by S_2 to 1994 and 1995. (S_2's 1996 separate NOL cannot be carried back because there was no consolidated NOL in 1996.) The $10,000 NOL offsets all of S_2's 1994 separate return taxable income of $8,000, and the remaining loss carryback of $2,000 reduces its 1995 separate return taxable income to $1,000. Alternatively, the P-S_1-S_2 affiliated group could elect to carry the loss forward to offset 1998's taxable income (see Chapter C3's discussion regarding why such an election would be advisable). ◀

CARRYFORWARD OF CONSOLIDATED NOL TO SEPARATE RETURN YEAR

If a corporation ceases to be a member of the affiliated group during the current year, the portion of the consolidated NOL that is allocable to the departing member becomes the member's separate carryforward. However, the allocation of the NOL to the departing group member cannot be made until the available carryover is absorbed in the current consolidated return year. This requirement exists even when all of the carryover is attributable to the departing member. The departing member's share of the NOL carryforward then may be used in its first separate return year.[46]

EXAMPLE C8-25 ▶ P, S_1, and S_2 Corporations form the P-S_1-S_2 affiliated group, with P owning all the S_1 and S_2 stock. The group files consolidated tax returns for several years. At the close of business on September 30, 1997, P sells its investment in S_1. S_1 must file a separate tax return covering the period October 1, 1997 through December 31, 1997. During pre-1997 tax years, P, S_1, and S_2 incur substantial NOLs. At the beginning of 1997, a consolidated NOL carryforward of $100,000 is still available. Two-thirds of this loss is allocable to S_1; the remainder is allocable to S_2. The affiliated group reports the following results (excluding NOL deductions) for 1997:

	Group Member	*Taxable Income*
P		$20,000
S_1:	January 1 through September 30	30,000
	October 1 through December 31	15,000
S_2		10,000
Total		$75,000

The consolidated NOL carryforward of $100,000 offsets the $60,000 of taxable income ($20,000 + $30,000 + $10,000) reported by P, S_1, and S_2 in their 1997 consolidated tax return. This leaves $40,000 of carryforward to be allocated between S_1 and S_2. S_1 receives $26,667 (0.667 × $40,000), and S_2 receives $13,333 (0.333 × $40,000) of the carryforward. $15,000 of S_1's carryforward can be used in its separate tax return for the period ending December 31, 1997. The remainder is carried over to S_1's 1998 separate tax return. The affiliated group can carry forward S_2's allocable share of the NOL to 1998 and subsequent years. ◀

TYPICAL MISCONCEPTION

In Example C8-25, it is important to understand that the group is entitled to use the consolidated NOL before S_1 determines its NOL carryforward. This can have an impact on negotiating an equitable purchase price for S_1.

OBJECTIVE 10

Determine how the special loss limitations restrict the use of separate and consolidated NOL carrybacks and carryovers

SPECIAL LOSS LIMITATIONS

Two special loss limitations, the **separate return limitation year (SRLY) rules** and the **Sec. 382 loss limitation rules**, are imposed on affiliated groups. The SRLY rules limit the separate return NOL amount that can be deducted as a NOL carryback or carryover by an affiliated group to a member's contribution to consolidated taxable income. This prevents the affiliated group from offsetting its current taxable income by purchasing loss corporations solely to use their NOLs. The Sec. 382 loss limitation rules, which were explained in Chapter C7 on a separate return basis, also apply to affiliated groups filing consolidated returns. The special consolidated return rules restrict an affiliated group from using NOLs following an ownership change that results from a purchase transaction or a tax-free reorganization. Each of these sets of rules is explained below.

KEY POINT

The SRLY rules are used to limit a group from acquiring already existing losses and offsetting those losses against the group's income.

SEPARATE RETURN LIMITATION YEAR RULES. A member incurring an NOL in a separate return year (that is available as a carryback or a carryforward to a consolidated return year) is subject to a limit on the use of the NOL when the loss year is designated a separate return limitation year. A **separate return limitation year** is defined as any separate return year, except

- A separate return year of the group member that is designated as the parent corporation for the consolidated return year to which the tax attribute (e.g., NOL) is carried, or

[46] Temp. Reg. Sec. 1.1502-21T(b)(2)(ii)(A).

ADDITIONAL COMMENT

These two exceptions to the SRLY rules exist because in both cases the group has not acquired already existing NOLs.

SELF-STUDY QUESTION

What is the consequence of having losses subject to the SRLY limitations?

ANSWER

The effect of having a loss tainted as a SRLY loss is that it can be used only to offset taxable income of the subsidiary member (or possibly loss subgroup) that created the NOL.

- A separate return year of any corporation that was a group member for every day of such loss year (i.e., a consolidated return was not elected or the corporation was an ineligible corporation in the loss year)

NOL Carryforwards. An NOL incurred in an SRLY may be used as a carryforward in a consolidated return year equal to the lesser of (1) the aggregate of the consolidated taxable income amounts for all consolidated return years of the group determined by taking into account only the loss member's items of income, gain, deduction, and loss minus any NOL carryovers previously absorbed, (2) consolidated taxable income, or (3) the amount of the NOL carryforward.[47] A SRLY carryover cannot be used when a member's cumulative contribution is less than zero. Any NOL carryovers or carrybacks that cannot be used currently because of the member's contribution to consolidated taxable income or the group's current year consolidated taxable income must be carried over to subsequent tax years.

EXAMPLE C8-26 ▶ P and S Corporations form the P-S affiliated group. P acquires the S stock shortly after its creation in mid-1997. P and S file separate tax returns for 1997 and begin filing a consolidated tax return in 1998. The group reports the following results (excluding NOL deductions) for 1997 through 2001:

	Taxable Income				
Group Member	*1997*	*1998*	*1999*	*2000*	*2001*
P	($ 9,000)	$17,000	$ 6,000	($6,000)	$ 2,000
S	(20,000)	(2,000)	5,000	5,000	16,000
Consolidated taxable income	$XXX	$15,000	$11,000	($1,000)	$18,000

ADDITIONAL COMMENT

It should be noted that S's 1997 NOL is subject not only to the SRLY limitations, but also to the Sec. 382 limitations. Some have suggested that this overlap of limitations causes unnecessary duplication.

Under the SRLY rules, the separate NOLs are used as follows:

- P's 1997 loss is offset against the group's $15,000 of 1998 consolidated taxable income (CTI). None of S's 1997 loss can be used because it incurred a separate NOL, which has already been offset against P's $17,000 profit.
- $3,000 of S's 1997 loss is offset against 1999 CTI: the smaller of S's $3,000 cumulative contribution to CTI [($2,000) + $5,000], its $20,000 loss carryover, or the $11,000 of CTI.
- None of the 1997 loss can be used in 2000 because the group reported a consolidated NOL. Assuming the 2000 NOL is carried back, 1998 CTI is reduced from $6,000 to $5,000 ($15,000 − $9,000 carryover from 1997 − $1,000 carryback from 2000).
- $17,000 of S's 1997 loss is offset against 2001 CTI: the smaller of S's $21,000 cumulative contributions to CTI in 1998–2001 ($24,000 net contributions to CTI in 1998–2001 − $3,000 NOL used in 1999), its $17,000 remaining loss carryover, or the $18,000 of CTI. Consolidated taxable income is reduced to $1,000 ($18,000 − $17,000), and no carryovers remain to 2002. ◀

The SRLY rules are generally applied to each individual corporation that has a loss carryover from a separate return limitation year. Under the new SRLY rules, the SRLY limitation must be determined for a subgroup of two or more corporations within an affiliated group that are continuously affiliated after ceasing to be members of a former affiliated group, that joined the affiliated group at the same time, and where at least one of the corporations carries over losses from the former group to the current group. If the

[47] Temp. Reg. Sec. 1.1502-21T(b)(1). Any unused NOLs that are carried to the consolidated return year from tax years ending before the separate return limitation year reduce the SRLY limitation on a first-in, first-out (FIFO) basis. Tax years ending on the same date reduce the SRLY limitations on a pro rata basis. A loss member's contribution to CTI is determined on a "with" and "without" basis. The difference between CTI "with" the loss member and "without" the loss member is the loss member's contribution to CTI.

subgroup has remained continuously affiliated up to the beginning of the year to which the loss is carried, the subgroup's loss carryovers can be used to the extent that the subgroup contributes to consolidated taxable income.[48]

EXAMPLE C8-27 ▶ P and S Corporations have filed consolidated tax returns together for a number of years. At the close of business on December 31, 1997, A Corporation purchases all of P's stock. The taxable income for P, S, and A Corporations for 1997 and 1998 are as follows:

	Taxable Income	
Group Member	*1997*	*1998*
A	xxx	$120
P	$100	40
S	(250)	30
CTI	($150)	$190

P and S are a subgroup when calculating the use of the SRLY losses in 1998. Their $150 NOL can be used to the extent of the smaller of their contribution to CTI ($70 = $40 + $30), the NOL carryover ($150), or CTI ($190), or $70. The remaining $80 NOL ($150 − $70) is carried over to 1999 and the subgroup rules are applied again. ◀

KEY POINT

The SRLY rules apply to both carryforwards and carrybacks. Remember that SRLYs stem from either a year in which a member files a separate return or a year in which a member joins in the filing of a consolidated return with a different affiliated group.

ADDITIONAL COMMENT

The built-in deduction rules eliminate the ability to circumvent the SRLY rules by acquiring a corporation with losses that have economically accrued and having these losses recognized after the subsidiary is a member of the group.

NOL Carrybacks. The SRLY rules also apply to NOL carrybacks from a separate return limitation year to a consolidated return year. For example, assume that S Corporation in the Example C8-26 leaves the P-S group at the end of 1999. Any NOL that S incurs in a subsequent separate return year that is carried back to the 1997 and 1998 consolidated return years is subject to the SRLY rules. (The carryback to 1997 is not limited since it is a separate return year.) Its use is restricted under the SRLY rules to S's contribution to consolidated taxable income for all consolidated return years.

The use of built-in deductions is also limited by the SRLY rules. A **built-in deduction** is a deduction that accrues in a separate return year but is recognized for tax purposes in a consolidated return year. One example of such a deduction is the depreciation connected with a subsidiary corporation's asset that declines in value between the time it was acquired in a separate return year and the beginning of the initial consolidated return year. Built-in deductions can also result from the sale of a capital or noncapital asset at a loss in a consolidated return year when the decline in value takes place in a separate return year. For example, S purchases inventory in a separate return year for $60,000. The inventory declines to a $45,000 FMV before the time P purchases the S stock and the two corporations start filing on a consolidated basis. The $15,000 ($60,000 − $45,000) built-in deduction can be deducted by S when it sells the inventory only if its SRLY limitation equals or exceeds the built-in deduction amount.[49]

TRANSITIONAL RULES. The SRLY rules described above apply to tax years beginning on or after January 1, 1997. These regulations were originally issued in proposed form to apply to acquisitions of subsidiaries occurring after January 28, 1991. The prior SRLY rules (or "old" SRLY rules) in general apply to tax years beginning before January 1, 1997. Affiliated groups can apply either the "new" SRLY rules or the "old" SRLY rules to losses incurred in consolidated return years ending after January 28, 1991 and before January 1, 1997 provided that the same set of rules is applied for all tax years open as of January 1, 1997.

Under the old SRLY rules, an NOL incurred in a SRLY can be used as a carryforward in a consolidated return year equal to the lesser of (1) the aggregate of the consolidated

[48] Temp. Reg. Sec. 1.1502-21T(c)(2)(i). This rule holds only if the losses were non-SRLY losses to the former affiliated group.

[49] Temp. Reg. Sec. 1.1502-15T(a).

taxable income of the group minus the consolidated taxable income of the group excluding the loss member's income, gain, deduction, and loss items for the carryover year, (2) the consolidated taxable income, or (3) the amount of the NOL carryforward. Thus, the ability to use an NOL from a separate return year is limited to the group member's contribution to consolidated taxable income within a single tax year.

SECTION 382 LOSS LIMITATION. Section 382 prevents the purchase of assets or stock of a corporation having loss carryovers (known as the loss corporation) where a substantial portion of the purchase price is related to the acquisition of the corporation's tax attributes.[50] Trafficking in NOLs and other tax attributes is prevented by applying the Sec. 382 loss limitation to any tax year ending after the ownership change. The 50 percentage point minimum stock ownership change needed to trigger the Sec. 382 rules can occur in acquisitive transactions involving a single corporation or a group of corporations that are filing separate or consolidated returns.

The consolidated Sec. 382 rules generally provide that the ownership change and Sec. 382 limitation are determined with respect to the entire affiliated group (or an affiliated subgroup) and not for individual entities.[51] Following an ownership change for a loss group, the consolidated taxable income for a post-change tax year that may be offset by a pre-change NOL cannot exceed the consolidated Sec. 382 limitation, which in some cases may be zero (see page C8-30). If the post-change tax year includes the ownership change date, the Sec. 382 limitation applies to the consolidated taxable income that is earned in the portion of the tax year following the ownership change date.

ADDITIONAL COMMENT

Section 382 adopts a single-entity approach in determining ownership changes and Sec. 382 limitations. This means that the members of a consolidated group are treated like divisions of a single taxpayer.

A loss group is an affiliated group that is entitled to use an NOL carryover (other than a SRLY carryover) to the tax year in which the ownership change occurs, or has a consolidated NOL for the tax year in which the ownership change occurs.[52] An affiliated group can have two forms of ownership changes: a parent ownership change and a subgroup ownership change. A parent ownership change occurs when (1) the loss group's common parent corporation has (a) a shift in stock ownership takes place involving a 5% or more shareholder, or (b) a tax-free reorganization takes place, and (2) the percentage of stock of the new loss corporation owned by one or more 5% shareholders has increased by more than 50 percentage points over the lowest percentage of stock owned in the old loss corporation by such shareholders during the preceding three-year (or shorter) testing period.[53] A parent ownership change is illustrated in the following example.

EXAMPLE C8-28 ▶ Dwayne owns all of the P Corporation stock. P owns 80% of the S Corporation stock. The remaining 20% of the S stock is owned by Mitzi. For 1997 the P-S group has a consolidated NOL that can be carried over to 1998. The P-S affiliated group is a loss group. On December 31, 1997, Dwayne sells 51% of the P stock to Carter, who has owned no P stock previously. The Sec. 382 stock ownership requirements are applied to P to determine whether an ownership change has occurred. The 51 percentage point increase in Carter's stock ownership is an ownership change that causes the Sec. 382 loss limitation to apply to the carryover of the 1997 NOL to 1998. If Carter had instead acquired only 49% of the P stock, the requisite ownership change would not have occurred and the Sec. 382 limit would not apply. ◀

The preceding example applied the ownership change rules to a parent corporation. An ownership change can also occur with respect to a loss subgroup. A loss subgroup generally consists of two or more corporations that are continuously affiliated after

[50] The Sec. 382 limitation rules apply to the tax attributes that are limited by Secs. 382-384 (e.g., NOLs, capital losses, foreign tax credits, general business credits, minimum tax credit, built-in gains, and built-in losses).

[51] Temp. Reg. Sec. 1.1502-91T(a)(1).

[52] Temp. Reg. Sec. 1.1502-91T(c).

[53] Temp. Reg. Sec. 1.1502-92T(b)(1)(i).

leaving one affiliated group when at least one of the corporations brings with it NOLs from the first group to the second group.[54] The loss subgroup can have an ownership change if, for example, the common parent of the loss subgroup has an ownership change (e.g., when an acquisition of subsidiaries from another affiliated group occurs). The 50 percentage point ownership change test is applied to the common parent of the loss subgroup. Further discussion of this type of ownership change is beyond the scope of an introductory text.

The consolidated Sec. 382 limitation (or subgroup limitation) for any post-change tax year equals the value of the loss group (or subgroup) times the highest adjusted federal long-term tax-exempt rate that applies with respect to the three-month period ending in the month of the ownership change. The value of the loss group is the value of the common and preferred stock of each member, other than stock owned by other group members, immediately before the ownership change.

EXAMPLE C8-29 ▶ Assume the same basic facts as in Example C8-28. In addition, the value of the P stock is \$1,000,000 and the value of the S stock is \$750,000. The value of the P-S affiliated group when applying the Sec. 382 limitation is \$1,150,000 [\$1,000,000 value of P stock + (0.20 × \$750,000 value of S stock owned by Mitzi)]. The \$1,150,000 value is multiplied by the appropriate federal long-term tax-exempt rate to determine the maximum amount of the 1997 consolidated NOL that can be used in 1998.[55] ◀

ADDITIONAL COMMENT

In Example C8-29, if S leaves the group, the loss that is attributable to S will be subject to whatever amount of the Sec. 382 limitation P apportions to S. S's Sec. 382 limitation is zero if P chooses not to apportion any of the group's Sec. 382 limitation to S.

A number of special Sec. 382 rules that apply to affiliated groups deserve brief recognition here.

- If the Sec. 382 limitation for a post-change tax year exceeds the consolidated taxable income that may be offset by a pre-change NOL, the excess amount is carried forward to the next tax year to increase that year's Sec. 382 limitation.[56]
- A loss group (or loss subgroup) is treated as a single entity for purposes of determining whether it satisfies the Sec. 382 continuity of enterprise requirement. Should the loss group not meet the continuity of enterprise requirement at any time in its first two years, the group's Sec. 382 limitation is zero.[57]
- The Sec. 382 rules can apply to a new corporation joining the affiliated group that brings with it a loss carryover from a separate return limitation year. The Sec. 382 ownership change requirement is tested on a separate entity basis to see whether the Sec. 382 limitation or the basic SRLY rules will apply to limit the use of the NOLs against consolidated taxable income.[58]
- When an affiliated group terminates or a member leaves the affiliated group, the Sec. 382 limitation is apportioned to the individual group members.[59]

The Sec. 382 limitation rules apply to ownership changes occurring on or after January 1, 1997. The three-year testing period applicable to Sec. 382 can cause the look-back rule to involve pre-1997 tax years. The consolidated return change of ownership (CRCO) rules apply to ownership changes occurring before January 29, 1991. A CRCO occurs when a more than 50 percentage point stock ownership change takes place within a two-year period due to a purchase or similar taxable transaction and one or more new corporations are added to the affiliated group. Loss carryovers are deductible only to the extent that the old members make a contribution to taxable income. An affiliated group can apply either the new Sec. 382 Temporary Regulations or the old CRCO rules to

[54] Temp. Reg. Sec. 1.1502-92T(b)(1)(ii).
[55] A daily allocation of the loss is not needed since the acquisition occurred on the last day of the loss corporation's tax year.
[56] Temp. Reg. Sec. 1.1502-93T(a).
[57] Temp. Reg. Sec. 1.1502-93T(d).
[58] Temp. Reg. Sec. 1.1502-94T(a).
[59] Temp. Reg. Sec. 1.1502-95T(a).

Topic Review C8-2

Rules Governing Affiliated Group NOL Carrybacks and Carryovers

Loss Year	Carryover/ Carryback Year	Rule and Special Limitations
CRY[a]	CRY	1. Consolidated NOLs are carried back three years and forward fifteen years. Election to forgo carryback period is made by the parent corporation. No special problems are encountered if the group members are the same in the loss year and carryback or carryover year. 2. Section 382 limitation can apply to the loss carryover if an ownership change has occurred.
CRY	SRY[b]	1. Carryback to a member's prior separate return year is possible only if part or all of the NOL is apportioned to the member. Offspring rule permits carryback of an offspring member's allocable share of consolidated NOL to a separate return year of the parent corporation or consolidated return year of the affiliated group. 2. The departing member is allocated part of the consolidated NOL carryover. The consolidated NOL is used first in the consolidated return year in which the departing member leaves the group before an allocation is made. The allocated share of the loss is then used in the departing member's first separate return year. The departing member may be allocated a portion of the Sec. 382 loss limitation by the common parent corporation.
SRY	CRY	1. A separate return year NOL can be carried over and used in a consolidated return year. SRLY rules will apply to NOLs other than those of a corporation that is the parent corporation in the carryover year or that is a group member on each day of the loss year. 2. Carryback of a loss of a departed group member to a consolidated return year is a SRLY loss.

[a]Consolidated return year.
[b]Separate return year.

ownership changes occurring after January 28, 1991 and before January 1, 1997. If a CRCO occurs, the use of prior NOLs is limited to the contribution of the group members at the time of the ownership change to consolidated taxable income.

Topic Review C8-2 presents a summary of the rules applying to carrybacks and carryovers of consolidated return and separate return NOLs. The general rules that apply to NOLs also apply to other tax attributes.

Consolidated Capital Gains and Losses

In the previous discussion of separate taxable income (see page C8-6), all capital gains and losses, Sec. 1231 gains and losses, and casualty and theft gains and losses were excluded. These three types of gains and losses are reported by the affiliated group on a consolidated basis. For a consolidated return year, the affiliated group's consolidated net capital gain or loss is composed of

- The aggregate amount of the capital gains and losses of the group members (without regard to any Sec. 1231 transactions or net capital loss carryovers or carrybacks)
- The net Sec. 1231 gain
- The net capital loss carryovers or carrybacks to the year[60]

Any capital gain net income that is part of consolidated taxable income is taxed at the regular corporate tax rates. Any consolidated net capital loss is carried back three years or forward five years as a short-term capital loss.

SECTION 1231 GAINS AND LOSSES

A group member's Sec. 1231 gains and losses exclude any such amounts deferred when an intercompany transaction occurs. These intercompany gains and losses are reported when a corresponding item triggers the recognition of the intercompany item. The consolidated Sec. 1231 net gain or loss for the tax year is determined by taking into account the aggregate gains and losses of the group members' Sec. 1231 results. If the group's total Sec. 1231 gains (including net gain from casualty and theft occurrences involving Sec. 1231 property and certain capital assets) exceed similar losses, the net gain from these transactions is the consolidated net Sec. 1231 gain and is eligible for long-term capital gain treatment unless recaptured as ordinary income because of prior net Sec. 1231 losses. If the group reports a net loss either from Sec. 1231 transactions or from its casualty and theft occurrences, the net Sec. 1231 loss is treated as an ordinary loss and is deductible in determining consolidated taxable income.

KEY POINT

Netting Sec. 1231 gains/losses on a consolidated basis rather than on a separate corporation basis can dramatically alter the amount of ordinary versus capital gain income.

CAPITAL GAINS AND LOSSES

DETERMINING THE AMOUNT OF GAIN OR LOSS. The amount of any group member's capital gains and losses excludes any such gains deferred when an intercompany transaction occurs. These intercompany gains and losses are reported when a corresponding item triggers the recognition of the intercompany item. Once the recognized gains and losses of each group member are determined, each member's short- and long-term transactions (including any consolidated Sec. 1231 net gain that is not treated as ordinary income) are combined into separate net gain or net loss positions. The sum of these separate positions then determines the amount of the affiliated group's aggregate short- or long-term capital gain or loss. These aggregate amounts are combined to determine the group's consolidated capital gain net income.

SELF-STUDY QUESTION

How do intercompany transactions affect the calculation of capital gains/losses?

ANSWER

Deferred intercompany gains/losses are included in the netting of capital gains/losses only when a corresponding item triggers the recognition of the intercompany item.

CARRYBACKS AND CARRYFORWARDS. The treatment of consolidated capital loss carrybacks and carryovers is similar to NOLs. The losses that are carried back or forward to other consolidated return years are treated as short-term capital losses and serve as a component of the consolidated capital gain or loss position.

The capital loss carrybacks or carryovers that can be used in a consolidated return year equal the sum of the affiliated group's unused consolidated capital loss carrybacks or carryovers and any unused capital loss carrybacks or carryovers of individual group members arising in separate return years. These capital loss carrybacks and carryovers are absorbed according to the same rules described above for NOLs (see pages C8-22 through C8-31).[61]

[60] Reg. Sec. 1.1502-22(a)(1).

[61] Reg. Sec. 1.1502-22(b).

EXAMPLE C8-30 ▶ P, S_1, and S_2 Corporations form the P-S_1-S_2 affiliated group. This group has filed consolidated tax returns for several years. During the current year the affiliated group reports $100,000 of ordinary income and the following property transaction results:

Group Member	Capital Gains and Losses: Short-Term	Capital Gains and Losses: Long-Term	Sec. 1231 Gains and Losses
P	$2,000	($1,000)	($2,500)
S_1	(1,000)	7,000	2,000
S_2	(2,000)	3,000	2,000
Total	($1,000)	$9,000	$1,500

In addition, the group carries over a consolidated capital loss of $3,000 from the preceding year. No net Sec. 1231 losses have been recognized in prior years. The P-S_1-S_2 affiliated group's $1,500 consolidated net Sec. 1231 gain is combined with the $8,000 aggregate amount of capital gains and losses ($9,000 − $1,000) and the $3,000 consolidated net capital loss carryover to obtain the current year consolidated capital gain net income of $6,500 ($1,500 + $8,000 − $3,000). This entire amount is taxed at the regular corporate tax rates. ◀

TYPICAL MISCONCEPTION

The allocation of net capital losses to the individual group members is based in part on each member's Sec. 1231 losses. Thus, it is possible for a member with only a Sec. 1231 loss to share in the net capital loss carryforward or carryback.

ADDITIONAL COMMENT

There is no election to forgo the three-year carryback for a net capital loss. This can complicate matters when the three prior years include separate tax return years of the members of the group.

Carryback of a Consolidated Net Capital Loss. A carryback of a member's apportionment of a consolidated capital loss to one of its preceding separate return years is required when capital gains are available in the carryback year against which the loss may be offset. Apportionment of the consolidated capital loss to the loss members occurs in a manner similar to that described for NOLs.

SRLY Limitation. Carryovers or carrybacks of capital losses from a separate return limitation year invoke the SRLY rules. The amount of the loss carryback or carryover from a separate return limitation year that may be used in a consolidated return year equals the lesser of the loss member's contribution to the consolidated capital gain net income and consolidated capital gain net income.[62]

Sec. 382 Limitation. The Sec. 382 loss limitation rules apply to consolidated and separate return capital loss carryovers as well as consolidated and separate return NOLs. Under Sec. 383, capital losses are subject to the general Sec. 382 limitation described earlier.

Taxable Income Limitation. In addition to the special capital loss limitations outlined above, Sec. 1212(a)(1)(A)(ii) contains a general limitation that prevents a capital loss from being carried back or over and creating or increasing the NOL for the tax year to which it is carried. Therefore, the use of a capital loss is also limited to the group's consolidated taxable income.

Departing Group Members' Losses. A member leaving the affiliated group may take with it an apportionment of any consolidated capital loss carryover and any of its unused capital loss carryovers that originated in a separate return year. These losses are used in subsequent years until they expire. Apportionment of the consolidated capital loss to the departing group member occurs in a manner similar to that described above for NOLs.

[62] As with a NOL, the SRLY rules can apply a single-year or multiple-year contribution comparison.

STOCK BASIS ADJUSTMENTS

KEY POINT

Positive stock basis adjustments will reduce the amount of gain that is reported when a sale of the stock of an affiliated group member occurs.

The basis for an investment in a subsidiary corporation is adjusted annually for its profits and losses as well as for distributions made to higher-tier subsidiaries, or its parent corporation. These rules parallel those used in the equity method of accounting, but use tax numbers instead of book income numbers. If the stock of a profitable subsidiary is sold, a "net" positive basis adjustment that is made produces a smaller capital gain than the gain that would otherwise have been recognized if separate tax returns were filed. The basis adjustment prevents the income earned by the subsidiary during the affiliation from being taxed a second time when the parent corporation disposes of the subsidiary's stock.

The starting point for the calculation is the original basis of the parent corporation's investment in the subsidiary, which, of course, depends on the acquisition method used to acquire the stock (e.g., purchase, tax-free corporate formation transfer, or tax-free reorganization). The following basis adjustments must be made to the original basis:

- Basis is increased for the subsidiary's income, gain, deduction, and loss items that are taken into account in determining consolidated taxable income. The adjustment includes net operating losses, but excludes deferred gains and losses, and unused capital losses.
- Basis is increased for income that is permanently excluded from taxation (e.g., tax-exempt bond interest and federal income tax refunds).
- Basis is decreased for NOLs used in the current year against other group members' taxable income or carried back and used in an earlier year. NOL carryovers and other suspended losses reduce basis in the year they are used. Expiring NOLs and capital losses reduce basis in the year that they expire.
- Basis is decreased for noncapital expenses that are not deductible (e.g., federal income taxes, the 50% of meals and entertainment expenses that are nondeductible, expenses related to tax-exempt income, and losses disallowed under Sec. 267).
- Basis is decreased for all distributions without regard to the E&P balance, or whether such amounts were accumulated in pre- or post-affiliation years.
- If the negative basis adjustments for losses and distributions, etc. are sufficiently large, the basis of the subsidiary's stock is reduced to zero. Additional basis reductions that occur create an excess loss account. No recognition of income or gain is triggered by the creation of this "negative basis account". Subsequent profits or additional capital contributions may reduce or eliminate the excess loss account and, if large enough, can produce a positive basis.

TAX PLANNING CONSIDERATIONS

100% DIVIDENDS-RECEIVED DEDUCTION ELECTION

KEY POINT

Note that a 100% dividends-received deduction may be necessary for intercompany dividends for state income tax purposes if the state doesn't allow the filing of consolidated tax returns.

Intercompany dividends are excluded when a consolidated tax return is filed. The 100% dividends-received deduction election may be used by the affiliated group to exempt from taxation any dividends received from corporations that are not eligible to be included in the consolidated return (e.g., a 100%-owned life insurance company).

If a state does not permit the filing of a consolidated tax return for state income tax purposes,[63] it may be necessary for an affiliated group to elect the 100% dividends-received deduction for both state and federal tax purposes. In such a case, the state requires the filing of separate tax returns by each member of the affiliated group. Generally, the state also permits the claiming of any dividends-received deduction elected for federal income tax purposes. When a consolidated tax return is not filed for state income tax purposes, no exclusion of the dividends is possible and the 100% dividends-received deduction (which was elected but not used on the federal tax return) is substituted on the state income tax return.

ESTIMATED TAX PAYMENTS

Once consolidated tax returns have been filed for two consecutive years, the affiliated group must pay estimated taxes on a consolidated basis.[64] The affiliated group is treated as a single corporation for this purpose. Thus, the estimated tax payments and any underpayment exceptions or penalties are based on the affiliated group's income for the current year and the immediately preceding tax year without regard to the number of corporations that comprise the affiliated group. This treatment can be advantageous if new, profitable corporations are added to the affiliated group.

EXAMPLE C8-31 ▶ The P-S_1 affiliated group files consolidated tax returns for several years. During 1996 the P-S_1 group reports a \$100,000 consolidated tax liability. The P-S_1 affiliated group acquires all of S_2 Corporation's stock during 1997. S_2 is very profitable and causes the P-S_1-S_2 group to report a \$300,000 consolidated tax liability in 1997. Assuming the P-S_1-S_2 group does not come under the large corporation rules outlined below, its 1997 estimated tax payments can be based on the P-S_1 group's \$100,000 consolidated tax liability for the prior tax year. No underpayment penalties are imposed provided the P-S_1-S_2 group makes \$25,000 (\$100,000 ÷ 4) estimated tax payments by the fifteenth day of the fourth, sixth, ninth, and twelfth months of the tax year, because the prior year's tax liability exception to the underpayment rules is satisfied. The balance of the consolidated tax liability must be paid by the due date for the consolidated tax return (without regard to any extensions) to avoid penalty. ◀

UNDERPAYMENT RULES. Affiliated groups are also subject to the special underpayment rules of Sec. 6655(d)(2) for large corporations (that is, corporations having taxable income of at least \$1 million in any one of the three immediately preceding tax years). An affiliated group is considered one corporation when applying the large corporation rules. Only the actual members of the affiliated group for the three preceding tax years are used in applying the \$1 million threshold. New members entering the group are ignored for the three-preceding-years test.[65]

CONSOLIDATED OR SEPARATE BASIS. For the first two years for which a group files consolidated tax returns, the affiliated group may elect to make estimated tax payments on either a consolidated or separate basis. Starting in the third year, however, the affiliated group must make consolidated estimated tax payments. It must continue to do so until separate tax returns are again filed. During the first two tax years for which the election is in effect, the affiliated group sometimes can reduce its quarterly payments by making separate estimated tax payments in the first year and consolidated estimated tax payments in the second year or vice versa. Application of the exceptions to the penalty for underpayment of estimated taxes depends on whether estimated taxes are paid on a

[63] Rev. Rul. 73-484, 1973-2 C.B. 78.
[64] Reg. Sec. 1.1502-5(a).
[65] Proposed Reg. Sec. 1.6655-4(e)(3) requires the \$1 million threshold to be applied to all members of the controlled group.

separate or consolidated basis. Different exceptions (e.g., prior year's liability or annualization of current year's income) to the underpayment rules should be used by the individual group members if it will reduce the amount of the estimated tax payments that are required. Determination of the actual separate or consolidated limitations, however, is beyond the scope of this book.

ADDITIONAL COMMENT

The final estimated tax payment for a member joining a consolidated group is due the fifteenth day of the last month of the short taxable year. If a member is acquired after the fifteenth, the final estimated tax payment is already overdue.

SHORT-PERIOD RETURN. If a corporation joins an affiliated group after the beginning of its tax year, a short-period return covering the pre-affiliation time period must generally be filed. The payment rules covering the short-period return are found in Reg. Sec. 1.6655-3. If a corporation leaves an affiliated group, it must make the necessary estimated tax payments required of a corporation filing a separate tax return for the post-affiliation, short-period tax year, unless it joins in the filing of a consolidated tax return with another affiliated group. No estimated tax payment is required for a short tax year that is less than four months.

COMPLIANCE AND PROCEDURAL CONSIDERATIONS

OBJECTIVE 11

Explain the procedures for making an initial consolidated return election

THE BASIC ELECTION AND RETURN

An affiliated group makes an election to use the consolidated method for filing its tax return by filing a consolidated tax return (Form 1120) that includes the income, expenses, etc. of all of its members. The election must be made no later than the due date for the common parent corporation's tax return, including any permitted extensions.[66] An affiliated group can change from a consolidated tax return to separate tax returns,[67] or from separate tax returns to a consolidated tax return, at any time on or before the last day for filing the consolidated tax return. Once that day has passed, no change can be made.

A sample Form 1120 is presented in Appendix B for reporting the current year's results for the Alpha affiliated group that is described in Example C8-32. The Form 1120 involves the five intercompany transactions mentioned in the example, and a worksheet which summarizes the income and expense items for the five companies illustrates the reporting of the intercompany transactions and presents the details of the consolidated taxable income calculation.

EXAMPLE C8-32 ▶ Alpha Manufacturing Corporation owns 100% of the stock of Beta, Charlie, Delta, and Echo Corporations. The affiliated group has filed consolidated returns for a number of years using the calendar year as their tax year. The components of the separate taxable income amounts of the four corporations are reported on the supporting schedule of the group's consolidated tax return contained in Appendix B. This return illustrates four common transactions involving members of an affiliated group. These are

- ▶ The sale of inventory from Alpha to Beta, which increases Alpha's deferred intercompany profit amount
- ▶ Intragroup dividends paid from Beta and Echo Corporations to Alpha
- ▶ Payment of interest from Delta to Alpha
- ▶ The sale of a truck from Alpha to Beta
- ▶ Beta's depreciation of the truck acquired in the intercompany transaction ◀

[66] Reg. Sec. 1.1502-75(a)(1).
[67] Such a change can take place only for the initial consolidated return year or for a tax year for which the IRS has granted permission to discontinue the consolidated return election.

ADDITIONAL COMMENT

If a group is considering making a consolidated return election, a properly executed Form 1122 should be obtained before any corporation is sold during the election year. After the sale, the consent form may be difficult to obtain.

Students should review this sample return to see how the transactions are reported and how the numbers from the consolidated taxable income schedule are reported in the affiliated group's Form 1120.

In addition to filing the necessary Form 1120 reflecting the consolidated results of operations, each corporation that is a member of the affiliated group during the initial consolidated return year must consent to the election. The parent corporation's consent is evidenced by its filing the consolidated tax return (Form 1120). Subsidiary corporations consent to the election by filing a Form 1122 (Authorization and Consent of Subsidiary to be Included in a Consolidated Income Tax Return) and submitting it as a part of the initial consolidated tax return. Only newly-acquired subsidiary corporations file Form 1122 with subsequent consolidated tax returns.

Each consolidated tax return must also include an Affiliations Schedule (Form 851). This form includes the name, address, and identification number of the corporations included in the affiliated group, the corporation's tax prepayments, the stock holdings at the beginning of the tax year, and all stock ownership changes occurring during the tax year.

The due date for the consolidated tax return is 2½ months after the end of the affiliated group's tax year. A six-month extension for filing the consolidated tax return is permitted if the parent corporation files Form 7004 and pays the estimated balance of the consolidated tax liability. The due date for the tax return of a subsidiary corporation that is not included in the consolidated return depends on whether the affiliated group's consolidated tax return has been filed by the due date for the subsidiary corporation's tax return. These rules are beyond the scope of this introductory text, but can be reviewed in Reg. Sec. 1.1502-76(c).

PARENT CORPORATION AS AGENT FOR THE AFFILIATED GROUP

The parent corporation acts as agent for each subsidiary corporation and for the affiliated group. As agent for each subsidiary, the parent corporation is authorized to act in its own name in all matters relating to the affiliated group's tax liability for the consolidated return year.[68]

No subsidiary corporation can act in its own behalf with respect to a consolidated return year except to the extent that the parent corporation is prohibited from acting in its behalf. Thus, a subsidiary corporation is prevented from making or changing any election that is used in computing separate taxable income, carrying on correspondence with the IRS regarding the determination of a tax liability, filing any requests for extensions of time in which to file a tax return, or filing a claim for a refund or credit relating to a consolidated return year.

ADDITIONAL COMMENT

Each member corporation is severally liable for the entire tax liability of the affiliated group. Anyone purchasing a corporation out of an affiliated group should consider this factor when negotiating the purchase price of the target corporation.

LIABILITY FOR TAXES DUE

The parent corporation and every other corporation that was a group member for any part of the consolidated return year are severally liable for that year's consolidated taxes.[69] Thus, the entire consolidated tax liability may be collected from one group member if, for example, the other group members are unable to pay their allocable portion. The IRS can ignore attempts made by the group members to limit their share of the liability by entering into agreements with one another or with third parties. Thus, the potential consolidated tax liability and any deficiencies could accrue to a corporation that is a member of an affiliated group for even a few days during a tax year.

An exception to this several liability principle occurs when a subsidiary corporation ceases to be a group member as a result of its stock being sold or exchanged before a deficiency is assessed against the affiliated group. Thus, the IRS can opt to assess a former

[68] Reg. Sec. 1.1502-77(a).

[69] Reg. Sec. 1.1502-6(a)

subsidiary corporation for only its allocable portion of the total deficiency if it believes that the assessment and collection of the balance of the deficiency from the other group members will not be jeopardized.

PROBLEM MATERIALS

DISCUSSION QUESTIONS

C8-1 What minimum level of stock ownership is required for a corporation to be included in an affiliated group?

C8-2 Which of the following equity items are considered to be stock for purposes of the stock ownership portion of the affiliated group definition?
- a. Common stock
- b. A second class of common stock
- c. Nonvoting preferred stock
- d. Voting preferred stock
- e. Nonvoting preferred stock convertible into common stock

C8-3 Which of the following corporations are includible in an affiliated group?
- a. C corporation
- b. S corporation
- c. Foreign corporation
- d. Real estate investment trust
- e. Regulated investment company
- f. Life insurance company taxed under Sec. 801

C8-4 Explain the difference between a controlled group and an affiliated group.

C8-5 P, S_1, S_2, and S_3 Corporations form a controlled group of corporations. Because S_3 Corporation is a nonincludible insurance corporation, only P, S_1, and S_2 Corporations are permitted to file their income tax returns on a consolidated basis. Explain to P Corporation's president the alternatives available for allocating the tax savings from the 15%, 25%, and 34% tax rates to the members of the controlled group.

C8-6 P Corporation has two subsidiaries, S_1 and S_2, both of which are 100%-owned. All three corporations are currently filing separate tax returns. P and S_1 have been profitable. S_2 is a start-up company that has reported losses for its first two years of existence. S_2 will eventually be selling cosmetics to S_1 for distribution to retailers. Explain to P Corporation's president the advantages (and disadvantages) of the three corporations filing a consolidated tax return.

C8-7 Briefly explain how consolidated taxable income is calculated starting with the financial accounting (book) income information for each individual group member. Explain how the consolidated taxable income calculation is different from the taxable income calculation for a corporation filing a separate tax return.

C8-8 Determine whether each of the following statements is true or false:
- a. One member of an affiliated group may elect to use the accrual method of accounting, even though another group member uses the cash receipts and disbursements method of accounting.
- b. A corporation that uses the calendar year as its tax year acquires all of the stock of another corporation that has for years used a fiscal year as its tax year. They both may continue to use their previous separate return tax years when filing their initial consolidated tax return.
- c. T Corporation, a calendar year taxpayer, becomes a member of the P-S affiliated group at the close of business on February 28 of a nonleap year. The P-S group has filed consolidated tax returns using the calendar year for a number of years. The P-S-T affiliated group's consolidated tax return includes 306/365ths of T's taxable income for the year.

C8-9 What events permit an affiliated group to terminate its consolidated tax return election?

C8-10 The P-S_1-S_2 affiliated group has filed consolidated tax returns using a calendar year for a number of years. At the close of business on July 15, P Corporation sells all of its S_1 Corporation stock to Mickey. P Corporation retains its investment in S_2 Corporation. Explain what tax returns are required of the three corporations for the current year. What effect does the sale have on the

P-S_1-S_2 group's prior year intercompany items and its charitable contributions carryover that is unused in the current year consolidated tax return?

C8-11 Assume the same facts as in Question C8-10 except that the original affiliated group was just P and S_1 Corporations and that the S_1 stock was sold to Mickey at the close of business on July 15. What affect does the sale have on the P-S_1 group's prior year intercompany items and its charitable contributions carryover that is unused in the final consolidated tax return?

C8-12 Define the following terms:
a. Intercompany transaction
b. Intercompany item
c. Corresponding item
d. Matching rule
e. Acceleration rule

C8-13 Explain how the rules governing depreciation recapture, basis, and depreciation operate when a seven-year recovery class property under the MACRS rules is sold at a profit by one group member to a second group member after the property has been held for three years. The purchasing group member will depreciate the property using the MACRS rules over a seven-year recovery period.

C8-14 Compare and contrast the reporting of interest income and interest expense by P and S Corporations for financial accounting and consolidated tax return purposes when P Corporation lends money to S Corporation on August 1 for a three-year period. Both corporations use the calendar year as their tax year and interest is paid on July 31 each year. First, assume both corporations use the accrual method of accounting, then assume that P and S Corporations use the cash and accrual methods of accounting, respectively.

C8-15 P and S_1 Corporations constitute the P-S_1 affiliated group on January 1. S_1 Corporation acquires all of the stock of S_2 Corporation at the close of business on April 1. Which of the following transactions are intercompany transactions?
a. P Corporation sells inventory to S_1 Corporation throughout the current year.
b. S_2 Corporation sells land (a capital asset) to P Corporation on March 15.
c. S_1 Corporation sells machinery (a Sec. 1245 property) to S_2 Corporation on September 1.
d. P Corporation sells inventory to the PS_1 Partnership, which is owned equally by P and S_1 Corporations on July 23.

C8-16 P, S_1, and S_2 Corporations constitute the P-S_1-S_2 affiliated group. The affiliated group members use the accrual method of accounting and the calendar year as their tax year. Determine whether each of the following transactions that take place during the current year are intercompany transactions. For each item indicate the intercompany item and corresponding item.
a. P Corporation lends S_1 Corporation money. The money remains unpaid at the end of the tax year.
b. S_1 Corporation sells inventory to P Corporation. P Corporation holds the inventory at year-end.
c. P Corporation sells land (a Sec. 1231 property) to S_2 Corporation. S_2 Corporation holds the land at year-end.
d. S_2 Corporation pays a cash dividend to P Corporation.
e. S_1 Corporation provides engineering services that are capitalized as part of the cost of S_2's new factory building.

C8-17 Indicate for each of the following dividend payments the tax treatment that is available in computing consolidated taxable income:
a. Dividend received from a C corporation that is 10%-owned by the parent corporation.
b. Dividend received from a C corporation that is 100%-owned by the parent corporation and included in the consolidated tax return election.
c. Dividend received from a foreign corporation that is 50%-owned by the parent corporation. The foreign corporation earns no U.S. source income.
d. Dividend received from an unconsolidated life insurance corporation that is 100%-owned by the parent corporation.

C8-18 Explain the circumstances in which a consolidated NOL can be carried back to a preceding separate return year.

C8-19 What advantages can accrue to an affiliated group or an individual group member by electing to forgo the carryback of an NOL that is incurred in a consolidated return year? A separate return year? Who makes the election to forgo the carryback?

C8-20 Define the term SRLY and explain its significance and application to an affiliated group filing a consolidated tax return.

C8-21 What is a Sec. 382 ownership change? What is the Sec. 382 loss limitation? Explain their significance and application to an affiliated group filing a consolidated tax return.

C8-22 Determine whether the following statements regarding the alternative minimum tax are true or false:

a. An affiliated group calculates its alternative minimum tax liability on a separate company basis.

b. Each member of an affiliated group receives a separate $40,000 statutory exemption.

c. An affiliated group must make an adjustment for 75% of the difference between its consolidated ACE and its consolidated preadjustment AMTI.

C8-23 P Corporation purchases 100% of the stock of S Corporation on January 1. Explain to the president of P Corporation what basis adjustment is required at year-end for its investment in S Corporation when S earns $350,000 of taxable income and $30,000 of tax-exempt interest income, while it distributes $150,000 to its parent corporation. Each company paid its own tax liability. Assume a 34% corporate tax rate.

C8-24 Explain why an affiliated group filing a consolidated tax return might make a federal tax election to claim a 100% dividends-received deduction for a tax year even though all dividends received during that year are received from other members of the affiliated group.

C8-25 During what time period can an affiliated group elect to file a consolidated tax return? How is the election made?

C8-26 Indicate for which of the following tax-related matters the parent corporation can act as the affiliated group's agent:

a. Making an initial consent for a subsidiary corporation to participate in a consolidated return election

b. Changing an accounting method election for a subsidiary corporation

c. Carrying on correspondence with the IRS during an audit regarding a transaction entered into by a subsidiary corporation that affects the group's determination of consolidated taxable income

d. Requesting an extension of time within which to file a consolidated tax return

C8-27 The consolidated tax return regulations represent an attempt by the taxing authorities to treat a group of separate but affiliated corporate entities as a single taxpaying entity. These regulations also permit the individual group members to retain a large degree of separate entity status. Provide at least two tax provisions that illustrate for an affiliated group filing a consolidated tax return each of these two opposing principles.

ISSUE IDENTIFICATION QUESTIONS

C8-28 Mark, a single individual, owns all of the stock of Red and Green Corporations. Red Corporation has been reporting $150,000 in taxable income for each of the past five years. Green Corporation has regularly been reporting $30,000 NOLs, which have accumulated to $120,000. Approximately one-third of Red's profits come from sales to Green. Intercompany sales between Red and Green have increased during each of the last five years. What tax issues should Mark consider with respect to his investments in Red and Green Corporations?

C8-29 Alpha and Baker Corporations, two accrual method of accounting corporations that use the calendar year as their tax year, have filed consolidated tax returns for a number of years. Baker Corporation, a 100-owned subsidiary of Alpha, is transferring a patent, equipment, and working capital to Charles Corporation in exchange for 100% of its stock. In 1997 the corporation will commence to produce parts for the automotive industry. Charles Corporation expects to incur organizational expenditures of $10,000 and start-up expenditures of $60,000. What tax issues should be considered by Charles Corporation with respect to the selection of its overall accounting method, inventory method, and tax year, and the proper reporting of its organizational and start-up expenditures?

C8-30 Crimson Tide Corporation is the parent corporation of a fourteen-member affiliated group that has filed consolidated tax returns for a number of years. Last year, the group sold all of the stock of Tiger Corporation to Mark Jones. Tiger Corporation reported a current year NOL of $300,000. Tiger's taxable income while a group member averaged $200,000 annually for the past three years, but is expected to be only $50,000 next year due to start-up costs that will be incurred with a new product line. What issues should Crimson Tide consider when trying to value Tiger's NOL prior to its sale? What tax issues should Tiger consider when deciding how to use its NOL?

PROBLEMS

C8-31 ***Affiliated Group Definition.*** Which of the following independent situations result in an affiliated group being created? In each case, indicate the corporations that are eligible to be included in the consolidated tax return election. All corporations are domestic corporations unless otherwise indicated.

a. Zeke, an individual, owns all of the stock of A and B Corporations.

b. Kelly, an individual, owns all of the stock of P and W Corporations. P Corporation owns all of the stock of both S_1 and S_2 Corporations.

c. P Corporation owns all of the stock of S_1 and S_2 Corporations. S_1 Corporation owns 40% of the stock of S_3 Corporation. P Corporation owns the remaining S_3 stock. S_2 Corporation is a foreign corporation.

C8-32 ***Affiliated Group Definition.*** Jane owns all of the stock of P Corporation. P Corporation owns all of S Corporation's stock. S Corporation owns all of the stock of F Corporation. P Corporation also owns all of T Corporation's stock and 70% of the U Corporation's stock. T Corporation owns the remaining 30% of U Corporation's stock and 80% of V Corporation's stock. F Corporation is a foreign corporation. All other corporations are domestic corporations. V Corporation is an insurance company taxed under Sec. 801 that has been 80%-owned by T for the past five years. All undisclosed minority interests are held by unrelated individuals. Which of the corporations can join in a consolidated tax return election?

C8-33 ***Stock Ownership Requirement.*** P Corporation is the parent corporation of the P-S_1-S_2 affiliated group. P Corporation is conducting negotiations to purchase the stock of T Corporation. The management of P would like to include T in the affiliated group's consolidated tax return. T Corporation's outstanding shares are as listed.

Type of Stock	*Shares Outstanding*	*Par Value*	*Market Value*
Common stock (1 vote per share)	50,000	$ 1	$30
Voting preferred stock (4 votes per share)	5,000	100	95
Nonvoting preferred stock	20,000	100	90

Determine a plan that permits P to acquire enough stock to include T in the affiliated group.

C8-34 ***Consolidated Return Election.*** P and S Corporations have been in existence for a number of years. P uses the calendar year as its tax year. S Corporation uses a fiscal year ending June 30 as its tax year. At the close of business on September 30, 1997, P acquires all of the S stock and elects to file a consolidated tax return for 1997.

a. What tax year must be used in filing the consolidated tax return?
b. What is the last date on which the election to file a consolidated tax return can be made?
c. What income of P and S is included in the consolidated tax return? in a separate return?

C8-35 ***Consolidated Return Election.*** The P-S_1 affiliated group has filed consolidated tax returns for several years. All P-S_1 returns have been filed using the calendar year as the tax year. At the close of business on August 8, 1997, P Corporation purchases all of the stock of S_2 Corporation. S_2 has been filing its separate tax returns using a fiscal year ending September 30. At the close of business on November 9, 1997, P Corporation sells all of its S_1 stock.
a. What tax year must S_2 Corporation use after joining the affiliated group?
b. What tax returns are required of S_2 Corporation to report its results from October 1, 1996 through December 31, 1997?
c. What tax year must S_1 Corporation use after leaving the affiliated group?
d. What action is needed (if any) should S_1 desire to change to a fiscal-year filing basis?

C8-36 ***Income Included in Consolidated Return.*** P and S_1 Corporations form the P-S_1 affiliated group, which has filed consolidated tax returns on a calendar-year basis for a number of years. At the close of business on February 25 of the current year, P Corporation sells all the stock of S_1 Corporation. P Corporation acquires all of the stock of S_2 Corporation at the close of business for both firms on September 25. S_2 Corporation has always used the calendar year as its tax year. The new P-S_2 affiliated group elects to file a consolidated tax return for this year. What tax returns are required of P, S_1, and S_2 Corporations with respect to reporting the current year's income?

C8-37 ***Alternative Minimum Tax.*** P and S Corporations are members of the P-S affiliated group, which has filed consolidated tax returns for a number of years. Consolidated adjusted current earnings is $700,000. Consolidated pre-adjustment alternative minimum taxable income is $400,000. Consolidated taxable income is $325,000. The consolidated general business credit amount (computed without regard to the overall limitation) is $10,000. What is the P-S group's federal tax liability?

C8-38 ***Intercompany Transactions.*** P, S_1, and S_2 Corporations form the P-S_1-S_2 affiliated group, with P Corporation owning all of the stock of S_1 and S_2 Corporations. The P-S_1-S_2 group has filed consolidated tax returns for several years. In 1997, S_1 sells land that it has held for a possible expansion to S_2 for $300,000. The land originally cost S_1 $120,000 in 1992. S_2 constructs a new plant facility on the land. The land and the plant facility are sold to a third party in 1998 with $400,000 of the sales price attributable to the land.
a. What are the amount and character of S_1's recognized gain or loss? In what year(s) is the gain or loss included in S_1's separate taxable income? In what year(s) is the gain or loss included in consolidated taxable income?
b. What are the amount and character of S_2's recognized gain or loss? In what year(s) is the gain or loss included in S_2's separate taxable income? In what year(s) is the gain or loss included in consolidated taxable income?

C8-39 ***Intercompany Transactions.*** P and S Corporations form the P-S affiliated group. The P-S group has filed consolidated tax returns for several years. S acquires some land from P Corporation in 1997 for $60,000. P acquired the land in 1986 as an investment at a cost of $20,000. S uses the land for four years as additional parking space for its employees. No improvements are made to the land. The land is sold by S to an unrelated party in 2000 for $180,000. Terms of the sale require a 20% down payment in the year of sale and four equal installments to be paid annually in the years 2002 through 2005. Interest is charged at a rate acceptable to the IRS. Assume all payments are made in a timely fashion.

a. What are the amount and character of P's recognized gain or loss? In what year(s) is the gain or loss included in P's separate taxable income? In what year(s) is it included in consolidated taxable income?
b. What are the amount and character of S's recognized gain or loss? In what year(s) is the gain or loss included in S's separate taxable income? In what year(s) is it included in consolidated taxable income?

C8-40 *Intercompany Transactions.* P and S Corporations form the P-S affiliated group, which has filed consolidated tax returns for several years. On June 10, 1995, P purchases a new machine (five-year MACRS property) for $20,000 cash. No special expensing elections under Sec. 179 were made. On April 4, 1997, P sells the machine to S for $15,000 cash. S uses the property for two years before selling it to an unrelated party on March 10, 1999, for $12,000.
a. What are the amount and character of P's recognized gain or loss? In what year(s) is the gain or loss included in P's separate taxable income? In what year(s) is the gain or loss included in consolidated taxable income?
b. What is S's basis for the equipment?
c. What depreciation method should S use for the equipment?
d. What are the amount and character of S's recognized gain or loss? In what year(s) is the gain or loss included in S's separate taxable income? In what year(s) is the gain or loss included in consolidated taxable income?

C8-41 *Intercompany Transactions.* P and S Corporations form the P-S affiliated group, which has filed consolidated tax returns for a number of years. On January 1, 1994 P Corporation purchased a new machine (seven-year MACRS property) for $50,000. $10,000 of the acquisition cost was expensed under Sec. 179. On June 30, 1997 P sells the machine to S for $35,000. The machine is still classified as seven-year MACRS property in S's hands. S holds the asset until March 15, 2000, when it is sold to an unrelated party for $20,000.
a. What are the amount and character of P's recognized gain or loss? In what year(s) is the gain or loss included in P's separate taxable income? In what year(s) is it included in consolidated taxable income?
b. What are the amount and character of S's recognized gain or loss? In what year(s) is the gain or loss included in S's separate taxable income? In what year(s) is it included in consolidated taxable income?

C8-42 *Intercompany Transactions.* P and S Corporations form the P-S affiliated group, which has filed consolidated tax returns for a number of years. During 1997 P Corporation commenced selling inventory items to S Corporation. P and S use the first-in, first-out inventory method. The intercompany profit on P's sales to S was $125,000 in 1997. Goods remaining in S's inventory at the end of 1997 accounted for $35,000 of the intercompany profit. During 1998 all of S's beginning inventory of goods acquired from P in 1997 was sold to unrelated parties and the intercompany profit on P's current sales of inventory to S amounted to $240,000. Goods remaining in S's inventory at the end of 1998 accounted for $60,000 of the intercompany profit. Taxable income for the P-S affiliated group (excluding the deferral and restoration of profits on intercompany inventory sales) is $100,000 in each year. What is consolidated taxable income for 1997 and 1998 for the P-S group?

C8-43 *Intercompany Transactions.* P and S Corporations form the P-S affiliated group. P has owned all of the S Corporation stock since 1992. The affiliated group has filed consolidated tax returns since 1992. No intragroup inventory sales occurred before 1997. During 1997 P sells S 100,000 widgets, earning $5 per unit profit on the sale. S uses the FIFO method to account for its inventories. On January 1, 1998, 25,000 widgets remain in S's inventory. During 1998 S sells the beginning widget inventory and purchases 175,000 additional widgets. P earns a $6 per unit profit on the sale. S retains 40,000 of these units in its 1998 ending inventory. No additional widgets are purchased in 1999. All widgets in beginning inventory are sold by S during 1999.

a. What intercompany profit amounts are deferred in 1997? in 1998? in 1999?

b. How would your answer to Part a change if the LIFO inventory method were instead used? (Assume the 1998 year-end LIFO inventory includes 25,000 units acquired in 1997 and 15,000 units acquired in 1998.)

C8-44 ***Intercompany Transactions.*** P Corporation has owned all of the stock of S Corporation since 1993. The P-S affiliated group commences filing a consolidated tax return in 1996 using the calendar year as its tax year. Both corporations use the accrual method of accounting. On July 1, 1997, P lends S $250,000 on a one-year note. Interest is charged at a 12% simple rate. The loan and interest are paid on June 30, 1998.

a. When does P report its interest income in its separate tax return? When does S report its interest expense in its separate tax return?

b. How would your answer to Part a change if P instead used the cash method of accounting?

C8-45 ***Dividends-Received Deduction.*** P and S Corporations form the P-S affiliated group. The P-S group has filed consolidated tax returns for several years. P and S report separate taxable income amounts (excluding any dividend payments, climinations, and dividends-received deductions) of $200,000 and ($70,000), respectively, for the current year. Cash dividend payments received by P and S this year are as follows:

Shareholder Corporation	*Distributing Corporation*	*Amount*
P	S	$100,000
P	100%-owned nonconsolidated domestic life insurance company	15,000
S	20%-owned domestic corporation	40,000

a. What is the amount of the gross income reported in the P and S separate tax returns as a result of the three distributions?

b. What is the amount of the dividends-received deduction?

c. Why might P elect to claim a 100% dividends-received deduction for the dividend received from S for federal income tax purposes, even though a consolidated tax return is being filed?

C8-46 ***Charitable Contributions Deduction.*** P and S Corporations form the P-S affiliated group. This group has filed consolidated tax returns for several years. The group reports consolidated taxable income (excluding charitable contributions) for the current year of $60,000. Included in this amount are a consolidated dividends-received deduction of $8,000 and an NOL deduction of $25,000 that represents a carryover of last year's consolidated NOL. P and S Corporations make cash contributions to public charities of $18,000 and $10,000, respectively, during this year.

a. What is the P-S group's consolidated taxable income?

b. What is the amount of the charitable contributions carryover?

C8-47 ***NOL Carryover.*** P, S_1, and S_2 Corporations form the P-S_1-S_2 affiliated group, which has filed consolidated tax returns since the creation of all three corporations in 1996. At the close of business on July 10, 1998, P Corporation sells its entire interest in S_2

Corporation. The affiliated group remains in existence after the sale because P Corporation still owns all of the S_1 stock. The P-S_1-S_2 group reports the following results for 1996 through 1998:

	Taxable Income		
Group Member	1996	1997	1998
P	$ 8,000	($12,000)	$16,000
S_1	9,000	(24,000)	(4,000)
S_2	10,000	(36,000)	6,000[a]
			8,000[b]
Consolidated taxable income (excluding NOL deduction)	$27,000	($72,000)	$18,000

[a] Taxable income earned from January 1, 1998 through July 10, 1998.
[b] Taxable income from July 11, 1998, through December 31, 1998, is included in S_2's separate tax return.

What amount of 1997's consolidated NOL can be carried over to 1999 by the P-S_1 affiliated group? By S_2?

C8-48 ***NOL Carrybacks and Carryovers.*** P and S Corporations form the P-S affiliated group, which files consolidated tax returns for the period 1996 through 1999. The affiliated group reports the following results for this period:

	Taxable Income			
Group Member	1996	1997	1998	1999
P	$10,000	($6,000)	$20,000	$15,000
S	2,000	2,000	(30,000)	10,000
Consolidated taxable income (excluding NOL deduction)	$12,000	($4,000)	($10,000)	$25,000

No elections were made to forgo the NOL carrybacks. What portion of the 1997 and 1998 consolidated NOLs can be carried back to 1996? Forward to 1999?

C8-49 ***NOL Carryovers and Carrybacks.*** P Corporation acquires S Corporation on January 1, 1998. Each company filed separate calendar-year tax returns for 1997. P and S report the following results for 1997 and 1998:

Group Member	1997	1998
P	$40,000	($30,000)
S	(30,000)	20,000
Taxable income	N/A	($10,000)

N/A = Not applicable

a. What are the 1998 tax consequences assuming a consolidated tax return is filed? What are the tax consequences if separate tax returns had instead been filed?
b. P and S report the following taxable income in 1999 before any NOL carryover: P, $20,000; S, $5,000. What is the consolidated taxable income assuming a consolidated return was filed in 1998?

C8-50 ***Special NOL Limitation.*** P, S_1, and S_2 Corporations form the P-S_1-S_2 affiliated group. P Corporation was created by Bart on January 1, 1997. P purchased all the S_1 and S_2 Corporation stock on September 1, 1997, after both corporations were in operation for about six months. All three corporations filed separate tax returns in 1997. The P-S_1-S_2 affiliated group elected to file a consolidated tax return starting in 1998. The P-S_1-S_2 group, which is still owned by Bart, reports the following results for 1997 through 1999:

Group Member	Taxable Income 1997	1998	1999
P	($8,000)	$50,000	$10,000
S_1	(24,000)	20,000	(18,000)
S_2	(16,000)	(10,000)	15,000
Consolidated taxable income (excluding NOL deduction)	XXX	$60,000	$ 7,000

a. What loss carryovers are available to be used in 2000? (Ignore the Sec. 382 loss limitation that might apply to the acquisitions of S_1 and S_2.)

b. How would your answer to Part a change if Bart instead created P, S_1, and S_2 Corporations as an affiliated group on January 1, 1997?

C8-51 ***Sec. 382 Loss Limitation.*** Mack owns all of the stock of P Corporation. P Corporation owns all of the stock of S_1 and S_2 Corporations. At the close of business on December 31, 1996, Mack sells his P Corporation stock to Jack for $9,000,000. The P-$S_1$-$S_2$ affiliated group has a consolidated NOL carryover to 1997 of $1,500,000 at the end of 1996.

a. Has a Sec. 382 ownership change occurred? Explain.

b. What is the P-S_1-S_2 affiliated group's consolidated Sec. 382 limitation for 1997 if the federal long-term tax-exempt rate is 5%?

c. How much of the consolidated NOL carryover can be used in 1997 if the affiliated group's taxable income is $750,000? in 1998 if the affiliated group's consolidated taxable income is $200,000?

C8-52 ***Consolidated Taxable Income.*** P and S Corporations have filed consolidated tax returns for a number of years. P is an accrual method of accounting taxpayer and S is a cash method of accounting taxpayer. P and S report separate return taxable income (before NOL and special deductions) for the current year of $100,000 and $150,000, respectively. These numbers include the following transactions or events accounted for appropriately on a separate return basis.

- P sold land held for investment purposes to S at a $25,000 profit three years ago. S sold the land (a Sec. 1231 asset) to an unrelated corporation this year for a $12,000 gain.
- P's separate taxable income includes a $15,000 dividend received from S Corporation.
- P sold inventory to S last year for which the deferred intercompany profit at year-end was $50,000. All of this inventory was sold outside the affiliated group this year. Additional inventory was sold by P to S this year that remained unsold at year-end. The deferred intercompany profit on this inventory is $80,000.
- The P-S group has a $20,000 NOL carryover available from last year.
- S receives a $10,000 dividend from an unrelated corporation. A $7,000 dividends-received deduction was claimed when determining S's separate return taxable income.
- P and S made charitable contributions of $16,000 and $12,000, respectively, this year.

a. What is consolidated taxable income for the P-S affiliated group for the current year?

b. What is the consolidated tax liability?

TAX FORM/RETURN PREPARATION PROBLEM

C8-53 The Flying Gator Corporation and it subsidiary, T Corporation, have filed consolidated tax returns for a number of years. Both corporations use the hybrid method of accounting. During the current year they report the operating results as listed in Table C8-2. Note the following additional information:

▼ **TABLE C8-2**

Flying Gator Corporation's Current Year Operating Results (Problem C8-53)

Income or Deductions	Flying Gator	T	Total
Gross receipts	$2,500,000	$1,250,000	$3,750,000
Cost of goods sold	(1,500,000)	(700,000)	(2,200,000)
Gross profit	$1,000,000	$ 550,000	$1,550,000
Dividends	100,000	50,000	150,000
Interest	15,000		15,000
Sec. 1231 gain		20,000	20,000
Sec. 1245 gain		25,000	25,000
Long-term capital gain (loss)	(5,000)	6,000	1,000
Short-term capital gain (loss)		(3,000)	(3,000)
Total income	$1,110,000	$ 648,000	$1,758,000
Salaries and wages	175,000	200,000	375,000
Repairs	25,000	40,000	65,000
Bad debts	10,000	5,000	15,000
Taxes	18,000	24,000	42,000
Interest	30,000	20,000	50,000
Charitable contributions	22,000	48,000	70,000
Depreciation (other than that included in cost of goods sold)	85,000	40,000	125,000
Other expenses	160,000	260,000	420,000
Total deductions	$ 525,000	$ 637,000	$1,162,000
Separate taxable income (before NOL and special deductions)	$ 585,000	$ 11,000	$ 596,000

- Flying Gator and T Corporations are the only members of their controlled group.
- Flying Gator's address is 2101 W. University Ave., Gainesburg, FL 32611. Its employer identification number is 38-2345678. Flying Gator was incorporated on June 11, 1986. Its total assets are $380,000. Flying Gator made estimated tax payments of $160,000 for the affiliated group in the current year. Stephen Marks is Flying Gator's president.
- No NOL or other carryovers from preceding years are available.
- Flying Gator uses the last-in, first-out (LIFO) inventory method. T commenced selling inventory to Flying Gator in the preceding year, which resulted in a $40,000 year-end deferred intercompany profit. An additional LIFO inventory layer was created by T's sales to Flying Gator during the current year that remained unsold at year-end. The intercompany profit on the additional inventory is $30,000. None of the original LIFO layer was sold during the current year.
- All of Flying Gator's dividends are received from T. T's dividends are received from a 15%-owned domestic corporation. All distributions are from E&P.
- Flying Gator's interest income is received from T. The interest is paid on March 31 of the current year on a loan that was outstanding from October 1 of the preceding year through March 31 of the current year. No interest income was accrued at the end of the preceding tax year.
- Officer's salaries are $80,000 for Flying Gator and $65,000 for T Corporation.
- Flying Gator's capital losses include a $10,000 long-term loss on a sale of land to T in the current year.

- There are no non-recaptured net Sec. 1231 losses from prior tax years.
- T's Sec. 1245 gains include $20,000 recognized on the sale of equipment to Flying Gator in the current year. The asset cost $100,000 and had been depreciated for two years by T as five-year property under the MACRS rules. One-half year depreciation was claimed by T in the current (second) year. Flying Gator commences depreciating the property in the current year by using the MACRS rules and a five-year recovery period. Flying Gator claimed one-half year's depreciation on the property in the current year.

Determine the affiliated group's current year consolidated tax liability. Prepare the front page of the affiliated group's current year corporate income tax return (Form 1120). Hint: Prepare a spreadsheet similar to the one included in Appendix B in order to arrive at consolidated taxable income.

CASE STUDY PROBLEMS

C8-54 P Corporation operates six fast-food restaurants in a metropolitan area. The restaurants have been a huge success in their first three years of operation and P's annual taxable income is in excess of $600,000. The real estate associated with the six restaurants is owned by J Corporation. P Corporation leases its restaurant locations from J Corporation. J Corporation is reporting large interest and MACRS depreciation deductions because of a highly leveraged operation. As a result J Corporation has reported NOLs in its first three years of operation.

Both corporations are owned by Carol, who is in her late 20s. Carol sees the idea for the restaurant chain starting to really develop and expects to add six more locations in each of the next two years. You and Carol have been friends for a number of years. Because of the rapid expansion that is planned, she feels that she has outgrown her father's accountant and needs to have new ideas to help her save tax dollars so that she can reinvest more monies in the business.

Required: The tax partner that you have been assigned to requests that you prepare a memorandum outlining your thoughts about Carol's tax problems and the suggested solutions to those problems in preparation for his meeting next week with Carol.

TAX RESEARCH PROBLEMS

C8-55 Angela owns all of the stock of A and P Corporations. P Corporation has owned all of the stock of S_1 Corporation for six years. The P-S_1 affiliated group has filed a consolidated tax return in each of these six years using the calendar year as its tax year. On July 10 of the current year, Angela sells her entire stock investment in A Corporation, which uses the calendar year as its tax year. At the close of business on November 25 of this year, S_1 Corporation purchases 90% of the common stock and 80% of the nonconvertible, nonvoting preferred stock (measured by value) of S_2 Corporation. A, P, S_1, and S_2 Corporations are domestic corporations that do not retain any special filing status. Which corporations are included in the affiliated group? In the controlled group? What income is included in the various tax returns? How is the allocation of the income between tax years made if the books are not closed on the sale or acquisition dates? If no special allocations are made, what portion of the reduced tax rate benefits of Sec. 11(b) can be claimed in the current year by the affiliated group? in future years?

CHAPTER 9

PARTNERSHIP FORMATION AND OPERATION

LEARNING OBJECTIVES

After studying this chapter, you should be able to

1. Differentiate between general and limited partnerships
2. Explain the tax results of a contribution of property or services in exchange for a partnership interest
3. Determine the permitted tax years for a partnership
4. Differentiate between items that must be separately stated and those that are included in ordinary income or loss
5. Calculate a partner's distributive share of partnership income, gain, loss, deduction, or credit items
6. Explain the requirements for a special partnership allocation
7. Calculate a partner's basis in a partnership interest
8. Determine the limitations on a partner's deduction of partnership losses
9. Determine the tax consequences of a guaranteed payment
10. Explain the requirements for recognizing the holder of a partnership interest as a partner in a family partnership
11. Determine the allocation of partnership income between a donor and a donee of a partnership interest
12. Determine the requirements for filing a partnership tax return

CHAPTER OUTLINE

Partnerships have long been one of the major entities for conducting business activities. Partnerships vary in complexity from the corner gas station owned and operated by two brothers to syndicated tax partnerships with their partnership interests traded on major security markets. Regardless of the simplicity or complexity of the partnership, a single set of rules determines the federal income tax consequences of its operations. These rules are found in Subchapter K of the Code, which includes the material from Secs. 701-761.

Chapters C9 and C10 discuss the income tax rules applying to partnership business operations. In this chapter, a partnership is defined and the two kinds of partnerships are described. The formation of a partnership is discussed next. The remainder of this chapter deals with the ongoing operations of a partnership, such as the annual taxation of partnership earnings, transactions between partners and the partnership, and a partner's basis in a partnership interest. Procedural matters are also considered, such as reporting the annual partnership income and IRS audit procedures for partnerships and their partners. Chapter C10 continues by discussing distributions to the partners and the tax implications of the numerous transactions that can be used to terminate a partner's interest in a partnership. Chapter C10 also includes discussions of adjustments that may be made to the bases of partnership assets and the unique problems of limited partnerships.

DEFINITION OF A PARTNERSHIP

ADDITIONAL COMMENT

Even though the formation of a partnership requires no legal documentation, to prevent subsequent disagreements and arguments, a formal written partnership agreement is recommended.

For tax purposes the definition of a partnership includes "a syndicate, group, pool, joint venture, or other unincorporated organization" that carries on a business or financial operation or venture. However, a trust, estate, or corporation cannot be taxed as a partnership. Unlike a corporation, which can exist only after incorporation documents are finalized, formation of a partnership requires no legal documentation. If two people (or business entities) work together to carry on any business or financial operation with the intention of making a profit and sharing that profit as co-owners, a partnership exists for federal income tax purposes.[1]

The Code and Regulations define a **partner** only as a member of a partnership. It is clear from years of case law and common business practice that a partner can be an individual, trust, estate, or corporation. The only restriction on the number of partners in a partnership is that there must be at least two partners, but there may be hundreds or even thousands of partners in a large syndicated partnership.

GENERAL AND LIMITED PARTNERSHIPS

OBJECTIVE 1

Differentiate between general and limited partnerships

KEY POINT

When deciding on the form in which to conduct a business, probably the strongest argument against a general partnership is that each partner has unlimited liability for partnership debts.

Each state has laws governing the rights and restrictions of partnerships. Almost all state statutes are modeled on the Uniform Partnership Act (UPA) or the Uniform Limited Partnership Act (ULPA) and so have strong similarities to each other. There are two legal forms a partnership can take: a general partnership or a limited partnership. The differences between the two forms are substantial and extend to the partners' legal rights and liabilities as well as the tax consequences to the partners of operations. Because of the importance of these differences, we examine these two partnership forms before proceeding with further discussion of the partnership tax rules.

GENERAL PARTNERSHIPS. A **general partnership** exists any time two or more partners join together and do not specifically provide that one or more of the partners is a

[1] Section 761(a) allows an election to avoid the Subchapter K rules for a very limited group of business owners.

limited partner (as defined below). In a general partnership, each partner has the right to participate in the management of the partnership. However, the general partnership form is flexible enough to allow the business affairs of the general partnership to be managed by a single partner chosen by the general partners.

While management may be exercised by only one (or a few) of the general partners, each general partner has the ability to make commitments for the partnership.[2] In a general partnership, each partner has unlimited liability for all partnership debts. If the partnership fails to pay its debts, each partner may have to pay far more than the amount he or she has invested in the venture. Thus, each partner faces the risk of losing personal assets if the partnership incurs business losses. This fact is the single biggest drawback to the general partnership form of doing business.

REAL-WORLD EXAMPLE

For 1994, 1.49 million partnership returns were filed. 1.16 million were general partnerships, 0.28 million were limited partnerships and 0.05 were limited liability companies. The average general partnership had 3.7 partners and the average limited partnership had 36 partners. More than 77% of partnership profits are reported by general partnerships.

SELF-STUDY QUESTION

Is it possible in a limited partnership to have all partners with limited liability?

ANSWER

No. A limited partnership must have at least one general partner. This general partner can be a corporation as long as it has a certain minimum amount of capitalization.

LIMITED PARTNERSHIPS. In a **limited partnership**, there are two classes of partners. There must be at least one general partner, who has essentially the same rights and liabilities as any general partner in a general partnership.[3] There must also be at least one limited partner. Even if a partnership becomes bankrupt, a limited partner can lose no more than his or her original investment plus any additional amount he or she has committed to contribute. However, a limited partner has no right to be active in the partnership's management.[4]

Even with this rudimentary explanation of the rights of general and limited partners, it is clear that a general partnership is an unwieldy form for operating a business with a large number of owners. A limited partnership having one (or a small number of) general partners, however, can be useful for a business operation that needs to attract a large amount of capital. In fact, one common form for a tax shelter investment is a limited partnership having a corporation with a small amount of capital as its sole general partner. Such an arrangement allows the tax advantages of the partnership form (detailed in the remainder of this chapter and in the next chapter) while retaining the limited liability feature for virtually every investor.

Many of these limited partnerships are so large and widely held that in many ways they appear more like corporations than partnerships. As discussed in Chapter C10, the tax laws provide that publicly traded partnerships may be reclassified for tax purposes as corporations.

LIMITED LIABILITY COMPANIES (LLCs). With the advent of LLCs, businesses have the chance to be taxed as a partnership while having limited liability protection for every owner. State law provides the limited liability. Unique tax rules for LLCs have not been developed. Instead, the check-the-box regulations (discussed in Chapter C2) permit each LLC to choose whether to be taxed as a partnership or as a corporation. If an LLC is considered a partnership for tax purposes, the same tax rules apply to the LLC that apply to a traditional partnership. Further discussion of the taxation of LLCs is found in Chapter C10.

LIMITED LIABILITY PARTNERSHIPS (LLPs). Initially professional organizations in certain fields (e.g., public accounting and law) were not permitted to operate as LLCs and therefore remained general partnerships. Many states have added LLPs to the list of business forms that can be formed. The primary difference between a general partnership and an LLP is that a partner is not liable for damages resulting from failures in the work of other partners or of people supervised by other partners. LLPs can be taxed under the

[2] Uniform Partnership Act

[3] Uniform Limited Partnership Act

[4] Under Sec. 9 of the Uniform Limited Partnership Act only general partners are empowered to manage the partnership's business.

check-the-box regulations as a partnership or as a corporation. Like an LLC, the default tax classification of an LLP is a partnership. The same tax rules apply to an LLP that apply to a traditional partnership. Further discussion of the taxation of LLPs is found in Chapter C10.

OVERVIEW OF TAXATION OF PARTNERSHIP INCOME

This overview gives a broad perspective of the taxation of partnership income. (A comparison of the tax characteristics of a partnership, a C corporation, and an S corporation is presented in Appendix F.) More detailed descriptions follow the overview.

PARTNERSHIP PROFITS AND LOSSES

SELF-STUDY QUESTION

Does a partnership pay taxes?

ANSWER

No. A partnership is an information-reporting entity. Any income/loss flows through to its partners, and the partners pay the necessary taxes.

ADDITIONAL COMMENT

Because most partnerships use the calendar year as their tax year, the K-1s are not due until April 15. Because a calendar-year corporate partner's return is due on March 15 and an individual partner's return is due on April 15, partners must often request extensions for filing their returns.

A partnership is not a taxpaying entity, and income earned by a partnership is not subject to two layers of federal income taxes. Instead, each partner reports a share of the partnership's income, gain, loss, deduction, and credit items as a part of his or her income tax return. The partnership, however, must file Form 1065 (U.S. Partnership Return of Income), an information return, which provides the IRS with information about partnership earnings as well as how the earnings are allocated among the partners. The partnership must elect a tax year and accounting methods to calculate its earnings. (Appendix B includes a completed partnership tax return that shows a Form 1065 and Schedule K-1 for a partner along with a set of supporting facts.)

Each partner receives a Schedule K-1 from the partnership, which informs the partner of the amount and character of his or her share of partnership income. The partner then combines his or her partnership earnings and losses with all other items of income or loss to be reported for the tax year, computes the amount of taxable income, and calculates the tax bill. Because each partner pays tax on a share of partnership income along with all other income and loss items, it is not reasonable to determine a tax rate for partnership earnings. Partnership income is taxed at the applicable tax rate for its partners, which can range from 15% to 39.6% for partners who are individuals, trusts, or estates. Corporate partners pay tax on partnership income at rates ranging from 15% to 39%.

One of the major advantages of the partnership form of doing business is that partnership losses are allocated among the partners. If the loss limitation rules (explained later in this chapter) do not apply, these losses are combined with the partners' other income, and the result is an immediate tax savings for the partners. The immediate tax saving that is available to the partner contrasts sharply with the net operating loss (NOL) carrybacks or carryforwards that result from a C corporation's tax loss.

SELF-STUDY QUESTION

Why does a partner need to know his or her basis in his or her partnership interest?

ANSWER

Three important reasons are to determine the gain/loss on a sale of the partnership interest, to determine the amount of partnership losses that a partner can deduct, and to determine the amount of distributions that are tax-free to the partner.

THE PARTNER'S BASIS

A partner's basis in his or her partnership interest is a crucial element in partnership taxation. When a partner makes a contribution to a partnership or purchases a partnership interest, he or she establishes the beginning basis. Because the partners are personally liable for partnership debts, a partner's basis in his or her partnership interest is increased by his or her share of any partnership liabilities. Accordingly, the partner's basis fluctuates as the partnership borrows and repays loans or increases and decreases its accounts payable. In addition, a partner's basis in his or her partnership interest is increased by the partner's share of partnership income and decreased by his or her share of partnership losses. Because a partner's basis in his or her partnership interest can never be negative, the basis serves as one limit on the amount of deductible partnership losses. (See the discussion on pages C9-26 through C9-29 about the various loss limitations.)

EXAMPLE C9-1 ▶ Tom purchases a 20% interest in the XY Partnership for $8,000 on January 1, 1996, and begins to materially participate in the partnership's business. The XY Partnership uses the calendar year as its tax year. At the time of the purchase, the XY Partnership has $2,000 in liabilities and Tom's share is 20%. Tom's basis in his partnership interest on January 1 is $8,400 [$8,000 + (0.20 × $2,000)]. ◀

EXAMPLE C9-2 ▶ Assume the same facts as in Example C9-1, except that the XY Partnership incurs $10,000 in losses and its liabilities increase by $4,000 during 1996. What is Tom's basis on December 31?

January 1 basis	$8,400
Plus: Share of liability increase ($4,000 × 0.20)	800
Minus: Share of partnership losses ($10,000 × 0.20)	(2,000)
December 31 basis	$7,200

◀

EXAMPLE C9-3 ▶ Assume the same facts as in Example C9-2, except that the XY Partnership incurs $50,000 in losses and its liabilities increase by $10,000 during 1997. Tom's share of the losses is $10,000 ($50,000 × 0.20). What is the maximum amount that he can deduct?

January 1 basis	$7,200
Plus: Share of liability increase	2,000
December 31 basis before losses	$9,200
Minus: Maximum loss to be deducted	(9,200)
December 31 basis	—0—

Tom's remaining $800 in losses must be carried over to a later year and are deducted when he has sufficient basis in his partnership interest. ◀

PARTNERSHIP DISTRIBUTIONS

When a partnership makes a current distribution, the distribution is generally tax-free to the partners because it represents the receipt of earnings that have already been taxed to the partners. Distributions reduce the partner's basis in his or her partnership interest. If a cash distribution is so large that it exceeds a partner's basis in his or her partnership interest, the partner will recognize gain equal to the amount of the excess. When the partnership goes out of business or when a partner withdraws from the partnership, liquidating distributions are paid to the partner. Like current distributions, these distributions generally cause the partner to recognize gain only if the cash that is received exceeds the partner's basis in his or her partnership interest. A loss may be recognized if the partner receives only cash, inventory, and unrealized receivables in complete liquidation of his or her partnership interest. (Distributions are discussed in Chapter C10.)

TYPICAL MISCONCEPTION

Many taxpayers think that partners pay taxes when they receive distributions from the partnership. However, distributions are generally tax-free because they are merely the receipt of earnings that have already been taxed to the partners.

TAX IMPLICATIONS OF FORMATION OF A PARTNERSHIP

When two or more individuals or entities decide to operate an unincorporated business together, a partnership is formed. In the following sections, the tax implications of property contributions, service contributions, and organization and syndication expenditures are examined.

CONTRIBUTION OF PROPERTY

OBJECTIVE 2

Explain the tax results of a contribution of property or services in exchange for a partnership interest

NONRECOGNITION OF GAIN OR LOSS. Formation of a partnership is governed by Sec. 721. In most cases, the statute provides that a partner who contributes property in exchange for a partnership interest does not recognize gain or loss on the transaction. Likewise, the partnership recognizes no gain or loss on the contribution of property. The partner's basis for his or her partnership interest and the partnership's basis for the property both reference the property's basis in the transferor partner's hands.[5]

The nonrecognition treatment is limited to transactions in which a partnership interest is received in exchange for a contribution of property. As in the corporate formation area, the term *property* includes cash, tangible property (e.g., buildings and land), and intangible property (e.g., franchise rights, trademarks, and leases).[6] Note that services are specifically excluded from the definition of property, so a contribution of services for a partnership interest is not a tax-free transaction.

KEY POINT

In order for contributions to a corporation to be nontaxable, the contributing shareholders must control (own at least 80%) the corporation immediately after the transaction. There is no such control requirement for contributions to a partnership to be nontaxable.

RECOGNITION OF GAIN OR LOSS. The general rule of Sec. 721(a) provides that no gain or loss is recognized by the partnership or any partner when property is contributed in exchange for a partnership interest. Three exceptions to this general rule may require a partner to recognize a gain (but never a loss) at the time a contribution of property to a partnership in exchange for a partnership interest occurs:

- Contribution of property to a partnership that would be treated as an investment company if it were incorporated
- Contribution of property followed by a distribution in an arrangement that may be considered a sale rather than a contribution
- Contribution of property to a partnership along with the partnership's assumption of liabilities previously owed by the partner

The investment company exception of Sec. 721(b) requires recognition of gain only if the exchange results in diversification of the transferor's property interest. This investment is taxed only when immediately after the exchange more than 80% of the value of the partnership's assets (excluding cash and nonconvertible debt obligations) is held for investment or is readily marketable stocks, securities, or interests in regulated investment companies or real estate investment trusts.[7] If the contribution of property is to an investment partnership, the contributing partner must recognize any gain realized on the property transfer as if the stocks or securities were sold.

Sections 707(a)(2)(A) and (B) set out the second exception, which holds that a property contribution followed by a distribution (or an allocation of income or gain) may have to be treated like a sale of property by the partner to the partnership rather than as a contribution made by the partner to the partnership. Under the Sec. 707 Treasury Regulations, sale treatment (and the recognition of gain or loss) may be required if the distribution would not have occurred except for the contribution.

EXAMPLE C9-4 ▶ In return for a 40% interest in the CD Partnership, Cara contributed a piece of land with a $100,000 fair market value (FMV). The partners agreed that they would distribute $100,000 in cash to Cara immediately after the contribution. Because the cash distribution would not have happened if Cara had not first contributed the land and become a partner, the transaction is likely to be treated as a sale of the land by Cara to the partnership. ◀

[5] Secs. 722 and 723.

[6] For an excellent discussion of the definition of the term *property*, see footnote 6 of *D.N. Stafford v. U.S.*, 45 AFTR 2d 80-785, 80-1 USTC ¶9218 (5th Cir., 1980).

[7] Reg. Sec. 1.351-1(c)(1).

If the distribution does not occur simultaneously with the contribution, the transaction is treated as a sale if the later distribution is not dependent on the normal business risk of the enterprise.

EXAMPLE C9-5 ▶ Elena received a 30% interest in the DEF Partnership in return for her contribution of land having a $60,000 FMV. The partnership waits six months and then distributes $60,000 in cash to Elena. If the $60,000 distribution was not contingent on the partnership's earnings or ability to borrow funds or other normal risks of doing business, the distribution and contribution will be treated as a sale of land by Elena to the partnership. ◀

KEY POINT

When a partner is relieved of debt, this is treated as if the partner receives a cash distribution. If a partner assumes debt, it is treated as if the partner makes a cash contribution. These two simple rules are critical to understanding transactions such as formations of partnerships, distributions from partnerships, and sales or liquidations of partnership interests.

EFFECTS OF LIABILITIES. The third condition that may cause gain to be recognized on the formation of a partnership is the contribution of property to a partnership along with the partnership's assumption of liabilities previously owed by the partner. Because each partner is liable for his or her share of partnership liabilities, increases and decreases in the partnership liabilities are reflected in each partner's basis. Specifically, Sec. 752 provides that two effects result from the contribution of property to a partnership if the partnership assumes any liabilities of the transferor.

- Each partner's basis is increased by his or her share of the partnership's liabilities as if he or she had contributed cash to the partnership in the amount of his or her share of partnership liabilities.
- The partner whose personal liabilities are assumed by the partnership has a reduction in the basis of his or her partnership interest as if the partnership distributed cash to him or her in the amount of the assumed liability.

The net effect of these two basis adjustments is seldom sufficiently large to cause a transferor partner to recognize gain when property is contributed to the partnership. The transferor partner is deemed first to have made a contribution of property plus a contribution of cash equal to the partner's share of any partnership liabilities existing prior to his or her entrance into the partnership (or contributed by other partners concurrently with this transaction). The partner is deemed then to have received a cash distribution equal to the total amount of his or her own liability that is assumed by the *other* partners. (No basis adjustment is required for the portion of the liability transferred to the partnership by the transferor that he or she will retain as a partner.) The following examples help clarify the necessary basis adjustments.

EXAMPLE C9-6 ▶ In return for a 20% partnership interest, Mary contributes land having a $60,000 FMV and a $30,000 basis to the XY Partnership. The partnership assumes Mary's $15,000 liability arising from her purchase of the land and Mary has a 20% share of partnership liabilities. The XY Partnership has $4,000 in liabilities immediately before her contribution. What is Mary's basis in her partnership interest?

Basis of contributed property		$30,000
Plus:	Mary's share of existing partnership liabilities ($4,000 × 0.20)	800
Minus:	Mary's liabilities that are assumed by the other partners ($15,000 × 0.80)	(12,000)
Mary's basis in her partnership interest		$18,800

Mary recognizes no gain on the partnership's assumption of her liability because the deemed cash distribution from the assumption of her $12,000 in liabilities by the partnership does not exceed her $30,800 basis in the partnership interest immediately preceding the fictional distribution. ◀

EXAMPLE C9-7 ▶ Assume the same facts as in Example C9-6, except that the amount of the liability assumed by the XY Partnership is $50,000. Mary's basis in her partnership interest is calculated as follows:

Basis of contributed property		$30,000
Plus:	Mary's share of existing partnership liabilities ($4,000 × 0.20)	800
Minus:	Mary's liabilities that are assumed by the other partners ($50,000 × 0.80)	(40,000)
Tentative basis for partnership interest		($9,200)
Basis (larger of zero or tentative basis)		—0—

The negative tentative basis amount means that Mary's deemed cash distribution from the assumption of her liability by the other partners exceeds her basis before the distribution. The cash that is deemed distributed in excess of Mary's basis requires her to recognize a $9,200 gain. No matter what negative number results from the distribution, the partner's basis in the partnership interest can never be less than zero. ◀

SELF-STUDY QUESTION

Why does Mary recognize a $9,200 gain in Example C9-7?

ANSWER

The reason that Mary has a $9,200 gain is that Mary receives a 20% partnership interest in exchange for the land. Thus, 80% of the debt is assumed by the other partners, which results in a deemed $40,000 cash distribution to Mary. Because the distribution exceeds her basis in the partnership interest, Mary recognizes a $9,200 gain.

STOP & THINK

Question: Assume the land Mary contributed in Example C9-6 has a $60,000 FMV and an $85,000 adjusted basis. Should Mary contribute it to the partnership?

Solution: If Mary contibutes the land, she will not be allowed to recognize her $25,000 ($60,000 FMV − $85,000 adjusted basis) loss until the partnership disposes of the property. Accordingly, Mary might prefer to sell the property and recognize her loss now. If the partnership can afford the $60,000 price and needs this property, Mary could sell the land to the partnership, recognize her loss on the sale, and then contribute the cash she receives from the partnership in exchange for her partnership interest. If the partnership does not need the property, Mary could sell the land to a third party, recognize her loss, and contribute the sales proceeds to the partnership in exchange for her partnership interest. However, a problem arises if the partnership needs this property and cannot afford to buy it from Mary. In that case, contributing the property to the partnership may be the best alternative in spite of the less-than-optimal tax results.

ADDITIONAL COMMENT

To contrast partnership formations with corporate formations, if Example C9-7 had involved a formation of the XY Corporation, Mary would have been treated as if relieved of the entire $50,000 of debt, which would have resulted in a $20,000 Sec. 357(c) gain to Mary.

Because the assumption of a partner's liabilities by the partnership is treated as a cash distribution, the character of any gain recognized by the partner is controlled by the partnership distribution rules. Cash distributions in excess of basis always result in gain recognition, and that gain is deemed to be gain from the sale of the partnership interest.[8] Because a partnership interest is usually a capital asset, the normal result is that gain arising from assumption of a partner's liabilities is a capital gain.

PARTNER'S BASIS IN THE PARTNERSHIP INTEREST (COMMONLY CALLED THE OUTSIDE BASIS). In general, the transferor partner's beginning basis in the partnership interest equals the sum of the money contributed plus his basis in the contributed property. If the partner recognizes any gain on the contribution because the partnership is an investment company, the amount of the recognized gain is added to his or her basis in the partnership interest.[9] Beginning basis is adjusted to reflect liability share. Any gain recognized because of the effects of liabilities on the partner's basis does not increase the basis for the partnership interest because the Code mandates that in this situation the basis is zero.

It should be noted that valuable property having little or no basis may be contributed. For example, the accounts receivable of a partner using the cash method of accounting

[8] Sec. 731(a).

[9] Sec. 722.

can be a valued contribution to a partnership, but if the receivables' bases are zero, the beginning basis of the partnership interest is also zero. Similarly, a note receivable from the contributing partner may be a valuable contribution to the partnership, but is likely to have a zero basis to carry over to the partnership interest.

TYPICAL MISCONCEPTION

If a partner contributes both ordinary income property and capital gain property to a partnership, the partner apparently has two different holding periods for his or her partnership interest. Once a partnership interest has been held twelve months, this becomes a moot point.

HOLDING PERIOD FOR PARTNERSHIP INTEREST. The holding period for the partnership interest includes the transferor's holding period for the contributed property if that property is a capital asset or a Sec. 1231 asset in the transferor's hands.[10] If the contributed property is an ordinary income asset (e.g., inventory) to the partner, the holding period for the partnership interest begins on the day after the date of the contribution.[11]

EXAMPLE C9-8 ▶ On April 1 Sue contributes a building (a Sec. 1231 asset) to the ST Partnership in exchange for a 20% interest. Sue purchased the building three years ago. Her holding period for her partnership interest includes her holding period for the contributed building. ◀

EXAMPLE C9-9 ▶ On April 1 Ted contributes inventory to the ST Partnership in exchange for a 20% interest. No matter when Ted acquired the inventory, his holding period for his partnership interest begins on April 2, the day after the date of his contribution. ◀

PARTNERSHIP'S BASIS IN PROPERTY. Under Sec. 723, the partnership's basis for contributed property is the same as the property's basis in the hands of the contributing partner. If, however, the contributing partner recognizes gain because the partnership is an investment company, such gain increases the partnership's basis in the contributed property. Gain recognized by the contributing partner because of the assumption of a partner's liability does not increase the partnership's basis in the property.[12]

TYPICAL MISCONCEPTION

Example C9-7 illustrates another difference between partnership and corporate formations. In the example, XY Partnership does not increase its basis in the property for the gain recognized by Mary, but if XY were a corporation, XY would increase its basis in the property by Mary's recognized gain.

Not only does the property's basis carry over to the partnership from the contributing partner, but for some properties the character of gain or loss on a subsequent disposition of the property by the partnership also references the character of the property in the contributing partner's hands. Section 724 prevents the transformation of ordinary income into capital gains (or capital losses into ordinary losses) when property is contributed to a partnership. Properties that were (1) unrealized receivables, inventory, or capital loss property in the hands of the contributing partner and (2) contributed to a partnership after March 31, 1984 retain their character for some subsequent partnership dispositions.[13]

Unrealized Receivables. The concept of unrealized receivables plays a key role for tax purposes in many different partnership transactions. An **unrealized receivable** is any right to payment for goods or services that has not been included in income because of the accounting method being used.[14] The most common examples of unrealized receivables are the accounts receivable of a cash method of accounting taxpayer.

If a property is an unrealized receivable in the hands of the contributing partner, any gain or loss recognized on the partnership's later disposition of the property is treated as ordinary income or loss. Ordinary income or loss treatment is mandated without regard to the period of time the partnership holds the property before disposition or the character of the property in the partnership's hands.

[10] Sec. 1223(1).
[11] Reg. Sec. 1.1223-1(a).
[12] Rev. Rul. 84-15, 1984-1 C.B. 158.
[13] Sec. 724. The determination of whether a property is an unrealized receivable, inventory, or a capital loss property in the contributing partner's hands occurs immediately before the contribution.
[14] Section 724(d)(1) references the unrealized receivables definition found in Sec. 751(c). For distributions and sale transactions, the unrealized receivables definition is broadened to include certain recapture items; this difference is discussed more fully in Chapter C10.

Inventory. If a property was inventory in the hands of the contributing partner, its character cannot be changed for five years. Any gain or loss recognized by the partnership on the disposition of such property during the five-year period beginning on the date of contribution is ordinary gain or loss. Ordinary gain or loss treatment is mandated even if the asset is a capital asset or Sec. 1231 asset in the partnership's hands.

EXAMPLE C9-10 ▶ On June 1, Jose, a real estate developer, contributes ten acres of land in an industrial park he developed to the Hi-Tech Partnership in exchange for a 30% interest in the partnership. Although Jose was holding the acreage in inventory, the land serves as the site for Hi-Tech's new research facility. Four years later Hi-Tech sells its research facility and the land. Gain on the sale of the land, which would ordinarily be taxed as Sec. 1231 gain, is reported as ordinary income under Sec. 724. ◀

ADDITIONAL COMMENT

Section 724 was enacted to eliminate the ability to transform the character of gain/loss on property by contributing the property to a partnership and having the partnership subsequently sell it.

Capital Loss Property. The final type of property whose character is fixed at the time of the contribution is property that would generate a capital loss if it were sold by the contributing partner rather than contributed to the partnership. A loss recognized by the partnership on the disposition of the property within five years of the date it is contributed to the partnership is a capital loss. However, the amount of loss that is characterized as capital may not exceed the capital loss the contributing partner would have recognized if the property had been instead sold on the contribution date. The character of any loss that exceeds the difference between the property's FMV and its adjusted basis on the contribution date is determined by the property's character in the hands of the partnership.

EXAMPLE C9-11 ▶ Pam holds investment land that she purchased for $50,000 in 1988. The FMV of the land is only $40,000 in 1993 when she contributes it to the PK Partnership, which is in the business of developing and selling lots. PK develops the contributed land and sells it in 1997 for $28,000, or at a loss of $22,000. The $10,000 loss that accrued while Pam held the land as a capital asset retains its character as a capital loss. The remaining $12,000 of loss that accrues while the land is part of the partnership's inventory is an ordinary loss. ◀

PARTNERSHIP'S HOLDING PERIOD. Under Sec. 1223(2), the partnership's holding period for its contributed assets includes the holding period of the contributing partner. This rule applies without regard to the character of the property in the contributing partner's hands or the partnership's hands.

KEY POINT

Unless gain is recognized by the transferor partner on the contribution of property to a partnership, the Sec. 1245 and Sec. 1250 recapture potential carry over to the partnership.

SECTION 1245 AND 1250 RECAPTURE RULES. Although the Sec. 1245 and Sec. 1250 depreciation recapture rules override most other nonrecognition of gain provisions in the Code, there is no depreciation recapture unless a gain is recognized when property is contributed in exchange for a partnership interest.[15] Instead, both the adjusted basis and depreciation recapture potential carry over to the partnership. If the property is later sold at a gain, the Sec. 1245 and 1250 provisions affect the character of the gain.

CONTRIBUTION OF PROPERTY AFTER FORMATION. Any time property is contributed in exchange for a partnership interest, the rules outlined above apply. They apply whether the contribution occurs during the formation of the partnership or at a

[15] Secs. 1245(b)(3) and 1250(d)(3). Property acquired as a capital contribution where gain is not recognized under Sec. 721 is subject to the MACRS anti-churning rules of Sec. 168(i)(7)(A). In general, the anti-churning rules require the partnership to use the same depreciation method as the partner who contributed the property. See Chapter C2 for a discussion of these rules in connection with a corporate formation transaction.

later point in time. This contrasts sharply with corporate contributions, where a tax-free contribution after formation is rare because of the 80% control requirement. Most contributions of property in exchange for a partnership interest are tax-free even if they occur years after the partnership was formed.

CONTRIBUTION OF SERVICES

A partner who receives a partnership interest in exchange for services has been compensated as surely as if he or she receives cash and must recognize ordinary income. The amount and timing of the income to be recognized are determined under Sec. 83. Consequently, receipt of an unrestricted interest in a partnership requires the service partner to immediately recognize income equal to the FMV of the partnership interest less any cash or property contributed by the partner. Generally, no income is recognized from the receipt of a restricted interest in a partnership until the restriction lapses or the interest can be freely transferred.

SELF-STUDY QUESTION

Does the contribution of services to a partnership in exchange for an unrestricted partnership interest qualify for Sec. 721 nontaxable treatment?

ANSWER

No. The service partner recognizes income to the extent of the FMV of the partnership interest received less any cash or other property contributed by the partner.

Although a partnership interest seems to be a unified interest, it is really made up of two components: a capital interest and a profits interest. A partner may receive both components or only a profits interest in exchange for his or her services. (It is rare to have a capital interest without a profits interest.) The Regulations indicate that a **capital interest** can be valued by determining the amount the partner would receive if the partnership liquidated on the day the partnership interest was received.[16] If the partner would receive proceeds from the sale of the partnership's assets or receive the assets themselves, then he or she is considered to own a capital interest. Alternatively, if the partner's only interest is in the future earnings of the partnership (with no interest in the current partnership assets), the partner owns a **profits interest** (but not a capital interest).

It has long been settled that receipt of a capital interest in a partnership in exchange for services is taxable under the rules outlined above. A profits interest is no more than a right to future income that will be taxed to the partner when it is earned. To the extent that the profits interest itself has a value, it is reasonable to expect that the value be taxed when the profits interest is received, as any other property received for services would be taxed.

EXAMPLE C9-12 ▶ Carl arranges favorable financing for the purchase of an office building and receives a 30% profits interest in a partnership formed to own and operate the building. Less than three weeks later Carl sells his profits interest to his partner for $40,000. Carl must recognize $40,000 as ordinary income from the receipt of a partnership profits interest in exchange for services. ◀

The facts in Example C9-12 approximate those of *Sol Diamond*, a landmark partnership taxation case, which was the first case to tax the partner when a profits interest was received.[17] The Tax Court pointed out that Sec. 61 included all compensation for services, and no other provision contained in the Code or Regulations removed this transaction from taxation. The Seventh Circuit Court of Appeals seemed to limit the inclusion of a profits interest to situations in which the market value of the profits interest could be determined. Much of the uncertainty in this area of tax law was resolved when Rev. Proc. 93-27 was issued, which provides that the IRS generally will not tax a profits interest received for services. Such a profits interest will be taxed upon receipt only in three specified instances in which a FMV is readily ascertainable.[18] In the general case, an

---

[16] Reg. Sec. 1.704-1(e)(1)(v). The capital interest definition that is referenced relates to family partnerships. There is no reason to believe that such definition differs from the one used for this purpose.

[17] 33 AFTR 2d 74-852, 74-1 USTC ¶9306 (7th Cir., 1974), *aff'g.* 56 T.C. 530 (1971).

[18] 1993-2 C.B. 343. The three exceptions involve receipt of a profits interest having a substantially certain and predictable income stream, the partner disposes of the profits interest within two years of receipt, or the profits interest is a limited interest in a publicly traded partnership.

income tax is not levied on the profits interest separately, but all partnership profits that accrue to the partner are, of course, taxed under the normal rules of partnership taxation.

KEY POINT

To the extent the service partner recognizes income, the partnership is entitled to a deduction or, if the services performed are a capital expenditure, the amount must be capitalized.

CONSEQUENCES TO THE PARTNERSHIP. Normally, payments made by the partnership for services are either deductible as an expense or capitalized. This result is unchanged when the partnership pays for services with an interest in the partnership. The timing of the partnership's deduction for the expense generally matches the timing for the partner to include the value of his or her partnership interest in income.[19]

Allocating The Expense Deduction. The expense deduction or the amortization of the capital expenditure is allocated among the partners other than the service partner. This allocation occurs because it is these partners who make the outlay by relinquishing part of their interest in the partnership.

EXAMPLE C9-13 ▶

In June of the current year Jay, a lawyer, receives a 1% capital and profits interest (valued at $4,000) in the JLK Partnership in return for providing legal services to JLK's employees during the first five months of the current year. The legal services were a fringe benefit for JLK's employees and were deductible by JLK. Jay must include $4,000 in his current year gross income and JLK can deduct the expense in the current year. ◀

If the service performed is of a nature that should be capitalized, the partnership capitalizes the amount and amortizes it as appropriate. The asset's basis is increased at the same time and in the same amount as the partner's gross income inclusion.[20]

EXAMPLE C9-14 ▶

In June of the current year Rob, an architect, receives a 10% capital and profits interest in the KLB Partnership for his services in designing a new building to house the partnership's operations. The June value of the partnership interest is $24,000. Rob must recognize $24,000 of ordinary income in the current year as a result of receiving the partnership interest. The KLB Partnership must capitalize the $24,000 as part of the building's cost and depreciate that amount (along with the building's other costs) over its recovery period. ◀

KEY POINT

The following is a summary of the tax consequences for both the service partner and the partnership when a contribution of services occurs:

- Income to the service partner to the extent of the FMV of an undivided interest in the partnership assets deemed received.
- Deduction (or capital expenditure) for the partnership's outlay.
- Gain/loss recognized by the partnership on the assets deemed transferred.
- Service partner's basis in his or her partnership interest equals the amount of income recognized by the service partner.
- The partnership adjusts its basis for the portion of the asset(s) deemed transferred. This adjustment reflects the gain/loss recognized by the partnership on the deemed asset transfer.

Note that the timing of the partner's recognition of income is not changed in the preceding two examples by the fact that the partnership could deduct one payment but had to capitalize the other.

Partnership Gain Or Loss. The partnership, in effect, pays its bill for services by transferring an interest in partnership property. Generally, when property is used to pay a debt, the payor must recognize gain or loss equal to the difference between the property's adjusted basis and FMV. Likewise, the partnership must recognize the gain or loss existing in the proportionate share of its assets deemed to be transferred to the service partner.[21] Furthermore, because the partnership must recognize gain or loss, the partnership's bases in its assets are changed.

EXAMPLE C9-15 ▶

On January 1 of the current year Maria is admitted as a 25% partner in the XYZ Partnership in exchange for services valued at $16,500. The partnership has no liabilities at the time but has assets with a basis of $50,000 and FMV of $66,000. The transaction is taxed as if Maria received an undivided one-fourth interest in each asset. She is taxed on the $16,500 FMV of the assets and takes a $16,500 basis in the partnership interest. The partnership must recognize $4,000 of gain [0.25 × ($66,000 FMV − $50,000 adjusted basis)] on the assets deemed paid to Maria. The partnership's original basis in its assets ($50,000) is increased by the $4,000 recognized gain. ◀

[19] Reg. Sec. 1.83-6(a)(1).

[20] Reg. Sec. 1.83-6(a)(4).

[21] Reg. Sec. 1.83-6(b).

ORGANIZATIONAL AND SYNDICATION EXPENDITURES

The costs of organizing a partnership are treated as capital expenditures. The capitalized amount can be amortized on a straight-line basis and deducted over a period of not less than sixty months beginning with the month in which the partnership begins business.[22] In order to amortize the organizational expenditures, the partnership must make an election that is included with the partnership tax return for the period including the month in which it begins business.

Organizational expenditures that can be capitalized and amortized must meet the same requirements as the costs incurred by a corporation making the Sec. 248 election to amortize organizational expenditures (see Chapter C3). The organizational expenditures must be incident to the creation of the partnership, chargeable to a capital account, and of a character that would be amortizable over the life of the partnership if the partnership had a limited life. Eligible expenditures include legal fees for negotiating and preparing partnership agreements, accounting fees for establishing the initial accounting system, and filing fees. Syndication expenditures for the issuing and marketing of interests in the partnership are not organizational expenditures and cannot be included in this election.[23] Unamortized organizational expenditures are deducted when the partnership is terminated or liquidated.

Topic Review C9-1 summarizes the tax consequences of the formation of a partnership.

SELF-STUDY QUESTION

What is the importance of the distinction between organizational expenditures and syndication expenditures?

ANSWER

Organizational expenditures can be amortized over a period of not less than sixty months, but syndication expenditures are *not* deductible or amortizable.

WHAT WOULD YOU DO IN THIS SITUATION?

Bob Krause, and his large family corporation, have been longtime clients of your accounting firm. During the current year Bob and his adult son, Tom, formed the BT Partnership to develop and sell vacation homes on the Suwanee River. Bob contributed a 1,000-acre tract of land in exchange for a 50% interest in BT Partnership's profits and losses. The land had a $300,000 FMV and a $30,000 adjusted basis. Tom contributed $150,000 in cash for the remaining 50% interest in the partnership. Two months after the partnership was formed, BT Partnership used the land as security for a $200,000 loan from a local bank. $50,000 of the loan proceeds were used to subdivide and plot the land. The partnership then distributed the other $150,000 of the loan proceeds to Bob. Bob plans not to report these transactions since property contributions in exchange for a partnership interest and distributions of money by a partnership which are not in excess of the partner's basis are tax-free transactions. What would you advise your client to do in this situation?

PARTNERSHIP ELECTIONS

OBJECTIVE 3

Determine the permitted tax years for a partnership

Once the partnership is formed, the partnership must make a number of elections. For example, partnerships must select a taxable year and elect accounting methods for all but a few items affecting the computation of partnership taxable income or loss.

PARTNERSHIP TAXABLE YEAR

The election of the partnership's taxable year is critical because it determines when each partner reports his or her share of partnership income or loss. Under Sec. 706(a), each

[22] Sec. 709(b).

[23] Reg. Sec. 1.709-2(a).

Topic Review C9-1

Formation of a Partnership

	Contribution to a Partnership: Property	Contribution to a Partnership: Services
Recognition of gain, loss, or income by partner	Tax-free unless (1) liabilities assumed by the partnership exceed partner's tentative basis in partnership interest (gain recognized is amount by which liabilities assumed by partnership exceed tentative basis), (2) the partnership formed is an investment partnership (gain recognized is excess of FMV of partnership interest over basis of assets contributed), or (3) a contribution is followed by a distribution that is treated as a sale (gain or loss recognized on sale transaction).	Taxable to partner equal to FMV of partnership interest received.
Basis of partnership interest	Substituted basis from property contributed plus share of partnership liabilities assumed minus the partner's liabilities assumed by the partnership. Gain recognized because of the investment company rules increases the basis of the partnership interest.	Amount of income recognized plus share of partnership liabilities assumed by the partner minus partner's liabilities assumed by the partnership.
Gain or loss recognized by the partnership	No gain or loss recognized by the partnership.	1. Deduction or capitalized expense is created depending on the type of service rendered. 2. Gain or loss recognized equals difference between FMV of portion of assets used to pay service partner and the basis of such portion of the assets.
Basis of assets to the partnership	Carryover basis is increased by gain recognized by the partner only if gain results from the formation of an investment partnership. No basis adjustment occurs when assumption of partner's liabilities results in gain recognition. In a sale transaction assets take a cost basis.	Increased or decreased to reflect the FMV of the assets paid to the service partner.

partner's tax return includes his or her share of partnership income, gain, loss, deduction, or credit items for any taxable year of the partnership ending within or with the partner's taxable year.

EXAMPLE C9-16 ▶

Vicki is a member of a partnership having a November 30 year-end. In her tax return for calendar year 1997, she must include her share of partnership items from the partnership tax year that ends November 30, 1997. Results of partnership operations in December 1997 are reported along with all other partnership items from the partnership year that ends on November 30, 1998 in Vicki's 1998 tax return. She receives, in essence, a one-year deferral of the taxes due on December's partnership income. ◀

KEY POINT

A partnership tax year is determined by the three rules in the following order:
1. The majority partner(s)' (own in aggregate more than 50%) tax year.
2. If (1) is not applicable, then the tax year of *all* principal partners (5% or more partners).
3. If neither (1) nor (2) is applicable, then the tax year that allows the least aggregate deferral.

SECTION 706 RESTRICTIONS. Because the choice of a tax year for a partnership can provide a substantial opportunity for tax deferral, it is no surprise that Sec. 706 severely restricts the available choices for a partnership's tax year. The partnership must use the same tax year as the one or more **majority partners** who have an aggregate interest in partnership profits and capital in excess of 50%. This rule must be used only if these majority partners have a common tax year and have had this tax year for the shorter of the three preceding years or the partnership's period of existence. If the tax year of the partner(s) owning a majority interest cannot be used, the partnership must use the tax year of all its principal partners (or the tax year to which all of its principal partners are concurrently changing). A **principal partner** is defined as one who owns a 5% or more interest in capital or profits.[24] If the principal partners do not have a common tax year, the partnership is required to use the tax year that allows the least aggregate deferral. The least aggregate deferral test provided in the Regulations[25] requires that for each possible tax year-end, each partner's ownership percentage be multiplied by the number of months that the partner would defer income (number of months from partnership year-end to partner year-end). The number arrived at for each partner is totaled across all partners. The same procedure is followed for each alternative tax year, and the tax year that produces the smallest total must be chosen.

EXAMPLE C9-17 ▶

Jane, Kerry Corporation, and Bob form the JKB Partnership. The three partners use tax years ending on December 31, June 30, and September 30, respectively. Jane, Kerry Corporation, and Bob own 40%, 40%, and 20%, respectively, of the partnership. What tax year-end is required for the partnership? Neither the majority partner rule nor the principal partner rule can be applied to determine JKB's tax year. To determine the least aggregate deferral, all three possible year-ends must be analyzed as follows:

			Possible Tax Year-Ends					
			6/30		*9/30*		*12/31*	
Partner	*Partnership Interest*	*Partner Tax Year*	*Months Deferred*[a]	*Total*[b]	*Months Deferred*	*Total*	*Months Deferred*	*Total*
Jane	40%	12/31	6	2.4	3	1.2	0	0
Kerry	40%	6/30	0	0	9	3.6	6	2.4
Bob	20%	9/30	3	0.6	0	0	9	1.8
				3.0		4.8		4.2

[a] Months from possible partnership tax year-end to partner tax year-end.
[b] Partnership interest × months deferred = Total.

The partnership must use a June 30 year-end because, with a total score of 3.0, that tax year-end it has the least aggregate deferral. ◀

[24] Sec. 706(b)(3).

[25] Temp. Reg. Sec. 1.706-1T.

KEY POINT

Partnerships that are able to satisfy the stringent requirements of Rev. Proc. 87-32 are permitted to use their natural business year for tax purposes.

If the partnership has a business purpose for using some tax year other than the year prescribed by these rules, the IRS may approve use of another tax year. Rev. Proc. 74-33[26] states that an acceptable business purpose for using a different tax year is to end the partnership's tax year at the end of the partnership's natural business year. This revenue procedure explains that a business having a peak period and a nonpeak period completes its natural business year at the end of its peak season (or shortly thereafter). For example, a ski lodge has a natural business year that ends in early spring. A second pronouncement, Rev. Proc. 87-32,[27] allows an alternate tax year if the following tests are met:

- 25% or more of the partnership's gross receipts for the twelve-month period in question are recognized in the last two months of the period.
- This requirement has been met for the prior three twelve-month periods.

Partnerships that do not have a peak period are not able to use the natural business year exception.

EXAMPLE C9-18 ▶ ABC Partnership is owned equally by Amy, Brad, and Chris. Each partner uses an October 31 tax year-end. ABC earns 30% of its gross receipts in July and August each year and has had this pattern of earnings for more than three years. The IRS would probably grant approval under the guidelines of Rev. Proc. 87-32 for the partnership to use an August 31 tax year-end. ◀

KEY POINT

Because of the Sec. 706 requirements, most partnerships are required to adopt a calendar year. As a compromise, a Sec. 444 election permits a fiscal tax year as long as no more than a three-month deferral exists and as long as the deferral is not increased from any deferral already approved.

HISTORICAL NOTE

Section 444 was enacted, in part, as a concession to tax return preparers who already have the majority of their clients with calendar year-ends.

The Revenue Act of 1987 provides an *election* in Sec. 444 that permits a partnership to use a year-end that results in a deferral of the lesser of the current deferral period or three months. The deferral period is the time from the beginning of the partnership's fiscal year to the close of the first required tax year ending within such year (i.e., usually December 31). The **Sec. 444 election** is available to both new partnerships making an initial tax year election or existing partnerships that are changing tax years. A partnership that satisfies the Sec. 706 requirements described above or has established a business purpose for its choice of a year-end (i.e., natural business year) does not need a Sec. 444 election.

A partnership that makes a Sec. 444 election must make a required payment under Sec. 7519 (see the Compliance and Procedural Considerations section of this chapter for a discussion of the Sec. 444 election and Sec. 7519 required payment). The required payment has the effect of collecting a tax on the partnership's deferred income at the highest individual marginal tax rate plus one percentage point.

Topic Review C9-2 presents a summary of the allowable partnership tax year elections.

OTHER PARTNERSHIP ELECTIONS

KEY POINT

Except for the three elections listed in this section, partnerships make the tax elections for the partnership rather than the partners.

With the exception of three specific elections that are reserved to the partners, Sec. 703(b) requires that all elections that can affect the computation of taxable income derived from the partnership be made by the partnership.[28] The three elections reserved to the individual partners relate to income from the discharge of indebtedness, deduction and recapture of certain mining exploration expenditures, and the choice between deducting or crediting foreign income taxes. Other than these elections, elections are generally made by the partnership as an entity. Accordingly, the partnership elects its overall accounting method, which can differ from the methods used by its partners. The partnership also elects its inventory and depreciation methods.

---

[26] 1974-2 C.B. 489. The IRS in Rev. Rul. 87-57, 1987-2 C.B. 224, has provided a series of situations illustrating the business purpose requirement.

[27] 1987-2 C.B. 396. Use of this test was endorsed by the Conference Committee Report for the 1986 Tax Reform Act. See H. Rept. No. 99-841, 99th Cong., 2d Sess., p. II-319 (1986).

[28] The partnership does not include any depletion from oil or gas wells in its computation of income (Sec. 703(a)(2)(F)). Instead each partner elects cost or percentage depletion (Sec. 613A(c)(7)(D)).

Topic Review C9-2

Allowable Tax Year For a Partnership

IRC Sec. 706 requires that a partnership select the highest ranked tax year-end from the ranking that follows:

1. The tax year-end used by the partners who own a majority of the partnership capital and profits.
2. The tax year-end used by all principal partners (i.e., a partner who owns at least 5% of the partnership capital or profits).
3. The tax year-end determined by the least aggregate deferral test.

The IRS may grant permission for the partnership to use a fiscal year-end if the partnership has a natural business year (for example, a tax year where 25% or more of the partnership's gross receipts for the twelve-month period are reported in the last two months of the period).

If the partnership does not have a natural business year, it must either

- Use the tax year-end required by Sec. 706 or
- Elect a fiscal year-end under Sec. 444 and make a required payment that approximates the tax due on the deferred income.

PARTNERSHIP REPORTING OF INCOME

OBJECTIVE 4

Differentiate between items that must be separately stated and those that are included in ordinary income or loss

PARTNERSHIP TAXABLE INCOME

Partnership taxable income is calculated in much the same way as the taxable income of individuals, with a few differences mandated by the statutes. First, taxable income is divided into separately stated items and ordinary income or loss. In Sec. 703(a), the Code specifies a list of deductions that are available to individuals but cannot be claimed by a partnership. The forbidden deductions include income taxes paid or accrued to a foreign country or U.S. possession, charitable contributions, oil and gas depletion, and net operating loss (NOL) carrybacks or carryovers. The first three items must be separately stated and may or may not be deductible by the partner. Because all losses are allocated to the partners for deduction on their tax returns, the partnership itself never has an NOL carryover or carryback. Instead, a single partner may have an NOL if his or her deductible share of partnership losses exceeds his or her other business income. These NOLs are used at the partner level without any further regard for the partnership entity.

SEPARATELY STATED ITEMS

Each partner's distributive share of partnership income must be reported. However, Sec. 702 establishes a list of items that must be separately stated at the partnership level so that their character can remain intact at the partner reporting level. Section 702(a) lists the following items that must be separately stated:

- Net short-term capital gains and losses
- Net long-term capital gains and losses
- Sec. 1231 gains and losses
- Charitable contributions

- Dividends that are eligible for a dividends-received deduction
- Taxes paid or accrued to a foreign country or to a U.S. possession
- Any other item provided by the Regulations

Regulation Sec. 1.702-1(a)(8) adds several other items to the list begun by the Code including:

- Tax-exempt or partially tax-exempt interest
- Any items subject to special allocations (discussed below)

As a general rule, an item must be separately stated if the income tax liability of any partner that would result from treating the item separately is different from the liability that would result if that item were included with partnership ordinary income.[29]

EXAMPLE C9-19

Amy and Big Corporation are equal partners in the AB Partnership, which purchases new equipment during the current year at a total cost of $100,000. In 1997 AB elects to expense $18,000 under the provisions of Sec. 179. Big Corporation has already expensed $9,000 under Sec. 179 this year. The Sec. 179 expense must be separately stated because Big Corporation is subject to a separate $18,000 limit of its own.

TYPICAL MISCONCEPTION

The amount and character of any gain/loss are determined at the partnership level. How the gain/loss will be taxed is determined at the partner level.

Once the item is separately stated and a distributive share is allocated to each partner, the separately stated items must be reported on each partner's tax return as if the partnership entity did not exist. The partner's share of partnership net long-term capital gains or losses is combined with the partner's personal long-term capital gains and losses to calculate the partner's net long-term capital gain or loss. Likewise, the partner's share of partnership charitable contributions is combined with the partner's own charitable contributions. The total is subject to the partner's charitable contribution limitations. In summary, Sec. 702(b) requires that the character of each separately stated item be determined at the partnership level. The amount is then passed down to the partners and reported in each partner's return as if the partner directly realized the amount.

PARTNERSHIP ORDINARY INCOME

TYPICAL MISCONCEPTION

Partnership ordinary income/loss is the sum of all taxable income/loss items not separately stated. This amount is reported as a residual number on line 22 of Form 1065. Partnership taxable income includes both the taxable separately stated items and the partnership ordinary income/loss. Students should not use these two terms interchangeably.

All taxable items of income, gain, loss, or deduction that do not have to be separately stated are combined into a total called Sec. 702(a)(8) income or loss or **partnership ordinary income** or **loss.** It must be noted that this ordinary income amount is sometimes incorrectly referred to as partnership taxable income. **Partnership taxable income** is the sum of all taxable items among the separately stated items plus the partnership ordinary income or loss. Therefore, partnership taxable income is often substantially greater than partnership ordinary income.

Included in the partnership's ordinary income are items such as gross profit on sales, administrative expenses, and employee salaries. Such items are always ordinary income or expenses that are not subject to special limitations. Income recognized under the Sec. 1245 or 1250 depreciation recapture rules is also included in the ordinary income total because it is not eligible for preferential treatment.

A share of partnership ordinary income or loss is allocated to each partner. Such an allocation is shown on Schedules K and K-1 of the partnership's Form 1065 (see the completed partnership tax return in Appendix B). If the partner is an individual, his or her distributive share of ordinary income, or the deductible portion of his or her distributive

[29] Reg. Sec. 1.702-1(a)(8)(ii).

share of ordinary loss, is reported on Schedule E of Form 1040. Schedule E includes rental and royalty income and income or losses from estates, trusts, S corporations, and partnerships. If the partner is a corporation, partnership ordinary income or loss is reported in the Other Income category on Form 1120.

PARTNER REPORTING OF INCOME

PARTNER'S DISTRIBUTIVE SHARE

OBJECTIVE 5

Calculate a partner's distributive share of partnership income, gain, loss, deduction, or credit items

After the partnership's separately stated income, gain, loss, deduction, or credit items, and partnership ordinary income or loss is determined, the totals must be allocated among the partners. Each partner must report and pay taxes on his or her distributive share. Under Sec. 704(b), the partner's distributive share is normally determined by the terms of the partnership agreement or, if the partnership agreement is silent, by the partner's overall interest in the partnership as determined by taking into account all facts and circumstances.

Note that the term **distributive share** is a misnomer because it has nothing to do with the amount actually distributed to a partner. A partner's distributive share is actually the portion of partnership taxable and nontaxable income that the partner has agreed to report for tax purposes. Actual distributions in a given year may be more or less than the distributive share reported by the partner.

KEY POINT

Once the amount and character of the partnership income/loss items have been determined, the distributive share, or amount each partner will report, must be determined for each item. The distributive share is usually determined by the partnership agreement.

PARTNERSHIP AGREEMENT. The **partnership agreement** may describe a partner's distributive share by indicating the partner's profits and loss interest, or it may indicate separate profits and loss interests. For example, the partnership agreement may state that a partner has a 10% interest in both partnership profits and losses or a partner has only a 10% interest in partnership profits (i.e., profits interest) but has a 30% interest in partnership losses (i.e., loss interest).

If only one interest percentage is stated, it is used to allocate both partnership profit and loss. If profit and loss percentages are stated separately, the partnership's taxable income for the year is first totaled to determine whether a net profit or net loss has been earned. Then the appropriate percentage (either profit or loss) is applied to each class of income for the year.[30]

EXAMPLE C9-20 ▶ The ABC Partnership reports the following income and loss items for the current year:

Net long-term capital loss	$100,000
Net Sec. 1231 gain	90,000
Ordinary income	220,000

Carmelia has a 20% profits interest and a 30% loss interest in the ABC Partnership.

What is her distributive share of current year income and loss? Because the partnership earns a $210,000 (− $100,000 + $90,000 + $220,000) net profit, Carmelia's distributive share is calculated using her 20% profits interest and is reported as follows:

Net long-term capital loss	$ 20,000
Net Sec. 1231 gain	18,000
Ordinary income	44,000

Her loss percentage is used only in years when the partnership has a net loss. ◀

[30] This rule is derived from the House and Senate reports on the original Sec. 704(b) provisions. The two reports are identical and read, "The income ratio shall be applicable if the partnership has taxable income . . . and the loss ratio shall be applicable [if] the partnership has a loss." H. Rept. No. 1337, 83d Cong., 2d Sess., p. A223 (1954); S. Rept. No. 1622, 83d Cong., 2d Sess., p. 379 (1954).

VARYING INTEREST RULE. If a partner's ownership interest changes during the partnership tax year, the income or loss allocation takes into account the partner's varying interest.[31] This varying interest rule is applied for changes occurring to a partner's interest as a result of buying an additional interest in the partnership, selling part (but not all) of a partnership interest, or giving or being given a partnership interest, or the admission of a new partner. The partner's ownership interest is generally applied to the income earned on a pro rata basis.

EXAMPLE C9-21 ▶

Maria owns 20% of the XYZ Partnership from January 1 through June 30 of the current year (not a leap year). On July 1 she buys an additional 10% interest in the partnership. During this year, XYZ Partnership has ordinary income of $120,000, which is earned evenly throughout the year. Maria's $30,049 ($11,901 + $18,148) distributive share of income is calculated as follows:

$$\text{Pre-July 1:} \quad \$120{,}000 \times \frac{181 \text{ days}}{365 \text{ days}} \times 0.20 = \$11{,}901$$

$$\text{Post-June 30:} \quad \$120{,}000 \times \frac{184 \text{ days}}{365 \text{ days}} \times 0.30 = \$18{,}148$$

Similar calculations would be made if the XYZ Partnership reported separately stated items such as capital gains and losses. ◀

SPECIAL ALLOCATIONS

OBJECTIVE 6

Explain the requirements for a special partnership allocation

Special allocations are unique to partnerships and allow tremendous flexibility in sharing specific items of income and loss among the partners. Special allocations can provide a specified partner with more or less of an item of income, gain, loss, or deduction than would be available using the partner's regular distributive share. There are two different kinds of special allocations. First, Sec. 704 requires certain special allocations with respect to contributed property. Second, other special allocations are allowed as long as they meet the tests laid out in the Regulations for having substantial economic effect. If the substantial economic effect test is not met, the special allocation is lost and the income, gain, loss, or deduction is allocated according to the partner's interest in the partnership as expressed in the actual operations and activities.

ALLOCATIONS RELATED TO CONTRIBUTED PROPERTY. As previously discussed, when property is contributed to a partnership, it takes a carryover basis that references the contributing partner's basis. If there were no special allocations, this carryover basis rule would require the partnership (and each of the partners) to accept the tax burden of any gain or loss that accrues to the property before its contribution.

EXAMPLE C9-22 ▶

In 1990, Elizabeth contributes land having a $4,000 basis and a $10,000 FMV to the DEF Partnership. Assuming the property continues to increase in value, or at least does not decline in value, DEF's gain on the ultimate sale of this property is $6,000 greater than the gain that actually accrues while the partnership owns the property. ◀

KEY POINT

Section 704(c) limits the ability to use a partnership to shift income/loss between taxpayers. This provision requires pre-contribution gains/losses to be allocated to the contributing partner when the gain/loss is recognized by the partnership.

Section 704(c) requires precontribution gains or losses to be allocated to the contributing partner for any property contributed to a partnership after March 31, 1984. Thus, the pre-contribution gain in Example C9-22 would be allocated to Elizabeth. In

[31] Sec. 706(d)(1).

addition, income and deductions reported with respect to contributed property must be allocated to take into account the difference between the property's basis and FMV at the time of contribution. The allocation of depreciation is a common example of the special deduction allocation related to contributed property that is necessary under these rules.

EXAMPLE C9-23 ▶ Kay and Sam form an equal partnership when Sam contributes cash of $10,000 and Kay contributes land having a $6,000 basis and a $10,000 FMV. If the partnership sells the land two years later for $12,000, the $4,000 precontribution gain ($10,000 FMV − $6,000 basis) is allocated only to Kay. The $2,000 gain that accrued while the partnership held the land ($12,000 sales price − $10,000 FMV at contribution) is allocated to Kay and Sam equally. Kay reports a total gain of $5,000 ($4,000 + $1,000) and Sam reports a $1,000 gain on the sale of the land. ◀

TYPICAL MISCONCEPTION

Special allocations are unique to partnerships and allow tremendous flexibility. Even so, for a special allocation to be recognized it must have substantial economic effect.

SUBSTANTIAL ECONOMIC EFFECT. Special allocations not related to contributed property must meet several specific criteria established by the Regulations. These criteria are designed to ensure that the allocations affect the partner's economic consequences and not just their tax consequences.

EXAMPLE C9-24 ▶ The AB Partnership earns $10,000 in tax-exempt interest income and $10,000 in taxable interest income each year. Andy and Becky each have 50% capital and profit interests in the partnership. An allocation of the tax-exempt interest income to Andy, a 39.6% tax bracket partner, and the taxable interest income to Becky, a 15% tax bracket partner, does not have substantial economic effect. ◀

The allocation described in Example C9-24 affects only the tax consequences to the partners, because a 50% distributive share would not really change the partner's economic position separate from the tax consequences.

KEY POINT

For an allocation to have economic effect, the regulations require that the allocation be reflected in the partner's capital account, liquidation proceeds be distributed in accordance with the capital account, and a partner be liable to the partnership for deficits in his or her capital account.

In order to separate transactions only affecting taxes from those affecting the partner's economic position, the Regulations look at whether the allocation has an economic effect and whether the economic effect is substantial. Under the Sec. 704 regulations, the allocation has economic effect if it meets all three of the following conditions:

- It results in the appropriate increase or decrease in the partner's capital account.
- The proceeds of any liquidation occurring at any time in the partnership's life cycle are distributed in accordance with positive capital account balances.
- Partners must make up negative balances in their capital accounts upon the liquidation of the partnership and these contributions are used to pay partnership debts or are allocated to partners having positive capital account balances.[32]

EXAMPLE C9-25 ▶ Arnie and Bonnie each contribute $100,000 to form the AB Partnership on January 1, 1996. These contributions plus a $1,800,000 mortgage are used to purchase a $2,000,000 office building. To simplify the calculations, assume the building is depreciated using the straight-line method over a forty-year life and that in each year income and expenses are equal before considering depreciation. AB makes a special allocation of depreciation to Arnie. The allocation reduces Arnie's capital account, and any liquidating distributions are made in accordance with the capital account balances.

[32] Reg. Sec. 1.704-1(b)(2)(ii). The Regulations provide other alternatives for meeting this portion of the requirements.

	Capital Account Balance	
	Arnie	*Bonnie*
January 1, 1996 balance	$100,000	$100,000
1996 loss	(50,000)	—0—
1997 loss	(50,000)	—0—
1998 loss	(50,000)	—0—
December 31, 1998 balance	($50,000)	$100,000

If we assume that the property has declined in value in an amount equal to the depreciation claimed and that the partnership is now liquidated, the need for the requirement to restore negative capital account balances becomes apparent.

Sales price of property on December 31, 1998	$ 1,850,000
Minus: Mortgage principal	(1,800,000)
Partnership cash to be distributed to partners	$ 50,000

If Arnie does not have to restore his negative capital account balance, there is only $50,000 in cash that Bonnie can receive, even though her capital account balance is $100,000. In effect, Bonnie has borne the economic burden of the 1998 depreciation. Without the requirement to restore the negative capital account balance, the special allocation to Arnie will be ignored for 1998 and Bonnie will receive the depreciation deduction. If Arnie must restore any negative capital account balance, he will contribute $50,000 when the partnership liquidates at the end of 1998, and Bonnie will receive her full $100,000 capital account balance. The 1998 special allocation to Arnie would then have economic effect. (Note that Arnie's allocation for 1996 and 1997 is acceptable even if there is no agreement to replace negative capital account balances. This result occurs in each of these two years because Arnie has sufficient capital to absorb the economic loss if the property declines in value in an amount equal to the depreciation that is allocated to him.)[33] ◀

The second requirement for a special allocation to be accepted under the Regulations is that the economic effect must be substantial, which requires that there be a reasonable possibility that the allocation will substantially affect the dollar amounts to be received by the partners independent of tax consequences.[34] For example, the allocation in Example C9-24 does not have a substantial effect. It is also highly unlikely that any special allocation of a tax credit can pass this test.

STOP & THINK

Question: The special allocation rules require that a partner who receives a special allocation of loss or expense receive less cash or property when the partnership liquidates. As we will see later in this chapter, losses reduce the partner's basis in the partnership interest, so a sale or liquidation of the partnership interest will cause a larger gain (or a smaller loss) to be recognized than would have resulted without this loss allocation. Because the basis is reduced, the partner is also more likely to recognize taxable gain on a distribution from the partnership. With these negative consequences, why would anyone want to be given a special allocation of partnership loss or expense?

Solution: The answer is a matter of timing. The specially allocated loss reduces taxable income now and saves more taxes now for the partner than would a "normal" loss

[33] Such allocations do not literally meet the three requirements outlined on page C9-20 for special allocations. However, allocations that meet the alternate standard—having sufficient capital to absorb the economic loss—will be allowed.

[34] Reg. Sec. 1.704-1(b)(2)(iii)(a). It should be noted that the substantial economic effect regulations go far beyond the rules covered in this text.

allocation. The negative consequences occur when the partner incurs a larger gain (or smaller loss) in a future period when the partnership interest is sold or liquidated. The special-allocation scenario may have a greater after-tax present value to the partner than the after-tax present value of receiving a normal share of losses and an increased liquidating distribution.

BASIS FOR PARTNERSHIP INTEREST

OBJECTIVE 7

Calculate a partner's basis in a partnership interest

The calculation of a partner's beginning basis in a partnership interest depends on the method used to acquire the interest, with different valuation techniques for a purchased interest, a gifted interest, and an inherited interest. The results of the partnership's operations and liabilities both cause adjustments to the beginning amount. Additional contributions to the partnership and distributions from the partnership further alter the partner's basis.

BEGINNING BASIS

A partner's beginning basis for a partnership interest received for a contribution of property or services has been discussed. It is possible to acquire a partnership interest by methods other than contributing property or services to the partnership. If the partnership interest is purchased from an existing partner, the new partner's basis is simply the price paid for the partnership interest, including assumption of partnership liabilities. If the partnership interest is inherited, the heir's basis is the FMV of the partnership interest on the decedent's date of death or, if elected by the executor, the alternate valuation date but not less than liabilities assumed. If a partnership interest is received as a gift, the donee's basis generally equals the donor's basis (including the donor's ratable share of partnership liabilities) plus the portion of any gift tax paid by the donor that relates to appreciation attaching to the gift property. In summary, the beginning basis for a partnership interest is calculated following the usual rules for the method of acquisition.

SELF-STUDY QUESTION

What are some of the more common methods of acquiring a partnership interest, and what is the beginning basis?

ANSWER

1. Purchase—cost basis
2. Inherit—FMV
3. Gift—usually donor's basis with a possible gift tax adjustment

EFFECTS OF LIABILITIES

The effect of partnership liabilities on the basis of a partnership interest was briefly discussed in connection with the contribution of property subject to a liability. However, a more complete explanation is necessary to fully understand the pervasive impact of liabilities on partnership taxation.

INCREASES AND DECREASES IN LIABILITIES. Two changes in a partner's liabilities are considered contributions of cash by the partner to the partnership. The first is an increase in the partner's share of partnership liabilities. This increase can arise from either an increase in the partner's profit or loss interests or from an increase in total partnership liabilities. Accordingly, if a partnership incurs a large debt, the partners' bases in their partnership interests increase. The second way to increase a partner's basis is to have the partner assume partnership liabilities in an individual capacity.[35]

There are also two liability changes that are treated for all purposes as distributions of cash from the partnership to the partner. These changes are a decrease in a partner's share of partnership liabilities and a decrease in the partner's individual liabilities caused by the

[35] Sec. 752(a).

partnership's assumption of a liability of the partner.[36] Often both an increase and a decrease result from a single transaction. The impact of these increases and decreases can be illustrated by the following example.

EXAMPLE C9-26 ▶ Juan, a 40% partner in the ABC Partnership, has a $30,000 basis in his partnership interest before receiving a partnership distribution of land. As part of the transaction, Juan agrees to assume a $10,000 mortgage on the land. The effect of the liabilities on Juan's basis in his partnership interest will first be a decrease of $4,000 for the decline in Juan's share of partnership liabilities resulting from the partnership no longer owing the $10,000 mortgage. His basis in the partnership interest is also increased by $10,000, which is the partnership liability that he assumes in his individual capacity. His net change in basis in his partnership resulting from the liabilities is $6,000 (−$4,000 + $10,000). Of course, his basis in his partnership interest must also be adjusted for the land distribution he receives. Distributions will be discussed further in Chapter C10. ◀

A PARTNER'S SHARE OF LIABILITIES. Once the general impact of liabilities as increases and decreases in a partner's basis for his or her partnership interest is understood, the specific amount of the partner's share of the partnership's liabilities must be determined. In all examples until now we have considered only general partners who have the same interest in profits and losses. It is common to have one or more limited partners in a partnership, and it is not unusual for partners to have differing profit and loss ratios. The Regulations provide guidelines for allocating partnership liabilities to the individual partners.

ADDITIONAL COMMENT

The fact that a partner gets basis for his or her share of recourse debt is not controversial. The fact that a partner gets basis for debt on which the partner is not personally liable seems questionable, yet other rules do limit the benefit of the basis created by the nonrecourse debt.

TYPICAL MISCONCEPTION

Nonrecourse debt is allocated among **all** partners primarily according to their profit ratios. Recourse debt is allocated to the limited partners to the extent that they bear an economic risk of loss but generally a limited partner's economic risk of loss is not greater than any additional amounts those partners pledged to contribute. The remaining recourse debt is allocated among the general partners according to their economic risk of loss.

Recourse And Nonrecourse Loans. A **recourse loan** is the usual kind of loan for which the borrower remains liable until the loan is paid. If the recourse loan is secured and payments are not made as scheduled, the lender can then sell the security. If the sales proceeds are insufficient to repay a recourse loan, the borrower must make up the difference. Under the regulations, a recourse loan is one for which any partner or a related party will stand an economic loss if the partnership cannot pay the debt.[37] A **nonrecourse loan** is one in which the lender may sell the security if the loan is not paid, but no partner is liable for any deficiency. The lender has no recourse against the borrower for additional amounts. Nonrecourse debts most commonly occur in connection with the financing of real property that is expected to substantially increase in value over the life of the loan.

General And Limited Partners. A limited partner is not normally liable to pay partnership debts beyond the original contribution (which is already reflected in basis) and any additional amount the partner pledged to contribute.[38] Therefore, recourse debt is added to a limited partner's basis only to the extent that the partner has a risk of economic loss. Nonrecourse debts increase a limited partner's basis based primarily on the profit ratio.[39]

A general partner's share of nonrecourse liabilities is also determined primarily by his or her profit ratio. Because limited partners seldom receive an allocated share of the recourse liabilities, the general partners share all recourse liabilities beyond any amounts that the limited partners can claim according to their economic loss potential.

---

[36] Sec. 752(b).

[37] Reg. Sec. 1.752-1(a).

[38] This may be modified by the limited partner agreeing to assume some of the risk of economic loss despite his or her limited partner status. For example, a limited partner may guarantee the debt or may agree to reimburse the general partner some amount if the general partner has to pay the debt. These arrangements mean that the limited partner shares the risk of loss.

[39] Some nonrecourse debt allocations involve two steps before an allocation according to profits interests. These two steps of the allocation process are beyond the scope of this explanation.

The Sec. 752 Regulations require that recourse liabilities be allocated to the partner who will bear the economic loss if the partnership can not pay the debt. The Regulations provide a complex procedure using a hypothetical liquidation to determine who would bear the loss. In this text, it is assumed that the hypothetical liquidation analysis has been completed for you, and the appropriate shares of economic loss as determined by the hypothetical liquidation procedure are stated as part of the problem or example information.

EXAMPLE C9-27 ▶ The ABC Partnership has one general partner (Anna) and a limited partner (Clay) with the following partnership interests:

	Anna (General)	*Clay (Limited)*
Loss interest	80%	20%
Profits interest	60%	40%
Basis before liabilities	$100,000	$100,000

Clay has an obligation to make an additional contribution of $5,000. He has made no other agreements or guarantees. The partnership has two liabilities at year-end: a $300,000 nonrecourse debt and a $400,000 debt with recourse to the partnership. Clay has a risk of economic loss only to the extent that he has agreed to make additional contributions. The partners' year-end bases are calculated as follows:

	Anna (General)	*Clay (Limited)*
Year-end basis (excluding liabilities)	$100,000	$100,000
Share of:		
Recourse debt	395,000	5,000
Nonrecourse debt	180,000[a]	120,000[b]
Year-end basis	$675,000	$225,000

[a] 60% × $300,000 = $180,000
[b] 40% × $300,000 = $120,000 ◀

EFFECTS OF OPERATIONS

KEY POINT

Basis in a partnership interest is increased by the partner's share of partnership income. This basis increase is necessary so that when the previously taxed earnings are distributed, the partner is not taxed a second time.

A partner's basis is a summary of his or her contributions and the partnership's liabilities, earnings, losses, and distributions. Basis serves the major role of preventing a second tax levy on income that was taxed as a partner's distributive share when that income is subsequently distributed. Section 705 mandates a basis increase for additional contributions made by the partner to the partnership plus the partner's distributive share for the current and prior tax years of the following items:

- Taxable income of the partnership (both separately stated items and partnership ordinary income)
- Tax-exempt income of the partnership

Basis is decreased (but not below zero) by distributions from the partnership to the partner plus the partner's distributive share for the current and prior tax years of the following items:

- Losses of the partnership (both separately stated items and partnership ordinary loss)
- Expenditures that are not deductible for tax purposes and that are not capital expenditures

The positive basis adjustment for tax-exempt income and the negative basis adjustment for nondeductible expenses are made to preserve that tax treatment for the partner. If these adjustments are not made, tax-exempt income would be taxable to the partner when a subsequent distribution is made or upon the sale or other disposition of the partnership interest.

OBJECTIVE 8

Determine the limitations on a partner's deduction of partnership losses

LOSS LIMITS. Each partner is allocated his or her distributive share of ordinary income or loss and separately stated income, gain, loss, or deduction items each year. The income and gain items are always reported in the partner's current tax year and increase the partner's basis in the partnership interest. However, the partner may not be able to use his or her full distributive share of losses because Sec. 704(d) allows losses to be deducted only up to the amount of the partner's basis in the partnership interest before the loss. All positive basis adjustments for the year and all reductions for actual or deemed distributions must be made before determining the amount of the deductible loss.[40]

EXAMPLE C9-28 ▶

On January 1 of the current year, Miguel has a $32,000 basis for his general interest in the MT Partnership. He materially participates in the partnership's business activities. On December 1, Miguel receives a $1,000 cash distribution. His distributive share of MT's current items are a $4,000 net long-term capital gain and a $43,000 ordinary loss. Miguel's deductible loss is calculated as follows:

January 1 basis	$32,000
Minus: Distribution	(1,000)
Basis before current year results	$31,000
Plus: Long-term capital gain	4,000
Limit for loss deduction	$35,000

Miguel can deduct $35,000 of the ordinary loss in the current year, which reduces his basis to zero. The remaining $8,000 of ordinary loss cannot be deducted currently but can be deducted in the following year if Miguel has sufficient basis in his interest. ◀

SELF-STUDY QUESTION

What happens to losses that are disallowed due to lack of basis in a partnership interest?

ANSWER

The losses are indefinitely suspended until that partner obtains additional basis.

Any distributive share of loss that cannot be deducted because of the basis limit is simply noted in the partner's financial records. It is not reported on the partner's tax return, nor does it reduce the partner's basis. However, the losses can be carried forward until the partner has positive basis again from capital contributions, additional partnership borrowings, or partnership earnings.[41]

EXAMPLE C9-29 ▶

Assume the same facts as in Example C9-28. Miguel makes no additional contributions in the following year, and the MT Partnership's liabilities are unchanged. Miguel's distributive share of MT's partnership items in the following year is $2,500 of net short-term capital gain and $14,000 of ordinary income. These items restore his basis to $16,500 (0 + $2,500 + $14,000), and he can deduct the $8,000 loss carryover. After taking these transactions into account, Miguel's basis is $8,500 ($16,500 − $8,000). ◀

Topic Review C9-3 summarizes the rules for determining the initial basis for a partnership interest and the annual basis adjustments required to determine the interest's adjusted basis.

SPECIAL LOSS LIMITATIONS

Three sets of rules limit the loss from a partnership interest that a taxpayer may deduct. The Sec. 704(d) rules explained above limit losses to the partner's basis in the partnership interest. Two other rules establish more stringent limits. The at-risk rules limit losses to

[40] Reg. Sec. 1.704-1(d)(2).

[41] Reg. Sec. 1.704-1(d)(1).

Topic Review C9-3

Basis of a Partnership Interest

Method of Acquisition	Beginning Basis
Property contributed	Substituted basis from property contributed plus gain recognized for contributions to an investment partnership
Services contributed	Amount of income recognized for services rendered (plus any additional amount that is contributed)
Purchase	Cost
Gift	Donor's basis plus gift tax on appreciation
Inheritance	Fair market value at date of death or alternatve valuation date
	Liability Impact
Increase basis for	Increases in the partner's share of partnership liabilities Liabilities of the partnership assumed by the partner in his or her individual capacity
Decrease basis for	Decreases in the partner's share of partnership liabilities Liabilities of the partner assumed by the partnership
	Operations Impact
Increase basis for	Partner's share of separately stated income and gain items (including tax-exempt items) and ordinary income Additional contributions to the partnership Precontribution gain recognized.
Decrease basis for	Partner's share of separately stated loss and deduction items (including items that are not deductible for tax purposes and are not capital expenditures) and ordinary loss Precontribution loss recognized Distributions from the partnership to the partner

an amount called *at-risk basis*. The passive activity loss or credit limitation rules disallow most net passive activity losses.

AT-RISK LOSS LIMITATION

The Sec. 704(d) loss limitation rules were the only loss limits for many years. However, Congress became increasingly uncomfortable with allowing partners to increase their basis by a portion of the partnership's nonrecourse liabilities and then offset this basis with partnership losses. Accordingly, Congress established the **at-risk rules**, which limit loss deductions to the partner's at-risk basis. The **at-risk basis** is essentially the same amount as the regular partnership basis with the exception that liabilities increase the at-risk basis only if the partner is at risk for such an amount. The at-risk rules apply to individuals and closely held C corporations. Widely held C corporations are not subject to these rules.

KEY POINT

Before a loss can be deducted by a partner, the partner may need to satisfy as many as three different limitation provisions. In order of application, these limitations are (1) adequate partnership basis under Sec. 704(d), (2) the at-risk loss limitations, and (3) the passive activity limitations.

Although much of the complexity of the *at-risk* term is beyond the scope of this text, a simplified working definition is possible: A partner is at risk for an amount if he or she would lose that amount should the partnership suddenly become worthless. Because a partner would not have to pay a partnership's nonrecourse liabilities even if the partnership became worthless, the usual nonrecourse liabilities cannot be included in any partner's at-risk basis. Under the at-risk rules, the loss that a partner may deduct may be substantially less than the amount that was deductible when only the Sec. 704(d) rules applied.[42]

EXAMPLE C9-30 ▶ Keesha is a limited partner in the KM Manufacturing Partnership. At the end of the partnership's tax year, her basis in the interest is $30,000 ($10,000 investment plus a $20,000 share of nonrecourse financing). Keesha's distributive share of partnership losses for the tax year is $18,000. The at-risk rules limit her deduction to $10,000 because she is not at risk for the nonrecourse financing. ◀

TYPICAL MISCONCEPTION

The at-risk rules severely limit the use of nonrecourse debt to obtain loss deductions except for certain qualified real estate financing, yet this real estate loophole is more apparent than real because of the final set of rules that must be satisfied: the passive activity limitations.

There is one significant exception to the application of the at-risk rules. At-risk rules do not apply to nonrecourse debt if it is qualified real estate financing. The partner is at risk for his or her share of nonrecourse real estate financing if all of the following requirements are met:

- The financing is secured by real estate used in the partnership's real estate activity.
- The debt is not convertible to any kind of equity interest in the partnership.
- The financing is from a qualified person or from any federal, state, or local government, or is guaranteed by any federal, state, or local government.[43] A qualified person is an unrelated party who is in the trade or business of lending money (e.g., bank, financial institution, or mortgage broker).

PASSIVE ACTIVITY LIMITATIONS

KEY POINT

Section 469 and its accompanying regulations are extremely complex. Their biggest impact in the partnership area is probably that limited partners generally are considered passive. Therefore, even if the limited partner has both Sec. 704(d) and at-risk basis, losses that are generated from passive activities may be used only to offset other passive activity income or gains.

The 1986 Tax Reform Act added still a third set of limits to the loss that a partner may deduct: the passive activity loss and credit limitations.

Under the passive activity limitation rules of Sec. 469, all income is divided into three categories: amounts derived from passive activities; active income such as salary, bonuses, and income from businesses in which the taxpayer materially participates; and portfolio income such as dividends and interest. Generally, losses of an individual partner from a passive activity cannot be used to offset either active income or portfolio income. However, passive losses can be carried over to future years. These passive losses are allowed in full when a taxpayer disposes of the entire interest in the passive activity. Passive losses generated by a passive rental activity in which an individual partner is an active participant may be deducted up to a maximum of $25,000 in a year. This deduction is phased out by 50% of the amount of the partner's adjusted gross income (AGI) in excess of $100,000, so that there is no deduction if the partner has AGI of $150,000 or more. (The phase-out begins at $200,000 for low-income housing or rehabilitation credits.) Losses disallowed under the phase-out are deductible to the extent of passive income.

A passive activity is any trade or business in which the taxpayer does not materially participate. A taxpayer who owns a limited partnership interest in any activity generally fails the material participation test. Accordingly, losses from most limited partnership interests can be used only to offset income from passive activities.[44]

Although passive activity limits may greatly affect the taxable income or loss reported by a partner, they have no unusual effect on basis. Basis is reduced (but not below zero) by the partner's distributive share of losses whether or not the losses may be deducted under the passive loss rules.[45] When the suspended passive losses later become deductible, the partner's basis in the partnership interest is not affected.

[42] Sec. 465(a).
[43] Sec. 465(b)(6).
[44] Sec. 469(h)(2).
[45] S. Rept. No. 99-313, 99th Cong., 2d Sess., p. 723, footnote 4 (1986).

EXAMPLE C9-31 ▶ Chris purchases a 20% capital and profits interest in the CJ Partnership in 1997, but he does not participate in CJ's business. Chris owns no other passive investments. Chris's distributive share of the CJ Partnership's loss for 1997 is $60,000. His Sec. 704(d) basis in CJ is $80,000, and his at-risk basis is $70,000. Chris's Sec. 704(d) basis is $20,000 ($80,000 − $60,000) and his at-risk basis is $10,000 ($70,000 − $60,000) after the results of 1997's operations are taken into account. However, Chris cannot deduct any of the CJ loss in 1997 because it is a passive activity loss. ◀

KEY POINT

The $60,000 loss in Example C9-31, which was disallowed because of the passive activity limitations, can be used in a subsequent year if passive income is generated. Because the $60,000 loss has already reduced basis for purposes of both Sec. 704(d) and the at-risk rules, the disallowed loss need not be tested against those rules a second time.

TRANSACTIONS BETWEEN A PARTNER AND THE PARTNERSHIP

The partner and the partnership are treated as separate entities for many transactions. Section 707(b) restricts the use of sales of property between the partner and partnership by disallowing certain losses and converting certain capital gains into ordinary income. Section 707(c) permits a partnership to make guaranteed payments for capital and services to a partner that are separate from the partner's distributive share. Each of these rules is explored below.

SALES OF PROPERTY

KEY POINT

Losses on sales between persons and certain related partnerships are disallowed, similar to the related party rules of Sec. 267. The concern is that tax losses can be artificially recognized without the property being disposed of outside the economic group.

KEY POINT

One of the complicating factors of the loss disallowance rules is the application of the attribution rules of Sec. 267(c) in determining what percentage a person is deemed to own in a partnership.

LOSS SALES. Without restrictions to prevent it, a controlling partner could sell property to the partnership to recognize a loss for tax purposes while retaining a substantial interest in the property through ownership of a partnership interest. Congress closed the door to such loss recognition with the Sec. 707(b) rules.

The rules for partnership loss transactions are quite similar to the Sec. 267 related party rules discussed in Chapter C3. Under Sec. 707(b)(1), no loss can be deducted on the sale or exchange of property between a partnership and a person who directly or indirectly owns more than 50% of the partnership's capital or profits interests. (Indirect ownership includes ownership by related parties such as members of the partner's family.[46]) Similarly, losses are disallowed on sales or exchanges of property between two partnerships in which the same persons own, directly or indirectly, more than 50% of the capital or profits interests. If a loss is disallowed under Sec. 707(b)(1), any subsequent gain realized on a sale of the property by the purchaser can be reduced by the previously disallowed loss.

EXAMPLE C9-32 ▶ Jamail, Kareem, and Takedra own equal interests in the JKT Partnership. Kareem and Takedra are siblings but Jamail is unrelated to the others. For purposes of Sec. 707, Kareem owns 66.66% of the partnership (33.33% directly and 33.33% indirectly from Takedra). Likewise, Takedra also owns 66.66%, but Jamail has only a direct ownership interest of 33.33%. ◀

EXAMPLE C9-33 ▶ Pat sold land having a $45,000 basis to the PTA Partnership for $35,000, its FMV. If Pat has a 60% capital and profits interest in the partnership, a $10,000 loss on the sale is realized, but not recognized by Pat. If Pat owns only a 49% interest, directly and indirectly, he can recognize the loss. ◀

[46] For purposes of Sec. 707, related parties include an individual and members of his or her family (spouse, brothers, sisters, lineal descendants, and ancestors), an individual and a more-than-50%-owned corporation, and two corporations that are members of the same controlled group.

EXAMPLE C9-34 ▶ Assume the same facts as in Example C9-33, except that the land is later sold by the partnership for $47,000. The partnership's realized gain is $12,000 ($47,000 − $35,000 basis). If Pat has a 60% capital and profits interest, his previously disallowed loss of $10,000 reduces the partnership's recognized gain to $2,000. This $2,000 gain is then allocated to the partners according to the partnership agreement. ◀

KEY POINT

If a gain is recognized on the sale of a capital asset between a partnership and a person who owns more than 50% of the partnership (or between two commonly controlled partnerships), and the property is not a capital asset to the transferee, then the character of the gain is ordinary.

GAIN SALES. When gain is recognized on the sale of a capital asset between a partnership and a related partner, Sec. 707(b)(2) requires that the gain be ordinary (and not capital gain) if the property will not be a capital asset to its new owner. Sales or exchanges resulting in the application of Sec. 707(b)(2) include transfers between (1) a partnership and a person who owns, directly or indirectly, more than 50% of the partnership's capital or profits interests, or (2) two partnerships in which the same persons own, directly or indirectly, more than 50% of the capital or profits interests.[47] This provision was added to prevent related parties from increasing the depreciable basis of assets (and therefore reducing future ordinary income) at the cost of recognizing a current capital gain.

EXAMPLE C9-35 ▶ Sharon and Tony have the following capital and profits interests in two partnerships:

Partner	*ST Partnership (%)*	*QRS Partnership (%)*
Sharon	42	58
Tony	42	30
Other unrelated partners	16	12
Total	100	100

The ST Partnership sells land having a $150,000 basis to the QRS Partnership for $180,000. The land was a capital asset for the ST Partnership, but QRS intends to subdivide and sell the land. Because the land is ordinary income property to the QRS Partnership and Sharon and Tony control both partnerships, the ST Partnership must recognize $30,000 of ordinary income on the land sale. ◀

GUARANTEED PAYMENTS

OBJECTIVE 9

Determine the tax consequences of a guaranteed payment

A corporate shareholder can be an employee of the corporation. However, a partner generally is not an employee of the partnership, and most fringe benefits are disallowed for a partner who is employed by his or her partnership.[48]

It is only reasonable that a partner who provides services to the partnership in an ongoing relationship might be compensated like any other employee. Code Sec. 707(c) provides for just this kind of payment and labels it a **guaranteed payment**. The term *guaranteed payment* also includes certain payments made to a partner for the use of invested capital that are similar to interest. Both types of guaranteed payments must be payments that are determined without regard to the partnership's income.[49] Conceptually, this requirement separates guaranteed payments from distributive shares. As indicated below, however, such a distinction may not be so clear in practice.

TYPICAL MISCONCEPTION

If a partner, acting in his or her capacity as a partner, receives payments from the partnership that are determined without regard to the partnership's income, the partner has received a guaranteed payment. If the partner is acting as a nonpartner, the partner is treated as any other outside contractor.

DETERMINING THE GUARANTEED PAYMENT. Sometimes the determination of the guaranteed payment is quite simple. For example, some guaranteed payments are expressed as specific amounts (e.g., $20,000 per year), with the partner also receiving his or her normal distributive share. Other times the guaranteed payment is expressed as a **guaranteed minimum**. However, these guaranteed minimum arrangements make it

[47] Sec. 707(b)(2).

[48] Rev. Rul. 91-26, 1991-1 C.B. 184, holds that accident and health insurance premiums paid for a partner by the partnership are guaranteed payments.

[49] Sec. 707(c).

difficult to distinguish the partner's distributive share and guaranteed payment amounts because there is no guaranteed payment under this arrangement unless the partner's distributive share is less than his or her guaranteed minimum.

EXAMPLE C9-36 ▶ Tina manages the real estate owned by the TAV Partnership, in which she is also a partner. She receives 30% of all partnership income before guaranteed payments, but no less than $60,000 per year. In the current year, the TAV Partnership reports $300,000 in ordinary income. Tina's 30% distributive share is $90,000 (0.30 × $300,000), which is greater than her $60,000 guaranteed minimum amount. Therefore, she has no guaranteed payment. ◀

EXAMPLE C9-37 ▶ Assume the same facts as in Example C9-36, except that the TAV Partnership reports $150,000 of ordinary income. Tina has a guaranteed payment of $15,000, which represents the difference between her $45,000 distributive share (0.30 × $150,000) and her $60,000 guaranteed minimum.[50] ◀

TAX IMPACT OF GUARANTEED PAYMENTS. Like salary or interest income, guaranteed payments are always ordinary income to the recipient. The guaranteed payment must be included in income for the recipient partner's tax year during which the partnership year ends and the partnership deducts or capitalizes the payments.[51]

EXAMPLE C9-38 ▶ In January 1998, a calendar-year taxpayer, Will, receives a $10,000 guaranteed payment from the WRS Partnership. WRS capitalizes the payment during its tax year ending on November 30, 1997. Will must report his guaranteed payment in his 1997 tax return because that return includes the 1997 partnership income that reflects the impact of the guaranteed payment. ◀

KEY POINT

The effect of a guaranteed payment is that the partner recognizes ordinary income and the partnership deducts or capitalizes the payments. A partner recognizes the income in the partner's tax year during which the partnership tax year ends regardless of when the payment is received. Example C9-38 illustrates this point.

For the partnership, the guaranteed payment is treated as if it is made to an outsider. If the payment is for a service that is a capital expenditure (e.g., architectural services for designing a building for the partnership), the guaranteed payment must be capitalized and, if allowable, amortized. If the payment is for a service that is deductible under Sec. 162, the payment can be deducted from ordinary income. Deductible guaranteed payments can offset the partnership's ordinary income but never its capital gains. If the guaranteed payment exceeds the partnership's ordinary income, the payment creates an ordinary loss that is allocated among the partners.[52]

EXAMPLE C9-39 ▶ Tarek is a partner in the STU Partnership. He is to receive a guaranteed payment for deductible services of $60,000 and 30% of partnership income computed after deducting the guaranteed payment. The partnership reports $40,000 of ordinary income and a $120,000 long-term capital gain before deducting the guaranteed payment. Tarek's income from the partnership is determined as follows:

		Tarek's Share	
	STU Partnership	*Ratable Share*	*Amount*
Ordinary income (before guaranteed payment)	$ 40,000		
Minus: Guaranteed payment	(60,000)	100%	$60,000
Ordinary loss	($20,000)	30%	(6,000)
Long-term capital gain	$120,000	30%	36,000 ◀

[50] Reg. Sec. 1.707-1(c), Exs. (1) and (2).
[51] Reg. Secs. 1.707-1(c) and 1.706-1(a).
[52] Reg. Sec. 1.707-1(c), Ex. (4).

FAMILY PARTNERSHIPS

CAPITAL OWNERSHIP

OBJECTIVE 10

Explain the requirements for recognizing the holder of a partnership interest as a partner in a family partnership

Because each partner reports and pays taxes on a distributive share of partnership income, a family partnership is an excellent way to spread income among family members and minimize the family's tax bill. However, in order to accomplish this tax minimization goal, the family members must be accepted by the IRS as real partners. The question of whether someone is a partner in a family partnership is often litigated, but there are safe-harbor rules that provide clear answers if a capital interest is owned in a family partnership. Under Sec. 704(e), three tests must be met: the partnership interest must be a capital interest, capital must be a material income-producing factor in the partnership's business activity, and the family member must be the true owner of the interest.

A capital interest gives the partner the right to receive assets if the partnership liquidates immediately upon the partner's acquisition of the interest. Capital is a material income-producing factor if substantial portions of gross income are derived from the use of capital. For example, capital is a material income-producing factor if the business has substantial inventory or significant investment in plant or equipment. Capital is seldom considered to be a material income-producing factor in a service business.[53]

KEY POINT

In certain situations, family partnerships provide an excellent tax-planning tool, but the family members must be real partners. The rules that determine who is a real partner in a family partnership are guided by the assignment-of-income principle.

The remaining question is whether the family member is the true owner of the interest. Ownership is seldom questioned if one family member purchases the interest at a market price from another family member. However, when the interest is gifted from one family member to another, the major question is whether the donor retains so much control over the partnership interest that the donor is still the owner of the interest. If the donor still controls the interest, the donor is taxed on the distributive share.

KEY POINT

A major problem in creating a family partnership is that when the donor gifts the partnership interest to the donee family member, the donor is often not willing to give up complete control of the gifted partnership interest.

DONOR RETAINED CONTROl. There is no mechanical test that indicates whether the donor has retained too much control, but there are several factors that may indicate a problem:[54]

- Retention of control over distributions of income can be a problem unless the retention occurs with the agreement of all partners or if the retention is for the reasonable needs of the business.
- Retention of control over assets that are essential to the partnership's business can indicate too much control by the donor.
- Limitation of the donee partner's right to sell or liquidate his or her interest may indicate that the donor has not relinquished full control over the interest.
- Retention of management control that is inconsistent with normal partnership arrangements can be another sign that the donor retains control. This situation is not considered a fatal problem unless it occurs in conjunction with a significant limit on the donee's ability to sell or liquidate his or her interest.

If the donor has not directly or indirectly retained too much control, the donee is a full partner. As a partner, the donee must report the distributive share of income.

KEY POINT

A valid family partnership is a useful method for splitting income between family members. However, the distributive share of income from a partnership interest to a partner under age 14 is subject to the "kiddie tax."

MINOR DONEES. When income splitting is the goal of a family, the appropriate donee for the partnership interest is often a minor. With the problem of donor-retained controls in mind, it becomes obvious that gifts to minors should be made with great attention to detail. Further, note that net unearned income of a child under age 14 is

[53] Reg. Sec. 1.704-1(e)(1)(iv).

[54] Reg. Sec. 1.704-1(e)(2)(ii).

taxed to the child at the parents' marginal tax rate. This provision removes much of the incentive to transfer family partnership interests to young children, but there are still significant tax advantages to gifting partnership interests to minors who are age 14 or older.

DONOR-DONEE ALLOCATIONS OF INCOME

OBJECTIVE 11

Determine the allocation of partnership income between a donor and a donee of a partnership interest

Partnership income must be properly allocated between a donor and a donee in order to be accepted by the IRS. Note that only the allocation between the donor and donee is questioned, and there is no impact on the distributive shares of any other partners.

There are two requirements for the donor-donee allocations. First, the donor must be allocated reasonable compensation for services rendered to the partnership. Then, after reasonable compensation is allocated to the donor, any remaining partnership income must be allocated based on relative capital interests.[55] Note that this allocation scheme apparently overrides the partnership's ability to make special allocations of income.

EXAMPLE C9-40

Andrew, a 40% partner in the ABC Partnership, gives one-half of his interest to his brother, John. During the current year Andrew performs services for the partnership for which reasonable compensation is $65,000, but for which he accepts no pay. Andrew and John are each credited with a $100,000 distributive share, all of which is ordinary income. Reallocation between Andrew and John is necessary to reflect the value of Andrew's services.

Total distributive shares for the brothers	$200,000
Minus: Reasonable compensation for Andrew	(65,000)
Income to allocate	$135,000

John's distributive share: $\frac{20\%}{40\%} \times \$135,000 = \$67,500$

Andrew's distributive share: $\left(\frac{20\%}{40\%} \times \$135,000\right) + \$65,000 = \$132,500$

ETHICAL POINT

CPAs have a responsibility to review an entity's conduct of its activities to be sure it is operating as a partnership. If a partnership interest is received as a gift and the donee is not the true owner of the interest (e.g., the donor retains too much control over the donee's interest), then the partnership return must be filed without a distributive share of income or loss being allocated to the donee.

TAX PLANNING CONSIDERATIONS

TIMING OF LOSS RECOGNITION

The loss limitation rules provide a unique opportunity for tax planning. For example, if a partner knows that his or her distributive share of active losses from a partnership for a tax year will exceed the Sec. 704 limit for deducting losses, he or she should carefully examine the tax situation for the current and upcoming tax years. Substantial current personal income may make immediate use of the loss desirable. Current income may be taxed at a higher marginal tax rate than future income because of, for example, an extraordinarily good current year, an expected retirement, or a decrease in future years' tax rates. If the partner chooses to use the loss in the current year, additional contributions can be made just before year-end (perhaps even from funds that the partner borrows, as long as the additional benefit exceeds the cost of the funds). Alternatively, one partner may convince the other partners to incur additional partnership liabilities so that each partner's basis increases. This last strategy should be exercised with caution unless there is a business reason (rather than solely a tax reason) for the borrowing.

KEY POINT

If a partner is unable to use all of his or her share of partnership losses due to a lack of basis, contributions to capital or increasing partnership liabilities may provide the additional needed tax basis. If the passive activity limitation rules are the reason that the partnership losses cannot be used, then the possibility of investing in passive activities that generate passive income may be the best planning alternative.

[55] Sec. 704(e)(2).

EXAMPLE C9-41 ▶ Ted, a 60% general partner in the ST Partnership, expects to be allocated partnership losses of $120,000 for 1997 from a partnership in which he materially participates, but where his partnership basis is only $90,000. Because he has a marginal tax rate of 39.6% for 1997 (and anticipates only a 28% marginal tax rate for 1998), Ted wants to use the ST Partnership losses to offset his 1997 income. He could make a capital contribution to raise his basis by $30,000. Alternatively, he could get the partnership to incur $50,000 in additional liabilities, which would increase his basis by his $30,000 ($50,000 × 0.60) share of the liability. The partnership's $50,000 borrowing must serve a business purpose for the ST Partnership. ◀

Alternatively, a partner may determine that it is better to delay the deduction of partnership losses that exceed the current year's loss limitation. This situation could occur if the partner has little current year income and expects substantial income in the following year. If the partner has loss, deduction, or credit carryovers that expire in the current year, a deferral of the distributive share of partnership losses to the following year may be desirable. If the partner opts to deduct the loss in a later year, he or she needs only to leave things alone so that the distributive share of losses exceeds the loss limitation for the current year.

COMPLIANCE AND PROCEDURAL CONSIDERATIONS

REPORTING TO THE IRS AND THE PARTNERS

OBJECTIVE 12

Determine the requirements for filing a partnership tax return

HISTORICAL NOTE

Turn to the partnership K-1 in Appendix B of this book. The large number of items that now have to be separately stated illustrates how certain tax laws, such as the passive activity limitation rules and the investment interest limitation rules, have complicated the preparation of Form 1065.

FORMS. Within 3½ months after the end of the partnership tax year, the partnership must file a Form 1065 with the IRS. (See Appendix B for a completed Form 1065.) The IRS can allow reasonable extensions of time of up to six months, although initial extensions are usually limited to sixty days. Penalties are imposed for failure to file a timely or complete partnership return. Because the partnership is only a conduit, Form 1065 is an information return and is not accompanied by any tax payment.[56] Included on the front page of Form 1065 are all the items of income, gain, loss and deduction that are not separately stated. Schedule K of Form 1065 reports both a summary of the ordinary income items and the partnership total of the items that are separately stated. Schedule K-1, which must be prepared for each partner, reflects that partner's distributive share of partnership income including his or her special allocations. The partner's Schedule K-1 is notification of his or her share of partnership items for use in calculating income taxes and self-employment taxes.

SEC. 444 ELECTION AND REQUIRED PAYMENTS. A partnership can elect to use a tax year other than a required year by filing an election under Sec. 444. This election is made by filing Form 8716 (Election to Have a Tax Year Other Than a Required Tax Year) by the earlier of the fifteenth day of the fifth month following the month that includes the first day of the tax year for which the election is effective or the due date (without regard to extension) of the income tax return resulting from the Sec. 444 election. In addition, a copy of the Form 8716 must be attached to the partnership's Form 1065 for the first tax year for which the Sec. 444 election is made.

[56] Reg. Sec. 301.6031-1(e)(2). Although the partnership pays no income tax, it still must pay the employer's share of social security taxes and any unemployment taxes as well as withhold income taxes from its employees' salaries.

A partnership making a Sec. 444 election needs to annually make a required payment under Sec. 7519. The required payment has the effect of collecting a deposit from the partnership equal to the tax (at the highest individual tax rate plus one percentage point) on the partnership's deferred income.

KEY POINT

Because the required payment is in the nature of a refundable deposit, the partnership is entitled to a refund, if the partnership terminates the Sec. 444 election, the partnership liquidates, or the required payment is less than last year's deposit.

A partnership can obtain a refund if past payments exceed the tentative payment due on the deferred income for the current year. Similar refunds are available if the partnership terminates a Sec. 444 election or liquidates. The required payments are not deductible by the partnership and are not passed through to a partner. The required payments are in the nature of a refundable deposit.

The Sec. 7519 required payment is due on or before May 15th of the calendar year following the calendar year in which the election year begins. The required payment is paid with Form 8752 (Required Payment or Refund Under Section 7519) along with a computational worksheet, which is illustrated in the instructions to the Form 1065. Refunds of excess required payments are also obtained by filing the Form 8752.

ESTIMATED TAXES. Because the partnership pays no income taxes, the partnership makes no estimated tax payments. However, the partners must make estimated tax payments based on their separate tax positions including their distributive share of partnership income or loss for the current year. It should be emphasized that the partners are not making separate estimated tax payments for their partnership income, but rather are including the effects of the partnership's results in the calculation of their normal estimated tax payments.

SELF-EMPLOYMENT INCOME. Every partnership must report the net earnings (or loss) for the partnership that constitute self-employment income to the partners. The instructions to the Form 1065 contain a worksheet to make such a calculation. The partnership's self-employment income includes both guaranteed payments, partnership ordinary income and loss, and separately stated items, but generally excludes capital gains and losses, Sec. 1231 gains and losses, interest, dividends, and rentals. The distributive share of the self-employment income for each partner is shown on a Schedule K-1 and is included with other self-employment income in determining a partner's self-employment tax liability (Schedule SE, Form 1040). The distributive share of partnership income allocable to a limited partner is not self-employment income.

EXAMPLE C9-42 ▶ Anwer is a general partner in the AB Partnership. Anwer's share of partnership items for the year includes ordinary income of $15,000 and short-term capital gains of $9,000. (The ordinary income does not include any ordinary losses from sales of Sec. 1231 property.) In addition, Anwer receives an $18,000 guaranteed payment for his work in the partnership's business. Anwer's self-employment income is $33,000 ($15,000 + $18,000). ◀

EXAMPLE C9-43 ▶ Assume the same facts as in Example C9-42 except that Anwer is a limited partner. His self-employment income includes only the $18,000 guaranteed payment. ◀

IRS AUDIT PROCEDURES

Any questions arising during an IRS audit about a partnership item must be determined at the partnership level (instead of at the partner level).[57] Section 6231(a)(3) defines **partnership items** as virtually all items that are reported by the partnership for the tax year including tax preference items, credit recapture items, guaranteed payments, and

[57] Sec. 6221.

the at-risk amount. In fact, almost every item that can appear on the partnership return is treated as a partnership item. Each partner must either report partnership items in a manner consistent with the Schedule K-1 received from the partnership or notify the IRS of the inconsistent treatment.[58]

KEY POINT

To alleviate the administrative nightmare of having to audit each partner of a partnership, Congress has authorized the IRS to conduct audits of partnerships in a unified proceeding at the partnership level. This process is more efficient and should provide greater consistency in the treatment of the individual partners than the previous system.

The IRS can bring a single proceeding at the partnership level to determine the characterization or tax impact of any partnership item. All partners have the right to participate in the administrative proceedings, and the IRS must offer a consistent settlement to all partners.

A **tax matters partner** is generally assigned to facilitate communication between the IRS and the partners of a large partnership and to serve as the primary representative of the partnership.[59] The tax matters partner is a partner designated by the partnership or, if no one is so designated, the general partner having the largest profits interest at the close of the partnership's tax year.

It should be noted, however, that these audit procedures do not apply to small partnerships. For this purpose, a small partnership is defined as one having no more than ten partners who must be either natural persons (but excluding nonresident aliens) or estates. In counting partners, a husband and wife (or their estates) count as a single partner. In addition, there can be no special allocations if the partnership is to qualify under these rules.[60] Further, the IRS has announced in Rev. Proc. 84-35 that a partnership can be excluded from the audit procedures only if it can be established that all partners fully reported their shares of partnership items on timely filed tax returns.[61]

PROBLEM MATERIALS

DISCUSSION QUESTIONS

C9-1 Yong and Li plan to begin a business that will grow plants for sale to retail nurseries. They expect to have substantial losses for the first three years of operations while they develop their plants and their sales operations. Both Yong and Li have substantial interest income, and both expect to work full-time in this new business. List three advantages for operating this business as a partnership instead of a C corporation.

C9-2 Bob and Carol want to open a bed and breakfast inn as soon as they buy and renovate a turn-of-the-century home. What would be the major disadvantage of using a general partnership rather than a corporation for this business?

C9-3 Sam, a 39.6% tax bracket taxpayer, wants to help his brother, Lou, start a new business. Lou is a capable auto mechanic, but has little business sense, so he needs Sam to help him make business decisions. Should this partnership be arranged as a general partnership or a limited partnership? Why?

C9-4 Doug contributes services but no property to the CD Partnership when it is being formed. What are the tax implications of his receiving only a profits interest versus his receiving a capital and profits interest?

C9-5 An existing partner wants to contribute property having a basis that is less than its FMV for an additional interest in a partnership.

a. Should he contribute the property to the partnership?

b. What are his other options?

c. Explain the tax implications for the partner of these other options.

---

[58] Sec. 6222.

[59] Sec. 6231(a)(7).

[60] Sec. 6231(a)(1)(B).

[61] 1984-1 C.B. 509.

C9-6 Jane contributes valuable property to a partnership in exchange for a general partnership interest. The partnership also assumes the recourse mortgage Jane incurred when she purchased the property two years ago.

a. How will the liability affect the amount of gain that Jane must recognize?
b. How will it affect her basis in the partnership interest?

C9-7 Which of the following items can be amortized as part of a partnership's organizational expenditures?

a. Legal fees for drawing up the partnership agreement
b. Accounting fees for establishing an accounting system
c. Fees for securing an initial working capital loan
d. Filing fees required under state law in initial year to conduct business in the state
e. Accounting fees for preparation of initial short-period tax return
f. Transportation costs for acquiring machinery essential to the partnership's business
g. Syndication expenses

C9-8 The BW Partnership reported the following current year earnings: $30,000 interest from tax exempt bonds, $50,000 long-term capital gain and, $100,000 in Sec. 702(a)(8) income. Bob saw these numbers and told his partner, Wendy, that the partnership had $100,000 of taxable income. Is he correct? Explain your answer.

C9-9 Which of the following items must be separately stated in determining partnership income?

a. Sec. 1245 gains
b. Tax-exempt interest
c. Dividends
d. Investment interest income
e. Specially allocated depreciation
f. Ordinary loss from operations
g. Sec. 1231 gains

C9-10 How will a partner's distributive share be determined if one-half of her beginning-of-the-year partnership interest is sold at the beginning of the tenth month of the partnership's tax year?

C9-11 Can a recourse debt of a partnership increase the basis of a limited partner's partnership interest? Explain.

C9-12 The ABC Partnership has a nonrecourse liability that it incurred by borrowing from an unrelated bank; it is secured by an apartment building owned and managed by the partnership. The liability is not convertible into an equity interest. How does this liability affect the at-risk basis of general partner Anna and limited partner Bob?

C9-13 Is the Sec. 704(d) loss limitation rule more or less restrictive than the at-risk rules? Explain.

C9-14 Jeff, a 10% limited partner in the recently formed JRS Partnership, expects to have losses from the partnership for several more years. He is considering the purchase of an interest in a profitable general partnership in which he will materially participate. Will the purchase allow him to use his losses from the JRS Partnership?

C9-15 Helen, a 55% partner in the ABC Partnership, owns land (a capital asset) having a $20,000 basis and a $25,000 FMV. She plans to sell the land tothe ABC Partnership, which will subdivide the land and sell the lots. Would you advise Helen to make the sale? Why or why not?

C9-16 What is the difference between a guaranteed payment that is a guaranteed amount and one that is a guaranteed minimum?

C9-17 The TUV Partnership is considering two compensation schemes for Tracy, the partner who runs the business on a daily basis. Tracy can be given a $10,000 guaranteed payment or she can be given a larger distributive share (and distribution) so that she receives about $10,000 more each year. From the standpoint of when the income must be reported in Tracy's tax return, are these two compensation alternatives the same?

C9-18 Roy's father gives him a capital interest in Family Partnership. Will the Sec. 704(e) family partnership rules apply to this interest?

C9-19 Andrew gives his brother Steve a 20% interest in the AS Partnership and he retains a 30% interest. Andrew works for the partnership but is not paid. How will this affect the income from the AS Partnership that is reported by Andrew and Steve?

ISSUE IDENTIFICATION QUESTIONS

C9-20 Bob and Kate form the BK Partnership, a general partnership, as equal partners. Bob contributes an office building with a $130,000 FMV and a $95,000 adjusted basis to the partnership along with a $60,000 mortgage which is assumed by the partnership. Kate contributes the land on which the building sits with a $50,000 FMV and a $75,000 adjusted basis. Kate will manage the partnership for the first five years of operations but will not receive a guaranteed payment for her work in the first year of partnership operations. Starting with the second year of partnership operations, Kate will receive a $10,000 guaranteed payment for each year she manages the partnership. What tax issues should Bob, Kate and the BK Partnership consider with respect to the formation and operation of the partnership?

C9-21 Suzanne and Laura form a partnership to market local crafts. In April, the women spent $400 searching for a retail outlet, $1,200 to have a partnership agreement drawn up, and $300 to have an accounting system established. During April, they signed contracts with a number of local crafters to feature their products in the retail outlet. The outlet was fitted and merchandise organized during May. In June, the store opened and the first crafts were sold. The partnership paid $100 to an accountant to prepare an income statement for the month of June. What tax issues should the partnership consider with regard to the beginning of this business?

C9-22 Cara, a CPA, established an accounting system for the ABC Partnership and received a 10% profits interest (but no capital interest) in the partnership in return for her services. Her usual fee for the services would be approximately $6,000. No sales of profits interests in the ABC Partnership occurred during the current year. What tax issues should Cara and the ABC Partnership consider with respect to the payment made for the services?

C9-23 George, a limited partner in the EFG Partnership, has a 20% interest in partnership capital, profits, and losses. His basis in the partnership interest is $15,000 before accounting for events of the current year. In December of the current year, the EFG Partnership repaid a $100,000 nonrecourse liability. The partnership earned $20,000 of ordinary income this year. What tax issues should George consider with respect to reporting the results of this year's activities for the EFG Partnership on his personal return?

C9-24 Katie works forty hours a week as a clerk in the mall and earns $20,000. In addition, she works five hours each week in the JKL Partnership's office. Katie, a 10% limited partner in the JKL Partnership, has been allocated a $2,100 loss from the partnership for the current year. The basis for her interest in JKL before accounting for current operations is $5,000. What tax issues should Katie consider with respect to her interest in, and employment by, the JKL Partnership?

C9-25 Daniel has no family to inherit his 80% capital and profits interest in the CD Partnership. To ensure the continuation of the business, he gives a 20% capital and profits interest in the partnership to David, his best friend's son, on the condition that David work in the partnership for at least five years. David receives guaranteed payments for his work. Daniel takes no salary from the partnership, but he devotes all of his time to the business operations of the partnership. What tax issues should Daniel and David consider with respect to the gift of the partnership interest and Daniel's employment arrangement with the partnership?

PROBLEMS

C9-26 ***Formation of a Partnership.*** Suzanne and Bob form the SB General Partnership as equal partners. They make the following contributions:

Individual	*Asset*	*Basis to Partner*	*FMV*
Suzanne	Cash	$45,000	$ 45,000
	Inventory (securities)	14,000	15,000
Bob	Land	45,000	40,000
	Building	50,000	100,000

The SB Partnership assumes the $80,000 recourse mortgage on the building that Bob contributes, and the partners share the economic risk of loss on the mortgage equally. Bob has claimed $40,000 in straight-line depreciation under the MACRS rules on the building. Suzanne is a stockbroker and contributed securities from her inventory. The partnership will hold them as an investment.

a. What are the amount and character of the gain or loss that each partner must recognize on the formation of the partnership?

b. What is each partner's basis in their partnership interest?

c. What is the partnership's basis in each asset?

d. The partnership holds the securities for two years and then sells them for $20,000. What are the amount and character of the gain that the partnership and each partner will report?

C9-27 ***Formation of a Partnership.*** On May 31, six brothers decided to form the Grimm Brothers Partnership to publish and print children's stories. The contributions of the brothers and their partnership interests are listed below. They share the economic risk of loss from liabilities according to their partnership interests.

Individual	*Asset*	*Basis to Partner*	*FMV*	*Partnership Interest*
Al	Cash	$15,000	$ 15,000	15%
Bob	Accounts receivable	—0—	20,000	20%
Clay	Office equipment	13,000	15,000	15%
Dave	Land	50,000	15,000	15%
Ed	Building	15,000	150,000	20%
Fred	Services	?	15,000	15%

Other information about the contributions may be of interest, as follows:

- Bob contributes accounts receivable from his proprietorship, which uses the cash method of accounting.
- Clay uses the office equipment in a small business he owns. When he joins the partnership, he sells the remaining business assets to an outsider. MACRS depreciation of $8,000 has been claimed on the office equipment.
- The partnership assumes a $130,000 mortgage on the building Ed contributes. Ed claimed $100,000 of straight-line MACRS depreciation on the commercial property.
- Fred, an attorney, drew up all the partnership agreements and filed the necessary paperwork. He receives a full 15% capital and profits interest for his services.

a. How much gain, loss, or income must each partner recognize as a result of the formation?

b. How much gain, loss, or income must the partnership recognize as a result of the formation?
c. What is each partner's basis in his partnership interest?
d. What is the partnership's basis in its assets?
e. What effects do the depreciation recapture provisions have on the property contributions?
f. How would your answer to Part a change if Fred received only a profits interest?
g. What are the tax consequences to the partners and the partnership when the land contributed by Dave, which has been held as an investment by the partnership for two years, is sold by the partnership for $9,000?

C9-28 *Formation of a Partnership.* On January 1, Julie, Kay, and Susan decide to form a partnership. The contributions of the three individuals are listed below. Julie and Susan each received a 30% partnership interest and Kay received a 40% partnership interest. They share the economic risk of loss from recourse liabilities according to their partnership interests.

Individual	*Asset*	*Basis to Partner*	*FMV*
Julie	Accounts receivable	$—0—	$ 30,000
Kay	Land	50,000	20,000
	Building	30,000	110,000
Susan	Services	?	30,000

Kay has claimed $60,000 of straight-line MACRS depreciation on the building. The building has a $90,000 mortgage, which is assumed by the partnership. Susan is an attorney and the services she contributes are the drawing-up of all partnership agreements.

a. What are the amount and character of the gain, loss, or income recognized by each partner on the formation of the partnership?
b. What is each partner's basis in her partnership interest?
c. What is the partnership's basis in each of its assets?
d. If the partnership sells the land contributed by Kay for $18,000, what is each partner's distributive share?

C9-29 *Contribution of Services.* Sean is admitted to the XYZ Partnership in December of the current year in return for his services managing the partnership's business during the year. The partnership reports ordinary income of $100,000 for the current year without considering this transaction.

a. What are the tax consequences to Sean and the XYZ Partnership if Sean receives a 20% capital and profits interest in the partnership with a $75,000 FMV?
b. What are the tax consequences to Sean and the XYZ Partnership if Sean receives only a 20% profits interest with no determinable FMV?

C9-30 *Contribution of Services and Property.* Marjorie works for a large firm whose business is to find suitable real estate, establish a limited partnership to purchase the property, and then sell the limited partnership interests. In the current year, Marjorie received a 5% limited partnership interest in the Eldorado Limited Partnership. Marjorie received this interest partially in payment for her services in selling partnership interests to others, but she was also required to contribute $5,000 in cash to the partnership. Similar limited partnership interests sold for $20,000 at approximately the same time that Marjorie received her interest. What are the tax consequences for Marjorie and the Eldorado Limited Partnership of Marjorie's receipt of the partnership interest?

C9-31 ***Partnership Tax Year.*** The BCD Partnership is being formed and will be owned equally by Beth, Cindy, and Delux Corporation. The partners' tax year-ends are June 30 for Beth, September 30 for Cindy, and October 31 for Delux. The BCD Partnership's natural business year ends on January 31.

a. What tax year(s) can the partnership elect without IRS permission?
b. What tax year(s) can the partnership elect with IRS permission?
c. How would your answers to Parts a and b change if Beth, Cindy, and Delux own 4%, 4%, and 92%, respectively, of the partnership?

C9-32 ***Partnership Tax Year.*** The BCD Partnership is formed in April of the current year. The three equal partners, Bipin, Carlos, and Damien have had tax years ending on December 31, August 30, and December 31, respectively, for the last five years. The BCD Partnership has no natural business year.

a. What tax year is required for the BCD Partnership under Sec. 706?
b. Can the BCD Partnership make a Sec. 444 election? If so, what are the alternative tax years that BCD could select?

C9-33 ***Reporting Partnership Income.*** The KLM Partnership, which uses the accrual method of accounting, is owned equally by Karen, who uses the cash method of accounting, and LM Corporation, which uses the accrual method of accounting. Karen is a real estate developer. Both materially participate in the business. KLM reported the following results for the current year:

Operating profit (excluding the items listed below)	$120,000
Dividends from a 10%-owned domestic corporation	19,000
Interest income:	
Municipal bonds (tax-exempt)	18,000
Corporate bonds	29,000
Gains and losses on property sales:	
Gain on sale of land contributed by Karen two years ago when its basis was $10,000 and FMV was $35,000. (The land was included in Karen's inventory but held by KLM as an investment property.)	40,000
Sec. 1231 loss	28,000
Long-term capital gains	17,000
Long-term capital losses	21,000
Short-term capital losses	5,000
Charitable contributions	23,000
Interest expense on loans to acquire taxable investments	16,000
Guaranteed payment to Karen for management services	37,000
MACRS depreciation	36,000
Rehabilitation expenditures on a certified historic dwelling placed in service on November 1 of the current year, as an office for the partnership.	164,000

Depreciation on the rehabilitation expenditures is included in the MACRS depreciation total.

a. What are KLM's separately stated items?
b. What is KLM's ordinary income (loss)?

C9-34 ***Reconciling Financial Accounting and Tax Income and Reporting Partnership Income.*** The JLK Partnership, which uses the accrual method of accounting, is owned equally by

Jim, Liz and Ken. All three materially participate in the business. JLK reports financial accounting income of $186,000 for the current year. The following information was used to determine financial accounting income.

Operating profit (excluding the items listed below)	$ 94,000
Rental income	30,000
Interest income:	
Municipal bonds (tax-exempt)	15,000
Corporate bonds	3,000
Dividend income (all from less-than-20%-owned domestic corporations)	20,000
Gains and losses on property sales:	
Gain on sale of land held as an investment (contributed by Jim six years ago when its basis was $9,000 and its FMV was $15,000)	60,000
Long-term capital gains	10,000
Short-term capital losses	7,000
Sec. 1231 gain	9,000
Sec. 1250 gain	44,000
Depreciation:	
Rental real estate	12,000
Machinery and equipment	27,000
Interest expense related to:	
Mortgages on rental property	18,000
Loans to acquire municipal bonds	5,000
Guaranteed payments to Jim	30,000
Low-income housing expenditures qualifying for credit	21,000

The following additional information is available about the current year's activities.

- A $1,000 prepayment of rent for the next year has been received, but not recorded as income for financial accounting purposes.
- The land was recorded for financial accounting purposes at $15,000.
- MACRS depreciation on the rental real estate and machinery and equipment were $12,000 and $29,000, respectively, in the current year.
- Depreciation on the low-income housing expenditures is included in the MACRS depreciation for the rental real estate.

a. What is JLK's taxable income? (See Appendix B for an example of a financial accounting-to-tax reconciliation.)
b. What are JLK's separately stated items?
c. What is JLK's ordinary income (loss)?

C9-35 ***Partner's Distributive Shares.*** On January of the current year, the BCD Partnership is owned 20% by Becky, 30% by Chuck, and 50% by Dawn. During the current year BCD reports the following results. All items occur evenly throughout the year unless otherwise indicated.

Ordinary income	$120,000
Long-term capital gain (recognized September 1)	18,000
Short-term capital loss (recognized March 2)	6,000
Charitable contribution (made October 1)	20,000

a. What are the distributive shares for each partner, assuming they all continue to hold their interests at the end of the year?

b. Assume that Becky purchases a 5% partnership interest from Chuck on July 1 so that Becky and Chuck each own 25% from that date through the end of the year. What are Becky and Chuck's distributive shares for the current year?

C9-36 ***Partner's Distributive Share.*** On January 1, the ABC Partnership is owned by Amy (25%), Brad (35%), and Craig (40%). During the year the partnership earned the following amounts. Assume earnings were even throughout the year and the year is not a leap year.

Ordinary loss	$120,000
Long-term capital gain	190,000
Sec. 1231 gains	40,000
Short-term capital losses	30,000

a. What is each partner's distributive share of partnership income assuming no change in ownership occurs during the year?
b. Assume that on July 1 Craig sold one-half of his partnership interest to Brad. What are the distributive shares of Brad and Craig?

C9-37 ***Allocation of Pre-Contribution Gain.*** In 1996, Patty contributed land with a $4,000 basis and a $10,000 FMV in exchange for a 40% profits, loss, and capital interest in the PD Partnership. Dave contributed land with an $8,000 basis and a $15,000 FMV for the remaining 60% interest in the partnership. During 1997, PD Partnership reported $8,000 of ordinary income and $10,000 of long-term capital gain from the sale of the land Patty contributed. What income or gain must Patty and Dave report from the PD Partnership in 1997?

C9-38 ***Special Allocations.*** Clark sold securities for a $40,000 capital loss during the current year but he has no personal capital gains to recognize. The C&L General Partnership, in which Clark has a 50% capital, profits, and loss interest, has reported a $60,000 capital gain this year. In addition, the partnership has $140,000 of ordinary income. Clark's only partner, Lois, agrees to divide the year's income as follows:

Type of Income	*Total*	*Clark*	*Lois*
Capital gain	$ 60,000	$50,000	$10,000
Ordinary income	140,000	50,000	90,000

The partners and partnership all report using a calendar year-end.
a. Has a valid special allocation of income been made?
b. What are the amount and character of income each partner must report on his/her tax return?

C9-39 ***Special Allocations.*** Diane and Ed have equal capital and profits interests in the DE Partnership and they share the economic risk of loss from recourse liabilities according to their partnership interests. In addition, Diane has a special allocation of all depreciation on buildings owned by the partnership. The buildings are financed with recourse liabilities. The depreciation reduces Diane's capital account, and liquidation is in accordance with the capital account balances. Depreciation for the DE Partnership is $50,000 annually. Diane and Ed each have $50,000 capital account balances on January 1, 1997. Will the special allocation be acceptable for 1997, 1998, and 1999 in the following independent situations?
a. There is no obligation to repay negative capital account balances, and the partnership's operations (other than depreciation) each year have no net effect on the capital accounts.
b. There is an obligation to repay negative capital account balances.

c. There is no obligation to repay negative capital account balances. The partnership operates at its break-even point (excluding any depreciation that is claimed) and borrows $200,000 on a full recourse basis on December 31, 1998.

C9-40 ***Basis in Partnership Interest.*** What is Kelly's basis for her partnership interest in each of the following independent situations? The partners share the economic risk of loss from recourse liabilities according to their partnership interests.

a. Kelly receives her 20% partnership interest for a contribution of property having a $14,000 basis and a $17,000 FMV. The partnership assumes her $10,000 recourse liability but has no other debts.

b. Kelly receives her 20% partnership interest as a gift from a friend. The friend's basis (without considering partnership liabilities) is $34,000. The FMV of the interest at the time of the gift is $36,000. The partnership has liabilities of $100,000 when Kelly receives her interest. No gift tax was paid with respect to the transfer.

c. Kelly inherits her 20% interest from her mother. Her mother's basis was $140,000. The FMV of the interest is $120,000 on the date of death and $160,000 on the alternate valuation date. The executor chooses the date of death for valuing the estate. The partnership has no liabilities.

C9-41 ***Basis in Partnership Interest.*** Yong received a 40% general partnership interest in the XYZ Partnership in each of the independent situations below. In each situation, assume that the general partners have agreed that their economic risk of loss related to recourse liabilities will be shared according to their loss interests. What is Yong's basis in his partnership interest?

a. Yong designs the building the partnership will use for its offices. Yong would normally charge a $20,000 fee for a similar building design. Based on the other partner's contributions, the 40% interest has a FMV of $25,000. There are no liabilities.

b. Yong contributes land with a $6,000 basis and an $18,000 FMV, a car (which he has used in his business since it was purchased) with a $15,000 adjusted basis and a $6,000 FMV, and $2,000 cash. The partnership has recourse liabilities of $100,000.

C9-42 ***Basis in Partnership Interest.*** Tina purchases an interest in the TP Partnership on January 1 of the current year for $50,000. The partnership uses the calendar year as its tax year and has only $200,000 in recourse liabilities when Tina acquires her interest. The partners share economic risk of loss associated with recourse debt according to their loss percentage. Her distributive share of partnership items for the year is as follows:

Ordinary income (excluding items listed below)	$30,000
Long-term capital gains	10,000
Municipal bond interest income	8,000
Charitable contributions	1,000
Interest expense related to municipal bond investment	2,000

TP reports the following liabilities on December 31:

Recourse debt	$100,000
Nonrecourse debt (not qualified real estate financing)	80,000

a. What is Tina's basis on December 31 if she has a 40% interest in profits and losses? TP is a general partnership and Tina has not guaranteed partnership debt nor has she made any other special agreements about partnership debt.

b. How would your answer to Part a change if Tina instead had a 40% interest in profits and a 30% interest in losses? Assume TP is a general partnership, and all other agreements continue in place.

c. How would your answer to Part a change if Tina were instead a limited partner having a 40% interest in profits and 30% interest in losses? There are no guarantees or special agreements.

C9-43 *At-Risk Loss Limitation.* The KC Partnership is a general partnership that manufactures widgets. The partnership uses a calendar year as its tax year and is owned equally by Kerry and City Corporation, a widely held corporation. On January 1 of the current year, Kerry and City Corporation each has a $300,000 basis in the partnership interest. Operations during the year provide the following results:

Ordinary loss	$900,000
Long-term capital loss	100,000
Short-term capital gain	300,000

The only change in KC's liabilities during the year is KC's first borrowing: a $100,000 nonrecourse loan (not qualified real estate financing) that is still outstanding at year-end.

a. What is each partner's deductible loss from the partnership's activities before any passive loss limitation?
b. What is each partner's basis in the partnership interest after the year's operations?
c. How would your answers to Parts a and b change if the KC Partnership's business were totally in real estate but not a rental activity? Assume the loan is qualified real estate financing.

C9-44 *At-Risk Loss Limitation.* Mary and Gary are partners in the MG Partnership. Mary owns a 40% capital, profits, and loss interest; Gary owns the remaining interest. Both materially participate in partnership activities. At the beginning of the current year, MG's only liabilities are $30,000 in accounts payable, which remain outstanding at year-end. In November, MG borrows $100,000 on a nonrecourse basis from First Bank. The loan is secured by property with a $200,000 FMV. These are MG's only liabilities at year-end. Basis for the partnership interests at the beginning of the year is $40,000 for Mary and $60,000 for Gary before considering the impact of liabilities and operations. MG has a $200,000 ordinary loss during the current year. How much loss can Mary recognize? Gary?

C9-45 *Passive Loss Limitation.* Eve and Tom own 40% and 60%, respectively, of the ET Partnership, which manufactures clocks. The partnership is a limited partnership and Eve is the only general partner. She works full-time in the business. Tom is essentially an investor in the firm and works full-time at another job. Tom has no other income except his salary from his full-time employer. During the current year, the partnership reports the following income, gain, and losses:

Ordinary loss	$140,000
Long-term capital gain	20,000

Before the current year's income, gains, and losses have been included, Eve and Tom had $46,000 and $75,000 bases for their partnership interests, respectively. There are no nonrecourse liabilities. Tom has no further obligation to make any additional investment in the partnership.

a. What income, gain, or loss should each partner report on their individual tax returns?
b. If the partnership borrowed an additional $100,000 of recourse liabilities, how would your answer to Part a change?

C9-46 ***Passive Loss Limitation.*** Kate, Chad, and Stan are partners in the KCS Partnership, which operates a manufacturing business. The partnership was formed in 1987 with Kate and Chad each as general partners with a 40% capital and profits interest. Kate materially participates; Chad does not. Stan has a 20% interest as a limited partner. At the end of the current year, the following information was available:

	Kate	*Chad*	*Stan*
Basis in partnership (immediately before year-end)	$100,000	$100,000	$50,000
Distributive share of:			
Nonrecourse liability (already included in basis and not qualified real estate financing)	50,000	50,000	25,000
Operating losses	(80,000)	(80,000)	(40,000)
Capital gains	20,000	20,000	10,000

a. How much operating loss can each partner deduct in the current year?

b. How much loss could each partner deduct if the KCS Partnership were engaged in rental activities? Assume Kate and Chad both actively participate but Stan does not.

C9-47 ***Related Party Transactions.*** Susan, Steve, and Sandy own 15%, 35%, and 50%, respectively, in the SSS Partnership. Susan sells securities for their $40,000 FMV to the partnership. What are the tax implications of the following independent situations?

a. Susan's basis in the securities is $60,000. The three partners are siblings.

b. Susan's basis in the securities is $50,000. Susan is unrelated to the other partners.

c. Susan's basis in the securities is $30,000. Susan and Sandy are sisters. The partnership will hold the securities as an investment.

C9-48 ***Related Party Transactions.*** Jack, Kyle, and Lynn are equal partners in the JKL Partnership. Jack sells the partnership some land he held as an investment for its $30,000 FMV. What are the tax implications of the sale in the following independent situations?

a. Jack's basis for the land is $40,000, and he is not related to either Kyle or Lynn.

b. Jack's basis for the land is $44,000. Jack and Kyle are brothers but Lynn is unrelated.

c. Jack's basis for the land is $20,000. Jack, Kyle, and Lynn are siblings. The partnership holds the land as investment property.

d. Assume the same facts as in Part c, except that the partnership subdivides the land and sells it as lots.

C9-49 ***Related Party Transactions.*** Kara owns 35% of the KLM Partnership and 45% of the KTV Partnership. Lynn owns 20% of KLM and 3% of KTV. Maura, Kara's daughter, owns 15% of KTV. There are no other partners who own an interest in both partnerships or who are related to other partners. The KTV Partnership sells the KLM Partnership 1,000 shares of stock, which KTV has held for investment purposes, for its $50,000 FMV. What are the tax consequences of the sale for each of the following independent situations?

a. KTV's basis for the stock is $80,000.

b. KTV's basis for the stock is $23,000 and KLM holds the stock as an investment.

c. KTV's basis for the stock is $35,000 and KLM holds the stock as inventory.

C9-50 *Guaranteed Payments.* Scott and Dave each invested $100,000 cash when the SD Partnership was formed and they became equal partners. They agreed that the partnership would pay each a 5% guaranteed payment on their $100,000 capital account. Before the two guaranteed payments, current year results were $23,000 of ordinary income and $14,000 of long-term capital gain. What are the amount and character of the income reported by Scott and Dave for the current year from their partnership?

C9-51 *Guaranteed Payments.* Allen and Bob are equal partners in the AB Partnership. Bob manages the business and receives a guaranteed payment. What are the amount and character of the income reported by Allen and Bob in each of the following independent situations?

a. The AB Partnership earns $160,000 of ordinary income before considering Bob's guaranteed payment. Bob is guaranteed a $90,000 payment plus 50% of all income remaining after the guaranteed payment.
b. Assume the same facts as Part a except that Bob's distributive share is 50% with a guaranteed minimum of $90,000.
c. The AB Partnership earns only a $140,000 long-term capital gain. Bob is guaranteed $80,000 plus 50% of all amounts remaining after the guaranteed payment.

C9-52 *Guaranteed Payments.* Pam and Susan own the PS Partnership. Pam takes care of daily operations and receives a guaranteed payment for her efforts. What are the amount and character of the income each partner reports in each of the following independent situations?

a. The PS Partnership reports only a $10,000 long-term capital gain. Pam receives a $40,000 guaranteed payment plus a 30% distributive share of all partnership income after deducting the guaranteed payment.
b. The PS Partnership reports $70,000 of ordinary income and $60,000 of Sec. 1231 gain. Pam receives a $35,000 guaranteed payment plus a 20% distributive share of all partnership income after deducting the guaranteed payment.
c. The PS Partnership reports $120,000 of ordinary income. Pam receives 40% of partnership income but no less than $60,000.

C9-53 *Family Partnership.* Dad gives Son a 20% capital and profits interest in the Family Partnership. Dad holds a 70% interest, and Fred, an unrelated individual, holds a 10% interest. Dad and Fred work in the partnership but Son does not. Fred and Dad receive reasonable compensation for their work. The partnership earns $100,000 ordinary income, and the partners agree to divide this amount based on their relative ownership interests. Fred does not know that Son has a partnership interest. What income must Father, Son, and Fred report if Family Partnership is a manufacturing firm with substantial inventories?

C9-54 *Family Partnership.* Steve wishes to pass his business on to his children, Tracy and Vicki, and gives each a 20% partnership interest to begin getting them involved. Steve retains the remaining 60% interest. Neither daughter is employed by the partnership, which buys and manages real estate. Steve draws only a $40,000 guaranteed payment for his work for the partnership. Reasonable compensation for his services would be $70,000. The partnership reports ordinary income of $120,000 after deducting the guaranteed payment. Distributive shares for the three partners are tentatively reported as: Steve, $72,000; Tracy, $24,000; and Vicki, $24,000. What is the proper distributive share of income for each partner?

▼ **TABLE C9-1**

Dapper-Dons Partnership Income Statement for the Twelve Months Ending December 31 of the Current Year (Problem C9-55)

Sales		$2,350,000
Returns and allowances		(20,000)
		$2,330,000
Beginning inventory (FIFO method)	$ 200,050	
Purchases	624,000	
Labor	600,000	
Supplies	42,000	
Other costs[a]	12,000	
Goods available for sale	$1,478,050	
Ending inventory[b]	(146,000)	(1,332,050)
Gross profit		$ 997,950
Salaries for employees other than partners	$51,000	
Guaranteed payment for Dapper	85,000	
Utilities expense	46,428	
Depreciation (MACRS depreciation is $74,311)[c]	49,782	
Automobile expense	12,085	
Office supplies expense	4,420	
Advertising expense	85,000	
Bad debt expense	2,100	
Interest expense (all trade- or business-related)	45,000	
Rent expense	7,400	
Travel expense (meals cost $4,050 of this amount)	11,020	
Repairs and maintenance expense	68,300	
Accounting and legal expense	3,600	
Charitable contributions[d]	16,400	
Payroll taxes	5,180	
Other taxes (all trade- or business-related)	1,400	
Total expenses		494,115
Operating profit		$ 503,835
Other income and losses:		
Gain on sale of AB stock[e]	$18,000	
Loss on sale of CD stock[f]	(26,075)	
Sec. 1231 gain (sale of land[g])	5,050	
Interest on U.S. treasury bills for entire year ($80,000 face amount)	9,000	
Dividends from 15%-owned domestic corporation	11,000	16,975
Net income		$ 520,810

[a] Additional Sec. 263A costs of $7,000 for the current year are included in other costs.
[b] Ending inventory includes the appropriate Sec. 263A costs, and no further adjustment is needed to properly state cost of sales and inventories for tax purposes.
[c] The tax depreciation includes depreciation adjustments of $8,000 and $2,000 on personal property and real property, respectively, placed in service after 1986. Dapper-Dons acquired and placed into service $40,000 of rehabilitation expenditures for a certified historical property this year. The appropriate MACRS depreciation on the rehabilitation expenditures is already included in the MACRS depreciation total.
[d] All contributions are made in cash to qualifying charities.
[e] The AB stock was purchased as an investment two years ago on December 1 for $40,000 and sold on June 14 of the current year for $58,000.
[f] The CD stock was purchased as an investment on February 15 of the current year for $100,000 and sold on August 1 for $73,925.
[g] The land was used as a parking lot for the business. It was purchased four years ago for $30,000 and sold on August 15 of the current year for $35,050.

▼ TABLE C9-2

Dapper-Dons Partnership Balance Sheet for January 1 and December 31 of the Current Year (Problem C9-55)

	Balance January 1	Balance December 31
Assets:		
Cash	$ 10,000	$ 40,000
Accounts receivable	72,600	150,100
Inventories	200,050	146,000
Marketable securities[a]	220,000	260,000
Building and equipment	374,600	465,000
Minus: Accumulated depreciation	(160,484)	(173,100)
Land	185,000	240,000
Total assets	$901,766	$1,128,000
Liabilities and equities:		
Accounts payable	$ 35,000	$ 46,000
Accrued salaries payable	14,000	18,000
Payroll taxes payable	3,416	7,106
Sales taxes payable	5,200	6,560
Mortgage and notes payable (current maturities)	44,000	52,000
Long-term debt	210,000	275,000
Capital:		
Dapper	236,060	289,334
Dons	354,090	434,000
Total liabilities and equities	$901,766	$1,128,000

[a] Short-term investment.

TAX FORM/RETURN PREPARATION PROBLEM

C9-55 The Dapper-Dons Partnership (employer identification no. 89-3456798) was formed ten years ago as a general partnership to custom tailor men's clothing. Dapper-Dons is located at 123 Flamingo Drive in Miami, Florida 33131. Bob Dapper (social security no. 654-32-1098) manages the business and has a 40% capital and profits interest. His address is 709 Brumby Way, Miami, Florida 33131. Jeremy Dons (social security no. 354-12-6531) owns the remaining 60% interest but is not active in the business. His address is 807 9th Avenue, North Miami, Florida 33134. The partnership values its inventory using the cost method and there was no change in the method used during the current year. The partnership uses the accrual method of accounting. Because of the simplicity of the partnership, it is not subject to the partnership audit procedures. There are no foreign partners, no foreign transactions, no interests in foreign trusts, and no foreign financial accounts. This partnership is neither a tax shelter nor a publicly traded partnership. There have been no distributions of property other than cash nor changes in ownership of partnership interests during the current year. Cash distributions of $155,050 and $232,576 were made to Dapper and Dons, respectively, on December 30 of the current year. Financial statements for the current year are presented in Tables C9-1 and C9-2.

Prepare a current year partnership tax return for Dapper-Dons Partnership.

CASE STUDY PROBLEMS

C9-56 Abe and Brenda formed the AB Partnership ten years ago and have been very successful with the business. However, in the current year, economic conditions caused them to lose significant amounts but they expect the economy and their business to return to profitable operations by next year or the year after. Abe manages the partnership business and works in it full-time. Brenda has a full-time job as an accountant for a $39,000 annual salary but she also works in the partnership occasionally. She estimates that she spent about 120 hours working in the partnership this year. Abe has a 40% profits interest, a 50% loss interest, and a basis in his partnership interest on December 31 (before considering this year's operations or outstanding liabilities) of $65,000. Brenda has a 60% profits interest, a 50% loss interest, and a basis of $80,000 on December 31 (before considering this year's operations or outstanding liabilities). The only liability outstanding on December 31 is a recourse debt of $40,000. Neither Abe nor Brenda currently has other investments. The AB Partnership earns the following amounts during the year.

Ordinary loss	$100,000
Sec. 1231 gain	10,000
Tax-exempt municipal bond income	14,000
Long-term capital loss	14,000
Short-term capital loss	136,000

Early next year, the AB Partnership is considering borrowing $100,000 from a local bank to be secured by a mortgage on a building owned by the partnership with $150,000 FMV.

Required: Prepare a presentation to be made to Abe and Brenda discussing this matter. Points that should be discussed include: What amounts should Abe and Brenda report on their income tax return for the current year from the AB Partnership? What are their bases in their partnership interests after taking all transactions into effect? What happens to any losses they cannot deduct in the current year? What planning opportunities are presented by the need to borrow money early next year? What planning ideas would you suggest for Brenda?

C9-57 On the advice of his attorney, Dr. Andres, a local pediatrician, contributed several office buildings, which he had previously owned as sole proprietor, to a new Andres Partnership in which he became a one-third general partner. He gave the remaining limited partnership interests to his two sons, Miguel and Esteban. Last year when the partnership was formed, the boys were 14 and 16. The real estate is well-managed and extremely profitable. Dr. Andres regularly consults with a full-time hired manager about the business, but neither of his sons has any dealings with the partnership. Under the terms of the partnership agreement, the boys can sell their partnership interest to no one but their dad. Distributions from the partnership have been large, and Dr. Andres has insisted that the boys put all of their distributions into savings accounts to pay for their college education.

Last year's return (the partnership's first) was filed by Mr. Jones, a partner in the local CPA firm of Wise and Johnson. Mr. Jones, who was Dr. Andres's accountant for a decade, retired last summer. Dr. Andres's business is extremely profitable and is an important part of the client base of this small-town CPA firm. Ms. Watson, the young partner who has taken over Dr. Andres's account, asked John, a second-year staff accountant, to prepare the current year's partnership return.

John has done considerable research and is positive that the Andres Partnership does not qualify as a partnership at all because the father has retained too much control over the sons' interests. John has briefly talked to Mr. Jones about his concerns. Mr. Jones said he was really rushed in the prior year when he filed the partnership return and admitted he never looked into the question of whether the arrangement met the requirements for being taxed as a partnership. After hearing more of the details, Mr. Jones stated that John was probably correct in his conclusion. Dr. Andres's tax bill will be significantly larger if he has to pay tax on all of the partnership's income. When John approached Ms. Watson with his conclusions, her response was, "Oh, no! Dr. Andres is already unhappy because Mr. Jones is no longer preparing his returns. He'll really be unhappy if we give him a big tax increase too." She paused thoughtfully, and then went on. "My first thought is just to leave well enough alone, and file the partnership return. Are you positive, John, that this won't qualify as a partnership? Think about it, and let me know tomorrow."

Required: Prepare a list of points you want to go over with the tax partner that would support finding that the business activity is a partnership. Prepare a second list of points that would support finding that the business activity is not a partnership.

Optional: Act out the final meeting between John and Ms. Watson.

TAX RESEARCH PROBLEMS

C9-58 Caitlin and Will formed the C & W Partnership on January 5 of the current year. Caitlin contributed cash of $150,000 and Will contributed office furniture with a FMV of $21,000. He bought the furniture for $20,000 on January 1 last year and has depreciated it using MACRS depreciation. Will did not claim a Sec. 179 expensing deduction when he bought it. He also contributed an office building and land with a combined FMV of $129,000. The land's FMV is $9,000. Will bought the land in 1990 for $8,000 and had the building constructed for $100,000. The building was placed in service in June 1992.

Required: Your tax manager has asked you to prepare a schedule for the file indicating the basis of property that Will contributed at the time of contribution, the depreciation for each piece of property that can be claimed by the partnership, and the allocation of the depreciation to the two partners. Also indicate the amount and type of any recapture to which the contributed property may be subject at the time of the contribution and at a later time when the property is sold by the partnership. Your tax manager knows that some recent changes have been made to Reg. Sec. 1.704-3 and that now there are several alternatives for allocating depreciation relating to contributed property. He remembers that there is a traditional method and a couple of others, but he's not sure what method applies in this situation. He wants you to check the alternatives and indicate what method should be used. Be certain to clearly label your schedule so that anyone who looks at the file later will be able to determine where your numbers came from and the authority for your calculations. The manager has asked you to consult, at a minimum, Code Sections 168, 704, 1231, 1245, and 1250 and the related regulations as well as Rev. Proc. 87-57. Consult other tax authorities if you do not obtain a complete answer from these sources.

C9-59 George is a general partner in the GS Partnership. He has a 40% capital, profits, and loss interest and also has a special allocation of all depreciation deductions on the partnership's office building. If the partnership sells the office building for a gain, George will receive a special allocation of gain up to the amount of depreciation he has claimed (a gain charge-back arrangement). Any loss recognized on the sale of the office building would be allocated based on the usual distributive share arrangement.

All allocations of income, gain, loss, and deductions affect the capital accounts whether they are distributive share items or special allocation items. Liquidation proceeds would be distributed based on capital accounts. George is obligated to repay any negative capital account balance at the time of liquidation.

The $1,100,000 purchase price of the office building was financed by a $1,000,000 recourse loan plus partner contributions. Only interest is paid until the building is sold. On the day the office building is purchased, George has a $100,000 capital account balance and a $500,000 basis for his partnership interest (his capital account plus his 40% share of the $1,000,000 liability). Annual depreciation expenses are calculated using the straight-line MACRS rules. The partnership operates at its break-even point (without considering depreciation), but always expects to make a profit. It is likely that the office building will be sold for an amount greater than its purchase price.

Required: Prepare a presentation to be made to the tax partner in charge of George's work explaining whether the special allocation will be acceptable to the IRS. The tax manager has suggested that in getting ready for the presentation, be sure to consult Code Sec. 704 and the related regulations. In addition to any other case law you might find, be sure to look at *Stanley C. Orrisch*. He said it was an early 1970s Tax Court decision that the partner feels may be relevant to your presentation.

C9-60 Almost two years ago, the DEF Partnership was formed when Demetrius, Ebony, and Farouk each contributed $100,000 in cash. They are equal general partners in the real estate partnership, which has a December 31 year-end. The partnership uses the accrual method of accounting for financial accounting purposes but uses the cash method of accounting for tax purposes. The first year of operations resulted in a $50,000 loss. Because the real estate market plummeted, the second year of operations is going to result in an even larger ordinary loss. On November 30, calculations reveal that the year's loss is likely to be $100,000 for financial accounting purposes. Financial accounting results for the year are as follows:

	Quarter			
	First	*Second*	*Third*	*Fourth**
Revenue	$40,000	$60,000	$80,000	$100,000
Maintenance expense	(30,000)	(58,000)	(70,000)	(85,000)
Interest expense	(10,000)	(30,000)	(35,000)	(50,000)
Utilities expense	(3,000)	(3,000)	(3,000)	(3,000)
Projected loss	($3,000)	($31,000)	($28,000)	($38,000)

* Fourth quarter results are the sum of actual October and November results along with estimates for December results. December estimates are revenue, $33,000; maintenance, $60,000; interest, $20,000; and utilities, $1,000.

Cash has been short throughout the second year of operations, so more than $65,000 of expenses for second year operations have resulted in bills that are currently due or overdue. The unpaid bills are for July 1 through November 30 interest on a loan from the bank. In addition, all but essential maintenance has been postponed during the fourth quarter so that most of the fourth quarter maintenance is scheduled to be completed during December.

The DEF partners wants to attract a new partner to obtain additional capital. Raj is interested in investing $100,000 as a limited partner in the DEF Partnership if a good deal can be arranged. Raj would have a 25% profits and loss interest in the partnership but would expect something extra for the current year. In the current tax year, Raj has passive income of more than $200,000 from other sources so he would like to have large passive losses allocated to him from DEF.

Required: Your tax partner has asked you to prepare a memorandum suggesting a plan to maximize the amount of current year loss that can be allocated to Raj. Assume none of the partners perform more than one-half of their personal service time in connection with real estate trades or businesses in which they materially participate. She reminded you to consider the varying interest rules for allocating losses to new partners found in Sec. 706, and to look into the possibilities of somehow capitalizing on the cash method of accounting or of using a special allocation. She wants you be sure to check all of the relevant case law for the plan you suggest.

[illegible] DH partner wants to attract a new partner to obtain additional capital [illegible] [illegible] ... \$300,000 ... limited partnership. [illegible] ... a good deal [illegible]

[illegible]

[illegible]

CHAPTER 10

SPECIAL PARTNERSHIP ISSUES

LEARNING OBJECTIVES

After studying this chapter, you should be able to

1. Determine the amount and character of the gain or loss recognized by a partner from a nonliquidating partnership distribution
2. Determine the basis of assets received by a partner from a nonliquidating partnership distribution
3. Identify the partnership's Sec. 751 assets
4. Determine the tax implications of a sale or cash distribution when the partnership has Sec. 751 assets
5. Determine the amount and character of the gain or loss recognized by a partner from a liquidating partnership distribution
6. Determine the basis of assets received in a liquidating distribution
7. Determine the amount and character of the gain or loss recognized when a partner retires from the partnership or dies
8. Explain the tax implications of a gift of a partnership interest
9. Determine whether a partnership has terminated for tax purposes
10. Determine the adjustment required by the sale of a partnership interest or a partnership distribution when the partnership elects to make optional basis adjustments

CHAPTER OUTLINE

Chapter C10 continues the discussion of the taxation of partnerships. Simple nonliquidating distributions are first explained, then more complex nonliquidating and liquidating distributions are discussed. Other methods of disposing of a partnership interest are explained next. Included in this discussion are sales and gifts of the partnership interest and the retirement or death of a partner. In addition, transactions that terminate the entire partnership are considered.

One topic unique to the partnership form of doing business is the **optional basis adjustment.** This elective partnership technique causes the basis of partnership assets to be adjusted up or down as a result of distributions from the partnership to partners or sales of partnership interests by existing partners.

The final topic in this chapter is an examination of special partnership forms. Publicly traded partnerships, limited liability companies, and limited liability partnerships are also discussed.

NONLIQUIDATING DISTRIBUTIONS

There are two categories of distributions from a partnership: liquidating distributions and nonliquidating (or current) distributions. A **liquidating distribution** is a single distribution, or one of a planned series of distributions, that terminates the partner's entire interest in the partnership. All other distributions, including those that substantially reduce a partner's interest in the partnership, are governed by the **nonliquidating (current) distribution** rules.

Although the tax consequences of the two types of distributions are quite similar in many respects, they are sufficiently different to require separate study. First, simple current distributions are discussed. Then complex current distributions involving Sec. 751 property and liquidating distributions are covered.

OBJECTIVE 1

Determine the amount and character of the gain or loss recognized by a partner from a nonliquidating partnership distribution

RECOGNITION OF GAIN

A current distribution that does not bring Sec. 751 into play cannot result in the recognition of a loss by either the partner who receives the distribution or the partnership. Gain cannot be recognized by the partnership on a current distribution (except for Sec. 751 properties). Partners who receive distributions can recognize a gain if they receive money distributions that exceed their basis.[1] For distribution purposes, money includes cash, deemed cash from reductions in a partner's share of liabilities, and the fair market value (FMV) of marketable securities if the securities are distributed after December 8, 1994.

EXAMPLE C10-1 ▶

Melissa is a 30% partner in the ABC Real Estate Partnership until Josh is admitted as a partner in exchange for a cash contribution. After Josh's admission, Melissa holds a 20% interest. Because of large loss deductions, Melissa's basis (before Josh's admission) is $20,000 including her 30% interest in the partnership liabilities of $250,000. She is deemed to receive a cash distribution equal to the $25,000 [(30% − 20%) × $250,000] reduction in her share of partnership liabilities. Because the cash distribution exceeds her basis, Melissa must recognize a $5,000 ($25,000 distribution − $20,000 basis) gain. ◀

KEY POINT

Remember that reductions in a partner's share of liabilities are treated as cash distributions (see Example C10-1).

[1] Secs. 731(a) and (b). The FMV of distributed securities is considered money if the distribution occurs after December 8, 1994.

SELF-STUDY QUESTION

Can gain/loss be recognized in a current distribution?

ANSWER

Current distributions with no Sec. 751 implications do not create losses to either the partner or partnership. Ignoring Sec. 751, gains are not recognized by the partnership. However, gains can be recognized by a partner if the partner receives a money distribution in excess of his or her basis in his or her partnership interest. A distribution may also trigger recognition of precontribution gain or loss for a partner.

Although a current distribution causes gain or loss to be recognized only in the conditions listed above, the distribution event may also trigger recognition of previously unrecognized precontribution gain or loss. Two different events may trigger recognition of precontribution gain or loss. First, if the contributed property is distributed to any partner (other than the contributing partner) within five years of the contribution date, the remaining precontribution gain or loss may be recognized by the contributing partner on the property he or she contributed to the partnership. Second, if the contributing partner receives a distribution with a FMV greater than his or her adjusted basis in his or her partnership interest, the remaining precontribution gain on any property he or she contributed in the preceding five years may have to be recognized.

If property is contributed to a partnership with a deferred precontribution gain or loss, the contributing partner must recognize the precontribution gain or loss when the property is distributed to any other partner within five years of the contribution. The amount of precontribution gain or loss that must be recognized by the contributing partner is determined by the amount of precontribution gain or loss remaining that would have been allocated to the contributing partner if the property had instead been sold for its FMV on the distribution date. The partnership's basis in the property immediately before the distribution and the contributing partner's basis in his or her partnership interest are both increased for any gain recognized or decreased for any loss recognized.[2]

EXAMPLE C10-2 ▶

Michael contributed land with a $4,000 basis and an $8,000 FMV to the AB Partnership in 1994. In 1997 the land was distributed to Stephen, another partner in the partnership. At the time of the distribution, the land had a $9,000 FMV. Stephen recognizes no gain on the distribution. Michael must recognize his $4,000 precontribution gain when the property is distributed to Stephen. Michael increases the basis in his partnership interest by $4,000 and the partnership's basis in the land immediately before the distribution is increased by $4,000. This increase in the partnership's basis for the land increases the land's basis to the distributee partner (Stephen). ◀

SELF-STUDY QUESTION

What type of abuse is this rule designed to eliminate?

ANSWER

This rule is designed to prohibit a taxpayer from using a partnership to avoid gain/loss recognition on the transfer of property to the other partner.

Property distributions made to a partner may cause a partner to recognize his or her remaining precontribution gain if the FMV of the distributed property exceeds the partner's basis in his or her partnership interest before the distribution.[3] The gain recognized under Code Sec. 737 is the lesser of the remaining precontribution net gain or the excess of the FMV of the distributed property over the adjusted basis of the partnership interest immediately before the property distribution (but after reduction for any money that is distributed at the same time).[4] The remaining precontribution gain is the excess net of all precontribution gains and losses for property contributed to the partnership in the five years immediately preceding the distribution to the extent that such precontribution gains and losses have not already been recognized. The character of the recognized gain is determined by referencing the type of property that had precontribution gains or losses. The gain recognized under Sec. 737 is in addition to any gain recognized on the same distribution under Sec. 731.

EXAMPLE C10-3 ▶

Sergio contributed land, a capital asset, with a $20,000 FMV and a $15,000 basis to the STU Partnership in 1995 in exchange for a 30% general interest in the partnership. The partnership still holds the land on January 31, 1997, and none of the $5,000 precontribution gain has been recognized. On January 31, 1997, Sergio has a $40,000 basis in his partnership interest when

[2] Sec. 704(c). See Chapter C9 for a discussion of precontribution gains and losses.

[3] Sec. 737.

[4] Section 737 does not apply if the property that is distributed was contributed by this same partner. Only the provisions of Sec. 731 would be considered in such a situation.

SELF-STUDY QUESTION

In Example C10-3, what is Sergio's basis in his partnership interest after the distribution?

ANSWER

$7,000. Sergio's precontribution basis of $40,000 is increased by the $5,000 Sec. 737 gain and decreased by the $8,000 of distributed cash and $30,000 adjusted basis for the distributed property.

he receives an $8,000 cash distribution plus property purchased by the partnership with a $45,000 FMV and a $30,000 basis. Under the Sec. 731 distribution rules, no gain is recognized because the cash distribution ($8,000) does not exceed the partner's predistribution basis in his partnership interest ($40,000). However, Sec. 737 mandates that he must recognize gain equal to the lesser of the $5,000 remaining precontribution gain or the $13,000 difference between the FMV of the property distributed ($45,000) and the basis of the partnership interest after the cash distribution but before any property distributions ($32,000 = $40,000 adjusted basis − $8,000 cash distributed). Sergio will recognize a $5,000 capital gain. ◀

EXAMPLE C10-4 ▶

Assume the same facts as in Example C10–3 except that the distribution was $20,000 in cash and $23,000 (FMV) in marketable securities plus the property. Sergio recognizes a $3,000 gain under Sec. 731 because he received a money distribution in excess of his basis in the partnership interest ($43,000 money distribution − $40,000 adjusted basis before distributions). Under Sec. 737 he must also recognize gain equal to the lesser of the remaining precontribution gain ($5,000) or the excess of the FMV of the property distributed ($45,000) over the zero basis of the partnership interest after money distributions but before property distributions ($0 = $40,000 adjusted basis − $43,000 money distributed). Sergio therefore recognizes both a $5,000 capital gain under Sec. 737 and a $3,000 capital gain under Sec. 731. ◀

If gain is recognized under Sec. 737, the partner's basis in his or her partnership interest is increased by the gain recognized (illustrated in the next section). Further, the partnership's basis in the property that was the source of the precontribution gain is also increased by the recognized gain.

EXAMPLE C10-5 ▶

Assume the same facts as in Example C10–3. At the time Sergio contributed the land, the partnership assumed Sergio's $15,000 basis in the land. Now, the partnership's basis in the land is increased to $20,000 by Sergio's $5,000 Sec. 737 gain. ◀

OBJECTIVE 2

Determine the basis of assets received by a partner from a nonliquidating partnership distribution

BASIS EFFECTS OF DISTRIBUTIONS

In general, the partner's basis for property distributed by the partnership carries over from the partnership. The partner's basis in the partnership interest is reduced by the amount of money received plus the carryover basis claimed for the distributed property.

EXAMPLE C10-6 ▶

TYPICAL MISCONCEPTION

In determining the tax consequences of partnership distributions, the basis, not the FMV, of the distributed property is most important. Partners take a carryover basis in the distributed property and a partner's basis in his or her partnership interest is reduced by the basis of the property distributed.

Jack has a $25,000 basis for his interest in the MLV Partnership before receiving a current distribution consisting of $4,000 in money, accounts receivable having a zero basis to the partnership, and land having a $14,000 basis to the partnership. Jack takes a carryover basis in the land and receivables. Following the distribution, his basis in the partnership interest is calculated as follows:

Predistribution basis in partnership interest		$25,000
Minus:	Money received	(4,000)
	Carryover basis in receivables	(—0—)
	Carryover basis in land	(14,000)
Postdistribution basis in partnership interest		$ 7,000

◀

The total bases of all distributed property in the partner's hands is limited to the partner's predistribution basis in his or her partnership interest plus the gain recognized on the distribution under Sec. 737.[5] If the partner's predistribution basis plus Sec. 737

[5] Secs. 732(a)(2) and 737(c). Marketable securities have a basis equal to their Sec. 732 basis plus any gain recognized under Sec. 731(c).

WHAT WOULD YOU DO IN THIS SITUATION?

You have done the personal and business tax work for Betty and Thelma for a number of years. Betty and Thelma are partners in a retail shop. In addition, the two have decided they want to exchange some property which is not associated with their partnership. Betty wants to exchange undeveloped land she personally holds as an investment, having a $40,000 FMV and a $10,000 adjusted basis, for machinery and office equipment that Thelma owns but no longer uses. Thelma's machinery and office equipment in total have a $40,000 FMV and a $28,000 adjusted basis. At a golf outing, a friend told Betty that several years ago he and an associate did a similar swap tax-free by contributing both pieces of property to be exchanged to a partnership, having the partnership hold the property for a few months, and then having the partnership distribute the property to the partner who wanted to receive it. The friend said the arrangement was tax-free because the initial transfer qualified as a tax-free contribution of property to the partnership in exchange for a partnership interest and the distribution was tax-free because it was simply a pro rata property distribution made by the partnership. Thelma and Betty have come to you asking that you structure their exchange using their retail shop partnership so that the transfer will be tax-free also. How should you respond to their request?

gain is less than the sum of the money received plus the carryover basis of any nonmoney property received, the order in which the basis is allocated is crucial. First, cash and deemed cash distributions reduce the partner's basis in his or her partnership interest. Next, the remaining basis is allocated to provide a carryover of the partnership's basis for receivables and inventory. If the partner's predistribution basis is not large enough to allow a carryover of the partnership's basis for these two property categories, the partner's remaining basis is allocated among the receivables and inventory items based on their relative bases.[6]

EXAMPLE C10-7 ▶

KEY POINT

If different types of property are distributed, the partnership distribution rules assume that the property is distributed in the following order: (1) cash, (2) receivables and inventory, and (3) other property. This ordering can affect both the recognition of gain to the partner and the basis the partner takes in the distributed property.

Tracy has a $15,000 basis in her interest in the TP Partnership and no remaining precontribution gain immediately before receiving a current distribution that consists of $6,000 in money, power tools held as inventory with a $4,000 basis to the partnership, and steel rod held as inventory with an $8,000 basis to the partnership. The basis of the distributed property in Tracy's hands is determined as follows:

Predistribution basis in partnership interest	$15,000
Minus: Money received	(6,000)
Plus: Sec. 737 gain	—0—
Amount to be allocated	$ 9,000

$$\text{Basis of power tools} = \frac{\$4,000}{\$4,000 + \$8,000} \times \$9,000 = \$3,000$$

$$\text{Basis of steel rod} = \frac{\$8,000}{\$4,000 + \$8,000} \times \$9,000 = \$6,000$$

◀

EXAMPLE C10-8 ▶

Assume the same facts as in Example C10-7 except that Tracy must recognize $1,000 of remaining precontribution gain under Sec. 737 as a result of the distribution. The basis of the distributed property in Tracy's hands is determined as follows:

[6] Sec. 732(c).

Predistribution basis in partnership interest	$15,000
Minus: Money received	(6,000)
Plus: Sec. 737 gain	1,000
Amount to be allocated	$10,000

$$\text{Basis of power tools} = \frac{\$4,000}{\$4,000 + \$8,000} \times \$10,000 = \$3,333$$

$$\text{Basis of steel rod} = \frac{\$8,000}{\$4,000 + \$8,000} \times \$10,000 = \$6,667$$

◀

If a partner's predistribution basis plus Sec. 737 gain recognized exceeds the sum of his or her money distribution plus the carryover basis for any receivables and inventory, a carryover basis is allocated to the other property received. If there is an insufficient basis for the partnership interest to provide a carryover basis for all the distributed property, the remaining basis for the partnership interest is allocated to the other property based on the relative bases of such properties in the partnership's hands.[7]

EXAMPLE C10-9 ▶

John has a $15,000 basis for his partnership interest and no remaining precontribution gain before receiving the following property as a current distribution:

Property	*Basis to the Partnership*
Money	$ 5,000
Inventory	4,000
Land parcel 1	4,500
Land parcel 2	3,000

John's basis in his distributed property is calculated as follows:

Predistribution basis	$15,000
Minus: Money received	(5,000)
Plus: Sec. 737 gain	—0—
Basis for nonmoney property	$10,000
Minus: Carryover basis for inventory	(4,000)
Remaining basis to be allocated	$ 6,000

$$\text{Basis of parcel 1} = \frac{\$4,500}{\$4,500 + \$3,000} \times \$6,000 = \$3,600$$

$$\text{Basis of parcel 2} = \frac{\$3,000}{\$4,500 + \$3,000} \times \$6,000 = \$2,400$$

John's basis in his partnership interest is zero after the distribution because all of its basis is allocated to the money and other property received. ◀

SELF-STUDY QUESTION

Assume the same facts as in Example C10-9 except that the basis in the two parcels of land is only $4,000 in total. What are the tax consequences of the distribution?

ANSWER

Example C10-9 is a good illustration of the three types of property that can be included in a partnership distribution. If the basis in the two parcels of land were only $4,000 in total, then the partner would take a $4,000 carryover basis in the land and retain a $2,000 basis in his partnership interest.

TYPICAL MISCONCEPTION

The partner's basis in his or her partnership interest cannot be less than zero. However, a partner's capital account can be less than zero. One must distinguish between references to a partner's basis in his or her partnership interest (his outside basis) and the balance in a partner's capital account.

Two other points should be noted. First, even when a partner's basis in the partnership interest is reduced to zero by a current distribution, an interest in the partnership is retained. If the partner has no remaining interest in the partnership (as opposed to a zero basis), the distribution would have been a liquidating distribution.

[7] Ibid.

Second, the basis of property distributed as a current distribution is always equal to or less than the carryover basis. Basis for distributed property cannot be increased above the carryover basis amount when it is received as a nonliquidating distribution.

HOLDING PERIOD AND CHARACTER OF DISTRIBUTED PROPERTY

The partner's holding period for property distributed as a current distribution includes the partnership's holding period for such property.[8] The length of time that the partner owns the partnership interest is irrelevant when determining the holding period for the distributed property. Thus, if a new partner receives a distribution of property that was held by the partnership for two years before he or she became a partner, the new partner's holding period for the distributed property is deemed to begin when the partnership purchased the property (i.e., two years ago), rather than on the more recent date when the partnership interest was purchased.

KEY POINT

Consistent with the discussion in Chapter C9, rules exist so that neither contributions to nor distributions from a partnership can be used to alter the character of certain gains and losses on property held by the partnership or by the individual partners.

A series of rules regulate the character of the gain or loss recognized when certain property distributed to a partner is subsequently sold or exchanged. These rules are similar to provisions regulating the character of gain or loss on contributed property.

If property that is an unrealized receivable in the partnership's hands is distributed, the income or loss recognized on a subsequent sale of that property by the distributee partner is ordinary income or loss. This ordinary income or loss treatment occurs without regard to the character of the property in the distributee partner's hands or the length of time the property is held by such a partner before its disposition.[9]

If property that is inventory in the hands of the partnership is distributed, the income or loss recognized on a subsequent sale by the distributee partner occurring within five years of the distribution date is ordinary income or loss.[10] Note that the inventory rule mandates the ordinary income or loss result only for the five-year period beginning on the distribution date. After five years, the character of the gain or loss recognized on the sale of such property is determined by its character in the hands of the distributee partner.

NONLIQUIDATING DISTRIBUTIONS WITH SEC. 751

So far, the discussion of current distributions has ignored the existence of the Sec. 751 property rules. Now, we must expand our discussion to include them.

OBJECTIVE 3

Identify the partnership's Sec. 751 assets

SECTION 751 ASSETS DEFINED

There are two categories of Sec. 751 assets: unrealized receivables and substantially appreciated inventory. These two categories encompass all property that is likely to produce ordinary income when sold or collected. Each of these categories must be carefully defined before further discussion of Sec. 751.

UNREALIZED RECEIVABLES. *Unrealized receivables* includes a much broader spectrum of property than the name implies. Unrealized receivables are certain rights to payments to be received by a partnership to the extent that they are not already included in income under the partnership's accounting methods. They include rights to payments for services performed or to be performed as well as rights to payment for goods delivered or to be delivered (other than capital assets). A common example

[8] Sec. 735(b).
[9] Sec. 735(a)(1).
[10] Sec. 735(a)(2).

KEY POINT

Section 751 property represents property in a partnership that is likely to produce ordinary income or loss. The application of Sec. 751 in conjunction with partnership distributions or sales of a partnership interest is of concern to individual partners because capital gains are subject to a preferential tax rate.

of unrealized receivables is the accounts receivable of a cash method of accounting partnership.

In addition to rights to receive payments for goods and services, the term *unrealized receivables* includes most potential ordinary income recapture items. A primary example of this type of unrealized receivable is the potential Sec. 1245 or 1250 gain on the partnership's depreciable property. The potential Sec. 1245 or 1250 gain is the amount of depreciation that would be recaptured as ordinary income under Sec. 1245 or 1250 if the partnership property were sold at its FMV.[11]

EXAMPLE C10-10 ▶ The LK Partnership has two assets: $10,000 cash and a machine having a $14,000 basis and a $20,000 FMV. Depreciation of $8,000 has been taken on the machine by the partnership since its purchase. If the machine is sold for its FMV, all $6,000 of the gain would be recaptured under Sec. 1245. Therefore, the LK Partnership has a $6,000 unrealized receivable item. ◀

SELF-STUDY QUESTION

What is included in the definition of unrealized receivables?

ANSWER

Unrealized receivables include not only the obvious cash-method accounts receivable that have yet to be recognized but also most of the potential ordinary income recapture provisions. Therefore, the term *unrealized receivables* is broader than it may appear.

The definition of unrealized receivables is not limited to Sec. 1245 and 1250 depreciation recapture. Among the other recapture provisions creating unrealized receivables are Sec. 617(d) (mining property), Sec. 1252 (farmland), and Sec. 1254 (oil, gas, and geothermal property). Assets covered by Sec. 1278 (market discount bonds) and Sec. 1283 (short-term obligations) generate unrealized receivables to the extent the taxpayer would recognize ordinary income if the asset were sold. This type of unrealized receivable is deemed to have a zero basis. It should be clear that only a rare partnership totally avoids dealing with the Sec. 751 complexities.

SUBSTANTIALLY APPRECIATED INVENTORY. ***Substantially appreciated inventory*** is equally surprising in its breadth. Inventory for purposes of Sec. 751 includes three major types of property:

- Items held for sale in the normal course of partnership business
- Any other property that, if sold by the partnership, would not be considered a capital asset or Sec. 1231 property
- Any other property held by the partnership that, if held by the selling or distributee partner, would be property of the two types listed above[12]

TYPICAL MISCONCEPTION

The definition of inventory is broadly construed by Sec. 751. In fact, for purposes of determining whether inventory is substantially appreciated, even unrealized receivables are treated as inventory items.

In short, cash, capital assets, and Sec. 1231 assets are the only properties that are not inventory. For purposes of testing whether the inventory is substantially appreciated (but *only* for that purpose), inventory also includes unrealized receivables. The inclusion of unrealized receivables in the definition of inventory makes it more likely that the inventory will be substantially appreciated.

The test to determine whether inventory is substantially appreciated (and therefore taxed under Sec. 751) is purely mechanical. Inventory is substantially appreciated if its FMV exceeds 120% of its adjusted basis to the partnership.

EXAMPLE C10-11 ▶ The ABC Partnership owns the following assets on December 31:

Assets	*Basis*	*FMV*
Cash	$10,000	$ 10,000
Unrealized receivables	—0—	40,000
Inventory	30,000	34,000
Land (Sec. 1231 property)	40,000	70,000
Total	$80,000	$154,000

[11] Sec. 751(c). Unrealized receivables may have basis if costs or expenses have been incurred but not taken into account under the partnership's method of accounting (e.g., the basis of property sold in a nondealer installment sale).

[12] Sec. 751(d)(2).

For purposes of the substantially appreciated inventory test, both ABC's unrealized receivables and inventory are included. The inventory's $74,000 FMV exceeds 120% of its adjusted basis [($30,000 + 0) × 1.20 = $36,000]. Therefore, the ABC Partnership has substantially appreciated inventory. ◀

OBJECTIVE 4

Determine the tax implications of a sale or cash distribution when the partnership has Sec. 751 assets

EXCHANGE OF SEC. 751 ASSETS AND OTHER PROPERTY

A current distribution is partially taxed under Sec. 751 only if the partnership has Sec. 751 assets and there is an exchange of Sec. 751 property for non-Sec. 751 property. Accordingly, if a partnership does not have *both* Sec. 751 property and other property, the rules discussed above for simple current distributions control the taxation of the distribution. Similarly, a distribution that is proportionate to all partners or (1) consists of only the partner's share of either Sec. 751 property or non-Sec. 751 property and (2) does not reduce the partner's interest in other property is not affected by the Sec. 751 rules.

However, any portion of the distribution that represents an exchange of Sec. 751 property for non-Sec. 751 property must be isolated and is not treated as a distribution at all. Instead, it is treated as a sale between the partnership and the partner, and any gain or loss realized on the sale transaction is fully recognized.[13] The character of the recognized gain or loss is determined by the character of the property deemed sold. For the party deemed the seller of the Sec. 751 assets, the gain or loss is ordinary income or loss.

Analyzing the transaction to determine what property was involved in the Sec. 751 transaction is best accomplished by using an orderly, step-by-step approach.

TYPICAL MISCONCEPTION

Even if a partnership has Sec. 751 property, Sec. 751 is not applicable as long as a partner's interest in the ordinary-income type assets is not altered. However, if a distribution of the partnership assets is disproportionate, then Sec. 751 treats that portion of the distribution as a deemed sale between the partnership and the distributee partner, with the corresponding income/loss being recognized.

STEP 1: DIVIDE THE ASSETS INTO SEC. 751 ASSETS AND NON-SEC. 751 ASSETS. Inventory must be tested at this time to see whether it is substantially appreciated in order to know whether it is a Sec. 751 asset.

STEP 2: DEVELOP A SCHEDULE, SUCH AS THE ONE IN TABLE C10-1, TO DETERMINE WHETHER THE PARTNER EXCHANGED SEC. 751 ASSETS FOR NON-SEC. 751 ASSETS OR VICE VERSA. This schedule must be based on the FMV of all the partnership's assets. To make the determination, it is necessary to compare the partner's interest in the partnership's assets before the distribution with his or her interest in the assets after the distribution. This part of our analysis assumes a fictional nontaxable pro rata distribution equal to the partner's decreased interest in the assets. We can see whether the partner exchanged Sec. 751 assets for non-Sec. 751 assets by comparing the fictional distribution with the actual distribution. Thus, in Table C10-1,

- Column 1 represents the partner's interest (valued at FMV) in each asset before the distribution.
- Column 2 represents the partner's interest (valued at FMV) in each asset after the distribution.
- Column 3 shows the amount of a fictional proportionate distribution that would have occurred if the partner's ownership interest were reduced by taking a pro rata share of each asset. (As such, the proportionate distribution would be nontaxable.)
- Column 4 shows the amounts actually distributed.
- Column 5 shows the difference between the fictional and actual distributions. This column contains the information that must be analyzed to see whether a Sec. 751 exchange has occurred.

KEY POINT

Steps 2 and 3 try to identify whether a disproportionate distribution of Sec. 751 assets has taken place. In Table C10-1, if the column 5 total for Sec. 751 assets is zero, Sec. 751 is not applicable. But as the table illustrates, Anne received $10,000 more than her share of the partnership cash without receiving any of her $10,000 share of Sec. 751 assets.

[13] Sec. 751(b).

STEP 3: ANALYZE COLUMN 5 TO DETERMINE WHETHER SEC. 751 ASSETS WERE EXCHANGED FOR NON-SEC. 751 ASSETS. If the column 5 total for the Sec. 751 assets section of Table C10-1 is zero, there is no Sec. 751 exchange. The partner simply received an additional amount of one type of Sec. 751 asset in exchange for relinquishing an interest in some other type of Sec. 751 asset. For example, no Sec. 751 exchange has occurred if a partner exchanged an interest in substantially appreciated inventory for an interest in unrealized receivables. However, if the column 5 total for the Sec. 751 assets is an amount other than zero, a Sec. 751 exchange has occurred. One (or more) Sec. 751 properties has been exchanged for one (or more) non-Sec. 751 properties.

EXAMPLE C10-12 ▶ The ABC Partnership holds the assets listed below on January 1 before making a $25,000 cash distribution to Anne that reduces her interest in the partnership from one-third to one-fifth.

Assets	*Basis*	*FMV*
Cash	$ 75,000	$ 75,000
Unrealized receivables	—0—	15,000
Inventory	30,000	60,000
Total	$105,000	$150,000

ABC owes no liabilities on January 1. Before the distribution, Anne has a $35,000 basis in her partnership interest. The following steps are needed to determine the tax effects of the distribution:

STEP 1. Determine ABC's Sec. 751 and non-Sec. 751 assets. ABC's Sec. 751 assets include the unrealized receivables and the substantially appreciated inventory. The cash is ABC's only non-Sec. 751 property.

STEP 2. Complete the table used to analyze the Sec. 751 distribution (see Table C10-1).

▼ **TABLE C10-1**

Analysis of Sec. 751 Nonliquidating Distribution (Example C10-12)

	Beginning Partnership Amount[a]	(1) Anne's Interest Before Distribution[a] (1/3)	(2) Anne's Interest After Distribution[a] (1/5)	(3) Fictional Proportionate Distribution (3) = (1) − (2)[a]	(4) Actual Distribution[a]	(5) Difference[b] (5) = (4) − (3)
Sec. 751 assets:						
Unrealized receivables	$15,000	$ 5,000	$ 3,000	$ 2,000	—0—	$ (2,000)
Inventory	60,000	20,000	12,000	8,000	—0—	(8,000)
Total Sec. 751 assets	$75,000	$25,000	$15,000	$10,000	—0—	$(10,000)
Non-Sec. 751 assets:						
Cash	$75,000	$25,000	$10,000[c]	$15,000	$25,000	$ 10,000
Total non-Sec. 751 assets	$75,000	$25,000	$10,000	$15,000	$25,000	$ 10,000

[a] Valued at fair market value.
[b] A negative amount means that Anne gave up her interest in a particular property. A positive amount means that she received more than her proportionate interest.
[c] One-fifth interest in remaining cash of $50,000.

TYPICAL MISCONCEPTION

Step 4 is crucial if a student is to understand the deemed sale that Sec. 751 creates. In Example C10-13, Anne is treated as if she had exchanged her $10,000 interest in the unrealized receivables and inventory for $10,000 of cash. Thus, Anne has a taxable gain/loss on the deemed sale. To determine Anne's gain/loss on the deemed sale, the adjusted basis of the unrealized receivables and inventory equals whatever her basis would have been if those assets had actually been distributed to her.

STEP 3. Analyze column 5 of Table C10-1 to see whether a Sec. 751 exchange has occurred. Because Anne's Sec. 751 asset total declined by $10,000, we know that $10,000 of her proportionate interest in ABC's Sec. 751 assets was given up in exchange for cash. ◀

STEP 4: DETERMINE THE GAIN OR LOSS ON THE SEC. 751 DEEMED SALE. It is necessary to assume that the exchange occurring in step 3 above was actually a sale of the exchanged property between the partnership and the partner. This step follows logically from the fact that the partner "bargained" to receive the amounts actually distributed rather than a proportionate distribution. She sold her interest in some assets to receive more than her proportionate interest in other assets. This sale is analyzed exactly the same way any other sale is analyzed. The gain (or loss) equals the difference between the FMV of the property received and the adjusted basis of the property given up. Note that up to this point we have been dealing only in terms of the FMV, so the adjusted basis of property given up must be determined as if that fictional distribution had actually been received.

EXAMPLE C10-13 ▶

Assume the same facts as in Example C10-12. The Sec. 751 sale portion of the distribution is analyzed as Anne receiving $10,000 more cash than her proportionate share and giving up a $2,000 (FMV) interest in the unrealized receivables and an $8,000 (FMV) interest in the inventory. By examining the balance sheet, we can see that the partnership's bases for the unrealized receivables and inventory are $0 and $4,000 [$8,000 × ($30,000 ÷ $60,000)]. If Anne received these properties in a current distribution, her basis would be the same as the property's basis in the partnership's hands, or $0 and $4,000, respectively. Therefore, Anne's deemed sale of the Sec. 751 assets is analyzed as follows:

Amount realized (cash)	$10,000
Minus: Adjusted basis of property sold	(4,000)
Realized and recognized gain	$ 6,000

KEY POINT

After determining the tax effects of the Sec. 751 exchange, the portion of the distribution that was not covered by Sec. 751 must be dealt with. Thus, the regular current distribution rules are applied to the remaining portion of the distribution.

The character of the recognized gain depends on the character of the property sold (in this case, the unrealized receivables and inventory). Therefore, Anne's $6,000 gain is ordinary income. ◀

STEP 5: DETERMINE THE IMPACT OF THE CURRENT DISTRIBUTION. The last step in analyzing the distribution's effect on the partner is to determine the impact of the portion of the distribution that is not a Sec. 751 exchange. This distribution is treated exactly like any other nonliquidating distribution.

EXAMPLE C10-14 ▶

Assume the same facts as in Examples C10-12 and C10-13. Examining the distribution, we see in column 4 of Table C10-1 that only $10,000 of the $25,000 money actually distributed is received as part of the Sec. 751 exchange. The remaining $15,000 that is distributed represents a current distribution. Under Sec. 731(a)(1), gain is recognized by a partner on a current distribution only if the money distributed exceeds his or her basis in the partnership interest. Anne recognizes no gain because she has a $16,000 basis in the partnership interest immediately after the current distribution. This basis is calculated as follows:

Predistribution basis for partnership interest	$35,000
Minus: Basis of property deemed distributed in Sec. 751 exchange ($0 unrealized receivables + $4,000 inventory)	(4,000)
Basis before current distribution	$31,000
Minus: Money distributed	(15,000)
Postdistribution basis of partnership interest	$16,000

After the entire distribution is complete, Anne owns a partnership interest with a basis of $16,000 and has $25,000 in money. She has recognized $6,000 in ordinary income. ◀

TERMINATING AN INTEREST IN A PARTNERSHIP

OBJECTIVE 5

Determine the amount and character of the gain or loss recognized by a partner from a liquidating partnership distribution

There are numerous ways to terminate an interest in a partnership. The two most common are receiving a liquidating distribution and selling the interest. Other possibilities include giving the interest away, exchanging the interest for corporate stock, and transferring the interest at death. Each of these methods of disposing of a partnership interest is considered.

LIQUIDATING DISTRIBUTIONS

A liquidating distribution is defined as a distribution, or one of a series of distributions, that terminates a partner's interest in the partnership.[14] If the partner's interest is drastically reduced but not terminated, the distribution is reported as a current distribution. A liquidating distribution can occur when only one member of a partnership terminates his or her interest, several partners terminate their interests but the partnership continues, or the entire partnership terminates and each partner receives a liquidating distribution. Rules for taxation of a liquidating distribution are the same whether one partner terminates his or her interest or the entire partnership liquidates.

KEY POINT

The rules for gain recognition are the same for liquidating and current distributions. However, in a liquidating distribution, the partner recognizes a loss if (1) the only assets distributed are cash, unrealized receivables, and inventory *and* (2) the adjusted basis in such assets is less than the partner's basis in his or her partnership interest. The loss is necessary because in a liquidating distribution, the partner does not retain a partnership interest.

GAIN OR LOSS RECOGNITION BY THE PARTNER. The rule for recognizing gain on a liquidating distribution is exactly the same rule used for a current distribution. Gain is recognized only if the money distributed (including money deemed distributed to the partner from a liability reduction or the FMV of marketable securities that are treated as money) exceeds the partner's predistribution basis in his or her partnership interest.[15]

Although loss can never be recognized from a current distribution, a loss can be recognized from a liquidating distribution. A loss is recognized only if the distribution consists of money (including money deemed distributed), unrealized receivables, and inventory, but no other property.[16] The amount of the loss is the difference between the partner's basis in the partnership interest before the distribution and the sum of money plus the bases of the receivables and inventory (to the partnership immediately before the distribution) that are received.

EXAMPLE C10-15 ▶

Qamar's interest in the ABC Partnership is terminated when her basis in the partnership is $35,000. She receives a liquidating distribution of $10,000 cash and inventory with a $12,000 basis to the partnership. Her recognized loss is $13,000 [$35,000 − ($10,000 + $12,000)]. The inventory has a $12,000 basis to Qamar. ◀

OBJECTIVE 6

Determine the basis of assets received in a liquidating distribution

TYPICAL MISCONCEPTION

The basis to a partner of distributed unrealized receivables or inventory can never be greater than the partnership's basis in those assets. Also, if the partner's basis in his or her partnership interest is not sufficient, the partner's basis in the distributed unrealized receivables and inventory is less than the partnership's basis in those assets.

BASIS IN ASSETS RECEIVED. The basis of an asset received by the partner from a liquidating distribution is determined using rules similar to those used to determine the basis of an asset received in a current distribution. For both kinds of distributions, the basis in unrealized receivables and inventory is generally the same as the property's basis in the partnership's hands. Under no condition is the basis of these two types of assets increased. Occasionally, however, the partner's basis in his or her partnership interest is so small that after making the necessary reduction for money (and deemed money) distributions, the basis in the partnership interest is smaller than the partnership's bases for the unrealized receivables and inventory that are distributed. In such cases, the remaining basis in the partnership interest must be allocated among the unrealized receivables and inventory items based on their relative bases on the partnership's books.[17] This means that the bases for the unrealized receivables and inventory are reduced, and

[14] Sec. 761(d).
[15] Sec. 731(a)(1).
[16] Sec. 731(a)(2).
[17] Sec. 732(c).

the amount of ordinary income to be recognized on their ultimate sale, exchange, or collection is increased.

Remember that a liquidating distribution of cash, unrealized receivables, and inventory with a total basis on the books of the partnership that is less than the partner's basis in his or her partnership interest results in the recognition of a loss. However, no loss is recognized if the distribution includes any property other than cash, unrealized receivables, and inventory. Instead, all of the remaining basis in the partnership interest must be allocated to the other property received regardless of that property's basis to the partnership or its FMV. Application of this rule can create strange results.

EXAMPLE C10-16 ▶ Assume the same facts as in Example C10-15, except that Qamar's distribution includes an office typewriter having a $50 basis to the partnership and a $100 FMV as part of the distribution. The allocation of basis proceeds as follows:

Predistribution basis for partnership interest	$35,000
Minus: Money received	(10,000)
Basis after money distribution	$25,000
Minus: Basis of inventory to partnership	(12,000)
Remaining basis of partnership interest	$13,000

The entire $13,000 remaining basis of the partnership interest is allocated to the typewriter. ◀

TYPICAL MISCONCEPTION

In a liquidating distribution, if a partner still has basis in his partnership interest after allocations to cash, unrealized receivables, and inventory, this remaining basis is allocated to the "other property" received by the partner. This rule can produce some unusual results. Example C10-16 illustrates this point.

The basis allocation procedure illustrated in Example C10-16 delays the loss recognition until the typewriter is either depreciated or sold. However, the allocation procedure may also change the character of the loss because Qamar would recognize a capital loss when she receives the liquidating distribution in Example C10-15. In Example C10-16, the character of Qamar's loss is determined by the character of the typewriter in her hands (or in some cases by a series of specific rules that are discussed below). Worst of all, if she converts the typewriter into personal-use property, the loss on its sale or exchange is nondeductible.

If two or more assets other than unrealized receivables or inventory are distributed together, the remaining basis in the partnership interest is allocated among them based on their relative bases in the partnership's hands. Note that such an allocation process can lead to either a decrease or increase in the total basis of these assets. This potential for increasing the assets' bases is unique to liquidating distributions.

EXAMPLE C10-17 ▶ Before receiving a liquidating distribution, Craig's basis in his interest in the BCD Partnership is $60,000. The distribution consists of $10,000 in money, inventory having a $2,000 basis to the partnership, and two parcels of undeveloped land (not held as inventory) having bases of $6,000 and $18,000 to the partnership. His bases in the assets received are calculated as follows:

Predistribution basis for partnership interest	$60,000
Minus: Money received	(10,000)
Basis of inventory to the partnership	(2,000)
Basis allocated to two parcels of land	$48,000

$$\text{Basis of parcel 1: } \frac{\$6,000}{\$6,000 + \$18,000} \times \$48,000 = \$12,000$$

$$\text{Basis of parcel 2: } \frac{\$18,000}{\$6,000 + \$18,000} \times \$48,000 = \$36,000$$

◀

KEY POINT

If neither gain nor loss is recognized in a liquidating distribution, the partner's basis in the distributed assets always equals the partner's former basis in his or her partnership interest.

In a liquidating distribution, the amount of money received plus the basis of the nonmoney property received in the hands of the distributee partner normally equals the partner's predistribution basis in the partnership interest. The only two exceptions to this rule occur when the money received exceeds the partner's basis in his or her partnership interest and a gain must be recognized or when money, unrealized receivables, and inventory are the only assets distributed and a loss must be recognized. In all other liquidating distributions, the distributee partner recognizes no gain or loss. Instead, that partner's predistribution basis in his or her partnership interest is transferred to the cash and other property received.

Holding Period in Distributed Assets. The distributee partner's holding period for any assets received in a liquidating distribution includes the partnership's holding period for such property.[18] If the partnership received the property as a contribution from a partner, the partnership's holding period may also include the period of time the contributing partner held the property (see Chapter C9). Note that the distributee partner's holding period for his or her partnership interest is irrelevant in determining the holding period of the assets received.

EXAMPLE C10-18 ▶

George purchases an interest in the DEF Partnership on June 1, 1997, but he cannot get along with the other partners. On July 1, 1997, he receives a liquidating distribution that terminates his interest in the partnership. George's distribution includes land that the partnership has owned since August 1, 1992. George's holding period for the land commences on August 1, 1992, even though his holding period for the partnership interest begins much later. ◀

The character of the gain or loss recognized on a subsequent sale of distributed property is determined using the same rules as for a current distribution.

KEY POINT

The main difference in how the mechanics of the Sec. 751 rules are applied to current versus liquidating distributions is that after a liquidating distribution, the partner always has a zero interest in the partnership assets because he or she is no longer a partner in the partnership.

EFFECTS OF SEC. 751. Section 751 has essentially the same impact on both liquidating and current distributions. To the extent that the partner's interest in Sec. 751 assets is exchanged for other assets (or vice versa), that portion of the transaction is removed from the distribution rules. Instead, this portion of the transaction is treated as a sale occurring between the partnership and the partner. There is one notable difference between liquidating distributions and current distributions having Sec. 751 implications: the postdistribution interest in partnership assets is zero for the liquidating distribution because it terminates the partner's interest in the partnership.

EXAMPLE C10-19 ▶

The ABC Partnership holds the assets listed below on December 31 before making a $50,000 cash distribution that reduces Al's one-third interest in the partnership to zero.

Assets	*Basis*	*FMV*
Cash	$75,000	$ 75,000
Unrealized receivables	—0—	15,000
Inventory	15,000	60,000
Total	$90,000	$150,000

The partnership has no liabilities, and Al's predistribution basis in his partnership interest is $30,000. The following steps are needed to determine the tax effects of the liquidating distribution:

STEP 1. Determine ABC's Sec. 751 and non-Sec. 751 assets. The Sec. 751 assets include the unrealized receivables and the substantially appreciated inventory. The cash is ABC's only non-Sec. 751 asset.

[18] Sec. 735(b).

STEP 2. Complete the table used to analyze the Sec. 751 distributions (see Table C10-2).

STEP 3. Analyze column 5 of Table C10-2 to see if a Sec. 751 exchange has occurred. Table C10-2 shows that Al exchanges $5,000 of unrealized receivables and $20,000 of inventory for $25,000 cash.

SELF-STUDY QUESTION

What is the deemed Sec. 751 exchange shown in Table C10-2?

ANSWER

Column 5 shows that Al received $25,000 of excess cash in lieu of $25,000 of Sec. 751 assets. Thus, the Sec. 751 exchange is a deemed sale by Al of $25,000 of unrealized receivables and inventory to the partnership in exchange for $25,000 of cash. With a table similar to Table C10-2, the Sec. 751 computations are much easier to understand.

STEP 4. Determine the gain or loss on the Sec. 751 deemed sale. Al is deemed to have sold unrealized receivables and inventory for cash. Assume Al first got the receivables and inventory in a current distribution. He obtains the partnership's bases for the assets of $0 and $5,000, respectively. The deemed sale results in Al recognizing a $20,000 gain.

Amount realized (cash)	$25,000
Minus: Adjusted basis of property sold	(5,000)
Realized and recognized gain	$20,000

Al's gain is ordinary income because it results from his deemed sale of receivables and inventory to the partnership.

STEP 5. Determine the impact of the non-Sec. 751 portion of the distribution. The liquidating distribution is only the $25,000 cash he receives that was *not* a part of the Sec. 751 transaction. To determine its impact, we must first find Al's basis in his partnership interest after the Sec. 751 transaction but before the $25,000 liquidating distribution.

Predistribution basis in the partnership interest	$30,000
Minus: Basis of receivables and inventory deemed distributed in Sec. 751 exchange	(5,000)
Basis before money distribution	$25,000
Minus: Money distribution	(25,000)
Gain recognized on liquidating distribution	$—0—

No further gain or loss is recognized from the liquidating distribution portion of the transaction. ◀

▼ **TABLE C10-2**

Analysis of Sec. 751 Liquidating Distribution (Example C10-19)

	Beginning Partnership Amount[a]	(1) Al's Interest Before Distribution[a] (1/3)	(2) Al's Interest After Distribution[a] (—0—)	(3) Fictional Proportionate Distribution[a] (3) = (1) − (2)	(4) Actual Distribution[a]	(5) Difference[b] (5) = (4) − (3)
Sec. 751 Assets:						
Unrealized receivables	$15,000	$ 5,000	—0—	$ 5,000	—0—	$ (5,000)
Inventory	60,000	20,000	—0—	20,000	—0—	(20,000)
Total Sec. 751 Assets	$75,000	$25,000	—0—	$25,000	—0—	$(25,000)
Non-Sec. 751 Assets:						
Cash	$75,000	$25,000	—0—	$25,000	$50,000	$25,000
Total Non-Sec. 751 Assets	$75,000	$25,000	—0—	$25,000	$50,000	$25,000

[a] Valued at fair market value.
[b] A negative amount means that Al gave up his interest in a particular property. A positive amount means that Al received more than his proportionate interest.

EFFECTS OF DISTRIBUTION ON THE PARTNERSHIP. A partnership recognizes no gain or loss on liquidating distributions made to its partners.[19] If a Sec. 751 deemed sale occurs, however, the partnership may be required to recognize gain or loss on assets deemed sold to its partner. A liquidating distribution normally does not itself terminate the partnership. The partnership terminates if none of the remaining partners continue to operate the business of the partnership in a partnership form. The partnership may also be affected by a liquidating distribution if the partnership has made a Sec. 754 election to make optional basis adjustments.

Topic Review C10-1 presents a summary of the tax consequences of current and liquidating distributions.

STOP & THINK

Question: Do most current distributions made by a partnership require a Sec. 751 calculation?

Solution: No, many current distributions are made pro rata to all partners so Sec. 751 is not involved. Often even if the distribution is not pro rata, the distribution does not create an exchange of an interest in Sec. 751 assets for an interest in other assets. This exchange happens only when (1) the partner is reducing his overall interest in the partnership, or (2) there is an explicit agreement that the distribution results in a partner giving up all or part of his interest in some asset(s) maintained by the partnership. Most current distributions do not involve Sec. 751.

SALE OF A PARTNERSHIP INTEREST

When a partner sells a partnership interest, capital gain or loss on the sale is recognized as if corporate stock were sold.[20] However, to the extent Sec. 751 applies, the partner must recognize ordinary income or loss from the sale of his or her interest in unrealized receivables and substantially appreciated inventory.[21] The sale of a partnership interest may have three other effects: the partner's share of the partnership's liabilities is acquired by the purchaser, an adjustment to the basis of the partnership's assets may be made if an optional basis adjustment election has been made, and the partnership may be terminated. Each of these situations related to the sale of a partnership interest is examined below.

SELF-STUDY QUESTION

What is the character of gain/loss on the sale of a partnership interest?

ANSWER

Because a partnership interest is generally a capital asset, the sale of a partnership interest results in a capital gain/loss being recognized. However, if a partnership has Sec. 751 assets, the partner is deemed to sell his or her share of Sec. 751 assets directly with a corresponding ordinary gain/loss being recognized.

SECTION 751 PROPERTIES. As with distributions, the effects of Sec. 751 should be calculated first so that the remainder of the transaction can be properly analyzed. The first step has two parts: determine the amount realized for the Sec. 751 property and calculate the adjusted basis of such property to the partner. The partner's adjusted basis for the Sec. 751 property equals the basis that the property would have if the partner received the property in a current distribution occurring just before the sale of the partnership interest. Next, the buyer and seller can allocate the price paid for the partnership interest among the Sec. 751 and non-Sec. 751 properties in any manner that they choose. If the allocation occurs at arm's length, it is generally acceptable to the IRS.[22] If no allocation is agreed upon, the amount allocated to each Sec. 751 property is based on the relative FMVs of the partnership's properties. The difference between the amount realized and adjusted basis for the Sec. 751 properties is the ordinary income or loss that must be recognized by the partner on the sale.

[19] Sec. 731(b).
[20] Sec. 741.
[21] Sec. 751(a).
[22] Reg. Sec. 1.751-1(a).

Topic Review C10-1

Current and Liquidating Distributions

Tax Consequences	Current Distributions	Liquidating Distributions
Impact on Partner:		
Money (or deemed money from liability changes or marketable securities) distributed	Recognize gain only if money distributed exceeds basis in partnership interest before distribution.	Recognize gain only if money distributed exceeds basis in partnership interest before distribution.
Unrealized receivables and/or inventory distributed	Carryover basis (limited to basis in partnership interest before distribution reduced by money distributed).	Carryover basis (limited to basis in partnership interest before distribution reduced by money distributed).
	No gain or loss is recognized.[a]	Loss recognized if only money, inventory and receivables are distributed with basis less than basis in partnership interest before distribution.[a]
Other property distributed	Carryover basis (limited to basis in partnership interest before distribution reduced by money and carryover basis in inventory and receivables).	Basis equal to basis in partnership interest before distribution reduced by money and carryover basis in inventory and receivables.
	No gain or loss is recognized.[a]	No gain or loss is recognized.[a]
Impact on Partnership:		
General rule	No gain or loss is recognized.	No gain or loss is recognized.
Other tax consequences:	If a Sec. 751 deemed sale or exchange occurs, gain or loss on the deemed sale may be recognized by the partner and/or the partnership.	If a Sec. 751 deemed sale or exchange occurs, gain or loss on the deemed sale may be recognized by the partner and/or the partnership.

[a] Precontribution gain (but not loss) may be recognized under Sec. 737 if there is remaining precontribution net gain and the FMV of the property distributed exceeds the adjusted basis of the partnership interest immediately before the property distribution (but after any money distribution). Precontribution gain or loss may also be recognized by the contributing partner if the contributed property is distributed to another partner within five years of the contribution (Sec. 704(c)).

EXAMPLE C10-20 ▶ Troy sells his one-fourth interest in the TV Partnership to Steve for $50,000 cash when the partnership's assets are as follows:

Assets	*Basis*	*FMV*
Cash	$ 40,000	$ 40,000
Unrealized receivables	—0—	36,000
Inventory	40,000	92,000
Land	40,000	32,000
Total	$120,000	$200,000

The partnership has no liabilities on the sale date. Troy's basis in his partnership interest is $30,000 on such date. Both the receivables and inventory are Sec. 751 assets. Assuming Troy and Steve do not agree to an allocation of the sales price, Troy's gain or loss for the Sec. 751 deemed sale is calculated as follows:

Amount realized for Sec. 751 assets	
[(0.25 × \$36,000) + (0.25 ×\$92,000)]	\$32,000
Minus: Adjusted basis of Sec. 751 assets	
[(0.25 × \$0) + (0.25 × \$40,000)][a]	(10,000)
Sec. 751 ordinary income	\$22,000

[a]Troy's basis for the receivables and inventory received in the deemed current distribution equals the partnership's basis for such properties unless Troy's basis in his partnership interest immediately before the distribution is less.

After the Sec. 751 portion of the sale is isolated, it is not difficult to analyze the remaining sale. The sales price minus the portion of the proceeds allocated to the Sec. 751 assets is the amount realized for the sale of the remaining partnership interest. For calculating gain or loss on the sale, the partner's basis in his or her partnership interest equals the predistribution basis for the partnership interest minus the amount of basis allocated to the Sec. 751 assets. Any gain or loss on the sale of the remaining partnership interest is considered to be gain or loss derived from the sale of a capital asset.

STOP & THINK

Question: Bill owns 20% of Kraco and plans to sell his ownership interest for a \$40,000 gain. Kraco has both unrealized receivables and substantially appreciated inventory. If Kraco is a corporation, Bill will report a \$40,000 capital gain. If Kraco is a partnership, part of the \$40,000 gain (the gain on his 20% share of the Sec. 751 assets) will be ordinary income and the remainder will be capital gain. Why did Congress decide to tax the gain on the sale of corporate stock differently from the gain on the sale of a partnership interest?

Solution: The corporation itself will pay tax on the ordinary income realized when unrealized receivables are collected or substantially appreciated inventory is sold, and the corporation's tax is unaffected by the identity of the shareholder. Under no conditions will the shareholder have to report any of the corporation's ordinary income. Accordingly, the sale of the corporate stock does not provide an opportunity to avoid ordinary income for the owner nor can the owner convert ordinary income into capital gain by selling the corporate stock.

Because the ordinary income earned by the partnership is reported by and taxed to the partners, a sale of a partnership interest that produces only capital gains would represent an opportunity for a partner to avoid recognizing ordinary income and recognize capital gains instead. Imagine, for example, that Kraco is a cash-basis service business whose only asset is a large account receivable where all work has been completed. If Bill stays in the partnership, he will recognize ordinary income when the receivable is collected by the partnership. If he were allowed to sell his partnership interest in this setting for a capital gain, he would be able to convert his ordinary income into capital gain. However, Sec. 751 prevents this from happening by causing him to recognize ordinary income on the sale of the partnership interest to the extent the sales proceeds are payments for Sec. 751 assets.

EXAMPLE C10-21 ▶

KEY POINT

Once the Sec. 751 gain/loss has been determined, the remaining gain/loss is a capital gain/loss. Example C10-21 illustrates that without Sec. 751 these two types of gains/losses would have been netted together.

Assume the same facts as in Example C10-20. Analyzing the non-Sec. 751 portion of the sale transaction occurs as follows:

		Sale of	
	Total	*Sec. 751 Assets*	*Remaining Partnership Interest*
Amount realized	$50,000	$32,000	$18,000
Minus: Adjusted basis	(30,000)	(10,000)	(20,000)
Recognized gain or loss	$20,000	$22,000	($2,000)
Ordinary income		$22,000	
Capital loss			($2,000)

The Sec. 751 portion of the sale remains the same as in Example C10-20. The $18,000 ($50,000 − $32,000) remainder of the purchase price is allocated to the remaining partnership interest along with the $20,000 ($30,000 − $10,000) remainder of the basis for the partnership interest. ◀

The separation of the sale of a partnership interest into its two components may yield both a gain and a loss as is illustrated by Example C10-21. If the entity theory prevailed instead, no assets would be separated out, and Troy would report a $20,000 capital gain. Because of Sec. 751, Troy must report both ordinary income and a capital loss.

LIABILITIES. When a partnership has liabilities, each partner's distributive share of any liabilities is always part of the basis for the partnership interest. When the partnership interest is sold, the partner is relieved of the liabilities. Accordingly, the amount realized on the sale of a partnership interest is made up of money plus the FMV of nonmoney property received plus the seller's share of partnership liabilities that are assumed or acquired by the purchaser.

EXAMPLE C10-22 ▶

Andrew is a 30% partner in the ABC Partnership when he sells his entire interest to Miguel for $40,000 cash. At the time of the sale, Andrew's basis is $27,000 (which, of course, includes his $7,000 share of partnership liabilities). The partnership has no Sec. 751 assets. Andrew's $20,000 gain on the sale is calculated as follows:

Amount realized:		
Cash	$40,000	
Liabilities assumed by purchaser	7,000	$47,000
Minus: Adjusted basis		(27,000)
Gain recognized on sale		$20,000 ◀

IMPACT ON THE PARTNERSHIP. When one partner sells his or her partnership interest, the sale usually has no more impact on the partnership than the sale of corporate stock by one shareholder has on the corporation. Only the partner and the purchaser of the interest are affected. However, the partnership itself is affected if the partnership elects under Sec. 754 to make optional basis adjustments or the partnership interest that is sold is sufficiently large that under Sec. 708 its sale terminates the partnership for tax purposes. Both of these effects are discussed later in this chapter.

OBJECTIVE 7

Determine the amount and character of the gain or loss recognized when a partner retires from a partnership or dies

RETIREMENT OR DEATH OF A PARTNER

If a partner dies or retires from a partnership, that partner's interest can be sold either to an outsider or to one or more existing partners.[23] The results of such a sale are outlined above. Often, however, a partner or a deceased partner's assignee departs from the partnership in return for payments made by the partnership itself. When the partnership buys out the partner's interest, the analysis of the tax results focuses on two types of payments: payments made in exchange for the partner's interest in partnership property and other payments.

PAYMENTS FOR PARTNERSHIP PROPERTY. Generally, the valuation placed on the retiring partner's interest in the partnership properties by the partners in an arm's-length transaction is accepted by the IRS. Payments made for the property interest are taxed under the liquidating distribution rules. Like any liquidating distribution made to a partner, payments made to a retiring partner or a deceased partner's successor-in-interest[24] in exchange for their property interest are not deductible by the partnership.[25]

If the retiring or deceased partner was a general partner and the partnership is a service partnership (i.e., capital is not a material income producing factor), payments made to a general partner for unrealized receivables and goodwill (when the partnership agreement does not provide for a goodwill payment on retirement or death) are not considered payments for property. Instead, any such payments are treated as other payments. The other payment treatment permits the partnership to deduct the amounts paid to the retiring or deceased partner or to reduce the distributive share allocable to the other partners.

TYPICAL MISCONCEPTION

The significance of the two different kinds of payments is not readily apparent to some taxpayers. The payments for partnership property are not deductible by the partnership and often are not income to the retiring partner. However, payments considered in the second category are deductible by the partnership (or they reduce the distributive shares that must be recognized by other partners) and usually are income to the retiring partner.

OTHER PAYMENTS. Payments made to a retiring partner or to a deceased partner's successor-in-interest that exceed the value of that partner's share of partnership property have a very different tax result for both the retiring partner and for the partnership. A few payments that do represent payments for property (e.g., payments to a general partner retiring from a service partnership for his or her interest in unrealized receivables and for his or her interest in partnership goodwill) are also taxed under these rules.

Under these rules, a payment is taxed as either a distributive share or a guaranteed payment. If the excess payment is determined as a function of partnership income (e.g., 10% of the partnership's net income), the income is considered a distributive share of partnership income.[26] Accordingly, the character of the income flows through to the partner, and each of the remaining partners is taxed on a smaller amount of partnership income. The income must be reported in the partner's tax year that includes the partnership year-end from which the distributive share arises, regardless of when the distribution is actually received.

If the amount of the excess payment is determined without regard to the partnership income, the payment is treated as a guaranteed payment.[27] If the payment is a guaranteed payment, the retiring partner recognizes ordinary income, and the partnership generally has an ordinary deduction. Like all guaranteed payments, the income is includible in the recipient's income for his or her tax year within which ends the partnership tax year in which the partnership claims its deduction (see Chapter C9).

TYPICAL MISCONCEPTION

The main difference between a payment being taxed as a distributive share or as a guaranteed payment is the character of the income recognized by the recipient partner. If the payment is taxed as a distributive share, the character of the income is determined by the type of income earned by the partnership. In contrast, the payment is always ordinary income if it is treated as a guaranteed payment.

EXAMPLE C10-23 ▶ When Shaka retires from the STU Partnership, he receives a cash payment of $30,000. At the time of his retirement, his basis for his one-fourth limited partnership interest is $25,000. The partnership has no liabilities and the following assets:

---

[23] Note that retirement from the partnership in this context has nothing to do with reaching a specific age and leaving the employ of the partnership but instead refers to the partner's withdrawal at any age from a continuing partnership.

[24] A deceased partner's successor-in-interest is the party that succeeds to the rights of the deceased partner's partnership interest (e.g., the decedent's estate or an heir or legatee of the deceased partner). A deceased partner's successor-in-interest is treated as a partner by the tax laws until his or her interest in the partnership has been completely liquidated.

[25] Sec. 736(b).

[26] Sec. 736(a)(1).

[27] Sec. 736(a)(2).

Assets	*Basis*	*FMV*	*Shaka's 1/4 FMV*
Cash	$ 40,000	$ 40,000	$10,000
Marketable securities	25,000	32,000	8,000
Land	35,000	48,000	12,000
Total	$100,000	$120,000	$30,000

In the absence of a valuation agreement, it is assumed that the partnership pays Shaka a ratable share of the FMV of each asset (and he receives no payment for any partnership goodwill). The $30,000 amount paid to Shaka equals the FMV of his one-fourth interest in the partnership assets. The $30,000 Shaka receives in exchange for his interest in partnership property is analyzed as a liquidating distribution in the following manner:

Basis in partnership interest	$25,000
Minus: Cash distributed	(30,000)
Gain recognized on liquidating distribution	$ 5,000

The gain is capital gain if Shaka held his partnership interest as a capital asset. Of course, the partnership gets no deduction for the distribution. ◀

EXAMPLE C10-24 ▶ Assume the same facts as in Example C10–23 except that the payment Shaka receives is $34,000. This represents payment for Shaka's one-fourth interest in partnership assets plus an excess payment of $4,000. Accordingly, this payment must either be a distributive share or a guaranteed payment. Because this $4,000 payment is not contingent on partnership earnings, it is taxed as a guaranteed payment. The partnership deducts the $4,000 payment and Shaka recognizes $4,000 of ordinary income.

In summary, Shaka receives $34,000 as a payment on his retirement from the STU Partnership. $4,000 of the payment is considered a guaranteed payment, which is ordinary income to Shaka and deductible by the partnership. The remaining $30,000 Shaka receives is in exchange for his interest in partnership property. Because the $30,000 cash payment exceeds his $25,000 basis in his partnership interest, he must recognize a $5,000 gain on the liquidating distribution. Of course, the partnership gets no deduction for the $30,000, which is considered a distribution. ◀

If the partnership has Sec. 751 assets, the calculations for a retiring partner are slightly more difficult. First, payments for substantially appreciated inventory and unrealized receivables are payments for property and must be analyzed using the liquidating distribution rules along with Sec. 751. The remainder of the transaction is analyzed as indicated above.

A retiring partner who receives payments from the partnership is considered to be a partner in that partnership for tax purposes until the last payment is received. Likewise, a deceased partner's successor-in-interest is a member of the partnership until the last payment is received.[28]

EXCHANGE OF A PARTNERSHIP INTEREST

EXCHANGE FOR ANOTHER PARTNERSHIP INTEREST. A partner may also terminate a partnership interest by exchanging it for either an interest in another partnership or a different interest in the same partnership. The Tax Reform Act of 1984 mandated that exchanges involving interests in different partnerships do not qualify for

[28] Reg. Sec. 1.736-1(a)(1)(ii).

like-kind exchange treatment.[29] Nevertheless, the IRS still allows exchanges of interests within a single partnership.[30]

EXAMPLE C10-25

SELF-STUDY QUESTION

Can the exchange of a partnership interest qualify for nonrecognition treatment as a like-kind exchange?

ANSWER

Yes, if the exchange of interests is within a single partnership. However, exchanges of partnership interests in different partnerships are not considered a like-kind exchange.

Pam and Dean are equal partners in the PD General Partnership, which owns and operates a farm. The two partners agree to convert PD into a limited partnership with Pam becoming a limited partner and Dean having both a general and a limited partnership interest in PD. Even though the partners exchange a general partnership interest for a limited partnership interest (plus an exchange of a general partnership interest for a general partnership interest for Dean), no gain or loss is recognized from the exchange. If, however, a partner's interest in the partnership's liabilities is changed, that partner's basis must be adjusted. If liabilities are reduced and a deemed distribution in excess of the basis for the partnership interest occurs, gain must be recognized. ◀

EXCHANGE FOR CORPORATE STOCK. A partnership interest may be exchanged for corporate stock in a transaction that qualifies under the Sec. 351 nonrecognition rules (see Chapter C2). For Sec. 351 purposes, a partnership interest is property. If the other Sec. 351 requirements are met, a single partner's partnership interest can be transferred for stock in a new or an existing corporation in a nontaxable exchange. This exchange is taxed to the partner as if he or she had exchanged any other property under the Sec. 351 rules. The basis in the corporate stock is determined by the partner's basis in the partnership interest. The holding period for the stock received in the exchange includes the holding period for the partnership interest. As a result of the exchange, one of the corporation's assets is an interest in a partnership, and the corporation (not the transferor) is now the partner of record. Thus, the corporation must report its distributive share of partnership income along with all of its other earnings.

SELF-STUDY QUESTION

If a partnership is incorporated, does the form of the transaction make a difference?

ANSWER

The form of an incorporation involving a partnership usually makes a difference. For example, if an existing corporation is an S corporation, the S election would be terminated if, as a result of the incorporation transaction, the partnership is a shareholder.

INCORPORATION. When limited liability is important, the entire partnership may choose to incorporate. Normally such an incorporation can be structured to fall within the Sec. 351 provisions and can be partially or totally tax exempt. When a partnership chooses to incorporate, there are three possible alternatives:

- The partnership contributes its assets and liabilities to the corporation in exchange for the corporation's stock. The stock is then distributed to the partners in a liquidating distribution of the partnership.
- The partnership liquidates by distributing its assets to the partners. The partners then contribute the properties to the new corporation in exchange for its stock.
- The partners contribute their partnership interests directly to the new corporation in exchange for its stock. The partnership is liquidated, with the corporation receiving all of the partnership's assets and liabilities.

The tax implications of the incorporation and the impact of partnership liabilities, gain to be recognized, basis in the corporate assets, and the new shareholders' bases in their stock and securities may be different depending on the form chosen for the transaction.[31]

FORMATION OF AN LLC OR LLP. A second option for obtaining limited liability protection for all owners is for the partnership to become an LLC. Under the new check-the-box rules, an LLC with more than one member is taxed as a partnership unless it elects to be taxed as a corporation (see Chapter C2). If the LLC elects to be taxed as a C or an S corporation, the transfer of the property to the LLC is taxed under the incorporation rules discussed above. If the LLC is taxed as a partnership, Rev.

[29] Sec. 1031(a)(2)(D).

[30] Rev. Rul. 84-52, 1984-1 C.B. 157.

[31] Rev. Rul. 84-111, 1984-2 C.B. 88.

Rul. 95-37[32] specifies that the transfer will be taxed as a partnership-to-partnership transfer. The property transfer does not cause the partners to recognize gain or loss nor does the transfer terminate the tax year for the partnership or any partner. The basis for the partners' interest in the partnership will be changed only if the liability shares for the partners change.

If a partnership chooses LLP status to reduce some of the liability risks facing the partners, the change from partnership to LLP status is also taxed under the partnership-to-partnership transfer rules described above. The transfer does not cause the partners to recognize gain or loss nor does the property transfer terminate the tax year for the partnership or any partner. Basis for the partners' interest in the partnership will be changed only if the liability shares for the partners change.[33]

OBJECTIVE 8

Explain the tax implications of a gift of a partnership interest

GIFT OF A PARTNERSHIP INTEREST

When a partner disposes of a partnership interest by giving away some or all of it, the role of partnership liabilities can lead to unusual results. The donee becomes liable for the distributive share of the partnership's liabilities associated with the gifted partnership interest. Accordingly, for tax purposes, the donor has a partial sale and a partial gift.[34]

The donor must recognize a gain on the sale portion of the transfer that is equal to the difference between the amount realized when the donee assumes the distributive share of the partnership liabilities and the donor's basis in the entire partnership interest on the date of transfer. If the basis of the partnership interest exceeds the distributive share of liabilities, no loss is recognized.

The gift tax is levied on the FMV of the transferred partnership interest on the date of the gift minus the amount realized on the partial sale resulting from the liability transfer. The donee's basis in the transferred partnership interest is equal to the greater of the liabilities assumed or the donor's basis in the partnership interest plus any gift tax paid on the appreciation.

KEY POINT

When a partnership interest is gifted, the partnership liabilities shifted from the donor to the donee are treated as a sale. If the amount of debt relief to the donor is greater than the adjusted basis of the partnership interest being transferred, the donor recognizes a gain.

EXAMPLE C10-26 ▶

Jack owns 40% of the JKL Partnership before giving away a 10% interest in the partnership to his son Andrew. Information about Jack's partnership interest before his gift and about Jack's gift of a 10% partnership interest to Andrew is listed below.

	Jack's Pre-Gift Interest	*Andrew's Gift*
Ownership percentage	40%	10%
FMV of interest	$250,000	$62,500
Adjusted basis to Jack	$240,000	$60,000
Liability share (included in basis)	$200,000	$50,000

Because Andrew in his role as a partner must assume his share of liabilities associated with the 10% interest, the transaction must be divided into a sale (for the liability amount) and a gift. The gift portion of the transaction is reported as follows:

FMV of interest transferred to Andrew	$62,500
Minus: Deemed sale for the liability assumed	(50,000)
Jack's gift to Andrew	$12,500

The portion of the transaction deemed to be a sale because of the liability assumption must be analyzed to see if Jack must recognize a gain. He is not allowed to recognize any loss on a gift.

Amount realized (liability assumed)	$50,000
Minus: Adjusted basis of gift to Jack	(60,000)
Realized loss (not recognized)	$10,000

[33] 1995-2 C.B. 313.
[32] 1995-1 C.B. 130.

[34] Reg. Sec. 1.1001-1(e).

Andrew's basis in his partnership interest is equal to the greater of the assumed liabilities ($50,000) or Jack's basis for the interest ($60,000) plus any gift tax Jack must pay on the appreciation. Thus, Andrew's basis is the $60,000 amount adjusted for any gift taxes Jack paid on the $12,500 gift. ◀

Topic Review C10-2 summarizes the tax consequences of a number of alternative methods for terminating an investment in a partnership.

INCOME RECOGNITION AND TRANSFERS OF A PARTNERSHIP INTEREST

The partnership tax year closes with respect to any partner who sells or exchanges his or her entire interest in a partnership or any partner whose interest in the partnership is liquidated. The partnership tax year closes on the sale or exchange date or the date of final payment on a liquidation. As a result, that partner's share of all items earned by the partnership must be reported in the partner's tax year that includes the transaction date.[35]

The partnership tax year does not close with respect to a partner whose interest is transferred by gift. The donor's share of income up to the date of the gift must be reported by the donor.[36] When a partner dies, the partnership tax year does not close with respect to the partner. The deceased partner's distributive share of income for the partnership tax year during which the partner's death occurs must be reported by the deceased partner's estate or successor-in-interest.[37]

TERMINATION OF A PARTNERSHIP

OBJECTIVE 9

Determine whether a partnership has terminated for tax purposes

EVENTS CAUSING A TERMINATION TO OCCUR. Because of the complex relationships among partners and their liability for partnership debts, state partnership laws provide for the termination of a partnership under a wide variety of conditions. Section 708(b) was enacted to avoid the tax complexity created by the wide variety of state laws and the numerous termination conditions. That section provides that a partnership terminates for tax purposes only if

- No part of any business, financial operation, or venture of the partnership continues to be carried on by any of its partners in a partnership or
- Within a twelve-month period there is a sale or exchange of at least 50% of the total interest in partnership capital and profits.

TYPICAL MISCONCEPTION

Taxpayers often do not understand the difference between a partnership tax year closing for a specific partner versus a partnership tax year closing for all partners due to a termination of the partnership itself. Obviously, the tax consequences of these two events are drastically different.

NO BUSINESS OPERATED AS A PARTNERSHIP. If no partner continues to operate any business of the partnership through the same or another partnership, the original partnership terminates. To avoid termination, the partnership must maintain both partners and business activity. For example, if one partner retires from a two-person partnership and the second partner continues the business alone, the partnership terminates. However, if one partner in a two-member partnership dies, the partnership does not terminate as long as the deceased's estate or successor-in-interest continues to share in the profits and losses of the partnership business.[38]

Likewise, a partnership terminates if it ceases to carry on any business or financial venture. The courts have allowed a partnership to continue under this rule even though the partnership sold all its assets and retained only a few installment notes.[39] Despite the courts' flexibility in these circumstances, it is wiser to maintain more than a nominal level of assets if continuation of the partnership is desired.

---

[35] Sec. 706(c)(2).

[36] Reg. Sec. 1.706-1(c)(5).

[37] Reg. Sec. 1.706-1(c)(3).

[38] Reg. Sec. 1.708-1(b)(1)(i)(a).

[39] For example, see *Max R. Ginsburg v. U.S.*, 21 AFTR 2d 1489, 68-1 USTC ¶9429 (Ct. Cls., 1968).

Topic Review C10-2

Terminating an Investment in a Partnership

Method	Tax Consequences to Partner
Death or retirement:	
Amounts paid for property[a]	Liquidating distribution tax consequences apply to the amount paid.
Amounts paid in excess of property values	
Amounts not determined by reference to partnership income	Ordinary income.
Amounts determined by reference to partnership income	Distributive share of partnership income.
Sale of partnership interest to outsider	Capital gain (loss) except for ordinary income (loss) reported on Sec. 751 assets.
Gift of partnership interest	Sale to extent of liability assumed by donee. Gain recognized equal to excess of liability assumed over adjusted basis of partnership interest.
Exchange for partnership interest:	
In same partnership	No tax consequences
In different partnership	Capital gain (loss) except for ordinary income (loss) on Sec. 751 assets.
Exchange for corporate stock	No gain or loss generally recognized if it qualifies for Sec. 351 tax-free treatment. Capital gain (loss) except for ordinary income (loss) on Sec. 751 assets if the exchange does not qualify for Sec. 351 treatment.
Incorporation of partnership	Tax consequences depend on form of transaction used for incorporation.
Formation of LLC/LLP	No tax consequences except for distributions/contributions deemed to occur if liability shares change.

[a]Only for a general partner departing from a service partnership, property excludes unrealized receivables and goodwill if it is not mentioned in the partnership agreement.

KEY POINT

In order for the 50% rule to terminate a partnership, there must be a *sale* or *exchange* of 50% or more of the capital *and* profits interests. Sales or exchanges occurring within a twelve-month period are aggregated; however, if the same interest is sold twice within twelve months, it is only counted once.

SALE OR EXCHANGE OF AT LEAST A 50% INTEREST. The second condition that leads to the termination of a partnership is the sale or exchange of at least a 50% interest in both partnership capital and profits within a twelve-month period. The relevant twelve-month period is determined without reference to the tax year of either the partnership or any partner but rather is any twelve consecutive months. To cause termination, the partnership interest must be transferred by sale or exchange. Transactions or occurrences that do not constitute a sale or exchange (e.g., the gifting of a partnership interest or the transferring of a partnership interest at death) cannot cause a partnership to terminate as long as partners continue the partnership business. Likewise, as long as at least two partners remain, the removal of a partner who owns more than

50% of the total partnership capital and profits interests can be accomplished without terminating the partnership by making a liquidating distribution.[40]

Measuring the portion of the total partnership capital and profits interest that has been transferred often presents difficulties. Multiple exchanges of the same partnership interest are counted only once for purposes of determining whether the 50% maximum is exceeded. When several different small interests are transferred within a twelve-month period, the partnership's termination occurs on the date of the transfer that first crosses the 50% threshold.[41]

EXAMPLE C10-27 ▶ On August 1, 1996, Miguel sells his 30% capital and profits interest in the LMN Partnership to Steve. On June 1, 1997, Steve sells the 30% interest acquired from Miguel to Andrew. For purposes of Sec. 708, the two sales are considered to be the transfer of a single partnership interest. Thus, the LMN Partnership does not terminate unless there are other sales of partnership interests totaling at least 20% of LMN's capital and profits interests during any twelve-month period that includes either August 1, 1996, or June 1, 1997. ◀

EXAMPLE C10-28 ▶ On July 15, 1996, Kelly sells Carlos a 37% capital and profits interest in the KRS Partnership. On November 14, 1996, Rick sells Diana a 10% capital and profits interest in the KRS Partnership. On January 18, 1997, Sherrie sells Evan a 5% capital and profits interest in the KRS Partnership. The KRS Partnership terminates on January 18, 1997 because the cumulative interest sold within the twelve-month period that includes January 18, 1997, first exceeds 50% on that date. ◀

EFFECTS OF TERMINATION.

KEY POINT

If the year-ends of the partners and the partnership are not the same, a termination of the partnership can result in more than twelve months of partnership income/loss being reported in the tax returns of some partners.

Importance of Timing. When a partnership terminates, its tax year closes, requiring the partners to include their share of partnership earnings for the short-period partnership tax year in their tax returns. If the termination is not properly timed, partnership income for a regular twelve-month tax year may already be included in the same return that must include the short tax year. As partners and partnerships are increasingly forced to adopt the same tax year, this will be less of a problem.

EXAMPLE C10-29 ▶ Joy is a calendar-year taxpayer who owns a 40% capital and profits interest in the ATV Partnership. ATV has a natural business year-end of March 31, and with IRS permission uses that date as its tax year-end. For the partnership tax year ending March 31, 1997, Joy has an $80,000 distributive share of ordinary income. Pat, who owns the remaining 60% capital and profits interests, sells his interest to Collin on November 30, 1997. Because more than 50% of the capital and profits interests have changed hands, the ATV Partnership terminates on November 30, 1997 and the partnership's tax year ends on that date.

Joy's tax return for the tax year ending on December 31, 1997, must include the $80,000 distributive share from the partnership tax year for the period April 1, 1996 through March 31, 1997 and the distributive share of partnership income for the short tax year including the period April 1, 1997 through November 30, 1997. ◀

SELF-STUDY QUESTION

What are the tax consequences of a partnership termination caused by a 50% change in ownership?

Liquidating Distributions and Contributions. When a termination occurs for tax purposes, a pro rata liquidating distribution is deemed to have been made to all partners. Gain or loss must be recognized by the partners under the liquidating distribution rules. An actual liquidating distribution may occur if the termination occurs because of the cessation of business. However, if the termination occurs because of a greater than 50% change in ownership of the capital and profits interests, an actual distribution usually

[40] Reg. Sec. 1.708-1(b)(1)(ii).
[41] Ibid.

does not occur. Nevertheless, gain or loss must be recognized, and the bases of assets deemed distributed must be adjusted as they would be in an actual liquidating distribution.[42]

If a termination occurs for tax purposes because of a greater than 50% change in ownership of the capital and profits interests, it is likely that the partnership's actual business activity will continue uninterrupted. If the partnership's business continues, a deemed contribution of property to the new partnership must follow the deemed distribution.[43] Generally, no gain is recognized on the contribution of the assets to the new partnership.[44] The partner's bases in these assets carry over to the partnership under Sec. 722.

ANSWER

When a partnership terminates as a result of a 50% change of ownership, the partnership is first treated as making a liquidating distribution. Because the partnership continues to operate, the partners are likewise treated as making a contribution of the liquidated assets back to the new partnership. This hypothetical distribution/contribution is subject to the regular partnership rules and could result in a gain/loss being recognized and a basis change taking place.

EXAMPLE C10-30 ▶

The ABC Partnership terminates for tax purposes on July 15, when Anna's 52% capital and profits interest is sold to Diane. Beth, who has a 20% interest in the partnership with a $70,000 basis at the time of the termination, is deemed to receive a pro rata liquidating distribution consisting of 20% of each partnership asset. The partnership's basis in the assets deemed distributed to Beth and her basis in the assets after the deemed distribution are as follows:

Assets	*20% of Partnership's Basis*	*Beth's Basis*
Cash	$ 5,000	$ 5,000
Receivables	—0—	—0—
Inventory	5,000	5,000
Building	30,000	45,000
Land	10,000	15,000
Total	$50,000	$70,000

The portion of Beth's total $70,000 basis allocable to the building and the land is determined as follows:

Beth's basis in old partnership interest before the distribution	$70,000
Minus: Cash	(5,000)
Carryover basis for unrealized receivables	—0—
Carryover basis for inventory	(5,000)
Basis to allocate to building and land	$60,000

Allocation of the total basis to the building and the land occurs as follows:

$$\text{Basis for building: } \$60,000 \times \frac{\$30,000}{\$30,000 + \$10,000} = \$45,000$$

$$\text{Basis for land: } \$60,000 \times \frac{\$10,000}{\$30,000 + \$10,000} = \$15,000$$

On the deemed contribution to the new partnership, the $70,000 total basis of the assets in Beth's hands carries over to the partnership, and the partnership's basis in her share of the building and land is increased from $40,000 to $60,000 by the termination. ◀

SELF-STUDY QUESTION

How does the new partnership depreciate the building?

ANSWER

To the extent of the $30,000 that carries over from the old partnership, the new partnership continues to depreciate the property as before. The $15,000 of new basis is treated as a new MACRS asset.

Changes in Accounting Methods. Not only does a termination result in a change to the basis of some partnership assets, but it may cause numerous other changes in the

[42] Proposed regulations for Sec. 708 were issued in May 1996 that would radically change this presumption. The proposed regulations provide that the terminated partnership is deemed to transfer all assets and liabilities to a new partnership. Then the terminated partnership distributes the interest in the new partnership as a liquidating distribution to the partners of the terminated partnership. As a result, the partners would not recognize gain nor loss, assets would not have their bases adjusted, and the bases of the partners' interests in the partnership would be unchanged.

[43] Reg. Sec. 1.708-1(b)(1)(iv).

[44] Sec. 721.

partnership's accounting methods. The termination ends all partnership elections. Thus, all partnership elections concerning its tax year and accounting methods must be made in the new partnership's first tax year.

The election that allows the partnership to make optional basis adjustments (discussed below) is also terminated. A partnership may find this to be a benefit of a termination because the optional basis adjustment is sometimes troublesome for a partnership and may be difficult to revoke.

KEY POINT

The principal concern when two or more partnerships are combined is which partnership's tax year, accounting methods, and elections will survive the merger. This determination is made by examining the capital and profits interests of the partners of the old partnerships.

MERGERS AND CONSOLIDATIONS

When two or more partnerships join together to form a new partnership, it is necessary to know which, if any, of the old partnerships are continued and which are terminated. An old partnership whose partner(s) own more than 50% of the profits and capital interests of the new partnership is considered to be continued as the new partnership.[45] Accordingly, the new partnership must continue with the tax year and accounting methods and elections of the old partnership that is considered to continue. All of the other old partnerships are considered to have been terminated.

EXAMPLE C10-31 ▶ The AB and CD Partnerships are merged to form the ABCD Partnership. April and Ben each own 30% of ABCD and Carole and David each own 20% of ABCD. The ABCD Partnership is considered a continuation of the AB Partnership because 60% of ABCD is owned by April and Ben, the former partners of AB. ABCD is bound by the tax year, accounting method, and other elections made by AB. CD, formerly owned by Carole and David, is considered to terminate on the merger date. ◀

It is possible that the partners of two or more of the old partnerships will hold the requisite profits and capital interest in the new partnership. When two or more old partnerships satisfy this requirement, the old partnership that is credited with contributing the greatest dollar value of assets to the new partnership is considered the continuing partnership and all other partnerships are terminated. Sometimes, none of the old partnerships account for more than 50% of the capital and profits of the new partnership. In that case, all of the old partnerships terminate, and the merged partnership is a new entity that can make its own tax year and accounting method elections.

EXAMPLE C10-32 ▶ Three partnerships are merged to form the ABCD Partnership. The AB Partnership (owned by Andy and Bill) contributes assets valued at $140,000 to ABCD; BC (owned by Bill and Cathy) and CD (owned by Cathy and Drew) Partnerships contribute assets valued at $180,000 and $120,000, respectively. The capital and profits interests of the partners in the new partnership are Andy, 20%; Bill, 35%; Cathy, 19%; and Drew, 26%. Both the AB and BC Partnerships had partners who now own more than 50% of the new partnership (Andy and Bill own 55%, and Bill and Cathy own 54%). The BC Partnership contributes more assets ($180,000) to the new partnership than the AB Partnership ($140,000). Therefore, the ABCD Partnership is a continuation of the BC Partnership. Both the AB and CD Partnerships terminate on the merger date. ◀

KEY POINT

The principal concern of a partnership division is to determine which of the new partnerships is the continuation of the prior partnership.

DIVISION OF A PARTNERSHIP

When a partnership is divided into two or more new partnerships, all of the new partnerships whose partners own collectively more than 50% of the profits and capital interests in the old partnerships are considered a continuation of the old partnership.[46] All partnerships that are continuations of the old partnership are bound by the old partnership's tax year and accounting method elections. Any other partnership that is created by the division is considered a new partnership eligible to make its own tax year

[45] Sec. 708(b)(2)(A).

[46] Sec. 708(b)(2)(B).

and accounting method elections. If no new partnership meets the criteria for continuation of the divided partnership, the divided partnership is terminated on the division date. The interest of any partner of the divided partnership who does not own an interest in a continuing partnership is considered to be liquidated on the division date.

EXAMPLE C10-33 ▶

The RSTV Partnership is in the real estate and insurance business. Randy owns a 40% interest and Sam, Tomas, and Vicki each own 20% of RSTV. The partners agree to split the partnership, with the RS Partnership receiving the real estate operations and the TV Partnership receiving the insurance business. Because Randy and Sam own more than 50% of the RSTV Partnership (40% + 20% = 60%), the RS Partnership is a continuation of the RSTV Partnership and must report its results using the same tax year and accounting method elections that RSTV used. Tomas and Vicki are considered to have terminated their interests in RSTV and to have received a liquidating distribution of the insurance business property. The TV Partnership makes its tax year and accounting method elections following the rules for a new partnership. ◀

OPTIONAL BASIS ADJUSTMENTS

In general, the partnership tax rules provide that no adjustment to the basis of partnership property occurs upon the sale or exchange of a partnership interest, when the partnership interest is transferred upon the death of a partner, or when a distribution is made to a partner. Sometimes, it could benefit the partnership or its partners to be able to adjust the partnership's basis in its assets.

EXAMPLE C10-34 ▶

OBJECTIVE 10

Determine the adjustment required by the sale of a partnership interest or a partnership distribution when the partnership elects to make optional basis adjustments

Eric purchases a 25% interest in the AB Partnership from Amy. Eric pays Amy $60,000 cash and assumes Amy's $20,000 share of partnership liabilities. At the time of Eric's purchase, the AB Partnership has the following balance sheet:

	Basis	*FMV*
Assets:		
Cash	$ 40,000	$ 40,000
Receivables	—0—	20,000
Inventory	30,000	40,000
Equipment[a]	140,000	180,000
Land	30,000	40,000
Total	$240,000	$320,000
Liabilities and capital:		
Liabilities	$ 80,000	$ 80,000
Capital—Amy	40,000	60,000
—Becky	120,000	180,000
Total	$240,000	$320,000

[a]If the equipment were sold, $40,000 of Sec. 1245 ordinary income would be recognized.

Eric pays an appropriate FMV price for the partnership interest, yet his share of the partnership's basis in its assets is only $60,000 (0.25 × $240,000) compared to his $80,000 basis in his partnership interest. The problem this creates is apparent when it is remembered that under Sec. 751(a) Amy's share of the ordinary income from the receivables and inventory assets is taxed to her when she sells her interest to Eric, whereas the asset's basis to the partnership is unchanged. Thus, when the partnership disposes of these assets, Eric's distributive share of this ordinary income (which actually has already been taxed to Amy) must be reported. ◀

TYPICAL MISCONCEPTION

The basis a partnership has in its assets (sometimes called inside basis) is not necessarily the same as the basis the partners have in their partnership interests (sometimes called outside basis). This difference usually results from a sale or exchange of a partnership interest, a transfer of a partnership interest at the death of a partner, or a distribution to a partner.

An election is available for a partnership to make an adjustment to the basis of its assets.[47] However, the blessing is a mixed one. Once the optional basis adjustment election is made, the partnership must make the required adjustments for *all* sales, exchanges, transfers on death, and distributions. Some of the required adjustments may decrease (rather than increase) the partnership's basis in its assets. In addition, the election can be revoked only with IRS permission.

KEY POINT

A Sec. 754 election allows a partnership to make special basis adjustments for its assets in certain circumstances. This election is a mixed blessing, for the adjustments can result in decreases to basis as well as increases to basis. Once the election is made, it can be revoked only with IRS permission.

ELECTION TO MAKE BASIS ADJUSTMENTS

Because the basis adjustments are optional, the partnership itself must file an election under Sec. 754 to make the adjustments. (See the Compliance and Procedural Considerations section of this chapter for a discussion of the election procedures.) The election applies to all transfers of a partnership interest by sale or exchange or upon the death of a partner under Sec. 743 and all distributions of partnership property under Sec. 734. The election is effective for all transfers and distributions for the year in which the election is made and for all subsequent years until the election is revoked.

OPTIONAL ADJUSTMENTS ON TRANSFERS

When a partner's interest is sold to an outsider, the outsider's basis in his or her partnership interest is the sum of the purchase price and the partner's share of partnership liabilities. The new partner's proportionate share of the partnership's basis in its assets seldom equals his or her basis in the partnership interest. A new partner is taxed on his or her share of gains and losses as the partnership recognizes them. Because the partner's distributive share of gains and losses recognized while he or she is a partner is reflected in his or her basis in the partnership interest, the difference is largely one of timing. However, if the partnership continues for many years, the timing difference may be quite significant.

EXAMPLE C10-35 ▶

Assume the same facts as in Example C10-34. The AB Partnership sells the equipment for its $180,000 FMV and recognizes a $40,000 ($180,000 − $140,000 basis) gain, which is characterized by Sec. 1245 as ordinary income. Eric recognizes a $10,000 (0.25 × $40,000) share of the ordinary income and also increases his basis for the partnership interest by $10,000. If nothing else has changed in the partnership since Eric purchased his interest, he has a $90,000 basis ($80,000 original basis + $10,000 income recognized), but the FMV of the interest remains unchanged at $80,000. Accordingly, Eric would recognize a $10,000 capital loss if he sells his partnership interest for its FMV. Eric recognizes $10,000 of ordinary income from partnership operations and a $10,000 loss (which would probably be a capital loss) if he sells his partnership interest. The loss recognition is, of course, delayed until he actually disposes of the partnership interest. ◀

KEY POINT

The partnership will increase/decrease the basis of its assets by the difference in the transferee's basis in the partnership interest and the transferee's share of the basis in the partnership assets. Adjustments are made with respect to the transferee partner only.

The result can be quite different if the partnership has an election to make optional basis adjustments in effect for the year of the transfer. The optional basis adjustment election permits the partnership's bases in its assets to be adjusted so that the new partner's initial basis in his or her partnership interest and his or her proportionate share of the partnership's basis for its assets are equal. If the partner's initial basis in his or her partnership interest exceeds his or her proportionate share of the partnership's basis for its assets, the partnership's basis for its assets is increased with respect to the transferee partner only. (Conversely, if the partner's basis in the partnership interest is less than his or her proportionate share of the partnership's basis for its assets, the partnership's basis for its assets is decreased.) Overall, the transferee's total basis in the partnership's assets after the optional basis adjustment is the same as if a direct interest were purchased in

---

[47] Sec. 754.

each individual asset. However, because Sec. 755 mandates a specific set of allocation rules, the partner's basis in an individual asset after the optional basis adjustment may not be the same as when a proportionate interest in that asset is purchased.

AMOUNT OF THE ADJUSTMENT. The amount of the optional basis adjustment equals the difference between the transferee partner's initial basis for his or her partnership interest and his or her share of the partnership's adjusted basis for all of its properties.[48] The transferee partner's share of the partnership's basis for its properties equals the sum of the partner's interest in the partnership capital plus the partner's share of the partnership's liabilities. The transferee partner's share of the adjusted basis of partnership property must also reflect any special allocations of gain or loss on contributed partnership property to the other partners. The calculation of the adjustment amount is illustrated in the following example.

EXAMPLE C10-36 ▶ Rosa purchases a one-third capital and profits interest in the PDK Partnership from Kyle for $22,000 in cash. At the time of the purchase, an election to make optional basis adjustments is in effect. No special allocations are mentioned in the partnership agreement. At the time of Rosa's purchase, PDK's balance sheet is as follows:

	Basis	*FMV*
Assets:		
Cash	$ 5,000	$ 5,000
Inventory	30,000	31,000
Depreciable assets	20,000	40,000
Total	$55,000	$76,000
Liabilities and capital:		
Liabilities	$10,000	$10,000
Capital—Pam	15,000	22,000
—Dan	15,000	22,000
—Kyle	15,000	22,000
Total	$55,000	$76,000

The $7,000 optional basis adjustment amount is calculated as follows:

Rosa's initial basis in the partnership interest:		
Cash purchase price	$22,000	
Plus: Share of liabilities (0.333 × $10,000)	3,333	$25,333
Minus: Rosa's share of partnership's basis in assets:		
Kyle's basis in partnership's assets	$15,000	
Plus: Share of liabilities (0.333 × $10,000)	3,333	(18,333)
Optional basis adjustment		$ 7,000 ◀

The calculation of the transferee's interest in the partnership's basis for its assets can be quite complex if there are special allocations among the partners or if the allocation of liabilities is complex, as might occur with a limited partnership interest. However, the general idea of equalizing basis for the partner and partnership is retained throughout the more complicated calculations.

The $7,000 adjustment is allocated to the basis of individual assets on the partnership's books under the rules of Sec. 755. The adjustment generally closes the gap between FMV and partnership adjusted basis in each asset.

[48] Sec. 743(b).

OPTIONAL ADJUSTMENTS ON DISTRIBUTIONS

As noted earlier, the general rule for distributions is that no basis adjustment is made at the partnership level even if a distributee partner does not take a carryover basis in the distributed property. The inequities caused by the no adjustment rule can be easily seen by considering an example.

EXAMPLE C10-37 ▶ Jennifer receives $6,000 cash as a liquidating distribution for her one-third interest in the XYZ Partnership. Jennifer's basis in her partnership interest is $4,000. XYZ's balance sheet immediately before the distribution is as follows:

	Basis	*FMV*
Assets:		
Cash	$ 6,000	$ 6,000
Land	6,000	12,000
Total	$12,000	$18,000
Partners' capital:		
Jennifer	$ 4,000	$ 6,000
Rick	4,000	6,000
Suzanne	4,000	6,000
Total	$12,000	$18,000

The XYZ Partnership has $6,000 of unrealized gain immediately before the distribution, all of which is attributable to the land. Each partner's share of the gain is $2,000. Because Jennifer receives cash in excess of her basis in the partnership interest, she must report a $2,000 ($6,000 − $4,000) gain. The two remaining partners, Rick and Suzanne, retain the land as their only remaining asset, and the land's basis is not adjusted under the general rules for partnership distributions. The partnership's remaining $6,000 of unrealized gain is divided between Rick and Suzanne. If the land is sold, Rick and Suzanne must each report a $3,000 gain. Jennifer's share of the unrealized gain on the land is shifted to Rick and Suzanne, even though Jennifer already paid a tax on the $2,000 gain inherent in liquidating her partnership interest. An optional basis adjustment will increase the basis of the land by $2,000 and restore each of the two remaining partners to the position of having $2,000 of unrealized gain. ◀

KEY POINT

Inequities can result from partnership distributions as well as from transfers of partnership interests. For example, if gain is recognized in a cash distribution or loss is recognized in a liquidating distribution, neither the gain nor the loss is reflected in the basis of the partnership assets. The optional basis adjustments that are allowed for these distributions affect all partners instead of just the transferee partner.

Once a Sec. 754 election is in effect, optional basis adjustments must be made on distributions as well as on transfers of partnership interests. Unlike basis adjustments made relative to the transferee partner when a sale or exchange of a partnership interest occurs, basis adjustments resulting from a partnership distribution apply to the common basis of partnership assets.[49] Accordingly, no special account is necessary for the basis adjustment, and all partners receive the benefit (or detriment) of the adjustment.

AMOUNT OF THE ADJUSTMENT. An optional basis adjustment is necessary when a distribution is made only if the distributee partner does not take a carryover basis for property that is received. If a partner recognizes a gain on a partnership distribution, the optional basis adjustment is to increase the basis of remaining partnership assets by the amount of the gain. If a partner recognizes a loss on a liquidating distribution, the optional basis adjustment is to decrease the basis of remaining partnership assets by the amount of the loss. If a partner increases (decreases) the basis of assets received in a

[49] Sec. 734(b).

property distribution from what the basis was in the partnership's hands, the optional basis adjustment is to decrease (increase) the basis of assets that remain in partnership hands by the same amount as the change in basis of the distributed assets.

EXAMPLE C10-38 ▶ Assume the same facts as in Example C10-37, except that a Sec. 754 election is in effect. The partnership increases the basis of its remaining asset (land) by $2,000. The unrealized gain remaining after the basis adjustment is made is reduced to $4,000, and each of the two remaining partners recognizes only a $2,000 gain if the land is sold. ◀

EXAMPLE C10-39 ▶ Jamal has a $10,000 basis in his JK Partnership interest before receiving a distribution of land having a basis of $12,000 on JK's books. Jamal's basis in the land is limited to $10,000 (Jamal's basis in his partnership interest). If a Sec. 754 election is in effect, JK must increase the basis of its remaining assets by $2,000 ($12,000 − $10,000). ◀

SPECIAL FORMS OF PARTNERSHIPS

Here, we examine a series of special partnership forms, including tax shelters that are organized as limited partnerships, publicly traded partnerships, limited liability companies, and limited liability partnerships.

TAX SHELTERS AND LIMITED PARTNERSHIPS

Tax shelters at their best are good investments that reduce the amount of an investor's tax bill. Traditionally, shelter benefits arise from leverage, income deferral, and tax credits.

Before the Tax Reform Act of 1986, limited partnerships were the primary vehicle for tax shelter investments. However, the Tax Reform Act of 1986 greatly reduced the benefits of limited partnerships as tax shelters by invoking the passive activity loss limitations for activity conducted in a limited partnership form. The limited partnership still allows an investor to limit liability while receiving the benefits of the shelter's tax attributes to save taxes on other passive income. Since the Tax Reform Act of 1986, limited partnerships that generate passive income rather than losses have become popular investments for investors who already hold loss-generating limited partnership interests.

HISTORICAL NOTE

Because partnerships are treated as flow-through entities, they have historically been popular for activities designed to produce tax losses (tax shelters). However, since the Tax Reform Act of 1986, profit partnerships are more in demand. This is due, in part, to the fact that many investors are now interested in generating passive income to offset their passive losses.

PUBLICLY TRADED PARTNERSHIPS

The Revenue Act of 1987 moved to restrict still further the benefits of tax shelter ownership by changing the taxation of **publicly traded partnerships** (PTPs). A PTP is a partnership whose interests are traded either on an established securities exchange or in a secondary market or the equivalent thereof. A partnership that meets the requirements is taxed as a C corporation under Sec. 7704.

There are two exceptions for partnerships that would otherwise be classified as PTPs:

- Partnerships that have 90% or more of their gross income being "qualifying income" continue to be taxed under the partnership rules.
- Partnerships that were in existence on December 17, 1987 and have not added a substantial new line of business since that date are grandfathered. In general, application of the PTP rules for these partnerships is delayed until tax years beginning after December 31, 1997.

REAL-WORLD EXAMPLE

The Chicago Board of Partnerships acts as a secondary market for limited partnership interests. Trades can range from less than $2,000 to in excess of $5 million. This market increases the liquidity of limited partnership investments. Some partnerships are publicly-traded on the major stock exchanges. For example, the Boston Celtics Limited Partnership is traded on the New York Stock Exchange. These limited partnerships have the same degree of liquidity for their investors as corporations.

For the 90% of gross income test, qualifying income is defined in Sec. 7704(d) as including certain interest, dividends, real property rents (but not personal property rents), income and gains from the sale or disposition of a capital asset or Sec. 1231(b) trade or business property that is held for the production of passive income, and gain from the sale or disposition of real property. It also includes gains from certain commodity trading and natural resource activities. It should be noted that any PTP that is not taxed as a corporation because of this 90% exception is subject to separate and more restrictive Sec. 469 passive loss rules than are partnerships that are not publicly traded.

If a partnership is first classified as a PTP that is taxed as a corporation during a tax year, there is a deemed contribution of all partnership assets and all partnership liabilities to a corporation in exchange for all the corporation's stock. The stock is then deemed distributed to the partners in complete liquidation of the partnership. This transaction is taxed exactly as if it had physically occurred.

LIMITED LIABILITY COMPANIES

A new form of business entity, the limited liability company (LLC), has emerged in the United States in recent years. This entity combines the legal and tax benefits of partnerships and S corporations. At the present time all fifty states have adopted LLC laws. The LLC business form combines the advantage of limited liability for all its owners with the ability of achieving the conduit treatment and the flexibility of being taxed as a partnership.

ADDITIONAL COMMENT

With the advantage of limited liability and the flexibility of being treated as a partnership, LLCs will be a popular choice of entity for conducting a business.

In the past, whether an LLC was characterized as a corporation or a partnership for federal tax purposes depended on the number of corporate characteristics that were present such as limited liability, free transferability of interests, centralized management, and continuity of life. The process of determining tax treatment was complex and time consuming. However, in December 1996, new regulations were adopted which allow entities (other than corporations and trusts) to choose whether to be taxed as a partnership or as an association. (An association is an unincorporated entity which is taxed as a corporation.) Accordingly, an LLC with two or more members can choose either partnership or association tax treatment. With a written and properly filed election, any LLC can choose to be taxed as an association. If no written election is made, an LLC with two or more members is considered to be a partnership for tax purposes, while a single member LLC with no written association election is generally taxed as a sole proprietorship.

ADDITIONAL COMMENT

The list of advantages of an LLC over an S corporation is substantial and suggests a decline in popularity of new S elections. However, one current, important advantage of an S corporation is that the shareholders are not subject to self-employment tax on the earnings of the entity.

An LLC with two or more members which does not elect association status is a partnership for tax purposes and is subject to all of the rules which apply to other partnerships. The formation of the LLC; income, gain, loss, and deductions which flow through to the LLC members; current and liquidating distributions; and sale, gift, or exchange of an interest in the LLC are all taxed under the partnership rules. An LLC taxed as a partnership is subject to the Sec. 704 rules for special allocations and allocations of precontribution gain or loss, to the Sec. 736 rules for retirement distributions, and to the Sec. 751 "hot asset" rules. For tax purposes, an LLC with two or more members which does not elect association status is fully taxed as a partnership.

Using the LLC form for a business with publicly traded ownership interests is likely to result in taxation as a corporation. Even if the LLC does not elect association status, the public trading of the ownership interest brings the LLC under the publicly traded partnership rules. As discussed above, these rules result in the business being taxed as a corporation unless 90% or more of the income is qualifying income or unless the LLC is covered under the grandfather rules. Given the recency of LLCs as a form for conducting business, the grandfather provisions are unlikely to apply.

If an LLC is taxed as a partnership, it offers greater flexibility than an S corporation in that there is no limit on the number of shareholders, the number of classes of stock, or the types of investments in related entities that can be made. Unlike S corporations, LLCs can use the special allocation rules of Sec. 704 to allocate income, gain, loss or deductions to their members. Each member's basis in the LLC interest includes that member's share of the organization's debts (and not just shareholder debt as with an S corporation).

LIMITED LIABILITY PARTNERSHIPS

REAL WORLD EXAMPLE

In 1994, all of the Big 6 accounting firms and a number of other national accounting firms became LLPs. Many local and regional professional accounting and law firms have also changed to LLPs.

Many states have added limited liability partnerships (LLPs) to the list of business forms that can be formed. Under the current state laws, the primary difference between a general partnership and a LLP is that in a limited liability partnership, a partner is not liable for damages resulting from failures in the work of other partners or of people supervised by other partners. For example, assume that a limited liability accounting partnership is assessed damages in a lawsuit that resulted from an audit partner in New York being negligent in an audit. The tax partner for the same firm, who is based in San Diego and who had no involvement with the audit or the auditor, should not be liable to pay damages resulting from the suit.

Like a general or limited partnership, this business form is a partnership for tax purposes. All of the partnership tax rules and regulations apply to this business form just as they do to any other partnership.

STOP & THINK

Question: What changes do you expect the "check-the-box" regulations to bring about for new businesses making their initial choice of entity decision? What changes do you expect these regulations to have on existing corporations?

Solution: Consider the options facing a new business. The business can be formed as a C corporation, which provides limited liability protection to owners but subjects the corporate income to double taxation. A business formed as a C corporation can make an S election for tax purposes, which keeps the limited liability protection for the owners and eliminates the double taxation by taxing all income directly to the owners. However, as you will see in Chapter C11, there are numerous restrictions that prevent a firm from being taxed as an S corporation. In addition, all income and loss of an S corporation must be allocated among the shareholders on a pro rata basis. A partnership offers the most flexible tax treatment with no double taxation of income, but the traditional partnership must have at least one general partner whose liability for partnership debts is not limited. An LLC, which is taxed as a partnership, provides limited liability protection to its owners while avoiding both the double taxation of income found in a regular corporation as well as the restrictions placed on S corporations. Because an LLC is taxed as a partnership, the income and loss shares reported by each partner is flexible, and the partner's basis for his partnership interest includes his or her share of the LLC's liabilities. In some senses, the LLC has the best attributes of both the corporation and the partnership.

There are strong reasons why a new entity would choose to form as an LLC and elect to be taxed as a partnership, but LLCs are a new business form. As such, statutes, case law, and regulations are still being developed. There remain many areas of uncertainty, which must be resolved over time.

The "check-the-box" regulations are likely to be of much less interest to existing C corporations and S corporations because an existing corporation must liquidate (with all the tax consequences of a liquidation, as described in Chapter C6) before it can form as an LLC. Potentially, the change in entity form has a very high tax cost for an existing corporation.

TAX PLANNING CONSIDERATIONS

LIQUIDATING DISTRIBUTION OR SALE TO PARTNERS

An unusual tax planning opportunity exists when one partner withdraws from a partnership and the remaining partners proportionately increase their ownership of the partnership. The partners can structure the ownership change as either a liquidating distribution made by the partnership or as a sale of the partnership interest to the remaining partners. In fact, the substance of the two transactions is the same, only the form is different. However, this difference in form can make a substantial difference in the tax consequences in a number of areas.

SELF-STUDY QUESTION

What difference does it make if the withdrawal of a partner is structured as a sale of a partnership interest rather than a liquidating distribution?

ANSWER

Two potential differences are that the optional basis adjustments are applied differently and a liquidating distribution of a 50% interest does not terminate the partnership.

- If the transferor partner receives payment for his or her interest in the partnership's Sec. 751 assets, ordinary income must be recognized no matter how the transaction is structured. The partnership's basis in Sec. 751 assets is increased in the case of a liquidating distribution. When a sale transaction takes place, the partnership's basis in Sec. 751 assets is increased only if the partnership has an optional basis adjustment election in effect.
- If the partnership has an optional basis adjustment election in effect, the allocation of the adjustment to the individual partnership assets can be different depending on whether the transaction is structured as a sale or as a liquidating distribution.
- If the interest being transferred exceeds 50% of the profits and capital interests, a sale to the remaining partners terminates the partnership. A liquidating distribution does not cause a termination to occur.

Because the tax implications of the sale transaction and liquidating distribution alternatives are both numerous and complex, the partners should make their choice only after careful consideration.

COMPLIANCE AND PROCEDURAL CONSIDERATIONS

SECTION 754 ELECTION

The Sec. 754 election brings the optional basis adjustments of Secs. 734 and 743 into play. Once the decision to file a Sec. 754 election is made, the procedure is simple. The election is filed along with a timely filed partnership return for the year in which a distribution or transfer occurs. If the election is properly filed, the partnership can make optional basis adjustments for distributions or transfers reported on the tax return filed with the election. The Sec. 754 election requires a written statement that must include the name and address of the partnership making the election, be signed by any one of the partners, and contain a declaration that the partnership elects under Sec. 754 to apply the optional basis adjustment provisions found in Secs. 734(b) and 743(b). The election remains in effect until it is revoked or until the partnership is terminated.[50]

HISTORICAL NOTE

If the date for making a Sec. 754 election is missed due to good cause, the IRS, at its discretion, may grant a reasonable extension. For example, the IRS has allowed an extension when a partner was misled by advice received from his tax accountant and an executor of an estate failed to mail the paperwork into the IRS.

REVOCATION OF THE ELECTION. The election to make optional basis adjustments is not easily revoked, but it is possible to do so with IRS approval. Approval can be given if there are sufficient grounds. Regulation Sec. 1.754-1(c) cites some examples that may be considered reason for revocation, including the following:

[50] Reg. Sec. 1.754-1(b).

- A change in the nature of the partnership's business
- A substantial increase in the partnership's assets
- A change in the character of the partnership's assets
- An increased frequency of retirements or shifts in partnership interests

These examples represent situations in which the administrative burden of having an election for optional basis adjustments would substantially increase and would make revocation of the election desirable. However, no application for revocation will be approved if its primary purpose is to avoid reducing the basis of partnership assets that would otherwise result from a distribution or transfer.

PROBLEM MATERIALS

DISCUSSION QUESTIONS

C10-1 Javier is retiring from the JKL Partnership. In January of the current year, he has a $100,000 basis in his partnership interest when he receives a $10,000 cash distribution. The partnership plans to distribute $10,000 each month this year, and Javier will cease to be a partner after the December payment. Is the January payment to Javier a current distribution or a liquidating distribution?

C10-2 Lia has a $40,000 basis in her partnership interest just before receiving a parcel of land as a current distribution. The land was purchased by the partnership. Lia has no precontribution gain. Under what conditions will Lia's basis in the land be $40,000? Under what conditions will Lia's basis in the land be a carryover basis from the partnership's basis in the land?

C10-3 Mariel has a $60,000 basis in her partnership interest just before receiving a parcel of land as a liquidating distribution. She has no remaining precontribution gain and will receive no other distributions. Under what conditions will Mariel's basis in the land be $60,000?

C10-4 Cindy has a $4,000 basis in her partnership interest before receiving a nonliquidating distribution of property having a $4,500 basis and a $6,000 FMV from the CDE Partnership. Cindy has a choice of receiving either inventory or a capital asset. She will hold the distributed property as an investment for no more than two years before she sells it. What tax difference (if any) will occur as a result of Cindy's selection of one property or the other to be distributed by the partnership?

C10-5 The AB Partnership purchases plastic components and assembles children's toys. The assembly operation requires a number of special machines which are housed in a building the partnership owns. The toys are sold on account to a number of retail establishments. The partnership uses the accrual method of accounting. Identify any items you think might be classified as unrealized receivables.

C10-6 Which of the following items are considered to be inventory for purposes of Sec. 751?
a. Supplies
b. Inventory
c. Notes receivable
d. Land held for investment purposes
e. Lots held for resale

C10-7 The AB Partnership has inventory items that have a $100,000 FMV. If the inventory is substantially appreciated for Sec. 751 purposes, what do you know about the basis of the partnership's inventory?

C10-8 Explain the conditions when Sec. 751 has an impact on nonliquidating (current) distributions.

C10-9 What conditions are required in order for a partner to recognize a loss when a distribution is received from a partnership?

C10-10 Can the basis of unrealized receivables and inventory received in a liquidating distribution be greater to the partner than to the partnership? Can the basis of unrealized receivables and inventory received in a distribution be smaller to the partner than to the partnership? Explain.

C10-11 Is it possible for a partner to recognize both a gain and a loss on the sale of a partnership interest? If so, under what conditions?

C10-12 Tyra has a zero basis in her partnership interest and a share in partnership liabilities, which are quite large. Explain how these facts will affect the taxation of her departure from the partnership using the following methods of terminating her interest in the partnership.
- **a.** A liquidating distribution of property
- **b.** A sale of the partnership interest to a current partner for cash
- **c.** A gift of the interest

C10-13 Tom is a 55% general partner in the RST Partnership. Tom wants to retire, and the other two partners, Stacy and Rich, want to continue the partnership business. They agree that the partnership will liquidate Tom's interest in the partnership by paying him 20% of partnership profits for each of the next ten years. Explain why Sec. 736 does (or does not) apply to the partnership's payments to Tom.

C10-14 Lucia has a $20,000 basis in her limited partnership interest before her retirement from the partnership. Her share of partnership assets have a $23,000 FMV, and the partnership has no Sec. 751 assets. In addition to being paid cash for her full share of partnership assets, Lucia will receive a share of partnership income for the next three years. Explain Lucia's tax treatment for the payments she receives.

C10-15 What are the advantages and disadvantages to the partnership and its partners when a partnership termination is caused by a sale of more than a 50% capital and profits interest?

C10-16 What are the advantages and disadvantages of a partnership electing under Sec. 754 to make optional basis adjustments?

C10-17 How is the amount of an optional basis adjustment calculated when a partnership interest is sold? when a partner receives a property distribution?

C10-18 What is a publicly traded partnership? Are all publicly traded partnerships taxed as corporations?

ISSUE IDENTIFICATION QUESTIONS

C10-19 When Kayla's basis in her interest in the JKL Partnership is $30,000, she receives a current distribution of office equipment. The equipment has an FMV of $40,000 and basis of $35,000. Kayla will not use the office equipment in a business activity. What tax issues should Kayla consider with respect to the distribution?

C10-20 Joel receives a $40,000 cash distribution from the JM Partnership which reduces his partnership interest from one-third to one-fourth. The JM Partnership is a general partnership which uses the cash method of accounting and has substantial liabilities. JM's inventory has appreciated substantially since it was purchased. What issues should Joel consider with regard to the distribution?

C10-21 Scott sells his one-third partnership interest to Sally for $40,000 when his basis is $35,000. On the date of the sale, the partnership has no liabilities and the following assets:

Assets	*FMV*	*Basis*
Cash	$ 30,000	$ 30,000
Inventory	21,000	12,000
Building	59,000	53,000
Land	10,000	10,000

The building is depreciated on a straight-line basis. What tax issues should Scott and Sally consider with respect to the sale transaction?

C10-22 David owns a 60% interest in the DDD Partnership, a general partnership, which he sells to the two remaining partners—Drew and Dana. The three partners have agreed that David will receive $150,000 in cash from the sale. David's basis in the partnership interest before the sale is $120,000 which includes his $30,000 share of partnership recourse liabilities. The partnership has assets with a $300,000 FMV and a $200,000 adjusted basis. What issues should David, Drew, and Dana consider before this sale takes place?

C10-23 Andrew and Beth are equal partners in the AB Partnership. On December 30 of the current year, the AB Partnership agrees to liquidate Andrew's partnership interest for a cash payment on December 30 of each of the next five years. What tax issues should Andrew and Beth consider with respect to the liquidation of Andrew's partnership interest?

C10-24 In the current year, Kent retires from the JKL Partnership in exchange for a $100,000 cash payment from the partnership. Kent purchased his partnership interest more than ten years ago. His partners, Jane and Lex, have been partners for more than twenty years and will continue the partnership. Before he receives the $100,000 payment, Kent's basis in his partnership interest is $40,000. The partnership has no liabilities and it has no Sec. 754 election. Distributions from the partnership have always been made in cash, and that policy is expected to continue. At the time that Kent retires, JKL has assets with a total basis of $120,000 and FMV of $300,000. What tax issues should Kent and the two remaining partners consider with respect to the liquidation of Kent's partnership interest?

C10-25 Alex owns 60% of the Hot Wheels LLC that is taxed as a partnership. He plans to give 15% of the LLC (one-fourth of his interest) to his daughter Haley for her high school graduation. He plans to put her interest in a trust and he will serve as the trustee until Haley is 21. The trust will receive any distributions from the LLC, but Haley is unlikely to be given any of the cash until she is age 21. Alex's 60% interest has a $120,000 FMV and an $80,000 adjusted basis including his $48,000 share of the LLC's liabilities. Alex works full time for the LLC for a small salary and his share of LLC income. Alex also has a special allocation of income from rental property he manages for the LLC. What issues should Alex consider before he completes the gift?

C10-26 Krypton Company has recently been formed as a limited liability company (LLC). Krypton Company is owned equally by three individuals—Jeff, Susan, and Richard—all of whom have substantial income from other sources. Krypton is a manufacturing firm and expects to earn approximately $130,000 of ordinary income and $30,000 of long-term capital gain each year for the next several years. Jeff will be a full time manager and will receive a salary of $60,000 each year. What tax issues should be considered by the owners regarding the LLC's initial year of operations?

PROBLEMS

C10-27 ***Current Distributions.*** In the following three independent situations, determine the partner's remaining basis in the partnership interest, the partner's recognized gain or loss, and the basis of any noncash property that is received. All distributions are current distributions, and any distribution involving Sec. 751 property is pro rata to all partners. All precontribution gains have been recognized before the distribution.

a. Lisa has a $25,000 basis in her partnership interest before receiving a distribution of $4,000 cash and land with a $30,000 FMV and a $14,000 basis to the partnership.

b. The RSTUV Partnership paid off a $100,000 liability. Rich's share of the liability was $20,000. The liability is included in Rich's $18,000 basis. The basis is smaller than his share of the liability because the basis has been properly reduced by large depreciation deductions.

c. Kara has a $32,000 basis in her partnership interest just before receiving a distribution of inventory with a $25,000 FMV and a $10,000 basis, receivables with a $3,000 FMV and a $0 basis, and $20,000 cash.

C10-28 ***Current Distributions.*** Complete the chart for each of the following independent distributions. Assume that all distributions are nonliquidating and pro rata to the partners, and no contributed property was distributed. All precontribution gain has been recognized before these distributions.

Partner's Basis and Gain/Loss		*Property Distributed*	*Property's Basis to Partnership*	*Property's FMV*	*Property's Basis to Partner*
a. Basis:					
Predistribution	$20,000	Cash	$ 6,000	$ 6,000	
Postdistribution	$_____	Land	4,000	15,000	$_____
Gain or loss	$_____	Machinery	3,000	2,000	$_____
b. Basis:					
Predistribution	$20,000	Land	$ 6,000	$ 4,000	$_____
Postdistribution	$_____	Inventory	7,000	7,500	$_____
Gain or loss	$_____	Cash	3,000	3,000	
c. Basis					
Predistribution	$26,000	Cash	$35,000	$35,000	
Postdistribution	$_____	Land—Parcel 1	6,000	10,000	$_____
Gain or loss	$_____	Land—Parcel 2	18,000	18,000	$_____
d. Basis:					
Predistribution	$28,000	Land—Parcel 1	$ 4,000	$ 6,000	$_____
Postdistribution	$_____	Land—Parcel 2	6,000	10,000	$_____
Gain or loss	$_____	Land—Parcel 3	4,000	10,000	$_____

C10-29 ***Current Distribution with Precontribution Gain.*** Three years ago, Mario joined the MN Partnership by contributing land with a $10,000 basis and an $18,000 FMV. On January 15 of the current year, Mario has a basis in his partnership interest of $20,000 and none of his precontribution gain has been recognized. On January 15, Mario receives a current distribution of a property other than the contributed land with a $15,000 basis and a $23,000 FMV.

a. Does Mario recognize any gain or loss on the distribution?

b. What is Mario's basis in his partnership interest after the distribution?

c. What is the partnership's basis in the land Mario contributed after Mario receives this distribution?

C10-30 ***Current Distribution of Contributed Property.*** In 1995, Andrew contributed investment land having an $18,000 basis and a $22,000 FMV and $4,000 in money to the ABC Partnership when it was formed. In December 1997, the investment land Andrew contributed was distributed by the partnership to Bob, another partner. At the time of the distribution, the land had a $21,000 FMV and Andrew and Bob's bases in their partnership interests were $21,000 and $30,000, respectively.

a. What gain or loss must be recognized on the distribution and who must recognize it?
b. What are the bases for Andrew and Bob's interests in the partnership after the distribution?
c. What is Bob's basis in the distributed land?

C10-31 ***Current Distribution of Contributed Property.*** The ABC Partnership made the following current distributions in the current year. (The dollar amounts listed are the amounts before any implications of the distribution are considered.)

	Property Received			
Partner	*Type of Property*	*Basis*	*FMV*	*Partner's Basis in Partnership Interest*
Alonzo	Land	$ 4,000	$10,000	$19,000
Beth	Inventory	1,000	10,000	15,000
Cathy	Money	10,000	10,000	18,000

The land Alonzo received had been contributed by Beth two years ago when its basis was $4,000 and its FMV was $8,000. The inventory Beth received had been contributed by Cathy two years ago when its basis was $1,000 and its FMV was $4,000. For each independent situation, what gain or loss must be recognized? What is the basis of the distributed property after the distribution? What are the bases of the partnership interests after the distribution? Assume that there are no Sec. 751 implications.

C10-32 ***Current Distribution with Sec. 751.*** The KLM Partnership owns the following assets on March 1 of the current year:

Assets	*Partnership's Basis*	*FMV*
Cash	$ 30,000	$ 30,000
Receivables	—0—	16,000
Inventory	50,000	52,000
Supplies	6,000	6,500
Equipment[a]	9,000	10,500
Land (investment)	40,000	65,000
Total	$135,000	$180,000

[a] Depreciation of $4,000 has been claimed on the equipment.

a. Which partnership items are unrealized receivables?
b. Is the partnership's inventory substantially appreciated?
c. Assume the KLM Partnership has no liabilities and that Kay's basis for her partnership interest is $33,750. On March 1 of the current year, Kay receives a $20,000 current distribution in cash, which reduces her partnership interest from one-third to one-fourth. What are the tax results of the distribution (i.e., the amount and character of any gain, loss, or income recognized and Kay's basis in her partnership interest)?

C10-33 ***Current Distribution with Sec. 751.*** The JAS Partnership owns the following assets on October 1 of the current year:

Assets	Partnership's Basis	FMV
Cash	$ 48,000	$ 48,000
Receivables	12,000	12,000
Inventory	21,000	24,000
Machinery[a]	190,000	240,000
Land	36,500	76,000
Total	$307,500	$400,000

[a] Sale of the machinery for its FMV would result in $50,000 of Sec. 1245 depreciation recapture.

a. Which partnership items are unrealized receivables?
b. Is the partnership's inventory substantially appreciated?
c. Assume the JAS Partnership has no liabilities and Jack's basis in his partnership interest is $76,875. On October 1 of the current year, Jack receives a $25,000 current distribution in cash, which reduces his partnership interest from one-fourth to one-fifth. What are the tax results of the distribution (i.e., the amount and character of any gain, loss, or income recognized and Jack's basis in his partnership interest)?

C10-34 *Liquidating Distributions.* Assume the same four independent distributions as in Question C10-28. Fill in the blanks in that problem assuming that the only change in the facts is that the distributions are now liquidating distributions instead of nonliquidating distributions.

C10-35 *Liquidating Distribution.* Marinda is a one-third partner in the MWH Partnership before she receives $100,000 cash as a liquidating distribution. Immediately before Marinda receives the distribution, the partnership has the following assets:

Assets	Partnership's Basis	FMV
Cash	$100,000	$100,000
Marketable securities	50,000	90,000
Investment land	90,000	140,000
Total	$240,000	$330,000

At the time of the distribution, the partnership has $30,000 of outstanding liabilities, which the three partners share equally. Marinda's basis in her partnership interest before the distribution was $80,000, which, of course, includes her share of liabilities. What are the amount and character of the gain or loss recognized by Marinda and the MWH Partnership on the liquidating distribution?

C10-36 *Liquidating Distributions.* The AB Partnership pays its only liability (a $100,000 mortgage) on April 1 of the current year and terminates that same day. Alison and Bob were equal partners in the partnership but have partnership bases immediately preceding these transactions of $110,000 and $180,000, respectively. Their bases, of course, include that partner's share of liabilities. The two partners receive identical distributions with each receiving the following assets:

Assets	Partnership's Basis
Cash	$ 20,000
Inventory	33,000
Receivables	10,000
Building	40,000
Land	15,000
Total	$118,000

There is no depreciation recapture on the building. What are the tax implications to Alison, Bob, and the AB Partnership of the April 1 transactions (i.e., basis of assets to Alison and Bob, amount and character of gain or loss recognized, etc.)?

C10-37 ***Sale of a Partnership Interest.*** The PKY Partnership is owned equally by Pat, Kelly and Yvette before Kelly sells her partnership interest. On January 1 of the current year, Kelly's basis in her partnership interest, which, of course, includes her share of liabilities, was $35,000. During January, the calendar-year partnership earned $15,000 ordinary income and $6,000 of tax-exempt income. The partnership has a $60,000 recourse liability on January 1 and throughout the tax year, and Kelly's share of that liability is $20,000. The partnership has no other liabilities. Kelly sells her interest on February 1 for a cash payment of $45,000. On the sale date the partnership had the following assets:

Assets	Partnership's Basis	FMV
Cash	$ 20,000	$ 20,000
Inventory	60,000	120,000
Building	36,000	40,000
Land	10,000	15,000
Total	$126,000	$195,000

The building has been depreciated using the straight-line method.

a. What is Kelly's basis in her partnership interest on February 1 just before the sale?

b. What are the amount and character of Kelly's gain or loss on the sale?

C10-38 ***Sale of Partnership Interest.*** Andrew has a $60,000 basis in his one-third interest in the JAS Partnership when he sells it to Miguel for $80,000. Andrew's basis includes his share of liabilities and his share of income up to the sale date. On the sale date, the general partnership reports $30,000 of liabilities and the following assets:

Assets	Partnership's Basis	FMV
Cash	$ 50,000	$ 50,000
Inventory	60,000	95,000
Land	70,000	125,000
Total	$180,000	$270,000

a. What are the amount and character of Andrew's recognized gain or loss on the sale?

b. What is Miguel's basis in his partnership interest?
c. Assuming no Sec. 754 election has been made, what is the partnership's basis in its assets after the sale?

C10-39 ***Sale of Partnership Interest.*** Clay owned 60% of the CAP Partnership and sold one-half of his interest (30%) to Steve for $75,000 cash. Before the sale, Clay's basis in his entire partnership interest was $96,000 including his $30,000 share of partnership liabilities and his share of income up to the sale date. Partnership assets on the sale date were

Assets	*Partnership's Basis*	*FMV*
Cash	$ 50,000	$ 50,000
Inventory	30,000	60,000
Land	80,000	190,000
Total	$160,000	$300,000

a. What are the amount and character of Clay's recognized gain on the sale? What is his remaining basis in his partnership interest?
b. What is Steve's basis in his partnership interest?
c. If no Sec. 754 election is in effect, how will the partnership's basis in its assets be affected? Should Steve make a Sec. 732(d) election if he receives a distribution of inventory one year after his purchase?
d. How would your answers to Parts a and c change if Clay sold his entire interest to Steve for $150,000 cash?

C10-40 ***Retirement of a Partner.*** Suzanne retires from the BRS Partnership when the basis of her one-third interest is $105,000, which, of course, includes her share of liabilities. At the time of her retirement, the partnership had the following assets:

Assets	*Partnership's Basis*	*FMV*
Cash	$145,000	$145,000
Receivables	40,000	40,000
Land	130,000	220,000
Total	$315,000	$405,000

The partnership has $60,000 of liabilities when Suzanne retires. The partnership will pay Suzanne cash of $130,000 to retire her partnership interest.

a. What are the amount and character of the gain or loss Suzanne must recognize?
b. Assuming no Sec. 754 election has been made, what is the impact of the retirement on the partnership and the remaining partners?

C10-41 ***Retirement of a Partner.*** Brian owns 40% of the ABC Partnership before his retirement on April 15 of the current year. On that date his basis in the partnership interest was $40,000 including his share of liabilities. The partnership's balance sheet on that date is as follows:

	Partnership's Basis	FMV
Assets:		
Cash	$ 60,000	$ 60,000
Receivables	24,000	24,000
Land	16,000	40,000
Total	$100,000	$124,000
Liabilities and capital:		
Liabilities	$ 20,000	$ 20,000
Capital—Abner	16,000	20,800
—Brian	32,000	41,600
—Charles	32,000	41,600
Total	$100,000	$124,000

What are the amount and character of the gain or loss that Brian and the ABC Partnership must recognize for the following independent retirement payments?

a. Brian receives $41,600 cash on April 15.

b. Brian receives $50,000 cash on April 15.

C10-42 ***Retirement of a Partner.*** Kim retires from the KLM Partnership on January 1 of the current year. At that time, her basis in the partnership is $75,000, which, of course, includes her share of liabilities. The partnership reports the following balance sheet:

	Partnership's Basis	FMV
Assets:		
Cash	$100,000	$100,000
Receivables	30,000	30,000
Inventory	40,000	40,000
Land	55,000	100,000
Total	$225,000	$270,000
Liabilities and capital:		
Liabilities	$ 75,000	$ 75,000
Capital—Kim	50,000	65,000
—Larry	50,000	65,000
—Michael	50,000	65,000
Total	$225,000	$270,000

Explain the tax consequences (i.e., amount and character of gain or loss recognized and Kim's basis for any assets received) of the partnership making the retirement payments described in the following independent situations. Kim's share of liabilities is $25,000.

a. Kim receives $65,000 cash on January 1.

b. Kim receives $75,000 cash on January 1.

C10-43 ***Death of a Partner.*** When Jerry dies on April 16 of the current year, he owns a 40% interest in the JM Partnership and Michael owns the remaining 60% interest. All of his assets are held in his estate for a two-year period while the estate is being settled. Jerry's estate is his successor-in-interest for the partnership interest. Under a formula contained in the partnership agreement, the partnership must pay Jerry's successor-in-interest $40,000 cash shortly after his death plus $90,000 for each of the two years immediately following a partner's death. The partnership agreement provides that all payments to a retiring partner will first be payments for the partner's share of assets and then any additional payments will be Sec. 736(a) payments. When Jerry died, the partnership had the following assets:

Assets	*Partnership's Basis*	*FMV*
Cash	$100,000	$100,000
Land	200,000	300,000
Total	$300,000	$400,000

Jerry's basis for the partnership interest on the date of his death was $120,000 including his $30,000 share of partnership liabilites.

a. How will the payments be taxed to Jerry's successor-in-interest?

b. What are the tax implications of the payments for the partnership?

C10-44 ***Death of a Partner.*** Bruce dies on June 1 of the current year. On the date of his death he holds a one-third interest in the ABC Partnership, which has a $100,000 basis including his share of liabilities. Under the partnership agreement, Bruce's successor-in-interest, his wife, is to receive the following amounts from the partnership: $130,000 cash, the partnership's assumption of Bruce's $20,000 share of partnership liabilities, plus 10% of partnership net income for the next three years. The partnership's assets immediately before Bruce's death are as follows:

Assets	*Partnership's Basis*	*FMV*
Cash	$100,000	$100,000
Receivables	90,000	90,000
Inventory	40,000	40,000
Land	70,000	220,000
Total	$300,000	$450,000

a. What are the amount and character of the gain or loss that Bruce's wife must recognize when the first year's payment is received?

b. What is the character of the gain recognized from the partnership interest when the payments are received in each of the following three years?

c. When does Bruce's successor-in-interest cease to be a member of the partnership?

C10-45 ***Liquidation or Sale of a Partnership Interest.*** John has a 60% capital and profits interest in the JAS Partnership with a basis of $331,200 (which includes his share of liabilities) when he decides to retire. Andrew and Stephen want to continue the partnership's business. On the date John retires, the partnership's balance sheet is as follows:

	Partnership's Basis	FMV
Assets:		
Cash	$160,000	$160,000
Receivables	60,000	60,000
Inventory	36,000	36,000
Equipment[a]	200,000	300,000
Land	96,000	180,000
Total	$552,000	$736,000
Liabilities and capital:		
Liabilities	$120,000	$120,000
Capital—John	259,200	369,600
—Andrew	86,400	123,200
—Stephen	86,400	123,200
Total	$552,000	$736,000

[a] Sale of the equipment will result in $80,000 of depreciation recapture under Sec. 1245.

a. What are the tax implications for John, Andrew, Stephen, and the JAS Partnership if Andrew and Stephen purchase one-half of John's partnership interest for a cash price of $184,800 each? (Include in your answer the amount and character of the recognized gain or loss, basis of the partnership assets, and any other relevant tax implications.)
b. What are the tax implications for John, Andrew, Stephen, and the JAS Partnership if the partnership pays John a liquidating distribution equal to 60% of each partnership asset?

C10-46 ***Liquidation or Sale of a Partnership Interest.*** Amy retires from the AJS Partnership on January 1 of the current year; her basis in her partnership interest is $120,000 including her share of liabilities. Amy receives $160,000 in cash from the partnership for her interest. On that date, the partnership balance sheet is as follows:

	Partnership's Basis	FMV
Assets:		
Cash	$180,000	$180,000
Receivables	60,000	60,000
Land	120,000	300,000
Total	$360,000	$540,000
Liabilities and capital:		
Liabilities	$ 60,000	$ 60,000
Capital—Amy	100,000	160,000
—Joan	100,000	160,000
—Stephanie	100,000	160,000
Total	$360,000	$540,000

a. What are the amount and character of Amy's recognized gain or loss?

b. How would your answers to Part a change if Joan and Stephanie each purchased one-half of Amy's partnership interest for $80,000 cash instead of having the partnership distribute the $160,000 in cash to Amy?

C10-47 ***Exchange of Partnership Interests.*** Josh holds a general partnership interest in the JLK Partnership having a $40,000 basis and a $60,000 FMV. The JLK Partnership is a limited partnership that engages in real estate activities. Diana has an interest in the CDE Partnership having a $20,000 basis and a $60,000 FMV. The CDE Partnership is a general partnership that also engages in real estate activities. Neither partnership has any Sec. 751 assets or liabilities.

a. What are the tax implications if Josh and Diana simply exchange their partnership interests?

b. What are the tax implications if instead Diana exchanges her general partnership interest in the CDE Partnership for a limited partnership interest in the same partnership (and Josh retains his general partnership interest in the JLK Partnership)?

C10-48 ***Gift of Partnership Interests.*** Tracy owns a one-half interest in the TU Real Estate Partnership and has a $90,000 basis in her partnership interest. Her share of partnership liabilities is $100,000. The FMV of the interest is $200,000. The partnership has no Sec. 751 assets. What are the amount and character of any recognized gain or loss and the basis of the partnership interest to the new owner if Tracy gives the interest to her son?

C10-49 ***Termination of a Partnership.*** Juanita, Carrie, and Robert owned 60%, 30%, and 10%, respectively, of the JCR Partnership immediately before Juanita sold her partnership interest to Molly for $54,000 cash. The partnership had the following balance sheet at the time of the sale:

	Partnership's Basis	*FMV*
Assets:		
Cash	$10,000	$ 10,000
Inventory	18,000	20,000
Land	42,000	70,000
Total	$70,000	$100,000
Liabilities and capital:		
Liabilities	$10,000	$ 10,000
Capital—Juanita	36,000	54,000
—Carrie	18,000	27,000
—Robert	6,000	9,000
Total	$70,000	$100,000

Juanita had a $42,000 basis in her partnership interest. Carrie and Robert have $23,000 and $7,000 bases in their partnership interests, respectively. The bases amounts include each partner's share of partnership liabilities.

a. What amount of gain or loss must be recognized by Juanita, Carrie, Robert, and Molly as a result of this sale?

b. What are the bases of the partnership assets after this sale?

C10-50 ***Termination of a Partnership.*** Wendy, Xenia, and Yancy own 40%, 8%, and 52%, respectively, of the WXY Partnership. For each of the following independent situations occurring in the current year determine whether the WXY Partnership terminates and, if so, the date on which the termination occurs.

a. Wendy sells her entire interest to Alan on June 1. Alan sells one-half of the interest to Beth on November 15.

b. Yancy receives a series of liquidating distributions totaling $100,000. He receives four equal annual payments on January 1 of the current year and the three subsequent years.

c. Wendy and Xenia each receive a liquidating distribution on September 14.

d. Yancy sells his interest to Karen on June 1 for $10,000 cash and a $90,000 installment note. The note will be paid in monthly installments of $10,000 principal plus interest (at a rate acceptable to the IRS) beginning on July 1.

e. The WXY and ABC Partnerships combine their businesses on December 30. Ownership of the new, combined partnership is as follows: Wendy, 20%; Xenia, 4%; Yancy, 26.5%; Albert, 20%; Beth, 19.5%; and Carl, 10%.

f. On January 1, the WXY Partnership divides its business into two new businesses. The WX Partnership is owned equally by Wendy and Xenia. Yancy continues his share of the business as a sole proprietorship.

C10-51 ***Termination of a Partnership.*** For each of the following independent situations determine which partnership(s) (if any) terminate and which partnership(s) (if any) continue.

a. The KLMN Partnership is created when the KL Partnership merges with the MN Partnership. The ownership of the new partnership is held 25% by Katie, 30% by Laura, 25% by Michael, and 20% by Neal.

b. The ABC Partnership, with $150,000 in assets, is owned equally by Amy, Beth, and Chuck. The CD Partnership, with $100,000 in assets, is owned equally by Chuck and Drew. The two partnerships merge and the resulting ABCD Partnership is owned as follows: Amy, 20%; Beth, 20%; Chuck, 40%; and Drew, 20%.

c. The WXYZ Partnership results when the WX and YZ Partnerships merge. Ownership of WXYZ is held equally by the four partners. WX contributes $140,000 in assets and YZ contributes $160,000 in assets to the new partnership.

d. The DEFG Partnership is owned 20% by Dawn, 40% by Eve, 30% by Frank, and 10% by Greg. Two new partnerships are formed by the division of DEFG. The two new partnerships, the DE and FG Partnerships, are owned in proportion to their relative interests in the DEFG Partnership by the individuals for whom they are named.

e. The HIJK Partnership is owned equally by its four partners, Hal, Isaac, Juan, and Kwangho, before its division. Two new partnerships, the HI and JK Partnerships, are formed out of the division with the new partnerships owned equally by the partners for whom they are named.

C10-52 ***Optional Basis Adjustment.*** Patty pays $100,000 cash for Stan's one-third interest in the STU Partnership. The partnership has a Sec. 754 election in effect. Just before the sale of Stan's interest, STU's balance sheet appears as follows:

	Partnership's Basis	FMV
Assets:		
Cash	$ 80,000	$ 80,000
Inventory	55,000	60,000
Land	105,000	160,000
Total	$240,000	$300,000
Partners' capital:		
Stan	$ 80,000	$100,000
Traffic Corporation	80,000	100,000
Union Corporation	80,000	100,000
Total	$240,000	$300,000

a. What is the total amount of the optional basis adjustment to be made?

b. If STU sells the land for its $160,000 FMV immediately after Patty purchases her interest, how much gain or loss will she report as a result of the land sale?

C10-53 ***Optional Basis Adjustment.*** Tom receives a current distribution from the TAD Partnership of inventory having a $14,000 basis and a $16,000 FMV. Before the distribution Tom has a $10,000 basis in his partnership interest. Assume that Sec. 751 does not apply to the distribution and that a Sec. 754 election is in effect.

a. What is the amount of the optional basis adjustment resulting from the distribution?

b. How would your answer to Part a change if Tom's basis in his partnership interest were $15,000 immediately preceding the distribution?

C10-54 ***Optional Basis Adjustment.*** Dave receives a distribution from the CDE Partnership. The partnership owns the following assets immediately before the distribution:

Assets	*Partnership's Basis*	*FMV*
Cash	$ 40,000	$ 40,000
Inventory	30,000	35,000
Land parcel 1	65,000	60,000
Land parcel 2	40,000	60,000
Total	$175,000	$195,000

Assuming the partnership has a Sec. 754 election in effect, what is the amount of the optional basis adjustment (if any) resulting from the following independent distributions? Assume Secs. 736 and 751 do not apply.

a. Dave's basis for his interest is $30,000 before he receives $34,000 cash as a current distribution.

b. Dave's basis for his interest is $30,000 before he receives land parcel 2 as a liquidating distribution.

c. Dave's basis for his interest is $18,000 before he receives inventory having a $20,000 basis to the partnership as a liquidating distribution.

C10-55 ***Disposal of a Tax Shelter.*** Maria buys an interest in a real estate tax shelter in 1985 and deducts losses from its operation for several years. The real property owned by the tax shelter when Maria made her investment has been fully depreciated on a straight-line basis. Her basis in her limited partnership interest is zero, but her share of partnership liabilities is $100,000. Explain the tax results for the following independent situations.

a. Maria sells her partnership interest for $5 cash.

b. Maria gives the interest to Fred, who works in the same office with her.

C10-56 ***Taxation of LLC Income.*** ABC Company, a limited liability company (LLC) organized in the state of Florida, reports using a calendar tax year-end. The LLC chooses to be taxed as a partnership. Alex, Bob, and Carrie (all calendar year-end taxpayers) own ABC equally, and each has a basis of $40,000 in his/her ABC interest on the first day of the current tax year. ABC has the following results for the current year's operation:

Operating income	$30,000
Short-term capital gain	12,000
Long-term capital loss	6,000

Each owner received a $12,000 cash distribution during the current year.

a. What are the amount and character of the income, gain, and loss that Alex must report on his tax return as a result of ABC's operations?

b. What is Alex's basis in his ownership interest in ABC after the current year's operations?

CASE STUDY PROBLEMS

C10-57 Mark Green and his brother Michael purchased land in Orlando, Florida in 1960. At that time they began their investing as Green Brothers Partnership with capital they obtained from placing second mortgages on their homes. Their investments have flourished both because of the prosperity and growth of the area and because they have shown an ability to select prime real estate for others to develop. Over the years, they have acquired a great amount of land and have sold some to developers.

Their tax year has just closed and the partnership has the following balance sheet:

	Partnership's Basis	*FMV*
Assets:		
Cash	$200,000	$ 200,000
Accounts receivable	90,000	90,000
Land held for investment	310,000	1,010,000
Total	$600,000	$1,300,000
Liabilities and capital:		
Mortgages	$400,000	$ 400,000
Capital—Mark	100,000	450,000
—Michael	100,000	450,000
Total	$600,000	$1,300,000

Mark and Michael each have a basis in their partnership interest of $300,000. They share the economic risk of loss from the liabilities equally. Last spring, Mark had a serious heart attack. On his doctor's advice, Mark wants to retire from all business activity and terminate his interest in the partnership. He is interested in receiving some cash now but is not averse to receiving part of his payment over time.

You have been asked to provide the brothers with information on how to terminate Mark's interest in the partnership. Several possibilities have occurred to Mark and Michael and they want your advice as to which is best for Mark from a tax standpoint. (Michael understands that the resulting choice may not be the best option for him.) The possibilities they have considered include the following:

- Michael has substantial amounts of personal cash and could purchase Mark's interest directly. However, the brothers think that it would probably take almost all the cash Michael could raise and they are concerned about any future cash needs Michael might have. They would prefer to have Mark receive $120,000 now plus $110,000 per year for each of the next three years. Mark would also receive interest at a market rate on the outstanding debt. This alternative would qualify for installment reporting. However, the installment sale rules for related parties would apply.
- The partnership could retire Mark's interest. They have considered the option of paying Mark $150,000 now plus 50% of partnership profits for the next three years. Alternatively, they could arrange for Mark to have a $150,000 payment now and a guaranteed payment of $100,000 per year for the next three years. They expect that the dollar amounts to be received by Mark would be approximately the same for the next three years under these two options.
- John Watson, a long-time friend of the family, has expressed an interest in buying Mark's interest for $450,000 cash immediately. Michael and John are comfortable that they could work well together.

Mark has substantial amounts of money in savings accounts and in stocks and bonds that have a ready market. He has invested in no other business directly. He always pays taxes at the highest marginal rates.

Prepare a memorandum summarizing the advice you would give the two brothers on the options that they have considered.

C10-58 In 1993 Miguel's long-time friend and attorney introduced him to Mr. Azul, a successful businessman who had just purchased some local land. Mr. Azul was planning to purchase a cattle feeding operation and sell limited partnership interests in the business. In order to sell the interests, he needed an accountant to prepare an opinion about the tax attributes of the operation for use in the prospectus. He told Miguel that he intended to use the same accountant to do all future partnership tax work. Even though he had previously used an accountant from his home state of New York, Mr. Azul said he wanted someone near the cattle feeding operation as the partnership's accountant.

Although Miguel had done previous work with local ranchers, he had no experience with a cattle feeding operation of the scope that Mr. Azul planned. He spent a little time studying the operations and was impressed with Mr. Azul's expertise in lining up interested investors and getting the operation organized. Although the tax advantages discussed in the prospectus looked generous to Miguel, Mr. Azul assured him that they were not unusual for the industry. Miguel's opinion letter was included in the prospectus and the limited partnership interests sold quickly.

At the end of the first year of operations, Miguel received the information for preparing the partnership's tax return and filed the return without question. The asset values looked a little high based on local land and cattle values, but Miguel figured that Mr. Azul knew what he was doing. During the second year of operations, local gossip is spreading that the cattle feeding operations are about to fold. However, when Miguel gets information to use in preparing the second year's tax return, the numbers look great and the investors will receive substantial tax benefits. Miguel's curiosity is aroused so he begins to investigate both Mr. Azul and the cattle feeding operation. Miguel soon realizes that values for the partnership assets were grossly overstated and that Mr. Azul has falsified much of the information he has given Miguel. Miguel believes that the IRS is very likely to start to investigate it. Further, he is concerned that the IRS may try to find him liable under Code Sec. 6694 for willful negligence if they start investigating the tax shelter.

Required: What should Miguel do now?

TAX RESEARCH PROBLEMS

C10-59 The ABC General Partnership is owned equally by Arnie, Becky, and Clay. The three individuals have bases in their partnership interests of $80,000, $120,000, and $160,000, respectively. For business reasons, the partnership needs to be changed into the ABC Corporation, and all three owners agree to the change. The only question to be resolved is how to best structure the transfer from a tax standpoint. The partnership is expected to have the following assets on the date that the change is to occur:

Assets	*Partnershp's Basis*	*FMV*
Cash	$ 50,000	$ 50,000
Accounts receivable	60,000	55,000
Inventory	150,000	200,000
Land	200,000	295,000
Total	$460,000	$600,000

Liabilities of $100,000 are currently outstanding and will be owed on the exchange date. Liabilities are shared equally and, of course, are already included in the bases of the partnership interest. Two possible structures are being considered for making the change:

a. ABC Partnership makes a liquidating distribution of a one-third interest in each asset to each of the partners. The partners then contribute their shares of each asset to the new ABC Corporation in exchange for stock.

b. ABC Partnership transfers all of its assets and liabilities to the new ABC Corporation in exchange for all of its stock. ABC Partnership then liquidates by distributing the ABC stock to Arnie, Becky, and Clay.

Required: The tax manager you work for has asked you to determine whether the differences in the form of these two transactions will affect the tax consequences. If the form makes a difference, describe the differences in tax treatments in a short memorandum to the partnership. Be sure to mention any relevant Code sections, Regulations, and revenue rulings.

C10-60 Della retires from the BCD General Partnership when her basis in her partnership interest is $60,000 including her $10,000 share of liabilities. The partnership is in the business of providing house-cleaning services for local residences. At the date of Della's retirement, the partnership's balance sheet is as follows:

	Partnership's Basis	*FMV*
Assets:		
Cash	$ 50,000	$ 50,000
Receivables	—0—	30,000
Equipment[a]	40,000	50,000
Building[b]	90,000	100,000
Land	30,000	40,000
Total	$210,000	$270,000
Liabilities and capital:		
Liabilities	$ 30,000	$ 30,000
Capital—Bruce	60,000	80,000
—Celia	60,000	80,000
—Della	60,000	80,000
Total	$210,000	$270,000

[a] If the equipment were sold for $50,000, the entire gain would be recaptured as Sec. 1245 ordinary income.
[b] The building has been depreciated using the straight-line method.

Della will receive payments of $20,000 cash plus 5% of partnership ordinary income for each of the next five years. The partnership agreement specifies that goodwill will be paid for when a partner retires. Bruce, Celia, and Della agree that the partnership has $21,000 in goodwill when Della retires and she will be paid for her one-third share.

Required: A tax manager in your firm has asked you to determine the amount and character of the income that Della must report for each of the next five years. In addition, he wants you to research the tax consequences of the retirement on the partnership for the next five years. (Assume the partnership earns $100,000 of ordinary income each year for the next five years.) Prepare an oral presentation to be made to Della explaining the tax consequences of the payments she will receive.

C10-61 Pedro owns a 60% interest in the PD General Partnership having a $40,000 basis and $200,000 FMV. His share of partnership liabilities is $100,000. Because he is nearing retirement age, he has decided to give away his partnership interest on June 15 of the current year. The partnership's tax year ends on December 31. Pedro's tax year ends on June 30. He intends to give a 30% interest to his son, Juan, and the remaining 30% interest to the American Red Cross.

Required: A tax manager in your firm has asked you to prepare a letter to Pedro explaining fully the tax consequences of this gift to him, the partnership, and the donees. She reminds you to be sure to include information about the allocation of the current year's partnership income.

CHAPTER 11

S CORPORATIONS

LEARNING OBJECTIVES

After studying this chapter, you should be able to

1. Explain the requirements for being taxed under Subchapter S
2. Explain the procedures for electing to be taxed under Subchapter S
3. Identify the events that will result in termination of the S election
4. Determine the permitted tax years for an S corporation
5. Calculate ordinary income or loss
6. Calculate the amount of any special S corporation tax levies
7. Calculate a shareholder's allocable share of ordinary income or loss and separately stated items
8. Determine the limitations on a shareholder's deduction of S corporation losses
9. Calculate a shareholder's basis in his or her S corporation's stock and debt
10. Determine the taxability of an S corporation's distributions to its shareholders
11. Explain the procedures for filing an S corporation tax return
12. Determine the estimated tax payments required of an S corporation and its shareholders

CHAPTER OUTLINE

KEY POINT

The S corporation rules are deceptively simple. Although taxed much like a partnership, an S corporation must also adhere to many of the corporate tax rules.

REAL-WORLD EXAMPLE

The 1986 Tax Act reduced the top individual tax rate below the top corporate tax rate for the first time in the history of the modern income tax. S corporation filings rose from 826,000 in 1986 to 1.90 million in 1993. C corporation filings declined from 2.60 million to 2.14 million during the same time period.

REAL-WORLD EXAMPLE

It is unlikely that large numbers of LLCs, partnerships, or proprietorships will elect to be taxed as an S corporation under the check-the-box regulations. It is more likely that an S election might be made following a conversion of one of these three entity forms into a corporation under state law.

This chapter discusses a special type of corporate entity known as an S corporation. The S corporation rules, located in Subchapter S of the Internal Revenue Code, were enacted in 1958 to permit small corporations to enjoy the nontax advantages of the corporate form of organization without being subject to the possible tax disadvantages of the corporate form (e.g., double taxation when corporate income is paid to shareholders as a dividend). Three purposes were stated for these rules:

- To permit businesses to select a particular form of business organization without being influenced by tax considerations
- To provide aid for small businesses by allowing the income of the business to be taxed to shareholders rather than being taxed at the corporate level
- To permit corporations realizing losses for a period of years to obtain a tax benefit of offsetting the losses against income at the shareholder level[1]

As discussed in Chapter C2, S corporations are treated as corporations for legal and business purposes. For federal income tax purposes, however, they are treated much like partnerships.[2] As in a partnership, the profits and losses of the S corporation are passed through to the shareholders, and the S corporation can make tax-free distributions of its previously taxed earnings. Although generally taxed like a partnership, the S corporation still follows many of the basic Subchapter C tax provisions (e.g., S corporations use the corporate tax rules regarding liquidations and tax-free reorganizations instead of the partnership rules). A tabular comparison of the S corporation, partnership, and C corporation rules is presented in Appendix F.

Recent changes have caused many businesses to reexamine the implications of an S election. First, the restrictive nature of the S corporation requirements has caused many new businesses, that were potential S corporations, to look at alternative business forms. All 50 states have now adopted limited liability company (LLC) legislation. LLCs offer many of the same tax advantages of S corporations because they are taxed as partnerships. LLCs are not subject to the same requirements that must be satisfied by an S corporation and its shareholder(s) to make and retain an S election. Partially because of the S corporation restrictions, some new businesses have organized as LLCs to take advantage of the greater operational flexibility that it provides the entity and its owners, as well as its liability protection. A number of small businesses, however, elected to be S corporations because of the greater certainty available within the legal system for corporate entities.

For many existing C corporations, the cost of liquidating the corporate entity and creating an LLC is a prohibitively expensive way to avoid the corporate level income tax (see Chapter C6). However, many of these C corporations have taken the next best alternative; that is, making an S election.

The 1993 Tax Act's increase in the top individual tax rates above the top corporate tax rate has caused some S corporations to terminate their S election to take advantage of the lower C corporation rates. In spite of tax cost for high-income taxpayers, the S election still remains a popular business form. The 1996 tax legislation brought with it about 20 changes to the S corporaton rules. Some of these changes eliminated requirements which reduced the S corporation's popularity (e.g., the 35 shareholder limit was increased to 75 and the prohibitions against certain entities and trusts becoming S corporation shareholders were lessened). These changes have reduced some of the differences between S corporations and LLCs and brought out renewed interest in S corporations.

This chapter examines the requirements for making an S election and the tax rules that apply to S corporations.

---

[1] S. Rept. No. 1983, 85th Cong., 2d Sess., p. 87 (1958).

[2] Some states do not recognize an S corporation as a conduit for state income tax purposes. Instead, they are taxed under the state income tax laws in the same manner as a C corporation.

Should an S Election Be Made?

Advantages of S Corporation Treatment

A number of advantages are available to a corporation that makes an S election.

- The corporation's income is exempt from the corporate income tax. An S corporation's income is taxed only to its shareholders, who may be in a lower tax bracket than the corporation.
- The corporation's losses are passed through to the shareholders and can be used to reduce the taxes owed on other types of income. This feature can be especially important for new businesses. An S election can be made, the start-up losses passed through to the owners, and the election terminated once it becomes advantageous to be taxed as a C corporation.
- Undistributed income that was taxed to the shareholder is not taxed when subsequently distributed unless the distribution exceeds the shareholder's basis for his or her stock.
- Capital gains and tax-exempt income are separately stated and pass through to the shareholders. Such amounts become commingled with other earnings and are taxed as dividends when distributed by the C corporation.
- Deductions, losses, and tax credits are separately stated and passed through to the shareholders. These amounts are subject to the various ceilings for the tax attribute at the shareholder level. This treatment can permit a tax benefit to be claimed by a shareholder when it would otherwise be denied to the corporation (e.g., a shareholder can claim the general business credit benefit even though the S corporation reports a substantial loss for the year).
- Splitting the S corporation's income between family members is possible. However, income splitting is restricted by the requirement that reasonable compensation be provided to family members who provide capital and services to the S corporation.
- An S corporation's earnings that flow through to the individual shareholders are not subject to the self-employment tax. A partnership must determine what portion of each general partner's net earnings constitutes self-employment income.

KEY POINT

Of all the advantages of an S election, possibly the most significant is that an S election generally avoids the double taxation inherent in our corporate tax system.

ADDITIONAL COMMENT

One advantage of an S corporation that is not often mentioned is the fact that S corporation earnings that flow through to the individual shareholders are not subject to self-employment taxes.

Disadvantages of S Corporation Treatment

A number of tax disadvantages also exist for a corporation that makes an S election.

- A C corporation is treated as a separate tax entity from its shareholders, thus permitting its first dollar of income to be taxed at a 15% marginal rate instead of the shareholder's marginal rate. In addition, the corporate rates are generally lower than the individual rates and may reduce the total tax burden if the earnings are to be retained in the business.
- The S corporation's earnings are taxed to the shareholders even though they are not distributed. This may require the corporation to make distributions or salary payments to permit the shareholder to pay the taxes owed on the S corporation's earnings.
- S corporations are subject to an excess net passive income tax and a built-in gains tax. Partnerships are not subject to either of these taxes.
- Dividends received by the S corporation are not eligible for the dividends-received deduction, as is the case for a C corporation.

TYPICAL MISCONCEPTION

The structure of an S corporation can create a real hardship for a shareholder if large amounts of income flow through without any compensation payments or distributions of cash to help pay the tax on the income.

- Allocation of ordinary income or loss and the separately stated items is based on the stock owned on each day of the tax year. Special allocations of particular items are not permitted, as they are in a partnership.
- The loss limitation for an S corporation shareholder is smaller than for a partner in a partnership. Shareholders can increase their loss limitations by the basis of any debt that they are owed by the S corporation. Partners, on the other hand, can increase their loss limitation by their ratable share of all partnership liabilities.
- S corporations and their shareholders are subject to the at-risk, passive activity limitation, and hobby loss rules. C corporations are not generally subject to these rules.
- An S corporation is restricted in the type and number of shareholders it can have and the capital structure it can use. Partnerships and C corporations are not so restricted.
- S corporations are restricted to using a calendar year as their tax year unless they can establish a business purpose for a fiscal year or they have made a special election to use a nonpermitted tax year. Similar restrictions are also applicable to partnerships.

Once the decision has been made to incorporate, there is no general rule that can be applied to determine whether an S election should be made. The management and shareholders should examine the long- and short-run tax and non-tax advantages and disadvantages of filing as a C corporation and as an S corporation before making a decision. Unlike a consolidated return election, the S election can be revoked or terminated at any time with minimal effort.

S CORPORATION REQUIREMENTS

OBJECTIVE 1

Explain the requirements for being taxed under Subchapter S

The S corporation requirements are divided into two categories: shareholder-related and corporation-related requirements. A corporation that satisfies all of the requirements is known as a small business corporation. Only small business corporations can make an S election. Each set of requirements is outlined below.

SHAREHOLDER-RELATED REQUIREMENTS

Three shareholder-related requirements must be satisfied on each day of the tax year.[3]

- The corporation must not have more than seventy-five shareholders.
- All shareholders must be individuals, estates, or certain kinds of trusts.
- None of the individual shareholders can be classified as a nonresident **alien**.

ADDITIONAL COMMENT

The Sec. 1244 stock rules (Ch. C2) and the S corporation rules both use the term *small business corporations.* The definitions have different requirements, although most S corporation stock can qualify as Sec. 1244 stock.

REAL-WORLD EXAMPLE

81% of all S corporations had 1 or 2 owners in 1993. Only 800 of the 1.9 million S corporations had greater than 30 owners.

75-SHAREHOLDER RULE. Section 1361(c)(1) treats a husband and wife (and their estates) as a single shareholder for purposes of applying the 75-shareholder limit. When stock is owned jointly by two unmarried individuals (e.g., as tenants in common or as joint tenants), each owner is considered a separate shareholder.

ELIGIBLE SHAREHOLDERS. Corporations and partnerships in general cannot own S corporation stock. This restriction prevents a corporation or a partnership having a large number of owners from avoiding the 75-shareholder limitation by purchasing S corporation stock and being treated as a single shareholder. Organizations that are exempt from the federal income tax under Sec. 501(a) (e.g., a tax-exempt public charity or private foundation) can hold S corporation stock starting in 1998. These organizations count as one shareholder when calculating the 75-shareholder limit.

[3] Secs. 1361(b)(1)(A)–(C).

ETHICAL POINT

Tax professionals must assist their clients in monitoring that the S corporation requirements are met on each day of the tax year. Failing to meet one of the requirements for even one day terminates the election. Ignoring the fact that a terminating event has occurred until it is discovered in an IRS audit will probably cause the corporation to be taxed as a C corporation and prevent it from having the termination treated as being inadvertent.

Seven types of trusts can own S corporation stock: grantor trusts, voting trusts,[4] testamentary trusts, **qualified Subchapter S trusts** (**QSSTs**),[5] qualified retirement plan trusts, small business trusts, and beneficiary-controlled trusts (i.e., trusts that distribute all of their income to a single income beneficiary who is treated as the owner of the trust). Grantor trusts, QSSTs, and beneficiary-controlled trusts can own S corporation stock only if the grantor or the beneficiary is a qualified shareholder. Each beneficiary of a voting trust must also be an eligible shareholder. A qualified retirement plan trust is one formed as part of a qualified stock bonus, pension, or profit sharing plan or employee stock ownership plan (ESOP) that are exempt from the federal income tax under Sec. 501(a).

Small business trusts can own S corporation stock starting in 1997. These trusts can be complex trusts, and are primarily used as estate planning devices. No interest in a small business trust can be acquired in a "purchase" transaction; that is, a transaction where the holder's interest takes a cost basis under Sec. 1012. Interests in small business trusts are generally acquired as a result of a gift or bequest. All current beneficiaries of a small business trust must be individuals or estates. Current beneficiaries are parties that can receive an income distribution for the period in question. In 1997, charitable organizations eligible to own S corporation stock can only own a contingent remainder interest. In 1998 and later years, charitable organizations can be current beneficiaries. Each beneficiary is counted for purposes of the 75-shareholder limit. QSSTs and tax-exempt trusts are ineligible to elect to be a small business trust. An affirmative election is required to obtain small business trust status.

A testamentary trust (i.e., a trust created under the terms of a will) that receives S corporation stock can hold the stock and continue to be an eligible shareholder for a two-year period, commencing on the date that the stock is transferred to the trust. A grantor trust that held S corporation stock immediately before the death of the deemed owner, and which continues in existence after the death of the deemed owner, can continue to hold the stock and be an eligible shareholder for the two-year period commencing on the date of the deemed owner's death.

EXAMPLE C11-1 ▶ Joan, a U.S. citizen, owns 25% of the stock of Waldo Corporation, an electing S corporation. At the time of her death in 1997, the Waldo stock passes to Joan's estate. The estate is a qualifying shareholder, and the transfer does not affect the S election. If the stock is subsequently transferred to a trust that is provided for in Joan's will, the testamentary trust can hold the Waldo stock for a two-year period before the election is terminated. ◀

The trust in Example C11-1 can hold the S corporation stock for an indefinite period of time only if an election is made by the trust's income beneficiary to have it treated as a QSST or small business trust. Otherwise, the S election will be terminated at the end of the two-year period.

ALIEN INDIVIDUALS. Individuals who are not U.S. citizens (i.e., alien individuals) can own S corporation stock only if they are U.S. residents or are married to a U.S. citizen or resident alien and make an election to be taxed as a resident alien. The S election is terminated if S corporation stock is purchased by an alien individual who does not reside in the United States or who has not made the appropriate election.

---

[4] A **voting trust** is an arrangement whereby the stock owned by a number of shareholders is placed under the control of a trustee, who exercises the voting rights possessed by the stock. One reason for creating a voting trust is to increase the voting power of a group of minority shareholders in the selection of corporate directors or the establishment of corporate policies.

[5] A QSST is a domestic trust that owns stock in one or more S corporations and distributes (or is required to distribute) all of its income to its sole income beneficiary. The income beneficiary must make an irrevocable election to have the QSST rules of Sec. 1361(d) apply. The beneficiary is treated as the owner (and, therefore, the shareholder) of the portion of the trust consisting of the S corporation stock. A separate election is made for each S corporation's stock owned by the trust.

CORPORATION-RELATED REQUIREMENTS

Three corporation-related requirements must be satisfied on each day of the tax year:

- The corporation must be a domestic corporation.
- The corporation must not be an "ineligible" corporation.
- The corporation must have only one class of stock.[6]

The first requirement precludes a foreign corporation from making an S election.

A corporation may be an ineligible corporation and thereby violate the second requirement in one of two ways:

- Corporations that maintain a special federal income tax status are not eligible to make an S election. For example, financial institutions (i.e., banks) that use the reserve method to account for bad debts and insurance companies are not eligible.
- Corporations that have elected the special Puerto Rico and U.S. possessions tax credit (Sec. 936) or the special Domestic International Sales Corporation tax exemption are ineligible to make the S election.

REAL-WORLD EXAMPLE

The 1996 Act changes to the S corporation stock ownership rules and the approval of the check-the-box regulations permit great flexibility in creating groups of entities that fit the business needs of their owners.

Starting in 1997, S corporations can own the stock of a C corporation or an S corporation without any limitation on the percentage of voting power or value that is held. The prohibition against a C corporation owning the stock of an S corporation remains. An S corporation that owns the stock of a C corporation cannot participate in the filing of a consolidated tax return. An S corporation can own the stock of a **Qualified Subchapter S Subsidiary** (QSSS). A QSSS is a domestic corporation that qualifies as an S corporation, is 100% owned by an S corporation, and for which an affirmative election to be treated as a QSSS is made. The assets, liabilities, income, deductions, losses, etc. of the QSSS are treated as those of its S corporation parent and reported on the parent's tax return.[7]

KEY POINT

A second class of stock does not exist if the only difference between the two classes of stock relates to voting rights.

A corporation that has two classes of stock issued and outstanding has violated the third requirement and cannot be an S corporation. The single class of stock determination has been made more difficult than it appears at first glance because of the many different financial arrangements that are possible between an S corporation and its shareholders. A corporation is treated as having only one class of stock if all of its outstanding shares of stock possess identical rights to distribution and liquidation proceeds and the corporation has not issued any instrument or obligation, or entered into any arrangement, that is treated as a second class of stock.[8] A second class of stock is not created if the only difference between the two classes of stock relates to voting rights.[9]

EXAMPLE C11-2 ▶ Kelly Corporation has two classes of common stock outstanding. The Class A and Class B common stock give the shareholders identical rights and interests in the profits and assets of the corporation. Class A stock has one vote per share. Class B stock is nonvoting. Kelly Corporation is treated as having only one class of stock outstanding and can make an S election. ◀

GENERAL RULES. The determination of whether all outstanding shares of stock confer identical rights to distribution and liquidation proceeds is based on the corporate charter, articles of incorporation, bylaws, applicable state law, and binding agreements relating to distribution and liquidation proceeds (i.e., the governing agreements).[10] The Regulations permit certain types of state laws, agreements, distributions, etc., to be disregarded in determining whether all of a corporation's outstanding shares confer identical rights to distribution and liquidation proceeds. These include

6 Sec. 1361(b)(1).
7 Sec. 1361(c)(2)(3).
8 Reg. Sec. 1.1361-1(l).
9 Sec. 1361(c)(4).
10 Reg. Sec. 1.1361-1(l)(2).

- Agreements to purchase stock at the time of death, divorce, disability, or termination of employment
- Distributions made on the basis of the shareholder's varying stock interests during the year
- Distributions that differ in timing (e.g., one shareholder receives a distribution in the current year and a second shareholder receives a similar dollar amount distribution shortly after the beginning of the next tax year)

Agreements to adjust upward cash or property distributions to shareholders who bear heavier state income tax burdens so as to provide equal after-tax distributions provide unequal distribution and liquidation rights. The unequal distributions will probably cause a second class of stock to be created. However, state laws that require a corporation to pay or withhold state income taxes on behalf of some or all of a corporation's shareholders are disregarded.

DEBT INSTRUMENTS. Debt instruments, corporate obligations, and deferred compensation arrangements are, in general, not treated as a second class of stock.[11] A number of safe harbors exist for characterizing corporate obligations as debt (and not as a second class of stock):

- Unwritten advances from a shareholder that do not exceed $10,000 during the tax year, are treated as debt by the two parties, and are expected to be repaid within a reasonable time.
- Obligations that are considered equity under the general tax laws, but are owned solely by the shareholders in the same proportion as the outstanding stock of the corporation.

KEY POINT

If debt instruments satisfy the safe-harbor rules, such instruments cannot be construed as equity. However, such debt must have been issued in an S corporation tax year.

A safe harbor is provided for straight debt instruments under Sec. 1361(c)(5) so that it is not treated as a second class of stock. For debt to qualify under the safe harbor, it must meet the following requirements if issued while an S election is in effect:

- The debt must represent an unconditional promise to pay a certain sum of money on a specified date or on demand.
- The interest rate and interest payment dates must not be contingent on profits, the borrower's discretion, or similar factors.[12]
- The debt must not be convertible directly or indirectly into stock.
- The creditor must be an individual, estate, or trust eligible to be an S corporation shareholder, or a nonindividual creditor that is actively and regularly engaged in the business of lending money.[13]

The safe harbor rules can apply to debt even if it would otherwise be considered a second class of stock under case law or other Code provisions. An obligation that originally qualifies as straight debt may no longer qualify if it is materially modified so that it no longer satisfies the safe harbor, or transferred to a third party who is not an eligible shareholder.[14]

---

[11] Reg. Sec. 1.1361-1(l)(4)(i). An exception applies to debt instruments, corporate obligations, and deferred compensation arrangements that are treated as stock under the general principles of the federal tax law where the principal purpose for the debt instrument, etc., is to circumvent the distribution or liquidation proceeds rights that are provided for by the outstanding stock or to circumvent the 75-shareholder limit.

[12] The fact that the interest rate is dependent on the prime rate or a similar factor not related to the debtor corporation will not disqualify the instrument from coming under the safe-harbor rules. If the interest being paid is unreasonably high, an appropriate portion may be treated as a payment other than interest that has been made to the holder.

[13] Sec. 1361(c)(5).

[14] Reg. Sec. 1.1361-1(l)(5)(ii) and (iii).

Election of S Corporation Status

OBJECTIVE 2

Explain the procedures for electing to be taxed under Subchapter S

The S election exempts a corporation from all taxes imposed by Chapter 1 of the Internal Revenue Code (Secs. 1-1399) except for the following:

- Sec. 1374 built-in gains tax
- Sec. 1375 excess net passive income tax
- Sec. 1363(d) LIFO recapture tax
- Recapture of previously claimed investment tax credits

This rule exempts the S corporation from the regular income tax, accumulated earnings tax, the personal holding company tax, and the corporate alternative minimum tax for the tax year in which the election is first effective and all subsequent tax years, until the election is revoked or terminated.

The S election affects the shareholders in three ways:

- The shareholders must report their pro rata share of the S corporation's ordinary income or loss as well as any separately stated items.
- Distributions made to the shareholders come under special rules that generally treat most distributions as a tax-free recovery of the shareholders' stock investments.
- The shareholders' bases in the stock are adjusted for their ratable share of the ordinary income or loss and any separately stated items.

MAKING THE ELECTION

The S election can be made only by small business corporations. In order for a small business corporation to make a valid S election, the election (Form 2553) must be filed in a timely manner and all of the corporation's shareholders must consent to the election. Existing corporations can make a timely S election at any time during the tax year preceding the year for which the election is to be effective or on or before the fifteenth day of the third month of the year for which the election is to be effective.[15]

EXAMPLE C11-3 ▶ Wilco Corporation, a calendar-year taxpayer, has been in existence for several years. Wilco wants to be taxed as an S corporation for 1997 and subsequent years. The election can be made any time during 1996 or between January 1 and March 15, 1997. If the election is made after March 15, 1997, it becomes effective in 1998. ◀

For a new corporation, the S election can be made at any time on or before the fifteenth day of the third month of its initial tax year. A new corporation's initial tax year commences with the first day on which the corporation has shareholders, acquires assets, or begins business.

If the S election is made during the first 2½ months of the tax year for which it is first to be effective, the corporation must also meet all of the small business corporation requirements on each day of the tax year that precedes the election date and on the election date. If one of the requirements is not met on any day that precedes the election date, the election becomes effective in the S corporation's next tax year.

SELF-STUDY QUESTION

Would the answer to Example C11-3 change if Wilco had been a member of an affiliated group through 1/15/97?

ANSWER

Yes. Because Wilco was an ineligible corporation for a portion of the 2½-month period of 1997, an S election would not be effective until 1/1/98.

CONSENT OF SHAREHOLDERS. Each person who is a shareholder on the date that the election is made must consent to the election.[16] The consent is binding on the current

[15] Sec. 1362(b)(1).

[16] Sec. 1362(a)(2).

tax year and all future tax years. No additional consents are required of shareholders who acquire the stock between the election date and its effective date or at any subsequent date.

Section 1362(b)(2) imposes a special rule on the shareholders when an election is made after the beginning of the tax year for which it is to be effective. Each shareholder who owned stock at any time during the portion of the year that precedes the time the election is made, and who is not a shareholder at the time the election is made, must also consent to the election.

EXAMPLE C11-4 ▶ Sara and Harry own all of the stock of Kraft Corporation. Sara sells all of her Kraft stock to Lisa on February 10. The next day Kraft makes an S election. For the election to apply in the current year, Sara, Harry, and Lisa must consent to the election. If Sara refuses to consent to the election, the election will not begin until next year. ◀

Each tenant (whether husband and wife or not) must consent to the S election if the stock is owned as tenants in common, joint tenants, or tenants in the entirety. If the S corporation stock is owned as community property, the consent must be made by each person having a community property interest. If the shareholder is a minor, the consent can be made by the minor or the minor's legal representative (e.g., a natural parent or legal guardian).

KEY POINT

The procedures for making an S election are very precise. Taxpayers must be careful to adhere to each requirement so as not to invalidate an S election inadvertently.

All of the appropriate procedures for making the S election and filing the necessary consents must be adhered to. Failure to do so will result in the S election being deferred or declared invalid. These procedures include the following:

- Make sure the election is filed on or before the fifteenth day of the third month of the tax year. Late elections will prevent the S corporation benefits from being claimed until the next tax year.
- Make sure that all of the small business corporation requirements are met when the election is filed. If the election is filed after the beginning of the tax year, planning is needed to ensure that the small business corporation requirements are met from the first day of the tax year on.
- Make sure that all of the necessary consents are obtained. Failure to obtain the consent of a shareholder (e.g., one spouse of a couple that jointly holds the S corporation stock) will invalidate the S election.

Topic Review C11-1 presents a summary of the S corporation requirements and procedures for making the S election.

OBJECTIVE 3

Identify the events that will result in termination of the S election

TERMINATION OF THE ELECTION

The S election is terminated when the corporation either revokes the election or terminates the election because it ceases to meet the small business corporation requirements. Each action is examined below. The requirements for making a new S election following a termination are also discussed.

REVOCATION OF THE ELECTION.

A corporation can revoke its S election in any tax year as long as it meets the requirements regarding shareholder consent and timeliness. Shareholders owning more than one-half of the corporation's stock (including nonvoting stock) on the day on which the revocation is made must consent to the revocation.[17] A revocation that is made on or before the fifteenth day of the third month of the tax year is effective on the first day of the S corporation's tax year. A revocation that is made after the first 2½ months of the tax year is effective on the first day of the

[17] Sec. 1362(d)(1)(B).

Topic Review C11-1

S Corporation Requirements and Election Procedures

Requirements

Shareholder-related:

1. The corporation may have no more than seventy-five shareholders. Husbands and wives and their estates count as one shareholder.
2. All shareholders must be individuals, estates, or certain kinds of trusts. Eligible trusts include grantor trusts, voting trusts, testamentary trusts, beneficiary-controlled trusts, qualified Subchapter S trusts, qualified retirement plan trusts, and small business trusts. Tax-exempt organizations (e.g., a tax-exempt public charity or private foundation) are eligible shareholders starting in 1998.
3. All of the individual shareholders must be U.S. citizens or resident aliens.

Corporation-related:

1. The corporation must be a domestic corporation or an unincorporated entity that makes an election to be taxed as a domestic corporation.
2. The corporation must not be an ineligible corporation (e.g., an ineligible bank or other financial institution, an insurance company, or a foreign corporation, etc.).
3. The corporation must have only one class of stock issued and outstanding. Differences in voting rights are ignored.

Making the Election

1. The S election can be made at any time during the tax year preceding the year for which the election is effective or on or before the fifteenth day of the third month of the tax year for which the election is effective. Late elections are effective with the next tax year.
2. Each shareholder who owns stock on the date that the election is made must consent to the election. If the election is made after the beginning of the tax year, each person who was a shareholder during the portion of the tax year preceding the election must also consent to the election.

SELF-STUDY QUESTION

Can the revocation of an S election ever be retroactive? Prospective?

next tax year. An exception is provided that permits the S corporation to select a prospective date for the revocation to be effective. The prospective date can be the date on which the revocation is made or any subsequent date.[18]

EXAMPLE C11-5 ▶

Adobe Corporation, a calendar-year taxpayer, has been taxed as an S corporation for several years. However, the corporation has become quite profitable, and management feels that it would be advantageous to make a public stock offering in order to obtain additional capital during 1997. Adobe can revoke its S election any time before March 16, 1997, and have the election terminated at the close of business on December 31, 1996. If the revocation election is made after March 15, 1997, it does not take effect until January 1, 1998. In either case, the corporation may specify a prospective 1997 revocation date as long as the date specified is on or after the date the revocation is made. ◀

ANSWER

A revocation can be retroactive to the beginning of the year if made within the first 2½ months of that year. A revocation can be prospective to any subsequent date.

TERMINATION OF THE ELECTION. The S election is terminated if the corporation fails one or more of the small business corporation requirements on any day after the first

[18] Secs. 1362(d)(1)(C) and (D).

ADDITIONAL COMMENT

When it is difficult to obtain the majority vote necessary for revocation, consideration should be given to purposely triggering a termination event.

HISTORICAL NOTE

Previously, a termination was deemed to be effective on the first day of the tax year in which the terminating event occurred. To stop this abuse, the rule was changed so that an S election is terminated on the day of the terminating event.

day that the election is effective.[19] The termination generally occurs on the day of the terminating event. Events that can terminate the election include

- Exceeding the 75-shareholder limit
- Having an ineligible shareholder own some of the stock
- Creating a second class of stock
- Retaining a prohibited tax status
- Selecting an improper tax year
- Failing the passive investment income test for three consecutive years

The passive investment income test is applied annually. It results in a termination of the S election if more than 25% of the corporation's gross receipts are passive investment income for each of three consecutive tax years *and* the corporation has Subchapter C earnings and profits (E&P) at the end of each of the three consecutive tax years.[20] If the test is failed for three consecutive tax years, the election is terminated on the first day of the next (fourth) tax year.

Passive investment income includes royalties, rents,[21] dividends, interest, annuities, and gains from the sale or exchange of stocks and securities. Regulation Sec. 1.1362-2(c)(5) holds that passive investment income excludes income derived from the active conduct of a trade or business. Subchapter C E&P include only earnings that have accrued in tax years in which an S election was not in effect (i.e., the corporation was taxed under the C corporation rules). An S corporation can avoid terminating its election and increase the portion of its gross receipts that is permitted to be passive income by distributing its Subchapter C E&P. This tax planning technique is discussed on page C11-39.

EXAMPLE C11-6 ▶ Silver Corporation is created in the current year and promptly makes an S election. Silver can earn an unlimited amount of passive income during a tax year without any fear of losing its S corporation status or being subject to the Sec. 1375 tax on excess net passive income because it has never been taxed as a C corporation nor has it acquired any accumulated E&P (e.g., by participating in the acquisition of a C corporation in a tax-free reorganization). (See page C11-17 for a discussion of this tax.) ◀

ALLOCATION OF INCOME. If a terminating event occurs at some time other than on the first day of the tax year, an S termination year is created. The **S termination year** is divided into an S short year and C short year. The **S short year** commences on the first day of the tax year and ends on the day preceding the day on which the termination is effective. The **C short year** commences on the day on which the termination is effective and continues through the last day of the corporation's tax year.[22]

EXAMPLE C11-7 ▶ Dixon Corporation has been taxed as an S corporation for several years. Paula and Frank each own one-half of Dixon's stock. Paula sells one-half of her Dixon stock to Eagle Corporation on July 1. The sale terminates the S election on July 1 because Eagle Corporation is an ineligible shareholder. Assuming that Dixon is a calendar-year taxpayer, the S short year includes the period January 1 through June 30. The C short year includes the period July 1 through December 31. ◀

The S short year income is reported by the S corporation's shareholders according to the normal reporting rules described below. The C corporation reports the income earned

[19] Sec. 1362(d)(2).
[20] Sec. 1362(d)(3).
[21] Regulation Sec. 1.1362-2(c)(5)(ii)(B)(2) excludes from rents payments received for the use or occupancy of property if the corporation provides significant services or incurs substantial costs in the rental business. See page C11-40 for additional explanations of the significant services and substantial costs definitions.
[22] Sec. 1362(e)(1).

KEY POINT

Income/loss can be allocated in the termination year under either of two methods. Careful consideration should be given to the possible tax advantages of a daily allocation versus an actual closing of the books.

ADDITIONAL COMMENT

In order to use an actual closing of the books to allocate the income/loss of Dixon in Example C11-7, Eagle Corporation must consent. Due to the consequences of such an election, the method of allocation should be considered in negotiating the Dixon stock sale.

during the C short year. The C short year income tax liability is calculated on an annualized basis (see Chapter C3). The S short year and C short year returns are due on the due date for the corporation's tax return for the tax year had the termination not occurred (including any extensions).[23]

Two rules can be used to allocate the termination year's income between the S short year and the C short year. The general rule of Sec. 1362(e)(2) allocates the ordinary income or loss and the separately stated items between the S short year and C short year based on the number of days in each year. A special election is available under Sec. 1362(e)(3) that permits the allocation to be made according to the corporation's normal tax accounting rules. The special allocation can be used only if all persons who were shareholders at any time during the S short year and all persons who are shareholders on the first day of the C short year consent to the election.[24] (See page C11-37 for further discussion of the tax planning considerations of this election.) A daily allocation cannot be used when an S termination year occurs and during such year sales or exchanges of 50 percent or more of the corporation's outstanding stock occur. In such a case, the corporation's normal accounting rules must be used to make the allocation.

INADVERTENT TERMINATION. Special rules permit the S election to continue if an inadvertent termination occurs by ceasing to be a small business corporation or by failing the passive investment income test for three consecutive years. If such a termination should occur, the S corporation or its shareholders must take the necessary steps, within a reasonable time period after discovering the event creating the termination, to restore its small business corporation status. If the Internal Revenue Service (IRS) determines that the termination was inadvertent, the corporation and all persons owning stock during the termination period must agree to make the adjustments necessary to report the income for this period as if the S election had been in effect continuously.[25]

EXAMPLE C11-8 ▶

Frye Corporation is created in 1994 and operates as a C corporation during that year. Frye makes an S election in 1995. During 1994, the corporation incorrectly computed its E&P and believed that no Subchapter C E&P existed for its only pre-S corporation tax year. From 1995 through 1997, Frye earns large amounts of passive income, but does not pay the Sec. 1375 excess net passive income tax or worry about termination of its election because it thinks that it does not have any accumulated E&P from 1994. Upon auditing Frye's tax returns, the IRS finds that Subchapter C E&P did, in fact, exist from 1994, and terminates the S election effective on January 1, 1998. If the E&P is distributed and the shareholders report the dividend income, the IRS will probably treat the occurrence as an inadvertent termination and not revoke the election. ◀

OTHER IRS WAIVERS. The IRS can not only waive a termination that it deems to be inadvertent, it also can validate certain invalid elections. Validation of an invalid election can occur when the election failed to meet the basic S corporation requirements of IRC Sec. 1361 or failed to provide the necessary shareholder consents. The IRS also can exercise this authority in situations where a corporation never filed an election.[26] In addition, the IRS can treat a late-filed S election as being timely-filed if the IRS determines that there was reasonable cause for failing to make a timely election.[27] In order to obtain relief for a late election, the IRS must issue a private letter ruling. These two changes were made in the 1996 tax legislation and are applicable to all invalid or late

---

[23] Sec. 1362(e)(6)(B).

[24] Sec. 1362(e)(3)(B).

[25] Sec. 1362(f)(1). Regulation Sec. 1.1362-4(b) holds that a termination will be inadvertent if the terminating event was not reasonably within the control of the corporation and was not part of a plan to terminate the election or it took place without the corporation's knowledge and reasonable safeguards were in place to prevent the event from occurring.

[26] Sec. 1362(f).

[27] Sec. 1362(b)(5). See Announcement 97-4, I.R.B. 1997-3, 14, for additional guidance and a special transition rule.

elections applying to tax years beginning after December 31, 1982 (the effective date of the last major S corporation revisions).[28] The committee reports indicate that Congress intended for the IRS to be reasonable in exercising this authority and apply standards similar to those applied to inadvertent terminations and other late or invalid elections.

NEW ELECTION FOLLOWING A TERMINATION. Section 1362(g) requires a corporation that terminates its S election to wait five tax years before making a new election.[29] This delay applies unless the IRS consents to an earlier reelection. Regulation Sec. 1.1362-5(a) indicates that permission for an early reelection can occur when more than 50% of the corporation's stock is owned by persons who did not own stock on the date of termination or the event causing the termination was not reasonably within the control of the corporation or the shareholders having a substantial interest in the corporation *and* was not part of a plan to terminate the election involving the corporation or such shareholders.

EXAMPLE C11-9 ▶ Victor Corporation, a calendar-year taxpayer, is owned by Terri and has been taxed as an S corporation for ten years. In January 1996, Terri sells all of the Victor stock to Michelle. Payments for the stock are to be made over a five-year period. In March 1998, Michelle fails to make the necessary payments and Terri repossesses the stock. During the time Michelle holds the stock, Victor Corporation revokes its S election. Victor Corporation should be able to immediately apply for reelection of S status because a more than 50% ownership change has occurred since the date of the termination. ◀

Congress enacted a special one-time waiver of the 5-year reelection waiting period for S corporation terminations occurring prior to August 20, 1996. These corporations can reelect S corporation status immediately without IRS consent.

AVOIDING THE TERMINATION OF AN S ELECTION. The termination of an S election generally carries with it substantial negative tax consequences in the form of increased corporate or shareholder taxes. The S corporation's owners, management, and tax advisor need to understand the various events that can cause the termination of the S election. Some of the steps that can be taken to prevent an untimely termination include the following:

- Monitor all transfers of S corporation stock. Make certain that the purchaser or transferee of the stock is not an ineligible shareholder (e.g., corporation, partnership, or nonresident alien) or that the total number of shareholders does not exceed seventy-five (e.g., a seventy-sixth shareholder resulting from creation of a joint interest).
- Establish procedures for the S corporation to purchase the stock of deceased shareholders to avoid the stock being acquired by a trust that is ineligible to be a shareholder.
- Establish restrictions on the transferability of the S corporation stock by having the shareholders enter into a stock purchase agreement. Such an agreement could provide that the stock cannot be transferred without the prior consent of all other shareholders and, if the necessary consent cannot be obtained, the stock will be repurchased by the corporation at a specified price (e.g., at book value).
- Monitor the passive income earned by an S corporation that has previously been taxed for one or more years as a C corporation. Make certain that the passive income requirement is not failed for three consecutive years by taking action to reduce the level of passive income or to distribute the Subchapter C E&P.

KEY POINT

The most common cause of inadvertent terminations is the sale of an S corporation's stock. Therefore, an S corporation should have a buy-sell agreement to guard itself against an ill-advised sale of its stock.

[28] See Announcement 97-4, I.R.B. 1997-3, 14, for additional guidance on when the IRS will permit the fixing of invalid or late S corporation elections or consents.

[29] *Termination* includes both revocation of the S election and loss of the election because one or more of the small business corporation requirements were not met.

S CORPORATION OPERATIONS

S corporations make the same accounting period and accounting method elections that are made by a C corporation. Each year, the S corporation must compute and report to the IRS and to its shareholders its ordinary income or loss and its separately stated items. The special S corporation rules are explained below.

OBJECTIVE 4

Determine the permitted tax years for an S corporation

TAXABLE YEAR

Section 1378(a) requires that the S corporation's taxable year be a permitted year. A permitted year is defined as

- A taxable year ending on December 31 (including a 52–53 week year)
- Any fiscal year for which the corporation establishes a business purpose[30]

Section 1378(b) specifically notes that an income deferral for the shareholders is not a necessary business purpose. An S corporation that adopts a fiscal year that coincides with its natural business year has satisfied the business purpose requirement. The natural business year for an S corporation depends on the type of business conducted. When a trade or business has nonpeak and peak periods of business, the natural business year is considered to end at, or soon after, the close of the peak business period. A business whose income is steady from month to month, year-round, does not have a natural business year. S corporations use the same natural business year definitions as were outlined for partnerships (see Chapter C9).

EXAMPLE C11-10 ▶ Sable Corporation, an electing S corporation, operates a ski resort and reports $1 million of gross receipts for each of its last three tax years. If at least $250,000 of the receipts are included in the months of February and March for each of the three consecutive years, Sable can adopt, or change to, or continue to use a natural business year ending on March 31. ◀

An S corporation's adoption of, or a change to, a fiscal year that is an ownership tax year is also permitted. An ownership tax year is the same tax year that is used by shareholders owning more than 50% of the corporation's outstanding stock. The 50% requirement must be met on the first day of the tax year to which the change relates. Failure to meet the 50% ownership requirement on the first day of any later tax year requires a change to a calendar year or other approved fiscal year. S corporations can also adopt or change to a fiscal year for which IRS approval is obtained based on the facts and circumstances of the situation.[31]

ADDITIONAL COMMENT

The requirement that all S corporations adopt calendar years (with March 15 return due dates) caused a hardship for tax return preparers. Section 444 is a compromise provision that allows a fiscal year for filing purposes, but mandates a special payment of the deferred taxes.

Section 444 permits an S corporation to elect to use a fiscal year other than a permitted year. The fiscal year elected under Sec. 444 must have a deferral period of three months or less (e.g., a September 30 or later fiscal year-end for an S corporation otherwise required to use a calendar year). An S corporation that is changing its tax year can elect to use a new fiscal year under Sec. 444 only if the deferral period is no longer than the shorter of three months or the deferral period of the tax year that is being changed.[32] A Sec. 444 election is not required of an S corporation that satisfies the business purpose exception.

S corporations that elect under Sec. 444 to use a fiscal year must make the necessary required payment under Sec. 7519 (see Chapter C9 for an explanation of these payment

[30] Some S corporations use a "grandfathered" fiscal year: a fiscal year for which IRS approval was obtained after June 30, 1974. Excluded are fiscal years that result in an income deferral of three months or less.

[31] Temporary Reg. Sec. 1.1378-1 and Rev. Proc. 87-32, 1987-2 C.B. 396, explain the procedures for an S corporation adopting a fiscal year or changing the tax year of a new or existing S corporation. The tests for a natural business year are found in Rev. Proc. 83-25, 1983-1 C.B. 689. Rev. Rul. 87-58, 1987-2 C.B. 224, examines eight situations concerning whether the tax year is a permitted year.

[32] Special Sec. 444 transitional rules for 1986 permitted many S corporations to retain a previously adopted fiscal year (e.g., January 31) even though the deferral period is longer than three months.

requirements). When the required payment is computed, the base year net income is the aggregate of all S corporation income, gain, loss, and deduction items that are described in Sec. 1366 (see page C11-16). Revocation or termination of the S election also terminates the Sec. 444 election unless the corporation becomes a personal service corporation. Termination of the Sec. 444 election permits the S corporation to obtain a refund of prior Sec. 7519 payments.

Topic Review C11-2 presents a summary of the alternative tax years that are available to an S corporation.

ACCOUNTING METHOD ELECTIONS

The accounting method elections used to compute ordinary income or loss and the separately stated items are made by the S corporation rather than the individual shareholders. As with a partnership, these elections are made independent of the accounting method elections made by its shareholders. Three elections generally reserved for the S corporation's shareholders are as follows:

- Sections 108(b)(5) or (c)(3) relating to income from the discharge of indebtedness
- Section 617 election relating to deduction and recapture of mining exploration expenditures
- Section 901 election to take a credit for foreign income taxes[33]

Topic Review C11-2

Alternative S Corporation Tax Years

Tax Year	*Requirements*
Calendar year (including certain 52–53 week years)	The permitted tax year that is required unless one of the other exceptions applies.
Permitted fiscal year:	IRS approval will be granted if
a. Ownership year	The same tax year is requested that is used by shareholders owing more than one-half of the corporation's outstanding stock. This test must be met on the first day of the year for which approval is requested as well as for each succeeding year.
b. Natural business year	25% or more of the gross receipts for each of the three most recent twelve-month periods are in the last two months of the requested tax year.
c. Facts and circumstances year	A business purpose (other than an ownership year or natural business year) is established using the facts and circumstances of the situation.
Nonpermitted fiscal year	A Sec. 444 election permits a nonpermitted tax year to be used if the deferral period is three months or less and the necessary required payments are made.

[33] Secs. 1363(c).

OBJECTIVE 5

Calculate ordinary income or loss

ORDINARY INCOME OR LOSS

S corporations do not compute their taxable income in the same manner as C corporations. Because S corporations are taxed like partnerships, they are treated as if they were individual taxpayers. Thus, they report both an ordinary income or loss amount and a series of separately stated items.

KEY POINT

S corporations are most like partnerships in their method of reporting income/losses. Both are flowthrough entities that provide K-1s to their owners with their respective shares of income/loss items.

The S corporation's separately stated items are the same ones that apply in partnership taxation under Sec. 702(a).[34] The items required to be separately stated by Sec. 702(a) include

- Net short-term capital gains and losses
- Net long-term capital gains and losses
- Sec. 1231 gains and losses
- Charitable contributions
- Dividends that are eligible for a dividends-received deduction[35]
- Taxes paid to a foreign country or to a U.S. possession
- Any other item provided by the Regulations

Regulation Sec. 1.702-1(a)(8) adds for partnerships several other items to the list begun by the Code. The same additions from the Regulations apply to S corporations and include the following:

- Tax-exempt or partially tax-exempt interest
- Soil and water conservation expenditures
- Intangible drilling and development costs
- Certain mining exploration expenditures

Additional items not mentioned in Sec. 702 or its regulations that are separately stated include

- Passive income and loss
- Portfolio income (e.g., dividends and interest)

(For a more complete list of the separately stated items see the Form 1120S Schedule K included in Appendix B.)

Section 1366(b) requires the character of any separately stated item to be determined as if the item were (1) realized directly by the shareholder from the same source from which it was realized by the corporation or (2) incurred by the shareholder in the same manner as it was incurred by the corporation. Thus, the character of an income, gain, deduction, loss, or credit item does not change merely because the item is passed through and taxed to the shareholders.

DEDUCTIONS THAT CANNOT BE CLAIMED. S corporations also have several deductions that cannot be claimed, including

KEY POINT

The dividends-received deduction is not permitted because the dividends flow through to the S corporation's shareholders and an S corporation cannot have a corporate shareholder.

- The 70%, 80%, or 100% dividends-received deduction (because dividends are passed through to the S corporation's shareholders)
- The same deductions that are disallowed to a partnership under Sec. 703(a)(2) (e.g., personal and dependency exemptions, additional itemized deductions for individuals, taxes paid or accrued to a foreign country or to a U.S. possession, charitable contributions, oil and gas depletion, and NOL carrybacks and carryforwards).[36]

---

[34] Sec. 1366(a).

[35] Partnerships are permitted to have C corporations as owners of partnership interests. Such is not the case with an S corporation who can not have a corporate shareholder.

[36] Sec. 1363(b)(2).

SIMILARITY TO C CORPORATION TREATMENT. S corporations are treated as corporations for certain tax matters. For example, an S corporation can elect to amortize its organizational expenditures under Sec. 248. Also, the 20% reduction in certain tax preference benefits under Sec. 291 applies to an S corporation if the corporation was a C corporation in any of its three preceding tax years.[37]

SELF-STUDY QUESTION

Because S corporations are conduits, can NOL carryforwards from a C corporation tax year flow through to the S corporation's shareholders?

ANSWER

No. C corporation NOLs are not a good reason to make an S election, because the NOLs cannot be carried to an S corporation tax year and passed through to the shareholder.

CARRYFORWARDS AND CARRYBACKS WHEN STATUS CHANGES. Some S corporations may operate as C corporations during a period of years that either precede the making of an S election or follow the termination of an S election. No carryforwards or carrybacks that originate in a C corporation tax year can be carried to an S corporation tax year other than carryforwards that can be used to offset the built-in gains tax (see page C11-18). Similarly, no carryforwards or carrybacks can be created in an S corporation tax year that can be taken to a C corporation tax year.[38] Losses from an S corporation tax year, of course, are passed through to the shareholder and, if in excess of the shareholder's income for the year, can create a NOL carryforward or carryback for the shareholder.

OBJECTIVE 6

Calculate the amount of any special S corporation tax levies

SPECIAL S CORPORATION TAXES

The S corporation is subject to four special tax levies: the excess net passive income tax, the built-in gains tax, the LIFO recapture tax, and the recapture of previously claimed investment tax credits. Each of these is explained below.

EXCESS NET PASSIVE INCOME TAX. The **excess net passive income (or Sec. 1375) tax** is levied when an S corporation has passive investment income for the tax year that exceeds 25% of its gross receipts and at the close of the tax year the S corporation has Subchapter C E&P. The excess net passive income tax equals the S corporation's excess net passive income times the highest corporate tax rate (35% for 1997).[39]

KEY POINT

The excess net passive income tax is of most concern to a former C corporation that has accumulated E&P. A corporation that has always been an S corporation is much less likely to have a passive income problem.

The **excess net passive income** is determined as follows:

$$\text{Excess net passive income} = \text{Net passive income} \times \frac{\text{Passive investment income} - 25\% \text{ of gross receipts}}{\text{Passive investment income}}$$

The excess net passive income is limited to the corporation's taxable income, which is defined as a C corporation's taxable income except with no reduction for the NOL deduction or the dividends-received and dividends-paid deductions. Net passive income equals passive investment income minus any deductions that are directly related to its production.[40]

Regulation Sec. 1.1362-2(c)(5) holds that passive investment income excludes income derived from the active conduct of a trade or business.

EXAMPLE C11-11 ▶ Paoli Corporation reports the following results for 1997:

Service (nonpassive) income	$35,000
Dividend income	37,000
Interest income	28,000
Passive income-related expenses	10,000
Other expenses	25,000

At the end of this year, Paoli's E&P for its C corporation tax years amounts to $60,000. Paoli's excess net passive income is determined as follows:

[37] Secs. 1363(b)(3) and (4).

[38] Sec. 1371(b).

[39] Sec. 1375(a). *Passive investment income* and *Subchapter C E&P* have the same definition here as when they were defined on page C11-11.

[40] Sec. 1375(b). Regulation Sec. 1.1375-1(f), Ex. (2) indicates that passive income that is subject to the Sec. 1375 tax includes municipal bond interest that is otherwise exempt from the federal income tax.

$$\$33{,}846 = (\$65{,}000 - \$10{,}000) \times \frac{\$65{,}000 - (0.25 \times \$100{,}000)}{\$65{,}000}$$

The excess net passive income tax (at 1997 rates) is $11,846 ($33,846 × 0.35). The special tax reduces (on a pro rata basis) the dividend income and interest income items that are passed through to the shareholders. The S election is not terminated at the end of 1997 unless Paoli was also subject to the tax in 1995 and 1996. Paoli Corporation can avoid the Sec. 1375 tax in future years (and the possibility of having its S election terminated) by distributing its $60,000 of Subchapter C E&P. This technique is discussed on page C11-39. ◀

KEY POINT

Section 1374 applies to an S corporation that made its S election after December 31, 1986. The motivation for this tax was the concern that C corporations would use the S election to avoid the imposition of the corporate level tax on liquidating distributions (see Chapters C4 and C6).

BUILT-IN GAINS TAX. The Tax Reform Act of 1986 added a second corporate level tax on gains that are recognized by an S corporation that was formerly a C corporation. This tax, called the **built-in gains (or Sec. 1374) tax,** is imposed on any income or gain that would have been included in gross income while a C corporation if the corporation had used the accrual method of accounting (known as a **built-in gain**) and that is reported during the ten-year period commencing on the date the S election took effect (known as the recognition period). Built-in losses reduce the amount of recognized built-in gains in determining the built-in gains tax liability. **Built-in losses** are any deductions or losses that would have been deductible while a C corporation if the corporation had used the accrual method of accounting and that are reported during the ten-year period commencing on the date the S election took effect.

Although this tax was enacted to prevent taxpayers from avoiding the imposition of the corporate level tax on liquidating distributions by making an S election before liquidating the corporation or selling its assets, the tax ramifications of the built-in gains tax extends far beyond corporations that are in the process of liquidating. The built-in gains tax applies to S corporation tax years beginning after December 31, 1986 where the S corporation was formerly a C corporation and the current S election was made after December 31, 1986.[41]

EXAMPLE C11-12 ▶

Tatum Corporation, a calendar-year taxpayer, was incorporated in 1984 and operated as a C corporation through the end of 1996. On February 3, 1997, Tatum Corporation filed an S election that was effective for 1997 and later tax years. Because Tatum's S election is filed after December 31, 1986, it is subject to the built-in gains tax for ten years starting with January 1, 1997. ◀

The Sec. 1374 tax is determined by using the following four-step calculation:

STEP 1: Determine the corporation's net recognized built-in gain for the tax year.

STEP 2: Reduce the net recognized built-in gain from Step 1 (but not below zero) by any NOL or capital loss carryovers from any prior C corporation tax years.

SELF-STUDY QUESTION

Can loss or credit carryforwards from a previous C corporation tax year help reduce the built-in gains tax?

ANSWER

Yes. Both NOL and capital loss carryforwards reduce the amount of recognized built-in gain taxed under Sec. 1374. The general business and minimum tax credit carryforwards reduce the actual built-in gains tax.

STEP 3: Compute a tentative tax by multiplying the amount determined in Step 2 by the highest corporate tax rate (35 percent in 1997).

STEP 4: Reduce the tax determined in Step 3 (but not below zero) by the amount of the general business credit and minimum tax credit carryovers from any prior C corporation tax years and the nonhighway use of gasoline and other fuels credit.

A recognized built-in gain or loss is any gain or loss recognized on an asset disposition during the ten-year recognition period unless the S corporation can establish that it did not hold the asset on the first day of the first tax year to which the S election applies. A recognized built-in gain cannot exceed the excess of a property's FMV over its adjusted basis on the first day of the ten-year recognition period. Dispositions include sales or exchanges and other events, including the collection of accounts receivable by a cash

[41] Sec. 1374(a).

method of accounting taxpayer, collection of an installment sale obligation, and the completion of a long-term contract by a taxpayer using the completed contract method.[42]

Built-in losses include not only losses originating from a disposition of property, but also any deductions claimed during the ten-year recognition period that are attributable to periods before the first S corporation tax year. A recognized built-in loss cannot exceed the excess of a property's adjusted basis over its FMV on the first day of the ten-year recognition period.[43] Built-in losses, however, do not include any loss, deduction, or carryforward originating from the disposition of an asset acquired before or during the recognition period where the principal purpose of such acquisition was avoiding the Sec. 1374 tax.

PRACTICAL APPLICATION

The application of the Sec. 1374 tax requires detailed records, which enable the taxpayer to track the built-in gain assets and determine when these gains are recognized.

The net recognized built-in gain for a tax year is limited to the smaller of:

- The excess of (1) the net unrealized built-in gain (i.e., excess of the FMV of the S corporation's assets at the beginning of its first tax year for which the S election is in effect over their total adjusted basis on such date) over (2) the total net recognized built-in gain for prior tax years beginning in the ten-year recognition period.[44]
- The S corporation's taxable income if it was taxed as a C corporation but was unable to claim any dividends-received deduction or NOL deduction.[45]

If the net of the recognized built-in gains and losses exceeds the corporation's taxable income and the S election was made after March 30, 1988, the excess built-in gain amount is carried over to the next tax year, where it may be subject to the Sec. 1374 built-in gains tax. The built-in gain carryover consists of a ratable share of each of the income categories (e.g., ordinary income, capital gains) making up the net recognized built-in gain amount for the tax year.

The built-in gains tax is passed on to the shareholders as if it were a loss. The loss must be allocated proportionately among the recognized built-in gains that resulted in the tax being imposed.

EXAMPLE C11-13 ▶

Assume the same facts as in Example C11-12, except that Tatum Corporation uses the accrual method of accounting and owns the following assets on January 1, 1997:

Assets	*Adjusted Basis*	*FMV*
Cash	$10,000	$10,000
Marketable securities	39,000	45,000
Accounts receivable	60,000	60,000
Inventory (FIFO)	60,000	75,000
Building	27,000	44,000
Land	10,000	26,000
Machinery and equipment[a]	74,000	140,000
Total	$280,000	$400,000

[a] $50,000 of the gain is subject to recapture under Sec. 1245.

ETHICAL POINT

A C corporation that has substantially appreciated assets and wants to make an S election should obtain an appraisal of its assets on or about the first day of the S election period. The S corporation's tax accountant must make sure that the appraiser does not assign an artifically low value of these assets to minimize the potential built-in gains tax burden.

During 1997, Tatum collects $58,000 of accounts receivable and declares $2,000 uncollectible. The FIFO inventory was sold at a $25,000 profit in the first quarter of 1997, and replaced with new inventory. Two machines were sold during 1997. One machine, having an $18,000

[42] Secs. 1374(d)(3) and (4). Income and gains can be taxed under both the excess net passive income (Sec. 1375) and built-in gains (Sec. 1374) taxes. Any such income or gain is fully taxed under the Sec. 1374 rules. The portion of the income or gain that is taxed under the Sec. 1374 tax is exempt from the Sec. 1375 tax.

[43] Sec. 1374(d)(5).

[44] Secs. 1374(c)(2) and (d)(1). The recognition period can be extended beyond ten years if property having a carryover basis is acquired in a tax-free transaction (e.g., a tax-free reorganization) from a C corporation. For such properties, the ten-year recognition period commences on the date the S corporation acquired the properties.

[45] Sec. 1374(d)(2).

FMV and an $11,000 adjusted basis on January 1, was sold for an $8,000 gain (Sec. 1245 income) on September 1. A second machine, having a $15,000 FMV and a $19,000 adjusted basis on January 1, was sold for a $7,000 loss on March 15.

- Tatum recognizes no built-in gain or loss on collecting the receivables because it is an accrual method taxpayer. The $2,000 uncollectible debt is not a built-in loss because the loss arose after January 1. It is deductible as part of the ordinary income/loss calculation.
- $15,000 ($75,000 − $60,000) of the $25,000 inventory profit is a built-in gain that is taxed under Sec. 1374. The entire $25,000 profit is included in ordinary income/loss.
- A $7,000 built-in gain ($18,000 − $11,000) and a $4,000 ($15,000 − $19,000) built-in loss, are recognized on the sale of the two machines. An $8,000 Sec. 1245 gain is included in ordinary income/loss and a $7,000 Sec. 1231 loss is passed through separately to the shareholders.

In total, an $18,000 ($15,000 + $7,000 − $4,000) net recognized built-in gain is taxed under Sec. 1374, subject, of course, to the taxable income ceiling. Assuming C corporation taxable income (without any NOL deduction and dividends-received deduction) is at least $18,000, the built-in gains tax is $6,300 ($18,000 × 0.35). The entire tax amount reduces the ordinary income from the inventory and machinery sales. ◀

LIFO RECAPTURE TAX. If a C corporation using the LIFO inventory method makes an S election, Sec. 1363(d)(3) requires the corporation to include its LIFO recapture amount in gross income for its last C corporation tax year. The LIFO recapture amount is the excess of the inventory's basis for tax purposes under the FIFO method over its basis under the LIFO method at the close of the final C corporation tax year. Any tax increase incurred in the final C corporation tax year is payable in four installments: on or before the due date for the final C corporation tax return and on or before the due date for the first three S corporation tax returns. The S corporation's inventory basis is increased by the LIFO recapture amount that is included in gross income.

EXAMPLE C11-14 ▶ Taylor Corporation, a calendar year C corporation since its inception in 1984, makes an S election on December 24, 1996, effective for its 1997 tax year. Taylor has used the LIFO inventory method for a number of years. Its LIFO inventory has a $400,000 adjusted basis, a $650,000 FIFO inventory value, and an $800,000 FMV. Taylor's LIFO recapture amount is $250,000 ($650,000 − $400,000). This amount is included in Taylor's gross income reported on its 1996 corporate tax return. Assuming a 34% corporate tax, Taylor's increased tax liability is $85,000 (0.34 × $250,000). $21,250 (0.25 × $85,000) is due with Taylor's 1996 C corporation tax return. An additional $21,250 is due with the 1997 through 1999 S corporation tax returns. Taylor increases the basis of its inventory by the $250,000 LIFO recapture amount. ◀

RECAPTURE OF PREVIOUSLY CLAIMED INVESTMENT TAX CREDITS. Making an S election does not trigger an investment tax credit recapture. The election is considered a mere change in the form of conducting the trade or business. S corporations are liable for the recapture of investment tax credits (e.g., the rehabilitation credit, energy credit, and reforestation credit) claimed while the S election was not in effect. Investment tax credits claimed while an S corporation, and the effects of any recapture, are accounted for at the shareholder level. Termination of the S election does not trigger any credit recapture.

STOP & THINK

Question: Former C corporations that are now taxed as S corporations are subject to three corporate level taxes—the LIFO recapture tax, the built-in gains tax, and the excess net passive income tax. What are the reasons behind enacting these three taxes?

Solution: In 1986, Congress debated making the conversion of a C corporation into an S corporation a taxable event subject to the corporate liquidation rules. All gains and losses would have been recognized by the corporation at the time of conversion. As a compromise, only LIFO users are subject to an "automatic" tax when conversion occurs, and this tax is only imposed on the LIFO recapture amount and not all inventory appreciation. The built-in gains tax is imposed only when assets are sold or exchanged during the corporation's first 10 years under the S election. Assets not sold or exchanged during this time period escape the tax. The excess net passive income tax is imposed to encourage S corporations to distribute their accumulated E&P. No tax is imposed if passive income is kept below the 25% of gross receipts threshold. Thus, former C corporations and their shareholders are generally better off under the current system than if a corporate liquidation were mandated.

TAXATION OF THE SHAREHOLDER

INCOME ALLOCATION PROCEDURES

OBJECTIVE 7

Calculate a shareholder's allocable share of ordinary income or loss and separately stated items

An S corporation's shareholders must report their pro rata share of the ordinary income or loss and separately stated items for the S corporation's tax year that ends with or within the shareholder's tax year.[46] Each shareholder's pro rata share of the aforementioned items is determined by

1. Allocating an equal portion of the item to each day in the tax year (by dividing the amount of the item by the number of days in the S corporation's tax year)
2. Allocating an equal portion of the daily amount for the item to each share of stock that is outstanding on each day (by dividing the daily amount for the item by the number of shares of stock outstanding on a particular day)
3. Totaling the daily allocations for each share of stock
4. Totaling the amounts allocated for each share of stock held by the shareholder

TYPICAL MISCONCEPTION

An S corporation's income/loss is allocated basically the same as a partnership's except that a partnership may have the added flexibility of making certain special allocations under Sec. 704(b).

These allocation rules are known as the "per day/per share" method. Special allocations (such as those that are found in Sec. 704 under the partnership tax rules) of the ordinary income or loss and separately stated items are not permitted.

If there is a sale of the S corporation stock during the year, the transferor reports the earnings allocated to the transferred shares through the day preceding the transfer date. The transferee's share of the earnings is reported from the transfer date through the end of the tax year.

EXAMPLE C11-15 ▶ Fox Corporation, an electing S corporation, is owned equally by Arnie and Bonnie during all of 1997. During this year, Fox reports ordinary income of $146,000 and a long-term capital gain of $36,500. Arnie and Bonnie each report $73,000 (0.50 × $146,000) of ordinary income and $18,250 (0.50 × $36,500) of long-term capital gain. ◀

EXAMPLE C11-16 ▶ Assume the same facts as in Example C11-15, except that Bonnie sells one-half of her shares to Clay on March 31, 1997 (the 90th day of Fox's tax year). Arnie reports the same ordinary income and long-term capital gain from his investment. Bonnie and Clay report ordinary income and long-term capital gain as follows:

[46] Sec. 1366(a). If the shareholder dies during the S corporation's tax year, the income earned during the portion of the tax year preceding death is reported on the shareholder's tax return. The income for the period of time that the estate holds the S corporation stock is reported on its fiduciary tax return.

Ordinary Income

$$\text{Bonnie:} \quad \left(\$146{,}000 \times \frac{1}{2} \times \frac{89}{365}\right) + \left(\$146{,}000 \times \frac{1}{4} \times \frac{276}{365}\right) = \$45{,}400$$

$$\text{Clay:} \quad \$146{,}000 \times \frac{1}{4} \times \frac{276}{365} = 27{,}600$$

$$\text{Total} \quad \$73{,}000$$

Long-Term Capital Gain

$$\text{Bonnie:} \quad \left(\$36{,}500 \times \frac{1}{2} \times \frac{89}{365}\right) + \left(\$36{,}500 \times \frac{1}{4} \times \frac{276}{365}\right) = \$11{,}350$$

$$\text{Clay:} \quad \$36{,}500 \times \frac{1}{4} \times \frac{276}{365} = 6{,}900$$

$$\text{Total} \quad \$18{,}250$$

◀

KEY POINT

Shareholders of an S corporation need to be aware that when they dispose of their stock, they have the option of having income/loss determined by an actual closing of the books rather than an allocation on a daily basis.

A special election is available for allocating the ordinary income or loss and separately stated items when the shareholder's interest in the S corporation is terminated during the tax year, or when the interest is substantially reduced, even if not completely terminated. If the election is made, the income is allocated according to the accounting methods used by the S corporation (instead of on a daily basis). The election divides the S corporation's tax year into two parts ending on

- The day the shareholder's interest in the corporation is terminated
- The last day of the S corporation's tax year

This election can only be made if all affected shareholders agree to the election.[47] An affected shareholder includes the shareholder whose interest was terminated, and all shareholders to whom the transferor transferred S corporation shares during the year. This election is explored in greater detail in the Tax Planning Considerations section of this chapter.

OBJECTIVE 8

Determine the limitations on a shareholder's deduction of S corporation losses

LOSS AND DEDUCTION PASS-THROUGH TO SHAREHOLDERS

The S corporation's ordinary loss and separately stated loss and deduction items pass through to the shareholders at the end of the corporation's tax year. These items are reported in the shareholder's tax year in which the S corporation's tax year ends.

ALLOCATION OF THE LOSS. Using the rules outlined above, allocation of the loss occurs on a daily basis. Thus, shareholders receive an allocation of the ordinary loss and separately stated items even if the stock is owned for only a portion of the year. If the ordinary loss and other separately stated loss and deduction pass-throughs exceed the shareholder's income, the excess may create an NOL for the shareholder and result in a carryback or carryover to the shareholder's other tax years.

EXAMPLE C11-17 ▶ Kauai Corporation, an electing S corporation, reports a $73,000 ordinary loss during 1997. At the beginning of 1997, Elvis and Frank own equally all of Kauai's stock. On June 30, 1997 (the 181st day of Kauai's tax year), Frank gives one-fourth of his stock to his son George. Elvis is allocated $36,500 of ordinary loss. Frank and George are allocated ordinary losses as follows:

[47] Sec. 1377(a)(2).

$$\text{Frank:} \quad \left(\$73{,}000 \times \frac{1}{2} \times \frac{180}{365}\right) + \left(\$73{,}000 \times \frac{3}{8} \times \frac{185}{365}\right) = \$31{,}875$$

$$\text{George:} \quad \$73{,}000 \times \frac{1}{8} \times \frac{185}{365} = 4{,}625$$

$$\text{Total} \quad \$36{,}500$$

All three shareholders can deduct these losses on their individual tax returns subject to the loss limitations described below. ◀

TYPICAL MISCONCEPTION

The amount of losses that can be deducted by a shareholder of an S corporation, unlike a partnership, is not increased by the S corporation's general liabilities unless the shareholder is the creditor.

SHAREHOLDER LOSS LIMITATIONS. Each shareholder's deduction for his or her share of the ordinary loss and the separately stated loss and deduction items is limited to the sum of the adjusted basis for his or her S corporation stock plus the adjusted basis of any indebtedness owed directly by the S corporation to the shareholder. Unlike the partnership taxation rules, a shareholder cannot increase his or her basis in the stock for purposes of determining the loss deduction limitation by a ratable share of the general S corporation liabilities.[48] However, a positive basis adjustment is made for any ordinary income or separately stated income or gain items reported in the "loss" year and the amount of capital contributions before the shareholder's loss limitation is determined.

Basis reductions for distributions are made before the shareholder's loss limitation is determined. Sequencing the basis reduction for distributions ahead of the absorption of the losses means that distributions reduce the deductibility of S corporation loss and deduction passthroughs, but losses do not change the taxability of S corporation distributions. Once the loss limitation is determined, the basis decreases occur in the following sequence.

1. Distributions that are not includible in the shareholder's income.[49]
2. Decreases attributable to nondeductible, noncapital expenditures.
3. Decreases attributable to ordinary losses and separately stated loss and deduction items.

Many S corporations are nothing more than incorporated forms of sole proprietorships or partnerships. As a result, banks and other lending institutions often require one or more of the shareholders to personally guarantee any loans made to the S corporation. In general, the IRS and the courts have held that this form of indirect borrowing by the S corporation does not create a corporate indebtedness to the shareholder. As a result, the shareholder's loss limitation is not increased as a result of his or her acting as a guarantor until the shareholder makes a payment of part or all of the corporation's liability or the shareholder executes a note at the bank in full satisfaction of the corporation's liability. Such an action on the part of the shareholder converts the guarantee into an indebtedness of the corporation to the shareholder, which increases the shareholder's loss limitation.[50]

The adjusted basis of the S corporation stock and debt is generally determined as of the last day of the S corporation's tax year. If the S corporation stock is disposed of before that date, the adjusted basis of the stock and debt is instead determined immediately prior to the disposition.

EXAMPLE C11-18 ▶ Tillis Corporation, an electing S corporation, is owned equally by Pat and Bill. During the current year Tillis reports an ordinary loss of $100,000. Tillis's liabilities at the end of the

[48] Sec. 1366(d)(1). Amounts owed by an S corporation to a conduit entity that has the shareholder as an owner or beneficiary will not increase the shareholder's loss limitation.

[49] Special basis adjustment rules apply to oil and gas depletion.

[50] Rev. Ruls. 70-50, 1970-1 C.B. 178; 71-288, 1971-2 C.B. 319; and 75-144, 1975-1 C.B. 277. See also *Estate of Daniel Leavitt v. CIR*, 63 AFTR 2d 89-1437, 89-1 USTC ¶9332 (4th Cir., 1989) among a series of decisions which uphold the IRS's position. However, see *Edward M. Selfe v. U.S.*, 57 AFTR 2d 86-464, 86-1 USTC ¶9115 (11th Cir., 1986) for a transaction where a guarantee was held to increase the shareholder's loss limitation because the transaction was structured so the bank looked primarily to the shareholder for repayment instead of the corporation.

current year include $100,000 of accounts payable, $150,000 of mortgage payable, and a $20,000 note owed to Bill. Pat and Bill each had a $40,000 adjusted basis for their Tillis stock on January 1. The ordinary loss is allocated equally to Pat and Bill. Pat's $50,000 loss allocation is only partially deductible this year (i.e., up to $40,000) because his $40,000 basis for the Tillis stock is exceeded. Bill's $50,000 loss allocation is fully deductible this year because his loss limitation is $60,000 ($40,000 + $20,000). ◀

The loss and deduction pass-through is allocated to each share of stock. If the pass-through for an individual share of stock exceeds that share's basis, the excess amount is allocated proportionately to all of the shareholder's remaining shares having basis based on their relative basis amounts. Once the losses and deductions have reduced the basis of all shares of stock to zero, they are applied against the basis of any amount owed by the S corporation to the shareholder.

TYPICAL MISCONCEPTION

If a shareholder sells his S corporation stock still having unused losses due to lack of stock basis, these losses do not transfer to the new shareholder. Instead, the unused losses lapse when the stock is sold.

Any loss or deduction pass-through that is not currently deductible is suspended until the shareholder has a basis in his stock or in an amount owed to him or her by the S corporation. The shareholder is permitted an unlimited carryover for the loss or deduction item.[51] The additional adjusted basis amount can originate from a number of sources, including subsequent profits earned by the S corporation, additional capital contributions or loans made by the shareholder to the corporation, or purchases of additional stock from other shareholders.

EXAMPLE C11-19 ▶

Assume the same facts as in Example C11-18, except that Tillis Corporation reports ordinary income of $20,000 in the next year. Pat and Bill are each allocated $10,000 of ordinary income. This income provides Pat with the necessary $10,000 basis for his Tillis stock to deduct the $10,000 loss carryover. ◀

SPECIAL SHAREHOLDER LOSS AND DEDUCTION LIMITATIONS. The S corporation's shareholders are subject to three special loss and deduction limitations. These limitations may prevent the S corporation's shareholder from using losses or deductions, even though the general loss limitation described above does not otherwise apply. Application of the special loss limitations occurs as follows:

KEY POINT

An oft-quoted advantage of an S election is that losses flow through to the shareholders. This advantage is significantly limited by the at-risk and passive activity rules.

- *At-Risk Rules:* The Sec. 465 at-risk rules are applied at the shareholder level. The loss from a particular S corporation activity is deductible only to the extent of the aggregate amount for which the taxpayer is at risk in the activity at the close of the S corporation's tax year.
- *Passive Activity Limitation Rules:* Losses and credits from a passive activity can be applied against income from that passive activity or other passive activities earned in the same or a subsequent tax year. An S corporation shareholder must personally meet the Sec. 469(h)(1) material participation standard for an activity in order to avoid the passive activity limitation. Material participation by the S corporation in an activity does not permit a passive investor to deduct the portion of the S corporation's loss against his or her salary and other "active" income.
- *Hobby Loss Rules:* Losses incurred by an S corporation are subject to the Sec. 183 hobby loss rules. Deductions incurred by the S corporation are limited to the activity's gross income unless the taxpayer can establish that the activity is a profit-making activity.

In addition, various separately stated loss and deduction items are subject to shareholder limitations (e.g., charitable contributions, long-term capital losses, and investment

[51] Sec. 1366(d)(2). If more than one type of loss or deduction item is passed through to the shareholder, the carryover amount is allocated to each of the passed-through items based on their relative amounts.

interest expense) but they are not subject to corporate limitations. Some separately stated items are subject to corporate limitations but not shareholder limitations (e.g., the 50% nondeductible portion of travel and entertainment expenses).

SELF-STUDY QUESTION

If losses are suspended due to the lack of basis in S corporation stock, do the losses expire when the S election terminates?

ANSWER

No. These loss carryovers may be deducted in the post-termination transition period (usually one year) if the shareholder creates additional stock basis in that period of time.

POST-TERMINATION LOSS CARRYOVERS. Loss and deduction carryovers that are incurred in S corporation tax years can be carried over even though the S election has been terminated. These carryovers can be deducted only in the **post-termination transition period.**[52] The length of the post-termination transition period depends upon the event causing the termination of the S election. The general rule is that the period commences on the day after the last day of the corporation's final S corporation tax year (generally the last day of the S short tax year) and ends on the later of one year after the last day or the due date for the final S corporation tax return (including any extensions). If the S election is terminated for a prior tax year as a result of a determination, the period runs for 120 days beginning on the determination date. Section 1377(b)(2) defines a determination as a court decision that becomes final, a closing agreement that is entered into, an audit determination that adjusts any Subchapter S item of income, loss, or deduction claimed by a former S corporation, a final disposition of a refund claim by the IRS, or an agreement between the corporation and the IRS that the corporation failed to qualify as an S corporation.

The loss and deduction carryovers can be deducted only up to the adjusted basis of the shareholder's stock at the end of the post-termination transition period.[53] Losses that cannot be deducted because of the basis limitation are lost forever. Losses that are deducted reduce the basis of the shareholder's stock.

Topic Review C11-3 presents a summary of the rules governing deductibility of S corporation losses and deductions that are passed through to the shareholders.

EXAMPLE C11-20 ▶ Pearson Corporation has been a calendar year S corporation for several years. Helen's basis for her stock is $45,000. On July 1, 1997, its S election is terminated when part of its stock is acquired by an ineligible shareholder. For the period ended June 30, 1997, Helen is allocated $60,000 of Pearson's ordinary loss. Only $45,000 of this loss can be deducted by Helen because the basis of her Pearson stock is reduced to zero by the loss. The $15,000 unused loss is carried over to the post-termination transition period, which ends on June 30, 1998 (assuming that Pearson does not extend the March 15, 1998 due date for the S short year tax return). Helen must have an adjusted basis for the Pearson stock of at least $15,000 at the close of business on June 30, 1998, in order to use the loss. Helen should consider making additional capital contributions of at least $15,000 between July 1, 1997 and June 30, 1998 to use the loss. ◀

FAMILY S CORPORATIONS

Family S corporations have been an important tax planning device. This type of tax planning quite often involves a high-tax-bracket taxpayer gifting stock to a minor child who generally has little other income. This results in income splitting among family members.

The IRS has the power to ignore such transfers when they appear to be primarily tax motivated. Regulation Sec. 1.1373-1(a)(2) indicates that "a donee or purchaser of stock in the corporation is not considered a shareholder unless such stock is acquired in a bona fide transaction and the donee or purchaser is the real owner of the stock." The IRS has enjoyed success in litigating cases dealing with intrafamily transfers of S corporation

[52] Sec. 1366(d)(3). The loss carryovers that are carried over include those disallowed by the at risk rules.

[53] Sec. 1366(d)(3)(B).

Topic Review C11-3

Deductibility of S Corporation Losses and Deductions

Allocation Process

1. Losses and deductions are allocated based on the number of shares of stock owned by each shareholder on each day of the tax year. Special allocations of losses and deductions are not permitted.
2. Termination of the S election requires the tax year to be divided into two parts. An election can be made to allocate the loss or deduction according to the accounting methods used by the corporation. This election is also available when the termination of a shareholder's interest in the S corporation occurs.

Loss Limitations

1. The loss or deduction pass-through is done on a per-share basis and is limited to the shareholder's basis in the stock. Once the basis for all the shareholder's stock is reduced to zero, the losses reduce the basis of any S corporation indebtedness to the shareholder.
2. Losses and deductions that are not deducted receive an unlimited carryover to a tax year in which the shareholder again has basis in his or her stock or S corporation debt.
3. S corporation shareholders are subject to three special loss limitations:
   - At-risk rules
   - Passive activity limitations
   - Hobby loss rules

   Some separately stated loss and deduction items are also subject to shareholder limitations (e.g., investment interest expense). Other separately stated items are subject to corporate limitations but not shareholder limitations (e.g., the 50% nondeductible portion of travel and entertainment expenses).

stock when the transferor (usually a parent) retains the economic benefits and control over the stock transferred to the transferee (usually a child).[54] The IRS has enjoyed less success when one family member purchases the stock from another family member at its market value.

The IRS also has the statutory authority under Sec. 1366(e) to adjust the income, loss, deduction, or credit items allocated to a family member to reflect the value of services rendered or capital provided to the corporation. Section 1366(e) defines family as including spouse, ancestors, lineal descendants, and trusts created for such individuals. This provision permits the reallocation of income to provide for full compensation of a shareholder or nonshareholder for services and capital provided to the corporation; it also reduces the residual income that is reported by the S corporation and allocated to the shareholders according to their stock ownership. Such a reallocation prevents not only the shifting of income from the family member providing the services or capital to other family members, but also the avoidance of employment taxes. Alternatively, the IRS can determine that too much compensation is paid to a shareholder and reduce that shareholder's salary and increase the residual income that is allocated based on stock ownership.

---

[54] See, for example, *Gino A. Speca v. CIR*, 47 AFTR 2d 81-468, 80-2 USTC ¶9692 (7th Cir., 1980) and *Henry D. Duarte*, 44 T.C. 193 (1965), where the IRS's position prevailed. See also *Gavin S. Millar*, 1975 PH T.C. Memo ¶75,113, 34 TCM 554, and *Donald O. Kirkpatrick*, 1977 PH T.C. Memo ¶77,281, 36 TCM 1122, where the taxpayers prevailed.

EXAMPLE C11-21 ▶ Harvey Corporation, an electing S corporation, reports ordinary income of $200,000 after a deduction of $20,000 is claimed for Sid Harvey's salary. The Harvey stock is owned equally by Sid and his three children. None of Sid's three children are employed by Harvey Corporation. It is subsequently determined that reasonable compensation for Sid is $80,000. This adjustment increases Sid's salary income and Harvey Corporation's compensation deduction by $60,000 ($80,000 − $20,000) and reduces Harvey Corporation's ordinary income to $140,000 ($200,000 − $60,000). Each shareholder's ratable share of ordinary income is reduced from $50,000 ($200,000 ÷ 4) to $35,000 ($140,000 ÷ 4). Alternatively, if the IRS can prove that the stock transfer to the three children is not a bona fide transfer, all $220,000 of Harvey Corporation's income is taxed to Sid—$80,000 as salary and $140,000 as an allocation of ordinary income. ◀

KEY POINT

The advantages of family S corporations have been somewhat curtailed. For example, income from stock of an S corporation gifted to a child under age 14 is subject to the "kiddie tax."

The use of family S corporations as a tax planning device was curtailed by the 1986 Tax Act. As mentioned earlier, gifts of S corporation stock have been used to enable part of the S corporation's income to be reported in the tax returns of minor children. Children under age 14 now must pay tax on their unearned income in excess of $1,300 (for 1997) at the top marginal tax rate of their parents, reducing the attractiveness of many gifts of S corporation stock from a tax planning perspective.[55]

BASIS ADJUSTMENTS

OBJECTIVE 9

Calculate a shareholder's basis in his or her S corporation's stock and debt

Adjustments must be made annually to the basis of the shareholder's S corporation stock. If the S corporation is indebted to the shareholder, the basis of the debt may need to be adjusted downward for loss or deduction pass-throughs and upward to reflect restoration of the basis when subsequent profits are earned. Each of these adjustments is described below.

BASIS ADJUSTMENTS TO S CORPORATION STOCK

The basis of the shareholder's stock is determined as follows:[56]

Initial investment (or basis at beginning of tax year)
Plus: Additional capital contributions made during the year
  Allocable share of ordinary income
  Allocable share of separately stated income and gain items
Minus: Allocable share of any expense that is not deductible in determining ordinary income (loss) and that cannot be charged to the capital account
  Allocable share of ordinary loss
  Allocable share of separately stated loss and deduction items
  Distributions excluded from the shareholder's gross income

Adjusted basis for stock (but not less than zero)

SELF-STUDY QUESTION

Why is the determination of stock basis in an S corporation important?

ANSWER

To determine gain/loss on the sale of the stock, to determine the amount of losses that can be deducted, and to determine the amount of distributions to shareholders that are tax-free.

The initial basis for the S corporation stock depends on the method by which it is acquired. Stock purchased from the corporation or another shareholder takes a cost basis. Stock received as part of a corporate formation transaction generally takes a substituted basis from the assets transferred. Stock acquired by gift will take the donor's

[55] Sec. 1(g)(1).

[56] Sec. 1367(a).

basis (adjusted for gift taxes paid) or FMV (if lower). Stock acquired at death will take its FMV on the decedent's date of death or the alternate valuation date (if elected). The basis of S corporation stock inherited from a deceased shareholder is its FMV minus any corporate income that would have been income in respect of a decedent (see Chapter C14) if the income had been acquired from the decedent. No basis adjustment occurs when the initial S election is made, nor does the basis include any portion of the entity's liabilities, as is the case with a partnership.

The basis adjustments made to the S corporation stock parallel those made to a partnership interest. The ordinary income and separately stated income and gain items increase the shareholder's basis whether they are taxable or tax-exempt, or receive preferential tax treatment.

EXAMPLE C11-22 ▶ Marlo Corporation, an electing S corporation, is owned by Cathy. At the beginning of the current year, Cathy's adjusted basis for the Marlo stock is $105,000. Marlo reports the following operating results this year:

Ordinary income	$70,000
Municipal bond interest income	15,000
Dividends from domestic corporations	6,000
Long-term capital gain	8,000
Short-term capital loss	17,000

Cathy's adjusted basis for the Marlo stock at the end of the year is $187,000 ($105,000 + $70,000 + $15,000 + $6,000 + $8,000 − $17,000). ◀

The basis adjustment is made at the end of the S corporation's tax year, when the results for the entire period are known. Because the profits and losses are allocated ratably on a daily basis to all shares held on each day of the tax year by the shareholder, a gain or loss realized on the sale of S corporation stock during the tax year is not determinable until the ordinary income or loss and separately stated items allocable to the shares sold are known. Similarly, when the S corporation stock becomes worthless during a tax year, the shareholder must make the necessary positive and negative basis adjustments before the amount of the worthless security loss can be determined.

EXAMPLE C11-23 ▶ Diaz Corporation, an electing S corporation, is owned equally by Mike, Carlos, and Juan. Mike's 100 shares of Diaz stock have a $25,000 adjusted basis at the beginning of 1997. Diaz Corporation reports ordinary income of $36,500 and municipal bond interest income of $14,600 in 1997. On January 31, Mike sells all of his Diaz stock for $30,000. Assuming the daily method is used to allocate the income items, Mike's basis for the Diaz stock is determined as follows:

$$\$26{,}400 = \$25{,}000 + \left(\$36{,}500 \times \frac{30}{365} \times \frac{1}{3}\right) + \left(\$14{,}600 \times \frac{30}{365} \times \frac{1}{3}\right)$$

Mike must report a $3,600 ($30,000 − $26,400) gain on the sale. ◀

KEY POINT

Losses first reduce the basis in the stock and then any amount of debt owed to the shareholder by the S corporation. Subsequent increases in basis are added first to the debt and then to the stock.

BASIS ADJUSTMENTS TO SHAREHOLDER DEBT

After the shareholder's basis in the S corporation stock is reduced to zero, the basis of any S corporation indebtedness to the shareholder still outstanding at the end of the S corporation's tax year is reduced (but not below zero) by the remainder of the available loss and deduction items.[57] If a shareholder has more than one loan outstanding at year-

[57] No basis reductions are made to debt repaid before the end of the tax year. Regulation Sec. 1.1367-2(d)(1) holds that restoration occurs immediately before any shareholder indebtednesses are repaid or disposed of during the tax year.

SELF-STUDY QUESTION

What happens when a debt owed to the shareholder is paid off after the basis of the debt has been reduced by previous losses?

ANSWER

The shareholder recognizes income to the extent of the excess of the debt payment over his or her basis in the debt.

end, the basis reduction is applied to all of the indebtednesses based on the relative adjusted basis for each loan. Any ordinary income or separately stated gain or income items allocated to the shareholder in subsequent tax years (net of distributions to the shareholders) first restores the basis of any S corporation indebtedness to the shareholder that is outstanding at the end of its tax year. Once all previous decreases to the basis of an S corporation's debt are restored, any additional positive basis adjustments increase the basis of the shareholder's stock.[58]

Repayment of a shareholder indebtedness results in gain being recognized by the shareholder if the payment amount exceeds the debt's adjusted basis. If the indebtedness is secured by a note, the difference is a gain that results from the exchange of the note. Ordinarily, such gain is characterized as a capital gain because it arises from the exchange of a capital asset. Generally, if the indebtedness is not secured by a note or other evidence of the indebtedness, the repayment is ordinary income.[59]

EXAMPLE C11-24 ▶ At the beginning of 1996, Betty owns one-half of the stock of Trailer Corporation, an electing S corporation. Betty's basis for the Trailer stock is $40,000. Trailer Corporation owes Betty $20,000 on January 1, 1996. During 1996 and 1997, Trailer reports an ordinary loss of $100,000 and ordinary income of $10,000, respectively. Betty's $50,000 loss pass-through from 1996 first reduces the basis of her Trailer stock from $40,000 to 0. Next, the $10,000 remainder of the loss pass-through reduces the basis of Trailer's note from $20,000 to $10,000. Betty's $5,000 allocation of 1997's ordinary income increases the basis for the Trailer note from $10,000 to $15,000. If the note is repaid before the end of 1997, Betty reports a $5,000 ($20,000 − $15,000) long-term capital gain resulting from the repayment plus any ordinary income or separately stated items resulting from Trailer's 1997 operations. If the debt were instead unsecured (i.e., an advance from the shareholder that is not secured by a note), the gain would be ordinary income. ◀

S CORPORATION DISTRIBUTIONS

OBJECTIVE 10

Determine the taxability of an S corporation's distributions to its shareholders

Two sets of rules apply to S corporation distributions. One applies to S corporations having accumulated E&P. Accumulated E&P may exist if an S corporation was subject to tax as a C corporation in a pre–S election tax year. Another set of distribution rules applies to S corporations that do not have E&P (e.g., a corporation that is formed after 1982 and makes a timely S election in its initial tax year). These rules are explained below.

CORPORATIONS HAVING NO EARNINGS AND PROFITS

KEY POINT

Two separate sets of rules exist for distributions depending on whether the S corporation has accumulated E&P.

For S corporations with no accumulated E&P, a two-tier rule applies. Distributions are initially tax-free and reduce the shareholder's adjusted basis in the stock (but not below zero). If the distribution exceeds the basis of the shareholder's stock, the "excess" is treated as a gain from the sale or exchange of the stock.[60]

All income, gain, loss, or deduction pass-throughs for the year must be reflected in the shareholder's basis before the taxability of the distribution can be determined. Thus, the sequencing of the income recognition and distribution steps permits the S corporation to

[58] Sec. 1367(b)(2)(B).

[59] Rev. Ruls. 64-162, 1964-1 (Part I) C.B. 304 and 68-537, 1968-2 C.B. 372.

[60] Sec. 1368(b).

make tax-free distributions throughout the tax year in anticipation of earning a specific profit amount by year-end.

EXAMPLE C11-25 ▶

Liberty Corporation, an electing S corporation, is owned entirely by Sandy. At the beginning of the current year, Sandy's adjusted basis in her Liberty stock (a capital asset) is $20,000. Liberty reports ordinary income of $30,000 and a long-term capital loss of $5,000 this year. Liberty makes a $35,000 cash distribution to Sandy on June 15. Sandy's basis for the stock must be adjusted for the ordinary income and capital loss before determining the taxability of the distribution. Because Sandy's $45,000 ($20,000 + $30,000 − $5,000) adjusted basis for the stock exceeds the $35,000 distribution amount, the entire distribution is excluded from her gross income. The distribution reduces the stock's basis to $10,000 ($45,000 − $35,000).

If Liberty instead reports only $5,000 of ordinary income and no capital loss, $10,000 of the distribution is taxable. The ordinary income increases the stock's basis to $25,000 ($20,000 + $5,000). Because the distribution exceeds the stock's adjusted basis by $10,000 ($35,000 − $25,000), the excess distribution is taxable to Sandy as a capital gain. The basis of the stock is zero at year-end. ◀

SELF-STUDY QUESTION

Can distributions in excess of stock basis be tax-free to the extent of shareholder loans?

ANSWER

No. Although the amount of deductible losses can be increased by the amount of shareholder loans, tax-free distributions are strictly limited to stock basis.

If an S corporation makes a distribution to its shareholders, the S corporation must recognize gain when appreciated property is distributed.[61] No loss is recognized when property that has declined in value is distributed. The gain recognized on the distribution may be taxed at the corporate level as part of the S corporation's built-in gains or the excess net passive income tax levy. The gain also becomes part of the S corporation's ordinary income or loss, or is passed through as a separately stated item, depending on the type of property distributed and the character of the gain recognized. After this adjustment is made, the property can be distributed tax-free provided the sum of the money plus the FMV of the nonmoney property distributed does not exceed the shareholder's basis for his or her stock. The shareholder's basis for his or her S corporation stock is reduced by the distribution amount.

EXAMPLE C11-26 ▶

Echo Corporation is owned entirely by Tad and has always been an S corporation. Tad's adjusted basis in the Echo stock at the beginning of the current year is $50,000. Echo reports $30,000 of ordinary income for this year (exclusive of the effects of a property distribution made to Tad). On December 1, Echo distributes some Cable Corporation stock to Tad. The stock, which cost $40,000 and has a $100,000 FMV, was held as an investment for three years. Echo reports $60,000 ($100,000 − $40,000) of capital gain from distributing the stock. Tad reports $30,000 of ordinary income and $60,000 of long-term capital gain from Echo's current year activities. Tad's adjusted basis for his Echo stock is increased to $140,000 ($50,000 + $30,000 + $60,000). The distribution is tax-free because the $140,000 basis for the Echo stock exceeds the $100,000 distribution amount. The basis of the Echo stock is $40,000 ($140,000 − $100,000) at year-end. The Cable stock has a $100,000 basis in Tad's hands. ◀

ADDITIONAL COMMENT

The distribution of the appreciated stock in Example C11-26 produced income only to Echo. A similar distribution by a C corporation would result in a double tax by causing income recognition to both Echo and Tad.

CORPORATIONS HAVING ACCUMULATED EARNINGS AND PROFITS

PRIOR RULES. Under pre-1983 rules, a corporation's undistributed taxable income was taxed to its shareholders as a deemed distribution at year-end. This income was accumulated in a **previously taxed income (PTI)** account. E&P earned in excess of PTI

[61] Sec. 311(b).

KEY POINT

Distributions that come out of the AAA and PTI also reduce the basis of the S corporation stock.

▼ TABLE C11-1

Source of Distributions Made by S Corporations Having Accumulated Earnings and Profits

		Types of Distributions Coming from Tier		
Tier	Classification	Money Distributions?	Property (Nonmoney) Distributions?	Taxable or Tax-Free Distributions?
1	Accumulated adjustments account	Yes	Yes	Tax-free[a]
2	Previously taxed income	Yes	No	Tax-free[a]
3	Accumulated E&P	Yes	Yes	Taxable
4	Basis of S corporation stock	Yes	Yes	Tax-free[a]

[a] These distributions reduce the basis of the S corporation stock. Although generally tax-free, gain can be recognized if the amount of money plus the FMV of the nonmoney property distributed exceeds the adjusted basis of the S corporation stock.

became part of a corporation's accumulated E&P account. Starting in 1997, pre-1983 accumulated E&P is no longer a source of S corporation distributions.

KEY POINT

The AAA represents the cumulative income/loss recognized in post-1982 S corporation years. To the extent that the AAA is positive and sufficient basis exists in the stock, distributions from an S corporation are tax-free.

CURRENT RULES. Under current (post-1982) rules, some S corporations still have PTI and post-1982 accumulated E&P balances, earned while a C corporation, from which part or all of a distribution may be treated as having been made. The current rules require S corporations that have accumulated E&P balances to maintain an **accumulated adjustments account (AAA)** from which most of their distributions are made. The existence of the PTI, accumulated E&P, and AAA earnings balances makes the tax treatment of cash and property distributions somewhat more complicated than the rules explained in the preceding section.

MONEY DISTRIBUTIONS. For corporations having an accumulated E&P balance, money distributions come from the three tiers of earnings illustrated in Table C11-1. Distributions are made from the first tier until it is exhausted. The distributions are then made from the second tier until that tier is used up, and so on. Amounts distributed after the three tiers of earnings are exhausted reduce the shareholder's remaining basis in his or her S corporation stock. Any additional amounts received once the stock basis has been reduced to zero are taxed as a gain recognized on the sale of the S corporation stock. Each of these four tiers is usually maintained as a working paper account and not as a general ledger account.

The AAA is the cumulative total of the ordinary income or loss and separately stated items accumulated for the S period but excluding tax-exempt income and the expenses related to its production. The S period is the most recent continuous period during which the corporation has been an S corporation. No tax years beginning before January 1, 1983 are included in this period.[62]

[62] Sec. 1368(e). An S corporation without accumulated E&P does not need to maintain the AAA to determine the tax effect of its distributions. If an S corporation having no E&P subsequently acquires E&P in a transaction where tax attributes are assumed under Sec. 381(a) (e.g., a merger), the corporation must calculate its AAA at the merger date to determine the tax effects of post-merger distributions. To accomplish this calculation, a firm may need to make calculations back to the orginal S election date. To reduce this hardship, the IRS, in the Form 1120S instructions, recommends that all S corporations maintain AAA information.

The year-end AAA balance is determined as follows:

AAA balance at the beginning of the year	
Plus:	Ordinary income
	Separately stated income and gain items (except for tax-exempt income)
Minus:	Ordinary loss
	Separately stated loss and deduction items (except for expenses or losses related to the production of tax-exempt income)
	Expenses that are not deductible in determining ordinary income (loss) and that cannot be charged to the capital account
	Distributions made from AAA
AAA balance at the end of the year	

Three differences exist between the positive and negative adjustments required for the AAA and the basis calculation for the S corporation stock:

- Tax-exempt income does not increase the AAA, but increases the basis of the S corporation stock.
- Nondeductible expenses that reduce the basis of the S corporation stock also reduce the AAA, except for expenses related to the production of tax-exempt income and federal income taxes related to a C corporation tax year.
- The AAA balance can be negative (e.g., when the cumulative losses exceed the cumulative profits), but the shareholder's basis in the S corporation stock cannot be less than zero.

TYPICAL MISCONCEPTION

Even though the basis of S corporation stock cannot be less than zero, the AAA can be negative if cumulative losses exceed cumulative profits.

An Other Adjustments Account (OAA) is maintained only by corporations having accumulated E&P at year-end. This account is increased for tax-exempt income earned and decreased by the expenses incurred in earning the tax-exempt income, distributions out of the OAA, and federal taxes paid by the S corporation that are attributable to C corporation tax years. The effect of creating a separate account for tax-exempt income earned by companies having accumulated E&P is that the AAA is determined by taking into account only the taxable portion of the S corporation's income and any expenses and losses other than those related to the production of the tax-exempt income. Although the OAA balance is reported on page 4 of the Form 1120S, it is not an accumulated earnings account. Municipal bond interest and other forms of tax-exempt income (net of related deductions) become part of the stock basis and are thus placed behind accumulated E&P when determining the distribution order. A company having an accumulated E&P balance might consider having the tax-exempt income-producing properties owned at the shareholder level rather than at the corporate level, or distributing the accumulated E&P.

EXAMPLE C11-27 ▶

Smith Corporation, an electing S corporation, reports the following results during the current year:

Ordinary income	$30,000
Long-term capital gain	15,000
Municipal bond interest income	5,000
Dividend from domestic corporation	3,000
Charitable contribution	8,000

LEARNING AID

Use "T" accounts to keep track of the stock basis and the one or more accumulated earnings account balances that are needed.

Smith's sole shareholder, Silvia, has a $60,000 stock basis on January 1. On January 1, Smith has a $40,000 AAA balance, a $25,000 accumulated E&P balance, and a $0 OAA balance. The stock basis, AAA, OAA, and accumulated E&P activity for the year (before any distributions) is summarized as follows:

	Stock Basis	AAA	E&P	OAA
Beginning balances	$60,000	$40,000	$25,000	$—0—
Ordinary income	30,000	30,000		
Long-term capital gain	15,000	15,000		
Municipal bond interest	5,000			$5,000
Dividend	3,000	3,000		
Charitable contribution	(8,000)	(8,000)		
Pre-distribution balance	$105,000	$80,000	$25,000	$5,000 ◀

TYPICAL MISCONCEPTION

If S corporation stock is sold, the AAA account remains with the S corporation. But if an S election terminates, other than for the post-termination transition period, the AAA is extinguished.

Allocation of the AAA balance to individual distributions occurs at year-end after taking into account current year income and loss items. In general, the AAA amount is allocated ratably to individual distributions within a tax year (other than distributions coming from E&P or PTI) based on the amount of money or FMV of nonmoney property distributed.

EXAMPLE C11-28 ▶

Assume the same facts as in Example C11-27, except that Smith makes $50,000 cash distributions to Silvia, its sole shareholder, on June 1 and December 1. The $80,000 AAA balance is allocated ratably to each of the distributions. The AAA allocation occurs as follows:

$$\$40,000 = \$50,000 \times \frac{\$80,000}{\$50,000 + \$50,000}$$

Accordingly, $40,000 of each distribution comes out of AAA. This portion of the distribution is tax-free because the AAA distributions in total are less than the stock's $105,000 pre-distribution basis.[63] The remaining $10,000 ($50,000 − $40,000) of each distribution comes out of accumulated E&P (tier 3) and is taxable as dividend income. Accumulated E&P is reduced to $5,000 ($25,000 − $20,000) at year-end. The OAA balance reported on Form 1120S is not affected by the distribution because the accumulated E&P has not been exhausted. The stock's basis is $25,000 ($105,000 − $80,000) at year-end because a dividend distribution does not reduce its basis. The effects of the distribution are summarized below:

	Stock Basis	AAA	E&P	OAA
Pre-distribution balance	$105,000	$80,000	$25,000	$5,000
AAA distribution	(80,000)	(80,000)		
E&P distribution	(—0—)		(20,000)	
Ending balance	$25,000	$—0—	$ 5,000	$5,000 ◀

PROPERTY DISTRIBUTIONS. Property distributions (other than money) made by an S corporation having accumulated E&P require the recognition of gain according to the general rules outlined on page C11-30. The FMV of the nonmoney property distributed will reduce AAA. Property distributions affect the earnings tiers differently than money distributions because the former can come only out of the AAA, accumulated E&P, and S corporation stock basis tiers. Distributions of PTI must be made in money. An S

[63] Special distribution rules apply when an S corporation incurs a "net loss" (i.e., excess of losses and deductions over income and gain) in a tax year in which a distribution is made from AAA. In this situation, AAA is reduced for the distribution before it is reduced for the net loss. This sequence preserves tax-free treatment for earnings accumulated in prior tax years that are distributed in the loss year. The AAA rules are similar to the basis adjustment rules, in which the stock basis would be reduced for the distribution before calculating the loss limitation and reducing the stock basis for the loss.

corporation's shareholders may find a money distribution more advantageous than a property distribution because money can be distributed tax-free if the corporation has a PTI balance, whereas a similar property distribution might be taxed as a dividend.

PRACTICAL APPLICATION

If a shareholder has NOL carryforwards that are about to expire, the election to treat distributions as dividend income to the extent of E&P (as opposed to AAA distributions) may make sense.

DISTRIBUTION ORDERING ELECTIONS. Two elections are available to change the distribution order. Separate elections are available to the S corporation to skip over the AAA and PTI accounts in determining the source of a cash or property distribution. If either election is made, distributions will normally come from accumulated E&P and then AAA and/or PTI. These elections permit Subchapter C E&P to be distributed so as to avoid the excess net passive income tax and termination of the S election. Further discussion of this election is contained in the Tax Planning Considerations section of the chapter.

POST-TERMINATION TRANSITION PERIOD. Distributions of money made during the S corporation's post-termination transition period can be made tax-free to those shareholders who owned S corporation stock at the time of the termination. These distributions come first from the former S corporation's AAA balance and then from current and accumulated E&P. The amounts from the AAA are tax-free and reduce the shareholder's basis for his or her stock.[64] The AAA balance disappears when the end of the post-termination period is reached. Even though the profits earned during the S election period can no longer be distributed tax-free from the AAA after the post-termination transition period ends, they can still be distributed tax-free from the shareholder's basis in his or her stock once the corporation's current and accumulated E&P has been distributed. Any distributions made from current or accumulated E&P and nonmoney distributions made during the post-termination transition period are taxable.

Topic Review C11-4 presents a summary of the taxation of S corporation income and gains that are passed through to the shareholders and S corporation distributions.

STOP & THINK

Question: Special earnings tracking rules apply to S corporations that were formerly C corporations. Why do we need to have these special rules which add to the complexity of the distribution topic?

Solution: Former C corporations that were profitable usually have an accumulated E&P balance when they become an S corporation. These earnings have never been taxed as a dividend to the corporation's shareholders. If separate tracking of the S corporation earnings (AAA) and C corporation earnings (accumulated E&P) did not occur, it would be impossible to determine which cash and property distributions came from S corporation earnings and which ones came from C corporation earnings. Therefore, the government could never collect the taxes due from the shareholders when accumulated E&P was distributed.

OTHER RULES

In addition to the differences discussed above, S corporations are treated differently from C corporations in a number of other ways. Some of these differences are examined below. They include tax preference items and other alternative minimum tax (AMT) adjustments, expenses owed by the S corporation to a shareholder, related party sales and exchanges, and fringe benefits paid by the S corporation to a shareholder-employee.

[64] Sec. 1371(e).

Topic Review C11-4

Taxation of S Corporation Income and Distributions

Taxation of Income to the Corporation

1. Unlike with a partnership, special corporate tax levies are imposed on an S corporation:
   a. Built-in gains tax: applicable to the net recognized built-in gain of an S corporation that has a history as a C corporation and made its S election after December 31, 1986.
   b. Excess net passive income tax: applicable to S corporations that have Subchapter C E&P at the close of the tax year and earn passive investment income in excess of 25% of gross receipts during the tax year.
   c. LIFO recapture tax: imposed when a C corporation that uses the LIFO inventory method in its final C corporation tax year makes an S election.

Allocation of Income to the Shareholders

1. Income and gains are allocated based on the number of shares of stock owned by each shareholder on each day of the tax year.
2. Termination of the S election or termination of the shareholder's interest in the S corporation during the tax year requires the tax year to be divided into two parts. An election can be made to allocate the income or gain according to the general rule in (1) or the accounting methods used by the corporation.

Shareholder Distributions

1. Income and gain allocated to the shareholder increase the basis of the S corporation stock. For any S corporation that does not have an E&P balance, the amount of money plus the FMV of any nonmoney property distributed is tax-free provided it does not exceed the shareholder's basis in the S corporation stock. Gain (but not loss) is recognized at the corporate level when nonmoney property is distributed.
2. If the S corporation has accumulated E&P, as many as three earnings tiers must be maintained: the AAA, PTI (pre-1983 earnings), and accumulated E&P. Distributions come from each tier in succeeding order until the tier is exhausted. Only distributions out of accumulated E&P are taxable to the shareholder, unless the stock basis is reduced to zero and then a capital gain may be recognized.

KEY POINT

An S corporation is not subject to the AMT, but instead the AMT adjustments and preferences flow through to the S corporation's shareholders.

TAX PREFERENCE ITEMS AND OTHER AMT ADJUSTMENTS

The S corporation is not subject to the corporate AMT. Instead, the S corporation computes and passes through all of its tax preference items contained in Sec. 57(a) to its shareholders. These tax preference items are then included in the shareholders' AMT calculations. Allocation of the tax preference items occurs on a daily basis, unless one of the two special elections is made to allocate the items based on the corporation's tax accounting methods.

Code Sec. 56(a) prescribes a number of adjustments to the tax reporting of certain transactions and occurrences for AMT purposes from that which is used for income tax purposes. The amount of these special AMT adjustments is also computed and passed through to the S corporation's shareholders and included in their individual AMT calculations.

S corporations do not have to make an adjustment for the difference between adjusted current earnings and pre-adjustment alternative minimum taxable income that is made by a C corporation in calculating its AMT liability. For certain corporations, this difference may make an S election attractive.[65]

TRANSACTIONS INVOLVING SHAREHOLDERS AND OTHER RELATED PARTIES

The Sec. 267(a)(2) related party transaction rules deny a payer a deduction for an expense paid to a related payee when a mismatching of the expense and income items occurs as a result of differences in accounting methods. A number of related party situations directly involve S corporations. Some of these transactions involve two S corporations or an S corporation and a C corporation where more than 50% of the value of each corporation's stock is directly or indirectly owned by the same persons. Section 267(a)(2), for example, prevents an S corporation using the accrual method of accounting from currently deducting a year-end expense accrued for an item that is owed to a second S corporation that uses the cash method of accounting when both corporations are owned by the same shareholders. The expense can be deducted by the first S corporation on the day that the income is includible in the second S corporation's gross income.

KEY POINT

An S corporation and *any* shareholder who owns stock directly or indirectly in the S corporation is considered a related party for purposes of deferring deductions under Sec. 267(a)(2).

The S corporation is considered a pass-through entity and is subject to Sec. 267(e), which extends the Sec. 267(a)(2) related party transaction rules described above to any payment made by the S corporation to *any* person who directly or indirectly owns S corporation stock. This prevents the S corporation from deducting a payment to be made to one of its shareholders or to someone who indirectly owns such stock until the payee reports the income. Payments made to the S corporation by a person who directly or indirectly owns S corporation stock are also similarly restricted.

EXAMPLE C11-29 ▶ Vassar Corporation, an electing S corporation, uses the accrual method of accounting. On September 1, 1997, Vassar borrows $50,000 from Joan, who owns 10% of the Vassar stock. Interest is charged at a 12% annual rate. Joan uses the cash method of accounting. At year-end, Vassar accrues $2,000 of interest expense on the loan. Six months of interest (including the $2,000 of accrued interest) is paid to Joan on March 1, 1998. Vassar cannot deduct the 1997 interest accrual when determining its ordinary income or loss until it is paid in 1998. ◀

Section 267(a)(1) denies a deduction for losses incurred on the sale or exchange of property directly or indirectly between related parties. The same definition of a related party is used for this purpose as is used in applying Sec. 267(a)(2) to expense transactions involving an S corporation. Any loss that is disallowed to the seller on the related party sale or exchange can be used to offset gains realized by the purchaser on a subsequent sale or exchange.

TYPICAL MISCONCEPTION

Most fringe benefits provided by a C corporation are deductible to the corporation and nontaxable to the employee. However, fringe benefits paid to a more-than-2% shareholder-employee of an S corporation are in many cases nondeductible unless taxable to the shareholder-employee as compensation.

FRINGE BENEFITS PAID TO A SHAREHOLDER-EMPLOYEE

The S corporation is not treated as a corporate taxpayer with respect to many fringe benefits paid to any 2% shareholder.[66] Instead, the S corporation is treated the same as a partnership, and the 2% shareholder is treated as a partner of such partnership.[67] Because of this restriction, many fringe benefits paid to a 2% shareholder-employee of an S corporation are taxable as compensation to the shareholder and deductible by the corporation if the benefit is not excludible from the gross income of a partner.

---

[65] Sec. 56(g)(6).

[66] Section 1372(b) defines a 2% shareholder as any person who directly or indirectly owns on any day of the S corporation's tax year more than 2% of its outstanding stock or stock possessing more than 2% of its voting power. The Sec. 318 stock attribution rules are used to determine if the 2% threshold has been exceeded.

[67] Sec. 1372(a).

Shareholders owning 2% or less of the S corporation stock are treated as ordinary employees.

The special fringe benefit rules apply only to statutory fringe benefits. They do not apply to stock options, qualified retirement plans, and nonqualified deferred compensation. The fringe benefits limited by the more-than-2%-shareholder rule include group term life insurance premiums (Sec. 79), accident and health benefit plan insurance premiums and payments (Secs. 105 and 106), meals and lodging furnished by the employer (Sec. 119), cafeteria plan benefits (Sec. 125), and employer-provided parking (Sec. 132). Fringe benefits that may be excluded by more-than-2%-shareholders include compensation for injuries and sickness (Sec. 104), educational assistance program benefits (Sec. 127), dependent care assistance program benefits (Sec. 129), and no-additional-cost benefits, qualified employee discounts, working condition fringe benefits, de minimis fringe benefits, and on-premises athletic facilities (Sec. 132). For purposes of the Sec. 162(l) above-the-line deduction for self-employed taxpayer's health insurance premiums, a more-than-2%-shareholder is deemed to be self-employed.

EXAMPLE C11-30 ▶ Edison Corporation, an electing S corporation, is owned equally by Billy and his wife Cathy. Billy and ten other individuals are employed by Edison. All employees receive group term life insurance benefits based on their annual salaries. All of the employees except for Billy can qualify for the Sec. 79 group term life insurance premium exclusion. Billy is treated as a partner and, therefore, does not qualify as an employee. Billy's premiums are treated as compensation and taxable to Billy. Edison can deduct the premiums paid to all of its employees, including Billy. Since Billy is treated as self-employed under the 2% shareholder rules, he can deduct a portion of the premiums paid on the health insurance as a "for" AGI deduction under the Sec.162(l) rules applicable to health insurance payments made by all self-employed individuals. ◀

TAX PLANNING CONSIDERATIONS

ELECTION TO ALLOCATE INCOME BASED ON THE S CORPORATION'S ACCOUNTING METHODS

KEY POINT

Shareholders of an S corporation should not overlook the planning possibilities available in the allocation of income/loss when an S election terminates or an S corporation shareholder terminates his or her interest.

As a general rule, the S corporation's ordinary income or loss and separately stated items are allocated based on the amount of stock owned by each shareholder on each day of the S corporation's tax year. A special election is available to allocate the income based on the S corporation's accounting methods when the S election is terminated or an S corporation shareholder terminates, or substantially reduces but does not terminate, his or her entire interest in the corporation.[68] The use of the S corporation's tax accounting method to allocate the year's profit or loss can permit an income shift between shareholders.

EXAMPLE C11-31 ▶ July Corporation, an electing S corporation, is owned equally by Rod and Dana at the beginning of 1997. During 1997, July reports ordinary income of $146,000. On April 1, 1997, Dana sells all of his July stock to Randy. July Corporation earns $125,000 of its ordinary income after March 31, 1997. Rod is allocated $73,000 ($146,000 × 0.50) of ordinary income. His income allocation is the same whether the daily allocation method or the special allocation election is used. In total, Dana and Randy are allocated $73,000 of ordinary income. Dana and Randy can allocate the ordinary income amount in the following ways:

[68] The shareholder, however, still can be a creditor, director, or employee of the corporation. Sections 1362(e) and 1377(a) prevent the daily allocation method from applying to any items resulting from a sale or exchange of 50% or more of the S corporation's stock during an S termination year.

	Daily Allocation	Special Election
Dana:	$\$146{,}000 \times \frac{1}{2} \times \frac{90}{365} = \$18{,}000$	$(\$146{,}000 - \$125{,}000) \times \frac{1}{2} = \$10{,}500$
Randy:	$\$146{,}000 \times \frac{1}{2} \times \frac{275}{365} = \$55{,}000$	$\$125{,}000 \times \frac{1}{2} = \$62{,}500$

The shifting of the $7,500 in income from Dana to Randy when the special election is made will also reduce Dana's adjusted basis for his July stock when determining his gain or loss on the sale. The $7,500 difference between the income allocations under the two methods may be a point for negotiation between Dana and Randy, particularly if their marginal tax rates are different. ◀

By electing to use the S corporation's tax accounting method to allocate profits or losses between the C short year and S short year in the year in which the S corporation election terminates, it is possible to shift losses into an S short year where an immediate benefit is obtained by the shareholders at a marginal tax rate of up to 39.6%, or shift to profits into a C short year to take advantage of the 15% and 25% marginal corporate tax rates. One such scenario is illustrated below.

EXAMPLE C11-32 ▶ Choe Corporation has been taxed as an S corporation for several years using a calendar year as its tax year. Their S election is terminated on July 1. The S short year includes January 1 through June 30 and the C short year includes July 1 through December 31. Total ordinary income this year is $10,000. If the books are closed on June 30, $40,000 of ordinary loss is allocable to the S short year and $50,000 of ordinary income is allocable to the C short year. Assuming each month has 30 days, the following income allocations are possible:

Period	*Daily Allocation*	*Closing of Books*
S short year	$5,000	($40,000)
C short year	5,000	50,000
Total	$10,000	$10,000

By closing the books, the $40,000 S short year loss is passed through to the shareholders and the $50,000 C short year income is taxed to the C corporation. With the daily allocation, one-half of the income is taxed to the shareholders and the other half is taxed to the C corporation.[69] Whether the special election is beneficial can be determined only by calculating the shareholder and corporate tax liabilities under each alternative. ◀

INCREASING THE BENEFITS FROM S CORPORATION LOSSES

At the shareholder level, the deduction that can be claimed for S corporation losses is restricted to the basis of the S corporation stock plus the basis of any amounts owed by the S corporation to the shareholder. Losses that are passed through in excess of this limitation are carried over to a subsequent tax year when the shareholder again has a basis for the stock investment or debt obligation. If the shareholder's marginal tax rate is expected to be the same or lower in a future tax year when the loss carryover can be used, the shareholder should consider either increasing the basis of his or her stock investment or loaning additional funds to the corporation before the end of the current tax year. Conversely, if the loans are never expected to be repaid, he or she should not lend the S corporation additional amounts just to secure an additional tax deduction, which is worth at most 39.6 cents (at 1997 rates) for each dollar that is loaned. If the

[69] Section 1362(e)(5)(A) requires calculation of the tax liability for the C short year to be based on the annualized income of the former S corporation (see Chapter C3).

shareholder's marginal tax rate is expected to be higher in future tax years, deferring additional capital contributions or loans until after the end of the current tax year should be considered.

EXAMPLE C11-33 ▶

KEY POINT

If an S corporation shareholder has losses that have been suspended due to lack of basis, either contributions to capital or bona fide loans to the corporation will create the necessary basis to use the losses.

Bailey Corporation, an S corporation, is owned entirely by Nancy. Bailey Corporation expects large losses in 1997 that will result in a $100,000 ordinary loss. Nancy's basis for her Bailey stock (before any adjustment for the current loss) is $35,000. Bailey also owes Nancy $25,000. Nancy's 1997 marginal tax rate is 39.6%. This marginal tax rate is expected to decline to 15% in 1998. Nancy should consider making $40,000 [$100,000 loss − ($35,000 stock basis + $25,000 loan basis)] of additional capital contributions or loans before the end of 1997 in order to obtain an additional $9,840 [(0.396 − 0.15) × $40,000] of tax benefits from deducting the anticipated loss carryover in the current year. If Nancy's 1997 and 1998 marginal tax rates are expected to be 15% and 39.6%, respectively, the $9,840 tax benefit (less the time value of money for one year) can be obtained by having Nancy merely defer her capital contributions or loans until 1998. Alternatively, Nancy could use the loss carryover to offset profits reported in 1998. These profits would restore part or all of the basis of the debt (and possibly increase the basis of the stock). The basis would then be partially or fully offset by the $40,000 loss carryover. ◀

The S corporation loss carryover is available only to the shareholder who held the stock when the loss was incurred. A shareholder should consider increasing the basis of the stock in order to take advantage of the carryover before the stock is sold. The purchasing shareholder does not acquire the carryover.

PASSIVE INCOME REQUIREMENTS

The S corporation can earn an unlimited amount of passive income each year without incurring any penalty provided it does not have any E&P accumulated in a C corporation tax year (known as Subchapter C E&P) at the end of its tax year. An S election thus can permit a corporation to avoid the personal holding company penalty tax.

Potentially, S corporations that have operated as C corporations and have accumulated Subchapter C E&P are liable for the excess net passive income tax. In addition, their S election may be terminated if the passive investment income exceeds 25% of gross receipts for three consecutive tax years. The S corporation can avoid both of these possible problems by making a special election under Sec. 1368(e)(3) to distribute its entire Subchapter C E&P balance to its shareholders. A corporation that makes the election to distribute Subchapter C E&P before its previously taxed income can make a second special election to distribute part or all of this distribution as a deemed dividend, which is distributed to the shareholders and immediately contributed by the shareholders to the corporation on the last day of the corporation's tax year. Such an election requires no cash outlay. The distribution results in a tax cost for the shareholders, who pay tax on the dividend income that results. To the shareholders, the cost of the election can be small if the accumulated E&P balance is insignificant or the shareholder has a current year NOL (excluding the distribution) or a NOL carryover. The ultimate long-run benefit, however, may be great because it permits the S corporation to earn an unlimited amount of passive investment income free from corporate taxes in subsequent tax years.

EXAMPLE C11-34 ▶

Hawaii Corporation is incorporated in 1985. It operates for a number of years as a C corporation, during which time it accumulates $30,000 of E&P. Most of Hawaii's gross income now comes from rentals and interest, constituting passive investment income. Hawaii makes an S election starting in 1997. The excess net passive income tax will apply in 1997 if Hawaii's rentals and interest exceed 25% of its gross receipts for the year, unless an election to distribute the accumulated E&P is made and the earnings are distributed by the end of Hawaii's first tax year as an S corporation. ◀

S corporations that earn rental income can also avoid the passive income tax and the possibility of having its election terminated if significant services are rendered to the occupant of the space or if significant costs are incurred in the rental business. According to Reg. Sec. 1.1362-2(c)(5)(ii)(B)(3), significant services are not rendered and substantial costs are not incurred in connection with net leases. Whether significant services are performed or substantial costs are incurred in the rental business is determined based on all the facts and circumstances including, but not limited to, the number of persons employed to provide the services and the types and amounts of costs and expenses incurred (other than depreciation).

EXAMPLE C11-35 ▶ Assume the same facts as in Example C11-34, except that Hawaii Corporation provides significant services to its tenants in connection with its rental activities. Because the services are significant, Hawaii Corporation has a passive income problem only if its interest income exceeds 25% of its gross receipts. If the 25% threshold is not exceeded. Hawaii can avoid having to distribute its Subchapter C E&P in 1997. ◀

KEY POINT

Because the existence of E&P in an S corporation can not only create a tax at the corporate level but can also cause the S election to be terminated, consideration should be given to having the S corporation elect to distribute its E&P.

Corporations that experience a passive income problem in two consecutive tax years should carefully monitor their passive income in the next year. If they see that their passive income for the third year will exceed the 25% threshold, they should make certain that they elect to distribute their accumulated Subchapter C E&P before year-end. This will not only prevent loss of the S election, but also avoid having to pay the Sec. 1375 tax.

COMPLIANCE AND PROCEDURAL CONSIDERATIONS

MAKING THE ELECTION

The S election is made by filing Form 2553 (Election by Small Business Corporation to Tax Corporation Income Directly to Shareholders). The election form can be signed by any person who is authorized to sign the S corporation's tax return under Sec. 6037. Form 2553 is filed with the IRS Service Center designated in the instructions. No extensions of time to file the S election are granted.[70]

Shareholder consents to the S election can be made either on Form 2553 or on a separate consent statement signed by the shareholder and attached to the corporation's election form. Regulation Sec. 1.1362-6(b) outlines the other information that must be provided with a separate consent. Extensions of time for filing shareholder consents to the S election can be granted by the IRS.[71]

A Sec. 444 election to use a fiscal year is made on Form 8716, which must be filed by the earlier of (1) the fifteenth day of the fifth month following the month that includes the first day of the tax year for which the election will be first effective or (2) the due date for the income tax return resulting from the election.[72] A copy of the Form 8716 must be attached to the Form 1120S for the first tax year for which the Sec. 444 election is effective. A corporation desiring to make a Sec. 444 election must also state its intention in a statement attached to its S election form (Form 2553).[73]

OBJECTIVE 11

Explain the procedures for filing an S corporation tax return

FILING THE CORPORATE TAX RETURN

All S corporations, whether they owe any taxes under Secs. 1374 or 1375 or not, must file a tax return if they are in existence for part or all of the tax year. An S corporation must file its corporate tax return not later than the fifteenth day of the third month following

[70] Rev. Rul. 60-183, 1960-1 C.B. 625.
[71] Reg. Sec. 1.1362-6(b)(3)(iii).
[72] Temp. Reg. Sec. 1.444-3T(b)(1).
[73] Temp. Reg. Sec. 1.444-3T(b)(3).

the end of the tax year.[74] The S corporation reports its results on Form 1120S (U.S. Income Tax Return for an S Corporation). A completed S corporation tax return and the facts supporting the return are illustrated in Appendix B. An S corporation is allowed an automatic six-month extension of time for filing its tax return by filing Form 7004 (Application for Automatic Extension of Time to File U.S. Corporation Income Tax Return), also illustrated in Appendix B.[75]

EXAMPLE C11-36 ▶ Simpson Corporation, an S corporation, uses the calendar year as its tax year. Its tax return is generally due on March 15. An automatic extension of six months is permitted for the return, thus extending its due date until September 15. ◀

KEY POINT

An S corporation must file Form 1120S, which is basically an informational return. The shareholders each receive a K-1 with their share of the income/loss/credit items for the year.

All S corporations that must file a tax return must furnish each person who is a shareholder at any time during the tax year with a copy of the tax return. The return must be made available to the shareholder not later than the day on which it is filed.[76] The S corporation's ordinary income or loss and certain passive income or loss items are reported on an individual shareholder's Form 1040, Schedule E. Most separately stated items are reported on other supporting schedules to Form 1040, as illustrated on the Form 1120S, Schedule K-1 presented in Appendix B.

An S corporation is subject to the same basic three-year statute of limitations that applies to other taxpayers. This three-year period applies for purposes of determining the time period during which

- The corporation remains liable for assessments of the excess net passive income tax and the built-in gains tax
- The IRS can question the correctness of an S election that was made for a particular tax year[77]

The limitation period for assessing the income tax liability of an S corporation shareholder (e.g., for an erroneous S corporation loss deduction claimed), however, runs from the date on which the shareholder's return is filed and not from the date that the S corporation's tax return is filed.[78]

Determination of the Sec. 7519 required payment is made on a computation worksheet provided in the instructions for the Form 1120S. A required payment does not have to be made if the total of such payments for the current year and all preceding years is $500 or less. Amounts less than the $500 threshold are carried over to succeeding years. The required payment amount is due on or before May 15 regardless of the fiscal year that is used. The required payment and the computation worksheet must accompany a Form 8752, which is also used to secure a refund of prior Sec. 7519 payments.[79]

OBJECTIVE 12

Determine the estimated tax payments required of an S corporation and its shareholders

ESTIMATED TAX PAYMENTS

S corporations are required to make estimated tax payments if their estimated tax liability is reasonably expected to be $500 or more. Estimated tax payments are required for the corporate liability attributable to the built-in gains tax (Sec. 1374), the excess net passive income tax (Sec. 1375), and recapture of investment tax credits claimed in tax years in which the corporation was taxed as a C corporation (Sec. 1371(d)(2)).[80] In addition, the S corporation's shareholders must include their income, gain, loss, deduction, and credit pass-throughs in their own estimated tax calculations.

SELF-STUDY QUESTION

Is an S corporation required to make estimated tax payments?

The corporate estimated tax payment requirements described for a C corporation in Chapter C3 also apply to an S corporation with respect to these three liabilities. The required quarterly installment is 25% of the lesser of (1) 100% of the tax shown on the return for the tax year and (2) the sum of 100% of the built-in gains tax and investment

[74] Sec. 6072(b).
[75] Reg. Sec. 1.6081-3.
[76] Sec. 6037(b).
[77] Sec. 6233.
[78] *Sheldon B. Bufferd v. CIR*, 71 AFTR 2d 93-573, 93-1 USTC ¶50,038 (USSC, 1993).
[79] Temp. Reg. Sec. 1.7519-2T.
[80] Sec. 6655(g)(4)(A).

ANSWER

Yes. An S corporation is required to pay estimated taxes if the corporation is subject to built-in gains, excess net passive income, or ITC recapture taxes. Also, shareholders are required to include their S corporation income/loss and credit pass-throughs in determining their estimated tax payments.

tax credit recapture amounts shown on the return for the tax year plus 100% of the excess net passive income tax shown on the return for the preceding tax year.[81]

An S corporation cannot use the prior year tax liability exception of Sec. 6655(d)(1)(B)(ii) when determining the required payment to be made with respect to the built-in gains tax and investment tax credit recapture amounts. This exception is available with respect to the excess net passive income tax portion of the required payment without regard to whether any tax was owed in the prior year.[82] All corporations can use the prior year tax liability exception for the excess net passive income tax whether they are "large" corporations under Sec. 6655(d)(2) or not. The annualization election of Sec. 6655(e) is also available when determining the quarterly estimated tax payment amounts.[83] An S corporation's failure to make timely estimated tax payments, or a timely final payment when the tax return is filed, will cause it to be subject to interest and penalties like other taxpayers.

The S corporation's shareholders must include their ratable share of the ordinary income or loss and separately stated items in determining their estimated tax liability. Such amounts are treated as having been received concurrently by the shareholders throughout the S corporation's tax year. Thus, ordinary income or loss and separately stated items for an S corporation tax year that ends with or within the shareholder's tax year are included in the estimated tax calculation to the extent they are attributable to months in the S corporation tax year that precede the month in which the installment is due.

CONSISTENCY RULES

KEY POINT

If the IRS is conducting an audit of an S corporation, the audit is conducted in a unified proceeding at the corporate level rather than in separate audits of each S corporation shareholder.

Section 6037(c) requires an S corporation shareholder to report on his or her return a Subchapter S item in a manner that is consistent with the treatment accorded the item on the S corporation's return. A Subchapter S item is any item (e.g., income, gain, deduction, loss, credit, accounting methods, tax year, etc.) of an S corporation where the reporting of the item is more appropriately determined at the corporation level than at the shareholder level. A shareholder must notify the IRS of any inconsistency when the corporation has filed a return but the shareholder's treatment on his return is (or may be) inconsistent with the treatment of the item on the corporation return. Failure to do so may result in the imposition of a negligence penalty under Sec. 6662. Any adjustment required to produce consistency with the corporate return is treated as a mathematical or clerical error for penalty calculation purposes. A similar notification is also required when the corporation has not filed a return. If a shareholder receives incorrect information from the S corporation regarding a Subchapter S item, the shareholder's consistent reporting of the item consistently with the information provided by the corporation will generally eliminate the imposition of any penalty.

SAMPLE S CORPORATION TAX RETURN

A sample S corporation Form 1120S and supporting Schedule K-1 are presented in Appendix B. The facts supporting the return are also presented. Two differences should be noted between the S corporation tax return and a partnership tax return. First, the S corporation tax return provides for the determination of a corporate tax liability and the payment of the three special taxes that can be levied on the S corporation. No such items are shown on the partnership return. Second, the S corporation return does not require a reconciliation of the shareholders' basis adjustments as occurs on a partnership tax return. Schedule M-1 and M-2 reconciliations similar to those required of a C corporation are required of an S corporation. The Schedule M-1 requires a reconciliation of book income with the income or loss reported on line 23 of Schedule K, which includes not only the ordinary income (loss) amount but also separately stated income and deduction items. The Schedule M-2 requires a reconciliation of the AAA, OAA, and

[81] Sec. 6655(g)(4)(C).

[82] Sec. 6655(g)(4)(B).

[83] Sec. 6655(g)(4)(E).

PTI accounts. The AAA reconciliation is required only of S corporations that have an accumulated E&P balance, although it is recommended that the AAA be maintained by all S corporations (see footnote 62 on page C11-31). The OAA balance is calculated and reported only by corporations that have an accumulated E&P balance at year-end. The account is adjusted for tax-exempt income and the related nondeductible expenses for the year.

PROBLEM MATERIALS

DISCUSSION QUESTIONS

C11-1 List five advantages and five disadvantages of making an S election. Briefly explain each item.

C11-2 Julio, age 50, is a U.S. citizen who has a 31% marginal tax rate. He has operated the A&B Automotive Parts Company for a number of years as a C corporation. A&B last year reported $200,000 of pre-tax profits, from which $50,000 in salary and $25,000 in dividends were paid to Julio. This year's pre-tax profits are expected to be $300,000. To date, no fringe benefits or pension plans have been created for Julio. Julio asks you to explain whether the corporation that is taxed like a partnership would reduce his taxes. How do you respond to Julio's inquiry?

C11-3 Celia, age 30, is leaving a major systems development firm to establish her own firm. She will design computer-based systems for small- and medium-sized businesses. Celia will invest $100,000 in the business. She hopes to operate near her breakeven point during her first year, although a small loss is possible. Profits will build up slowly over the next four years until she is earning $150,000 a year in her fifth year. Celia has heard some of the tax people who worked for her former employer talk about S corporations. She comes to you to ask whether the S corporation form would be advisable for her new business. How do you respond to Celia's inquiry?

C11-4 Lance and Rodney are contemplating starting a new business to manufacture computer software games. Losses are expected to be encountered in the initial years. Lance's CPA has talked to them about using an S corporation. Rodney, while reading a business publication, encounters a discussion on limited liability companies (LLCs). The article talks about the advantages of using an LLC instead of an S corporation. How would you respond to their inquiry?

C11-5 Which of the following classifications make a shareholder ineligible to own the stock of an S corporation?

a. U.S. citizen
b. Domestic corporation
c. Partnership where all the partners are U.S. citizens
d. Estate of a deceased U.S. citizen
e. Grantor trust created by a U.S. citizen
f. Nonresident alien individual

C11-6 Which of the following taxes do not apply to an S corporation?

a. Regular (income) tax
b. Accumulated earnings tax
c. Corporate alternative minimum tax
d. Investment tax credit recapture
e. Built-in gains tax
f. Personal holding company tax
g. Excess net passive income tax
h. LIFO recapture tax

C11-7 Which of the following events will cause an S election to be terminated?

a. The S corporation earning 100% of its gross receipts in its first tax year from passive sources
b. The S corporation issuing nonvoting stock that has a dividend preference
c. The S corporation purchasing 100% of the single class of stock of a second domestic corporation that has conducted business activities for four years
d. An individual shareholder donating 100 shares of S corporation stock to a charity that is exempt from tax under IRC Sec. 501(c)(3)
e. The S corporation earning tax-exempt interest income

C11-8 What is an inadvertent termination? What actions on the part of the S corporation and its shareholders are needed to correct an inadvertent termination?

C11-9 An S corporation has revoked its S election. How long must the corporation wait in order to make a new election? What circumstances permit an early reelection?

C11-10 What tax years can be adopted by a newly created corporation that makes an S election for its first tax year? If a fiscal year is permitted, does it require IRS approval?

C11-11 At the time Cable Corporation makes its S election it elects to use a fiscal year based on a Sec. 444 election. What other requirement(s) must be satisfied in order for Cable Corporation to continue to use its fiscal year election for future tax years?

C11-12 What are Subchapter C earnings and profits? How does the existence of such earnings affect the S corporation's ability to earn passive income?

C11-13 Which of the following items are included in an S corporation's ordinary income or loss?
- **a.** Long-term capital gains
- **b.** Sec. 1231 losses
- **c.** Sec. 1245 gains
- **d.** Dividend income received from a domestic corporation
- **e.** Interest income from corporate bonds
- **f.** Interest income from State of Florida bonds
- **g.** Charitable contributions
- **h.** Salary expense paid to a shareholder-employee
- **i.** Investment interest expense
- **j.** Straight-line depreciation on real property used in manufacturing activities

C11-14 Explain the procedures for allocating an S corporation's ordinary income or loss to each of the shareholders. What special allocation elections are available?

C11-15 What are the limitations on the amount of the loss pass-through that can be deducted by an S corporation's shareholder? What happens to any losses in excess of this limitation?

C11-16 What actions can be taken before year-end by an S corporation's shareholder to increase the amount of the S corporation's losses that can be deducted in the year that they are incurred?

C11-17 What is a post-termination transition period? What loss carryovers can be deducted by an S corporation's shareholder during this period?

C11-18 Which of the following deduction or loss provisions may apply to an S corporation or its shareholders?
- **a.** Dividends-received deduction
- **b.** Amortization of organizational expenditures
- **c.** Sec. 291 restriction on certain tax preferences
- **d.** Hobby loss rules
- **e.** At-risk rules
- **f.** Investment interest limitation
- **g.** Passive activity limitation

C11-19 Explain the positive and negative adjustments that are made to the basis of an S corporation shareholder's stock investment and the basis of an S corporation debt that is owed to the shareholder.

C11-20 Explain the differences between the tax treatment accorded nonliquidating property distributions made by S corporations and partnerships.

C11-21 What nonliquidating distributions made by an S corporation are taxable to its shareholders? tax-free to its shareholders?

C11-22 What is an accumulated adjustments account? What income, gain, loss, and deduction items *do not* affect this account assuming that the S corporation has an accumulated E&P balance?

C11-23 Explain the differences between the way the following items are reported by a C corporation and an S corporation:
- **a.** Ordinary income or loss
- **b.** Capital gains and losses
- **c.** Tax-exempt interest income
- **d.** Charitable contributions
- **e.** Nonliquidating property distributions
- **f.** Fringe benefits paid to a shareholder-employee

C11-24 When is the S corporation's tax return due? What extensions are available for filing the return?

C11-25 What S corporation tax levies must be prepaid by having the corporation make quarterly estimated tax payments? Can a shareholder owning S corporation stock use the corporation's estimated tax payments to reduce the amount of his or her individual estimated tax payments? Explain.

C11-26 Review the completed C corporation, partnership, and S corporation tax returns presented in Appendix B. List three major tax reporting similarities and three major tax reporting differences in either content or format among the three tax returns.

ISSUE IDENTIFICATION QUESTIONS

C11-27 J & P Corporation is to be owned equally by Jennelle and Paula. The corporation will be formed by exchanging the assets and liabilities of the J & P Manufacturing Partnership for all of its stock on September 1 of the current year. Both shareholders use the calendar year as their tax year, and desire to make an S election. What tax issues should be considered by Jennelle and Paula with respect to the incorporation?

C11-28 Williams Corporation has operated as a C corporation since 1990. The corporation has assets with a $450,000 adjusted basis and an $800,000 FMV. Liabilities amount to $100,000. All of the Williams Corporation stock is owned by Dan Williams, who uses a calendar year as his tax year. The corporation uses the accrual method of accounting and a June 30 year-end. Dan has been told by his CPA to convert to S corporation status to reduce his total corporate/personal federal income tax lability. Dan would like to complete the conversion on the last day of the firm's tax year. What tax issues should be considered by Dan and his CPA with respect to the S election?

C11-29 Peter owns 50% of Air South Corporation, an air charter service. His beginning of the year basis for the S corporation's stock is $100,000. Air South has not done well this year and will report an ordinary loss of $375,000. Peter's marginal tax rate for the current year is 36%. What tax issues should be considered by Peter with respect to the loss?

C11-30 Glacier Smokeries has been an S corporation since its inception in 1991. On January 1, the corporation's two equal shareholders, Adam and Rodney, had adjusted bases of $175,000 and $225,000, respectively, for their S corporation's stock. The shareholders are planning on having the corporation distribute land with a $75,000 adjusted basis and a $300,000 FMV in 1997. Ordinary income is expected to be $125,000 in the current year. What tax issues should be considered by Adam and Rodney with respect to the distribution?

PROBLEMS

C11-31 ***Comparison of Entity Forms.*** King Corporation is 100%-owned by Ken Munro, a single taxpayer. During the current year, King reports $100,000 of taxable income. Ken Munro reports no income other than that which is earned from King.

a. What is King Corporation's income tax liability assuming none of the earnings are withdrawn from the C corporation by Ken? What is Ken's income tax liability? What is the total tax liability for the corporation and its shareholder?

b. Assume that King Corporation instead distributes 100% of its after-tax earnings to Ken as a dividend in the current year. What is the total income tax liability for the C corporation and its shareholder?

c. How would your answer to Part a change if Ken withdrew $50,000 from the business in salary? Are there any taxes other than corporate and individual income taxes that must be considered now that a salary is paid?

d. How would your answers to Parts a–c change if King Corporation were instead an S corporation?

C11-32 ***Making the Election.*** Voyles Corporation, a calendar-year taxpayer formed in 1992, desires to make an S election commencing with 1997. Sue and Andrea each own one-half of the Voyles stock.

a. How does Voyles Corporation make the S election?

b. When can Voyles Corporation file its election form?

c. If the election in Part b is not filed in a timely manner, when will it first take effect?

C11-33 ***Termination of the Election.*** Orlando Corporation, a calendar-year taxpayer, has been taxed as an S corporation for several years. On July 10, 1997, Orlando Corporation authorizes a second class of nonvoting preferred stock that pays a 10% annual dividend. The stock is sold to Sid on September 15, 1997 to raise additional equity capital. Sid owns no other Orlando stock.

a. Does Orlando Corporation's S election terminate? If so, when is the termination first effective?
b. What tax returns must be filed by Orlando Corporation for 1997? When are they due?
c. How would your answer to Parts a and b change if the second class of stock were instead nonvoting Class B common stock?

C11-34 ***Revocation of the Election.*** Tango Corporation, a calendar-year taxpayer, has been taxed as an S corporation for several years. Tango's business activities have become very profitable in recent years. On June 15, 1997, its sole shareholder, who is in the 39.6% marginal tax bracket, desires to revoke the S election.
a. How does Tango revoke its S election? When does the revocation take effect?
b. Assume the revocation is effective July 1, 1997. What tax returns are required of Tango for 1997? for 1998? When are these returns due?
c. If a new S election is made after the revocation, when does it first take effect?

C11-35 ***Sale of S Corporation Interest.*** Peter and his wife, Alice, own all of the stock of Galleon Corporation. Galleon Corporation made its S election in January 1986. Peter and Alice sold one-half of their Galleon stock to a partnership owned by Rob and Susan (not husband and wife) at the close of business on December 31, 1997 for a $75,000 profit. What are the tax consequences of the sale transaction for Peter and Alice? for the corporation? As Peter and Alice's CPA, do you have any advice for them if all parties would like the S election to continue?

C11-36 ***Selecting a Tax Year.*** Indicate in each of the following situations whether the taxpayer can accomplish what is proposed. Provide adequate authority for your answer, including any special elections that are needed or requirements that must be satisfied. Assume that all individuals use the calendar year as their tax year unless otherwise indicated.
a. Will and Carol form the Classic Corporation. They want the corporation to adopt a fiscal year ending January 31 as its tax year to provide a maximum deferral for their income. An S election is made for its initial tax year ending January 31, 1998.
b. Mark and Dennis have owned and operated the Plastic Corporation for several years. Plastic Corporation has used a fiscal year ending June 30 since its organization as a C corporation because it conforms to the corporation's natural business year. An S election is made for its tax year beginning July 1, 1997.
c. Edith owns all the stock of Elite Corporation, an electing S corporation. Elite Corporation uses a fiscal year ending January 31 as its tax year. The IRS approved Elite Corporation's use of the fiscal year in 1980. A Sec. 444 election was made in 1986 commencing with the 1987 tax year. The appropriate required payments have been made since that date.

C11-37 ***Passive Income Tax Levy.*** North Corporation was organized in 1984 by Oliver. An S election is made by North Corporation for 1994 after it accumulates $60,000 of E&P as a C corporation. None of the accumulated E&P has been distributed as of December 31, 1997. In 1997 North Corporation reports the following results:

Dividends from domestic corporations	$ 60,000
Rental income	100,000
Services income	50,000
Expenses related to rental income	30,000
Expenses related to services income	15,000
Other expenses	5,000

Significant services are not provided nor are substantial costs incurred in connection with earning the rental income. The services income are the gross receipts derived from the active conduct of a trade or business.
a. Is North Corporation subject to the excess net passive income tax? If so, what is its tax liability?
b. What is the effect of the excess net passive income tax liability on North's pass-throughs of ordinary income and separately stated items?
c. What advice would you give North Corporation regarding its activities?

C11-38 ***Built-in Gains Tax.*** Tad Corporation was created in 1984. In its first year, it elected to use the cash method of accounting and adopted a calendar year as its tax year. An S election was made on August 15, 1996 effective for Tad's 1997 tax year. At the beginning of 1997, Tad has assets with a $600,000 FMV and a $180,000 adjusted basis. During 1997 Tad reports taxable income of $400,000.

- Tad collects all accounts receivables outstanding on January 1, 1997 in the amount of $200,000. The receivables had a zero adjusted basis.
- Tad sells an automobile on February 1, 1997 for $3,500. The automobile had a $2,000 adjusted basis and a $3,000 FMV on January 1, 1997. $1,000 of MACRS depreciation was claimed on the automobile in 1997.
- Tad sells land (a Sec. 1231 asset) that it held three years in anticipation of building its own office building for a $35,000 gain. The land had a $45,000 FMV and a $25,000 adjusted basis on January 1, 1997.
- Tad paid accounts payable outstanding on January 1, 1997 of $125,000. All of the payables are deductible expenses.

What is the amount of Tad's built-in gains tax liability?

C11-39 ***Determination of Pass-Throughs.*** West End Corporation, an S corporation using an accrual method of accounting, is owned by Amelia. Amelia uses the cash method of accounting. West End reports the following results for the current year:

Operating profit (excluding the items indicated below)	$275,000
Dividend income:	
From a domestic corporation 25%-owned by West End	12,000
From a foreign corporation 1%-owned by West End	6,000
Interest income:	
Installment sales of merchandise	9,000
Municipal bonds	7,000
Corporate bonds	3,000
Gains and losses on property sales:	
Sec. 1231 gain	9,000
Long-term capital gain	11,000
Long-term capital loss	6,000
Short-term capital gain	8,000
Sec. 1245 gain	10,000
MACRS depreciation on plant, equipment, and office equipment	46,000
Charitable contributions	25,000
Salary expense (all paid to Amelia this year)	60,000
Rental expense on building leased from Amelia ($6,000 of the rentals remained unpaid at year-end)	36,000
Repairs expense	36,000
State and local taxes	6,000
Interest on loans taken out to acquire stock investments	10,000
Foreign taxes withheld on dividend from foreign corporation	1,200

a. What is West End's ordinary income?
b. What are West End's separately stated items?

C11-40 ***Allocation of Income to Shareholders.*** John owns all of the stock of Lucas Corporation, an electing S corporation. John's basis for the 1,000 shares is $125,000. On June 11 of the current year (a non-leap year), John gifts 100 shares of stock to his younger brother Michael, who has been working in the buisness for one year. Lucas Corporation reports $125,000 of ordinary income for the current year. What amount of income is allocated to John? to Michael?

C11-41 ***Sale of S Corporation Interest.*** Al and Ruth each own one-half of the stock of Chemical Corporation, an electing S corporation. During the current year (a non-leap year),

Chemical Corporation earns $15,000 per month of ordinary income. On April 5 Ruth sells her entire stock interest to Patty. A business asset is sold on August 18 and a $75,000 Sec. 1231 gain is recognized. What alternatives (if any) exist for allocating Chemical Corporation's current year income?

C11-42 ***Allocation of Income to Shareholders.*** Toyland Corporation, an electing S corporation, uses the calendar year as its tax year. Bob, Alice, and Carter own 60, 30, and 10 shares, respectively, of the Toyland stock. Carter's basis for his stock is $26,000 on January 1 of the current year (a non-leap year). On July 1, Alice gifted one-half of her stock to Mike. On December 1, Carter sold his stock to Mike for $45,000. Toyland reports the following results for the current year:

Ordinary income	$120,000
Long-term capital loss	10,000
Charitable contributions	6,000

a. What amounts of income, loss, or deduction are reported by the four shareholders (assuming that no special elections are made)?

b. What gain or loss is recognized by Carter when the Toyland stock is sold?

C11-43 ***Allocation of Income to Shareholders.*** Redfern Corporation, a calendar-year taxpayer, has been an S corporation for several years. The Redfern stock is owned equally by Rod and Ken. On July 1 of the current year (a non-leap year), Redfern Corporation issues additional common stock that is purchased by Blackfoot Corporation. Rod, Ken, and Blackfoot Corporation each end up owning one-third of the Redfern stock. Redfern Corporation reports ordinary income of $125,000 and a short-term capital loss of $15,000 in the current year. Eighty percent of the ordinary income and all of the capital loss are accrued after Blackfoot Corporation purchases its stock. Redfern makes no distributions to its shareholders in the current year. What income and losses are reported by Redfern and Blackfoot Corporations and Rod and Ken as a result of the current year's activities?

C11-44 ***Allocation of Income Between Family Members.*** Bright Corporation, an electing S corporation, has been 100% owned by Betty since it was created in 1986. The corporation has been quite profitable in recent years, and in the current year (a non-leap year) it reports ordinary income of $240,000 after paying Betty a $60,000 salary. On January 1, Betty gifts 15% of the Bright stock to each of her three sons, John, Andrew, and Stephen, in the hope that they will work in the family business. Gift taxes are paid on the transfers. The sons are ages 16, 9, and 2 at present and are not currently active in the business. Bright distributes $7,500 in cash to each son and $27,500 in cash to Betty in the current year.

a. What income is reported by Betty, John, Andrew, and Stephen for the current year as a result of Bright's activities, assuming the sons are considered bona fide owners of the stock? How will the income be taxed to the children?

b. Assuming that the IRS determines a reasonable salary for Betty to be $120,000, how would your answer to Part a change?

c. How would your answer to Part a change if the sons were not considered bona fide owners of the stock?

C11-45 ***Allocation of Losses to Shareholders.*** Raider Corporation, an electing S corporation, is owned equally by Monte and Allie. Both individuals actively participate in Raider's activities. On January 1, Monte and Allie have adjusted bases for their Raider stock of $80,000 and $90,000, respectively. During the current year (a non-leap year), Raider Corporation reports the following results:

Ordinary loss	$175,000
Tax-exempt interest income	20,000
Long-term capital loss	32,000

Raider's balance sheet at year-end shows the following liabilities: accounts payable, $90,000; mortgage payable, $30,000; and note payable to Allie, $10,000.

a. What income and deductions will Monte and Allie report from Raider's current year activities?

b. What basis does Monte have in his stock investment on December 31?
c. What basis does Allie have in her stock investment and note on December 31?
d. What loss carryovers are available for Monte and Allie?
e. Explain how the use of the losses in Part a would change if Raider Corporation were instead a partnership and Monte and Allie were equal partners who shared profits, losses, and liabilities equally.

C11-46 *Use of Loss Carryovers.* Assume the same facts as in Problem C11-45 except that Raider Corporation reports $75,000 of ordinary income, $20,000 of tax-exempt income, and a $25,000 long-term capital gain in the next year.
a. What income and deductions will Monte and Allie report from this year's activities?
b. What basis does Monte have in his stock investment on December 31?
c. What basis does Allie have in her stock investment and note on December 31?
d. What loss carryovers (if any) are available to Monte and Allie?

C11-47 *Allocation of Losses to Shareholders.* Hammer Corporation, an electing S corporation, is owned by Tommy, who has a $100,000 basis for his investment on January 1. Tommy actively participates in Hammer's activities. The Hammer Corporation operating results were not good in the current year (a non-leap year), with an ordinary loss of $175,000 being reported. The size of the loss required Tommy to lend Hammer Corporation $50,000 on August 10 of the current year, to provide funds needed for operations. The loan is secured by a Hammer Corporation note. Hammer Corporation rebounds during the next year (also a non-leap year) and reports ordinary income of $60,000. The $50,000 note is repaid on December 15.
a. What amount of Hammer's current year loss can Tommy report on his income tax return?
b. What is Tommy's basis for the Hammer stock and note at the end of the loss year?
c. What income and deductions will Tommy report in the next year from Hammer's activities and the loan repayment?

C11-48 *Post-Termination Loss Use.* Stein Corporation, an electing S corporation, has 400 shares of stock outstanding. The shares are owned equally by Chuck and Linda. Both individuals actively participate in Stein's activities. Each shareholder contributed $60,000 when Stein was organized on September 10, 1996. Start-up losses during 1996 result in Stein reporting a $210,000 ordinary loss. Stein's activities have since become profitable, and the S election is voluntarily revoked on March 1, 1997, with no prospective revocation date being specified. In 1997, Stein reports $360,000 of taxable income ($30,000 per month). Stein makes no distributions to its shareholders in either year.
a. What amount of loss is deductible by Chuck and Linda in 1996?
b. What amount of loss must be carried over by Chuck and Linda to 1997?
c. If Chuck reported only $5,000 of other business income in 1996, what happens to the "excess" S corporation losses that are deducted?
d. What portion of the loss carryover from Part b can be deducted in 1997? What happens to any unused portion of the loss?
e. What advice can you offer to Chuck and Linda to enhance their use of the Stein loss?

C11-49 *Use of Loss Pass-Throughs by Shareholders.* Rocket Corporation, an electing S corporation, is owned by Tina, who has an $80,000 basis for her investment on January 1. During the first eleven months of the current year (a non-leap year), Rocket Corporation reports an ordinary loss of $100,000. An additional $20,000 loss is expected for December. Tina earns $250,000 of ordinary income from her other activities in the current year. Her other income is expected to decline to $75,000 next year and continue at that level in future years. Next year's losses for Rocket Corporation are expected to be only $20,000. Rocket Corporation projects a $50,000 profit for the following year and each of the next four years. What advice can you offer Tina about using her Rocket Corporation losses and retaining S corporation status in future years? How would your answer change if Tina's income from her other activities were expected to be $75,000 in the current year and $250,000 next year.

C11-50 ***Use of Loss Pass-Throughs by Shareholders.*** Morning Corporation is being formed by Alice, a single taxpayer, in the current year. Alice is planning to purchase all of Morning's common stock for $100,000. Morning will obtain additional capital by borrowing $75,000 from a local bank. Morning will conduct a variety of service activities with little need to retain its capital in the business. Start-up losses of $90,000 are expected during Morning's first year of operation. Pretax operating profits of $250,000 (before reduction for Alice's salary) are expected to be earned starting next year. Alice expects to withdraw $100,000 of Morning's profits as a salary. Her other income consists primarily of dividends and interest and is expected to amount to $100,000 annually. What advice can you provide Alice about the advisability of making an S election in the initial tax year? in a later tax year? How would your answers change if the Morning Corporation's expected annual income were instead $350,000? $500,000? (Hint: A comparison of the total tax liability for Alice and Morning Corporation as both an S and C corporation might be helpful.)

C11-51 ***Stock Basis Adjustment.*** For each of the following items, indicate whether they will increase, decrease, or cause no change in the S corporation's ordinary income (loss), AAA, and in the shareholder's stock basis. The corporation in question was formed in 1993, and made its S election in 1995. During the time period it was a C corporation, $30,000 of E&P was accumulated. This amount has not been distributed.

a. Operating profit
b. Dividend income received from domestic corporation
c. Interest income earned on corporate bond held as an investment
d. Life insurance proceeds paid on death of corporate officer
e. Long-term capital gain
f. Sec. 1231 loss
g. Sec. 1245 gain
h. Charitable contributions
i. Fines paid for having overweight trucks
j. Depreciation
k. Pension plan contributions for employees
l. Salary paid to owner
m. Premiums paid on life insurance policy in Part d
n. Distribution of money (but not in excess of current year's earnings)

C11-52 ***Taxability of Distributions.*** Sweets Corporation is organized in January of the current year and immediately elects to be taxed as an S corporation. All of the Sweets stock is owned by Tammy, who contributes $40,000 in cash to start the business. Sweets' current year results are reported below:

Ordinary income	$36,000
Short-term capital loss	4,000
Charitable contributions	1,000

On July 10, Sweets Corporation makes a $10,000 cash distribution to Tammy.

a. What income is recognized as a result of the distribution?
b. What is the basis for the Sweets stock on December 31?
c. How would your answers to Parts a and b change if Sweets' distribution were instead $75,000?

C11-53 ***Taxability of Distributions.*** Vogel Corporation is incorporated on January 15 of the current year by Curt, who makes a $60,000 capital contribution. Vogel makes a timely S election for this year. Vogel reports $60,000 of ordinary income, $40,000 of Sec. 1231 gain, $5,000 of tax-exempt interest income, and $3,000 of charitable contributions this year. On December 1 Vogel distributes $5,000 cash and land contributed by Curt that is no longer needed in the business. The land, which had a $10,000 basis and a $12,000 FMV when contributed to the corporation in January, has an $18,000 FMV when distributed.

a. What income is reported by Vogel Corporation and Curt as a result of the distribution?

b. What is the basis for the Vogel stock on December 31?
c. What are Vogel's earnings balances on December 31?

C11-54 ***Taxability of Distributions.*** Stable Corporation was organized in 1980 by Hal, who has continued to own all of its stock. An S election was made in 1981. At the beginning of 1997, Stable Corporation reports the following earnings accumulations:

Accumulated adjustments account	$85,000
Accumulated E&P	20,000

Hal's basis for his Stable stock on January 1, 1997 is $120,000. During 1997, Stable reports the following results from its operations:

Ordinary income	$30,000
Tax-exempt interest income	15,000
Long-term capital loss	20,000

Stable Corporation makes a $65,000 cash distribution to Hal on August 8.
a. What income, gain, or loss is recognized as a result of the distribution?
b. What is the basis of the Stable stock on December 31?
c. What are Stable's earnings balances on December 31?
d. How would your answers to Parts a through c change if Stable instead distributed $115,000?

C11-55 ***Comprehensive Problem—Comparison of Entity Formations.*** Cara, Bob, and Steve want to begin a business on January 1, 1997. The individuals are considering three business forms—C corporation, partnership, and S corporation.

- Cara has investment land with a $40,000 adjusted basis and a $50,000 FMV which she is willing to contribute. The land has a rundown building on it having a $25,000 basis and a $15,000 FMV. Cara has never used the building nor rented it. She would like to get rid of the building. Because she needs cash, Cara will take out a small ($25,000) mortgage on the property before the formation of the new business and have the new business assume the debt.
- Bob will contribute machinery and equipment which he purchased for his sole proprietorship in January 1993. He paid $100,000 for the equipment and has used the MACRS rules with a half-year convention on this 7-year recovery period property. He did not make a Sec. 179 expensing election for this property. The FMV of the equipment and machinery is $39,000.
- Steve will contribute cash of $1,600 and services worth $20,400 for his interest in the business. The services he will contribute include drawing up the necessary legal documentation for the new business and setting up the initial books.

To begin operations, the new business plans to borrow $50,000 on a recourse basis from their local bank. Each owner will guarantee their ownership share of the debt.

What are the tax and nontax consequences for the new business and its owners under each alternative? Assume that any corporation will have 200 shares of common stock authorized and issued. How would your answer to the basic facts change if Bob's contribution was instead valued at $40,000 and the services contributed by Steve were valued at $18,400?

C11-56 ***Comprehensive Problem—Comparison of Operating Activities.*** RST business entity reported the following items during 1997:

Dividends from 25%-owned domestic corporation	$19,000
State of Florida bond interest	18,000
General Electric Corporation bond interest	29,000
Gain on land contributed by Karen	40,000[a]
Operating profit (excluding depreciation)	120,000
MACRS depreciation	36,000

Section 1245 gain	5,000
Section 1231 loss	28,000
Net long-term capital losses	4,000
Short-term capital losses	5,000
Charitable contributions	23,000
Investment interest expense (related to General Electric bonds)	16,000
Salary (guaranteed payment)	37,000

[a] The land was held by Karen as an investment prior to contributing it to RST business entity in 1994 in exchange for her ownership interest. When Karen contributed the land, it had a basis of $15,000 and a FMV of $40,000. The land was sold in the current year for $55,000. RST business entity held the land as an investment. Assume that Sec. 351 applied to any corporate formation transaction.

a. What is the corporate taxable income and income tax liability for 1997 if RST is taxed as a C corporation?

b. What is the ordinary income and separately stated items for 1997 if RST elects to be taxed as an S corporation? Assume that RST has never operated as a C corporation.

c. What is the ordinary income and separately stated items if RST is taxed as a partnership?

C11-57 ***Comprehensive Problem—Comparison of Nonliquidating Distributions.*** Tampa Corporation was organized in 1980 and has always been equally owned by Jeff and John. In 1997, Tampa reports ordinary income/taxable income of $40,000. On April 5, Tampa distributes $100,000 cash to Jeff and land with a $100,000 FMV and a $70,000 adjusted basis to John. The land distributed to John was purchased as an investment by Tampa in 1994. What are the tax implications to Tampa, Jeff, and John of the land distribution in each of the four situations that follow?

a. Tampa has been a C corporation since its formation. On January 1, 1997, Jeff's basis in his stock is $50,000 and John's basis is $45,000. Tampa has accumulated E&P of $155,000 on January 1, 1997.

b. Tampa was formed as a C corporation, but made an S election in 1983. On January 1, 1997, Jeff's basis in his stock is $100,000 and John's basis is $80,000. Tampa had the following earnings balances on January 1, 1997:

Accumulated Adjustments Account	$125,000
Accumulated E&P	30,000

c. Tampa was formed as a partnership and continues to operate in that form. On January 1, 1997, Jeff's basis in his partnership interest is $100,000 and John's basis is $80,000. The partnership has no liabilities and no precontribution gain which has not been recognized.

d. How would your answers to Parts a–c change if the land held as an investment that was distributed to John had been contributed to Tampa by Jeff in 1995? At the time of Jeff's contribution, the land a FMV of $95,000.

TAX FORM/RETURN PREPARATION PROBLEM

C11-58 Bottle-Up, Inc., was organized on January 8, 1987 and made its S election on January 24, 1987. The necessary consents to the election were filed in a timely manner. Its federal tax identification number is 38-1507869. Its address is 1234 Hill Street, Gainesville, FL 32607. Bottle-Up, Inc., uses the calendar year as its year, the accrual method of accounting, and the first-in, first-out (FIFO) inventory method. Bottle-Up manufactures ornamental glass bottles. No changes to its inventory costing methods were made this year. The specific identification method is used for bad debts for book and tax purposes. Herman Hiebert (S.S. no. 123-45-6789) and Melvin Jones (S.S. no. 100-67-2000) own 500 shares each. Both individuals materially participate in Bottle-Up's single activity. Herman Hiebert is the tax matters person. Financial statements for Bottle-Up for the current year are shown in Tables C11-2 through C11-4. Prepare a current-year S corporation tax return for Bottle-Up, showing yourself as the paid preparer.

▼ TABLE C11-2

Bottle-Up, Inc. Income Statement for the Year Ended December 31 of the Current Year (Problem C11-58)

Sales		$2,500,000
Returns and allowances		(15,000)
Net sales		$2,485,000
Beginning inventory	$ 102,000	
Purchases	900,000	
Labor	200,000	
Supplies	80,000	
Utilities	100,000	
Other manufacturing costs	188,000[a]	
Goods available for sale	$1,570,000	
Ending inventory	(96,000)	1,474,000[b]
Gross profit		$1,011,000
Salaries[c]	$ 451,020	
Utilities expense	54,000	
Depreciation (MACRS depreciation is $36,311)	11,782	
Automobile and truck expense	26,000	
Office supplies expense	9,602	
Advertising expense	105,000	
Bad debts expense	620	
Rent expense	30,000	
Interest expense[d]	1,500	
Meals and entertainment expense	21,000	
Selling expenses	100,000	
Repairs and maintenance expense	38,000	
Accounting and legal expense	4,500	
Charitable contributions[e]	9,000	
Insurance expense[f]	24,500	
Hourly employees' fringe benefits	11,000	
Payroll taxes	36,980	
Other taxes	2,500	
Penalties (fines for overweight trucks)	1,000	(938,004)
Operating profit		$ 72,996
Other income and losses:		
Long-term gain on sale of capital assets	$ 48,666	
Sec. 1231 loss	(1,100)	
Interest on U.S. Treasury bills	1,200	
Interest on State of Florida bonds	600	
Dividends from domestic corporations	11,600	
Investment expenses	(600)	60,366
Net income		$ 133,362

[a] Total MACRS depreciation is $74,311. Assume that $38,000 of depreciation has been allocated to cost of sales for both book and tax purposes so that the book and tax inventory and cost of sales amounts are the same. The depreciation adjustment on personal property is $9,000.

[b] The cost of goods sold amount reflects the Uniform Capitalization Rules of Sec. 263A. The appropriate restatements have been made in prior years.

[c] Officer salaries of $120,000 are included in the total.

[d] Investment interest expense is $500. All other interest expense is trade- or business-related. None of the interest expense relates to the production of tax-exempt income.

[e] All contributions were made in cash to qualifying charities.

[f] Includes $3,000 of premiums paid for policies on lives of corporate officers. Bottle-Up is the beneficiary for both policies.

▼ TABLE C11-3

Bottle-Up, Inc. Balance Sheet for January 1 and December 31 of the Current Year (Problem C11-58)

	January 1	December 31
Assets:		
Cash	$ 15,000	$116,948
Accounts receivable	41,500	45,180
Inventories	102,000	96,000
Stocks	103,000	74,000
Treasury bills	15,000	16,000
State of Florida bonds	10,000	10,000
Building and equipment	374,600	375,000
Minus: Accumulated depreciation	(160,484)	(173,100)
Land	160,000	190,000
Total	$660,616	$750,028
Liabilities and equities:		
Accounts payable	$ 36,000	$ 10,000
Accrued salaries payable	12,000	6,000
Payroll taxes payable	3,416	7,106
Sales taxes payable	5,200	6,560
Due to Mr. Hiebert	10,000	5,000
Mortgage and notes payable (current maturities)	44,000	52,000
Long-term debt	210,000	260,000
Capital stock	10,000	10,000
Retained earnings	330,000	393,362
Total	$660,616	$750,028

▼ TABLE C11-4

Bottle-Up, Inc. Statement of Change in Retained Earnings, for the Current Year Ended December 31 (Problem C11-58)

Balance, January 1		$330,000[a]
Plus: Net income	$133,362	
Minus: Dividends	(70,000)	63,362
Balance, December 31		$393,362

[a]The January 1 accumulated adjustments account balance is $274,300. [The AAA balance is different from retained because it is based on tax numbers rather than book numbers.]

CASE STUDY PROBLEMS

C11-59 Debra has operated a family counseling practice for a number of years as a sole proprietor. She owns the condominium office space that she occupies in addition to her professional library and office furniture. She has a limited amount of working capital and little need to accumulate additional business assets. Her total business assets are about $150,000, with an $80,000 mortgage on the office space being her only liability. Typically she has withdrawn any unneeded assets at the end of the year. Debra has used her personal car for business travel and charged the business for the mileage at the appropriate mileage rate provided by the IRS. Over the last three years Debra's practice has grown so that she now forecasts $80,000 of income being earned this year. Debra has contributed small amounts to an Individual Retirement Annuity each year, but has never reached the $2,000 annual limit. Although she has never been sued, Debra has recently become more concerned about legal liability. An attorney friend of hers has suggested that she incorporate her business in order to protect herself against being sued and to save taxes.

Required: You are a good friend of Debra's and a CPA; she asks your opinion on incorporating her business. You are to meet with Debra tomorrow for lunch. Prepare a draft of the points you feel should be discussed over lunch about incorporating the family counseling practice.

C11-60 One way to compare the accumulation of income by alterative business entity forms is to use mathematical equations. The following equations are provided which express the investment accumulation calculation for a particular entity form:

Conduit entities (S corporations, partnerships, and LLCs): $A_n = [1 + R(1 - t_p)]^n$

C corporation: $A_n = [1 + R(1 - t_c)]^n(1 - gt_p) + gt_p$

where: $R =$ pre-tax rate of return;

$t_p =$ owner's marginal tax rate

$t_c =$ corporation's marginal tax rate

$g =$ portion of capital gain subject to tax

$n =$ number of periods

For each alternative business form, an initial investment of $1 is made. The following operating assumptions apply:

Marginal tax rate for owner (t_p): 0.396

Corporate tax rate (t_c): 0.34

Capital gains rate: 0.28

Portion of capital gain subject to tax (g) = 0.70707

Investment horizon (n): 1, 5, 10, 20 years

A partnership distributes only enough cash each year for the partners to pay the taxes. The corporation pays no dividends. The shareholders sell their stock at the end of the investment horizon and all profits are taxed at the capital gains rates.

Required: What is the after-tax accumulation if the business is operated for the investment horizon and then sold for the amount of the accumulation? What nontax variables might influence your decision about the best entity form? How would your calculations change if the C corporation was a qualified small business corporation eligible for the tax benefits contained in Code Sec. 1202?

TAX RESEARCH PROBLEMS

C11-61 Cato Corporation is incorporated on July 1, 1992 in California, with Tim and Elesa, husband and wife, owning all of the Cato stock. On August 15, 1992, Cato Corporation makes an S election effective for tax year 1992. Tim and Elesa file the necessary consents to the election. On March 10, 1996, Tim and Elesa transfer 15% of the Cato stock to the Reid and Susan Trust, an irrevocable trust created three years earlier for the benefit of their two minor children. In early 1997, Tim and Elesa's tax accountant learns about the transfer and advises the couple that the transfer of the stock to the trust may have terminated Cato's S election. Prepare a memorandum for your tax manager indicating any action Tim and Elesa can take that will permit Cato Corporation to retain its S election? Research sources suggested by the tax manager include Secs. 1361(c)(2), 1362(d)(2), and 1362(f).

C11-62 One of your wealthy clients, Cecile, invests $100,000 in the stock of an electing S corporation. The corporation, which is solely owned by Cecile, is in the process of developing a new food product. It is anticipated that the new business will need approximately $200,000 in capital (other than trade payables) during the first two years of its operations before it starts to earn sufficient profits to pay a return on the shareholder's investment. The first $100,000 of this total is to come from Cecile's contributed capital. The remaining $100,000 of funds will come from one of the following three sources:

- Have the corporation borrow the $100,000 from a local bank. Cecile is required to act as a guarantor for the loan.
- Have the corporation borrow $100,000 from the estate of Cecile's late husband. Cecile is the sole beneficiary of the estate.
- Have Cecile lend $100,000 to the corporation from her personal funds.

Interest at a rate acceptable to the IRS is to be paid by the S corporation. During the first two years of operations, the corporation anticipates losing $125,000 before it begins to earn a profit. The tax manager that you work for has asked you to evaluate the tax ramifications of each of the three financing alternatives. Prepare a memorandum to the tax manager outlining the information you found in your research.

C11-63 Andy and Karen are 30 year-old engineering school graduates who are starting a new business to manufacture and sell digital circuits. One year ago they left a large digital circuit manufacturer and obtained a patent on a new circuitry design. They intend to start a business with $500,000 of their own capital and $2 million obtained from 20 other investors. Each outside investor has committed to contribute $100,000. Organizational and start-up expenditures of $125,000 are expected to be incurred in the corporation's first year.

Andy and Karen have already spent $200,000 to develop their idea. They plan to contribute the patent to the new business as part of their $500,000 commitment. All research and development (R&D) costs have been capitalized. Losses of $500,000 are expected to be incurred in each of the first two years of operations. The company expects to breakeven in the third year, and be profitable at the end of the fourth year even though the nature of the digital circuit business requires continual R&D activities. If losses exceed expectations, monies will be obtained from additional investors.

Andy is an absolute genius, who has always succeeded at whatever he has attempted. However, Andy is a bit sloppy with his attention to detail. Karen, on the other hand, is a methodical organizer who intends to oversee the business operations. They feel that they will be a successful team.

Karen is married to a successful author, who earns approximately $500,000 a year from his writing. Andy is single, and his only income will come from the business. Both individuals will devote full time to the business. If needed, Karen has indicated she may be able to contribute more than her original $250,000 commitment, and possibly guarantee some bank loans.

Andy and Karen have approached Stan about helping them promote their business. Stan has connections in the electronics industry and feels that the new circuitry will be quite successful. Stan is willing to work in the business on a full-time basis drawing only a small salary until the business gets on its feet. Unfortunately, Stan does not have any monies to invest in the business at the present time.

Required: Your tax manager has asked you to prepare a presentation to be delivered to Andy and Karen about what entity form you would recommend and any particular tax issues they will face on the formation of the entity. Karen has heard about using a limited liability company from a friend, and wonders if it would be better than the S corporation that she and Andy have been considering. She recommends that you examine, at a minimum, the following articles:

- Richard M. Lipton, "Choice of Entity: How to Choose, How to Change," *Taxes* (June 1994), pp. 309-326.
- Kent H. McMahan, "The Limited Liability Company Part One: Fundamentals," *Estate Planning Studies,* April 1995, pp. 1-8.

CHAPTER 12

THE GIFT TAX

LEARNING OBJECTIVES

After studying this chapter, you should be able to

1. Understand the concept of a unified transfer tax system
2. Explain the gift tax formula
3. Identify a number of transfers subject to the gift tax
4. Determine whether an annual gift tax exclusion is available
5. Identify deductions available for gift tax purposes
6. Apply the gift-splitting rules
7. Calculate the gift tax liability
8. Understand how basis affects the overall tax consequences
9. Recognize the filing requirements for gift tax returns

CHAPTER OUTLINE

The **gift tax** is a **wealth transfer tax** that applies if a property transfer occurs during a person's lifetime. It is similar to the estate tax, which applies to transfers associated with death. Both the gift tax and the estate tax are part of the unified transfer tax system under which gratuitous transfers of property between persons are subject to taxation. The vast majority of all property transfers are exempt from these transfer taxes as a result of the annual exclusion and the various deductions and credits. However, planning for reducing these transfer taxes is a significant matter for wealthy or moderately wealthy individuals.

This chapter discusses both the structure of the gift tax (including the exclusion, deduction, and credit provisions) and exactly which property transfers fall within its purview. The income tax basis rules are reviewed in the context of their implications for selecting properties to transfer by gift instead of at death.

CONCEPT OF TRANSFER TAXES

OBJECTIVE 1

Understand the concept of a unified transfer tax system

KEY POINT

The person liable for the gift tax is the person who makes the gift: the donor.

ADDITIONAL COMMENT

The IRS reports that 215,010 gift tax returns were filed in 1995. Total gift tax collections in fiscal year 1995 were $1.82 billion.

KEY POINT

Reasons for the gift tax are to raise revenues, to prevent the avoidance of estate taxes, to make up for the fact that income produced from gifted property is often taxed at a lower marginal income tax rate to the donee than to the donor; and to redistribute wealth.

IRC Sec. 102 explicitly excludes gifts and inheritances from the recipient's gross income.[1] Thus, the recipient of a gift incurs no income tax liability. The donor, however, is primarily obligated to pay the gift tax, a type of excise tax. The gift tax applies to the act of transferring property to a recipient who pays either no consideration or consideration with a value lower than that of the property received. The gift tax is levied on the donor, the person who transferred the property.

HISTORY AND PURPOSE OF TRANSFER TAXES

The United States has had an estate tax since 1916 and a gift tax since 1932.[2] The structure of the gift and estate taxes has remained fairly constant, but details such as the amount of the exclusion and the rate schedules have changed numerous times. Very significant changes were made by the Tax Reform Act of 1976 (the 1976 Act), which adopted a unified rate schedule for gift and estate tax purposes. The Economic Recovery Tax Act of 1981 (the 1981 Act) increased the amount of the annual exclusion and removed the ceiling on the amount deductible for gifts or bequests to one's spouse.

There are several purposes for the gift tax, one of the most important of which is to raise revenue. However, because of the fairly generous annual exclusion and unified credit legislated by Congress, the gift tax yields only a small fraction of the federal government's total revenues. Only donors making relatively large gifts owe any gift taxes. Another purpose of the gift tax is to serve as a backstop to the estate tax and to prevent individuals from avoiding a significant amount—not all—of estate taxes by disposing of property before death. For example, without the gift tax, persons who know they are terminally ill could dispose of property "on their deathbed" and escape the transfer tax. In addition, the gift tax is a source of revenue to make up for some of the income tax revenue lost because income produced by the gifted property sometimes is taxed to a person in a lower income tax bracket. Another purpose for levying gift and estate taxes is to redistribute wealth.

There is no way to know what the distribution of wealth would have been if Congress had not enacted transfer taxes. However, one study estimates that more than 41% of this nation's net wealth is concentrated in the hands of the top 1% of the population.[3] Such concentration has remained relatively constant since the 1950s.

[1] The income earned from property received as a gift or an inheritance, however, is not exempt from the income tax.

[2] A gift tax was also in existence from 1924 to 1926.

[3] U.S., Congress, Joint Economic Committee, *The Concentration of Wealth in the United States* (Washington, DC: U.S. Government Printing Office, July 1986), p. 24. Pension benefits, automobiles, and household durables were not included in the estimates of net wealth. Another study concluded that the percentage of national net worth held by the top 1% of U.S. families rose from 31% in 1983 to 36% in 1989. See Gene Koretz, "Would the Economy Gain From Spreading Inherited Wealth?" *Business Week* (May 18, 1992), p. 22. The article cites a study done by the Federal Reserve.

THE UNIFIED TRANSFER TAX SYSTEM

The 1976 Act greatly revamped the transfer tax system by combining the separate estate and gift tax systems into one unified transfer tax system. Although Chapters C12 and C13 use the terms *gift tax* and *estate tax*, these taxes are actually components of the same unified transfer tax system. The system also includes the generation-skipping transfer tax, a topic discussed in Chapter C13. The unification of the transfer tax system removes the previous law's bias favoring tax treatment of lifetime gifts in comparison with transfers at death. The three most significant elements of the unified system—the unified rate schedule, the inclusion of taxable gifts in the death tax base, and the unified credit—are discussed below.

KEY POINT

The purpose of the five percentage point surtax is to phase out the benefits of both the progressive rate structure and the unified credit (to be discussed later in this chapter).

SELF-STUDY QUESTION

Use the rate schedule in Code Sec. 2001 to determine the amount of gift tax (before credits) on 1997 taxable gifts of the following:

(1) $4,000,000. The tax is: On the first $3.0 million, $1,290,800; plus 55% of the excess over $3.0 million, or $550,000. Gross tax equals $1,840,800.

(2) $30,000,000. The tax is: On the first $3.0 million, $1,290,800; plus 55% of the excess over $3.0 million, $14,850,000; plus 5% of excess over $10,000,000 but not in excess of $21,040,000, or $552,000. Gross tax equals $16,692,800.

KEY POINT

At the taxpayer's death, the unified tax is computed on the sum of the taxable estate plus the adjusted taxable gifts. The tax on this sum is reduced by the tax that would have been payable (at current rates) on the taxable gifts made after December 31, 1976.

UNIFIED RATE SCHEDULE

Before the 1976 Act mandated a **unified rate schedule** applicable to both lifetime transfers and transfers at death, the gift tax rates were only 75% of the estate tax rates on a transfer of the same size. The unified rate schedule is effective for gifts made after 1976 and deaths occurring after 1976. The rates are progressive and have varied over the years. The rate schedule reaches a peak of 55% (see the inside back cover for the unified transfer tax rates), but it also contains a phase-out provision whereby, the benefit of the rates below the highest rate is phased out, as is the benefit of the unified credit. The phase-out is accomplished by imposing an additional 5 percentage point surtax on tax bases in excess of $10,000,000 but not in excess of $21,040,000. Thus, if in 1997 a donor makes a taxable gift of $30,000,000, such gift will, in effect, be taxed at a 55% flat rate even if this is the first gift the donor makes.

IMPACT OF TAXABLE GIFTS ON DEATH TAX BASE

Before 1977, lifetime gifts were viewed separately from dispositions at death. By making gifts, an individual could shift the taxation of properties from the top of the estate tax rate schedule to the bottom of the gift tax rate schedule. Few taxpayers could take advantage of this shifting, however, because only people with a relatively large amount of property could afford to part with sizable amounts of their assets while alive.

Under today's unified system, taxable gifts affect the size of the tax base at death. Any taxable gifts (other than gifts included in the gross estate) made after 1976 are called **adjusted taxable gifts**, and such gifts are included in the donor's death tax base. They are valued at their fair market value (FMV) on the date of the gift. The addition of such taxable gifts to the tax base at death can result in the donor-decedent's estate being taxed at a higher marginal tax rate. However, such gifts are not taxed for a second time upon the donor's death because gift taxes (computed at current rates) on these gifts are subtracted in determining the estate tax liability.

EXAMPLE C12-1 ▶ In 1982, Dan makes taxable gifts totaling $500,000. When Dan dies in the current year, the value of the gifted property has tripled. Dan's death tax base includes the $500,000 of post-1976 taxable gifts. They are valued for estate tax purposes at their FMV on the date of the gift; the post-gift appreciation escapes the transfer tax system. Thus, the transfer tax value is fixed or frozen at the date-of-gift value. ◀

Note that unification (including taxable gifts that become part of the tax base at death) extends only to gifts made after 1976. Congress exempted gifts made before 1977 from unification because it did not want to retroactively change the two separate transfer tax systems that previously existed.

UNIFIED CREDIT

The **unified credit** reduces dollar for dollar a certain amount of the tax computed on the taxable gifts or the taxable estate. The amount of the credit varies depending on the year of the transfer. With respect to the gift and estate tax formulas, the full credit is available for lifetime transfers and again in determining the tax payable at death. In concept, however, an individual's estate does not receive the benefit of this unified credit amount at death to the extent the credit has already been used against lifetime transfers (as explained in Chapter C13). The gift tax formula, including the unified credit, is discussed below.

GIFT TAX FORMULA

OBJECTIVE 2

Explain the gift tax formula

The formula described in this section is used to calculate a donor's gift tax liability for the year of the transfer. As with income taxes, gift tax reporting is done on an annual basis. Figure C12-1 illustrates the formula for determining the donor's annual gift tax liability. This formula is discussed in detail later in the chapter.

ADDITIONAL COMMENT

The gift tax applies to cumulative lifetime gifts made since the enactment of the gift tax in 1932. The unified gift and estate tax, enacted in 1976, applies only to cumulative lifetime gifts made after 1976. This means that a taxable gift of $75,000 made in 1970 would not be included in the unified tax base of a decedent but would affect the gift tax payable by that person.

DETERMINATION OF GIFTS

The starting point in the process is to determine which, if any, of the taxpayer's transfers constitute gifts. The next section discusses the various types of transfers that the statute views as gifts. All gifts are valued at their FMVs on the date of the gift. Next, the aggregate amount of gifts for the period is determined. The aggregate gifts are then reduced by any exclusions and deductions. Finally, the tax is computed according to the formula illustrated in Figure C12-1.

EXCLUSIONS AND DEDUCTIONS

The maximum amount that is excludible annually is $10,000 per donee.[4] If the gifts made to a donee do not equal at least $10,000, the amount excludible is limited to the amount of the gift made to such a donee. Exclusions may be claimed for transfers to an unlimited number of donees.

TYPICAL MISCONCEPTION

Individuals often think they can make only up to $10,000 in gifts each year that would not be subject to the gift tax. Actually, the $10,000 exclusion applies to each *donee* per year; therefore, the total amount of tax-free gifts in a given year can be much greater than $10,000.

Two types of deductions are available for reducing the amount of the taxable gifts. Most transfers to one's spouse generate a marital deduction; there is no ceiling on the amount of this deduction. Similarly, most transfers to charitable organizations are cancelled out by the charitable contribution deduction.

GIFT-SPLITTING ELECTION

Congress authorized gift-splitting provisions to achieve more comparable tax consequences between taxpayers of community property and noncommunity property (common law) states.[5] Under **community property law**, assets acquired after marriage are community property unless they are acquired by gift or inheritance. Typically, in a **community property state**, a large portion of the spouses' assets is community property, property in which each spouse has a one-half interest. One-half of a community property gift is automatically considered to be given by each spouse. By contrast, in a **common law state**, all assets acquired during the marriage are the property of the acquiring spouse. The other spouse does not automatically acquire an interest in the property. Thus, often only one spouse owns enough assets to make gifts.

KEY POINT

Some advantages of gift-splitting are doubling the excluded amount per donee (up to $20,000), using a spouse's lower gift tax rate, and using a spouse's unified credit.

Section 2513 authorizes spouses to elect gift splitting. As a result of this election, gifts made by each spouse to third parties are treated as if each spouse made one-half of the

[4] Sec. 2503(b).

[5] The eight traditional community property states are Louisiana, Texas, New Mexico, Arizona, California, Washington, Idaho, and Nevada. Wisconsin's marital property law, though not providing for community property, is basically the same as community property.

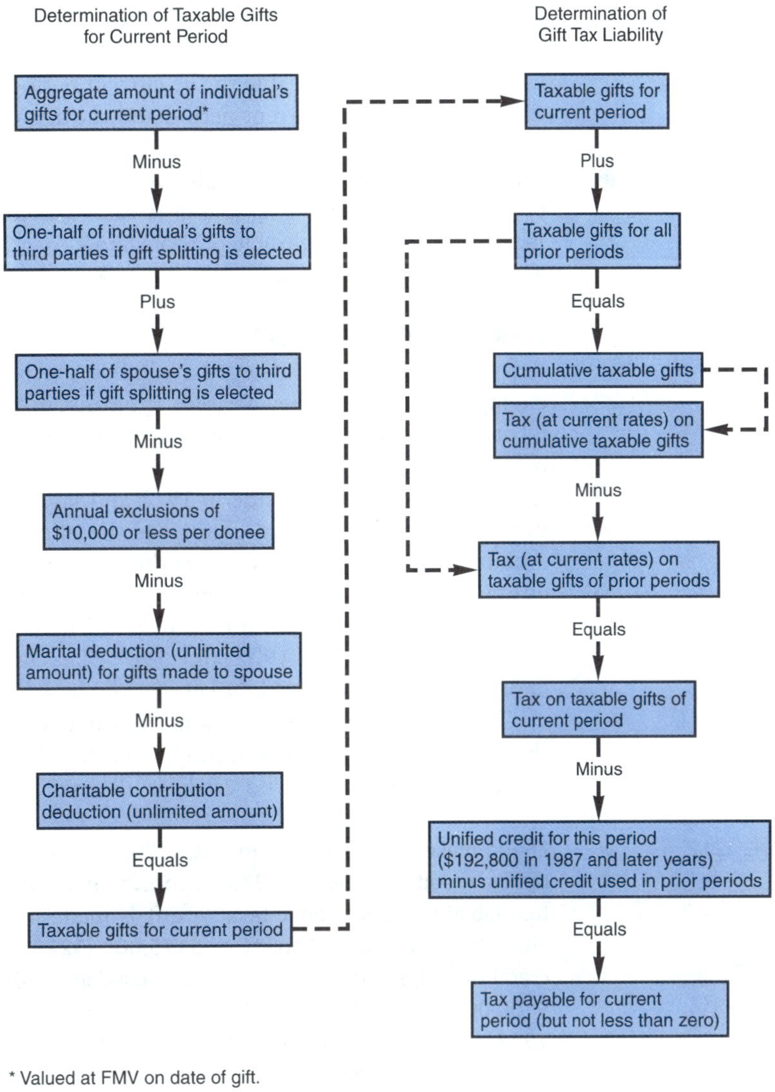

SELF-STUDY QUESTION

Al and Beth, husband and wife, live in a common law state. Al makes a gift of $620,000 to each of two children by a previous spouse. Al and Beth agree to split the gift. Neither Al nor Beth has made taxable gifts in any prior year. What are Al's and Beth's taxable gifts?

ANSWER

One-half of each gift, a total of $620,000, is reported on each taxpayer's gift tax return. Neither Al nor Beth has any gift tax liability for the current year due to the annual exclusions and the unified credit. Al has effectively used some of Beth's unified credit without Beth ever having ownership or control over Al's property.

FIGURE C12-1 ▶ THE GIFT TAX FORMULA

gift. The gift-splitting election allows spouses in common law states to achieve the same benefits as those that apply automatically for gifts of community property. Thus, both spouses can claim a $10,000 per donee exclusion although only one spouse actually makes the gift. As a result, each donee may receive up to $20,000 before a taxable gift is made.

EXAMPLE C12-2 ▶ Andy and Bonnie, residents of a common law state, are married throughout the current year. In the current year Andy gives his brother $100,000 cash. Andy and Bonnie may elect gift splitting and thereby treat the $100,000 gift as if $50,000 had been given by each. As a result, the excludible portion of the gift totals $20,000 ($10,000 per donee for each of the two deemed donors). If they elect gift splitting, each donor's $40,000 taxable gift may be taxed at a lower marginal tax rate. In addition, Bonnie is able to use a unified credit amount that she might not otherwise be able to use. As a result of gift splitting, the tax consequences are the same as if Andy and Bonnie were residents of a community property state and gave $100,000 of community property to Andy's brother. ◀

CUMULATIVE NATURE OF GIFT TAX

Unlike the income tax, computations of gift tax liabilities are cumulative in nature. The marginal tax rate applicable to the current period's taxable gifts is a function of both the taxable gifts for the current period and the aggregate taxable gifts for all earlier periods.

EXAMPLE C12-3 ▶ Sandy and Jack each make taxable gifts in the current year totaling $200,000. However, for previous periods Sandy's taxable gifts total $100,000 and Jack's total $1,500,000. Because Jack's cumulative total taxable gifts are larger than Sandy's, Jack's current year gifts are taxed at a higher marginal tax rate (45% for Jack vs. 34% for Sandy). ◀

UNIFIED CREDIT

Before 1977, the Code allowed a $30,000 specific exemption. Donors could deduct this exemption whenever they desired. Typically, donors claimed it as early as they needed to in order to reduce the amount of gifts that would otherwise be taxable. The 1976 Act repealed this exemption and replaced it with the unified credit.[6] Consequently, the gift tax computed for gifts made in 1977 and later years is reduced dollar for dollar by the unified credit. The unified credit has the effect of allowing donors to make a certain amount of taxable gifts (known as the **exemption equivalent**) without needing to pay the gift tax. Beginning with 1987, the unified credit has been $192,800, which is equivalent to a $600,000 exemption from the gift tax. The maximum amount of the credit increased progressively between 1977 and 1987. The unified credit amount for various years appears on the inside back cover.

The amount creditable for a particular year is the credit amount for that year minus the credit that could have been claimed for the taxable gifts made by the individual in earlier years. Recall that no credit is allowed for gifts made before 1977.

EXAMPLE C12-4 ▶ Zheng makes her first taxable gift,[7] $200,000 in amount, in 1978. Zheng used the $34,000 unified credit available for 1978 (as shown on the inside back cover) to reduce her $54,800 gift tax liability. Zheng's next taxable gift is made in 1984. The taxable amount is $500,000. Zheng's 1984 gift tax liability of $175,000 ($229,800 − $54,800) was reduced by a unified credit of $62,300 ($96,300 − $34,000 used in 1978). The $175,000 represents the tax on the $700,000 of cumulative taxable gifts, which is $229,800, minus the tax on the $200,000 of 1978 taxable gifts, which is $54,800. If she makes taxable gifts in the current year, the maximum credit she can claim against her current tax is $96,500 ($192,800 − $96,300 used already). ◀

KEY POINT

The gift tax (before credits) on a $30 million gift made in 1997 is $16,692,800 (see page C12-3 annotation). This amount is a flat 55% of the $30 million gift plus an add back of the $192,800 unified credit. At this level, all gifts made by the taxpayer have been taxed at a 55% rate, and the taxpayer has not been given the advantage of either the progressive rate structure or the unified credit.

As mentioned earlier, the benefit of the unified credit is phased out for taxable amounts between $10,000,000 and $21,040,000 by the imposition of an additional 5% tax.

After the passage of the 1976 Act, prospective donors quickly realized the advantages of making gifts in 1976 to avoid the unification provisions. Some prospective donors had made such small gifts in the past that they had used none or only part of their specific exemption. Congress adopted a special rule that affects donors who used any portion of their specific exemption between September 9, 1976 and December 31, 1976.[8] The amount of unified credit otherwise available to such donors is reduced by 20% of the amount of the specific exemption they claimed between September 9 and December 31, 1976. The maximum reduction in the unified credit as a result of this provision is $6,000 (0.20 × $30,000).

EXAMPLE C12-5 ▶ In November 1976 Maria makes a large taxable gift, her first gift. Maria uses her $30,000 specific exemption to reduce the taxable gift amount. As a result, the unified credit that Maria

[6] Sec. 2505.

[7] No credit is used for a gift that is completely nontaxable.

[8] Sec. 2505(b).

could otherwise claim after 1976 is reduced by $6,000 (0.20 × $30,000). Moreover, her 1976 taxable gifts are not includible in her death tax base. ◀

OBJECTIVE 3

Identify a number of transfers subject to the gift tax

SELF-STUDY QUESTION

Consider two points: The gift tax is a tax on *cumulative* lifetime gifts, and the unified credit is reduced by 20% of the pre-1977 specific exemption used on gifts made between September 9 and December 31, 1976. What implications do these two points have for recordkeeping?

ANSWER

Taxpayers must keep track of all gifts previously made because previous gifts are part of the calculation for current gift tax due and any estate tax liability. In addition, taxpayers must keep a record of how much of the specific exemption they used between September 9 and December 31, 1976 in order to determine how much of the unified credit is available to them. Such information appears on the gift tax forms.

KEY POINT

The amount of the gift made is the FMV of property transferred reduced by the FMV of any consideration received by the donor.

TRANSFERS SUBJECT TO THE GIFT TAX

In general, property transferred for less than adequate consideration in money or money's worth is deemed to be a gift in the gift tax context. The gift occurs when the donor gives up all control over the transferred property. Congress has legislated several provisions that exempt various property transfers that might otherwise be viewed as gifts from the scope of the gift tax. These exemptions include direct payments of medical expenses and tuition, transfers to political organizations, property settlements in conjunction with a divorce, and qualified disclaimers.

TRANSFERS FOR INADEQUATE CONSIDERATION

As mentioned earlier, the initial step in determining the donor's gift tax liability is deciding which transfers constitute gifts for gift tax purposes. Section 2501(a) states that a gift tax is imposed on "the transfer of property by gift." Thus, if *property* is transferred *by gift,* the transferor potentially incurs a gift tax liability. Perhaps surprisingly, the Code does not define the term *gift.* Section 2511(a) expands on Sec. 2501(a) by indicating that the tax is applicable "whether the transfer is in trust or otherwise, whether the gift is direct or indirect, and whether the property is real or personal, tangible or intangible."

A transaction is subject to the gift tax even though not entirely gratuitous if "the value of the property transferred by the donor exceeds the value in money or money's worth of the consideration given therefor."[9] In such circumstances the amount of the gift is the difference between the value of the property the donor gives up and the value of the consideration in money or money's worth received. The following discussion examines in more depth the scope of the rule regarding transfers for less than adequate consideration.

BARGAIN SALES. Often an individual wants to sell an asset to a family member, but the prospective buyer cannot afford to pay the full FMV of the property. If the buyer pays consideration of less than the FMV of the transferred property, the seller makes a gift to the buyer. The amount of the gift is the bargain element of the transaction; that is, the excess of the property's FMV over its sales price.

EXAMPLE C12-6 ▶ Martha sells her ranch, having a $1,000,000 FMV, to her son Stan. Stan can afford to pay only $300,000 of consideration. In the year of the sale, Martha makes a gift to Stan of $700,000, the excess of the ranch's FMV over the consideration received. ◀

TRANSFERS IN NORMAL COURSE OF BUSINESS. There is an exception to the general rule that a transfer for inadequate consideration triggers a gift. According to the Regulations, a transaction arising "in the ordinary course of business (a transaction which is bona fide, at arm's length, and free from any donative intent)" is considered to have been made for adequate consideration.[10] Thus, no gift arises when a buyer acquires property for less than its FMV if the acquisition is in the ordinary course of business.

[9] Reg. Sec. 25.2512-8.

[10] Ibid.

EXAMPLE C12-7 ▶ John, a merchant, has a clearance sale and sells a diamond bracelet valued at $30,000 to Bess. Bess pays $12,000, the clearance sale price. Because the clearance sale arose in the ordinary course of John's business, the bargain element ($18,000) does not constitute a gift to Bess. ◀

STATUTORY EXEMPTIONS FROM THE GIFT TAX

For various reasons, including simplifying the administration of the gift tax, Congress has enacted several provisions that exempt certain transactions from the purview of the gift tax. In the absence of these statutory rules, some of these transactions could constitute gifts.

SELF-STUDY QUESTION

Ben's adult son Clarence, who is not Ben's dependent, needs a liver transplant. Because Clarence cannot afford the surgical procedure, Ben pays the $100,000 medical fee directly to the hospital. Is the payment for Clarence's benefit a taxable gift?

ANSWER

The payment is not a taxable gift because of Sec. 2503(e).

PAYMENT OF MEDICAL EXPENSES OR TUITION. Section 2503(e) states that a qualified transfer is not treated as a transfer of property by gift. The term *qualified transfer* is defined as an amount paid on behalf of an individual to an educational organization for tuition or to any person who provides medical care as payment for such medical care. Such payments are exempt from gift treatment only if made *directly* to the educational organization or to the person providing the medical care. *Educational organization* has the same definition as for charitable contribution purposes,[11] and *medical care* has the same definition as for medical expense deduction purposes.[12] Note that only tuition—not room, board, and books—is addressed by this rule. Note also that the identity of the person whose expenses are paid is not important. The special exemption applies even if the payments are made on behalf of an individual who is not a relative.

If one makes payments on behalf of another and the expenditures constitute support that the payor must furnish under state law, such payments are support, not gifts. State law determines the definition of support. Generally, payments of medical expenses for one's minor child would be categorized as support and not a gift, even in the absence of Sec. 2503(e). On the other hand, state law does not generally require parents to pay medical expenses or tuition for an adult child. Thus, the enactment of Sec. 2503(e) removed such payments from the gift tax.

According to the Staff of the Joint Committee on Taxation, special rules concerning tuition and medical expense payments were enacted because

> Congress was concerned that certain payments of tuition made on behalf of children who have attained their majority, and of special medical expenses on behalf of elderly relatives, technically could be considered gifts under prior law. The Congress believed such payments should be exempt from gift taxes.[13]

EXAMPLE C12-8 ▶ Sergio pays $9,000 for his adult grandson's tuition at medical school and $11,000 for the grandson's room and board in the medical school's dormitory. All payments are made directly to the educational organization. The direct payment of the tuition to the medical school is exempted by Sec. 2503(e) from being treated as a gift. Sergio is not required under state law to pay room and board for an adult grandson. Thus, such payments are not support. Sergio has made an $11,000 gift to the grandson. ◀

EXAMPLE C12-9 ▶ Assume the same facts as in Example C12-8, except that Sergio pays the money to his grandson, who in turn pays the money to the medical school. Sergio has made a $20,000 gift. Because Sergio does not pay the tuition directly to the school, Sergio does not meet all of the conditions for exempting the tuition payments from gift tax treatment. ◀

---

[11] Section 170(b)(1)(A)(ii) defines *educational organization* in the context of the charitable contribution deduction.

[12] Section 213(d) defines *medical care* in the context of the medical expense deduction.

[13] U.S., Congress, Staff of the Joint Committee on Taxation, *General Explanation of the Economic Recovery Tax Act of 1981* (Washington, DC: U.S. Government Printing Office, 1981), p. 273.

WHAT WOULD YOU DO IN THIS SITUATION?

You are a CPA and your tax preparation client is a very wealthy elderly woman named Ms. Atsushi Trong. She is a model of the U.S. success story. Having struggled in her native country, she immigrated to the United States as a teenager and studied clothing trends among her peers in both high school and college. She started her own clothing company and over the years has led the way by promoting such trends as miniskirts, bell-bottom pants, the so-called "Mature Elvis" look, and the hip-hop-rap grunge fashion. She has a net worth of over $100 million and no immediate family.

She has decided to plow some of her good fortune back into the educational system, which provided the intellectual foundation for her success. She selected the current class of her old high school, P.S. 101, and gave each of 100 graduating students $100,000. This money was to be used to pay tuition costs for four years at her college alma mater, the prestigious Other League College of I Owe University (IOU). Each of the 100 student donees was admitted to IOU and used the $100,000 to prepay the four-year tuition costs. All these transactions took place during the current tax year.

You have now been asked to report these transactions to the federal government on Ms. Trong's tax returns. What position would you take after considering the requirements of the Code and Treasury Department Circular 230?

TRANSFERS TO POLITICAL ORGANIZATIONS. Congress adopted a provision specifically exempting transfers to political organizations from being deemed to be a transfer of property by gift.[14] In the absence of this special rule, these transfers would generally be subjected to gift tax treatment.

EXAMPLE C12-10 ▶ Ann transfers $2,000 to a political organization founded to promote the campaign of Thomas for governor. Ann's $2,000 transfer does not fall within the statutory definition of a gift. ◀

KEY POINT

Property transfers resulting from a divorce agreement generally are not gifts.

PROPERTY SETTLEMENTS IN CONJUNCTION WITH DIVORCE. To reduce litigation, Congress enacted special rules addressing property transfers in the context of a divorce. Earlier, the courts were often called on to resolve the issue of whether the transferee gave up consideration in money or money's worth in exchange for receiving property as part of a divorce settlement. Section 2516 specifies circumstances in which property settlements in connection with a divorce are automatically exempted from being treated as gifts. Thus, for qualifying transfers it is not necessary to deliberate whether the transferee furnished consideration in money or money's worth.

For Sec. 2516 to be applicable, the spouses must adopt a written agreement concerning their marital and property rights and the divorce must occur during a three-year period beginning one year before the agreement is made. No gift arises from any transfer made in accordance with such agreement if property is transferred to settle a spouse's marital or property rights or to provide reasonable support for the children while they are minors.

EXAMPLE C12-11 ▶ In June 1996, Hal and Wanda sign a property agreement whereby Hal is to transfer $750,000 to Wanda in settlement of her property rights. Hal makes the transfer in May 1997. Hal and Wanda receive a divorce decree in July 1997. Hal is not deemed to have made a gift to Wanda by making the transfer. ◀

QUALIFIED DISCLAIMERS. Sometimes a person who is named to receive property under a decedent's will prefers not to receive such property and would like to disclaim (not accept) it. Typically, the person is quite ill and/or elderly or very wealthy. State

[14] Sec. 2501(a)(5).

SELF-STUDY QUESTION

Harry dies, willing his entire estate equally to his three children. Angela, one of the children, has accumulated a substantial estate due to a successful writing career and wishes to have her share of Harry's estate go to her siblings. Can Angela's share go to one of her siblings without Angela's making a taxable gift?

ANSWER

By making a *qualified disclaimer* under Sec. 2518, Angela can refuse to accept the property, and the property will pass under another clause of the will or under state law to someone else, perhaps a sibling. Angela will not be considered to have made a taxable gift.

disclaimer statutes allow individuals to say "no thank you" to the property willed to them. State law or another provision in the will addresses how to determine who will receive the property after the original beneficiary declines to accept it.

Section 2518(a) states that people making a qualified disclaimer are to be treated as if the disclaimed property were never transferred to them. Thus, the person making the disclaimer is not deemed to have made a gift to the person who receives the asset as a result of the disclaimer.

A **qualified disclaimer** must meet the following four tests:

- It is an irrevocable, unqualified, written refusal to accept property.
- The transferor or his or her legal representative receives the refusal no later than nine months after the later of the day the transfer is made and the day the person named to receive the property becomes age 21.
- The disclaiming person has not accepted the property interest or any of its benefits.
- As a result of the disclaimer, the property passes to the decedent's spouse or a person other than the one disclaiming it. In addition, the person disclaiming the property cannot direct who is to receive the property.[15]

EXAMPLE C12-12 ▶

Doug dies on February 1, 1997 and wills 500 acres of land to Joan. If Joan disclaims the property in a manner that meets all four of the tests for a qualified disclaimer, Joan will not be treated as making a gift to the person who receives the property as a result of her disclaimer. ◀

EXAMPLE C12-13 ▶

Assume the same facts as in Example C12-12, except that Joan instead disclaims the property on January 2, 1998. Joan's action arose too late to meet the second qualified disclaimer test above. Joan makes a gift to the person who receives the property as a result of her disclaimer. ◀

CESSATION OF DONOR'S DOMINION AND CONTROL

A gift does not occur until a transfer becomes complete. The gift is valued as of the date the transfer becomes complete. Thus, the concept of a completed transfer is important in two contexts: determination of whether a gift has arisen and, if so, the amount of its value. According to the Regulations, a gift becomes complete—and is thus deemed made and valued—when the donor "has so parted with dominion and control as to leave in him no power to change its disposition, whether for his own benefit or for the benefit of another."[16] A gift is not necessarily complete just because the transferor is not entitled to any further personal benefits from the property. If the transferor still has influence over the benefits others may receive from the transferred property, the transfer is incomplete with respect to the portion of the property over which the transferor retained control.

REVOCABLE TRUSTS. A transferor who conveys property to a revocable trust has made an incomplete transfer because the creator of a revocable trust can change the trust provisions, including the identity of the beneficiaries. Moreover, the creator may demand the return of the trust property. Because the transferor does not give up any control over property conveyed to a revocable trust, the individual does not make a gift upon funding the trust. Once the trustee distributes trust income to a beneficiary, however, the creator of the trust loses control over the distributed funds. The creator then makes a completed gift of the distributed income amounts.

[15] Sec. 2518(b).

[16] Reg. Sec. 25.2511-2(b).

EXAMPLE C12-14 ▶ On May 1, 1997, Ted transfers $500,000 to a revocable trust with First National Bank as trustee. The trustee must pay out all the income to Ed during Ed's lifetime. At Ed's death, the property is to be paid to Ed, Jr. On December 31, 1997, the trustee distributes $35,000 of income to Ed. The May 1 transfer is incomplete because Ted may revoke the trust; thus, no gift arises upon the funding of the trust. A $35,000 gift to Ed occurs on December 31, 1997, because Ted no longer has control over the distributed income. ◀

EXAMPLE C12-15 ▶ Assume the same facts as in Example C12-14, except that Ted amends the trust instrument on July 7, 1998 to make the trust irrevocable. By this date, the trust property has appreciated to $612,000. Ted makes a completed gift of $612,000 on July 7, 1998 because he gives up his powers over the trust. ◀

KEY POINT

If the donor of property retains control over any portion of such property, no gift is considered to have been made with respect to the portion of the property that the donor still controls.

OTHER RETAINED POWERS. Even transfers to an irrevocable trust can be deemed incomplete with respect to the portion of the trust over which the creator kept control. The Regulations state that if "the donor reserves any power over its [the property's] disposition, the gift may be wholly incomplete, or may be partially complete and partially incomplete, depending upon all the facts in the particular case."[17] They add that one must examine the terms of the power to determine the scope of the donor's retention of control. The Regulations elaborate by indicating that "[a] gift is . . . incomplete if and to the extent that a reserved power gives the donor the power to name new beneficiaries or to change the interests of the beneficiaries."[18]

EXAMPLE C12-16 ▶ On May 3, 1997, Art transfers $300,000 of property in trust with a bank as trustee. Art names his friends Bob and/or Sue to receive the trust income for fifteen years and Karl to receive the trust property at the end of fifteen years. Art reserves the power to determine how the income is to be divided between Bob and Sue each year. Because Art reserves the power over payment of the income for the fifteen-year period, this portion of the transfer is incomplete on May 3. The valuation of the completed gift to Karl is determined from actuarial tables discussed in the next section of the chapter. ◀

EXAMPLE C12-17 ▶ Assume the same facts as in Example C12-16, except that on December 31, 1997, Art instructs the trustee to distribute the trust's $30,000 of income as follows: $18,000 to Bob and $12,000 to Sue. Once the income is paid out, Art loses control over it. Thus, Art makes an $18,000 gift to Bob and a $12,000 gift to Sue on December 31. ◀

EXAMPLE C12-18 ▶ Assume the same facts as in Example C12-16, except that on May 3, 1998, when the trust assets are valued at $360,000, Art relinquishes his powers over payment of income and gives this power to the trustee. Art's transfer of the income interest (with a remaining term of fourteen years) becomes complete on May 3, 1998. The valuation of the gift of a fourteen-year income interest is determined from actuarial tables in Appendix H. ◀

A summary of various complete, incomplete, and partially complete transfers can be found in Topic Review C12-1.

KEY POINT

Because the determination of value is such a subjective issue, it is not surprising that a large number of the tax controversies involving gift taxes are nothing more than valuation disagreements.

VALUATION OF GIFTS

GENERAL RULES. All gifts are valued at their FMV as of the date of the gift (i.e., the date the transfer becomes complete). The Regulations state that a property's value is "the price at which such property would change hands between a willing buyer and a willing seller, neither being under any compulsion to buy or to sell, and both having reasonable

[17] Ibid.

[18] Reg. Sec. 25.2511-2(c).

Topic Review C12-1

Examples of Complete and Incomplete Transfers

1. Complete Transfers, Subject to Gift Tax:
   a. Property transferred outright to donee
   b. Property transferred in trust with donor retaining no powers over the trust
2. Incomplete Transfers, Not Subject to Gift Tax:
   a. Property transferred to a revocable trust
   b. Property transferred to an irrevocable trust for which the donor has discretionary powers over income and the remainder interest
3. Partially Complete Transfers, Only a Portion Subject to Gift Tax:
   a. Property transferred to an irrevocable trust for which the donor has discretionary powers over income but not the remainder interest[a]

[a]The gift of the remainder interest constitutes a completed transfer.

knowledge of relevant facts."[19] According to the Regulations, stocks and bonds traded on a stock exchange or over the counter are valued at the mean of the highest and lowest selling price on the date of the gift.[20] In general, the guidelines for valuing properties are the same, regardless of whether the property is conveyed during life or at death. However, life insurance policies are less valuable while the insured is alive. Valuation of life insurance policies is discussed in a later section of this chapter, as well as in Chapter C13's coverage of the estate tax.

KEY POINT

The value of the life estate plus the value of the remainder interest equals the total FMV of the property.

LIFE ESTATES AND REMAINDER INTERESTS. Often one may transfer less than his or her entire interest in an asset. For example, an individual may transfer property in trust and reserve the right to the trust's income for life. Another individual will be named to receive the property upon the transferor's death. In such a situation, the transferor is said to have retained a **life estate** and given a **remainder interest**. Only the remainder interest is subject to the gift tax unless the gift is to a family member, as discussed in the estate freeze section below. If the transferor keeps an annuity (a fixed amount) for life and names another person to receive the remainder at the transferor's death, in all situations the gift is of just the remainder interest.

ADDITIONAL COMMENT

If a life estate is retained by the donor and a remainder interest is transferred on the donor's death, the FMV of the property will be drawn back into the decedent/donor's gross estate. At this point, the entire interest in the property passes to the remainderman who obtains a date-of-death FMV basis in the property, rather than a carryover gift basis.

A grantor may also transfer property in trust with the promise that another person is to receive the income for a certain number of years and at the end of that time period the property will revert to the grantor. In this case, the donor retains a reversionary interest, whereas the other party receives a **term certain interest**.[21] Unless the donee is a family member, only the term certain interest is subject to the gift tax. Trusts whereby the grantor retains a reversionary interest have disadvantageous income tax consequences to the grantor if they are created after March 1, 1986. Chapter C14 discusses the income tax treatment of such trusts.

Life estates, annuity interests, remainders, and term certain interests are valued from actuarial tables that incorporate the Sec. 7520 interest rate. In general, these tables must be used regardless of the actual earnings rate of the transferred assets. Excerpts from the tables appear in Appendix H. Table S is used for valuing life estates and remainders and

[19] Reg. Sec. 25.2512-1.

[20] Reg. Sec. 25.2512-2.

[21] *Term certain interest* means that a particular person has an interest in the property held in trust for a specified time period. The person having such interest does not own or hold title to the property, but has a right to receive the income from such property for a specified time period. At the end of the time period, the property reverts to the grantor (or passes to another person).

Table B for term certain interests. The factor for a life estate or term certain interest is 1.0 minus the remainder factor. The remainder factor simply represents the present value of the right to receive a property at the end of someone's life (in the case of Table S) or at the end of a specified time (in the case of Table B). The value of the income interest plus the remainder interest is 1.0. The factor for an annuity is the life estate or the term factor divided by the Sec. 7520 interest rate. Code Sec. 7520 calls for the interest rate to be revised every month to the rate, rounded to the nearest 0.2%, that is 120% of the Federal midterm rate applicable for the month of the transfer.[22] Revisions to the tables to reflect mortality experience are to be made at least once every ten years. Use of the actuarial tables is illustrated with the following examples.

EXAMPLE C12-19 ▶ Refer to Example C12-16, wherein Art transfers $300,000 of property in trust with a bank as trustee. Art names his friends Bob and Sue to receive the trust income for fifteen years but reserves the power to determine how the income is to be divided between them each year. Art specifies that Karl is to receive the trust property at the end of the fifteenth year. Only the gift of the remainder interest is a completed transfer. The gift is valued from Table B. If the interest rate is 10%, the amount of the gift is $71,818 (0.239392 × $300,000). This amount represents the present value of the property to be received at the end of 15 years. ◀

EXAMPLE C12-20 ▶ Assume the same facts as in Example C12-19, except that three years later, when the trust assets are valued at $360,000, Art transfers his power over the payment of trust income to the trustee. The income interest has a remaining term of twelve years. The gift is the present value of the twelve-year income interest, which is valued from Table B by subtracting the factor for a remainder interest (0.318631 if the interest rate is 10%) from 1.0. Thus, the amount of the gift is $245,293 [(1.0 − 0.318631) × $360,000]. ◀

EXAMPLE C12-21 ▶ On July 5 of the current year, Don transfers $100,000 of property in trust and names his friends Larry (age 60) to receive all of the income for the rest of Larry's life and Ruth (age 25) to receive the trust assets upon Larry's death. Don names a bank as the trustee. The amount of each donee's gift is determined from Table S. If the interest rate is 10% and Larry is age 60, the value of the gift to Ruth, as calculated from the single life remainder factors column of Table S, is $22,674 (0.226740 × $100,000). This amount represents the present value of the property to be received after the death of a person age 60. The remaining portion of the $100,000 of property, $77,326 ($100,000 − $22,674), is the value of the life estate transferred to Larry. The total value of the income plus remainder interests is 1.0. ◀

STOP & THINK

Question: In which scenario would the amount of the gift be larger: (1) a gift of a remainder interest to a friend if a 68-year-old donor retained the income for life or (2) a gift of a remainder interest to a friend if an 86-year-old donor retained the income for life? Assume that the two gifts are made on the same day so that the applicable interest rates are the same for each scenario.

Solution: The gift of the remainder interest would be larger if the donor is 86, instead of 68, because the actuarial value of the income interest the donor retains would be smaller if the donor is older. Older donors generally have shorter life expectancies.

[22] The applicable rate for determining the present value of an annuity, an interest for life or a term of years, or a remainder or reversionary interest for January 1997 is 7.6% (Rev. Rul. 96-57, I.R.B. 1996-50, 5).

KEY POINT

In estate freeze transfers, Congress has shifted its emphasis to providing rules that will generally increase the amount classified as a gift at the time of the actual transfer.

SPECIAL VALUATION RULES: ESTATE FREEZES. In recent years Congress became concerned that individuals were able to shift wealth to other individuals, usually in a younger generation, without paying their fair share of the transfer taxes. An approach they commonly used was to recapitalize a corporation (by exchanging common stock for both common and preferred shares) and then to give the common stock to individuals in the younger generation. This technique was one of a variety of transactions known as estate freezes.

In 1990 Congress decided to address the perceived problem of estate freezes by writing new valuation rules that apply when a gift occurs. The thrust of these rules—new Chapter 14 (Secs. 2701 through 2704) of the Code—is to ensure that gifts are not undervalued. A couple of the more common situations governed by the new rules are described below, but the rules are too complicated to warrant a complete discussion. If a parent owns 100% of the stock of a corporation and then gives the common stock to his or her children and retains the preferred, the value of the right to the preferred dividends is treated as zero unless the stock is cumulative preferred. If the donor creates a trust in which he or she retains an interest and in which he or she gives an interest to a family member, the value of the transferor's interest is treated as zero unless the retained interest is an annuity interest (fixed payments) or a unitrust interest (calling for distributions equal to a specified percentage of the current FMV of the trust). Thus, the donor is treated as having kept nothing. The effect of these rules is to increase the gift amount unless the transferor structures the transaction to avoid having a zero value assigned to his or her retained interest.[23]

GIFT TAX CONSEQUENCES OF CERTAIN TRANSFERS

SELF-STUDY QUESTION

Madge deposits $50,000 in a joint bank account in the name of herself and Susan, her niece. During the current year, the bank credited the account with interest of $4,000. No withdrawals are made during the year. Has Madge made a gift to Susan?

ANSWER

Madge has not made a gift to Susan because Susan has not withdrawn anything from the account. The interest earned by the account is reported by Madge on her personal income tax return because none of the money in the account is owned by Susan.

Some transactions that cause the transferor to have made a gift are straightforward. It is easy to see that the disposition is within the scope of the gift tax if, for example, an individual places the title to stock or real estate solely in another person's name and receives less than adequate consideration in return. The Regulations include the following examples of transactions that may be subject to the gift tax: forgiving of a debt, assignment of the benefits of a life insurance policy, transfer of cash, and transfer of federal, state, or municipal bonds.[24] The gratuitous transfer of state and local bonds falls within the scope of the gift tax, even though interest on such bonds is exempt from federal income taxation. The following discussion concerns the gift tax rules for several transfers that are more complicated than, for example, putting the title to realty or stock solely in the name of another person.

CREATION OF JOINT BANK ACCOUNTS. There are gift tax consequences for parties maintaining a bank account that is jointly owned. Funding a joint bank account is an incomplete transfer because the depositor is free to withdraw the amount deposited into the account. A gift occurs when one party withdraws an amount in excess of the amount he or she deposited.[25] The transfer is complete at that time because the withdrawn money is subject to only the withdrawing person's control.

EXAMPLE C12-22 ▶ On May 1, 1997, Connie deposits $100,000 into a joint bank account in the names of Connie and Ben. Her friend Ben makes no deposits. On March 1, 1998, Ben withdraws $20,000 from the joint account and purchases an auto. No gift arises upon the creation of the bank account.

---

[23] See Reg. Secs. 25.2701-1 through -6 and 25.2702-1 through -6 for guidance concerning the estate freeze provisions.

[24] Reg. Sec. 25.2511-1(a).

[25] Reg. Sec. 25.2511-1(h)(4).

However, on March 1, 1998, Connie makes a gift to Ben in the amount of $20,000, the excess of Ben's withdrawal over Ben's deposit. ◀

CREATION OF OTHER JOINT TENANCIES. A completed gift arises when the transferor titles real estate or other properties in the names of himself or herself and another (e.g., a spouse, a sibling, or a child) as joint tenants. **Joint tenancy** is a popular form for the ownership of property from a convenience standpoint because it serves as a substitute for a will. Each joint tenant is deemed to have an equal interest in the property. The person furnishing the consideration to acquire the property is deemed to have made a gift to the other joint tenant in an amount equal to the value of donee's pro rata interest in the property.[26]

EXAMPLE C12-23 ▶ Kwame purchases land for $250,000 and immediately has it titled in the names of Kwame and Kesha, as joint tenants with right of survivorship. Kwame and Kesha are not husband and wife. Kwame makes a gift to Kesha of $125,000, or one-half the value of the property. ◀

TRANSFER OF LIFE INSURANCE POLICIES. The mere naming of another as the beneficiary of a life insurance policy is an incomplete transfer. The owner of the policy can change the beneficiary designation at any time. However, if an individual irrevocably assigns all ownership rights in an insurance policy to another party, this event constitutes a gift of the policy to the new owner.[27] Ownership rights include the ability to change the beneficiary, borrow against the policy, and cash the policy in for its cash surrender value.

The payment of a premium on an insurance policy owned by another is considered a gift to the policy's owner. The amount of the gift is the amount of the premium paid. The tax result is the same as if cash were transferred to the policy owner and used by the owner to pay the premium.

Regulation Sec. 25.2512-6 describes the technique for valuing gifts of life insurance policies. The transferred policy is valued at the amount it would cost to purchase a comparable policy on the gift date. The Regulations point out, however, that if the policy is several years old, the cost of a comparable policy is not readily ascertainable. In such a situation the policy is valued at its interpolated terminal reserve (i.e., an amount similar to the policy's cash surrender value) plus the amount of any unexpired premiums. The insurance company will furnish information concerning the interpolated terminal reserve.

EXAMPLE C12-24 ▶ On September 1, 1997, Bill transfers all of his ownership rights in a $300,000 life insurance policy on his own life to his sister Susan. The policy's interpolated terminal reserve is $24,000 as of September 1. On July 1, 1997, Bill paid the policy's $4,800 annual premium. Bill makes a gift to Susan on September 1, 1997 in the amount of $28,000 [$24,000 + (10/12 × $4,800)]. ◀

EXAMPLE C12-25 ▶ Assume the same facts as in Example C12-24. On July 1, 1998, Bill pays the $4,800 annual premium on the policy now owned by Susan. As a result of the premium payment, Bill makes a $4,800 gift to Susan. ◀

EXAMPLE C12-26 ▶ Assume the same facts as in Examples C12-24 and C12-25, except that Susan, who now owns the policy, changes the beneficiary of the policy from Frank to John. This event is not a gift because Susan has not given up control; she can change the beneficiary again in the future. ◀

---

[26] Reg. Sec. 25.2511-1(h)(5). If the two joint tenants are husband and wife, no taxable gift will arise because of the unlimited marital deduction.

[27] Reg. Sec. 25.2511-1(h)(8).

EXERCISE OF A GENERAL POWER OF APPOINTMENT. Section 2514 provides the rules concerning powers of appointment. A **power of appointment** exists when a person transfers property (perhaps in trust) and grants someone else the power to specify who eventually will receive the property. Thus, possession of a power of appointment has some of the same benefits as ownership of the property. Powers can be general or special. *Potential* gift tax consequences are associated with the powerholder's exercise of a **general power of appointment**. A person possesses a general power of appointment if he or she has the power to appoint the property (have the property paid) to him- or herself, his or her creditors or estate, or the creditors of his or her estate. The words *his or her estate* mean that there are no restrictions concerning to whom the individual may bequeath the property.

A gift occurs when a person exercises a general power of appointment and names some other person to receive the property.[28] The gift is made to the person named to receive the property. The exercise of a general power of appointment in favor of the holder of the power is not a gift (i.e., one cannot make a gift to him- or herself).

EXAMPLE C12-27 ▶ In 1997, Tina creates an irrevocable trust and names Van to receive the income for life. In addition, Tina gives Van a general power of appointment exercisable during his life as well as at his death. Tina made a gift to Van at the time that the property was transferred to the trust in 1997. In 1998 Van instructs the bank trustee to distribute $50,000 of trust property to Kay. Through the exercise of his general power of appointment in favor of Kay, Van makes a $50,000 gift to Kay in 1998. ◀

NET GIFTS. A **net gift** occurs when an individual makes a gift to a donee who agrees to pay the gift tax as a condition to receiving the gift. The amount of the gift is the excess of the FMV of the transferred property over the amount of the gift tax paid by the donee. The donee's payment of the gift tax is treated as consideration paid to the donor. Because the amount of the gift is dependent on the amount of gift tax payable, which in turn is a function of the amount of the gift, the calculations require the use of simultaneous equations.[29]

The net gift strategy is especially attractive for people who would like to remove a rapidly appreciating asset from their estate but are unable to pay the gift tax because of liquidity problems. However, there is one potential disadvantage to a net gift; the Supreme Court has ruled that the donor must recognize as a gain the excess of the gift tax payable over his or her adjusted basis in the property.[30] The Court's rationale is that the donee's payment of the donor's gift tax liability constitutes an "amount realized" for purposes of determining the gain or loss realized on a sale, exchange, or other disposition. From a practical standpoint, this decision affects only donors who transfer property that is so highly appreciated that its adjusted basis is less than the amount of gift tax liability triggered by its disposition.

EXAMPLE C12-28 ▶ Mary transfers land with a $3,000,000 FMV to her son, Sam, who agrees to pay the gift tax liability. Mary's adjusted basis in the land is $15,000. Earlier in the year she gave him $10,000. The amount of the taxable gift is $3,000,000, less the gift tax paid by Sam. Simultaneous equations are used to calculate the amount of the gift and the gift tax liability. Mary must

---

[28] In general, the exercise of a special power of appointment is free of gift tax consequences. In the case of special powers of appointment, the holder of the power does not have an unrestricted ability to name the persons to receive the property. For example, he or she may be able to appoint to only his or her descendants.

[29] In Rev. Rul. 75-72 (1975-1 C.B. 310), the IRS explained how to calculate the amount of the net gift and the gift tax. In Ltr. Rul. 7842068 (July 20, 1978), the IRS stated that the donor's available unified credit, not the donee's, is used to calculate the gift tax payable.

[30] *Victor P. Diedrich v. CIR*, 50 AFTR 2d 82-5054, 82-1 USTC ¶9419 (USSC, 1982).

recognize gain equal to the excess of the gift tax liability paid by Sam minus Mary's $15,000 basis in the property.

ADDITIONAL COMMENT

As a general rule, substantially appreciated property should not be transferred by gift. It should be transferred at death to take advantage of the step-up in basis to the estate tax value (usually FMV at date of death). If Mary in Example C12-28 were elderly, it might be better to transfer an asset other than the land so as to obtain the basis increase for the land.

Assume that because of sizable previous taxable gifts, any additional gifts Mary makes will be subject to the 55% gift tax rate. If G represents the amount of the gift and T is the amount of the tax, then

$$G = \$3,000,000 - T$$
$$T = .55G$$

Substituting .55G for T in the first equation and solving for G, we get G = $1,935,484, the amount of the gift. The tax is 55% of this amount, or $1,064,516. The calculation becomes more difficult when, because of splitting brackets, more than one gift tax rate applies. Mary's gain equals the $1,064,516 gift tax paid by Sam minus the $15,000 basis she has in the property, or $1,049,516. ◀

EXCLUSIONS

OBJECTIVE 4

Determine whether an annual gift tax exclusion is available

In many instances a portion or all of a transfer by gift is tax-free because of the annual exclusion authorized by Sec. 2503(b). The purpose of the **annual exclusion** was explained by the Senate Finance Committee in 1932 as follows:

> Such exemption . . . is to obviate the necessity of keeping an account of and reporting numerous small gifts, and . . . to fix the amount sufficiently large to cover in most cases wedding and Christmas gifts and occasional gifts of relatively small amount.[31]

As a result of the availability of the annual exclusion, most gift transactions result in the donor's making no taxable gift. Consequently, administration of the gift tax provisions is a much simpler task than it would otherwise be.

AMOUNT OF THE EXCLUSION

The amount of this exclusion, which is analogous to an exclusion from gross income for income tax purposes, is currently $10,000.[32] It is available each year for an unlimited number of donees. For transfers made in trust, each beneficiary is deemed to be a separate donee. Any number of donors may make a gift to the same donee, and each is eligible to claim the exclusion. The only limitations on the annual exclusion are the donor's wealth, generosity, and imagination in identifying donees.

EXAMPLE C12-29 ▶

In 1997, Ann and Bob each give $10,000 cash to each of Tad and Liz. Ann and Bob again make $10,000 cash gifts to Tad and Liz in 1998. For both 1997 and 1998, Ann receives $20,000 of exclusions ($10,000 for the gift to Tad and $10,000 for the gift to Liz). The same result applies to Bob. ◀

ADDITIONAL COMMENT

The income that would have been received by the donor on the property given away goes to the donee. This also helps, over time, to reduce the donor's estate. It might also reduce the total income taxes paid by the economic (family) unit.

The annual exclusion is a significant tax planning device that has no estate tax counterpart. So long as a donor's gifts to a particular donee do not exceed the excludable amount, the donor will never make any taxable gifts or have any gift tax liability. Because taxable gifts will be zero, the donor's estate tax base will not include any adjusted taxable gifts. A donor who each year for 10 years gives $10,000 per donee to each of 10 donees removes $1 million (10 × $10,000 × 10) from being taxed in his or her estate. The donor

[31] S. Rept. No. 665, 72nd Cong., 1st Sess. (1932), reprinted in 1939-1 C.B. (Part 2), pp. 525–526.

[32] On January 1, 1982, the annual exclusion was increased from $3,000 to $10,000.

does this without making any taxable gifts or paying any gift tax. If retained, the $1 million would have been taxed in the donor's estate, at perhaps a 55% rate, unless the gifts were made to, or the property was willed to, the donor's surviving spouse.

PRESENT INTEREST REQUIREMENT

Although we generally speak of the annual exclusion as if it were available automatically for all gifts, in actuality it is not. A donor receives an exclusion only for gifts that constitute a present interest.

KEY POINT

It is extremely important to distinguish between gifts that are present interests and those that are future interests because the $10,000 exclusion per donee applies only to gifts that are present interests.

DEFINITION OF PRESENT INTEREST. A **present interest** is defined as "an unrestricted right to the immediate use, possession, or enjoyment of property or the income from property (such as a life estate or term certain)."[33] Only such interests qualify for the annual exclusion. If only a portion of a transfer constitutes a present interest, the excluded portion of the gift may not exceed the value of the present interest.

DEFINITION OF FUTURE INTEREST. A future interest is the opposite of a present interest. A **future interest** "is a legal term, and includes reversions, remainders, and other interests . . . which are limited to commence in use, possession, or enjoyment at some future date or time."[34] Gifts of future interests are ineligible for the annual exclusion. The following examples help demonstrate the attributes of present and future interests.

EXAMPLE C12-30 ▶ Nancy transfers $500,000 of property to an irrevocable trust with a bank serving as trustee. Nancy names Norm (age 55) to receive all of the trust income quarterly for the rest of Norm's life. At Norm's death, the property is to pass to Ellen (age 25) or Ellen's estate. Norm has an unrestricted right to immediate enjoyment of the income. Thus, Norm has a present interest. Ellen, however, has a future interest because Ellen cannot enjoy the property or any of the income until Norm dies. ◀

EXAMPLE C12-31 ▶ Greg transfers $800,000 of property to an irrevocable trust with a bank serving as trustee and instructs the trustee to distribute all of the trust income semiannually to Greg's three adult children, Jill, Katy, and Laura. The trustee is to use its discretion in deciding how much to distribute to each beneficiary. Moreover, it is authorized to distribute nothing to a particular beneficiary if it deems such action to be in the beneficiary's best interest. Although all of the income must be paid out, the trustee has complete discretion to determine how much to pay to a particular beneficiary. None of the beneficiaries have the assurance that they will receive a trust distribution. Thus, no present interests are created. ◀

SPECIAL RULE FOR TRUSTS FOR MINORS. Congress realized that many parents would not find it desirable to require trusts created for minor children to distribute all of their income to the young children. It enacted Sec. 2503(c), which contains provisions that authorize special trusts for minors, to address parents' concerns about the distribution of trust income to minors. Section 2503(c) allows parents (and other donors) to obtain an annual exclusion for gifts to trusts for children under age 21 that need not distribute all of their income annually. Such trusts, known as **Section 2503(c) trusts**, allow donors to claim the annual exclusion if the following two conditions are met:

- Until the beneficiary becomes age 21, the trustee may pay the income and/or the underlying assets to the beneficiary.

[33] Reg. Sec. 25.2503-3(b).

[34] Reg. Sec. 25.2503-3(a).

ADDITIONAL COMMENT

The donor may serve as trustee of a Sec. 2503(c) trust, but this is generally not advisable. If the donor's powers are not sufficiently limited, the trust property will be included in the donor's estate if the donor's death occurs while the trust is in force.

- Any income and underlying assets that are not paid to the beneficiary will pass to that beneficiary when he or she reaches age 21. If the beneficiary should die before becoming age 21, the income and underlying assets are payable to either the beneficiary's estate or any person the minor may appoint if the minor possesses a general power of appointment over the property.

If the trust instrument contains the provisions listed above, no part of the trust is considered to be a gift of a future interest. Therefore, the entire transfer is eligible for the annual exclusion.

As a result of Sec. 2503(c), donors creating trusts for donees under age 21 can get an exclusion, even though the trustee has discretion over paying out the trust income. However, the trustee must distribute the assets and accumulated income to the beneficiary at age 21.

CRUMMEY TRUST. The **Crummey trust** is yet another technique that allows the donor to obtain an annual exclusion upon funding a discretionary trust. The trust can terminate at whatever age the donor specifies and can be created for a beneficiary of any age. Thus, the *Crummey* trust is a much more flexible arrangement than the 2503(c) trust.

ADDITIONAL COMMENT

The holder of a *Crummey* power must be given notice of a contribution to the trust to which the power relates and must be given a reasonable time period within which to exercise the power. The donor receives the annual exclusion regardless of whether the donee exercises the power.

The *Crummey* trust is named for a Ninth Circuit Court of Appeals decision holding that the trust beneficiaries had a present interest as a result of certain language in the trust instrument.[35] That language, which is referred to interchangeably as a *Crummey* power, *Crummey* demand power, or *Crummey* withdrawal power, entitled each beneficiary to demand a distribution of the lesser of $4,000 or the amount transferred to the trust that year. If such power was not exercised by a specified date, it expired. The reason for the "lesser of" language with respect to the demand power is as follows: The largest present interest needed by the donor is equal to the annual exclusion amount. In years in which the gift is smaller than the annual exclusion amount, the donor simply needs to be able to exclude the amount of that year's gift. In addition, the donor wants to restrict the amount to which the beneficiary can have access. Today, the maximum amount that the beneficiary can withdraw is likely to be set at $10,000 (the amount of the annual exclusion) or $20,000 if gift splitting is anticipated.

The court held that the demand power provided each beneficiary with a present interest; the amount of the present interest was the maximum amount that the beneficiary could require the trustee to pay over to him or her that year. Use of the *Crummey* trust technique entitles the donor to receive the annual exclusion while creating a discretionary trust that terminates at whatever age the donor deems appropriate. The donor thereby avoids the more restrictive rules of Sec. 2503(c). Generally, the donor hopes the beneficiary will not exercise the demand right.

EXAMPLE C12-32 ▶ Al funds two $100,000 irrevocable trusts and names First Bank the trustee. The first trust is for the benefit of Kay, his 15-year-old daughter. The trustee is to distribute income and/or principal to Kay until she reaches age 21. If she dies before age 21, the trust assets are payable to whomever she appoints in her will or to her estate if she dies without a will. The second trust is for the benefit of Bob, Al's 25-year-old son. Income or principal are payable to Bob in the trustee's discretion until Bob reaches age 35, whereupon Bob will receive the trust assets. Bob may demand by December 31 of each year that the trustee pay him the lesser of $10,000 and the amount transferred to the trust that calendar year. The trust for Kay is a 2503(c) trust, and the one for Bob is a *Crummey* trust. An annual exclusion is available for each trust. ◀

[35] *D. Clifford Crummey v. CIR*, 22 AFTR 2d 6023, 68-2 USTC ¶12,541 (9th Cir., 1968).

STOP & THINK

Question: For which of the following gifts would the donor receive an annual exclusion:

- A gift of a remainder interest in land if the donor retains the income interest for life
- A gift outright of a life insurance policy that has a cash surrender value
- A gift to a discretionary trust that is classified as a 2503(c) trust
- A gift to a Crummey trust?

Solution: All of the transfers except the gift of the remainder interest are eligible for the annual exclusion. Even though the gift to the 2503(c) trust does not literally involve a gift of a present interest (the right to current income or enjoyment), the Code explicitly allows this kind of transfer to qualify for the annual exclusion.

GIFT TAX DEDUCTIONS

OBJECTIVE 5

Identify deductions available for gift tax purposes

The formula for determining taxable gifts allows two types of deductions: marital and charitable contribution. The **marital deduction** is for transfers to one's spouse. The **charitable contribution deduction** is for gifts to charitable organizations. Section 2524 states that the deductible amount in either case may not exceed the amount of the "includible gift"— that is, the amount of the gift in excess of the annual exclusion. Thus, the taxable amount of the gift is zero, not a negative number, as would be the case if the deduction equalled the amount of the gift.

MARITAL DEDUCTION

KEY POINT

The marital deduction is allowed because a taxpayer who transfers property to his or her spouse has not made a transfer outside the economic (husband/wife) unit.

Generally, the marital deduction results in tax-free interspousal transfers, but an exception discussed below applies to gifts of certain terminable interests. Congress first enacted the marital deduction in 1948 to provide more uniform treatment of community property and noncommunity property donors. To recap, in community property states, most property acquired after marriage is owned equally by each spouse. In noncommunity property states, however, the spouses' wealth is often divided unequally, and such spouses can equalize each individual's share of the wealth only by engaging in a gift-giving program. As a result of the marital deduction, spouses can shift wealth between themselves completely free of any gift tax consequences.

UNLIMITED AMOUNT. Over the years, the maximum marital deduction has varied. For gifts made after 1981, the rules are very favorable; there is an unlimited marital deduction whereby one spouse may deduct up to 100% of the amount of gifts made to the other spouse. The amount of the marital deduction, however, is limited to the amount of the gift that is in excess of the annual exclusion.[36] For gifts made after 1981, transfers of community property are eligible for the marital deduction; earlier such gifts did not qualify for the deduction.

EXAMPLE C12-33 ▶ A wife gives her husband stock valued at $450,000. She excludes $10,000 of this transfer using her annual exclusion and claims a $440,000 marital deduction. Thus, no taxable gift arises from her gift to her husband. ◀

[36] Sec. 2524.

GIFTS OF TERMINABLE INTERESTS: GENERAL RULE.

Nondeductible Terminable Interests. A **terminable interest** is an interest that ends or is terminated when some event occurs (or fails to occur) or a specified amount of time passes. Some, but not all, terminable interests are ineligible for the marital deduction.[37] A marital deduction is denied only when the transfer is of a nondeductible terminable interest. A nondeductible terminable interest has one of the following characteristics:

- The donor keeps an interest or conveys an interest to a third party who does not pay adequate consideration. The donee-spouse's interest ceases at a set time (such as at death) and the property then passes to either the donor or a third party.
- Immediately after making the gift, the donor has the power to name someone else to receive an interest in the property, and the person named may possess the property upon the termination of the donee-spouse's interest.[38]

The following three examples illustrate some of the subtleties of the definition of nondeductible terminable interests. In Example C12-34, a marital deduction is available because the interest transferred is not a nondeductible terminable interest.

EXAMPLE C12-34 ▶ A patent is a terminable interest because the property interest terminates at the end of the patent's legal life. Nevertheless, the patent does not constitute a nondeductible terminable interest; when the patent's legal life expires, a third party will not possess an interest in the patent. Thus, a donor will receive a marital deduction for a patent transferred to a spouse. ◀

In Example C12-35, a marital deduction is denied because the first of the two alternative characteristics of a nondeductible terminable interest is present.

EXAMPLE C12-35 ▶ A donor transfers property in trust and (1) names his wife to receive trust income, at the trustee's discretion, annually for the next fifteen years and (2) states that at the end of the fifteen-year period the trust's assets are to be distributed to their child. The donor has given his wife a nondeductible terminable interest. When the spouse's interest ceases, the property passes to their child, a recipient who did not pay adequate consideration. Thus, the donor receives no marital deduction. ◀

In Example C12-36, a marital deduction is available. In this case, the donee-spouse has a general power of appointment over the trust's assets in addition to having a lifetime income interest. The donee-spouse determines the persons to eventually receive the property.

EXAMPLE C12-36 ▶ The donor gives his wife the right to all the income from a trust annually for life plus a general power of appointment over the trust's assets. He has transferred an interest eligible for the marital deduction. The general power of appointment may be exercisable during life, at death, or at both times. In addition, the donee-spouse is entitled to receive the income annually. ◀

ADDITIONAL COMMENT

In 1978 Brad transferred property to a trust, income to be distributed annually to his wife Sonia until her death, with a general power of appointment in Sonia over the remainder. The general power of appointment in Sonia was necessary so the transfer would be eligible for the gift tax marital deduction.

The rationale behind the nondeductible terminable interest rule is that a donor should obtain a marital deduction only if an interest that will have transfer tax significance to the donee-spouse is conveyed. In other words, when a spouse makes a lifetime gift of a property that was received as a result of an interspousal transfer, a transfer subject to the gift tax occurs. If the donee-spouse retains such property until death, the item is included in the donee-spouse's gross estate.

[37] Sec. 2523(b).

[38] Ibid.

ADDITIONAL COMMENT

Assume the same facts as in the previous annotation except that Brad has been married twice. He had two children by his first wife and three children with Sonia. Brad could not be sure his first two children would ever receive anything from the trust because Sonia could exercise her general power of appointment in favor of her three children (or someone else). If this transfer were to occur after the enactment of the QTIP provisions, Brad would not have to give Sonia a general power of appointment over the trust corpus; the trust instrument could specify that the remainder, on Sonia's death, would go equally to all five children. Brad could thus control the ultimate disposition of the remainder and still receive a marital deduction.

QTIP PROVISIONS. Commencing in 1982, a major change was made to the nondeductible terminable interest rule. Under the new rule, transfers of qualified terminable interest property are eligible for the marital deduction.[39] Such transfers are commonly referred to as *QTIP transfers*. **Qualified terminable interest property** is property

- That is transferred by the donor-spouse,
- In which the donee has a "qualifying income interest for life," and
- For which a special election has been made.

A spouse has the necessary "qualifying income interest for life" if

- The spouse is entitled to all of the income from the property annually or more often and
- No person has a power to appoint any part of the property to any person other than the donee-spouse unless the power cannot be exercised while the spouse is alive.

The QTIP rule enhances the attractiveness of making transfers to one's spouse. A donor can now receive a marital deduction—and thereby make a nontaxable transfer—without having to grant the spouse full control over the gifted property. The QTIP rule is especially attractive for a donor who wants to ensure that the children by a previous marriage will receive the property upon the donee-spouse's death.

The donor does not have to claim a marital deduction even though the transfer otherwise qualifies as a QTIP transfer. Claiming the deduction on such transfers is elective.[40] If the donor elects to claim a marital deduction, the donee-spouse must include the QTIP trust property in his or her estate at its value as of the donee-spouse's date of death. Thus, as with other transfers qualifying for the marital deduction, the interspousal transfer is tax-free, and the taxable event is postponed until the donee-spouse transfers the property.

EXAMPLE C12-37 ▶ Jo transfers $1 million of property in trust with a bank acting as trustee. All of the trust income is payable to Jo's husband, Ed, quarterly for the rest of his life. Ed is age 64 at the time of the transfer. Upon Ed's death, the property will pass to Jo's nieces. This gift is eligible for a marital deduction. If Jo elects to claim the marital deduction, she will receive a $990,000 ($1,000,000 − $10,000) marital deduction. The deduction is limited to the amount of the includible gift. ◀

Note that Jo's marital deduction in the preceding example is for $990,000 and not for the value of Ed's life estate. If Jo elects to claim the marital deduction, Ed's gross estate will include the value of the entire trust. The trust is valued as of the date of Ed's death. The QTIP provision permits Jo to receive a marital deduction while still being able to specify who will receive the property upon her husband's death.

A summary of the eligibility of a transfer for the marital deduction and the amount of the marital deduction that can be claimed is presented in Topic Review C12-2.

CHARITABLE CONTRIBUTION DEDUCTION

Charitable contributions in excess of $10,000 per recipient organization must be reported on a gift tax return. Such transfers will not create taxable gifts, however, if they meet the requirements for a charitable contribution deduction. Claiming an income tax deduction for a charitable contribution does not preclude the donor from also obtaining a gift tax deduction. In contrast with the income tax provisions, there is no percentage

[39] Sec. 2523(f).

[40] The donor might decide not to claim the marital deduction if the donee-spouse has substantial assets already or a short life expectancy, especially if the gifted property's value is expected to appreciate at a high annual rate.

Topic Review C12-2

Eligibility for and Amount of the Marital Deduction

Examples of Transfers Eligible for the Marital Deduction

Property transferred to spouse as sole owner

Property transferred in trust with all of the income payable to the spouse for life and over which the donee-spouse has a general power of appointment

Property transferred in trust with all of the income payable to the spouse for life and for which the donor-spouse named the remainderman—marital deduction available if elected under QTIP rule

Examples of Transfers Ineligible for the Marital Deduction

Property transferred in trust with the income payable to the spouse for life, but in the trustee's discretion, and for which the donor-spouse named the remainderman

Property transferred in trust with all of the income payable to the spouse for a specified number of years and for which the donor-spouse named the remainderman

Amount of the Marital Deduction

The amount of the transfer minus the portion eligible for the annual exclusion

limitation for the gift tax charitable contribution deduction. The only ceiling on the deduction is imposed by Sec. 2524, which limits the deduction to the amount of the gift that is in excess of the excluded portion.

EXAMPLE C12-38 ▶ Julio gives stock valued at $75,000 to State University. Julio receives a $10,000 annual exclusion and a $65,000 charitable contribution deduction when computing his taxable gifts. ◀

ADDITIONAL COMMENT

A charitably minded taxpayer could avoid the gift (and the estate) tax entirely by giving all of his or her property to a qualified charitable organization. Actually, the taxpayer could give (or will) up to $600,000 to noncharitable donees as long as the balance of his or her property was given (or willed) to charity and still pay no gift (or estate) tax.

TRANSFERS ELIGIBLE FOR THE DEDUCTION. To be deductible, the gift must be made to a charitable organization. The rules defining charitable organizations are quite similar for income, gift, and estate tax purposes.[41] According to Sec. 2522, a gift tax deduction is available for contributions to the following:

- The United States or any subordinate level of government within the United States as long as the transfer is solely for public purposes
- A corporation, trust fund, etc., that is organized exclusively for religious, charitable, scientific, literary, or educational purposes, or to foster amateur sports competition, including the encouragement of art and the prevention of cruelty to children or animals
- A fraternal society or similar organization operating under the lodge system if the gifts are to be used in the United States only for religious, charitable, scientific, literary, or educational purposes
- A war veterans' post or organization organized in the United States or one of its possessions if no part of their net earnings accrues to the benefit of private shareholders or individuals

SPLIT-INTEREST TRANSFERS. Specialized rules apply when a donor makes a transfer for both private (i.e., an individual) and public (i.e., a charitable organization)

[41] In contrast to the income tax rules, a charitable contribution deduction is available under the gift tax rules for transfers made to foreign charitable organizations. No deduction is available, however, for gifts made to foreign governments.

purposes. Such arrangements are known as **split-interest transfers.** An example of a split-interest transfer is the gift of a residence to one's sister for life with the remainder interest to a college or university. If a donor gives a charitable organization a remainder interest, the charitable contribution deduction is forfeited unless the remainder interest is in either a personal residence (not necessarily the donor's principal residence), a farm, a charitable remainder annuity trust or unitrust, or a pooled income fund.[42] A split-interest gift of a present interest that is made to a charity qualifies for a charitable contribution deduction only if the charity receives a guaranteed annuity interest or a unitrust interest.

EXAMPLE C12-39 ▶ Al transfers $800,000 of property to a charitable remainder annuity trust. He reserves an annuity of $56,000 per year for his remaining life and specifies that upon his death the trust property will pass to the American Red Cross. In the same year, Al gives a museum a remainder interest in his antique furniture collection and reserves a life estate for himself.

Each of these is a split-interest transfer. Unfortunately for the donor, only the remainder interest in the charitable remainder annuity trust is eligible for a charitable contribution deduction. Consequently, Al makes a taxable gift in an amount equal to the value of the remainder interest in the antique furniture. Even though the furniture is not an income-producing property, the value of the remainder interest is determined from the actuarial tables found in Appendix H.

Assume that Al was age 60 at the time of the gifts and that the appropriate interest rate was 10%. What is the amount of Al's charitable contribution deduction?

Answer: The portion of the annuity trust retained by Al is $433,026 {[(1.0 − 0.226740) ÷ 0.10] × $56,000}. The charitable deduction on the gift tax return is $366,974 ($800,000 − $433,026). The same amount is also allowable as a charitable contribution deduction on Al's income tax return for that year. ◀

SELF-STUDY QUESTION

In Example C12-39, does Al receive an annual exclusion for the gift of the furniture?

ANSWER

No. The remainder interest is a future interest.

THE GIFT-SPLITTING ELECTION

OBJECTIVE 6

Apply the gift-splitting rules

The gift-splitting provisions of Sec. 2513 allow spouses to treat a gift that is actually made by one of them to a third party as if each spouse had made one-half of the gift. This election offers several advantages, as follows:

- If only one spouse makes a gift to a particular donee, the election enables $20,000 (instead of $10,000) to be given to the donee before a taxable gift arises.
- If per-donee transfers exceed $20,000 and taxable gifts occur, the election may lower the applicable marginal gift tax rate.
- Each spouse's unified credit may be used to reduce the gift tax payable.

To take advantage of the gift-splitting election, the spouses must meet certain requirements at the time of the transfer:

- The spouses must be U.S. citizens or residents.
- At the time of the gift(s) for which the election is made, the donor-spouse must be married to the person who consents to gift splitting. In addition, the donor-spouse must not remarry before the end of the year.

The gift-splitting election is effective for all transfers to third parties made during the portion of the year that the spouses were married to each other.

If a spouse living in a community property state makes a gift of separate property (e.g., an asset received by inheritance), gift splitting may be desired. If this is the case, the

KEY POINT

A wife makes a gift of $40,000 to a child in March and a gift of $60,000 to another child in November of the same year. If the election is made, it will apply to both gifts because the election to gift split applies to all gifts made during the year. If her husband so elects, he will report one-half of each gift on his own gift tax return.

[42] In a **charitable remainder annuity trust**, an individual receives trust distributions for a certain time period or for life. The annual distributions are a uniform percentage (5% or higher) of the value of the trust property, valued on the date of the transfer. For a **charitable remainder unitrust**, the distributions are similar, except that they are a uniform percentage (5% or higher) of the value of the trust property, revalued at least annually. Thus, the annual distributions from a unitrust, but not an annuity trust, vary from one year to the next. A **pooled income fund** is similar in concept to a mutual fund. The various individual beneficiaries receive annual distributions of their proportionate shares of the fund's total income.

election automatically extends to gifts of community property even though splitting each spouse's gifts of community property has no impact on the amount of the taxable gifts.

Note that gift splitting is an all-or-nothing proposition. Spouses electing it for one gift must elect it for all gifts to third parties for that year. Each year's election stands alone, however, and is not binding on future years.[43] The procedural aspects of the gift-splitting election are discussed in the Compliance and Procedural Considerations section of this chapter.

EXAMPLE C12-40 ▶ Eli marries Joy on April 1 of the current year. They are still married to each other at the end of the year. In March, Eli gave Amy $60,000. In July, Eli gave Barb $48,000 and Joy gave Claire $20,000. If the couple elects gift splitting, the election is effective only for the July gifts. Each spouse is treated as giving $24,000 and $10,000 to Barb and Claire, respectively. Because they may not elect gift splitting for the gift Eli makes before their marriage, Eli is treated as giving $60,000—the amount he actually transfers—to Amy. Under gift splitting, both Eli and Joy exclude $10,000 of gifts to both Barb and Claire, or a total of $40,000. Eli also excludes $10,000 of his gift to Amy. ◀

ADDITIONAL COMMENT

The gift-splitting election is a year-by-year election. For example, a husband and wife could elect to gift split in 1992, 1994, and 1996, but elect not to gift split in 1993, 1995, and 1997.

Upon the death of the actual donor or the spouse who consented to gift splitting, the amount of such decedent's adjusted taxable gifts must be included in the estate tax base. By electing gift splitting, a couple can reduce the amount of the taxable gifts the donor-decedent is deemed to have made. Under gift splitting, the adjusted taxable gifts include only the portions of the gifts that are taxable on the gift tax returns filed by the donor-decedent. Of course, a portion is also reported by the nondonor-spouse's estate.

STOP & THINK

Question: One spouse (Bob) has made taxable gifts of $4,000,000, and the other spouse (Betty) has not made any taxable gifts. Betty inherited a large fortune last year and is contemplating making $500,000 in gifts this year to each of her two children. Bob does not anticipate making any taxable gifts this year. Should they elect gift splitting for Betty's gifts?

Solution: They should not necessarily elect gift splitting because the only advantage of the election will be that the aggregate annual exclusions will be $40,000 instead of $20,000. An adverse effect will be that Bob, who has exhausted his unified credit and is in a higher marginal tax bracket, will be the deemed donor of $480,000 [(0.50 × $1,000,000) − $20,000] of taxable gifts.

COMPUTATION OF THE GIFT TAX LIABILITY

OBJECTIVE 7

Calculate the gift tax liability

EFFECT OF PREVIOUS TAXABLE GIFTS

The gift tax computation involves a cumulative process. All of the donor's previous taxable gifts (i.e., those made in 1932 or later years) plus the donor's taxable gifts for the current year affect the marginal tax rate at which current gifts are taxed. Thus, two donors making the same taxable gifts in the current period may incur very different gift tax liabilities because one may have made substantially larger taxable gifts in earlier

[43] If the nondonor-spouse has made substantial taxable gifts relative to those made by the donor-spouse, the gift tax liability for the period in question may be lower if the spouses do not elect gift splitting because the nondonor-spouse may have no unified credit left and may have reached the highest marginal transfer tax rate.

periods than the other donor. The process outlined below must be used to compute the gross tax levied on the current period's taxable gifts.

1. Determine the gift tax liability (at current rates) on the donor's cumulative taxable gifts (taxable gifts of current period plus aggregate taxable gifts of previous periods).
2. Determine the gift tax liability (at current rates) on the donor's cumulative taxable gifts made through the end of the preceding period.
3. Subtract the gift tax determined in Step 2 from that in Step 1. The difference equals the gross gift tax on the current period's taxable gifts.

This calculation process is needed in order to tax the gifts on a progressive basis over the donor's lifetime.

Note that although the gift tax rates have varied over the years, the current rate schedules are used in the calculation. This rule holds even when some or all of the gifts are made when different rates are in effect. This process ensures that the taxable gifts of the current period are taxed at the appropriate rate, given the donor's earlier gift history.

EXAMPLE C12-41 ▶ In 1975, Tony makes $2 million in taxable gifts. These gifts are the first Tony ever made. The tax imposed under the 1975 rate schedule is $564,900. Tony's next taxable gifts are made in 1997. The taxable amount of these gifts is $400,000. The tax on Tony's 1997 taxable gifts is calculated as follows:

Tax at current rates on $2,400,000 of cumulative taxable gifts	$976,800
Minus: Tax at current rates on $2,000,000 of prior period taxable gifts	(780,800)
Tax on $400,000 of taxable gifts made in the current period	$196,000 ◀

This cumulative process results in the $400,000 gift in Example C12-41 being taxed at a 49% rate, the marginal gift tax rate applicable to taxable transfers ranging between $2,000,000 and $2,500,000. If the gift tax computations were not cumulative, the tax on the $400,000 of gifts would be determined by using the lowest marginal rates and would have been only $121,800. Because the tax on taxable transfers made in previous periods is determined by reference to the current rate schedule, Tony's 1975 gift tax liability, incurred when the gift tax rates were lower, is not relevant to the determination of his current gift tax. As discussed below, the unified credit will reduce the tax liability.

UNIFIED CREDIT AVAILABLE

Congress enacted a unified credit for both gift and estate tax purposes commencing in 1977. The unified credit reduces the amount of the gross gift tax that is owed on current period gifts. The amount of the credit increased over the years (see inside back cover) until it reached a maximum of $192,800 for 1987 and later years. Donors who have already made taxable gifts in the post-1976 period have already used some of their credit. In such situations, the amount of the credit available for the current year is reduced by the aggregate amount allowable as a credit in all preceding years. If after 1987 the donor's cumulative taxable transfers exceed $10,000,000, the benefit of the unified credit begins to be phased out.

EXAMPLE C12-42 ▶ Hu makes her first taxable gift in 1978. The taxable amount of the 1978 gift is $100,000, which results in a gross gift tax of $23,800. Hu claims $23,800 (of the $34,000 credit then available) on her 1978 return to reduce her net gift tax liability to zero. Hu makes her next taxable gift in 1984. The taxable amount of the gift is $400,000. The tax on the $400,000 gift equals (1) the tax on $500,000 of total gifts (at 1984 gift tax rates) of $155,800 minus (2) the tax on $100,000 of previous gifts (at 1984 gift tax rates) of $23,800, or $132,000. The credit amount for 1984 is $96,300. Hu's gift tax is reduced by a credit of only $72,500 ($96,300 − $23,800), because $23,800 was allowable as a credit against her 1978 gift tax liability. If Hu is planning to make additional taxable gifts, $96,500 [$192,800 −($23,800 + $72,500)] of unified credit will be available to reduce the gift tax liability in the future. ◀

STOP & THINK

Question: You are reviewing a gift tax return that a co-worker prepared. The tax return reflects current taxable gifts of $250,000 and taxable gifts made in 1992 in the amount of $625,000. You note that on the return your colleague (a new staff member) claimed a unified credit of $70,800 and, thus, reported zero gift tax payable. What should you discuss with your colleague?

Solution: You should explain that the unified credit of $192,800 (which is equal to the tax on the first $600,000 of taxable gifts) is not an annual credit maximum, but rather is the credit available during a donor's lifetime. Because in 1992 the donor made $625,000 of taxable gifts, he exhausted his unified credit. In addition, you should explain the cumulative nature of the gift tax calculations. $70,800 is the tax calculated on the first $250,000 of taxable gifts. If the colleague claimed a $70,800 unified credit and showed zero tax payable, he did not calculate the tax on the current taxable gift of $250,000 by performing the cumulative calculations that take into effect the $625,000 of earlier taxable gifts.

COMPREHENSIVE ILLUSTRATION

The following comprehensive illustration demonstrates the computation of one donor's gift tax liability for the situation where the donors elect gift splitting. Computation of one of the spouse's gift tax liability is shown.

BACKGROUND DATA

Hugh and Wilma Brown are married to each other throughout 1996. Hugh made no taxable gifts in earlier periods. Wilma's previous taxable gifts are $300,000 in 1975 and $200,000 in 1978. In 1996 Wilma makes the following gratuitous transfers:

- $80,000 in cash to son Billy
- $24,000 in jewelry to daughter Betsy
- $30,000 in medical expense payments to Downtown Infirmary for medical care of grandson Tim
- Remainder interest in vacation cabin to friend Ruth Cain. Wilma (age 60) retains a life estate. The vacation cabin is valued at $100,000.
- $600,000 of stocks to a bank in trust with all of the income payable semiannually to husband Hugh (age 62) for life and remainder payable at Hugh's death to Jeff Bass, Wilma's son by an earlier marriage, or Jeff's estate. Wilma wants to elect the marital deduction.

In 1996 Hugh's only gifts were

- $80,000 of stock to State University
- $600,000 of land to daughter Betsy

Assume the applicable interest rate for valuing life estates and remainders is 10%.

CALCULATION OF TAX LIABILITY

The medical expense payments are exempt from the gift tax under Sec. 2503(e). The vacation cabin is valued at $100,000, and the remainder interest therein at $22,674 (0.226740 ×$100,000) (see Table S, age 60 in Appendix H) for gift tax purposes. The stock is transferred to a QTIP trust, and election of the marital deduction treats the entire interest (not just the life estate) as having been given to Hugh Brown.

Table C12-1 shows the computation of Wilma's gift tax liability for 1996. These same facts are used for the sample United States Gift Tax Return, Form 709, in Appendix B.

BASIS CONSIDERATIONS FOR A LIFETIME GIVING PLAN

OBJECTIVE 8

Understand how basis affects the overall tax consequences

Prospective donors should consider the tax-saving features of making a series of lifetime gifts (discussed in the Tax Planning Considerations section of this chapter). Lifetime

▼ **TABLE C12-1**

Comprehensive Gift Tax Illustration

Wilma's actual 1996 gifts:			
Billy, cash			$ 80,000
Betsy, jewelry			24,000
Ruth, remainder interest in vacation cabin (future interest)			22,674
Husband Hugh and son Jeff, transfer to QTIP trust			600,000
Total gifts made by Wilma			$726,674
Minus:	One-half of Wilma's gifts made to third parties that are deemed made by Hugh [0.50 × ($726,674 − $600,000)]		(63,337)
Plus:	One-half of Hugh's gifts made to third parties (State University and Betsy) that are deemed made by Wilma [0.50 × ($600,000 + $80,000)]		340,000
Minus:	Annual exclusions for gifts of present interests ($10,000 each for gifts made to Billy, Betsy, Hugh, and State University)		(40,000)
Minus:	Marital deduction ($600,000 − $10,000 exclusion)		(590,000)
Minus:	Charitable contribution deduction ($40,000 − $10,000 exclusion)		(30,000)
Taxable gifts for current period			$343,337
Tax on cumulative taxable gifts of $843,337[a]			$284,701
Minus:	Tax on previous taxable gifts of $500,000 (current rate schedule)		(155,800)
Tax on taxable gifts of $343,337 for the current period			$128,901
Minus:	Unified credit:		
	Credit for 1996	$192,800	
	Minus: Credit allowable for prior periods	(34,000)[b]	(158,800)[c]
Tax payable for 1996			$ —0—

[a] $300,000 (in 1975) + $200,000 (in 1978) + $343,337 (in 1996).
[b] 0 (for 1975) + $34,000 (for 1978).
[c] Actually, for 1996 Wilma uses only $128,901 of her remaining credit. In a later year she will have a credit of $29,899 [$192,800 − ($128,901 + $34,000)] available.

giving plans can remove income from the donor's income tax return and transfer it to the donee's income tax return, where it may be taxed at a lower marginal tax rate. A series of gifts may permit property to be transferred to a donee without incurring a gift tax liability and thus enable the donor to eliminate part or all of his or her estate tax liability. These two advantages must be weighed against the unattractive basis rules (discussed below) applicable for such transfers.

SELF-STUDY QUESTION

Barkley purchased land in 1955 for $90,000. In 1974, when the FMV of the land was $300,000, he gave the land to his son Tracy. He paid gift taxes of $23,000 on the gift. What is Tracy's basis in the land? What if the gift had been made in 1984?

ANSWER

If the gift was made in 1974, Tracy's basis is $90,000 plus the $23,000 gift tax, or $113,000. Had Barkley made the gift in 1984, Tracy's basis would be $90,000 plus [($210,000/$300,000) × $23,000], or $106,100.

SELF-STUDY QUESTION

Betty gave property to Mary when its FMV was $75,000. Betty's basis in the property was $100,000, and Betty paid gift taxes of $16,000. What is Mary's basis in the gifted property?

ANSWER

Mary's basis for determining gain is $100,000; her basis for determining loss is $75,000. None of the gift taxes paid can increase the basis of the property. Had Betty instead sold the property, she could have recognized the $25,000 loss for income tax purposes and gifted Mary $75,000 in cash.

ADDITIONAL COMMENT

Phil owns investment property worth $350,000 in which his adjusted basis is $500,000. Unless there are reasons why the property should be kept in the family, Phil should sell the property and recognize an income tax loss. If he gifts the property to his child, the loss basis in the child's hands is $350,000. Thus, the income tax loss for the $150,000 decline in market value will never be taken. If he dies holding the loss property, his heirs will take the estate tax return value (FMV) as their basis, and the potential income tax loss will not be recognized.

PROPERTY RECEIVED BY GIFT

The carryover basis rules apply to property received by gift. Provided the property's FMV on the date of the gift exceeds its adjusted basis, the donee's basis in such property is the same as the donor's basis. In addition, the donee's basis may be increased by some or all of the gift tax that is paid by the donor. In the case of pre-1977 gifts, all of the gift taxes paid by the donor may be added to the donor's adjusted basis. For post-1976 transfers, however, only the portion of the gift taxes represented by the following fraction may increase the donor's adjusted basis:

$$\frac{\text{Amount of property's appreciation from acquisition date through date of gift}}{\text{FMV of property on the date of the gift}}$$

In no event, however, can the gift tax adjustment increase the donee's basis above the property's FMV on the date of the gift.[44]

If the gifted property's FMV on the date of the gift is less than the donor's adjusted basis, the basis rules are more complicated. For purposes of determining gain, the donee's basis is the same as the donor's adjusted basis. For purposes of determining loss, the donee's basis is the property's FMV on the date of the gift. If the donee sells the property for an amount between its FMV as of the date of the gift and the donor's adjusted basis, the donee recognizes no gain or loss. The property's basis cannot be increased by any gift taxes paid in circumstances where the donor's adjusted basis exceeds the property's FMV as of the date of the gift. Prospective donors should dispose of property that has declined in value by selling it instead of gifting it.

PROPERTY RECEIVED AT DEATH

In general, the basis rules that apply to property received as a result of another's death call for a step up or step down to the property's FMV as of the decedent's date of death. The recipient's basis is the same as the amount at which the property is valued on the estate tax return, which is its FMV on either the decedent's date of death or the alternate valuation date. Generally the alternate valuation date is six months after the date of death. Although these rules are generally thought of as providing for a step-up in basis, if the property has declined in value before the transferor's death, the basis is stepped-down to its date of death or alternate valuation date value.

In certain circumstances there is no step up in basis for appreciated property transferred at death.[45] This exception applies if the following two conditions are present:

- The decedent receives the appreciated property as a gift during the one-year period preceding his or her death.
- The property passes to the donor or to the donor's spouse as a result of the donee-decedent's death.

[44] See Reg. Sec. 1.1015-5(b) for a discussion of how to allocate the gift tax liability among several taxable gifts made during the period.

[45] Sec. 1014(e).

Before the enactment of the rule, a widely publicized planning technique was the transfer of appreciated property to an ill spouse who, in turn, could will the property back to the donor-spouse, who would receive the property at a stepped-up basis. The interspousal transfers by gift and at death are tax-free because of the unlimited marital deduction that is available under both the gift tax and estate tax rules. Consequently, before the change in the statute the property received a step-up in basis at no transfer tax cost.

EXAMPLE C12-43 ▶ In June 1996, Sarah makes a gift of property valued at $700,000 to Tom, her husband. Sarah's adjusted basis in the property is $120,000. Tom dies in March 1997. At this time, the property is worth $740,000. If the property passes back to Sarah under Tom's will upon Tom's death, Sarah's basis will be $120,000. However, if the property passes to someone other than Sarah at Tom's death, its basis will be stepped-up to $740,000. If Tom lives for more than one year after receiving the gift, the basis is stepped-up to its FMV as of Tom's date of death regardless of whether the property passes to Sarah or someone else. If Tom (the donee) sold the property a few months before his death, Tom's basis would be the same as Sarah's was, or $120,000. ◀

BELOW-MARKET LOANS: GIFT AND INCOME TAX CONSEQUENCES

GENERAL RULES

Section 7872 provides definitive rules concerning both the gift and income tax consequences of below-market loans. In general, it treats the lender as both making a gift to the borrower and receiving interest income. The borrower is treated as paying interest expense. Congress enacted Sec. 7872 to answer unresolved issues left by a Supreme Court case[46] that held that the transfer of the right to use money without paying sufficient interest is a transfer of property for purposes of the gift tax.

In the case of a demand loan, the lender is treated as having made a gift in each year in which the loan is outstanding.[47] The amount of the gift equals the forgone interest income for the portion of the year that the loan is outstanding. The forgone interest income is calculated by referring to the difference between the interest rate the lender charged and the federal short-term rate of Sec. 1274(d), for the period in question.[48]

For income tax purposes, the forgone interest is treated as being retransferred from the borrower to the lender on the last day of each calendar year in which the loan is outstanding. The amount of the forgone interest is the same as for gift tax purposes and is reported by the lender as income for the year in question. The borrower gets an interest expense deduction for the same amount unless one of the rules limiting the interest deduction applies (e.g., personal interest or investment interest limitations).

EXAMPLE C12-44 ▶ On July 1 Frank lends $500,000 to Susan, who signs an interest-free demand note. The loan is still outstanding on December 31. Assume that 10% is the applicable annual interest rate. Frank is deemed to have made a gift to Susan on December 31 of $25,000 (0.10 × $500,000 × 6/12). Frank must report $25,000 of interest income. Susan deducts $25,000 of interest expense provided the deduction is not otherwise limited or disallowed. ◀

DE MINIMIS RULES

Under one of the *de minimis* rules of Sec. 7872, neither the income nor the gift tax rules apply to any gift loan made directly between individuals for any day on which the

[46] *Esther C. Dickman v. CIR*, 53 AFTR 2d 84-1608, 84-1 USTC ¶9240 (USSC, 1984).
[47] Sec. 7872(a).
[48] For January 1997, the short-term federal rate, compounded semiannually, is 3.79%.

aggregate loans outstanding between the borrower and the lender are $10,000 or less. All loans are counted in determining whether the $10,000 amount has been exceeded, irrespective of their interest rate. The *de minimis* exception cannot be used to exempt any loan directly attributable to the purchase or carrying of income-producing assets.

A second *de minimis* exception potentially permits loans of $100,000 or less to receive more favorable income tax treatment. The exception is not applicable for gift tax purposes, however. This *de minimis* exception treats the amount considered retransferred to the lender as not exceeding the borrower's net investment income (as defined in Sec. 163(d)(3)) for the year. Moreover, if the borrower's net investment income for the year is $1,000 or less, such amount is treated as being zero. Thus, the lender would not have to report any interest income.

The provisions just discussed are inapplicable when the interest arrangements for any loan have the avoidance of any federal tax as one of their principal purposes. Should such a purpose be present, the general income tax rules of Sec. 7872 apply to such loans. The *de minimis* rules do not apply to any day on which the total outstanding loans between the borrower and the lender exceed $100,000. In determining whether the taxpayer meets the $100,000 or $10,000 loan limitations, a husband and wife are treated as one person.

EXAMPLE C12-45 ▶ On August 1 Mike lends $100,000 to Don. No other loans are outstanding between the parties. Avoidance of federal taxes is not a principal purpose of the loan. Don signs a demand note providing for the payment of simple interest at a 6% annual rate. Assume 10% is the applicable interest rate. The loan is still outstanding on December 31. Mike is treated as having made a gift to Don on December 31 in the amount of $1,667 [$100,000 × (0.10 − 0.06) × 5/12]. This gift is not taxable and need not be reported unless Mike's aggregate gifts to Don in the current year exceed the $10,000 annual exclusion.

For income tax purposes, three alternative reporting treatments are available depending on Don's net investment income. If Don's net investment income for the year exceeds $1,667, Mike reports both the $1,667 of imputed interest income under Sec. 7872 and the interest actually received. Subject to rules that may disallow some or all of the interest expense deduction, Don deducts both the $1,667 interest expense under Sec. 7872 and the interest expense he actually paid. If Don's net investment income is between $1,001 and $1,667, each party reports interest income or expense under Sec. 7872 equal to Don's net investment income. Mike and Don report no interest income or expense under Sec. 7872 if Don's net investment income is $1,000 or less. ◀

TAX PLANNING CONSIDERATIONS

Although the tax law's bias in favor of lifetime transfers was reduced by the 1976 tax law changes that introduced the unification concept, lifetime gifts still provide many more advantages than disadvantages. Many factors, including the expected appreciation rate, affect the decision of whether to make gifts. The optimal result is not always clear. The pros and cons of lifetime gifts from an estate planning perspective are discussed below.

TAX-SAVING FEATURES OF *INTER VIVOS* GIFTS

USE OF ANNUAL EXCLUSION. The annual exclusion offers the opportunity for donors who start making gifts to several donees per year relatively early in their lifetime to keep substantial amounts of property off the transfer tax rolls. The tax-free amount can be doubled if a husband and wife use the gift-splitting election.

ADDITIONAL COMMENT

Laura, who is always in the 28% marginal income tax bracket, makes a gift of $10,000 to each of her six grandchildren each year for eight years. At the inception of the gift program, all of the grandchildren are under age 6. The gift monies are invested at 10%. The grandchildren have no income during the eight-year period except the investment return on the gift monies. Assume Laura's estate will be taxed at a 39% marginal estate tax rate and the parents of the grandchildren are always in the 28% marginal income tax bracket. Given these facts, the after-tax amount retained by the family unit through Laura's eight-year gift program exceeds by $271,937 the amount the family unit would retain in the absence of the gift program.

There is no estate tax counterpart to the annual gift tax exclusion. Consequently, a terminally ill person whose will includes bequests of approximately $10,000 to each of several individuals would realize substantial transfer tax savings if gifts—instead of bequests—were made to these individuals.

REMOVAL OF POST-GIFT APPRECIATION FROM TAX BASE. Another very important advantage of lifetime gifts is that their value is frozen at their date-of-gift value. That is, any post-gift appreciation escapes the transfer tax rolls. Consequently, transfer tax savings are maximized if the donor gives away the assets that appreciate the most.

REMOVAL OF GIFT TAX AMOUNT FROM TRANSFER TAX BASE. With one exception, gift taxes paid by the donor are removed from the transfer tax base. The lone exception applies to gift taxes paid on gifts the donor makes within three years of dying. Under the gross-up rule (discussed in Chapter C13), the donor's gross estate includes gift taxes paid on gifts made within three years of the donor's death.

INCOME SHIFTING. Originally, one of the most favorable consequences of lifetime gifts was income shifting, but the compression of the income tax rate schedules beginning in 1987 has lessened these benefits. The income produced by the gifted property is taxed to the donee, who may have a lower marginal income tax rate, and if income tax savings do arise, they accrue each year during the post-gift period. Thus, the income tax savings can be quite sizable over a span of several years.

ADDITIONAL COMMENT

If a terminally ill spouse, Sam, has no property, an election to gift split can effectively use up Sam's unified credit. Another method of using Sam's unified credit is to give Sam property in trust that meets the following requirements: income from the trust must go to Sam for life, remainder is subject to a general power of appointment in Sam, and if the general power of appointment is not exercised during Sam's lifetime (or by will on Sam's death), the remainder must pass to specified beneficiaries other than the donor.

GIFT IN CONTEMPLATION OF DONEE-SPOUSE'S DEATH. At times, a terminally ill spouse may have very few assets. If such a spouse died, a sizable portion of his or her unified credit would be wasted because the decedent's estate would be well below the amount of the exemption equivalent provided by the unified credit. If the healthier spouse is relatively wealthy, he or she could make a gift to the ill spouse to create an estate in an amount equal to the estate tax exemption equivalent. Because of the unlimited marital deduction, the gift would be tax-free. Upon the death of the donee-spouse, no estate tax would be payable because the estate tax liability would not exceed the unified credit. The donee-spouse should not transfer his or her property back to the donor-spouse at death. Otherwise, the donee-spouse's unified credit would be wasted, and the original tax planning would be negated. Moreover, the returned property would be included in the surviving spouse's estate.

A gift of appreciated property in contemplation of the donee-spouse's death provides an additional advantage. If the property does not pass back to the donor-spouse, its basis is increased to its value on the donee's date of death. In the event the property is willed to the donor-spouse, a step-up in basis still occurs if the date of the gift precedes the donee-spouse's date of death by more than one year.

KEY POINT

A charitable gift before death removes the property from the estate of the donor *and* provides an income tax deduction. A charitable gift made at death reduces the estate tax liability but does not provide an income tax deduction to the decedent.

LESSENING STATE TRANSFER TAX COSTS. All states levy a death tax, but only six states impose a gift tax.[49] Therefore, in most states the tax cost of lifetime transfers is lower than that for transfers at death.

INCOME TAX SAVINGS FROM CHARITABLE GIFTS. Some individuals are inclined to dispose of a portion of their property by transferring it to charitable organizations. Assuming the disposition is of a type eligible for a charitable contribution deduction, the transfer tax implications are the same—no taxable transfer—irrespective

[49] The six states that impose a gift tax are Connecticut, Delaware, Louisiana, New York, North Carolina, and Tennessee.

of whether the transfer occurs *inter vivos* or at death. From an income tax standpoint, however, a lifetime transfer is preferable because only lifetime transfers produce an income tax deduction for charitable contributions.

NEGATIVE ASPECTS OF GIFTS

LOSS OF STEP-UP IN BASIS. People deliberating about whether to make gifts or which properties to give should keep in mind that the donee receives no step-up in basis for property acquired by gift. From a practical standpoint, sacrifice of the step-up in basis is insignificant if the donee does not plan to sell the property or if the property is not of a character subject to an allowance for depreciation.

PREPAYMENT OF ESTATE TAX. A donor who makes taxable gifts in an amount in excess of the exemption equivalent must pay a gift tax. Upon such a donor's death, the taxable gift is included in his or her estate tax base as an adjusted taxable gift. Because the gift tax paid during the donor's lifetime reduces the donor's estate tax liability, in a sense, the donor's payment of the gift tax results in prepayment of a portion of the estate tax.

COMPLIANCE AND PROCEDURAL CONSIDERATIONS

OBJECTIVE 9

Recognize the filing requirements for gift tax returns

FILING REQUIREMENTS

Section 6019 specifies the circumstances in which a gift tax return should be filed. In general, the donor will file Form 709 (United States Gift Tax Return). In certain circumstances, however, the donor may file a simpler return, Form 709A (United States Short Form Gift Tax Return). A completed Form 709 appears in Appendix B. The facts used in the preparation of the completed Form 709 are the same as the facts of the comprehensive illustration.

As is the case for income tax returns, a return is often required even though the taxable amount and the tax payable are both zero. A donor must file a gift tax return for any calendar year in which gifts are made other than

- Gifts to one's spouse that qualify for the marital deduction
- Gifts that are fully shielded from taxation because they fall within the annual exclusion amount or are for excludable educational or medical expenses

However, if the gift to the spouse is of qualified terminable interest property (QTIP), the gift must be reported on the gift tax return. The marital deduction is not available for these transfers unless the donor makes the necessary election, which is done by claiming a marital deduction on the gift tax return.

United States persons who receive aggregate amounts in excess of $10,000 a year that they treat as gifts or bequests must report such amounts as prescribed in the Regulations. The $10,000 amount is to be indexed for inflation.[50]

DUE DATE

All gift tax returns must be filed on a calendar-year basis. Under the general rule, gift tax returns are due no later than April 15 following the close of the year of the gift.[51] An extension of time granted for filing an individual income tax return is deemed to

[50] Sec. 6039F.

[51] Sec. 6075(b).

automatically extend the filing date for the individual's gift tax return for that year. At present, such extensions are until August 15.

KEY POINT

Normally a gift tax return is due April 15 of the following year. However, if a donor dies during the year, the gift tax return is due no later than the due date of the donor's estate tax return (generally nine months after the date of death).

If the donor dies early in the year in which a gift is made, the due date for the donor's final gift tax return may be earlier than April 15. Because information concerning the decedent's taxable gifts is necessary in order to complete the estate tax return, the gift tax return for the year of death is due no later than the due date (including extensions) for the donor's estate tax return.[52] Estate tax returns are due nine months after the date of death.

Receipt of an extension for filing a gift tax return does not postpone the due date for payment of the tax. Interest is imposed on any gift tax that is not paid by April 15. Unlike with the income tax, estimated payments of gift taxes throughout the reporting period are not required.

GIFT-SPLITTING ELECTION

In order for taxable gifts to be computed under the gift-splitting technique, both spouses must indicate their consent to gift splitting in one of the following ways:[53]

- Each spouse signifies his or her consent on the other spouse's gift tax return.
- Each spouse signifies his or her consent on his or her own gift tax return.
- Both spouses signify their consent on one of the gift tax returns.

The Regulations state that the first approach listed above is the preferred manner for designating consent.

SHORT-FORM GIFT TAX RETURN

A gift tax return is necessary in order to elect gift splitting, even if no gift tax is due. Thus, if one spouse makes a gift to a third party of an amount between $10,001 and $20,000, the spouse must still file a gift tax return. Spouses may file a simpler gift tax form, Form 709A (United States Short Form Gift Tax Return), if after gift splitting their gifts are nontaxable and they made no terminable interest gifts to the other spouse. This form cannot be filed, however, if the donor gives something other than tangible personal property, cash, or stocks and bonds listed on an exchange.

LIABILITY FOR TAX

KEY POINT

Similarly to a husband and wife filing a joint income tax return, if gift splitting is elected, the husband and wife have joint and several liability for the entire gift tax liability regardless of who made the actual gifts.

The gift tax is to be paid by the donor,[54] and if the spouses consent to gift splitting, the entire gift tax liability is a joint and several liability of the spouses.[55] Thus, if spouses do not pay the tax voluntarily, the IRS may attempt to collect whatever amount it deems appropriate from either spouse, irrespective of the size of the gift that spouse actually made.

In the rare event that the donor does not pay the gift tax, the donee becomes personally liable for the gift tax.[56] However, a donee's liability is limited to the value of the gift.

DETERMINATION OF VALUE

One of the most difficult problems encountered by donors and their tax advisors is the determination of the FMV of the gifted property. This task is especially difficult if the gifted property is stock in a closely held business, an oil and gas property, or land in an area where few sales occur.

---

[52] The decedent's post-1976 taxable gifts affect the size of his or her estate tax base, as discussed in the next chapter.

[53] Reg. Sec. 25.2513-2(a)(1).

[54] Sec. 2502(c).

[55] Sec. 2513(d).

[56] Reg. Sec. 301.6324-1.

ETHICAL POINT

A CPA who advises a client about the tax consequences of making a gift also has a responsibility to make sure that the property is correctly valued. Otherwise, if the valuation claimed is too low, a penalty can be levied on the donor. For example, a gift of noncash property (e.g., land) may require that an appraisal be obtained. Failure to obtain an appraisal, or failure to investigate an appraisal that seems too low, may result in an undervaluation of the gift property, which may lead to additional gift taxes, interest, and penalties being imposed.

If the transfer involves a sale, the IRS can argue that the asset's value exceeds its sales price and, thus, there is a gift to the extent of the bargain element. This problem is especially common with sales to family members. In situations where the donor is giving a property whose value is not readily determinable, it is advisable for the donor to have the property appraised before filing the gift tax return.

PENALTY FOR UNDERVALUATION. Penalties can apply for undervaluations of properties for gift and estate tax purposes. Section 6662 imposes a penalty, at one of two rates, on underpayments of gift or estate taxes resulting from a valuation understatement. The amount on which the penalty is imposed is the underpayment of the transfer tax attributable to the valuation understatement.

No penalty applies if the valuation shown on the return exceeds 50% of the amount determined during an audit or court trial to be the correct value. If the value reported on the return is 50% or less of the correct value, the penalty rate is as shown below.

Ratio of Value Per Return to Correct Value	*Penalty Rate*
More than 25% but 50% or less	20%
25% or less	40%

Section 6662(g)(2) exempts a taxpayer from paying the penalty if the underpayment is less than $5,000. In addition, the penalty will not be levied if the taxpayer shows good faith and a reasonable cause for the valuation claimed.

EXAMPLE C12-46 ▶

Donna has already used her available unified credit. She gives land to her son and reports its value at $400,000 on her gift tax return. Donna's return is audited, and she agrees that $900,000 was the correct value of the property. Because the value stated on the return is only 44.44% [($400,000 ÷ $900,000) × 100] of the correct value, a 20% penalty is levied on the underpayment attributable to the valuation understatement. If Donna is in the 55% marginal gift tax bracket, the gift tax underpayment is $275,000 [0.55 × ($900,000 − $400,000)]. Thus, the penalty is $55,000 (0.20 × $275,000) in the absence of a demonstration of reasonable cause and good faith. ◀

STATUTE OF LIMITATIONS

ADDITIONAL COMMENT

Even if a taxpayer questions whether a taxable gift has been made, it is probably a good idea to file a gift tax return. The filing of the return causes the statute of limitations to start and limits the amount of time during which the IRS may question the valuation of the gift. However, if the donor did not pay any gift tax, the IRS can argue for adjusting the value of the gift for purposes of arriving at the donor's cumulative taxable gifts when the donor later makes a substantial gift.

In general, the statute of limitations for gift tax purposes is three years after the later of the date the return was filed and the return's due date.[57] The statute of limitations is extended from three to six years if the donor omits from the gift tax return gifts whose value in total is more than 25% of the gifts reported on the return. If the donor files no return because, for example, he or she is unaware that he or she made any gifts, the tax may be assessed at any time.

The cumulative nature of the gift tax causes the taxable gifts of earlier years to affect the gift tax owed in subsequent periods. Once the statute of limitations has expired, the IRS cannot argue that taxable gifts of prior periods were undervalued (and thus that the current period's gifts should be taxed at a higher rate than that used by the donor) as long as a gift tax was paid on the earlier gifts. In such circumstances, for purposes of the cumulative computations of the gift tax, the value of a gift made in the prior period is "the value of such gift which was used in computing the tax for the last preceding calendar period for which a tax was assessed or paid."[58]

Notice the language "or paid" in the preceding quotation. Because of the unified credit, many donors do not owe any gift tax, even though they make taxable gifts. Although the IRS cannot collect additional tax on such gifts after the expiration of the

[57] Sec. 6501.

[58] Sec. 2504(c).

statute of limitations, it can increase the value of such gifts for purposes of calculating the cumulative taxable gifts and the tax thereon. As a result, the marginal tax rate applicable to the gifts of the current period may be increased.[59]

EXAMPLE C12-47 ▶ Andy files a gift tax return for 1990, reporting taxable gifts of $250,000. The unified credit reduces Andy's gift tax payable to zero. In 1998, Andy files a gift tax return to report gifts made in 1997. The IRS examines Andy's 1997 return, and in the process reviews the values reported on Andy's 1990 return. The IRS may not collect any additional tax with respect to the 1990 gifts. Because no tax was paid on such gifts, however, the IRS can contend that, for purposes of calculating the tax owed on the 1997 taxable gifts, the 1990 taxable gifts exceed $250,000. ◀

PROBLEM MATERIALS

DISCUSSION QUESTIONS

C12-1 Describe two ways in which the transfer tax (estate and gift tax) system is a unified system.

C12-2 What was the Congressional intent for enacting the gift-splitting provisions?

C12-3 Determine whether the following statement is true or false: Every donor who makes a taxable gift incurs a gift tax liability. Explain your answer.

C12-4 Under what circumstances must the unified credit that is usually available be reduced (by a maximum amount of $6,000) even though the donor has never claimed any unified credit?

C12-5 Is a grandfather's direct payment of his grandchild's college tuition treated differently for gift tax purposes than his direct payment of a neighbor's medical expenses? Explain.

C12-6 Steve is considering the following actions. Explain to him which actions will constitute gifts for gift tax purposes.

a. Transferring all of his ownership rights in a life insurance policy to another person
b. Depositing funds into a joint bank account in the names of Steve and another party (who deposits nothing)
c. Paying for land and having it titled in the names of Steve and his son as joint tenants with right of survivorship
d. Paying a hospital for the medical expenses of a neighbor
e. Making a $1,000,000 demand loan to an adult child and charging no interest

C12-7 Dick wants to transfer property with a $400,000 FMV to an irrevocable trust with a bank as the trustee. Dick will name his distant cousin Earl to receive all of the trust income annually for the next thirteen years. Then the property will revert to Dick. In the last few years, the income return (yield) on the property has been 7%. Assume this yield is not likely to increase and that the rate for the actuarial tables is 10%.

a. What will be the amount of Dick's gift to Earl?
b. Would you recommend that Dick transfer the property yielding 7% to this type of a trust? Explain. If not, what type of property would you recommend that Dick transfer to the trust?

C12-8 Antonio would like to make a gift of a life insurance policy. Explain to him what he must do to make the gift.

C12-9 When might a potential donor be interested in making a net gift? Explain the potential income tax problem with making a net gift.

[59] Reg. Sec. 25.2504-2.

C12-10 What is the purpose of the gift tax annual exclusion?

C12-11 A client is under the impression that all gifts are eligible for the gift tax annual exclusion. Is the client correct? Explain.

C12-12 Compare and contrast a 2503(c) trust and a *Crummey* trust.

C12-13 From a nontax standpoint, would a parent probably prefer to make a transfer to a minor child by using a 2503(c) trust or a *Crummey* trust?

C12-14 Explain the requirements for classifying a transaction as a transfer of a qualified terminable interest property.

C12-15 Why is the qualified terminable interest property transfer an especially attractive arrangement for some donors who make gifts to their spouses?

C12-16 A client is under the impression that a donor cannot incur a gift tax liability if his or her only gifts are gifts to a U.S. charitable organization. What would you say to the client?

C12-17 Describe to a married couple three advantages of making the gift-splitting election.

C12-18 Both Damien and Latoya make taxable gifts of $250,000 in the current year. Will their current year gift tax liabilities necessarily be identical? Explain.

C12-19 A donor made his first taxable gift a number of years ago and his second taxable gift in the current year. In the intervening years, the gift tax rates increased. In calculating the tax on taxable gifts of previous periods, which rate schedule is used: the one applicable in the year in which the earlier taxable gift was made or the one for the current period?

C12-20 A mother is trying to decide which of the two assets listed below to give to her adult daughter.

Asset	*FMV*	*Adjusted Basis*	*Annual Net Income from the Asset*
Apartment	$2,400,000	$1,500,000	($10,000)
Stock	2,400,000	2,200,000	240,000

The mother has a higher marginal income tax rate than her daughter. Describe the pros and cons of giving each of the two properties.

C12-21 Phil and Marcy have been married for a number of years. Marcy is very wealthy, but Phil is not. In fact, Phil has only $10,000 of property. Phil has been very ill recently, and his doctor feels it is likely that he will die within the next year. Make one (or more) tax planning suggestions for the couple.

C12-22 Assume that the facts remain the same as in Problem C12-21, except that Marcy has decided to give Phil property valued at $590,000. Phil will probably leave the gifted property to their children under his will.

a. What are the gift tax consequences to Marcy and the estate tax consequences to Phil of the transfer (assuming the property does not appreciate before his death)?

b. Assume Marcy is trying to decide whether to give Phil stock with an adjusted basis of $10,000 or land with an adjusted basis of $500,000. Each asset is valued at $590,000. Which asset would you recommend she give and why?

C12-23 Carlos has heard about the unified transfer tax system and does not understand how making gifts can be beneficial. Explain to Carlos how a lifetime gift fixes or freezes the gifted property's value for transfer tax purposes.

C12-24 Describe for a client five advantages and two disadvantages of disposing of property by gift instead of at death.

C12-25 In general, what is the due date for the gift tax return? What circumstances permit a donor either more or less time to file the return?

C12-26 In 1991, Frank sells realty to Stu, his son, for $400,000. Frank does not report this transaction as a gift. In 2000, the IRS audits Frank's 1998 income tax return and somehow finds out about the sale. The IRS then contends that the property sold was worth $700,000 in 1991, and that Frank made a $300,000 gift to Stu in 1991.

a. Can the IRS collect the gift tax on the 1991 gift? If not, will the 1991 gift affect the tax due on later gifts that may be made by Frank?

b. Assume instead that the IRS conducted its audit in 1994. Would Frank potentially be subject to any penalty? Explain.

ISSUE IDENTIFICATION QUESTIONS

C12-27 Kwambe is thinking of making a substantial gift to his fiancée, Maya. The wedding is scheduled for October 1 of the current year. Kwambe has already exhausted his unified credit. He is also considering giving $20,000 cash this year to each of his three children by a previous marriage. What tax issues should Kwambe consider with respect to the gifts he plans to make to Maya and his three children?

C12-28 Janet is considering transferring assets valued at $300,000 to an irrevocable trust with Farmers Bank as trustee. The trust would be for the benefit of her son, Gordon, age 15. Her attorney has drafted a trust agreeement that provides that Gordon is to receive income in the trustee's discretion for the next twenty years, and that at age 35 the trust assets will be distributed equally between Gordon and his sister Joanna. Janet anticipates that her husband will consent to gift splitting. What tax issues should Janet and her husband consider with respect to the trust she is creating?

C12-29 Melvin funds an irrevocable trust with Holcomb Bank as trustee and reserves the right to receive the income for seven years. He provides that at the end of the seventh year the trust assets will pass outright to his adult daughter, Pamela, or to Pamela's estate should Pamela not be alive. Melvin transfers assets valued at $1,000,000 to the trust; the assets at present are producing income of about 6.5% per year. Assume that the Sec. 7520 rate per the actuarial tables for the month of the transfer is 10%. What tax issues should Melvin consider regarding the trust?

PROBLEMS

C12-30 ***Calculation of Gift Tax.*** In the current year, Latesha makes taxable gifts aggregating $5 million. Her only other taxable gifts amount to $1 million, all of which were made in 1985.

a. What is Latesha's current gift tax liability?

b. What is her current gift tax liability under the assumption that she made the $1 million of taxable gifts in 1974 instead of 1985?

C12-31 ***Calculation of Gift Tax.*** Amir made taxable gifts as follows: $100,000 in 1974, $650,000 in 1978, and $200,000 in the current year. What is Amir's current year gift tax liability?

C12-32 ***Determination of Taxable Gifts.*** In the current year, Beth, who is single, sells stock valued at $40,000 to Linda for $18,000. Later that year, Beth gives Linda $12,000 in cash.

a. What is the amount of Beth's taxable gifts?

b. How would your answer to Part a change if Beth instead gave the cash to Patrick?

C12-33 ***Determination of Taxable Gifts.*** In the current year, Clay gives $30,000 cash to each of his eight grandchildren. His wife makes no gifts during the current year.

a. What are Clay's taxable gifts, assuming Clay and his wife do *not* elect gift splitting?

b. How would your answer to Part a change if gift splitting were elected?

C12-34 ***Determination of Taxable Gifts.*** In the current year, Diane gives $50,000 of stock to Mel and $120,000 of bonds to Nan. In the current year, Diane's husband gives $150,000 of land to Opal. Assume the couple elects gift splitting for the current year.

a. What are the couple's taxable gifts?

b. How would your answer to Part a change if Diane gave the $50,000 of stock to Opal (instead of to Mel)?

C12-35 ***Recognition of Transactions Treated as Gifts.*** In the current year, Emily, a widow, engages in the following transactions. Determine the amount of the completed gift, if any, arising from each of the following occurrences.

a. Emily names Lauren the beneficiary of a $100,000 life insurance policy on Emily's life. The beneficiary designation is not irrevocable.

b. Emily deposits $50,000 cash into a checking account in the joint names of herself and Matt, who deposits nothing to the account. Later that year, Matt withdraws $12,000 from the account.

c. Emily pays $22,000 of nephew Noah's medical expenses directly to County Hospital.

d. Emily transfers the title to land valued at $60,000 to Olive.

C12-36 ***Calculation of Gift Tax.*** Assume the same facts as in Problem C12-35. Emily's history of prior gifts is as follows:

Year	*Amount of Taxable Gifts*
1974	$500,000
1984	2,000,000

What is the gift tax liability with respect to Emily's current year gifts?

C12-37 ***Recognition of Transactions Treated as Gifts.*** In the current year, Marge (age 67) engages in the following transactions. Determine the amount of the completed gift, if any, arising from each of the following events. Assume 10% is the applicable interest rate.

a. Marge transfers $100,000 of property in trust and irrevocably names herself to receive $8,000 per year for life and daughter Joy (age 37) to receive the remainder.

b. Marge pays her grandson's $15,000 tuition to State University.

c. Marge gives the same grandson stock valued at $72,000.

d. Marge deposits $150,000 into a revocable trust. Later in the year the bank trustee distributes $18,000 of income to the named beneficiary, Gail.

C12-38 ***Recognition of Transactions Treated as Gifts.*** Determine the amount of the completed gift, if any, arising from each of the following occurrences.

a. A parent sells real estate valued at $1.8 million to an adult child, who pays $1 million in consideration.

b. Before marriage, Al transfers $800,000 of stocks to Barb, his fiancée. Barb signs an agreement waiving her future marital rights in Al's property. Such rights are estimated to be worth $800,000.

c. A furniture store holds a clearance sale and sells a customer a $5,000 living room suite for $1,500.

d. A father purchases food and clothing costing $8,500 for his minor child.

e. A citizen contributes $1,500 cash to a political organization.

f. Zeke lends $600,000 interest free to Henry, who signs a demand note on August 1. Assume 10% is the applicable interest rate and the note remains unpaid at year-end.

C12-39 ***Determination of Unified Credit.*** In November 1976, Mike makes a taxable gift of $100,000. In arriving at the amount of his taxable gift, Mike elects to deduct the $30,000 specific exemption formerly available. In the current year Mike makes his next gift; the taxable amount is $600,000.

a. What unified credit can Mike claim on his current year's return?

b. What unified credit can Mike claim on his current year's if the 1976 gift is made in May instead of November?

C12-40 ***Valuation of Gifts.*** On September 1 of the current year, Mario irrevocably transfers a $100,000 whole life insurance policy on his life to Mario, Jr. as owner. On September 1, the policy's interpolated terminal reserve is $30,000. Mario paid the most recent annual premium ($1,800) on June 1. What is the amount of the gift Mario made in the current year?

C12-41 ***Determination of Gift Tax Deductions.*** Tina makes cash gifts of $400,000 to her husband and $60,000 to the City Art Museum. What are the amounts of the deductions available for these gifts when calculating Tina's income tax and gift tax liabilities?

C12-42 ***Determination of Annual Exclusion.*** For each of the following situations, determine the amount of the annual exclusion that is available. Explain your answer.

a. Tracy creates a trust in the amount of $300,000 for the benefit of her 8-year-old daughter, May. She names a bank as trustee. Before May reaches age 21, the trustee in its discretion is to pay income or corpus (trust assets) to May or for her benefit. When May reaches age 21, she will receive the unexpended portion of the trust income and corpus. If May dies before reaching age 21, the unexpended income and corpus will be paid to her estate or a party (or parties) she appoints under a general power of appointment.

b. Assume the same facts as in Part a, except Tracy's daughter is age 28 when Tracy creates the trust and that the trust agreement contains age 41 wherever age 21 appears in Part a.

c. Assume the same facts as in Part b, except that the trust instrument allows May to demand by December 31 of each year the lesser of $10,000 or the amount transferred to the trust that year.

C12-43 ***Determination of Annual Exclusion.*** During the current year Will gives $40,000 cash to Will, Jr. and a remainder interest in a few acres of land to his friend Suzy. The remainder interest is valued at $32,000. Will and his wife, Helen, elect gift splitting, and during the current year Helen gives Joyce $8,000 of stock. What is the total amount of the annual gift tax exclusions available to Will and Helen?

C12-44 ***Determination of Annual Exclusion.*** Bonnie, a widow, irrevocably transfers $1 million of property to a trust with a bank named as trustee. For as long as Bonnie's daughter Carol is alive, Carol is to receive all of the trust income annually. Upon Carol's death, the property is to be distributed to Carol's children. Carol is age 32 and has three children. How many gift tax exclusions does Bonnie receive for the transfer?

C12-45 ***Calculation of Gift Tax.*** Before last year neither Hugo nor Wanda, his wife, made any gifts. Last year Hugo gave $10,000 cash to each of his 30 nieces, nephews, and grandchildren. This year Wanda gives $30,000 of stock to each of the same people. What is the *minimum* legal gift tax liability (before reduction for the unified credit) for each spouse for each year?

C12-46 ***Calculation of Marital Deduction.*** Hugh makes the gifts listed below to Winnie, his wife, age 37. What is the amount of the marital deduction, if any, that is attributable to each?

a. $500,000 is transferred to a trust with a bank named as trustee. All of the income must be paid to Winnie monthly for life. At Winnie's death the property passes to Hugh's sisters or their estates.

b. $300,000 is transferred to a trust with a bank named as trustee. Income is payable at the trustee's discretion to Winnie annually until the earlier of her death or her remarriage. When payments to Winnie cease, the property is to be distributed to Hugh's children by a previous marriage or their estates.

C12-47 ***Calculation of the Marital Deduction.*** In the current year Meg makes the transfers described below to Pete, her husband, age 47. What is the amount of her marital deduction, if any, attributable to each transfer?

a. In June she gives him land valued at $45,000.
b. In October she gives him a fifteen-year income interest in a trust with a bank named as trustee. She names their daughter to receive the remainder interest. The irrevocable trust is funded with $400,000 in assets, and 10% is the applicable interest rate.

C12-48 ***Charitable Contribution Deduction.*** Tien (age 67) transfers a remainder interest in a vacation cabin (with a total value of $100,000) to a charitable organization. She retains a life estate in the cabin for herself.

a. What is the amount of the gift tax charitable contribution deduction, if any, attributable to this transfer? Assume that 10% is the applicable interest rate.
b. How will your answer to Part a change if Tien instead gives a remainder interest in a valuable oil painting (worth $100,000) to the organization?

C12-49 ***Calculation of Gift Tax.*** In the current year Homer and his wife, Wilma (residents of a non–community property state) make the gifts listed below. Homer's previous taxable gifts consist of $200,000 made in 1970 and $800,000 made in 1984. Wilma has made no previous taxable gifts.

Wilma's current year gifts were	
to Art	$500,000
to Bart	8,000
Homer's current year gifts were	
to Linda	$700,000
to a charitable organization	60,000
to Norma (future interest)	460,000

a. What are the gift tax liabilities of Homer and Wilma for the current year, assuming gift splitting is elected?
b. How would the gift tax liabilities for each spouse in Part a change if gift splitting were not elected?

C12-50 ***Calculation of Gift Tax.*** In the current year Henry and his wife, Wendy, made the gifts shown below. All gifts are of present interests. What is Wendy's gift tax payable for the current year if the couple elects gift splitting and Wendy's previous taxable gifts (made in 1985) total $1,000,000?

Wendy's current gifts were	
to Janet	$80,000
to Cindy	70,000
to Henry	40,000
Henry's current gifts were	
to Janet	30,000

C12-51 ***Basis Rules.*** In June 1996, Karen transfers property with a $75,000 FMV and a $20,000 adjusted basis to Hal, her husband. Hal dies in March 1997; the property has appreciated to $85,000 in value by then.

a. What is the amount of Karen's taxable gift?
b. What gain would Hal recognize if he sells the property for $95,000 in July 1996?
c. If Hal wills the property to Dot, his daughter, what would be Dot's basis for the property?
d. How would your answer to Part c change if Hal instead willed the property to Karen?
e. How would your answer to Part d change if Hal did not die until August 1997?

C12-52 ***Basis Rules.*** Siu is considering giving away stock in Ace Corporation or Gold Corporation. Each has a current FMV of $500,000, and each has the same estimated appreciation rate. Siu's basis in the Ace stock is $100,000, and her basis in the Gold stock is $450,000. Which stock would you suggest that she give away and why, or does it make any difference?

C12-53 ***Below-Market Loans.*** On October 1, Sam lends Tom $10 million. Tom signs an interest-free demand note. The loan is still outstanding on December 31. Explain the income tax and gift tax consequences of the loan to both Sam and Tom. Assume that the federal short-term rate is 9%.

C12-54 ***Below-Market Loans.*** Assume the same facts as in Problem C12-53, except the amount of the loan is $42,000. This is the only loan between Sam and Tom. Tom's net investment income for the year is $600.

C12-55 ***Filing Requirements.*** In the current year, Germana gives $15,000 cash to Paulo and $12,000 cash to Mario. Placido, her husband, makes identical gifts in the current year. May Germana file Form 709A (the short form) instead of Form 709?

TAX FORM/RETURN PREPARATION PROBLEMS

C12-56 Dave and Sara Moore, of 10,105 Lake View Lane, Chicago, Illinois 60108, engage in the transactions described below in the current year. Use this information to prepare a gift tax return (Form 709) for Dave. He and Sara want to use gift splitting. Both are U.S. citizens. His Social Security number is 477-11-1333 and hers is 272-92-4403. For simplicity, assume the rate for the actuarial tables used is 10%. Dave's transactions are summarized below.

		Amount
1.	Tuition paid to Harvard University for son-in-law, Jim Smith.	$ 12,000
2.	Room and board paid to Harvard University for Jim Smith.	11,000
3.	Sports car purchased for Jim Smith.	18,000
4.	Premium paid on life insurance policy on Dave's life. The policy was transferred to Dave's sister, Amy Lane, as owner in 1979.	11,000
5.	Land given to daughter, Glenda Muñoz.	68,000
6.	Remainder interest in personal residence given to State University. Dave (age 70) retains a life estate. The total value of the residence is $80,000.	
7.	Stocks transferred to an irrevocable trust with First National Bank as trustee. The trust income is payable to Sara (age 60) semiannually for life. The remainder is payable at Sara's death to daughter, Amanda Webb, or her estate.	350,000

Sara's only gift was $42,000 of cash paid to Dave's sister, Amy Lane. Dave's gift history includes a $600,000 taxable gift made in 1975 and a $400,000 taxable gift made in 1982.

C12-57 Alice Arnold, Social Security number 572-13-4409, a widow, engages in the transactions listed below in the current year. Use this information to prepare a gift tax return (Form 709) for Alice.

		Amount
1.	Cash given to daughter, Brenda Bell.	$ 70,000
2.	Stock transferred to son, Al Arnold.	300,000
3.	$400,000 interest-free demand loan made to Brenda Bell on July 1. The loan is still outstanding on December 31.	

Assume 8% is the applicable interest rate. Alice has made only one previous taxable gift: $100,000 (taxable amount) in 1983. Alice, a U.S. citizen, resides at 105 Peak Rd., Denver, Colorado 80309.

CASE STUDY PROBLEMS

C12-58 Your client, Karen Kross, recently married Larry Kross; she is age 72 and quite wealthy and in reasonably good health. To date, Karen has not made any taxable gifts, but Larry made taxable gifts totaling $700,000 in 1988. Karen is considering giving each of her five college-age grandchildren approximately $22,000 of cash for them to use to pay their college expenses of tuition and room and board for the year. In addition, she is considering giving her three younger grandchildren $3,000 each to use for orthodontic bills. Karen wants to give her daughter property valued at $400,000. She is trying to choose between giving her daughter cash or stock with a basis of $125,000. As for her son, she would like to give him $400,000 of property also, but would like for the property to be kept in a discretionary trust with a bank as trustee for at least 15 years. Karen has been approached by an agricultural museum about making a contribution to it and, as a result, is contemplating deeding her family farm to the museum but retaining a life estate in the farm.

Required: Prepare a memorandum to the tax partner of your firm that discusses the transfer tax and income tax consequences of the proposed transactions described above. Also, make any recommendations that you deem appropriate.

C12-59 Morris Jory, a long-time tax client of the firm you work for, has made substantial gifts during his lifetime. Mr. Jory transferred Jory Corporation stock to several donees in December 1996. Each donee received shares valued at $10,000. Two of the donees were Mr. Jory's adult children, Amanda and Peter. The remaining twelve donees were employees of Jory Corporation who are not related to Mr. Jory. Mr. Jory, a widower, advised the employees that within two weeks of receiving the stock certificates they must endorse such certificates over to Amanda and Peter. Six of the donees were instructed to endorse their certificates to Amanda and six to Peter. During 1996, Mr. Jory also gave $35,000 cash to his favorite grandchild, Robin. Your firm has been engaged to prepare Mr. Jory's 1996 gift tax return. In January 1997 you have a meeting with Mr. Jory. At this meeting Mr. Jory insists that his 1996 taxable gifts will be $25,000 ($35,000 − $10,000 annual exclusion). After your meeting with Mr. Jory you are uncertain about his position regarding the amount of his 1996 gifts and have scheduled a meeting with your firm's senior tax partner, who has worked with Mr. Jory for more than twenty years. In preparation for the meeting, prepare a summary of the tax and ethical considerations (with supporting authority where possible) regarding whether you should prepare a gift tax return that reports the taxable gifts in accordance with Mr. Jory's wishes.

TAX RESEARCH PROBLEMS

C12-60 Karl Kremble funded an irrevocable trust in March 1997 with oil and gas properties valued at $400,000; assume that the Sec. 7520 interest rate for the actuarial tables was 10% on the date of funding. Karl named a bank trustee and provided that his distant cousin, Louise Lane, will receive all of the trust income annually for the next thirty-four years. Then the assets will revert (pass back) to Karl or his estate. The trust instrument specifically states that the trust is not to maintain a reserve for depletion. (That is, no portion of the royalties received from the oil and gas properties is to be transferred to the trust's principal account to account for the wasting nature of the trust assets.) Your manager has requested that you research whether the amount of Karl's gift to Louise may be determined by using the actuarial tables and that you write a memo summarizing your conclusions. Your manager indicated, further, that your memo should address the amount of the gift Karl is deemed to have made.

C12-61 On March 13, 1987, Harold filed a gift tax return for 1986 on which he reported taxable gifts in the amount of $700,000. He paid the applicable gift tax at the time that he filed his return. Harold died on January 3, 1995 and his estate tax return was filed on September 30, 1995. The return showed a taxable estate of $2,500,000 and adjusted taxable gifts of $700,000. (Harold's only taxable gifts were made in 1986.) The IRS audited Harold's estate tax return in 1997, and the agent contended that the 1986 gifts were incorrectly valued on the gift tax return. The agent further contended that such gifts should be reported on the estate tax return as adjusted taxable gifts of $1,500,000 instead of $700,000. Adopt the role of either the IRS agent or the estate's executor and present arguments about why the adjusted taxable gifts are $1,500,000 or $700,000, respectively. Also present arguments about the additional estate tax liability resulting from the audit of the estate tax return. That is, what additional estate tax (if any) will be owed if the adjusted taxable gifts are revalued? A suggested starting point is Sec. 2504.

C12-62 Carrie Chen owns 100% of the outstanding stock of Carrie's Clothier's, a C corporation. The corporation has only common stock outstanding; there are 1,000 outstanding shares. An appraiser recently valued the corporation at $1,000,000. Carrie has five adult children, and she would like to give each child 150 shares of stock; thus, she would be giving away 750 shares in total. Because she is proposing to give away 75% of the stock in the firm, the tax manager you report to wonders whether a control premium should be applied in determining the value of the gifts. If so, the total value of the 750 shares given away would exceed 75% of the $1,000,000 value of the business. Prepare a memo to your manager in which you address the issue of the valuation of the gift.

Your manager indicates that you should start with Sec. 2512.

CHAPTER 13

THE ESTATE TAX

LEARNING OBJECTIVES

After studying this chapter, you should be able to

1. Explain the formula for the estate tax
2. Describe the methods for valuing interests
3. Determine which interests are includible in the gross estate
4. Identify deductions available for estate tax purposes
5. Calculate the estate tax liability
6. Identify tax provisions that alleviate liquidity problems
7. Recognize the filing requirements for estate tax returns

CHAPTER OUTLINE

Gift taxes and estate taxes, wealth transfer taxes that are part of the unified transfer tax system, account for only a small portion of the federal government's collections from taxation. Their history and purposes were discussed in Chapter C12.

As previously noted, the term *gift taxes* applies to lifetime transfers and the term *estate taxes* applies to dispositions of property that occur as a result of the transferor's death. This chapter discusses the structure of the federal estate tax. It examines in detail the types of interests and transactions that result in inclusions in the decedent's gross estate. The various deductions and credits affecting the federal estate tax liability and the rules concerning the taxable gifts that affect the estate tax base are also discussed.

It is essential to keep in mind that the estate tax is a *wealth transfer tax,* not a property or an income tax. Understanding this point makes it easier to understand the rules surrounding the estate tax.

ESTATE TAX FORMULA

OBJECTIVE 1

Explain the formula for the estate tax

The tax base for the federal estate tax is the total of the decedent's taxable estate (i.e., the gross estate less the deductions discussed below) and adjusted taxable gifts (post-1976 taxable gifts). After the gross tax liability on the tax base is determined, various credits—including the unified credit—are subtracted to arrive at the net estate tax payable. The estate tax formula appears in Figure C13-1.

GROSS ESTATE

KEY POINT

Both the gift and the estate tax are taxes on the *transfer of wealth* and are part of the unified transfer tax system.

REAL-WORLD EXAMPLE

The IRS reports that 82,860 estate tax returns were filed in 1995. Total estate tax collections in fiscal year 1995 were $13.3 billion. More than half of the assets in the estate tax returns were stock and real estate.

As illustrated in Figure C13-1, calculation of the decedent's estate tax liability begins with determining which items are included in the gross estate. Such items are valued at either the decedent's date of death or the alternate valuation date.[1] As a transfer tax, the estate tax is levied on dispositions that are essentially testamentary in nature. Transactions are viewed as being essentially **testamentary transfers** if the transferor's control or enjoyment of the property in question ceases at death, not before death.[2]

Inclusions in the gross estate extend to a much broader set of properties than merely those to which the decedent holds title at the time of death. Making a lifetime transfer that generates a taxable gift does not guarantee that the transferred property will be removed from the decedent's gross estate. Although an individual usually removes property from his or her gross estate by giving it to another before death, the donor's gross estate must include the gifted property if either the right to receive the income generated by such property or control over the property is retained during the donor's lifetime.

EXAMPLE C13-1 ▶

In the current year, Ted transfers stocks to an irrevocable trust with a bank named as trustee. Under the terms of the trust agreement, Ted is to receive the trust income annually for the rest of his life and Ted's cousin Ed (or Ed's estate) is to receive the remainder. In the current year, Ted makes a taxable gift of the remainder interest (but not the income interest) in the trust. If, for example, Ted has already used all of his unified credit, he incurs a gift tax liability. When Ted dies, the entire value of the trust is included in Ted's gross estate, even though Ted does not

[1] Under Sec. 2032, the alternate valuation date is the earlier of six months after the date of death and the date the property is disposed of.

[2] An example of a transaction that is essentially **testamentary** in nature is a situation where the donor transfers property in trust but reserves a lifetime right to receive the trust income and, thus, continues to enjoy the economic benefits.

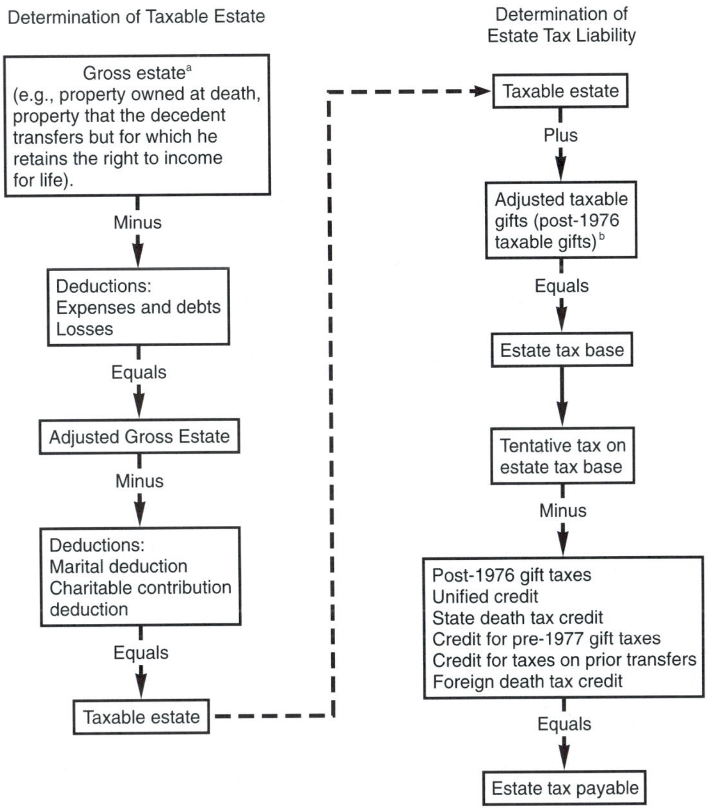

[a] Valued at decedent's date of death or alternate valuation date.
[b] Valued at date of gift.

FIGURE C13-1 ▶ ESTATE TAX FORMULA

have legal title to the property. Because the shift in the enjoyment of the right to the income does not occur until Ted's death, the transfer is testamentary in nature. ◀

SELF-STUDY QUESTION

In 1987 Barb transferred $500,000 in trust, income for life to herself, remainder to her daughter. What part, if any, of the value of the trust's assets will be included in Barb's estate?

ANSWER

The value of the entire trust will be included in Barb's estate, because she retained the income from the trust until her death.

The categories of items that are included in the gross estate and their valuation are examined in detail later in this chapter. Once the components of the gross estate have been determined and valued, the deductions from the gross estate are calculated.

DEDUCTIONS

The Code authorizes four categories of items that may be deducted in arriving at the amount of the taxable estate:

- ▶ Expenses and debts
- ▶ Casualty and theft losses
- ▶ Transfers to the decedent's spouse
- ▶ Transfers to charitable organizations

Deductible expenses include funeral expenses and expenses of administering the decedent's property. As is true for gift tax purposes, there is no ceiling on the marital deduction. Thus, the death of the first spouse is free of estate taxes if all the decedent's property, or all the property except for an amount equal to the exemption equivalent, is

ADDITIONAL COMMENT

If a decedent leaves all of his or her property to his or her spouse, the decedent's exemption equivalent is wasted. In addition, the estate of the surviving spouse is increased and may be pushed into higher tax brackets.

left to the decedent's spouse.[3] Property passing to charitable organizations qualifies, in general, for a charitable contribution deduction. There is no ceiling on the amount of such deductions.

ADJUSTED TAXABLE GIFTS AND TAX BASE

Under the unified transfer tax concept, certain gifts (i.e., adjusted taxable gifts) are added to the taxable estate to determine the amount of the estate tax base. Section 2001(b) defines adjusted taxable gifts as taxable gifts made after 1976 other than gifts that are included in the gross estate. Very few gifts are included in the gross estate; thus, almost every post-1976 taxable gift is classified as an adjusted taxable gift.

Adjusted taxable gifts are valued at their date-of-gift values; therefore, any post-gift appreciation escapes both the gift tax and estate tax. Allowable deductions and exclusions are subtracted from the gift's value in determining the adjusted taxable gifts amount. The potential effect of having to increase the taxable estate by any adjusted taxable gifts is to force the estate into a higher marginal tax rate.

EXAMPLE C13-2 ▶

In 1982, Amy makes $5,000,000 of taxable gifts, none of which are included in her gross estate. In 1997, Amy dies with a taxable estate of $4,000,000. The property Amy gives away in 1982 appreciates to $7,000,000 in value by the date of death. Amy's estate tax base is calculated as follows:

Taxable estate	$4,000,000
Plus: Adjusted taxable gifts (valued at date-of-gift values)	5,000,000
Estate tax base	$9,000,000

The $2,000,000 of post-gift appreciation escapes transfer taxation. Amy's $9,000,000 tax base includes the gifted property, which is valued on the date of the gift. ◀

ADDITIONAL COMMENT

Income earned by gifted property is the donee's and is not included in the donor's estate.

TENTATIVE TAX ON ESTATE TAX BASE

KEY POINT

If the taxable estate is $21,040,000, the estate is taxed at a flat 55% rate. The estate tax (before credits) is $11,764,800. This amount reflects a flat 55% tax ($21,040,000 × 0.55) plus the phase-out of the unified credit ($192,800).

Once the amount of the tax base has been determined, the next step is to calculate the tax on this base. Section 2001(c) contains the unified tax rates; they are reproduced on the inside back cover. The top marginal tax rate of 55% applies to tax bases in excess of $3 million. The benefits of the marginal tax rates below 55% and the unified credit are phased out for larger estates. This phase-out is accomplished by imposing an additional 5 percentage point surtax on tax bases in excess of $10,000,000 but not in excess of $21,040,000. In effect, the marginal rate is 60% for tax bases between $10,000,000 and $21,040,000. As described below, the tax determined from the rate schedules is reduced by the decedent's post-1976 gift taxes.

EXAMPLE C13-3 ▶

Assume the same facts as in Example C13-2. The gross tax on Amy's $9,000,000 tax base is $4,590,800. The estate is taxed at a 55% marginal tax rate, the highest rate applicable (ignoring the 5 percentage point additional tax). ◀

KEY POINT

Example C13-3 refers to the 55% marginal tax rate as the highest *marginal* tax rate. The 55% rate does not include the 5 percentage point additional tax levied to phase-out the unified credit and the lower marginal rates.

REDUCTION FOR POST-1976 GIFT TAXES

Adjusted taxable gifts, in effect, are not taxed twice because Sec. 2001(b)(2) allows a reduction to the estate tax for gift taxes imposed on post-1976 taxable gifts. If the rate schedule for the year of death differs from the schedule applicable for the year of the gift, the tax on post-1976 taxable gifts is determined by using the rate schedule in effect for

[3] The exemption equivalent of $600,000, as explained in Chapter C12, is the size of the tax base for which the gift tax or estate tax liability is exactly cancelled by the unified credit of $192,800.

the year of death. This rule works to the disadvantage of decedents who make taxable gifts and pay taxes at a higher rate than the rate in effect on the date of death. The rationale for this rule is to ensure that the estate pays a transfer tax at the current marginal tax rate applicable for the decedent's amount of taxable estate and adjusted taxable gifts.

EXAMPLE C13-4

Assume the same facts as in Examples C13-2 and C13-3. Recall that in 1982 Amy made $5,000,000 of taxable gifts. The tax on $5,000,000 of 1982 taxable gifts is $2,530,800. Amy is entitled to a $62,800 unified credit and pays $2,468,000 of gift taxes. Amy's 1982 gifts are taxed at a 65% marginal rate. For the year of Amy's death (1997), the marginal rate for $5,000,000 of transfers is 55%. Consequently, the reduction for gift taxes on post-1976 taxable gifts is limited to the amount of gift taxes that would be payable if the 1997 rate schedule were in effect in the year of the gift. This amount is calculated as follows:

Tax on $5,000,000 at 1997 rates	$2,390,800
Minus: Unified credit for 1982 (the year of the gift)	(62,800)
Tax that would have been payable on $5,000,000 if 1997 rates were in effect	$2,328,000

Note that the only change to the gift tax computation is that the 1997 transfer tax rates are used. The actual credit applicable for the year of the gift (and not the credit for the year of death) is subtracted.

EXAMPLE C13-5

From Examples C13-3 and C13-4, Amy's estate tax, before reduction for any credits, is calculated as follows:

Tax on $9,000,000 tax base (Example C13-3)	$4,590,800
Minus: Tax that would have been payable on $5,000,000 of post-1976 taxable gifts, at 1997 rates (Example C13-4)	(2,328,000)
Estate tax, before reduction for credits (discussed below)	$2,262,800

SELF-STUDY QUESTION

Taxpayer made $3,000,000 of taxable gifts in 1987 and paid gift taxes of $1,098,000 (gross tax of $1,290,800 minus the unified credit of $192,800). Taxpayer died in the current year with a taxable estate of $100,000. At current rates the gift taxes payable on $3,000,000 would still be $1,098,000. Determine the amount of her estate tax liability.

ANSWER

The unified transfer tax base is $3,100,000, the sum of the $3,000,000 of 1987 taxable gifts and the $100,000 estate. The current tax on $3,100,000 is $1,345,800. The unified credit of $192,800 and the credit for gift taxes of $1,098,000 reduce the tax liability to $55,000. The tax due equals the additional tax base of $100,000 times the 55% marginal tax rate.

UNIFIED CREDIT

For decedents dying after 1986, the unified credit of Sec. 2010 is $192,800, which is equivalent to a $600,000 exemption. The unified credit enables a $600,000 tax base, referred to as the exemption equivalent, to be completely free of transfer taxes. (The tax on $600,000 equals $192,800.) Like the situation for gift tax purposes, the unified credit has increased over the years. The amount of the unified credit for earlier years is reproduced on the inside back cover.

The estate tax computation permits an estate to subtract the entire unified credit applicable for the year of death (reduced by any phaseout for certain pre-1977 gifts) regardless of the amount of the unified credit that the decedent claimed for gift tax purposes. As a conceptual matter, however, only one unified credit is available. Under the unification concept, the estate tax is computed on a tax base consisting of the taxable estate plus the adjusted taxable gifts. The tentative tax on the tax base is reduced not by the amount of the "gross" tax on the adjusted taxable gifts, but by the "gross" tax on such gifts minus the unified credit. This computation achieves the same result as allowing the unified credit amount to be subtracted only once against all of a person's transfers but allowing a reduction to the estate tax for the gift tax liability *before* reduction for the unified credit.

OTHER CREDITS

In addition to the unified credit—the only credit available for gift tax purposes—the Code authorizes four credits for estate tax purposes. These additional credits are discussed in more detail on pages C13-25 thru C13-28.

THE GROSS ESTATE: VALUATION

DATE-OF-DEATH VALUATION

OBJECTIVE 2

Describe the methods for valuing interests

All property included in the gross estate is valued at either its fair market value (FMV) on the date of death or the alternate valuation date. The valuation date election is an all-or-nothing proposition. Each item included in the gross estate must be valued as of the same date; in other words, the executor (called the personal representative in some states) may not value some items as of the date of death and others as of the alternate valuation date).

TYPICAL MISCONCEPTION

The basis of inherited property is the value of the property on the decedent's date of death which could be higher or lower than the decedent's basis. This change is referred to as a step-up or a step-down in basis. Many taxpayers hear so much about step-up that they forget that a step-down may also occur.

Fair market value is defined as "the price at which the property would change hands between a willing buyer and a willing seller, neither being under any compulsion to buy or to sell and both having reasonable knowledge of relevant facts."[4] In general, the FMV of a particular asset on a certain date is the same regardless of whether the property is being valued for gift or estate tax purposes. Life insurance on the life of the transferor is an exception to this rule. Upon the death of the insured, the policy is valued at its face value, whereas it is valued at a lesser amount while the insured is alive. Generally, this lesser amount is either the cost of a comparable contract or the policy's interpolated terminal reserve plus the unexpired portion of the premium.

For certain types of properties the Regulations contain detailed descriptions of the valuation approach. However, the valuation of interests in closely held businesses is described in only very general terms. More detailed rules can often be found in supplementary sources (e.g., revenue rulings and judicial decisions). Valuation rules for several interests are discussed below. For purposes of this discussion, it is assumed that date-of-death valuation is elected.

ETHICAL POINT

Valuation of interests in closely held corporations and real estate is an area where a CPA or attorney may need to engage a qualified appraiser. Because appraisals are subjective, two appraisers may arrive at different values. Using the highest appraisal may mean additional estate taxes, but also provide a greater step-up in basis. Using too low an appraisal may subject the estate to undervaluation penalties (see page C13-39).

LISTED STOCKS. Stocks traded on a stock exchange are valued at the average of their highest and lowest selling prices on the date of death.[5] If no sales occur on the date of death, but sales do take place within a few days of such date, the estate tax value is a weighted average of the high and low sales prices on the nearest trade dates before and after the date of death. The average is weighted inversely in relation to the number of days separating the sales dates and the date of death.

EXAMPLE C13-6 ▶ Juan, who dies on November 15, owns 100 shares of Jet Corporation stock. Jet stock is traded on the New York Stock Exchange. It trades at a high of $120 and a low of $114 on November 15. On Juan's estate tax return the stock is valued at $117 per share, the average of $120 and $114. The total value of the block of Jet stock is $11,700 (100 × $117). ◀

EXAMPLE C13-7 ▶ Susan, who dies on May 7, owns 100 shares of Top Corporation stock. Top stock is traded on the New York Stock Exchange. On May 7 there are no sales of Top stock. The sales occurring closest to May 7 take place two business days before May 7 and three business days after May 7. On the earlier date, the stock trades at a high of $500 and a low of $490, with an average of $495. On the later date, the high is $492 and the low is $490, for an average of $491. The date-of-death per-share valuation of the stock is computed under the inverse weighted average approach, as follows:

$$\frac{[3 \times \$495] + [2 \times \$491]}{5} = \$493.40$$

The total value of the block of Top stock is $49,340 (100 × $493.40). ◀

[4] Reg. Sec. 20.2031-1(b).

[5] Reg. Sec. 20.2031-2(b).

SELF-STUDY QUESTION

Elwood's estate consisted of cash of $60,000, life insurance of $150,000, NYSE stocks valued at $90,000, and a lot and building. The real estate was appraised by two independent real estate appraisers. One valued the property at $150,000 and the second valued it at $200,000. Which value should the estate report?

ANSWER

The higher value, $200,000. Because the gross estate is less than the equivalent exemption, no estate tax will be due. Therefore, valuing the property at $200,000 will not increase the tax. In addition, the heirs receive a higher basis that decreases (increases) the gain (loss) recognized when they dispose of the property. Because an estate tax return (Form 706) need not be filed, the IRS may challenge the higher $200,000 appraisal when the real estate is sold or exchanged.

KEY POINT

Larry's father created a trust and named Larry the income beneficiary for thirty years. At the time of Larry's death, he or his estate was entitled to receive the income for twelve more years. The present value of the right to receive income for twelve years will be included in Larry's gross estate. Actuarial tables will be used to value the income interest.

In certain circumstances, the decedent may own such a large block of stock that the price at which the stock is traded in the market may not represent the FMV per share for the decedent's number of shares. The regulations allow a departure from the traditional valuation rule for stocks in such circumstances. These regulations, referred to as the blockage regulations, state,

> In certain exceptional cases, the size of the block of stock to be valued in relation to the number of shares changing hands in sales may be relevant in determining whether selling prices reflect the fair market value of the block of stock to be valued. If the executor can show that the block of stock to be valued is so large in relation to the actual sales on the existing market that it could not be liquidated in a reasonable time without depressing the market, the price at which the block could be sold as such outside the usual market, as through an underwriter, may be a more accurate indication of value than market quotations.[6]

INTERESTS IN FIRMS WHOSE STOCK IS NOT PUBLICLY TRADED. Often the decedent owns stock in a firm whose shares are not publicly traded. No regulations specifically address the valuation rules for this type of an interest. Rather detailed guidelines about relevant factors, including book value and earning capacity, are found in Rev. Rul. 59-60, however.[7] If the stock is a minority interest in a closely held firm, the courts often recognize a discount for the minority interest.

REAL ESTATE. Perhaps surprisingly, the Regulations do not specifically address the valuation approach for real estate. Thus, the general valuation principles concerning a price that would be acceptable to a willing buyer and a willing seller must be implemented without the benefit of more specific guidance. Appraisal literature discusses three techniques for valuing realty: comparable sales, reproduction cost, and capitalization of earnings.[8] Unfortunately, it may be difficult to locate a comparable real estate sale. The reproduction cost, of course, is not applicable to valuing land. Capitalization of earnings is often used in valuing commercial realty. At times, all three approaches may be used.

ANNUITIES, INTERESTS FOR LIFE OR A TERM OF YEARS, REVERSIONS, REMAINDERS. Actuarial tables are used to value annuities, interests for life or a term of years, reversions, and remainders that are included in the gross estate.[9] The same tables apply for both estate and gift tax purposes. (See Chapter C12 for a discussion of the use of these tables.) The following example illustrates a situation when the actuarial tables must be used to value an inclusion in the decedent's estate.

EXAMPLE C13-8 ▶ Tony gives property to a trust with a bank named as trustee and his cousin named to receive all of the trust income for the next fifteen years (i.e., a term certain interest). At the end of the fifteenth year, the property reverts to Tony or his estate. Tony dies exactly four years after creating the trust; the trust property is valued at $100,000 at Tony's death. At Tony's death, the trust has eleven years to continue until the property reverts to Tony's estate. The inclusion in Tony's estate is the value of a reversionary interest following a term certain interest with eleven remaining years. If 10% is the applicable rate for the actuarial tables, the reversionary

[6] Reg. Sec. 20.2031-2(e). As examples of cases dealing with the blockage discount, see *Horace Havemeyer v. U.S.*, 33 AFTR 1069, 45-1 USTC ¶10,194 (Ct. Cls., 1945); *Estate of Charles M. Prell*, 48 T.C. 67 (1967); and *Estate of David Smith*, 57 T.C. 650 (1972). The *Smith* case extended the blockage concept to large holdings of works of art.

[7] 1959-1 C.B. 237.

[8] For a discussion of techniques for appraising real estate, see The Appraisal Institute, *The Appraisal of Real Estate*, 10th ed. (Chicago, IL: The Appraisal Institute, 1992).

[9] Section 7520 provides that the interest rate potentially changes every month. Regulation Sec. 20.7520-1(a)(2) provides these tables. An excerpt from these tables is included in Appendix H.

interest is valued at $35,049 (0.350494 × $100,000) by using the excerpt from Table B of the actuarial tables included in Appendix H. ◀

ALTERNATE VALUATION DATE

Section 2032 authorizes the executor to elect to value all property included in the gross estate at its FMV on the alternate valuation date. Congress enacted this provision in response to the stock market crash of 1929 to make sure that an entire estate could not be confiscated for taxes because of a sudden, substantial drop in values.

In general, the **alternate valuation date** is six months after the date of death. However, if the property is distributed, sold, exchanged, or otherwise disposed of within six months of the date of death, the alternate valuation date is the date of sale or other disposition.

EXAMPLE C13-9 ▶

Ron dies on March 3. Ron's estate includes two items: stock and land. The stock is still owned by the estate on September 3, but the land is sold on August 20. If Ron's executor elects the alternate valuation date, the stock is valued as of September 3. The land, however, is valued as of August 20 because it is disposed of before the end of the six-month period. Of course, the value of land generally would change very little, if any, between August 20 and September 3. ◀

If the executor elects the alternate valuation date, generally any changes in value that occur *solely* because of a "mere lapse of time" are to be ignored in determining the property's value.[10] In a limited number of situations, one must concentrate on this rule concerning the mere passage of time. One example of such a situation involves valuing patents. If the executor elects the alternate valuation date, he or she must ignore any change in value that is attributable to the fact that the patent's remaining life is six months shorter on the alternate valuation date than it was on the date of death.

KEY POINT

The alternate valuation date cannot be elected unless both the gross estate and the estate tax are reduced by the election. Thus, it cannot be elected if it is not necessary to file an estate tax return.

The alternate valuation date election can be made only if it decreases the value of the gross estate and the estate tax liability (after reduction for credits).[11] As a result of this provision, electing the alternate valuation date cannot accomplish a higher step-up in basis. Congress enacted this strict rule because the alternate valuation date formerly offered a substantial tax planning advantage in situations where no estate tax was owed because the decedent took advantage of the unlimited marital deduction. If the property appreciated between the date of death and the alternate valuation date, the recipient could receive an increased basis by having the executor elect the alternate valuation date.[12] With the unlimited marital deduction, the estate could achieve an additional step-up in basis without increasing the estate tax liability.

STOP & THINK

Question: Joan died on April 1. Her estate consisted of three assets: an apartment building valued at $1,200,000 on April 1, stock valued at $700,000 on April 1, and $400,000 of cash. On October 1 the values were as follows: apartment building—$1,500,000, stock—$100,000, and cash of $400,000. Joan willed all of her property to her son, who anticipates owning the properties for a long time. Assume that the deductions for Joan's estate are negligible. Is there an estate tax benefit in electing the alternate valuation date? Is there an income tax benefit in electing the alternate valuation date?

[10] Reg. Sec. 20.2032-1(f).
[11] Sec. 2032(c).
[12] Sec. 1014(a).

Solution: There is an estate tax benefit to using the alternate valuation date. The estate tax liability is less given that the taxable estate would be $300,000 smaller if the alternate valuation date value ($2,000,000 minus deductions) were used instead of the date of death value ($2,300,000 minus deductions). There is also some income tax benefit to using the alternate valuation date. By using the alternate valuation date value, the tax basis for calculating cost recovery on the apartment building is $300,000 higher, ignoring any allocation of value to the land. However, there is a related detriment in that the basis of the stock is $600,000 less when the alternate valuation date value is used. If it is anticipated that the stock will be sold in the near future, the $600,000 capital loss that would be available by using the date of death value might permit Joan's son to recognize tax-free some unrealized capital gains.

THE GROSS ESTATE: INCLUSIONS

OBJECTIVE 3

Determine which interests are includible in the gross estate

SELF-STUDY QUESTION

Which of the following properties will be included in (1) the probate estate, (2) the gross estate, (3) both the probate and gross estate, or (4) neither estate?
1. Realty held in joint tenancy with the decedent's spouse. (The answer is 2.)
2. Realty held as a tenant in common with the decedent's spouse. (The answer is 3.)
3. A life insurance policy owned by the decedent in which the decedent's spouse is named the beneficiary. (The answer is 2.)
4. A life insurance policy always owned by the decedent's spouse in which the decedent's children are named the beneficiaries. (The answer is 4.)

As Figure C13-1 illustrates, the process of calculating the decedent's estate tax liability commences with determining the components of the gross estate. The **gross estate** is analogous to gross income. Once the components of the gross estate have been identified, they must be valued. As previously mentioned, the gross estate encompasses a much wider array of items than merely those to which the decedent held title at death. For example, under certain statutory provisions, referred to as the *transferor sections,* the gross estate includes items previously transferred by the decedent. For decedents other than nonresident aliens, the fact that property is located in a foreign country does not preclude it from being included in the gross estate. Table C13-1 provides an overview of the inclusions in the gross estate.

COMPARISON OF GROSS ESTATE WITH PROBATE ESTATE

The gross estate is a federal tax law concept. The probate estate is a state law concept. To oversimplify, the **probate estate** can be defined as encompassing properties that pass subject to the will (or under an intestacy statute) and are subject to court administration. Often, a decedent's gross estate is substantially larger than his or her probate estate. For example, suppose that at the time of death, a decedent owns a life insurance policy on his own life with his daughter as the beneficiary. The policy is not a part of the decedent's probate estate because it is payable directly to the daughter, but it is included in the gross estate.

STOP & THINK

Question: Karl died recently, and Karl's executor has included the following properties in Karl's gross estate: life insurance payable to the beneficiary, Karl's wife; savings account solely in Karl's name; land titled in the names of Karl and his spouse as joint tenants with right of survivorship; and a trust created under the will of Karl's mother. Karl had an income interest in the trust for his lifetime and complete power to choose the owners of the property on his death. With the exception of the trust assets (willed to his children), Karl's will leaves all of his property to his beloved cousin, Karla. Which assets pass under the terms of Karl's will? Which assets will Karla receive?

Solution: This scenario illustrates the difference between the property included in a decedent's gross estate and in the probate estate. Karl's gross estate is larger than his probate estate. Only two assets—the savings account and the trust property—pass under the terms of Karl's will. Karla will receive only the savings account.

SELF-STUDY QUESTION

When Dorothy died on April 10, she owned Z Corporation bonds, that paid interest on April 1 and October 1, and stock in X and Y Corporations. X Corporation had declared a dividend on March 15 payable to stockholders of record on April 1. Y Corporation had declared a dividend on March 31 payable to stockholders of record on April 15. Dorothy's estate received the interest and dividends on the payment dates. Should any of the interest or dividends be included in Dorothy's gross estate?

ANSWER

The X Corporation dividend must be included because the date of record preceded Dorothy's death. The Y Corporation dividend will not be included because the date of record was after her death. The Z Corporation bond interest that must be included is the interest that accrued between the April 1 payment date and the April 10 date of death.

▼ **TABLE C13-1**
Inclusions in the Gross Estate

Code Section	Type of Property or Transaction Included
2033	Property in which the decedent had an interest
2035	Gift taxes on property given away within three years of death <u>plus</u> certain property (primarily life insurance) given away within three years of death
2036	Property that the decedent transferred but in which the decedent retained economic benefits or the power to control enjoyment
2037	Property that the decedent transferred but for which the decedent has too large a reversionary interest
2038	Property that the decedent transferred but over which the decedent held the power to alter, amend, revoke, or terminate an interest
2039	Annuities
2040	Jointly owned property
2041	Property over which the decedent possessed a general power of appointment
2042	Life insurance on the decedent's life
2044	QTIP trust for which a marital deduction was claimed by the decedent's spouse

PROPERTY IN WHICH THE DECEDENT HAD AN INTEREST

Section 2033, which is sometimes called the *generic section,* provides that the gross estate includes the value of all property the decedent beneficially owned at the time of death. Its broad language taxes such items as a personal residence, automobile, stocks, and any other asset titled in the decedent's name. Because the rule refers to beneficial ownership, however, its scope extends beyond assets to which the decedent held title. For example, such items as remainder interests are also included in the gross estate.

EXAMPLE C13-10 ▶ At the time of his death, the following assets are in Raj's name: personal residence, mountain cabin, Zero Corporation stock, checking account, and savings account. Raj beneficially owns each of these items when he dies. Under Sec. 2033, each item is included in Raj's gross estate. ◀

EXAMPLE C13-11 ▶ Ken's will named Ann to receive trust income for life and Raj or Raj's estate to receive the trust remainder upon Ann's death. Raj's gross estate, therefore, includes the value of the remainder interest if Raj predeceases Ann. If Raj does not outlive Ann, the passage of the remainder is controlled by Raj's will. The transfer is associated with Raj's death, and, hence, is subject to the estate tax. ◀

DOWER OR CURTESY RIGHTS

KEY POINT

Any property that passes outright to the decedent's spouse, due to dower or curtesy rights under state law, is eligible for the marital deduction and will not be included in the unified tax base.

Certain state laws provide wealth protection to surviving spouses through dower or curtesy rights.

- Dower is a widow's interest in her deceased husband's property.
- Curtesy is a widower's interest in his deceased wife's property.

Dower or curtesy rights entitle the surviving spouse to a certain portion of the decedent spouse's estate, even though the decedent may have willed a smaller portion to this person. Because the decedent spouse does not have complete control over the portion of his or her estate that is subject to dower or curtesy rights, some might argue that the portion of the estate that must go to the surviving spouse is excluded from the gross estate. Thus, Congress made it crystal clear that the decedent's gross estate is not reduced for the value of the property in which the surviving spouse has a dower or curtesy interest or some other statutory interest.[13]

EXAMPLE C13-12 ▶ The laws of a certain state provide that widows are entitled to receive one-third of their deceased husband's property. The husband's gross estate does not exclude his widow's dower rights (one-third interest) in his property. ◀

TRANSFEROR PROVISIONS

Sections 2035 through 2038 are called the transferor provisions. They apply if the decedent earlier made a transfer of a type specified in the Code section in question, *and* the decedent did not receive adequate consideration in money or money's worth for the transferred interest. If one of the transferor provisions applies, the transferred property is included in the gross estate at its date-of-death or alternate valuation date value.

GIFTS MADE WITHIN THREE YEARS OF DEATH. Section 2035(d) specifies the circumstances in which a gift that a decedent makes within three years of death triggers an inclusion in the gross estate. The scope of this provision, which is relatively narrow, encompasses the following two types of transfers made by the donor-decedent within three years before death:

- A life insurance policy on the decedent's life that would have been taxed under Sec. 2042 had it not been given away
- An interest in property that would have been taxed under Sec. 2036 (transfers with a retained life estate), 2037 (transfers taking effect at death), or 2038 (revocable transfers) had it not been transferred

Of these situations, the most common involves the insured's gifting a life insurance policy on his or her own life and dying within three years of the transfer. In the case of new insurance policies, the potential for an inclusion can be avoided if the decedent never owns the new policy. In other words, instead of the insured purchasing a new policy and then giving it to a transferee as owner, the other party should buy the new policy. A common planning technique involves a transfer of cash by an individual to a trust, and the trust (a life insurance trust) using the cash to purchase an insurance policy on the transferor's life.

EXAMPLE C13-13 ▶ On April 1, 1994, Roy transfers to Sally ownership of a $400,000 life insurance policy on his own life purchased in 1984. Sally is the policy's beneficiary. Roy dies on February 3, 1997. Because Roy dies within three years of giving away the policy, the policy is included in Roy's gross estate. The estate tax value of the policy is its $400,000 face value. If Roy had lived until at least April 2, 1997, the policy transfer would have fallen outside the three-year rule, and the policy would not have been included in Roy's gross estate. ◀

EXAMPLE C13-14 ▶ Roy makes a gift of stock to Troy on May 1, 1996. Roy dies on February 3, 1997. The stock is worth $80,000 on the gift date and $125,000 at the time of Roy's death. The gifted property is not included in Roy's gross estate because it is not life insurance on Roy's life, nor is it

[13] Sec. 2034.

property that would have been taxed in Roy's estate under Secs. 2036 through 2038 had he kept such property. ◀

GROSS-UP RULE. The donor-decedent's gross estate is increased by any gift tax that he or she, or his or her estate pays on any gift that the decedent or his or her spouse makes during the three-year period ending with the decedent's death.[14] This provision, known as the gross-up rule, applies to the gift tax triggered by a gift of any type of property during the three-year look-back period.

The purpose of the gross-up rule is to foreclose the opportunity that existed under pre-1977 law to reduce one's gross estate (and thereby one's taxable estate) by removing the gift tax on "deathbed" gifts from the gross estate. Because the donor's estate received a credit for some or all of the gift tax paid, under the pre-1977 rules a person on his or her deathbed could prepay a portion of his or her estate tax and at the same time reduce his or her gross estate by the amount of the gift tax.

The effect of the gross-up rule, as illustrated in the two examples below, is to reinstate the estate to the position it would be in if no gift tax liability were incurred.

EXAMPLE C13-15 ▶ In late 1994 Cheron makes a $1,000,000 taxable gift of stock and pays a gift tax of $153,000 ($345,800 gross tax − $192,800 unified credit). Cheron dies in early 1997. Cheron's gross estate does not include the stock, but it does include the $153,000 gift tax paid because the gift is made within three years of her death. ◀

EXAMPLE C13-16 ▶ In late 1994 Hal makes a gift of stock having a $2,020,000 FMV, and he and Wanda, his wife, elect gift splitting. Each is deemed to have made a $1,000,000 [($2,020,000 ÷ 2) − $10,000 annual exclusion] taxable gift, and each pays $153,000 ($345,800 gross tax − $192,800 unified credit) of gift tax. Wanda dies in early 1997. Wanda's gross estate includes the $153,000 in gift tax she paid on the portion of her husband's gift that she is deemed to have made within three years of her death. Her cash balance had declined because of paying the gift tax, and the gross-up replenishes the reduction to her estate. ◀

SELF-STUDY QUESTION

Refer to Example C13-16. Assume that Hal, the spouse who actually made the gift, paid Wanda's $153,000 gift tax as well as his own $153,000 gift tax. Would Wanda's $153,000 gift tax be included in her gross estate?

ANSWER

No, it would not be included because it did not reduce her cash balance and gross estate when it was paid.

TRANSFERS WITH RETAINED LIFE ESTATE. Section 2036, although titled "Transfers with Retained Life Estate,"extends beyond taxing solely lifetime transfers made by the decedent in which he or she retained a life estate (the right to income or use for life). The two primary types of transfers that are taxed under Sec. 2036 are those for which the decedent

- Kept possession or enjoyment of the property or the right to its income
- Retained the power to designate the person who is to possess or enjoy the property or to receive its income

Thus, Sec. 2036 applies when the transferor kept the income or enjoyment or the right to control other individuals' income or enjoyment.

The direct or indirect retention of voting rights in stock of a controlled corporation that has been transferred can also cause the gifted stock to be included in the transferor's gross estate.[15] A controlled corporation is one in which the decedent owned (directly, indirectly, or constructively), or had the right to vote, stock that possessed at least 20% of the voting power.[16]

The retention of income, control, or voting rights for one of the three retention periods listed below causes the transferred property to be included in the transferor's gross estate. The three periods are

SELF-STUDY QUESTION

Mary owns a $500,000 life insurance policy on her life. Dick is the named beneficiary. The cash value of the policy is $70,000. How can Mary make a gift of the policy to Dick and keep the amount of the gift within the $10,000 gift tax exclusion?

[14] Sec. 2035(c).
[15] Sec. 2036(b)(1).
[16] Sec. 2036(b)(2).

ANSWER

One way is to borrow $60,000 from the insurance company against the value of the policy, thus reducing the value of the policy to $10,000. If Mary continues to pay the premiums and wishes to pay off the policy loan, the total amount of premiums and loan payments paid by Mary in each year following the year of the gift should not exceed $10,000. A second way is to have the insurance company rewrite the policy into separate policies, each having a value of less than $10,000. She could then gift one policy each year for several years.

- The transferor's lifetime
- A period that cannot be determined without referring to the transferor's death (e.g., the transferor retained the right to quarterly payments of income, but payments ceased with the last quarterly payment before the transferor's death)
- A period that does not end before the transferor's death

An implied agreement or understanding is sufficient to trigger inclusion. For example, if a mother gives a residence to her daughter and continues to occupy the residence alone and rent free, the residence will probably be included in the mother's gross estate. The rationale is that there was an implied understanding that the mother could occupy the residence for life.

If Sec. 2036 applies to a transfer, and the decedent's retention of enjoyment or control extends to all of the transferred property, 100% of the value of the transferred property is included in the transferor's gross estate.[17] However, if the transferor keeps the right to only one-third of the income for life and retains no control over the remaining two-thirds, his estate includes just one-third of the date-of-death value of the property. The following three examples illustrate some of the transactions that cause Sec. 2036 to apply.

EXAMPLE C13-17 ▶ In 1992 David (age 30) transfers an office building to Ellen but retains the right to collect all of the income from the building for life. David dies in 1997. Because David retained the income right for life, there is a Sec. 2036 inclusion. The amount included is 100% of the building's date-of-death value. ◀

EXAMPLE C13-18 ▶ Assume the same facts as in Example C13-17, except that David retains the right to income for only fifteen years. David dies five years after the transfer; therefore, David has the right to receive the income for the remaining ten-year period. Because the retention period does not *in fact* end before David's death, his gross estate includes 100% of the property's date-of-death value. ◀

EXAMPLE C13-19 ▶ Tracy creates a trust and names Alice, Brad, and Carol to receive the trust income for their joint lives and Dick to receive the remainder upon the death of the first among Alice, Brad, and Carol to die. Tracy reserves the right to designate the portion of the income to be paid to each income beneficiary each year. Only the gift to Dick was a completed transfer and subject to gift taxes. Tracy dies before any of the other parties. Because the control over the flow of income does not end before Tracy's death, the date-of-death value of the trust assets is included in Tracy's estate even though a portion of the transfer was subject to gift taxes. If Tracy had instead "cut the string" and not kept control over the income flow, she could have removed the trust property from her estate. ◀

SELF-STUDY QUESTION

Refer to Example C13-19. Assume the same facts except that the trust is directed to distribute its annual income equally to Alice, Brad, and Carol for their joint lives. Also assume that Tracy names Dick and Eva the remaindermen. Will the value of the trust be included in Tracy's gross estate?

ANSWER

No, because Tracy retained no power to control the enjoyment of the property.

REVERSIONARY INTERESTS. If there is the chance that the property will pass back to the transferor under the terms of the transfer, the transferor has a **reversionary interest**. Under Sec. 2037 the transferor's gross estate includes earlier transferred property if the decedent stipulates that another person must survive him or her in order to own the property and the value of the decedent's reversionary interest exceeds 5% of the value of the transferred property. Actuarial techniques are used to value the reversionary interest.[18] Section 2037 does not apply if the value of the reversionary interest does not exceed the 5% *de minimis* amount.

---

[17] Reg. Sec. 20.2036-1(a).

[18] The **reversionary interest** is the interest that will return to the transferor; often it will return only if certain contingencies occur. The value of Beth's reversionary interest in Example C13-20 is a function of the present value of the interest Beth would receive after the deaths of Tammy and Doug, valued as from actuarial tables (see Appendix H) and coupled with the probability that Tammy and Doug would die before Beth.

EXAMPLE C13-20 ▶ Beth transfers an asset to Tammy for life and then to Doug for life. The asset is to revert to Beth, if Beth is still alive, upon the death of either Tammy or Doug, whoever dies second. If Beth is not alive upon the death of the survivor of Tammy and Doug, the asset is to pass to Don or to a charitable organization if Don is not alive. Thus, Don must live longer than Beth in order to receive the property. The property is included in Beth's estate if the value of Beth's reversionary interest exceeds 5% of the property's value. The amount that is included is not the value of Beth's reversionary interest, but rather the date-of-death value of the gifted property less the value of Tammy's and Doug's intervening life estates. ◀

ADDITIONAL COMMENT

Sections 2036-2038 draw back into the gross estate certain previously transferred property and include it in the gross estate at its FMV on the date of the decedent's death. For income tax purposes, if the property has appreciated in value, donees will obtain a stepped-up basis rather than a carryover gift tax basis.

REVOCABLE TRANSFERS. Section 2038 covers the rules for revocable transfers (i.e., revocable trusts). However, this provision also taxes all transfers over which the decedent has, at the time of his or her death, the power to change the enjoyment by altering, amending, revoking, or terminating an interest. Section 2038 can apply even though the decedent does not originally retain powers over the property. The crucial factor is that the transferor possesses the powers at the time of death regardless of whether such powers were retained originally.

The estate must include only the value of the interest that is subject to the decedent's power to change. Sections 2038 and 2036 overlap greatly, and if one amount is taxable under one section and a different amount is taxable under the other section, the gross estate includes the larger amount. Two types of transfers taxed by Sec. 2038 are illustrated in the following examples.

EXAMPLE C13-21 ▶ Joe creates and funds a revocable trust. Joe names his son to receive the income for life and his grandson to receive the property upon the son's death. Because the trust is revocable, Joe may change the terms of the trust or take back the trust property during his lifetime. Joe's power to revoke the transfer extends to the entire amount of the trust. Thus, Joe's gross estate includes the date-of-death value of the entire trust. ◀

EXAMPLE C13-22 ▶ Vicki creates a trust and names Gina to receive the income for life and Matt to receive the remainder. Vicki, however, retains the right to substitute Liz (for Matt) as remainderman. When Vicki dies, she has the authority to change the enjoyment of the remainder. Thus, the value of the trust's remainder interest is includible in Vicki's estate. ◀

SELF-STUDY QUESTION

Reggie purchased a fifteen-year term certain annuity. If Reggie dies before the end of the fifteen-year term of the annuity, his estate will be entitled to the remaining payments. Reggie died after receiving nine of the fifteen payments. Will the value of the remaining six payments be included in Reggie's estate?

ANSWER

Yes, Sec. 2039 requires that the cost of a comparable contract of six payments be included in his gross estate.

ANNUITIES AND OTHER RETIREMENT BENEFITS

Section 2039 explicitly addresses the estate tax treatment of annuities. Even if this section had not been enacted, some annuities would probably have been taxable under the more general language of Sec. 2033, because the decedent would have been viewed as having an interest in the property. For an annuity to be included in the gross estate, it must involve payments made under a contract or an agreement. In addition, the decedent must be receiving such payments at the time of his or her death or must have the right to collect such payments alone or with another person. If the annuity simply ceases with the death of the decedent in question, nothing is to be received by another party and nothing is included in the gross estate. For the payments to be included in the decedent's estate, they must be paid for the decedent's life, a period that may not be determined without referring to the decedent's date of death or for a period that does not actually end before the decedent's death.

ANNUITIES NOT RELATED TO EMPLOYMENT. The purchase of an annuity designed to pay benefits to the purchaser and then to a named survivor upon the purchaser's death, or to both parties simultaneously and then to the survivor, is a form of wealth shifting. The other party receives wealth that originates with the purchaser. This type of transfer is different from most other wealth transfers because it involves a series of annuity payments instead of a transfer of a tangible property.

The amount included in the gross estate with respect to annuities or other retirement benefits is a fraction (described below) of the value of the annuity or lump-sum payment to be received by the surviving beneficiary. Annuities are valued at the cost of a comparable contract.[19] To determine the figure to be included in the gross estate, this cost is multiplied by a fraction that represents the portion of the purchase price that the decedent has contributed.

EXAMPLE C13-23 ▶

In 1983 Jim purchases a joint and survivor annuity to pay benefits to himself and his son and then to the survivor. Jim and his son start collecting payments in 1989. Jim dies in the current year, survived by his son. At the time of Jim's death, the cost of a comparable contract providing the same benefits to the son is $180,000. Because Jim provided all of the consideration to purchase the annuity, his gross estate includes 100% of the $180,000 cost of a comparable contract. This annuity arrangement represents a shifting of wealth from Jim to his son upon Jim's death. ◀

EMPLOYMENT-RELATED RETIREMENT BENEFITS. Recall that to determine the amount of an annuity that is includible in the decedent's gross estate, the cost of a comparable contract is multiplied by a fraction representing the portion of the purchase price contributed by the decedent. Section 2039(b) states that contributions from the decedent's employer (or former employer) are treated as contributions made by the decedent, provided such payments are made as a result of the employment relationship. Thus, 100% of the benefits from an employment-related annuity are included in the gross estate.[20]

EXAMPLE C13-24 ▶

Pat was employed by Wheel Corporation at the time of his death. Wheel Corporation maintains a qualified retirement plan to which it makes 60% of the contributions and its employees contribute 40%. Pat's spouse is to receive an annuity valued at $350,000 from the retirement plan. Because the employer's contributions are considered to have been made by the employee, Pat is deemed to have provided all of the consideration for the retirement benefits. Consequently, Pat's gross estate includes 100% of the annuity's $350,000 date-of-death value. ◀

SELF-STUDY QUESTION

On his retirement at age 65, Winslow elected to take a joint and survivor annuity from his qualified pension plan. The plan provided Winslow and his wife with a monthly pension of $2,500 until the death of the survivor. Winslow died seven years later. What amount (if any) must be included in Winslow's gross estate?

JOINTLY OWNED PROPERTY

Section 2040 addresses the estate tax treatment of jointly owned property (i.e., property owned in a joint tenancy with right of survivorship or tenancy by the entirety arrangement).[21] An important characteristic of such a form of ownership is that, upon the

[19] Reg. Sec. 20.2031-8(a).

[20] Section 4980A imposes a 15% tax on "excess accumulations" attributable to a qualified retirement plan as of an employee's death. This tax, which is an addition to the regular estate tax, may not be reduced by the unified credit. "Excess accumulations" equal the excess of (1) the value of the decedent's interest in the retirement benefits over (2) the present value of an annuity of $160,000 per year in 1997 (a number subject to indexing for inflation) for the life of someone the decedent's age. The companion 15% tax on excess distributions from retirement plans and IRAs has been suspended for distributions made 1997–1999.

[21] Both joint tenancies with right of survivorship and tenancies by the entirety have the feature of survivorship. When one joint owner dies, his or her interest passes by right of survivorship to the remaining joint owner(s). Only spouses may use the tenancy by the entirety arrangement, whereas any persons may own as joint tenants with right of survivorship. A joint tenancy with right of survivorship may be severed by the action of any joint owner, whereas a tenancy by the entirety arrangement continues unless severed by the joint action of both joint owners.

The following definitions are from Henry Campbell Black, *Black's Law Dictionary*, Rev. 6th ed., Ed. by Joseph R. Nolan and Jacqueline M. Nolan-Haley (St. Paul, MN: West Publishing Co., 1990), p. 1,465.

Joint tenancy with right of survivorship: The primary incident of joint tenancy is survivorship, by which the entire tenancy on the decease of any joint tenant remains to the survivors, and at length to the last survivor.

Tenancy by the entirety: A tenancy which is created between husband and wife and by which together they hold title to the whole with right of survivorship so that upon death of either, other takes whole to exclusion of deceased heirs. It is essentially a "joint tenancy" modified by the common-law theory that husband and wife are one person, and survivorship is the predominant and distinguishing feature of each. Neither party can alienate or encumber the property without the consent of the other.

death of one joint owner, the decedent's interest passes automatically (by right of survivorship) to the surviving joint owner(s). Thus, the property is not part of the probate estate and does not pass under the will. Section 2040 contains two sets of rules, one for property jointly owned by spouses and one for all other jointly owned properties.

ANSWER

You would include the cost of a comparable contract providing $2,500 a month for the rest of the spouse's life. The age of the spouse would affect this amount.

OWNERSHIP INVOLVING PERSONS OTHER THAN SPOUSES. When persons other than spouses or persons in addition to spouses own property as joint owners, a test to determine the amount of consideration furnished is used to ascertain the amount includible.[22] Under this test, property is included in a joint owner's gross estate in accordance with the portion of the consideration he or she furnished to acquire the property. Obviously, this portion can range between 0% and 100%.

EXAMPLE C13-25 ▶

In 1987 Fred and Jack provide $10,000 and $30,000 of consideration, respectively, to purchase realty titled in the names of Fred and Jack as joint tenants with right of survivorship. Fred dies in the current year and is survived by Jack. The realty is valued at $60,000. Fred's gross estate includes $15,000 (0.25 × $60,000) because Fred furnished 25% of the consideration to acquire the property. If Jack instead predeceases Fred, his estate would include $45,000 (0.75 × $60,000). ◀

KEY POINT

Property held in joint tenancy at the time of death will not be included in the probate estate. Joint tenancies are sometimes called the poor man's will.

If part of the consideration furnished by one joint tenant is originally received gratuitously from another joint tenant, the consideration is attributable to the joint tenant who made the gift. If all joint owners acquire their interests by gift, devise, bequest, or inheritance, the decedent joint owner's estate includes his or her proportionate share of the date-of-death value of the jointly owned property.

ADDITIONAL COMMENT

The tracing rule is easy to understand, but difficult to implement. Suppose that a joint tenancy between a parent and a child was created in a parcel of real estate thirty years ago when the parent purchased the property. The child has just died of a heart attack and the parent is senile. Nothing should be included in the child's gross estate. Unfortunately the burden of proof to keep a portion of the property out of the estate is on the estate, not the IRS.

EXAMPLE C13-26 ▶

Ray gives stock valued at $50,000 to Sandy. Three years later Sandy uses this stock (now valued at $60,000) as partial consideration to acquire realty costing $120,000. Ray furnishes the remaining $60,000 of consideration. The realty is titled in the names of Ray and Sandy as joint tenants with right of survivorship. Because Sandy received the asset that he used as consideration as a gift from Ray (the other joint tenant), Sandy is treated as having furnished no consideration. If Sandy dies before Ray, Sandy's estate will include none of the realty's value. But if Ray predeceases Sandy, Ray's estate will include the entire date-of-death value. ◀

OWNERSHIP INVOLVING ONLY SPOUSES. If spouses are the only joint owners, the property is classified as a **qualified joint interest**. Section 2040(b)(1) provides that in the case of qualified joint interests, the decedent's gross estate includes one-half the value of the qualified joint interest. The 50% inclusion rule applies automatically regardless of the relative amount of consideration provided by either spouse.

EXAMPLE C13-27 ▶

Wilma provides all of the consideration to purchase stock costing $80,000. She has the stock registered in her name and her husband's name as joint tenants with right of survivorship. The estate of the first spouse to die, regardless of which spouse it is, will include 50% of the value of the jointly owned stock. Of course, upon the second spouse's death, all of the property will be included in the gross estate because it will no longer be jointly owned property. ◀

SELF-STUDY QUESTION

Fred and Myrtle, husband and wife, hold title to their home in joint tenancy with right of survivorship. They have three children. Fred is killed in an airplane crash. What part of the value of the residence will be included in Fred's gross estate? Who will own the residence if Fred wills his property to the children?

GENERAL POWERS OF APPOINTMENT

Section 2041 requires certain property interests that the decedent never owns in a legal sense to be included in the gross estate. This occurs because the decedent had the power to designate who would eventually own the property. The authority to designate the owner—a significant power—is called a power of appointment. There are both general and special (i.e., more restricted) powers of appointment.

[22] Sec. 2040(a).

ANSWER

One-half the value of the residence will be included in Fred's gross estate. Myrtle will own the residence after Fred's death because it passes to her by right of survivorship.

Only a general power of appointment results in an addition to the gross estate. If a general power was created before October 22, 1942, however, there is no inclusion unless the decedent exercised the power. For a post-1942 general power of appointment, there is an inclusion regardless of whether the power is exercised. A general power of appointment exists if the holder can exercise the power in favor of him- or herself, his or her estate or creditors, or the creditors of his or her estate. Being exercisable in favor of the decedent's estate means that there are no restrictions on the powerholder's ability to specify the person(s) to receive the property. The power may be exercisable during the decedent's life, by his or her will, or both.

If the appointment power is limited by an ascertainable standard, it is not a general power. Appointment powers are governed by an ascertainable standard and are free of estate tax consequences if they may be exercised solely for purposes of the decedent's health, support, maintenance, or education.

EXAMPLE C13-28 ▶ When Kathy dies in 1950, her will creates a trust from which Doris is to receive the income for life. In addition, Doris is granted the power to designate by will the person or persons to receive the trust's assets. Doris has a testamentary general power of appointment. The trust's assets are included in Doris's gross estate regardless of whether Doris exercises the power. If Kathy had instead died in 1940, Doris would have had a pre-1942 power of appointment. Such powers are taxed only if exercised. ◀

EXAMPLE C13-29 ▶ Assume the same facts as in Example C13-28, except that Kathy's will merely empowers Doris to name which of her descendants would receive the trust assets. Doris now has only a special power of appointment because she does not have the power to leave the property to whomever she desires (e.g., the power to appoint the property to her estate). Because Doris's power of appointment is only a special power, the value of the trust is not included in Doris's gross estate. ◀

LIFE INSURANCE

Section 2042 addresses the estate tax treatment of life insurance policies on the life of the decedent. Life insurance policies owned by the decedent on the lives of others are taxed under the more general language of Sec. 2033. According to Sec. 2042, a decedent's gross estate includes the value of policies on his or her own life if the proceeds are receivable by the executor or for the benefit of the estate, or the decedent had any "incidents of ownership" in the policy at the time of death. The Regulations list the following powers as a partial inventory of the incidents of ownership:

TYPICAL MISCONCEPTION

Many taxpayers who own life insurance policies on their own lives believe that their estates will not owe estate taxes on the life insurance proceeds if they name someone other than their estate as the beneficiary. Life insurance will be included in the gross estate of the decedent if, at the time of death, the decedent held *any* (one) of the incidents of ownership in the policy.

- To change the beneficiary
- To surrender or cancel the policy
- To borrow against the policy
- To pledge the policy for a loan
- To revoke an assignment of the policy[23]

The examples in the Regulations of incidents of ownership involve economic rights over the insurance policies. Judicial decisions have also been important in defining what constitutes incidents of ownership. In some jurisdictions, the phrase has been interpreted to be broader than simply relating to economic powers.[24]

If the decedent could have exercised the incidents of ownership only in conjunction with another party, the policy is nevertheless included in the gross estate. Moreover, it is

[23] Reg. Sec. 20.2042-1(c)(2).

[24] See, for example, *Estate of James H. Lumpkin, Jr. v. CIR*, 31 AFTR 2d 73-1381, 73-1 USTC ¶12,909 (5th Cir., 1973), wherein the court held that the right to choose how the proceeds were to be paid—in a lump sum or in installments—was an incident of ownership.

the legal power to exercise ownership rights, not the practical ability to do so, that leads to an inclusion. The Supreme Court in the *Estate of Marshal L. Noel* emphasized the decedent-insured's legal powers in a situation where the insured was killed in a plane crash and the policies he owned on his life were in his spouse's possession on the ground. The Court held that the decedent possessed incidents of ownership and thus the policies were includible in his gross estate.[25]

EXAMPLE C13-30 ▶ Tracy purchases an insurance policy on her life in 1980. In 1990 she transfers all of her incidents of ownership in the policy to her daughter. Seven years after the transfer, Tracy dies. Tracy's niece has always been the policy's beneficiary. The policy is not included in Tracy's gross estate because Tracy did not have any incidents of ownership in the policy at the time of her death, nor is her estate the beneficiary. ◀

EXAMPLE C13-31 ▶ Assume the same facts as in Example C13-30, except that Tracy's estate is instead designated as the policy's beneficiary. Because Tracy's estate is designated as the beneficiary, the policy is included in her gross estate. The policy is valued at its face value. ◀

It is not sufficient to consider only Sec. 2042 in determining whether a life insurance policy on the decedent's life is includible in the gross estate. Recall from the discussion on page C13-11 that a life insurance policy is includible in a decedent's gross estate if the individual makes a gift of a life insurance policy on his or her own life within three years of dying.[26]

EXAMPLE C13-32 ▶ In 1995 Peng gives all of his incidents of ownership in a life insurance policy on his own life to his son, Phong. The face value of the policy is $400,000. Phong has always been the beneficiary. Peng dies in 1997. Because Peng dies within three years of giving Phong the policy, Peng's gross estate includes the policy. The policy is valued at its date-of-death value of $400,000. The potential problem of making a transfer of a life insurance policy within three years of death could have been avoided if Phong had been the one who originally owned the policy. In that case, Peng would not have made a transfer and need not have been concerned with the three-year rule. ◀

SELF-STUDY QUESTION

In reviewing his estate tax plan, Farmer Brown is concerned the estate will not have sufficient cash to pay its estate taxes. He could buy life insurance so his estate will have cash to pay the estate taxes. However, if he owns the policy or if he names his estate the beneficiary of the policy, the proceeds of the policy will also be taxed in his gross estate. What should he do to keep the life insurance out of his gross estate?

CONSIDERATION OFFSET

Section 2043 allows an offset against inclusions in the gross estate for consideration that was received with respect to certain transactions.[27] This offset is allowed only if the decedent received some, but less than adequate, consideration with respect to an earlier transaction. The gross estate is reduced by an offset for the partial consideration received. The offset is for the actual dollars received, not for the pro rata portion of the cost paid by the decedent. This offset, called the consideration offset, serves the same function as a deduction in that it reduces the taxable estate. If the decedent receives consideration equal to the value of the property transferred, the property in question is not included in the gross estate. No offset is permitted if the property is excluded from the decedent's gross estate.

The consideration offset is designed to prevent a double counting of property in the decedent's estate. For example, if an individual makes a transfer that is includible in the gross estate and receives partial consideration in return, the consideration received is part of the gross estate unless it has been consumed. Sections 2035 through 2038 also require the transferred property to be included in the gross estate, even though it is not owned on the date of death.

---

[25] *CIR v. Estate of Marshal L. Noel,* 15 AFTR 2d 1397, 65-1 USTC ¶12,311 (USSC, 1965).

[26] The gifted insurance policy is included under the rules of Sec. 2035(d)(2).

[27] Section 2043 provides a consideration offset for items included in the gross estate under Secs. 2035 through 2038 and 2041.

EXAMPLE C13-33 ▶

ANSWER

Farmer Brown should have his children (or an irrevocable life insurance trust) buy the life insurance and name themselves the beneficiaries, even if he has to provide the funds for the premiums (by making gifts). If the children are the beneficiaries, they can use the policy proceeds to buy an asset from the estate so that the estate can raise money needed to pay the estate taxes.

In 1995, Steve transfers a $300,000 life insurance policy on his life to Earl. The policy is worth $75,000 at the time of transfer, but Earl pays only $48,000 for the policy. Steve dies in 1997 with the $48,000 still in his savings account. Steve's gross estate includes both the amount in the savings account and the $300,000 face value of the insurance policy. Under Sec. 2043, Steve's gross estate is reduced by the $48,000 consideration received on the transfer of the insurance policy. The insurance policy on Steve's life would be excluded from Steve's estate if Steve survived the transfer by more than three years. No consideration offset would be permitted in the second situation because the property for which the consideration is received is not included in the gross estate. ◀

RECIPIENT SPOUSE'S INTEREST IN QTIP TRUST

Chapter C12 contains a discussion of the gift tax consequences of transferring qualified terminable interest property (QTIP) to one's spouse. The estate tax rules for QTIP interests are explained at pages C13-24 and C13-25. Claiming a marital deduction with respect to QTIP interests is voluntary. If the donor or the executor elects to claim a marital deduction for QTIP interests transferred to the spouse during life or at death, the transferred property is generally included in the recipient spouse's gross estate.[28] A QTIP interest included in the gross estate, like other property included in the gross estate, is valued at its date-of-death or alternate valuation date value.

The QTIP interest is excluded from the gross estate of the surviving spouse if the transferor spouse does not elect to claim a marital deduction. If the recipient spouse has a life estate, has no general power of appointment, and was not the transferor, no Code sections other than Sec. 2044 (dealing with QTIPs) cause the property to be includible in the gross estate.

There is no inclusion in the gross estate for QTIP interests for which a marital deduction is elected if the recipient spouse disposes of all or a portion of his or her income interest during his or her lifetime. Dispositions of all or a portion of one's income interest in a QTIP are treated under Sec. 2519 as a transfer of all interests in the QTIP other than the qualifying income interest. Thus, such dispositions are subject to the gift tax.

EXAMPLE C13-34 ▶

Henry dies in 1986. His will creates a $650,000 QTIP trust for his widow, Wendy, age 75. Henry's executor elects to claim a marital deduction for the QTIP trust. Wendy dies in the current year. By then, the assets in the QTIP trust have appreciated to $850,000. Wendy's gross estate includes the QTIP trust, which is valued at $850,000. If Henry's executor did not claim a marital deduction for the QTIP trust, the value of the trust would be excluded from Wendy's estate. If Henry's executor had made a partial QTIP election for 70% of the trust, then only 70% of the $850,000 value would be in Wendy's estate. ◀

DEDUCTIONS

OBJECTIVE 4

Identify deductions available for estate tax purposes

As mentioned earlier in this chapter, there are four categories of deductions from the gross estate. Two of these categories (debts and funeral and administration expenses and casualty and theft losses) cause the tax base to reflect the net wealth passed to the decedent's heirs, legatees, or devisees. The two remaining deduction categories provide the estate with a reduction in the tax base for transfers to one's spouse (the marital deduction) or to charitable organizations (the charitable contribution deduction). There is no deduction, however, for the amount of wealth that is diverted to the government in

[28] Sec. 2044.

▼ **TABLE C13-2**
Estate Tax Deductions

Code Section	Type of Deduction
2053	Funeral and administration[a] expenses and debts
2054	Casualty and theft losses[a]
2055	Charitable contributions[b]
2056	Marital deduction[b]

[a] Deductible on the estate tax return or on the estate's income tax return.
[b] No limit on deductible amount.

the form of estate taxes. Each deduction category is examined below. Table C13-2 provides an overview of the estate tax deductions.

DEBTS AND FUNERAL AND ADMINISTRATION EXPENSES

TYPICAL MISCONCEPTION

Most taxpayers are so used to dealing with the fact that expenses for income tax purposes must be paid or accrued in order to be deductible that they do not recognize that the expenses of administering an estate can be estimated at the time the estate tax return is filed. Estimation is necessary because the administration of the estate can go on long after the estate tax return is filed.

Section 2053 authorizes deductions for mortgages and other debts owed by the decedent, as well as for the decedent's funeral and administration expenses. Mortgages and all other debts of the decedent are deductible provided they represent bona fide contracts for an adequate and full consideration in money or money's worth. Even debts relating to an expenditure for which no income tax deduction would be allowable are deductible. Interest, state and local taxes, and trade or business expenses that are accrued at the date of death are deductible on both the estate tax return (as a debt of the decedent) and on the estate's income tax return (as an expense known as a deduction in respect of a decedent) when they are paid. (See Chapter C14 for a discussion of the income tax implications.)

Examples of administration expenses include executor's commissions, attorneys' fees, court costs, accountants' fees, appraisers' fees, and expenses of preserving and distributing the estate. The executor must decide whether to deduct administration expenses on the estate tax return (Form 706) or the estate's income tax return (Form 1041). Such expenses cannot be deducted twice, although some may be deducted on the estate tax return and others on the estate's income tax return.

An estate that does not owe any estate tax (e.g., because of the unlimited marital deduction or the unified credit) should deduct administration expenses on its income tax return because no tax savings will result if they are deducted on the estate tax return. If an estate owes estate taxes, its marginal estate tax rate will be at least 37% because the tax base will exceed the $600,000 exemption equivalent, and taxable estates above $1,000,000 will be in a 41% or higher marginal tax bracket. The highest income tax rate for an estate is 39.6%; thus, for taxable estates in excess of $1 million, administration expenses should be deducted on the estate tax return.

Funeral expenses are deductible only on the estate tax return. The estate may deduct any funeral expenses that are allowable under local law including "[a] reasonable expenditure for a tombstone, monument, or mausoleum, or for a burial lot, either for the decedent or his family, including a reasonable expenditure for its future care."[29] The transportation costs of the person bringing the body to the burial place are also deductible as funeral expenses.

[29] Reg. Sec. 20.2053-2.

EXAMPLE C13-35 ▶ At Ed's date of death, Ed owes a $75,000 mortgage on his residence, plus $280 of interest accrued thereon, and $320 of personal expenditures charged to a department store charge card. The estate's administration expenses are estimated to be $32,000. His funeral expenses total $12,000. Under Sec. 2053, Ed's estate can deduct $75,600 ($75,000 + $280 + $320) for debts and $12,000 for funeral expenses. The $32,000 of administration expenses are deductible on the estate tax return, on the estate's income tax return for the year in which they are paid, or some on each return. Ed's estate will get an income tax deduction for the accrued interest whenever it is paid. ◀

KEY POINT

The executor should elect to deduct any casualty or theft loss, when such loss is allowable, from the estate tax return if the taxable estate will be in excess of $1 million. The highest marginal income tax rate is 39.6% and the marginal estate tax rate is at least 41% when the taxable estate is in excess of $1 million; the deduction should be taken on the return with the highest marginal tax rate.

LOSSES

Section 2054 authorizes a deduction for losses incurred from theft or casualty while the estate is being settled. Just as in the context of the income tax, examples of casualties include fires, storms, and earthquakes. The amount of the loss takes into consideration the amount of any insurance compensation received. If the alternate valuation date is elected, the loss may not be used to reduce the alternate value and then used again as a loss deduction. As with administration expenses, the executor must decide whether to deduct the loss on the estate tax return or the estate's income tax return. There is no double deduction for these losses and no nondeductible floor for estate tax purposes.

EXAMPLE C13-36 ▶ Sam dies on May 3. One of the items included in Sam's gross estate is a mountain cabin valued at $35,000. The uninsured cabin is totally destroyed in a landslide on August 18. If the date-of-death valuation is chosen, the cabin is included in the gross estate at $35,000. The executor must choose between claiming a Sec. 2054 deduction on the estate tax return or a casualty loss deduction on the estate's income tax return. ◀

EXAMPLE C13-37 ▶ Assume the same facts as in Example C13-36, except that Sam's executor elects the alternate valuation date. The cabin is valued at zero when determining the value of the gross estate. No loss deduction is available for the casualty on the estate tax return. The estate cannot claim an income tax deduction for the casualty loss either, because the property's adjusted basis in its hands is zero. ◀

CHARITABLE CONTRIBUTION DEDUCTION

Section 2055 authorizes a deduction for transfers to charitable organizations. The rules concerning eligible donee organizations are the same as for gift tax purposes.

Because there is no ceiling on the amount of the estate tax charitable contribution deduction, a decedent could eliminate his or her estate tax liability by willing all of his or her property (or all of his or her property except for an amount equal to the exemption equivalent) to a charitable organization. Similarly, an estate tax liability could be eliminated if an amount equal to the exemption equivalent is willed to the decedent's children and the rest of the estate is willed to the surviving spouse and a charitable organization (e.g., in equal shares).[30] People who desire to leave property to a charity at their death should be encouraged to give the property before death, so they can obtain an income tax deduction for the gift and also reduce their gross estate by the amount of the gift.

COMPUTING THE DEDUCTION. Computation of the estate tax charitable contribution deduction can be somewhat complicated in certain circumstances. Suppose the decedent (a widow) has a $5 million gross estate and no Sec. 2053 or 2054 deductions.

[30] Another way the estate could owe no taxes is if all of the property, or all of the property except for the exemption equivalent, is shielded from taxation by the marital deduction.

The decedent's will specifies that her son is to receive $3 million and a charitable organization is to receive the residue (the rest not explicitly disposed of). Assume that state law specifies that death taxes are payable from the residue. Because $3 million of property passes to the decedent's child, the estate will definitely owe some estate taxes. The charitable organization will receive $2 million, less the estate taxes payable therefrom. The estate tax liability depends on the amount of the charitable contribution deduction, which in turn depends on the amount of the estate tax liability. Simultaneous equations are required in order to calculate the amount of the charitable contribution deduction.[31]

EXAMPLE C13-38 ▶ Ahmed, a widower, dies with a gross estate of $6,000,000. Ahmed wills State University $1,000,000 and the residue of his estate to his children. Under state law, death taxes are payable from the residue. Ahmed's estate receives a charitable contribution deduction for $1,000,000 bequest because the estate taxes are charged against the children's share. ◀

SPLIT-INTEREST TRANSFERS. If the decedent's will provides for a split-interest transfer (i.e., a transfer of interests to both an individual and a charitable organization), the rules concerning whether a charitable contribution deduction is available are very technical. Basically, the rules are the same as for gift tax purposes.

EXAMPLE C13-39 ▶ Jane dies in the current year with a gross estate of $2,500,000. Under Sec. 2036, one of the items included in Jane's gross estate is her personal residence, valued at $350,000. She gave City Art Museum a remainder interest in the residence in 1986 but retained the right to live there rent-free for the rest of her life. Upon Jane's death, no other individuals have an interest in the residence. Jane received an income tax deduction in 1986 for the transfer of the remainder interest. Her estate receives a $350,000 charitable contribution deduction.

There is no added estate tax cost attributable to her lifetime transfer. The residence is included in her gross estate, but the inclusion is a wash because of the charitable contribution deduction claimed for the value of the residence. ◀

MARITAL DEDUCTION

The fourth category of deductions is the marital deduction for certain properties passing to the decedent's surviving spouse.[32] For estates of decedents dying after 1981, there is no ceiling on the marital deduction. Thus, the decedent's estate does not owe any federal estate taxes if all of the items includible in the gross estate (or all items except an amount equal to the exemption equivalent) pass to the surviving spouse.[33] If the surviving spouse is not a U.S. citizen, however, a marital deduction is not available unless the decedent's property passes to a special trust called a qualified domestic trust.

ADDITIONAL COMMENT

Advantages of the marital deduction include that the estate tax is deferred until the death of the surviving spouse, the surviving spouse can reduce the overall estate tax through personal consumption and a lifetime gifting program, and the liquidity problems that might exist when the first spouse dies are generally avoided.

The marital deduction is intended to provide equal treatment for decedents of common law and community property states. As mentioned in Chapter C12, marital property is treated differently under each type of state law. In community property states, for example, a large portion of the assets acquired after a couple marries constitutes community property (i.e., property owned equally by each spouse). On the other hand, in common law states, one spouse may own the majority of the assets acquired after marriage. Thus, if there were no marital deduction, the progressive estate tax rates could cause the combined estate tax liability to be higher for a couple living in a noncommunity property state. Nevertheless, a marital deduction is available even to a decedent dying after 1981 who owns nothing but community property.

[31] The simultaneous equation problem does not generally occur if a charity is willed a specific dollar amount. See Reg. Sec. 20.2055-3 for a discussion of death taxes payable from charitable transfers.

[32] Sec. 2056.

[33] Some states have not adopted an unlimited marital deduction; therefore, some estates may owe state death taxes, even though no federal liability would otherwise exist. Passage of substantial sums to a state as taxes will reduce the amount passing to the spouse as a marital deduction and can cause federal taxes to be owed.

Only certain transfers to the surviving spouse are eligible for the marital deduction. The estate does not receive a marital deduction unless the interest conveyed to the surviving spouse will be subject to either the estate tax in the recipient spouse's estate or to the gift tax if transferred while the surviving spouse is alive. In other words, the surviving spouse can generally escape transfer taxation on the transferred property only by consuming it.

The following three tests must be met before an interest qualifies for the marital deduction:

- The property must be included in the decedent's gross estate.
- The property must pass to the recipient spouse in a qualifying manner.
- The interest conveyed must not be a nondeductible terminable interest.

TEST 1: INCLUSION IN THE GROSS ESTATE. No property passing to the surviving spouse is eligible for the marital deduction unless the property is included in the decedent's gross estate. The reason for this rule is obvious: Something that is excluded from the gross estate cannot generate a deduction.

EXAMPLE C13-40 At the time of Gail's death there is a life insurance policy on her life for which her husband, Al, is the beneficiary. Gail's sister always had the incidents of ownership in the policy. Gail held the title to the personal residence in which she and Al lived. The residence is willed to Al. The residence qualifies for the marital deduction. Even though the insurance proceeds are payable to Al, Gail's estate receives no marital deduction for the insurance. The policy is excluded from Gail's gross estate because she had no incidents of ownership, her estate was not the beneficiary, and the policy was not transferred within three years of her death.

TEST 2: THE PASSING REQUIREMENT. Property is not eligible for the marital deduction unless it passes to the decedent's spouse in a qualifying manner. According to Sec. 2056(c), property is deemed to pass from one spouse to the other if the recipient-spouse receives the property as a result of the following:

- A bequest or devise under the decedent's will
- An inheritance resulting from the decedent dying intestate
- Dower or curtesy rights
- An earlier transfer from the decedent
- Right of survivorship
- An appointment by the decedent under a general power of appointment or in default of appointment
- A designation as the beneficiary of a life insurance policy on the decedent's life

In addition, a surviving spouse's interest in a retirement benefit plan is considered to have passed from the decedent to the survivor to the extent the retirement benefits are included in the gross estate.[34]

TEST 3: THE TERMINABLE INTEREST RULE. The last statutory test requires that the recipient-spouse's interest not be classified as a nondeductible terminable interest.[35] A terminable interest is one that ceases with the passage of time or the occurrence of some event. Some terminable interests qualify for the marital deduction, however, because only *nondeductible* terminable interests fail to generate a marital deduction. Nondeductible terminable interests have the following features:

[34] Reg. Sec. 20.2056(e)-1(a)(6).

[35] Nondeductible terminable interests are also precluded from eligibility for the marital deduction for gift tax purposes.

- An interest in the property must pass or have passed from the decedent to a person other than the surviving spouse, and such person must have paid less than adequate consideration in money or money's worth.
- The other person may possess or enjoy any part of the property after the termination of the surviving spouse's interest.

Thus, if the decedent makes a transfer whereby the surviving spouse receives the right to receive all of the income annually for life and a general power of appointment over the property, the property is eligible for the marital deduction. As discussed below, as a result of the QTIP provisions a marital deduction is available for certain transfers that would otherwise be disqualified.

EXAMPLE C13-41 At the time of Louis's death he wills a copyright with a ten-year remaining life to his wife, Tina, age 42. His will also sets up a trust for the benefit of Tina, whom he entitles to receive all of the income semiannually until the earlier of her remarriage or her death. Upon Tina's remarriage or death, the trust property is to be distributed to the couple's children or their estates. Both the copyright and the trust are terminable interests. The copyright is eligible for the marital deduction because it is not a nondeductible terminable interest. No person other than Tina receives an interest in the copyright. No marital deduction is available for the trust because it is a nondeductible terminable interest. Upon the termination of Tina's interest, the children will possess the property, and they receive their interests from Louis without paying adequate consideration

SELF-STUDY QUESTION

A decedent, by will, creates a trust with income to the surviving spouse for twenty-five years, the remainder to their children. The surviving spouse's life expectancy is sixteen years. Does the property qualify for the marital deduction?

ANSWER

The property does not qualify because the surviving spouse's interest terminates at the end of twenty-five years. The fact that the spouse's life expectancy is shorter is immaterial.

QTIP TRANSFERS. For the estates of persons dying after 1981, Sec. 2056(b)(7) authorizes a marital deduction for transfers that were previously ineligible for the deduction. The eligible transfers are of qualified terminable interest property (called QTIP transfers). The QTIP provisions are somewhat revolutionary because they allow a marital deduction in situations where the recipient spouse is not entitled to designate which parties eventually receive the property.

Qualified terminable interest property is defined as property that passes from the decedent in which the surviving spouse has a qualifying income interest for life, and to which an election applies. A spouse has a qualifying income interest for life if the following are true:

- He or she is entitled to all of the income from the property, payable at least annually.
- No person has a power to appoint any portion of the property to anyone other than the surviving spouse unless the power cannot be exercised during the spouse's lifetime (e.g., it is exercisable only at or after the death of the surviving spouse).

SELF-STUDY QUESTION

How does the donor spouse or decedent spouse who establishes a QTIP trust control the disposition of the trust corpus?

ANSWER

The donor or decedent spouse states in the trust instrument or in his or her will who will receive the remainder interest on the death of the recipient spouse.

Claiming the marital deduction with respect to QTIP transfers is not mandatory. In the event the executor elects to claim a marital deduction for all of the QTIP transfer, the marital deduction is for the entire amount of the QTIP transfer. In other words, the deduction is not limited to the value of the surviving spouse's life estate.

If the marital deduction is elected in the first spouse's estate, the property is taxed in the surviving spouse's estate under Sec. 2044 or is subject to the gift tax in such spouse's hands if disposed of during the spouse's lifetime.[36] Thus, as with other interspousal transfers, the QTIP provisions allow a postponement of the taxable event until the second spouse dies or disposes of the interest by gift. If the taxable event is postponed, the property is valued at its FMV as of the date of the second spouse's transfer by gift or at death. See the Tax Planning Considerations section of this chapter for a discussion of planning opportunities (including partial QTIP elections) with the marital deduction.

[36] Section 2519 states that if a recipient spouse disposes of a qualifying income interest for life for which the donor or the executor elected a marital deduction under the QTIP rules, the recipient spouse is treated as having made a gift of everything except the qualifying income interest. Under the generic gift rules of Sec. 2511, the gift of the income interest is treated as a gift.

EXAMPLE C13-42 ▶

Tom dies in 1987. He is survived by his wife, Mary, who lives until the current year. Tom's will calls for setting up a $1,000,000 trust from which Mary would receive all of the income quarterly for the rest of her life. Upon Mary's death, the property is to be distributed to Tom's children by a previous marriage. At Mary's death, the trust assets are valued at $1,300,000. If Tom's executor elects to claim a marital deduction, Tom's estate receives a $1,000,000 marital deduction. Section 2044 includes $1,300,000 in Mary's gross estate. If Tom's executor forgoes electing the marital deduction, Mary's gross estate excludes the value of the trust. The trust assets will be taxed in the estate of one of the spouses. ◀

ADDITIONAL COMMENT

Refer to Example C13-42. The executor may elect QTIP status for less than the entire property in the trust. For example, the executor might elect QTIP treatment for only 60% of the $1,000,000 placed in the trust. If this is done, on Mary's death, 60% of $1,300,000, or $780,000, is included in her estate.

The aggregate amount of the four categories of deductions is subtracted from the gross estate amount to determine the taxable estate.

COMPUTATION OF TAX LIABILITY

OBJECTIVE 5

Calculate the estate tax liability

As mentioned earlier, the estate tax base is the aggregate of the decedent's taxable estate and his or her adjusted taxable gifts. Figure C13-1 on page C13-3 illustrates how these two concepts are combined in the estate tax formula.

TAXABLE ESTATE AND TAX BASE

The gross estate's value is reduced by the deductions to arrive at the amount of the taxable estate. Before 1977, the taxable estate was the tax base for the estate tax. Under the unification provisions effective after 1976, however, the estate tax base consists of the taxable estate plus the adjusted taxable gifts, defined as *all* taxable gifts made *after 1976 other than* gifts included in the gross estate. The addition of the adjusted taxable gifts to the estate tax base may cause an estate to be taxed at a higher marginal tax rate. If the decedent elects gift splitting, the decedent's adjusted taxable gifts equal the amount of the taxable gifts the individual is deemed to have made after applying the gift-splitting provisions. Adjusted taxable gifts can arise from consenting to gift splitting, even though the decedent never actually gives away any property.

Adjusted taxable gifts are valued at date-of-gift values; therefore, any post-gift appreciation is exempt from the transfer taxes. The estate tax computations for decedents who never made any gifts in excess of the excludable amount reflect no adjusted taxable gifts.

SELF-STUDY QUESTION

Verda died penniless. Because of consenting to gift splitting, her taxable gifts made after 1976 were $750,000. She paid $55,500 of gift taxes on these gifts. What is her unified tax base?

ANSWER

Her unified tax base is $750,000, the amount of her lifetime taxable gifts. Note that the gifts are valued at what they were worth on the date of the gift.

TENTATIVE TAX AND REDUCTION FOR POST-1976 GIFT TAXES

The tentative tax is computed on the estate tax base, which is the sum of the taxable estate and the adjusted taxable gifts, if any.[37] The unified transfer tax rates are found in Sec. 2001(c) and are reproduced on the inside back cover. The tentative tax is reduced by the decedent's post-1976 gift taxes. In determining the tax on post-1976 taxable gifts, the effect of gift splitting is taken into consideration. That is, the amount of the post-1976 gift taxes is usually the levy imposed on the taxable gifts that the decedent is deemed to have made after applying any gift-splitting election.

If the tax rates change between the time of the gift and the time of death, the subtraction for gift taxes equals the amount of gift taxes that would have been payable on post-1976 gifts if the rate schedule applicable in the year of death had been in effect in the year of the gift. The only "as if" computation is for the gross tax amount; the unified credit actually used on the gift tax return is subtracted to determine the amount of gift tax that would have been payable.

SELF-STUDY QUESTION

Refer to the previous self-study question. What is the amount of the unified tax before credits? after credits?

ANSWER

The unified tax before credits is $248,300. This tax is reduced by the unified credit of $192,800 and by post-1976 gift taxes of $55,500, which leaves zero tax due.

---

[37] Sec. 2001(b).

UNIFIED CREDIT

The excess of the tentative tax over the post-1976 gift taxes is reduced by the unified credit of Sec. 2010. The amount of this credit has changed over the years and after 1986 has been $192,800 (see inside back cover). With a credit of $192,800, the tax on a $600,000 tax base is completely eliminated. The unified credit never generates a refund; the most relief it can provide is to eliminate an estate's federal estate tax liability. The credit begins to phase-out when the tax base exceeds $10,000,000.

Section 2010(c) provides that the unified credit otherwise available for estate tax purposes must be reduced because of certain pre-1977 gifts. Before 1977, a $30,000 lifetime exemption was available for the gift tax. Donors could claim some or all of this exemption whenever they so desired. The exemption was repealed and replaced with the unified credit effective with 1977 and later years. If the decedent claimed any portion of the $30,000 exemption with respect to gifts made after September 8, 1976 and before January 1, 1977, the unified credit is reduced by 20% of the amount of the exemption claimed.

EXAMPLE C13-43 ▶ Carl dies in the current year with a tax base of $2,000,000. In October 1976, Carl made his first taxable gift. Carl claimed the $30,000 exemption in order to reduce the amount of his taxable gifts. Thus, Carl's $192,800 unified credit is reduced by $6,000 (0.20 × $30,000). If Carl claimed the exemption by making a gift on or before September 8, 1976, his estate would be entitled to the full $192,800 credit. ◀

OTHER CREDITS

The Code authorizes four additional credits: a state death tax credit, a gift tax credit on pre-1977 gifts, a credit on estate taxes paid on prior transfers, and a credit on foreign death taxes. The last three credits apply less often than the unified credit and the state death tax credit. These credits, like the unified credit, cannot exceed the amount of the estate tax actually owed.

STATE DEATH TAX CREDIT. All states levy some form of death tax: an inheritance tax, an estate tax, or both. Many states have enacted a simple system whereby the state death tax liability equals the credit for state death taxes allowed on the federal estate tax return.

KEY POINT

The amount of the credit allowed is the lesser of the state death taxes actually paid or the amount stated in Sec. 2011(b).

The maximum credit allowable on the federal return is calculated in accordance with the schedule contained in Sec. 2011(b). Appendix G reproduces the schedule. In order to claim this maximum credit, the estate must have paid state death taxes equal to or in excess of the credit calculated using the schedule.

To use the Sec. 2011(b) schedule, you must first determine the size of the decedent's adjusted taxable estate. The "adjusted taxable estate" terminology appears only in Sec. 2011 and means the taxable estate reduced by $60,000. Thus, adjusted taxable gifts have no impact on the state death tax credit. Section 2011(f) limits the state death tax credit to the amount of the estate tax (after reduction for the unified credit).

EXAMPLE C13-44 ▶ John dies in the current year with a taxable estate of $3,600,000 and adjusted taxable gifts of $1,000,000. John's estate pays $250,000 of state death taxes. John's adjusted taxable estate is $3,540,000 ($3,600,000 − $60,000) and John's maximum state death tax credit (from the Sec. 2011(b) schedule in Appendix G) is $238,800. ◀

EXAMPLE C13-45 ▶ Assume the same facts as in Example C13-44, except that John's estate pays state death taxes of $230,000. The credit for state death taxes is limited to the smaller of the state death tax credit from Appendix G ($238,800) or the actual death taxes that were paid ($230,000), or $230,000. ◀

CREDIT FOR PRE-1977 GIFT TAXES. Section 2012(a) authorizes a credit for gift taxes paid by the decedent on pre-1977 gifts that must be included in the gross estate. Remember that Sec. 2001(b)(2) allows a reduction for gift taxes paid on post-1976 gifts. The following transaction involves a situation in which the credit for pre-1977 gift taxes is applicable.

EXAMPLE C13-46 ▶ In 1975 Yuji creates a trust from which he is to receive the income for life and his son, Yuji, Jr., is to receive the remainder. Yuji pays a gift tax on the gift of the remainder. Upon Yuji's death in the current year, the date-of-death value of the trust's assets is included in his estate under Sec. 2036. Yuji's estate receives a credit for some or all of his 1975 gift taxes. ◀

In general, the credit for pre-1977 gift taxes equals the amount of gift taxes paid with respect to transfers included in the gross estate. Because of a ceiling rule, however, the amount of the credit is sometimes lower than the amount of gift taxes paid. A discussion of the credit ceiling computation is beyond the scope of this text.

CREDIT FOR TAX ON PRIOR TRANSFERS. The credit available under Sec. 2013 for the estate taxes paid on prior transfers reduces the cost of having property taxed in more than one estate in quick succession. Without this credit, the overall tax cost could be quite severe if the legatee dies soon after the original decedent. The credit applies if the person who transfers the property (i.e., the transferor-decedent) to the decedent in question (i.e., the transferee-decedent) dies no more than ten years before, or within two years after, the date of the transferee-decedent's death. The potential credit is the smaller of the federal estate tax of the transferor-decedent that is attributable to the transferred interest or the federal estate tax of the transferee-decedent that is attributable to the transferred interest.

To determine the final credit, the potential credit is multiplied by a percentage that varies inversely with the period of time separating the two dates of death. If the transferor dies no more than two years before or after the transferee, the credit percentage is 100%. As specified in Sec. 2013(a), the other percentages are as follows:

Number of Years by Which Transferor's Death Precedes the Transferee's Death	*Credit Percentage*
More than 2, but not more than 4	80
More than 4, but not more than 6	60
More than 6, but not more than 8	40
More than 8, but not more than 10	20

The following two examples illustrate situations in which the credit for the taxes paid on prior transfers is applicable.

EXAMPLE C13-47 ▶ Mary dies on March 1, 1992. All of Mary's property passes to Debra, her daughter. Debra dies on June 1, 1997. All of Debra's property passes to her son. Both Mary's and Debra's estates pay federal estate taxes. Debra's estate is entitled to a credit for a percentage of some, or all, of the taxes paid by Mary's estate. Because Mary's death precedes Debra's death by five years and three months, the credit for the tax paid on prior transfers is 60% of the potential credit. ◀

EXAMPLE C13-48 ▶ Ed dies on May 7, 1996. One of the items included in Ed's estate is a life insurance policy on Sam's life. Sam had given Ed all of his incidents of ownership in this policy on December 13, 1995. Sam dies on June 15, 1997, which is within three years of making a gift of the insurance policy on his own life. The policy is included in Sam's gross estate under Sec. 2035. Because Sam dies within two years of Ed's death, Ed's estate is entitled to a credit for 100% of the potential credit and an amended return must be filed to claim this credit. ◀

SELF-STUDY QUESTION

What is the effect of the maximum credit provision for the foreign death tax credit?

ANSWER

The effect is to tax the property located in the foreign country at the higher of the U.S. estate tax rate or the foreign death tax rate.

FOREIGN DEATH TAX CREDIT. Under Sec. 2014, the estate is entitled to a credit for some or all of the death taxes paid to a foreign country for property located in that foreign country and included in the gross estate. The maximum credit is the smaller of the foreign death tax attributable to the property situated in the foreign country that imposed the tax or the federal estate tax attributable to the property situated in the foreign country and taxed by such country.

COMPREHENSIVE ILLUSTRATION

The following comprehensive illustration demonstrates the computation of the estate tax liability.

BACKGROUND DATA

Herman Estes dies on October 13, 1996. Herman, an Ohio resident, is survived by his widow, Ann, and three adult children. During his lifetime, Herman makes three gifts, as follows:

- In 1974, he gives his son Billy $103,000 cash. Herman claims the $30,000 exemption (then available) and a $3,000 annual exclusion available then. The taxable gift is thus $70,000.
- In 1978, he gives his daughter, Dotty, $203,000 cash. He claims a $3,000 annual exclusion available then and makes a $200,000 taxable gift on which he pays a $28,000 gift tax.
- In December 1994, he gives his son Johnny land then worth $490,000. Herman claims a $10,000 annual exclusion and makes a $480,000 taxable gift on which he claims the available unified credit and he pays an $11,900 gift tax. On October 13, 1996, the land is worth $550,000.

Properties discovered after Herman's death appear below. All amounts represent date-of-death values.

- Checking account containing $10,000.
- Savings account containing $75,000.
- Land worth $400,000 held in the names of Herman and Ann, joint tenants with right of survivorship. Herman provided all of the consideration to buy the land in January 1982.
- Life insurance policy 123-A with a face value of $200,000. Herman had incidents of ownership; Johnny is the beneficiary.
- A personal residence titled in Herman's name worth $325,000.
- Stock in Ajax Corporation worth $600,000.
- Qualified pension plan to which Herman's employer made 60% of the contributions and Herman made 40%. Ann is to receive a lump-sum distribution of $240,000.
- A trust created under the will of Herman's mother, Amelia, who died in 1970. Herman was entitled to receive all of the income quarterly for life. In his will, Herman could appoint the trust assets to such of his descendants as he desired. The trust assets are valued at $375,000.

At his death, Herman owes a $25,200 bank loan, including accrued interest. Balances due on his various charge cards total $6,500. Herman's funeral expenses are $15,000, and his administration expenses are estimated to be $70,000. Assume that tax savings will be maximized if the administration expenses are deducted on the estate tax return.

Herman's will contains the following provisions:

- "To my wife, Ann, I leave my residence and my checking and savings accounts."
- "I leave $200,000 of property in trust with First Bank as trustee. My wife, Ann, is to receive all of the income from this trust fund quarterly for the rest of her life. Upon Ann's death, the trust property is to be divided equally among our three children."
- "To the American Cancer Society I leave $10,000."
- "I appoint the property in the trust created by my mother, Amelia Estes, to my daughter, Dotty."
- "The residue of my estate is to be divided equally between my two sons, Johnny and Billy."

CALCULATION OF TAX LIABILITY

The computation of Herman's estate tax liability is illustrated in Table C13-3. These same facts are used for the sample Estate Tax Return (Form 706) included in Appendix B. For illustration purposes, it is assumed that the executor elects to claim the marital deduction on the QTIP trust and Herman's state death taxes equal the maximum federal credit for state death taxes.

Note that the computation set out in Table C13-1 is affected by several factors:

- Herman had only a special power of appointment over the assets in the trust created by his mother. Therefore, the trust property is not included in his estate.
- Assets that pass to the surviving spouse outside the will, such as by survivorship and by beneficiary designation, can qualify for the marital deduction.
- Only post-1976 taxable gifts are added to the taxable estate as adjusted taxable gifts.
- The estate tax payable is not reduced by pre-1977 gift taxes unless the gifted property is included in the gross estate.
- Because the highest marginal income tax rate for the estate is less than the 41% marginal estate tax rate and an estate tax liability is owed (even with the available credits), administration expenses should be deducted on the estate tax return.

LIQUIDITY CONCERNS

OBJECTIVE 6

Identify tax provisions that alleviate liquidity problems

Liquidity is one of the major problems facing individuals planning their estates and eventually executors that are managing the estates. Life insurance is one source often used to help address this problem. In general, the entire amount of the estate tax liability is due nine months after the decedent's death. Certain provisions, however, allow the executor to pay some or all of the estate tax liability at a later date. Deferral of the payment of part or all of the estate taxes and three other provisions aimed at alleviating a liquidity problem are discussed below.

DEFERRAL OF PAYMENT OF ESTATE TAXES

REASONABLE CAUSE. Section 6161(a)(1) authorizes the Secretary of the Treasury to extend the payment date for the estate taxes for a reasonable period. The term *reasonable period* is defined as a period of not longer than twelve months. Moreover, the

▼ **TABLE C13-3**
Comprehensive Estate Tax Illustration

Gross estate:	
Checking account (Sec. 2033)	$ 10,000
Savings account (Sec. 2033)	75,000
Land held in joint tenancy with wife (0.50 × $400,000) (Sec. 2040)	200,000
Life insurance (Sec. 2042)	200,000
Personal residence (Sec. 2033)	325,000
Stock (Sec. 2033)	600,000
Qualified pension plan (Sec. 2039)	240,000
Gross-up for gift tax paid on 1994 gift (Sec. 2035)	11,900
Total gross estate	$1,661,900
Minus:	
Debts (Sec. 2053):	
Bank loan, including accrued interest	(25,200)
Charge cards	(6,500)
Funeral expenses (Sec. 2053)	(15,000)
Administration expenses (Sec. 2053)	(70,000)
Marital deduction (Sec. 2056):	
Residence	(325,000)
Checking account	(10,000)
Savings account	(75,000)
QTIP trust	(200,000)
Land	(200,000)
Qualified pension plan	(240,000)
Charitable contribution deduction (Sec. 2055)	(10,000)
Total reductions to gross estate	($1,176,700)
Taxable estate	$ 485,200
Plus adjusted taxable gifts (Sec. 2001(b)):	
1978	200,000
1994	480,000
Estate tax base	$1,165,200
Tentative tax on tax base (Sec. 2001)	$ 413,532
Minus:	
Reduction for post-1976 gift taxes (Sec. 2001(b))	(39,900)[a]
Unified credit (Sec. 2010)	(192,800)
State death tax credit (Sec. 2011)	(9,526)[b]
Estate tax payable	$ 171,306

[a] $28,000 (for 1978) + $11,900 (for 1994) = $39,900.
[b] This figure is calculated based on the table reproduced in Appendix G and a $425,200 adjusted taxable estate.

IRS may extend the payment date for a maximum period of ten years if the executor shows reasonable cause for not being able to pay some, or all, of the estate tax liability on the regular date.[38]

[38] Sec. 6161(a)(2).

Whenever the executor pays a portion of the estate tax after the regular due date, the estate owes interest on the portion of the tax for which payment is postponed. In general, the interest rate, which is governed by Sec. 6621, is the same as that applicable to underpayments. The interest rate on underpayments potentially fluctuates quarterly with changes in the rate paid on short-term U.S. Treasury obligations.[39]

REMAINDER OR REVERSIONARY INTERESTS. If the gross estate includes a relatively large remainder or reversionary interest, liquidity problems could result if the estate has to pay the entire estate tax liability soon after the decedent's death. The estate might not gain possession of the assets until many years after the decedent's death. For example, the estate might include a remainder interest in an asset in which a healthy, thirty-year-old person has a life estate. Section 6163 permits the executor to elect to postpone payment of the tax attributable to a remainder or reversionary interest until six months after the other interests terminate. In addition, upon being convinced of reasonable cause, the Secretary of the Treasury may grant an additional extension of not more than three years.

SELF-STUDY QUESTION

Why might a person who owns a substantial interest in a small business choose to gift property other than the business interest?

ANSWER

If this person is aware of the five-year deferral, ten-installment option of Sec. 6166, he or she may want to retain the business interest in his or her estate so that his or her estate will qualify for Sec. 6166 treatment.

INTERESTS IN CLOSELY HELD BUSINESSES. Section 6166 authorizes the executor to pay a portion of the estate tax in as many as ten annual installments in certain situations. Executors may elect to apply Sec. 6166 if

- The gross estate includes an interest in a closely held business.
- The value of the closely held business exceeds 35% of the value of the adjusted gross estate.

Closely held businesses are defined as proprietorships and partnerships or corporations having no more than fifteen owners.[40] If a corporation or partnership has more than fifteen owners, it can be classified as closely held if the decedent's gross estate includes 20% or more of the capital interest (in the partnership) or the voting stock (in the corporation).[41]

The adjusted gross estate is defined as the gross estate less *allowable* Sec. 2053 and 2054 deductions. Consequently, in determining whether the estate meets the 35% requirement, all administration expenses and casualty and theft losses are subtracted, regardless of whether the executor elects to deduct them on the estate tax return or the estate's income tax return.

Once the election is chosen, certain restrictions regarding its use must be met, including

- The portion of the estate tax that can be paid in installments is the ratio of the value of the closely held business interest to the value of the adjusted gross estate.
- The first of the ten allowable installments is generally not due until five years after the due date for the return. (This defers the last payment for as many as fifteen years.)
- Interest on the tax due is payable annually, even during the first five years.

Some or all of the installment payments may accrue interest at a rate of only 4%. The maximum amount of deferred tax to which the 4% rate applies is $345,800 minus the amount of the unified credit available for the year of death.[42] The interest rate on any additional deferred tax amounts is the same as the rate applicable to underpayments (discussed in footnote 39).

---

[39] Sec. 6621. The interest rate is discussed in Chapter C15. For the first quarter of 1997, the interest rate is 9%.

[40] Sec. 6166(b)(1).

[41] Ibid.

[42] Sec. 6601(j).

EXAMPLE C13-49 ▶ Frank dies on March 1, 1997. Frank's gross estate, which includes a proprietorship interest valued at $1,000,000, is $2,600,000. The executor deducts all $100,000 of the potential Sec. 2053 and 2054 deductions on the estate tax return. Frank has no marital or charitable contribution deductions and makes no taxable gifts. Frank's adjusted gross estate, taxable estate, and tax base are $2,500,000. His estate tax payable is $833,000 ($1,025,800 − $192,800). Frank's closely held business interest makes up 40% ($1,000,000 ÷ $2,500,000) of his adjusted gross estate.

Thus, $333,200 (0.40 × $833,000) may be paid in ten equal annual installments. The first installment payment is due on December 1, 2002. The 4% interest rate applies to $153,000 ($345,800, the tax on $1,000,000, minus the unified credit of $192,800) of Frank's deferred tax liability. Interest accrues on the remaining $180,200 ($333,200 − $153,000) at the rate for underpayments. ◀

STOCK REDEMPTIONS TO PAY DEATH TAXES

It is difficult for a shareholder to receive cash or other property in his or her role as a shareholder and avoid reporting dividend income equal to the amount of the cash or the FMV of the other property received. (Chapter C4 provides more details concerning this topic.) At a shareholder's death, however, Sec. 303 provides a chance for the estate to treat a stock redemption as a sale or exchange of the property. Thus, the amount of gain recognized is limited to the excess of the redemption price over the adjusted basis of the stock surrendered. Generally, this excess is minimal because of the step-up in basis that occurs at the time of the decedent's death.

To qualify for Sec. 303 treatment, the stock in the corporation that is redeeming the shares must make up more than 35% of the value of the decedent's gross estate, less any *allowable* Sec. 2053 and 2054 deductions. The maximum amount of redemption proceeds eligible for exchange treatment is the total of the estate's death taxes and funeral and administration expenses, regardless of whether they are deducted on the estate tax return or the estate's income tax return.

WHAT WOULD YOU DO IN THIS SITUATION?

You are a CPA specializing in wealth transfer taxation. You have established your practice in Aspen, Colorado because there is a lot of wealth situated in that ski resort. You client is a long-time resident of Aspen, and his health has recently taken a downhill turn. His doctor told him to consider putting his affairs in order because he will probably not ski any moguls for more than six months.

Your client is a merchant who owns a number of assets with FMVs totaling $1.0 million under some estimates. His largest single asset is his Victorian era store building situated in the desirable and exclusive West End of Aspen. Based on comparable fair market sales in the area, your client's building appears to be worth approximately $760,000 in the current real estate market. Because your client is in poor health, he does not use all of the store space and occasionally rents out some space in his building to vendors for selling crafts and gifts. During the ski season, the full price fair market rental value of the space would be over $1,000 per week. Your client's only son has indicated that he is not interested in moving to Aspen. The son is independently wealthy, does not really need to liquidate the building, and plans to continue the rental practices initiated by his father.

You are interested in saving your client some estate taxes. Would you propose to him that this asset be listed in the estate as Special Use Value property pursuant to IRC Sec. 2032A? Would it be ethical to propose a valuation method based on the historical income generated by this property for the estate tax return of your client? Using the historical income stream, the capitalized value would be $350,000. With this value, no tax would be owed because of an overall valuation of under $600,000 for the entire estate.

SELF-STUDY QUESTION

Why might an heir to farmland not want an estate to use the special valuation method of Sec. 2032A?

ANSWER

The heir may prefer the higher basis he or she would get if FMV is used rather than the special farmland value, especially if the estate taxes are payable out of the residual estate and the heir does not share in that residual.

SPECIAL USE VALUATION OF FARM REALTY

In 1976 Congress became concerned that farms sometimes had to be sold to generate funds to pay estate taxes. This situation was attributable, in part, to the fact that the FMV of the farm land in many areas was relatively high, perhaps because suburban housing was being built nearby. Congress enacted Sec. 2032A, which allows a property used for farming or in a trade or business other than farming to be valued using a formula approach that attempts to value the property at what it is worth for farming purposes. The lowest valuation that is permitted is $750,000 less than the property's FMV.

A number of requirements must be met before the executor can elect the special valuation rules.[43] Moreover, if during the ten-year period after the decedent's death the new owner of the property disposes of it or no longer uses it as a farm, in general, an additional tax equal to the estate tax savings that arose from the lower Sec. 2032A valuation is levied.

GENERATION-SKIPPING TRANSFER TAX

The Tax Reform Act of 1976 enacted a third transfer tax—the generation-skipping transfer tax (GSTT)—to fill a void in the gift and estate tax structure. In 1986 Congress repealed the original GSTT retroactive to its original effective date and replaced it with a revised GSTT. The new GSTT is generally applicable to *inter vivos* transfers made after September 25, 1985 and transfers at death made after October 22, 1986.

KEY POINT

The purpose of the GSTT is to ensure that a family's wealth is subject to a transfer tax for each generation. Generally, a generation is determined along family lines.

For years, a popular estate planning technique, especially among the very wealthy, involved giving people in several generations an interest in the same property. For example, a decedent might set up a testamentary trust creating successive life estates for a child and a grandchild and a remainder interest for a great grandchild. Under this arrangement, an estate tax would be imposed at the death of the person establishing the trust but not again until the great grandchild's death. The GSTT's purpose is to ensure that some form of transfer taxation is imposed one time a generation. It accomplishes its purpose by subjecting transfers that escape gift or estate taxation for one or more generations to the GSTT.

The GSTT is levied at a flat rate: the highest rate under the estate and gift tax rate schedule, which is 55%.[44] The tax applies to taxable terminations of and taxable distributions from generation-skipping transfers. A **generation-skipping transfer** involves a disposition that

- Provides interests for more than one generation of beneficiaries who are in a younger generation than the transferor, or
- Provides an interest solely for a person two or more generations younger than the transferor.[45]

For family members, generation assignments are made according to the family tree. The second type of arrangement listed above is known as a direct skip, because it skips one or more generations.

EXAMPLE C13-50 ▶ Tom creates a trust with income payable to Tom, Jr., for life and a remainder interest distributable to Tom, III, upon the death of Tom, Jr. (his father). This is a generation-skipping transfer because Tom, Jr., and Tom, III, are one and two generations younger, respectively, than the transferor (Tom). ◀

---

[43] For example, the farm real and personal property must make up at least 50% of the adjusted value of the gross estate, and the farm real property must make up 25% or more of the adjusted value of the gross estate.

[44] Sec. 2641.

[45] Sec. 2611.

EXAMPLE C13-51 ▶ Tom transfers an asset directly to Tom, III, his grandson. This is a direct skip type of generation-skipping transfer because the transferee (Tom, III) is two generations younger than the transferor (Tom). ◀

The termination of an interest in a generation-skipping arrangement is known as a taxable termination.[46] This event triggers imposition of the GSTT. The tax is levied on the before-tax amount transferred. The trustee pays the tax.

EXAMPLE C13-52 ▶ A taxable termination occurs with respect to a generation-skipping trust valued at $2,000,000. The tax is $1,100,000 (0.55 × $2,000,000). The trustee pays the tax and distributes the $900,000 of remaining assets to the beneficiary. ◀

In the case of a direct skip, the amount subject to the GSTT is the value of the property received by the transferee.[47] The transferor is liable for the tax. If the direct skip occurs *inter vivos*, the GSTT paid by the transferor is treated as an additional transfer subject to the gift tax.[48] As a result, the total transfer tax liability (GSTT plus gift tax) can exceed the value of the property received by the donee.

EXAMPLE C13-53 ▶ Susan gives $1,000,000 to her granddaughter. Susan has used all of her unified credit and is in the 55% marginal gift tax bracket; ignore the annual exclusion. The GSTT is $550,000 (0.55 × $1,000,000). The amount subject to the gift tax is the value of the property transferred ($1,000,000) plus the GSTT paid ($550,000). Thus, the gift tax is $775,000 (0.50 × $1,550,000). It costs $1,325,000 ($550,000 + $775,000) to shift $1,000,000 of property to the granddaughter. ◀

Every grantor is entitled to a $1 million exemption from the GSTT.[49] The grantor elects when, and against which transfers, to apply this exemption. Appreciation on the property for which the exemption is elected is also exempt from the GSTT.

TAX PLANNING CONSIDERATIONS

The effectiveness of many of the pre-1977 transfer tax-saving strategies has been diluted. This reduced effectiveness is attributable to the unification of the transfer tax system in general, the adoption of a unified rate schedule, and the concept of adjusted taxable gifts in particular. To some extent, the enactment of provisions that allow a higher tax base to be free of estate taxes and permit most interspousal transfers to be devoid of transfer tax consequences counterbalances unification. Various tax planning considerations that should be explored in the process of trying to reduce the transfer taxes applicable to a family unit are discussed below.

USE OF *INTER VIVOS* GIFTS

KEY POINT

Gifting of income-producing property transfers the future income on such property to the donee. The removal of this future income from the donor's possession can be important in limiting the future growth of the donor's estate.

One of the most significant strategies for reducing transfer taxes is a well-designed, long-term gift program. As long as the gifts to each donee do not exceed the $10,000 per donee annual exclusion, there will be no additions to the gross estate and no adjusted taxable gifts. Thousands of dollars of property may be passed to others free of any transfer tax consequences if enough donees are selected and gifts are made over a substantial number of years. If taxable gifts do occur, the post-gift appreciation is removed from the estate tax base. Moreover, if the donor lives more than three years after the date of the gift, the gift tax paid is removed from the gross estate.

[46] Sec. 2612(a).
[47] Sec. 2623.
[48] Sec. 2515.
[49] Sec. 2631(a).

SELF-STUDY QUESTION

What types of property should one consider gifting?

ANSWER

Gift property that either is expected to appreciate substantially in future years, produces substantial amounts of income, or is a family heirloom that will probably be passed from the donee to the donee's heirs and not sold.

The opportunities for reducing transfer taxes through the use of lifetime gifts should be weighed against the income tax disadvantage of foregoing the step up in basis that occurs if the property is retained until death. However, unless the donee is the donor's spouse, income taxes on the income produced by the gifted property may be reduced, although not as significantly as was possible before the compression of the income tax rates effective for 1987 and later tax years.

USE OF EXEMPTION EQUIVALENT

As a result of the exemption equivalent, a certain amount of property—$600,000 currently—may pass to people other than the decedent's spouse without any estate taxes being extracted therefrom. There is no limit on the amount of property that can be transferred to the spouse tax-free. Thus, because the spouse presumably will die before any children or grandchildren (i.e., individuals to whom people often will property), a wealthy person should contemplate leaving at least an amount equal to the exemption equivalent to people other than his or her spouse. (If one leaves this amount of property in trust, the trust is often called a credit shelter or bypass trust.) Otherwise, he or she will waste some or all of the exemption equivalent, and the property will be taxed when the surviving spouse dies.

Making full use of the exemption equivalent enables a husband and wife to transfer to third parties an aggregate of $1,200,000 without incurring any estate taxes. The strategy of making gifts to an ill spouse, who is not wealthy, to keep the donee-spouse's exemption equivalent from being wasted was discussed earlier (see Chapter C12). Under this technique the wealthier spouse makes gifts to the other spouse free of gift taxes because of the marital deduction. The recipient spouse then has an estate that can be passed tax-free to children, grandchildren, or other individuals because of the exemption equivalent.

STOP & THINK

Question: Sol made $600,000 in taxable gifts six years before his death. Sol's taxable estate (gross estate minus estate tax deductions) coincidentally was $600,000 also. Because of the $600,000 exemption equivalent, would Sol's estate tax payable be zero?

Solution: No. In concept, the unified credit of $192,800, which cancels out the tax on the $600,000 exemption equivalent, is available only once. Calculation of Sol's estate tax payable would be as follows:

Taxable estate	$ 600,000
Plus: Adjusted taxable gifts	600,000
Estate tax base	$1,200,000
Tentative tax on estate tax base	$ 427,800
Minus:	
Post-1976 gift tax (on $600,000 gift)	(—0—)
Unified credit	(192,800)
Estate tax payable	$ 235,000

The $235,000 represents the tax on the second $600,000 (the taxable portion of Sol's estate), which, because of the progressive rates, is a higher tax than the tax on the first $600,000.

WHAT SIZE MARITAL DEDUCTION IS BEST?

To reiterate, there is no ceiling on the amount of property eligible for the marital deduction. Even so, the availability of an unlimited marital deduction does not necessarily mean that it should be used. From a tax perspective wealthier people should leave an amount equal to the exemption equivalent to someone other than the spouse. Alternatively, they could leave the spouse an income interest in the exemption equivalent amount of property along with the power to invade such property for reasons of health, support, maintenance, or education.

In certain circumstances, it may be preferable for an amount in excess of the exemption equivalent to pass directly to third parties. It might be beneficial for the first spouse's estate to pay some estate taxes if the surviving spouse already has substantial property and has a relatively short life expectancy, especially if the decedent spouse's assets are expected to rapidly increase in value.

EXAMPLE C13-54 ▶ Paul dies in the current year with a $3,000,000 gross estate and no deductions other than the marital deduction. At the time of Paul's death, his wife has a life expectancy of two years. The assets she owns in the current year are estimated to be worth $6,000,000 in two years. Paul's property is expected to increase in value by 25% during the two-year period following his death. Paul wills his wife, Jill, $1,000,000 and his children the rest. The estate tax payable for each spouse's estate is as follows:

	Paul	*Jill*
Gross estate	$3,000,000	$7,250,000[a]
Minus: Marital deduction	(1,000,000)	—0—
Taxable estate and tax base	$2,000,000	$7,250,000
Estate tax, after unified credit	$ 588,000	$3,435,500
Combined estate tax	→ $4,023,500 ←	

[a]$6,000,000 + (1.25 × $1,000,000) = $7,250,000. ◀

EXAMPLE C13-55 ▶ Assume the same facts as in Example C13-54 except that Paul wills everything except $600,000 to Jill. The estate tax payable for each spouse's estate is as follows:

	Paul	*Jill*
Gross estate	$3,000,000	$9,000,000[a]
Minus: Marital deduction	(2,400,000)	—0—
Taxable estate and tax base	$ 600,000	$9,000,000
Estate tax, after unified credit	—0—	$4,398,000
Combined estate tax	→ $4,398,000 ←	

[a]$6,000,000 + (1.25 × $2,400,000) = $9,000,000. ◀

SELF-STUDY QUESTION

Given the facts of Examples C13-54 and C13-55, which of the two estate plans would you advise Paul and Jill to adopt?

ANSWER

For any after (income) tax rate of return of up to 27.94%, Paul and Jill should select the plan in Example C13-54. This outcome assumes that Jill will live only two years longer than Paul.

The combined estate tax liability is $374,500 higher in Example C13-55 than in Example C13-54. However, in Example C13-55, no tax is owed upon the first spouse's death. Because the estate taxes for the second spouse's estate are not payable until some later date, their discounted present value should also be considered. It should be noted that if Paul's will had created a $1,000,000 trust instead of leaving the property to Jill outright, the arrangement would have been more flexible because of partial QTIP elections.

STOP & THINK

Question: Tarik died recently at the age of 78. He was survived by his wife, Saliah, and several children and grandchildren. Saliah is 54 and in excellent health. Tarik's adjusted gross estate is \$6,200,000, and his will leaves \$600,000 outright to his children and the rest to a trust for Saliah. The trust is eligible for the QTIP election. An investment advisor believes that the trust assets will likely appreciate annually at the rate of at least 10%. Name two advantages and one disadvantage in electing the marital deduction on the entire trust.

Solution: One advantage is that the tax on the trust will be deferred, perhaps for a long time, given the wife's age and health. Another advantage is that, by not paying any tax at Tarik's death, the assets are left intact to appreciate and produce more income for Saliah. That is, there is no current capital drain to pay transfer taxes. A disadvantage is that because of the anticipated appreciation and the long time before Saliah's death, the amount taxed in Saliah's estate will likely be much greater than \$6,200,000.

USE OF DISCLAIMERS

Because a **qualified disclaimer** is not treated as a gift, disclaimers can be valuable estate planning tools (see Chapter C12). For example, if all of a decedent's property is willed to the surviving spouse, such spouse could disclaim an amount at least equal in size to the exemption equivalent and thereby enable the decedent's estate to take full advantage of the unified credit. Alternatively, a decedent's children might disclaim some bequests if, as a result of their disclaimer, the property would pass instead to the surviving spouse. This approach might be desirable if the estate otherwise would receive a relatively small marital deduction. Another scenario where a disclaimer could be appropriate is where the disclaimant is elderly and in poor health and wishes to preclude the property from being taxed again relatively soon. (Of course, the credit for tax on prior transfers would provide some relief from double taxation.) Bear in mind, however, that the person making the qualified disclaimer has no input concerning which people receive the disclaimed property.

ROLE OF LIFE INSURANCE

Life insurance is an important asset with respect to estate planning for the following reasons:

- It can help provide the liquidity for paying estate taxes and other costs associated with death.
- It has the potential for large appreciation. If the insured gives away his or her incidents of ownership and survives the gift by more than three years, his or her estate benefits by keeping the appreciation out of the estate.

Assume an individual is contemplating purchasing a new insurance policy on his or her life and transferring it to another individual as a gift. The insured must live for more than three years after making the gift in order to exclude the face amount of the policy from his or her gross estate. Should the insured die within three years of gifting the policy, the policy's face amount is included in his or her gross estate. If the donee instead purchased the policy, the insured will not make a gift of the policy, and the three-year rule will not be of concern.

QUALIFYING THE ESTATE FOR INSTALLMENT PAYMENTS

ADDITIONAL COMMENT

The payment of estate taxes can be deferred as much as fourteen years if the benefits of Sec. 6166 are timely elected. The interest that is charged on the deferred taxes is at a very favorable rate.

It can be quite beneficial for an estate owning an interest in a closely held business to qualify for installment payment of estate taxes under Sec. 6166. In a sense, the estate can borrow a certain amount of dollars from the government at 4% and the rest at a higher, but still favorable, rate.

Judicious selection of the properties that are disposed of by lifetime gifts can raise the odds that the estate will qualify for such treatment. Retaining closely held business interests and gifting other assets will increase the likelihood of the estate's being able to elect the installment payments. However, closely held business interests often have a potential for great appreciation and, consequently, from the standpoint of reducing the size of the estate are good candidates for gifts.

It is not possible for people to make gifts to restructure their estates and thereby qualify for Sec. 6166 if they wait until soon before their death to do so. If the decedent makes gifts within three years of dying, the closely held business interest must make up more than 35% of the adjusted gross estate in both of the following scenarios:

1. Calculate the ratio of the closely held business to the actual adjusted gross estate.
2. Redo the calculations after revising the ratio to include (at date-of-death values) any property given away within three years of death.

EXAMPLE C13-56 ▶

Joe dies in 1997. Joe's gross estate includes a closely held business interest valued at $400,000 and other property valued at $650,000. Joe's allowable Sec. 2053 and 2054 deductions total $50,000. In 1995, partly in hopes of qualifying his estate for Sec. 6166 treatment, Joe made gifts of listed securities of $300,000 (at 1997 valuations) and paid no gift tax on the gift. The two tests for determining whether Joe's estate is eligible for Sec. 6166 are as follows.

Excluding gifts: $400,000 ÷ $1,000,000 = 40%
Including gifts: $400,000 ÷ $1,300,000 = 30.77%

The estate may not elect Sec. 6166 treatment because it meets the more than 35% test in only one of the two computations. ◀

WHERE TO DEDUCT ADMINISTRATION EXPENSES

Another tax planning opportunity concerns the choice of where to deduct administration expenses: on the estate tax return, on the estate's income tax return, or some in each place. The decision should be made based on where the deduction will yield the greatest tax savings. Thus, if the marginal estate tax rate exceeds the estate's marginal income tax rate, which it will if the estate tax base exceeds $1,000,000, the executor should deduct the expenses on the estate tax return. If no estate taxes are owed because of the exemption equivalent or the marital deduction, administration expenses should be deducted on the estate's income tax return.

COMPLIANCE AND PROCEDURAL CONSIDERATIONS

OBJECTIVE 7

Recognize the filing requirements for estate tax returns

FILING REQUIREMENTS

Section 6018 indicates the circumstances in which estate tax returns are necessary. In general, no return is necessary unless the value of the gross estate exceeds the $600,000 exemption equivalent. An exception applies, however, if the decedent makes any post-1976 taxable gifts or claims any portion of the $30,000 specific exemption after September 8, 1976 and before January 1, 1977. In such circumstances, a return must be filed if the value of the gross estate exceeds the amount of the exemption equivalent minus the total of the decedent's adjusted taxable gifts and the amount of the specific exemption claimed against gifts made after September 8, 1976 and before January 1, 1977.

A completed sample Estate Tax Return (Form 706) appears in Appendix B. The facts on which the preparation of the return is premised are the same as for the comprehensive illustration appearing on pages C13-28 through C13-29.

ADDITIONAL COMMENT

In fiscal 1994, the IRS audited 48% of the estate tax returns filed for estates of $5 million or greater taxable estate.

DUE DATE

Estate tax returns generally must be filed within nine months after the decedent's death.[50] The Secretary of the Treasury is authorized to grant a reasonable extension of time for filing.[51] The maximum extension period is six months. Obtaining an extension does not extend the time for paying the estate tax. Section 6601 imposes interest on any portion of the tax that is not paid by the due date of the return, determined without regard to the extension period. Thus, to avoid interest, the tax must be paid by the original due date.

VALUATION

One of the most difficult tasks of preparing estate tax returns is valuing the items included in the gross estate. Some items (e.g., one-of-a-kind art objects) may truly be unique. For many properties the executor should arrange for appraisals by experts.

If the value of any property reported on the return is 50% or less of the amount determined to be the proper value during an audit or court case, an undervaluation penalty is imposed.[52] The penalty will not be imposed, however, with proof that there is a reasonable cause for the valuation claimed and that the claim is made in good faith. This penalty is increased if a gross valuation misstatement occurs; that is, the estate tax valuation is 25% or less than the amount determined to be the proper value.[53] These penalties are discussed in more detail in Chapter C12.

ELECTION OF ALTERNATE VALUATION DATE

The executor may elect to value the gross estate on the alternate valuation date instead of on the date of death. The executor must make this irrevocable election on the estate tax return. The election does not necessarily have to be made on a timely return, but no election is possible if the return is filed more than a year after the due date (including extensions).

DOCUMENTS TO BE INCLUDED WITH RETURN

The instructions for the Estate Tax Return (Form 706) indicate that numerous documents and other papers must be filed with the return. Some of the more important items that should accompany the form include

- A certified copy of the will if the decedent died testate (i.e., having made and left a valid will)
- A listing of the qualified terminable interest property and its value if the executor wishes to make the QTIP election
- Copies of appraisals for real estate
- A Form 712 (obtained from the insurance companies) for each life insurance policy on the decedent's life
- Copies of written trust and other instruments with respect to lifetime transfers made by the decedent

---

[50] Sec. 6075(a).
[51] Sec. 6081(a).
[52] Sec. 6662(g).
[53] Sec. 6662(h).

- Certified or verified copies of instruments granting the decedent a power of appointment, even if the power is not a general one
- A certified copy of the order admitting the will to probate if the will makes bequests for which a marital deduction or charitable contribution deduction is claimed

In addition, the executor should submit at the time of filing the return (or as soon thereafter as possible) a certificate from the proper officer of the taxing state that denotes the amount of the state death taxes and the payment date.

PROBLEM MATERIALS

DISCUSSION QUESTIONS

C13-1 In general, at what amount are items includible in the gross estate valued? (Answer in words.) Indicate one exception to the general valuation rules and the reason for this exception.

C13-2 A client requests that you explain the valuation rules used for gift tax and estate tax purposes. Explain the similarities and differences of the two sets of rules.

C13-3 Compare the valuation for gift and estate tax purposes of a $150,000 group term life insurance policy on the transferor's life.

C13-4 Explain how shares of stock traded on a stock exchange are valued. What is the blockage rule?

C13-5 Assume that the properties included in Alex's gross estate have appreciated during the six-month period immediately after his death. May Alex's executor elect the alternate valuation date and thereby achieve a larger step-up in basis? Explain.

C13-6 Explain to an executor an advantage and a disadvantage of electing the alternate valuation date.

C13-7 Is stock transferred by gift with no strings attached two weeks before death included in the decedent's gross estate? In the estate tax base?

C13-8 From a tax standpoint, which of the following alternatives would a client prefer?

a. Buying a new insurance policy on his life and soon thereafter giving it to another person
b. Encouraging the other person to buy the policy with funds previously accumulated

Explain your answer.

C13-9 Explain the difference between the estate tax treatment for gift taxes paid on gifts made two years before death and on gifts made ten years before death.

C13-10 A client is considering consenting to gift splitting. She wants to know whether the gross-up rule can apply to her if she consents to gift splitting for gifts her spouse made. Explain.

C13-11 A widow owns a valuable eighteenth-century residence that she would like the state historical society to have someday. Explain to her the estate tax consequences of the following two alternatives:

a. She deeds the state historical society a remainder interest in the residence and reserves the right to live there for the rest of her life.
b. She gifts her entire interest in the house to the society and moves to another home for the rest of her life.

C13-12 Which three retention periods can cause Sec. 2036 (transfers with retained life estate) to apply to a transferor's estate?

C13-13 What characteristics do Secs. 2035-2038 have in common?

C13-14 When does the consideration furnished test apply to property that the decedent held as a joint tenant with right of survivorship?

C13-15 What are the two circumstances in which life insurance on the decedent's life is includible in the gross estate under Sec. 2042? If insurance policies on the decedent's life escape being included under Sec. 2042, are they definitely excluded from the gross estate? Explain.

C13-16 Indicate two situations in which property that has previously been subject, at least in part, to gift taxation is nevertheless included in the donor-decedent's gross estate.

C13-17 Al died in the current year. Under Al's will, property is put in trust with a bank as trustee. Al's will names his sister Pam to receive the trust income annually for life and empowers Pam to will the property to whichever of her brothers, sisters, or descendants she so desires. Pam plans to leave the property by will to two of her children in equal shares. Pam seeks your advice about whether the trust will be included in her estate. Respond to Pam.

C13-18 Determine the accuracy of the following statement: The gross estate includes a general power of appointment possessed by the decedent only if the decedent exercised the power.

C13-19 Carlos dies in 1985. His will calls for the creation of a trust to be funded with $1,000,000 of property. The bank trustee must distribute all of the trust income semiannually to Carlos's widow for the rest of her life. Upon the widow's death, the trust assets are to be distributed to the couple's children. The widow dies in the current year; by then the trust assets have appreciated to $1,300,000. Are the trust assets included in the widow's gross estate? Explain.

C13-20 List the various categories of estate tax deductions, and compare them with the categories of gift tax deductions. What differences exist?

C13-21 Compare the tax treatment of administration expenses with that of debts of the decedent.

C13-22 Mona dies survived by her husband, Matt, who receives the following interests as a result of his wife's death. Does Mona's estate receive a marital deduction for them? Explain.

a. $400,000 of life insurance proceeds, Matt is the beneficiary; their son Sam has held the incidents of ownership for ten years.

b. $700,000 trust fund with income payable to Matt until the earlier of his death or remarriage. When Matt's income interest ceases, the property passes to their daughter.

C13-23 Compare the credits available for estate tax purposes with the credits available for gift tax purposes. What differences exist?

C13-24 Explain to a client the tax policy reason for allowing installment payments of the estate taxes attributable to closely held business interests.

C13-25 Assume that Larry is wealthier than Jane, his wife, and that he is likely to die before her. From an overall tax standpoint (considering transfer taxes and income taxes), is it preferable for Larry to transfer property to Jane *inter vivos* or at death, or does it matter? Explain.

C13-26 Bala desires to freeze the value of his estate. Explain which of the following assets you would recommend that Bala transfer during his lifetime (more than one asset may be suggested):

a. Life insurance on his life

b. Cash

c. Corporate bonds (assume interest rates are expected to rise)

d. Stock in a closely held business with a bright future

e. Land in a boom town

C13-27 Refer to Problem C13-26. Explain the negative considerations (if any) with respect to Bala's making gifts of the assets that you recommended.

C13-28 From a tax standpoint, why is it advisable for a wealthy married person to dispose of an amount equal to the exemption equivalent to people other than his or her spouse?

C13-29 When is the estate tax return due? In general, when is the estate tax due?

ISSUE IDENTIFICATION QUESTIONS

C13-30 Henry Arkin (a widower) is quite elderly and is beginning to do some estate planning. His goal is to reduce his transfer taxes. He is considering purchasing land with a high potential for appreciation and owning it with his grandson as joint tenants with rights of survivorship. Henry would provide all of the consideration, estimated to be about $4,500,000. What tax issues should Henry Arkin consider with respect to the purchase of the land?

C13-31 Annie James died early this year. All of her property passed subject to her will, which provides that her surviving husband, Dave James, is to receive all of the property outright. Her will further states that if Dave disclaims something, such property will pass instead to their children in equal shares. Annie's gross estate is about $5,000,000, and her Sec. 2053 deductions are very small. Dave, who is in poor health, already owns about $3,000,000 of property. What tax issues should Dave James consider with respect to the property bequested to him by his wife?

C13-32 Assume the same facts as in Problem C13-31 except that Annie's will leaves all of her property to a QTIP trust for Dave for life with the remainder to their children. What tax issues should Dave James and the estate's executor consider with respect to the property that passes to the QTIP trust?

C13-33 Jeung Hong, a widower, died in March of this year. His gross estate is $1,000,000 and he owed debts at the time of his death of $40,000. His will made a charitable bequest of $330,000 and left the rest of his property to his children. His administrative expenses are estimated to be about $55,000. What tax issues should the estate's CPA consider when preparing Jeung's estate tax return and his estate's income tax return?

PROBLEMS

C13-34 ***Valuation.*** Kay dies on May 5 of the current year. Her executor elects date-of-death valuation. Kay's gross estate includes the items listed below. What is the estate tax value of each item?

a. 1,000 shares of Milwaukee Corporation stock, traded on a stock exchange on May 5 at a high of 47, a low of 40, and a close of 46.

b. Life insurance policy on the life of Kay having a face value of $500,000. The cost of a comparable policy immediately before Kay's death is $125,250.

c. Life insurance policy on the life of Kay's son having a face value of $100,000. The interpolated terminal reserve immediately before Kay's death is $27,230. Unexpired premiums are $1,325.

d. Personal residence appraised at a FMV of $175,000 and valued for property tax purposes at $135,000.

C13-35 ***Valuation.*** Mary dies on April 3 of the current year. As of this date, Mary's gross estate is valued at $2,800,000. On October 3, Mary's gross estate is valued at $2,500,000. No assets are distributed or sold before October 3. Mary's estate has no deductions or adjusted taxable gifts. What is Mary's *lowest* possible estate tax liability? Ignore the state death tax credit.

C13-36 ***Estate Tax Formula.*** Sue dies on May 3, 1997. On March 1, 1996, Sue gave Tom some land valued at $810,000. Sue applied a unified credit of $192,800 against the tax due on this transfer. On Sue's date of death the land is valued at $600,000.

a. What is the amount included in Sue's gross estate?

b. What is the amount of Sue's adjusted taxable gifts as a result of making the 1996 gift?

C13-37 ***Transferor Provisions.*** Val dies on May 13, 1997. On October 3, 1996, she gave a $400,000 life insurance policy on her own life to Ray. Because the value of the policy was relatively low, the transfer did not cause any gift tax to be payable.

a. What amount is included in Val's gross estate as a result of the 1996 gift?

b. What amount is included in Val's gross estate if the property given is land instead of a life insurance policy?

c. Refer to Part a. What amount would be included in Val's gross estate if she instead dies on May 13, 2001?

C13-38 ***Transferor Provisions.*** In 1995 Jody transferred stock having a $1,010,000 FMV to her daughter Joan. Jody paid $153,000 of gift taxes on this transfer. When Jody died in 1997, the stock was valued at $1,500,000. Jody made no other gifts during her lifetime. With respect to the stock, what amount is included in Jody's gross estate and what amount is reported as adjusted taxable gifts?

C13-39 *Transferor Provisions.* In 1995 Curt and Kate elected gift splitting to report $2,020,000 of gifts made by Curt. Each paid gift taxes of $153,000 by spending his or her own funds. Kate died in 1997 and was survived by Curt. Her only taxable gift was the one reported for 1995. When Kate died in 1997 the gifted property had appreciated to $2,500,000. With respect to her 1995 gift, what amount is included in Kate's gross estate and what amount is reported as adjusted taxable gifts?

C13-40 *Transferor Provisions.* What amount, if any, is included in Doug's gross estate in each of the following situations:

a. In 1982 Doug creates an irrevocable trust and funds it with $400,000 of assets. He names a bank as trustee. The trust instrument provides that the income is payable to Doug annually for life. Upon Doug's death, the assets are to be divided equally among Doug's descendants. Doug dies at the age of 72. The trust assets are then worth $560,000.

b. In 1983 Doug transfers title to his personal residence to his daughter. The residence is worth $50,000 on the transfer date. Doug continues to live alone in the residence until his death and pays no rent. At Doug's death, the residence is worth $85,000.

c. In 1983 Doug creates an irrevocable trust and funds it with $200,000 of assets. Doug names himself trustee. According to the trust agreement, all the trust income is to be paid out annually for twenty-five years. The trustee, however, is to decide how much income to pay each year to each of the three beneficiaries (Doug's children). Upon termination of the trust, the assets are to be distributed equally among Doug's three children or their estates. The trust's assets are worth $310,000 when Doug dies.

d. Assume the same facts as in Part c, except that the trustee is a bank.

e. In 1984 Doug creates a revocable trust with a bank named as trustee. He names his grandson Joe as the beneficiary for life. Upon Joe's death, the property is to be distributed equally among Joe's descendants. The trust assets are worth $400,000 when Doug dies.

C13-41 *Transferor Provisions.* Latoya transfers property to an irrevocable trust in 1988 with a bank named as trustee. Latoya names Al to receive the trust income annually for life and Pat or Pat's estate to receive the remainder upon Al's death. Latoya reserves the power to designate Mike or Mike's estate (instead of Pat or Pat's estate) to receive the remainder. Upon Latoya's death, the trust assets are valued at $200,000; Al is age 50; Mike, age 27; and Pat, age 32. Assume a 10% rate for the actuarial tables.

a. How much, if any, is included in Latoya's gross estate?

b. How much would have been included in Latoya's gross estate if she had *not* retained any powers over the trust? (Assume that Latoya survives for more than three years after the transfer.)

C13-42 *Annuities.* Maria dies in the current year, two years after her retirement. At the time of her death at age 67, she is covered by the two annuities listed below.

- An annuity purchased by Maria's father providing benefits to Maria upon her reaching age 65. Upon Maria's death, survivor benefits are payable to her sister. The sister's benefits are valued at $45,000.
- An annuity purchased by Maria's former employer under a qualified plan to which only the employer contributes. Benefits are payable to Maria upon her retirement. Upon Maria's death an annuity valued at $110,000 is payable to her son.

a. What is the amount of the inclusion in Maria's gross estate with respect to each annuity?

b. How would your answer for the first annuity change if Maria had instead purchased the annuity?

c. How would your answer for the second annuity change if the employer had instead made 70% of the contributions to the qualified plan and Maria had made the remaining 30%?

C13-43 ***Jointly Owned Property.*** In 1983 Art purchases land for $60,000 and immediately titles it in the names of Art and Bart, joint tenants with right of survivorship. Bart pays no consideration. In 1997 Art dies and is survived by Bart. The land's value has appreciated to $300,000.

a. What is the amount of the inclusion in Art's gross estate?
b. If Bart died before Art, what amount would be included in Bart's gross estate?
c. Assume that Art dies in 1997 and Bart dies in 1999, when the land is worth $320,000. What amount is included in Bart's gross estate?

C13-44 ***Jointly Owned Property.*** In 1983 Fred and Gail, who are not married, pool their resources and purchase a mountain cabin. Fred provides $10,000 of consideration, and Gail furnishes $30,000. Gail dies and is survived by Fred. The property, which they had titled in the names of Fred and Gail, joint tenants with right of survivorship, is valued at $90,000 when Gail dies. What amount is included in Gail's gross estate?

C13-45 ***Jointly Owned Property.*** Mrs. Cobb buys land costing $80,000 in 1983. She has the land titled in the names of Mr. and Mrs. Cobb, joint tenants with right of survivorship. Mrs. Cobb dies and is survived by Mr. Cobb. At Mrs. Cobb's death the land's value is $200,000.

a. What amount is included in Mrs. Cobb's gross estate?
b. What is the amount, if any, of the marital deduction that Mrs. Cobb's estate can claim with respect to the land?
c. Assume Mr. Cobb dies after Mrs. Cobb and the land is worth $240,000 at his death. What amount is included in his gross estate?

C13-46 ***Powers of Appointment.*** Tai, who dies in the current year, is the income beneficiary for life of each of the trusts described below. For each trust indicate whether and why it is includible in Tai's gross estate.

a. A trust created under the will of Tai's mother, who died in 1968. Upon Tai's death, the trust assets are to pass to those of Tai's descendants whom Tai directs by his will. Should Tai fail to appoint the trust property, the trust assets are to be distributed to the Smithsonian Institution. Tai wills the property to his twin daughters in equal shares.
b. An irrevocable *inter vivos* trust created in 1960 by Tai's father. The trust agreement authorizes Tai to appoint the property to whomever he so desires. The appointment could be made only by his will. Tai appoints the property to an elderly neighbor.
c. An irrevocable trust funded by Tai in 1963. Upon Tai's death, the property is to pass to his children.
d. A trust created under the will of Tai's grandmother, who died in 1937. Her will authorizes Tai to appoint the property by his will to whomever he so desires. In default of appointment, the property is to pass to Tai's descendants in equal shares. Tai's will does not mention this trust.
e. Assume the same facts as in Part b, except that Tai's will does not mention the trust property.

C13-47 ***Life Insurance.*** Joy dies on November 5, 1997. Soon after Joy's death, the following insurance policies on Joy's life are discovered. Indicate the amount includible in Joy's gross estate for each policy.

Policy Number	*Owner*	*Beneficiary*	*Face Value*
123	Joy	Joy's husband	$400,000
757	Joy's son	Joy's estate	225,000
848	Joy's son	Joy's son	300,000
414	Joy's daughter	Joy's husband	175,000

Joy transferred policies 757 and 848 to her son in 1987. She transferred policy 414 to her daughter in 1996.

C13-48 ***Life Insurance.*** Refer to Problem C13-47. What is the net addition to Joy's *taxable estate* with respect to the insurance policies listed above if the property passing under Joy's will goes to Joy's son?

C13-49 ***Deductions.*** When Yuji dies in 1997, his gross estate is valued at $3,400,000. He owes debts totaling $500,000. Funeral and administration expenses are estimated at $15,000 and $50,000, respectively. It is estimated that the marginal estate tax rate will exceed his estate's marginal income tax rate. Yuji wills his church $30,000. What is Yuji's adjusted gross estate?

C13-50 ***Marital Deduction.*** Assume the same facts as in Problem C13-49 and that Yuji wills to his wife his stock and cash (total value of $800,000). His will also provides for setting up a trust to be funded with $400,000 of property with a bank named as trustee. His wife is to receive all of the trust income semiannually for life, and upon her death the trust assets are to be distributed equally among Yuji's children and grandchildren.

a. What is the amount of Yuji's taxable estate? Provide two possible answers.

b. Assume Yuji's widow dies in 2000. With respect to Yuji's former assets, which items will be included in the widow's gross estate? Provide two possible answers.

C13-51 ***Marital Deduction.*** Assume the same facts as in Problems C13-49 and C13-50 and that before Yuji's death his wife already owns property valued at $300,000. Assume that each asset owned by each spouse increases 20% in value by 2000 and that Yuji's executor elects to claim the maximum marital deduction possible. From a tax standpoint, was the executor's strategy of electing the marital deduction on the QTIP trust a wise decision? Support your answer with computations.

C13-52 ***Adjusted Taxable Gifts.*** Will, a bachelor, dies in the current year. At the time he dies, his sole asset is cash of $1,000,000. Assume no debts or funeral and administration expenses. His gift history is as follows:

Date	*Amount of Taxable Gifts*	*FMV of Gift Property at Date of Death*
October 1977	$270,000	$290,000
October 1981	90,000	65,000

a. What is Will's estate tax base?

b. How would your answer to Part a change if the first gift were made in 1974 (instead of 1977)?

C13-53 ***Estate Tax Base.*** Bess dies in 1997. Her gross estate, which totals $3,000,000, includes a $100,000 life insurance policy on her life that she gave away in 1996. The taxable gift that arose from giving away the policy was $15,000. In 1995 Bess made a $40,000 taxable gift of stock whose value increased to $75,000 by the time Bess died. Assume her estate tax deductions total $80,000.

a. What is her estate tax base?

b. What unified credit may her estate claim?

C13-54 ***Installment Payments.*** Claire dies on May 1, 1997. Her gross estate consists of the following items:

Cash	$ 40,000
Stocks traded on a stock exchange	410,000
Personal residence	175,000
25% capital interest in six-person partnership	325,000

Claire's Sec. 2053 deductions total $30,000. She has no other deductions.

a. What fraction of Claire's federal estate taxes may be paid in installments under Sec. 6166? When is the first installment payment due?
b. May Claire's estate elect Sec. 6166 treatment if the stocks are valued at $2,000,000 instead of $410,000?

C13-55 ***State Death Tax Credit.*** Demetrius dies with a taxable estate of $680,000 and a tax base of $710,000. His estate pays state death taxes of $20,000. What is the credit for state death taxes?

COMPREHENSIVE PROBLEMS

C13-56 Bonnie dies on June 1, 1997. Bonnie is survived by her husband, Abner, and two sons, Carl and Doug. Bonnie's only lifetime taxable gift is made in October 1995 in the taxable amount of $700,000. She does not elect gift splitting. By the time of her death, the value of the gifted property (stock) has risen to $820,000.

Bonnie's executor discovers the items shown below. Amounts shown are the FMVs of the items as of June 1, 1997.

Cash in checking account in her name	$100,000
Cash in savings account in her name	430,000
Stock in names of Bonnie and Doug, joint tenants with right of survivorship. Bonnie provided all the consideration ($3,000) to purchase the stock.	25,000
Land in names of Bonnie and Abner, joint tenants with right of survivorship. Abner provided all the consideration to purchase the land.	360,000
Personal residence in only Bonnie's name	250,000
Life insurance on Bonnie's life; Bonnie is owner and Bonnie's estate is beneficiary (face value)	210,000
Trust created by will of Bonnie's mother (who died in 1965). Bonnie is entitled to all the trust income for life, and she could will the trust property to whomever she desired. She wills it to her sons in equal amounts.	700,000

Bonnie's debts, as of her date of death, are $60,000. Her funeral and administration expenses total $80,000. The executor deducts the administration expenses on the estate tax return.

Bonnie's will includes the following:

"I leave my residence to my husband Abner."

"$250,000 of property is to be transferred to a trust with First Bank named as trustee. All of the income is to be paid to my husband, Abner, semiannually for the rest of his life. Upon his death the property is to be divided equally between my two sons or their estates."

"I leave $47,000 to the American Cancer Society."

Assume that the executor elects to claim the maximum marital deduction possible. Compute the following with respect to Bonnie's estate:

a. Gross estate
b. Adjusted gross estate
c. Taxable estate
d. Adjusted taxable gifts
e. Estate tax base
f. Tentative tax on estate tax base
g. Federal estate tax payable (assume her state death taxes exactly equal the amount of the credit for state death taxes)

C13-57 Assume the same facts as in Problem C13-56, except that the joint tenancy land is held in the names of Bonnie and Doug, joint tenants with right of survivorship, and Bonnie provided 55% of the consideration to buy the land; Bonnie's executor does not elect to claim the marital deduction on the QTIP trust; and the administration expenses ($65,000) are deducted on the estate's income tax return. (Assume that there is no taxable gift on the purchase of the joint tenancy land.)

TAX FORM/RETURN PREPARATION PROBLEMS

C13-58 Prepare an Estate Tax Return (Form 706) for Judy Griffin (464-55-3434), who dies on June 30, 1996. Judy is survived by her husband, Greg, and her daughter, Candy. Judy was a resident of 17 Fiddlers Way, Nashville, Tennessee 37205. She was employed as a corporate executive with Sounds of Country, Inc., a recording company, at the time of her death. The assets discovered at Judy's death are listed below. Amounts shown are date-of-death values.

Savings account in Judy's name	$190,000
Checking account in Judy's name	10,000
Personal residence (having a $200,000 mortgage)	500,000
Household furnishings	75,000
400 shares of stock in Omega Corporation (quotes on June 30, 1996 are high of 70, low of 60, close of 67)	?
Land in New York (inherited from her mother in 1970)	140,000
Porsche purchased by Greg in 1991 as an anniversary gift to Judy	45,000

Other items include the following:

1. Life insurance policy 1: Judy purchased a $200,000 life insurance policy on her life on August 1, 1993 and paid the first annual premium of $2,500. The next day, she transferred the policy to her brother, Todd Williams, who is also the beneficiary. Judy paid the premium on August 1, 1994 and 1995.
2. Life insurance policy 2: A $150,000 whole life policy on Greg's life. Judy purchased the policy in 1980 and has always paid the $1,200 semiannual premium due on March 30 and September 30. Interpolated terminal reserve is $25,000. The beneficiary is Judy or her estate. Judy is the owner of the policy.
3. Employer annuity: Judy's employer established a qualified pension plan in 1980. The employer contributes 60% and the employee pays 40% of the required annual contributions. Judy chose a settlement option that provides for annual payments to Greg until his death. The annuity receivable by Greg is valued at $600,000.

Other information includes the following:

1. In October 1994, Judy transferred to her brother, Todd, $1,520,000 of stock that she received as a gift. Judy and Greg elected gift splitting. This was the first taxable gift for each spouse, and they paid their own portion of the gift tax from their own funds. When Judy dies, the stocks have appreciated to $1,600,000.
2. Unpaid bills at death include $2,500 owed on a bank credit card.
3. The cost of Judy's funeral and tombstone totals $25,000.
4. Judy's administration expenses are estimated at $55,000. Her estate's marginal transfer tax rate will be higher than the estate's marginal income tax rate.
5. Judy's will includes the following dispositions of property:

   "I leave $60,000 of property in trust with Fourth Bank named as trustee. All income is to be paid semiannually to my husband, Greg, for life or until he remarries, whichever occurs first. At the termination of Greg's interest, the property will pass to my daughter, Candy, or her estate."

   "To my beloved husband, Greg, I leave my Omega stock. The rest of my property I leave to my daughter, Candy, except that I leave $10,000 to the University of Tennessee."

6. Assume the state estate tax payable equals the maximum credit available on the federal return for state death taxes.
7. Make the QTIP election if possible.

C13-59 Prepare an Estate Tax Return (Form 706) for Joe Blough (177-47-3217) of 1412 Robin Lane, Birmingham, Alabama 35208. Joe died on November 12, 1996; he was survived by his wife, Joan, and their daughter, Katy. Joe was a bank vice president. Date-of-death values of the assets discovered at Joe's death are listed below.

Checking and savings accounts in names of Joe and Joan, joint tenants with right of survivorship	$800,000
Second home, in Joe's name	450,000
Life insurance policy on Joe's life; his estate is the beneficiary and Joan is the owner	250,000

Other pertinent information is as follows:

1. In 1985 Joe gave his sister land then valued at $220,000. He and Joan elected gift splitting. This was Joe's first taxable gift. The land was worth $350,000 when Joe died.
2. Joan owns the house that had been the couple's principal residence. Its value is $750,000.
3. Joe willed all of his property to their daughter, Katy.
4. For simplicity, assume there are no administration expenses and that funeral expenses are $11,000.
5. Assume that state death taxes are equal to the federal credit for state death taxes.

CASE STUDY PROBLEMS

C13-60 Your clients, Matt and Mindy Mason, have come to you for estate planning advice. Each is age 66 and in reasonably good health. Mr. and Mrs. Mason have no children by their marriage, but Mrs. Mason has two children (Brett and Becky) by her previous marriage. Mr. and Mrs. Mason, residents of a non-community property state, own the assets with the FMVs listed below:

	Mr. Mason	*Mrs. Mason*
Cash	$1,000,000	$1,500,000
Life insurance on self	1,300,000	—0—
Stocks in public companies	2,000,000	800,000
Residence	—0—	400,000
Stock in solely owned company	125,000	—0—

In addition, Mrs. Mason is the beneficiary of a trust created under the will of her mother, who died in 1975. The trust is currently valued at $350,000. Under the trust instrument, Mrs. Mason is entitled to receive all of the trust income for life and may specify in her will the person(s) to receive the remainder interest. Mr. Mason's nephew (Norman) is the beneficiary of the insurance policy on Mr. Mason's life.

Fortunately, both Mr. and Mrs. Mason are free of debt.

Mr. Mason's will includes the following provisions at present:

> "I leave all of my property to my wife, Mindy Mason, if she survives me. If she does not survive me, I leave all of my property to my favorite charitable organization, the Humane Society of Louisville."

Mrs. Mason's will includes the following provisions at present:

"I leave each of my grandchildren [five people are named] and each of my nieces and nephews [twenty-five people are named] $15,000 each."

"I leave assets valued at $600,000 to my son and daughter (Brett and Becky) in equal shares."

"I appoint the property of the trust created under my mother's will to my sister, Helen Adams, or her descendants."

"The rest of my estate I leave to a trust with First Bank as trustee. My husband, Matt, is to receive all of the trust income annually until the earlier of his death or remarriage. The remainder is to pass in equal shares to my son and daughter, or their descendants. Should my spouse predecease me, all of the rest of my estate is to be divided equally between my son and daughter, or their descendants."

For simplicity, assume that there will be no funeral or administration expenses for either spouse and that no death taxes are payable from property eligible for the marital or charitable contribution deductions. Assume also that state death taxes are equal to the credit for state death taxes available on the federal estate tax return.

Required:

a. Prepare a memorandum to the tax partner of your firm that calculates the total estate taxes payable by the two estates under the situations listed below. Ignore further appreciation. Assume that:

1. Matt dies first.

2. Mindy dies first.

b. Make estate planning recommendations in your memorandum that would reduce the couple's estate tax liability. Assume that Matt will die first.

c. In making your suggestions to the clients, what factors besides tax consequences should you consider?

C13-61 Your client is Jon Jake, the executor of the Estate of Beth Adams. Mrs. Adams died a widow, eleven years after the death of her husband Sam. Mr. Jake wants assistance in the preparation of the estate tax return for Mrs. Adams, whose estate consists primarily of real estate. Mrs. Adams's estate will be divided among her three adult children except that a small amount of property is willed to charity. The real estate has been appraised at $2,000,000 by her son-in-law (who is married to one of Mrs. Adams's three children), an experienced real estate appraiser. You have a number of real estate clients and have considerable familiarity with property values for real estate located in the same general area as the estate's property. Your "gut feeling" is that the appraised values may be somewhat understated. What responsibilities do you have as a tax adviser to make additional inquiries? What information should you give Mr. Jake concerning possible penalties?

TAX RESEARCH PROBLEMS

C13-62 Roy, a Texas resident, dies in the current year, at the age of 80, survived by his bachelor son, Ted. At the time of his death, Roy is living in a residence that he purchased in 1970 and that he and Ted occupy as their personal residence. In 1975, Roy deeded the residence to Ted, but until his death Roy continues to live in the house with Ted without paying rent. After deeding the house to Ted, Roy never has any visitors unless he first receives Ted's permission. On many occasions, Roy mentions to his friends that he fears Ted will commit him to a nursing home. After the transfer, Ted pays all of the property taxes on the residence. The residence is valued at $150,000 at Roy's death. Your senior asked that you write a memorandum addressing the amount (if any) that is included in Roy's gross estate with respect to the residence.

Your senior suggested that you begin your research with the following authorities:

- Reg. Sec. 20.2036-1

- Rev. Rul. 70-155, 1970-1 C.B. 189
- *Estate of Allen D. Gutchess*, 46 T.C. 554 (1966)
- *Estate of Emil Linderme, Sr.*, 52 T.C. 305 (1969)
- *Estate of Sylvia H. Roemer*, 1983 PH T.C. Memo ¶83,509, 46 TCM 1176

C13-63 Val, a resident of Illinois, dies on June 12 of the current year. On May 5 she writes four checks for $10,000 each, payable to each of her four grandchildren. Val mails the checks on May 6, and each donee receives the check on or before May 9. None of the donees deposit their checks until after Val's death. As of Val's date of death, the balance in her checking account is $52,127. This balance includes the $40,000 of outstanding checks issued to her grandchildren. Assume the executor will elect date-of-death valuation.

Your senior requested that you prepare a memorandum concerning whether the checks will be able to be subtracted from the $52,127 cash balance in arriving at the cash includible in Val's gross estate. Your senior indicates that you should start with the following authorities:

- Sec. 2031(a)
- Reg. Secs. 20.2031-5 and 25.2511-2(b)

C13-64 Randy died on June 10 of the current year. His will created a trust from which his surviving spouse is entitled to receive all of the trust income quarterly for life; however, any income accumulated between the last quarterly payment date and his spouse's date of death is to be paid to the remainderman, Randy, Jr. Prepare a memorandum in which you address whether the trust is eligible for the marital deduction under the QTIP rules.

CHAPTER 14

INCOME TAXATION OF TRUSTS AND ESTATES

LEARNING OBJECTIVES

After studying this chapter, you should be able to

1. Understand the basic concepts concerning trusts and estates
2. Distinguish between principal and income
3. Explain how to calculate the tax liability of a trust or an estate
4. Understand the significance of distributable net income
5. Determine the taxable income of a simple trust
6. Determine the taxable income of a complex trust
7. Recognize the significance of income in respect of a decedent
8. Explain the effect of the grantor trust provisions
9. Recognize the filing requirements for fiduciary returns

CHAPTER OUTLINE

Chapters C12 and C13 examined two components of the transfer tax system: the gift tax and the estate tax. We return to income taxation by exploring the basic rules for the taxation of trusts and estates, two special tax entities, often called **fiduciaries**. Income generated by property owned by an estate or a trust is reported on an income tax return for that entity. In general, the tax rules governing estates and trusts are identical. Unless the text states that a rule applies to only one of these entities, the discussion concerns both estates and trusts. Subchapter J (Secs. 641-692) contains the special tax rules applicable to estates and trusts. This chapter describes the basic provisions of Subchapter J.

This chapter also discusses principles of fiduciary accounting, a concept that influences the tax consequences. The major focus of the chapter is on the determination of the taxable income of the fiduciary and the amount taxable to the beneficiaries. Comprehensive examples concerning the computations are included, and Appendix B includes completed tax returns (Form 1041) for both a simple and a complex trust. The chapter also explores the circumstances that cause the grantor (transferor) to be taxed on the trust's income.

BASIC CONCEPTS

OBJECTIVE 1

Understand the basic concepts concerning trusts and estates

INCEPTION OF TRUSTS

Often a relatively wealthy person (one for whom gift and estate taxes are relevant) will create trusts for tax and other reasons (e.g., conserving assets). Trusts may be created at any point in time by transferring property to the trusts. The property in the trust is administered by a **trustee** (named by the transferor) for the benefit of the beneficiary. The trustee may be either an individual or an institution, such as a bank, and there can be more than one trustee.

If the transfer occurs during the transferor's lifetime, the trust is called an **inter vivos trust**. The transferor is known as the **grantor** or the **trustor**. A trust created under the direction of a decedent's will is called a **testamentary trust**. The assets used to fund a testamentary trust were formerly held by the decedent's estate. A trust may continue to exist for whatever time is specified in the trust instrument or the will, subject to the constraints of the **Rule Against Perpetuities.**[1]

KEY POINT

Trusts and estates (fiduciaries) are treated as taxable entities separate from their beneficiaries. This chapter deals with the determination of the federal income tax liability of fiduciaries.

INCEPTION OF ESTATES

Estates come into being only upon the death of the person whose assets are being administered. The estate continues in existence until the duties of the executor[2] (i.e., the person(s) named in the will to manage the property and distribute the assets) have been completed. An executor's duties include collecting the assets, paying the debts and taxes, and distributing the properties. The time to perform the duties may vary from a year or two to over a decade, depending on many factors (e.g., whether anyone contests the will).

ADDITIONAL COMMENT

The IRS reports that 3.19 million fiduciary income tax returns (Forms 1041 and 1041S) were filed in 1995.

Sometimes the decedent's survivors can reduce their personal income taxes by preserving the estate's existence. The estate is a separate tax entity. Thus, continuing the estate's existence achieves having some income taxed to yet another taxpayer, even though the estate's tax rates are very compressed. The Regulations provide, however, that if the IRS considers the administration of an estate to have been unreasonably

[1] The Rule against Perpetuities addresses how long property may be tied up in trust and is the "principle that no interest in property is good unless it must vest, if at all, not later than 21 years, plus period of gestation, after some life or lives in being at time of creation of interest." Henry C. Black, *Black's Law Dictionary,* Rev. 6th ed., Ed. by Joseph R. Nolan and Jacqueline M. Nolan-Haley (St. Paul, MN: West Publishing Co., 1990), p. 1,331.

[2] In some states this individual is called a personal representative.

KEY POINT

A trust is a contract between two parties: the grantor and the trustee. The grantor gives the trustee legal title to property, which the trustee then holds for the benefit of a third party(ies), called the beneficiary(ies). The trustee, acting in a fiduciary capacity, manages the property for the duration of the trust. Beneficiaries of a trust may have an income interest, which means that they receive part or all of the trust's income, or they may have a remainder interest, which means that they will receive the property held by the trust on some specified future date. A beneficiary may hold both an income interest and a remainder interest. The grantor may be a beneficiary and/or the trustee.

prolonged, it will view the estate as having been terminated for federal tax purposes after the expiration of a reasonable period for performance of the administrative duties.[3] In such a situation, the income is taxed directly to the individuals entitled to receive the assets of the estate. These people may have a higher marginal tax rate than the estate.

REASONS FOR CREATING TRUSTS

A myriad of reasons—both tax and nontax—exist for creating trusts. Some of these reasons are discussed here.

TAX SAVING ASPECTS OF TRUSTS. If the trust is irrevocable, meaning the grantor cannot require the trustee to return the assets, one of the primary tax purposes for establishing the trust has traditionally been to achieve income splitting. With income splitting, the income from the trust assets is taxed to at least one taxpayer (i.e., the trust or the beneficiary) at a lower marginal tax rate than the grantor. Because of the compression of the rate schedules after 1986, trusts do not offer the same benefits from income shifting now that they originally did. The accumulation distribution rules also reduce the effectiveness of using trusts to decrease taxes. Sometimes the trust instrument authorizes the trustee to use his or her discretion in "sprinkling" the income among several beneficiaries or accumulating it within the trust. In such circumstances, the trustee must consider the tax effects of making a distribution of income to one beneficiary rather than another or retaining income in the trust.

Individuals may also create trusts in order to minimize their estate taxes. As discussed in Chapter C13, in order for the transferor to exclude the property conveyed to the trust from the gross estate, the transferor must not retain the right to receive the trust income or the power to control which other people receive the income[4] or have, at the time of death, the power to alter the identity of any people named earlier to receive such assets.[5]

NONTAX ASPECTS OF TRUSTS. Reduction of taxes is not always the foremost reason for establishing trusts. Trusts, including Sec. 2503(c) trusts and *Crummey* trusts, are often used when minors are the donees so that a trustee can manage the assets. (See Chapter C12 for a discussion of such trusts.) Even when the donee is an adult, donors may sometimes prefer that the assets be managed by a trustee deemed to have better management skills than the donee. Other donors may want to avoid conveying assets directly to a donee if they fear the donee would soon consume most of them. In addition, trusts are sometimes used to protect assets from creditors.

The creation of a **revocable trust** (i.e., one in which the grantor may demand that the assets be returned) does not yield any income or estate tax savings for the grantor. Nevertheless, revocable trusts, including ones in which the grantor is also the beneficiary, are often created for nontax purposes such as having the properties managed by an individual or an institution with superior management skills. In states in which the probate costs for administering a decedent's estate are high, use of a revocable trust reduces probate costs because assets in a revocable trust avoid probate. In this text, a trust is deemed to be an **irrevocable trust** unless it is explicitly denoted as being revocable.

BASIC PRINCIPLES OF FIDUCIARY TAXATION

Throughout the rest of this chapter several basic principles of fiduciary taxation should be kept in mind. These features are discussed below. They apply to all trusts other than

[3] Reg. Sec. 1.641(b)-3(a).
[4] Sec. 2036.
[5] Sec. 2038.

grantor trusts. (See pages C14-36 through C14-40 for a description of the tax treatment of grantor trusts.)

TRUSTS AND ESTATES AS SEPARATE TAXPAYERS. An estate or a trust is a separate taxpaying entity. If the estate or trust has any taxable income, it pays an income tax. Such tax is calculated by using Form 1041. The 1997 tax rates applicable to estates and trusts are reproduced on the inside back cover. These rates became indexed for inflation beginning in 1989. The rates are very compressed in comparison with the rates for individuals. As is true for individuals, an estate's or trust's long-term capital gains are taxed at a top tax rate of 28%.

EXAMPLE C14-1 ▶ For calendar year 1997, a trust reports taxable income of $10,000. Its tax liability is $3,039. An unmarried individual not qualifying as a head of household would owe taxes of $1,500 on $10,000 of taxable income. ◀

KEY POINT

Essentially, an estate or a trust is taxed only on income it retains. Taxable income that it passes on (distributes) to the income beneficiaries is taxable to those beneficiaries.

NO DOUBLE TAXATION. Unlike the situation for corporations, there is no double taxation of the income earned by an estate or trust. The estate or trust receives a deduction for the income it distributes to its beneficiaries. The beneficiaries, in turn, report the taxable portion of their receipts as income on their individual returns. Thus, the current income is taxed once, to the fiduciary or to the beneficiary or some to each, depending on whether it is distributed. In total, all of the estate or trust's current income is taxed, perhaps some to the fiduciary and the remaining amount to the beneficiary. One of the primary purposes of the Subchapter J rules is to determine exactly where the estate or trust's current income is taxed.

EXAMPLE C14-2 ▶ In the current year, the Lopez Trust receives total dividend income of $25,000, of which $15,000 is distributed at the trustee's discretion to Lupe. Lupe is taxed on $15,000, the amount of the distribution. The trust is taxed on the income it retains or accumulates, $10,000 in this case, less a $100 personal exemption (discussed on page C14-10). ◀

CONDUIT APPROACH. A conduit approach governs for fiduciary income taxation. Under this approach, the distributed income has the same character in the hands of the beneficiary as it has to the trust. Thus, if the trust distributes tax-free interest income on state and local bonds, such income retains its tax-free character at the beneficiary level.

EXAMPLE C14-3 ▶ In the current year, the Lopez Trust receives $15,000 of dividends and $10,000 of tax-free interest. It distributes all of its receipts to its beneficiary. The beneficiary is deemed to receive $15,000 of dividend income and $10,000 of tax-free interest. ◀

SELF-STUDY QUESTION

King Trust receives interest on a savings account. All of the trust income is distributed to Anne. Because the trust is treated as a conduit, the interest is reported by Anne as taxable interest. Why might this be important?

ANSWER

For purposes of the limitation on the investment interest deduction, the interest from the trust is part of Anne's investment income. For purposes of the passive loss limitations, it is classified as portfolio income.

SIMILARITY TO RULES FOR INDIVIDUALS. Section 641(b) states "[T] he taxable income of an estate or trust shall be computed in the same manner as in the case of an individual, except as otherwise provided in this part." Sections 641–683 appear in this part (Part I) of Subchapter J. Thus, the tax effect for fiduciaries is the same as for individuals if the provisions of Secs. 641–683 do not specify rules that differ from those applicable for individual taxpayers. Sections 641–683 do not contain any special treatment for interest income from state and local bonds or for state and local tax payments. Consequently, an estate or trust is entitled to an exclusion for state and local bond interest and the same deductions as individuals for state and local taxes. On the other hand, Sec. 642(b) specifies the amount of the personal exemption to which fiduciaries are entitled. Thus, this subsection preempts the Sec. 151 rule concerning the amount of the personal exemption for individuals.

PRINCIPLES OF FIDUCIARY ACCOUNTING

OBJECTIVE 2

Distinguish between principal and income

For a better understanding of the special tax treatment of fiduciary income, especially the determination of to whom the estate or trust's current income is taxed, one needs a general knowledge of the principles of fiduciary accounting. In a sense, fiduciary accounting is similar to fund accounting for government entities. Instead of having separate funds, all receipts and disbursements are classified as either income or principal (or corpus).

THE IMPORTANCE OF IDENTIFYING INCOME AND PRINCIPAL

When computing taxable income, we are generally concerned with whether a particular item is included in or deducted from gross income. When answering fiduciary tax questions, however, we also need to consider whether an item is classified as principal (corpus) or income for fiduciary accounting purposes. For example, certain items (e.g., interest on state bonds) may constitute **fiduciary accounting income** but are not included in the gross income calculation. Other items (e.g., capital gains) may be included in gross income but classified as principal for fiduciary accounting purposes.

One of the most difficult aspects of feeling comfortable with the fiduciary taxation rules is to appreciate the difference between fiduciary accounting income and income in the general tax sense. To understand and apply the Code, one has to know in which context the word *income* is used. Section 643(b) provides guidance for this matter. It states, "[F]or purposes of this subpart and subparts B, C and D [Secs. 641–668], the term 'income' when not preceded by the words 'taxable,' 'distributable net,' 'undistributed net,' or 'gross,' means the amount of income of the estate or trust for the taxable year determined under the terms of the governing instrument and applicable local law." In other words, in most of Subchapter J, the word *income* refers to income in the fiduciary accounting context unless other words modify the word *income.* In this text, the term *net accounting income* is used to refer to the excess of accounting gross income over expenses charged to accounting income.

SELF-STUDY QUESTION

A trust agreement provides that all trust income is to be distributed to Janet until Joe's thirty-fifth birthday, at which time the trust is to terminate and distribute all of its corpus to Joe. Stock is the only property owned by the trust. The stock, purchased for $15,000 by the trust fifteen years ago, is worth $100,000. If the trust sells the stock before it terminates, is Janet entitled to the $85,000 profit and Joe to the $15,000 original investment?

ANSWER

This question stresses the reason why income and principal must be differentiated. The trustee, in his or her fiduciary capacity, must follow the definitions of income and corpus as stated in the trust agreement, or if not there, under state law. Janet receives nothing if the proceeds are classified as corpus.

The categorization of a receipt or disbursement as principal or income generally affects the amount taxed to the fiduciary or the beneficiary. For example, if a gain is classified as principal and the trustee can distribute only income, the trust is taxed on the gain. Even though an item may constitute gross income for tax purposes, it cannot be distributed to a beneficiary if it constitutes principal under the fiduciary accounting rules unless the trustee is authorized to distribute principal. If the trust instrument stipulates that the trustee can distribute only income prior to the termination of the trust, the amount of fiduciary accounting income sets the ceiling on the current distribution that the trustee can make to a beneficiary.

EXAMPLE C14-4 ▶

In the current year, the Bell Trust reports net accounting income of $18,000. In addition, it sells stock for a $40,000 capital gain. Under state law the gain is allocated to principal. The trust instrument requires the trustee to distribute all of the trust's income to Beth annually until she reaches age 45. The trust assets are to be held and paid to Beth on her forty-fifth birthday (five years from now). The trustee must distribute $18,000 to Beth in the current year. The capital gain cannot be distributed currently because it is allocated to principal, and the trustee is not empowered to make distributions of principal. The trust will pay tax on the gain. ◀

EFFECTS OF STATE LAW OR TERMS OF TRUST INSTRUMENT

Recall that for purposes of Subchapter J, *income* generally refers to income as determined under the governing instrument and applicable local law. Grantors can influence the tax consequences to trusts and their beneficiaries because they can define income and principal in the trust instrument in whatever manner they desire. For example, they can specify that gains are to be included in income. Under state law, the definitions in the trust instrument preempt any definitions contained in state statutes. In the absence of definitions in the trust instrument, the applicable state statute controls for classifying items as principal or income. For purposes of defining principal and income, many states have adopted the *Revised Uniform Principal and Income Act* (hereafter referred to as the *Uniform Act*) in its entirety or with minor modifications.[6]

PRINCIPAL AND INCOME: THE UNIFORM ACT

INCOME RECEIPTS. The Uniform Act defines *income* as "the return in money or property derived from the use of principal." It lists income as including the following: rent, interest, corporate distributions of dividends, distributions by a regulated investment company from ordinary income, and the net profits of a business. The rules are more detailed for receipts from the disposition of natural resources. A portion (27.5%) of the receipts from royalties is added to principal as a depletion allowance. The remainder of the royalties constitutes income.

SELF-STUDY QUESTION

Why does the Uniform Act allocate to principal some part of the royalty from a property such as a gravel pit?

ANSWER

A property such as the one described is a wasting asset, which means that the removal of the mineral eventually uses up the property. The principal of the trust would be reduced by such removal if some part of the property removed were not added back into principal, ostensibly to be used to replace whatever was removed.

PRINCIPAL RECEIPTS. ***Principal*** is defined in the Uniform Act as "the property which has been set aside by the owner or the person legally empowered so that it is held in trust eventually to be delivered to the **remainderman** while the return or use of the principal is in the meantime taken or received by or held for accumulation for an **income beneficiary**." Among the categories of receipts included in principal are the following: consideration received on the sale or other transfer of principal or on repayment of a loan, stock dividends, receipts from disposition of corporate securities, and 27.5% of royalties received from natural resources.

SELF-STUDY QUESTION

A person contemplating establishing a trust needs to understand the definitions of income and expense as defined in the state in which he or she is domiciled. Why?

ANSWER

There might be substantial differences between what the person thinks is included in fiduciary accounting income and what the law defines as that income.

EXPENDITURES. The Uniform Act provides guidance for expenditures also. Among the important charges for which income is to be reduced are the following:

- Ordinary expenses, including regularly recurring property taxes, insurance premiums, interest, and ordinary repairs
- A reasonable allowance for depreciation
- Tax payable by the trustee if it is levied on receipts classified as income

Some of the more significant expenditures chargeable to principal are

- Principal payments on an indebtedness
- Extraordinary repairs or expenses incurred in making a capital improvement
- Any tax levied on gain or other receipts allocated to principal even if the tax is described as an income tax

Generally, the agreement with the trustee specifies the respective portions of the trustee's fee that are chargeable to income and corpus.

EXAMPLE C14-5 ▶ The governing instrument for the Wang Trust contains no definitions of income and principal. The state in question has adopted the Uniform Act. In the current year the trust reports the following receipts and disbursements:

[6] The *Revised Uniform Principal and Income Act* is a model set of rules proposed by the Uniform Commission on State Laws. States can voluntarily adopt such provisions verbatim or in amended form.

Dividends	$12,000
Proceeds from sale of stock, including $20,000 of gain	70,000
Trustee's fee, all charged to income	1,000
CPA's fee for preparation of tax return	500

The trust's net accounting income is $10,500 ($12,000 − $1,000 − $500). The gain on the sale of stock and the rest of the sales proceeds constitute corpus. ◀

SELF-STUDY QUESTION

Wilson Trust, which owns a commercial building, is required to distribute all of its income each year. The building is leased to a tenant on a net lease, so the only expense the trust has is depreciation. The rental income is $25,000 and the depreciation is $11,000. If depreciation is chargeable to income, the distribution to the income beneficiary will be $14,000 and $11,000 of the income will be set aside for the remainderman. What is the impact if depreciation is chargeable to principal?

ANSWER

The income distribution will be $25,000. If the trust holds the building to the end of its useful life, the building will theoretically "turn to dust" overnight and the remainderman would receive nothing (as far as the building is concerned) because there was no depreciation reserve.

CATEGORIZATION OF DEPRECIATION

As mentioned above, depreciation is charged to income under the Uniform Act; it thereby reduces net accounting income and the maximum amount that can be distributed to a beneficiary if the trust instrument does not authorize the distribution of corpus. Many states have departed from the Uniform Act's treatment of depreciation by providing that depreciation is a charge against principal (instead of against income). If depreciation is charged against principal, the maximum amount that can be distributed to the income beneficiaries is not reduced by the depreciation deduction. This result is advantageous to the income beneficiary. (See page C14-9 for a discussion of the tax treatment of depreciation.)

A statement in the trust instrument concerning the accounting treatment for depreciation overrides a provision of state law. Some trust instruments require the trustee to set aside (and not distribute) a certain amount of income as a depreciation reserve.

EXAMPLE C14-6 ▶

Park Trust, whose trust instrument is silent with respect to depreciation, collects rental income of $17,000 and pays property taxes of $1,000. Its depreciation expense is $4,000. Under state law, all depreciation is charged to principal. Therefore, the trust's net accounting income is $16,000 ($17,000 − $1,000). If the trust instrument mandates current distribution of all the income, the beneficiary receives $16,000. If the trust instrument states that depreciation is charged against income, the income distribution is limited to $12,000. ◀

Topic Review C14-1 summarizes the treatment under the Uniform Act of the major receipts and expenditures of fiduciaries.

FORMULA FOR TAXABLE INCOME AND TAX LIABILITY

OBJECTIVE 3

Explain how to calculate the tax liability of a trust or an estate

The formula for determining a fiduciary's taxable income and income tax liability is very similar to the formula applicable to individuals. There are three major differences, though. A fiduciary's deductions are not divided between deductions *for* and *from* adjusted gross income (AGI). Instead, a fiduciary's deductions are simply deductible in arriving at taxable income. A fiduciary receives no standard deduction. A type of deduction inapplicable to individuals—the distribution deduction—is available in computing a fiduciary's taxable income. Figure C14-1 illustrates the formula for computing a fiduciary's taxable income and tax liability.

GROSS INCOME

The items included in a trust or estate's gross income are the same as those included in an individual's gross income. However, the categorization of income is not identical for tax and accounting purposes. For example, a gain usually constitutes principal for accounting purposes, but it is part of gross income for tax purposes.

Topic Review C14-1

Classification of Receipts and Expenditures as Principal or Income Under the Uniform Act

Income Account	Principal Account
Income:	Receipts:
Rent	Consideration (including gains) received upon disposition or property
Interest	Stock dividends
Dividends	27½% of royalties
Net profits of a business	
72½% of royalties	
Expenses:	Expenditures:
Ordinary expenses (e.g., property taxes, insurance, interest, and ordinary repairs)	Principal payments on debt
Taxes levied on accounting income	Extraordinary repairs and capital improvements
Depreciation[a]	Taxes levied on gains and other items of principal

[a]Many state laws depart from the Uniform Act and characterize depreciation as a charge to principal.

EXAMPLE C14-7 ▶ In the current year, Duke Trust receives $8,000 interest on corporate bonds, $20,000 interest on state bonds, and a $50,000 capital gain. The trust reports gross income of $58,000 ($8,000 + $50,000). Its accounting income is $28,000 ($8,000 + $20,000) because the gain is part of principal. ◀

DEDUCTIONS FOR EXPENSES

Fiduciaries incur numerous deductible expenses for their expenditures. These expenses, which parallel those of individuals, include interest, taxes (e.g., state and local income taxes and property taxes), fees for investment advice, fees for tax return preparation, expenses associated with producing income, and trade or business expenses. In addition, fiduciaries may deduct the trustee's fee. This fee, which is similar to a property management fee incurred by an individual, is deductible under Sec. 212 as an expense incurred for the management of property held for the production of income.

Miscellaneous itemized deductions are deductible only to the extent the aggregate amount of such deductions exceeds 2% of the taxpayer's AGI. Although estates and trusts do not literally have AGI, according to Sec. 67(e), a hypothetical AGI amount for an estate or trust is determined in the same fashion as for an individual *except* that expenses paid or incurred in connection with the administration of the estate or trust *that would not have been incurred if the property were not held in such trust or estate*, the personal exemption, and the distribution deduction are not treated as miscellaneous itemized deductions. Thus, these deductions are not subject to the 2% floor; in addition, they are subtracted to arrive at hypothetical AGI and thereby reduce the amount of disallowed miscellaneous deductions. The trustees' or executors' fees and the cost of preparation of a fiduciary return would have been avoided had the trust or estate not existed, and thereby are excepted from the 2% floor. In *William J. O'Neill, Jr. Irrevocable Trust*[7] the Sixth Circuit reversed the Tax Court's decision that amounts paid

KEY POINT

Trustees' and executors' fees, as well as tax return preparation fees, are *not* subject to the 2% miscellaneous itemized deduction floor.

[7] 71 AFTR 2d 93-2052, 93-1 USTC ¶50,332 (6th Cir., 1993), reversing 98 T.C. 227 (1992), nonacq., I.R.B. 1994-38, 4.

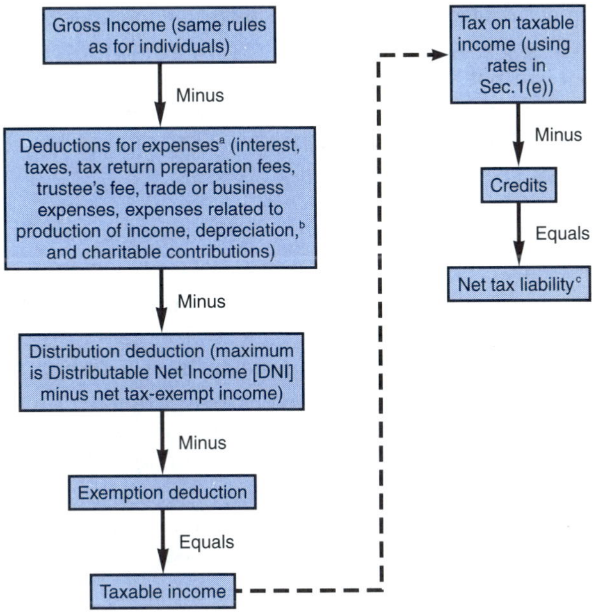

[a] No deduction is available for expenses allocable to tax-exempt income.

[b] When the trust instrument is silent, depreciation is allocated between the fiduciary and the beneficiary according to the portion of income attributable to each.

[c] Trusts and estates are also subject to the alternative minimum tax (AMT). The AMT may be owed by a trust or estate in addition to the income tax levy described in this figure. The AMT is calculated in the same way as for individual taxpayers. Trusts and estates, however, are allowed only a $22,500 statutory exemption. This exemption is phased-out from $75,000 to $165,000 of alternative minimum taxable income.

FIGURE C14-1 ▶ FORMULA FOR DETERMINING THE TAXABLE INCOME AND TAX LIABILITY OF A FIDUCIARY

for investment counsel fees were subject to the floor because they were not unique to the administration of estates and trusts.

An executor can deduct administration expenses on the estate's income tax return if such items are not deducted on the estate tax return. Unlike the situation for individuals, there is no limit on a fiduciary's charitable contribution deduction. A deduction is not allowed, however, unless a charitable contribution is authorized in the trust instrument.[8]

A depreciation or depletion deduction is available to an estate or trust only to the extent it is not allowable to beneficiaries under Secs. 167(h) or 611(b).[9] According to Sec. 167(h), the depreciation deduction for trusts is to be apportioned between the income beneficiaries and the trust pursuant to the terms of the trust instrument. If the instrument is silent, the depreciation is to be divided between the parties on the basis of the trust income allocable to each. For estates, however, the depreciation must always be apportioned according to the share of the income allocable to each party. The Sec. 611(b) rules for depletion parallel those described above for the allocation of depreciation.

EXAMPLE C14-8 ▶ In the current year, Nunn Trust distributes 20% of its income to Bob and 50% to Clay. It accumulates the remaining 30%. The trust's current year depreciation is $10,000. The trust

[8] Sec. 642(c)(1).

[9] Sec. 642(e).

instrument is silent concerning the depreciation deduction. Under state law, depreciation is charged to principal. Even though net accounting income and the maximum distributable amount are not reduced by the depreciation deduction, Bob receives a $2,000 (0.20 × $10,000) depreciation deduction and Clay receives a $5,000 (0.50 × $10,000) depreciation deduction. The remaining $3,000 (0.30 × $10,000) of depreciation is deducted in calculating the trust's taxable income. ◀

DISTRIBUTION DEDUCTION

TYPICAL MISCONCEPTION

The definition of *simple trust* is commonly misunderstood. If a trust *must* distribute all of its income currently, has no charitable beneficiary, and does *not* distribute corpus during the year, it is a simple trust for that year. *Income,* as used here, is fiduciary accounting income.

SIMPLE TRUSTS. Some trusts must distribute all of their income currently and are not empowered to make charitable contributions. The Regulations refer to such trusts as **simple trusts.**[10] According to Sec. 651(a), these trusts receive a distribution deduction for the income required to be distributed currently; that is, 100% of the trust income. No words modify the word *income;* therefore, *income* means accounting income. If the accounting income that must be distributed exceeds the trust's distributable net income (see page C14-11), the distribution deduction may not exceed the distributable net income. As used in this context, the distributable net income amount does not include any tax-free income (net of related deductions) that may have been earned by the trust.[11] Whatever amount is deductible at the trust level is taxed to the beneficiaries, and they are taxed on all of the income, irrespective of the amount they receive.

COMPLEX TRUSTS. Trusts that are not required to distribute all of their income currently are referred to as **complex trusts.**[12] The distribution deduction for complex trusts and all estates is the sum of the income required to be distributed currently and any other amounts (such as discretionary payments) properly paid, credited, or required to be distributed for the year. As is the case for simple trusts, the distribution deduction may not exceed the trust or estate's distributable net income (reduced by its tax-exempt income net of any related deductions).[13] The complex trust or estate's beneficiaries report, in the aggregate, gross income equal to the amount of the distribution deduction.[14]

EXAMPLE C14-9 ▶

Green Trust must distribute 25% of its income annually to Amy. In addition, the trustee in its discretion may distribute additional income to Amy or Brad. In the current year the trust has accounting income and distributable net income of $100,000, none from tax-exempt sources. The trust makes a $25,000 mandatory distribution to Amy and $10,000 discretionary distributions each to Amy and Brad. The trust's distribution deduction is $45,000 ($25,000 + $10,000 + $10,000). Amy and Brad report trust income of $35,000 and $10,000, respectively, on their individual returns. ◀

PERSONAL EXEMPTION

One of the differences between the rules for individuals and for fiduciaries is the amount of the personal exemption. Under Sec. 151, individuals are allowed personal exemptions. Section 642(b) authorizes an exemption for fiduciaries that applies in lieu of the amount for individuals. There is no exemption for a trust or estate in the year of termination.

KEY POINT

A trust, whether it is a simple or a complex trust, is eligible for the $300 personal exemption if it is required to distribute all of its income.

Estates are entitled to a $600 exemption. The exemption amount for trusts differs, depending on the terms of the trust. If the trust instrument requires that the trustee distribute all of the income annually, the trust receives a $300 exemption. Otherwise, $100 is the exemption amount. Some trusts may be required to make current distributions of all their income in certain years, whereas in other years they may be

[10] Reg. Sec. 1.651(a)-1.
[11] Sec. 651(b).
[12] Reg. Sec. 1.661(a)-1.
[13] Secs. 661(a) and (c).
[14] Sec. 662(a).

directed to accumulate the income or to make distributions at the trustee's discretion. For such trusts the exemption amount is $300 in some years and $100 in other years.

EXAMPLE C14-10 ▶ Gold Trust is established in 1996 with Jack as the beneficiary. The trust instrument instructs the trustee to make discretionary distributions of income to Jack during the years 1996 through 2000. Beginning in 2001, the trustee is to pay all of the trust income to Jack currently. For 1996 through 2000, the trust's exemption is $100. Beginning in 2001, it rises to $300. ◀

Recall that a trust receives a distribution deduction for income currently distributed to its beneficiaries. At first blush, it appears that the distribution deduction balances out the income of trusts that must distribute all of their income currently, and such trusts receive no tax benefits from their exemption deduction. True, the exemption produces no tax savings for such trusts if they have no gains credited to principal. Tax savings result from the personal exemption, however, if the trust has gains that are not distributed. The exemption reduces the amount of gain otherwise taxed at the trust level.

EXAMPLE C14-11 ▶ Rizzo Trust is required to distribute all of its income currently. Capital gains are characterized as principal. In the current year, Rizzo Trust has $25,000 of interest income from corporate bonds and a $10,000 capital gain. It has no expenses. It receives a distribution deduction of $25,000 and a $300 personal exemption. Its taxable income is $9,700 ($25,000 + $10,000 − $25,000 − $300). ◀

SELF-STUDY QUESTION

A trust, although not required to do so, distributes all of its income for the year. In the same year, it has a long-term capital gain. The trust agreement allocates the gain to principal. The trust does not distribute corpus and none of its beneficiaries are charities. Is the trust a simple trust? What is its personal exemption?

ANSWER

It is a complex trust because it is not required to distribute all of its income. The exemption is $100 because distributions are discretionary.

The personal exemption amount for individuals is adjusted annually for changes in the consumer price index, but no comparable provision exists for the personal exemption for fiduciaries. The Committee Reports do not discuss why indexing of the exemption for fiduciaries was not proposed. The rate schedules for both fiduciaries and individuals are indexed for inflation.

CREDITS

In general, the rules for tax credits for fiduciaries are the same as those for individuals. A fiduciary does not generally incur expenditures of the type that trigger some of the personal credits, such as the credit for household and dependent care expenses. Trusts and estates are allowed a foreign tax credit determined in the same manner as for individual taxpayers, except that the credit is limited to the amount of foreign taxes not allocable to the beneficiaries.[15]

DISTRIBUTABLE NET INCOME

OBJECTIVE 4

Understand the significance of distributable net income

As stated earlier in this chapter, the primary function of Subchapter J is to determine to whom—the fiduciary, the beneficiary, or some to each—the estate or the trust's current income is to be taxed. **Distributable net income (DNI)** plays a key role in determining the amount taxed to each party. In fact, DNI has been called the pie to be cut for tax purposes.[16]

SIGNIFICANCE OF DNI

DNI sets the ceiling on the amount of distributions taxed to the beneficiaries. As mentioned earlier, beneficiaries are taxed on the lesser of the amount of their

---

[15] Sec. 642(a)(1).

[16] M. Carr Ferguson, James L. Freeland, and Richard B. Stephens, *Federal Income Taxation of Estates and Beneficiaries* (Boston, MA: Little, Brown, 1970), p. 1x.

SELF-STUDY QUESTION

What functions does distributable net income (DNI) serve?

ANSWER

1. It establishes the maximum amount on which the beneficiaries may be taxed.
2. It establishes the maximum amount the trust or estate may deduct as a distribution deduction.
3. It establishes the character of the income or expense in DNI that flows to the beneficiaries (income or expense flows to the beneficiaries in proportion to the part each different type of income or expense bears to DNI).

distributions or their share of the amount of DNI (reduced by net tax-exempt income). These statements assume that the trust makes no distributions of income accumulated in a prior period; therefore, the accumulation distribution rules of Secs. 665 through 668 are inapplicable (see pages C14-30 through C14-32).

Just as the total amount taxed to the beneficiaries equals the fiduciary's distribution deduction, DNI represents not only the maximum that can be taxed to the beneficiaries but also the maximum that can be deducted at the fiduciary level. Recall from the preceding section that the distribution deduction is the smaller of the amount distributed or the fiduciary's DNI. The distribution deduction may not, however, include any portion of tax-exempt income (net of any related deductions) that is deemed to have been distributed.

DNI also determines the character of the beneficiaries' income. Under the conduit approach, each beneficiary's distribution is deemed to consist of various categories of income (net of deductions) in the same proportion as the total of each class of income bears to the total DNI. For example, if 40% of the trust's income consists of dividends, 40% of each beneficiary's distribution is deemed to consist of dividends.

An exception applies, however, if the governing instrument or local law specifically allocates particular types of income to certain beneficiaries. Allocations prescribed in the trust instrument are honored for tax purposes only to the extent that they have an economic effect independent of the tax results.[17] For example, an allocation of all of a trust's dividend income to Amy, irrespective of the total amount of income earned, and an allocation of the remainder of the trust's income to Bob would have economic implications independent of the tax consequences.

EXAMPLE C14-12 ▶

Sun Trust has $30,000 of DNI for the current year; its DNI includes $10,000 of rental income and $20,000 of corporate bond interest. The trust instrument requires that each year the trustee distribute 30% of the trust's income to Jose and 70% to Petra. The trust instrument does not require an allocation of the different types of income to the two beneficiaries. Because the trust has no tax-exempt income and must distribute all of its income, it receives a $30,000 distribution deduction.

Jose reports $9,000 (0.30 × $30,000) of trust income, and Petra reports $21,000 (0.70 × $30,000) of trust income. Because rents make up one-third ($10,000 ÷ $30,000) of DNI, the composition of the income reported by Jose and Petra is one-third rental income and two-thirds corporate bond interest. ◀

DEFINITION OF DNI

Section 643(a) defines *DNI* as the fiduciary's taxable income, adjusted as follows:

- No distribution deduction is subtracted.
- No personal exemption is subtracted.
- Capital gains are not included and capital losses are not subtracted unless such gains and losses are allocated to accounting income instead of to principal.
- Extraordinary dividends and taxable stock dividends are not included if they are allocable to principal.
- An addition is made for tax-exempt interest (minus the expenses allocable thereto).

Because one purpose of DNI is to set a ceiling on the distribution deduction, the distribution deduction is not subtracted from taxable income in determining DNI. If capital gains and extraordinary dividends are allocated to corpus, they are excluded from DNI because they cannot be distributed. Tax-exempt interest is part of accounting income and can be distributed even though it is excluded from gross income.

[17] Reg. Secs. 1.652(b)-2(b) and 1.662(b)-1.

Consequently, DNI includes tax-exempt income (net of the nondeductible expenses allocable to such income). Even though net tax-exempt income is included in DNI, no distribution deduction is available for the portion of the distribution that is deemed to consist of tax-exempt income.

KEY POINT

The difference between net accounting income and DNI is that DNI is reduced by certain expenses that are charged to principal. These expenses do not decrease net accounting income, nor do they decrease the amount of money that can be distributed.

In general, net accounting income and DNI are the same, with one exception. If some expenses (e.g., trustee's fees) are charged to principal, such expenses reduce DNI even though they do not lessen net accounting income. The trustee's fees (whether charged to income or to principal) are deductible in arriving at taxable income. But taxable income is not adjusted upward for such expenses to arrive at DNI. Reduction of DNI by the expenses charged to principal provides a tax advantage for the income beneficiary because these fees lessen the amount that is taxable to the beneficiary. However, they do not decrease the money that can be distributed to the beneficiary.

MANNER OF COMPUTING DNI

The amount of taxable income is in large measure a function of the distribution deduction, and the distribution deduction depends on the amount of DNI. The distribution deduction cannot exceed DNI. Thus, the Sec. 643(a) definition of DNI, which involves making adjustments to a fiduciary's taxable income, is not a workable definition from a practical standpoint. Under the definition, the computation is circular because the distribution deduction must be computed in order to know the amount of income taxable to the fiduciary.

However, there are two other, practical means of determining DNI. Under the first approach you begin with taxable income exclusive of the distribution deduction and make the adjustments to taxable income that the Code specifies. Of course, an adjustment for the distribution deduction is not necessary.

EXAMPLE C14-13 ▶ In the current year, Darby Trust reports the following results. The trust must distribute all of its income annually.

	Amounts Allocable to	
	Income	*Principal*
Corporate bond interest	$20,000	
Rental income	30,000	
Gain on sale of investment land		$40,000
Property taxes	5,000	
Trustee's fee charged to corpus		2,000
Distribution to beneficiary	45,000	

The trust's taxable income exclusive of the distribution deduction is computed as follows:

Corporate bond interest		$20,000
Rental income		30,000
Capital gain		40,000
Minus:	Property taxes	(5,000)
	Trustee's fee	(2,000)
	Personal exemption	(300)
Taxable income exclusive of distribution deduction		$82,700

Now that taxable income exclusive of the distribution deduction has been determined, DNI can be computed in the following manner:

Taxable income exclusive of distribution deduction	$82,700
Plus: Personal exemption	300
Minus: Capital gain	(40,000)
DNI	$43,000 ◀

A second method that can generally be used for determining DNI is to calculate the amount of net accounting income and reduce such amount by any expenses charged to corpus. In a few situations, however, DNI is a larger amount than the amount arrived at under this approach, but the discussion of such situations is beyond the scope of this book.

EXAMPLE C14-14 ▶ Assume the same facts as in Example C14-13. The following steps illustrate the second approach to calculating the DNI amount.

Corporate bond interest	$20,000
Rental income	30,000
Minus: Property taxes	(5,000)
Net accounting income	$45,000
Minus: Trustee's fee charged to corpus	(2,000)
DNI	$43,000 ◀

Note that although the beneficiary receives a cash distribution of $45,000 (net accounting income), he or she reports only $43,000 (DNI) as income. The beneficiary receives $2,000 tax-free. Thus, an income beneficiary benefits in the form of lower gross income from trustee's fees charged to principal. The trust's distribution deduction is limited to $43,000 (DNI), even though the amount paid to the beneficiary is higher.

STOP & THINK

Question: Wei is the beneficiary of a number of unrelated simple trusts. His marginal tax rate is 28%. From which simple trust would Wei have the larger after-tax cash flow?

- Trust A collects dividend income of $40,000 and pays a trustee's fee of $1,000. The trustee's fee is charged to corpus.
- Trust B collects corporate bond interest of $40,000 and pays a trustee's fee of $800. The trustee's fee is charged to income.

Solution: Wei would receive $40,000 in cash from Trust A. He would pay federal income taxes on only $39,000, which is the trust's DNI. The trust's cash flows are based on net accounting income, which is not reduced by the trustee's fee. Wei's gross income is based on the trust's DNI, which is reduced by the trustee's fee. Wei would receive $39,200 in cash from Trust B. He would pay federal income taxes on the same $39,200 amount, which is the trust's DNI. The trustee's fee paid by Trust B reduces both net accounting income and DNI. Even though the trust's economic income is larger with Trust B, Wei would have a larger amount of after-tax cash flow from Trust A.

DETERMINING A SIMPLE TRUST'S TAXABLE INCOME

OBJECTIVE 5

Determine the taxable income of a simple trust

The term *simple trust* does not appear in the Code. The Regulations interpreting Secs. 651 and 652—the statutory rules for trusts that distribute current income only—introduce the term *simple trust*. The provisions of Secs. 651 and 652 are applicable only to trusts whose trust agreements require that all income be distributed currently and do not authorize charitable contributions. Moreover, such provisions are inapplicable if the trust makes distributions of principal.

Some trusts may be required to pay out all of their income currently in certain years but permitted to retain a portion of their income in other years. In some of the years in which they must distribute all of their income, they may also make mandatory or discretionary distributions of principal. These trusts are simple trusts in some years and complex trusts in others. The amount of the personal exemption, however, turns not on whether the trust is simple or complex but on whether it must pay out all of its income currently. Suppose, for example, a trust must pay out all of its current income and one-fourth of its principal. Because the trust distributes principal, it is a complex trust. It claims a $300 personal exemption because of the mandate to distribute all of its income. Table C14-1 highlights the trust classification rules and the $300 or $100 exemption dichotomy.

ALLOCATION OF EXPENSES TO TAX-EXEMPT INCOME

Recall that expenses related to producing tax-exempt income are not deductible.[18] Thus, if a trust has income from both taxable and tax-exempt sources and it incurs expenses that are not directly attributable to the production of taxable income, a portion of such expenses may not be deducted. Regulation Secs. 1.652(b)-3 and 1.652(c)-4(e) address the issue of the allocation of deductions. An expense that is directly attributable to one type of income, such as a repair expense for rental property, is allocated thereto. Expenses not directly related to a particular item of income, such as a trustee's fee for administering the trust's assets, may be allocated to any type of income that is included in computing DNI, provided that a portion of the expense is allocated to nontaxable income. Regulation Sec. 1.652(b)-3 sets forth the following formula for determining the amount of indirect expenses allocable to nontaxable income:

$$\frac{\text{Tax-exempt income (net of expenses directly attributable thereto)}}{\text{Accounting income (net of all direct expenses)}^{19}} \times \begin{array}{c}\text{Expenses not directly}\\ \text{attributable to any}\\ \text{item of income}\end{array} = \begin{array}{c}\text{Indirect}\\ \text{expenses}\\ \text{allocable to}\\ \text{nontaxable}\\ \text{income}\end{array}$$

▼ **TABLE C14-1**
Trust Classification Rules and the Size of the Exemption

Situation	Classification	Exemption Amount
Required to pay out all of its income, makes no charitable contributions, distributes no principal	Simple	$300
Required to pay out all of its income, makes no charitable contributions, distributes principal	Complex	$300
Required to pay out all of its income, authorized to make charitable contributions, distributes no principal	Complex	$300
Authorized to make discretionary distributions of income, makes no charitable contributions, distributes no principal	Complex	$100
Authorized to make discretionary distributions of income and principal, makes no charitable contributions	Complex	$100

[18] Sec. 265(a)(1).

[19] A discrepancy exists in the Regulations with respect to how to allocate expenses to tax-exempt income. According to Reg. Sec. 1.652(b)-3(b), the denominator is accounting income net of direct expenses. Regulation Sec. 1.652(c)-4(e) makes computations where accounting income is not reduced by direct expenses to arrive at the denominator. The latter approach is used in the text.

EXAMPLE C14-15 ▶ In the current year, the Mason Trust reports the following results:

Dividends	$12,000
Interest from corporate bonds	6,000
Tax-exempt interest from state bonds	18,000
Capital gain (allocated to corpus)	20,000
Trustee's fee	4,000

Accounting gross income is $36,000 ($12,000 + $6,000 + $18,000). The trustee's fee is an indirect expense that must be allocated to the tax-exempt income as follows:

$$\frac{\$18{,}000}{\$36{,}000} \times \$4{,}000 = \$2{,}000$$

Thus, the Mason Trust cannot deduct $2,000 of its trustee's fee. The remaining $2,000 may be allocated to dividends or corporate bond interest in whatever amounts the return preparer desires. ◀

SELF-STUDY QUESTION

A trust can allocate indirect expenses arbitrarily (after the appropriate allocation is made to tax-exempt income). Hill Trust has rental income, taxable interest income, and dividend income this year. To which income would you suggest allocating the trustee's fee?

ANSWER

If possible the trust should take into consideration the tax status of its beneficiaries. In a situation where the sole beneficiary has nondeductible rental losses of his or her own, it would be beneficial to charge the fee to interest or dividend income, thus reducing the beneficiaries' portfolio income.

DETERMINATION OF DNI AND THE DISTRIBUTION DEDUCTION

As mentioned above, DNI is defined as taxable income with several adjustments, including a subtraction for capital gains credited to principal. According to the methods described above, a practical technique for determining DNI involves beginning with taxable income exclusive of the distribution deduction. Once DNI has been determined, the distribution deduction and the trust's taxable income can both be calculated.

A simple trust must distribute all of its net accounting income currently. Thus, a simple trust generally receives a distribution deduction equal to the amount of its net accounting income.[20] There are two exceptions to this general rule:

- The distribution deduction may not exceed DNI. Therefore, if a trust has expenses that are charged to corpus (as in Example C14-14), the distribution deduction is limited to the DNI amount because DNI is smaller than net accounting income.
- Because tax-exempt income is not included in the trust's gross income, no distribution deduction is available with respect to tax-exempt income (net of the expenses allocable thereto) included in DNI.[21]

TAX TREATMENT FOR BENEFICIARY

The aggregate gross income reported by the beneficiaries equals the trust's net accounting income, subject to the constraint that the aggregate of their gross income amount does not exceed the trust's DNI. If DNI is lower than net accounting income and there is more than one beneficiary, each beneficiary's share of gross income is the following fraction of total DNI:[22]

$$\frac{\text{Income required to be distributed to such beneficiary}}{\text{Income required to be distributed to } \textit{all} \text{ beneficiaries}}$$

The income received by the beneficiaries retains the character that it had at the trust level. Thus, if the trust receives tax-exempt interest, the beneficiaries are deemed to have received tax-exempt interest. Unless the trust instrument specifically allocates particular types of income to certain beneficiaries, the income of each beneficiary is viewed as consisting of the same fraction of each category of income as the total of such category bears to total DNI.

[20] Sec. 651(a).
[21] Sec. 651(b).
[22] Sec. 652(a).

EXAMPLE C14-16 ▶ In the current year, Crane Trust's DNI is $80,000: $20,000 of net tax-exempt interest and $60,000 of net dividends. Net accounting income for the current year is $88,000 ($22,000 + $66,000), and $8,000 of trustee's fees are charged to corpus. The trust instrument requires that one-eighth of the income be distributed annually to Matt and the remaining seven-eighths of the income to Pat. The distributions to Matt and Pat are $11,000 and $77,000, respectively. The distribution deduction and the aggregate gross income of the beneficiaries are limited to $60,000 ($80,000 DNI − $20,000 net tax-exempt interest). Matt and Pat will report gross income of $7,500 (0.125 × $60,000) and $52,500 (0.875 × $60,000), respectively. Dividends make up 75% ($60,000 ÷ $80,000) of DNI and 100% ($60,000 ÷ $60,000) of taxable DNI; therefore, all of Matt's and Pat's *gross* income is deemed to consist of dividends. Matt and Pat are also viewed as having received $2,500 (0.125 × $20,000) and $17,500 (0.875 × $20,000), respectively, of tax-exempt interest. ◀

KEY POINT

The beneficiaries of a simple trust are taxed on their distributable share of their trust's income, whether or not it is distributed.

Because a simple trust must distribute all of its income currently, trustees cannot defer the taxation of trust income to the beneficiaries by postponing distributions until the beginning of the next year. Beneficiaries of simple trusts are taxed currently on their pro rata share of taxable DNI regardless of the actual amount distributed to them during the year.[23]

SHORT-CUT APPROACH TO PROVING CORRECTNESS OF TAXABLE INCOME

A short-cut approach may be used to verify the correctness of the amount calculated as a simple trust's taxable income. Because a simple trust must distribute all of its income currently, the only item taxable at the trust level should be the amount of gains (net of losses) credited to principal, reduced by the personal exemption. The taxable income calculated under the short-cut approach should equal the taxable income determined under the formula illustrated in Figure C14-1. The steps of the short-cut approach are as follows:

1. Start with the excess of gains over losses credited to principal.
2. Subtract the $300 personal exemption.

EXAMPLE C14-17 ▶ In the current year West Trust, which must distribute all of its income currently, reports $25,000 of corporate bond interest, a $44,000 long-term capital gain, and a $4,000 long-term capital loss. Under the short-cut approach, its taxable income is calculated as $39,700 [($44,000 − $4,000) − $300 personal exemption]. In the actual calculation of taxable income the trust also reports $25,000 of gross income from interest and a $25,000 distribution deduction. ◀

EFFECT OF A NET OPERATING LOSS

If a trust incurs a net operating loss (NOL), the loss is not passed through currently to the beneficiaries unless the loss arises in the year the trust terminates. Trusts are allowed to carry an NOL back and forward. In determining the amount of the NOL, deductions are not allowed for charitable contributions or the distribution deduction.[24] In the year a trust terminates, any loss that would otherwise qualify for a loss carryover at the trust level passes through to the individual return of the beneficiary(ies) succeeding to the trust's property.[25]

EXAMPLE C14-18 ▶ In 1997, the year it terminates, New Trust incurs a $10,000 NOL. In addition, it has a $40,000 NOL carryover from 1995 and 1996. At termination, New Trust distributes 30% of its assets to

[23] Reg. Sec. 1.652(a)-1.

[24] Reg. Sec. 1.642(d)-1(b).

[25] Reg. Sec. 1.642(h)-1. A trust is never categorized as a simple trust in the year it terminates because in its final year it always makes distributions of principal.

Kay and 70% to Liz. Because 1997 is the termination year, Kay may report a $15,000 (0.30 × $50,000) NOL on her 1997 return and Liz may report a $35,000 (0.70 × $50,000) NOL on her 1997 return. Before 1997, the beneficiaries are ineligible to report any of the trust's NOLs on their returns. ◀

SELF-STUDY QUESTION

In its first year, Bell Trust has $800 of operating income and $2,000 in operating expenses. It has a $1,200 NOL. For tax purposes, the loss is carried forward. Is the loss deductible in the second year in determining the *fiduciary accounting income?*

ANSWER

One would have to rely on the state law or the trust agreement for such an interpretation. If the loss is not deductible from future income, the remainderman is the eventual loser. The NOL can pass through to the remainderman if the trust terminates.

EFFECT OF A NET CAPITAL LOSS

The maximum capital loss that a trust can deduct is the lesser of $3,000 or the excess of its capital losses over capital gains.[26] Because simple trusts must distribute all of their accounting income currently and the distribution deduction reduces their taxable income to zero, they receive no tax benefit from capital losses that exceed capital gains. Nevertheless, the trust's taxable income for the year of the loss is reduced by its net capital loss, up to $3,000. In determining the capital loss carryover, capital losses that produced no tax benefit are deemed to be available as a carryover to offset capital gains realized by the trust in subsequent years. In addition, if all of the capital loss carryovers have not been absorbed by capital gains before the trust's termination date, the remaining capital loss is passed through in the termination year to the beneficiaries succeeding to the trust's property.[27]

EXAMPLE C14-19 ▶

Old Trust, which must distribute all of its income currently, makes two sales of capital assets during its existence. In 1995 it sells an asset at a $20,000 loss. In 1996 it sells an asset for a $6,000 gain. In 1997 it terminates and distributes its assets equally between its two beneficiaries, Joy and Tim. The trust is not a simple trust in 1997 because it distributes principal that year. Because the $20,000 loss provided no benefit on the 1995 return, the carryover to 1996 is $20,000, and $6,000 of it is offset against 1996's $6,000 capital gain. The remaining $14,000 is carried forward to 1997. Because 1997 is the termination year, a $7,000 (0.50 × $14,000) capital loss is passed through to both Joy's and Tim's individual returns for 1997. Joy experiences a $12,000 capital gain by selling assets in 1997. Joy offsets the $7,000 trust loss against her own gain. Tim sells no assets in 1997. Therefore, Tim may deduct $3,000 of the loss from the trust against his other income. His remaining $4,000 loss is carried over to 1998. ◀

SELF-STUDY QUESTION

Why do the regulations (see footnotes 25 and 27) allow unused NOLs and capital losses to be used by the remainderman on the termination of a trust?

ANSWER

Losses that cannot be offset against future gains (either income or corpus) have, in effect, depleted the corpus of the trust. Because the remainderman's interest has been depleted by these losses, it seems reasonable to allow the trust to pass these losses through to the remainderman at the end of its life.

Topic Review C14-2 describes how to calculate the taxable income of a trust.

COMPREHENSIVE ILLUSTRATION: DETERMINING A SIMPLE TRUST'S TAXABLE INCOME

A number of the points discussed previously are reviewed in the comprehensive illustration that follows. The facts for this illustration are used to complete the Form 1041 for a simple trust, which appears in Appendix B.

BACKGROUND DATA

The Bob Adams Trust was established by a gift from Zed Brown in 1982. Its trust instrument requires that the trustee (First Bank) distribute all of the trust income at least annually to Bob Adams for life. Capital gains are credited to principal. The 1996 results of the trust are as follows:

[26] Sec. 1211(b).

[27] Reg. Sec. 1.642(h)-1.

Topic Review C14-2

Calculation of Trust Taxable Income

Gross income[a]	
Minus:	Deductions for expenses[a]
	Distribution deduction[b]
	Personal exemption ($300 or $100)
Taxable income	

[a] Rules for calculating these amounts are generally the same as for individual taxpayers.
[b] Deduction cannot exceed the amount of DNI from taxable sources.

	Amounts Allocable	
	Income	*Principal*
Dividends	$30,000	
Rental income from land	5,000	
Tax-exempt interest	15,000	
Rental expenses (realtor's commission on rental income)	1,000	
Trustee's fee		$ 1,200
Fee for preparation of tax return	500	
Long-term capital gain on sale of stock		12,000
Distribution of net accounting income to Bob	48,500	
Payments of estimated tax		2,600

TRUSTEE'S FEE

As mentioned earlier, a portion of the trustee's fee is nondeductible because it must be allocated to tax-exempt income. The trust receives $50,000 ($30,000 + $5,000 + $15,000) of gross accounting income, of which $15,000 is tax-exempt. Therefore, $360 [($15,000 ÷ $50,000) × $1,200] of the trustee's fee is allocated to tax-exempt income and is nondeductible. All of the return preparation fee is deductible because no such fee would have been incurred if the trust's income had been entirely from tax-exempt sources.

DISTRIBUTION DEDUCTION AND DNI

One of the key amounts affecting taxable income is the distribution deduction. Taxable income exclusive of the distribution deduction can be the starting point for determining the amount of DNI, a number crucial in quantifying the distribution deduction. The trust's taxable income, exclusive of the distribution deduction, is calculated as follows:

Dividends	$30,000
Rental income	5,000
Long-term capital gain	12,000
Minus: Rental expenses	(1,000)
Deductible portion of trustee's fee	(840)
Fee for tax return preparation	(500)
Personal exemption	(300)
Taxable income, exclusive of distribution deduction	$44,360

DNI can now be calculated by making the adjustments shown below to taxable income, exclusive of the distribution deduction.[28]

Taxable income, exclusive of distribution deduction		$44,360
Plus:	Personal exemption	300
Minus:	Long-term capital gain	(12,000)
Plus:	Tax-exempt interest, net of $360 of allocable expenses	14,640
DNI		$47,300

Recall that the distribution deduction cannot exceed the DNI, as reduced by tax-exempt income (net of any allocable expenses). The distribution deduction may be computed as follows:

Smaller of:	Net accounting income ($48,500) or DNI ($47,300)		$47,300
Minus:	Tax-exempt interest	$15,000	
	Minus: Allocable expenses	(360)	(14,640)
Distribution deduction			$32,660

TRUST'S TAXABLE INCOME

Once the amount of the distribution deduction has been determined, the trust's taxable income can be calculated. Table C14-2 illustrates this calculation.

CATEGORIZING A BENEFICIARY'S INCOME

In addition to taxable income, the amount of each category of income received by the beneficiary must be determined. Income reported by the beneficiary retains the same character it had at the trust level. Thus, Bob is deemed to have received dividends, rents, and tax-exempt interest. Rental expenses are, of course, charged against rental income. The deductible portion of the trustee's fee and the tax return preparation fee can be allocated in full to rents or dividends, or some to each. If they are allocated to rental income, the character of Bob's income is determined as follows:

	Dividends	*Rents*	*Tax-Exempt Interest*	*Total*
Accounting income	$30,000	$ 5,000	$15,000	$50,000
Minus: Expenses:				
Rental expenses		(1,000)		(1,000)
Trustee's fee		(840)	(360)	(1,200)
Tax return preparation fee		(500)		(500)
DNI	$30,000	$ 2,660	$14,640	$47,300

Bob reports $30,000 of dividend income and $2,660 of rental income on his individual return.

[28] Another way of determining the amount of DNI is to reduce the net accounting income of $48,500 by the $1,200 of expenses charged to principal. The resulting amount is $47,300.

▼ TABLE C14-2

Comprehensive Illustration: Determining a Simple Trust's Taxable Income and Tax Liability

Gross income:	
Dividends	$30,000
Rental income	5,000
Long-term capital gain	12,000
Minus: Expense deductions:	
Rental expenses	(1,000)
Deductible portion of trustee's fee	(840)
Fee for tax return preparation	(500)
Minus: Distribution deduction	(32,660)
Minus: Personal exemption	(300)
Taxable income	$11,700[a]
Tax liability (1996 rates)	$3,068[b]
Minus: Estimated tax payments	(2,600)
Tax owed	$468

[a] The short-cut approach to verifying taxable income is as follows:

Long-term capital gain	$12,000
Minus: Personal exemption	(300)
Taxable income	$11,700

[b] The taxable income consists of a long-term capital gain, which is taxed at a maximum rate of 28%.

KEY POINT

The short-cut approach to computing taxable income used in Table C14-2 consists of all of the income allocated to corpus minus the personal exemption.

DETERMINING TAXABLE INCOME FOR COMPLEX TRUSTS AND ESTATES

OBJECTIVE 6

Determine the taxable income of a complex trust

The caption to Subpart C of Part I of Subchapter J (Secs. 661 through 664) is titled "Distribution for Estates and Trusts Accumulating or Distributing Corpus." In general, the rules applicable to estates and these trusts (complex trusts) are the same. The Code does not contain the term *complex trust,* but according to the Regulations, "A trust to which subpart C is applicable is referred to as a 'complex' trust."[29] Recall from the discussion about simple trusts that a trust that must distribute all of its income currently can be classified as a complex trust for a particular year if it also pays out some principal during the year. Trusts that can accumulate income are categorized as complex trusts, even in years in which they make discretionary distributions of all of their income. A trust is also a complex trust if the trust instrument provides for amounts to be paid to, or set aside for, charitable organizations (see Table C14-1).

Many of the rules are the same for simple and complex trusts, but some differences exist. Different rules are used to determine the distribution deduction for the two types of trusts. The rules for determining an estate's distribution deduction are the same as those applicable to complex trusts. The personal exemption differs, however; it is $600 for an estate and $300 or $100 for a complex trust. The $300 amount applies for years in which a trust must pay out all of its income; otherwise, the exemption is $100.

[29] Reg. Sec. 1.661(a)-1.

DETERMINATION OF DNI AND THE DISTRIBUTION DEDUCTION

Section 661(a) defines the distribution deduction for complex trusts and estates as being the sum of the total current income *required* to be paid out currently plus any other amounts "properly paid or credited or required to be distributed" (i.e., discretionary distributions) to the beneficiary during the year. If the fiduciary has the option of making mandatory distributions from either income or principal, distributions are counted as "current income required to be paid" if paid out of the trust's income. Just as in the case of simple trusts, the amount of the trust's DNI acts as a ceiling on the amount of the distribution deduction.

EXAMPLE C14-20 ▶ In the current year, Able Trust has net accounting income and DNI of $30,000, all from taxable sources. It makes a $15,000 mandatory distribution of income to Kwame and a $4,000 discretionary distribution to Kesha. Its distribution deduction is computed as follows:

Income required to be distributed currently	$15,000
Plus: Other amounts properly paid, etc.	4,000
Tentative distribution deduction	$19,000
DNI	$30,000
Distribution deduction (lesser of tentative distribution deduction or DNI)	$19,000 ◀

As is the case for simple trusts, there is an additional constraint on the amount of the distribution deduction. No distribution deduction is allowed with respect to tax-exempt income (net of allocable expenses).

EXAMPLE C14-21 ▶ Assume the same facts as in Example C14-20, except that net accounting income and DNI consist of $20,000 of corporate bond interest and $10,000 of tax-exempt interest. Because one-third ($10,000 ÷ $30,000) of the DNI is from tax-exempt sources, tax-exempt income is deemed to make up one-third of the distributions. Thus, the distribution deduction is only $12,667 (0.667 × $19,000). ◀

DNI is not reduced by the charitable contribution deduction when determining the maximum distribution deduction for mandatory distributions of income. However, DNI is reduced by the charitable contribution deduction when calculating the deductible discretionary distributions.

EXAMPLE C14-22 ▶ Assume the same facts as in Example C14-20, except that the trust has net accounting income and DNI (exclusive of the charitable contribution deduction) of $15,000. The trust makes a $15,000 mandatory distribution to Kwame and a $4,000 discretionary distribution to Kesha. In addition, the trust, in accordance with its trust instrument, pays $3,000 to a charitable organization.

Tentative distribution deduction (see calculation in Example C14-20)	$19,000
DNI (excluding charitable contribution deduction)	15,000
Distribution deduction (lesser of tentative distribution deduction or DNI)	15,000

If the distributions to Kwame and Kesha instead were both discretionary, the $3,000 charitable contribution would first reduce DNI to $12,000. The distribution deduction would be limited to $12,000. ◀

The DNI concept is summarized in Topic Review C14-3.

TAX TREATMENT FOR BENEFICIARY

GENERAL RULES. In general, the amount of any distributions from estates or complex trusts includible in a beneficiary's gross income equals the sum of the amount of

SELF-STUDY QUESTION

Is DNI reduced by the charitable contribution deduction in calculating the portion of DNI to be included in each beneficiary's gross income?

ANSWER

DNI is not reduced by charitable contributions in determining the DNI to be included in the gross income of mandatory beneficiaries, but it is reduced in arriving at the DNI to be included in the gross income of discretionary beneficiaries.

Topic Review C14-3

The Distributable Net Income (DNI) Concept

Significance of DNI:

DNI, exclusive of net tax-exempt interest included therein, sets the ceiling on:

1. the distribution deduction, and
2. the aggregate amount of gross income reportable by the beneficiaries.

Calculation of DNI:

Taxable income, exclusive of distribution deduction[a]	
Plus:	Personal exemption
Minus:	Capital gains (or plus deductible capital losses)
Plus:	Tax-exempt interest (net of allocable expenses)
DNI[b]	

[a] Gross income (dividends, taxable interest, rents, capital gains) minus deductible expenses and the personal exemption.

[b] In general, DNI is the same amount as net accounting income minus trustee's fees charged to corpus.

income required to be distributed currently to the beneficiary, plus any other amounts properly paid or credited, or required to be distributed (i.e., discretionary distributions) to the beneficiary during the year.[30] There are three exceptions to this general rule. Exceptions are authorized for the tier system and separate share rules of trusts and for specific bequests of estates.

KEY POINT

Distributions to beneficiaries retain the same character that the income has at the fiduciary level; for example, the character of rents, interest, dividends, or tax-exempt income flows through to the beneficiary.

Because income retains the character it has at the fiduciary level, beneficiaries do not include distributions of tax-exempt income in their gross income. Each beneficiary's distribution is deemed to consist of tax-exempt income in the proportion that total tax-exempt income bears to total DNI.[31] Thus, if 30% of DNI is from tax-exempt income, 30% of each beneficiary's distribution is deemed to consist of tax-free income.

Even in the absence of distributions of principal, mandatory payments to beneficiaries can exceed DNI because at times accounting income may exceed DNI. When the total income required to be distributed currently exceeds DNI (before reduction for the charitable contribution deduction), each beneficiary reports as gross income the following ratio of DNI attributable to taxable sources:

$$\frac{\text{Income required to be distributed currently to the beneficiary}}{\text{Aggregate income required to be distributed to all beneficiaries currently}^{32}}$$

In calculating the portion of DNI includible in the gross income of each beneficiary receiving mandatory distributions, DNI is not reduced for the charitable contribution deduction.

EXAMPLE C14-23 ▶ In the current year, Yui Trust reports net accounting income of $125,000 but DNI of only $100,000 because certain expenses are charged to principal. The trust must distribute $100,000 of income to Tai and $10,000 to Tien. It makes no discretionary distributions or charitable contributions. Because the trust's mandatory distributions exceed its DNI, the amount each beneficiary reports as gross income is as follows:

[30] Sec. 662(a).

[31] Sec. 662(b).

[32] Sec. 662(a)(1).

Beneficiary	*Gross Income*
Tai	\$90,909 = (\$100,000 ÷ \$110,000) × \$100,000
Tien	\$9,091 = (\$10,000 ÷ \$110,000) × \$100,000 ◀

KEY POINT

If income distributions for the year exceed DNI, the amount taxable to each beneficiary is calculated under a tier system. Beneficiaries are assigned to tiers based on whether they receive mandatory or discretionary payments.

THE TIER SYSTEM. If both principal and income are distributed, distributions will exceed income even if net accounting income and DNI are equal. If the sum of current income required to be distributed currently and all other amounts properly paid or required to be distributed (e.g., discretionary payments of income or any payments of corpus) exceed DNI, the amount taxable to each beneficiary is calculated under a tier system. Beneficiaries to whom income distributions must be made are commonly called **tier-1 beneficiaries.**[33] All other beneficiaries are known as **tier-2 beneficiaries.** An individual can be both a tier-1 and a tier-2 beneficiary if both mandatory and discretionary payments are received in the same year.

Under the tier system, tier-1 beneficiaries are the first to absorb income. The total income taxed to this group is the lesser of aggregate mandatory distributions or DNI, which is determined without reduction for charitable contributions. If required income distributions plus all other payments exceed DNI, each tier-2 beneficiary includes in income a fraction of the excess of DNI over the income required to be distributed currently. Section 662(a)(2) states that the fraction is as follows:

$$\frac{\text{Other amounts properly paid or required to be distributed to the beneficiary}}{\text{Aggregate of amounts properly paid or required to be distributed to } \textit{all} \text{ beneficiaries}}$$

EXAMPLE C14-24 ▶

In the current year, Eagle Trust reports net accounting income and DNI of \$80,000, all from taxable sources. The trustee is required to distribute \$30,000 of income to Holly currently. In addition, the trustee makes \$60,000 of discretionary distributions, \$15,000 to Holly and \$45,000 to Irene. \$10,000 of the discretionary distributions are from corpus. The gross income reported by each beneficiary is determined as follows.

1. Gross income from mandatory distributions:	
Lesser of:	
a. Amount required to be distributed, or	\$30,000
b. DNI	80,000
Amount reportable by Holly	30,000
2. Gross income from other amounts paid:	
Lesser of:	
a. All other amounts paid, or	60,000
b. DNI minus amount required to be distributed (\$80,000 − \$30,000)	50,000
Amount reportable by Holly and Irene	50,000
3. Total amount reportable (1) + (2) = (3)	80,000

The portions of the \$50,000 from Step 2 to be reported by each beneficiary are calculated as follows:

Holly's: \$50,000 × (\$15,000 ÷ \$60,000) = \$12,500
Irene's: \$50,000 × (\$45,000 ÷ \$60,000) = \$37,500

Recapitulation of the beneficiaries' gross income is calculated as follows:

[33] The terms *tier-1* and *tier-2* do not appear in the Code or Regulations.

	Amount Reported by	
Type of Distribution	*Holly*	*Irene*
Mandatory distributions	$30,000	$—0—
Discretionary distributions	12,500	37,500
Total	$42,500	$37,500

Tier-1 beneficiaries are generally taxed on their total distributions, whereas tier-2 beneficiaries are more likely to receive a portion of their distributions tax-free. Thus, Tier-2 beneficiaries can receive more favorable tax treatment than tier-1 beneficiaries.

SELF-STUDY QUESTION

What is the ultimate effect of the separate share rule?

ANSWER

It has the effect of treating the trust as two or more separate trusts, each with its own DNI. This "separate" DNI is allocated to the specific beneficiary of each share of the trust.

SEPARATE SHARE RULE. Some trusts with more than one beneficiary can be treated as consisting of separate trusts for purposes of determining the amount of the trust's distribution deduction and the beneficiaries' gross income.[34] In calculating the trust's income tax liability, however, these trusts are treated as one entity. Trusts eligible for this treatment, known as the **separate share rule**, must have governing instruments that require that distributions be made in substantially the same manner as if separate trusts had been created.[35] If the separate share rule is applicable, the amount of the income taxable to a beneficiary can differ from the amount that otherwise would be taxable to such beneficiary. Beneficiaries generally receive favorable tax treatment from this rule.

EXAMPLE C14-25

Berry Trust is created for the benefit of Dale and John. According to the trust instrument, no income is to be distributed until a beneficiary reaches age 21. Moreover, income is to be divided into two equal shares. Once a beneficiary reaches age 21, the trustee may make discretionary distributions of income and principal to such beneficiary, but distributions may not exceed a beneficiary's share of the trust. Each beneficiary is to receive his remaining share of the trust assets on his thirtieth birthday. Earlier distributions of income and principal will be taken into account in determining each beneficiary's final distribution.

On January 1 of the current year, Dale reaches age 21; John is age 16. In the current year, the trust has DNI and net accounting income of $50,000, all from taxable sources. During the current year, the trustee distributes $25,000 of income (Dale's 50% share) and $80,000 of principal to Dale. No distribution of income or corpus is made to John. Under the separate share rule, the trust's distribution deduction and Dale's gross income inclusion are limited to his share of DNI, or $25,000. Dale receives the remaining $80,000 distribution tax-free. Berry Trust is taxed on John's separate share of the income (all accumulated), or $25,000. In the absence of the separate share rule, Dale would be taxed on $50,000 (the lesser of DNI and his total distributions).

SPECIFIC BEQUESTS. Recall that a beneficiary is taxed on other amounts properly paid, credited, or required to be distributed,[36] subject to the constraint that the maximum amount taxed to all beneficiaries is the fiduciary's DNI. Thus, a beneficiary can be required to report gross income, even though a distribution is received from the principal account.

EXAMPLE C14-26

Doug dies in 1996, leaving a will that bequeaths all of his property to his sister Tina. During 1997, Doug's estate reports $50,000 of DNI, all from taxable sources. During 1997, the executor distributes Doug's coin collection, valued at $22,000, to Tina. The adjusted basis of the coin collection is $22,000, its value at the date of death. The distribution of the coin collection is classified as an other amount properly paid and, even though the executor

[34] Sec. 663(c).
[35] Reg. Sec. 1.663(c)-3(a).
[36] Sec. 662(a)(2).

ADDITIONAL COMMENT

The executor of an estate should carefully consider the timing of property distributions where the property being distributed is not the subject of a specific bequest. If possible, property (other than specific bequests) should be distributed in a year when there is little or no DNI.

distributes no income, Tina reports $22,000 of gross income. If the coin collection's adjusted basis and FMV exceed $50,000 (DNI), Tina's gross income would be limited to the $50,000 DNI amount. ◀

Properties that are distributed do not trigger a distribution deduction at the estate level or the recognition of gross income at the beneficiary level if such properties constitute a bequest of a specific sum of money or of specific property to be paid at one time or in not more than three installments.[37] If Doug's will in Example C14-26 includes specific bequest language (e.g., "I bequeath my coin collection to Tina"), Tina would not report any gross income upon receiving the coin collection.

More income is generally taxed at the estate level (and less at the beneficiary level) if the decedent's will includes numerous specific bequests. If the estate has a lower marginal tax rate than its beneficiaries' marginal tax rates, the optimal tax result is to have the income taxed to the estate because the tax liability is lower.

EXAMPLE C14-27 ▶

Dick dies in 1996. Dick bequeaths $100,000 cash to Fred. Dick's residence, valued at $300,000, is devised to Gary. The executor distributes the cash and the residence in 1997, when the estate has $475,000 of DNI, all from taxable sources. Because the cash and residence constitute specific bequests, the estate gets no distribution deduction and the beneficiaries report no gross income. ◀

STOP & THINK

Question: Sally is the sole beneficiary of her uncle Harry's estate. In the current year, the estate had DNI of $36,000, all from dividends and corporate interest. During the current year, the estate's executor distributed to Sally $12,200 of cash and her uncle Harry's rare book collection, valued at $5,400. Uncle Harry's will made a specific bequest of the rare book collection to Sally. How much gross income should Sally report as a result of the distributions from the estate during the current year? What is the amount of the estate's distribution deduction?

Solution: A beneficiary does not have to report gross income as a result of receiving a specific bequest. Sally's cash distribution does not exceed the estate's DNI. Thus, Sally should report gross income equal to the cash distributed from the estate to her ($12,200). The estate's distribution deduction equals the amount included in Sally's gross income ($12,200). If the book collection were not a specific bequest, its distribution by the estate would be taxable to Sally because the $17,600 ($12,200 + $5,400) distributed by the estate is less than the estate's $36,000 DNI.

EFFECT OF A NET OPERATING LOSS

KEY POINT

Generally, the tax consequences of both NOLs and net capital losses are the same for estates, complex trusts, and simple trusts.

As with simple trusts, an NOL of an estate or complex trust can be carried back and carried forward. In the year the trust or estate terminates, any remaining NOL is passed through to the beneficiaries who succeed to the assets. In addition, in its year of termination the estate passes through to its beneficiaries any excess of current nonoperating expenses (e.g., executor's fees) over current income. If the estate incurs NOLs over a series of years, a tax incentive exists for terminating the estate as early as possible so that the beneficiaries can reap the benefit of the loss deductions.

EFFECT OF A NET CAPITAL LOSS

The tax effect of having capital losses in excess of capital gains is generally the same for estates and complex trusts as for simple trusts. As in the case of an individual taxpayer,

[37] Sec. 663(a)(1).

the maximum capital loss deduction is the lesser of $3,000 or the excess of its capital losses over capital gains.[38] Simple trusts, however, receive no immediate tax benefit when capital losses exceed capital gains. Estates and complex trusts often do not distribute all of their income and, thus, have taxable income against which a capital loss may be offset.

EXAMPLE C14-28 ▶ For 1996, Gold Trust reports $30,000 of net accounting income and DNI, all from taxable sources. It makes discretionary distributions totaling $7,000 to Amy. Its one sale of a capital asset results in an $8,000 long-term capital loss. The trust can deduct $3,000 of capital losses in arriving at its taxable income. The trust can carry over the remaining $5,000 of capital loss to 1997. Suppose that in 1997, Gold Trust sells a capital asset for a $5,000 long-term capital gain. It will offset the $5,000 loss carryover against the $5,000 capital gain. ◀

COMPREHENSIVE ILLUSTRATION: DETERMINING A COMPLEX TRUST'S TAXABLE INCOME

The comprehensive illustration below enables us to review a number of points discussed earlier. A sample Form 1041 for a complex trust appears in Appendix B; it is prepared on the basis of the facts in this illustration.

BACKGROUND DATA

The Cathy and Karen Stephens Trust was established by Ted Tims in 1983. Its trust instrument empowers the trustee (Merchants Bank) to distribute income in its discretion to Cathy and Karen for the next fifteen years. The trust will then be terminated, and the trust assets will be divided equally between Cathy and Karen, irrespective of the amount of distributions each has previously received. In other words, separate shares are not to be maintained. Under state law, capital gains are part of principal.

The 1996 income and expenses of the trust are reported below. With the exception of the information concerning distributions and payments of estimated tax, the amounts are the same as in the comprehensive illustration for a simple trust discussed previously in the chapter.

	Amounts Allocable to	
	Income	*Principal*
Dividends	$30,000	
Rental income from land	5,000	
Tax-exempt interest	15,000	
Rental expenses (realtor's commissions on rental income)	1,000	
Trustee's fee		$ 1,200
Fee for preparation of tax return	500	
Long-term capital gain on sale of stock		12,000
Distribution of net accounting income to:		
Cathy	14,000	
Karen	7,000	
Payments of estimated tax	5,240	3,360

TRUSTEE'S FEE

Recall that a portion of the trustee's fee must be allocated to tax-exempt income. The expenses so allocated are nondeductible. Of the trust's $50,000 ($30,000 + $5,000 +

[38] Sec. 1211(b).

$15,000) gross accounting income, $15,000 is from tax-exempt sources. Consequently, the nondeductible trustee's fee is $360 [($15,000 ÷ $50,000) × $1,200]. The remaining $840 of the fee is deductible, as are the $500 of tax return preparation fees.

DISTRIBUTION DEDUCTION AND DNI

The primary function of the Subchapter J rules is to provide guidance for calculating the amounts taxable to the beneficiaries and to the fiduciary. One of the crucial numbers in the process is the distribution deduction. The amount of DNI must be known in order to arrive at the amount of the distribution deduction. Taxable income, exclusive of the distribution deduction, is the starting point for calculating DNI, and is computed as follows:

Dividends		$30,000
Rental income		5,000
Long-term capital gain		12,000
Minus:	Rental expenses	(1,000)
	Deductible portion of trustee's fee	(840)
	Fee for tax return preparation	(500)
	Personal exemption	(100)
Taxable income, exclusive of distribution deduction		$44,560

DNI is calculated by adjusting taxable income, exclusive of the distribution deduction, as follows:

Taxable income, exclusive of distribution deduction		$44,560
Plus:	Personal exemption	100
Minus:	Long-term capital gain	(12,000)
Plus:	Tax-exempt interest (net of $360 of allocable expenses)	14,640
DNI		$47,300

The distribution deduction is the lesser of (1) amounts required to be distributed, plus other amounts properly paid or credited, or required to be distributed, or (2) DNI. This lesser-of amount must be reduced by tax-exempt income (net of allocable expenses). DNI, exclusive of net tax-exempt income, is calculated as follows:

DNI		$47,300
Minus:	Tax-exempt income (net of $360 of allocable expenses)	(14,640)
DNI, exclusive of net tax-exempt income		$32,660

In no event may the distribution deduction exceed $32,660, the DNI, exclusive of net tax-exempt income. The DNI ceiling is of no practical significance in this example, however, because the total amount distributed is only $21,000.

ADDITIONAL COMMENT

This example dealing with a complex trust clearly illustrates the computational complexity that exists in situations with multiple categories of income and multiple beneficiaries.

Because a portion of the payments to each beneficiary is deemed to consist of tax-exempt income, the distribution deduction is less than the $21,000 distributed. The actual amount of each beneficiary's tax-exempt income is determined by dividing DNI into categories of income. In this categorization process, rental expenses are direct expenses that must be charged against rental income, and $360 of the trustee's fees must be charged against tax-exempt income. In this example the deductible trustee's fee and the tax return preparation fee are charged against rental income. They could, however, be charged against dividend income or some against each income category. Total DNI of $47,300 is categorized as follows:

	Dividends	*Rents*	*Tax-Exempt Interest*	*Total*
Accounting income	$30,000	$5,000	$15,000	$50,000
Minus: Expenses:				
Trustee's fee		(840)	(360)	(1,200)
Rental expenses		(1,000)		(1,000)
Fee for tax return preparation		(500)		(500)
DNI	$30,000	$2,660	$14,640	$47,300

Because the complex trust illustration involves two beneficiaries and three categories of income, we must calculate the amount of each beneficiary's distribution that comes from each income category. These steps were not needed in the simple trust illustration because it involved only one beneficiary.

Category of Income	*Proportion of DNI*	
Dividends	63.4249%	= $30,000 ÷ $47,300
Rental income	5.6237%	= $ 2,660 ÷ $47,300
Tax-exempt income	30.9514%	= $14,640 ÷ $47,300
Total	100.0000%	

As a result, 30.9514% of each beneficiary's distribution represents tax-exempt interest and is ineligible for a distribution deduction. The amount of the distribution deduction (which cannot exceed the $32,660 DNI, exclusive of net tax-exempt income) is determined as follows:

Amount distributed	$21,000
Minus: Net tax-exempt income deemed distributed (0.309514 × $21,000)	(6,500)
Distribution deduction	$14,500

The distributions received by the beneficiaries are deemed to consist of three categories of income in the amounts shown below.

Components of Distributions	*Cathy*	*Karen*	*Total*
Dividends (63.4249%)	$8,879	$4,440	$13,319
Plus: Rental income (5.6237%)	788	393	1,181
Gross income (69.0486%)	$9,667	$4,833	$14,500
Plus: Tax-exempt interest (30.9514%)	4,333	2,167	6,500
Total income (100.0000%)	$14,000	$7,000	$21,000

TRUST'S TAXABLE INCOME

Once the amount of the taxable and tax-exempt distributions has been quantified, the trust's taxable income can be calculated. Table C14-3 illustrates this calculation. Unlike the simple trust situation, there is no short-cut approach to verifying taxable income for complex trusts and estates except in the years when such entities distribute all of their income.

ADDITIONAL OBSERVATIONS

A few additional observations are in order concerning the Stephens Trust:

- If the entity is an estate instead of a trust, all amounts except the personal exemption are the same. The estate's personal exemption would be $600, instead of $100.

- Assume that (1) the trust owns a building instead of land and incurs $2,000 of depreciation expense, chargeable against principal under state law, and (2) the trust instrument does not require a reserve for depreciation. Because approximately 56% of the trust's income is accumulated (i.e., $26,300 of its $47,300 DNI), $1,120 (0.56 × $2,000) of the depreciation is deductible by the trust and its taxable income is $1,120 lower. The remaining $880 (0.44 × $2,000) is deductible on the beneficiaries' returns. The $880 of depreciation is then divided between the two beneficiaries in accordance with their pro rata share of the total distributions. Cathy deducts $587 [$880 × ($14,000 ÷ $21,000)], and Karen deducts $293 [$880 × ($7,000 ÷ $21,000)]. In summary, the depreciation is deductible as follows:

Trust	$1,120
Cathy	587
Karen	293
Total	$2,000

- If the trust instrument had mandated a reserve for depreciation equal to the depreciation expense for tax purposes, accounting income would have been reduced by the depreciation. In addition, the entire $2,000 of depreciation would have been deducted by the trust, and DNI would have been $45,300 instead of $47,300.

ACCUMULATION DISTRIBUTION RULES

PURPOSE

This section discusses the concept of the **accumulation distribution rules**, also known as the throwback rules. These rules are an exception to the general rule that DNI serves as a ceiling on the amount taxable to a beneficiary, and the beneficiary excludes from his or her gross income the portion of any distribution that exceeds DNI. If there were no exceptions to the general rule, great opportunities would have existed before 1987 for reducing taxes through the timing of distributions from complex trusts.[39] For example, assume that

- A beneficiary, Jeff, is in the top marginal tax bracket for many years before 1987.
- The discretionary trust accumulates $10,000 of its income each year from 1979 through 1986; the accumulated income totals $80,000, net of taxes. After 1986 the trust no longer accumulates income.
- In 1997, the trust has DNI and net accounting income of $12,000, all from taxable sources.
- In 1997, the trust distributes $92,000 ($12,000 + $80,000).

If the accumulation distribution rules did not exist, Jeff would receive a $92,000 distribution and pay taxes on only $12,000. Considerable savings would have arisen from having the income for the earlier years accumulated and taxed at the trust's lower rates. In the post-1986 era, because trusts reach the top tax bracket very quickly, the tax incentive for trusts to accumulate income is lessened substantially. Nontax reasons for retaining income (e.g., the need to reinvest monies in repairing a building owned by a trust) continue to apply, however.

KEY POINT

The theory behind the throwback rules is to put the trust beneficiary in the same after-tax position he or she would have been in had the accumulated income been distributed in the year it was received by the trust.

[39] Because of the compression of the income tax rate schedules for fiduciary taxpayers beginning in 1987, there is little incentive for trustees to accumulate income in order to reduce income taxes.

▼ **TABLE C14-3**

Comprehensive Illustration: Determining a Complex Trust's Taxable Income and Tax Liability

Gross income:	
Dividends	$30,000
Rental income	5,000
Long-term capital gain	12,000
Minus: Expense deductions:	
Rental expenses	(1,000)
Deductible portion of trustee's fee	(840)
Fee for tax return preparation	(500)
Minus: Distribution deduction	(14,500)
Minus: Personal exemption	(100)
Taxable income	$30,060
Tax liability (1996 rates)[a]	$9,616
Minus: Estimated taxes	(8,600)
Tax owed	$1,016

[a] $18,060 of taxable income is taxed at the fiduciary ordinary income rates and $12,000 of long-term capital gain is taxed at the 28% maximum tax rate on capital gains.

The accumulation distribution rules preclude the beneficiary in the example from being taxed on only $12,000 in 1997. Under the *concept* of these rules, Jeff would pay a tax for 1997 on the $80,000 of accumulated income and $12,000 of current income that he received. The amount of the tax on the previously accumulated income would equal the additional tax he would have paid for 1979 through 1986, had the trust distributed all of its income as earned, minus the tax the trust paid on such income. The statutory provisions governing throwbacks adopted a somewhat simplified approach that does not completely mesh with the concept. The statute does, however, ensure that the beneficiary is taxed on more than the current period's DNI.

WHEN APPLICABLE

KEY POINT

The throwback rules do not apply to distributions made out of a Sec. 2503(c) minor's trust. This rule allows the trust to accumulate the trust income up to the time the minor child reaches 21 years of age without concern about the throwback rules. At age 21, the accumulated trust income must be distributed to the child. Note also that estates are exempt from the throwback rules.

Because estates are exempt from the throwback rules, a beneficiary of an estate is never taxed on more than the estate's current DNI. A trust that has never accumulated income is also exempt from the throwback rules. Any distribution in excess of DNI that such a trust makes is classified as a tax-free distribution of principal. If a trust's net accounting income exceeds its DNI because of expenses that are charged against principal, the trust is exempt from the throwback rules when it distributes no more than its net accounting income, even though the distribution exceeds DNI.[40]

Distributions of income accumulated before the birth of the distributee/beneficiary, or before such beneficiary reaches age 21, are exempt from the throwback rules. At the time this provision was enacted, the Code did not contain the rule taxing unearned income of children under age 14 at their parents' top tax rate. The probable reason for this exemption is that at the time of enactment, beneficiaries younger than 21 generally were in a low marginal tax bracket and the opportunity for saving taxes was probably not the motivating factor for accumulating the income. Subsequent to 1986, this exception can present an opportunity for saving taxes by accumulating some income within a trust, provided such income if distributed would be taxed at the beneficiary's parents' rates.

[40] Sec. 665(b).

EXAMPLE C14-29 ▶ Bell Trust is formed in 1992 for the benefit of Brenda, then age 16. The trustee in its discretion accumulates all of the income until 1997, when it distributes the accumulated income to Brenda on her twenty-first birthday. It also distributes the current income for 1997. Because the income is accumulated while Brenda was under age 21, it is exempt from the throwback rules. Otherwise, such rules would apply. ◀

SECTION 644 TAX

PURPOSE

Section 644 was enacted to eliminate a tax-planning opportunity available to trusts. Before its enactment, taxpayers were able to convey highly appreciated assets to trusts, let the trusts sell the assets shortly after receiving them, and have the gains taxed to a new taxpayer (the trust) in a lower tax bracket. Under Sec. 644, if a trustee sells appreciated property soon (not more than two years) after receiving it, the tax on the gain is the same as if the donor had sold the asset.

WHEN APPLICABLE

Section 644 is applicable if the following two conditions are present:

- The trust sells property at a gain within two years of the transfer of the property in trust.
- The FMV of the property at the time of the transfer exceeds the property's adjusted basis immediately after the transfer.[41]

The adjusted basis immediately after the transfer is the donor's adjusted basis, increased by a portion of the gift taxes paid by the donor. Note that sales will fall outside the purview of Sec. 644 if they occur more than two years after the date of transfer. Also, Sec. 644 does not apply if the trust acquires property as the result of a death or if the trust is one of several types of charitable trusts.[42]

COMPUTATION OF THE TAX

The Sec. 644 tax is imposed on the trust's *includible gain,* which is the lesser of the gain recognized by the trust or the excess of the property's FMV at the time it is transferred to the trust over the property's adjusted basis immediately after the transfer.[43] Thus, post-transfer appreciation is not taxed under Sec. 644. If the trust and the transferor have the same tax year, the Sec. 644 tax is the additional tax (including any alternative minimum tax) the transferor would have owed had the includible gain been included in his or her own income for the year of the sale.[44] Because trusts must now use a calendar year, most trusts and transferors will have the same tax year.

Although the amount of the Sec. 644 tax is a function of the transferor's income, the trust pays the tax. The amount of the includible gain (net of any allocable deductions) is not included in the fiduciary's taxable income.[45] Thus, the includible gain is subject to the Sec. 644 tax, but not the regular income tax.

ADDITIONAL COMMENT

Because fiduciaries reach the maximum income tax rate of 39.6% at only $8,100 of taxable income (in 1997), the ability to reduce income taxes by shifting appreciated property to trusts is limited even without the application of Sec. 644.

EXAMPLE C14-30 ▶ In 1996, Dana forms York Trust and transfers to it, among other items, Major Corporation stock valued at $26,000. Dana purchased the stock for $20,000 several years earlier. Dana paid no gift tax on the transfer. The trust instrument allocates gains to principal and requires all

[41] Sec. 644(a)(1).
[42] Sec. 644(e). The types of charitable trusts exempted from the scope of Sec. 644 are pooled income funds and charitable remainder annuity trusts and unitrusts.
[43] Sec. 644(b).
[44] Sec. 644(a)(2).
[45] Sec. 641(c)(1).

income to be distributed currently. In 1997, the trustee sells the Major stock for $27,000, or a $7,000 ($27,000 − $20,000) long-term capital gain. The trust's only other income for 1997 is $3,000 of dividends. There are no expenses. Both the trust and Dana are calendar-year taxpayers. Dana's marginal tax rate for 1997 is 39.6%.

The Sec. 644 tax owed by the trust is computed as follows. To simplify the analysis, it is assumed that Dana does not owe any alternative minimum tax for 1997.

Includible gain [lesser of $7,000 realized gain or $6,000 ($26,000 − $20,000) pre-transfer gain]	$6,000
Times: Transferor's marginal tax rate (limited to 28% for long-term capital gains)	× 0.28
Sec. 644 tax liability	$1,680

The trust's taxable income is determined in the computations below.

Dividends	$3,000
Plus: Long-term capital gain (in excess of amount taxed under Sec. 644)	1,000
Minus: Distribution deduction	(3,000)
Personal exemption	(300)
Taxable income	$700

The $700 of taxable income is taxed at the fiduciary tax rate of 15%, for a tax of $105. The total tax owed is $1,785 ($1,680 Sec. 644 tax + $105). Had Sec. 644 not applied, $6,700 would have been taxed at the fiduciary tax rates—$1,650 at 15% and the remaining $5,050 long-term capital gain at 28%. The total tax would have been $1,661.50 ($247.50 + $1,414). Thus, Sec. 644 caused the tax liability to increase. ◀

INCOME IN RESPECT OF A DECEDENT

OBJECTIVE 7

Recognize the significance of income in respect of a decedent

DEFINITION AND COMMON EXAMPLES

Section 691 specifies the tax treatment for specific types of income known as income in respect of a decedent. **Income in respect of a decedent** (IRD) is gross income that the decedent earned before death, but such income was not includible on the decedent's income tax return for the tax year ending with the date of his or her death or for an earlier tax year because the decedent (a cash basis taxpayer) had not collected the income. Because most individuals use the cash method of accounting, IRD generally consists of income earned, but not actually or constructively received, before death. Common examples of IRD include the following:

- Interest earned, but not received, before death
- Salary, commission, or bonus earned, but not received, before death
- Dividend collected after the date of death, for which the record date precedes the date of death
- Gain portion of collections on an installment sale that took place before the date of death

SIGNIFICANCE OF IRD

DOUBLE TAXATION. Recall from Chapter C13 that a decedent's gross estate includes properties to the extent of his or her interest therein. The decedent has an interest in any income earned but not actually or constructively received before death. Thus, the decedent's gross estate includes income accrued as of the date of death. Assuming the

SELF-STUDY QUESTION

Roger, a cash method taxpayer, is a medical doctor. At the time of Roger's death, patients owe him $150,000. These accounts receivable are "property" in which Roger has an interest at the time of his death and are included in his gross estate. Why are the accounts receivable income in respect of a decedent?

ANSWER

Because they are income Roger earned while alive, but did not report as income due to his accounting method, they constitute income to his estate (or his heirs) when they are collected. Thus, they are income in respect of a decedent (IRD).

SELF-STUDY QUESTION

Karl receives his regular monthly paycheck on May 1 and deposits the paycheck in his savings account. He dies on May 10. He did not make any withdrawals from the account before his death. On June 1, Karl's employer pays Karl's estate one-third of Karl's monthly salary (the amount Karl had earned prior to his death on May 10). What are the tax consequences?

ANSWER

Karl's gross estate will include his savings account. Karl's final income tax return will include his salary through April 30 (i.e., his May 1 check is subject to both the income and the estate tax). The income taxes owed on the April salary are deductible as a debt on his estate tax return.

Karl's gross estate will include the one-third of his May salary. His estate will also report this amount as income. The salary is income in respect of a decedent, so the estate will receive some relief under Sec. 691(c) from the double tax.

decedent used the cash method of accounting, this accrued income is not included in gross income until it is collected. The income is taxed to the party (i.e., the estate or a named individual) entitled to receive it. Thus, IRD is taxed under both the transfer tax system and the income tax system. The income is also taxed twice if the decedent collects a dividend check, deposits it into his or her bank account, and dies before consuming the cash. In the latter case, the dividend is included in the decedent's individual income tax return, and the cash (from the dividend check) is included in the decedent's gross estate. The income taxes owed on the dividend income are deductible as a debt on the estate tax return.

EXAMPLE C14-31 ▶ Doug dies on July 1. Included in Doug's gross estate is an 8%, $1,000 corporate bond that pays interest each September 1 and March 1. Doug's gross estate also includes accrued interest for the period March 2 through July 1 of $27 ($1,000 × 0.08 × 4/12). On September 1, Doug's estate collects $40 of interest, of which $27 constitutes IRD. The income tax return for Doug's estate includes $40 of interest income. ◀

SECTION 691(c) DEDUCITON. Some relief for the double taxation of IRD is provided by the Sec. 691(c) deduction. This deduction equals the federal estate taxes attributable to the net IRD included in the gross estate. The total Sec. 691(c) deduction is the excess of the decedent's actual federal estate tax over the federal estate tax that would be payable if the net IRD were excluded from the decedent's gross estate. Net IRD means IRD minus deductions in respect of a decedent (DRD). If the IRD is collected in more than one tax year, the Sec. 691(c) deduction for a particular tax year is determined by the following formula:[46]

$$\text{Sec. 691(c) deduction for the year} = \text{Total Sec. 691(c) deduction} \times \frac{\text{Net IRD included in gross income for the year}}{\text{Total Net IRD}}$$

EXAMPLE C14-32 ▶ Latoya dies in 1996 with a taxable estate and estate tax base of $1,000,000. Latoya's estate owes no state death taxes. Latoya's gross estate includes $250,000 of IRD, none of which is received by her surviving spouse. Her estate has no DRD. The estate collects $200,000 of the IRD during its 1997 tax year. The Sec. 691(c) deduction for Latoya's estate for 1997 is calculated as shown below.

Actual federal estate tax liability (on base of $1,000,000)	$153,000
Minus: Federal estate tax on base ($750,000) determined by excluding net IRD from gross estate	(55,500)
Total Sec. 691(c) deduction	$ 97,500
Sec. 691(c) deduction available in 1997: ($200,000 ÷ $250,000) × $97,500 =	$ 78,000

◀

DEDUCTIONS IN RESPECT OF A DECEDENT. Section 691(b) authorizes **deductions in respect of a decedent (DRD)**. Such deductions include trade or business expenses, expenses for the production of income, interest, taxes, depletion, etc. that are accrued before death but are not deductible on the decedent's final income tax return because the decedent used the cash method of accounting. Because some of these accrued expenses have not been paid before death, they may also be deductible as debts on the estate tax return. The accrued expenses are also deductible on the estate's income tax return when paid by the estate. Thus, a double benefit can be obtained for DRD.

[46] Sec. 691(c)(1).

EXAMPLE C14-33 ▶ Dan dies on September 20. At the time of his death, Dan owes $18,000 of salaries to the employees of his proprietorship. The executor pays the total September payroll of $29,000 on September 30. The $18,000 of accrued salaries is deductible as a debt on the estate tax return. As a trade or business (Sec. 162) expense, the salaries also constitute DRD. The $18,000 of DRD, plus any other amounts paid, is deductible on the estate's income tax return for the period of payment. ◀

NO STEP-UP IN BASIS. Most property received as the result of a decedent's death acquires a basis equal to its FMV on the date of death or the alternate valuation date, except for properties classified as IRD. Items of IRD retain the same basis that they had in the decedent's hands.[47]

This carryover basis rule for IRD items is especially unfavorable when the decedent sells a highly appreciated asset soon before death, collects a relatively small portion of the sales price before death, and reports the sale under the installment method of accounting. For example, if the gain is 80% of the sales price, 80% of each principal payment in the post-death period will continue to be characterized as gain. If the sale is instead postponed until after the date of death, the gain is restricted to the post-death appreciation (if any) because the step-up in basis rules apply to the asset.

EXAMPLE C14-34 ▶ On June 3, 1997, Joel sells a parcel of investment land for $40,000. The land has a $10,000 adjusted basis in Joel's hands. The buyer pays $8,000 down and signs a $32,000 note at an interest rate acceptable to the IRS. The note is payable June 3, 1998. Joel uses the installment method for reporting the $30,000 ($40,000 − $10,000) gain. The gross profit ratio is 75% ($30,000 gain ÷ $40,000 contract price). Joel dies on June 13, 1997. A gain of $6,000 (0.75 × $8,000) is reported on Joel's final individual income tax return. The estate reports a gain of $24,000 (0.75 × $32,000) on its 1998 tax return because it collects the $32,000 balance due on June 3, 1998. Had the sale contract been entered into a few days after Joel's death, the gain would have been zero because the land's basis would have been its $40,000 FMV at the date of death. ◀

SELF-STUDY QUESTION

Roger died leaving $150,000 of zero basis accounts receivable. What basis does his estate have in these accounts receivable?

ANSWER

Zero. The accounts receivable constitute IRD. If they were stepped-up in basis, they would never be subject to an income tax.

STOP & THINK

Question: Isaac, a cash-basis, calendar-year taxpayer, died on May 12 of the current year. On which income tax return—Isaac's or his estate's—should the following income and expenses be reported? Assume the estate's tax year is the calendar year.

- Dividends declared in January and paid in February
- Interest income on a corporate bond that pays interest each June 30 and December 31
- Rent collected in June for a vacation home rented to tenants for the month of March, but the tenants were allowed to pay after occupying the property
- Balance due on Isaac's state income taxes for the previous year, paid in July because the return was extended
- Federal estimated income tax that Isaac paid in January for the previous year

Solution: Income received before death and deductible expenses paid before death should be reported on his individual return, in this case the dividends and nothing more. Income received after Isaac's death, even though earned before his death, is to be reported on the estate's income tax return. The same is true for deductible expenses paid by the estate. Items to be reported on the estate's income tax return include the interest income, the rental income, and the state income taxes. The federal income taxes are not deductible on the federal income tax return of either taxpayer.

[47] Sec. 1014(c).

GRANTOR TRUST PROVISIONS

OBJECTIVE 8

Explain the effect of the grantor trust provisions

This portion of the chapter examines the provisions affecting a special type of trust known as a **grantor trust**, which is governed by Secs. 671-679. As discussed previously, income of a regular (or nongrantor) trust or an estate is taxed to the beneficiary or the fiduciary in accordance with the portion that is distributed or accumulated. In the case of a grantor trust, however, the trust's grantor (creator) is taxed on some or all of the trust's income even though such income may have been distributed to the beneficiary. In certain circumstances, a person other than the grantor or the beneficiary (e.g., a person with powers over the trust) must pay taxes on the trust's income.

PURPOSE AND EFFECT

KEY POINT

The purpose of the grantor trust rules is to prevent tax avoidance through the use of transfers in trust where the grantor has not given up enough control over the transferred assets. Under the grantor trust rules the grantor reports all or part of the trust's income on his or her individual tax return.

The grantor trust rules are intended to require grantors who do not give up enough control or economic benefits when they create a trust to pay a price by being taxed on part or all of the trust's income. A grantor must report some or all of a trust's income on his or her individual tax return if he or she does not part with enough control over the trust assets or give up the right to income produced by the assets for a sufficiently long time period. For transfers after March 1, 1986, the grantor is generally taxed on the trust's income if the trust property will return to the grantor or the grantor's spouse at any time. According to the Tax Court, the grantor trust rules have the following purpose and result:

> This subpart [Secs. 671-679] enunciates the rules to be applied where, in described circumstances, a grantor has transferred property to a trust but has not parted with complete dominion and control over the property or the income which it produces. . . . [48]

Sections 671-679 use the term *treated as owner*. Section 671 specifies that when a grantor is treated as owner, the income, deductions, and credits attributable to the portion of the trust with respect to which the grantor is treated as owner are reported directly on the grantor's tax return and not on the trust's return. The fiduciary return contains only the items attributable to the portion of the trust for which the grantor is not treated as the owner.[49]

ADDITIONAL COMMENT

Many trust provisions can cause the grantor trust rules to apply. A trust need *not* be a revocable trust to be a grantor trust.

Unfortunately, the rules governing when a transfer is complete for income tax purposes (meaning the grantor avoids being taxed on the trust's income) do not agree completely with the rules concerning whether the transfer is complete for gift tax purposes or the transferred property is removed from the donor's gross estate. In certain circumstances, a donor can make a taxable gift and still be taxed on the income from the transferred property. For example, assume a donor makes a transfer to a trust with the income payable annually to the donor's cousin for six years and a reversion of the property to the donor at the end of the sixth year. The donor makes a gift, subject to the gift tax, of the value of an income interest for six years. Under the grantor trust rules, however, the donor continues to be taxed on the trust's income.

Retention of certain powers over property conveyed in trust can cause the trust assets to be included in the donor's gross estate even though these powers do not cause the donor to be taxed on the trust income. Assume that a donor has the discretionary power to pay out or accumulate trust income until the beneficiary reaches age 21. The trust assets, including any accumulated income, are to be distributed to the beneficiary on his or her twenty-first birthday. The donor is not taxed on the trust income, but if the donor

[48] *William Scheft,* 59 T.C. 428, at 430-431 (1972).

[49] For trusts created before March 2, 1986, the grantor may be treated as the owner with respect to the trust's capital gains but not its ordinary income because the property returns to the grantor after a period of more than ten years. In such a situation the grantor is taxed on the capital gains and the trust and/or the beneficiary on the ordinary income.

ADDITIONAL COMMENT

A common use of the revocable trust is to avoid probate for the property held by the trust. On the death of the grantor, the trustee of the revocable trust distributes the trust property in accordance with the trust agreement. Because the trustee holds legal title to the property, he or she can distribute the property without going through the probate process.

dies before the beneficiary attains age 21, the donor's gross estate will include the trust property because of Sec. 2036 (see Chapter C13).

REVOCABLE TRUSTS

The grantor of a revocable trust is able to control the assets conveyed to the trust by altering the terms of the trust (including changing the identity of the beneficiaries) and/or withdrawing assets from the trust. Not surprisingly, Sec. 676 provides that the grantor is taxed on the income generated by a revocable trust. As Chapter C12 points out, a transfer of assets to a revocable trust is an incomplete transfer and not subject to the gift tax.

EXAMPLE C14-35 ▶ In the current year, Tom transfers property to a revocable trust and names Ann to receive the income for life and Beth to receive the remainder. The trust's income for the current year consists of $15,000 of dividends and an $8,000 long-term capital gain. The dividends are distributed to Ann. The gain is credited to principal and not distributed. Because the trust is revocable, the dividend and capital gain income are taxed directly to Tom on his current year individual tax return. Nothing is taxed to the trust or its beneficiaries. ◀

CLIFFORD TRUSTS

Certain irrevocable trusts are subject to the grantor trust rules if, for example, the grantor has a reversionary interest that reverts (passes back) too soon. Before its amendment in 1986, Sec. 673(a) provided that the grantor is taxed on the trust's accounting income if the trust assets revert to the grantor within ten years of the transfer date. However, if the reversion date is more than ten years from the transfer date, the grantor is not taxed on the accounting income. Regardless of when the trust terminates, the grantor is always taxed on capital gains credited to principal because such gains are held for distribution to the grantor upon termination of the trust.[50] The gains are taxed in the year realized, not at the termination of the trust.

If the trust period was long enough for the grantor to escape being taxed on the trust's accounting income, the trust was often referred to as a ***Clifford*** or **short-term trust**. The phrase *Clifford trust* relates to the *Clifford* case, a case decided before the adoption of the statutory rules concerning reversionary interest trusts.[51] In *Clifford,* however, the Supreme Court concluded that the grantor was taxable on the trust income because the reversion would occur too soon after the transfer.

Example C14-36 involves a trust for which the grantor successfully shifts the taxability of the accounting income.

EXAMPLE C14-36 ▶ In June 1985, Ted transferred property to a trust whose trust instrument specifies that all of its income is payable annually to Amy for the next twelve years. At the end of twelve years, the property reverts to Ted. Amy is taxed on the trust's accounting income. Ted is taxed currently on any capital gains because he will regain the property when the trust ends. ◀

The next example concerns a reversion within ten years.

EXAMPLE C14-37 ▶ Assume the same facts as in Example C14-36, except the term of the trust was instead eight years. During the existence of the trust, Ted was taxed on the accounting income because the assets reverted to Ted in ten years or less. Ted was also taxed on any capital gains. ◀

---

[50] Sec. 677(a).

[51] *Helvering v. George B. Clifford, Jr.*, 23 AFTR 1077, 40-1 USTC ¶9265 (USSC, 1940).

POST-1986 REVERSIONARY INTEREST TRUSTS

KEY POINT

The *Clifford,* or short-term, trust cannot be used as an income shifting device any longer. The reversion of corpus to the grantor at the end of the term of the trust now causes the trust to be treated as a grantor trust unless the reversion occurs many, many years after the funding of the trust.

The 1986 Tax Reform Act sounded the death knell for *Clifford* trusts. It amended Sec. 673(a) for transfers made after March 1, 1986 to provide that the grantor is taxed on the accounting income of the trust if he or she has a reversionary interest in either income or principal. Under Sec. 672(e), a grantor is treated as holding any interest held by his or her spouse.

There are two exceptions to the provision taxing the grantor who holds a reversionary interest or whose spouse holds a remainder interest. The grantor trust rules do not apply if, as of the inception of the trust, the value of the reversionary interest does not exceed 5% of the value of the trust. The second exception applies when the reversion would occur only if the beneficiary dies before reaching age 21 and the beneficiary is a lineal descendant of the grantor.

EXAMPLE C14-38 ▶ In the current year, Paul establishes a trust with income payable to his elderly parents for 15 years. The assets of the trust will then revert to Paul. The value of Paul's reversionary interest exceeds 5%. Because Paul has a reversionary interest valued at above 5% and the transfer arises after March 1, 1986, Paul is taxed currently on the trust's accounting income and capital gains. ◀

The next example illustrates the application of one of the exceptions.

EXAMPLE C14-39 ▶ In the current year, Paul transfers property to a trust with income payable to his daughter Ruth until Ruth reaches age 21. On Ruth's twenty-first birthday, she is to receive the trust property outright. In the event Ruth dies before reaching age 21, the trust assets will revert to Paul. Paul is not taxed on the accounting income because his reversion is contingent on the death of the beneficiary (a lineal descendant) before age 21. ◀

RETENTION OF ADMINISTRATIVE POWERS

Under the rules of Sec. 675, the grantor is taxed on the accounting income and gains if he or she or his or her spouse holds certain administrative powers. Such powers include, but are not limited to, the following:

- The power to purchase or exchange trust property for less than adequate consideration in money or money's worth
- The power to borrow from the trust without adequate interest or security except where the trustee (who is someone other than the grantor) is empowered under a general lending power to make loans irrespective of interest or security
- The power exercisable in a nontrustee capacity to (1) vote stock of a corporation in which the holdings of the grantor and the trust are significant from the standpoint of voting control and (2) reacquire the trust property by substituting other property of equal value

RETENTION OF ECONOMIC BENEFITS

Under the rules of Sec. 677, the grantor is taxed on the portion of the trust with respect to which the income may be

- Distributed to the grantor or his or her spouse
- Held or accumulated for future distribution to the grantor or his or her spouse
- Used to pay premiums on life insurance policies on the life of the grantor or his or her spouse

Use of trust income to provide support for a child whom the grantor is legally obligated to support also yields obvious economic benefits to the grantor. A grantor is taxed on any trust income that is distributed by the trustee and used to support people whom the grantor is legally obligated to support (e.g., children). However, the mere existence of the discretionary power to use trust income for support purposes does not cause the grantor to be taxed on the trust income. Taxation turns on whether the trust income is actually used to meet the support obligation.

The following example deals with the payment of premiums on an insurance policy on the grantor's life.

EXAMPLE C14-40 ▶ One of the assets of Martinez Trust is a life insurance policy on the life of Maria, the trust's grantor. The trust instrument requires that $1,000 of trust income be used to pay the insurance premiums and that the rest be distributed to Juan. Section 677 requires Maria (the grantor) to be taxed on $1,000 of accounting income. The remaining income is taxed to Juan under the general trust rules. ◀

The rule concerning income held for eventual distribution to the grantor is illustrated in the next example.

EXAMPLE C14-41 ▶ Judy created a trust in January 1985 with all the income payable to Eric for fifteen years. The trust assets will then revert to Judy. Section 677 taxes Judy on the capital gains provided they are credited to corpus. Eric is taxed on the accounting income because the trust was funded before March 1986. ◀

The next example concerns use of trust income to support the grantor's minor child.

EXAMPLE C14-42 ▶ Hal creates a trust and empowers the bank trustee to distribute income to his minor son, Louis, until the son reaches age 21. When Louis reaches age 21, the trust assets including accumulated income are to be paid over to the child. In the current year, when Louis is age 15, the trustee distributes $5,000 that is used to support Louis and $8,000 that is deposited into Louis's savings account. The remaining $12,000 of income is accumulated. Hal (the grantor) is taxed on the $5,000 used to support his son. Louis includes $8,000 in his gross income, and the trust pays tax on $12,000 less its $100 exemption. ◀

TYPICAL MISCONCEPTION

Keep in mind that the discussion in Example C14-40 covers trusts created by the grantor, who is the insured. If the trust were created by a person other than the insured, say a parent, the income required to be used for the payment of life insurance would not be taxed to the grantor because the insured is not the grantor or the grantor's spouse.

CONTROL OF OTHERS' ENJOYMENT

Section 674 requires the grantor to be taxed on trust income if he or she, his or her spouse, or someone without an interest in the trust (e.g., a trustee) has the power to control others' beneficial enjoyment such as by deciding how much income to distribute. Many exceptions, including exceptions for independent trustees, exist for Sec. 674's general rule of taxing the grantor.

EXAMPLE C14-43 ▶ Otto is grantor and trustee of a trust over which the trustee has complete discretion to pay out the income or corpus in any amount he deems appropriate to some or all of its three beneficiaries, Kay, Fay, and May. In the current year, the trustee distributes all of the income to Kay. Otto, the grantor, is taxed on the income. Kay would have been taxed if there had been an independent trustee. ◀

Under Sec. 678, an individual other than the trust's grantor or beneficiary can be required to report the trust income. The other individual is taxed on the trust income if he or she has the power under the trust instrument to vest the trust principal or the income in him- or herself, provided such power is exercisable solely by such individual.

Topic Review C14-4 summarizes the grantor trust rules.

Topic Review C14-4

Grantor Trust Rules

Factual Situation	Tax Treatment
1. Trust is revocable.	Ordinary income and capital gains are taxed to grantor.
2. Irrevocable trust (funded before March 2, 1986) pays income to third-party beneficiary for more than ten years and property then reverts to grantor.	Ordinary income is taxed to beneficiary, and capital gains are taxed to grantor.
3. Same as number 2, except trust is funded on or after March 2, 1986, and the value of the reversionary interest exceeds 5% of the value of the trust.	Ordinary income and capital gains are taxed to grantor.
4. The grantor of an irrevocable trust retains administrative powers described in the Code.	Ordinary income and capital gains are taxed to grantor.
5. The income of an irrevocable trust is disbursed to meet the grantor's obligation to support his or her children.	Ordinary income used for support is taxed to grantor.
6. The income of an irrevocable trust is disbursed to pay the premium on a life insurance policy on the life of the grantor or the grantor's spouse.	Ordinary income and capital gains are taxed to grantor to the extent they may be used to pay the premiums.

TAX PLANNING CONSIDERATIONS

ADDITIONAL COMMENT

In 1997, the first $1,650 of trust income is taxed at 15%. If the trust is a complex trust, it is entitled to a personal exemption of $100. In other words, a trust pays no tax on $100 of income and only 15% on the next $1,650 of income. If the trust distributes dividend or interest income to a child under age 14 who is a dependent and has no other unearned income, the child pays no tax on the first $650 of that income and pays taxes at his or her own rate on the next $650. If the child's parents are continually in the 36% or 39.6% income tax bracket, some income tax savings can still be achieved by using a trust to spread income over different taxpayers. For the situation described here, a Sec. 2503(c) trust (trust for minors) is commonly used.

Many tax planning opportunities exist with respect to estates and trusts, including the ability to shift income to the fiduciary and/or the beneficiaries and the opportunity for executors or trustees of discretionary trusts to consider the tax consequences of the timing of distributions. These and other tax planning considerations are discussed below.

ABILITY TO SHIFT INCOME

Before 1987, one of the primary tax advantages of using trusts was the ability to shift income from the grantor to the trust or the beneficiary. Two changes have reduced the tax advantages of shifting income. First, the tax rate schedules for all taxpayers—but especially for fiduciaries—are very compressed. In fact, an estate or trust has only $1,650 of income subject to the 15% tax rate. Second, unearned income in excess of $1,300 of children under age 14 is taxed at the higher of the parents' or the child's tax rate, even if distributed from a trust or estate. Depending on whether the income is distributed or retained, it is taxed to the trust or the beneficiary or a portion to each. Because the trust is a separate taxpayer, income taxed to the trust is taxed under the trust's rate schedule. If the beneficiary has income from other sources, the income shifted to the beneficiary may not be taxed at the lowest rates. An income tax savings can nevertheless occur whenever a portion of the shifted income is taxed at a rate lower than the rate the grantor would pay on that income. The accumulation distribution provisions lessen the overall tax-saving effects of using trusts.

TIMING OF DISTRIBUTIONS

KEY POINT

When you consider that one often cannot determine the exact amount of income a trust (or any other entity) has earned until after the end of the tax year, you can see that the 65-day rule is extremely helpful for distribution planning.

People managing estates and discretionary trusts can reduce taxes by carefully planning the timing of distributions. From a tax standpoint, the executor or trustee should consider the beneficiary's income from other sources and make distributions in amounts that equalize the marginal tax rates of the beneficiary and the fiduciary. If the trust is a **sprinkling trust** (a discretionary trust with several beneficiaries), the trustee can accomplish tax savings for the beneficiaries by making distributions to the beneficiaries who have the lowest marginal tax rate that year. Of course, nontax reasons might require a trustee to distribute income to other beneficiaries also. A special 65-day rule allows trustees of complex trusts to treat distributions made during the first sixty-five days of the trust's tax year as if they had been made on the last day of the preceding tax year. If the trustee does not make the election, the distributed income is deducted by the trust and taxed to the beneficiary in the year the actual distribution is made.

PROPERTY DISTRIBUTIONS

A special tax saving election is available for trusts that make noncash (property) distributions. Under the general rule affecting property distributions, the trust gets a distribution deduction equal to the lesser of the fiduciary's adjusted basis in the property or the property's FMV.[52] If the trust distributes appreciated property, the trustee can elect, however, to recognize a gain on the distribution. The gain is the excess of the property's FMV over its adjusted basis on the distribution date. If the election is not made, the trust recognizes no gain as a result of distributing the property.

If the trustee elects to recognize the gain, the distribution deduction equals the property's FMV. The beneficiary, in turn, takes a basis equal to the property's adjusted basis to the trust plus the gain recognized by the trust on the distribution. If property will probably be sold soon after distribution, the election provision allows the trustee to choose where the appreciation will be taxed: at the trust level or the beneficiary level. If the distribution involves appreciated capital gain property, the capital gain that is recognized may offset the trust's capital loss carryovers from prior tax years.

CHOICE OF YEAR-END FOR ESTATES

Before 1987, a fiduciary taxpayer had the freedom to choose its original tax year as long as it made the choice on a timely filed return. Proper timing of the estate or trust's year-end deferred the reporting of income by a beneficiary from one tax year to the next because distributions from an estate or trust are taxed to the beneficiaries in the beneficiaries' tax year in which the fiduciary's year ends.[53]

KEY POINT

Generally, a trust must now use the calendar year as its tax year.

Because of the ability to defer the taxation of trust distributions to beneficiaries by choosing a noncalendar year, Congress in 1986 required all trusts (even existing fiscal-year trusts) other than tax-exempt and wholly charitable trusts to use a calendar year as their tax year.[54] Estates, however, are completely free to choose a year-end, probably because death is a high price to pay to achieve favorable tax treatment for a beneficiary.

EXAMPLE C14-44 ▶ Madison Estate adopts a fiscal year ending on January 31. During the period February 1, 1996 through January 31, 1997, Madison Estate distributes $30,000 to Bob, a calendar-year beneficiary. The estate's DNI exceeds $30,000. Bob reports $30,000 of estate income on his individual return for 1997, Bob's tax year during which the estate's tax year ended. By choosing the January 31 year-end (instead of a calendar year-end), the executor postpones the taxation of income to Bob from 1996 to 1997. ◀

[52] Sec. 643(d).
[53] Secs. 652(c) and 662(c).
[54] Sec. 645.

DEDUCTION OF ADMINISTRATION EXPENSES

Chapter C13 points out that the executor elects where to deduct administration expenses: on the estate tax return, the estate's income tax return, or some on each return. Unlike the situation for deductions in respect of a decedent, Sec. 642(g) provides that there is no double deduction for administration expenses. Such expenses should be deducted where they will yield the greatest tax savings. Of course, if the surviving spouse receives all of the decedent's property or all except for an amount equal to the exemption equivalent, deducting administration expenses on the estate tax return will produce no tax savings because the estate will owe no estate taxes.

COMPLIANCE AND PROCEDURAL CONSIDERATIONS

OBJECTIVE 9

Recognize the filing requirements for fiduciary returns

FILING REQUIREMENTS

GENERAL RULE. Every estate that has gross income of at least $600 for the tax year must file an income tax return (Form 1041-U.S. Fiduciary Income Tax Return). A trust income tax return (also generally Form 1041) is required for every trust that has taxable income or has gross income of $600 or more.[55] In addition, every estate or trust that has a nonresident alien as a beneficiary must file a return.[56] A simplified trust form, Form 1041S, is available for use by simple trusts with no taxable income. This form may be prepared for simple trusts that have no capital gains or losses and have an income distribution deduction equal to the amount of income that must be distributed currently.

ETHICAL POINT

Individual beneficiaries report their share of income from trusts and estates on Schedule E of Form 1040. CPAs have a responsibility to monitor the beneficial interests that clients have in trusts and estates to prevent underreporting. Some clients may unintentionally forget to report income from a fiduciary simply because they received no cash distributions from the fiduciary during the year.

KEY POINT

Both estates and trusts must generally make estimated tax payments. Estates, however, are exempted for their first two tax years.

DUE DATE FOR RETURN AND TAX

The due date for fiduciary returns (Form 1041) is the same as for individuals, the fifteenth day of the fourth month following the end of the tax year.[57] If an extension is desired, Form 2758 must be filed. The extension period is for four months, but an additional extension for two months may be requested.

Both trusts and estates must generally make estimated tax payments using the general rules applicable to individual taxpayers.[58] Estates, however, are exempted from making estimated tax payments for their first two tax years. If the fiduciary's tax liability exceeds the estimated tax payments, the balance of the tax is due on or before the due date for the return.[59] Estimated tax payments for a trust or an estate are made by using Form 1041-ES (Estimated Income Tax for Fiduciaries).

DOCUMENTS TO BE FURNISHED TO IRS

Although the executor or the trustee need not file a copy of the will or the trust instrument with the return, at times the IRS may request a copy of such documents. If the IRS makes such a request, the executor or the trustee should also transmit the following:

- A statement signed under penalty of perjury that the copy is true and complete
- A statement naming the provisions of the will or trust agreement that the executor or the trustee believes control how the income is to be divided among the fiduciary, the beneficiaries, and the grantor (if applicable)

---

[55] Secs. 6012(a)(3) and (4). A special grantor trust rule permits a revocable trust's income to be reported on the grantor's tax return. See Reg. Sec. 1.671-4(b).

[56] Sec. 6012(a)(5).

[57] Sec. 6072(a).

[58] Sec. 6654(l).

[59] Sec. 6151(a).

SAMPLE SIMPLE AND COMPLEX TRUST RETURNS

Appendix B contains samples of simple and complex trust returns (Form 1041). The Appendix illustrates the completion of Schedule K-1 for the reporting of income, etc. to the beneficiary. One copy of Schedule K-1 for each beneficiary is filed with Form 1041. In addition, each beneficiary receives a copy of his or her Schedule K-1, so that he or she knows the amount and type of gross income to report for the distributions received. If the beneficiary is entitled to a deduction for depreciation, information concerning the amount appears on lines 4(b) and 5(b) of Schedule K-1.

The Sec. 644 tax is not owed in the two sets of facts illustrated in the sample returns. When such tax is owed, the amount should be entered on line 1b of Schedule G of Form 1041. In addition, a schedule should be attached for disclosing the computation of the tax. Moreover, only the gain in excess of the Sec. 644 gain should be included in the trust's taxable income and taxed at the trust's tax rates.

The alternative minimum tax is not owed on the two sets of facts illustrated in the sample returns. When such tax is owed, the amount is reported on Schedule I of Form 1041.

PROBLEM MATERIALS

DISCUSSION QUESTIONS

C14-1 Explain to a client whether the income of an estate or trust is subject to double taxation.

C14-2 Given the nature of the tax rate schedule for trusts, what reasons exist today for creating a trust?

C14-3 Is the taxable income of a trust calculated more like the taxable income of an individual or a corporation? Explain.

C14-4 Explain to a client the significance of the income and principal categorization scheme used for fiduciary accounting purposes.

C14-5 List some common examples of principal and income items.

C14-6 A client asks about the relevance of state law with respect to the classification of items as principal or income. Explain the relevance.

C14-7 A trust from which Irene is entitled to receive only distributions of income and from which Beth will receive the remainder interest sells property at a gain. Income and corpus are classified in accordance with the Uniform Act. Will Irene receive a distribution of an amount equal to the gain? Explain.

C14-8 Refer to Question C14-7. Which taxpayer (the trust, Irene, or Beth) pays the tax on the gain?

C14-9 A trust owns some properties on which depreciation is claimed. The trust distributes all of its income to its sole income beneficiary. Whose taxable income is reduced by the depreciation?

C14-10 What is the amount of the personal exemption for trusts and estates?

C14-11 A client inquires about the significance of distributable net income (DNI). Explain.

C14-12
- **a.** Are net accounting income and DNI always the same amount?
- **b.** If not, explain a common reason for a difference.
- **c.** Are capital gains usually included in DNI?

C14-13 Explain how to determine the deductible portion of trustee's fees.

C14-14 Assume that a trust collects rental income and interest income on tax-exempt bonds. Will a portion of the rental expenses be nondeductible because of having to be allocated to tax-exempt income? Explain.

C14-15
- **a.** Describe the short-cut approach for verifying that the amount calculated as a simple trust's taxable income is correct.
- **b.** Can a short-cut verification process be applied with respect to trusts and estates that accumulate some of their income? Explain.

C14-16 When does the NOL of a trust or estate produce tax deductions for the beneficiaries?

C14-17 The Mary Morgan Trust, a simple trust, sells one capital asset in the current year. The sale results in a loss.

a. When will the capital loss produce a tax benefit for the trust or its beneficiary? Explain.

b. Would the result necessarily be the same for a complex trust? Explain.

C14-18 A client is under the impression that complex trusts always receive a $100 personal exemption. Is the client correct?

C14-19 Describe the tier system for trust beneficiaries.

C14-20 Determine the accuracy of the following statement: Under the tier system, beneficiaries who receive mandatory distributions of income are more likely to be taxed on the distributions they receive than are beneficiaries who receive discretionary distributions.

C14-21 a. What is the purpose of the accumulation distribution rules?

b. Are the accumulation distribution rules an exception to the general rule that DNI sets the ceiling on the amount taxable to the beneficiary? If so, explain.

c. List two situations in which the accumulation distribution rules do not apply even though the fiduciary earlier accumulated income and the current year's distributions exceed the current year's DNI.

C14-22 Answer the following questions relating to the Sec. 644 tax.

a. What does the term *includible gain* mean?

b. Who pays the tax on a trust's includible gain?

C14-23 Indicate whether, and why, you agree with the following statement: If the current tax rate structure had always existed, there would not be much of a policy reason for imposing the Sec. 644 tax.

C14-24 a. Describe to a client what income in respect of a decedent (IRD) is.

b. Describe to the client one tax disadvantage and one tax advantage that occur as a result of the classification of a receipt as IRD.

C14-25 Describe three situations that cause trusts to be subject to the grantor trust rules.

C14-26 A client is under the impression that the tax treatment is the same for all trusts in which the grantor has a reversionary interest. Is the client correct? Explain.

C14-27 A client is under the impression that if the grantor trust rules apply to a trust, the grantor is always taxed on both the trust's ordinary income and its gains. Is the client correct? Explain.

C14-28 a. What is the due date for fiduciary income tax returns?

b. Must estates and trusts make payments of estimated income taxes?

ISSUE IDENTIFICATION QUESTIONS

C14-29 Art Rutter sold an apartment building in May 1996 for a small amount of cash and a note payable over five years. Principal and interest payments are due annually on the note in April of 1997 through 2001. Art died in August 1996. He willed all of his assets to his daughter Amelia. Art's gross estate is about $2 million, and his estate tax deductions are very small. What tax issues should the executor of his estate consider with respect to the reporting of the sale of the building and the collection of the installments?

C14-30 For the first five months of its existence (August through December 1997), the Estate of Amy Ennis had gross income (net of expenses) of $7,000 per month. For January through July 1998, it is estimated that the estate will have gross income (net of expenses) totaling $5,000. The estate's sole beneficiary is Amy's son, Joe, who is a calendar-year taxpayer. Joe incurred a large NOL from his sole proprietorship years ago, and $34,000 of the NOL carryover remains but expires at the end of 1997. During 1997, Joe received only $5,000 of income from part-time employment. What tax issues should be considered by the executor of Amy's estate with respect to the reporting of the estate's income?

C14-31 Raj Kothare funded an irrevocable trust in May 1996. One of the assets he transferred to the trust was Webbco stock, which had a FMV on the transfer date of $35,000. Raj's basis in the stock was $30,000, and he paid no gift tax on the transfer. The stock's value has risen to $37,000, and the trustee thinks that now (October 1997) might be the time to realize the gain. For 1997 the trust will have $20,000 of income exclusive of any gain. Raj's taxable income is approximately $15,000. What tax issues should be considered by the trustee with respect to the possible sale of the stock?

PROBLEMS

C14-32 ***Calculation of the Tax Liability.*** A trust has taxable income of $18,000 in the current year. What is its income tax liability?

C14-33 ***Determination of Taxable Income.*** A simple trust has the following receipts and expenditures for the current year. The long-term capital gain and trustee's fees are part of principal.

Dividends	$30,000
Long-term capital gain	12,000
Trustee's fees	1,500
Distribution to beneficiary	30,000

a. What is the trust's taxable income under the formula approach of Figure C14-1?
b. What is the trust's taxable income under the short-cut approach?

C14-34 ***Determination of Taxable Income.*** Refer to Problem C14-33. How would your answer to Part a change if the trust in addition received $10,000 interest from tax-exempt bonds, and it distributed $40,000 instead of $30,000?

C14-35 ***Determination of Taxable Income and Tax Liability.*** A simple trust has the following receipts and expenditures for the current year. Assume the trust instrument is silent with respect to capital gains and that state law concerning trust accounting income follows the Uniform Act. Assume the trustee's fee is charged to principal.

Corporate bond interest	$30,000
Tax-exempt interest	20,000
Long-term capital gain	8,000
Trustee's fee	2,000
Distribution to beneficiary	50,000

a. What is the trust's taxable income under the formula approach of Figure C14-1?
b. What is the trust's tax liability?
c. How (if at all) would the tax and nontax consequences differ if the trustee's fee were charged to income instead of principal?

C14-36 ***Determination of Taxable Income.*** During the current year a simple trust has the following receipts and expenditures. Assume that trustee's fees are charged to income and that the Uniform Act governs for accounting.

Dividends	$40,000
Long-term capital gain	15,000
Trustee's fees	2,000

a. How much must be distributed to the beneficiary?
b. What is the trust's taxable income under the short-cut approach?

C14-37 ***Determination of Distribution Deduction.*** A trust has net accounting income of $18,000 and DNI of $16,000. What is its distribution deduction under the following situations:

a. It distributes $18,000, and all of its income is from taxable sources.
b. It distributes $18,000, and it has tax-exempt income (net of allocable expenses) of $2,000.
c. It distributes $9,000, and all of its income is from taxable sources.

C14-38 ***Determination of Beneficiary's Income.*** A trust is authorized to make discretionary distributions of income and principal to its two beneficiaries, Roy and Sandy. For the current year it has DNI and net accounting income of $36,000, all from taxable sources. It distributes $20,000 to Roy and $40,000 to Sandy. How much gross income does each beneficiary report, assuming that the accumulation distribution rules do not apply?

C14-39 ***Determination of Beneficiary's Income.*** Refer to Problem C14-38. How would your answer change if the trust instrument required that $10,000 per year be distributed to Sandy and the trustee also made discretionary distributions of $20,000 to Roy and $30,000 to Sandy?

C14-40 ***Determination of Accounting Income and Distribution.*** A trust has the receipts and expenditures listed below for the current year. Assume the Uniform Act governs an item's classification as principal or income. What is the trust's net accounting income and the maximum distribution possible? Assume the trust cannot pay out principal.

Dividends	$12,000
Interest on tax-exempt bonds	5,000
Gain on sale of capital asset	20,000
Rental income from land	3,000
Property taxes on rental property	200
Trustee's fee charged to principal in accordance with agreement with trustees	1,200

C14-41 ***Determination of Taxable Income.*** Refer to Problem C14-40. Assume the trustee must pay out all of its income currently to its beneficiary, Julio.

a. What is the deductible portion of the trustee's fee?
b. What is the trust's taxable income exclusive of the distribution deduction?
c. What is the trust's DNI?
d. What is the trust's taxable income using the formula approach of Figure C14-1?

C14-42 ***Determination of Taxable Income.*** Refer to Problem C14-41. How would your answers change if the trust were a discretionary trust that distributes $8,000 to its beneficiary, Julio?

C14-43 ***Calculation of Deductible Expenses.*** The Ellen Levinson Trust reports the receipts and expenditures listed below. What are the trust's *deductible* expenses?

Dividends	$15,000
Rental income	6,000
Interest from tax-exempt bonds	7,000
Property taxes on rental property	500
Maintenance of rental property	1,300
CPA's fee for tax return preparation	700
Trustee's fee	1,800

C14-44 ***Tax Treatment of Capital Losses.*** A simple trust had a long-term capital loss of $10,000 for 1996 and a long-term capital gain of $15,000 for 1997. Its net accounting income and DNI are equal. Explain the tax treatment for the 1996 capital loss assuming the trust is in existence at the end of 1998.

C14-45 ***Tax Treatment of Capital Losses.*** Refer to Problem C14-44. How would your answer change if the trust were instead a complex trust that makes no distributions in 1996 and 1997? Assume the trust earns $8,000 of corporate bond interest income each year.

C14-46 ***Section 644 Tax.*** Last year Chris transferred stock valued at $60,000 to a trust. The stock's adjusted basis is $10,000. Chris pays no gift tax on the transfer. The trust sells the stock in the current year for $150,000. Both Chris and the trust report on a calendar-year basis. Chris, who is single, claims the standard deduction and has $300,000 of taxable income in the current year.

a. What is the Sec. 644 tax? (Ignore any alternative minimum tax implications.)
b. What gain (if any) is included in the trust's taxable income?

C14-47 *Section 644 Tax.* Refer to Problem C14-46. Explain how your answer would change for each of the two independent situations indicated below:
a. Chris instead makes the transfer four years before the sale.
b. Chris's adjusted basis for the property is instead $80,000.

C14-48 *Revocable Trusts.* A revocable trust created by Amir realizes $12,000 of dividend income and a $40,000 capital gain. It distributes $12,000 to Ali, its beneficiary. How much income is taxed to the trust, the grantor, and the beneficiary?

C14-49 *Reversionary Interest Trusts.* The Holly Marx Trust is created by Holly in January 1986. Starting in 1986, the trust income is payable to her son, Jack (age 17 in 1986), for a period of fourteen years. At the end of the fourteenth year (2000), the trust assets are to revert to Holly. In the current year, the trust realizes $20,000 of dividend income and an $18,000 long-term capital gain. How much income is taxed to the trust, the grantor, and the beneficiary in the current year?

C14-50 *Reversionary Interest Trusts.* Refer to Problem C14-49. Explain how your answers would change for each independent situation indicated below:
a. The term of the trust is nine years (instead of twelve).
b. Holly creates the trust in October 1997 for a term of thirteen years.

C14-51 *Income in Respect of Decedent.* The following items are reported on the first income tax return for the Ken Kimble Estate. Mr. Kimble died on July 1, 1997.

Dividends	$10,000
Interest on corporate bonds	18,000
Collection on installment note from sale of investment land	24,000

The record date was June 14 for $6,000 of the dividends and October 31 for the remaining $4,000 of dividends. The bond interest is payable annually on October 1. Mr. Kimble's basis in the land was $8,000. He sold it in 1996 for a total sales price of $48,000 and reported his gain under the installment method. What amount of IRD is reported on the estate's income tax return?

C14-52 *Income in Respect of Decedent.* Julie Brown died on May 29 of the current year. She was employed before her death, and her gross salary was $2,000 per month. Her pay day was the last day of each month and her employer did not pro rate her last monthly salary payment. She owned stock that paid quarterly dividends of $800 per quarter each March 31, June 30, September 30, and December 31. The record date for the June dividend was June 10. Assume her estate chooses a calendar year as its tax year. What amount of gross income should be reported on the estate's first income tax return? Identify the IRD included in gross income.

C14-53 *Income Recognition by Beneficiary.* Joan died April 17, 1996. Joan's executor chose a tax year for the estate that ends on March 31. The estate's only beneficiary, Kathy, reports on a calendar year. The executor of Joan's estate makes the following distributions to Kathy:

June 1996	$ 5,000
August 1996	10,000
March 1997	12,000
August 1997	14,000

The 1996 and 1997 distributions do not exceed DNI. How much income should Kathy report on her 1996 return as a result of the distributions from the estate? On her 1997 return?

TAX FORM/RETURN PREPARATION PROBLEMS

C14-54 Marion Mosley creates the Jenny Justice Trust in 1986 with First Bank named as trustee. For twenty years the trust is to pay out all of its income semiannually to the beneficiary, Jenny Justice. At the end of the twentieth year, the trust assets are to be distributed to Jenny's descendants. Capital gains are credited to principal, and depreciation is charged to principal. For the current year the trust reports the following results:

	Amounts Allocable to	
	Income	*Principal*
Rental income	$15,000	
Dividend income	27,000	
Interest on tax-exempt (non-private activity) bonds	8,000	
Long-term capital gain on sale of stock		30,000[a]
Maintenance and repairs of rental property	1,500	
Property taxes on rental property	700	
Fee for tax return preparation	500	
Trustee's fee		2,000
Depreciation		2,400
Estimated federal income taxes paid		9,000

[a] The sales price and adjusted basis are $110,000 and $80,000, respectively. Mrs. Mosley acquired the stock in 1970.

Prepare a Form 1041, including any needed Schedule K-1s, for the Jenny Justice Trust. The trustee's address is P.O. Box 100, Dallas, TX 75202. The identification number of the trust is 74-6224343. Jenny, whose Social Security number is 252-37-1492, resides at 2 Mountain View, Birmingham, AL 35205.

C14-55 Mark Wilson created an irrevocable trust in 1986 by transferring to it appreciated assets. Because of the unified credit, he owed no gift tax on the transfer. The trustee in its discretion is to pay out income or corpus to Doug Weldon (017-22-1344) until Doug becomes age 33. Then the property is to be distributed to Doug or his estate. The trustee is Yankee Bank, 20 State St., Boston, MA 02111. Doug resides at 38 Walden Ln., Boston, MA 02115.

During the current year, the following events occurred with respect to the trust:

Dividends received	$ 9,000
Rent received on raw land	1,200
Interest received from City of Salem bonds	13,000
Accountant's fee paid for prior year's return	275
Trustee's fee paid:	
Charged to income	250
Charged to corpus	400
Property taxes paid on land	140
Proceeds received from sale of stock	18,000

The stock was valued at $7,000 when transferred to the trust in 1986. Mark Wilson had paid $9,200 for the stock in 1982. The trustee distributed $5,100 to Doug during the current year and paid $4,000 of estimated federal income taxes on behalf of the trust. The City of Salem bonds are not private activity bonds. Prepare a Form 1041 and accompanying Schedule K-1 for the Mark Wilson Trust (74-9871234).

C14-56 Mark Meadows creates a trust in 1985 with Merchants Bank named as trustee. The trustee in its discretion is to pay out income to Mark's children, Angela and Barry, for fifteen years. Then the trust will terminate, and its assets, including accumulated income, will be paid to Angela and Barry in equal amounts. (Separate shares are *not* to be maintained.) In the current year the trustee distributes $3,000 to Angela and $9,000 to Barry. The trust paid estimated federal income taxes of $15,000 and reported the following additional results for the current year.

	Amounts Allocable to	
	Income	*Principal*
Dividends	$50,000	
Interest on corporate bonds	4,000	
Interest on City of Cleveland (non-private activity) bonds	9,000	
Long-term capital loss on sale of stock		$12,000[a]
Trustee's fee		2,400
CPA's fee for tax return preparation	400	

[a] Mr. Meadows purchased the stock for $30,000 in 1970. It was valued at $44,000 when he transferred it to the trust in 1985. The trust sold the stock for $18,000.

Prepare a Form 1041, including any needed Schedule K-1s, for the trust established by Mr. Meadows. The trustee's address is 201 Fifth Ave., New York, NY 10017. The trust's identification number is 74-5271322. Angela (127-14-1732) and Barry (127-14-1733) reside at 3 East 246th St., Huntington, NY 11743.

CASE STUDY PROBLEMS

C14-57 Arthur Rich, a widower, is considering setting up a trust (or trusts) with a bank as trustee for each of his three minor children. The trust will be funded at $900,000 (or $300,000 each in the case of three trusts). A friend suggested that he might want to consider a January 31 year-end for the trusts. The friend also suggested that Arthur might want to make each trust a complex discretionary trust. Arthur is a little apprehensive about the idea of a trust that would be complex. Arthur's friend warned him that the trust income should not be spent on providing support for Arthur's children. The friend also said, "In 1985 I set up a trust for my minor child for fifteen years and specified that at the end of the fifteenth year the property would pass back to me. Why don't you do the same? You might need the income from the $900,000 of property in your golden years."

Required: Prepare a memorandum to the tax partner of your firm concerning the above client matter. As part of your analysis, consider the following:

a. What tax reasons, if any, can you think of for having three trusts instead of one?
b. Why did the friend suggest a January 31 year-end?
c. What is your reaction to the friend's suggestion about the year-end?
d. Which taxpayer, the beneficiary or the trust, is taxed on the income from a discretionary trust?
e. To what extent do trusts serve as income-shifting arrangements?
f. What can you advise Arthur concerning his apprehension about a complex trust?
g. Why did the friend warn against spending income for support?
h. What is your opinion about the friend's suggestion for a fifteen-year trust?

C14-58 You are in the process of preparing a 1996 individual tax return for Robert Lucca, a real estate developer. Robert is a long-time client. In the process of preparing Robert's individual return you learn that he has income from a trust his 75-year-old father created in 1995. His 1996 income from the trust is properly reflected on a Schedule K-1 prepared by the accounting firm that prepared the trust's 1996 return. Robert prepared the trust's return for 1995, and decided that he should not be taxed on any of the trust's income because the trust distributed nothing to him. Upon reviewing Robert's copy of the trust instrument, you learn that the instrument calls for mandatory distributions of all of the income to Robert every year. Assume that the trust reported only $3,300 of taxable income for 1995, and that Robert was in the highest marginal tax bracket for 1995.

a. What is your responsibility in 1997 with respect to correcting the error made for tax year 1995? Refer to the *Statements on Responsibilities in Tax Practice* in Appendix E.
b. Assume instead that an IRS agent has just begun to audit Robert's 1995 individual tax return. What is your responsibility if you have discovered the error on the 1995 trust return, and you are representing Robert in the audit?

TAX RESEARCH PROBLEMS

C14-59 A simple trust incurs a trustee's fee of $3,000 for the current year. Its receipts during the current year are as follows:

	Amounts Allocable to	
	Income	*Principal*
Dividends from listed stocks	$22,000	
Interest on tax-exempt (non-private activity) bonds	5,000	
Corporate distribution from a closely held firm; amount is not treated as a dividend because the firm has no earnings and profits	12,000	
Long-term capital gain on sale of land		32,000

Your manager requests that you prepare a memorandum addressing the *deductible* portion of the trustee's fee. Your manager suggests that you consider at a minimum these research sources:

- Reg. Secs. 1.652(b)-3(b) and 1.652(c)-4(e)
- Rev. Rul. 77-355, 1977-2 C.B. 82
- Rev. Rul. 80-165, 1980-1 C.B. 134

C14-60 In 1996, Bill Ames dies at the age of 48. One of the items included in his gross estate is the principal residence where he and his widow, Lynn (age 46), lived for twenty years. Its FMV in 1996 was $200,000. In accordance with Bill's will, the residence and numerous other assets pass to a trust. Lynn is entitled to all of the trust income for the rest of her life.

In 1997, the trust sells the residence for $300,000 and later that year pays $310,000 for a "replacement" house that Lynn moves into as her principal residence. Your manager asks that you draft a letter to the trustee and in the letter explain whether the trust may use the nonrecognition rules of Sec. 1034.

Your manager suggests that you consider at a minimum the following research sources:

- Sec. 1034
- Rev. Rul. 54-583, 1954-2 C.B. 158

You should attach to the letter a list of additional relevant authorities and their citations.

C14-61 Prepare a memorandum to your manager in which you address whether the Jacobs Trust, a revocable trust funded in May 1996, must use a calendar year as its tax year. Its grantor, Joni Jacobs, has used a March 31 year-end for a number of years.

CHAPTER 15

ADMINISTRATIVE PROCEDURES

LEARNING OBJECTIVES

After studying this chapter, you should be able to

1. Understand the role of the IRS in our tax system
2. Discuss how returns are selected for audit and the alternatives available to people whose returns are audited
3. Describe the IRS's ruling process
4. Recognize the due dates for tax returns and the penalties associated with not abiding by such dates
5. Explain the penalty for not paying estimated taxes
6. Describe more severe penalties, including the fraud penalty
7. Understand the statute of limitations
8. Explain from whom the government may collect unpaid taxes
9. Understand the government-imposed standards affecting tax advisors

CHAPTER OUTLINE

This chapter provides an overview of the administrative and procedural aspects of tax practice, an area with which all tax advisors should have some familiarity. The specific matters discussed include the role of the Internal Revenue Service (IRS), the manner in which tax returns are chosen for audit, taxpayers' alternatives to immediately agreeing to pay a proposed deficiency, due dates for returns, penalties potentially affecting taxpayers, and the statute of limitations. In Chapter C1 we explored the American Institute of CPAs' *Statements on Responsibilities in Tax Practice,* which guide CPAs engaged in tax practice. Here we examine additional tax practice topics, including the Internal Revenue Code penalty provisions that affect tax advisors and tax return preparers.

ROLE OF THE INTERNAL REVENUE SERVICE

OBJECTIVE 1

Understand the role of the IRS in our tax system

The IRS is a part of the Treasury Department. The top IRS official, called the commissioner, is appointed by the president. The IRS employs almost 100,000 people in civil service (as opposed to political) positions. The responsibilities of the IRS include enforcing and interpreting tax laws.

ENFORCEMENT AND COLLECTION

KEY POINT

The U.S. tax structure is based on a self-assessment system. The level of voluntary compliance is actually quite high, but one of the principal purposes of the IRS is to enforce compliance with the federal tax laws by taxpayers who willfully or inadvertently fail to pay their fair share of the tax burden.

One of the most significant functions of the IRS is the enforcement of the tax laws.[1] The IRS is responsible for ensuring that taxpayers file returns, report their tax liabilities correctly, and pay any tax due.

The United States enjoys a high level of voluntary compliance with its tax laws. However, because some people do not comply voluntarily, it is necessary for the IRS to perform audits on selected taxpayers' returns and investigate certain nonfilers. In addition, because a number of ambiguities (gray areas) exist with respect to the proper interpretation of the tax laws, taxpayers and the IRS do not always agree on the tax treatment of certain transactions. As part of its enforcement duties, the IRS must attempt to discover situations where taxpayers report these ambiguous transactions in their tax returns differently from the manner in which the IRS would have treated them. As a later discussion points out, taxpayers who do not agree with the position advanced by the IRS in auditing their returns may litigate.

Not only must the IRS try to ensure that taxpayers report the correct tax liability, it must also make sure that taxpayers pay their taxes. For various reasons, some taxpayers file returns without paying any or all of the tax owed. The IRS's collection personnel are responsible for collecting as much as possible from such persons or entities.

INTERPRETATION OF THE STATUTE

As noted in Chapter C1, generally the statutory language is of such a general nature that administrative and judicial interpretations are necessary. The IRS is charged with making some of the administrative interpretations. Its most important administrative interpretations are revenue rulings, revenue procedures, notices, and information releases. Each of these interpretations is available to the general public. In addition, the IRS also issues interpretations to specific taxpayers in the form of letter rulings. Letter rulings, however, have no precedential value. These interpretations are discussed in detail in Chapter C1.

[1] The IRS does not have enforcement duties, however, with respect to the taxes on guns and alcohol.

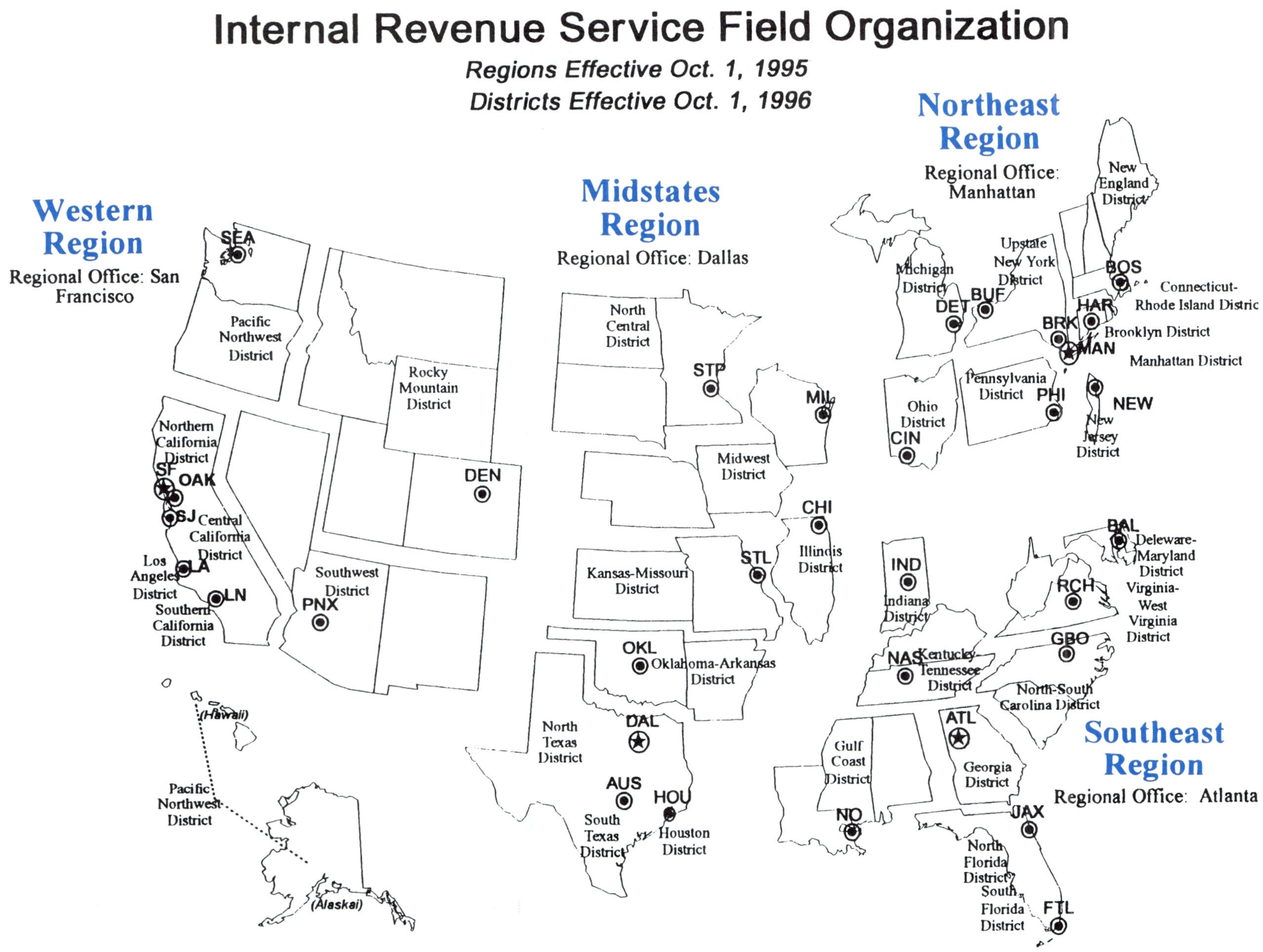

Source: Bureau of National Affairs, Inc., *BNA Daily Tax Report,* Special Supplement, July 17, 1995, p. S-182.

FIGURE C15-1 ▶ INTERNAL REVENUE SERVICE FIELD ORGANIZATION

ORGANIZATION OF THE IRS

The IRS must perform its responsibilities on a nationwide basis. For purposes of easier administration, the IRS is divided into four geographic regions, each headed by a regional commissioner. The regions are further subdivided into thirty-three districts, for whom the chief administrative officer is the district director. Some districts (e.g., Kansas-Missouri) include more than one state while some states (e.g., New York, California, and Texas) have more than one district. Figure C15-1 shows the regions and districts. The IRS also operates ten service centers throughout the nation that are responsible for receiving and processing tax returns.[2] At the national level, in addition to the commissioner, other top officials include the senior deputy commissioner, a series of assistants to the commissioner and deputy commissioner, a chief inspector, and the chief counsel. The chief counsel's office prepares regulations and represents the government in Tax Court cases.

AUDITS OF TAX RETURNS

OBJECTIVE 2

Discuss how returns are selected for audit and the alternatives available to people whose returns are audited

REAL-WORLD EXAMPLE

The IRS issued 33 million penalty notices in 1994 for 140 different reasons.

ADDITIONAL COMMENT

Although individual tax returns increased by 15% from 102 million to 116 million between 1984 and 1995, the number of returns examined increased by 44% from 1.34 to 1.92 million.

KEY POINT

Arithmetic checks and the matching of figures reported by taxpayers with those reported by employers and other payers is sufficient to ensure proper compliance by most taxpayers. Because these procedures are not considered audits, the statistics about the low percentage of returns audited is somewhat misleading.

One of the IRS's most significant enforcement activities is auditing tax returns. All returns are subject to some verification. For example, one job the IRS service centers perform is verifying the arithmetic and checking whether amounts are properly carried from one line of a return to another. Also, the IRS checks to determine whether any items, such as signatures and Social Security numbers, are missing. Computers also compare (or "match") by Social Security number the amounts reported on a taxpayer's return with employer- or payer-filed documents (Forms W-2 and 1099) filed with the service center.[3] To date, however, a 100% matching of these documents with tax return information has not been possible.

If the service center detects an error in the tax liability reported on the return, the center transmits to the taxpayer a notice outlining the additional tax or refund due. If the information reported on a return does not agree with Forms W-2 or 1099 submitted by an employer or payer that contain the taxpayer's Social Security number, the taxpayer will be requested to provide a written explanation of the discrepancy or pay some additional tax.

PERCENTAGE OF RETURNS EXAMINED

Only a small fraction of all returns are examined. For example, for fiscal 1995, the IRS examined only 1.67% of all individual returns, 2.05% of all C corporation returns, 0.46% of all partnership returns, 0.92% of all S corporation returns, and 0.14% of all fiduciary returns. For individuals with total positive income (i.e., gross income before losses and other deductions) of $100,000 or more, the audit rate was 2.79%, and corporations with assets of at least $250 million had a 51.77% rate. As a result of its audit process, the IRS recommended additional taxes and penalties totaling $27.87 billion in that year.[4]

The examination percentages described above may be misleading because over half of the returns filed are subjected to a computerized "instant audit" in which the IRS compares the tax return information with documents (Forms 1099 and W-2) submitted by payers and employers. According to a former commissioner of the IRS, "[M]ore than half of the individual returns filed are simple enough so that a matching with forms filed by employers and interest payors is sufficient to insure compliance."[5]

[2] IRS Service Centers are located in Andover, Massachusetts; Chamblee, Georgia; Austin, Texas; Holtsville, New York; Covington, Kentucky; Fresno, California; Kansas City, Missouri; Memphis, Tennessee; Ogden, Utah; and Philadelphia, Pennsylvania. The Chamblee, Holtsville, and Covington Service Centers are known as the Atlanta, Brookhaven, and Cincinnati Service Centers, respectively. There are plans to reduce the number of service centers and have more centralization.

[3] Form W-2 reports employees' salaries and withholding tax, and Form 1099 reports income such as interest and dividends.

[4] *Internal Revenue Service 1995 Data Book* (Washington, DC: U.S. Government Printing Office, 1996), Table 11. Examinations are done by revenue agents, tax auditors, and service center personnel.

[5] Bureau of National Affairs, *BNA Daily Tax Reports*, June 20, 1984, p. G-1.

SELECTION OF RETURNS FOR AUDIT

Returns are chosen for audit in a variety of ways, with many being selected under the *discriminant function (DIF)* process described below. The IRS's objective in using the DIF process is to make the audit process as productive as possible by minimizing the number of audits that result in the collection of no additional taxes. The DIF process has improved the IRS's ability to select returns for audit. In recent years the IRS failed to collect additional taxes on only about 10 to 15 percent of the individual returns audited by its revenue agents and tax auditors. By comparison, in the late 1960s, before the advent of the DIF program, the IRS failed to collect additional taxes in 45 to 50 percent of its audits.[6] Recently the IRS began an audit approach known as the Market Segment Specialization Program (MSSP). Under the MSSP, IRS personnel develop industry expertise, and the IRS prepares MSSP audit guides. Examples of market segments include manufacturing, wholesale trade, retail trade (auto and boat dealers and service stations), and services (medical and health).[7] It is expected that as IRS personnel become more familiar with industries, their ability to spot issues for which the taxpayer may have handled the tax treatment incorrectly will improve.

HISTORICAL NOTE

Several attempts have been made by taxpayers to make the actual DIF program public information. However, so far the courts have refused to require the IRS to provide such detailed information. The basic thrust of the DIF program is that a return will be flagged if enough items on the return are out of the norm for a taxpayer in that particular income bracket.

DISCRIMINANT FUNCTION (DIF) PROGRAM. Two-thirds of the individual returns audited in 1982 were chosen under the **DIF** program, but for 1994 only 20% were selected under the DIF program, with the rest being selected under 12 different audit initiatives, some of which involve nonfilers, tax-shelter related write-offs, computer matches of third-party information, claims for refund, return preparers, and unallowable items.[8] The IRS began laying the groundwork for the DIF program in the mid-1960s in an effort to

- Reduce the staff and computer time necessary to screen returns
- Identify the returns most likely to contain errors
- Reduce the number of audited returns for which an examination results in little or no additional tax[9]

An assistant commissioner described the DIF selection process in the following manner:

> DIF is a type of statistical analysis, using multiple variables or criteria to differentiate between two populations. For the IRS, those populations are tax returns needing examination versus those returns not needing examination. DIF essentially identifies items on tax returns having predictive power; that is, the selected items on returns in the "need to examine" group show up differently than those in the "no need to examine" group. DIF takes several items on a tax return and reduces them to a single score, which is then used as a major determinant as to whether a particular return will be examined.[10]

Returns with a relatively high DIF score have characteristics in common with returns for which the IRS earlier assessed a deficiency upon audit (e.g., the return may have reported a relatively high casualty loss or charitable contribution deduction). Because the IRS does not have the resources to audit all returns with a relatively high DIF score, IRS managers choose which of the higher scored returns should receive top priority for an audit.

The IRS has developed its DIF formulas based on information from the Taxpayer Compliance Measurement Program (TCMP), discussed below. As part of its TCMP examination, the IRS divided returns into two groups: those with significant tax changes

---

[6] Letter from Sheldon S. Cohen, former IRS Commissioner, to Representative Nancy L. Johnson, Chairman of House Ways and Means Subcommittee on Oversight Regarding the TCMP, dated July 20, 1995, reprinted in *Tax Notes Today*, August 10, 1995, Document 95 TNT 156-63.

[7] K. D. Bakhai and G. E. Bowers, "A New Era in IRS Auditing," *Florida CPA Today*, November 1994, pp. 26–30.

[8] J. L. Wedick, Jr., "Looking for a Needle in a Haystack—How the IRS Selects Returns for Audit," *The Tax Adviser*, November 1983, p. 673, and Commerce Clearing House, *1996 Standard Federal Tax Reporter*, "New Audit Stats Give Clues to Audit Selection Process," ¶48,775, citing report by U.S. General Accounting Office.

[9] Ibid., pp. 673–674.

[10] Ibid., p. 674.

and those with small tax changes. The only items on the tax returns that are used in the DIF program are those that are most valuable in distinguishing between the returns with a significant change in taxes and those with little or no change.

KEY POINT

The TCMP generated the information that the IRS used to build its DIF program. Thus, taxpayers from all income levels were randomly selected for a TCMP audit. In a TCMP audit, the IRS was more interested in the information it gathered than the additional taxes it might collect.

In the past, a small fraction of audited returns were selected at random under the **Taxpayer Compliance Measurement Program**, which was instigated to improve the selection process of the DIF program. Before 1994, every three years about 50,000 individual returns were audited. TCMP audits were also conducted for other entities, such as corporations. In a TCMP audit, the IRS agent audited every item on the tax return. Because of expected budget cuts, in 1995 the IRS "indefinitely postponed" TCMP audits.[11]

On returns chosen for audit, the IRS is expanding its financial status ("economic reality" or "lifestyle") audits under which IRS agents investigate differences between a taxpayer's reported income and apparent standard of living.[12] In these audits, which are designed to detect unreported income, the IRS agents consider the taxpayer's entire economic situation. The agents may ask questions about where the taxpayer goes on vacation, where the children go to school, and the cost and kind of automobiles that the taxpayer owns, for example. Under IRS policy, the agents are not to make such inquiries at the commencement of an audit if there is no suggestion of unreported income.

OTHER METHODS. The IRS uses several other methods for selecting returns for audit, but the percentage of returns chosen under these other methods is relatively small. Some returns are chosen because the taxpayer filed a claim for refund of taxes paid previously, and the IRS decides to audit the tax return before issuing a refund of the requested amount. A few returns are audited because the IRS receives a tip from one taxpayer (perhaps a disgruntled former employee) that another taxpayer did not file a correct return. If the IRS does collect additional taxes as a result of such an audit, it is empowered to pay a reward to the individual furnishing the tip. The reward is completely discretionary, although it cannot exceed 10% of the additional tax and penalties found due.[13] Sometimes the process of examining the return of an entity (e.g., a corporation) will suggest an audit of a related party's return (e.g., a major stockholder).

REAL WORLD EXAMPLE

Examination rates vary from region to region. In a recent year, the Mid-Atlantic region's 0.69% rate was the lowest, while the Western region's 1.76% rate was the highest.

From time to time, the IRS carries on special investigatory projects to gain some indication of the degree of tax compliance with respect to certain transactions. Some returns are chosen for audit as a result of these pilot programs. For example, during 1989 the IRS sampled 3,000 to 4,000 individual returns to determine whether certain expenses were misclassified in order to avoid the 2% floor applicable to miscellaneous itemized deductions. In 1992 information from Form 8300 (concerning cash transactions of above $10,000) was cross-referenced by computer to income tax returns of businesses and self-employed individuals to determine whether the cash transactions were correctly reported for income-tax purposes.[14]

ALTERNATIVES FOR A TAXPAYER WHOSE RETURN IS AUDITED

KEY POINT

Depending on the expected complexity of an audit, a correspondence audit, an office audit, or a field audit will be performed. On average, a revenue agent spent 24 hours on each audit in 1994.

When a taxpayer is notified of an impending audit, such notice will indicate whether the audit is a correspondence audit, an office audit, or a field audit. In correspondence audits, all of the communication, such as providing documentation or indicating why certain income was not reported, can be handled through the mail. An office audit results in the taxpayer and/or his or her tax advisor meeting with an IRS employee at a nearby IRS office. The notice informing the taxpayer about the audit indicates which items will be examined and what information should be brought to the audit. Field examinations are

[11] "Rare Reprieve: IRS Postpones Its Superaudits," *Wall Street Journal*, October 24, 1995, p. B1.

[12] Bureau of National Affairs, *BNA Daily Tax Reports*, October 27, 1995, p. G-6.

[13] Reg. Sec. 301.7623-1(c).

[14] "Tax Report," *Wall Street Journal*, November 4, 1992, p. 1.

WHAT WOULD YOU DO IN THIS SITUATION?

One of the most positive social, economic, and legal trends that has emerged in the late twentieth century is the emphasis on cultural and ethnic diversity at every level in our society. Despite the many growing pains that have followed, our society is far more inclusive today than ever before. But are there limits to this movement?

Consider the case of Mr. Jung Yul Yu and his difficulties with the IRS (*United States v. Yu,* 954 F.2d 951 (3rd Cir., 1993)). Mr. Yu was born, raised, and educated as a lawyer in Korea. His employment experience included working for the Korean counterpart of the U.S. IRS. Mr. Yu immigrated to the United States at age forty-six and was self-employed as a tax preparer. He became a naturalized U.S. citizen, and his tax practice flourished.

Mr. Yu's personal tax returns were audited by the IRS, and the audit resulted in an assessment of $27,000 additional taxes and penalties. Mr. Yu proceeded to pay the auditing IRS agent $5,000 in return for a "no-change" letter. Unbeknownst to Mr. Yu at the time, the transaction was secretly taped. Mr. Yu was convicted of violating a U.S. law (18 USC 201(5)(1)(A)) in his attempt to bribe a government official.

At his sentencing hearing, pursuant to the U.S. Sentencing Guidelines, Mr. Yu argued that his national origin should be taken into account in the determination of his sentence. Mr. Yu posited that it is expected practice in Korea to offer tax officials an "honorarium" in order to settle tax controversies. Not to do so would be considered an insult to the tax official's authority in Korea.

Do you believe that the payment of $5,000 to the IRS agent was appropriate in these circumstances? Assume that you were acting as Mr. Yu's representative. How should you have responded to your client when he initially proposed to make the offer to the IRS agent?

common for business returns and more complex individual returns. The IRS employee conducts these audits at either the taxpayer's place of business or residence or at his or her tax advisor's office.

ADDITIONAL COMMENT

This special relief rule was designed to reduce the likelihood that the IRS could harass a taxpayer by repeatedly auditing a taxpayer on the same issue.

SPECIAL RELIEF RULE. A special relief rule exists for repetitive audit examinations for the same item. A taxpayer who receives an audit notice can request that the examination be suspended while a review is conducted to determine whether the audit should proceed if (1) his or her return was audited for the same item in at least one of the two previous years and (2) the earlier audit did not result in a change to his or her tax liability. To request the suspension, the taxpayer should call the person whose name and telephone number appear on the audit notice.

EXAMPLE C15-1 ▶ In October 1997, Tony receives notice that the IRS will audit the medical expense deduction claimed on his 1995 return. Tony's 1993 return was audited with respect to medical expenses, but the IRS did not assess any additional tax. Tony may request that the audit of his 1995 return be suspended pending a review of whether the audit should continue. ◀

EXAMPLE C15-2 ▶ Assume the same facts as in Example C15-1, except that Tony's 1993 return was audited for employee business expenses. Because that audit dealt with a different item, Tony may not ask for a suspension of the audit. ◀

The next few pages discuss taxpayers' rights during an examination of their returns. The various alternatives are illustrated in Figure C15-2.

MEETING WITH A REVENUE AGENT. Generally, the first step in the audit process involves a meeting between the IRS agent and the taxpayer or the taxpayer's advisor. If the taxpayer is fortunate, the agent will agree that the return was correct as filed or, even better, that the taxpayer is entitled to a refund. In most instances,

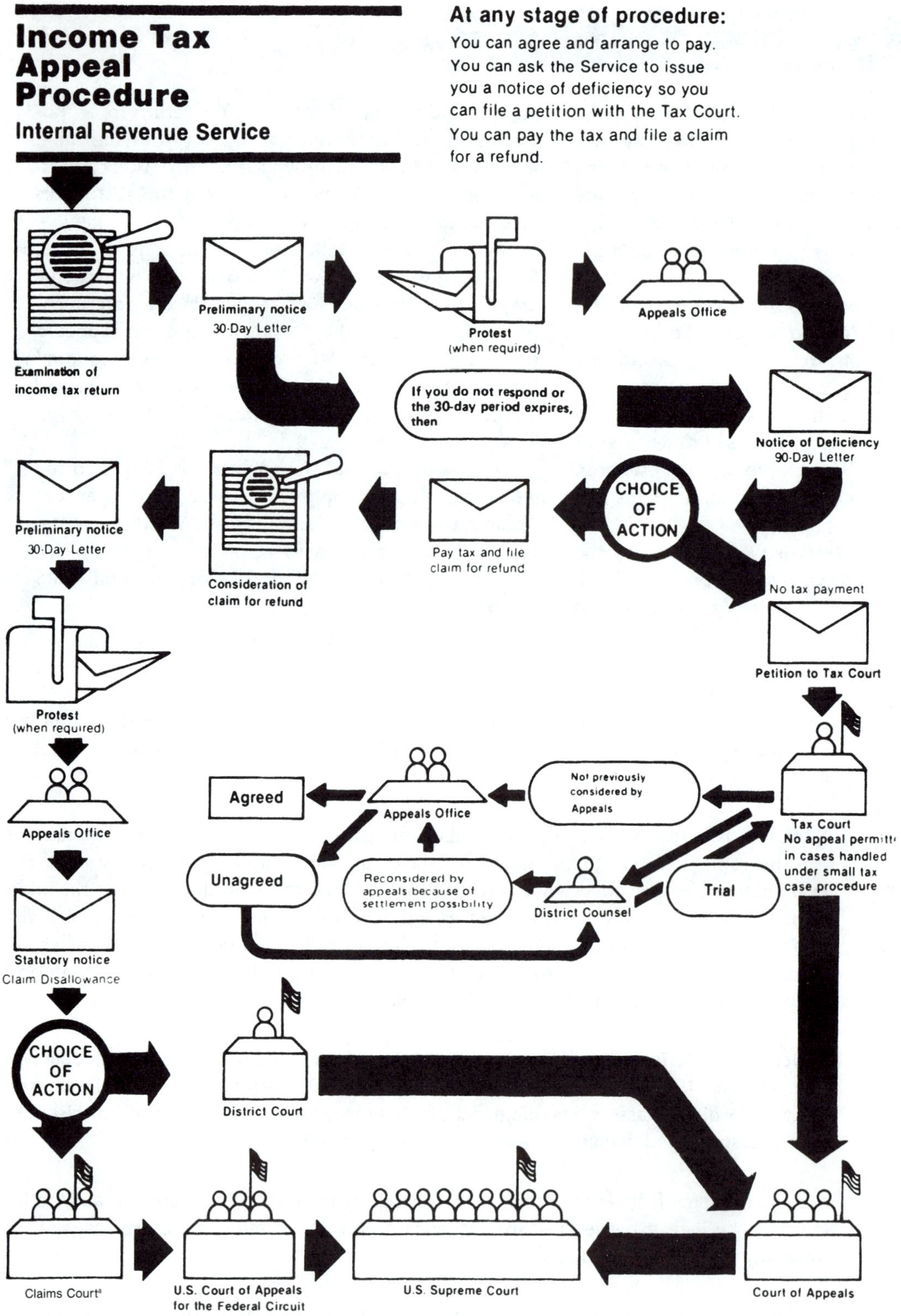

[a]Renamed the *U.S. Court of Federal Claims* effective November 1, 1992.

FIGURE C15-2 ▶ ALTERNATIVES AVAILABLE TO TAXPAYERS FOR WHOM IRS PROPOSES A DEFICIENCY

Source: IRS, *Publication No. 556* [Examination of Returns, Appeal Rights, and Claims for Refund], (1990), p. 9.

ADDITIONAL COMMENT

From the perspective of the tax practitioner, taxpayers should be encouraged to allow the tax practitioner to handle the audit. Because taxpayers usually have a limited understanding of the complexities of the tax law and its administration, having the taxpayer present at the audit generally is not a good idea.

TYPICAL MISCONCEPTION

Taxpayers should be cautioned about signing a Form 870 too quickly. Once this form is properly executed, the taxpayer is no longer permitted to administratively pursue the items under audit.

however, the agent contends that the taxpayer owes additional taxes. Taxpayers who do not agree with the outcome of their meeting with the IRS agent may ask to meet with the agent's supervisor. A meeting with the supervisor may or may not lead to an agreement concerning the additional tax due.

Should the taxpayer agree and the agent's supervisor concur in the amount owed, the taxpayer must sign Form 870 (Waiver of Statutory Notice). This indicates the taxpayer's agreement to waive any restrictions on the IRS's ability to assess tax and consent to the IRS's collecting the tax. However, signing Form 870 does not preclude the taxpayer from filing a refund suit later.

If the taxpayer agrees that additional tax is owed and pays the tax upon signing the Form 870, interest is due on the tax deficiency from the due date of the return through the payment date. The taxpayer can wait to pay the extra tax. In such a situation, interest ceases to accrue thirty days after the Form 870 was signed, and no additional interest is charged if the taxpayer pays the tax due within ten days of the billing date.

TECHNICAL ADVICE MEMORANDA. From time to time, the issue in question may be a complex, highly technical one with which the IRS employee has little or no experience. Regardless of the level of the audit, an IRS employee may request advice from the IRS's National Office. Sometimes, the taxpayer may urge the IRS employee to seek such advice. The advice given, called a Technical Advice Memorandum, is made public in the form of letter rulings. If the advice is favorable to the taxpayer, the agent or appeals officer must follow it. Even if the advice is pro-IRS, the appeals officer may still consider the hazards of litigation in deciding whether to compromise.

APPEAL TO APPEALS DIVISION. If the taxpayer does not sign the Form 870, the IRS will send the taxpayer a report, known as a **thirty-day letter**, detailing the proposed changes and advising the taxpayer of his right to pursue the matter with the Appeals Office. The taxpayer has thirty days from the date on the letter in which to request a conference with an appeals officer.

If the audit was a field audit and the amount of additional tax plus penalties and interest in question exceeds $10,000, the taxpayer must submit a **protest letter** within the thirty-day period. Only a brief written statement is necessary if the amount is between $2,501 and $10,000. An oral request is acceptable for office audits, regardless of the amount of the additional tax, penalties, and interest. If the taxpayer does not respond to the thiry-day letter, the IRS will follow up with a ninety-day letter, which is discussed below.

Protest letters are submitted to the district director and should include the following information:

- The taxpayer's name and address
- A statement that the taxpayer wishes to appeal the findings of the IRS agent to the Appeals Office
- The date and symbols from the letter showing the proposed adjustments
- The tax years involved
- An itemized schedule of the proposed changes with which the taxpayer disagrees
- A statement of facts supporting the taxpayer's position with respect to any issues with which he or she disagrees
- A statement indicating the law or other authority on which the taxpayer relied[15]

---

[15] IRS, *Publication No. 556* [Examination of Returns, Appeal Rights, and Claims for Refund], November, 1990, pp. 3 and 4. A sample protest letter is contained in Robert E. Meldman and Richard A. Petrie, *Federal Taxation Practice and Procedure* (Chicago: Commerce Clearing House, Inc., 1992), p. 262.

The taxpayer must declare, under penalties of perjury, that the statement of facts is true. If the taxpayer's representative prepares the protest letter, the representative must declare whether he or she knows personally that the statement of facts is true and correct.

KEY POINT

The appeals officer currently has the authority to settle or compromise issues with the taxpayer. To help alleviate some of the workload and to make the audit process more efficient, the IRS is currently considering giving more of this settlement authority to revenue agents.

Appeals officers are relatively experienced and sophisticated IRS personnel. Unlike IRS agents, appeals officers have the authority to settle (compromise) cases after considering the hazards of litigation. Their settlement authority extends to both questions of fact and questions of law. Thus, if the appeals officer feels that the IRS has approximately a 40% chance of winning in court, the appeals officer may agree to close the case if the taxpayer will pay an amount equal to 40% of the originally proposed deficiency.

In some situations, however, an appeals officer does not have settlement authority. For example, if the matter involves an appeals coordinated issue, the appeals officer must obtain concurrence or guidance from the regional director of appeals in order to reach a settlement. An example of an **appeals coordinated issue** is the matter of whether the taxpayer has in substance made a disposition of excess inventory and, thus, is entitled to claim a tax deduction for the loss on disposition.[16]

If, after the appeals conference, the taxpayer completely agrees with the IRS's contentions, he or she signs Form 870. However, if the appeals officer makes some concessions and the parties agree that the additional tax is smaller than that originally proposed, the taxpayer will sign Form 870-AD (Waiver of Restrictions on Assessment and Collection). Unlike the situation for Form 870, taxpayers generally may not later file a claim for refund for a year for which they executed Form 870-AD. Also, Form 870-AD is effective only if it is accepted by the IRS. If no agreement is reached, the IRS will issue a ninety-day letter.

NINETY-DAY LETTER

KEY POINT

If a taxpayer fails to respond to a thirty-day letter or to reach an agreement with the appeals officer, the taxpayer will receive a ninety-day letter. The taxpayer must petition the Tax Court within ninety days or pay the deficiency. This ninety-day time limit is strictly enforced. Therefore, if a taxpayer desires to pursue the issue in the Tax Court, he or she should take the ninety-day letter seriously.

If the taxpayer does not file a protest letter within thirty days of the date of the thirty-day letter, the IRS issues a **ninety-day letter** (officially called a Statutory Notice of Deficiency).[17] A ninety-day letter is also sent when the taxpayer has met with an appeals officer and no agreement was reached. The ninety-day letter includes information concerning the amount of the deficiency, an explanation of how the amount was arrived at, and a statement that the IRS will assess a deficiency unless the taxpayer files a petition with the Tax Court within ninety days of the date the letter is mailed.[18] Thus, the letter advises taxpayers that they may either file a petition with the Tax Court during the ninety-day period or be billed for the deficiency by the IRS. Taxpayers who pay the deficiency can sue for a refund in a U.S. district court or the U.S. Court of Federal Claims.

The ninety-day time limit is strictly enforced. The Tax Court cannot consider a case if a taxpayer's petition is filed late. During the ninety-day period, the IRS is precluded from assessing a deficiency and attempting to make any collections. If the taxpayer petitions the Tax Court, the IRS may not assess a deficiency and try to collect until the court decision becomes final.

LITIGATION

Taxpayers who disagree with the deficiency proposed by the IRS can, of course, litigate. As discussed in Chapter C1, litigation can begin in one of the three trial courts: the Tax Court, a U.S. district court, or the U.S. Court of Federal Claims (formerly the U.S. Claims

---

[16] *Internal Revenue Manual,* Sec. 8776.(14). An appeals coordinated issue is a specially designated tax matter for which the IRS desires consistent treatment of the appeals across its regions. Therefore, these appeals are generally coordinated by the Director of Appeals for a particular region that has been so designated by the national Director of the IRS Appeals Division. Guidance is provided to the local region in the handling of the matter by the regional Director of Appeals in accordance with Rev. Proc. 79-34 (1979-2 C.B. 498).

[17] Upon request, the IRS may grant an extension of time for filing a protest letter.

[18] Sec. 6213(a). If the notice is addressed to a person outside the United States, the time period is 150 days instead of 90.

Court). After considering the time and expense of litigation, however, some taxpayers may pay the deficiency even though they strongly believe that their position is correct. If a taxpayer does decide to litigate, the precedents, if any, of the various courts should be considered before deciding where to litigate. Chapter C1 explores the topic of which cases each court must follow.

KEY POINT

Litigating in the Tax Court has the advantages of no payment of the deficiency beforehand and the option of the more informal small tax case procedures if the amount in question does not exceed $10,000 for the year. The disadvantage: The small tax case procedure does not offer an opportunity for appeal.

TAX COURT. Taxpayers desiring to litigate in the Tax Court must file their petition with the Tax Court within ninety days of the date the Statutory Notice of Deficiency is mailed. Before the scheduled trial date, however, taxpayers may still reach an agreement with the IRS. There are some advantages of going the Tax Court route, including not having to pay the deficiency as a prelude to filing suit. If the amount in question does not exceed $10,000 for a year, the taxpayer may use the more informal small tax case procedures, an alternative not available in other courts. The small tax case procedures can have a potential disadvantage for the taxpayer, however, because there is no chance for appeal.

In general, the taxpayer has the burden of proof in Tax Court cases. The IRS, however, bears the burden of proof for any new issues that it raises after the issuance of the Statutory Notice of Deficiency (ninety-day letter).[19] The burden of proof also lies with the IRS in fraud cases. Frequently, the taxpayer and the IRS stipulate a number of tax treatment items before going to trial. Because agreement was reached on these stipulated matters, such issues may not be reopened in court.

Taxpayers must pay the additional tax, plus any interest and penalties, if they lose in Tax Court and choose not to appeal their case. In some situations, the Tax Court leaves the computation of the additional tax up to the litigating parties. When this happens, the phrase "Entered under Rule 155" appears at the end of the Tax Court's opinion.

KEY POINT

To litigate in a district court or in the U.S. Court of Federal Claims, the taxpayer must first pay the deficiency and then file a claim for a refund. After filing the claim for refund, the taxpayer can initiate a suit for refund after the earlier of six months or the date on which the IRS denies the claim for refund.

DISTRICT COURT OR U.S. COURT OF FEDERAL CLAIMS. As a condition of going to either a federal district court or the U.S. Court of Federal Claims, the taxpayer must pay the deficiency and then file a claim for refund. The IRS will deny the refund claim because it just finished arguing that such an amount of additional tax was due. After receiving the notice of denial, the taxpayer may file a refund suit. If a denial of the refund is not received within six months of filing a refund claim, the taxpayer may go ahead and file a suit. The latest possible time for filing suit is two years after the IRS disallows the claim.

APPEAL OF A LOWER COURT'S DECISION. Whichever party loses—the taxpayer or the government—may appeal the lower court's decision to an appellate court. If the case began in the Tax Court or a federal district court, the case is appealable to the circuit court of appeals for the taxpayer's geographical jurisdiction. For individuals, the taxpayer's place of residence generally controls which court of appeals has jurisdiction. In the case of corporations, the firm's principal place of business or office determines which court has jurisdiction. Cases originating in the U.S. Court of Federal Claims are appealable to the Circuit Court of Appeals for the Federal Circuit. That is, all cases are heard by the same circuit, irrespective of the taxpayer's residence or principal place of business.

Either the taxpayer or the government can request that the Supreme Court review an appellate court's decision. If the Supreme Court decides to hear a case, it grants **certiorari**. In a given year, however, the Supreme Court hears only a few cases dealing with tax matters.

[19] Tax Court Rule No. 142.

STOP & THINK

Question: Two years ago Pete made a large expenditure and deducted it in full in the year paid. Recently, the IRS began an audit of Pete's return for that year and contended that the expenditure is not deductible. Pete is a resident of California, which is in the Ninth Circuit. In a very similar case a few years ago the Tax Court held that the expenditure was deductible, and the IRS did not appeal the decision. In another similar case litigated in a district court in California the taxpayer won, but the government won the appeal to the Ninth Circuit. If Pete decides to litigate, in which forum (trial court) should he bring his case, and why?

Solution: He probably would like to litigate in the Tax Court because there, unlike the other courts, he would not have to pay the contested tax in advance. However, under the *Golsen* rule, the Tax Court will depart from its earlier pro-taxpayer decision and rule for the government because Pete's case would be appealable to the Ninth Circuit, and the Ninth Circuit has adopted a pro-government position. Because the district court for his district in California would follow the Ninth Circuit precedent, he should not start his litigation in the district court. This situation would disappoint Pete if he believed that a jury would rule in his favor, because only the district courts allow for jury trials. The only forum in which he could win is the U.S. Court of Federal Claims. There is no case law that this court must follow because neither the Supreme Court, the Circuit Court of Appeals for the Federal Circuit, nor the U.S. Court of Federal Claims have previously ruled on this issue.

REQUESTS FOR RULINGS

OBJECTIVE 3

Describe the IRS's ruling process

As discussed in Chapter C1, the taxpayer can learn how the IRS characterizes the tax effects of a transaction by requesting that it rule on the transaction. The IRS answers the taxpayer's request in the form of a letter ruling (sometimes referred to as a private letter ruling) addressed to the taxpayer. A letter ruling is "a written statement issued to a taxpayer by the National Office that interprets and applies the tax laws to the taxpayer's specific set of facts."[20] Letter rulings are also a matter of public record, but all confidential information is eliminated before they are made public. Legislation enacted in 1987 allows the IRS to charge a user fee for issuing rulings. The fees range from a low of $75 for computation of an exclusion for an annuitant under Sec. 72, for example, to $25,000 for requests for advance pricing agreements.[21] The fee for a ruling on a proposed transaction is $3,650.

ADDITIONAL COMMENT

The information requirements for requesting a letter ruling are very precise (see Rev. Proc. 97-1). In general, a tax professional experienced in dealing with the National Office of the IRS should be consulted. Also, a good blueprint of what should be included in a ruling request can often be found by locating an already-published letter ruling and examining its format.

INFORMATION TO BE INCLUDED IN TAXPAYER'S REQUEST

Early each calendar year, the IRS issues a revenue procedure that details how to request a ruling and the information to be contained in the ruling request. Taxpayers or tax advisors should consult the appropriate revenue procedure before requesting a ruling. Appendix B of this procedure contains a checklist that may be used to ensure that the taxpayer's request is in order. The IRS has issued additional detailed guidelines about the data to be included in the request for a ruling. For example, the IRS has specified the information to be included in a ruling request concerning the tax effects of transfers to a controlled corporation under Sec. 351. Each ruling request must contain a statement of all the relevant facts, including the following:

[20] Rev. Proc. 97-1, I.R.B. 1997-1, 11, Sec. 2.01.
[21] Rev. Procs. 97-1, I.R.B. 1997-1, 11, Sec. 15 and Appendix A, and 97-8, I.R.B. 1997-1, 187.

- Names, addresses, telephone numbers, and taxpayer identification numbers of all interested parties
- The annual accounting period and the overall accounting methods for maintaining the accounting books and filing the federal income tax returns of all interested parties
- Location of the IRS District Office that has or will have examination jurisdiction over the return
- A description of the taxpayer's business operations
- A complete statement of the business reasons for the transaction
- A detailed description of the transaction[22]

The taxpayer should also submit copies of the contracts, agreements, deeds, wills, instruments, and other documents that affect the transaction. The taxpayer must include an explicit statement of all the relevant facts and not merely incorporate by reference the language from the documents. The taxpayer should also indicate what confidential data should be deleted from the ruling before its release to the public.

If the taxpayer advocates that the IRS reach a particular conclusion, the basis of this assertion and the authorities relied on must be indicated. Even if the taxpayer is not arguing for any particular tax treatment, an opinion about the tax results must be furnished along with a statement of authorities supporting this position. Moreover, the taxpayer is urged to disclose and discuss any authorities to the contrary. The IRS also indicates that if there are no authorities to the contrary, it would be helpful if the taxpayer made a statement to this effect.

The person on whose behalf a ruling is requested should sign the following declaration: "Under penalties of perjury, I declare that I have examined this request, including accompanying documents, and to the best of my knowledge and belief, the request contains all the relevant facts relating to the request, and such facts are true, correct, and complete."[23]

TYPICAL MISCONCEPTION

It is easy to be confused about the difference between letter rulings, which pertain to either prospective transactions or completed transactions for which a return has not yet been filed, and Technical Advice Memoranda, which pertain to completed transactions for which the return has been filed and is under audit.

WILL THE IRS RULE?

With respect to income tax and gift tax matters, the IRS will rule only on proposed transactions and on completed transactions for which a return has not yet been filed.[24] For estate tax matters, a ruling generally will not be issued if the estate tax return has been filed. The IRS will issue rulings concerning the estate tax consequences of a living person.[25] If no temporary or final regulations have been issued for a particular statutory provision, the following policies generally govern the issuance of a ruling:

- If the answer seems clear by applying the statute to the facts, a ruling will be issued under the usual procedures.
- If the answer seems reasonably certain by applying the statute to the facts but not entirely free from doubt, the IRS will rule.
- If the answer does not seem reasonably certain, the IRS will rule if issuance of a ruling is in the best interests of tax administration.
- If the issue cannot be readily resolved in the absence of regulations, a ruling will not be issued.[26]

[22] Rev. Proc. 97-1, I.R.B. 1997-1, 11, Sec. 8.01(1). Certain revenue procedures provide a checklist of information to be included for frequently occurring transactions. See, for example, Rev. Proc. 83-59, 1983-2 C.B. 575, which includes guidelines for requesting rulings regarding a corporate formation coming under Sec. 351.

[23] Ibid., Sec. 8.01(13).

[24] Ibid., Secs. 5.01.

[25] Ibid., Sec. 5.05.

[26] Ibid., Sec. 5.14.

The IRS will not rule on a set of alternative ways of designing a proposed transaction or on the tax consequences of hypothetical transactions. Generally, the IRS will not rule on certain issues because of the factual nature of the problem involved or for other reasons.[27]

From time to time, the IRS discloses, by means of a revenue procedure, a list of the topical areas in which it definitely will not rule. The list is not all-inclusive; the IRS may refuse to issue a ruling in additional areas whenever, in its opinion, the facts and circumstances justify its refusal to rule.

SELF-STUDY QUESTION

How are letter rulings different from other IRS administrative interpretations (i.e., revenue rulings, revenue procedures, notices, and information releases)?

ANSWER

Letter rulings are written for specific taxpayers (not the general public) and have no precedential value.

According to Rev. Proc. 97-3, the matters on which the IRS will not rule include the following:

- Whether property qualifies as the taxpayer's principal residence
- Whether compensation is reasonable in amount
- Whether a capital expenditure for an item ordinarily used for personal purposes (e.g., a swimming pool) has medical care as its primary purpose
- The determination of the amount of a corporation's earnings and profits[28]

In addition, the revenue procedure lists a number of issues on which rulings will not ordinarily be issued. The revenue procedure also enumerates topics on which the IRS will not rule until it resolves the issue through publishing regulations or a revenue ruling, a revenue procedure, or otherwise.

The IRS has announced that it will discontinue granting letter rulings addressing "issues that are clearly and adequately addressed by published authorities."[29] The reason for restricting the scope of its rulings policy was to allow the IRS to use its resources to address more matters of concern to the general public and to be able to issue letter rulings on a more timely basis. Tax practitioners did not react favorably to the "no comfort rulings" policy, and the IRS decided not to fully implement the "no rule" policy. Instead, the IRS will specify certain no-rule areas, design model documents, and publish ruling checklists.[30]

ADDITIONAL COMMENT

Requesting a letter ruling makes most sense for transactions that would not be undertaken without certain tax consequences being assured. For example, certain divisive reorganizations are structured to be tax-free under Sec. 355. Taxpayers often request a ruling that a proposed transaction does in fact satisfy the intricate requirements of Sec. 355.

WHEN RULINGS ARE DESIRABLE

In certain circumstances it is especially helpful to gain insight into the IRS's assessment of the tax effects of a transaction. In other circumstances, however, the taxpayer might prefer not to request a ruling. If the state of the law is unclear and there is a possibility that the tax results could be disastrous, obtaining a ruling would be desirable, especially if the transaction in question has not been finalized. If the IRS has earlier ruled favorably in a practically identical set of facts, the taxpayer might want to request a letter ruling as an "insurance policy" concerning how the IRS interprets this taxpayer's tax results.

A taxpayer would not want to request a ruling if the IRS's position, as expressed in earlier letter rulings or revenue rulings, is unfavorable to taxpayers. At times, taxpayers have no flexibility concerning how to structure a transaction. Because of the possibility that the IRS would rule unfavorably to the taxpayer, it would not be in the taxpayer's best interest to request a ruling. Similarly, a taxpayer generally should not seek a ruling for an issue if the IRS might also issue an unrequested ruling on related matters. This contingency is especially significant if the taxpayer feels vulnerable on the related matters.

---

[27] Ibid., Secs. 7.01 and 7.02.

[28] Rev. Proc. 97-3, I.R.B. 1997-1, 84.

[29] Rev. Proc. 89-34, 1989-1 C.B. 917.

[30] Ann. 90-65, I.R.B. 1990-20, 23. This change has been accomplished in part by additional guidance that the IRS has included in Rev. Proc 97-3 (and its predecessors) over the last seven years on whether it will continue to rule or not rule on a particular issue (or subissue).

DUE DATES AND PENALTIES

DUE DATES FOR RETURNS

OBJECTIVE 4

Recognize the due dates for tax returns and the penalties associated with not abiding by such dates

Returns for individuals, fiduciaries, and partnerships are due on or before the fifteenth day of the fourth month following the year-end of the individual or entity.[31] C corporation and S corporation tax returns, however, are due no later than the fifteenth day of the third month after the firm's year-end. Individuals and fiduciaries must have a certain level of gross income during a year before needing to file a return, but all corporations subject to tax under Subtitle A (income taxes) and all partnerships must file a return each year.[32]

EXTENSIONS

Congress realized that in some instances it would be difficult or impossible for taxpayers to gather their information and complete the return by the designated due date for filing the return. Thus, it authorized extensions of time for filing returns. Extensions may be granted for a reasonable period of time. Unless the taxpayer is abroad, the extension period cannot exceed six months.[33]

INDIVIDUALS. Individuals may request an automatic extension until four months after the original due date by filing Form 4868 (Application for Automatic Extension of Time to File U.S. Individual Income Tax Return). An extension is not available, however, unless the taxpayer executes Form 4868. The extension is automatic in the sense that the taxpayer need not convince the IRS that an extension is necessary.

If a taxpayer still needs additional time as the end of the four-month extension period draws near, an additional extension of up to two months may be requested by filing Form 2688 (Application for Additional Extension of Time to File U.S. Individual Income Tax Return). The taxpayer must state detailed reasons for needing more time, because the additional extension is not automatic. However, even if the IRS denies the request, it often grants the taxpayer a brief grace period for filing.

EXAMPLE C15-3 ▶ Bob and Alice, his wife, are calendar-year taxpayers. They may automatically get an extension for filing their 1997 return until August 15, 1998[34] by executing Form 4868. Suppose that both have been quite ill throughout 1998. As August 15 draws near, they may submit Form 2688 and request an additional extension until no later than October 15, 1998. They must explain their reasons when requesting an additional extension. ◀

CORPORATIONS. Corporations request an automatic extension for filing by submitting Form 7004 (Application for Automatic Extension of Time to File Corporation Income Tax Return) by the original due date of the return. Although the Code states that three months is the automatic extension period, the Regulations and the Form 7004 instructions state that the automatic extension period is for six months.[35] Because the automatic extension period is for six months, no further discretionary extensions are available.

EXAMPLE C15-4 ▶ Lopez Corporation reports on a fiscal year ending March 31. The regular due date for its return is June 15. It may file Form 7004 and request an automatic six-month extension that postpones the due date for the return until December 15. ◀

---

[31] Sec. 6072(a). Section 6072(c), however, extends the due date for returns of nonresident alien individuals to the fifteenth day of the sixth month after the end of their tax year.

[32] Secs. 6012(a)(2) and 6031(a).

[33] Sec. 6081(a).

[34] All due dates are stated in terms of the 15th day of the month. This ignores Saturdays, Sundays, and holidays when determining the due dates.

[35] Sec. 6081(b) and Reg. Sec. 1.6081-3(a).

TYPICAL MISCONCEPTION

Obtaining an extension defers the date by which the return must be filed, but it does *not* defer payment of the tax liability. Therefore, an extension for filing must be accompanied by a payment of an estimate of the taxpayer's tax liability. Computing this estimated tax liability can be difficult because much of the information necessary to complete the return may be incomplete or not yet available.

DUE DATES FOR PAYMENT OF THE TAX

It is important to understand that obtaining an extension merely postpones the due date for the return. It does not extend the time for paying the tax. In general, the due date for the tax payment is the same as the due date for the return (determined without regard to extensions).[36] In addition, the first estimated tax installment for an individual taxpayer is due on the due date for the preceding year's return, and the additional payments are due two, five, and nine months later. Taxpayers who elect to let the IRS compute their tax must pay within thirty days of the date the IRS mails a notice stating the amount of tax payable.[37]

Interest is imposed on any tax that is not paid by the return's due date, as determined ignoring extensions. When individuals request an automatic extension, they should project their tax liability to the best of their ability. Any tax owed, after all withholding tax and estimated tax payments are subtracted from the projected amount, should be remitted with the extension request. In addition, if an extension for filing a gift tax return is also requested (on the same form), the estimated amount of gift tax liability should be remitted. Similarly, corporations should remit the amount of the tax liability they anticipate, reduced by any estimated tax already paid, with their automatic extension request.

INTEREST ON TAX NOT TIMELY PAID

Any tax not paid by the original due date for the return is subject to an interest charge.[38] Basically, taxpayers incur interest expense in four contexts.

- They file late, without having requested an extension, and pay late.
- They request an extension for filing but inaccurately estimate their tax liability and, thus, must pay some additional tax when they file their return.
- They file on time but are not financially able to pay some, or all, of their tax liability.
- Their return is audited, and it is determined that they owe additional taxes.

DETERMINATION OF RATE. The IRS's interest rate is determined under the rules of Sec. 6621. The rate varies with fluctuations in the federal short-term rates; potentially the interest rate changes at the beginning of each calendar quarter. In general, the interest rate for underpayments of tax is three percentage points higher than the federal short-term rate, and the rate for overpayments is two percentage points higher. For corporate tax overpayments in excess of $10,000, the interest rate is reduced to the federal short-term rate plus one-half percentage point. For corporate underpayments exceeding $100,000, the rate for underpayments is five percentage points above the federal short-term rate if the deficiency is not paid before a certain date. Rates are rounded to the nearest full percent. Interest rates recently applicable are as follows:

Period	*General Rate for Underpayments*	*Rate for Overpayments*
July 1, 1996 through March 31, 1997	9%	8%
April 1 through June 30, 1996	8%	7%
January 1 through March 31, 1996	9%	8%

[36] Sec. 6151(a).

[37] Sec. 6151(b)(1). The special estimated tax payment rules for C corporations, S corporations, and trusts and estates are described in Chapters C3, C11, and C14, respectively, of this volume.

[38] Secs. 6601(a) and (b)(1).

EXAMPLE C15-5 ▶ Ann's 1995 individual return is filed in a timely manner and is audited in March 1997. Ann is a calendar-year taxpayer. The IRS contends that Ann owes $2,700 of additional taxes. Ann pays the additional taxes on March 31, 1997. Ann must also pay interest on the $2,700 deficiency for the period April 16, 1996, through March 31, 1997. The interest rate is 8% from April 16, 1996 through June 30, 1996. The interest rate is 9% from July 1, 1996 through the March 31, 1997 payment date. The interest rate is compounded daily (see discussion below). ◀

HISTORICAL NOTE

Probably two of the most significant changes in tax administration have been the daily compounding of interest and tying the interest rate charged to the federal short-term rate, which has resulted in a higher rate being used to calculate the interest charge than in years past. Before these two changes, taxpayers who played the "audit lottery" and took aggressive positions incurred little risk.

DAILY COMPOUNDING. Daily compounding of interest applies to both the interest that taxpayers owe the government and interest that the government owes taxpayers who have overpaid their taxes. The task of computing interest under daily compounding rules has been facilitated greatly because the IRS has issued Rev. Proc. 95-17 containing tables to be used for calculating the interest.[39] These tables are reproduced in the major tax services. In addition, software packages are available for the interest calculations.

PERIOD FOR WHICH INTEREST IS IMPOSED. Interest is usually imposed from the original due date of the return until the date of payment. In certain instances, however, an exception applies for the interest levied on a deficiency. If the IRS does not issue a notice and demand for payment within thirty days after the taxpayer signs a Form 870 (Waiver of Statutory Notice), no interest can be charged for the period between the end of the thirty-day period and the date the IRS issues its notice and demand.[40] Taxpayers litigating in the Tax Court may make a deposit to reduce the interest potentially owed. If the court decides that the taxpayer owes a deficiency, interest will not accrue on the amount of the deposit.

EXAMPLE C15-6 ▶ Cindy receives an automatic extension for filing her 1997 return. She submits her return, along with the $700 balance she owes on her 1997 tax, on June 24, 1998. She owes interest on $700 for the period April 16 through June 24, 1998. Interest is compounded daily using the interest rate for underpayments determined under Sec. 6621. ◀

EXAMPLE C15-7 ▶ Raj files his 1994 individual return on March 17, 1995. The return is audited in 1997, and on January 24, 1997, Raj signs a Form 870, on which he agrees that he owes a $780 deficiency. The IRS does not issue a notice and demand for payment until March 19, 1997. Raj pays the deficiency two days later. Raj owes interest, compounded daily at the Sec. 6621 underpayment rate, for the period April 16, 1995 through February 23, 1997. No interest can be levied for the period February 24 through March 19, 1997 because the IRS did not issue its notice and demand for payment until more than thirty days after Raj signed Form 870. ◀

PENALTIES

Penalties for failure to file on time and failure to pay by the due date are two commonly encountered penalties for income, estate, and gift tax purposes. These penalties are assessed in addition to the interest charged on taxes paid after the due date. Some penalties bear interest.

FAILURE TO FILE. Taxpayers who do not file a return by the due date generally are liable for a penalty of 5% per month (or fraction thereof) of the amount of the net tax due.[41] A fraction of a month, even just a day, counts as a full month. In general, the maximum penalty for failing to file is 25%. If the taxpayer receives an extension, the

---

[39] 1995-1 C.B. 556.

[40] Sec. 6601(c).

[41] Sec. 6651(a).

extended due date counts as the due date. In determining the amount of the net tax due (i.e., the amount subject to the penalty), the taxpayer's tax is reduced by any taxes paid by the return's due date (e.g., withholding and estimated tax payments) and tax credits claimed on the return.[42] If any failure to file is fraudulent, the penalty rate is 15% per month with a maximum penalty of 75%.[43]

ADDITIONAL COMMENT

The most common reason given to support reasonable cause for failing to file a timely tax return is reliance on one's tax advisor. Other possible arguments include severe illness or serious accident. Reliance on a tax advisor is not always sufficient cause to obtain a waiver of the penalties.

Penalties are not levied if a taxpayer can prove that he or she failed to file a timely return because of a reasonable cause (as opposed to willful neglect). According to the Regulations, reasonable cause exists if "the taxpayer exercised ordinary business care and prudence and was nevertheless unable to file the return within the prescribed time."[44] It is not surprising that much litigation deals with the issue of reasonable cause.

Note that the penalty imposed for not filing on time is generally a function of the net tax due. However, a minimum penalty applies to some income tax returns.[45] The minimum penalty was enacted because of the cost to the IRS of identifying nonfilers. If an income tax return is not filed within sixty days of the due date (including any extensions), the penalty will be no less than the smaller of $100 or 100% of the tax due on the return. Taxpayers who owe no tax are not subject to the **failure-to-file penalty**. The penalty is waived if the taxpayer shows reasonable cause for not filing.

EXAMPLE C15-8 ▶ Earl files his 1997 individual income tax return on July 4, 1998. No extension was requested, and Earl did not have reasonable cause for his late filing but fraud did not occur. Earl's 1997 return shows a balance due of $400. Under the regular rules, the late filing penalty would be $60 (0.05 × 3 months × $400). Earl's penalty is $100 because of the minimum penalty provisions invoked by his failure to file the return within sixty days of the due date. ◀

In general, interest is not imposed on any penalty that is paid within ten days of the date that notification of the penalty is given. Interest is levied under Sec. 6601(e)(2)(B) on the failure-to-file penalty, however, from the due date of the return (including any extensions) until the payment date.

FAILURE TO PAY. The **failure-to-pay penalty** is imposed at a rate of 0.5% per month (or fraction thereof).[46] The maximum penalty is 25%. The penalty is imposed on the amount of tax shown on the return less any tax payments (e.g., withholding, estimated tax, other payments, and credits) made before the beginning of the month for which the penalty is being calculated.[47] The term *other payments* is relevant when computing the penalty for months subsequent to months in which the taxpayer pays part of the tax liability. As with the failure-to-file penalty, the failure-to-pay penalty is waived if the taxpayer shows reasonable cause for not paying.

Because the tax is due on the original due date for the return, taxpayers who request an extension without paying 100% of their tax liability potentially owe a failure-to-pay penalty. The Regulations provide some relief by exempting a taxpayer from the penalty if the additional tax due with the filing of the extended return does not exceed 10% of the tax owed for the year.[48]

EXAMPLE C15-9 ▶ Gary requests an extension for filing his 1997 individual income tax return. His 1997 tax payments include withholding of $4,500, estimated tax payments of $2,000, and $1,000 submitted with his request for an automatic extension. He files his return on June 7, 1998, showing a total tax of $8,000 and a balance due of $500. Gary is exempt from the failure-to-pay penalty because the $500 balance due does not exceed 10% of

[42] Sec. 6651(b)(1).
[43] Sec. 6651(f).
[44] Reg. Sec. 301.6651-1(c)(1).
[45] Sec. 6651(a).
[46] Sec. 6651(a)(2).
[47] Sec. 6651(b)(2).
[48] Reg. Sec. 301.6651-1(c)(3) and (4).

his 1997 liability (0.10 × $8,000 = $800). Had Gary's 1997 tax instead been $9,000, he would have owed an additional tax of $1,500 and a failure-to-pay penalty of $15 (0.005 × 2 months × $1,500). ◀

The 0.5% penalty rises to 1% a month, or fraction thereof, in certain circumstances. The rate is 1% for any month beginning after the earlier of

- Ten days after the date the IRS gives the taxpayer notice that it plans to make a levy on the taxpayer's salary or property and
- The day the IRS gives notice and demand for immediate payment because it believes that collection is in jeopardy

EXAMPLE C15-10 ▶ Ginny files her 1994 individual income tax return on April 11, 1995. However, Ginny does not pay her tax liability. On October 5, 1997, the IRS notifies Ginny of its plans to levy on her property. The failure-to-pay penalty is 0.5% per month for the period April 16, 1995 through October 15, 1997. Beginning on October 16, 1997, the penalty rises to 1% per month, or fraction thereof. ◀

SELF-STUDY QUESTION

If a taxpayer does not have sufficient funds to pay his or her tax liability by the due date, should the taxpayer wait until the funds are available before filing the tax return?

ANSWER

No. He or she should file the return on a timely basis. This avoids the 5% per month failure-to-file penalty. The taxpayer will still be liable for the failure-to-pay penalty, but at least this penalty is only 0.5% per month.

Some taxpayers file on time to avoid the failure-to-file penalty, even though they cannot pay the balance of their taxes. Barring a showing of reasonable cause, such taxpayers will still incur the failure-to-pay penalty. Because taxpayers who do not file a timely return are likely to owe additional taxes, in many instances, both the failure-to-file and the failure-to-pay penalties are owed.

The statute contains a special rule for calculating the 5% per month failure-to-file penalty for periods in which both penalties are applicable. The 5% per month failure-to-file penalty is reduced by the failure-to-pay penalty.[49] Thus, the total penalties for a given month will not exceed 5%; for months when both penalties are incurred, the failure-to-file penalty generally becomes a 4½% effective rate (0.05 − 0.005). Note, however, that there is no reduction if the minimum penalty for failure to file is applicable.

EXAMPLE C15-11 ▶ Tien files her 1997 individual income tax return on August 5, 1998, without having requested an extension. Her total tax is $20,000. Tien pays $15,000 in a timely manner and the $5,000 balance when she files the return. No reasonable cause can be shown for Tien's late filing and late payment, but she did not engage in fraud. Tien's penalties are computed as follows:

Failure-to-pay penalty:		
$5,000 × 0.005 × 4 months		$ 100
Failure-to-file penalty:		
$5,000 × 0.05 × 4 months	$1,000	
Minus: Reduction for failure-to-pay penalty imposed for same period	(100)	900
Total penalties		$1,000 ◀

EXAMPLE C15-12 ▶ Assume the same facts as in Example C15-11 except that Tien instead pays the $5,000 balance on November 17, 1998. The penalties are as follows:

Failure-to-pay penalty:		
$5,000 × 0.005 × 8 months (April 16 through November 17)		$ 200
Failure-to-file penalty:		
$5,000 × 0.05 × 4 months (April 16 through August 5)	$1,000	
Minus: Reduction for failure-to-pay penalty levied for April 16 through August 5 ($5,000 ×0.005 × 4 months)	(100)	900
Total penalties		$1,100 ◀

[49] Sec. 6651(c)(1).

ESTIMATED TAXES

OBJECTIVE 5

Explain the penalty for not paying estimated taxes

In general, individuals receiving income from sources other than salaries and wages should pay quarterly estimated tax installments. As a result, the balance due with the filing of their return is usually relatively small. C corporations, S corporations (if they owe taxes), and trusts also have to pay estimated taxes. Estates, however, are exempt from paying estimated taxes for their first two tax years. S corporations pay estimated taxes only on their corporate tax levies—the built-in gains tax and excess net passive income tax—and any investment tax credit recapture amount. The C corporation, S corporation, and fiduciary estimated tax payment requirements are discussed in Chapters C3, C11, and C14, respectively.

PAYMENT REQUIREMENTS

KEY POINT

In general, individuals who are self-employed or have substantial income other than from salaries or wages (i.e., interest, dividends, K-1 income from partnerships, S corporations, estates, or trusts) are the taxpayers who should be most concerned about making timely estimated tax payments.

In general, individuals should make quarterly estimated tax payments if they have more than a relatively small amount of income from sources other than salary and wages. Assuming an individual's income other than from salary and wages is earned fairly uniformly throughout the year, four equal quarterly payments of estimated taxes should be made. To avoid imposition of a penalty, the estimated payments generally should be calculated as follows:

Step 1: Determine the lesser of
- a. 90% of the taxpayer's regular tax, alternative minimum tax (if any), and self-employment tax for the current year, or
- b. 100% of the taxpayer's prior year regular tax, alternative minimum tax (if any), and self-employment tax if a return was filed for the prior year and the year was not a short tax year.

Step 2: Calculate the total of
- a. Tax credits for the current year
- b. Taxes withheld on the current year's wages
- c. Overpayments of the prior year's tax liability that the taxpayer requests be credited against the current year's tax

Step 3: Multiply the excess of the amount from Step 1 over the amount from Step 2 by 25%.[50]

For calendar-year individual taxpayers, the quarterly payments are due April 15, June 15, September 15, and January 15.

For tax years beginning after December 31, 1993, individuals must substitute a 110%-of-prior-year's-liability safe harbor for the 100% safe harbor if their AGI for the prior tax year exceeds $150,000 ($75,000 for married filing separate returns).[51]

EXAMPLE C15-13 ▶ Mike's regular tax on his 1997 taxable income is $35,000. Mike also owes $2,000 of self-employment tax but no alternative minimum tax. Mike's 1996 total tax liability, for both income and self-employment taxes, is $24,000. His 1996 AGI did not exceed $150,000. Taxes withheld from Mike's wages in 1997 are $8,000. Mike does not have an overpayment of his 1996 tax or any 1997 credits. Mike should have made quarterly estimated tax payments of $4,000, as calculated below.

Lesser of:	90% of current year's tax (0.90 × $37,000 = $33,300) or 100% of prior year's tax ($24,000)	$24,000
Minus:	Taxes withheld from 1997 wages	(8,000)
Minimum estimated tax payment to avoid penalty under general rule		$16,000
Quarterly estimated tax payments (0.25 × $16,000)		$ 4,000 ◀

[50] Secs. 6654(d), (f), and (g).

[51] Sec. 6654(d)(1)(C). Included in the definition of *individual taxpayers* are estates and trusts. AGI for estates and trusts is defined under Sec. 67(e). (See Chapter C14.)

ADDITIONAL COMMENT

Although it is simpler to use the amount of tax paid (or, if necessary, 110% of the amount of tax paid) in the preceding year as a safe harbor, the estimate of the current year's tax liability is clearly preferable if the current year's tax liability is expected to be significantly less than the preceding year's tax liability.

The ability to make estimated tax payments based on the preceding year's income is especially significant for taxpayers with rising levels of income. To protect themselves against a penalty, these taxpayers generally need to pay in only an amount equal to the prior year's tax liability. Using this safe harbor eliminates the need for a high degree of accuracy in estimating the current year's tax liability.

EXAMPLE C15-14 ▶

Peter, a single calendar-year taxpayer, incurs a regular tax liability of $76,000 in 1997. Peter owes no alternative minimum tax liability nor can he claim any tax credits. No overpayments of 1996 taxes are available to offset the 1997 tax liability. Taxes withheld evenly from Peter's wages throughout 1997 are $68,000. Peter's 1996 AGI exceeded $150,000 and his regular tax liability was $60,000. Because Peter's $17,000 of withholding for each quarter exceeds the $16,500 minimum required quarterly payments, as calculated below, no underpayment penalty is incurred.

Lesser of:	90% of current year's (0.90 × $76,000 = $68,400) or	
	110% of prior year's $60,000 tax liability	$66,000
Minus:	Taxes withheld from 1997 wages	(68,000)
Minimum estimated tax payment to avoid penalty under general rule		$—0—

The $8,000 ($76,000 − $68,000) balance of the 1997 taxes is due on or before April 15, 1998. ◀

PENALTY FOR UNDERPAYING ESTIMATED TAXES

With the exceptions discussed in the next section, taxpayers who do not pay in the requisite amount of estimated tax by the appropriate date are generally subject to a penalty for underpayment of estimated taxes. The penalty is at the same rate as the interest rate applicable under Sec. 6621 to late payments of tax.[52] The penalty for each quarter is calculated separately.

ADDITIONAL COMMENT

If a taxpayer is having taxes withheld and making estimated tax payments, a certain amount of tax planning is possible. Withholdings are deemed to have occurred equally throughout the year. Thus, disproportionately large amounts could be withheld in the last quarter to allow the taxpayer to avoid the underpayment penalty.

The amount subject to the penalty is the excess of the total tax that should have been paid during the quarter (e.g., $6,000 [$24,000 prior year's tax liability ÷ 4] in Example C15-13) over the sum of the estimated tax actually paid during that quarter on or before the installment date plus the withholding that is attributable to that quarter. Unless the taxpayer proves otherwise, the withholding is deemed to take place equally during each quarter. This rule creates a planning opportunity. People who have not paid sufficient amounts of estimated tax in the first three quarters can foreclose the imposition of the penalty by having large amounts of tax withheld during the last quarter.

The penalty is assessed for the time period beginning with the due date for the quarterly installment and ending on the earlier of the date the underpayment is actually paid or the due date for the return (April 15 assuming a calendar-year taxpayer). The next example illustrates the computation of the underpayment penalty.

EXAMPLE C15-15 ▶

Assume the same facts as in Example C15-13, except that Mike pays only $3,000 of estimated tax payments on April 15, June 15, and September 15 of 1997, and January 15 of 1998, and, for simplicity, that 10% is the Sec. 6621 underpayment rate for the entire time period. Mike files his 1997 return on March 30, 1998, and pays the $17,000 ($37,000 − $8,000 withholding − $12,000 estimated taxes) balance due at that time. Mike's underpayment penalty is determined as follows:

[52] Daily compounding is not applicable in calculating the penalty.

TYPICAL MISCONCEPTION

Many self-employed taxpayers assume they are not liable for estimated taxes if they have sufficient itemized deductions and exemptions to create zero taxable income or a taxable loss. However, a self-employment tax liability may exist even if there is no taxable income. Thus, taxpayers in this situation can end up with an overall tax liability and an accompanying estimated tax penalty.

	Quarter			
	First	*Second*	*Third*	*Fourth*
Amount that should have been paid ($24,000 ÷ 4)	$6,000	$6,000	$6,000	$6,000
Minus: Withholding	(2,000)	(2,000)	(2,000)	(2,000)
Estimated tax payment	(3,000)	(3,000)	(3,000)	(3,000)
Underpayment	$1,000	$1,000	$1,000	$1,000
Number of days of underpayment; ends with earlier of March 30 or April 15, 1998	349	288	196	74
Penalty at 10% assumed annual rate for number of days of underpayment	$ 96	$ 79	$ 54	$ 20

The total penalty equals $249 ($96 + $79 + $54 + $20). The $249 penalty is not deductible. ◀

Interest is not assessed on underpayments of estimated tax.[53] But if the entire tax is not paid by the due date for the return, interest and perhaps a failure-to-pay penalty will be levied on the unpaid amount.

EXCEPTIONS TO THE PENALTY

In certain circumstances, individuals who have not paid in the requisite amount of estimated tax will nevertheless be exempted from the underpayment penalty. No penalty is imposed if the taxpayer's tax exceeds the taxes withheld from wages for the year in question by less than $500. Similarly, the taxpayer will not owe a penalty, regardless of the size of the underpayment, if the taxpayer owed no taxes for the prior year, the prior year consisted of twelve months, and the taxpayer was a U.S. citizen or resident alien for the entire preceding year. The Secretary of the Treasury is empowered to waive the penalty otherwise due in the case of "casualty, disaster, or other unusual circumstances" or for newly retired or disabled individuals.[54]

EXAMPLE C15-16 ▶ Paul's 1997 tax is $2,200, the same amount as his 1996 tax. His withholding tax is $1,730, and Paul does not pay any estimated taxes. Paul pays the $470 balance due on March 15, 1998. Under the general rules, Paul is subject to the underpayment penalty because he does not meet either the 90% of 1997 tax or 100% of 1996 tax minimums. However, because Paul's tax exceeds the withholding from his wages by less than $500, he does not owe any penalty for underpaying his estimated tax. ◀

In certain circumstances, taxpayers may be exempt from the underpayment penalty in some quarters but not in others. These additional exceptions to the underpayment penalty are beyond the scope of this text.[55] (Additional coverage on the other exceptions (e.g., the annualization of income exception) is contained in Chapter I14 of *Prentice Hall's Federal Taxation: Individuals* and *Comprehensive* texts.)

---

[53] Sec. 6601(h).

[54] Sec. 6654(e).

[55] Section 6654(d)(2) allows for computation of the underpayments, if any, by annualizing income. Relief from the underpayment penalty may result from applying the annualization rules. Corporations, but not individuals, are permitted a seasonal adjustment to the annualization rules.

OTHER MORE SEVERE PENALTIES

OBJECTIVE 6

Describe more severe penalties, including the fraud penalty

In addition to the penalties for failure to file, failure to pay, and underpayment of estimated tax, taxpayers can be subject to other more severe penalties. These include the so-called accuracy-related penalty (applicable in several contexts) and the fraud penalty, each of which is discussed below.[56] An accuracy-related penalty of 20% applies to the portion of any underpayment that is attributable to negligence, any substantial understatement of income tax, and several errors beyond the scope of this text. An accuracy-related penalty is not levied, however, if the fraud penalty is imposed or if no return was filed.

NEGLIGENCE

ADDITIONAL COMMENT

Because the IRS's determination is presumptively correct, the taxpayer has the burden of proof.

The accuracy-related **negligence penalty** applies whenever the IRS determines that taxpayers have underpaid any part of their taxes as a result of negligence or disregard of the rules or regulations (but without intending to defraud).[57] The penalty amount is 20% of the underpayment attributable to negligence. Interest is levied on the negligence penalty at the rates applicable to underpayments.[58]

EXAMPLE C15-17 ▶ Ted's 1996 individual return is audited. Ted agrees to the assessment of a $7,500 deficiency, of which $2,500 is attributable to negligence. Ted pays the $7,500 of additional tax on October 13, 1999. Ted incurs a negligence penalty of $500 (0.20 × $2,500). ◀

The Code defines ***negligence*** as "any failure to make a reasonable attempt to comply with the provisions" of the Code. Disregard of the rules or regulations is defined as "any careless, reckless, or intentional disregard."[59] According to the Regulations, there is a strong indication of negligence if the taxpayer does not include in gross income an amount of income shown on an information return or does not reasonably attempt to ascertain the correctness of a deduction, credit, or exclusion that a reasonable and prudent person would think was "too good to be true."[60]

A taxpayer is careless if he or she does not diligently try to determine the correctness of his or her position. He or she is reckless if he or she exerts little or no effort to determine whether a rule or regulation exists. His or her disregard is intentional if he or she knows about the rule or regulation he or she disregards.[61]

The penalty will not be imposed for any portion of an underpayment for which the taxpayer had reasonable cause for his or her position and acted in good faith.[62] Failure to follow a regulation must be disclosed, however, on Form 8275-R (Regulation Disclosure Statement).

EXAMPLE C15-18 ▶ Mario's current year individual return is audited, and he agrees to the assessment of a $4,000 deficiency. Assume that Mario had reasonable cause for adopting his tax return positions (which were not contrary to any rules or regulations) and acted in good faith. Mario will not be liable for a penalty for negligence. ◀

SUBSTANTIAL UNDERSTATEMENT

Taxpayers who substantially understate their income tax liability will be liable for an accuracy-related penalty for their substantial understatements. The Code defines a

[56] Secs. 6662(a) and (b).
[57] Secs. 6662(b) and (c).
[58] Sec. 6601(e)(2)(B).
[59] Sec. 6662(c).
[60] Reg. Sec. 1.6662-3(b)(1).
[61] Reg. Sec. 1.6662-3(b)(2).
[62] Sec. 6664(c).

ADDITIONAL COMMENT

Theoretically, penalties are used to deter taxpayers from willfully disregarding federal tax laws. Some taxpayers have been concerned that the IRS has used the multitude of tax penalties primarily as a source of revenue. This was accomplished by "stacking" penalties (i.e., applying several penalties to a single underpayment). Recent legislation has attempted to alleviate some of this concern.

substantial understatement as an understatement of tax exceeding the greater of 10% of the tax required to be shown on the return or $5,000 (or $10,000 in the case of a C corporation).[63] Thus, this penalty cannot apply unless the taxpayer's tax is understated—at a minimum—by more than $5,000 (or $10,000 if a C corporation). If the penalty applies, it is equal to 20% of the amount of the underpayment of tax that is attributable to the substantial understatement. The penalty does not apply to understatements for which the taxpayer demonstrates reasonable cause and good faith for his or her position.

SELF-STUDY QUESTION

How is an understatement different from an underpayment?

ANSWER

An underpayment can be bigger than an understatement. Understatements do not include underpayments for which there was either substantial authority or adequate disclosure.

UNDERSTATEMENT VERSUS UNDERPAYMENT. The amount of tax classified as attributable to the substantial understatement may be less than the amount of the underpayment. In general, the amount of the understatement is calculated as the amount by which the amount of tax required to be shown (e.g., the correct tax) exceeds the amount of tax shown on the return. However, because the amount of tax attributable to certain items is not treated as an understatement, the additional tax attributed to such items is not subject to the penalty. An underpayment for a transaction other than a tax shelter item is *not* treated as an understatement if either of the following is true:

- There is or was substantial authority for the tax treatment the taxpayer adopted.
- The taxpayer discloses, either on the return or in a statement attached to the return, the relevant facts affecting the tax treatment for the transaction and there is a reasonable basis for such treatment.

The adequate disclosure exception will be met if the taxpayer properly completes a form attached to the tax return or discloses information on the tax forms in a manner prescribed in an annual revenue procedure.[64] Proposed Reg. Sec. 1.6662-3(b)(3) explains that reasonable basis is "significantly higher" than not frivolous and that the standard will generally be satisfied if the position is based on one or more of the authorities applicable for assessing whether substantial authority exists.

EXAMPLE C15-19 ▶

Val's current year individual income tax return is examined, and Val agrees to the assessment of a $9,000 deficiency, which increases her taxes from $25,000 to $34,000. Val neither made adequate disclosure concerning the transactions for which the deficiency is assessed nor had substantial authority for the tax treatment used. Thus, Val's understatement is also $9,000. This deficiency is a substantial understatement because it exceeds both 10% of her correct tax ($3,400 = 0.10 × $34,000) and the $5,000 minimum. She incurs a substantial understatement penalty of $1,800 (0.20 × $9,000). ◀

EXAMPLE C15-20 ▶

Assume the same facts as in Example C15-19 except that Val has substantial authority for the tax treatment adopted for a transaction that results in a $1,000 additional assessment. In addition, she makes adequate disclosure for a second transaction on which the IRS assesses additional taxes of $1,500. Although Val's total deficiency is $9,000, her understatement is $6,500 [$9,000 − ($1,000 + $1,500)]. This $6,500 amount is a substantial understatement (more than the greater of 10% of Val's tax or $5,000). Because of the substantial authority and adequate disclosure, the penalty is only $1,300 (0.20 × $6,500). ◀

ADDITIONAL COMMENT

Even though the substantial understatement penalty is a taxpayer penalty, tax preparers must make their clients aware of the potential risk. In some situations, failure to do so has resulted in the client's attempting to collect the amount of the substantial understatement penalty from the preparer.

Like the negligence penalty, the substantial understatement penalty bears interest. The interest rate is the rate applicable to underpayments, and the interest is incurred for the period beginning with the due date of the return.

---

[63] Sec. 6662(d)(1).

[64] Reg. Secs. 1.6662-4(f)(1) and (2). See Rev. Proc. 95-55, 1995-2 C.B. 457, where Treasury identifies circumstances where disclosure of a position on a taxpayer's return is adequate to reduce the understatement penalty of Sec. 6662(d) and tax preparer penalties of Sec. 6694(a).

CONCEPT OF SUBSTANTIAL AUTHORITY. Recall that except for tax-shelter items, the penalty is not imposed for transactions where the taxpayer has substantial authority for the tax treatment adopted. Defining *substantial authority*, however, is quite difficult. According to the Committee Reports, Congress adopted this standard, in part, because it was new. The Committee Reports elaborate on this concept in the following manner:

> [T]he courts will be free to look at the purpose of this new provision in determining whether substantial authority existed . . . such a standard should be less stringent than a "more likely than not" standard and more stringent than a "reasonable basis" standard. Thus, it is anticipated that this new standard will require that a taxpayer have stronger support for a position than a mere "reasonable basis" (a "reasonable basis" being one that is arguable, but fairly unlikely to prevail in court . . .) . . . the weight of the authorities that support the taxpayer's position should be substantial when compared with those supporting other positions.[65]

The Committee Reports also give the following guidance concerning the process for evaluating whether substantial authority exists in a particular situation.

> It will be necessary to weigh court opinions, Treasury regulations and official administrative pronouncements (such as revenue rulings and revenue procedures) that involve the same or similar circumstances and are otherwise pertinent, as well as the Congressional intent reflected in the committee reports, to determine whether the position is supported by present law and may be taken with the good faith expectation that it reflects the proper treatment of the item.[66]

Regulations offer some guidance with respect to interpreting the term *substantial authority*, stating that "substantial authority"

- Is a less stringent standard than the "more likely than not" test applicable to tax-shelter items but a stronger test than the "reasonable basis" standard that the taxpayer must meet to avoid the negligence penalty
- Only exists if "the weight of authorities supporting the treatment is substantial in relation to the weight of authorities supporting contrary positions"
- Involves a situation where the taxpayer's position is stronger than one that is arguable but fairly unlikely to prevail in court[67]

According to the Regulations, the following are considered authority: statutory provisions; proposed, temporary and final regulations; court cases; revenue rulings; revenue procedures; tax treaties; Congressional intent as reflected in committee reports and floor statements of a bill's managers; private letter rulings; technical advice memoranda; information or press releases; notices; and any other similar documents published by the IRS in the *Internal Revenue Bulletin* and the *General Explanation of the Joint Committee on Taxation* (also known as the Blue Book). The time for assessing substantial authority is either the date the return is filed or the last day of the tax year covered by the return. An authority does not continue to have weight if it is overruled or modified, implicitly or explicitly, by a body that has the power to overrule or modify.

In general, the Regulations do not allow decisions of the taxpayer's geographical jurisdiction to be awarded additional weight in assessing whether substantial authority exists. A taxpayer does have substantial authority, however, if he or she follows a decision of the Court of Appeals for his or her circuit.

---

[65] Conf. Rept. 97-760, 97th Cong., 2d Sess., p. 575 (1982).

[66] Ibid.

[67] Reg. Sec. 1.6662-4(d)(2).

EXAMPLE C15-21 ▶ Authorities addressing a particular issue are as follows:

- For the government: Tax Court and Fourth Circuit Court of Appeals
- For taxpayers: U.S. District Court for Rhode Island and First Circuit Court of Appeals

The taxpayer (Tina) is a resident of Rhode Island, which is in the First Circuit. Tina would be deemed to have ''substantial authority'' for a pro-taxpayer position because such an interpretation is supported by the Circuit Court of Appeals for Tina's geographical jurisdiction. ◀

No doubt, it will take years for the meaning of the term *substantial authority* to be clarified through the judicial system. In the meantime, taxpayers need to realize that adopting a pro-taxpayer position with respect to a relatively sizable gray-area transaction can result in incurring a 20% penalty. If their return involving a nontax-shelter item is audited and they agree to a deficiency, they will owe a 20% penalty unless they had substantial authority for their tax treatment or they disclosed adequate information concerning the transaction. However, making a disclosure on a tax return may create a red flag that increases the probability of an audit.

TAX SHELTERS. Different rules apply to transactions that constitute tax shelters in determining whether there is an understatement. If a deficiency is assessed for a tax-shelter transaction, adequate disclosure cannot prevent the deficiency from being classified as an understatement. Instead of needing substantial authority, the taxpayer must meet a more stringent test to prevent a deficiency from being classified as an understatement. Here, the taxpayer must reasonably believe that the tax treatment used was more likely than not the proper tax treatment. *More likely than not* means a greater than 50% probability.[68] A *tax shelter* is defined as an arrangement for which the principal purpose is the avoidance or evasion of federal income tax.[69]

EXAMPLE C15-22 ▶ Assume the same facts as in Example C15-20, except that Val's entire deficiency is related to tax-shelter items and Val does not reasonably believe that the tax treatment used is more likely than not the proper tax treatment for the transaction in question. Val's understatement is the full $9,000 because the disclosure provides no relief for tax-shelter items and Val does not reasonably believe that the tax treatment used was more likely than not correct. Val's penalty is $1,800 (0.20 × $9,000). ◀

CIVIL FRAUD

The IRS may contend that errors on a taxpayer's return are attributable to fraudulent acts. At times criminal charges may also be filed against a taxpayer; taxpayers found guilty of such charges may receive a prison sentence. At other times the IRS may not press the criminal charges but will attempt to have the taxpayer held liable for only taxes, interest, and a civil fraud penalty. In both civil and criminal cases, the IRS has the burden of proof when it charges fraud. However, in civil cases, proof consists of "clear and convincing evidence,"whereas for criminal purposes, the standard is "beyond a reasonable doubt."

Fraud differs from simple, honest mistakes and negligence: It involves a deliberate attempt to deceive. Because the IRS cannot establish intent per se, it attempts to prove intent in an indirect fashion by emphasizing some of the taxpayer's actions. One leading authority describes fraud cases as having some of the following elements:

---

[68] Reg. Sec. 1.6661-5(d)(1).

[69] Sec. 6662(d)(2)(C)(iii). Special, more stringent, rules apply to substantial underpayments for corporations attributable to tax-shelter activities. See Sec. 6662(d)(2)(C)(ii) for details.

> Fraud cases ordinarily involve systematic omissions from gross income or fictitious deductions or dependency claims, accompanied by the falsification or destruction of records or false or inconsistent statements to the investigating agents, especially where records are not kept by the taxpayer. The taxpayer's education and business experience are also relevant.[70]

If part of a tax underpayment is the result of fraud, a fraud penalty equal to 75% of the portion of the underpayment attributable to fraud will be levied under Sec. 6663. However, if the IRS establishes that any portion of the underpayment is due to fraud, the entire underpayment is treated as resulting from fraud unless the taxpayer establishes by a preponderance of the evidence the portion that is not attributable to fraud. Like the negligence penalty, the fraud penalty bears interest.[71]

EXAMPLE C15-23 ▶ Ned's 1997 individual return is audited in 1999, and the IRS postulates that Ned's underpayment is due to fraud. Ned agrees to the $40,000 deficiency but establishes that only $32,000 of the deficiency is attributable to fraudulent acts. The rest results from mistakes that the IRS did not feel were due to negligence. Ned's civil fraud penalty is $24,000 (0.75 × $32,000). ◀

KEY POINT

The amount of the civil fraud penalty is 75% of the portion of the underpayment attributable to fraud. Once any portion of the underpayment is held to be due to fraud, the entire underpayment is treated as resulting from fraud, unless the taxpayer establishes otherwise.

The fraud penalty can be assessed with respect to income, gift, and estate tax returns. However, if the fraud penalty is imposed, the negligence and substantial understatement penalties are not levied on the portion of the underpayment resulting from fraud.[72]

On a joint return, no fraud penalty can be collected from a spouse who has not committed a fraudulent act.[73] In other words, one spouse is not liable for the other spouse's fraudulent acts.

STOP & THINK

Question: A few years ago Joyce filed her individual income tax return, reporting $250,000 of taxable income. She paid all the tax shown on the return on the day she filed. She fraudulently omitted an additional $100,000 of gross income from her tax return for that year. Of course, she does not have substantial authority for this fraudulent omission. She did not make a disclosure about the omitted income. If the IRS proves that fraud occurred, will Joyce be liable for both the civil fraud penalty and the substantial understatement penalty? What are the rates for the two penalties?

Solution: The penalties will not be stacked. Thus, she will not owe both penalties. If the IRS is successful in proving fraud, she will owe a penalty of 75% of the tax levied on the omitted income. She will not owe the 20% penalty for substantial understatements.

CRIMINAL FRAUD

KEY POINT

Few taxpayers are charged with criminal fraud, but for taxpayers who are accused, the government's conviction rate is high. Fines range up to $100,000 and five years in prison.

No distinct lines separate the activities that trigger criminal fraud charges from those that bring only civil fraud charges. Few taxpayers, however, are charged with fraud under the criminal provisions in any one year.

The Department of Justice must agree with the IRS's contention that criminal tax fraud charges should be filed against the taxpayer in question. The government's conviction rate in criminal fraud cases is high, and the government wants to keep it that way so the public will feel that such charges are only brought when the outcome is fairly certain. Thus, in fiscal 1995, the IRS initiated 3,698 criminal fraud investigations, and it

---

[70] Boris I. Bittker, *Federal Taxation of Income, Estates, and Gifts* (Boston, MA: Warren, Gorham & Lamont, 1981), vol. 4, pp. 114–119.

[71] Sec. 6601(e)(2)(B).

[72] Sec. 6662(b).

[73] Sec. 6663(c).

referred 2,470 for prosecution. During fiscal 1995, there were 2,948 convictions. Prison sentences were handed down in 1,387 of those cases.[74]

BURDEN OF PROOF. As mentioned earlier, the government must prove beyond a reasonable doubt that the taxpayer actually committed the crime of which he or she is accused. The proof standard is quite stringent. In fact, it is the same standard the plaintiff must meet in any other type of criminal case (e.g., a murder case).

CRIMINAL FRAUD INVESTIGATIONS. Criminal fraud investigations are carried out by the Criminal Investigation Division of the IRS. The agents responsible for the investigation are called **special agents**. Under IRS policy, at the first meeting between the special agent and the taxpayer, the special agent must

- Identify himself or herself as such
- Advise the taxpayer that he or she is the subject of a criminal investigation
- Advise the taxpayer of his or her rights to remain silent and consult legal counsel

PENALTY PROVISIONS. Provisions concerning the penalties associated with various tax crimes are contained in Chapter 75, Subchapter A, of the Code (Secs. 7201 through 7216). Some of the more important penalties are discussed below.

Section 7201. Section 7201 provides for the assessment of a penalty against any person who "willfully attempts . . . to evade or defeat any tax." The maximum penalty is $100,000 ($500,000 for corporations), a prison sentence of up to five years, or both. In order to obtain a conviction under this section, the IRS must prove that the taxpayer paid less tax than was actually owed. Because this is so difficult to prove, the government may decide to file charges under another Code section. It is easier for the government to prove beyond a reasonable doubt that a taxpayer willfully failed to pay tax or file a return or willfully filed a false return than it is to prove that the taxpayer paid less than the correct amount of taxes.

ADDITIONAL COMMENT

Any time a tax professional learns a client has engaged in activities that may constitute tax fraud, such client should be immediately referred to qualified legal counsel. Taxpayers are usually granted privileged communication only within an attorney–client relationship.

Section 7203. Section 7203 imposes a penalty on people who willfully fail to pay tax or file a return. The maximum fine is $25,000 ($100,000 for corporations), a prison sentence of no more than one year, or both. If the government charges the taxpayer with willfully failing to prepare a return, it need not also prove that the taxpayer owes additional tax in order to impose the penalty.

Section 7206. People other than the taxpayer can be charged under Sec. 7206. This section addresses any person who willfully makes and subscribes any return "which he does not believe to be true and correct as to *every material matter*" (emphasis added). Litigation has arisen over what constitutes a material matter.[75] The scope of Sec. 7206 extends beyond just the taxpayer because it applies to any person who

> [W]illfully aids or assists in, or procures, counsels, or advises the preparation or presentation under, or in connection with any matter arising under the internal revenue laws, of a return, affidavit, claim, or other document, which is fraudulent or is false as to any material matter, whether or not such falsity or fraud is with the knowledge or consent of the person authorized or required to present such return, affidavit, claim, or document.[76]

---

[74] *Internal Revenue Service, 1995 Data Book [Publication 55B]* (Washington, DC: U.S. Government Printing Office, 1996), p. 23.

[75] See, for example, *U.S. v. Joseph DiVarco,* 32 AFTR 2d 73-5605, 73-2 USTC ¶9607 (7th Cir., 1973), wherein the court held that the source of the taxpayer's income as stated on the tax return is a material matter.

[76] Sec. 7206(2).

WHAT WOULD YOU DO IN THIS SITUATION?

You have just begun your practice as a sole practitioner CPA, after working eight years for a large CPA firm. Your practice has not been as profitable as you had expected, and you are considering how you might attract more clients. One idea is to obtain bigger refunds for your clients than they had been anticipating. Your reputation for knowing all the tax-saving tips might spread, and likewise your profits would increase. You think more deeply and decide that maybe you could claim itemized deductions for charitable contributions that were not made and for business expenses that were not paid. You are aware that Sec. 7206, regarding false and fraudulent statements, is in the Code, but you think that you can avoid the "as to any material matter" language if you keep the overstatements of deductions to rather small amounts. Would you try this technique for increasing your profits? If you would, do you think that you would escape the scope of Sec. 7206? What ramifications might these actions have on your standing as a CPA under the AICPA's Statements of Responsibilities in Tax Practice and Code of Professional Conduct?

The maximum penalty under Sec. 7206 is $100,000 ($500,000 for corporations), a prison sentence of up to three years, or both. The government need not prove that more tax is owed.

Topic Review C15-1 summarizes the penalty provisions that potentially affect taxpayers.

STATUTE OF LIMITATIONS

OBJECTIVE 7

Understand the statute of limitations

The statute of limitations has the same practical implications in the tax area as in other contexts. It stipulates a time limit during which the government must assess tax or be barred from either assessing such tax or filing a court proceeding to collect the tax. The statute of limitations also limits the time during which a taxpayer may claim a refund of an overpayment of tax.

GENERAL THREE-YEAR RULE

Under the general rule of Sec. 6501(a), the statute of limitations is three years after the return is filed, regardless of whether the return is timely filed. A return that is filed before its due date is treated as if it was filed on the due date.[77]

EXAMPLE C15-24 ▶ Ali files his 1997 individual return on March 3, 1998. The government may not assess additional taxes for 1997 after April 15, 2001. ◀

EXAMPLE C15-25 ▶ Ali files his 1997 individual return on October 4, 1998. The statute of limitations for this return expires on October 4, 2001. ◀

KEY POINT

For purposes of the 25% omission test, gross income means the total of the amounts received or accrued from the sale of goods or services before deduction of the cost of those sales and services.

SIX-YEAR RULE FOR SUBSTANTIAL OMISSIONS

INCOME TAX RETURNS. In the case of substantial omissions from returns, the statute of limitations is six years after the later of the date the return is filed or the return's due date. For income tax purposes, the six-year statute is applicable if the

[77] Sec. 6501(b)(1).

Topic Review C15-1

Penalties Levied on Taxpayers

Penalty	Code Section
Failure to File:	
General rule—5% per month or fraction thereof; 25% maximum[a]	6651(a)
Minimum penalty if late more than 60 days—Smaller of $100 or 100% of tax due	6651(a)
Fraudulent reason for not filing—15% per month or fraction thereof; 75% maximum	6651(f)
Failure to Pay:	
Failure to Pay Taxes—0.5% per month or fraction thereof; 25% maximum[a]	6651(a)
Failure to Pay Estimated Tax—Penalty at same rate as interest rate for deficiency; imposed for period between due date for estimated tax payments and earlier of date paid or due date for return	6654
Accuracy-Related Penalties:	
Negligence—20% of underpayment due to negligence	6662(c)
Substantial Understatement of Income Tax—20% of underpayment attributable to substantial understatement (portion for which no substantial authority and no disclosure exists)	6662(d)
Civil Fraud:	
75% of portion of underpayment attributable to fraud	6663
Criminal Fraud:	
Willful attempt to evade tax—$100,000 ($500,000 for corporations) and/or up to five years in prison	7201
Willful failure to pay tax or file return—$25,000 ($100,000 for corporations) and/or up to one year in prison	7203
Willful making of false return—$100,000 ($500,000 for corporations) and/or up to three years in prison	7206

[a] If the taxpayer owes both the failure-to-file and the failure-to-pay penalties for a given month, the total penalty for such month is limited to 5%.

taxpayer omits from gross income an amount exceeding 25% of the gross income shown on the return. If an item is disclosed either on the return or in a statement attached to the return, it is not treated as an omission if the disclosure is "adequate to apprise the Secretary of the nature and amount of such item."[78] In the case of taxpayers operating a trade or business, gross income for purposes of the 25% omission test means the taxpayer's sales revenues (not the taxpayer's gross profit).[79] Taxpayers benefit from this special meaning of gross income because it allows the 25% test to be applied to a larger number.

EXAMPLE C15-26 ▶ Peg files her 1997 return on March 31, 1998. Her return shows $6,000 of interest from corporate bonds and $30,000 of salary. Peg attaches a statement to her return that indicates why she thinks a $2,000 receipt is nontaxable. However, as a result of an oversight, she does not report an $8,000 capital gain. Instead of the $10,000 literally omitted from the return, Peg is deemed to have omitted only $8,000, because the $2,000 receipt is disclosed.

---

78 Sec. 6501(e).

79 Generally, *gross income* is defined by Reg. Sec. 1.61-3(a) as sales less cost of goods sold.

KEY POINT

A 25% omission of gross income extends the basic statute to six years, whereas a 25% overstatement of deductions is still subject to the basic three-year statute. However, if fraud can be shown, there is no statute of limitations.

The $8,000 omitted gain is 22.22% ($8,000/$36,000) of gross income. Because the omission does not exceed 25% of Peg's reported gross income, the statute of limitations expires on April 15, 2001. ◀

Note that the six-year rule applies only to omitted income; thus, claiming excessive deductions will not result in a six-year statute of limitations. If fraud can be shown with the omission in Example C15-25, there will be an unlimited statute of limitations.

EXAMPLE C15-27 ▶

Assume the same facts as in Example C15-26, except that Peg does not make adequate disclosure concerning the $2,000 receipt. Thus, $10,000 is considered to have been omitted from gross income. The $10,000 omission is 27.77% ($10,000/$36,000) of gross income; therefore, the six-year statute of limitations applies. ◀

EXAMPLE C15-28 ▶

Rita operates a sole proprietorship. Rita's 1997 return, filed on March 17, 1998, shows sales of $100,000 and cost of goods sold of $70,000. Rita inadvertently fails to report $9,000 of interest income received on a loan made to a relative. For purposes of the 25% omission test, her gross income is deemed to be $100,000, not $30,000. The omitted income is 9% ($9,000/$100,000) of gross income shown on the return. Because the $9,000 omitted interest does not exceed 25% of the gross income shown on her return, the statute of limitations expires on April 15, 2001. ◀

GIFT AND ESTATE TAX RETURNS. A similar six-year statute of limitations applies for gift and estate tax purposes. If items that exceed 25% of the gross estate or the total amount of gifts stated on the return are omitted from the gross estate or the total amount of gifts, the statute of limitations expires six years after the later of the date the return is filed or the due date. Items disclosed on the return or in a statement attached to the return "in a manner adequate to apprise the Secretary of the nature and amount of such item" do not count as omissions.[80] Understatements of the value of assets disclosed on the return are not treated as omissions.

EXAMPLE C15-29 ▶

John files a gift tax return for 1997 on April 1, 1998. The return reports a cash gift of $600,000. In 1997, John sells land to his son for $700,000. At the time, John thinks that the land's FMV is $700,000 and does not disclose the sale on the gift tax return. Upon audit, it is determined that the FMV of the land on the sale date is $900,000. Thus, a $200,000 gift to the son arose. The $200,000 gift not disclosed is 33⅓% ($200,000/$600,000) of the gifts reported. The six-year statute of limitations applies. ◀

WHEN NO RETURN IS FILED

There is no statute of limitations if the taxpayer does not file a return.[81] That is, the government may assess tax or initiate a court proceeding for collection at any point in time.

EXAMPLE C15-30 ▶

Jill does not file a tax return for 1997. The statute of limitations never expires for 1997. Consequently, if the government discovers twenty years later that the return was not filed, it is able to assess a 1997 tax against Jill. ◀

OTHER EXCEPTIONS TO THREE-YEAR RULE

EXTENSION OF THE THREE-YEAR PERIOD. There are many other exceptions to the general three-year statute of limitations, some of which are discussed here. The taxpayer and the IRS can mutually agree in writing to extend the statute of limitations for

[80] Sec. 6501(e)(2).

[81] Sec. 6501(c)(3).

SELF-STUDY QUESTION

Should a taxpayer ever agree to extend the statute of limitations?

ANSWER

When an audit is already in progress, if a taxpayer refuses to extend the statute, the agent may assert a deficiency for each item in question. Had the taxpayer granted an extension, perhaps many of the items in question would never have been included in the revenue agent's report.

taxes other than the estate tax.[82] In such situations, the statute of limitations is extended until the date agreed on by the two parties. Such agreements are usually executed when a return is being audited near the time the general statute of limitations is set to expire. Taxpayers may agree to extend the statute of limitations because they think that if they do not agree, the IRS will assess a higher deficiency than it would if it had a longer time to spend on the audit.

CARRYBACKS. In the case of a year to which net operating losses (NOLs) are carried back, the statute of limitations is open until the statute expires with respect to the year in which the NOL arises.[83]

WHEN FRAUD IS PROVEN.

Deficiency and Civil Fraud Penalty. If the government is successful in proving that a taxpayer's return was "false or fraudulent . . . with the intent to evade tax" or that the taxpayer engaged in a "willful attempt . . . to defeat or evade tax," there is no statute of limitations.[84] In other words, the government may assess the tax or begin a court proceeding to collect the tax and the interest thereon at any time. In addition, if fraud is proven, the government can also collect the civil fraud penalty. If fraud is not proven, and the regular three-year statute and the special six-year statute for 25% omissions have expired, no additional taxes can be assessed. Often the fraud issue is very significant in litigated matters because the government must prove fraud to be able to assess a deficiency for that year.

EXAMPLE C15-31 ▶

The IRS audits Trey's 2001 return late in 2004. It also looks at some prior years' returns and contends that Trey has willfully attempted to evade tax on his timely filed 1997 return. Trey's litigation in the Tax Court on the fraud issue is successful. Because the IRS does not prove fraud, additional taxes may not be assessed for 1997. However, if the IRS had proven fraud, the statute of limitations for the 1997 return would have still been open and the additional taxes could be assessed. ◀

KEY POINT

Even though a taxpayer is home free after six years with respect to being prosecuted under the criminal provision, he or she is still subject to possible civil fraud penalties if fraud is proven at any time after the six-year period.

Criminal Provisions. Taxpayers must be indicted for criminal violations of the tax law within a certain period or they are home free. For most criminal offenses in the tax area, the maximum time period for indictment is six years after the commission of the offense.[85] Taxpayers cannot be prosecuted, tried, or punished unless an indictment is made during that time period. Note that the six-year period refers to the date of the commission of the offense, not to the date the return is filed. People who file fraudulent returns can commit offenses related to the returns at a subsequent date. An example of an offense that is often committed after the filing of a return is depositing money into a new bank account under a fictitious name.

EXAMPLE C15-32 ▶

In March 1998, Tony files a fraudulent 1997 return in which he attempts to evade tax. Before filing, Tony keeps a double set of books. In 1997 Tony deposits some funds into a bank account under a fictitious name. In 1999 he moves to another state, and on May 3, 1999, he transfers these funds to a new bank account under a different fictitious name. Depositing money into the new account is an offense relating to the fraudulent return. Provided Tony engages in no additional offenses, the statute of limitations for indictment expires on May 3, 2005. ◀

REFUND CLAIMS

After a certain amount of time has expired, taxpayers are precluded from obtaining a refund. Taxpayers are generally not entitled to a refund of overpayments of tax unless

[82] Sec. 6501(c)(4).
[83] Sec. 6501(h).
[84] Secs. 6501(c)(1) and (2).
[85] Sec. 6531.

they file a claim for refund by the later of three years from the date the return is filed and two years from the date the tax is paid.[86] A return filed before the due date is deemed to have been filed on the due date. The due date is determined without regard to extensions. In most cases taxpayers pay the tax concurrently with filing the return. Generally, if the later of the two dates is two years after the payment of the tax, the taxpayer's return has been audited, a deficiency proposed, and additional taxes assessed and paid. The additional taxes may have been paid, for example, two years after the due date for the return. In such a situation the taxpayer may file for a refund of these taxes at any time within two years after making the additional payment (or a total of four years after the filing date). If the taxpayer does not file a claim until more than three years after the date of filing the return, the maximum refund is the amount of tax paid during the two-year period immediately preceding the date the claim for refund is filed.

SELF-STUDY QUESTION

Suppose a taxpayer incorrectly includes a receipt in a tax return and then, after the statute of limitations has run for that year, correctly includes the receipt in a subsequent return. Is it equitable for the taxpayer to have to pay tax on the same income twice?

ANSWER

No. A complicated set of provisions (Secs. 1311-1314) allows, in specific situations, otherwise closed years to be opened if a position taken in an open year is inconsistent with a position taken in a closed year.

EXAMPLE C15-33 ▶

Pat files his 1997 return on March 11, 1998. The return shows taxes of $5,000, and Pat pays this entire amount when he files his return. No additional tax is paid. Pat must file a claim for refund by April 15, 2001. The maximum refundable amount is $5,000. ◀

EXAMPLE C15-34 ▶

Assume the same facts as in Example C15-33, except that Pat's 1997 return is audited, and Pat pays a $1,200 deficiency on October 3, 2000. Pat may file a claim for refund as late as October 3, 2002. If Pat's refund claim is filed later than April 15, 2001, however, the refund may not exceed $1,200 (the amount of tax paid during the two-year period immediately preceding the filing of the claim). ◀

LIABILITY FOR TAX

Taxpayers have the primary liability for payment of their tax. Transferees, however, can also be liable for the tax, as discussed below.

OBJECTIVE 8

Explain from whom the government may collect unpaid taxes

JOINT RETURNS

If spouses file a joint income tax return, the liability for taxes is joint and several, even if only one of the spouses had income.[87] Consequently, the government may collect a deficiency from either spouse, regardless of whether the underpayment relates to that spouse's income or deductions. This rule perhaps has its most practical significance when the spouse to whom the deficiency is attributable has left the country and the IRS can more easily locate the other spouse.

If spouses originally file a joint return, they cannot amend their return and file separate returns after the due date for the return.[88] This rule is intended to prevent a spouse from escaping the joint and several liability aspect of having filed a joint return. In other words, a married individual may not substitute a separate return for the joint return if he or she learns after the due date that the other spouse omitted gross income from their return.

VALIDITY OF JOINT RETURN. In general, a joint return must include the signatures of both spouses to be recognized as valid. If one spouse cannot sign because of a disability, the return is viewed as valid if that spouse orally consents to the other spouse's signing for him or her.[89] A joint return is deemed to be invalid if one spouse forces the other to file jointly under duress.

[86] Sec. 6511(a).

[87] Sec. 6013(d)(3).

[88] Reg. Sec. 1.6013-1(a)(1).

[89] Reg. Sec. 1.6012-1(a)(5).

KEY POINT

Spouses filing joint returns have joint and several liability. However, the innocent spouse provisions provide equitable relief in certain situations.

INNOCENT SPOUSE PROVISION. Congress enacted the **innocent spouse provision** in order to provide relief from liability for additional taxes in certain circumstances.[90] In order for a spouse to be relieved of liability for certain additional taxes, the following four conditions must be met:

- A joint return must have been filed.
- The return must have included "a substantial understatement of tax attributable to grossly erroneous items of one spouse."
- The spouse contending for relief must establish that he or she did not know about, and had no reason to know about, the substantial understatement.
- Based on all the facts and circumstances, it must be inequitable for the other spouse to be liable for the deficiency attributable to the substantial understatement.

Test for Substantial Understatement of Tax. Relief from liability first involves the objective test of a substantial understatement of tax. The Code defines *substantial understatement* as an understatement in excess of $500.[91]

For relief to be granted, such understatement must be attributed to a grossly erroneous item of the other spouse. The following two situations each meet the definition of a grossly erroneous item:

- An item of gross income attributable to the other spouse is omitted from gross income.
- The other spouse makes any claim for a deduction, credit, or basis in an amount for which there is no basis in fact or law.

The would-be innocent spouse must also meet the subjective tests of proving that he or she had no reason to know about the understatement and that it would be inequitable for him or her to have to pay the tax resulting from the understatement.

EXAMPLE C15-35 ▶

For the current year, Bill omitted $4,500 of his income from the joint return he filed with May, his spouse. The IRS audited the return, discovered the omitted income, and assessed $1,782 in additional tax. The understatement, which exceeds the $500 minimum, is a result of an omission of Bill's gross income. The IRS cannot collect the $1,782 of tax from May, provided she did not know about and had no reason to know about the omission, and it would be inequitable to hold her liable. ◀

No Basis in Fact or Law. Originally, innocent spouse relief was available only if the other spouse omitted gross income. Congress extended relief for certain situations involving improper deductions, credits, or basis. Thus, the "no basis in fact or law" requirement is relatively new terminology. In many instances, the courts must also decide whether there is a basis in fact or law for an item (e.g., deduction, etc.) claimed.

The understatement attributable to deductions, credits, or basis for which there is no basis in fact or law must exceed a certain percentage of the would-be innocent spouse's adjusted gross income (AGI) in order for the innocent spouse provisions to apply. (There is no comparable minimum threshold for gross income omissions.) If the would-be innocent spouse's AGI for the preadjustment year is $20,000 or less, the understatement must be more than 10% of such spouse's AGI. If the would-be innocent spouse has preadjustment year AGI over $20,000, the understatement must exceed 25% of that spouse's AGI. **Preadjustment year** is defined as the most recent tax year of the spouse ending before the date the deficiency notice is mailed.

[90] Sec. 6013(e).

[91] Sec. 6013(e)(3).

EXAMPLE C15-36 ▶

Jim and Joy file a joint return for 1997. Jim claims tax deductions of $8,000 for items that clearly constitute personal expenses. The IRS mails a deficiency notice for $3,168 of additional tax in 1999. The understatement is attributable to deductions that had no basis in fact or law. Joy's AGI for 1998 (the preadjustment year) is $19,000. Because the understatement exceeds $1,900 ($0.10 \times \$19,000$), Joy potentially qualifies for relief from the $3,168 additional tax liability if she also has no reason to know about the understatement and it is considered inequitable for her to be liable. ◀

EXAMPLE C15-37 ▶

Assume the same facts as in Example C15-36, except that Joy's AGI for 1998 is $28,000. Joy is ineligible for innocent spouse relief because the understatement ($3,168) does not exceed 25% of her preadjustment year AGI ($\$7,000 = 0.25 \times \$28,000$). ◀

The Effect of Community Property Laws. Community property laws are ignored in determining to whom income (other than income from property) is attributable. Thus, if one spouse living in a community property state wins money by gambling, for example, the gambling earnings are not viewed as community property for purposes of the innocent spouse provisions. If the gambling winnings are omitted from a joint return, they are deemed to be solely the income of the spouse who gambled. Thus, if the conditions discussed above are met, the other spouse qualifies as an innocent spouse.

TRANSFEREE LIABILITY

TYPICAL MISCONCEPTION

A taxpayer cannot escape payment of taxes by transferring assets to a transferee (donees, heirs, legatees, etc.) or a fiduciary (estate of the taxpayer, decedent, donor, etc.).

Section 6901 indicates that the IRS may collect taxes from people other than the taxpayer. The two categories of people from whom the taxes may be collected are transferees and fiduciaries. Transferees include donees, heirs, legatees, devisees, shareholders of dissolved corporations, parties to a reorganization, and other distributees.[92] Fiduciaries include the estate of a taxpayer, decedent, or donor, as the case may be. In general, the statute of limitations with respect to a transferee expires one year after the statute of limitations would have run out with respect to the taxpayer in the case of income taxes, the executor for estate taxes, and the donor for gift taxes.

EXAMPLE C15-38 ▶

Lake Corporation is liquidated in the current year and all of its assets are distributed to its sole shareholder, Leo. If the IRS audits Lake's return and assesses a deficiency, Leo (the distributee) is responsible for paying the deficiency. ◀

TAX PRACTICE ISSUES

OBJECTIVE 9

Understand the government-imposed standards affecting tax advisors

A number of statutes and guidelines address what constitutes proper behavior of CPAs and others engaged in tax practice.[93] The Code also provides for the assessment of penalties against tax return preparers and tax advisors in certain circumstances.

STATUTORY PROVISIONS CONCERNING TAX RETURN PREPARERS

Sections 6694-6696 regulate tax return preparers by imposing penalties on them in certain circumstances. Section 7701(a)(36) defines an income tax return preparer as a

---

[92] Reg. Sec. 301.6901-1(b).

[93] Chapter C1 discusses the AICPA's *Statements on Responsibilities in Tax Practice,* which provide guidelines concerning model behavior of CPAs in tax practice. See Appendix E for a reproduction of the Statements.

KEY POINT

As evidenced by the formidable list of possible penalties, an individual considering becoming a tax return preparer needs to be aware of certain procedures that are required by the Code.

"person who prepares for compensation, or who employs one or more persons to prepare for compensation, any return of tax imposed by subtitle A [income tax] or any claim for refund of tax imposed by subtitle A." Preparation of a substantial portion of a return or refund claim is treated as preparation of such return or claim. Note that preparers of estate and gift tax returns and claims for refund of such taxes are not affected by these statutory provisions.

Section 6695 imposes penalties for

- Failure to furnish the taxpayer with a copy of the return or claim ($50 per failure)
- Failure to sign a return or claim ($50 per failure)
- Failure to furnish one's identification number ($50 per failure)
- Failure to keep a copy of a return or claim or, in lieu thereof, to maintain a list of taxpayers for whom returns or claims were prepared ($50 per failure, up to a maximum of $25,000 for a return period)
- Failure to file the return disclosing the names, identification numbers, and places of work of each income tax return preparer employed ($50 per return plus $50 for each failure to set forth an item in the return)
- Endorsement or other negotiation of an income tax refund check made payable to anyone other than the preparer ($500 per check)

The first five penalties described above will not be levied if the preparer shows that the failure is due to reasonable cause.[94]

The penalties just described relate to procedural matters. However, a preparer will owe a $250 penalty under Sec. 6694 as a result of understating the taxpayer's tax liability if any of the understatement is due to a position that does not have a realistic possibility of being sustained on its merits provided the preparer knew, or reasonably should have known of, the position and the position either was frivolous or was not disclosed. If any of the understatement results from the preparer's willful attempt to understate taxes or reckless or intentional disregard of rules or regulations, the penalty is $1,000.

REAL WORLD EXAMPLE

In addition to these penalties, the IRS has the ability to suspend or bar a tax practitioner from practicing before the IRS. Each week the IRS publishes a list of suspended practitioners. In 1994 N.T. Nordbruck, a tax practitioner, was barred for life for "continually or repeatedly" engaging in prohibited conduct.

Regulation Sec. 1.6694-2(b)(2) states that the relevant authorities for the realistic-possibility-of-being-sustained test are the same as the authorities that apply in the substantial authority context. The IRS "will treat a position as having a realistic possibility of being sustained on 'its merits' if a reasonable and well-informed analysis by a person knowledgeable in the tax law would lead such a person to conclude that the position has approximately a one in three, or greater, likelihood of being sustained on its merits."[95]

Regulation Sec. 1.6694-3 addresses the willful understatement penalty. It states that preparers are considered to have willfully understated taxes if they have attempted to wrongfully reduce taxes by disregarding pertinent information. A preparer generally is deemed to have recklessly or intentionally disregarded a rule or regulation if he or she adopts a position that is contrary to a rule or regulation that he or she knows about or is reckless in not knowing about. There is no problem, however, in adopting a position contrary to a revenue ruling if there is a realistic possibility that the position can be sustained on its merits. A preparer may depart from following a regulation without penalty if he or she has a good faith basis for challenging its validity and adequately discloses his or her position on Form 8275-R (Regulation Disclosure Statement).

[94] Regulation Sec. 1.6695-1(b)(5) states that reasonable cause is "a cause which arises despite ordinary care and prudence exercised by the individual preparer."

[95] Reg. Sec. 1.6694-2(b).

Topic Review C15-2

Penalties Levied on Tax Return Preparers

Penalty	Amount	Code Section
Procedural matters:		
Failure to provide copy to taxpayer of return or claim	$ 50	6695(a)
Failure to sign return or claim	50	6695(b)
Failure to furnish identification number	50	6695(c)
Failure to keep copy of return or claim or list of taxpayers	50	6695(d)
Failure to file return regarding preparers employed	50	6695(e)
Endorsement of another's tax refund check	500	6695(f)
Understatement of tax because of taking a position that lacks a realistic possibility of being sustained	250	6694(a)
Willful attempt to understate taxes and reckless or intentional disregard of rules or regulations	1,000	6694(b)

Note: The amounts shown above are per item or per return; most of the penalties provide for a maximum that can be imposed in the event of numerous violations.

Topic Review C15-2 summarizes the penalty provisions applicable to tax return preparers.

KEY POINT

In addition to the standards imposed on most tax practitioners by their respective professional organizations, the IRS has promulgated a set of practice requirements that must be adhered to by persons practicing before the IRS.

ETHICS ANNOTATION

In deciding whether to adopt a pro-taxpayer position on a tax return or in rendering tax advice, a tax advisor should keep in mind his or her responsibilities under the tax return preparer rules of the Code, *Treasury Department Circular 230,* and the *Statements of Responsibilities in Tax Practice,* especially Statement No. 1. Statement No. 1 (discussed in Chapter C1 and reproduced in Appendix E) requires that a CPA have a good faith belief that the position adopted on the tax return is supported by existing law or by a good faith argument for extending, modifying, or reversing existing law.

RULES OF *CIRCULAR 230*

Treasury Department Circular 230 (or *Circular 230*) regulates the practice of attorneys, CPAs, enrolled agents, and enrolled actuaries before the IRS. Practice before the IRS includes representing taxpayers in meetings with IRS agents and appeals officers. People who do not comply with the rules and regulations of *Circular 230* can be barred from practicing before the IRS. Such people are entitled to an administrative hearing, however, before being barred.

The following are among the duties and restrictions applicable to people practicing before the IRS.[96]

- If the practitioner knows that a client has not complied with federal tax laws or has made an error in or omissions from any return, the practitioner should promptly advise the client of the error or omission.
- Each person practicing before the IRS is expected to exercise due diligence in preparing returns, determining the correctness of representations made to the Treasury Department, and determining the correctness of representations made to clients about tax matters.

Like Sec. 6694, *Treasury Department Circular 230* provides that a tax practitioner should not give advice or prepare a return taking a position unless the position has a realistic possibility of being sustained on its merits or the position is not frivolous and is disclosed (or, a practitioner simply giving advice should inform the client of the ability to avoid a penalty by making a disclosure). The realistic possibility standard is deemed to be met if a person knowledgeable in the tax law would conclude that the position has approximately a one in three, or greater, chance of being sustained on its merits.[97]

Circular 230 also contains a detailed discussion of practices people must follow in conjunction with issuing tax-shelter opinions.[98]

[96] *Treasury Department Circular 230* (1994), Secs. 10.21 and 10.22.

[97] Ibid., Sec. 10.34.

[98] Ibid., Sec. 10.33.

PROBLEM MATERIALS

DISCUSSION QUESTIONS

C15-1 Describe the verifications of tax returns performed at the IRS Service Centers.

C15-2 Name some of the administrative interpretations that the IRS is responsible for issuing.

C15-3 **a.** Describe three ways in which the IRS has selected returns for audit.
b. Explain the difference between how returns were selected for audit and the scope of the audit for returns selected under both the DIF and the TCMP procedures.

C15-4 What was the purpose of TCMP audits?

C15-5 Critique the following comment: "There's only about a 1% chance that any individual tax return will be audited."

C15-6 Al's individual return shows salary income and exemptions for himself and seven dependents; his itemized deductions consist of mortgage interest, real estate taxes, and a large loss from breeding dogs. Ben's individual return reports self-employment income, a large loss from a partnership, a casualty loss deduction equal to 25% of his AGI, charitable contribution deductions equal to 30% of his AGI, and an exemption for himself. Al's return shows higher taxable income than Ben's. Which return is more likely to be selected for audit under the DIF program? Which return was more likely to be chosen under the TCMP program? Explain your answers.

C15-7 Tom receives a notice that the IRS has decided to audit his 1996 return with respect to his deduction for interest expense. His 1994 return was audited for his charitable contribution deduction. The IRS did not, however, assess a deficiency for Tom's 1994 return. Is any potential relief available to Tom with respect to the audit of his 1996 return?

C15-8 Brad's 1996 return is chosen for audit on the employee business expense issue. Brad has just finished meeting with a revenue agent who contends that Brad owes $775 of additional taxes. Discuss briefly the alternatives available to Brad.

C15-9 A client wants to know the difference between a thirty-day letter and a ninety-day letter. Explain.

C15-10 List the trial courts in which a taxpayer can begin litigation concerning a tax matter.

C15-11 Why is the Tax Court so popular as a forum for beginning litigation?

C15-12 In what situations is a protest letter necessary?

C15-13 What general types of information should be included in a request for a ruling?

C15-14 In what circumstances will the IRS rule on estate tax issues?

C15-15 What recent changes took place in the IRS's policy concerning letter rulings?

C15-16 Tracy wants to take advantage of a "terrific business deal" by entering into a transaction with Homer. Homer, quite domineering and impatient, wants Tracy to finalize the transaction within two weeks and under the exact terms proposed by Homer. Otherwise, Homer will offer the deal to another party. Tracy is unsure about the tax consequences of the proposed transaction. Would you advise Tracy to request a ruling? Explain.

C15-17 Answer the following for both individuals and corporations:
a. Due date for the income tax return, assuming no extension is requested
b. Due date for the return assuming an automatic extension request is filed
c. Latest possible due date for the return

C15-18 Your client wants to know whether she must execute any paperwork in order to take advantage of the automatic extension provision. Explain.

C15-19 A client is under the impression that obtaining an extension for filing an income tax return would give him an additional amount of time to pay the tax at no interest cost. Is the client correct?

C15-20 Briefly explain the rules that determine what interest rate will be charged for tax underpayments. Is the rate the same for overpayments as for underpayments? In which months does the interest rate for underpayments potentially change?

C15-21 Stan does not have sufficient assets in April 1997 to pay his 1996 tax liability. However, he does anticipate paying the tax by August 1997. He wonders if he should request an extension of time for filing instead of simply filing his return and paying the tax in August. What is your response?

C15-22 What is the rate at which the penalty for underpaying estimated taxes is imposed? How is the amount of the penalty calculated?

C15-23 Tony's return was audited, and Tony agreed that he owed additional taxes plus the negligence penalty. Is the negligence penalty necessarily imposed on the total additional taxes that Tony owes? Explain.

C15-24 Assume that a taxpayer owes substantial additional taxes as a result of an audit. Nevertheless, the IRS may decide not to argue for applying the substantial understatement penalty. Explain two reasons why the IRS might not argue for imposing such a penalty.

C15-25 Maria's correct tax liability is determined to be $40,000 upon audit. She agrees that she owes a $7,000 deficiency. Will she necessarily have to pay the substantial understatement penalty? Explain.

C15-26 Distinguish between the circumstances that would lead to the imposition of the civil fraud penalty as opposed to the negligence penalty.

C15-27 Distinguish between the burden of proof the government must meet for imposition of the civil fraud and criminal fraud penalties.

C15-28 Explain why the government might bring criminal tax fraud charges against a taxpayer under Sec. 7206 instead of Sec. 7201. How do the maximum penalties under Secs. 7201, 7203, and 7206 compare?

C15-29 In general, when does the statute of limitations expire? List four exceptions to the general rule.

C15-30 What is the purpose of the innocent spouse provisions?

C15-31 For purposes of the tax return preparer provisions of the Code, when should a CPA sign a tax return as a preparer?

C15-32 List five penalties that can be assessed against tax return preparers under the Code. Does the Internal Revenue Code require a CPA to audit the information a client furnishes?

C15-33 According to *Treasury Department Circular 230,* what standard should be met in order for a CPA to take a position on a tax return?

ISSUE IDENTIFICATION QUESTIONS

C15-34 You are preparing the tax return for Bold Corporation, which had sales of $60,000,000. Bold made a $1,000,000 expenditure for which the appropriate tax treatment—deductible or capitalizable—is a gray area. Bold's Director of Federal Taxes and the Chief Financial Officer are pushing you to deduct the expenditure on the return that you are in the process of completing. What tax compliance issues should be considered in deciding whether to deduct the expenditure?

C15-35 Your client, Hank Goedert, collected $100,000 of salary and $40,000 of dividends in the current year. His itemized deductions total $37,000. In addition, Hank received $42,000 during the year from a relative who was his former employer. You have researched whether the $42,000 should be classified as a gift or compensation and are confident that substantial authority exists for classifying the receipt as a gift. You have almost finished Hank's current year tax return. What tax compliance issues should be considered in deciding whether to report or exclude the receipt?

C15-36 Baseball player Darryl Strawberry, major league outfielder, had his 1986 through 1990 tax returns examined by IRS auditors. The IRS contended that Strawberry earned $422,250 for autograph signings, appearances, and product endorsements, but reported only $59,685. The shortfall was alleged to be largely due to his receipt of cash for autograph sessions and promotional events. The cash payments were allegedly concealed in separate bank accounts that were not known to his CPA. What tax compliance issues regarding the alleged underreporting are pertinent to the CPA?

PROBLEMS

C15-37 ***Calculation of Penalties.*** Amy files her 1997 calendar-year return and pays the balance due on August 13, 1998 without having requested an extension. The tax shown on her return is $20,000. Her 1997 withholding tax is $12,000. Amy pays no estimated taxes and does not claim any tax credits on her 1997 return.

a. What penalties will Amy owe (ignoring the penalty for underpayment of estimated taxes)? Assume there is no fraud.

b. On what dollar amount, and for how many days, will Amy owe interest?

C15-38 ***Calculation of Penalties.*** Refer to Problem C15-37. How will your answers change if Amy instead files her return on June 18 and pays the balance of her taxes on September 8, 1998, and her withholding tax is

a. $19,000?

b. $20,500?

c. How will your answer to Part a change if Amy requests an automatic extension?

C15-39 ***Calculation of Penalties.*** The taxes shown on Hu's tax returns for 1996 and 1997 were $5,000 and $8,000, respectively. Hu's withholding tax for 1997 was $5,200, and she paid no estimated taxes. Hu filed her 1997 return on March 17, 1998, but she did not have sufficient funds to pay any taxes at the time she filed her return. She paid the $2,800 balance due on June 19, 1999. Hu's AGI for 1997 did not exceed $150,000. Calculate the penalties Hu owes.

C15-40 ***Calculation of Penalties.*** Ted's 1997 return reported tax of $1,800. Ted's withholding for 1997 was $2,200. Because of his poor memory, Ted did not file his 1997 return until May 28, 1998. What is the amount of any penalties Ted owes?

C15-41 ***Calculation of Penalties.*** Bob, a calendar year taxpayer, files his 1997 individual return on July 17, 1998 without having requested an extension. His return shows a balance due of $4,000. Bob pays the balance due on November 3, 1998. What are Bob's penalties for his failure to file and his failure to pay his tax on time? Assume there is no fraud.

C15-42 ***Calculation of Penalties.*** Carl, a calendar year taxpayer, requests an automatic extension for filing his 1997 return. By April 15, 1998, he has paid $20,000 of taxes in the form of withholding and estimated taxes. He does not pay any additional tax with his extension request. Carl files his return and pays the balance of the taxes due on June 19, 1998. For 1996 his tax liability was $19,000, and his AGI did not exceed $150,000. What penalties will Carl owe if his 1997 tax is $23,000? $20,800?

C15-43 ***Determination of Interest.*** Refer to Problem C15-42.

a. Will Carl owe any interest? If so, on what amount and for how many days?

b. Assume the applicable interest rate is 11%. Compute Carl's interest payable if his 1997 tax is $23,000. (See Rev. Proc. 95-17, 1995-1 C.B. 556, or a major tax service, for the compounding tables.)

C15-44 ***Penalty for Underpayment of Estimated Taxes.*** Ed's tax liability for 1996 was $24,000. Ed projects that his tax for 1997 will be $34,000. Ed is self-employed and, thus, will have no withholding. His AGI for 1996 did not exceed $150,000. How much estimated tax should Ed pay for 1997 to avoid the penalty for underpaying estimated taxes?

C15-45 ***Penalty for Underpayment of Estimated Taxes.*** Refer to Problem C15-44. Assume that Ed expects that his income for 1997 will decline and that his tax liability for 1997 will be only $15,000. How much in estimated taxes, at a minimum, should Ed pay for 1997? What problem will Ed encounter if he pays in the minimum amount of estimated taxes projected earlier and his income exceeds 1996's because of a large capital gain in December 1997?

C15-46 ***Penalty for Underpayment of Estimated Taxes.*** Pam's 1996 income tax liability was $23,000. Her 1996 AGI did not exceed $150,000. Pam, a calendar year taxpayer, files her 1997 individual return showing a $30,000 income tax liability (before reduction for withholding) on April 1, 1998. In addition, Pam owes self-employment taxes of $2,600. Taxes withheld from Pam's salary total $20,000; she has paid no estimated taxes.

a. Will Pam owe a penalty for not paying estimated taxes? Explain.

b. How many dollars (if any) per quarter are subject to the penalty? For what period will the penalty be imposed for each quarter's underpayment?

c. How would your answers to Parts a and b change if Pam's 1997 tax liability (including self-employment taxes) were instead $17,000?

C15-47 ***Penalty for Underpayment of Estimated Taxes.*** Amir's 1997 projected tax liability is $20,000. Although Amir has substantial dividend and interest income, he does not pay any estimated taxes. Amir's withholding for January through November 1997 is $1,300 per month. For December 1997 he wants to increase the amount of his withholding to avoid the penalty for underpaying estimated taxes. Amir's 1996 liability (exclusive of his withholding) is $19,000. His 1996 AGI did not exceed $150,000. What amount should Amir have withheld from his December check? Explain.

C15-48 ***Negligence Penalty.*** Tan's 1997 individual return is audited, and the IRS assesses a $9,000 deficiency, $3,000 of which results from Tan's negligence. What is Tan's negligence penalty? Does the penalty bear interest?

C15-49 ***Negligence Penalty.*** Pearl's current year individual return is audited. The IRS determines that, among other errors, she negligently did not report dividend income of $8,000. The deficiency with respect to the dividends is $2,240. The IRS argues for an additional $12,000 deficiency for various other errors that do not involve negligence. What is Pearl's negligence penalty for the $14,240 of deficiencies?

C15-50 ***Substantial Understatement Penalty.*** Carmen's current year individual return shows a $6,000 deduction for a questionable item that is not a tax-shelter item. Carmen does not make a disclosure regarding this item. Carmen's return is audited, and she concedes to the assessment of a deficiency. As a result, her tax liability increases from $20,000 to $21,860. Assume Carmen lacks substantial authority for claiming the deduction.

a. What is the substantial understatement penalty (if any) that will be levied?

b. Will the penalty bear interest?

c. How would your answer to Parts a and b change if the deduction were instead for $20,000, and her tax liability increased by $6,200 to $26,200?

C15-51 ***Substantial Understatement Penalty.*** Refer to Part c of Problem C15-50. Assume that Carmen has substantial authority and discloses the transaction. How would your original answer change if

a. The transaction does not involve a tax-shelter item?

b. The transaction does involve a tax-shelter item?

C15-52 ***Fraud Penalty.*** Luis, a bachelor, owes $60,000 of additional taxes, all because of fraudulent acts.

a. What is the amount of the civil fraud penalty?

b. What criminal fraud penalty might be levied under Sec. 7201?

C15-53 ***Fraud Penalty.*** Hal and Wanda, his wife, are in the 39.6% marginal tax bracket for the current year. Wanda fraudulently omits $50,000 of gross income from their joint return. Hal does not participate in or know about her fraudulent acts. Hal, however, overstates his deductions by $10,000 because of an oversight.

a. If the government is successful in proving fraud in a civil case, what fines and/or penalties will Wanda owe? If Hal and Wanda establish that the overstatement of deductions is not attributable to fraud, can the government collect the civil fraud penalty from Hal?

b. If the government is successful in proving fraud in a criminal case, what fines or penalties will Wanda owe? Can she or Hal receive a prison sentence?

C15-54 ***Statute of Limitations.*** Frank, a calendar year taxpayer, reports $100,000 of gross income and $60,000 of taxable income on his 1997 return, which he files on March 10, 1998. He omits a $52,000 long-term capital gain and a $10,000 short-term capital loss from his return. When does the statute of limitations concerning the government's ability to collect the taxes expire if

a. His omission results from an oversight?

b. His omission of the gain arose because of an attempt to evade tax?

C15-55 ***Statute of Limitations.*** Refer to Problem C15-54. Assume Frank commits fraudulent acts with respect to his 1997 return as late as November 4, 1999. When does the statute of limitations for indicting Frank for criminal tax fraud expire?

C15-56 ***Claim for Refund.*** Maria, a calendar year taxpayer, files her 1997 individual return on March 17, 1998 and pays the balance of her taxes on that date. She later discovers that she overlooked some deductions that she should have claimed on the return. By what date must she file a claim for refund?

C15-57 ***Innocent Spouse Provisions.*** Wilma has no income for 1997, but she files a joint return with her husband, Hank. Their 1997 return shows $40,000 of gross income and AGI and $24,000 of taxable income. Hank also has $12,000 of gambling winnings (no losses) in 1997, but he omits them from the return. Wilma does not know about Hank's gambling activities, much less his winnings. The IRS audits their 1997 return and assesses additional taxes.

a. Does Wilma satisfy the objective tests for relief under the innocent spouse provisions?

b. What subjective tests must Wilma also meet in order to qualify as an innocent spouse?

C15-58 ***Innocent Spouse Provisions.*** Joe and Joan filed a joint return for 1997. They are in the 31% marginal tax bracket. Joan omitted from the return a prize valued at $8,000 that she won. Does Joe meet the objective tests for relief under the innocent spouse provisions?

CASE STUDY PROBLEM

C15-59 A long-time client, Horace Haney, wishes to avoid recognizing revenue currently for a particular transaction. A recently finalized Treasury Regulation provides, however, that revenue should be recognized in the current year for such a transaction. Horace insists that you report no revenue from the transaction and, furthermore, that you make no disclosure about going against the regulation. The Internal Revenue Code is unclear about whether the income should be recognized currently. No relevant cases, revenue rulings, or letter rulings deal specifically with the transaction in question.

Required: Discuss whether you, a CPA, can prepare Horace's tax return and abide by his wishes. Assume that recognizing the income in question would increase Horace's tax liability by about 25%.

TAX RESEARCH PROBLEMS

C15-60 Art is named executor of the Estate of Stu Stone, his father, who dies on February 3, 1997. Art engages Larry to serve as the estate's attorney. Larry advises Art that the estate must file an estate tax return but does not mention the due date. Art, a pharmacist, has no experience with tax matters other than the preparation of his own income tax returns. Art provides Larry with all the necessary information by June 15, 1997. On six occasions Art contacts Larry to check on the progress on the estate tax return. Each time, Larry assures Art that "everything is under control." On November 15, 1997, Art contacts Larry for the seventh time. He learns that because of a clerical oversight, the return—due on November 2, 1997—has not been filed. Larry apologizes and says he will make sure that an associate finishes the return promptly. The return, showing an estate tax liability of $75,200, is filed on December 7, 1997. Your manager requests that you prepare a memorandum addressing whether the estate will owe the failure-to-file penalty. Your manager suggests that you consult, at a minimum,

- Sec. 6151(a)
- *U.S. v. Robert W. Boyle,* 55 AFTR 2d 85-1535, 85-1 USTC ¶13,602 (USSC, 1985)

C15-61 Harold and Betty, factory workers who until 1996 prepared their own individual tax returns, purchased an investment from an investment advisor in 1995. They reviewed some of the legal description of the investment, and the advisor explained the more complicated features to them. In early 1996 they struggled to prepare their 1995 individual return but, because of the investment, found it too complicated to complete the return. Thus, they engaged a CPA to prepare the return for them. The CPA deducted losses from the investment against income that Harold and Betty had from other sources. The IRS audited the 1995 return and contended that the loss was not deductible; Harold and Betty, after consulting with their CPA who investigated the investment further, agreed that the loss was not deductible and agreed to pay the deficiency. The IRS also contended that the couple owes the substantial understatement penalty because no disclosure about the investment was made on their return, and they did not have substantial authority for their position. Adopt the position of representing the taxpayers in their arguments before the IRS that they should be exempted from the substantial understatement penalty. Your tax manager reminds you to consult Code Sec. 6662 when doing your research.

C15-62 Gene employed his attorney to draft identical trust instruments for trusts for each of his three minor children. Before he signs the instruments, Gene wishes to receive a ruling from the IRS concerning whether the trusts will qualify for the gift tax annual exclusion. Your task is to prepare a request for a letter ruling. Each trust instrument names the Fourth City Bank as trustee and states the trust is irrevocable. It further provides that until the beneficiary reaches age 21, the trustee in its discretion is to pay income and/or principal (corpus) to the beneficiary. Upon reaching age 21, the beneficiary has sixty days in which to request that the trust assets be paid over to him. Otherwise, the assets will stay in the trust until the beneficiary reaches age 35. The beneficiary is also granted a general testamentary power of appointment over the trust assets. If the beneficiary dies before the trust terminates and does not exercise his power of appointment (because, for example, he dies without a will), the trust property will be distributed to family members in accordance with state intestacy laws. The three beneficiaries are Judy (age 5), Terry (age 7), and Grady (age 11). Each trust will be funded with property valued at $100,000.

A partial list of research sources is

- Secs. 2503(b) and (c)
- Reg. Sec. 25.2503-4
- Rev. Rul. 67-270, 1967-2 C.B. 349
- Rev. Rul. 74-43, 1974-1 C.B. 285
- Rev. Rul. 81-7, 1981-1 C.B. 474

CHAPTER 16

U.S. TAXATION OF FOREIGN-RELATED TRANSACTIONS

LEARNING OBJECTIVES

After studying this chapter, you should be able to

1. Understand the characteristics used to determine the U.S. taxes owed on a foreign-related transaction
2. Determine the foreign tax credit available to a U.S. taxpayer
3. Calculate the earned income exclusion available to U.S. taxpayers employed abroad
4. Determine whether a foreign individual is a resident or nonresident alien
5. Determine the U.S. tax liability for a nonresident alien
6. Calculate the deemed paid tax credit available for an investor in a foreign corporation
7. Determine whether a foreign corporation is a controlled foreign corporation
8. Explain the special tax provisions applying to a controlled foreign corporation
9. Explain the special tax benefits accruing to a foreign sales corporation
10. Explain the special tax benefits accruing to a domestic international sales corporation

CHAPTER OUTLINE

Taxes imposed by the U.S. government on international transactions must be considered when making many kinds of business decisions. For example, U.S. income tax considerations affect whether a foreign business should be conducted directly by a U.S. corporation or indirectly through a foreign subsidiary corporation. The placement and compensation of U.S. employees in businesses operated outside the United States also requires careful consideration because, in many cases, such individuals can exempt part or all of their foreign salaries and allowances from U.S. taxation.

This chapter is intended to provide a general awareness of the U.S. tax laws in an international setting. The discussion is limited to coverage of the U.S. taxation of international operations because of the impracticality of examining the laws of individual foreign countries in the space provided.

JURISDICTION TO TAX

OBJECTIVE 1

Understand the characteristics used to determine the U.S. taxes owed on a foreign-related transaction

The U.S. income tax laws use the following four characteristics to determine the tax treatment accorded foreign-related transactions:

- The taxpayer's country of citizenship
- The taxpayer's country of residence
- The type of income earned
- The location where the income is earned

An overview of the importance of each of these four characteristics to the operation of the U.S. tax laws is presented in the next section of this chapter.

The U.S. tax laws provide different tax treatments according to the taxpayer's country of citizenship or country of organization. U.S. citizens and domestic corporations[1] are taxed by the United States on their worldwide income. Individuals who are not U.S. citizens and foreign corporations are taxed according to their country of residence.

Individuals who are not U.S. citizens are called aliens. The U.S. income tax laws divide aliens into two classes: resident aliens and nonresident aliens. A **resident alien** is an individual who resides in the United States *but* is not a U.S. citizen. A **nonresident alien** is an individual who resides outside the United States *and* is not a U.S. citizen.

TYPICAL MISCONCEPTION

Many people believe that income earned outside the United States is not subject to taxation by the United States. This is incorrect. U.S. citizens, resident aliens, and domestic corporations are taxed by the United States on their worldwide income.

U.S. citizens, resident aliens, and domestic corporations generally receive the same tax treatment for the various kinds of income they earn. They are taxed on their worldwide income. In general, the same rules apply whether the income is earned in the United States, a foreign country, or a U.S. possession. Some special treatments are available for income earned in foreign countries or U.S. possessions.

- Compensation received by a U.S. citizen or resident alien who works in a foreign country for an extended period of time is eligible for a special exclusion of up to $70,000 annually.
- The income taxes paid to a foreign country or a U.S. possession can be credited against the U.S. tax liability.

The tax treatment accorded nonresident aliens and foreign corporations depends on whether they conducted a trade or business in the United States at some time during the year. If no such activities are conducted, the nonresident aliens and foreign corporations are taxed only on their U.S.-source investment income. If they conduct a trade or

[1] Secs. 7701(a)(3) and (4). A domestic corporation is defined as a corporation created or organized under federal law or the laws of one of the fifty states or the District of Columbia. All other corporations are **foreign corporations**.

▼ **TABLE C16-1**
Overview of Important International Tax Issues

Entity Form	U.S. Tax Base	U.S. Tax Issues
Individuals:		
U.S. citizen	Worldwide income	1, 2
U.S. resident alien	Worldwide income	1, 2
U.S. nonresident alien	U.S. territorial	3, 4
Corporations:		
U.S. parent with foreign branch	Worldwide income	1
U.S. parent with foreign subsidiary	Worldwide income	1, 5, 6
Foreign parent with U.S. branch	U.S. territorial	3, 4, 6, 7
Foreign parent with U.S. subsidiary	Worldwide	1, 4, 6

U.S. Tax Issues Listing

1. Foreign tax credit
2. Foreign earned income exclusion
3. U.S. income tax liability
4. Withholding of U.S. taxes on payments made to non-U.S. persons
5. Deferral of foreign profits
6. Transfer pricing
7. Branch profits tax

KEY POINT

The place where income is earned or sourced (either U.S. or foreign) is determined under a complex set of rules, depending on the type of income. For example, with certain exceptions, interest income is sourced in the country of residence of the obligor.

business in the United States at some time during the year, the nonresident aliens and foreign corporations are taxed on both their U.S.-source investment income and their U.S.-source (and limited foreign-source) income that is connected with the conduct of the U.S. trade or business. Trade or business and investment income earned by aliens and foreign corporations in foreign countries is generally exempt from U.S. taxation.

An overview of the important international tax issues to the various tax entity forms that operate in, or from within, the United States is presented in Table C16-1. Hopefully, this table will provide some structure to the discussion of the many U.S. tax rules that are applied to foreign-related transactions.

TAXATION OF U.S. CITIZENS AND RESIDENT ALIENS

OBJECTIVE 2

Determine the foreign tax credit available to a U.S. taxpayer

This portion of the chapter examines the two most common foreign tax provisions applicable to U.S. citizens and resident aliens: the foreign tax credit and the foreign-earned income exclusion. Both provisions reduce the burden of having income taxed both in the foreign country in which it is earned and in the United States.

FOREIGN TAX CREDIT

The **foreign tax credit** permits U.S. taxpayers to avoid double taxation by crediting income taxes paid or accrued to a foreign country (including political subdivisions such as provinces and cities) or a U.S. possession[2] against the U.S. income tax liability. The foreign tax credit reduces a U.S. taxpayer's total worldwide tax rate on income earned in foreign countries or U.S. possessions to the higher of the U.S. or the foreign tax rates.

STOP & THINK

Question: The United States uses the foreign tax credit system as its primary mechanism for reducing double taxation. What are the advantages and disadvantages of the foreign tax credit system?

Solution: The foreign tax credit system is linked with the concept that all income is subject to tax no matter where it is earned, unless it is excluded by the statute. Foreign source income is taxed by the U.S. government and a credit is allowed for foreign income taxes paid or accrued up to the amount of the U.S. taxes owed on all foreign-source income. The credit system requires that a taxpayer must report the income, file a tax return, and claim the credit to reduce his or her U.S. tax liability. This ensures the reporting of non-U.S. income to the U.S. tax authorities and provides additional U.S. tax revenues to the extent that the U.S. tax rates are higher than the foreign tax rates. The reporting requirement, however, increases compliance costs for U.S. taxpayers. The credit system provides an incentive for foreign governments to raise their tax rates to level of the U.S. tax rates. Such increases will not increase a taxpayer's worldwide tax costs, but will shift tax revenues from the United States to the foreign country.

KEY POINT

This double taxation is caused by two different jurisdictions taxing the same income, rather than one jurisdiction taxing the same income twice (such as dividends from a C corporation). The foreign-earned income exclusion and income tax treaties, as well as the foreign tax credit, are all ways of mitigating the double tax.

REAL-WORLD EXAMPLE

The foreign tax credit is the largest U.S. tax credit. In 1993 U.S. corporations claimed $22.9 billion in foreign tax credits, which is 7.5 times larger than their general business credits.

ADDITIONAL COMMENT

Recognize that foreign income taxes are also deductible under Sec. 164. However, taxpayers may not both deduct and credit the same foreign income taxes. Whether a taxpayer credits or deducts the foreign income taxes is an annual election.

CREDITABLE TAXES. The foreign tax credit benefits are available only for income taxes paid or accrued to a foreign country or a U.S. possession. Other foreign taxes are deductible according to the rules of Code Sec. 164, which are explained in Chapter I7 of the companion volume, *Prentice Hall's Federal Taxation: Individuals.*

The IRS regularly promulgates information as to the creditability of specific foreign tax levies.[3] These notices save time and effort in determining whether a specific tax levy is creditable. Some foreign tax levies have been the subject of litigation. Summaries of these promulgations and judicial decisions can be found in the major tax services.

ELIGIBILITY FOR THE CREDIT. Section 901(a) permits U.S. citizens and resident aliens to elect to claim a foreign tax credit for income taxes paid or accrued to a foreign country or a U.S. possession. This type of tax credit is known as a *direct credit.* Most taxpayers annually elect to credit their foreign income taxes. As will be discussed later, a limited number of taxpayers may choose to deduct their foreign income taxes.

Taxpayers who use the accrual method of accounting must claim the foreign tax credit in the year in which the tax levy accrues. A taxpayer who uses the cash method of accounting claims the foreign tax credit in the year in which the tax is paid unless a special election is made to accrue the taxes (the advantages of this election are discussed in the Tax Planning Considerations section of this chapter).

TRANSLATION OF THE FOREIGN TAX PAYMENTS. Determining the amount of the credit necessitates translating the tax payment made in a foreign currency into U.S. dollars. Cash-method taxpayers use the exchange rate on the payment date to do this. Accrual-method taxpayers use the exchange rate on the date the foreign tax accrues to calculate a tentative foreign tax credit amount. Generally, this is the last day of the tax year that is used for foreign tax purposes. If the exchange rate changes between the accrual date and the payment date, an accrual-method taxpayer must make an

---

[2] U.S. Possessions include, for Sec. 901 purposes, Puerto Rico, the Virgin Islands, Guam, the Northern Mariana Islands, and American Samoa.

[3] Reg. Sec. 1.901-2. See, for example, Rev. Rul. 91-45, 1991-2 C.B. 336, relating to the creditability of the Mexican asset tax and the Mexican income tax.

adjustment to the amount of the credit for the increase or decrease in the translated tax amount.[4]

EXAMPLE C16-1 ▶ U.S. citizen Bill is a resident of Country A during 1996. Country A permits its residents to make a single tax payment on the first day of the third month following the close of the taxpayer's tax year. Bill's tax year for both U.S. and Country A tax reporting is the calendar year. Bill remits a 60,000 pirog payment for 1996's Country A taxes on March 1, 1997. The exchange rate between the pirog and the U.S. dollar on December 31, 1996 is 1 pirog = $0.50 (U.S.). The exchange rate on the March 1, 1997 payment date is 1 pirog = $0.60 (U.S.). If Bill uses the cash method of accounting (and does not elect to accrue his foreign taxes), a $36,000 (60,000 pirogs × $0.60) foreign tax credit can be claimed. If Bill uses the accrual method of accounting, the year-end foreign tax credit amount is $30,000 (60,000 pirogs × $0.50). This tentative credit amount increases to $36,000 (60,000 pirogs × $0.60) because of the exchange rate change that takes place between the accrual and payment dates. ◀

ADDITIONAL COMMENT

The numerator of the limiting fraction is U.S. taxable income from foreign sources. The foreign taxes actually paid or accrued are computed using the tax laws of the foreign jurisdiction. Because these tax laws may differ significantly from the U.S. tax laws, determining whether the fraction is a limiting factor cannot necessarily be determined by simply comparing the stated tax rates of the two countries.

FOREIGN TAX CREDIT LIMITATION.

Calculation of the General Limitation. The foreign tax credit limitation was instituted to prevent the credit from being used to reduce taxes levied on income earned in the United States. This limit, which sets the maximum foreign tax credit as that portion of the gross U.S. tax liability originating from foreign source taxable income, is calculated as follows:

$$\begin{array}{c}\text{Overall foreign}\\ \text{tax credit}\\ \text{limitation}\end{array} = \begin{array}{c}\text{U.S. tax}\\ \text{liability}\end{array} \times \frac{\text{Taxable income from all foreign countries}}{\text{Total worldwide taxable income}}$$

The foreign tax credit equals the lesser of the creditable taxes paid or accrued to all foreign countries and U.S. possessions or the overall foreign tax credit limitation. The overall limitation permits taxpayers to offset "excess" foreign taxes paid in one country against "excess" limitation amounts that result from activities in other countries during the same tax year. The only caveat is that the total foreign taxes paid or accrued on foreign source taxable income may not exceed the total U.S. tax due on such income.[5]

EXAMPLE C16-2 ▶ U.S. citizen Theresa has $10,000 of taxable income (wages) from U.S. sources and $20,000 of taxable income (wages) from Country B in the current year. Theresa pays $6,400 of taxes to Country B in the current year. Assuming a 28% U.S. tax rate, Theresa's gross U.S. tax liability can be determined as follows:

Source of Income	*Taxable Income*	*U.S. Tax Liability*
United States	$10,000	$2,800
Country B	20,000	5,600
Total	$30,000	$8,400

Theresa's foreign tax credit limitation is determined as follows:

$$\$5,600 = \$8,400 \times \frac{\$20,000}{\$30,000}$$

SELF-STUDY QUESTION

Kathy Richards, a U.S. citizen, earns $100,000 in Country X, $200,000 in Country Z, and $200,000 in the United States. She pays $10,000 in taxes to X and $90,000 in taxes to Z. Assume a 36% U.S. tax rate. What is Richards's post-credit U.S. tax liability?

[4] Temp. Reg. Sec. 1.905-3T. If the taxpayer has filed his or her U.S. tax return by the date the foreign tax is paid, an amended U.S. tax return must be filed to report the increase or decrease in the credit amount.

[5] Sec. 904(a). An "excess" foreign tax amount is the excess of the foreign taxes paid or accrued over the foreign tax credit limitation. An "excess" limitation amount is the excess of the foreign tax credit limitation over the foreign taxes paid or accrued.

ANSWER

Pre-credit U.S. tax = $180,000 ($500,000 × 0.36). The credit is the lesser of the $100,000 ($10,000 + $90,000) of foreign taxes paid or the $108,000 ($180,000 × 300/500) foreign tax credit limitation. Note that although Richards pays taxes to Country Z at a much higher rate than the U.S. rate, all of the foreign taxes are creditable. All taxes are creditable because the limit is computed on an overall basis and the Country X tax rate is so low.

Without any limit on the foreign tax credit, Theresa could take a $6,400 credit for foreign taxes paid, which would reduce her tax on U.S. income to $2,000 ($8,400 − $6,400). The foreign tax credit limitation reduces the foreign tax credit to the amount of U.S. taxes owed on the Country B income, or $5,600. This limit ensures that $2,800 of U.S. taxes are paid on the U.S. income. The $800 ($6,400 − $5,600) excess credit amount can be carried back and over to other tax years. ◀

Determining the Income Amounts. The income amounts used in the credit limitation calculation are determined according to the source of income rules found in Secs. 861-865. These rules can be summarized as follows:

- Personal service income: Compensation for personal services is earned in the location where the personal services are performed.
- Sales of personal property (other than inventory property): Income from this category of property sales involving a U.S. resident is earned in the United States. Income from such sales earned by a nonresident is earned outside the United States.[6]
- Sales of inventory property: Income derived from inventory property that is purchased and sold is earned in the country where the sale occurs. Income from inventory property that is produced and sold is earned partially in the country where the production occurs and partially where the sale occurs.[7]
- Rents and royalties: Rental or royalty income is earned in the place where the tangible and intangible property is located or used. For intangible properties (e.g., patents, copyrights, and trademarks) this rule applies if the income is contingent on the productivity, use, or disposition of the intangible property.
- Sales of real property: Income derived from the sale of real property is earned in the country where the property is located.
- Interest: Interest income is generally earned in the obligor's country of residence. For this purpose, a U.S. resident includes U.S. citizens, resident aliens, domestic corporations, and foreign partnerships and foreign corporations that conduct a U.S. trade or business during the tax year.
- Dividends: Dividend income is generally earned in the distributing corporation's country of incorporation.

Deductions and losses are allocated to the foreign-source gross income according to the rules outlined in Treas. Reg. Sec. 1.861-8 and reduce foreign-source taxable income. For individual taxpayers, taxable income is computed for foreign tax credit limitation purposes without any reduction for personal exemptions. Itemized deductions are allocated between U.S.- and foreign-source income. In general, deductions follow the income associated with them. Deductions not associated with a specific type of income (such as charitable contributions and standard deductions) are allocated to all classes of gross income.

Foreign Tax Credit Carrybacks and Carryovers. Excess foreign tax credits can be carried back two years and forward five years to a tax year in which the taxpayer has an excess foreign tax credit limitation. The total of the foreign taxes paid or accrued in a tax year, plus any carryback or carryover of excess credits to the tax year, cannot exceed the

[6] Sec. 865(a). Income from sales of personal property (including inventory) by a nonresident that is attributable to an office or place of business located in the United States is earned in the United States. Section 865(g) defines the terms *resident* and *nonresident* for personal property sales. The definition used is generally based on the individual's domicile.

[7] Sec. 865(b) and Reg. Secs. 1.863-3(b) and (c). For tax purposes an inventory sale generally takes place in the location where the title passes from the buyer to the seller. The IRS may depart from this general rule where the sale is arranged in a particular manner for tax-avoidance purposes.

taxpayer's foreign tax credit limitation. When a taxpayer reports excess credits in more than one year, the excess credits are used in a first-in, first-out (FIFO) manner.[8]

EXAMPLE C16-3 ▶ U.S. citizen Kathy accrues $125,000 of creditable foreign taxes in 1997. Kathy's 1997 foreign tax credit limitation is $80,000. The $45,000 of 1997 excess credits can be carried back to 1995 and 1996 and forward to 1998 through the year 2002. The use of the credit carryback is illustrated below.

	1995	*1996*	*1997*
Foreign tax accrual	$80,000	$ 90,000	$125,000
Foreign tax credit limitation	85,000	100,000	80,000
Excess credits			45,000
Excess limitation	5,000	10,000	

The excess credits are first carried back to 1995 and then to 1996. Amended tax returns must be filed for both 1995 and 1996 to claim the $15,000 of credit carryback that can be used in those two years. The remaining $30,000 ($45,000 − $15,000) of excess credits can be carried forward and are lost if not used by the end of the year 2002. ◀

ADDITIONAL COMMENT

Since 1988, U.S. corporate tax rates tend to be lower than the tax rates of many foreign jurisdictions. This fact, coupled with the imposition of separate limitation baskets, has caused about 70% of all U.S. multinational corporations to remain in an excess foreign tax credit position.

Special Foreign Tax Credit Limitations. For some taxpayers, more than one foreign tax credit calculation is required. The Sec. 904 foreign tax credit limitation rules create ten baskets of income, for which separate foreign tax credit limitation calculations must be made.[9] The more common baskets include:

- Passive income: Income classified as foreign personal holding company income (see page C16-27). This basket generally includes dividends, interest, annuities, rents, and royalties.
- High withholding tax interest: Interest income that is subject to a withholding tax (or similar gross-basis tax) of a foreign country or U.S. possession where the tax rate is at least 5%.
- Financial services income: Income that is (1) derived from the active conduct of a banking, financing, or similar business, or the investment activities of an insurance company, or (2) derived from insurance under the Subpart F income (see page C16-27) rules.
- Foreign oil and gas income.
- Income other than the income included in the items listed above.

TYPICAL MISCONCEPTION

A separate limitation applies to the dividends received from each separate noncontrolled foreign corporation. This is explained on page C16-23.

Dividends, interest, rents, and royalties received by a U.S. taxpayer from a controlled foreign corporation (i.e., a majority-U.S.-owned foreign corporation) in which the U.S. taxpayer is a 10% or more shareholder are treated as income earned in the separate baskets on a look-through basis (i.e., as if the foreign corporation were a conduit entity).

For some taxpayers, their compensation or manufacturing income falls only into the "other income" category. These taxpayers must make only one foreign tax credit calculation. Other taxpayers may have to make only two or three foreign tax credit calculations. Many large multinational corporations, of course, must make every one of the calculations.

Excess foreign taxes paid or accrued in a particular foreign tax credit basket cannot be used to offset excess limitation amounts in another basket. Because the calculation of the foreign tax credit limitation is divided into separate pools, taxpayers are prevented

---

[8] Sec. 904(c).

[9] Sec. 904(d)(1). Other less-common baskets include foreign base company shipping income taxed under the Subpart F rules (see page C16-29), dividends from a Domestic International Sales Corporation (see page C16-36), taxable income attributable to a foreign sales corporation [FSC] (see page C16-34), and distributions from an FSC or former FSC.

Topic Review C16-1

Foreign Tax Credit

- Foreign income taxes paid or accrued to a foreign country or a U.S. possession are deducted or credited by U.S. taxpayers.
- The election to deduct or credit foreign taxes is made annually. Generally a taxpayer will elect to credit foreign taxes.
- Cash method of accounting taxpayers can elect to accrue their foreign taxes. This election generally accelerates by one year the time for claiming the credit and may reduce the need to carry back or carry over excess credits.
- A direct credit is available for foreign taxes paid or accrued by the taxpayer as well as for foreign taxes withheld by a foreign payer.
- Foreign taxes are translated at the exchange rate for the date on which they are accrued or paid depending on the taxpayer's accounting method.
- The foreign tax credit limitation prevents foreign taxes from offsetting the U.S. tax liability on U.S. source income. The foreign tax credit that can be claimed is the lesser of (a) the creditable taxes paid or accrued to all foreign countries and U.S. possessions, or (b) the overall foreign tax credit limitation. Excess credits can be carried back two years and forward five years. Several special foreign tax credit baskets apply to some taxpayers. Excess credits from one basket cannot be used against an excess limitation available in another basket.

from using excess credits arising from foreign taxes paid or accrued on income taxable at a high rate in a foreign country (e.g., salary or business profits) to offset U.S. taxes owed on income taxed at a low tax rate in a foreign country or not taxed at all (e.g., interest, dividends, or shipping income).

EXAMPLE C16-4 ▶

SELF-STUDY QUESTION

Do any limitations apply to the carryback or carryforward of excess foreign taxes?

ANSWER

Yes. The carryback and carryover provision is available only within the separate baskets. In Example C16-4, the $800 of excess foreign taxes can be offset only against an excess limitation in the ''other income'' basket for a carryback or carryover year.

Assume the same facts as in Example C16-2, except that Theresa also earns $15,000 of interest income in Country C that is not subject to local taxation. The additional U.S. tax liability resulting from this interest income is $4,200 ($15,000 × 0.28). Two foreign tax credit limitations must be calculated for Theresa:

Interest income $\quad \$4{,}200 = \$12{,}600 \times \dfrac{\$15{,}000}{\$45{,}000}$

Wages income $\quad \$5{,}600 = \$12{,}600 \times \dfrac{\$20{,}000}{\$45{,}000}$

Theresa can claim a $5,600 foreign tax credit—the lesser of the $5,600 foreign tax credit limitation and the $6,400 tax accrual—with respect to the Country B wages. No foreign tax credit can be claimed with respect to the Country C interest income because no foreign taxes were paid on this income. Even though the interest income is foreign-source income and the worldwide method of calculating the foreign tax credit limitation is used by the United States, the $800 of excess taxes paid with respect to the Country B wages cannot be used to offset the U.S. taxes owed on the Country C interest income. This inability to offset the two amounts occurs because the interest income is included in the passive income basket and the salary income is included in the ''other income'' basket. Theresa can carry the excess foreign taxes attributable to the ''other income'' basket back to the second preceding tax year. ◀

Topic Review C16-1 presents a summary of the foreign tax credit provisions.

OBJECTIVE 3

Calculate the earned income exclusion available to U.S. taxpayers employed abroad

REAL-WORLD EXAMPLE

In 1991, 221,000 U.S. taxpayers excluded $9.7 billion of foreign-earned income and $1.0 billion of housing cost exclusion. 44% of the exclusion originated in the United Kingdom, Japan, and Canada.

ADDITIONAL COMMENT

The foreign income exclusion is elective and is made by filing Form 2555 with the income tax return (or amended return) for the first taxable year for which the election is to be effective.

KEY POINT

Whether a U.S. citizen has established foreign residency is based on all the pertinent facts and circumstances. This is different from the determination of whether a foreign citizen has established U.S. residency. The latter is based on either the green card test or the substantial physical presence test (discussed later in this chapter).

FOREIGN-EARNED INCOME EXCLUSION

Special earned income exclusions exist for individuals working in foreign countries, Puerto Rico, and certain U.S. possessions. These exclusions are examined in the next two sections of this chapter.

U.S. CITIZENS AND RESIDENT ALIENS EMPLOYED ABROAD.

U.S. citizens and resident aliens employed abroad are taxed by the United States on their worldwide income. The individuals may incur additional costs when living abroad in order to maintain the same standard of living they had in the United States. In addition, overseas employment may involve inconveniences, substandard living conditions, and hazardous duty. These individuals are generally paid special allowances to compensate for the higher foreign living costs and the inconveniences encountered. These special allowances may be taxed by both the United States and the country of residence. The U.S. employer generally compensates U.S. employees for these additional tax costs so individuals do not bear any increased tax burden. All of these costs can make hiring a U.S. national more expensive than hiring a non-U.S. national who has the same skills.

To help U.S. firms compete abroad, the U.S. government established a policy of reducing the U.S. tax burden on U.S. citizens and resident aliens living abroad for an extended period of time. Taxpayers who are bona fide residents of a foreign country (or countries) for an entire tax year, or who are physically present in a foreign country (or countries) for 330 full days[10] out of a twelve-month period, can exclude $70,000 of foreign-earned income. This benefit, which is known as the *foreign-earned income exclusion,* is available to taxpayers who meet the bona fide resident test or the physical presence test.

BONA FIDE RESIDENT TEST.

A U.S. citizen (but not a resident alien) satisfies the bona fide resident test of Sec. 911(d)(1)(A) if that individual has been a resident of a foreign country (or countries) for an uninterrupted period that includes an entire tax year and has maintained a tax home in a foreign country (or countries) during the period of residence.

For Sec. 911 purposes, an individual's tax home is defined in the same way it is for determining the deductibility of travel expenses incurred while away from home.[11] In other words, an individual's tax home is his or her regular or principal place of business. Temporary absences from the foreign country for trips back to the United States or to other foreign countries normally do not interrupt an individual's foreign residency period.

An individual is not a bona fide resident of a foreign country if that person submits a statement to the taxing authorities of that country claiming to be a nonresident and receives a tax exemption for earned income from that country's taxing authorities based on being a nonresident.[12]

An individual does not qualify for the earned income exclusion until he or she has been a foreign resident for an *entire tax year.* At the end of that time, the individual can retroactively claim the Sec. 911 benefits from the date he or she became a foreign resident.

EXAMPLE C16-5 ▶ U.S. citizen Mark, who uses the calendar year as his tax year, is transferred by his employer to Country P. Mark becomes a Country P resident upon his arrival at noon on July 15, 1994. At that time Mark's tax home is established in P's capital city. Mark's residency in P is maintained until his return to the United States at 2 p.m. on January 10, 1998. Mark first qualifies for the

[10] A full day is a continuous twenty-four-hour period beginning with midnight and ending with the following midnight.

[11] Sec. 911(d)(3).

[12] Sec. 911(d)(5). The Sec. 911 residency test is different from the Sec. 7701(b) test which is used to determine whether an alien individual is a resident or nonresident alien of the United States and is described on page C16-14.

TYPICAL MISCONCEPTION

A day is not just any twenty-four-hour period. In order to count a day, the taxpayer must be in a foreign country for a period of twenty-four hours beginning and ending at midnight.

Sec. 911 benefits as a bona fide resident of a foreign country on December 31, 1995. This permits Mark to claim the earned income exclusion starting with July 15, 1994. Mark can continue to claim the exclusion through January 10, 1998. ◀

PHYSICAL PRESENCE TEST. A taxpayer who cannot satisfy the bona fide resident requirements can still qualify for the Sec. 911 benefits by satisfying the physical presence test of Sec. 911(d)(1)(B). To qualify, the taxpayer must meet two requirements:

- Be physically present in a foreign country (or countries) for at least 330 *full* days during a twelve-month period.
- Maintain a tax home in a foreign country (or countries) during the period of presence.

The 330 days do not need to be consecutive, nor does the taxpayer need to be in the same country at all times. The twelve-month period may begin on any day of the calendar year. The period ends on the day before the corresponding calendar day in the twelfth succeeding month.

SELF-STUDY QUESTION

During a twelve-month period, U.S. citizen Robert's work requires him to be physically present in a foreign country for 317 days. If Robert delays his return to the U.S. by vacationing overseas for thirteen more days, will he qualify for the foreign-earned income exclusion?

ANSWER

Yes. The foreign physical presence can be for any reason.

EXAMPLE C16-6 ▶

Assume the same facts as in Example C16-5. The 330 days of physical presence commence with the first full day Mark is present in Country P (July 16, 1994) and includes a total of 169 days through the end of 1994. The 161 additional days needed to reach 330 days include January 1, 1995 through June 10, 1995. One possible twelve-month period for Mark thus commences on July 16, 1994 and runs through July 15, 1995. An alternative twelve-month period could include June 11, 1994 through June 10, 1995, whereby the 330 days of physical presence are at the end of the time period. ◀

ADDITIONAL COMMENT

Note that in Example C16-6, Mark would prefer to use the twelve-month period of June 11, 1994 through June 10, 1995 when computing the exclusion for 1994 in order to have more days of the year in the qualifying period and, hence, a larger exclusion.

FOREIGN-EARNED INCOME DEFINED. Earned income means wages, salaries, professional fees, and other amounts received as compensation for personal services actually rendered.[13] Earned income is excludable only if it is foreign source income. The source of income rules described above are used to determine whether income is earned in the United States or a foreign country. In general, income is allocated to the location where the services are performed. If services are performed in more than one location during the tax year, allocation between the two or more locations is based on the number of days worked in each location.[14]

Fringe benefits that are excluded from gross income under a Code provision other than Sec. 911 (e.g., meals and lodging furnished for the convenience of the employer and excluded under Sec. 119) do not diminish the annual dollar ceiling for the exclusion. Items that generally are taxable to the recipient, but which are excluded from the definition of earned income for Sec. 911 purposes, include pensions and annuities, amounts paid by the United States or one of its agencies to an employee,[15] and amounts received more than one tax year after the tax year in which the services are performed.

AMOUNT OF THE EXCLUSION. The earned income exclusion is available only for the number of days in the tax year during which the taxpayer meets either the bona fide resident requirement or the physical presence requirement. Section 911(b)(2)(A) limits the earned income exclusion to the lesser of the following:

- The individual's foreign-earned income
- The amount of the daily exclusion times the number of days during the tax year that the individual qualifies for the exclusion

The annual and daily limits are $70,000 and $191.78 ($191.26 in leap years), respectively.

[13] Sec. 911(d)(2).

[14] Sec. 911(b)(1)(A).

[15] Civilian officers and employees of the U.S. government who are employed abroad can exclude from gross income certain foreign area allowances and cost-of-living allowances under Sec. 912. No further coverage of these rules is presented because of their limited applicability.

EXAMPLE C16-7 ▶ U.S. citizen Lee, who uses the calendar year as his tax year, establishes a tax home and residency in Country A on November 1, 1995 (the 305th day of the year). Lee maintains his tax home and residency there until March 31, 1997 (the 90th day), when Lee returns to the United States. Lee earns salary and allowances at a $15,000 monthly rate while employed abroad. Lee's available exclusion is determined as follows:

Taxable Year	*Foreign-Earned Income*	*Qualifying Days (1)*	*Daily Exclusion Amount (2)*	*Amount Excluded (3) = (1) × (2)*
1995	$ 30,000	61	191.78	$11,699
1996	180,000	366	191.26	70,000
1997	45,000	90	191.78	17,260 ◀

Individuals satisfying the residency requirement can claim the exclusion for each day they are a resident of the foreign country whether or not they are physically present in a foreign country on that day. Individuals satisfying the physical presence requirement can claim the exclusion for each day of a twelve-month period that falls within the tax year whether or not they are physically present in a foreign country on that day. Because an individual needs only to be physically present in a foreign country for 330 days out of the twelve-month period (365 days), it is possible that an individual might qualify for the exclusion for as many as 35 days before arrival in the foreign country, or for as many as 35 days after departure from the foreign country. Such an extension of the qualifying period in the year of arrival or departure may be a reason for calculating the exclusion using the physical presence requirement in these years.[16]

EXAMPLE C16-8 ▶ Assume the same facts as in Example C16-7, except that it is also known that Lee was physically present in Country A at all times from his arrival in 1995 to his departure in 1997. Lee's first 330 full days in Country A run from November 2, 1995 through September 27, 1996. Lee's last 330 full days in Country A run from May 6, 1996 through March 30, 1997. Lee's two corresponding twelve-month periods run from September 28, 1995 (the 271st day of 1995) through September 27, 1996, and from May 6, 1996 through May 5, 1997 (the 125th day of 1997). The amount of Lee's available exclusion is determined below:

Taxable Year	*Foreign-Earned Income*	*Qualifying Days (1)*	*Daily Exclusion Amount (2)*	*Amount Excluded (3) = (1) × (2)*
1995	$ 30,000	95[17]	$191.78	$18,219
1996	180,000	366	191.26	70,000
1997	45,000	125[18]	191.78	23,972

Lee obtains a larger exclusion in 1995 and 1997 under the physical presence test. The additional benefits of using this tax planning device are diminished to the extent that Lee is physically present in the United States during his period of foreign residence. ◀

KEY POINT

A taxpayer may elect to use or not use the foreign-earned income exclusion and the housing cost exclusion. Once an election to take an exclusion is made, it is effective for that year and all subsequent years.

HOUSING COST EXCLUSION OR DEDUCTION. Section 911 permits a taxpayer who is eligible for the foreign-earned income exclusion to exclude or deduct a **housing cost amount**, which is determined as follows:

$$\text{Housing cost amount} = \text{Housing expenses incurred} - \text{Base housing amount}$$

[16] Reg. Sec. 1.911-3(d).

[17] September 28, 1995 through December 31, 1995 is 95 days.

[18] January 1, 1997 through May 5, 1997 is 125 days.

$$\text{Base housing amount} = 0.16 \times \begin{array}{c}\text{Salary of a federal}\\ \text{employee compensated at}\\ \text{Step 1, GS-14 rate}\end{array} \times \frac{\text{Number of qualifying days in the tax year}}{\text{Number of days in the tax year}}$$

The annual rate of pay for an individual having the federal government Step 1, GS-14 pay classification is determined as of January 1 of the year in which the taxpayer's tax year begins. For 1995 and 1996 these amounts are $56,625 and $57,760, respectively. This makes the base housing amount equal to $9,060 for 1995 and $9,242 for 1996 for taxpayers qualifying for the Sec. 911 benefits for the entire tax year. The daily base housing amount is $24.82 in 1995 and $25.25 in 1996.

Housing expenses include any reasonable expenses paid or incurred for housing in a foreign country for the taxpayer, his or her spouse, and any dependents during the portion of the year that the taxpayer qualifies for the Sec. 911 benefits. Housing expenses also include expenses incurred for a second home if the taxpayer must maintain a separate home outside the United States for his or her spouse and dependents at a location other than their tax home because of adverse living conditions.[19]

ADDITIONAL COMMENT

Employer-provided amounts include all compensation provided by the employer (salary, bonus, allowances, etc.), not just the amount identified as the housing allowance.

The exclusion is limited to the lesser of the employer-provided amount or the individual's foreign-earned income. Any amount excluded as a housing cost amount reduces the taxpayer's foreign-earned income for purposes of computing the basic exclusion. Employer-provided amounts include any amounts that are foreign-earned income and included in the employee's gross income for the tax year (without regard to Sec. 911). Such amounts include, but are not limited to, salary or allowances paid by the employer (including allowances other than housing allowances), reimbursements made for housing, in-kind housing (other than that excluded under Sec. 119), and reimbursements made to third parties on behalf of the employee.

EXAMPLE C16-9 ▶

U.S. citizen John is a bona fide resident of Country M for all of 1996. John, who uses the calendar year as his tax year, receives $120,000 in salary and allowances from his employer. Included in this total is $15,000 in housing allowances. Eligible housing expenses incurred by John in 1996 are $18,000. John's housing cost amount is $8,758 ($18,000 − $9,242). Because John's employer-provided amount is $120,000, all of the housing cost amount can be excluded. In addition, John can exclude the lesser of his foreign-earned income exclusion ceiling ($70,000, because he qualified for all of 1996) or his foreign-earned income (after a reduction for the housing cost amount exclusion) [$111,242 = $120,000 − $8,758]. Therefore, his total exclusion is $78,758 ($8,758 + $70,000). Only $41,242 of John's total compensation is subject to U.S. taxation. ◀

KEY POINT

If an individual has only W-2 income (no self-employment income), he or she is eligible for only the housing cost exclusion because the entire housing cost amount is attributable to employer-provided amounts. The housing cost exclusion and deduction can both be taken only in situations where an individual has both W-2 income and self-employment income. Proration of the housing cost amount between a deduction and an exclusion is based on the relative amounts of the taxpayer's W-2 income and self-employment income.

Any portion of the housing cost amount that is not attributable to employer-provided amounts is a *for*-AGI deduction.[20] Thus, if an individual has only self-employment income, the entire housing cost amount is deducted. Such would be the case in Example C16-9 if John were self-employed and the $120,000 represented commission income. His $8,758 housing cost amount could only be claimed as a *for*-AGI deduction.

The housing cost deduction is limited to the taxpayer's foreign-earned income minus the sum of the foreign-earned income and housing cost amount exclusions. If the deduction for housing costs exceeds its limitation, the excess amount can be carried forward to the next year and deducted (subject to that year's limitation).

DISALLOWANCE OF DEDUCTIONS AND CREDITS. Section 911(d)(6) prohibits taxpayers from claiming deductions or credits with respect to their excluded income. The rules used to determine the nondeductible portion of an individual's employment-

[19] Sec. 911(c)(2).

[20] Sec. 911(c)(3)(A).

related expenses and the noncreditable portion of an individual's foreign taxes are presented below.

Employment-related Expenses. Any employment-related expenses that are allocated to a taxpayer's excluded foreign-earned income are nondeductible. Expenses that are related to other forms of income are deductible in full.[21] Although housing expenses are related to overseas employment, no restriction is placed on deducting the housing cost amount.

EXAMPLE C16-10 ▶ Don reports $150,000 of foreign-earned income and $15,000 of employment-related expenses in the current year that are subject to the 2% of AGI floor. Don also incurs $12,000 of other itemized deductions that are not directly related to foreign-earned income and that are not subject to the 2% of AGI floor. Don may exclude $70,000 of his foreign-earned income. The calculation below illustrates that the exclusion prevents Don from deducting $7,000 ($15,000 total expenses − $8,000 deductible expenses) of employment-related expenses. All $12,000 of the itemized deductions can be deducted.

$$\$8{,}000 \text{ (Deductible expenses)}^{a} = \$15{,}000 \text{ (Expenses directly attributable to foreign-earned income)} \times \left[1 - \frac{\$70{,}000 \text{ (Excluded foreign-earned income)}}{\$150{,}000 \text{ (Total foreign-earned income)}}\right]$$ ◀

[a] Subject to the 2% nondeductible floor.

The employment-related expenses are deductible only to the extent that they exceed 2% of Don's $80,000 AGI ($150,000 − $70,000). Don may deduct $6,400 [$8,000 − ($80,000 × 0.02)] of employment-related expenses plus the $12,000 of other itemized deductions not subject to the 2% floor.

Foreign Income Taxes. Foreign income taxes that are paid or accrued with respect to excluded foreign-earned income cannot be credited or deducted. The creditable foreign taxes are determined by using the following formula.[22]

$$\text{Creditable taxes} = \text{Foreign income taxes paid or accrued} \times \left[1 - \frac{\text{Excluded foreign-earned income (minus nondeductible foreign employment-related expenses)}}{\text{Total foreign-earned income (minus expenses related to foreign-earned income) subject to tax in the foreign country}}\right]$$

If a taxpayer's income taxes are paid or accrued on earned income and other income and the taxes owed on the two amounts cannot be separated, the denominator of the fraction must include the total of all income amounts subject to tax in the foreign country (minus all related expenses).

EXAMPLE C16-11 ▶ Assume the same facts as in Example C16-10, except that Don also incurs $33,750 of Country F income taxes on his earned income. Don's $18,000 of creditable foreign taxes are computed as follows:

$$\$18{,}000 = \$33{,}750 \times \left[1 - \frac{\$70{,}000 - \$7{,}000}{\$150{,}000 - \$15{,}000}\right]$$ ◀

[21] Sec. 911(d)(6) and Reg. Sec. 1.911-6(a). Miscellaneous itemized expenses are subject to the 2% nondeductible floor, whether the taxpayer is eligible for the Sec. 911 exclusion or not.

[22] Reg. Sec. 1.911-6(c).

Topic Review C16-2

Foreign-Earned Income and Housing Cost Amount Exclusions

1. U.S. citizens can qualify under the bona fide resident test; that is, they must have been a resident of a foreign country(ies) for an uninterrupted period including an entire tax year and have maintained a tax home in a foreign country(ies) during the residence period.
2. U.S. citizens and resident aliens can qualify under the physical presence test. They must (a) be physically present in a foreign country(ies) for at least 330 full days during a twelve-month period and (b) maintain a tax home in a foreign country(ies) during the period of presence.
3. The earned income exclusion equals the lesser of the taxpayer's foreign earned income or the $191.78 daily exclusion ($191.26 in leap years) times the number of days in the tax year that the taxpayer qualifies for the exclusion.
4. For the residence test, qualifying days includes the number of days during the tax year that the taxpayer met the residency and tax home tests. For the physical presence test, the taxpayer can claim the exclusion for the number of days in any twelve-month period(s) that fall within the tax year whether the taxpayer is physically present in the foreign country(ies) on that day or not.
5. Employees can exclude a housing cost amount in addition to the basic earned income exclusion. Self-employed individuals can deduct the housing cost amount. The housing cost amount equals the housing expenses incurred minus the base housing amount ($9,060 for 1995 and $9,242 for 1996) for the portion of the tax year for which the taxpayer qualifies for the earned income exclusion.
6. Taxpayers qualifying for the earned income exclusion are unable to claim deductions or credits with respect to their excluded income. A similar rule applies to the foreign tax credit.

Topic Review C16-2 presents a summary of the foreign-earned income and housing cost amount exclusions.

TAXATION OF NONRESIDENT ALIENS

Whether an alien individual is a U.S. resident or a nonresident determines the U.S. tax treatment of that person's income. Under Sec. 871, U.S. taxation of nonresident aliens is limited to their U.S.-source investment income and any U.S. income (and limited foreign income) that is effectively connected with the conduct of a U.S. trade or business.

OBJECTIVE 4

Determine whether a foreign individual is a resident or nonresident alien

DEFINITION OF NONRESIDENT ALIEN

With certain specific exceptions,[23] aliens who do not satisfy the Sec. 7701(b) definition of resident aliens below are considered nonresident aliens. Aliens are U.S. residents if they meet one of the following tests:

- *Lawful permanent resident test:* They are lawful permanent residents of the United States at any time during the tax year. An alien having a green card visa status for immigration purposes is considered a permanent resident.

[23] A nonresident alien can also become a resident alien by being married to a U.S. citizen or resident alien and electing to be treated as a resident alien under Sec. 6013(g). (See the Tax Planning Considerations section of this chapter.)

- *Substantial presence test:* They are present in the United States for 31 or more days during the current calendar year *and* present in the United States for a total of 183 or more days during the current tax year and the two preceding tax years when using a weighted-average calculation. The weighted average counts each day in the current year as 1, each day in the immediately preceding year as 1/3, and each day in the year before that as 1/6.

EXAMPLE C16-12

Marco, an alien individual, is present in the United States for 122 days in 1997 and 122 days each in 1995 and 1996. In determining his alien status, Marco counts all 122 days from 1997, one-third of the 122 days from 1996 (40.67 = 0.3333 × 122), and one-sixth of the 122 days from 1995 (20.33 = 0.1667 × 122), or a total 183 days (122 + 40.67 + 20.33). He satisfies both the 31-day and 183-day requirements.

KEY POINT

A citizen of another country generally is considered a U.S. resident if one of two tests are met: the green card test (the individual is granted legal permission to reside permanently in the U.S.) or a substantial presence test (the individual is present in the U.S. for at least (a) 31 days during the current year and (b) the sum of 183 days during the current tax year and the two preceding years (counting current-year days as 1, last-year days as 1/3, and the preceding-year days as 1/6).

Individuals who satisfy the physical presence test can be nonresident aliens if they establish that they have a nominal presence in the United States (i.e., physically present in the United States for less than 30 days in the current year even though the three-year total is 183 or more days) or a closer connection to a foreign country than to the United States. This requires that the individual be present in the United States for less than 183 days in the current year, maintain a tax home in a foreign country for all of the current year, and have a closer connection to the single foreign country in which the tax home is maintained than to the United States. A closer connection to the foreign country is achieved if the individual has maintained more significant contacts with the foreign country than with the United States.

Aliens typically maintain a dual status in their first and last years in which they maintain residency. This dual status means that their tax computation is based on nonresident alien status for part of the tax year and resident alien status for the remainder of the tax year. An individual who is in his or her first year and who satisfies the lawful permanent resident test (but not the substantial presence test) commences his or her residency period on the first day of the first year that he or she is physically present in the United States as a lawful permanent resident. An individual who satisfies the substantial presence test commencing with his or her first year in the United States becomes a resident on the first day of the first year that he or she is physically present in the United States.

Aliens terminate their residence on the last day of the last year that they are lawful permanent residents in the United States. Aliens who satisfy the physical presence test for a particular year maintain residency through the last day of such year that they were physically present in the United States (ignoring periods of nominal U.S. presence).

The United States amended its tax laws to reduce the incentive for U.S. citizens and long-term U.S. residents to give up their U.S. citizenship or residency. The U.S. government can impose expatriation taxes as part of the income, estate, and gift tax rules when a tax avoidance motive is established for the change in citizenship or residency. A basic presumption of tax avoidance has been added to the IRC, which references the individual's average taxes for the five-year period preceding the change, and the individual's net worth. The expatriation tax is based on an expanded U.S. source of income definition that applies to nonresident aliens who are subject to the additional income tax levy.[24] The estate and gift tax levies are modified to bring certain properties transferred within 10 years of the event triggering the loss of citizenship or residency back into the gift and estate tax returns.[25]

OBJECTIVE 5

Determine the U.S. tax liability for a nonresident alien

INVESTMENT INCOME

Passive or investment income is taxed to a nonresident alien only when it is U.S.-source income. Section 871(a)(1)(A) includes the following types of income in this classification:

[24] IRC, Sec. 877.

[25] IRC, Secs. 2107 and 2501.

TYPICAL MISCONCEPTION

Alien individuals who are U.S. residents are taxed on their worldwide income, just as U.S. citizens are. They file Form 1040. Nonresident aliens who are subject to U.S. taxation file Form 1040NR.

interest, dividends, rents, salaries,[26] premiums; annuities; compensation; and other fixed or determinable annual or periodical gains, profits, or income. Capital gains earned in the United States (other than in the conduct of a U.S. trade or business) are only taxed to nonresident aliens if they are physically present in the United States for at least 183 days during the tax year.[27] Some exceptions to this general rule reduce the nonresident alien's U.S. tax burden:

- Interest income earned by a nonresident alien from deposits maintained with a U.S. or foreign office of a U.S. bank or other financial institution is exempt from U.S. taxation provided it is not effectively connected with the alien's conduct of a U.S. trade or business.
- Portfolio interest (interest paid on registered and unregistered obligations issued by U.S. taxpayers and held by a nonresident alien as a portfolio investment) is exempt from U.S. taxation.[28]
- Income derived from the sale of personal property in the United States is not fixed or determinable annual or periodic income. As a result, casual sales of inventory that are not extensive enough to constitute a trade or business are not taxed in the United States.
- Gain from the sale of intangible assets (e.g., patents, copyrights, trademarks, etc.) is taxed as ordinary income to the extent that the payments are contingent on the productivity, use, or disposition of the intangible asset. Income that is not a contingent payment is a capital gain that is sourced inside the United States if it is sold by a U.S. resident and is sourced outside the United States if sold by a nonresident.

REAL-WORLD EXAMPLE

$77.5 billion of U.S. source income was paid to foreign people in 1992. Interest amounted to $49.1 billion; dividends were $13.7 billion. The effective U.S. withholding rate was 2.6%. 74% of the income went to foreign corporations, and 87% of the monies went to treaty countries. $60 billion was exempt from withholding while only $2.1 billion was taxed at a 30% rate.

EXAMPLE C16-13 ▶ Paula, a citizen and resident of Country A, licenses a patent to a U.S. corporation in return for a $2 fee for each unit produced in the United States. During the current year, Paula receives $18,000 from the U.S. corporation as a licensing fee. Paula is not physically present in the United States during the current year. The $18,000 is a contingent payment and is taxed as ordinary income. If a single $18,000 payment were instead received in exchange for all rights to the patent, a sale of the patent would be deemed to have occurred outside the United States and is therefore exempt from U.S. taxation. ◀

ADDITIONAL COMMENT

Many tax treaties reduce this flat 30% rate for specific types of income.

Ordinary investment income and capital gains earned by a nonresident alien are taxed at a 30% rate.[29] The rate is applied to the gross income amount. No deductions or losses can reduce the income that is taxed. Collection of the tax levy is accomplished by having the last U.S. payer withhold the tax levy from the amount paid to the alien. When the U.S. payer fails to withhold the proper amount of U.S. taxes, the payer becomes liable for the taxes if the alien does not pay them, as well as any penalties that are attributable to the failure to withhold.[30]

EXAMPLE C16-14 ▶ First State Bank issues the dividend checks for a domestic corporation. One of the corporation's shareholders is Kelly, a nonresident alien, who is to receive a $30,000 dividend. If the dividend is investment income to Kelly, First State Bank must withhold $9,000 ($30,000 × 0.30) in U.S. taxes from Kelly's payment. It must then remit these taxes to the U.S.

[26] Income earned from the performance of personal services is ordinarily trade or business income. Salary income is trade or business income even if the alien does not conduct a U.S. trade or business in the tax year in which the income is reported for tax purposes (e.g., no services are performed in the United States in the year in which a final paycheck is collected by a cash method of accounting taxpayer) if it is attributable to an earlier tax year and would have been treated as effectively connected with the conduct of a U.S. trade or business in that year.

[27] Sec. 871(a)(2). The capital gains can be reduced by U.S. capital losses, and only the net gain is taxed.

[28] Portfolio obligations might include, for example, obligations issued by a domestic corporation in the Eurobond market.

[29] Sec. 871(a). The 30% tax rate applies to capital gains of a nonresident alien only if they are present in the United States for at least 183 days during a tax year. In most cases such a time period means that the individual is not a nonresident alien at all, but a resident alien.

[30] Secs. 1441(a) and 1461.

government. Kelly need not make any other tax payments with respect to the dividend. The 30% rate that is applied to investment income is reduced by the terms of many tax treaties that the United States has entered into (see the discussion under Tax Planning Considerations section later in this chapter). ◀

TRADE OR BUSINESS INCOME

A nonresident alien who owns or operates a business in the United States involving the sale of services, products, merchandise, and so on is considered to be engaged in the conduct of a U.S. trade or business. A partner in a partnership or a beneficiary of a trust or estate is considered to be conducting a U.S. trade or business if the partnership, trust, or estate is engaged in the conduct of a U.S. trade or business.

Nonresident aliens who are in the United States for less than 90 days in a year; are employed by a nonresident alien, foreign partnership, or foreign corporation that does not engage in the conduct of a U.S. trade or business or by a foreign place of business maintained by a U.S. party; and do not earn more than $3,000 for their services are considered not to have engaged in the conduct of a U.S. trade or business. Their wages are exempt from U.S. taxation because such wages are classified as foreign source income.

Nonresident aliens who invest in stocks, securities, and so on through a broker are also considered not to have conducted a U.S. trade or business. As a result, their capital gains are exempt from U.S. taxation unless they are present in the United States for more than 183 days during the tax year.

SPECIAL ELECTION FOR REAL ESTATE INVESTORS. A special election is available for investors in U.S. real estate. This election permits an alien's real estate activities to be considered a trade or business even though they would not otherwise meet the trade or business requirements (e.g., a passive investment in real estate). This election permits the taxpayer to claim all deductions and losses associated with the activities. If the election is not made and the activity does not constitute a trade or business, the rental income is taxed at a 30% rate (without any reduction for deductions and losses).[31] Gains from the sale of U.S. real property interests (whether capital or ordinary in nature) are taxed as effectively connected with the conduct of a U.S. trade or business. A U.S. real property interest can be a direct or indirect (e.g., an investment in a corporation or a partnership) interest in real property that is located in the United States.[32]

PRACTICAL APPLICATION

Paula operates a U.S. business and qualifies as a nonresident alien. Paula invests the excess cash from the business in short-term securities. The investment income is effectively connected with the business under the asset-use test.

EFFECTIVELY CONNECTED TEST. Income is effectively connected with the conduct of a U.S. trade or business if either an asset-use or business-activities test is satisfied. The asset-use test is satisfied if an asset is held or used in the conduct of a U.S. trade or business. The income that is generated by the asset is thus effectively connected with the conduct of a U.S. trade or business. For example, interest income earned by an alien from a certificate of deposit (CD) can be either investment income or trade or business income depending on the relationship between the funds used to purchase the CD and the taxpayer's U.S. trade or business. The business-activities test is met if the activities of the U.S. trade or business are a material factor in the realization of the income. Capital gain income that is effectively connected with the conduct of a U.S. trade or business under either test is taxable without regard to the number of days that the individual is physically present in the United States.

Income from the sale of inventory and other personal property by a nonresident alien is U.S.-source and, therefore, taxable if the alien has a U.S. office and the sale is attributable to that office. This rule does not apply, however, and the income is exempt from U.S. taxation as foreign-source income, if the property is for foreign use or

[31] Sec. 871(d).

[32] Secs. 897(a) and (c).

disposition and if a non-U.S. office participated materially in the sale. When personal property is produced in the United States and then sold abroad by an alien, a portion of the income is allocated to the U.S. production and subject to U.S. taxation. The remainder is allocated to the location where the sale occurred and may or may not be taxed in the United States.

CALCULATING THE TAX. An alien who conducts a U.S. trade or business may have to make two separate tax calculations. Investment income that is unrelated to the U.S. trade or business activities is taxed at a 30% rate (unless the rate is reduced by a tax treaty). This tax is collected through the withholding process. Trade or business income is reduced by all related expenses and losses. Nonresident aliens cannot use the standard deduction otherwise available for individual taxpayers. They must itemize their deductions. In addition, nonresident aliens are generally limited to a single personal exemption.[33]

Regular individual tax rates apply to taxable income. The trade or business income for an unmarried nonresident alien is taxed using the tax rate schedules for a single taxpayer. A married nonresident alien uses the tax rate schedule for married individuals filing separately unless an election to file a joint return is made under Sec. 6013(g) (see the Tax Planning Considerations section of this chapter). The individual alternative minimum tax applies to nonresident aliens on their U.S. trade or business activities. The taxes that are owed on the trade or business income can be reduced by any available tax credits. The net U.S. tax liability is then paid through estimated tax payments or a remittance that is made when the return is filed.

EXAMPLE C16-15 ▶

Maria is single and a citizen and resident of Country D. In 1997 Maria reports $40,000 of dividend income from a U.S. corporation that is unrelated to Maria's U.S. trade or business and $1,000 of itemized deductions. Maria's U.S. trade or business reports $300,000 of gross income from sales activities, $20,000 of interest income, $225,000 of expenses, and $500 of tax credits. Maria's tax liability on her dividend income is $12,000 ($40,000 × 0.30) unless a tax treaty reduces the 30% rate. The taxes owed on Maria's trade or business income are determined as follows:

Gross income:	
Sales	$300,000
Interest	20,000
Total gross income	$320,000
Minus: Trade or business expenses	(225,000)
Adjusted gross income	$ 95,000
Minus: Personal exemption	(2,650)
Itemized deductions	(1,000)
Taxable income	$ 91,350
Gross tax liability (single rate schedule)	$ 23,321
Minus: Tax credits	(500)
Net tax liability	$ 22,821

Maria's total U.S. tax liability is $34,821 ($12,000 + $22,821). ◀

SELF-STUDY QUESTION

In Example C16-15, assume Maria also earned $10,000 of capital gain income on the sale of investment property she had owned in the United States. How would this change Maria's total U.S. tax liability?

ANSWER

Maria's U.S. tax liability would not increase unless it was connected with a U.S. trade or business, or it was investment gain and Maria was present in the U.S. for 183 days or more, and the gain was U.S. source income.

Topic Review C16-3 presents a summary of the tax rules applicable to nonresident alien individuals.

[33] Section 873(b) permits certain personal deductions not directly related to trade or business activities to reduce the trade or business income.

Topic Review C16-3

Taxation of Nonresident Aliens

1. Nonresident aliens are alien individuals who do not maintain U.S. residency. Resident alien status can be obtained by satisfying either the lawful permanent resident test or the substantial presence test.
2. Aliens generally maintain a dual status in their first and last years of U.S. residency. The alien is taxed as a resident alien for part of each year and as a nonresident alien for the remainder of the year. Two different tax computations are required in these years.
3. Passive or investment income (e.g., dividends, interest, etc.) is taxed to a nonresident alien only when it is U.S. source income. The income is taxed at a 30% rate with no deductions or exemptions permitted. A lower tax rate is permitted under many of the tax treaties involving the United States and a foreign country.
4. Capital gains earned in the United States (other than those related to the conduct of a U.S. trade or business) are taxed at the 30% rate only if the alien is physically present in the United States for 183 or more days during the tax year.
5. The U.S. income tax on the passive or investment income and capital gains is collected by means of withholding at the basic 30% tax rate or at the lower rate specified in a tax treaty. The U.S. tax liability is withheld by the U.S. payer who makes the income payment to the nonresident alien.
6. Ordinary income and capital gains earned by a nonresident alien are taxed in the United States if they are effectively connected with the conduct of a U.S. trade or business. Business expenses and losses are deductible against effectively connected income. Individuals claim a single personal exemption, and cannot claim a standard deduction. Regular individual rates apply to taxable income. The tax owed on the effectively connected income is paid by means of estimated tax payments.
7. A special election is available to nonresident aliens to file a joint return with their U.S.-citizen or resident-alien spouse. This election requires the nonresident alien to be subject to worldwide taxation as if a resident alien.

Taxation of U.S. People Doing Business Abroad

This section examines the tax laws that apply to U.S. people who engage in overseas business activities. These activities can involve the exportation of U.S.-produced products, the performance of services overseas, or even the establishment of manufacturing or selling activities in one or more foreign countries. These overseas activities receive a number of favorable tax breaks, including the following:

- Foreign subsidiary corporations (also known as controlled foreign corporations [CFCs]) are generally exempt from U.S. taxation unless they conduct a U.S. trade or business or make U.S. investments. This tax exemption extends to the foreign corporation's U.S. owners, who generally are not taxed on their share of the earnings until they are received as a dividend.
- Foreign sales corporations (FSCs) are partially exempt from the U.S. corporate income tax, and their shareholders can claim a dividends-received deduction that exempts part or all of their distributions from U.S. taxation.
- Domestic international sales corporations (DISCs) are exempt from the corporate income tax, and their shareholders are taxed on actual or deemed distributions of the

KEY POINT

Note that the first two activities (foreign subsidiary corporations and FSCs) are foreign corporations, while the last two activities (DISCs and possessions corporations) are U.S. (domestic) corporations.

DISC's taxable income. An interest charge is levied on the portion of the DISC's taxable income that is not actually or deemed distributed to its shareholders.

- Corporations that conducted a trade or business in Puerto Rico or a U.S. possession prior to January 1, 1996, can qualify for a special tax credit that can exempt part or all of their non-U.S. income from U.S. taxation. This credit is being phased-out for tax years 1996 through 2005. These complex phase-out rules are beyond the scope of an introductory text.

The remainder of this chapter looks at the ways in which overseas business activities can be conducted and the special tax privileges that apply to them.

DOMESTIC SUBSIDIARY CORPORATIONS

Domestic subsidiary corporations provide two nontax advantages for making sales to foreign purchasers. First, the foreign sales activities can be operationally separate from any domestic activities. Second, the subsidiary corporation's liabilities are separate from those of its parent corporation. Thus, the parent corporation's assets are protected from foreign creditors if there are large overseas losses.

Profits from the overseas sales activities are taxed when they are earned. Losses are deductible when they are incurred. Because the overseas sales activities are conducted by a domestic corporation, the foreign activities can be reported as part of a consolidated tax return including both the parent and its domestic subsidiary corporations. Thus, foreign losses can be used to reduce the tax liability on domestic profits and vice versa.

FOREIGN BRANCHES

A domestic corporation may elect to conduct its overseas sales or manufacturing activities through a foreign branch. A **foreign branch** is an office or other establishment (e.g., a manufacturing plant) of a domestic entity that operates in a foreign country. A branch is treated as an extension of the domestic corporation. Profits from the overseas activities are reported by the domestic corporation in the year they are earned. It does not matter whether they have been remitted to the United States. Foreign income taxes paid or accrued on these profits are creditable under the Sec. 901 direct credit rules described earlier.

Losses from overseas activities are reported in the year they are incurred. Losses can reduce the taxes due on domestic profits. The deductibility of these losses is a major advantage of using a foreign branch to establish the initial overseas activities. By using a branch activity, a domestic corporation can deduct start-up losses when they are incurred. Once the overseas activities become profitable, the domestic corporation can incorporate the foreign branch as a foreign corporation and defer any U.S. income taxes owed on the profits until they are remitted to the United States.

FOREIGN CORPORATIONS

There are four advantages to conducting overseas business activities through a foreign corporation:

- The foreign corporation's liabilities are separate from the assets of the parent corporation, thus limiting the domestic corporation's losses to its capital investment in the foreign corporation.
- The U.S. income tax levy on the domestic corporation's ratable share of the foreign corporation's earnings is postponed until the earnings are remitted to the United States.
- A domestic corporation receiving a dividend from a foreign corporation in which it has at least a 10% stock interest can claim a deemed paid tax credit for a ratable share of the foreign income taxes paid or accrued by the foreign corporation.

- A domestic corporation receiving a dividend from a foreign corporation in which it has at least a 10% stock interest can claim a dividends-received deduction with respect to the portion of the dividend paid from the corporation's undistributed profits that are effectively connected with the conduct of a U.S. trade or business. A dividends-received deduction is not available for dividends paid by a foreign corporation out of its earnings from a non-U.S. trade or business or its investments.

The last three of these advantages are explored below along with the tax treatment accorded the foreign corporation's U.S. activities.

ADDITIONAL COMMENT

This deferral privilege is eliminated for certain types of income of controlled foreign corporations. This is discussed later in the chapter.

DEFERRAL PRIVILEGE. For tax purposes, foreign corporations are considered separate entities from their shareholders. A tax exemption known as the **deferral privilege** is provided by the U.S. government for the foreign corporation's earnings. The corporation's earnings are taxed as dividend income when they are remitted to the United States.

EXAMPLE C16-16 ▶ Adobe Corporation, a U.S. corporation, owns all of the stock of Delta Corporation, a foreign corporation. In 1993, Delta Corporation reported $300,000 in after-tax profits. These profits were reinvested in active assets and are remitted to the United States as a dividend in 1997. No U.S. income taxes are due on Delta Corporation's profits until 1997. This result can be contrasted to a foreign branch activity, where the earnings would be taxed to Adobe Corporation in 1993. The value of the tax deferral equals the amount of U.S. taxes that are deferred times the time value of money for four years. ◀

Losses incurred by a foreign corporation cannot be deducted by any of its shareholders. Instead, the losses reduce profits reported by the foreign corporation in other years that can be distributed as dividend income to its shareholders.

EXAMPLE C16-17 ▶ Boston Corporation, a U.S. corporation, owns all of the stock of Gulf Corporation, a foreign corporation. In the current year, Gulf Corporation reports $125,000 in losses. None of Gulf Corporation's losses can be used to reduce Boston's current year taxable income. Instead, they can reduce profits earned in other years that are reported as dividends if distributed to Boston. Had the $125,000 of losses instead been reported by a foreign branch activity, Boston could have used the loss to offset the profits earned on its U.S. operations in the current year. ◀

FOREIGN TAX CREDIT. A U.S. corporation that uses a foreign branch to operate overseas and incurs a foreign tax liability can claim a direct foreign tax credit to offset the U.S. taxes that are due on its profits. If the U.S. corporation conducts its foreign operations indirectly through a foreign subsidiary corporation, the foreign subsidiary incurs the foreign tax liability and the U.S. corporation can only claim a direct foreign tax credit for the income taxes that are withheld from the foreign corporation's dividend remittances. Because most foreign countries impose higher income tax levies on a foreign corporation's profits than are withheld on its dividend remittances, the foreign tax credit rules could discourage the use of foreign subsidiary corporations by denying a tax credit for most of the foreign income taxes incurred. To remedy this inequity, Congress enacted the Sec. 902 **deemed paid foreign tax credit** for non-U.S. income taxes paid or accrued by a foreign corporation.

KEY POINT

The foreign corporation's earnings and profits must be calculated using U.S. tax concepts.

In order to claim a deemed paid foreign tax credit, corporations must meet two conditions:

- The foreign corporation must make a dividend payment to the domestic corporation out of its earnings and profits (E&P).

▶ The domestic corporation must own at least 10% of the foreign corporation's voting stock on the date of the distribution.[34]

OBJECTIVE 6

Calculate the deemed paid tax credit available for an investor in a foreign corporation

TYPICAL MISCONCEPTION

The deemed paid foreign tax credit is available from first-, second-, and third-tier foreign corporations (but not lower-tier corporations). The credit becomes available only as an *actual* dividend is paid from each subsidiary to its parent. The U.S. corporation actually takes the credit when the first-tier foreign corporation pays a dividend to the U.S. corporation.

Calculating the Deemed Paid Credit. The deemed paid credit for post-1986 tax years of a domestic corporate distributee is calculated using the following formula.[35]

$$\text{Deemed paid foreign tax credit} = \frac{\text{Dividend paid to domestic corporation out of post-1986 undistributed earnings}}{\text{Undistributed earnings accumulated in post-1986 tax years}} \times \text{Creditable taxes paid or accrued by the foreign corporation in post-1986 tax years}$$

The undistributed earnings amounts are based on the foreign corporation's E&P for its post-1986 tax years. The dividend definition used in calculating the numerator is the same one that is used for domestic corporations (see Chapter C4).

Both the deemed paid tax credit and the amount of the actual dividend paid to the domestic corporation are included in gross income.[36] Such a step prevents the domestic corporation from benefiting from both a tax deduction and a tax credit for the income taxes that are paid or accrued by the foreign corporation.

EXAMPLE C16-18 ▶

KEY POINT

The deemed paid foreign tax credit is available only to corporate U.S. shareholders. Individual U.S. shareholders are not eligible.

Coastal Corporation, a U.S. corporation, owns 40% of the stock of Bay Corporation, a foreign corporation. During the current year, Bay Corporation reports $200,000 of E&P, pays $50,000 in foreign income taxes, and remits $60,000 in dividends to Coastal Corporation. Foreign country M withholds $6,000 in foreign income taxes from the dividend payment. In prior post-1986 tax years, Bay Corporation reported $100,000 of E&P, paid $40,000 in foreign income taxes, and paid no dividends. Coastal's calculation for the deemed paid foreign tax credit for the current year dividend is as follows:

$$\$18{,}000 = \frac{\$60{,}000}{\$200{,}000 + \$100{,}000} \times (\$50{,}000 + \$40{,}000)$$

The $18,000 deemed paid credit is included in Coastal Corporation's gross income and enters into the calculation of its U.S. tax liability:

Dividend	$60,000
Plus: Deemed paid credit	18,000
Gross income	$78,000
Times: Corporate tax rate	× 0.34
Gross U.S. tax liability	$26,520
Minus: Deemed paid credit	(18,000)
Direct credit	(6,000)
Net U.S. tax liability	$ 2,520

◀

Translating the Dividend and Foreign Taxes into U.S. Dollars. Normally the foreign corporation's books and records are maintained in the local currency. To report the remittance to the U.S. taxing authorities, the dividend must be translated into U.S. dollars. If the distributee is a domestic corporation eligible for the deemed paid credit,

[34] Secs. 902(a) and 902(b)(1)–(3). The deemed paid credit benefits are also available for foreign taxes paid by subsidiary corporations of the foreign corporation.

[35] Sec. 902(a). Deemed paid foreign taxes are not deductible under Sec. 164.

[36] Sec. 78.

the foreign corporation's E&P and foreign taxes must also be translated into U.S. dollars. The current exchange rate for the date that the dividend distribution is taken into income is used to translate a dividend paid by a noncontrolled foreign corporation and the related E&P.[37] Translation of foreign taxes for purposes of the deemed paid credit takes place using the exchange rate in effect for the date the taxes are paid.[38]

EXAMPLE C16-19 ▶ Houston Corporation, a U.S. corporation, owns 40% of the stock of Far East Corporation, a foreign corporation that commenced operations in 1996. During 1997, Far East Corporation pays a 70,000 pira dividend to Houston Corporation. In 1996 and 1997, Far East earns a total of 400,000 pira in pretax profits. It pays 30,000 and 20,000 pira, respectively, in home country taxes in 1996 and 1997. The exchange rate between the pira and the dollar is 1 pira = $0.22 (U.S.) on the dividend payment date. The 1996 and 1997 foreign taxes were paid when the exchange rates were 1 pira = $0.20 (U.S.) and 1 pira = $0.25 (U.S.), respectively. Far East's E&P is 350,000 (400,000 − 50,000) pira. The translated dividend amount is 70,000 pira × $0.22 = $15,400. The translated foreign taxes amount is $11,000 [(30,000 pira × $0.20) + (20,000 pira × $0.25)]. The translated foreign taxes amount attributable to the dividend is $2,200 [$11,000 × (70,000 pira ÷ 350,000 pira)]. ◀

MULTIPLE FOREIGN TAX CREDIT BASKETS. A separate foreign tax credit limitation is required for noncontrolled foreign corporation (Sec. 902) dividends received by a corporate shareholder owning at least 10% of the foreign corporation's stock. Coastal must calculate a separate foreign tax credit limitation for the dividends received from Bay Corporation in Example C16-18 and each other noncontrolled (Sec. 902) foreign corporation. The separate foreign tax credit basket prevents cross-crediting of foreign taxes from occurring between the dividends received from two or more noncontrolled foreign corporations.

TAXATION OF A FOREIGN CORPORATION'S U.S. ACTIVITIES

Regular and Alternative Minimum Taxes. A foreign corporation that earns investment income in the United States or conducts a U.S. trade or business is taxed by the U.S. government. In general the rules governing U.S. taxation of a foreign corporation's income parallel those for nonresident aliens described earlier.

Section 881(a) taxes the U.S.-source investment income of a foreign corporation at a 30% rate. Capital gains that are not effectively connected with the conduct of a U.S. trade or business are exempt from taxation. The U.S. taxes on the investment income are collected through the withholding process.[39]

Section 882(a) taxes the portion of the foreign corporation's income that is effectively connected with the conduct of a U.S. trade or business. The 15% to 39% corporate tax rates and the 20% corporate alternative minimum tax rate are used to determine the corporate tax liability. The earnings from the conduct of a U.S. trade or business are not taxed to the foreign corporation's U.S. shareholders until they are distributed.

ADDITIONAL COMMENT

Dividends received from a foreign corporation that come from E&P created in a U.S. trade or business are eligible for a dividends-received deduction.

Section 245(a) permits a domestic corporation receiving a dividend from a foreign corporation in which it has at least a 10% stock interest to claim a 70%, 80%, or 100% dividends-received deduction with respect to the portion of the dividend made from the corporation's undistributed profits that are effectively connected with the conduct of a U.S. trade or business. This deduction is available because these earnings were already subject to the U.S. corporate income tax.

Branch Profits Tax. Foreign corporations that conduct their U.S. activities by using a U.S. subsidiary corporation are subject to a second level of taxation when the

---

[37] Reg. Secs. 1.301-1(b) and 1.902-1(g) and *The Bon Ami Co.*, 39 B.T.A. 825 (1939).

[38] Sec. 986(b).

[39] Sec. 1442.

ADDITIONAL COMMENT

The objective of the branch profits tax is to afford comparable treatment to income earned by a U.S. corporation controlled by a foreign corporation and to income earned by other U.S. operations controlled by a foreign corporation.

subsidiary corporation's profits are distributed in the form of a dividend. This additional levy is in the form of a withholding tax at a 30% rate or at a lower rate that is specified in a tax treaty. U.S. branches of foreign corporations are subject to a second tax levy, the **branch profits tax,** that is similar to the withholding described for distributions made by a U.S. subsidiary of a foreign corporation.[40] U.S. branches are taxed on their dividend equivalent amount and their allocable interest under the branch profits tax rules.

The dividend equivalent portion of the tax equals 30% (or a lower rate specified in a tax treaty) times the dividend equivalent amount. The dividend equivalent amount equals the foreign corporation's E&P for the tax year that are effectively connected with the conduct of its U.S. trade or business increased by the decrease (or decreased by the increase) in the foreign corporation's net equity in its branch assets during the year. Thus, the branch profits tax base is increased by earnings remitted to the foreign corporation during the year that reduce the branch's U.S. trade or business assets and is decreased by earnings that are reinvested in the branch's U.S. trade or business assets during the year. The allocable interest portion of the branch profits tax provides that certain interest paid by the U.S. branch is taxed as if it were paid by a U.S. corporation. Hence, the interest is U.S. source income and subject to a 30% U.S. withholding tax (or a lower rate specified in a tax treaty).

CONTROLLED FOREIGN CORPORATIONS

REAL-WORLD EXAMPLE

The 7,500 largest CFCs (in total assets) controlled by U.S. multinational corporations had $1.22 trillion in assets and $970 billion in receipts in 1992. These CFCs paid $41.4 billion in dividends to their U.S. parent corporations, who reported $13.2 billion of Subpart F income.

BEFORE THE SUBPART F RULES. Before the enactment of the controlled foreign corporation (CFC) provisions (known as the Subpart F rules) in 1962, U.S. corporations used foreign subsidiaries located in "tax-haven" nations to minimize their tax liability on overseas operations. The usual scenario worked this way:

1. A U.S. manufacturing corporation formed a sales subsidiary in a foreign country that either imposed no corporate income tax or had a low corporate tax rate.
2. The goods were shipped directly by the U.S. corporation that had produced them to the foreign purchasers.
3. The tax haven sales subsidiary was billed for the goods by the U.S. corporation.
4. The tax haven sales subsidiary, in turn, billed the foreign purchasers at a higher price.
5. The tax haven sales subsidiary's profits largely escaped U.S. and local taxation.

A similar scenario could be used for services performed by a U.S. firm for foreign clients.

EXAMPLE C16-20 ▶

Under pre-CFC rules, Chicago Corporation, a U.S. corporation, forms a foreign branch to handle its overseas widget sales. The foreign country in which the branch operates imposes no branch income taxes. Assume that Chicago's overseas widget sales annually result in a $1,000,000 profit. Chicago will pay a $340,000 ($1,000,000 × 0.34) U.S. tax liability and no foreign income taxes in the year the income is earned. The branch rules are a benchmark against which the benefits of the deferral privilege can be illustrated. If the same profit is instead divided equally between Chicago and Island Corporations, their worldwide tax cost is reduced substantially if the foreign government does not impose a corporate income tax. Chicago's $500,000 share of the profit results in a $170,000 ($500,000 × 0.34) U.S. tax liability. Island Corporation owes no U.S. or local income tax liability on its $500,000 share of the profit. Chicago owes no U.S. taxes on Island's share of the profits since they have not been remitted to the United States as a dividend. Figure C16-1 illustrates this. An attempt by Chicago to maximize its tax deferral by selling its widgets to Island at its cost would probably be challenged by the IRS under Sec. 482 (see page C16-31). These rules would limit Island's profit to the portion of the $1,000,000 total profit that it had earned based on the services it had

[40] Sec. 884(a).

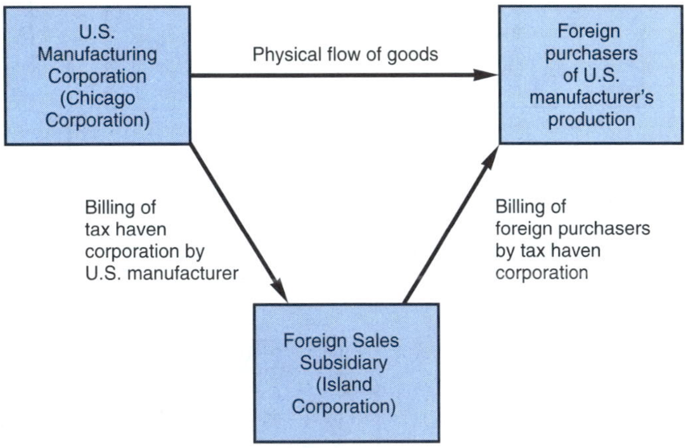

Sale by foreign branch:
$1,000,000 profit x 0.34 = $340,000 U.S. tax liability for Chicago. No foreign taxes.

Indirect sale by Chicago and Island with profit divided equally and no Subpart F rules:
Chicago: $500,000 profit x 0.34 = $170,000 U.S. tax liability.
Island: $500,000 profit x 0 = 0 Local country tax liability (and no U.S. tax liability for Chicago until profit is remitted to the U.S.)

Indirect sale by Chicago and Island with profit divided equally and Subpart F rules:
Chicago: $500,000 profit on sales to Island x 0.34 = $170,000 U.S. tax liability.
$500,000 constructive distribution x 0.34 = $170,000 U.S. tax liability.
No U.S. tax liability when Island's profits are remitted to the U.S.
Island: $500,000 profit x 0 = $-0- Local country tax liability and no U.S. tax liability.

FIGURE C16-1 ▶ ILLUSTRATION OF USE OF TAX-HAVEN SALES SUBSIDIARY (EXAMPLE C16-20)

provided. This amount may be less than the amount allocated under the 50–50 split currently used. ◀

UNDER THE SUBPART F RULES. The Subpart F rules short-circuit this scenario by accelerating U.S. taxation of certain forms of tainted income (see Figure C16-2 for a summary of the Subpart F tainted income categories).

EXAMPLE C16-21 ▶ Assume the same facts as in Example C16-20, except that Island Corporation is a CFC. Under the U.S. tax laws, Island's profit on sales of widgets to both related and unrelated parties located outside of Island's country of incorporation is considered tainted or Subpart F income. It is constructively distributed to Chicago Corporation on the last day of Island Corporation's tax year. Only the portion of Island Corporation's profits attributable to widget sales in Island's country of incorporation is exempt from current U.S. taxation. If all of Island Corporation's sales are made outside its country of incorporation, its $500,000 of profits would be taxed to Chicago Corporation under the Subpart F rules. This result is basically the same as if a foreign branch had been used to accomplish the sales. ◀

KEY POINT

The tainted income is taxable to Chicago (the CFC's U.S. parent) as a deemed dividend, rather than being taxed directly to the CFC.

Because of the increased tax cost incurred when the Subpart F rules are triggered, one of the major tax planning objectives of U.S. investors is structuring overseas activities to avoid CFC status, or structuring the transaction to avoid reporting tainted Subpart F income.

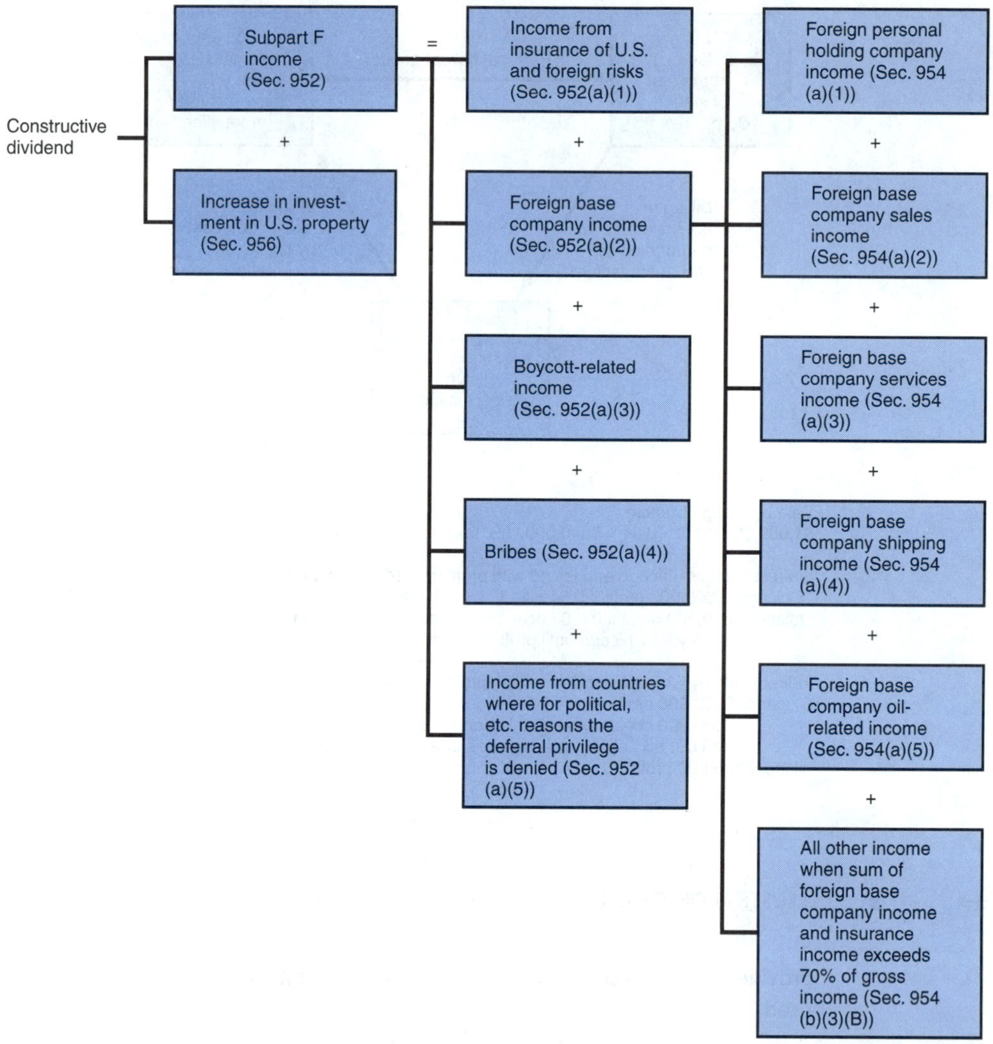

FIGURE C16-2 ▶ AMOUNT OF INCOME OF CONTROLLED FOREIGN CORPORATION CONSTRUCTIVELY INCLUDED IN GROSS INCOME OF U.S. SHAREHOLDERS

OBJECTIVE 7

Determine whether a foreign corporation is a controlled foreign corporation

CFC DEFINED. A **CFC** is a foreign corporation having more than 50% of its voting stock or more than 50% of the value of its outstanding stock owned by U.S. shareholders on any day of the foreign corporation's tax year.[41] A **U.S. shareholder** is a U.S. person who owns at least 10% of the foreign corporation's voting stock.[42] An individual is treated as owning all of the stock that he or she owns directly, indirectly, or constructively. Constructive ownership is determined by applying the stock attribution rules of Sec. 318 (see Chapter C4) with some technical modifications that are found in Sec. 958(b).

[41] Sec. 957(a). A CFC must adopt the same tax year as their majority U.S. shareholder if on the first day of the CFC's tax year (or other days as prescribed by the IRS) 50% or more of the voting power or value of all classes of the CFC's stock is directly, indirectly, or constructively owned by a single U.S. shareholder.

[42] Sec. 951(b). A U.S. person includes individual citizens or resident aliens of the United States, a domestic corporation, a domestic partnership, or a domestic trust or estate.

EXAMPLE C16-22 ▶ Europa Corporation, a foreign corporation, is owned by five unrelated individuals. Al, Bill, and Connie are U.S. citizens who own 24%, 20%, and 9%, respectively, of Europa Corporation's single class of stock. Duane and Elaine are nonresident aliens who own 40% and 7%, respectively, of Europa's stock. Only Al and Bill are considered U.S. shareholders because they are the only U.S. people who own at least 10% of Europa's stock. Europa Corporation is not a CFC because Al and Bill together own only 44% of its stock. If Al were instead Connie's father, Connie would now be a U.S. shareholder because she would own 33% (9% directly + 24% constructively from Al) of Europa's stock after applying the family attribution rules. Europa then is a CFC because its three U.S. shareholders own in total 53% (24% + 20% + 9%) of its stock. Double-counting of Al's 24% interest for both Al and Connie is not permitted. ◀

OBJECTIVE 8

Explain the special tax provisions applying to a controlled foreign corporation

KEY POINT

One of the purposes of enacting Subpart F was to prevent the use of holding companies created in tax-haven nations to shelter foreign profits from U.S. taxation. Thus, Subpart F income is taxed to the U.S. shareholder as a constructive distribution in the year the income is earned.

TYPICAL MISCONCEPTION

This election to be taxed as a domestic corporation allows an individual to take the deemed paid foreign tax credit. However, the election is seldom made because the income is taxed again when it is actually distributed rather than being distributed tax-free.

CONSTRUCTIVE DISTRIBUTIONS OF SUBPART F INCOME. U.S. shareholders must report their ratable shares of the CFC's Subpart F income each year. A U.S. shareholder is taxed on the Subpart F income items only when the foreign corporation is a CFC for at least thirty days during its tax year. If this requirement is met, each U.S. shareholder's ratable share of the Subpart F income items must be reported as a deemed dividend that is distributed on either the last day of the CFC's tax year or the last day on which CFC status is retained.[43]

The constructive distribution is included in the U.S. shareholder's gross income and increases the shareholder's basis in the CFC stock. If the U.S. shareholder is a domestic corporation, a deemed paid foreign tax credit is available under Sec. 960 for a ratable share of the CFC's foreign income taxes. An individual shareholder may elect under Sec. 962 to have the constructive distribution taxed as if he or she were a domestic corporation, or be taxed as an individual taxpayer.

Subpart F income includes five categories of income: income from the insurance of U.S. and foreign risks that originate outside the country of organization, foreign base company income, boycott-related income, income equal to the amount of any bribes or other illegal payments paid by or on behalf of the CFC, and income from countries where for political or other reasons the deferral privilege is denied. These items are discussed below.

Insurance of U.S. and Foreign Risks. Income derived by the CFC from the insurance of certain U.S. and foreign risks is Subpart F income. Included in this category are premiums for property insurance on property located in, a liability arising out of an activity in, or in connection with the lives or health of residents of a country other than the one in which the CFC is organized. Such premiums must be of a type that would be taxed by the United States if they were instead earned by a domestic (U.S.) insurance company.

Foreign Base Company Income. This income category is the largest of the Subpart F income categories. It is composed of the following five subcategories of income.

1. *Foreign personal holding company income* (FPHCI) includes passive income such as dividends, interest, royalties, annuities, rents, and gains from the sale of a property producing one of these passive income forms; gain from the sale of a property that does not produce income; gain from commodities transactions; and foreign exchange gains. It excludes rents and royalties received from a related corporation for the use of property within the CFC's country of incorporation, or an unrelated person if such payments are connected with the CFC's active conduct of a trade or business. Dividends and interest are not FPHCI if received from a related corporation created or

[43] Sec. 951(a).

organized in the CFC's country of incorporation having a substantial part of its assets involved in a trade or business in that country.[44]

EXAMPLE C16-23 ▶

Time Corporation is a CFC incorporated in Country X. Time receives interest and dividends from its two foreign subsidiary corporations, East Corporation and West Corporation. East is incorporated in Country V and conducts all of its activities in that country. West is incorporated in Country X and conducts all of its activities in that country. Only the interest and dividend payments received from East represent FPHCI. East Corporation's interest and dividends are FPHCI since it is not incorporated in Country X. West Corporation's interest and dividends are not FPHCI since it is incorporated in Country X and conducts all of its activities in that country. ◀

KEY POINT

The goods must be both manufactured and sold for use outside the CFC's country of incorporation. If the goods are manufactured or sold in the CFC's country of incorporation, the assumption is that a good business reason exists for having set up the CFC in that country. Thus, the CFC has no foreign base company sales income.

2. *Foreign base company sales income* includes any fees and profits earned from the sale, or purchase and sale, of personal property when a related party is involved in the transaction *and* the property is manufactured and sold outside the CFC's country of incorporation. The related party transactions that result in foreign base company sales income are[45]

- The purchase of personal property from a related person and its sale to any person
- The sale of personal property to any person on behalf of a related person (e.g., commission income)
- The purchase of personal property from any person and its sale to a related person
- The purchase of personal property from any person on behalf of a related person

Foreign base company sales income excludes the profit earned when the product is manufactured in the CFC's country of incorporation, sold for use in the CFC's country of incorporation, or manufactured by the CFC itself in its country of incorporation.[46]

EXAMPLE C16-24 ▶

Dublin Corporation is a CFC incorporated in Country F that purchases machine tools from its U.S. parent corporation for sale to unrelated parties. Dublin sells 70% of the tools in Country E and 30% in Country F. Only the profit earned from the tools sold in Country E constitutes foreign base company sales income. If Dublin Corporation manufactured the machine tools itself in Country F, none of its profit from the Country E or Country F sales would be foreign base company sales income. ◀

ADDITIONAL COMMENT

Goods are deemed to have been manufactured by the CFC if it substantially transforms the product (such as making screws and bolts from steel rods) or if its direct labor and factory overhead account for 20% or more of the total cost of goods sold.

3. *Foreign base company services income* includes compensation earned from performing service activities for or on behalf of a related person outside of the country in which the CFC is created or organized. In general, compensation for personal services is earned at the location where the services are performed.[47]

EXAMPLE C16-25 ▶

Andes Corporation, incorporated in Country A, is 100% owned by Hi-Tech Corporation, a U.S. corporation. Hi-Tech sells industrial machines to Amazon Corporation, an unrelated user, for use in Country B. The portion of the sales contract covering installation and maintenance of the machines is assigned by Hi-Tech to Andes. Andes is to be paid for these services by Hi-Tech. The installation and maintenance performed by Andes is foreign base company services income because it is performed for a related party (Hi-Tech) outside of its country of incorporation (Country A). ◀

---

[44] Sec. 954(c). Section 954(d)(3) defines a related person for Subpart F purposes as (a) any individual, corporation, partnership, trust, or estate that controls, or is controlled by, the CFC, or (b) any corporation, partnership, trust, or estate controlled by the same people who control the CFC. Control is defined as direct, indirect, or constructive ownership of 50% or more of the total voting power or total value of the CFC's stock.

[45] Sec. 954(d)(1).

[46] Sec. 954(d).

[47] Sec. 954(e).

4. *Foreign base company shipping income* includes compensation earned from the use of any aircraft or vessel in foreign commerce and the hiring or leasing of such a vessel for use in foreign commerce by another person.[48] Foreign base company shipping income excludes income earned from the use of an aircraft or vessel in commerce between two points within the foreign country in which the CFC is created or organized and in which the aircraft or vessel is registered.

5. *Foreign base company oil-related income* includes amounts earned from oil- and gas-related activities (other than any activities involving the extraction of oil and gas) located in a foreign country. Activities producing this type of income include the transportation, shipping, processing, and distribution of oil and gas and any related service activities. These types of income are not taxed under Subpart F if they are earned in the foreign country in which the oil and gas were extracted.[49]

Exceptions to the definition of foreign base company income or insurance income reduce the burden of Subpart F. Subpart F income excludes

- Income earned by the CFC in its conduct of a U.S. trade or business that is taxed by the United States[50]
- Foreign base company income or insurance income that is subject to an effective foreign tax rate that is greater than 90% of the maximum U.S. corporate tax rate specified in IRC Sec. 11[51]
- Foreign base company income and insurance income that in total is less than the smaller of 5% of the CFC's gross income or $1 million[52]
- Income earned by the CFC that cannot be repatriated to the United States because of currency or other restrictions[53]

When foreign base company income and insurance income exceed 70% of the CFC's gross income, all of the CFC's gross income is foreign base company income or insurance income as appropriate.[54]

The Subpart F income is reduced by any related deductions. Allocation of the deductions to the Subpart F income takes place using the rules found in Reg. Sec. 1.861-8.[55] These regulations are beyond the scope of this chapter.

KEY POINT

A *de minimis* rule provides that if the sum of the foreign base company income and insurance income is less than the smaller of 5% of the CFC's gross income or $1 million, none of its gross income is foreign base company income for the tax year. This *de minimis* rule does not apply to any other Subpart F income.

Boycott-related Income. This category includes any income derived by the CFC from the participation in, or cooperation with, an international boycott against a particular nation (or group of nations). The portion of the CFC's profits that are boycott-related is determined by a rather detailed set of rules found in IRC Sec. 999, which are beyond the scope of this chapter.

ADDITIONAL COMMENT

Countries that participate in, or cooperate with, international boycotts include Iraq, Kuwait, Lebanon, Libya, Oman, Qatar, Saudi Arabia, Syria, United Arab Emirates, and Yemen.

Bribes, Kickbacks, and Other Illegal Payments. Payments made by or for the CFC of bribes, kickbacks, and other illegal payments result in a loss of the CFC's deferral privilege for a portion of the CFC's earnings equal to the sum of all such payments.

Earnings Derived in Certain Foreign Countries. For political reasons certain tax benefits are denied to taxpayers doing business in a selected group of countries. U.S. shareholders of a CFC are denied the deferral privilege on earnings derived in these countries. These countries include those the U.S. government does not recognize, those with whom the U.S. government has severed diplomatic relations, those with whom the U.S. government

ADDITIONAL COMMENT

Income derived from the following countries is not eligible for the deferral privilege: Cuba, Iran, Iraq, Libya, North Korea, Sudan, and Syria.

[48] Secs. 951(a)(1)(A)(iii) and 954(f).
[49] Sec. 954(h).
[50] Sec. 952(b).
[51] Sec. 954(b)(4).
[52] Sec. 954(b)(3)(A).
[53] Sec. 964(b).
[54] Sec. 954(b)(3)(B).
[55] Sec. 954(b)(5).

has not severed diplomatic relations but does not conduct such relations, and those the U.S. government believes support international terrorism.

INVESTMENTS IN U.S. PROPERTY. Special rules were enacted to prevent CFCs from avoiding U.S. taxation and the foreign income tax withholding rules by either investing funds directly in assets located in the United States or making loans to a U.S. shareholder instead of paying dividends. Under these rules, each U.S. shareholder receives a constructive distribution of the lesser of the U.S. shareholder's share of the average amount of U.S. property held at the close of each quarter over E&P previously taxed under IRC Sec. 956 or the shareholder's ratable share of the CFC's earnings for the year.[56] Earnings that have been taxed as Subpart F income may be invested in U.S. property without incurring any additional tax liability. Such amounts, if distributed, would not constitute a dividend.

ADDITIONAL COMMENT

If the CFC guarantees an obligation of a U.S. person, it is deemed to hold that obligation. Thus, if a CFC guarantees a loan of its U.S. parent, the guarantee constitutes the acquisition of U.S. property. This can be a tax trap for the unwary.

The U.S. property investment is an average measured on the last day of each quarter of the CFC's tax year and includes only the property's adjusted basis (minus any liability to which it is subject). U.S. property includes any tangible property located in the United States, stock of domestic corporations, obligations of U.S. people or any patents, copyrights, and so on that are developed by the CFC for use in the United States.[57] Exceptions to the U.S. property definition include U.S. government obligations, U.S. bank deposits, stock of domestic corporations that are not a U.S. shareholder of the CFC or more than 25% owned by one of the CFC's U.S. shareholders, and U.S. property acquired before the first day on which CFC status is retained or after the last day on which CFC status is retained.

EXAMPLE C16-26 ▶

Forco, a foreign corporation, is a CFC that is in its initial year of operation. Forco reports $1,000,000 of earnings during the current year, none of which is taxed as Subpart F income. On December 31, Forco has an aggregate U.S. property investment of $400,000. By making this investment, Forco loses its tax deferral for these earnings and causes the $400,000 to be taxed ratably to its U.S. shareholders. ◀

SELF-STUDY QUESTION

If $500,000 of the $1,000,000 in Example C16-26 had been Subpart F income (and thus currently taxed to the CFC's U.S. shareholders), would the acquisition of the U.S. property also be taxed currently?

ANSWER

The E&P invested in U.S. property comes first out of the E&P that has previously been taxed. Therefore, no additional tax levy would be incurred as a result of the investment.

DISTRIBUTIONS FROM A CFC. Distributions made by a CFC are deemed to be paid first from its earnings invested in U.S. property, and its most recently accumulated Subpart F income. Distributions of any tax-deferred earnings are not deemed to have been made until after these two forms of previously taxed income have been distributed. Distributions of previously taxed income (i.e., earnings invested in U.S. property, and Subpart F income) are tax-free to the U.S. shareholder and reduce the basis of his or her CFC stock investment.[58]

EXAMPLE C16-27 ▶

Bulldog Corporation, a domestic corporation, owns all of the stock of Marine Corporation, a CFC. Bulldog's cost basis for the Marine stock is $600,000. Marine reports $400,000 of E&P since Bulldog made its investment, of which $175,000 is taxed to Bulldog under the Subpart F rules. Marine makes a $200,000 cash distribution to Bulldog. Of this distribution, $175,000 is tax-free as a distribution of previously taxed Subpart F income. The remaining $25,000 is taxable as a dividend because it represents a distribution of earnings that were not previously taxed under Subpart F. Bulldog's basis for the Marine stock is $600,000 ($600,000 + $175,000 − $175,000) immediately after the distribution. ◀

KEY POINT

Section 1248 is a backstop to the Subpart F rules in that it prevents the gain from the disposition of CFC stock from escaping taxation as ordinary income to the extent that it previously has not been taxed.

DISPOSITION OF CFC STOCK. Section 1248 prevents the stock of a CFC from being sold or exchanged at capital gains rates. These rules apply only to a U.S. person who

[56] Sec. 951(a)(2).

[57] Secs. 956(a)(3) and (b).

[58] Secs. 959(c) and 961(b).

owns at least 10% of the foreign corporation's voting stock when the foreign corporation retained CFC status within five years of the disposition date. The gain recognized on the sale or exchange of a CFC's stock is taxed as a dividend to the extent that the gain is attributable to E&P accumulated in a tax year beginning after December 31, 1962 (the effective date of the Subpart F rules), during a time period that the stock sold or exchanged was held by the U.S. person, and while the foreign corporation was a CFC.[59] Any gain exceeding this amount is taxed as a capital gain. The dividend portion of the gain reported by a corporate shareholder qualifies for the deemed paid foreign tax credit.

EXAMPLE C16-28 ▶ Texas Corporation, a domestic corporation, purchases 200 of the 500 outstanding shares of Le Chien Corporation's stock on October 30, 1995. Texas holds the shares continuously until March 31, 1997, when it sells the stock for a $60,000 gain. Le Chien is a CFC at all times while the stock is owned. Le Chien's E&P amounts are as follows: 1995, $60,000; 1996, $30,000; and 1997, $70,000. The E&P attributable to the stock sold or exchanged is determined using the following formula:

$$\text{E\&P for tax year} \times \frac{\text{Number of shares sold or exchanged}}{\text{Number of shares outstanding}} \times \frac{\text{Number of days shares are owned and corporation is a CFC}}{\text{Number of days in CFC's tax year}} = \text{E\&P attributable to shares sold or exchanged}$$

$$1995\text{: } \$60{,}000 \times \frac{200}{500} \times \frac{61}{365} = \$\ 4{,}011$$

$$1996\text{: } \$30{,}000 \times \frac{200}{500} \times \frac{366}{366} = 12{,}000$$

$$1997\text{: } \$70{,}000 \times \frac{200}{500} \times \frac{91}{365} = 6{,}981$$

$$\text{Total} \qquad \$22{,}992$$

Thus, $22,992 of the gain is dividend income and $37,008 ($60,000 − $22,992) is capital gain. Texas can claim a deemed paid foreign tax credit with respect to the dividend income. ◀

TYPICAL MISCONCEPTION

Section 482 applies to transactions involving two U.S. entities as well as to transactions involving a U.S. entity and a foreign entity.

SECTION 482 RULES. Transactions involving a domestic corporation and a foreign subsidiary present an increased opportunity for tax avoidance. One method of tax avoidance is to have the domestic corporation sell goods and services to the subsidiary at a price that is less than the price that would be arrived at in arm's-length dealings (see Figure C16-1 and related text). Another method is to have the foreign subsidiary pay a less-than-arm's-length charge for the use of intangibles (such as patents or trademarks). Both situations cause an increased amount of profits to be earned by the foreign subsidiary that are exempt from U.S. taxation.

EXAMPLE C16-29 ▶ Taylor Corporation, a domestic corporation, sells widgets to its wholly owned foreign subsidiary Wheeler. Wheeler Corporation is incorporated in and pays taxes to Country Z. Taylor Corporation normally sells widgets to a U.S. wholesaler providing services similar to those provided by Wheeler at a price of $10 per unit. If Taylor Corporation sells the widgets to

[59] Sec. 1248(a).

Wheeler for $8 per unit, Wheeler's profits are increased by $2 per unit and Taylor's profits are decreased by $2 per unit. Unless the additional profit is Subpart F income, it is not taxed by the United States until Wheeler remits it to Taylor as a dividend. ◀

EXAMPLE C16-30 ▶ Assume the same facts as in Example C16-29, except that Taylor Corporation instead licenses Wheeler to manufacture the widgets and charges a $1 per-unit royalty for each unit produced and sold. A royalty arrangement with an unrelated foreign producer of widgets provides for a $3 per-unit royalty to be paid to Taylor Corporation. The reduced royalty payment increases Wheeler's profits by an additional $2 per unit. Because the profit is derived from manufacturing performed by the CFC, it is unlikely that the additional profit will be taxed as Subpart F income. Such profits are exempt from U.S. taxation until Wheeler remits it to Taylor as a dividend. ◀

Under Code Sec. 482, the IRS has the power to distribute, apportion, or allocate gross income, deductions, credits or allowances between or among controlled entities to prevent tax evasion and to clearly reflect the income of the entities. For Sec. 482 to be used, the following conditions must exist:

- There must be two or more organizations, trades, or businesses.
- These entities must be owned or controlled by the same parties.
- A transaction taking place between the entities does not reflect the income that would have been reported had an arm's-length standard been used.

The Sec. 482 rules can apply to transactions taking place between two unincorporated entities, two incorporated entities, or one incorporated entity and one unincorporated entity. The related parties can be either domestic or foreign and do not have to be part of an affiliated group of corporations that files a consolidated tax return.

The Sec. 482 regulations provide rules for determining an arm's-length standard for a number of types of transactions, including

- Loans or advances
- Performance of services
- Sales or transfers of intangible properties
- Use of intangible properties
- Sales or transfers of tangible properties
- Use of tangible properties
- Cost sharing arrangements[60]

These rules provide a number of safe havens for the related parties' transactions. If the price charged for the property meets one of the acceptable standards found in the Sec. 482 regulations, it will not be subject to challenge by the IRS.

ADDITIONAL COMMENT

Under the temporary regulations, a special priority order exists for the transfer pricing methods used for the sale of tangible property: (1) comparable uncontrolled price method, (2) resale method, (3) cost plus method, (4) comparable profits method, (5) profit split method, and (6) any appropriate method approved by the IRS.

New Sec. 482 Regulations were finalized in 1994. Under these Regulations the IRS has become much more specific in its application of the Sec. 482 rules. For example, Reg. Sec. 1.482-3(b)(2) holds that a transaction involving the transfer of tangible property (as in Example C16-29) between controlled taxpayers meets the arm's-length standard if the transaction results are consistent with the outcome that would have occurred if uncontrolled taxpayers had engaged in a *comparable* transaction under *comparable* circumstances. The tangible property and circumstances of an uncontrolled transaction are considered substantially the same as those of a controlled transaction only if minor differences between the transactions have no effect on the amount charged, or can be accounted for by a reasonable number of adjustments to the uncontrolled transaction. If comparability cannot be obtained, then the resale price method, cost plus method,

[60] Reg. Sec. 1.482-1 through -6 and -8.

PRACTICAL APPLICATION

The IRS entered into thirty-one new advance pricing agreements (APAs) with taxpayers in 1996 bringing the total number of APAs to 72. As of September 30, 1996, 142 APAs are pending. APAs provide advance Sec. 482 approval for the transfer pricing procedures used by the taxpayer on transfers of tangible personal property or financial instruments. Firms that have taken advantage of APAs include Apple Computer, Matsushita (makers of Panasonic and Qasar products), and Barclays Bank.

comparable profits method, profit split method, or appropriate other method approved by the IRS can be used.

For intangibles (as in Example C16-30), the arm's-length consideration for a controlled transfer of an intangible is the same amount charged or incurred in a comparable uncontrolled transfer. An uncontrolled transaction is comparable to a controlled transfer if it involves comparable intangible property and takes place under comparable circumstances, as defined under Reg. Sec. 1.482-4(c)(2). If differences exist between the controlled and uncontrolled transfers that do not make them comparable, then the comparable profits method may not be used. The comparable profits method determines the arm's-length consideration for a controlled transfer of property by referring to objective measures of profitability (e.g., profit level indicators such as rates of return) derived from uncontrolled taxpayers that engage in similar business activities with other uncontrolled taxpayers under similar circumstances. If the comparable profits method cannot be used, then the taxpayer can petition to use an appropriate other method approved by the IRS.

Section 482 permits the IRS to adjust the payments made for the use of an intangible over time and to not have the question of appropriateness of the royalty be determined only at the time of the initial transfer. Thus, the actual profit experience, including changes in the income attributed to the intangible over time, of the parties must be considered in determining the royalty rate.

A net Sec. 482 transfer pricing adjustment for the sale of property or services, or the use of property, can constitute a substantial valuation misstatement under Sec. 6662(e)(1)(B) if it exceeds the lesser of $5 million or 10% of the taxpayer's gross receipts. As such, an accuracy-related penalty equal to 20% of the amount of the tax underpayment attributable to the transfer pricing violation is imposed.

SPECIAL FOREIGN CORPORATION FORMS

Foreign corporations have been used by individuals to conduct investment-related activities while avoiding both the U.S. and foreign tax laws. The shareholders of two

WHAT WOULD YOU DO IN THIS SITUATION?

You are a tax manager in your first year on the U.S. Manufacturing and Export Corporation (USM&E) engagement. USM&E manufactures machine tools for shipment throughout North and South America. The USM&E sells its products to six 100%-owned foreign subsidiaries that have sales responsibilities for various geographical areas. In reviewing the profit margins on the sales to the six subsidiaries, you notice that the sales to the U.S. and Canadian sales subsidiaries provide USM&E the largest profit margin. Sales to the four Central and South American foreign subsidiaries are made at different prices that are barely above the parent company's manufacturing costs. In reviewing prior year information, you find that the income tax rates incurred by USM&E in Canada are similar to the U.S. rates, while the income tax rates in the other four countries are substantially below the U.S. rates. The sales manager at USM&E tells you that this pricing structure has been used for a number of years and the services provided by the six sales subsidiaries are substantially identical. He also informs you that none of the tax people on the prior year engagements have ever questioned USM&E's transfer pricing. In reviewing USM&E's costs, you find some additional costs being incurred to ship the goods from the United States to Central and South America, but these costs do not account for the price differences. You suspect that there is a transfer pricing problem here. What advantages could be accruing to USM&E from their current pricing arrangements? Can you provide advice to your client about the possible negative consequences of using incorrect transfer prices? Are there any alternatives available to USM&E under the U.S. tax laws which might permit them to use different transfer pricing methods or non-arm's length transfer prices? Can USM&E obtain guidance from the IRS about their transfer pricing methods?

foreign corporate forms used for investment purposes, however, do not receive the tax deferral that is normally available for their share of a foreign corporation's earnings. U.S. citizens and resident aliens owning stock in a **foreign personal holding company (FPHC)** must report their share of the entity's undistributed FPHC income annually. A foreign corporation is a FPHC if at least 60% of its income is passive income and at some time during the corporation's tax year more than 50% of the value of its outstanding stock is owned by five or fewer individuals who are U.S. citizens or residents.[61] A U.S. person must pay U.S. tax and an interest charge based on the value of the tax deferral received on accumulated foreign earnings when he or she disposes of the stock of a **passive foreign investment company (PFIC)** or receives an excess distribution from the PFIC.[62] A foreign corporation is a PFIC if 75% or more of its gross income for the tax year is passive income, or at least 50% of the average value of its assets during the tax year produces or is held for producing passive income.

OBJECTIVE 9

Explain the special tax benefits accruing to a foreign sales corporation

FOREIGN SALES CORPORATIONS

The **foreign sales corporation (FSC)** provisions represent the U.S. government's reaction to a determination by an international tribunal that the portion of the U.S. tax laws regarding the domestic international sales corporation (DISC) violated the General Agreement on Tariffs and Trade (GATT). FSCs were created to rebut these arguments and to satisfy the GATT requirements that tax benefits for export activities be permitted only if the income is earned through economic activity outside the home country.

KEY POINT

As opposed to a DISC, an FSC must be a *foreign* corporation.

An FSC is a corporation created or organized in a foreign country that is a party to either an exchange of information agreement or a tax treaty with the United States or a qualified U.S. possession and that has made the necessary election to be taxed as an FSC.[63]

FSCs provide exporters with three major tax incentives:

- Exemption of a portion of the FSC's foreign trade income from the U.S. corporate income tax
- Special transfer pricing rules that permit the FSC to use other than arm's-length pricing methods
- Dividend distributions that are eligible for a 70%, 80%, or 100% dividends-received deduction

Each of these advantages is explained below.

REAL-WORLD EXAMPLE

In the most recent IRS study there were 2,613 FSC tax returns filed for the twelve-month period ending June 30, 1988. These returns reported exports of $20.3 billion, FSC taxable income of $1.2 billion, and exempt income (net of losses) of $2.1 billion. The total number of FSCs has increased to about 4,500 in 1995.

TAXATION OF AN FSC's ACTIVITIES. A FSC's income is divided into two major categories: foreign trade income and other income. Foreign trade income is again subdivided into exempt and nonexempt foreign trade income. Exempt foreign trade income is exempt from the U.S. corporate income tax. The percentage of foreign trade income that is exempt (from 30% to almost 70%) depends on the transfer pricing method used and whether the FSC has corporate shareholders. Nonexempt foreign trade income is taxed differently depending on the transfer pricing method used to price the goods or services purchased by the FSC. If an administrative pricing method is used, the nonexempt foreign trade income is U.S. source income that is effectively connected with the conduct of a U.S. trade or business. If the arm's-length transfer pricing method is used, the nonexempt foreign trade income is either taxed as being effectively connected with the conduct of a U.S. trade or business, tax-exempt as unrelated to a U.S. trade or business, or taxed to the FSC's shareholders as Subpart F income.

Investment income (e.g., interest, dividends, royalties, annuities, rentals, and gains on the sale of stocks or securities) and carrying charges are taxed as U.S. source income.

[61] Sec. 551(a).

[62] Sec. 1296(a).

[63] Secs. 922(a) and 927(f).

Such income is considered to be effectively connected with the conduct of a U.S. trade or business.

EXAMPLE C16-31 ▶ Jetstone Products FSC, a qualifying commission FSC, was organized during 1995 and is 100%-owned by Jetstone Products, a domestic corporation. The FSC sells medical products throughout South America. In 1997, the FSC earned taxable income of $920,000 from commissions on sales of Jetstone products and $40,000 of investment income. Commissions are earned only on sales producing foreign trade income and are determined using an administrative pricing method. FSCs with a corporate shareholder can exempt 16/23 of their foreign trade income from U.S. taxation if they use an administrative pricing method, or, in this case, $640,000 (16/23 × $920,000). The nonexempt foreign trade income is $280,000 ($920,000 − $640,000). This income, and any investment income, are both U.S. source income that is effectively connected with the conduct of a U.S. trade or business. ◀

KEY POINT

Note that these requirements are all in line with the basic purpose of the FSC legislation: to stimulate U.S. exports of goods and services.

DETERMINATION OF FOREIGN TRADE INCOME. **Foreign trade income** is the FSC's gross income that is attributable to foreign trading gross receipts. Section 924(a) defines foreign trading gross receipts as including receipts from

- The sale, exchange, or other disposition of export property (i.e., property that is manufactured, produced, grown, or extracted in the United States by a person other than an FSC).
- The lease or rental of export property for use by the lessee outside the United States
- Services related to the sale or lease of export property
- Engineering or architectural services performed for non-U.S. construction projects
- Managerial services performed for an unrelated FSC or DISC

An FSC's gross receipts are foreign trading gross receipts only if (1) it performs outside the United States (a) the necessary management activities (i.e., location for directors' meetings; location of principal bank account; and payment of dividends, directors' fees and certain other expenses) during the tax year and (b) the necessary economic activities (i.e., solicitation, negotiation, or making of the sales contract) related to a particular transaction, and (2) the non-U.S. direct costs attributable to the transaction are at least 50% of the total direct costs attributable to the transaction.

ADDITIONAL COMMENT

Most FSCs operate as commission FSCs. Rather than buying an item from the parent and reselling it, they receive a commission for arranging the sale by the parent.

TRANSFER PRICING RULES. Two types of FSCs are commonly encountered when export property is being sold. The first type, the *sales FSC,* generally involves the FSC stocking the export property and performing the various services (e.g., warehousing, delivery, extending of credit) that are associated with a wholesaler or distributor. The second type, the *commission FSC,* generally involves the FSC selling the export property for a related or unrelated producer company and earning a sales commission.

With either type of FSC, its taxable income is determined by using either the arm's-length or administrative (non-arm's-length) transfer pricing methods. In the case of the sales FSC, the transfer pricing rules are used to determine the minimum price that the FSC can be charged for the export property. In the case of the commission FSC, the transfer pricing rules are used to determine the maximum commission that can be earned by the FSC when it sells the export property.

Administrative Transfer Pricing Methods. The administrative methods permit the taxable income attributable to a transaction (or a group of transactions) to be any amount that does not exceed the ceiling for the pricing method used. The taxable income that can be earned by a FSC is an amount not exceeding the larger of

- 1.83% of the foreign trading gross receipts derived by the FSC from the sale
- 23% of the combined taxable income of the FSC and the related supplier attributable to the foreign trading gross receipts derived by the FSC from the sale

KEY POINT

The arm's-length transfer pricing rules of Sec. 482 permit an FSC to report only the amount of income that would be reported if the goods were purchased from a related supplier at an arm's-length price and sold by the FSC to a related or unrelated person at an arm's-length price.

Arm's-length Transfer Pricing Method. Transactions involving a sale by an FSC of export property acquired from a related person can also be based on the sales price actually charged the FSC by the related person (or commission paid the FSC by the related person) if the amount satisfies the arm's-length transaction requirements of Sec. 482. Transactions involving export property produced by an unrelated party are always based on the price that the FSC actually pays for the export property, or the commission the FSC actually is paid.

EXAMPLE C16-32 ▶

Assume the same facts as in Example C16-31. The $920,000 of taxable income from FSC commissions is the larger of 1.83% of the FSC's foreign trading gross receipts or 23% of the combined taxable income of the FSC and its related supplier (Jetstone Products). Once taxable income is determined, the maximum commission the FSC can charge Jetstone Products on any transactions producing foreign trade income can be determined. It is $920,000 plus the expenses that Jetstone Products FSC incurs from the transactions on which it earns commissions. ◀

SELF-STUDY QUESTION

How is exempt foreign trade income never subject to U.S. income tax?

ANSWER

At the FSC, it is foreign-source income earned by a foreign corporation—thus, no U.S. tax is imposed. Then, when the FSC pays dividends to its U.S. corporate shareholders, the dividend is subject to a 100% dividends-received deduction. The U.S. tax exemption may or may not extend to the nonexempt foreign trade income depending on which pricing method is used.

Exemption of FSC Dividends from Taxation. Distributions to a U.S. corporation of foreign trade income earned by a FSC that uses the administrative pricing rules are eligible for the 100% dividends-received deduction. As a result, the exempt foreign trade income is never subject to the U.S. corporate income tax. Nonexempt foreign trade income is taxed only to the FSC. Only the exempt portion of the foreign trade income determined by using the arm's-length pricing rules is eligible for the 100% dividends-received deduction. No dividends-received deduction is available for the nonexempt foreign trade income determined by using the arm's-length pricing rules unless the income is effectively connected with the conduct of a U.S. trade or business.[64] A 70% or 80% dividends-received deduction is available for dividends paid out of investment income or carrying charges earned by the FSC.

EXAMPLE C16-33 ▶

Assume the same facts as in Examples C16-31 and C16-32 except that Jetstone Products FSC pays a $200,000 dividend to its parent corporation. FSC dividends initially come from foreign trade income E&P and then from any other E&P. In this case, all of the FSC's dividends are from foreign trade income E&P. Because the administrative pricing rules were used, a 100% dividends-received deduction is available to Jetstone Products on the entire dividend. ◀

OBJECTIVE 10

Explain the special tax benefits accruing to a domestic international sales corporation

KEY POINT

A domestic corporation can no longer elect to be a DISC without agreeing to pay the interest charge on the tax-deferred income. Most interest-charge DISCs that still exist made their elections before 1985.

DOMESTIC INTERNATIONAL SALES CORPORATIONS

The special **domestic international sales corporation** (**DISC**) tax laws were created in 1971 to encourage U.S. companies to engage in export activities. The DISC rules originally provided four special tax advantages:

- The DISC was exempt from the corporate income tax.
- The DISC's shareholders could defer up to one-half of the DISC's profits from taxation until they were distributed, the DISC stock was sold or exchanged, or the DISC election was terminated.
- Special pricing rules could be used to determine the DISC's taxable income.
- The DISC could lend money to a related producer (known as a *producer's loan*) without the transaction being considered a dividend.

The 1984 Tax Act reduced the tax advantage of a DISC by eliminating the tax deferral for annual DISC receipts in excess of $10 million, levying an interest charge on each shareholder's portion of the DISC's post-1984 tax-deferred earnings, eliminating the

[64] Sec. 245(c).

ability to make new DISC elections after December 31, 1984 except where the DISC's shareholders agree to pay the appropriate interest charge, and revoking an existing DISC election whenever an FSC election is made by a corporation in the DISC's controlled group. Despite these restrictions, a number of interest-charge DISCs remain active today.

REAL-WORLD EXAMPLE

In 1991 there were approximately 980 interest-charge DISCs (down from 1,185 in 1988) that reported 3.5 billion dollars of export receipts and 222.3 million dollars of taxable income.

DISC REQUIREMENTS AND TAXABLE INCOME. Because of the reduced importance DISCs have today, only a brief summary of their tax characteristics is presented. Like an FSC, a DISC must satisfy a series of organizational requirements (i.e., domestic corporation, one class of stock outstanding, not a member of a controlled group that includes an FSC, and a timely election with the consent of all shareholders). In addition, at least 95% of the DISC's assets must be qualified export assets, and at least 95% of the DISC's receipts must be qualified export receipts.

A DISC can elect one of three methods to compute its taxable income: the Section 482 (or arm's-length) method, the gross receipts method, and the combined taxable income method. These methods parallel the FSC methods explained above.

TAXATION OF DISC DISTRIBUTIONS. DISCs are exempt from the U.S. corporate income tax. DISC shareholders are taxed on both actual and constructive distributions made by the DISC. DISC shareholders are taxed on the following types of constructive distributions: gross interest income derived from producer's loans, taxable income attributable to qualified export receipts in excess of $10 million in a tax year, and 1⁄17 of the DISC's remaining taxable income.[65]

EXAMPLE C16-34 ▶ Alpha Corporation, which has been a DISC for a number of years, is owned entirely by Total Corporation, a domestic corporation taxed at a 34% rate. Both corporations use the calendar year as their tax years. During 1996, Alpha Corporation reports taxable income of $267,000. Included in this total is $12,000 of producer's loan interest. Total Corporation receives a constructive distribution of $27,000 [$12,000 + 1⁄17 ($267,000 − $12,000)] from Alpha Corporation on December 31, 1996. Total Corporation must pay an interest charge in 1997 on the $240,000 ($267,000 − $27,000) of tax-deferred DISC profits from 1996 that are not actually or constructively distributed by Alpha Corporation as well as the cumulative tax-deferred DISC profits from all prior post-1984 tax years. The interest charge is paid with Total's 1997 corporate tax return. ◀

All DISC shareholders must pay an interest charge on their DISC-related deferred tax liability. The interest charge that is owed for a particular tax year is based on the DISC's cumulative tax-deferred profits earned through the end of the preceding tax year. The DISC-related deferred tax liability equals the additional amount of tax that would be owed by a shareholder whose gross income includes his or her ratable share of the DISC's tax-deferred profits that were earned in post-December 31, 1984 tax years. The interest charge is based on a rate published annually by the IRS.[66]

A DISC's distributions are tax-free if they come out of its previously taxed income. A DISC's previously taxed income is the total of its constructive distributions for the current and preceding tax years that have not been distributed to its shareholders. As part of the enactment of the FSC provisions, the DISC's tax-deferred income balance on December 31, 1984 was frozen and can be distributed tax-free to its shareholders. Tax-deferred DISC income accumulated after December 31, 1984 is taxed when distributed.[67]

The tax-deferred DISC income does not receive a permanent tax exemption. Shareholders who sell or exchange part or all of their DISC stock may have to recognize some or all of the gain as ordinary income.[68]

[65] Sec. 995(b).
[66] Sec. 995(f).
[67] Sec. 996(a)(1).
[68] Sec. 996(d).

Topic Review C16-4 presents a summary of the tax treatment accorded the primary means for doing business abroad.

TAX PLANNING CONSIDERATIONS

DEDUCTION VERSUS CREDIT FOR FOREIGN TAXES

An election to deduct or credit any paid or accrued foreign income taxes is available to taxpayers annually.[69] Nearly all taxpayers who pay foreign taxes claim them as a credit. This advantage is illustrated in the following example.

EXAMPLE C16-35 ▶ Phil, a U.S. citizen, earns $100 of foreign income. Phil pays $25 in foreign income taxes. Two separate calculations comparing Phil's U.S. tax liability when the foreign taxes are deducted and credited are presented in the following table:

Topic Review C16-4

Taxation of U.S. People Doing Business Abroad

Type of Entity Used	Tax Treatment
Domestic subsidiary corporation	Profits are taxed in the year earned. A direct foreign tax credit is available for foreign taxes paid or accrued. Losses are deducted in the year they are incurred.
Foreign branch	Foreign branches are unincorporated extensions of the domestic taxpayer. Tax rules similar to those for a domestic subsidiary corporation are used.
Foreign corporation (less than 50% U.S.-owned)	A tax deferral is available for a foreign corporation's earnings until repatriated to the United States. A domestic corporation can claim a deemed paid credit with respect to dividends received from foreign corporations that are 10% or more owned.
Controlled foreign corporation (CFC) (more than 50% U.S.-owned)	Same rules as for previous entry. Some income forms of the CFC are taxed in the year in which they are earned. Tax-deferred earnings can be taxed under Subpart F when invested in U.S. property. Previously taxed income is distributed tax-free. Special rules apply to the sale or exchange of CFC stock.
Foreign sales corporation (FSC)	Special export entity that must meet certain mandated administrative and economic activity requirements. Part or all of the FSC's foreign trade income is exempt from U.S. taxation based on the transfer pricing method used. Administrative transfer pricing methods permit the FSC to use other-than-arm's-length pricing. Dividend distributions may be eligible for a 100% dividends-received deduction. Foreign tax credit is also available for taxes withheld on dividends.
Domestic international sales corporation (DISC)	Special export entity that is exempt from the U.S. corporate income tax if it meets certain procedural requirements. Constructive distributions are required annually. U.S. shareholders are taxed on actual and constructive distributions. An interest charge is levied on the U.S. shareholder's portion of the tax deferred earnings. Administrative transfer pricing methods can be used to determine DISC taxable income. DISCs can lend money tax-free to a related producer (usually a member of its controlled group).

[69] Sec. 901(a).

	Deduction	*Credit*
Gross income	$100	$100
Minus: Foreign income tax deduction	(25)	
Taxable income	$75	$100
Times: Marginal tax rate	× 0.31	× 0.31
Gross U.S. tax liability	$23	$31
Minus: Foreign tax credit		(25)
Net U.S. tax liability	$23	$6

REAL WORLD EXAMPLE

Seldom will it be advantageous to a taxpayer to deduct the foreign taxes paid when such taxes can be claimed as a foreign tax credit. Some taxpayers deduct their foreign taxes, when they are a small dollar amount, because of the complexity of complying with the foreign tax credit rules (e.g., figuring out the law and filing the necessary form(s)).

If the foreign income taxes are deducted, Phil's total U.S. and foreign tax liability is $48 ($25 + $23). By claiming the credit, Phil reduces his total U.S. and foreign tax liability to $31 ($25 + $6). ◀

Some taxpayers deduct their foreign income taxes when they have incurred foreign losses, and they feel that the foreign tax payment will not be used as a credit in either the current year or the seven-year carryback or carryover period. The deduction election provides a taxpayer with current tax benefits if he or she has U.S. profits in excess of his or her foreign losses. If such U.S. profits have not been earned, the foreign taxes will increase the taxpayer's NOL.

ELECTION TO ACCRUE FOREIGN TAXES

Cash method of accounting taxpayers can elect to claim their foreign tax credit by using either the cash or accrual method of accounting. This election is not available if the foreign taxes are deducted. The election is binding on all tax years and can be revoked only with IRS consent.[70]

This election permits a cash method of accounting taxpayer to credit foreign income taxes that have been accrued but not yet paid. The election does not affect the application of the cash method of accounting to other income or expense items. Two advantages result from this election.

- The election accelerates the time that the foreign tax credit is claimed by one or more tax years from the time the credit would otherwise be claimed.
- The election eliminates the problem of matching income and foreign taxes for foreign tax credit limitation purposes and in many cases obviates the need for a carryback or carryover of excess credits.

EXAMPLE C16-36 ▶ Tulsa Corporation, a domestic corporation, commenced to conduct foreign activities in Country Z in 1994. Tulsa has used the cash method of accounting for several years. Z's tax laws require the use of a calendar year as the reporting period. Taxes that are owed on income earned in a year must be paid by the first day of the third month following the year-end. Tulsa operates overseas in 1994–1996 before closing its business on December 31, 1996. Its results are as follows:

	1994	*1995*	*1996*	*1997*
Foreign source taxable income	$1,000	$1,000	$1,000	$—0—
Foreign taxes accrued	300	300	300	—0—
Foreign taxes paid	—0—	300	300	300
Foreign tax credit limitation (34% corporate tax rate)	340	340	340	—0—
Foreign tax credit:				
Cash method of accounting	—0—	300	300	300
Accrual method of accounting	300	300	300	—0—

[70] Sec. 905(a).

Under the cash method of accounting, Tulsa pays its 1994 U.S. taxes without the benefit of any foreign tax credit. Excess credits of $300 are reported in 1997 because of the mismatching of the reporting of the income and the making of the tax payments. $40 of the 1997 tax payment can be carried back to each 1995 and 1996, but $220 [$300 − ($40 + $40)] of the foreign tax credit would be lost because Tulsa has discontinued its foreign activities. If such activities had not been discontinued, they could be carried over and used in later years when the foreign tax credit limitation exceeds the foreign taxes paid. No mismatching occurs if the accrual method of accounting is elected for reporting the foreign tax credit. ◀

SPECIAL EARNED INCOME ELECTIONS

Taxpayers may choose to either break a previously made election to exclude foreign-earned income or not make the initial election, if they find themselves in one of the following two situations:

- They are employed in a foreign country where the foreign tax rate exceeds the U.S. tax rate (e.g., Canada or West Germany).
- They incur a loss from overseas employment or trade or business activities.

In the first situation, the available foreign tax credits exceed the taxpayer's gross U.S. tax liability. The foreign-earned income exclusion causes part of the excess credits to be lost. By not electing to use Sec. 911, the taxpayer can use the entire amount of excess credits as a carryback or carryover to another tax year (subject, of course, to the separate basket concepts). These excess credits might prove beneficial if, for example, income was earned in another year in a country where the local tax rate is lower than the U.S. tax rate.

In the second situation, taxpayers who incur losses have an excess of deductions over gross income. If they exclude part or all of their foreign-earned income, a similar proportion of the related expenses will be disallowed. Such an action reduces the amount of any available NOL carryback or carryover. A decision not to elect Sec. 911 preserves the full amount of the excess deductions.

Taxpayers do not have an election to either exclude or deduct the housing cost amount. A qualifying taxpayer who earns entirely employer-provided amounts (W-2 income) must exclude the housing cost amount. If only self-employment income is earned, then the housing cost amount can only be deducted. If a combination of the two types of income is earned, then the housing cost amount is divided up between an exclusion and a deduction based on the relative amounts of the two types of income that were earned.

An election not to use the Sec. 911 benefits is made on the taxpayer's tax return or on an amended tax return. Taxpayers should be cautious when revoking this election because a new election to claim the Sec. 911 benefits cannot be made until five years have passed or until the IRS consents to an earlier reelection.[71] Thus, a taxpayer who revokes an election while residing in a country that has a tax rate higher than the United States may not be able to elect to exclude earned income if he or she moves to a country that has a low tax rate.

TAX TREATIES

KEY POINT

With certain exceptions, whenever a treaty and the Internal Revenue Code are in conflict, the treaty takes precedence.

A treaty is an agreement negotiated between two sovereign nations. The United States has entered into income tax treaties covering about fifty nations. Income **tax treaties** have two primary objectives:

- To reduce or eliminate the burden of double taxation
- To establish cooperation between the taxing authorities of the two nations

In addition to income tax treaties, the United States has entered into estate and gift tax treaties and totalization agreements for Social Security taxes.

[71] Sec. 911(e)(2).

The first objective represents the major use of an income tax treaty in tax planning. An income tax treaty involving the United States, however, cannot be used by a U.S. citizen or domestic corporation to reduce their U.S. income tax liability. U.S. citizens and domestic corporations are still taxed on their worldwide income at the regular U.S. tax rates. However, the treaty can reduce the income taxes paid to the foreign country and may reduce or eliminate any problem that U.S. taxpayers have with excess foreign tax credits. Nonresident aliens and foreign corporations generally can avail themselves of the treaty provisions to reduce the U.S. withholding rate on most forms of investment income. For some types of investment income, the U.S. tax is eliminated.

ADDITIONAL COMMENT

Tax treaties designate a competent authority to represent each country. The U.S. competent authority is the Assistant Commissioner (International) of the IRS.

The second objective is achieved by providing for an exchange of information between the taxing authorities of the two nations to prevent tax evasion and by establishing a mechanism by which taxpayers of one nation can settle tax disputes with the taxing authorities of the second nation.

A taxpayer who takes a position based on a treaty to which the U.S. is a party that overrules an internal revenue law (for example, the Internal Revenue Code) is required by Code Sec. 6114 to disclose such a position on his or her tax return or on a statement attached to his or her return.

SPECIAL RESIDENT ALIEN ELECTIONS

Two special elections are available to nonresident alien individuals that permit them to be classified as resident aliens. The first election permits them to be treated as resident aliens in situations where they move to the United States too late in the year to qualify for that year under the substantial presence test (see page C16-15).

This election is available if the alien

- Does not qualify as a resident alien under the lawful resident test or substantial presence test for the calendar year for which the election is being made (i.e., election year)
- Does not qualify as a resident alien for the calendar year preceding the election year
- Qualifies as a resident alien under the substantial presence test in the calendar year immediately following the election year, and
- a. Was present in the United States for at least 31 consecutive days in the election year and

  b. Was present in the United States for at least 75% of the days in the period beginning with the first day of the thirty-one-consecutive-day or longer period and ending with the last day of the election year.

The election is irrevocable (except with the IRS's consent) and is made on the alien's tax return for the election year, but cannot be made before the alien satisfies the substantial presence test for the calendar year following the election year.[72]

ADDITIONAL COMMENT

The special resident alien election is made by attaching to a joint return a statement to the effect that the Sec. 6013(g) election is being made. This election must be made within the time period designated for filing a claim for credit or refund.

Code Sec. 6013(g) permits nonresident aliens who are married to U.S. citizens or resident aliens to elect to be taxed as resident aliens. Such an election requires both individuals to agree to be taxed on their worldwide income and to provide all books, records, and information necessary to ascertain either spouse's tax liability. This election permits nonresident aliens to file a joint tax return with their spouses. By filing the joint return, the couple can take advantage of the lower tax rates for married couples filing jointly.

A special election is available under Sec. 6013(h) for the tax year that a nonresident alien becomes a resident alien. This election permits the alien to be treated as a resident alien for income tax and withholding (on wages only) purposes. This election is available if an individual is a nonresident alien at the beginning of the tax year and a resident alien

[72] Sec. 7701(b)(4).

at the end of the year, the individual is married to a U.S. citizen or resident alien at the end of the tax year, and both individuals make a timely election. This election permits the same tax benefits as a Sec. 6013(g) election and eliminates the need to be taxed as a nonresident alien for part of the year and a resident alien for the remainder of the year.

COMPLIANCE AND PROCEDURAL CONSIDERATIONS

REPORTING THE FOREIGN TAX CREDIT

The foreign tax credit is claimed on the taxpayer's income tax return by filing Form 1116 (for noncorporate taxpayers) or Form 1118 (for corporations). Separate forms are filed for each of the separate foreign tax credit limitations for which the taxpayer must make a foreign tax credit calculation. A completed Form 1116 is illustrated in Appendix B. The form is based on the following example:

EXAMPLE C16-37 ▶ Andrew Roberts, a married U.S. resident who files jointly with his wife, having social security number 123-45-6789, reports $30,000 of dividend income from France on which 24,840 FF (French francs) in French income taxes are withheld on December 31, 1996. Roberts owns 3% of the distributing foreign corporation's outstanding stock. The French taxes are translated at the exchange rate for the date on which they were withheld (December 31, 1996). The $30,000 of gross income is reduced by an allocable portion of Roberts's $12,000 of itemized deductions. The entire $4,500 foreign tax amount can be claimed as a foreign tax credit because it is less than the $7,098 applicable foreign tax credit limit for passive income. ◀

REPORTING THE EARNED INCOME EXCLUSION

KEY POINT

Taxpayers who regularly reside in a foreign country generally qualify under both the physical presence and bona fide resident tests. Tax practitioners must indicate on Form 2555 which one of the two tests has been met when claiming the foreign earned exclusion. Determining whether one is a foreign resident is more difficult than merely determining one's physical presence during the tax year. If a taxpayer fails the physical presence test, documentation should be retained by the client (e.g., rent receipts, employment contract, visas, etc.) to support the bona fide resident claim should an IRS inquiry occur.

The elections for the foreign earned income and housing cost amount exclusions are made separately on Form 2555. Each election must be made with an income tax return that is timely filed (including any extensions), a later amended return filed within the statute of limitations, or an original income tax return filed within one year after the return's due date. Once an election is made, it remains in effect for that year and all subsequent tax years unless the IRS consents to revoke the election. Thus, a new election is not required when an individual either moves from one foreign country to another or moves to the United States and then returns to a foreign country some years later.[73]

Taxpayers whose tax homes are outside the United States and Puerto Rico are permitted a special two-month extension of time to file the return.[74] Any return filed before the end of the Sec. 911 qualifying period must be filed without claiming its benefits. If a taxpayer subsequently qualifies for the Sec. 911 benefits, an amended return or refund claim can be filed to recover any overpaid taxes. A taxpayer can avoid having to file an amended return or refund claim by obtaining an additional extension of time for filing the return until after the Sec. 911 qualifying period ends.[75]

A completed Form 2555 is illustrated in Appendix B based on the following example.

EXAMPLE C16-38 ▶ Lawrence Smith, a U.S. citizen, social security number 234-56-7890, is employed in 1996 by the Very Public Corporation in Paris, France. Smith is eligible for the Sec. 911 earned income exclusion for all of 1996 even though he spent five business days in the United States. For 1996, Smith can exclude $70,000 under the basic earned income exclusion and an additional $12,058 ($21,300 qualifying expenses − $9,242 base housing amount) under the housing

[73] Reg. Sec. 1.911-7(a).
[74] Reg. Sec. 1.6081-5(a).
[75] Reg. Secs. 1.911-7(c) and 1.6081-5.

cost amount exclusion. This $82,058 amount is not reduced by any disallowed for AGI deductions because all of Smith's employment-related expenses are deducted as miscellaneous itemized deductions.

FILING REQUIREMENTS FOR ALIENS AND FOREIGN CORPORATIONS

A nonresident alien must file his or her income tax return on or before the fifteenth day of the sixth month following the close of the tax year. A nonresident alien files a Form 1040-NR. If the nonresident alien has wages that are subject to the withholding of income taxes, then Form 1040-NR must be filed on or before the fifteenth day of the fourth month following the close of the tax year.[76]

The due date for a foreign corporation's income tax return is extended to the fifteenth day of the sixth month following the close of its tax year if the foreign corporation does not maintain a U.S. office or place of business. If a U.S. office or place of business is maintained, the due date is the fifteenth day of the third month following the close of the tax year. A foreign corporation files Form 1120-F.[77]

FSC AND DISC FILING REQUIREMENTS

The U.S. income tax return of an FSC is due by the fifteenth day of the third month following the close of its tax year. The FSC files a Form 1120-FSC.[78] An interest-charge DISC's income tax return is due by the fifteenth day of the ninth month following the close of its tax year. An interest-charge DISC files a Form 1120-IC-DISC.[79]

PROBLEM MATERIALS

DISCUSSION QUESTIONS

C16-1 What four primary characteristics have been used by the drafters of the U.S. tax laws to determine the taxability of foreign-related transactions? Explain the importance of each characteristic.

C16-2 Why is it important for an alien taxpayer to determine whether he or she is a resident of the United States?

C16-3 Explain the alternatives available to individual taxpayers for reporting foreign income taxes that have been paid or accrued.

C16-4 What types of foreign taxes are eligible to be credited?

C16-5 Why did Congress feel that it was necessary to enact the foreign tax credit limitation rules?

C16-6 Explain how the separate basket approach to determining the foreign tax credit limitation has created excess foreign tax credit problems for some U.S. taxpayers.

C16-7 What advantages accrue to a cash method of accounting taxpayer who elects to accrue his or her foreign taxes for foreign tax credit purposes?

C16-8 What requirements must be satisfied in order for a U.S. citizen or resident alien living abroad to qualify for the foreign-earned income exclusion?

C16-9 Tony, a U.S. citizen, uses the calendar year as his tax year. Tony is transferred to foreign country C on June 15, 1995 and he immediately becomes a resident of that country. His employer transfers him back to the United States on March 10, 1997. Does Tony qualify for the foreign-earned income exclusion as a bona fide resident? If not, is there any other way he can qualify?

C16-10 Explain the reasons why a taxpayer might prefer to calculate his or her foreign-earned income exclusion by using the physical presence rules instead of the bona fide foreign resident rules.

C16-11 Why might a taxpayer not elect to use the foreign-earned income exclusion benefits? If

[76] Reg. Sec. 1.6072-1(c).

[77] Reg. Secs. 1.6072-2(a) and (b) and 1.6081-5(a).

[78] Ibid.

[79] Reg. Sec. 1.6072-2(e).

such a decision is made in the current tax year, what negative consequences might it have on future tax years?

C16-12 Compare the U.S. tax treatment of a nonresident alien and a resident alien, both of whom earn U.S. trade or business and U.S. investment income.

C16-13 Explain how a nonresident alien is taxed in the year of arrival and departure if he or she arrives in the United States on July 1, 1995 and immediately establishes U.S. residency and departs from the United States on October 1, 1997, thereby terminating his or her U.S. residency.

C16-14 How is a nonresident alien's U.S. source investment income taxed? What means are used to collect the tax?

C16-15 Why is the effectively connected concept important to the taxation of a nonresident alien's trade or business income?

C16-16 Manuel, a nonresident alien, conducts a trade or business in the United States during the current year. He earns $25,000 of interest income in the United States during the current year. What factors or tests are used to determine whether the interest income is taxed as investment income or trade or business income by the U.S. taxing authorities?

C16-17 What are the advantages of a U.S. corporation conducting foreign business activities through a foreign branch? through a foreign subsidiary?

C16-18 What is the deferral privilege? What tax provisions can produce current U.S. taxation for part or all of a foreign corporation's earnings?

C16-19 Why did Congress feel that it was necessary to enact the deemed paid foreign tax credit provisions?

C16-20 Kilarney Corporation, a foreign corporation, is incorporated in Country J and is 100% owned by Maine Corporation, a domestic corporation. During the current year Kilarney earns $500,000 from its Country J operations and $100,000 from its U.S. operations. None of the Country J income is Subpart F income. None of Kilarney's after-tax profits are distributed as a dividend to Maine. Explain how Kilarney is taxed by the U.S. taxing authorities and whether any of Kilarney's income is taxed to Maine. How would your answer change if none of the income were earned from U.S. operations and a $50,000 dividend were instead paid to Maine?

C16-21 What is the branch profits tax? Explain the Congressional intent behind its enactment.

C16-22 What is a controlled foreign corporation (CFC)? How does the tax treatment of its U.S. owner(s) share of the distributed and undistributed profits differ from a noncontrolled foreign corporation?

C16-23 Explain the concept of Subpart F income. What are the two major income forms that are taxed under the Subpart F rules?

C16-24 One of the purposes of enacting Subpart F was to prevent the use of holding companies created in tax-haven nations to shelter foreign profits from U.S. taxation. Explain how the following income concepts accomplish this purpose:
a. Foreign personal holding company income
b. Foreign base company sales income
c. Foreign base company services income

C16-25 What are investments in U.S. property? Explain why Congress made the amount of such investments taxable to U.S. shareholders.

C16-26 Explain the tax consequences of a U.S. shareholder receiving a distribution of previously taxed Subpart F income from a CFC.

C16-27 How does the taxation of the gain recognized when the stock of a CFC is sold differ from when the stock of a non-CFC is sold?

C16-28 Explain how the Sec. 482 and CFC rules work together to reduce tax avoidance in a domestic corporation's use of a foreign sales subsidiary.

C16-29 List the major advantages of using a foreign sales corporation (FSC) to conduct export activities.

C16-30 What restrictions have been placed on domestic international sales corporations (DISCs) that reduce their tax incentives?

C16-31 King Corporation, a U.S. corporation, owns 25% of each of two foreign corporations. King's foreign business activities are taxed at local tax rates that are higher than in the United States so it is in an excess foreign tax credit situation. Corporation A is located in a country that is a partner with the United States in a tax treaty. The treaty reduces the withholding on any dividend payments made to a U.S. corporation from 15% to 5%. Corporation B is located in a non-treaty country where the withholding rate is 15%. A and B both pay approximately the same local income taxes. If King wants to repatriate profits from one or both of the corporations, which corporation should pay the dividend in order to minimize the repatriation cost? Can such a dividend payment be used to reduce King's excess foreign tax credits that are incurred on its other foreign income?

ISSUE IDENTIFICATION QUESTIONS

C16-32 George Kratzer has been assigned by his U.S. employer to their Brussels office since January of the current year. This year he earned salary, a cost-of-living allowance, a housing allowance, a home leave allowance that permitted him to return home once each year, and an education allowance to pay for U.S. schooling for his daughter. George and his wife, Geneva, have rented an apartment in Brussels and paid Belgian income taxes. What tax issues does George need to consider when preparing his tax return?

C16-33 Bailey Corporation, a domestic corporation, commenced operating overseas in the current year. This year Bailey sold machine tools that it manufactured in the United States to Canadian companies from a branch office located in Toronto, purchased a 40% investment in a Brazilian corporation from which it received a dividend, and received royalties from an English firm who is the licensee of machine tool patents held by Bailey. The patents are used by the English firm to manufacture machine tools that are sold in England. What international tax issues should Bailey's Director of Taxes consider with respect to these activities?

C16-34 Sanders Corporation created a foreign subsidiary in Country Z this year. The subsidiary receives components from Sanders, assembles the components into a finished product using local labor, and sells them to unrelated wholesalers in Countries X, Y, and Z using its own sales force. No dividends have been paid by the foreign subsidiary to the parent this year. What tax issues should Sanders' Director of Taxes consider with respect to these activities?

PROBLEMS

C16-35 ***Translation of Foreign Tax Payments.*** Arnie, a U.S. citizen who uses the calendar year as his tax year, operates a proprietorship in Country Z. Arnie uses the cash method of accounting. During 1996 he reports 500,000 dubles of pretax profits. Country Z income taxes for calendar year 1996 in the amount of 150,000 dubles are paid on June 1, 1997. Exchange rates between the duble and the U.S. dollar at various times in 1996 and 1997 are as follows:

December 31, 1996	4.00 dubles = $1 (U.S.)
1996 average	3.75 dubles = $1 (U.S.)
June 1, 1997	4.25 dubles = $1 (U.S.)

a. What is the amount of Arnie's translated foreign tax credit? In what year can the credit be claimed?

b. How would your answer to Part a change if Arnie elected to accrue his foreign income taxes and filed his U.S. income tax return on April 15, 1997?

c. What type of adjustment to the credit claimed in Part b would be required when Arnie pays his Country Z taxes on June 1, 1997?

C16-36 ***Foreign Tax Credit Limitation.*** Jackson Corporation, a domestic corporation, engages in both U.S. and foreign activities during the current year. All of its overseas activities are conducted by a branch office in Country S. Jackson Corporation uses the accrual method of accounting. The results of Jackson's current year operations are as follows:

U.S. source taxable income	$2,000,000
Foreign source taxable income	1,500,000
Country S income taxes accrued	600,000

a. What is Jackson Corporation's foreign tax credit amount (assuming that the corporate tax rate is 34% and all foreign activities fall into a single basket)?
b. Are any foreign tax credit carrybacks or carryovers available to be used in other years? If so, in what years can they be used?

C16-37 ***Foreign Tax Credit Limitation.*** Tucson Corporation, a domestic corporation organized in 1995, reports the following information about its activities for the period 1995–1997.

	1995	*1996*	*1997*
Foreign tax accrual	$100,000	$120,000	$140,000
Foreign source taxable income	400,000	300,000	500,000
Worldwide taxable income	1,000,000	1,000,000	1,000,000

The foreign source and worldwide taxable income amounts are determined under U.S. law.

a. What is Tucson Corporation's foreign tax credit limitation for the years 1995–1997 (assume a 34% U.S. corporate tax rate and all foreign activities fall into a single basket)?
b. What happens to Tucson's excess foreign tax credits (if any) during this period? Do any carryovers remain after 1997?
c. How would your answers to Parts a and b change if as part of an IRS audit $100,000 of expenses thought to be U.S.-source when determining taxable income were required to be reported as foreign-source in each year?

C16-38 ***Foreign-Earned Income Exclusion.*** Julia, a U.S. citizen, leaves the United States at noon on August 1, 1995 and arrives in Country P at 8:00 a.m. the next day. She immediately establishes a permanent residence in Country P, which she maintains until her return to the United States at 3:00 p.m. on April 5, 1997. Her only trips outside Country P are related to temporary employment in Country B from November 1, 1995 through December 10, 1995 and a U.S. vacation commencing at 5:00 p.m. on June 1, 1996 and ending at 10:00 p.m. on June 30, 1996. Can Julia qualify for the Sec. 911 benefits? If so, what is the amount of her foreign earned income exclusion for the years 1995 through 1997?

C16-39 ***Foreign-Earned Income Exclusion.*** Fred, a U.S. citizen, arrives in Country K on July 15, 1995, and proceeds to a construction site in the oil fields, where he takes up residence in employer-provided housing where he is required to reside. He remains at the site until his departure on December 1, 1997, except for local travel and the months of July and August 1996, when he is on vacation in the United States. No services are provided while he is in the United States. Fred earns $10,000 per month in salary and allowances while employed overseas. In addition, he receives meals and lodging valued at $1,750 per month while in Country K. What is the amount of Fred's earned income exclusions for the years 1995 through 1997?

C16-40 ***Foreign-Earned Income Exclusion.*** Dillon, a U.S. citizen, resides overseas in Country K for all of 1996. Dillon is married, files a joint return with his wife, and claims two exemptions. He reports the following information about his 1996 activities:

Salary and allowances (other than for housing)[a]	$175,000
Housing allowance	28,000
Employment-related expenses[b]	7,500
Housing costs	30,000
Other itemized deductions	4,000
Country K income taxes	12,000

[a] All Dillon's salary and allowances are attributable to services performed in Country K.
[b] The employment-related expenses are itemized deductions.

What is Dillon's net U.S. tax liability for 1996 (assume that Dillon excludes his earned income and housing cost amount)?

C16-41 ***Tax Calculation for a Nonresident Alien.*** Tien is a citizen of Country C. During the current year, while she is a nonresident alien for U.S. tax purposes, Tien earns the following amounts:

Dividend paid by a U.S. corporation	$ 2,500
Rentals from a U.S. building	10,000
Interest paid by a foreign corporation	5,000

Tien does not conduct a U.S. trade or business during the current year. Her interest and depreciation expenses from leasing the building under a net lease arrangement are $7,000.

a. What is Tien's U.S. tax liability assuming the real estate income is investment income? How is the tax collected?

b. How does the answer to Part a change if an election is made by Tien to treat the real estate as a trade or business?

C16-42 ***Taxation of a Nonresident Alien.*** Pierre, a single nonresident alien, is in the United States for eighty days in the current year engaging in the conduct of a U.S. trade or business. Pierre reports the following income from his U.S. activities. Indicate how each of the following independent items will be taxed and how the tax will be collected.

a. $25,000 of dividend income paid by a U.S. corporation on a portfolio stock investment that is unrelated to Pierre's trade or business.

b. $75,000 of sales commissions earned by Pierre as an employee of a foreign corporation. $50,000 is earned on sales made while in the United States, and $25,000 is earned on non-U.S. sales while outside the United States.

c. A $10,000 capital gain earned on the sale of stock in a U.S. corporation while Pierre was in the United States.

d. $3,000 of interest income earned on a bank account in Pierre's home country.

C16-43 ***Deemed Paid Foreign Tax Credit.*** Paper Corporation, a domestic corporation, owns 40% of the stock of Sud Corporation, a foreign corporation. Sud Corporation reports earnings and profits of $200,000 for its post-1986 tax years. Its post-1986 foreign income taxes are $50,000. Sud pays a $90,000 dividend in the current year to its shareholders. A 15% income tax levied by Country T on nonresident shareholders is withheld by Sud Corporation from the dividend payment.

a. What amount of gross income does Paper Corporation report as a result of receiving the dividend?

b. What is Paper Corporation's net increase in its U.S. tax liability as a result of receiving the dividend (assume a 34% U.S. corporate tax rate)?

c. How would your answer to Parts a and b change if the post-1986 foreign income taxes had instead been $80,000?

C16-44 ***Deemed Paid Foreign Tax Credit.*** Duke Corporation, a domestic corporation, owns all of the stock of Taiwan Corporation, a foreign corporation. Taiwan Corporation pays a $160,000 dividend in the current year to Duke Corporation. Taiwan Corporation's post-1986 operating results show $1,000,000 of earnings and profits and $300,000 of foreign income taxes. Foreign income taxes of $8,000 are withheld on the dividend. Assume Duke Corporation has no other foreign source income and its U.S. taxable income (excluding the dividend) is $1 million.

a. What is the amount of Duke Corporation's deemed paid foreign tax credit?

b. What is Duke Corporation's additional U.S. tax liability as a result of receiving the dividend?

c. How would your answers to Parts a and b change if the $160,000 dividend were instead paid to U.S. citizen Donna (instead of to Duke Corporation), who has a 39.6% marginal tax rate?

C16-45 ***Translation of a Dividend.*** Dayton Corporation, a domestic corporation, owns all of the stock of Fiero Corporation, a foreign corporation. Assume Dayton Corporation has no other foreign source income and its U.S. taxable income (excluding the dividend) is $1 million. Fiero Corporation is formed in early 1997. During 1997, Fiero Corporation earns 400,000 pirogs of pretax profits and accrues 100,000 pirogs in Country Z income taxes. On August 25, 1997, Fiero Corporation pays a 150,000 pirog dividend to Dayton Corporation. Country Z income taxes for 1997 are paid by Fiero Corporation on March 1, 1998. The exchange rates between the pirog and the U.S. dollar at various times during 1997 and 1998 are as follows:

January 1, 1997	9.0 pirogs = $1 (U.S.)
August 25, 1997	10.0 pirogs = $1 (U.S.)
1997 average	9.5 pirogs = $1 (U.S.)
March 1, 1998	10.5 pirogs = $1 (U.S.)

a. What are the translated amounts of Dayton Corporation's dividend and deemed paid credit?

b. What is Dayton Corporation's net U.S. tax liability as a result of receiving the dividend?

C16-46 ***Worldwide Tax Rates.*** Young Corporation operates in both the United States and a foreign country. What is Young Corporation's worldwide (combined U.S. and foreign) tax rate on the foreign branch income it earns in the foreign country in each of the following independent situations assuming that it elects to claim the maximum foreign tax credit for any foreign income taxes:

Situation	*U.S. Tax Rate*	*Foreign Tax Rate*
1	34%	0%
2	34%	15%
3	34%	34%
4	34%	40%

What incentive exists for the foreign nation to increase its tax rates if the foreign income is taxed by the United States when it is earned? if it is earned in one year by a foreign subsidiary but taxed in a later year when it is repatriated to the United States as a dividend?

C16-47 ***Foreign Tax Credit Carrybacks and Carryovers.*** Hamilton Corporation, a domestic corporation, reports the following results from its current year activities:

U.S.-source taxable income	$1,000,000
Foreign-source taxable income from manufacturing branch activity in Country M	1,000,000
Foreign taxes accrued on branch income	280,000
Cash dividend payment from India Corporation, a foreign corporation	212,500
Foreign taxes withheld by India Corporation and remitted to Country X government	37,500

India Corporation is 15% owned by Hamilton and pays its dividend on April 20. Its pretax profits from post-1986 tax years are $6,000,000 and its Country X taxes from post-1986 tax years are $1,500,000. India's E&P is $4,500,000 under U.S. rules. Hamilton Corporation has excess foreign tax credit limitations of $20,000 and $40,000 from its two preceding tax years, respectively. Assume that the foreign tax credit carryovers originated from prior dividend distributions received by Hamilton Corporation from India Corporation.

a. What is Hamilton Corporation's foreign tax credit (assuming a 34% U.S. corporate tax rate)? *Hint:* The Sec. 904 foreign tax credit rules have a separate limitation for Sec. 902 dividends.

b. Are any foreign tax credit carrybacks or carryovers available to be used? If so, in what years can they be used?

C16-48 ***Definition of a CFC.*** In the following independent situations, determine whether a foreign corporation, having a single class of stock outstanding, is characterized as a controlled foreign corporation.

a. The foreign corporation's stock is equally owned by Alpha Corporation, a domestic corporation, and Bart, a U.S. citizen. Bart owns none of the Alpha Corporation stock.

b. Assume the same facts as in Part a, except Bart is instead a nonresident alien.

c. The foreign corporation's stock is owned 7% by Art, 49% by Phong, 29% by Colleen, and 15% by Danielle. Art, Colleen, and Danielle are U.S. citizens and Phong is a nonresident alien. All four individuals are unrelated.

d. Assume the same facts as in Part c, except that Danielle is instead Art's daughter.

C16-49 ***Definition of Foreign Base Company Income.*** Manila Corporation, a foreign corporation, is incorporated in Country J. All of Manila Corporation's stock is owned by Simpson Corporation, a domestic corporation. Determine which of the following transactions produce Subpart F income.

a. Manila Corporation purchases a product from Simpson Corporation and sells it to unrelated parties in Countries J and X.

b. Manila Corporation receives a dividend from foreign corporation Manila-Sub. All of Manila-Sub's stock has been owned by Manila Corporation since its creation. Manila-Sub is incorporated and operates exclusively in Country J.

c. Manila Corporation purchases raw materials locally and manufactures a product in Country J. The product is sold to an unrelated purchaser for use in Country Z.

d. Manila Corporation services machinery manufactured by an unrelated Country J corporation. Service activities conducted outside of Country J on this machinery constitute 80% of Manila Corporation's gross income.

e. Manila Corporation purchases a product from a related U.S. corporation and sells it to unrelated people in Country Z.

C16-50 ***Definition of Foreign Base Company Income.*** Apache Corporation, a domestic corporation, owns 80% of the stock of Burrito Corporation, a foreign corporation. Burrito Corporation is incorporated in Country Y. Burrito Corporation reports the following results for the current year:

	Gross Income	*Deductions*
Foreign base company sales income	$300,000	$120,000
Foreign base company services income	150,000	90,000
Dividend from Kane Corporation, a 70%-owned Country Y corporation	70,000	—0—
Rental income earned in Country Y	280,000	220,000

Kane Corporation performs substantially all of its activities in Country Y.

a. What amount of income does Apache Corporation have to recognize as a result of Burrito's activities?

b. How would your answer to Part a change if Kane Corporation were instead a 70%-owned Country M corporation?

c. How would your answer to Part b change if the foreign base company sales income before reduction for deductions were instead $500,000?

C16-51 ***Transfer Pricing Rules.*** Arrow Corporation, a domestic corporation, annually sells 1,000,000 starter motors to Bentley Corporation, a foreign corporation. Bentley is organized in Country K, is 100% owned by Arrow, and sells the starters as replacement equipment through auto dealers in Country K. The statutory Country K tax rate is 20%.

a. What is the value of the annual U.S. tax deferral available to Arrow Corporation if the starters are sold to Bentley for $40, cost Arrow $30 to produce, and are sold to the auto dealers for $60? Assume Bentley's operating expenses are $4,000,000.

b. What additional benefit would accrue to Arrow annually if it reduced the price it sold each starter to Bentley from $40 to $30? What mechanisms are likely to be used by U.S. tax authorities to prevent the $30 amount from being charged?

c. How would your answer to Part a change if the starters were sold by Bentley to auto dealers in Country M?

C16-52 ***Sale of CFC Stock.*** Irvan Corporation, a domestic corporation, acquires all of the stock of DeLeon Corporation, a foreign corporation, on April 1, 1995 for $300,000. Irvan Corporation sells the DeLeon stock at the close of business on December 31, 1997 for $825,000. $25,000 of Subpart F income has been reported by Irvan as a result of DeLeon's 1995–1997 activities. DeLeon Corporation reports E&P balances during the period 1995 through 1997 as follows (assume all months have thirty days):

Year	*E&P*
1995	$120,000
1996	110,000
1997	144,000

What are the amount and character of Irvan Corporation's gain on the sale of the DeLeon stock?

TAX FORM/RETURN PREPARATION PROBLEMS

C16-53 Stephen R. and Rachel K. Bates, both U.S. citizens, lived in Country K for all of the current year except when Stephen was temporarily assigned to his employer's home office in the United States. They file a joint return and use the calendar year as their tax year. Their taxpayer identification number is 123-45-6789. The Bateses report the following current-year income and expense items:

Salary and allowances:	United States	$ 10,000
	Country K	150,000
Dividends:	From U.S. corporation	2,000
	From Country K corporation	10,000
Unreimbursed foreign business expenses (directly allocable to Country K earned income and deductible as a miscellaneous itemized deduction)		5,000
Charitable contributions paid to U.S. charities (not directly allocable to any income)		8,000
Country K income taxes paid on April 1 of current year		12,500
Personal and dependency exemptions		2

Last year the Bateses elected to accrue their foreign income taxes for foreign tax credit purposes. No foreign tax credit carryovers are available to the current year. Stephen Bates estimates that they will owe 75,000 tesos in Country K income taxes for this year on the Country K salary and dividends. On December 31 of the current year, 4 tesos equal $1 (U.S.). The exchange rate between the teso and the dollar did not change between year-end and the date the Country K taxes are paid. No Country K taxes are withheld on the foreign corporation dividend.

Complete the two Form 1116s the Bateses must file with their current year return in order to claim the foreign tax credit on the salary and dividends. Ignore the implications of the Sec. 911 earned income exclusion, itemized deduction reduction, personal exemption phase-out, and alternative minimum tax provisions.

C16-54 John Lawrence Bailey (social security number 234-56-7890) is employed by American Conglomerate Corporation in Country T. Bailey has resided in Country T with his wife and three children for seven years. He made one five-day business trip back to the United States in the current year. $1,500 of salary (but none of the allowances) is allocable to Bailey's U.S. business trip. Bailey reports the following tax information about the current year:

Income:	
Base salary	$75,000
Overseas premium	9,000
Cost-of-living allowance	37,500
Housing allowance	30,000
Education allowance	12,750
Home leave travel allowance	11,000
Income tax reimbursement from employer for preceding tax year	18,000
Expenditures:	
Tuition at U.S. school	12,000
Housing expenses (rental of home and related expenses)	32,500
Itemized deductions (including $3,000 of unreimbursed employee expenses)	10,000
Foreign income taxes	9,000

Complete a Form 2555 for the Baileys' 1996 tax year. Assume that all prior tax returns are filed claiming that Mr. Bailey is a bona fide foreign resident.

CASE STUDY PROBLEMS

C16-55 Mark Pruett, a U.S. citizen, is being transferred abroad by his employer. You have done his tax work for a number of years. His 1997 salary and allowances in Country M will be $175,000 which is substantially above his 1996 salary. This increase is due to the higher cost of living in Country M and his added responsibilities. $30,000 of the allowances are housing allowances. His housing costs are expected to run $36,000 for 1997. The statutory Country M income tax rate is 40%. His employer has a second location in Country T, where Mark probably will be transferred in three or four years. The statutory Country T income tax rate is 20%.

The anticipated transfer date is February 1. Mark will be accompanied by his wife and three-year-old daughter. Mark anticipates returning to the United States for one week of training during September.

Required: Your tax manager has asked you to draft a memorandum (to Mark) for his review explaining the tax consequences of the relocation, whether he should elect to use the foreign earned income exclusion, and what records he will need when filing his tax return for the year of transfer.

C16-56 Ralph Sampson was hired last year by a small international trading company. You have done Ralph's tax returns for a number of years while he worked in the U.S. offices of a large international bank and have continued to handle his tax work while he is overseas on assignment to manage the trading company's Country T (a nontreaty country) office. Ralph has been assigned abroad since November 1, 1995 and has resided in a company-provided apartment continuously in T's capital. His wife and child have maintained their old residence in the United States to enable Mrs. Sampson to continue her career as a university professor and their son to finish high school. During 1995, Ralph was in Country T and other foreign countries for all of November and December. During 1996, Ralph was in the United States for ninety-three days and in Country T and other foreign countries for the remainder of his time. The ninety-three days spent in the United States occurred evenly throughout the four quarters of 1996. Ralph has been quite busy this year and wants you to file an amended 1995 tax return and initial 1996 tax return claiming the maximum possible foreign-earned income exclusion on each return. (The 1995 return was originally filed with no foreign-earned income exclusion because Ralph did not meet either requirement when the return was due.) Ralph knows that he does not meet the physical presence requirement, but he has assured you that he meets the residency requirements. However, because of his heavy travel schedule during 1996, he has not yet been able to accumulate the needed information to document that he is a Country T resident.

Required: Should you file the Sampson's amended 1995 tax return and new 1996 income tax returns claiming the maximum foreign-earned income for which Ralph has asked? What ethical issues do you face if you file the return based on Ralph's promise to obtain the information before the IRS ever gets around to auditing the returns?

TAX RESEARCH PROBLEMS

C16-57 Spike "Spitball" Weaver was a hard-throwing pitcher who was reaching the end of his major league baseball career. After becoming a free agent, he signed a rather lucrative three-year contract (which included a substantial signing bonus) to play for the Tokyo Bombers in the fledgling World Baseball League. This league included twelve teams, only four of which were located in the United States. Although Spike's salary is paid over a twelve-month period, he resides in Japan only for the seven-month regular season, the preseason training period, and the postseason playoffs (if his team makes the playoffs). The remainder of his time is spent at his home in Fitzgerald, Georgia. The tax manager for whom you regularly work has asked you to prepare a memorandum to the file indicating what factors should be considered in allocating Spike's bonus and salary between the U.S. and non-U.S. locations?

She suggests that at a minimum you should consider

- Reg. Sec. 1.861-4
- Rev. Rul. 76-66, 1976-1 C.B. 189
- Rev. Rul. 87-38, 1987-1 C.B. 176
- *Peter Stemkowski v. CIR*, 50 AFTR 2d 82-5739, 82-2 USTC ¶9589 (2nd Cir., 1982)

C16-58 Determine whether the taxes levied under each of the Acts listed below are creditable under Sec. 901.

a. Mexican assets tax and Mexican income tax
b. Canadian Branch Tax Act (imposed on Canadian branches of foreign companies)
c. Ontario (Canada) Corporations Tax Act
d. Japan Corporation Tax Law

A partial list of research sources is

- Rev. Rul. 91-45, 1991–2 C.B. 336
- Research Institute of America, *United States Tax Reporter,* ¶9015.03
- Commerce Clearing House, *Standard Federal Tax Reporter,* ¶28466.318
- Bureau of National Affairs, *Tax Management Portfolios,* individual country portfolios on Mexico, Canada, and Japan

Authors' note: One might also consult the tax treaties that the United States has signed with each of the three nations for further authority.

C16-59 Kiwi Corporation, a sales FSC, is created on January 1 of the current year. Kiwi Corporation meets all of the FSC requirements for the current year. It sells a product that is produced by its U.S. parent corporation. During the current year Kiwi sells 20,000 units of the product at a $10.00 per-unit price. All of the sales produced foreign trading gross receipts. The per-unit costs incurred by Kiwi and its U.S. parent corporation are parent's manufacturing costs, $2.50; FSC's promotion and sales expenses, $3.00; and FSC's general and administrative expenses, $2.00. An arm's-length transfer price for the product would have been $4.60.

Prepare a memorandum for your boss, the Director of Worldwide Taxes at Kiwi, explaining:

a. What are Kiwi's maximum per-unit profit under all three transfer pricing alternatives?

b. What are the amount and tax treatment for Kiwi's exempt foreign trade income and nonexempt foreign trade income under each of the alternative pricing methods?

APPENDIX A

TAX RESEARCH WORKING PAPER FILE

George Dunn

Tax File

December 19XX

INDEX TO WORKING PAPERS

Item	Page Reference
Draft of Client Letter	A–1
Memo to File, Patsy Partner	B–1
Summary of Questions and Conclusions	C–1
Detailed Questions and Conclusions	D–1

CARTER, PARKER, & ADAMS, CPAs
1011 Sunshine Blvd.
Tampa, Florida 33602

December 20, 19XX

Mr. George Dunn
15 Coral Court
Tampa, Florida 33611

We are pleased to report the results of our research concerning whether you will have to report any gain on the sale of your former residence. Before discussing our conclusions, I would like to restate briefly the facts that you related to me in our phone conversation of December 15. Please review these facts carefully because our conclusions depend upon an accurate understanding of all the relevant facts.

- - - (Summary of facts goes here.) - - -

Assuming that the preceding paragraphs constitute an accurate statement of all the relevant facts, we conclude that authority exists for viewing 105 Orange St. as your principal residence as of the date of sale. Accordingly, because the cost of your new residence exceeded the sales price (net of expenses) of your former residence, you may defer all of the gain. Deferral of the gain will reduce the basis of your new property. Whether a property constitutes your principal residence depends on all the facts and circumstances and your failure to occupy a house at the sale date does not automatically disqualify the house from being classified as your principal residence. We have a good faith belief that classification of 105 Orange St. as your principal residence on the sale date has a realistic possibility of being sustained administratively or judicially if challenged. However, if your return is audited, the Internal Revenue Service may argue that you are ineligible for deferral because, in their opinion, you had abandoned 105 Orange St. as your principal residence by the sale date. We will be happy to discuss this matter with you in more detail.

Thank you for consulting us. It is important that this letter be kept confidential. If you have any questions concerning our conclusions, please call.

Sincerely,

Patsy Partner

D-R-A-F-T

December 15, 19XX

MEMO TO FILE

FROM: Patsy Partner

SUBJECT: George Dunn-Tax Engagement

Today George Dunn called to inquire about the tax results of the sale of his former residence, 105 Orange St., Tampa, Florida. Basically, he wants to know whether he will have to report any gain on the sale.

Dunn purchased the house in 1963 for $75,000. He made no improvements to the house. In 1965 he married Linda Graves but continued to hold the house solely in his name. This is the first house that Dunn has owned. George and Linda occupied the house as their only residence until February 14, 19XX, when they decided to get a divorce. Mr. Dunn moved into an apartment on February 14, 19XX, and Mrs. Dunn continued to live in the house while she contemplated relocating to her hometown of Ponca City, Oklahoma. Dunn thought that if Mrs. Dunn did move back to Oklahoma, he would move back into the house after the divorce, provided Mrs. Dunn did not receive the house as part of her property settlement in connection with the divorce.

The divorce became final on September 13, 19XX, and Mrs. Dunn received stocks and bonds, but not the house, as her property settlement. She moved backed to Oklahoma on September 15, 19XX, and Mr. Dunn started making plans to move back into the house. Time pressures from business kept him too busy to move immediately. On September 25, 19XX, George decided to spend some of his free time touring model homes in a new development in Tampa. One of the homes, 15 Coral Court, turned out to be the house he had always dreamed of owning. He anticipated he could sell 105 Orange St. for almost as much as the asking price of 15 Coral Court.

Dunn thought about the new house for several days, and on October 4 he contracted to buy 15 Coral Court for $250,000. That same day he listed 105 Orange St. with the realtor who sold him his new house. On December 13, 19XX, Dunn sold his Orange St. house for $235,000 cash. There was no debt on his property. He incurred no fixing-up expenses, but his selling expenses totaled $15,000. Dunn will move to Coral Court by the end of this month. Subsequent to the move, he anticipates that this property will be his only residence.

Dunn hopes that his sale will be eligible for rollover of the gain under Sec. 1034. He is not 55 years old; consequently, he will not be eligible for the special rules affecting "older persons" who sell their homes.

We need to determine whether 105 Orange St. still qualifies as Dunn's principal residence, given that he did not live there for the period (approximately 10 months) between the date of the couple's decision to get a divorce and the sale date. I told Dunn we'd try to finish our research within a week. I have assigned Steve Staff the responsibility of researching this matter and drafting a client letter. Steve is to finish this assignment within 5 days. (He already has several other projects on which he is working.)

GEORGE DUNN

SUMMARY OF QUESTIONS AND CONCLUSIONS

	Work Paper Reference
1. Does Dunn's sale qualify for a deferral of his realized gain?	
Conclusion: It qualifies for deferral *provided* the house meets the principal residence test as of the sale date.	D–1
2. Did the house constitute Dunn's principal residence as of the sale date?	
Conclusion: We have a good faith belief that classification of the house as his principal residence on the sale date, even though he did not occupy it on the date, is a position warranted in existing law. The IRS may, however, contend that he had abandoned this house as his principal residence. We should advise Dunn of the IRS's possible position and determine whether he wants us to file his return on the basis that he qualifies for deferral.	D–3

GEORGE DUNN

WORK PAPERS

1. Does Dunn's sale qualify for deferral of recognition of the gain?

 Conclusion: Yes, provided 105 Orange St. meets the test of being Dunn's principal residence as of the sale date. Section 1034 is the controlling authority. It reads as follows:

SEC. 1034. ROLLOVER OF GAIN ON SALE OF PRINCIPAL RESIDENCE.

(a) **Nonrecognition of Gain.**—If property (in this section called "old residence") used by the taxpayer as his principal residence is sold by him, and, within a period beginning 2 years before the date of such sale and ending 2 years after such date, property (in this section called "new residence") is purchased and used by the taxpayer as his principal residence, gain (if any) from such sale shall be recognized only to the extent that the taxpayer's adjusted sales price (as defined in subsection (b)) of the old residence exceeds the taxpayer's cost of purchasing the new residence.

See ques. 2

See ques. 1(a)

(b) **Adjusted Sales Price Defined.**—

(1) **In general.**—For purposes of this section, the term "adjusted sales price" means the amount realized, reduced by the aggregate of the expenses for work performed on the old residence in order to assist in its sale.

See ques. 1(b)

(2) **Limitations.**

(c) **Rules for Application of Section.**

(d) **Limitation.**

Not Applicable

(e) **Basis of New Residence.**—Where the purchase of a new residence results, under subsection (a) or under section 112(n) of the Internal Revenue Code of 1939, in the nonrecognition of gain on the sale of an old residence, in determining the adjusted basis of the new residence as of any time following the sale of the old residence, the adjustments to basis shall include a reduction by an amount equal to the amount of the gain not so recognized on the sale of the old residence. For this purpose, the amount of the gain not so recognized on the sale of the old residence includes only so much of such gain as is not recognized by reason of the cost, up to such time, or purchasing the new residence.

If gain is deferred, the basis of the "new" house is affected.

(f) **Tenant-Stockholder in a Cooperative Housing Corporation.**

(g) **Husband and Wife.**

(h) **Members of Armed Forces.**

(i) **Special Rule for Condemnation.**

Not Applicable

(j) **Statute of Limitations.**-If the taxpayer during a taxable year sells at a gain property used by him as his principal residence, then-

(1) the statutory period for the assessment of any deficiency attributable to any part of such gain shall not expire before the expiration of 3 years from the date the Secretary is notified by the taxpayer (in such manner as the Secretary may be regulations prescribe) of-

(A) the taxpayer's cost of purchasing the new residence which the taxpayer claims results in nonrecognition of any part of such gain,

(B) the taxpayer's intention not to purchase a new residence within the period specified in subsection (a), or

(C) a failure to make such purchase within such period; and

(2) such deficiency may be assessed before the expiration of such 3-year period notwithstanding the provisions of any other law or rule of law which would otherwise prevent such assessment.

Cost will be reported on 19XX return.

(k) **Individual Whose Tax Home is Outside the United States.**

(l) **Cross Reference.**

Not Applicable

1 (a) What gain is recognized if 105 Orange St. constitutes his principal residence?

Conclusion: No gain is recognized *if* the old house is still Dunn's principal residence because the cost of the replacement residence exceeds the adjusted sales price of the old residence.

Adjusted sales price	$220,000	*See ques. 1(b)*
Minus: Cost of replacement residence	(250,000)	
Recognized gain (but not less than 0)	$ -0-	

1 (b) What is the adjusted sales price of the old residence?

Conclusion: The adjusted sales price is $220,000.

Amount realized	$220,000	*See ques. 1(c)*
Minus: Expenses for work performed to assist with sale	(-0-)	
Adjusted sales price	$220,000	

1 (c) What is the amount realized?

Conclusion: The amount realized is $220,000.

Section 1001(b) defines amount realized as follows:

(b) **Amount Realized.**—The amount realized from the sale or other disposition of property shall be the sum of any money received plus the fair market value of the property (other than money) received. In determining the amount realized—

(1) there shall not be taken into account any amount received as reimbursement for real property taxes which are treated under section 164(d) as imposed on the purchaser, and

(2) there shall be taken into account amounts representing real property taxes which are treated under section 164(d) as imposed on the taxpayer if such taxes are to be paid by the purchaser.

Money received ($235,000 − $15,000)	$220,000	*See ques. 1(d)*
Plus: FMV of other property received	-0-	
Amount realized	$220,000	

1 (d) How do the selling expenses affect the amount realized?

Conclusion: The selling expenses are subtracted from the sale price to compute the amount realized. Regulation Sec. 1.1034-1(b)(4) states that items that "are properly an offset against the considerations received upon the sale (such as commissions and expenses of advertising the property for sale, of preparing the deed, and of other legal services in connection with the sale)" are to be subtracted from the consideration received to arrive at the amount realized.

2 Did 105 Orange St. constitute Dunn's principal residence as of the date of disposition?

Conclusion: Reasonable authority exists to treat 105 Orange St. as his principal residence on the disposition date. However, because Dunn had not occupied the house for the approximate 10 month period immediately preceding its sale, the IRS may contend that he had abandoned the house as his principal residence.

2 (a) What is the definition of "principal residence"? Section 1034 does not define "principal residence," but Regulation Sec. 1.1034-1(c)(3) provides some guidance concerning the definition.

(3) **Property used by the taxpayer as his principal residence.**—(i) Whether or not property is used by the taxpayer as his residence, and whether or not property is used by the taxpayer as his principal residence (in the case of a taxpayer using more than one property as a residence), depends upon all the facts and circumstances in each case, including the good faith of the taxpayer. The mere fact that property is, or has been, rented is not determinative that such property is not used by the taxpayer as his principal residence. For example, if the taxpayer purchases his new residence before he sells his old residence, the fact that he temporarily rents out the new residence during the period before he vacates the old residence may not, in the light of all the facts and circumstances in the case, prevent the new residence from being considered as property used by the taxpayer as his principal residence. Property used by the taxpayer as his principal residence may include a houseboat, a house trailer, or stock held by a tenant-stockholder in a cooperative housing corporation (as those terms are defined in section 216(b)(1) and (2)), if the dwelling which the taxpayer is entitled to occupy as such stockholder is used by him as his principal residence (section 1034(f)). Property used by the taxpayer as his principal residence does not include personal property such as a piece of furniture, a radio, etc., which, in accordance with the applicable local law, is not a fixture.

Thus, whether a property constitutes one's principal residence is a factual issue, and property can be rented to another without its automatically being disqualified from principal residence status. The statement concerning renting property indicates that a property may still be a taxpayer's principal residence even though he does not live in such property as of the date of the sale.

According to the Committee Reports (H. Rept. No. 586, 82d Cong., 1st Sess., 109 (1951); S. Rept. No. 781 (Pt. 2), 82d Cong., 1st Sess., 32 (1951), accompanying the legislation that added the predecessor of Sec. 1034 to the Code, the word "residence" is used "in contradistinction to property used in trade or business and property held for the production of income." The Committee Reports also state that renting out either the old or the new residence will *not necessarily* prevent deferral of the gain.

Dunn did not hold 105 Orange St. for the production of income or use it in his trade or business. Thus, the argument can be made that treating 105 Orange St. as his principal residence is within the spirit of the legislation that authorized deferral of gain in certain situations.

2 (b) Do any judicial or administrative authorities address the availability of deferral under Sec. 1034 to taxpayers not occupying the property on the date of sale? If so, what result do such authorities reach?

Conclusion: There are numerous authorities, several of which are summarized below, that address the issue. The holdings differ, based upon the applicable facts. An analysis of such authorities leads to the conclusion that we have a good faith belief for adopting the position that the 105 Orange St. house was still his principal residence on the date of sale. Special emphasis is placed on *Clapham* and *Barry* (decided for the taxpayer) and *Young* (decided for the IRS).

Cases in Favor of Principal Residence Status:

Ralph L. Trisko, 29 T.C. 515 (1957), *acq.* 1959-1 C.B. 5. The taxpayer (T) leased his residence while working abroad. He intended to reoccupy the house upon his return but could not because of rent controls and a lease obligation. He later sold the house to generate funds to use for buying a replacement house. The court allowed deferral of the gain even though T had moved from the house several years earlier. The IRS stated it will follow *Trisko* only in cases which are "factually similar."

Robert W. Aagaard, 56 T.C. 191 (1971), *acq.* 1971-2 C.B. 1. Here the Tax Court held that Sec. 1034 was applicable, even though the taxpayer did not occupy the old residence at the time of sale *or intend to return* to the house.

Robert G. Clapham, 63 T.C. 505 (1975), *acq.* 1979-2 C.B. 1. Here the taxpayers (T) offered their old house for sale about 4 months prior to moving to rental property located in another city. T rented the old house (with an option to buy) for a year because of lack of offers. T leased it again for a short time and then let it stay vacant. T bought and moved into the new house about 9 months before finally selling the old one. T did not plan to return to the old house.

The Tax Court held that Sec. 1034 was available. It placed emphasis on the fact that T's *only desire* with respect to the old house *was to sell* it as soon as possible and that he accepted his first offer. The court stressed that T rented the old house because of "the *exigencies* of the real estate *market*."

Arthur R. Barry, 1971 PH T.C. Memo ¶ 71,179, 30 TCM 757. In this case taxpayer (T), a military officer, occupied a house in Maryland from August 1955 through July 1960. Then he was stationed in Germany and Colorado. At the time he moved from Maryland he planned to return to his home there upon his retirement from the military. He rented the home on a yearly basis until September 1965, when he listed it for sale because he had decided to live in Colorado after his retirement from the military in November 1965. He sold the Maryland house in August 1966 and in November 1966 occupied the house he had purchased in Colorado.

The Tax Court concluded that the Maryland house retained its status as T's principal residence until the sale date. It emphasized that T *at all times intended to occupy* this home and that he did not offer it for sale prior to his changing his principal residence to Colorado. It characterized the *change* in his principal residence in 1966 as resulting from "an *unexpected change of plans*." It added that he could not have adopted his temporary military quarters as "new" principal residence because his scheduled retirement time was in the near future.

Lee D. Andrews, 1981 PH T.C. Memo ¶ 81,247, 41 TCM 1533 (aff'd. by Fourth Circuit in unpublished opinion 7/6/82). In Andrews the taxpayers (T) lived in Washington D.C., during 1973 and the first half of 1974. In July 1974 they moved to North Carolina. In June 1974, in anticipation of their move, they listed their D.C. home for rent. In August 1974 they purchased a home in North Carolina. They sold their D.C. home in April 1975.

In allowing Sec. 1034 treatment, the Tax Court stressed that deferral is not automatically precluded just because the seller does not occupy the property on the date of the sale. In deciding that T had not abandoned the D.C. house as his principal residence, the Tax Court was influenced by the fact that when T moved to North Carolina, he was *uncertain whether he would stay* there or return to D.C. Because of the uncertainty of his plans, it was appropriate for him to keep the D.C. house.

Cases Denying Principal Residence Status:

William C. Stolk, 40 T.C. 345 (1963), *acq.* 1964-2 C.B. 7. In this case, Mr. Stolk (T) moved out of his old house located outside New York City in June 1953. Having no intention to return to the house, he had all of his furniture moved from it. T moved to an apartment in Manhattan. His old house stood vacant until its sale in July 1955. In September 1955 he purchased a house in Virginia. T then began spending his weekends in Virginia.

The Tax Court held that from about May 1953 until July 1955, at least, T's principal residence was his Manhattan apartment. It concluded that he had *abandoned* the old house as his principal residence. Although in *Trisko* the seller received deferral of gain with respect to a house he did not occupy at the time of sale, the court found *Stolk* to be distinguishable from *Trisko*. It stated that *Trisko* does not stand for the broad proposition that the taxpayer does not have to live in the property as of its sale date.

Richard T. Houlette, 48 T.C. 350 (1967). In *Houlette*, the taxpayer (T) was a Coast Guard Officer. In July 1955 he was transferred from Oregon to Alaska. For a few months prior to moving he tried to sell his house but could not do so without incurring a loss. Thus, he rented the property under a 2-year lease that he later extended for another year. Upon the expiration of the second lease, T again tried to sell. Having no success in selling, T rented the property again. In September, 1960, T purchased a new home. In the interim period he had lived in rental property. In May, 1961 T finally sold his old home.

The Tax Court denied Sec. 1034 treatment because it decided the old house no longer constituted T's principal residence. It recognized that actual occupancy on the sale date is not a universal requirement for qualifying for Sec. 1034. In its opinion, "however, the facts and circumstances must be exceptional and unusual to permit the conclusion that a principal residence is being used by the taxpayer at the time of sale if he is not in possession thereof and occupying same at that time." The court placed importance on the fact that T had *not occupied* the old house for almost *6 years*, that it was rented during the entire period, that T *persistently tried to sell it*, and that he had *no* intentions to reoccupy the house.

Claud R. Young, 1985 PH T.C. Memo ¶ 85,122, 49 TCM 981. Here Mr. Young (T) was divorced in October 1975. In the divorce proceedings he was awarded 25% interest in the house that he and his ex-wife had occupied. On the day of the divorce he moved into an apartment, and his ex-wife and child continued to live in the house. In November 1976 T and his ex-wife entered into an agreement whereby he conveyed to her his 25% interest in the house in exchange for being released from the obligation to pay alimony and the mortgage and other fees related to the house. In November 1977 T bought a new house.

The Tax Court declined to allow a deferral of the gain. It concluded that the old house ceased to be T's principal residence after he ceased to live there and the court awarded exclusive use to his ex-wife and child. It stated, "generally, cases in which taxpayers have been allowed the benefits of section 1034(a) even though they were not in possession of the old residence at the time of sale involve either the temporary rental of the property or . . . exceptional and unusual facts and circumstances over which the taxpayer had no control." It added that, "a divorce while often unpleasant and unwanted, is uniquely personal and is not the type of external objective circumstances that allows a taxpayer not in possession of a home to be deemed a resident therein for purposes of section 1034(a)."

See below

Curtis B. Perry V. CIR, 78 AFTR 2d 96-5797, 96-2 USTC 50,405 (CA-9, 1996) also involved the sale of a home by a divorced taxpayer. Here, when his marriage broke up in June 1984, the taxpayer moved out of the house with no intention to return. The divorce was final in December 1985, and in accordance with the divorce settlement, the former wife and the child were given exclusive use of the home until the end of 1987, after which the house was to be sold as soon as possible and the sales proceeds divided equally between the two former spouses. The house was sold in March 1988, and the taxpayer treated the transaction as eligible for Sec. 1034. The court ruled that Sec. 1034 is not applicable in a situation such as here when the taxpayer leaves the home "permanently and with no intention to return, pursuant to a divorce settlement which gives the other spouse exclusive occupancy and which does not mandate that the house immediately be sold."

Application of the Cases to Dunn's Facts:

Dunn thought that he would move back to his old house unless his ex-wife received it as a property settlement. He did not place the home on the market until he had contracted to buy a new home. His purchase of a new home was a spur-of-the-moment decision. He sold his old home about 10 months after moving out of it and about 3 months after it was determined which spouse would receive the house in the property settlement. It was not possible, from an emotional standpoint, for him to occupy the house with his ex-wife after their final decision to seek a divorce.

A taxpayer is not unconditionally required to live in a property on the sale date in order for it to receive principal residence status. Whether a house is the taxpayer's principal residence depends on all the facts and circumstances. Dunn's move from his old house was a result of the "exigencies" (*Clapham*) of his pending divorce. Unlike *Stolk*, he never abandoned the old house; rather, like *Barry* his decision to sell resulted from an "unexpected change of plans." Dunn's facts meet the "exceptional and unusual circumstances" test described in *Houlette* as being a precondition to getting Sec. 1034 treatment for a property not occupied at the sale date.

If Dunn's return is audited, the IRS may argue that he had abandoned his old house. In fact, it may cite *Young* as holding that a divorce situation never meets the "exceptional and unusual" facts and circumstances test for qualifying a house that the taxpayer does not live in for nonrecognition under Sec. 1034. Our counterargument is that the language concerning divorce situations (page D-6) is not a holding to be applied across the board but, rather, is restricted to factual situations similar to those in *Young*. Unlike Dunn, Young knew when he moved from the house that he could not reoccupy it. His sale occurred 2 years after he moved in contrast with 10 months for Dunn's sale. Furthermore, Dunn sold his property about 2 months after his decision not to reoccupy it.

The recent case of *Perry* should not pose a problem because, unlike Mr. Perry, Dunn did not leave the house with no intention to return, and the ownership or use of the house was not addressed in Dunn's divorce.

We have a good faith belief for classifying 105 Orange St. as Dunn's principal residence on the sale date that is warranted in existing law. We should, however, advise Dunn of the position the IRS might take if it audits his return and inquire concerning what position he wants us to take.

APPENDIX B

COMPLETED TAX FORMS

SCHEDULE C (Form 1040)

Department of the Treasury Internal Revenue Service (98)

Profit or Loss From Business

(Sole Proprietorship)

▶ Partnerships, joint ventures, etc., must file Form 1065.

▶ Attach to Form 1040 or Form 1041. ▶ See Instructions for Schedule C (Form 1040).

OMB No. 1545-0074 | 1996 | Attachment Sequence No. 09

Name of proprietor: Andrew Lawrence	Social security number (SSN): 297 63 2110
A Principal business or profession, including product or service (see page C-1): Manufacturing Furniture	B Enter principal business code (see page C-6) ▶ 2506
C Business name. If no separate business name, leave blank.	D Employer ID number (EIN), if any: 59 2029763

E Business address (including suite or room no.) ▶ 1234 University Avenue
City, town or post office, state, and ZIP code: Gainesville, FL 32611

F Accounting method: (1) ☐ Cash (2) ☒ Accrual (3) ☐ Other (specify) ▶

G Did you "materially participate" in the operation of this business during 1996? If "No," see page C-2 for limit on losses. ☒ Yes ☐ No

H If you started or acquired this business during 1996, check here ▶ ☐

Part I Income

		Line	Amount
1	Gross receipts or sales. **Caution:** *If this income was reported to you on Form W-2 and the "Statutory employee" box on that form was checked, see page C-2 and check here* ▶ ☐	1	869,658
2	Returns and allowances	2	29,242
3	Subtract line 2 from line 1	3	840,416
4	Cost of goods sold (from line 42 on page 2)	4	540,204
5	**Gross profit.** Subtract line 4 from line 3	5	300,212
6	Other income, including Federal and state gasoline or fuel tax credit or refund (see page C-2)	6	
7	**Gross income.** Add lines 5 and 6 ▶	7	300,212

Part II Expenses. Enter expenses for business use of your home only on line 30.

		Line	Amount
8	Advertising	8	13,000
9	Bad debts from sales or services (see page C-3)	9	4,000
10	Car and truck expenses (see page C-3)	10	10,400
11	Commissions and fees	11	
12	Depletion	12	
13	Depreciation and section 179 expense deduction (not included in Part III) (see page C-3)	13	12,476
14	Employee benefit programs (other than on line 19)	14	4,000
15	Insurance (other than health)	15	
16	Interest:		
a	Mortgage (paid to banks, etc.)	16a	
b	Other	16b	8,000
17	Legal and professional services	17	
18	Office expense	18	16,000
19	Pension and profit-sharing plans	19	2,000
20	Rent or lease (see page C-4):		
a	Vehicles, machinery, and equipment	20a	36,000
b	Other business property	20b	
21	Repairs and maintenance	21	
22	Supplies (not included in Part III)	22	
23	Taxes and licenses	23	9,840
24	Travel, meals, and entertainment:		
a	Travel	24a	4,000
b	Meals and entertainment: 8,000		
c	Enter 50% of line 24b subject to limitations (see page C-4): 4,000		
d	Subtract line 24c from line 24b	24d	4,000
25	Utilities	25	
26	Wages (less employment credits)	26	52,000
27	Other expenses (from line 48 on page 2)	27	8,650
28	**Total expenses** before expenses for business use of home. Add lines 8 through 27 in columns ▶	28	184,366
29	Tentative profit (loss). Subtract line 28 from line 7	29	115,846
30	Expenses for business use of your home. Attach **Form 8829**	30	
31	**Net profit or (loss).** Subtract line 30 from line 29. • If a profit, enter on **Form 1040, line 12,** and ALSO on **Schedule SE, line 2** (statutory employees, see page C-5). Estates and trusts, enter on Form 1041, line 3. • If a loss, you MUST go on to line 32.	31	115,846

32 If you have a loss, check the box that describes your investment in this activity (see page C-5).
• If you checked 32a, enter the loss on **Form 1040, line 12,** and ALSO on **Schedule SE, line 2** (statutory employees, see page C-5). Estates and trusts, enter on Form 1041, line 3.
• If you checked 32b, you MUST attach **Form 6198.**

32a ☒ All investment is at risk.
32b ☐ Some investment is not at risk.

Schedule C (Form 1040) 1996 Page **2**

Part III Cost of Goods Sold (see page C-5)

33 Method(s) used to value closing inventory: a ☒ Cost b ☐ Lower of cost or market c ☐ Other (attach explanation)

34 Was there any change in determining quantities, costs, or valuations between opening and closing inventory? If "Yes," attach explanation . . . ☐ Yes ☒ No

35 Inventory at beginning of year. If different from last year's closing inventory, attach explanation	35	64,000
36 Purchases less cost of items withdrawn for personal use	36	340,800
37 Cost of labor. Do not include salary paid to yourself	37	143,204
38 Materials and supplies	38	90,000
39 Other costs	39	7,000
40 Add lines 35 through 39	40	645,004
41 Inventory at end of year	41	104,800
42 **Cost of goods sold.** Subtract line 41 from line 40. Enter the result here and on page 1, line 4	42	540,204

Part IV Information on Your Vehicle.

Complete this part **ONLY** if you are claiming car or truck expenses on line 10 and are not required to file Form 4562 for this business. See the instructions for line 13 on page C-3 to find out if you must file.

43 When did you place your vehicle in service for business purposes? (month, day, year) ▶ 03 / 12 / 95.

44 Of the total number of miles you drove your vehicle during 1996, enter the number of miles you used your vehicle for:

a Business 17,000 b Commuting 4,500 c Other 12,000

45 Do you (or your spouse) have another vehicle available for personal use? . . . ☒ Yes ☐ No

46 Was your vehicle available for use during off-duty hours? . . . ☒ Yes ☐ No

47a Do you have evidence to support your deduction? . . . ☒ Yes ☐ No

b If "Yes," is the evidence written? . . . ☒ Yes ☐ No

Part V Other Expenses.

List below business expenses not included on lines 8–26 or line 30.

Repairs	4,800
General and administrative	3,000
Miscellaneous	850
48 **Total other expenses.** Enter here and on page 1, line 27 . . . 48	8,650

FACTS FOR SOLE PROPRIETORSHIP (SCHEDULE C)

Andrew Lawrence is the sole proprietor of a business that operates under the name Andrew Lawrence Furniture (Business Code 2500). The proprietorship is located at 1234 University Ave., Gainesville, FL 32611. Its employer identification number is 59-2029763. Andrew started the business with a $200,000 capital investment on June 1, 1990. The business uses the calendar year as its tax year (the same as its proprietor), and the accrual method of accounting. The following information has been gathered about its 1996 activities:

A trial balance is included as part of the accompanying worksheet. Notes accompanying the account balances are presented below.

1. Cost of goods sold is determined as follows:

Inventory at beginning of year	$ 64,000
Plus: Purchases	340,800
Cost of labor	143,204
Additional Sec. 263A adjustment	7,000
Overhead	90,000
Goods available for sale	$645,004
Minus: Inventory at end of year	(104,800)
Cost of goods sold	$540,204

Inventory is valued using the first-in, first-out method and historical costs. The Sec. 263A rules apply to the proprietorship. There was no change in valuing inventories between the beginning and end of the tax year.

2. MACRS depreciation is used for tax purposes. The current year tax depreciation is $27,476. $15,000 of this amount is included in cost of goods sold and inventory. The AMT depreciation adjustment on post-1986 personal property is $4,514. This amount is reported on Andrew Lawrence's Form 6251 (Alternative Minimum Tax—Individuals) which is not reproduced here.

3. Various temporary investments have been purchased with proprietorship funds. These include a 2% investment in Plaza Corporation stock, 50 shares of Service Corporation stock, and some tax-exempt municipal bonds. The Plaza stock was held for two years and sold for $4,500 more than its $7,000 adjusted basis. Prior to the sale, Plaza paid a $1,000 dividend. The 50 shares of Service stock, which had been purchased during the year, was declared worthless during the year. None of its $2,100 adjusted basis was recovered.

4. Employees other than Andrew Lawrence receive limited fringe benefits. One employee also receives a $2,000 contribution to an Individual Retirement Annuity that is paid by the proprietorship.

5. Miscellaneous expenses includes $150 of expenses related to the production of the dividend income.

6. No estimated taxes were paid by the proprietorship.

7. Balance sheet information is not provided for the sole proprietorship since it is not reported on the Schedule C. Balance sheet information can be found on page 4 of the C corporation tax return.

Andrew Lawrence, Sole Proprietorship Reconciliation of Book and Taxable Income For Year Ending December 31, 1996

	Book Income		Adjustments		Taxable Income		Schedule	Other Tax	
Account Name	Debit	Credit	Debit	Credit	Debit	Credit	C	Forms	
Sales		869,658				869,658	869,658		
Sales returns & allowances	29,242				29,242		−29,242		
Cost of sales	540,204				540,204		−540,204		
Dividends		1,000				1,000		1,000	(Sched. B)
Tax-exempt interest		18,000	18,000			0			
Gain on stock sale		4,500				4,500		4,500	(Sched. D)
Worthless stock loss	2,100				2,100			−2,100	(Sched. D)
Proprietor's salary[a]	36,000			36,000	0		0	0	
Other salaries	52,000				52,000		−52,000		
Rentals	36,000				36,000		−36,000		
Bad debts	4,000				4,000		−4,000		
Interest:									
Working capital loans	8,000				8,000		−8,000		
Purchase tax-exempt bonds	2,000			2,000	0				
Employment taxes	8,320				8,320		−8,320		
Taxes	1,520				1,520		−1,520		
Repairs	4,800				4,800		−4,800		
Depreciation[b]	12,000		476		12,476		−12,476		
Charitable contributions	12,000				12,000			−12,000	(Sched. A)
Travel	4,000				4,000		−4,000		
Meals and entertainment[c]	8,000			4,000	4,000		−4,000		
Office expenses	16,000				16,000		−16,000		
Advertising	13,000				13,000		−13,000		
Transportation expense	10,400				10,400		−10,400		
General and administrative	3,000				3,000		−3,000		
Pension plans[d]	2,000				2,000		−2,000		
Employee benefit programs[e]	4,000				4,000		−4,000		
Miscellaneous	1,000				1,000		−850	−150	(Form 4952)
Net profit/Taxable income	83,572		23,524		107,096				
Total	893,158	893,158	42,000	42,000	875,158	875,158	115,846		

[a] The $3,000 monthly salary for Andrew Lawrence is treated as a withdrawal from the proprietorship and is not deducted on Schedule C. The salary does not reduce Schedule C income, and is therefore taxed as self-employment income.

[b] MACRS depreciation $12,476 − $12,000 = $476

[c] 50% of the meals and entertainment expense is not deductible for tax purposes.

[d] The pension plan expense is the same for book and tax purposes for this firm. No pension expenses relate to pensions for the proprietor.

[e] The employee benefit expense is the same for book and tax purposes for this firm. None relate to proprietor benefits.

Form **1120** Department of the Treasury Internal Revenue Service

U.S. Corporation Income Tax Return

For calendar year 1996 or tax year beginning ...., 1996, ending ...., 19 ...
▶ Instructions are separate. See page 1 for Paperwork Reduction Act Notice.

OMB No. 1545-0123 — **1996**

A Check if a:
1 Consolidated return (attach Form 851) ☐
2 Personal holding co. (attach Sch. PH) ☐
3 Personal service corp. (as defined in Temporary Regs. sec. 1.441-4T—see instructions) ☐

Use IRS label. Otherwise, print or type.

Name: Johns and Lawrence, Inc.
Number, street, and room or suite no. (If a P.O. box, see page 6 of instructions.): 1234 University Avenue
City or town, state, and ZIP code: Gainesville, FL 32611

B Employer identification number: 76 3457689
C Date incorporated: 6/1/90
D Total assets (see page 6 of instructions): $ 479,324

E Check applicable boxes: (1) ☐ Initial return (2) ☐ Final return (3) ☐ Change of address

Income

Line	Description		Amount
1a	Gross receipts or sales 869,658 — b Less returns and allowances 29,242 — c Bal ▶	1c	840,416
2	Cost of goods sold (Schedule A, line 8)	2	540,204
3	Gross profit. Subtract line 2 from line 1c	3	300,212
4	Dividends (Schedule C, line 19)	4	1,000
5	Interest	5	
6	Gross rents	6	
7	Gross royalties	7	
8	Capital gain net income (attach Schedule D (Form 1120)) Not reproduced	8	2,400
9	Net gain or (loss) from Form 4797, Part II, line 20 (attach Form 4797)	9	
10	Other income (see page 7 of instructions—attach schedule)	10	
11	**Total income.** Add lines 3 through 10 ▶	11	303,612

Deductions (See instructions for limitations on deductions.)

Line	Description		Amount
12	Compensation of officers (Schedule E, line 4)	12	36,000
13	Salaries and wages (less employment credits)	13	52,000
14	Repairs and maintenance	14	4,800
15	Bad debts	15	4,000
16	Rents	16	36,000
17	Taxes and licenses	17	16,000
18	Interest	18	8,000
19	Charitable contributions (see page 8 of instructions for 10% limitation)	19	7,694
20	Depreciation (attach Form 4562) — 20: 27,476		
21	Less depreciation claimed on Schedule A and elsewhere on return — 21a: 15,000	21b	12,476
22	Depletion	22	
23	Advertising	23	13,000
24	Pension, profit-sharing, etc., plans	24	2,000
25	Employee benefit programs	25	4,000
26	Other deductions (attach schedule)	26	38,400
27	**Total deductions.** Add lines 12 through 26 ▶	27	234,370
28	Taxable income before net operating loss deduction and special deductions. Subtract line 27 from line 11	28	69,242
29	**Less:** a Net operating loss deduction (see page 10 of instructions) — 29a: ; b Special deductions (Schedule C, line 20) — 29b: 700	29c	700

Tax and Payments

Line	Description		Amount
30	**Taxable income.** Subtract line 29c from line 28	30	68,542
31	**Total tax** (Schedule J, line 10)	31	12,136
32	**Payments:** a 1995 overpayment credited to 1996 — 32a:		
b	1996 estimated tax payments — 32b: 14,000		
c	Less 1996 refund applied for on Form 4466 — 32c: ( ) d Bal ▶ 32d:		
e	Tax deposited with Form 7004 — 32e:		
f	Credit from regulated investment companies (attach Form 2439) — 32f:		
g	Credit for Federal tax on fuels (attach Form 4136). See instructions — 32g:	32h	14,000
33	Estimated tax penalty (see page 11 of instructions). Check if Form 2220 is attached ▶ ☐	33	
34	**Tax due.** If line 32h is smaller than the total of lines 31 and 33, enter amount owed	34	
35	**Overpayment.** If line 32h is larger than the total of lines 31 and 33, enter amount overpaid	35	1,864
36	Enter amount of line 35 you want: **Credited to 1997 estimated tax** ▶ **Refunded** ▶	36	

Sign Here

Under penalties of perjury, I declare that I have examined this return, including accompanying schedules and statements, and to the best of my knowledge and belief, it is true, correct, and complete. Declaration of preparer (other than taxpayer) is based on all information of which preparer has any knowledge.

Signature of officer: Andrew Lawrence — Date: 3/15/97 — Title: Vice-President

Paid Preparer's Use Only

Preparer's signature: Michael Kramer — Date: 3/14/97 — Check if self-employed ☒ — Preparer's social security number: 375 49 6339

Firm's name (or yours if self-employed) and address: Michael S. Kramer, 1110 McMillan, Gainesville, FL — EIN ▶ 59 2029763 — ZIP code ▶ 32611

Cat. No. 11450Q

Form 1120 (1996) Page **2**

Schedule A **Cost of Goods Sold** (See page 11 of instructions.)

1	Inventory at beginning of year	1	64,000
2	Purchases	2	340,800
3	Cost of labor	3	143,204
4	Additional section 263A costs (attach schedule)	4	7,000
5	Other costs (attach schedule)	5	90,000
6	**Total.** Add lines 1 through 5	6	645,004
7	Inventory at end of year	7	104,800
8	**Cost of goods sold.** Subtract line 7 from line 6. Enter here and on page 1, line 2	8	540,204

9a Check all methods used for valuing closing inventory:

(i) ☒ Cost as described in Regulations section 1.471-3

(ii) ☐ Lower of cost or market as described in Regulations section 1.471-4

(iii) ☐ Other (Specify method used and attach explanation.) ▶

b Check if there was a writedown of subnormal goods as described in Regulations section 1.471-2(c) ▶ ☐

c Check if the LIFO inventory method was adopted this tax year for any goods (if checked, attach Form 970) ▶ ☐

d If the LIFO inventory method was used for this tax year, enter percentage (or amounts) of closing inventory computed under LIFO | 9d |

e If property is produced or acquired for resale, do the rules of section 263A apply to the corporation? ☒ Yes ☐ No

f Was there any change in determining quantities, cost, or valuations between opening and closing inventory? If "Yes," attach explanation ☐ Yes ☒ No

Schedule C **Dividends and Special Deductions** (See page 12 of instructions.)	**(a)** Dividends received	**(b)** %	**(c)** Special deductions **(a)** × **(b)**
1 Dividends from less-than-20%-owned domestic corporations that are subject to the 70% deduction (other than debt-financed stock)	1,000	70	700
2 Dividends from 20%-or-more-owned domestic corporations that are subject to the 80% deduction (other than debt-financed stock)		80	
3 Dividends on debt-financed stock of domestic and foreign corporations (section 246A)		see instructions	
4 Dividends on certain preferred stock of less-than-20%-owned public utilities		42	
5 Dividends on certain preferred stock of 20%-or-more-owned public utilities		48	
6 Dividends from less-than-20%-owned foreign corporations and certain FSCs that are subject to the 70% deduction		70	
7 Dividends from 20%-or-more-owned foreign corporations and certain FSCs that are subject to the 80% deduction		80	
8 Dividends from wholly owned foreign subsidiaries subject to the 100% deduction (section 245(b))		100	
9 **Total.** Add lines 1 through 8. See page 12 of instructions for limitation			
10 Dividends from domestic corporations received by a small business investment company operating under the Small Business Investment Act of 1958		100	
11 Dividends from certain FSCs that are subject to the 100% deduction (section 245(c)(1))		100	
12 Dividends from affiliated group members subject to the 100% deduction (section 243(a)(3))		100	
13 Other dividends from foreign corporations not included on lines 3, 6, 7, 8, or 11			
14 Income from controlled foreign corporations under subpart F (attach Form(s) 5471)			
15 Foreign dividend gross-up (section 78)			
16 IC-DISC and former DISC dividends not included on lines 1, 2, or 3 (section 246(d))			
17 Other dividends			
18 Deduction for dividends paid on certain preferred stock of public utilities			
19 **Total dividends.** Add lines 1 through 17. Enter here and on line 4, page 1 ▶			
20 **Total special deductions.** Add lines 9, 10, 11, 12, and 18. Enter here and on line 29b, page 1 ▶			700

Schedule E **Compensation of Officers** (See instructions for line 12, page 1.)

Complete Schedule E only if total receipts (line 1a plus lines 4 through 10 on page 1, Form 1120) are $500,000 or more.

	(a) Name of officer	**(b)** Social security number	**(c)** Percent of time devoted to business	Percent of corporation stock owned: **(d)** Common	**(e)** Preferred	**(f)** Amount of compensation
1	Stephen Johns	386-05-9174	100 %	50 %	%	18,000
	Andrew Lawrence	297-63-2110	100 %	50 %	%	18,000
			%	%	%	
			%	%	%	
			%	%	%	
2	Total compensation of officers					36,000
3	Compensation of officers claimed on Schedule A and elsewhere on return					
4	Subtract line 3 from line 2. Enter the result here and on line 12, page 1					36,000

Form 1120 (1996) Page **3**

Schedule J Tax Computation (See page 13 of instructions.)

1	Check if the corporation is a member of a controlled group (see sections 1561 and 1563) . . . . . ▶ ☐ **Important:** Members of a controlled group, see instructions on page 13.		
2a	If the box on line 1 is checked, enter the corporation's share of the $50,000, $25,000, and $9,925,000 taxable income brackets (in that order): **(1)** $ **(2)** $ **(3)** $		
b	Enter the corporation's share of: **(1)** Additional 5% tax (not more than $11,750) $ **(2)** Additional 3% tax (not more than $100,000) $		
3	Income tax. Check this box if the corporation is a qualified personal service corporation as defined in section 448(d)(2) (see instructions on page 13) . . . ▶ ☐	3	12,136
4a	Foreign tax credit (attach Form 1118) . . . **4a**		
b	Possessions tax credit (attach Form 5735) . . . **4b**		
c	Check: ☐ Nonconventional source fuel credit ☐ QEV credit (attach Form 8834) **4c**		
d	General business credit. Enter here and check which forms are attached: ☐ 3800 ☐ 3468 ☐ 5884 ☐ 6478 ☐ 6765 ☐ 8586 ☐ 8830 ☐ 8826 ☐ 8835 ☐ 8844 ☐ 8845 ☐ 8846 ☐ 8820 ☐ 8847 **4d**		
e	Credit for prior year minimum tax (attach Form 8827) . . . **4e**		
5	**Total credits.** Add lines 4a through 4e	5	0
6	Subtract line 5 from line 3	6	12,136
7	Personal holding company tax (attach Schedule PH (Form 1120))	7	
8	Recapture taxes. Check if from: ☐ Form 4255 ☐ Form 8611	8	
9	Alternative minimum tax (attach Form 4626)	9	
10	**Total tax.** Add lines 6 through 9. Enter here and on line 31, page 1	10	12,136

Schedule K Other Information (See page 15 of instructions.)

		Yes	No
1	Check method of accounting: **a** ☐ Cash **b** ☒ Accrual **c** ☐ Other (specify) ▶		
2	See page 17 of the instructions and state the principal: **a** Business activity code no. ▶ 2500 **b** Business activity ▶ Manufacturing **c** Product or service ▶ Furniture		
3	Did the corporation at the end of the tax year own, directly or indirectly, 50% or more of the voting stock of a domestic corporation? (For rules of attribution, see section 267(c).) If "Yes," attach a schedule showing: (a) name and identifying number, (b) percentage owned, and (c) taxable income or (loss) before NOL and special deductions of such corporation for the tax year ending with or within your tax year.		X
4	Is the corporation a subsidiary in an affiliated group or a parent-subsidiary controlled group? If "Yes," enter employer identification number and name of the parent corporation ▶		X
5	Did any individual, partnership, corporation, estate or trust at the end of the tax year own, directly or indirectly, 50% or more of the corporation's voting stock? (For rules of attribution, see section 267(c).) If "Yes," attach a schedule showing name and identifying number. (Do not include any information already entered in **4** above.) Enter percentage owned ▶ 50%*	X	
6	During this tax year, did the corporation pay dividends (other than stock dividends and distributions in exchange for stock) in excess of the corporation's current and accumulated earnings and profits? (See secs. 301 and 316.) If "Yes," file Form 5452. If this is a consolidated return, answer here for the parent corporation and on **Form 851,** Affiliations Schedule, for each subsidiary.		X
7	Was the corporation a U.S. shareholder of any controlled foreign corporation? (See sections 951 and 957.) If "Yes," attach Form 5471 for each such corporation. Enter number of Forms 5471 attached ▶		X
8	At any time during the 1996 calendar year, did the corporation have an interest in or a signature or other authority over a financial account (such as a bank account, securities account, or other financial account) in a foreign country? If "Yes," the corporation may have to file Form TD F 90-22.1. If "Yes," enter name of foreign country ▶		X
9	During the tax year, did the corporation receive a distribution from, or was it the grantor of, or transferor to, a foreign trust? If "Yes," see page 16 of the instructions for other forms the corporation may have to file		X
10	Did one foreign person at any time during the tax year own, directly or indirectly, at least 25% of: **(a)** the total voting power of all classes of stock of the corporation entitled to vote, or **(b)** the total value of all classes of stock of the corporation? If "Yes," **a** Enter percentage owned ▶ N/A **b** Enter owner's country ▶ N/A **c** The corporation may have to file Form 5472. Enter number of Forms 5472 attached ▶		X
11	Check this box if the corporation issued publicly offered debt instruments with original issue discount . ▶ ☐ If so, the corporation may have to file Form 8281.		
12	Enter the amount of tax-exempt interest received or accrued during the tax year ▶ $ 18,000		
13	If there were 35 or fewer shareholders at the end of the tax year, enter the number ▶ 2		
14	If the corporation has an NOL for the tax year and is electing to forego the carryback period, check here ▶ ☐		
15	Enter the available NOL carryover from prior tax years (Do not reduce it by any deduction on line 29a.) ▶ $ None		

* See Schedule E

Form 1120 (1996) Page **4**

Schedule L Balance Sheets per Books

		Beginning of tax year		End of tax year	
	Assets	(a)	(b)	(c)	(d)
1	Cash		60,000		72,600
2a	Trade notes and accounts receivable	25,000		24,000	
b	Less allowance for bad debts	(1,000)	24,000	(1,000)	23,000
3	Inventories		64,000		104,800
4	U.S. government obligations				
5	Tax-exempt securities (see instructions)		200,000		200,000
6	Other current assets (attach schedule)		7,000		
7	Loans to stockholders				
8	Mortgage and real estate loans				
9	Other investments (attach schedule)				
10a	Buildings and other depreciable assets	151,600		151,600	
b	Less accumulated depreciation	(45,200)	106,400	(72,676)	78,924
11a	Depletable assets				
b	Less accumulated depletion	( )		( )	
12	Land (net of any amortization)				
13a	Intangible assets (amortizable only)				
b	Less accumulated amortization	( )		( )	
14	Other assets (attach schedule)				
15	Total assets		461,400		479,324
	Liabilities and Stockholders' Equity				
16	Accounts payable		26,000		19,000
17	Mortgages, notes, bonds payable in less than 1 year		4,000		4,000
18	Other current liabilities (attach schedule)		3,600		3,600
19	Loans from stockholders				
20	Mortgages, notes, bonds payable in 1 year or more		130,000		119,724
21	Other liabilities (attach schedule)				
22	Capital stock: **a** Preferred stock				
	b Common stock	200,000	200,000		200,000
23	Paid-in or capital surplus				
24	Retained earnings—Appropriated (attach schedule)				
25	Retained earnings—Unappropriated		97,800		133,000
26	Less cost of treasury stock		( )		( )
27	Total liabilities and stockholders' equity		461,400		479,324

Note: *You are not required to complete Schedules M-1 and M-2 below if the total assets on line 15, column (d) of Schedule L are less than $25,000.*

Schedule M-1 Reconciliation of Income (Loss) per Books With Income per Return (See page 16 of instructions.)

1	Net income (loss) per books	63,412	7	Income recorded on books this year not included on this return (itemize): Tax-exempt interest $ 18,000	
2	Federal income tax	14,000			
3	Excess of capital losses over capital gains				
4	Income subject to tax not recorded on books this year (itemize):		8	Deductions on this return not charged against book income this year (itemize):	
5	Expenses recorded on books this year not deducted on this return (itemize):			**a** Depreciation $ 476	
	a Depreciation $			**b** Contributions carryover $	
	b Contributions carryover $ 4,306				
	c Travel and entertainment $ 4,000				
	Interest on loans to acquire municipal bonds 2,000	10,306	9	Add lines 7 and 8	18,476
6	Add lines 1 through 5	87,718	10	Income (line 28, page 1)—line 6 less line 9	69,242

Schedule M-2 Analysis of Unappropriated Retained Earnings per Books (Line 25, Schedule L)

1	Balance at beginning of year	97,800	5	Distributions: **a** Cash	28,212
2	Net income (loss) per books	63,412		**b** Stock	
3	Other increases (itemize):			**c** Property	
			6	Other decreases (itemize):	
			7	Add lines 5 and 6	28,212
4	Add lines 1, 2, and 3	161,212	8	Balance at end of year (line 4 less line 7)	133,000

FACTS FOR C CORPORATION (FORM 1120)

The same basic facts that were presented for the Andrew Lawrence proprietorship are used for the C corporation except for the following:

1. Andrew Lawrence and Stephen Johns are the two 50% shareholders of Johns and Lawrence, Inc., a furniture manufacturer (Business Code 2500). Johns and Lawrence is located at 1234 University Ave., Gainesville, FL 32611. Its employer identification number is 76-3456789. The following information has been gathered about the 1996 corporate tax return:

Compensation of Officers

Name	S.S. No.	Shares	Title	Compensation
Stephen Johns	386-05-9174	1,000	President	$18,000
Andrew Lawrence	297-63-2110	1,000	V.P.	18,000
Total		2,000		$36,000

All salaries owed to the shareholders were paid in 1996. None of the interest or rentals are paid to the shareholders.

2. The book income for the corporation is presented in the attached worksheet which reconciles the corporation's book income and its taxable income.

3. The company was incorporated on June 1, 1990. One-half of the stock is held by each of the two officers and was acquired on that date for a total cash and property contribution of $200,000. There has been no change in the stockholdings since incorporation. Johns and Lawrence each devote 100% of their time to the business. No expense allowances are provided. Properly substantiated expenses, however, are reimbursed. Both officers are U.S. citizens. Johns and Lawrence is not a member of a controlled group.

4. Addresses for the officers are: Andrew Lawrence, 436 N.W. 24th Ave., Gainesville, FL 32607; Stephen Johns, 1250 N.E. 12th Ave., Gainesville, FL 32601.

5. Estimated taxes of $14,000 were paid for tax year 1996.

6. Other deductions include:

Travel	$4,000
Meals and entertainment	8,000
Minus: 50% disallowance	(4,000)
Office expenses	16,000
Transportation	10,400
General and administrative	3,000
Miscellaneous	1,000
Total	$38,400

7. The charitable contributions deduction limitation is $7,694 {[$303,612 gross income −$244,200 book expenses − ($12,000 + $4,000 + $2,000 − $476)] × 0.10}. A carryover of $4,306 ($12,000 − $7,694) to 1997 and the four succeeding tax years is available.

8. The $28,212 of withdrawals made by the two owners are dividends coming from the corporation's earnings and profits. They are reported as gross income on the shareholders' individual tax returns.

9. The beginning-of-the-year balance sheets for all entity forms are the same. This permits a direct comparison of the 1996 tax differences. In actuality, tax differences would have been reported in all prior years (1990 through 1995) which would have been included in the January 1, 1996 balance sheet. If these differences were so included, the direct comparisons would be much more difficult.

Johns and Lawrence, Inc. (C Corporation) Book Income to Taxable Income Reconciliation For Year Ending December 31, 1996

	Book Income		Adjustments		Taxable Income	
Account Name	Debit	Credit	Debit	Credit	Debit	Credit
Sales		869,658				869,658
Sales returns & allowances	29,242				29,242	
Cost of sales	540,204				540,204	
Dividends		1,000				1,000
Tax-exempt interest		18,000	18,000			0
Gain on stock sale		4,500				4,500
Worthless stock loss	2,100				2,100	
Officers' salaries	36,000				36,000	
Other salaries	52,000				52,000	
Rentals	36,000				36,000	
Bad debts	4,000				4,000	
Interest:						
Working capital loans	8,000				8,000	
Purchase tax-exempt bonds	2,000			2,000	0	
Employment taxes	14,480				14,480	
Taxes	1,520				1,520	
Repairs	4,800				4,800	
Depreciation[(a)]	12,000		476		12,476	
Charitable contributions[(b)]	12,000			4,306	7,694	
Travel	4,000				4,000	
Meals and entertainment[(c)]	8,000			4,000	4,000	
Office expenses	16,000				16,000	
Advertising	13,000				13,000	
Transportation expense	10,400				10,400	
General and administrative	3,000				3,000	
Pension plans	2,000				2,000	
Employee benefit programs	4,000				4,000	
Miscellaneous	1,000				1,000	
Federal income taxes	14,000			14,000	0	
Taxable income b/4 spec. dedns.			18,476	24,306	69,242	
Div. recd. dedn. (10%-owned)[(d)]			700		700	
NOL deduction					0	
Net profit/Taxable income	63,412		5,130		68,542	
Total	893,158	893,158	24,306	24,306	875,158	875,158

[(a)] MACRS depreciation $12,476 − $12,000 = $476

[(b)] Charitable contribution deduction limitation:

Gross income	$843,816
Minus: Deductions other than char. cont. & DRD	(766,880)
Charitable contribution base	$ 76,936
Times: 10%	× 0.10
Charitable contribution deduction	$ 7,694

[(c)] $8,000 × 0.50 disallowance rate = $4,000 disallowed expenses

[(d)] Dividends-received deduction: $1,000 × 0.70 = $700.

Form **7004** (Rev. June 1995) Department of the Treasury Internal Revenue Service

Application for Automatic Extension of Time To File Corporation Income Tax Return

OMB No. 1545-0233

Name of corporation: Perry Corporation

Employer identification number: 38-1505286

Number, street, and room or suite no. (If a P.O. box or outside the United States, see instructions.): 1631 W. University Avenue

City or town, state, and ZIP code: Gainesville, FL 32601

Check type of return to be filed:

☒ Form 1120	☐ Form 1120-FSC	☐ Form 1120-ND	☐ Form 1120-REIT	☐ Form 1120-SF
☐ Form 1120-A	☐ Form 1120-H	☐ Form 1120-PC	☐ Form 1120-RIC	☐ Form 990-C
☐ Form 1120-F	☐ Form 1120-L	☐ Form 1120-POL	☐ Form 1120S	☐ Form 990-T

Form 1120-F filers: Check here if you do not have an office or place of business in the United States . . . . ▶ ☐

1a I request an automatic 6-month (or, for certain corporations, 3-month) extension of time until June 15, 1998, to file the income tax return of the corporation named above for ▶ ☐ calendar year 19...... or ▶ ☒ tax year beginning October 1, 1996, and ending September 30 1997.

b If this tax year is for less than 12 months, check reason:
☐ Initial return ☐ Final return ☐ Change in accounting period ☐ Consolidated return to be filed

2 If this application also covers subsidiaries to be included in a consolidated return, complete the following:

Name and address of each member of the affiliated group	Employer identification number	Tax period

3 Tentative tax (see instructions)	3	72,000
4 Credits:		
a Overpayment credited from prior year	4a	
b Estimated tax payments for the tax year	4b	68,000
c Less refund for the tax year applied for on Form 4466	4c	( )
Bal ▶	4d	68,000
e Credit from regulated investment companies	4e	
f Credit for Federal tax on fuels	4f	
5 Total. Add lines 4d through 4f	5	68,000
6 Balance due. Subtract line 5 from line 3. **Deposit this amount electronically or with a Federal Tax Deposit (FTD) Coupon** (see instructions)	6	4,000

Signature.—Under penalties of perjury, I declare that I have been authorized by the above-named corporation to make this application, and to the best of my knowledge and belief, the statements made are true, correct, and complete.

E. Stephens Boeland (Signature of officer or agent) President (Title) 12/15/97 (Date)

For Paperwork Reduction Act Notice, see instructions. Cat. No. 13804A Form **7004** (Rev. 6-95)

Form **2220**

Department of the Treasury
Internal Revenue Service

Underpayment of Estimated Tax by Corporations

▶ See separate instructions.
▶ Attach to the corporation's tax return.

OMB No. 1545-0142

1996

Name	Employer identification number
Globe Corporation	38 : 1505087

Note: *In most cases, the corporation* **does not** *need to file Form 2220. The IRS will figure any penalty owed and bill the corporation. File Form 2220* **only** *if any of the boxes or the* **Note** *in Part I applies to the corporation. If the corporation does not need to file Form 2220, it may still use it to figure the penalty. Enter the amount from line 36 on the penalty line of the corporation's income tax return, but do not attach Form 2220.*

Part I **Reasons For Filing**—Check the boxes below that apply to the corporation. If any box is checked or the **Note** below applies, the corporation must file Form 2220 with the corporation's tax return, even if it does not owe the penalty. If the box on line 1 or line 2 applies, the corporation may be able to lower or eliminate the penalty. See page 2 of the instructions.

1 ☐ The corporation is using the annualized income installment method.
2 ☐ The corporation is using the adjusted seasonal installment method.
3 ☐ The corporation is a "large corporation" figuring its first required installment based on the prior year's tax.

Note: *The corporation must also file Form 2220 if it is claiming a waiver of the penalty. See* ***Waiver of penalty*** *on page 3 of the instructions.*

Part II **Figuring the Underpayment**

4	Total tax (see page 2 of the instructions)		4	100,000
5a	Personal holding company tax included on line 4 (Schedule PH (Form 1120), line 26)	5a		
b	Interest due under the look-back method of section 460(b)(2) for completed long-term contracts included on line 4	5b		
c	Credit for Federal tax paid on fuels (see page 2 of the instructions)	5c		
d	**Total.** Add lines 5a through 5c		5d	-0-
6	Subtract line 5d from line 4. If the result is less than $500, **do not** complete or file this form. The corporation does not owe the penalty		6	100,000
7	Enter the tax shown on the corporation's 1995 income tax return. (**CAUTION:** ***See page 2 of the instructions before completing this line.***)		7	125,000
8	Enter the **smaller** of line 6 or line 7. If the corporation must skip line 7, enter the amount from line 6 on line 8		8	100,000

			(a)	(b)	(c)	(d)
9	**Installment due dates.** Enter in columns (a) through (d) the 15th day of the 4th, 6th, 9th, and 12th months of the corporation's tax year ▶	9	4/15/96	6/15/96	9/15/96	12/15/96
10	**Required installments.** If the box on line 1 or line 2 above is checked, enter the amounts from Schedule A, line 41. If the box on line 3 (but not 1 or 2) is checked, see page 2 of the instructions for the amounts to enter. If none of these boxes are checked, enter 25% of line 8 above in each column	10	25,000	25,000	25,000	25,000
11	Estimated tax paid or credited for each period (see page 2 of the instructions). For column (a) only, enter the amount from line 11 on line 15	11	16,000	16,000	16,000	16,000
	Complete lines 12 through 18 of one column before going to the next column.					
12	Enter amount, if any, from line 18 of the preceding column	12		0	0	0
13	Add lines 11 and 12	13		16,000	16,000	16,000
14	Add amounts on lines 16 and 17 of the preceding column	14		9,000	18,000	27,000
15	Subtract line 14 from line 13. If zero or less, enter -0-	15	16,000	7,000	0	0
16	If the amount on line 15 is zero, subtract line 13 from line 14. Otherwise, enter -0-	16		0	2,000	
17	**Underpayment.** If line 15 is less than or equal to line 10, subtract line 15 from line 10. Then go to line 12 of the next column. Otherwise, go to line 18 (see page 3 of the instructions)	17	9,000	18,000	27,000	36,000
18	**Overpayment.** If line 10 is less than line 15, subtract line 10 from line 15. Then go to line 12 of the next column	18				

Complete Part III on page 2 to figure the penalty. If there are no entries on line 17, no penalty is owed.

For Paperwork Reduction Act Notice, see page 1 of the instructions. Cat. No. 11746L Form **2220** (1996)

Form 2220 (1996) Page 2

Part III Figuring the Penalty

	Line	(a)	(b)	(c)	(d)
19 Enter the date of payment or the 15th day of the 3rd month after the close of the tax year, whichever is earlier (see page 3 of the instructions). *(Form 990-PF and Form 990-T filers:* Use 5th month instead of 3rd month.)	19	6/15/96	9/15/96	12/15/96	3/15/97
20 Number of days from due date of installment on line 9 to the date shown on line 19	20	61	92	91	90
21 Number of days on line 20 after 4/15/96 and before 7/1/96	21	61	15		
22 Underpayment on line 17 × $\frac{\text{Number of days on line 21}}{366}$ × 8%	22	$ 120	$ 59	$	$
23 Number of days on line 20 after 6/30/96 and before 1/1/97	23		77	91	16
24 Underpayment on line 17 × $\frac{\text{Number of days on line 23}}{366}$ × 9%	24	$	$ 341	$ 604	$ 142
25 Number of days on line 20 after 12/31/96 and before 4/1/97.	25				74
26 Underpayment on line 17 × $\frac{\text{Number of days on line 25}}{365}$ × 9%	26	$	$	$	$ 655
27 Number of days on line 20 after 3/31/97 and before 7/1/97	27				
28 Underpayment on line 17 × $\frac{\text{Number of days on line 27}}{365}$ × *%	28	$	$	$	$
29 Number of days on line 20 after 6/30/97 and before 10/1/97.	29				
30 Underpayment on line 17 × $\frac{\text{Number of days on line 29}}{365}$ × *%	30	$	$	$	$
31 Number of days on line 20 after 9/30/97 and before 1/1/98	31				
32 Underpayment on line 17 × $\frac{\text{Number of days on line 31}}{365}$ × *%	32	$	$	$	$
33 Number of days on line 20 after 12/31/97 and before 2/16/98	33				
34 Underpayment on line 17 × $\frac{\text{Number of days on line 33}}{365}$ × *%	34	$	$	$	$
35 Add lines 22, 24, 26, 28, 30, 32, and 34	35	$ 120	$ 400	$ 604	$ 797

36 **Penalty.** Add columns (a) through (d), of line 35. Enter the total here and on Form 1120, line 33; Form 1120-A, line 29; or the comparable line for other income tax returns	36	$ 1,921

*If the corporation's tax year ends after December 31, 1996, see **Lines 28, 30, 32,** and **34** on page 3 of the instructions.

Form **4626**

Department of the Treasury
Internal Revenue Service

Alternative Minimum Tax—Corporations

▶ See separate instructions.
▶ Attach to the corporation's tax return.

OMB No. 1545-0175

1996

Name: Glidden Corporation

Employer identification number: 38 : 1505786

Line	Description	Box	Amount	Box	Amount
1	Taxable income or (loss) before net operating loss deduction			1	128,278
2	**Adjustments and preferences:**				
a	Depreciation of post-1986 property	2a	7,500		
b	Amortization of certified pollution control facilities	2b			
c	Amortization of mining exploration and development costs	2c			
d	Amortization of circulation expenditures (personal holding companies only)	2d			
e	Adjusted gain or loss	2e	<6,918>		
f	Long-term contracts	2f			
g	Installment sales	2g			
h	Merchant marine capital construction funds	2h			
i	Section 833(b) deduction (Blue Cross, Blue Shield, and similar type organizations only)	2i			
j	Tax shelter farm activities (personal service corporations only)	2j			
k	Passive activities (closely held corporations and personal service corporations only)	2k			
l	Loss limitations	2l			
m	Depletion	2m			
n	Tax-exempt interest from specified private activity bonds	2n			
o	Charitable contributions	2o			
p	Intangible drilling costs	2p			
q	Accelerated depreciation of real property (pre-1987)	2q			
r	Accelerated depreciation of leased personal property (pre-1987) (personal holding companies only)	2r			
s	Other adjustments	2s			
t	Combine lines 2a through 2s			2t	582
3	Preadjustment alternative minimum taxable income (AMTI). Combine lines 1 and 2t			3	128,860
4	**Adjusted current earnings (ACE) adjustment:**				
a	Enter the corporation's ACE from line 10 of the worksheet on page 8 of the instructions	4a	316,750		
b	Subtract line 3 from line 4a. If line 3 exceeds line 4a, enter the difference as a negative amount (see examples beginning on page 4 of the instructions)	4b	187,890		
c	Multiply line 4b by 75% (.75). Enter the result as a positive amount	4c			
d	Enter the excess, if any, of the corporation's total increases in AMTI from prior year ACE adjustments over its total reductions in AMTI from prior year ACE adjustments (see page 5 of the instructions). **Note:** *You **must** enter an amount on line 4d (even if line 4b is positive)*	4d	140,917		
e	ACE adjustment: • If you entered a positive number or zero on line 4b, enter the amount from line 4c here as a positive amount. • If you entered a negative number on line 4b, enter the smaller of line 4c or line 4d here as a negative amount.			4e	140,917
5	Combine lines 3 and 4e. If zero or less, stop here; the corporation does not owe alternative minimum tax			5	269,777
6	Alternative tax net operating loss deduction (see page 5 of the instructions)			6	-0-
7	**Alternative minimum taxable income.** Subtract line 6 from line 5			7	269,777

For Paperwork Reduction Act Notice, see separate instructions. Cat. No. 12955I Form **4626** (1996)

Form 4626 (1996) Page **2**

8	Enter the amount from line 7 (alternative minimum taxable income)	8	269,777
9	**Exemption phase-out computation** (if line 8 is $310,000 or more, skip lines 9a and 9b and enter -0- on line 9c):		
a	Subtract $150,000 from line 8 (if you are completing this line for a member of a controlled group, see page 5 of the instructions). If zero or less, enter -0- **9a** 119,777		
b	Multiply line 9a by 25% (.25) **9b** 29,944		
c	Exemption. Subtract line 9b from $40,000 (if you are completing this line for a member of a controlled group, see page 5 of the instructions). If zero or less, enter -0-	9c	10,056
10	Subtract line 9c from line 8. If zero or less, enter -0-	10	259,721
11	Multiply line 10 by 20% (.20)	11	51,944
12	Alternative minimum tax foreign tax credit. See page 5 of the instructions for limitations	12	-0-
13	Tentative minimum tax. Subtract line 12 from line 11	13	51,944
14	Regular tax liability before all credits except the foreign tax credit and possessions tax credit	14	33,278
15	**Alternative minimum tax.** Subtract line 14 from line 13. Enter the result on the appropriate line of the corporation's income tax return (e.g., Form 1120, Schedule J, line 9). If zero or less, enter -0-	15	18,666

Form **1120** — Department of the Treasury, Internal Revenue Service

U.S. Corporation Income Tax Return

For calendar year 1996 or tax year beginning ...., 1996, ending ...., 19 ...

▶ Instructions are separate. See page 1 for Paperwork Reduction Act Notice.

OMB No. 1545-0123 — **1996**

A Check if a:
1. Consolidated return (attach Form 851) ☑
2. Personal holding co. (attach Sch. PH) ☐
3. Personal service corp. (as defined in Temporary Regs. sec. 1.441-4T—see instructions) ☐

Use IRS label. Otherwise, print or type.

Name: Alpha Manufacturing Corp. and Subsidiaries

Number, street, and room or suite no. (If a P.O. box, see page 6 of instructions.): 820 N.W. 1ST Place

City or town, state, and ZIP code: Gainesville, FL 32601

B Employer identification number: 38 0000001

C Date incorporated: 9-15-73

D Total assets (see page 6 of instructions): $ 3,976,492

E Check applicable boxes: (1) ☐ Initial return (2) ☐ Final return (3) ☐ Change of address

Income	1a	Gross receipts or sales 6,147,000; b Less returns and allowances -0-; c Bal ▶	1c	6,147,000
	2	Cost of goods sold (Schedule A, line 8)	2	2,301,000
	3	Gross profit. Subtract line 2 from line 1c	3	3,846,000
	4	Dividends (Schedule C, line 19)	4	40,000
	5	Interest	5	156,000
	6	Gross rents	6	195,000
	7	Gross royalties	7	
	8	Capital gain net income (attach Schedule D (Form 1120))	8	67,939
	9	Net gain or (loss) from Form 4797, Part II, line 20 (attach Form 4797)	9	37,080
	10	Other income (see page 7 of instructions—attach schedule)	10	10,000
	11	**Total income.** Add lines 3 through 10 ▶	11	4,352,019
Deductions (See instructions for limitations on deductions.)	12	Compensation of officers (Schedule E, line 4)	12	165,000
	13	Salaries and wages (less employment credits)	13	1,356,000
	14	Repairs and maintenance	14	83,000
	15	Bad debts	15	48,500
	16	Rents	16	179,000
	17	Taxes and licenses	17	138,000
	18	Interest	18	58,000
	19	Charitable contributions (see page 8 of instructions for 10% limitation)	19	15,000
	20	Depreciation (attach Form 4562) — 20: 246,093		
	21	Less depreciation claimed on Schedule A and elsewhere on return — 21a: 77,400	21b	168,693
	22	Depletion	22	
	23	Advertising	23	269,140
	24	Pension, profit-sharing, etc., plans	24	140,000
	25	Employee benefit programs	25	105,000
	26	Other deductions (attach schedule)	26	1,284,000
	27	**Total deductions.** Add lines 12 through 26 ▶	27	4,009,333
	28	Taxable income before net operating loss deduction and special deductions. Subtract line 27 from line 11	28	342,686
	29	**Less:** a Net operating loss deduction (see page 10 of instructions) — 29a; b Special deductions (Schedule C, line 20) — 29b: 32,000	29c	32,000
Tax and Payments	30	**Taxable income.** Subtract line 29c from line 28	30	310,686
	31	**Total tax** (Schedule J, line 10)	31	104,417
	32	**Payments:** a 1995 overpayment credited to 1996 — 32a		
	b	1996 estimated tax payments — 32b: 146,000		
	c	Less 1996 refund applied for on Form 4466 — 32c ( ) d Bal ▶ 32d: 146,000		
	e	Tax deposited with Form 7004 — 32e		
	f	Credit from regulated investment companies (attach Form 2439) — 32f		
	g	Credit for Federal tax on fuels (attach Form 4136). See instructions — 32g	32h	146,000
	33	Estimated tax penalty (see page 11 of instructions). Check if Form 2220 is attached ▶ ☐	33	
	34	**Tax due.** If line 32h is smaller than the total of lines 31 and 33, enter amount owed	34	
	35	**Overpayment.** If line 32h is larger than the total of lines 31 and 33, enter amount overpaid	35	41,583
	36	Enter amount of line 35 you want: **Credited to 1997 estimated tax ▶** **Refunded ▶**	36	41,583

Sign Here

Under penalties of perjury, I declare that I have examined this return, including accompanying schedules and statements, and to the best of my knowledge and belief, it is true, correct, and complete. Declaration of preparer (other than taxpayer) is based on all information of which preparer has any knowledge.

Signature of officer: U. R. Stuck — Date: 3/15/97 — Title: President

Paid Preparer's Use Only

Preparer's signature: John A. Kramer — Date: 3/15/97 — Check if self-employed ☒ — Preparer's social security number: 241 69 3967

Firm's name (or yours if self-employed) and address: Kramer and Associates, 2250 N.W. 24th Ave., Gainesville, FL — EIN ▶ 01 0000001 — ZIP code ▶ 32605

Cat. No. 11450Q

Form 1120—Consolidated Taxable Income Computation

Line	Title	Consolidated	Adjustments and Eliminations	1 Alpha Mfg. Corp.	2 Beta Corp.	3 Charlie Corp.	4 Delta Corp.	5 Echo Corp.
1	Gross Receipts	$6,147,000	($109,000)[1]	$1,566,000	$2,680,000	$676,000		$1,249,000
	Returns/Allowances		85,000[2]					
2	Cost Goods/Operations	(2,301,000)		(783,000)	(1,390,000)	(128,000)		—0—
3	Gross Profit	$3,846,000	($24,000)	$ 783,000	$1,290,000	$548,000	—0—	$1,249,000
4	Dividends (Sch. C)	40,000	(170,000)[3]	210,000				
5	Interest	156,000		46,000	89,000			21,000
6	Gross Rents	195,000					$195,000	
7	Gross Royalties							
8	Capital Gain Net Income (Sch. D)	67,939		67,939				
9	Net Gain or Loss from Form 4797	37,080	(14,600) 2,920[5]	52,760	(4,000)			
10	Other Income	10,000[4]		10,000				
11	Total Income	$4,352,019	($205,680)	$1,169,699	$1,375,000	$548,000	$195,000	$1,270,000
12	Compensation of Officers	$ 165,000		$ 165,000				
13	Salaries and Wages	1,356,000		138,000	$ 240,000	$377,000	$ 36,000	$ 565,000
14	Repairs	83,000		19,000	18,000	7,000	18,000	21,000
15	Bad Debts	48,500			36,500	4,000		8,000
16	Rents	179,000		93,000	39,000	11,000		36,000
17	Taxes	138,000[4]		36,000	27,000	10,000	16,000	49,000
18	Interest	58,000		27,000			29,000	2,000
19	Contributions	15,000[4]		9,000	4,000			2,000
20	Depreciation	246,093		101,900	62,930	24,370	24,043	32,850
21a	Depreciation shown elsewhere on return	(77,400)		(77,400)				
21b	Depreciation	168,693		24,500	62,930	24,370	24,043	32,850
22	Depletion	—0—						
23	Advertising	269,140			223,140	27,000		19,000
24	Pension, Profit Sharing, etc. plans	140,000		39,000	21,000	35,000		45,000
25	Employee Benefit Programs	105,000		26,000	16,000	29,000		34,000
26	Other Deductions	1,284,000[4]		409,000	401,000	72,000	49,000	353,000
27	Total Deductions	$4,009,333	—0—	$ 985,500	$1,088,570	$596,370	$172,043	$1,166,850

Line	Title	Consolidated	Adjustments and Eliminations	1 Alpha Mfg. Corp.	2 Beta Corp.	3 Charlie Corp.	4 Delta Corp.	5 Echo Corp.
28	Taxable Income Before NOL Dedn. and Special Deductions	$ 342,686	($205,680)	$ 184,199	$ 286,430	($48,370)	$ 22,957	$ 103,150
29a	NOL Deduction							
29b	Special Deductions	(32,000)	(32,000)					
30	Taxable Income	$ 310,686	($237,680)					

Explanatory Notes

[1] Increase in deferred intercompany profits on the sale of inventory items (intercompany item) from Alpha to Beta during 1996 are eliminated from the revenues. The amount is reported when Beta sells the inventory outside the affiliated group or some other corresponding item occurs.

[2] Restoration of deferred intercompany profits arising from the sale of inventory items from Alpha to Beta in 1996 and prior years. These goods were sold outside the affiliated group in 1996. The increased intercompany profit deferral for 1996 is $24,000 ($109,000 − $85,000). This amount is reflected in the reduced gross profit.

[3] Intragroup dividends of $100,000 and $70,000 paid by Beta and Echo, respectively, to Alpha are an adjustment to consolidated taxable income since they were included in Alpha's separate tax return. The remaining $40,000 of dividends are from unaffiliated domestic corporations that are more than 20%-owned and eligible for an 80% dividends-received deduction (see Line 29b).

[4] The supporting schedule of component items is not reproduced here.

[5] Alpha sells a truck to Beta on June 27, 1996 for $25,000. The truck (a five-year MACRS property) cost $26,000 when purchased new on June 1, 1994. Depreciation of $13,520 [$26,000 × (0.2000 + 0.3200)] is claimed on the truck in 1994 and 1995. Depreciation of $2,080 ($26,000 × 0.1920 × 5/12) is claimed by Alpha in 1996. Alpha claims a total of $15,600 ($13,520 + $2,080) in depreciation prior to the sale. Alpha's deferred gain (intercompany item) on the sale is $14,600 [$25,000 − ($26,000 − $15,600)]. The truck is recorded as two separate MACRS properties on Beta's tax books. The original $26,000 basis for the truck is depreciated by Beta using the remainder of Alpha's 5-year recovery period. Depreciation on this portion of the basis is $2,912 ($26,000 × 0.1920 × 7/12) in 1996. Beta can also depreciate the second MACRS property; that is, the step-up in basis that results from the intercompany sale. Beta elects to depreciate this portion of the basis as a 5-year MACRS property and claims an additional $2,920 ($14,600 × 0.2000) of depreciation in 1996. The $2,920 is the portion of the deferred gain (Sec. 1245 income) that is reported by Alpha in 1996.

Form **1065** | Department of the Treasury | Internal Revenue Service

U.S. Partnership Return of Income

For calendar year 1996, or tax year beginning ...., 1996, and ending ...., 19 ....
▶ See separate instructions.

OMB No. 1545-0099 | **1996**

A Principal business activity: Manufacturing	Name of partnership: Johns and Lawrence	D Employer identification number: 76 3456789
B Principal product or service: Furniture	Number, street, and room or suite no. If a P.O. box, see page 10 of the instructions.: 1234 University Avenue	E Date business started: 6-1-90
C Business code number: 2500	City or town, state, and ZIP code: Gainesville, FL 32611	F Total assets (see page 10 of the instructions): $ 499,484

Use the IRS label. Otherwise, please print or type.

G Check applicable boxes: (1) ☐ Initial return (2) ☐ Final return (3) ☐ Change in address (4) ☐ Amended return

H Check accounting method: (1) ☐ Cash (2) ☒ Accrual (3) ☐ Other (specify) ▶

I Number of Schedules K-1. Attach one for each person who was a partner at any time during the tax year ▶ 2

Caution: *Include **only** trade or business income and expenses on lines 1a through 22 below. See the instructions for more information.*

Income

1a	Gross receipts or sales	1a 869,658		
b	Less returns and allowances	1b 29,242	1c	840,416
2	Cost of goods sold (Schedule A, line 8)		2	540,204
3	Gross profit. Subtract line 2 from line 1c		3	300,212
4	Ordinary income (loss) from other partnerships, estates, and trusts *(attach schedule)*		4	
5	Net farm profit (loss) *(attach Schedule F (Form 1040))*		5	
6	Net gain (loss) from Form 4797, Part II, line 20		6	
7	Other income (loss) *(attach schedule)*		7	
8	**Total income (loss).** Combine lines 3 through 7		8	300,212

Deductions (see page 11 of the instructions for limitations)

9	Salaries and wages (other than to partners) (less employment credits)		9	52,000
10	Guaranteed payments to partners		10	36,000
11	Repairs and maintenance		11	4,800
12	Bad debts		12	4,000
13	Rent		13	36,000
14	Taxes and licenses (8,320 + 1,520)		14	9,840
15	Interest		15	8,000
16a	Depreciation (if required, attach Form 4562)	16a 27,476		
b	Less depreciation reported on Schedule A and elsewhere on return	16b 15,000	16c	12,476
17	Depletion **(Do not deduct oil and gas depletion.)**		17	
18	Retirement plans, etc.		18	2,000
19	Employee benefit programs		19	4,000
20	Other deductions *(attach schedule)*		20	51,250
21	**Total deductions.** Add the amounts shown in the far right column for lines 9 through 20		21	220,366
22	**Ordinary income (loss)** from trade or business activities. Subtract line 21 from line 8		22	79,846

Please Sign Here

Under penalties of perjury, I declare that I have examined this return, including accompanying schedules and statements, and to the best of my knowledge and belief, it is true, correct, and complete. Declaration of preparer (other than general partner or limited liability company member) is based on all information of which preparer has any knowledge.

▶ Andrew Lawrence — Signature of general partner or limited liability company member | ▶ 4/10/97 — Date

Paid Preparer's Use Only

Preparer's signature ▶ Michael S. Kramer	Date 4/7/97	Check if self-employed ▶ ☒	Preparer's social security no. 375 49 6339
Firm's name (or yours if self-employed) and address ▶ Michael S. Kramer 1110 McMillan Gainesville, FL		EIN ▶	59 2029763
		ZIP code ▶	37611

Schedule A **Cost of Goods Sold** (see page 13 of the instructions)

1	Inventory at beginning of year	1	64,000
2	Purchases less cost of items withdrawn for personal use	2	340,800
3	Cost of labor	3	143,204
4	Additional section 263A costs *(attach schedule)*	4	7,000
5	Other costs *(attach schedule)*	5	90,000
6	**Total.** Add lines 1 through 5	6	645,004
7	Inventory at end of year	7	104,800
8	**Cost of goods sold.** Subtract line 7 from line 6. Enter here and on page 1, line 2	8	540,204

9a Check all methods used for valuing closing inventory:
- **(i)** ☒ Cost as described in Regulations section 1.471-3
- **(ii)** ☐ Lower of cost or market as described in Regulations section 1.471-4
- **(iii)** ☐ Other (specify method used and attach explanation) ▶

b Check this box if there was a writedown of "subnormal" goods as described in Regulations section 1.471-2(c) ▶ ☐

c Check this box if the LIFO inventory method was adopted this tax year for any goods *(if checked, attach Form 970)* ▶ ☐

d Do the rules of section 263A (for property produced or acquired for resale) apply to the partnership? ☒ **Yes** ☐ **No**

e Was there any change in determining quantities, cost, or valuations between opening and closing inventory? ☐ **Yes** ☒ **No**
If "Yes," attach explanation.

Schedule B **Other Information**

		Yes	No
1	What type of entity is filing this return? Check the applicable box: **a** ☐ General partnership **b** ☒ Limited partnership **c** ☐ Limited liability company **d** ☐ Other (see page 14 of the instructions) ▶		
2	Are any partners in this partnership also partnerships?		X
3	Is this partnership a partner in another partnership?		X
4	Is this partnership subject to the consolidated audit procedures of sections 6221 through 6233? If "Yes," see **Designation of Tax Matters Partner** below		X
5	Does this partnership meet **ALL THREE** of the following requirements? **a** The partnership's total receipts for the tax year were less than $250,000; **b** The partnership's total assets at the end of the tax year were less than $600,000; **AND** **c** Schedules K-1 are filed with the return and furnished to the partners on or before the due date (including extensions) for the partnership return. If "Yes," the partnership is not required to complete Schedules L, M-1, and M-2; Item F on page 1 of Form 1065; or Item J on Schedule K-1		X
6	Does this partnership have any foreign partners?		X
7	Is this partnership a publicly traded partnership as defined in section 469(k)(2)?		X
8	Has this partnership filed, or is it required to file, **Form 8264,** Application for Registration of a Tax Shelter?		X
9	At any time during calendar year 1996, did the partnership have an interest in or a signature or other authority over a financial account in a foreign country (such as a bank account, securities account, or other financial account)? See page 14 of the instructions for exceptions and filing requirements for Form TD F 90-22.1. If "Yes," enter the name of the foreign country. ▶		X
10	During the tax year, did the partnership receive a distribution from, or was it the grantor of, or transferor to, a foreign trust? If "Yes," see page 14 of the instructions for other forms the partnership may have to file		X
11	Was there a distribution of property or a transfer (e.g., by sale or death) of a partnership interest during the tax year? If "Yes," you may elect to adjust the basis of the partnership's assets under section 754 by attaching the statement described under **Elections Made By the Partnership** on page 5 of the instructions		X

Designation of Tax Matters Partner (see page 15 of the instructions)
Enter below the general partner designated as the tax matters partner (TMP) for the tax year of this return: (Not required)

Name of designated TMP ▶ Andrew Lawrence Identifying number of TMP ▶ 297-63-2110

Address of designated TMP ▶ 436 NW 24th Ave
Gainesville, FL 32607

Form 1065 (1996) Page **3**

Schedule K Partners' Shares of Income, Credits, Deductions, etc.

Section	(a) Distributive share items	Line	(b) Total amount
Income (Loss)	1 Ordinary income (loss) from trade or business activities (page 1, line 22)	1	79,846
	2 Net income (loss) from rental real estate activities *(attach Form 8825)*	2	
	3a Gross income from other rental activities (3a)		
	b Expenses from other rental activities *(attach schedule)* (3b)		
	c Net income (loss) from other rental activities. Subtract line 3b from line 3a	3c	
	4 Portfolio income (loss): a Interest income	4a	
	b Dividend income	4b	1,000
	c Royalty income	4c	
	d Net short-term capital gain (loss) *(attach Schedule D (Form 1065))* (not reproduced)	4d	(2,100)
	e Net long-term capital gain (loss) *(attach Schedule D (Form 1065))* (not reproduced)	4e	4,500
	f Other portfolio income (loss) *(attach schedule)*	4f	
	5 Guaranteed payments to partners	5	36,000
	6 Net gain (loss) under section 1231 (other than due to casualty or theft) *(attach Form 4797)*	6	
	7 Other income (loss) *(attach schedule)*	7	
Deductions	8 Charitable contributions *(attach schedule)*	8	12,000
	9 Section 179 expense deduction *(attach Form 4562)*	9	
	10 Deductions related to portfolio income (itemize)	10	150
	11 Other deductions *(attach schedule)*	11	
Investment Interest	12a Interest expense on investment debts	12a	
	b (1) Investment income included on lines 4a, 4b, 4c, and 4f above	12b(1)	1,000
	(2) Investment expenses included on line 10 above	12b(2)	150
Credits	13a Low-income housing credit:		
	(1) From partnerships to which section 42(j)(5) applies for property placed in service before 1990	13a(1)	
	(2) Other than on line 13a(1) for property placed in service before 1990	13a(2)	
	(3) From partnerships to which section 42(j)(5) applies for property placed in service after 1989	13a(3)	
	(4) Other than on line 13a(3) for property placed in service after 1989	13a(4)	
	b Qualified rehabilitation expenditures related to rental real estate activities *(attach Form 3468)*	13b	
	c Credits (other than credits shown on lines 13a and 13b) related to rental real estate activities	13c	
	d Credits related to other rental activities	13d	
	14 Other credits	14	
Self-Employment	15a Net earnings (loss) from self-employment	15a	115,846
	b Gross farming or fishing income	15b	
	c Gross nonfarm income	15c	
Adjustments and Tax Preference Items	16a Depreciation adjustment on property placed in service after 1986	16a	1,514
	b Adjusted gain or loss	16b	
	c Depletion (other than oil and gas)	16c	
	d (1) Gross income from oil, gas, and geothermal properties	16d(1)	
	(2) Deductions allocable to oil, gas, and geothermal properties	16d(2)	
	e Other adjustments and tax preference items *(attach schedule)*	16e	
Foreign Taxes	17a Type of income ▶ .... b Foreign country or U.S. possession ▶		
	c Total gross income from sources outside the United States *(attach schedule)*	17c	
	d Total applicable deductions and losses *(attach schedule)*	17d	
	e Total foreign taxes (check one): ▶ ☐ Paid ☐ Accrued	17e	
	f Reduction in taxes available for credit *(attach schedule)*	17f	
	g Other foreign tax information *(attach schedule)*	17g	
Other	18 Section 59(e)(2) expenditures: a Type ▶ .... b Amount ▶	18b	
	19 Tax-exempt interest income	19	18,000
	20 Other tax-exempt income	20	
	21 Nondeductible expenses	21	6,000
	22 Distributions of money (cash and marketable securities)	22	
	23 Distributions of property other than money	23	28,212
	24 Other items and amounts required to be reported separately to partners *(attach schedule)*		
Analysis	25a Income (loss). Combine lines 1 through 7 in column (b). From the result, subtract the sum of lines 8 through 12a, 17e, and 18b	25a	107,096

b Analysis by type of partner:	(a) Corporate	(b) Individual i. Active	(b) Individual ii. Passive	(c) Partnership	(d) Exempt organization	(e) Nominee/Other
(1) General partners		107,096				
(2) Limited partners						

Form 1065 (1996) Page **4**

Note: *If Question 5 of Schedule B is answered "Yes," the partnership is not required to complete Schedules L, M-1, and M-2.*

Schedule L — Balance Sheets per Books

Assets	Beginning of tax year (a)	(b)	End of tax year (c)	(d)
1 Cash		60,000		92,760
2a Trade notes and accounts receivable	25,000		24,000	
b Less allowance for bad debts	1,000	24,000	1,000	23,000
3 Inventories		64,000		104,800
4 U.S. government obligations				
5 Tax-exempt securities		200,000		200,000
6 Other current assets *(attach schedule)*		7,000		
7 Mortgage and real estate loans				
8 Other investments *(attach schedule)*				0
9a Buildings and other depreciable assets	151,600		151,600	
b Less accumulated depreciation	45,200	106,400	72,676	78,924
10a Depletable assets				
b Less accumulated depletion				
11 Land (net of any amortization)				
12a Intangible assets (amortizable only)				
b Less accumulated amortization				
13 Other assets *(attach schedule)*				
14 **Total** assets		461,400		499,484
Liabilities and Capital				
15 Accounts payable		26,000		19,000
16 Mortgages, notes, bonds payable in less than 1 year		4,000		4,000
17 Other current liabilities *(attach schedule)*		3,600		3,600
18 All nonrecourse loans				
19 Mortgages, notes, bonds payable in 1 year or more		130,000		119,724
20 Other liabilities *(attach schedule)*				
21 Partners' capital accounts		297,800		353,160
22 **Total** liabilities and capital		461,400		499,484

Schedule M-1 — Reconciliation of Income (Loss) per Books With Income (Loss) per Return (see page 23 of the instructions)

1 Net income (loss) per books	83,572	6 Income recorded on books this year not included on Schedule K, lines 1 through 7 (itemize): a Tax-exempt interest $ 18,000	18,000
2 Income included on Schedule K, lines 1 through 4, 6, and 7, not recorded on books this year (itemize):			
3 Guaranteed payments (other than health insurance)	36,000	7 Deductions included on Schedule K, lines 1 through 12a, 17e, and 18b, not charged against book income this year (itemize): a Depreciation $ 476	476
4 Expenses recorded on books this year not included on Schedule K, lines 1 through 12a, 17e, and 18b (itemize): a Depreciation $ b Travel and entertainment $ 4,000 Interest on loans to buy tax exempt bonds $2,000	6,000	8 Add lines 6 and 7	18,476
5 Add lines 1 through 4	125,572	9 Income (loss) (Schedule K, line 25a). Subtract line 8 from line 5	107,096

Schedule M-2 — Analysis of Partners' Capital Accounts

1 Balance at beginning of year	297,800	6 Distributions: a Cash	28,212
2 Capital contributed during year		b Property	
3 Net income (loss) per books	83,572	7 Other decreases (itemize):	
4 Other increases (itemize):		8 Add lines 6 and 7	28,212
5 Add lines 1 through 4	381,372	9 Balance at end of year. Subtract line 8 from line 5	353,160

SCHEDULE K-1 (Form 1065)
Department of the Treasury
Internal Revenue Service

Partner's Share of Income, Credits, Deductions, etc.

▶ See separate instructions.

For calendar year 1996 or tax year beginning , 1996, and ending , 19

OMB No. 1545-0099

1996

Partner's identifying number ▶ 297-63-2110

Partnership's identifying number ▶ 76 : 3456789

Partner's name, address, and ZIP code

Andrew Lawrence
436 NW 24th Ave
Gainesville, FL 32607

Partnership's name, address, and ZIP code

Johns and Lawrence
1234 University Avenue
Gainesville, FL 32611

A This partner is a ☒ general partner ☐ limited partner ☐ limited liability company member

B What type of entity is this partner? ▶ Individual

C Is this partner a ☐ domestic or a ☐ foreign partner?

D Enter partner's percentage of:

	(i) Before change or termination	(ii) End of year
Profit sharing	%	50 %
Loss sharing	%	50 %
Ownership of capital	%	50 %

E IRS Center where partnership filed return: Atlanta

F Partner's share of liabilities (see instructions):

Nonrecourse . . . $
Qualified nonrecourse financing . $
Other . . . $ 73,162

G Tax shelter registration number ▶ N/A

H Check here if this partnership is a publicly traded partnership as defined in section 469(k)(2) . . . ☐

I Check applicable boxes: **(1)** ☐ Final K-1 **(2)** ☐ Amended K-1

J **Analysis of partner's capital account:**

(a) Capital account at beginning of year	(b) Capital contributed during year	(c) Partner's share of lines 3, 4, and 7, Form 1065, Schedule M-2	(d) Withdrawals and distributions	(e) Capital account at end of year (combine columns (a) through (d))
148,900	0	41,786	(14,106)	176,580

		(a) Distributive share item		(b) Amount	(c) 1040 filers enter the amount in column (b) on:
Income (Loss)	1	Ordinary income (loss) from trade or business activities	1	39,923	See pages 5 and 6 of Partner's Instructions for Schedule K-1 (Form 1065).
	2	Net income (loss) from rental real estate activities	2		
	3	Net income (loss) from other rental activities	3		
	4	Portfolio income (loss):			
	a	Interest	4a		Sch. B, Part I, line 1
	b	Dividends	4b	500	Sch. B, Part II, line 5
	c	Royalties	4c		Sch. E, Part I, line 4
	d	Net short-term capital gain (loss)	4d	(1,050)	Sch. D, line 5, col. (f) or (g)
	e	Net long-term capital gain (loss)	4e	2,250	Sch. D, line 13, col. (f) or (g)
	f	Other portfolio income (loss) *(attach schedule)*	4f		Enter on applicable line of your return.
	5	Guaranteed payments to partner	5	18,000	See page 6 of Partner's Instructions for Schedule K-1 (Form 1065).
	6	Net gain (loss) under section 1231 (other than due to casualty or theft)	6		
	7	Other income (loss) *(attach schedule)*	7		Enter on applicable line of your return.
Deductions	8	Charitable contributions (see instructions) *(attach schedule)*	8	6,000	Sch. A, line 15 or 16
	9	Section 179 expense deduction	9		See page 7 of Partner's Instructions for Schedule K-1 (Form 1065).
	10	Deductions related to portfolio income *(attach schedule)*	10	75	
	11	Other deductions *(attach schedule)*	11		
Investment Interest	12a	Interest expense on investment debts	12a		Form 4952, line 1
	b	(1) Investment income included on lines 4a, 4b, 4c, and 4f above	b(1)	500	See page 7 of Partner's Instructions for Schedule K-1 (Form 1065).
		(2) Investment expenses included on line 10 above	b(2)	75	
Credits	13a	Low-income housing credit:			
		(1) From section 42(j)(5) partnerships for property placed in service before 1990	a(1)		Form 8586, line 5
		(2) Other than on line 13a(1) for property placed in service before 1990	a(2)		
		(3) From section 42(j)(5) partnerships for property placed in service after 1989	a(3)		
		(4) Other than on line 13a(3) for property placed in service after 1989	a(4)		
	b	Qualified rehabilitation expenditures related to rental real estate activities	13b		See page 8 of Partner's Instructions for Schedule K-1 (Form 1065).
	c	Credits (other than credits shown on lines 13a and 13b) related to rental real estate activities	13c		
	d	Credits related to other rental activities	13d		
	14	Other credits	14		

For Paperwork Reduction Act Notice, see Instructions for Form 1065. Cat. No. 11394R **Schedule K-1 (Form 1065) 1996**

Second schedule K-1 for Stephen Johns is similar to this one, but is not reproduced here.

Schedule K-1 (Form 1065) 1996 Page 2

		(a) Distributive share item		(b) Amount	(c) 1040 filers enter the amount in column (b) on:
Self-employment	15a	Net earnings (loss) from self-employment	15a	57,923	Sch. SE, Section A or B
	b	Gross farming or fishing income	15b		See page 8 of Partner's Instructions for Schedule K-1 (Form 1065).
	c	Gross nonfarm income	15c		
Adjustments and Tax Preference Items	16a	Depreciation adjustment on property placed in service after 1986	16a	757	See pages 8 and 9 of Partner's Instructions for Schedule K-1 (Form 1065) and Instructions for Form 6251.
	b	Adjusted gain or loss	16b		
	c	Depletion (other than oil and gas)	16c		
	d	**(1)** Gross income from oil, gas, and geothermal properties	d(1)		
		(2) Deductions allocable to oil, gas, and geothermal properties	d(2)		
	e	Other adjustments and tax preference items *(attach schedule)*	16e		
Foreign Taxes	17a	Type of income ▶			Form 1116, check boxes
	b	Name of foreign country or U.S. possession ▶			Form 1116, Part I
	c	Total gross income from sources outside the United States *(attach schedule)*	17c		
	d	Total applicable deductions and losses *(attach schedule)*	17d		
	e	Total foreign taxes (check one): ▶ ☐ Paid ☐ Accrued	17e		Form 1116, Part II
	f	Reduction in taxes available for credit *(attach schedule)*	17f		Form 1116, Part III
	g	Other foreign tax information *(attach schedule)*	17g		See Instructions for Form 1116.
Other	18	Section 59(e)(2) expenditures: **a** Type ▶			See page 9 of Partner's Instructions for Schedule K-1 (Form 1065).
	b	Amount	18b		
	19	Tax-exempt interest income	19	9,000	Form 1040, line 8b
	20	Other tax-exempt income	20		See page 9 of Partner's Instructions for Schedule K-1 (Form 1065).
	21	Nondeductible expenses	21	3,000 *	
	22	Distributions of money (cash and marketable securities)	22	28,212	
	23	Distributions of property other than money	23		
	24	Recapture of low-income housing credit:			
	a	From section 42(j)(5) partnerships	24a		Form 8611, line 8
	b	Other than on line 24a	24b		

Supplemental Information

25 Supplemental information required to be reported separately to each partner *(attach additional schedules if more space is needed)*:

* $1,000 of interest expense incurred to purchase tax-exempt bonds and $2000 of meals and entertainment expenses that were disallowed by Sec. 274.

FACTS FOR GENERAL PARTNERSHIP (FORM 1065)

The same basic facts that were presented for the Andrew Lawrence proprietorship are used for the partnership except for the following:

1. Johns and Lawrence is instead a general partnership. Andrew Lawrence and Stephen Johns are both general partners and have equal capital and profits interests. The partnership was created on June 1, 1990. Johns and Lawrence each exchanged their $100,000 of property for a 50% interest in capital and a 50% interest in profits.

2. The book income for Johns and Lawrence is presented in the attached worksheet which reconciles book income and partnership taxable income.

3. The $18,000 salaries paid to each partner are stipulated in the partnership agreement and are treated as guaranteed payments.

4. Federal and state employment taxes are paid on the wages paid to employees other than the partners Johns and Lawrence. The employment tax expense is $52,000 × 0.16 = $8,320. The guaranteed payments made to Johns and Lawrence are treated as self-employment income by the two partners.

5. No estimated federal income taxes were paid by the partnership.

6. The $28,212 in withdrawals were paid equally to the two partners.

7. Other deductions include:

Travel	$4,000
Meals and entertainment	8,000
Minus: 50% disallowance	(4,000)
Office expenses	16,000
Transportation	10,400
General and administrative	3,000
Advertising	13,000
Miscellaneous	850
Total	$51,250

   $150 of the miscellaneous expenses are related to the production of the dividend income and are separately stated.

8. Reconciliation of net income for the C corporation and the partnership occurs as follows:

Net income for C corporation	$63,412
Plus: Federal income taxes	14,000
Employment tax adjustment ($14,480 − $8,320)	6,160
Net income for partnership	$83,572

9. Total paid-in capital and accumulated profits were divided equally between the two partners in accordance with the actual contributions and allocation of partnership profits in the partnership agreement. Actual business operations may provide for an unequal allocation.

10. The balance sheet for Johns and Lawrence is presented on page 4 of Form 1065.

Johns and Lawrence General Partnership Reconciliation of Book and Taxable Income For Year Ending December 31, 1996

							Form 1065 Schedule K	
	Book Income		Adjustments		Taxable Income			
Account Name	Debit	Credit	Debit	Credit	Debit	Credit	Ordinary Income	Separately Stated Items
Sales		869,658				869,658	869,658	
Sales returns & allowances	29,242				29,242		−29,242	
Cost of sales	540,204				540,204		−540,204	
Dividends		1,000				1,000		1,000
Tax-exempt interest		18,000	18,000			0		18,000
Gain on stock sale		4,500				4,500		4,500
Worthless stock loss	2,100				2,100			−2,100
Guaranteed payments[a]	36,000			36,000	0		−36,000	
Other salaries	52,000				52,000		−52,000	
Rentals	36,000				36,000		−36,000	
Bad debts	4,000				4,000		−4,000	
Interest:								
Working capital loans	8,000				8,000		−8,000	
Purchase tax-exempt bonds	2,000			2,000	0			−2,000
Employment taxes	8,320				8,320		−8,320	
Taxes	1,520				1,520		−1,520	
Repairs	4,800				4,800		−4,800	
Depreciation[b]	12,000		476		12,476		−12,476	
Charitable contributions	12,000				12,000			−12,000
Travel	4,000				4,000		−4,000	
Meals and entertainment[c]	8,000			4,000	4,000		−4,000	
Meals and ent. nondeductible								−4,000
Office expenses	16,000				16,000		−16,000	
Advertising	13,000				13,000		−13,000	
Transportation expense	10,400				10,400		−10,400	
General and administrative	3,000				3,000		−3,000	
Pension plans[d]	2,000				2,000		−2,000	
Employee benefit programs[e]	4,000				4,000		−4,000	
Miscellaneous	1,000				1,000		−850	−150
Net profit/Taxable income	83,572		23,524		107,096			
Total	893,158	893,158	42,000	42,000	875,158	875,158	79,846	

[a] Note that guaranteed payments have no net effect on taxable income. The guaranteed payments both reduce ordinary income and increase separately stated income items that are taxable.
[b] MACRS depreciation $12,476 − $12,000 = $476
[c] 50% of the meals and entertainment expense is not deductible for tax purposes but must be separately stated on the Schedule K and K-1s.
[d] The pension plan expense is the same for book and tax purposes for this firm. No pension expenses relate to pensions for the partners.
[e] The employee benefit expense is the same for book and tax purposes for this firm. None relate to partner benefits.

Form **1120S** — Department of the Treasury, Internal Revenue Service

U.S. Income Tax Return for an S Corporation

▶ **Do not file this form unless the corporation has timely filed Form 2553 to elect to be an S corporation.**
▶ **See separate instructions.**

OMB No. 1545-0130 — **1996**

For calendar year 1996, or tax year beginning , 1996, and ending , 19

A Date of election as an S corporation: 6/13/90	Use IRS label. Otherwise, please print or type. Name: Johns and Lawrence, Inc.	**C** Employer identification number: 76 3456789
	Number, street, and room or suite no. (If a P.O. box, see page 9 of the instructions.): 1234 University Avenue	**D** Date incorporated: 6/1/90
B Business code no. (see Specific Instructions): 2500	City or town, state, and ZIP code: Gainesville, FL 32611	**E** Total assets (see Specific Instructions): $ 493,324

F Check applicable boxes: (1) ☐ Initial return (2) ☐ Final return (3) ☐ Change in address (4) ☐ Amended return

G Check this box if this S corporation is subject to the consolidated audit procedures of sections 6241 through 6245 (see instructions before checking this box) ▶ ☐

H Enter number of shareholders in the corporation at end of the tax year ▶ 2

Caution: *Include **only** trade or business income and expenses on lines 1a through 21. See the instructions for more information.*

Income	1a	Gross receipts or sales 869,658 **b** Less returns and allowances 29,242 **c** Bal ▶		1c	840,416
	2	Cost of goods sold (Schedule A, line 8)		2	540,204
	3	Gross profit. Subtract line 2 from line 1c		3	300,212
	4	Net gain (loss) from Form 4797, Part II, line 20 *(attach Form 4797)*		4	
	5	Other income (loss) *(attach schedule)*		5	
	6	**Total income (loss).** Combine lines 3 through 5 ▶		6	300,212
Deductions (see page 10 of the instructions for limitations)	7	Compensation of officers		7	36,000
	8	Salaries and wages (less employment credits)		8	52,000
	9	Repairs and maintenance		9	4,800
	10	Bad debts		10	4,000
	11	Rents		11	36,000
	12	Taxes and licenses		12	16,000
	13	Interest		13	8,000
	14a	Depreciation *(if required, attach Form 4562)*	14a: 27,476		
	b	Depreciation claimed on Schedule A and elsewhere on return	14b: 15,000		
	c	Subtract line 14b from line 14a		14c	12,476
	15	Depletion **(Do not deduct oil and gas depletion.)**		15	
	16	Advertising		16	13,000
	17	Pension, profit-sharing, etc., plans		17	2,000
	18	Employee benefit programs		18	4,000
	19	Other deductions *(attach schedule)*		19	38,250
	20	**Total deductions.** Add the amounts shown in the far right column for lines 7 through 19 ▶		20	226,526
	21	Ordinary income (loss) from trade or business activities. Subtract line 20 from line 6		21	73,686
Tax and Payments	22	**Tax: a** Excess net passive income tax *(attach schedule)*	22a		
	b	Tax from Schedule D (Form 1120S)	22b		
	c	Add lines 22a and 22b (see page 13 of the instructions for additional taxes)		22c	None
	23	**Payments: a** 1996 estimated tax payments and amount applied from 1995 return	23a		
	b	Tax deposited with Form 7004	23b		
	c	Credit for Federal tax paid on fuels *(attach Form 4136)*	23c		
	d	Add lines 23a through 23c		23d	None
	24	Estimated tax penalty. Check if Form 2220 is attached ▶ ☐		24	
	25	**Tax due.** If the total of lines 22c and 24 is larger than line 23d, enter amount owed. See page 3 of the instructions for depository method of payment ▶		25	None
	26	**Overpayment.** If line 23d is larger than the total of lines 22c and 24, enter amount overpaid ▶		26	
	27	Enter amount of line 26 you want: **Credited to 1997 estimated tax** ▶ **Refunded** ▶		27	

Please Sign Here

Under penalties of perjury, I declare that I have examined this return, including accompanying schedules and statements, and to the best of my knowledge and belief, it is true, correct, and complete. Declaration of preparer (other than taxpayer) is based on all information of which preparer has any knowledge.

Signature of officer	Date	Title
Andrew Lawrence	3/15/97	Vice-President

Paid Preparer's Use Only

Preparer's signature: Michael Kramer	Date: 3/14/97	Check if self-employed ▶ ☒	Preparer's social security number: 375 49 6339
Firm's name (or yours if self-employed) and address: Michael S. Kramer, 1110 McMillan, Gainesville, FL		EIN ▶	59 2029763
		ZIP code ▶	32611

Form 1120S (1996) Page 2

Schedule A **Cost of Goods Sold** (see page 14 of the instructions)

1	Inventory at beginning of year	1	64,000
2	Purchases	2	340,800
3	Cost of labor	3	143,204
4	Additional section 263A costs *(attach schedule)*	4	7,000
5	Other costs *(attach schedule)*	5	90,000
6	**Total.** Add lines 1 through 5	6	645,004
7	Inventory at end of year	7	104,800
8	**Cost of goods sold.** Subtract line 7 from line 6. Enter here and on page 1, line 2	8	540,204

9a Check all methods used for valuing closing inventory:
(i) ☒ Cost as described in Regulations section 1.471-3
(ii) ☐ Lower of cost or market as described in Regulations section 1.471-4
(iii) ☐ Other (specify method used and attach explanation) ▶

b Check if there was a writedown of "subnormal" goods as described in Regulations section 1.471-2(c) ▶ ☐

c Check if the LIFO inventory method was adopted this tax year for any goods *(if checked, attach Form 970)*. ▶ ☐

d If the LIFO inventory method was used for this tax year, enter percentage (or amounts) of closing inventory computed under LIFO | 9d |

e Do the rules of section 263A (for property produced or acquired for resale) apply to the corporation? ☒ Yes ☐ No

f Was there any change in determining quantities, cost, or valuations between opening and closing inventory? ☐ Yes ☒ No
If "Yes," attach explanation.

Schedule B **Other Information**

		Yes	No
1	Check method of accounting: **(a)** ☐ Cash **(b)** ☒ Accrual **(c)** ☐ Other (specify) ▶		
2	Refer to the list on page 24 of the instructions and state the corporation's principal: **(a)** Business activity ▶ Manufacturing **(b)** Product or service ▶ Furniture		
3	Did the corporation at the end of the tax year own, directly or indirectly, 50% or more of the voting stock of a domestic corporation? (For rules of attribution, see section 267(c).) If "Yes," attach a schedule showing: **(a)** name, address, and employer identification number and **(b)** percentage owned.		X
4	Was the corporation a member of a controlled group subject to the provisions of section 1561?		X
5	At any time during calendar year 1996, did the corporation have an interest in or a signature or other authority over a financial account in a foreign country (such as a bank account, securities account, or other financial account)? (See page 14 of the instructions for exceptions and filing requirements for Form TD F 90-22.1.)		X
	If "Yes," enter the name of the foreign country ▶		
6	During the tax year, did the corporation receive a distribution from, or was it the grantor of, or transferor to, a foreign trust? If "Yes," see page 14 of the instructions for other forms the corporation may have to file		X
7	Check this box if the corporation has filed or is required to file **Form 8264,** Application for Registration of a Tax Shelter ▶ ☐		
8	Check this box if the corporation issued publicly offered debt instruments with original issue discount ▶ ☐ If so, the corporation may have to file **Form 8281,** Information Return for Publicly Offered Original Issue Discount Instruments.		
9	If the corporation: **(a)** filed its election to be an S corporation after 1986, **(b)** was a C corporation before it elected to be an S corporation **or** the corporation acquired an asset with a basis determined by reference to its basis (or the basis of any other property) in the hands of a C corporation, and **(c)** has net unrealized built-in gain (defined in section 1374(d)(1)) in excess of the net recognized built-in gain from prior years, enter the net unrealized built-in gain reduced by net recognized built-in gain from prior years (see page 14 of the instructions) ▶ $		
10	Check this box if the corporation had subchapter C earnings and profits at the close of the tax year (see page 15 of the instructions) ▶ ☐		

Designation of Tax Matters Person (see page 15 of the instructions)

Enter below the shareholder designated as the tax matters person (TMP) for the tax year of this return:

Name of designated TMP ▶ Andrew Lawrence

Identifying number of TMP ▶ 297-63-2110

Address of designated TMP ▶ 436 N.W. 24th Avenue Gainesville, FL 32607

Form 1120S (1996) Page 3

Schedule K Shareholders' Shares of Income, Credits, Deductions, etc.

	(a) Pro rata share items		(b) Total amount
Income (Loss)	1 Ordinary income (loss) from trade or business activities (page 1, line 21)	1	73,686
	2 Net income (loss) from rental real estate activities *(attach Form 8825)*	2	
	3a Gross income from other rental activities — 3a		
	b Expenses from other rental activities *(attach schedule)* — 3b		
	c Net income (loss) from other rental activities. Subtract line 3b from line 3a	3c	
	4 Portfolio income (loss):		
	a Interest income	4a	
	b Dividend income	4b	1,000
	c Royalty income	4c	
	d Net short-term capital gain (loss) *(attach Schedule D (Form 1120S))*	4d	(2,100)
	e Net long-term capital gain (loss) *(attach Schedule D (Form 1120S))*	4e	4,500
	f Other portfolio income (loss) *(attach schedule)*	4f	
	5 Net gain (loss) under section 1231 (other than due to casualty or theft) *(attach Form 4797)*	5	
	6 Other income (loss) *(attach schedule)*	6	
Deductions	7 Charitable contributions *(attach schedule)*	7	12,000
	8 Section 179 expense deduction *(attach Form 4562)*	8	
	9 Deductions related to portfolio income (loss) (itemize)	9	150
	10 Other deductions *(attach schedule)*	10	
Investment Interest	11a Interest expense on investment debts	11a	
	b (1) Investment income included on lines 4a, 4b, 4c, and 4f above	11b(1)	1,000
	(2) Investment expenses included on line 9 above	11b(2)	150
Credits	12a Credit for alcohol used as a fuel *(attach Form 6478)*	12a	
	b Low-income housing credit:		
	(1) From partnerships to which section 42(j)(5) applies for property placed in service before 1990	12b(1)	
	(2) Other than on line 12b(1) for property placed in service before 1990	12b(2)	
	(3) From partnerships to which section 42(j)(5) applies for property placed in service after 1989	12b(3)	
	(4) Other than on line 12b(3) for property placed in service after 1989	12b(4)	
	c Qualified rehabilitation expenditures related to rental real estate activities *(attach Form 3468)*	12c	
	d Credits (other than credits shown on lines 12b and 12c) related to rental real estate activities	12d	
	e Credits related to other rental activities	12e	
	13 Other credits	13	
Adjustments and Tax Preference Items	14a Depreciation adjustment on property placed in service after 1986	14a	1,514
	b Adjusted gain or loss	14b	
	c Depletion (other than oil and gas)	14c	
	d (1) Gross income from oil, gas, or geothermal properties	14d(1)	
	(2) Deductions allocable to oil, gas, or geothermal properties	14d(2)	
	e Other adjustments and tax preference items *(attach schedule)*	14e	
Foreign Taxes	15a Type of income ▶		
	b Name of foreign country or U.S. possession ▶		
	c Total gross income from sources outside the United States *(attach schedule)*	15c	
	d Total applicable deductions and losses *(attach schedule)*	15d	
	e Total foreign taxes (check one): ▶ ☐ Paid ☐ Accrued	15e	
	f Reduction in taxes available for credit *(attach schedule)*	15f	
	g Other foreign tax information *(attach schedule)*	15g	
Other	16 Section 59(e)(2) expenditures: a Type ▶		
	b Amount	16b	
	17 Tax-exempt interest income	17	18,000
	18 Other tax-exempt income	18	
	19 Nondeductible expenses	19	6,000*
	20 Total property distributions (including cash) other than dividends reported on line 22 below	20	28,212
	21 Other items and amounts required to be reported separately to shareholders *(attach schedule)*		
	22 Total dividend distributions paid from accumulated earnings and profits	22	
	23 **Income (loss).** (Required only if Schedule M-1 must be completed.) Combine lines 1 through 6 in column (b). From the result, subtract the sum of lines 7 through 11a, 15e, and 16b	23	64,936

* $4,000 travel and entertainment expenses disallowed and $2000 of interest expenses incurred to purchase tax-exempt bonds.

Form 1120S (1996) Page **4**

Schedule L — Balance Sheets per Books

Assets	Beginning of tax year (a)	(b)	End of tax year (c)	(d)
1 Cash		60,000		86,600
2a Trade notes and accounts receivable	25,000		24,000	
b Less allowance for bad debts	1,000	24,000	1,000	23,000
3 Inventories		64,000		104,800
4 U.S. Government obligations				
5 Tax-exempt securities		200,000		200,000
6 Other current assets *(attach schedule)*		7,000		
7 Loans to shareholders				
8 Mortgage and real estate loans				
9 Other investments *(attach schedule)*				
10a Buildings and other depreciable assets	151,600		151,600	
b Less accumulated depreciation	45,200	106,400	72,676	78,924
11a Depletable assets				
b Less accumulated depletion				
12 Land (net of any amortization)				
13a Intangible assets (amortizable only)				
b Less accumulated amortization				
14 Other assets *(attach schedule)*				
15 Total assets		461,400		493,324
Liabilities and Shareholders' Equity				
16 Accounts payable		26,000		19,000
17 Mortgages, notes, bonds payable in less than 1 year		4,000		4,000
18 Other current liabilities *(attach schedule)*		3,600		3,600
19 Loans from shareholders				
20 Mortgages, notes, bonds payable in 1 year or more		130,000		119,724
21 Other liabilities *(attach schedule)*				
22 Capital stock		200,000		200,000
23 Paid-in or capital surplus				
24 Retained earnings		97,800		147,000
25 Less cost of treasury stock		( )		( )
26 Total liabilities and shareholders' equity		461,400		493,324

Schedule M-1 — Reconciliation of Income (Loss) per Books With Income (Loss) per Return (You are not required to complete this schedule if the total assets on line 15, column (d), of Schedule L are less than $25,000.)

1 Net income (loss) per books	77,412	5 Income recorded on books this year not included on Schedule K, lines 1 through 6 (itemize): a Tax-exempt interest $ 18,000	18,000
2 Income included on Schedule K, lines 1 through 6, not recorded on books this year (itemize):			
3 Expenses recorded on books this year not included on Schedule K, lines 1 through 11a, 15e, and 16b (itemize): a Depreciation $ b Travel and entertainment $ 4,000 Interest on loans for municipal bonds 2,000	6,000	6 Deductions included on Schedule K, lines 1 through 11a, 15e, and 16b, not charged against book income this year (itemize): a Depreciation $ 476	476
		7 Add lines 5 and 6	18,476
4 Add lines 1 through 3	83,412	8 Income (loss) (Schedule K, line 23). Line 4 less line 7	64,936

Schedule M-2 — Analysis of Accumulated Adjustments Account, Other Adjustments Account, and Shareholders' Undistributed Taxable Income Previously Taxed (see page 22 of the instructions)

	(a) Accumulated adjustments account	(b) Other adjustments account	(c) Shareholders' undistributed taxable income previously taxed
1 Balance at beginning of tax year	86,100	11,700	
2 Ordinary income from page 1, line 21	73,686		
3 Other additions	5,976*	18,000	
4 Loss from page 1, line 21	( )		
5 Other reductions	(18,250**)	(2,000)	
6 Combine lines 1 through 5	147,512		
7 Distributions other than dividend distributions	28,212		
8 Balance at end of tax year. Subtract line 7 from line 6	119,300	27,700	

* $1,000 + $4,500 + $476 = $5976

** $12,000 + $4,000 + $150 + $2,100 = $18,250

SCHEDULE K-1 (Form 1120S)

Department of the Treasury
Internal Revenue Service

Shareholder's Share of Income, Credits, Deductions, etc.

▶ See separate instructions.

For calendar year 1996 or tax year beginning , 1996, and ending , 19

OMB No. 1545-0130

1996

Shareholder's identifying number ▶ 297-63-2110

Corporation's identifying number ▶ 76 3456789

Shareholder's name, address, and ZIP code

Andrew Lawrence *
436 N.W. 24th Avenue
Gainesville, FL 32607

Corporation's name, address, and ZIP code

Johns and Lawrence, Inc.
1234 University Avenue
Gainesville, FL 32611

A Shareholder's percentage of stock ownership for tax year (see instructions for Schedule K-1) . . . ▶ 50 %

B Internal Revenue Service Center where corporation filed its return ▶ Atlanta, GA

C Tax shelter registration number (see instructions for Schedule K-1) . . . ▶ N/A

D Check applicable boxes: (1) ☐ Final K-1 (2) ☐ Amended K-1

	(a) Pro rata share items		(b) Amount	(c) Form 1040 filers enter the amount in column (b) on:
Income (Loss)	1 Ordinary income (loss) from trade or business activities	1	36,843	See pages 4 and 5 of the Shareholder's Instructions for Schedule K-1 (Form 1120S).
	2 Net income (loss) from rental real estate activities	2		
	3 Net income (loss) from other rental activities	3		
	4 Portfolio income (loss):			
	a Interest	4a		Sch. B, Part I, line 1
	b Dividends	4b	500	Sch. B, Part II, line 5
	c Royalties	4c	<1,050>	Sch. E, Part I, line 4
	d Net short-term capital gain (loss)	4d	2,250	Sch. D, line 5, col. (f) or (g)
	e Net long-term capital gain (loss)	4e		Sch. D, line 13, col. (f) or (g)
	f Other portfolio income (loss) *(attach schedule)*	4f		(Enter on applicable line of your return.)
	5 Net gain (loss) under section 1231 (other than due to casualty or theft)	5		See Shareholder's Instructions for Schedule K-1 (Form 1120S).
	6 Other income (loss) *(attach schedule)*	6		(Enter on applicable line of your return.)
Deductions	7 Charitable contributions *(attach schedule)*	7	6,000	Sch. A, line 15 or 16
	8 Section 179 expense deduction	8		See page 6 of the Shareholder's Instructions for Schedule K-1 (Form 1120S).
	9 Deductions related to portfolio income (loss) *(attach schedule)*	9	75	
	10 Other deductions *(attach schedule)*	10		
Investment Interest	11a Interest expense on investment debts	11a		Form 4952, line 1
	b (1) Investment income included on lines 4a, 4b, 4c, and 4f above	b(1)	500	See Shareholder's Instructions for Schedule K-1 (Form 1120S).
	(2) Investment expenses included on line 9 above	b(2)	75	
Credits	12a Credit for alcohol used as fuel	12a		Form 6478, line 10
	b Low-income housing credit:			
	(1) From section 42(j)(5) partnerships for property placed in service before 1990	b(1)		Form 8586, line 5
	(2) Other than on line 12b(1) for property placed in service before 1990	b(2)		
	(3) From section 42(j)(5) partnerships for property placed in service after 1989	b(3)		
	(4) Other than on line 12b(3) for property placed in service after 1989	b(4)		
	c Qualified rehabilitation expenditures related to rental real estate activities	12c		See page 7 of the Shareholder's Instructions for Schedule K-1 (Form 1120S).
	d Credits (other than credits shown on lines 12b and 12c) related to rental real estate activities	12d		
	e Credits related to other rental activities	12e		
	13 Other credits	13		
Adjustments and Tax Preference Items	14a Depreciation adjustment on property placed in service after 1986	14a	2,257	See page 7 of the Shareholder's Instructions for Schedule K-1 (Form 1120S) and Instructions for Form 6251
	b Adjusted gain or loss	14b		
	c Depletion (other than oil and gas)	14c		
	d (1) Gross income from oil, gas, or geothermal properties	d(1)		
	(2) Deductions allocable to oil, gas, or geothermal properties	d(2)		
	e Other adjustments and tax preference items *(attach schedule)*	14e		

For Paperwork Reduction Act Notice, see page 1 of Instructions for Form 1120S. Cat. No. 11520D **Schedule K-1 (Form 1120S) 1996**

* A second schedule K-1 for Stephen Johns is similar to this one, but is not reproduced here.

Schedule K-1 (Form 1120S) (1996) Page 2

		(a) Pro rata share items		(b) Amount	(c) Form 1040 filers enter the amount in column (b) on:
Foreign Taxes	15a	Type of income ▶			Form 1116, Check boxes
	b	Name of foreign country or U.S. possession ▶			
	c	Total gross income from sources outside the United States *(attach schedule)*	15c		Form 1116, Part I
	d	Total applicable deductions and losses *(attach schedule)*	15d		
	e	Total foreign taxes (check one): ▶ ☐ Paid ☐ Accrued	15e		Form 1116, Part II
	f	Reduction in taxes available for credit *(attach schedule)*	15f		Form 1116, Part III
	g	Other foreign tax information *(attach schedule)*	15g		See Instructions for Form 1116
Other	16	Section 59(e)(2) expenditures: **a** Type ▶			See Shareholder's Instructions for Schedule K-1 (Form 1120S).
	b	Amount	16b		
	17	Tax-exempt interest income	17	9,000	Form 1040, line 8b
	18	Other tax-exempt income	18		See pages 7 and 8 of the Shareholder's Instructions for Schedule K-1 (Form 1120S).
	19	Nondeductible expenses	19	3,000*	
	20	Property distributions (including cash) other than dividend distributions reported to you on Form 1099-DIV	20	14,106	
	21	Amount of loan repayments for "Loans From Shareholders"	21		
	22	Recapture of low-income housing credit:			
	a	From section 42(j)(5) partnerships	22a		Form 8611, line 8
	b	Other than on line 22a	22b		

Supplemental Information

23 Supplemental information required to be reported separately to each shareholder *(attach additional schedules if more space is needed)*:

* $1,000 of interest expense incurred to purchase tax-exempt bonds and $2000 of meals and entertainment expenses that were disallowed by Sec. 274.

FACTS FOR S CORPORATION (FORM 1120S)

The same basic facts that were presented for the Andrew Lawrence proprietorship are used for the S corporation except for the following:

1. Johns and Lawrence, Inc. made an S corporation election on June 13, 1990. The election was effective for its initial tax year.

2. The book income for Johns and Lawrence is presented in the attached worksheet which reconciles book income and S corporation taxable income.

3. The $18,000 salaries paid to each employee are subject to the same employment tax requirements as when paid by the C corporation. The total employment taxes ($14,480) are the same as for the C corporation.

4. No estimated federal income taxes were paid by the S corporation.

5. The $28,212 distribution was paid equally to the two shareholders. It is not included in the shareholder's gross income, but instead reduces the basis for their stock.

6. Other deductions include:

Travel	$4,000
Meals and entertainment	8,000
Minus: 50% disallowance	(4,000)
Office expenses	16,000
Transportation	10,400
General and administrative	3,000
Miscellaneous	850
Total	$38,250

   $150 of the miscellaneous expenses are related to the production of the dividend income and are separately stated.

7. Reconciliation of net income for the C corporation and the S corporation occurs as follows:

Net income for C corporation	$63,412
Plus: Federal income taxes	14,000
Net income for S corporation	$77,412

   The S corporation return can be tied back to the partnership return. The only difference between the two returns is that the S corporation pays an additional $6,160 in employment taxes with respect to the shareholder-employee salaries, as compared to the partnership's guaranteed payments. This dollar difference is reflected in the net income numbers, the ordinary income numbers, capital account balances, and total asset amounts.

8. The balance sheet for Johns and Lawrence is presented on page 4 of Form 1120S.

Johns and Lawrence, Inc. (S Corporation) Reconciliation of Book and Taxable Income For Year Ending December 31, 1996

	Book Income		Adjustments		Taxable Income		Form 1120S Schedule K	
Account Name	Debit	Credit	Debit	Credit	Debit	Credit	Ordinary Income	Separately Stated Items
Sales		869,658				869,658	869,658	
Sales returns & allowances	29,242				29,242		−29,242	
Cost of sales	540,204				540,204		−540,204	
Dividends		1,000				1,000		1,000
Tax-exempt interest		18,000	18,000			0		18,000
Gain on stock sale		4,500				4,500		4,500
Worthless stock loss	2,100				2,100			−2,100
Officers salaries[a]	36,000				36,000		−36,000	
Other salaries	52,000				52,000		−52,000	
Rentals	36,000				36,000		−36,000	
Bad debts	4,000				4,000		−4,000	
Interest:								
Working capital loans	8,000				8,000		−8,000	
Purchase tax-exempt bonds	2,000			2,000	0			−2,000
Employment taxes	14,480				14,480		−14,480	
Taxes	1,520				1,520		−1,520	
Repairs	4,800				4,800		−4,800	
Depreciation[b]	12,000		476		12,476		−12,476	
Charitable contributions	12,000				12,000			−12,000
Travel	4,000				4,000		−4,000	
Meals and entertainment[c]	8,000			4,000	4,000		−4,000	
Meals and ent. nondeductible								−4,000
Office expenses	16,000				16,000		−16,000	
Advertising	13,000				13,000		−13,000	
Transportation expense	10,400				10,400		−10,400	
General and administrative	3,000				3,000		−3,000	
Pension plans[d]	2,000				2,000		−2,000	
Employee benefit programs[e]	4,000				4,000		−4,000	
Miscellaneous	1,000				1,000		−850	−150
Net profit/Taxable income	77,412			12,476	64,936			
Total	893,158	893,158	18,476	18,476	875,158	875,158	73,686	

[a] Salaries for the S corporation's shareholder-employees are deductible by the S corporation, and subject to the same employee taxes as are imposed on nonshareholder-employees.
[b] MACRS depreciation $12,476 − $12,000 = $476
[c] 50% of the meals and entertainment expense is not deductible for tax purposes but must be separately stated on the Schedule K and K-1s.
[d] The pension plan expense is the same for book and tax purposes for this firm. No pension expenses relate to pensions for the shareholder-employees.
[e] The employee benefit expense is the same for book and tax purposes for this firm. None relate to shareholder-employee benefits.

Form **709** (Rev. December 1996)
Department of the Treasury Internal Revenue Service

United States Gift (and Generation-Skipping Transfer) Tax Return

(Section 6019 of the Internal Revenue Code) (For gifts made after December 31, 1991)

Calendar year 19 96

▶ **See separate instructions. For Privacy Act Notice, see the Instructions for Form 1040.**

OMB No. 1545-0020

Part 1—General Information

1 Donor's first name and middle initial: Wilma	2 Donor's last name: Brown	3 **Donor's social security number**: 123 45 6789
4 Address (number, street, and apartment number): 2 Main Street		5 Legal residence (domicile) (county and state): U.S.A.
6 City, state, and ZIP code: Dalton, GA 35901		7 Citizenship: U.S.A.

Line	Item	Yes	No
8	If the donor died during the year, check here ▶ ☐ and enter date of death ...., ...		
9	If you received an extension of time to file this Form 709, check here ▶ ☐ and attach the Form 4868, 2688, 2350, or extension letter		
10	Enter the total number of separate donees listed on Schedule A—count each person only once. ▶ 4		
11a	Have you (the donor) previously filed a Form 709 (or 709-A) for any other year? If the answer is "No," do not complete line 11b	X	
11b	If the answer to line 11a is "Yes," has your address changed since you last filed Form 709 (or 709-A)?		X
12	Gifts by husband or wife to third parties.—Do you consent to have the gifts (including generation-skipping transfers) made by you and by your spouse to third parties during the calendar year considered as made one-half by each of you? (See instructions.) (If the answer is "Yes," the following information must be furnished and your spouse must sign the consent shown below. **If the answer is "No," skip lines 13–18 and go to Schedule A.**)	X	
13	Name of consenting spouse: Hugh Brown — **14** SSN: 987-65-4321		
15	Were you married to one another during the entire calendar year? (see instructions)	X	
16	If the answer to 15 is "No," check whether ☐ married ☐ divorced or ☐ widowed, and give date (see instructions) ▶		
17	Will a gift tax return for this calendar year be filed by your spouse?	X	

18 Consent of Spouse—I consent to have the gifts (and generation-skipping transfers) made by me and by my spouse to third parties during the calendar year considered as made one-half by each of us. We are both aware of the joint and several liability for tax created by the execution of this consent.

Consenting spouse's signature ▶ Hugh Brown **Date** ▶ 3/2/97

Part 2—Tax Computation

Line	Item		Amount
1	Enter the amount from Schedule A, Part 3, line 15	1	343,337
2	Enter the amount from Schedule B, line 3	2	500,000
3	Total taxable gifts (add lines 1 and 2)	3	843,337
4	Tax computed on amount on line 3 (see Table for Computing Tax in separate instructions)	4	284,701
5	Tax computed on amount on line 2 (see Table for Computing Tax in separate instructions)	5	155,800
6	Balance (subtract line 5 from line 4)	6	128,901
7	Maximum unified credit (nonresident aliens, see instructions)	7	192,800 00
8	Enter the unified credit against tax allowable for all prior periods (from Sch. B, line 1, col. C)	8	34,000
9	Balance (subtract line 8 from line 7)	9	158,800
10	Enter 20% (.20) of the amount allowed as a specific exemption for gifts made after September 8, 1976, and before January 1, 1977 (see instructions)	10	
11	Balance (subtract line 10 from line 9)	11	158,800
12	Unified credit (enter the smaller of line 6 or line 11)	12	128,901
13	Credit for foreign gift taxes (see instructions)	13	
14	Total credits (add lines 12 and 13)	14	128,901
15	Balance (subtract line 14 from line 6) (do not enter less than zero)	15	0
16	Generation-skipping transfer taxes (from Schedule C, Part 3, col. H, Total)	16	
17	Total tax (add lines 15 and 16)	17	0
18	Gift and generation-skipping transfer taxes prepaid with extension of time to file	18	
19	If line 18 is less than line 17, enter BALANCE DUE (see instructions)	19	0
20	If line 18 is greater than line 17, enter AMOUNT TO BE REFUNDED	20	

Attach check or money order here.

Under penalties of perjury, I declare that I have examined this return, including any accompanying schedules and statements, and to the best of my knowledge and belief it is true, correct, and complete. Declaration of preparer (other than donor) is based on all information of which preparer has any knowledge.

Donor's signature ▶ Wilma Brown Date ▶ 3/2/97

Preparer's signature (other than donor) ▶ Sally Preparer Date ▶ 3/2/97

Preparer's address (other than donor) ▶ 110 Last Bank Tower, Dalton, GA 35901

For Paperwork Reduction Act Notice, see page 1 of the separate instructions for this form. Cat. No. 16783M Form **709** (Rev. 12-96)

Form 709 (Rev. 12-96) Page **2**

SCHEDULE A Computation of Taxable Gifts

Does the value of any item listed on Schedule A reflect any valuation discount? If the answer is "Yes," see instructions . . . Yes ☐ No ☐

Part 1—Gifts Subject Only to Gift Tax. *Gifts less political organization, medical, and educational exclusions—see instructions*

A Item number	B • Donee's name and address • Relationship to donor (if any) • Description of gift • If the gift was made by means of a trust, enter trust's identifying number and attach a copy of the trust instrument • If the gift was of securities, give CUSIP number	C Donor's adjusted basis of gift	D Date of gift	E Value at date of gift
1	Billy Brown, cash	80,000	1996	80,000
2	Betsy Brown, jewelry	18,000	1996	24,000
3	Ruth Cain, remainder interest in vacation cabin (0.22674x 100,000)	15,000	1996	22,674
4.	Trust at First Bank, income to Hugh Brown for life. Remainder to Jeff Brown (QTIP Trust)	480,000	1996	600,000

Total of Part 1 (add amounts from Part 1, column E) . . . . ▶

Part 2—Gifts That are Direct Skips and are Subject to Both Gift Tax and Generation-Skipping Transfer Tax. You must list the gifts in chronological order. *Gifts less political organization, medical, and educational exclusions—see instructions. (Also list here direct skips that are subject only to the GST tax at this time as the result of the termination of an "estate tax inclusion period." See instructions.)*

A Item number	B • Donee's name and address • Relationship to donor (if any) • Description of gift • If the gift was made by means of a trust, enter trust's identifying number and attach a copy of the trust instrument • If the gift was of securities, give CUSIP number	C Donor's adjusted basis of gift	D Date of gift	E Value at date of gift
1				

Total of Part 2 (add amounts from Part 2, column E) . . . . ▶

Part 3—Taxable Gift Reconciliation

1	Total value of gifts of donor (add totals from column E of Parts 1 and 2)			1	726,674
2	One-half of items 1, 2, 3 attributable to spouse (see instructions)			2	63,337
3	Balance (subtract line 2 from line 1)			3	663,337
4	Gifts of spouse to be included (from Schedule A, Part 3, line 2 of spouse's return—see instructions) . .			4	340,000
	If any of the gifts included on this line are also subject to the generation-skipping transfer tax, check here ▶ ☐ and enter those gifts also on Schedule C, Part 1.				
5	Total gifts (add lines 3 and 4)			5	1,003,337
6	Total annual exclusions for gifts listed on Schedule A (including line 4, above) (see instructions) . . .			6	40,000
7	Total included amount of gifts (subtract line 6 from line 5)			7	963,337
	Deductions (see instructions)				
8	Gifts of interests to spouse for which a marital deduction will be claimed, based on items 4 of Schedule A	8	600,000		
9	Exclusions attributable to gifts on line 8	9	10,000		
10	Marital deduction—subtract line 9 from line 8	10	590,000		
11	Charitable deduction, based on items gifts of spouse less exclusions	11	30,000		
12	Total deductions—add lines 10 and 11			12	620,000
13	Subtract line 12 from line 7			13	343,337
14	Generation-skipping transfer taxes payable with this Form 709 (from Schedule C, Part 3, col. H, Total) .			14	
15	Taxable gifts (add lines 13 and 14). Enter here and on line 1 of the Tax Computation on page 1			15	343,337

(If more space is needed, attach additional sheets of same size.)

Form 709 (Rev. 12-96) Page **3**

SCHEDULE A Computation of Taxable Gifts *(continued)*

16 Terminable Interest (QTIP) Marital Deduction. (See instructions for line 8 of Schedule A.)

If a trust (or other property) meets the requirements of qualified terminable interest property under section 2523(f), and

a. The trust (or other property) is listed on Schedule A, and

b. The value of the trust (or other property) is entered in whole or in part as a deduction on line 8, Part 3 of Schedule A,

then the donor shall be deemed to have made an election to have such trust (or other property) treated as qualified terminable interest property under section 2523(f).

If less than the entire value of the trust (or other property) that the donor has included in Part 1 of Schedule A is entered as a deduction on line 8, the donor shall be considered to have made an election only as to a fraction of the trust (or other property). The numerator of this fraction is equal to the amount of the trust (or other property) deducted on line 10 of Part 3, Schedule A. The denominator is equal to the total value of the trust (or other property) listed in Part 1 of Schedule A.

If you make the QTIP election (see instructions for line 8 of Schedule A), the terminable interest property involved will be included in your spouse's gross estate upon his or her death (section 2044). If your spouse disposes (by gift or otherwise) of all or part of the qualifying life income interest, he or she will be considered to have made a transfer of the entire property that is subject to the gift tax (see Transfer of Certain Life Estates on page 3 of the instructions).

17 Election Out of QTIP Treatment of Annuities

☐ ◀ Check here if you elect under section 2523(f)(6) **NOT** to treat as qualified terminable interest property any joint and survivor annuities that are reported on Schedule A and would otherwise be treated as qualified terminable interest property under section 2523(f). (See instructions.) Enter the item numbers (from Schedule A) for the annuities for which you are making this election ▶

SCHEDULE B Gifts From Prior Periods

If you answered "Yes" on line 11a of page 1, Part 1, see the instructions for completing Schedule B. If you answered "No," skip to the Tax Computation on page 1 (or Schedule C, if applicable).

A Calendar year or calendar quarter (see instructions)	B Internal Revenue office where prior return was filed		C Amount of unified credit against gift tax for periods after December 31, 1976	D Amount of specific exemption for prior periods ending before January 1, 1977	E Amount of taxable gifts
1975	Atlanta, Georgia		0	0	300,000
1978	Atlanta, Georgia		34,000	0	200,000
1 Totals for prior periods (without adjustment for reduced specific exemption)		**1**	34,000	0	500,000
2 Amount, if any, by which total specific exemption, line 1, column D, is more than $30,000				**2**	0
3 Total amount of taxable gifts for prior periods (add amount, column E, line 1, and amount, if any, on line 2). (Enter here and on line 2 of the Tax Computation on page 1.)				**3**	500,000

(If more space is needed, attach additional sheets of same size.)

Form 709 (Rev. 12-96) Page **4**

SCHEDULE C Computation of Generation-Skipping Transfer Tax

Note: *Inter vivos direct skips that are completely excluded by the GST exemption must still be fully reported (including value and exemptions claimed) on Schedule C.*

Part 1—Generation-Skipping Transfers

A Item No. (from Schedule A, Part 2, col. A)	B Value (from Schedule A, Part 2, col. E)	C Split Gifts (enter ½ of col. B) (see instructions)	D Subtract col. C from col. B	E Nontaxable portion of transfer	F Net Transfer (subtract col. E from col. D)
1					
2					
3					
4					
5					
6					

If you elected gift splitting and your spouse was required to file a separate Form 709 (see the instructions for "Split Gifts"), you must enter all of the gifts shown on Schedule A, Part 2, of your spouse's Form 709 here. In column C, enter the item number of each gift in the order it appears in column A of your spouse's Schedule A, Part 2. We have preprinted the prefix "S-" to distinguish your spouse's item numbers from your own when you complete column A of Schedule C, Part 3. In column D, for each gift, enter the amount reported in column C, Schedule C, Part 1, of your spouse's Form 709.	Split gifts from spouse's Form 709 (enter item number)	Value included from spouse's Form 709	Nontaxable portion of transfer	Net transfer (subtract col. E from col. D)
	S-			
	S-			
	S-			
	S-			
	S-			
	S-			
	S-			
	S-			

Part 2—GST Exemption Reconciliation (Section 2631) and Section 2652(a)(3) Election

Check box ▶ ☐ if you are making a section 2652(a)(3) (special QTIP) election (see instructions)

Enter the item numbers (from Schedule A) of the gifts for which you are making this election ▶ ....

1	Maximum allowable exemption	1	$1,000,000
2	Total exemption used for periods before filing this return	2	
3	Exemption available for this return (subtract line 2 from line 1)	3	
4	Exemption claimed on this return (from Part 3, col. C total, below)	4	
5	Exemption allocated to transfers not shown on Part 3, below. **You must attach a Notice of Allocation.** (See instructions.)	5	
6	Add lines 4 and 5	6	
7	Exemption available for future transfers (subtract line 6 from line 3)	7	

Part 3—Tax Computation

A Item No. (from Schedule C, Part 1)	B Net transfer (from Schedule C, Part 1, col. F)	C GST Exemption Allocated	D Divide col. C by col. B	E Inclusion Ratio (subtract col. D from 1.000)	F Maximum Estate Tax Rate	G Applicable Rate (multiply col. E by col. F)	H Generation-Skipping Transfer Tax (multiply col. B by col. G)
1					55% (.55)		
2					55% (.55)		
3					55% (.55)		
4					55% (.55)		
5					55% (.55)		
6					55% (.55)		
					55% (.55)		
					55% (.55)		
					55% (.55)		
					55% (.55)		
Total exemption claimed. Enter here and on line 4, Part 2, above. May not exceed line 3, Part 2, above			**Total generation-skipping transfer tax.** Enter here, on line 14 of Schedule A, Part 3, and on line 16 of the Tax Computation on page 1				

(If more space is needed, attach additional sheets of same size.)

Form **706** (Rev. August 1993) Department of the Treasury Internal Revenue Service

United States Estate (and Generation-Skipping Transfer) Tax Return

Estate of a citizen or resident of the United States (see separate instructions). To be filed for decedents dying after October 8, 1990. For Paperwork Reduction Act Notice, see page 1 of the instructions.

OMB No. 1545-0015 Expires 12-31-95

Part 1.—Decedent and Executor

1a Decedent's first name and middle initial (and maiden name, if any): Herman	1b Decedent's last name: Estes		2 Decedent's social security no.: 999 11 4444
3a Domicile at time of death (county and state, or foreign country): Ohio	3b Year domicile established: 1934	4 Date of birth: 1917	5 Date of death: 10-13-96
6a Name of executor (see instructions): John Johnson	6b Executor's address (number and street including apartment or suite no. or rural route; city, town, or post office; state; and ZIP code): 10 Main Place Dayton, OH 45347		
6c Executor's social security number (see instructions): 998 12 5732			
7a Name and location of court where will was probated or estate administered			7b Case number
8 If decedent died testate, check here ▶ ☒ and attach a certified copy of the will.	9 If Form 4768 is attached, check here ▶ ☐		
10 If Schedule R-1 is attached, check here ▶ ☐			

Part 2.—Tax Computation

Line	Description			Line	Amount
1	Total gross estate (from Part 5, Recapitulation, page 3, item 10)			1	1,661,900
2	Total allowable deductions (from Part 5, Recapitulation, page 3, item 20)			2	1,176,700
3	Taxable estate (subtract line 2 from line 1)			3	485,200
4	Adjusted taxable gifts (total taxable gifts (within the meaning of section 2503) made by the decedent after December 31, 1976, other than gifts that are includible in decedent's gross estate (section 2001(b))			4	680,000
5	Add lines 3 and 4			5	1,165,200
6	Tentative tax on the amount on line 5 from Table A in the instructions			6	413,532
7a	If line 5 exceeds $10,000,000, enter the lesser of line 5 or $21,040,000. If line 5 is $10,000,000 or less, skip lines 7a and 7b and enter -0- on line 7c	7a			
b	Subtract $10,000,000 from line 7a	7b			
c	Enter 5% (.05) of line 7b			7c	0
8	Total tentative tax (add lines 6 and 7c)			8	413,532
9	Total gift tax payable with respect to gifts made by the decedent after December 31, 1976. Include gift taxes by the decedent's spouse for such spouse's share of split gifts (section 2513) only if the decedent was the donor of these gifts and they are includible in the decedent's gross estate (see instructions)			9	39,900
10	Gross estate tax (subtract line 9 from line 8)			10	373,632
11	Maximum unified credit against estate tax	11	192,800 00		
12	Adjustment to unified credit. (This adjustment may not exceed $6,000. See page 6 of the instructions.)	12			
13	Allowable unified credit (subtract line 12 from line 11)			13	192,800
14	Subtract line 13 from line 10 (but do not enter less than zero)			14	180,832
15	Credit for state death taxes. Do not enter more than line 14. Compute the credit by using the amount on line 3 less $60,000. See Table B in the instructions and **attach credit evidence** (see instructions)			15	9,526
16	Subtract line 15 from line 14			16	171,306
17	Credit for Federal gift taxes on pre-1977 gifts (section 2012) (attach computation)	17			
18	Credit for foreign death taxes (from Schedule(s) P). (Attach Form(s) 706CE)	18			
19	Credit for tax on prior transfers (from Schedule Q)	19			
20	Total (add lines 17, 18, and 19)			20	171,306
21	Net estate tax (subtract line 20 from line 16)			21	
22	Generation-skipping transfer taxes (from Schedule R, Part 2, line 10)			22	
23	Section 4980A increased estate tax (from Schedule S, Part I, line 17) (see instructions)			23	
24	Total transfer taxes (add lines 21, 22, and 23)			24	171,306
25	Prior payments. Explain in an attached statement	25			
26	United States Treasury bonds redeemed in payment of estate tax	26			
27	Total (add lines 25 and 26)			27	
28	Balance due (or overpayment) (subtract line 27 from line 24)			28	171,306

Under penalties of perjury, I declare that I have examined this return, including accompanying schedules and statements, and to the best of my knowledge and belief, it is true, correct, and complete. Declaration of preparer other than the executor is based on all information of which preparer has any knowledge.

John Johnson — Signature(s) of executor(s) — Date 2/14/97

Mary Wilson — Signature of preparer other than executor — 100 Tower Building Austin, TX 78703 — Address (and ZIP code) — Date 2/14/97

Cat. No. 20548R

Note: Instructions on blank pages 5, 6, 7, 14, 16, 18, 20, 24, 28, 29, 30, 37 and 41 are omitted.

Form 706 (Rev. 8-93)

Estate of: Herman Estes

Part 3.—Elections by the Executor

Please check the "Yes" or "No" box for each question.	Yes	No
1 Do you elect alternate valuation?		X
2 Do you elect special use valuation? If "Yes," you must complete and attach Schedule A-1		X
3 Do you elect to pay the taxes in installments as described in section 6166? If "Yes," you must attach the additional information described in the instructions.		X
4 Do you elect to postpone the part of the taxes attributable to a reversionary or remainder interest as described in section 6163?		X

Part 4.—General Information (**Note:** *Please attach the necessary supplemental documents.* **You must attach the death certificate.)**

Authorization to receive confidential tax information under Regulations section 601.504(b)(2)(i), to act as the estate's representative before the Internal Revenue Service, and to make written or oral presentations on behalf of the estate if return prepared by an attorney, accountant, or enrolled agent for the executor:

Name of representative (print or type)	State	Address (number, street, and room or suite no., city, state, and ZIP code)
John Johnson	Ohio	10 Main Place Dayton, OH 45347

I declare that I am the ☐ attorney/ ☐ certified public accountant/ ☐ enrolled agent (you must check the applicable box) for the executor and prepared this return for the executor. I am not under suspension or disbarment from practice before the Internal Revenue Service and am qualified to practice in the state shown above.

Signature	CAF number	Date	Telephone number
John Johnson	111-2222	2-14-97	(512)-444-4444

1 Death certificate number and issuing authority (attach a copy of the death certificate to this return).
1246 County Coroner

2 Decedent's business or occupation. If retired, check here ▶ ☐ and state decedent's former business or occupation.
Executive

3 Marital status of the decedent at time of death:
☒ Married
☐ Widow or widower—Name, SSN, and date of death of deceased spouse ▶
☐ Single
☐ Legally separated
☐ Divorced—Date divorce decree became final ▶

4a Surviving spouse's name	4b Social security number	4c Amount received (see instructions)
Ann Estes	555 77 9999	1,050,000

5 Individuals (other than the surviving spouse), trusts, or other estates who receive benefits from the estate (do not include charitable beneficiaries shown in Schedule O) (see instructions). For Privacy Act Notice (applicable to individual beneficiaries only), see the Instructions for Form 1040.

Name of individual, trust, or estate receiving $5,000 or more	Identifying number	Relationship to decedent	Amount (see instructions)
Johnny Estes	555-61-4107	Son	342,600*
Billy Estes	556-63-4437	Son	142,600
*Their daughter, Dorothy Estes, receives the trust corpus of the trust established by Amelia Estes			
All unascertainable beneficiaries and those who receive less than $5,000 ▶			
Total			485,200

(Continued on next page)

Form 706 (Rev. 8-93)

Part 4.—General Information *(continued)*

Please check the "Yes" or "No" box for each question.		Yes	No
6	Does the gross estate contain any section 2044 property (qualified terminable interest property (QTIP) from a prior gift or estate) (see page 5 of the instructions)?		X
7a	Have Federal gift tax returns ever been filed? If "Yes," please attach copies of the returns, if available, and furnish the following information:	X	
7b	Period(s) covered 1974, 1978, 1994 — **7c** Internal Revenue office(s) where filed Cincinnati, Ohio		
If you answer "Yes" to any of questions 8-16, you must attach additional information as described in the instructions.			
8a	Was there any insurance on the decedent's life that is not included on the return as part of the gross estate?		X
b	Did the decedent own any insurance on the life of another that is not included in the gross estate?		X
9	Did the decedent at the time of death own any property as a joint tenant with right of survivorship in which (a) one or more of the other joint tenants was someone other than the decedent's spouse, and (b) less than the full value of the property is included on the return as part of the gross estate? If "Yes," you must complete and attach Schedule E		X
10	Did the decedent, at the time of death, own any interest in a partnership or unincorporated business or any stock in an inactive or closely held corporation?		X
11	Did the decedent make any transfer described in section 2035, 2036, 2037, or 2038 (see the instructions for Schedule G)? If "Yes," you must complete and attach Schedule G	X	
12	Were there in existence at the time of the decedent's death:		
a	Any trusts created by the decedent during his or her lifetime?		X
b	Any trusts not created by the decedent under which the decedent possessed any power, beneficial interest, or trusteeship?	X	
13	Did the decedent ever possess, exercise, or release any general power of appointment? If "Yes," you must complete and attach Schedule H		X
14	Was the marital deduction computed under the transitional rule of Public Law 97-34, section 403(e)(3) (Economic Recovery Tax Act of 1981)? If "Yes," attach a separate computation of the marital deduction, enter the amount on item 18 of the Recapitulation, and note on item 18 "computation attached."		X
15	Was the decedent, immediately before death, receiving an annuity described in the "General" paragraph of the instructions for Schedule I? If "Yes," you must complete and attach Schedule I	X	
16	Did the decedent have a total "excess retirement accumulation" (as defined in section 4980A(d)) in qualified employer plans and individual retirement plans? If "Yes," you must complete and attach Schedule S		X

Part 5.—Recapitulation

Item number	Gross estate	Alternate value	Value at date of death
1	Schedule A—Real Estate		325,000
2	Schedule B—Stocks and Bonds		600,000
3	Schedule C—Mortgages, Notes, and Cash		85,000
4	Schedule D—Insurance on the Decedent's Life (attach Form(s) 712)		200,000
5	Schedule E—Jointly Owned Property (attach Form(s) 712 for life insurance)		200,000
6	Schedule F—Other Miscellaneous Property (attach Form(s) 712 for life insurance)		
7	Schedule G—Transfers During Decedent's Life (attach Form(s) 712 for life insurance)		11,900
8	Schedule H—Powers of Appointment		
9	Schedule I—Annuities		240,000
10	Total gross estate (add items 1 through 9). Enter here and on line 1 of the Tax Computation		1,661,900

Item number	Deductions	Amount
11	Schedule J—Funeral Expenses and Expenses Incurred in Administering Property Subject to Claims	85,000
12	Schedule K—Debts of the Decedent	31,700
13	Schedule K—Mortgages and Liens	
14	Total of items 11 through 13	116,700
15	Allowable amount of deductions from item 14 (see the instructions for item 15 of the Recapitulation)	116,700
16	Schedule L—Net Losses During Administration	
17	Schedule L—Expenses Incurred in Administering Property Not Subject to Claims	
18	Schedule M—Bequests, etc., to Surviving Spouse	1,050,000
19	Schedule O—Charitable, Public, and Similar Gifts and Bequests	10,000
20	Total allowable deductions (add items 15 through 19). Enter here and on line 2 of the Tax Computation	1,176,700

Form 706 (Rev. 8-93)

Estate of: Herman Estes

SCHEDULE A—Real Estate

(For jointly owned property that must be disclosed on Schedule E, see the instructions for Schedule E.)

(Real estate that is part of a sole proprietorship should be shown on Schedule F. Real estate that is included in the gross estate under section 2035, 2036, 2037, or 2038 should be shown on Schedule G. Real estate that is included in the gross estate under section 2041 should be shown on Schedule H.)

(If you elect section 2032A valuation, you must complete Schedule A and Schedule A-1.)

Item number	Description	Alternate valuation date	Alternate value	Value at date of death
1	Personal residence, house and lot located at 105 Elm Court, Dayton, Ohio			325,000
	Total from continuation schedule(s) (or additional sheet(s)) attached to this schedule . .			
	TOTAL. (Also enter on Part 5, Recapitulation, page 3, at item 1.)			325,000

(If more space is needed, attach the continuation schedule from the end of this package or additional sheets of the same size.)

(See the instructions on the reverse side.)

Form 706 (Rev. 8-93)

Estate of: | **Decedent's Social Security Number**

SCHEDULE A-1—Section 2032A Valuation

Part 1.—Type of Election (Before making an election, see the checklist on page 7.):

☐ **Protective election (Regulations section 20.2032A-8(b)).—**Complete Part 2, line 1, and column A of lines 3 and 4. (See instructions.)

☐ **Regular election.—**Complete all of Part 2 (including line 11, if applicable) and Part 3. (See instructions.)

Before completing Schedule A-1, see the checklist on page 7 for the information and documents that must be included to make a valid election.

The election is not valid unless the agreement (i.e., Part 3-Agreement to Special Valuation Under Section 2032A)—

- Is signed by each and every qualified heir with an interest in the specially valued property, and
- Is attached to this return when it is filed.

Part 2.—Notice of Election (Regulations section 20.2032A-8(a)(3))

Note: *All real property entered on lines 2 and 3 must also be entered on Schedules A, E, F, G, or H, as applicable.*

1 Qualified use—check one ▶ ☐ Farm used for farming, or
▶ ☐ Trade or business other than farming

2 Real property used in a qualified use, passing to qualified heirs, and to be specially valued on this Form 706.

A Schedule and item number from Form 706	B Full value (without section 2032A(b)(3)(B) adjustment)	C Adjusted value (with section 2032A(b)(3)(B) adjustment)	D Value based on qualified use (without section 2032A(b)(3)(B) adjustment)
Totals			

Attach a legal description of all property listed on line 2.

Attach copies of appraisals showing the column B values for all property listed on line 2.

3 Real property used in a qualified use, passing to qualified heirs, but not specially valued on this Form 706.

A Schedule and item number from Form 706	B Full value (without section 2032A(b)(3)(B) adjustment)	C Adjusted value (with section 2032A(b)(3)(B) adjustment)	D Value based on qualified use (without section 2032A(b)(3)(B) adjustment)
Totals			

If you checked "Regular election," you must attach copies of appraisals showing the column B values for all property listed on line 3.

(Continued on next page)

Form 706 (Rev. 8-93)

4 Personal property used in a qualified use and passing to qualified heirs.

A Schedule and item number from Form 706	**B** Adjusted value (with section 2032A(b)(3)(B) adjustment)	**A (continued)** Schedule and item number from Form 706	**B (continued)** Adjusted value (with section 2032A(b)(3)(B) adjustment)
		"Subtotal" from Col. B, below left	
Subtotal		**Total adjusted value**	

5 Enter the value of the total gross estate as adjusted under section 2032A(b)(3)(A). ▶

6 Attach a description of the method used to determine the special value based on qualified use.

7 Did the decedent and/or a member of his or her family own all property listed on line 2 for at least 5 of the 8 years immediately preceding the date of the decedent's death? ☐ **Yes** ☐ **No**

8 Were there any periods during the 8-year period preceding the date of the decedent's death during which the decedent or a member of his or her family:

	Yes	No
a Did not own the property listed on line 2 above?		
b Did not use the property listed on line 2 above in a qualified use?		
c Did not materially participate in the operation of the farm or other business within the meaning of section 2032A(e)(6)?		

If "Yes" to any of the above, you must attach a statement listing the periods. If applicable, describe whether the exceptions of sections 2032A(b)(4) or (5) are met.

9 Attach affidavits describing the activities constituting material participation and the identity and relationship to the decedent of the material participants.

10 Persons holding interests. Enter the requested information for each party who received any interest in the specially valued property. **(Each of the qualified heirs receiving an interest in the property must sign the agreement, and the agreement must be filed with this return.)**

	Name	Address
A		
B		
C		
D		
E		
F		
G		
H		

	Identifying number	Relationship to decedent	Fair market value	Special use value
A				
B				
C				
D				
E				
F				
G				
H				

You must attach a computation of the GST tax savings attributable to direct skips for each person listed above who is a skip person. (See instructions.)

11 Woodlands election.—Check here ▶ ☐ if you wish to make a woodlands election as described in section 2032A(e)(13). Enter the Schedule and item numbers from Form 706 of the property for which you are making this election ▶
You must attach a statement explaining why you are entitled to make this election. The IRS may issue regulations that require more information to substantiate this election. You will be notified by the IRS if you must supply further information.

Schedule A-1—Page 9

Form 706 (Rev. 8-93)

Part 3.—Agreement to Special Valuation Under Section 2032A

Estate of:	Date of Death	Decedent's Social Security Number

There cannot be a valid election unless:

- The agreement is executed by each and every one of the qualified heirs, and
- The agreement is included with the estate tax return when the estate tax return is filed.

We (list all qualified heirs and other persons having an interest in the property required to sign this agreement)

____

____,

being all the qualified heirs and ____

____,

being all other parties having interests in the property which is qualified real property and which is valued under section 2032A of the Internal Revenue Code, do hereby approve of the election made by ______________________________,

Executor/Administrator of the estate of ______________________________,

pursuant to section 2032A to value said property on the basis of the qualified use to which the property is devoted and do hereby enter into this agreement pursuant to section 2032A(d).

The undersigned agree and consent to the application of subsection (c) of section 2032A of the Code with respect to all the property described on line 2 of Part 2 of Schedule A-1 of Form 706, attached to this agreement. More specifically, the undersigned heirs expressly agree and consent to personal liability under subsection (c) of 2032A for the additional estate and GST taxes imposed by that subsection with respect to their respective interests in the above-described property in the event of certain early dispositions of the property or early cessation of the qualified use of the property. It is understood that if a qualified heir disposes of any interest in qualified real property to any member of his or her family, such member may thereafter be treated as the qualified heir with respect to such interest upon filing a Form 706-A and a new agreement.

The undersigned interested parties who are not qualified heirs consent to the collection of any additional estate and GST taxes imposed under section 2032A(c) of the Code from the specially valued property.

If there is a disposition of any interest which passes or has passed to him or her or if there is a cessation of the qualified use of any specially valued property which passes or passed to him or her, each of the undersigned heirs agrees to file a **Form 706-A,** United States Additional Estate Tax Return, and pay any additional estate and GST taxes due within 6 months of the disposition or cessation.

It is understood by all interested parties that this agreement is a condition precedent to the election of special use valuation under section 2032A of the Code and must be executed by every interested party even though that person may not have received the estate (or GST) tax benefits or be in possession of such property.

Each of the undersigned understands that by making this election, a lien will be created and recorded pursuant to section 6324B of the Code on the property referred to in this agreement for the adjusted tax differences with respect to the estate as defined in section 2032A(c)(2)(C).

As the interested parties, the undersigned designate the following individual as their agent for all dealings with the Internal Revenue Service concerning the continued qualification of the specially valued property under section 2032A of the Code and on all issues regarding the special lien under section 6324B. The agent is authorized to act for the parties with respect to all dealings with the Service on matters affecting the qualified real property described earlier. This authority includes the following:

- To receive confidential information on all matters relating to continued qualification under section 2032A of the specially valued real property and on all matters relating to the special lien arising under section 6324B.
- To furnish the Service with any requested information concerning the property.
- To notify the Service of any disposition or cessation of qualified use of any part of the property.
- To receive, but not to endorse and collect, checks in payment of any refund of Internal Revenue taxes, penalties, or interest.
- To execute waivers (including offers of waivers) of restrictions on assessment or collection of deficiencies in tax and waivers of notice of disallowance of a claim for credit or refund.
- To execute closing agreements under section 7121.

(continued on next page)

Form 706 (Rev. 8-93)

Part 3.—Agreement to Special Valuation Under Section 2032A *(Continued)*

Estate of:	Date of Death	Decedent's Social Security Number

• Other acts (specify) ▶ ____________________

By signing this agreement, the agent agrees to provide the Service with any requested information concerning this property and to notify the Service of any disposition or cessation of the qualified use of any part of this property.

Name of Agent	Signature	Address

The property to which this agreement relates is listed in Form 706, United States Estate (and Generation-Skipping Transfer) Tax Return, and in the Notice of Election, along with its fair market value according to section 2031 of the Code and its special use value according to section 2032A. The name, address, social security number, and interest (including the value) of each of the undersigned in this property are as set forth in the attached Notice of Election.

IN WITNESS WHEREOF, the undersigned have hereunto set their hands at ____________________,

this __________ day of __________ .

SIGNATURES OF EACH OF THE QUALIFIED HEIRS:

Signature of qualified heir	Signature of qualified heir
Signature of qualified heir	Signature of qualified heir
Signature of qualified heir	Signature of qualified heir
Signature of qualified heir	Signature of qualified heir
Signature of qualified heir	Signature of qualified heir
Signature of qualified heir	Signature of qualified heir

Signatures of other interested parties

Signatures of other interested parties

Form 706 (Rev. 8-93)

Estate of: Herman Estes

SCHEDULE B—Stocks and Bonds

(For jointly owned property that must be disclosed on Schedule E, see the instructions for Schedule E.)

Item number	Description including face amount of bonds or number of shares and par value where needed for identification. Give CUSIP number if available.	Unit value	Alternate valuation date	Alternate value	Value at date of death
1	Stock in Ajax Corporation, 1000 shares, $10 par value	600			600,000
	Total from continuation schedule(s) (or additional sheet(s)) attached to this schedule . .				
	TOTAL. (Also enter on Part 5, Recapitulation, page 3, at item 2.)				600,000

(If more space is needed, attach the continuation schedule from the end of this package or additional sheets of the same size.)

(The instructions to Schedule B are in the separate instructions.)

Form 706 (Rev. 8-93)

Estate of: Herman Estes

SCHEDULE C—Mortgages, Notes, and Cash

(For jointly owned property that must be disclosed on Schedule E, see the instructions for Schedule E.)

Item number	Description	Alternate valuation date	Alternate value	Value at date of death
1	Checking account			10,000
2.	Savings account (includes accrued interest through date of death)			75,000
	Total from continuation schedule(s) (or additional sheet(s)) attached to this schedule .			
	TOTAL. (Also enter on Part 5, Recapitulation, page 3, at item 3.)			85,000

(If more space is needed, attach the continuation schedule from the end of this package or additional sheets of the same size.)
(See the instructions on the reverse side.)

Form 706 (Rev. 8-93)

Estate of: Herman Estes

SCHEDULE D—Insurance on the Decedent's Life

You must list **all** policies on the life of the decedent and attach a Form 712 for each policy.

Item number	Description	Alternate valuation date	Alternate value	Value at date of death
1	Life insurance policy No. 123-A issued by the Life Insurance Company of Ohio Beneficiary - Johnny Estes			200,000
	Total from continuation schedule(s) (or additional sheet(s)) attached to this schedule .			
	TOTAL. (Also enter on Part 5, Recapitulation, page 3, at item 4.)			200,000

(If more space is needed, attach the continuation schedule from the end of this package or additional sheets of the same size.)

(See the instructions on the reverse side.)

Form 706 (Rev. 8-93)

Estate of: Herman Estes

SCHEDULE E—Jointly Owned Property

(If you elect section 2032A valuation, you must complete Schedule E and Schedule A-1.)

PART 1.—Qualified Joint Interests—Interests Held by the Decedent and His or Her Spouse as the Only Joint Tenants (Section 2040(b)(2))

Item number	Description For securities, give CUSIP number, if available.	Alternate valuation date	Alternate value	Value at date of death
	Land			400,000
	Total from continuation schedule(s) (or additional sheet(s)) attached to this schedule			
1a	Totals			400,000
1b	Amounts included in gross estate (one-half of line 1a)			200,000

PART 2.—All Other Joint Interests

2a State the name and address of each surviving co-tenant. If there are more than three surviving co-tenants, list the additional co-tenants on an attached sheet.

	Name	Address (number and street, city, state, and ZIP code)
A.		
B.		
C.		

Item number	Enter letter for co-tenant	Description (including alternate valuation date if any) For securities, give CUSIP number, if available.	Percentage includible	Includible alternate value	Includible value at date of death
		Total from continuation schedule(s) (or additional sheet(s)) attached to this schedule			
2b		Total other joint interests			
3		**Total includible joint interests** (add lines 1b and 2b). Also enter on Part 5, Recapitulation, page 3, at item 5			

(If more space is needed, attach the continuation schedule from the end of this package or additional sheets of the same size.)
(See the instructions on the reverse side.)

Form 706 (Rev. 8-93)

Estate of: Herman Estes

SCHEDULE F—Other Miscellaneous Property Not Reportable Under Any Other Schedule

(For jointly owned property that must be disclosed on Schedule E, see the instructions for Schedule E.)
(If you elect section 2032A valuation, you must complete Schedule F and Schedule A-1.)

	Yes	No
1 Did the decedent at the time of death own any articles of artistic or collectible value in excess of $3,000 or any collections whose artistic or collectible value combined at date of death exceeded $10,000? . . . . If "Yes," submit full details on this schedule and attach appraisals.		X
2 Has the decedent's estate, spouse, or any other person, received (or will receive) any bonus or award as a result of the decedent's employment or death? . . . . If "Yes," submit full details on this schedule.		X
3 Did the decedent at the time of death have, or have access to, a safe deposit box? . . . . If "Yes," state location, and if held in joint names of decedent and another, state name and relationship of joint depositor. If any of the contents of the safe deposit box are omitted from the schedules in this return, explain fully why omitted.		X

Item number	Description For securities, give CUSIP number, if available.	Alternate valuation date	Alternate value	Value at date of death
1				
Total from continuation schedule(s) (or additional sheet(s)) attached to this schedule. .				
TOTAL. (Also enter on Part 5, Recapitulation, page 3, at item 6.)				0

(If more space is needed, attach the continuation schedule from the end of this package or additional sheets of the same size.)
(See the instructions on the reverse side.)

Form 706 (Rev. 8-93)

Estate of: Herman Estes

SCHEDULE G—Transfers During Decedent's Life

(If you elect section 2032A valuation, you must complete Schedule G and Schedule A-1.)

Item number	Description For securities, give CUSIP number, if available.	Alternate valuation date	Alternate value	Value at date of death
A.	Gift tax paid by the decedent or the estate for all gifts made by the decedent or his or her spouse within 3 years before the decedent's death (section 2035(c))	X X X X X		11,900
B.	Transfers includible under section 2035(a), 2036, 2037, or 2038:			
1				
	Total from continuation schedule(s) (or additional sheet(s)) attached to this schedule .			
	TOTAL. (Also enter on Part 5, Recapitulation, page 3, at item 7.).			11,900

SCHEDULE H—Powers of Appointment

(Include "5 and 5 lapsing" powers (section 2041(b)(2)) held by the decedent.)

(If you elect section 2032A valuation, you must complete Schedule H and Schedule A-1.)

Item number	Description	Alternate valuation date	Alternate value	Value at date of death
1				
	Total from continuation schedule(s) (or additional sheet(s)) attached to this schedule .			
	TOTAL. (Also enter on Part 5, Recapitulation, page 3, at item 8.).			

(If more space is needed, attach the continuation schedule from the end of this package or additional sheets of the same size.)
(The instructions to Schedules G and H are in the separate instructions.)

Form 706 (Rev. 8-93)

Estate of: Herman Estes

SCHEDULE I—Annuities

Note: *Generally, no exclusion is allowed for the estates of decedents dying after December 31, 1984 (see instructions).*

	Yes	No
A Are you excluding from the decedent's gross estate the value of a lump-sum distribution described in section 2039(f)(2)? . . . . . If "Yes," you must attach the information required by the instructions.		X

Item number	Description Show the entire value of the annuity before any exclusions.	Alternate valuation date	Includible alternate value	Includible value at date of death
1	Qualified pension plan issued by Buckeye Corporation Beneficiary - Ann Estes - spouse			240,000
	Total from continuation schedule(s) (or additional sheet(s)) attached to this schedule .			
	TOTAL. (Also enter on Part 5, Recapitulation, page 3, at item 9.)			240,000

(If more space is needed, attach the continuation schedule from the end of this package or additional sheets of the same size.)

(The instructions to Schedule I are in the separate instructions.)

Form 706 (Rev. 8-93)

Estate of: Herman Estes

SCHEDULE J—Funeral Expenses and Expenses Incurred in Administering Property Subject to Claims

Note: *Do not list on this schedule expenses of administering property not subject to claims. For those expenses, see the instructions for Schedule L.*

If executors' commissions, attorney fees, etc., are claimed and allowed as a deduction for estate tax purposes, they are not allowable as a deduction in computing the taxable income of the estate for Federal income tax purposes. They are allowable as an income tax deduction on Form 1041 if a waiver is filed to waive the deduction on Form 706 (see the Form 1041 instructions).

Item number	Description	Expense amount	Total Amount
	A. Funeral expenses:	15,000	
1			
	Total funeral expenses		15,000
	B. Administration expenses:		
1	Executors' commissions—amount estimated/agreed upon/paid. (Strike out the words that do not apply.)		} 70,000
2	Attorney fees—amount estimated/agreed upon/paid. (Strike out the words that do not apply.) . . .		
3	Accountant fees—amount estimated/agreed upon/paid. (Strike out the words that do not apply.) . .		
4	Miscellaneous expenses:	Expense amount	
	Total miscellaneous expenses from continuation schedule(s) (or additional sheet(s)) attached to this schedule		
	Total miscellaneous expenses		

TOTAL. (Also enter on Part 5, Recapitulation, page 3, at item 11.) 85,000

(If more space is needed, attach the continuation schedule from the end of this package or additional sheets of the same size.)
(See the instructions on the reverse side.)

Form 706 (Rev. 8-93)

Estate of: Herman Estes

SCHEDULE K—Debts of the Decedent, and Mortgages and Liens

Item number	Debts of the Decedent—Creditor and nature of claim, and allowable death taxes	Amount unpaid to date	Amount in contest	Amount claimed as a deduction
1	Bank loan (including interest accrued through date of death)	25,200		25,200
2	American Express, Visa, and Master Card credit cards	6,500		6,500
	Total from continuation schedule(s) (or additional sheet(s)) attached to this schedule			
	TOTAL. (Also enter on Part 5, Recapitulation, page 3, at item 12.)			31,700

Item number	Mortgages and Liens—Description	Amount
1		
	Total from continuation schedule(s) (or additional sheet(s)) attached to this schedule	
	TOTAL. (Also enter on Part 5, Recapitulation, page 3, at item 13.)	

(If more space is needed, attach the continuation schedule from the end of this package or additional sheets of the same size.)
(The instructions to Schedule K are in the separate instructions.)

Form 706 (Rev. 8-93)

Estate of:

SCHEDULE L—Net Losses During Administration and Expenses Incurred in Administering Property Not Subject to Claims

Item number	Net losses during administration (**Note:** *Do not deduct losses claimed on a Federal income tax return.*)	Amount
1		
	Total from continuation schedule(s) (or additional sheet(s)) attached to this schedule	
	TOTAL. (Also enter on Part 5, Recapitulation, page 3, at item 16.)	

Item number	Expenses incurred in administering property not subject to claims (Indicate whether estimated, agreed upon, or paid.)	Amount
1		
	Total from continuation schedule(s) (or additional sheet(s)) attached to this schedule	
	TOTAL. (Also enter on Part 5, Recapitulation, page 3, at item 17.)	

(If more space is needed, attach the continuation schedule from the end of this package or additional sheets of the same size.)

 (The instructions to Schedule L are in the separate instructions.)

Form 706 (Rev. 8-93)

Estate of: Herman Estes

SCHEDULE M—Bequests, etc., to Surviving Spouse

Election To Deduct Qualified Terminable Interest Property Under Section 2056(b)(7).—If a trust (or other property) meets the requirements of qualified terminable interest property under section 2056(b)(7), and

a. The trust or other property is listed on Schedule M, and

b. The value of the trust (or other property) is entered in whole or in part as a deduction on Schedule M,

then unless the executor specifically identifies the trust (all or a fractional portion or percentage) or other property to be excluded from the election the executor shall be deemed to have made an election to have such trust (or other property) treated as qualified terminable interest property under section 2056(b)(7).

If less than the entire value of the trust (or other property) that the executor has included in the gross estate is entered as a deduction on Schedule M, the executor shall be considered to have made an election only as to a fraction of the trust (or other property). The numerator of this fraction is equal to the amount of the trust (or other property) deducted on Schedule M. The denominator is equal to the total value of the trust (or other property).

Election To Deduct Qualified Domestic Trust Property Under Section 2056A.—If a trust meets the requirements of a qualified domestic trust under section 2056A(a) and this return is filed no later than 1 year after the time prescribed by law (including extensions) for filing the return, and

a. The entire value of a trust or trust property is listed on Schedule M, and

b. The entire value of the trust or trust property is entered as a deduction on Schedule M,

then unless the executor specifically identifies the trust to be excluded from the election, the executor shall be deemed to have made an election to have the entire trust treated as qualified domestic trust property.

		Yes	No
1	Did any property pass to the surviving spouse as a result of a qualified disclaimer? *If "Yes," attach a copy of the written disclaimer required by section 2518(b).*		X
2a	In what country was the surviving spouse born? United States		
b	What is the surviving spouse's date of birth? 3-12-37		
c	Is the surviving spouse a U.S. citizen?	X	
d	If the surviving spouse is a naturalized citizen, when did the surviving spouse acquire citizenship? N/A		
e	If the surviving spouse is not a U.S. citizen, of what country is the surviving spouse a citizen? N/A		
3	**Election out of QTIP Treatment of Annuities.—**Do you elect under section 2056(b)(7)(C)(ii) **not** to treat as qualified terminable interest property any joint and survivor annuities that are included in the gross estate and would otherwise be treated as qualified terminable interest property under section 2056(b)(7)(C)? (see instructions)		X

Item number	Description of property interests passing to surviving spouse	Amount
1	Residence	325,000
2	Checking Account	10,000
3	Savings Account	75,000
4	Land, held in joint tenancy	200,000
5	Qualified pension plan	240,000
6	Trust with First Bank as trustee	200,000
	Total from continuation schedule(s) (or additional sheet(s)) attached to this schedule	

4	**Total** amount of property interests listed on Schedule M		4	1,050,000
5a	Federal estate taxes (including section 4980A taxes) payable out of property interests listed on Schedule M	5a		
b	Other death taxes payable out of property interests listed on Schedule M	5b		
c	Federal and state GST taxes payable out of property interests listed on Schedule M	5c		
d	Add items a, b, and c		5d	0
6	Net amount of property interests listed on Schedule M (subtract 5d from 4). Also enter on Part 5, Recapitulation, page 3, at item 18		6	1,050,000

(If more space is needed, attach the continuation schedule from the end of this package or additional sheets of the same size.)

(See the instructions on the reverse side.)

Form 706 (Rev. 8-93)

Estate of: Herman Estes

SCHEDULE O—Charitable, Public, and Similar Gifts and Bequests

		Yes	No
1a	If the transfer was made by will, has any action been instituted to have interpreted or to contest the will or any of its provisions affecting the charitable deductions claimed in this schedule? . . . . If "Yes," full details must be submitted with this schedule.		X
b	According to the information and belief of the person or persons filing this return, is any such action planned? If "Yes," full details must be submitted with this schedule.		X
2	Did any property pass to charity as the result of a qualified disclaimer? . . . . If "Yes," attach a copy of the written disclaimer required by section 2518(b).		X

Item number	Name and address of beneficiary	Character of institution	Amount
1	American Cancer Society	Charity	10,000
	Total from continuation schedule(s) (or additional sheet(s)) attached to this schedule		

3	Total		3	10,000
4a	Federal estate tax (including section 4980A taxes) payable out of property interests listed above	4a		
b	Other death taxes payable out of property interests listed above	4b		
c	Federal and state GST taxes payable out of property interests listed above	4c		
d	Add items a, b, and c		4d	
5	Net value of property interests listed above (subtract 4d from 3). Also enter on Part 5, Recapitulation, page 3, at item 19		5	10,000

(If more space is needed, attach the continuation schedule from the end of this package or additional sheets of the same size.)
(The instructions to Schedule O are in the separate instructions.)

Form 706 (Rev. 8-93)

Estate of:

SCHEDULE P—Credit for Foreign Death Taxes

List all foreign countries to which death taxes have been paid and for which a credit is claimed on this return.

If a credit is claimed for death taxes paid to more than one foreign country, compute the credit for taxes paid to one country on this sheet and attach a separate copy of Schedule P for each of the other countries.

The credit computed on this sheet is for the ....
(Name of death tax or taxes)

.... imposed in ....
(Name of country)

Credit is computed under the ....
(Insert title of treaty or "statute")

Citizenship (nationality) of decedent at time of death

(All amounts and values must be entered in United States money)

1 Total of estate, inheritance, legacy, and succession taxes imposed in the country named above attributable to property situated in that country, subjected to these taxes, and included in the gross estate (as defined by statute)	
2 Value of the gross estate (adjusted, if necessary, according to the instructions for item 2)	
3 Value of property situated in that country, subjected to death taxes imposed in that country, and included in the gross estate (adjusted, if necessary, according to the instructions for item 3)	
4 Tax imposed by section 2001 reduced by the total credits claimed under sections 2010, 2011, and 2012 (see instructions)	
5 Amount of Federal estate tax attributable to property specified at item 3. (Divide item 3 by item 2 and multiply the result by item 4.)	
6 Credit for death taxes imposed in the country named above (the smaller of item 1 or item 5). Also enter on line 18 of Part 2, Tax Computation	

SCHEDULE Q—Credit for Tax on Prior Transfers

Part 1.—Transferor Information

	Name of transferor	Social security number	IRS office where estate tax return was filed	Date of death
A				
B				
C				

Check here ▶ ☐ if section 2013(f) (special valuation of farm, etc., real property) adjustments to the computation of the credit were made (see instructions).

Part 2.—Computation of Credit (see instructions)

Item	Transferor			Total A, B, & C
	A	B	C	
1 Transferee's tax as apportioned (from worksheet, (line 7 ÷ line 8) × line 35 for each column)				
2 Transferor's tax (from each column of worksheet, line 20)				
3 Maximum amount before percentage requirement (for each column, enter amount from line 1 or 2, whichever is smaller)				
4 Percentage allowed (each column) (see instructions)	%	%	%	
5 Credit allowable (line 3 × line 4 for each column)				
6 TOTAL credit allowable (add columns A, B, and C of line 5). Enter here and on line 19 of Part 2, Tax Computation				

 (The instructions to Schedules P and Q are in the separate instructions.)

Form 706 (Rev. 8-93)

SCHEDULE R—Generation-Skipping Transfer Tax

Note: *To avoid application of the deemed allocation rules, Form 706 and Schedule R should be filed to allocate the GST exemption to trusts that may later have taxable terminations or distributions under section 2612 even if the form is not required to be filed to report estate or GST tax.*

The GST tax is imposed on taxable transfers of interests in property located ***outside the United States*** *as well as property located inside the United States.*

Part 1.—GST Exemption Reconciliation (Section 2631) and Section 2652(a)(3) (Special QTIP) Election

Check box ▶ ☐ if you are making a section 2652(a)(3) (special QTIP) election (see instructions)		
1 Maximum allowable GST exemption	1	$1,000,000
2 Total GST exemption allocated by the decedent against decedent's lifetime transfers	2	
3 Total GST exemption allocated by the executor, using Form 709, against decedent's lifetime transfers	3	
4 GST exemption allocated on line 6 of Schedule R, Part 2	4	
5 GST exemption allocated on line 6 of Schedule R, Part 3	5	
6 Total GST exemption allocated on line 4 of Schedule(s) R-1	6	
7 Total GST exemption allocated to intervivos transfers and direct skips (add lines 2–6)	7	
8 GST exemption available to allocate to trusts and section 2032A interests (subtract line 7 from line 1)	8	
9 Allocation of GST exemption to trusts (as defined for GST tax purposes):		

A Name of trust	B Trust's EIN (if any)	C GST exemption allocated on lines 2–6, above (see instructions)	D Additional GST exemption allocated (see instructions)	E Trust's inclusion ratio (optional—see instructions)
9D Total. May not exceed line 8, above		9D		

10 GST exemption available to allocate to section 2032A interests received by individual beneficiaries (subtract line 9D from line 8). You must attach special use allocation schedule (see instructions)	10	

(The instructions to Schedule R are in the separate instructions.)

Form 706 (Rev. 8-93)

Estate of:

Part 2.—Direct Skips Where the Property Interests Transferred Bear the GST Tax on the Direct Skips

Name of skip person	Description of property interest transferred	Estate tax value

1	Total estate tax values of all property interests listed above	1	
2	Estate taxes, state death taxes, and other charges borne by the property interests listed above	2	
3	GST taxes borne by the property interests listed above but imposed on direct skips other than those shown on this Part 2. (See instructions.)	3	
4	Total fixed taxes and other charges. (Add lines 2 and 3.)	4	
5	Total tentative maximum direct skips. (Subtract line 4 from line 1.)	5	
6	GST exemption allocated	6	
7	Subtract line 6 from line 5	7	
8	GST tax due. (Divide line 7 by 2.818182)	8	
9	Enter the amount from line 8 of Schedule R, Part 3	9	
10	**Total GST taxes payable by the estate.** (Add lines 8 and 9.) Enter here and on line 22 of the Tax Computation on page 1	10	

Form 706 (Rev. 8-93)

Estate of:

Part 3.—Direct Skips Where the Property Interests Transferred Do Not Bear the GST Tax on the Direct Skips

Name of skip person	Description of property interest transferred	Estate tax value

1 Total estate tax values of all property interests listed above	**1**	
2 Estate taxes, state death taxes, and other charges borne by the property interests listed above	**2**	
3 GST taxes borne by the property interests listed above but imposed on direct skips other than those shown on this Part 3. (See instructions.)	**3**	
4 Total fixed taxes and other charges. (Add lines 2 and 3.)	**4**	
5 Total tentative maximum direct skips. (Subtract line 4 from line 1.)	**5**	
6 GST exemption allocated	**6**	
7 Subtract line 6 from line 5	**7**	
8 GST tax due (multiply line 7 by .55). Enter here and on Schedule R, Part 2, line 9	**8**	

SCHEDULE R-1 (Form 706)
(August 1993)
Department of the Treasury
Internal Revenue Service

Generation-Skipping Transfer Tax

Direct Skips From a Trust

Payment Voucher

OMB No. 1545-0015
Expires 12-31-95

Executor: File one copy with Form 706 and send two copies to the fiduciary. Do not pay the tax shown. See the separate instructions.
Fiduciary: See instructions on following page. Pay the tax shown on line 6.

Name of trust		**Trust's EIN**
Name and title of fiduciary	Name of decedent	
Address of fiduciary (number and street)	Decedent's SSN	Service Center where Form 706 was filed
City, state, and ZIP code	Name of executor	
Address of executor (number and street)	City, state, and ZIP code	
Date of decedent's death	Filing due date of Schedule R, Form 706 (with extensions)	

Part 1.—Computation of the GST Tax on the Direct Skip

Description of property interests subject to the direct skip	Estate tax value

1 Total estate tax value of all property interests listed above	1	
2 Estate taxes, state death taxes, and other charges borne by the property interests listed above.	2	
3 Tentative maximum direct skip from trust. (Subtract line 2 from line 1.)	3	
4 GST exemption allocated	4	
5 Subtract line 4 from line 3	5	
6 **GST tax due from fiduciary.** (Divide line 5 by 2.818182) **(See instructions if property will not bear the GST tax.)**	6	

Under penalties of perjury, I declare that I have examined this return, including accompanying schedules and statements, and to the best of my knowledge and belief, it is true, correct, and complete.

Signature(s) of executor(s) — Date

Date

Signature of fiduciary or officer representing fiduciary — Date

Form 706 (Rev. 8-93)

Estate of:

SCHEDULE S—Increased Estate Tax on Excess Retirement Accumulations

(Under section 4980A(d) of the Internal Revenue Code)

Part I Tax Computation

1 Check this box if a section 4980A(d)(5) spousal election is being made . . . ▶ ☐
You must attach the statement described in the instructions.

2 Enter the name and employer identification number (EIN) of each qualified employer plan and individual retirement account in which the decedent had an interest at the time of death:

	Name	EIN
Plan #1		
Plan #2		
Plan #3		
IRA #1		
IRA #2		
IRA #3		

	A Plan #1	B Plan #2	C Plan #3	D All IRAs
3 Value of decedent's interest . . .				
4 Amounts rolled over after death . . .				
5 Total value (add lines 3 and 4) . . .				
6 Amounts payable to certain alternate payees (see instructions) . . .				
7 Decedent's investment in the contract under section 72(f)				
8 Excess life insurance amount . . .				
9 Decedent's interest as a beneficiary . . .				
10 Total reductions in value (add lines 6, 7, 8, and 9) . . .				
11 Net value of decedent's interest (subtract line 10 from line 5) . . .				

12 Decedent's aggregate interest in all plans and IRAs (add columns A–D of line 11) . . . ▶			12	
13 Present value of hypothetical life annuity (from Part III, line 4) . . .	13			
14 Remaining unused grandfather amount (from Part II, line 4) . . .	14			
15 Enter the greater of line 13 or line 14 . . .			15	
16 Excess retirement accumulation (subtract line 15 from line 12) . . .			16	
17 Increased estate tax (multiply line 16 by 15%). Enter here and on line 23 of the Tax Computation on page 1 . . .			17	

(The instructions to Schedule S are in the separate instructions.)

Form 706 (Rev. 8-93)

Part II Grandfather Election

1 Was a grandfather election made on a previously filed Form 5329? . . . . ▶ ☐ Yes ☐ No
If "Yes," complete lines 2–4 below. **You may not make or revoke the grandfather election after the due date (with extensions) for filing the decedent's 1988 income tax return.** If "No," enter -0- on line 4 and skip to Part III.

2 Initial grandfather amount	**2**	
3 Total amount previously recovered	**3**	
4 Remaining unused grandfather amount (subtract line 3 from line 2). Enter here and on Part I, line 14, on page 38	**4**	

Part III Computation of Hypothetical Life Annuity

1 Decedent's attained age at date of death (in whole years, rounded down)	**1**	
2 Applicable annual annuity amount (see instructions)	**2**	
3 Present value multiplier (see instructions)	**3**	
4 Present value of hypothetical life annuity (multiply line 2 by line 3). Enter here and on Part I, line 13, on page 38	**4**	

Form 706 (Rev. 8-93) (Make copies of this schedule before completing it if you will need more than one schedule.)

Estate of:

CONTINUATION SCHEDULE

Continuation of Schedule ______________
(Enter letter of schedule you are continuing.)

Item number	Description For securities, give CUSIP number, if available.	Unit value (Sch B, E, or G only)	Alternate valuation date	Alternate value	Value at date of death or amount deductible
TOTAL. (Carry forward to main schedule.)					

See the instructions on the reverse side.

Form **1041** Department of the Treasury—Internal Revenue Service

U.S. Income Tax Return for Estates and Trusts 1996

For calendar year 1996 or fiscal year beginning , 1996, and ending , 19 — OMB No. 1545-0092

A Type of entity:
- ☐ Decedent's estate
- ☒ Simple trust
- ☐ Complex trust
- ☐ Grantor type trust
- ☐ Bankruptcy estate–Ch. 7
- ☐ Bankruptcy estate–Ch. 11
- ☐ Pooled income fund

B Number of Schedules K-1 attached (see instructions) ▶

Name of estate or trust (If a grantor type trust, see page 7 of the instructions.): Bob Adams Trust (Simple Trust)

Name and title of fiduciary: First Bank

Number, street, and room or suite no. (If a P.O. box, see page 7 of the instructions.): Post Office Box 100

City or town, state, and ZIP code: Nashville, TN 37203

C Employer identification number: 74 : 1237211

D Date entity created: 1982

E Nonexempt charitable and split-interest trusts, check applicable boxes (see page 8 of the instructions):
- ☐ Described in section 4947(a)(1)
- ☐ Not a private foundation
- ☐ Described in section 4947(a)(2)

F Check applicable boxes: ☐ Initial return ☐ Final return ☐ Amended return ☐ Change in fiduciary's name ☐ Change in fiduciary's address

G Pooled mortgage account (see page 9 of the instructions): ☐ Bought ☐ Sold Date:

Income

Line	Description		Amount
1	Interest income	1	
2	Dividends	2	30,000
3	Business income or (loss) (attach Schedule C or C-EZ (Form 1040))	3	
4	Capital gain or (loss) (attach Schedule D (Form 1041))	4	12,000
5	Rents, royalties, partnerships, other estates and trusts, etc. (attach Schedule E (Form 1040))	5	4,000
6	Farm income or (loss) (attach Schedule F (Form 1040)) ↖ (see below)	6	
7	Ordinary gain or (loss) (attach Form 4797)	7	
8	Other income. List type and amount	8	
9	**Total income.** Combine lines 1 through 8 ▶	9	46,000

Deductions

Line	Description		Amount
10	Interest. Check if Form 4952 is attached ▶ ☐	10	
11	Taxes	11	
12	Fiduciary fees ($1,200 - $360)	12	840
13	Charitable deduction (from Schedule A, line 7)	13	
14	Attorney, accountant, and return preparer fees	14	500
15a	Other deductions NOT subject to the 2% floor (attach schedule)	15a	
b	Allowable miscellaneous itemized deductions subject to the 2% floor	15b	
16	**Total.** Add lines 10 through 15b	16	1,340
17	Adjusted total income or (loss). Subtract line 16 from line 9. Enter here and on Schedule B, line 1 ▶	17	44,660
18	Income distribution deduction (from Schedule B, line 17) (attach Schedules K-1 (Form 1041))	18	32,660
19	Estate tax deduction (including certain generation-skipping taxes) (attach computation)	19	
20	Exemption	20	300
21	**Total deductions.** Add lines 18 through 20 ▶	21	32,960

Tax and Payments

Line	Description		Amount
22	Taxable income. Subtract line 21 from line 17. If a loss, see page 13 of the instructions	22	11,700
23	**Total tax** (from Schedule G, line 8)	23	3,068
24	**Payments: a** 1996 estimated tax payments and amount applied from 1995 return	24a	2,600
b	Estimated tax payments allocated to beneficiaries (from Form 1041-T)	24b	
c	Subtract line 24b from line 24a	24c	
d	Tax paid with extension of time to file: ☐ Form 2758 ☐ Form 8736 ☐ Form 8800	24d	
e	Federal income tax withheld. If any is from Form(s) 1099, check ▶ ☐	24e	
	Other payments: **f** Form 2439 ; **g** Form 4136 ; Total ▶	24h	
25	**Total payments.** Add lines 24c through 24e, and 24h ▶	25	2,600
26	Estimated tax penalty (see page 13 of the instructions)	26	
27	**Tax due.** If line 25 is smaller than the total of lines 23 and 26, enter amount owed	27	468
28	**Overpayment.** If line 25 is larger than the total of lines 23 and 26, enter amount overpaid	28	
29	Amount of line 28 to be: **a Credited to 1997 estimated tax** ▶ ; **b Refunded** ▶	29	

Please Sign Here

Under penalties of perjury, I declare that I have examined this return, including accompanying schedules and statements, and to the best of my knowledge and belief, it is true, correct, and complete. Declaration of preparer (other than fiduciary) is based on all information of which preparer has any knowledge.

▶ Tom Trusty — Signature of fiduciary or officer representing fiduciary | Date: 3/16/97 | ▶ 38 : 1505087 — EIN of fiduciary if a financial institution (see page 4 of the instructions)

Paid Preparer's Use Only

Preparer's signature ▶ Karen Certified | Date: 3/16/97 | Check if self-employed ▶ ☒ | Preparer's social security no.: 444 : 17 : 1313

Firm's name (or yours if self-employed) and address ▶ Karen Certified, One Opryland Place, Nashville, TN | EIN ▶ 74 : 1234567 | ZIP code ▶ 37204

For Paperwork Reduction Act Notice, see page 1 of the separate instructions. Cat. No. 11370H Form **1041** (1996)

Line 4: Net rental income = Rental income ($5,000) - Rental expenses-- Realtor's commissions ($1,000) = Net rental income ($4,000)

Schedule A Charitable Deduction. Do not complete for a simple trust or a pooled income fund.

1	Amounts paid for charitable purposes from gross income	1	
2	Amounts permanently set aside for charitable purposes from gross income	2	
3	Add lines 1 and 2	3	
4	Tax-exempt income allocable to charitable contributions (see page 14 of the instructions)	4	
5	Subtract line 4 from line 3	5	
6	Capital gains for the tax year allocated to corpus and paid or permanently set aside for charitable purposes	6	
7	**Charitable deduction.** Add lines 5 and 6. Enter here and on page 1, line 13	7	None

Schedule B Income Distribution Deduction

1	Adjusted total income (from page 1, line 17) (see page 14 of the instructions)	1	44,660
2	Adjusted tax-exempt interest ($15,000 − $360)	2	14,640
3	Total net gain from Schedule D (Form 1041), line 17, column (a) (see page 15 of the instructions)	3	
4	Enter amount from Schedule A, line 6	4	
5	Long-term capital gain for the tax year included on Schedule A, line 3	5	
6	Short-term capital gain for the tax year included on Schedule A, line 3	6	
7	If the amount on page 1, line 4, is a capital loss, enter here as a positive figure	7	
8	If the amount on page 1, line 4, is a capital gain, enter here as a negative figure	8	(12,000)
9	**Distributable net income (DNI).** Combine lines 1 through 8. If zero or less, enter -0-	9	47,300
10	If a complex trust, enter accounting income for the tax year as determined under the governing instrument and applicable local law — 10: 48,500		
11	Income required to be distributed currently	11	48,500
12	Other amounts paid, credited, or otherwise required to be distributed	12	
13	Total distributions. Add lines 11 and 12. If greater than line 10, see page 15 of the instructions	13	48,500
14	Enter the amount of tax-exempt income included on line 13	14	14,640
15	Tentative income distribution deduction. Subtract line 14 from line 13	15	33,860
16	Tentative income distribution deduction. Subtract line 2 from line 9. If zero or less, enter -0-	16	32,660
17	**Income distribution deduction.** Enter the smaller of line 15 or line 16 here and on page 1, line 18	17	32,660

Schedule G Tax Computation (see page 16 of the instructions)

1	**Tax:** a ☐ Tax rate schedule or ☒ Schedule D (Form 1041)	1a	3,068		
	b Other taxes	1b			
	c Total. Add lines 1a and 1b ▶			1c	3,068
2a	Foreign tax credit (attach Form 1116)	2a			
b	Check: ☐ Nonconventional source fuel credit ☐ Form 8834	2b			
c	General business credit. Enter here and check which forms are attached: ☐ Form 3800 or ☐ Forms (specify) ▶	2c			
d	Credit for prior year minimum tax (attach Form 8801)	2d			
3	**Total credits.** Add lines 2a through 2d ▶			3	
4	Subtract line 3 from line 1c			4	3,068
5	Recapture taxes. Check if from: ☐ Form 4255 ☐ Form 8611			5	
6	Alternative minimum tax (from Schedule I, line 41)			6	
7	Household employment taxes. Attach Schedule H (Form 1040)			7	
8	**Total tax.** Add lines 4 through 7. Enter here and on page 1, line 23 ▶			8	3,068

Other Information

		Yes	No
1	Did the estate or trust receive tax-exempt income? If "Yes," attach a computation of the allocation of expenses. Enter the amount of tax-exempt interest income and exempt-interest dividends ▶ $ 15,000 (see below)	X	
2	Did the estate or trust receive all or any part of the earnings (salary, wages, and other compensation) of any individual by reason of a contract assignment or similar arrangement?		X
3	At any time during calendar year 1996, did the estate or trust have an interest in or a signature or other authority over a bank, securities, or other financial account in a foreign country? See page 17 of the instructions for exceptions and filing requirements for Form TD F 90-22.1. If "Yes," enter the name of the foreign country ▶		X
4	During the tax year, did the estate or trust receive a distribution from, or was it the grantor of, or transferor to, a foreign trust? If "Yes," see page 17 of the instructions for other forms the estate or trust may have to file		X
5	Did the estate or trust receive, or pay, any seller-financed mortgage interest? If "Yes," see page 17 of the instructions for required attachment		X
6	If this is a complex trust making the section 663(b) election, check here (see page 17 of the instructions) ▶ ☐		
7	To make a section 643(e)(3) election, attach Schedule D (Form 1041), and check here (see page 17) ▶ ☐		
8	If the decedent's estate has been open for more than 2 years, check here ▶ ☐		

Line 2: Allocation of expenses: $\frac{\$15,000}{\$50,000} \times \$1,200 = \$360$ of trustee's fee allocated to tax-exempt income

Form 1041 (1996) Page 3

Schedule I Alternative Minimum Tax (see pages 18 through 22 of the instructions)

Part I—Estate's or Trust's Share of Alternative Minimum Taxable Income

1	Adjusted total income or (loss) (from page 1, line 17)			1	44,660
2	Net operating loss deduction. Enter as a positive amount			2	
3	Add lines 1 and 2			3	44,660
4	**Adjustments and tax preference items:**				
a	Interest	4a			
b	Taxes	4b			
c	Miscellaneous itemized deductions (from page 1, line 15b)	4c			
d	Refund of taxes	4d	( )		
e	Depreciation of property placed in service after 1986	4e			
f	Circulation and research and experimental expenditures	4f			
g	Mining exploration and development costs	4g			
h	Long-term contracts entered into after February 28, 1986	4h			
i	Amortization of pollution control facilities	4i			
j	Installment sales of certain property	4j			
k	Adjusted gain or loss (including incentive stock options)	4k			
l	Certain loss limitations	4l			
m	Tax shelter farm activities	4m			
n	Passive activities	4n			
o	Beneficiaries of other trusts or decedent's estates	4o			
p	Tax-exempt interest from specified private activity bonds	4p			
q	Depletion	4q			
r	Accelerated depreciation of real property placed in service before 1987	4r			
s	Accelerated depreciation of leased personal property placed in service before 1987	4s			
t	Intangible drilling costs	4t			
u	Other adjustments	4u			
5	Combine lines 4a through 4u			5	
6	Add lines 3 and 5			6	44,660
7	Alternative tax net operating loss deduction (see page 21 of the instructions for limitations)			7	
8	Adjusted alternative minimum taxable income. Subtract line 7 from line 6. Enter here and on line 13			8	44,660
	Note: *Complete Part II before going to line 9.*				
9	Income distribution deduction from line 27	9	32,660		
10	Estate tax deduction (from page 1, line 19)	10			
11	Add lines 9 and 10			11	32,660
12	Estate's or trust's share of alternative minimum taxable income. Subtract line 11 from line 8			12	12,000

If line 12 is:

- $22,500 or less, stop here and enter -0- on Schedule G, line 6. The estate or trust is not liable for the alternative minimum tax.
- Over $22,500, but less than $165,000, go to line 28.
- $165,000 or more, enter the amount from line 12 on line 34 and go to line 35.

(continued on page 4)

Form 1041 (1996) Page 4

Part II—Income Distribution Deduction on a Minimum Tax Basis

13	Adjusted alternative minimum taxable income (from line 8)	13	44,660
14	Adjusted tax-exempt interest (other than amounts included on line 4p)	14	14,640
15	Total net gain from Schedule D (Form 1041), line 17, column (a). If a loss, enter -0-	15	
16	Capital gains for the tax year allocated to corpus and paid or permanently set aside for charitable purposes (from Schedule A, line 6)	16	
17	Capital gains paid or permanently set aside for charitable purposes from current year's income (see page 21 of the instructions)	17	
18	Capital gains computed on a minimum tax basis included on line 8	18	(12,000)
19	Capital losses computed on a minimum tax basis included on line 8. Enter as a positive amount	19	
20	Distributable net alternative minimum taxable income (DNAMTI). Combine lines 13 through 19	20	47,300
21	Income required to be distributed currently (from Schedule B, line 11)	21	48,500
22	Other amounts paid, credited, or otherwise required to be distributed (from Schedule B, line 12)	22	
23	Total distributions. Add lines 21 and 22	23	48,500
24	Tax-exempt income included on line 23 (other than amounts included on line 4p)	24	14,640
25	Tentative income distribution deduction on a minimum tax basis. Subtract line 24 from line 23	25	33,860
26	Tentative income distribution deduction on a minimum tax basis. Subtract line 14 from line 20	26	32,660
27	**Income distribution deduction on a minimum tax basis.** Enter the smaller of line 25 or line 26. Enter here and on line 9	27	32,660

Part III—Alternative Minimum Tax

28	Exemption amount			28	$22,500
29	Enter the amount from line 12	29	12,000		
30	Phase-out of exemption amount	30	$75,000		
31	Subtract line 30 from line 29. If zero or less, enter -0-	31	0		
32	Multiply line 31 by 25% (.25)			32	0
33	Subtract line 32 from line 28. If zero or less, enter -0-			33	22,500
34	Subtract line 33 from line 29			34	0
35	If line 34 is: • $175,000 or less, multiply line 34 by 26% (.26). • Over $175,000, multiply line 34 by 28% (.28) and subtract $3,500 from the result			35	0
36	Alternative minimum foreign tax credit (see page 21 of instructions)			36	
37	Tentative minimum tax. Subtract line 36 from line 35			37	0
38	Regular tax before credits (see page 22 of instructions)	38	3,068		
39	Section 644 tax included on Schedule G, line 1b	39			
40	Add lines 38 and 39			40	3,068
41	**Alternative minimum tax.** Subtract line 40 from line 37. If zero or less, enter -0-. Enter here and on Schedule G, line 6			41	0

SCHEDULE D (Form 1041)
Department of the Treasury
Internal Revenue Service

Capital Gains and Losses

▶ Attach to Form 1041 (or Form 5227). See the separate instructions for Form 1041 (or Form 5227).

OMB No. 1545-0092

1996

Name of estate or trust	Employer identification number
Bob Adams Trust	74 1237211

Note: *Form 5227 filers need to complete ONLY Parts I and II.*

Part I — Short-Term Capital Gains and Losses—Assets Held One Year or Less

(a) Description of property (Example, 100 shares 7% preferred of "Z" Co.)	(b) Date acquired (mo., day, yr.)	(c) Date sold (mo., day, yr.)	(d) Sales price	(e) Cost or other basis (see instructions)	(f) Gain or (loss) (col. (d) less col. (e))
1					

2 Short-term capital gain or (loss) from Forms 4684, 6252, 6781, and 8824	2	
3 Net short-term gain or (loss) from partnerships, S corporations, and other estates or trusts	3	
4 Net gain or (loss). Combine lines 1 through 3	4	
5 Short-term capital loss carryover from 1995 Schedule D, line 28	5	( )
6 Net short-term gain or (loss). Combine lines 4 and 5. Enter here and on line 15 below ▶	6	

Part II — Long-Term Capital Gains and Losses—Assets Held More Than One Year

(a) Description of property	(b) Date acquired	(c) Date sold	(d) Sales price	(e) Cost or other basis	(f) Gain or (loss)
7 1000 shares of ABC Corporation Stock	1-2-1971	6-9-1996	15,000	3,000	12,000

8 Long-term capital gain or (loss) from Forms 2439, 4684, 6252, 6781, and 8824	8	
9 Net long-term gain or (loss) from partnerships, S corporations, and other estates or trusts	9	
10 Capital gain distributions	10	
11 Gain from Form 4797	11	
12 Net gain or (loss). Combine lines 7 through 11	12	12,000
13 Long-term capital loss carryover from 1995 Schedule D, line 35	13	( )
14 Net long-term gain or (loss). Combine lines 12 and 13. Enter here and on line 16 below ▶	14	12,000

Part III — Summary of Parts I and II

		(a) Beneficiaries' (see instructions)	(b) Estate's or trust's	(c) Total
15 Net short-term gain or (loss) from line 6, above	15			
16 Net long-term gain or (loss) from line 14, above	16		12,000	12,000
17 Total net gain or (loss). Combine lines 15 and 16 ▶	17		12,000	12,000

Note: *If line 17, column (c), is a net gain, enter the gain on Form 1041, line 4. If lines 16 and 17, column (b) are net gains, go to Part VI, and DO NOT complete Parts IV and V. If line 17, column (c), is a net loss, complete Parts IV and V, as necessary.*

For Paperwork Reduction Act Notice, see page 1 of the Instructions for Form 1041. Cat. No. 11376V **Schedule D (Form 1041) 1996**

Schedule D (Form 1041) 1996 Page 2

Part IV **Capital Loss Limitation**

18 Enter here and enter as a (loss) on Form 1041, line 4, the smaller of: **a** The loss on line 17, column (c); **or** **b** $3,000	**18**	(	)

If the loss on line 17, column (c) is more than $3,000, OR if Form 1041, page 1, line 22, is a loss, complete Part V to determine your capital loss carryover.

Part V **Capital Loss Carryovers From 1996 to 1997**

Section A.—Carryover Limit

19 Enter taxable income or (loss) from Form 1041, line 22	**19**		
20 Enter loss from line 18 as a positive amount	**20**		
21 Enter amount from Form 1041, line 20	**21**		
22 Adjusted taxable income. Combine lines 19, 20, and 21, but do not enter less than zero	**22**		
23 Enter the smaller of line 20 or line 22	**23**		

Section B.—Short-Term Capital Loss Carryover
(Complete this part only if there is a loss on line 6 and line 17, column (c).)

24 Enter loss from line 6 as a positive amount			**24**		
25 Enter gain, if any, from line 14. If that line is blank or shows a loss, enter -0-	**25**				
26 Enter amount from line 23	**26**				
27 Add lines 25 and 26			**27**		
28 **Short-term capital loss carryover to 1997.** Subtract line 27 from line 24. If zero or less, enter -0-. If this is the final return of the trust or decedent's estate, also enter on Schedule K-1 (Form 1041), line 12b			**28**		

Section C.—Long-Term Capital Loss Carryover
(Complete this part only if there is a loss on line 14 and line 17, column (c).)

29 Enter loss from line 14 as a positive amount			**29**		
30 Enter gain, if any, from line 6. If that line is blank or shows a loss, enter -0-			**30**		
31 Enter amount from line 23	**31**				
32 Enter amount, if any, from line 24	**32**				
33 Subtract line 32 from line 31. If zero or less, enter -0-			**33**		
34 Add lines 30 and 33			**34**		
35 **Long-term capital loss carryover to 1997.** Subtract line 34 from line 29. If zero or less, enter -0-. If this is the final return of the trust or decedent's estate, also enter on Schedule K-1 (Form 1041), line 12c			**35**		

Part VI **Tax Computation Using Maximum Capital Gains Rate** (Complete this part only if both lines 16 and 17, column (b) are gains, and Form 1041, line 22 is more than $3,800.)

36 Enter taxable income from Form 1041, line 22			**36**	11,700	
37a **Net capital gain.** Enter the smaller of line 16 or 17, column (b)	**37a**	11,700			
b If you are filing Form 4952, enter the amount from Form 4952, line 4e	**37b**	-0-			
c Subtract line 37b from line 37a. If zero or less, stop here; you cannot use Part VI to figure the tax for the estate or trust. Instead, use the 1996 Tax Rate Schedule			**37c**	11,700	
38 Subtract line 37c from line 36. If zero or less, enter -0-			**38**	-0-	
39 Enter the greater of line 38 or $1,600			**39**	1,600	
40 Tax on amount on line 39 from the 1996 Tax Rate Schedule. If line 39 is $1,600, enter $240.00			**40**	240	
41 Subtract line 39 from line 36. If zero or less, enter -0-			**41**	10,100	
42 Multiply line 41 by 28% (.28)			**42**	2,828	
43 Maximum capital gains tax. Add lines 40 and 42			**43**	3,068	
44 Tax on amount on line 36 from the 1996 Tax Rate Schedule			**44**	3,737	
45 **Tax.** Enter the smaller of line 43 or line 44 here and on line 1a of Schedule G, Form 1041			**45**	3,068	

SCHEDULE K-1 (Form 1041)

Department of the Treasury Internal Revenue Service

Beneficiary's Share of Income, Deductions, Credits, etc.

for the calendar year 1996, or fiscal year

beginning ...., 1996, ending ...., 19 ......

▶ Complete a separate Schedule K-1 for each beneficiary.

OMB No. 1545-0092

1996

☐ Amended K-1
☐ Final K-1

Name of trust or decedent's estate: Bob Adams Trust

Beneficiary's identifying number ▶ 389-16-4001

Estate's or trust's EIN ▶ 74 : 1237211

Beneficiary's name, address, and ZIP code:
Bob Adams
3 Andrew Jackson Highway
Nashville, TN 37211

Fiduciary's name, address, and ZIP code:
First Bank
Post Office Box 100
Nashville, TN 37203

(a) Allocable share item		**(b)** Amount	**(c)** Calendar year 1996 Form 1040 filers enter the amounts in column (b) on:
1 Interest	**1**	30,000	Schedule B, Part I, line 1
2 Dividends	**2**		Schedule B, Part II, line 5
3a Net short-term capital gain	**3a**		Schedule D, line 5, column (g)
b Net long-term capital gain	**3b**		Schedule D, line 13, column (g)
4a Annuities, royalties, and other nonpassive income before directly apportioned deductions	**4a**		Schedule E, Part III, column (f)
b Depreciation	**4b**		Include on the applicable line of the appropriate tax form
c Depletion	**4c**		
d Amortization	**4d**		
5a Trade or business, rental real estate, and other rental income before directly apportioned deductions (see instructions)	**5a**	2,660*	Schedule E, Part III
b Depreciation	**5b**		Include on the applicable line of the appropriate tax form
c Depletion	**5c**		
d Amortization	**5d**		
6 Income for minimum tax purposes	**6**	32,660	
7 Income for regular tax purposes (add lines 1 through 3b, 4a, and 5a)	**7**	32,660	
8 Adjustment for minimum tax purposes (subtract line 7 from line 6)	**8**		Form 6251, line 12
9 Estate tax deduction (including certain generation-skipping transfer taxes)	**9**		Schedule A, line 27
10 Foreign taxes	**10**		Form 1116 or Schedule A (Form 1040), line 8
11 Adjustments and tax preference items (itemize):			
a Accelerated depreciation	**11a**		Include on the applicable line of Form 6251
b Depletion	**11b**		
c Amortization	**11c**		
d Exclusion items	**11d**		1997 Form 8801
12 Deductions in the final year of trust or decedent's estate:			
a Excess deductions on termination (see instructions)	**12a**		Schedule A, line 22
b Short-term capital loss carryover	**12b**		Schedule D, line 5, column (f)
c Long-term capital loss carryover	**12c**		Schedule D, line 13, column (f)
d Net operating loss (NOL) carryover for regular tax purposes	**12d**		Form 1040, line 21
e NOL carryover for minimum tax purposes	**12e**		See the instructions for Form 6251, line 20
f	**12f**		Include on the applicable line of the appropriate tax form
g	**12g**		
13 Other (itemize):			
a Payments of estimated taxes credited to you	**13a**		Form 1040, line 53
b Tax-exempt interest	**13b**	14,640	Form 1040, line 8b
c	**13c**		Include on the applicable line of the appropriate tax form
d	**13d**		
e	**13e**		
f	**13f**		
g	**13g**		
h	**13h**		

For Paperwork Reduction Act Notice, see page 1 of the Instructions for Form 1041. Cat. No. 11380D **Schedule K-1 (Form 1041) 1996**

*$5,000 – ($1,000 + $840 + $500) = $2,660.

Form **1041** Department of the Treasury—Internal Revenue Service

U.S. Income Tax Return for Estates and Trusts 1996

For calendar year 1996 or fiscal year beginning , 1996, and ending , 19 | OMB No. 1545-0092

A Type of entity:
- ☐ Decedent's estate
- ☐ Simple trust
- ☒ Complex trust
- ☐ Grantor type trust
- ☐ Bankruptcy estate–Ch. 7
- ☐ Bankruptcy estate–Ch. 11
- ☐ Pooled income fund

B Number of Schedules K-1 attached (see instructions) ▶ 2

Name of estate or trust (If a grantor type trust, see page 7 of the instructions.)
Cathy and Karen Stephens Trust (Complex Trust)

Name and title of fiduciary
Merchants Bank

Number, street, and room or suite no. (If a P.O. box, see page 7 of the instructions.)
3000 Sun Plaza I

City or town, state, and ZIP code
Tampa, FL 32843

C Employer identification number: 74 : 5727422

D Date entity created: 3/12/83

E Nonexempt charitable and split-interest trusts, check applicable boxes (see page 8 of the instructions):
- ☐ Described in section 4947(a)(1)
- ☐ Not a private foundation
- ☐ Described in section 4947(a)(2)

F Check applicable boxes: ☐ Initial return ☐ Final return ☐ Amended return ☐ Change in fiduciary's name ☐ Change in fiduciary's address

G Pooled mortgage account (see page 9 of the instructions): ☐ Bought ☐ Sold Date:

	Line	Description	No.	Amount
Income	1	Interest income	1	
	2	Dividends	2	30,000
	3	Business income or (loss) (attach Schedule C or C-EZ (Form 1040))	3	
	4	Capital gain or (loss) (attach Schedule D (Form 1041))	4	12,000
	5	Rents, royalties, partnerships, other estates and trusts, etc. (attach Schedule E (Form 1040)) ↖ (see below)	5	4,000
	6	Farm income or (loss) (attach Schedule F (Form 1040))	6	
	7	Ordinary gain or (loss) (attach Form 4797)	7	
	8	Other income. List type and amount	8	
	9	**Total income.** Combine lines 1 through 8 ▶	9	46,000
Deductions	10	Interest. Check if Form 4952 is attached ▶ ☐	10	
	11	Taxes	11	
	12	Fiduciary fees	12	840
	13	Charitable deduction (from Schedule A, line 7)	13	
	14	Attorney, accountant, and return preparer fees	14	500
	15a	Other deductions NOT subject to the 2% floor (attach schedule)	15a	
	b	Allowable miscellaneous itemized deductions subject to the 2% floor	15b	
	16	**Total.** Add lines 10 through 15b	16	1,340
	17	Adjusted total income or (loss). Subtract line 16 from line 9. Enter here and on Schedule B, line 1 ▶	17	44,660
	18	Income distribution deduction (from Schedule B, line 17) (attach Schedules K-1 (Form 1041))	18	14,500
	19	Estate tax deduction (including certain generation-skipping taxes) (attach computation)	19	
	20	Exemption	20	100
	21	**Total deductions.** Add lines 18 through 20 ▶	21	14,600
Tax and Payments	22	Taxable income. Subtract line 21 from line 17. If a loss, see page 13 of the instructions	22	30,060
	23	**Total tax** (from Schedule G, line 8)	23	9,616
	24	**Payments: a** 1996 estimated tax payments and amount applied from 1995 return	24a	8,600
	b	Estimated tax payments allocated to beneficiaries (from Form 1041-T)	24b	
	c	Subtract line 24b from line 24a	24c	8,600
	d	Tax paid with extension of time to file: ☐ Form 2758 ☐ Form 8736 ☐ Form 8800	24d	
	e	Federal income tax withheld. If any is from Form(s) 1099, check ▶ ☐	24e	
		Other payments: f Form 2439 ; g Form 4136 ; Total ▶	24h	
	25	**Total payments.** Add lines 24c through 24e, and 24h ▶	25	8,600
	26	Estimated tax penalty (see page 13 of the instructions)	26	
	27	**Tax due.** If line 25 is smaller than the total of lines 23 and 26, enter amount owed	27	1,016
	28	**Overpayment.** If line 25 is larger than the total of lines 23 and 26, enter amount overpaid	28	
	29	Amount of line 28 to be: **a Credited to 1997 estimated tax ▶ ; b Refunded ▶**	29	

Please Sign Here

Under penalties of perjury, I declare that I have examined this return, including accompanying schedules and statements, and to the best of my knowledge and belief, it is true, correct, and complete. Declaration of preparer (other than fiduciary) is based on all information of which preparer has any knowledge.

Fred Fidus | 3/20/97 | ▶ 38 : 4371419

Signature of fiduciary or officer representing fiduciary | Date | EIN of fiduciary if a financial institution (see page 4 of the instructions)

Paid Preparer's Use Only

Preparer's signature ▶ Sarah Public | Date 3/15/97 | Check if self-employed ▶ ☒ | **Preparer's social security no.** 127 : 84 : 3978

Firm's name (or yours if self-employed) and address ▶ Sarah Public, 2000 Sun Plaza III, Tampa, FL | EIN ▶ 38 : 9876543 | ZIP code ▶ 32843

For Paperwork Reduction Act Notice, see page 1 of the separate instructions. Cat. No. 11370H Form **1041** (1996)

Line 4: Net rental income
Rental income $5,000 - Rental Expenses ($1,000) = Net Rental Income $4,000

Schedule A **Charitable Deduction.** Do not complete for a simple trust or a pooled income fund.

1	Amounts paid for charitable purposes from gross income	1	
2	Amounts permanently set aside for charitable purposes from gross income	2	
3	Add lines 1 and 2	3	
4	Tax-exempt income allocable to charitable contributions (see page 14 of the instructions)	4	
5	Subtract line 4 from line 3	5	
6	Capital gains for the tax year allocated to corpus and paid or permanently set aside for charitable purposes	6	
7	**Charitable deduction.** Add lines 5 and 6. Enter here and on page 1, line 13	7	None

Schedule B **Income Distribution Deduction**

1	Adjusted total income (from page 1, line 17) (see page 14 of the instructions)	1	44,660
2	Adjusted tax-exempt interest (15,000 - 360)	2	14,640
3	Total net gain from Schedule D (Form 1041), line 17, column (a) (see page 15 of the instructions)	3	
4	Enter amount from Schedule A, line 6	4	
5	Long-term capital gain for the tax year included on Schedule A, line 3	5	
6	Short-term capital gain for the tax year included on Schedule A, line 3	6	
7	If the amount on page 1, line 4, is a capital loss, enter here as a positive figure	7	
8	If the amount on page 1, line 4, is a capital gain, enter here as a negative figure	8	(12,000)
9	**Distributable net income (DNI).** Combine lines 1 through 8. If zero or less, enter -0-	9	47,300
10	If a complex trust, enter accounting income for the tax year as determined under the governing instrument and applicable local law — 10: 48,500		
11	Income required to be distributed currently	11	
12	Other amounts paid, credited, or otherwise required to be distributed	12	21,000
13	Total distributions. Add lines 11 and 12. If greater than line 10, see page 15 of the instructions	13	21,000
14	Enter the amount of tax-exempt income included on line 13	14	6,500
15	Tentative income distribution deduction. Subtract line 14 from line 13	15	14,500
16	Tentative income distribution deduction. Subtract line 2 from line 9. If zero or less, enter -0-	16	32,660
17	**Income distribution deduction.** Enter the smaller of line 15 or line 16 here and on page 1, line 18	17	14,500

Schedule G **Tax Computation** (see page 16 of the instructions)

1	**Tax: a** ☐ Tax rate schedule or ☒ Schedule D (Form 1041)	1a	9,616		
	b Other taxes	1b			
	c Total. Add lines 1a and 1b ▶			1c	9,616
2a	Foreign tax credit (attach Form 1116)	2a			
b	Check: ☐ Nonconventional source fuel credit ☐ Form 8834	2b			
c	General business credit. Enter here and check which forms are attached: ☐ Form 3800 or ☐ Forms (specify) ▶	2c			
d	Credit for prior year minimum tax (attach Form 8801)	2d			
3	**Total credits.** Add lines 2a through 2d ▶			3	0
4	Subtract line 3 from line 1c			4	9,616
5	Recapture taxes. Check if from: ☐ Form 4255 ☐ Form 8611			5	
6	Alternative minimum tax (from Schedule I, line 41)			6	
7	Household employment taxes. Attach Schedule H (Form 1040)			7	
8	**Total tax.** Add lines 4 through 7. Enter here and on page 1, line 23 ▶			8	9,616

Other Information

		Yes	No
1	Did the estate or trust receive tax-exempt income? If "Yes," attach a computation of the allocation of expenses. Enter the amount of tax-exempt interest income and exempt-interest dividends ▶ $ 15,000 (see below)	X	
2	Did the estate or trust receive all or any part of the earnings (salary, wages, and other compensation) of any individual by reason of a contract assignment or similar arrangement?		X
3	At any time during calendar year 1996, did the estate or trust have an interest in or a signature or other authority over a bank, securities, or other financial account in a foreign country? See page 17 of the instructions for exceptions and filing requirements for Form TD F 90-22.1. If "Yes," enter the name of the foreign country ▶		X
4	During the tax year, did the estate or trust receive a distribution from, or was it the grantor of, or transferor to, a foreign trust? If "Yes," see page 17 of the instructions for other forms the estate or trust may have to file		X
5	Did the estate or trust receive, or pay, any seller-financed mortgage interest? If "Yes," see page 17 of the instructions for required attachment		X
6	If this is a complex trust making the section 663(b) election, check here (see page 17 of the instructions) ▶ ☐		
7	To make a section 643(e)(3) election, attach Schedule D (Form 1041), and check here (see page 17) ▶ ☐		
8	If the decedent's estate has been open for more than 2 years, check here ▶ ☐		

Line 1: Allocation of expense $\frac{\$15,000}{\$50,000} \times \$1,200 = \$360$ of trustee's fees allocated to tax exempt income

Form 1041 (1996) Page **3**

Schedule I **Alternative Minimum Tax** (see pages 18 through 22 of the instructions)

Part I—Estate's or Trust's Share of Alternative Minimum Taxable Income

1	Adjusted total income or (loss) (from page 1, line 17)			1	44,660
2	Net operating loss deduction. Enter as a positive amount			2	
3	Add lines 1 and 2			3	44,660
4	**Adjustments and tax preference items:**				
a	Interest	4a			
b	Taxes	4b			
c	Miscellaneous itemized deductions (from page 1, line 15b)	4c			
d	Refund of taxes	4d	( )		
e	Depreciation of property placed in service after 1986	4e			
f	Circulation and research and experimental expenditures	4f			
g	Mining exploration and development costs	4g			
h	Long-term contracts entered into after February 28, 1986	4h			
i	Amortization of pollution control facilities	4i			
j	Installment sales of certain property	4j			
k	Adjusted gain or loss (including incentive stock options)	4k			
l	Certain loss limitations	4l			
m	Tax shelter farm activities	4m			
n	Passive activities	4n			
o	Beneficiaries of other trusts or decedent's estates	4o			
p	Tax-exempt interest from specified private activity bonds	4p			
q	Depletion	4q			
r	Accelerated depreciation of real property placed in service before 1987	4r			
s	Accelerated depreciation of leased personal property placed in service before 1987	4s			
t	Intangible drilling costs	4t			
u	Other adjustments	4u			
5	Combine lines 4a through 4u			5	
6	Add lines 3 and 5			6	44,660
7	Alternative tax net operating loss deduction (see page 21 of the instructions for limitations)			7	
8	Adjusted alternative minimum taxable income. Subtract line 7 from line 6. Enter here and on line 13			8	44,660
	Note: *Complete Part II before going to line 9.*				
9	Income distribution deduction from line 27	9	14,500		
10	Estate tax deduction (from page 1, line 19)	10			
11	Add lines 9 and 10			11	14,500
12	Estate's or trust's share of alternative minimum taxable income. Subtract line 11 from line 8			12	30,160

If line 12 is:

- $22,500 or less, stop here and enter -0- on Schedule G, line 6. The estate or trust is not liable for the alternative minimum tax.
- Over $22,500, but less than $165,000, go to line 28.
- $165,000 or more, enter the amount from line 12 on line 34 and go to line 35.

(continued on page 4)

Form 1041 (1996) Page **4**

Part II—Income Distribution Deduction on a Minimum Tax Basis

13	Adjusted alternative minimum taxable income (from line 8)	13	44,660
14	Adjusted tax-exempt interest (other than amounts included on line 4p)	14	14,640
15	Total net gain from Schedule D (Form 1041), line 17, column (a). If a loss, enter -0-	15	
16	Capital gains for the tax year allocated to corpus and paid or permanently set aside for charitable purposes (from Schedule A, line 6)	16	
17	Capital gains paid or permanently set aside for charitable purposes from current year's income (see page 21 of the instructions)	17	
18	Capital gains computed on a minimum tax basis included on line 8	18	(12,000)
19	Capital losses computed on a minimum tax basis included on line 8. Enter as a positive amount	19	
20	Distributable net alternative minimum taxable income (DNAMTI). Combine lines 13 through 19	20	47,300
21	Income required to be distributed currently (from Schedule B, line 11)	21	0
22	Other amounts paid, credited, or otherwise required to be distributed (from Schedule B, line 12)	22	21,000
23	Total distributions. Add lines 21 and 22	23	21,000
24	Tax-exempt income included on line 23 (other than amounts included on line 4p)	24	6,500
25	Tentative income distribution deduction on a minimum tax basis. Subtract line 24 from line 23	25	14,500
26	Tentative income distribution deduction on a minimum tax basis. Subtract line 14 from line 20	26	32,660
27	**Income distribution deduction on a minimum tax basis.** Enter the smaller of line 25 or line 26. Enter here and on line 9	27	14,500

Part III—Alternative Minimum Tax

28	Exemption amount			28	$22,500
29	Enter the amount from line 12	29	30,160		
30	Phase-out of exemption amount	30	$75,000		
31	Subtract line 30 from line 29. If zero or less, enter -0-	31	0		
32	Multiply line 31 by 25% (.25)			32	0
33	Subtract line 32 from line 28. If zero or less, enter -0-			33	22,500
34	Subtract line 33 from line 29			34	7,660
35	If line 34 is: • $175,000 or less, multiply line 34 by 26% (.26). • Over $175,000, multiply line 34 by 28% (.28) and subtract $3,500 from the result			35	1,992
36	Alternative minimum foreign tax credit (see page 21 of instructions)			36	
37	Tentative minimum tax. Subtract line 36 from line 35			37	1,992
38	Regular tax before credits (see page 22 of instructions)	38	9,616		
39	Section 644 tax included on Schedule G, line 1b	39			
40	Add lines 38 and 39			40	9,616
41	**Alternative minimum tax.** Subtract line 40 from line 37. If zero or less, enter -0-. Enter here and on Schedule G, line 6			41	0

SCHEDULE D (Form 1041)

Department of the Treasury
Internal Revenue Service

Capital Gains and Losses

▶ **Attach to Form 1041 (or Form 5227). See the separate instructions for Form 1041 (or Form 5227).**

OMB No. 1545-0092

1996

Name of estate or trust: Cathy and Karen Stephens Trust

Employer identification number: 74 5724722

Note: *Form 5227 filers need to complete ONLY Parts I and II.*

Part I Short-Term Capital Gains and Losses—Assets Held One Year or Less

(a) Description of property (Example, 100 shares 7% preferred of "Z" Co.)	(b) Date acquired (mo., day, yr.)	(c) Date sold (mo., day, yr.)	(d) Sales price	(e) Cost or other basis (see instructions)	(f) Gain or (loss) (col. (d) less col. (e))
1					

2 Short-term capital gain or (loss) from Forms 4684, 6252, 6781, and 8824	2	
3 Net short-term gain or (loss) from partnerships, S corporations, and other estates or trusts	3	
4 Net gain or (loss). Combine lines 1 through 3	4	
5 Short-term capital loss carryover from 1995 Schedule D, line 28	5	( )
6 Net short-term gain or (loss). Combine lines 4 and 5. Enter here and on line 15 below ▶	6	

Part II Long-Term Capital Gains and Losses—Assets Held More Than One Year

(a) Description of property	(b) Date acquired	(c) Date sold	(d) Sales price	(e) Cost or other basis	(f) Gain or (loss)
7 1,000 Shares TST Corporation stock	10/1/71	3/6/96	32,000	20,000	12,000

8 Long-term capital gain or (loss) from Forms 2439, 4684, 6252, 6781, and 8824	8	
9 Net long-term gain or (loss) from partnerships, S corporations, and other estates or trusts	9	
10 Capital gain distributions	10	
11 Gain from Form 4797	11	
12 Net gain or (loss). Combine lines 7 through 11	12	12,000
13 Long-term capital loss carryover from 1995 Schedule D, line 35	13	( )
14 Net long-term gain or (loss). Combine lines 12 and 13. Enter here and on line 16 below ▶	14	12,000

Part III Summary of Parts I and II

		(a) Beneficiaries' (see instructions)	(b) Estate's or trust's	(c) Total
15 Net short-term gain or (loss) from line 6, above	15			
16 Net long-term gain or (loss) from line 14, above	16		12,000	12,000
17 Total net gain or (loss). Combine lines 15 and 16 ▶	17		12,000	12,000

Note: *If line 17, column (c), is a net gain, enter the gain on Form 1041, line 4. If lines 16 and 17, column (b) are net gains, go to Part VI, and DO NOT complete Parts IV and V. If line 17, column (c), is a net loss, complete Parts IV and V, as necessary.*

Schedule D (Form 1041) 1996 Page **2**

Part IV **Capital Loss Limitation**

18 Enter here and enter as a (loss) on Form 1041, line 4, the smaller of: **a** The loss on line 17, column (c); **or** **b** $3,000	18	( )

If the loss on line 17, column (c) is more than $3,000, OR if Form 1041, page 1, line 22, is a loss, complete Part V to determine your capital loss carryover.

Part V **Capital Loss Carryovers From 1996 to 1997**

Section A.—Carryover Limit

19 Enter taxable income or (loss) from Form 1041, line 22	19	
20 Enter loss from line 18 as a positive amount	20	
21 Enter amount from Form 1041, line 20	21	
22 Adjusted taxable income. Combine lines 19, 20, and 21, but do not enter less than zero	22	
23 Enter the smaller of line 20 or line 22	23	

Section B.—Short-Term Capital Loss Carryover
(Complete this part only if there is a loss on line 6 and line 17, column (c).)

24 Enter loss from line 6 as a positive amount			24	
25 Enter gain, if any, from line 14. If that line is blank or shows a loss, enter -0-	25			
26 Enter amount from line 23	26			
27 Add lines 25 and 26			27	
28 **Short-term capital loss carryover to 1997.** Subtract line 27 from line 24. If zero or less, enter -0-. If this is the final return of the trust or decedent's estate, also enter on Schedule K-1 (Form 1041), line 12b			28	

Section C.—Long-Term Capital Loss Carryover
(Complete this part only if there is a loss on line 14 and line 17, column (c).)

29 Enter loss from line 14 as a positive amount			29	
30 Enter gain, if any, from line 6. If that line is blank or shows a loss, enter -0-			30	
31 Enter amount from line 23	31			
32 Enter amount, if any, from line 24	32			
33 Subtract line 32 from line 31. If zero or less, enter -0-			33	
34 Add lines 30 and 33			34	
35 **Long-term capital loss carryover to 1997.** Subtract line 34 from line 29. If zero or less, enter -0-. If this is the final return of the trust or decedent's estate, also enter on Schedule K-1 (Form 1041), line 12c			35	

Part VI **Tax Computation Using Maximum Capital Gains Rate** (Complete this part only if both lines 16 and 17, column (b) are gains, and Form 1041, line 22 is more than $3,800.)

36 Enter taxable income from Form 1041, line 22			36	30,060
37a **Net capital gain.** Enter the smaller of line 16 or 17, column (b)	37a	12,000		
b If you are filing Form 4952, enter the amount from Form 4952, line 4e	37b			
c Subtract line 37b from line 37a. If zero or less, stop here; you cannot use Part VI to figure the tax for the estate or trust. Instead, use the 1996 Tax Rate Schedule			37c	12,000
38 Subtract line 37c from line 36. If zero or less, enter -0-			38	18,060
39 Enter the greater of line 38 or $1,600			39	18,060
40 Tax on amount on line 39 from the 1996 Tax Rate Schedule. If line 39 is $1,600, enter $240.00			40	6,256
41 Subtract line 39 from line 36. If zero or less, enter -0-			41	12,000
42 Multiply line 41 by 28% (.28)			42	3,360
43 Maximum capital gains tax. Add lines 40 and 42			43	9,616
44 Tax on amount on line 36 from the 1996 Tax Rate Schedule			44	11,007
45 **Tax.** Enter the smaller of line 43 or line 44 here and on line 1a of Schedule G, Form 1041			45	9,616

SCHEDULE K-1 (Form 1041)

Department of the Treasury
Internal Revenue Service

Beneficiary's Share of Income, Deductions, Credits, etc.

for the calendar year 1996, or fiscal year

beginning .... **, 1996, ending** .... **, 19** ....

▶ Complete a separate Schedule K-1 for each beneficiary.

OMB No. 1545-0092

1996

Name of trust or decedent's estate: Cathy and Karen Stephens Trust

☐ Amended K-1
☐ Final K-1

Beneficiary's identifying number ▶ 411-36-4761

Estate's or trust's EIN ▶ 74 5727422

Beneficiary's name, address, and ZIP code:
Cathy Stephens
13 Sunny Shores
Miami Beach, FL 33131

Fiduciary's name, address, and ZIP code:
Merchants Bank
3000 Sun Plaza I
Tampa, FL 32843

	(a) Allocable share item		**(b)** Amount	**(c)** Calendar year 1996 Form 1040 filers enter the amounts in column (b) on:
1	Interest	1		Schedule B, Part I, line 1
2	Dividends	2	8,879	Schedule B, Part II, line 5
3a	Net short-term capital gain	3a		Schedule D, line 5, column (g)
b	Net long-term capital gain	3b		Schedule D, line 13, column (g)
4a	Annuities, royalties, and other nonpassive income before directly apportioned deductions	4a		Schedule E, Part III, column (f)
b	Depreciation	4b		Include on the applicable line of the appropriate tax form
c	Depletion	4c		
d	Amortization	4d		
5a	Trade or business, rental real estate, and other rental income before directly apportioned deductions (see instructions)	5a	788	Schedule E, Part III
b	Depreciation	5b		Include on the applicable line of the appropriate tax form
c	Depletion	5c		
d	Amortization	5d		
6	Income for minimum tax purposes	6	9,667	
7	Income for regular tax purposes (add lines 1 through 3b, 4a, and 5a)	7	9,667	
8	Adjustment for minimum tax purposes (subtract line 7 from line 6)	8		Form 6251, line 12
9	Estate tax deduction (including certain generation-skipping transfer taxes)	9		Schedule A, line 27
10	Foreign taxes	10		Form 1116 or Schedule A (Form 1040), line 8
11	Adjustments and tax preference items (itemize):			
a	Accelerated depreciation	11a		Include on the applicable line of Form 6251
b	Depletion	11b		
c	Amortization	11c		
d	Exclusion items	11d		1997 Form 8801
12	Deductions in the final year of trust or decedent's estate:			
a	Excess deductions on termination (see instructions)	12a		Schedule A, line 22
b	Short-term capital loss carryover	12b		Schedule D, line 5, column (f)
c	Long-term capital loss carryover	12c		Schedule D, line 13, column (f)
d	Net operating loss (NOL) carryover for regular tax purposes	12d		Form 1040, line 21
e	NOL carryover for minimum tax purposes	12e		See the instructions for Form 6251, line 20
f		12f		Include on the applicable line of the appropriate tax form
g		12g		
13	Other (itemize):			
a	Payments of estimated taxes credited to you	13a		Form 1040, line 53
b	Tax-exempt interest	13b	4,333	Form 1040, line 8b
c		13c		Include on the applicable line of the appropriate tax form
d		13d		
e		13e		
f		13f		
g		13g		
h		13h		

SCHEDULE K-1 (Form 1041)

Department of the Treasury
Internal Revenue Service

Beneficiary's Share of Income, Deductions, Credits, etc.

for the calendar year 1996, or fiscal year

beginning ...., 1996, ending ...., 19 ......

► Complete a separate Schedule K-1 for each beneficiary.

OMB No. 1545-0092

1996

☐ Amended K-1
☐ Final K-1

Name of trust or decedent's estate: Cathy and Karen Stephens Trust

Beneficiary's identifying number ► 456-78-1230

Estate's or trust's EIN ► 74 5727422

Beneficiary's name, address, and ZIP code:
Karen Stephens
1472 Ski Run
Vail, Colorado 74820

Fiduciary's name, address, and ZIP code:
Merchants Bank
3000 Sun Plaza I
Tampa, FL 32843

	(a) Allocable share item		(b) Amount	(c) Calendar year 1996 Form 1040 filers enter the amounts in column (b) on:
1	Interest	1		Schedule B, Part I, line 1
2	Dividends	2	4,440	Schedule B, Part II, line 5
3a	Net short-term capital gain	3a		Schedule D, line 5, column (g)
b	Net long-term capital gain	3b		Schedule D, line 13, column (g)
4a	Annuities, royalties, and other nonpassive income before directly apportioned deductions	4a		Schedule E, Part III, column (f)
b	Depreciation	4b		Include on the applicable line of the appropriate tax form
c	Depletion	4c		
d	Amortization	4d		
5a	Trade or business, rental real estate, and other rental income before directly apportioned deductions (see instructions)	5a	393	Schedule E, Part III
b	Depreciation	5b		Include on the applicable line of the appropriate tax form
c	Depletion	5c		
d	Amortization	5d		
6	Income for minimum tax purposes	6	4,833	
7	Income for regular tax purposes (add lines 1 through 3b, 4a, and 5a)	7	4,833	
8	Adjustment for minimum tax purposes (subtract line 7 from line 6)	8		Form 6251, line 12
9	Estate tax deduction (including certain generation-skipping transfer taxes)	9		Schedule A, line 27
10	Foreign taxes	10		Form 1116 or Schedule A (Form 1040), line 8
11	Adjustments and tax preference items (itemize):			
a	Accelerated depreciation	11a		Include on the applicable line of Form 6251
b	Depletion	11b		
c	Amortization	11c		
d	Exclusion items	11d		1997 Form 8801
12	Deductions in the final year of trust or decedent's estate:			
a	Excess deductions on termination (see instructions)	12a		Schedule A, line 22
b	Short-term capital loss carryover	12b		Schedule D, line 5, column (f)
c	Long-term capital loss carryover	12c		Schedule D, line 13, column (f)
d	Net operating loss (NOL) carryover for regular tax purposes	12d		Form 1040, line 21
e	NOL carryover for minimum tax purposes	12e		See the instructions for Form 6251, line 20
f		12f		Include on the applicable line of the appropriate tax form
g		12g		
13	Other (itemize):			
a	Payments of estimated taxes credited to you	13a		Form 1040, line 53
b	Tax-exempt interest	13b	2,167	Form 1040, line 8b
c		13c		Include on the applicable line of the appropriate tax form
d		13d		
e		13e		
f		13f		
g		13g		
h		13h		

For Paperwork Reduction Act Notice, see page 1 of the Instructions for Form 1041. Cat. No. 11380D **Schedule K-1 (Form 1041) 1996**

Form **1116**

Department of the Treasury
Internal Revenue Service

Foreign Tax Credit

(Individual, Estate, Trust, or Nonresident Alien Individual)

▶ Attach to Form 1040, 1040NR, 1041, or 990-T.

▶ See separate instructions.

OMB No. 1545-0121

1996

Attachment Sequence No. **19**

Name	Identifying number as shown on page 1 of your tax return
Andrew Roberts	123-45-6789

Report all amounts in U.S. dollars except where specified in Part II. Use a separate Form 1116 for each category of income listed below. Check only **one** *box. Before you check a box, read* **Categories of Income** *on page 3 of the instructions. Complete this form for credit for taxes on:*

- **a** ☒ Passive income
- **b** ☐ High withholding tax interest
- **c** ☐ Financial services income
- **d** ☐ Shipping income
- **e** ☐ Dividends from a DISC or former DISC
- **f** ☐ Certain distributions from a foreign sales corporation (FSC) or former FSC
- **g** ☐ Lump-sum distributions (see page 3 of the instructions before completing form)
- **h** ☐ General limitation income—all other income from sources outside the United States (including income from sources within U.S. possessions)

i Resident of (name of country) ▶ United States

Note: *If you paid taxes to only one foreign country or U.S. possession, use column A in Part I and line A in Part II. If you paid taxes to* **more than one** *foreign country or U.S. possession, use a separate column and line for each country or possession. However, see the exception under* **How To Complete Form 1116** *on page 1 of the instructions.*

Part I Figuring Taxable Income or Loss From Sources Outside the United States for Category Checked Above

	Foreign Country or U.S. Possession A	B	C		Total (Add cols. A, B, and C.)
j **Enter the name of the foreign country or U.S. possession** ▶	France				
1 Gross income from sources within country shown above and of the type checked above. See page 5 of the instructions: Dividends	30,000			1	30,000
Deductions and losses (*Caution: See pages 5 and 6 of the instructions*):					
2 Expenses **definitely related** to the income on line 1 (attach statement)	0				
3 Pro rata share of other deductions **not definitely related:**					
a Certain itemized deductions or standard deduction. See instructions	12,000				
b Other deductions (attach statement)					
c Add lines 3a and 3b	12,000				
d Gross foreign source income. See instructions	30,000				
e Gross income from all sources. See instructions	210,000				
f Divide line 3d by line 3e. Do not enter more than "1"	.1428571				
g Multiply line 3c by line 3f	1,714				
4 Pro rata share of interest expense. See instructions:					
a Home mortgage interest. (Use worksheet on page 6 of the instructions)					
b Other interest expense					
5 Losses from foreign sources					
6 Add lines 2, 3g, 4a, 4b, and 5	1,714			6	1,714
7 Subtract line 6 from line 1. Enter the result here and on line 14, page 2 ▶				7	28,286

Part II Foreign Taxes Paid or Accrued (See page 6 of the instructions.)

Country	Credit is claimed for taxes (you must check one) (k) ☒ Paid (l) ☐ Accrued — (m) Date paid or accrued	Foreign taxes paid or accrued — In foreign currency — Taxes withheld at source on: (n) Dividends	(o) Rents and royalties	(p) Interest	(q) Other foreign taxes paid or accrued	In U.S. dollars — Taxes withheld at source on: (r) Dividends	(s) Rents and royalties	(t) Interest	(u) Other foreign taxes paid or accrued	(v) Total foreign taxes paid or accrued (add cols. (r) through (u))
A	12/31/96	24840FF				4,500			None	4,500
B										
C										

8 Add lines A through C, column (v). Enter the total here and on line 9, page 2 ▶ **8** 4,500

For Paperwork Reduction Act Notice, see page 1 of separate instructions. Cat. No. 11440U Form **1116** (1996)

Form 1116 (1996) Page **2**

Part III **Figuring the Credit**

Line	Description	Box	Amount	Box	Amount
9	Enter amount from line 8. These are your total foreign taxes paid or accrued for the category of income checked above Part I	9	4,500		
10	Carryback or carryover (attach detailed computation)	10			
11	Add lines 9 and 10	11	4,500		
12	Reduction in foreign taxes. See page 7 of the instructions	12			
13	Subtract line 12 from line 11. This is the total amount of foreign taxes available for credit			13	4,500
14	Enter amount from line 7. This is your taxable income or (loss) from sources outside the United States (before adjustments) for the category of income checked above Part I. See page 7 of the instructions	14	28,286		
15	Adjustments to line 14. See page 7 of the instructions	15	0		
16	Combine the amounts on lines 14 and 15. This is your net foreign source taxable income. (If the result is zero or less, you have no foreign tax credit for the category of income you checked above Part I. Skip lines 17 through 21.)	16	28,286		
17	**Individuals:** Enter amount from Form 1040, line 35. If you are a nonresident alien, enter amount from Form 1040NR, line 34. **Estates and trusts:** Enter your taxable income without the deduction for your exemption	17	159,000		
	Caution: *If you figured your tax using the maximum tax rate on capital gains, see page 8 of the instructions.*				
18	Divide line 16 by line 17. If line 16 is more than line 17, enter the figure "1"			18	0.1778994
19	**Individuals:** Enter amount from Form 1040, line 38, **less** any amounts on Form 1040, lines 39, 40, and any mortgage interest credit (from Form 8396) on line 42. If you are a nonresident alien, enter amount from Form 1040NR, line 37, less any amount on Form 1040NR, line 38 and any mortgage interest credit (from Form 8396) on line 40. **Estates and trusts:** Enter amount from Form 1041, Schedule G, line 1c, or Form 990-T, lines 36 and 37			19	39,899 *
20	Multiply line 19 by line 18 (maximum amount of credit)			20	7,098
21	Enter the amount from line 13 or line 20, whichever is **smaller.** If this is the only Form 1116 you are completing, skip lines 22 through 29 and enter this amount on line 30. Otherwise, complete the appropriate line in Part IV ▶			21	4,500

Part IV **Summary of Credits From Separate Parts III** (See page 8 of the instructions.)

Line	Description	Box	Amount	Box	Amount
22	Credit for taxes on passive income	22	4,500		
23	Credit for taxes on high withholding tax interest	23			
24	Credit for taxes on financial services income	24			
25	Credit for taxes on shipping income	25			
26	Credit for taxes on dividends from a DISC or former DISC	26			
27	Credit for taxes on certain distributions from a FSC or former FSC	27			
28	Credit for taxes on lump-sum distributions	28			
29	Credit for taxes on general limitation income (all other income from sources outside the United States)	29			
30	Add lines 22 through 29			30	4,500
31	Reduction of credit for international boycott operations. See instructions for line 12 on page 7			31	
32	Subtract line 31 from line 30. This is your foreign tax credit. Enter here and on Form 1040, line 41; Form 1040NR, line 39; Form 1041, Schedule G, line 2a; or Form 990-T, line 39a ▶			32	4,500

* Tax on $153,900

Form **2555**

Department of the Treasury
Internal Revenue Service

Foreign Earned Income

▶ See separate instructions. ▶ Attach to Form 1040.

OMB No. 1545-0067

1996

Attachment Sequence No. **34**

For Use by U.S. Citizens and Resident Aliens Only

Name shown on Form 1040: Lawrence E. Smith

Your social security number: 234 56 7890

Part I General Information

1 Your foreign address (including country): 123 Rue de Harve 75011 Paris France

2 Your occupation: Financial Vice-President

3 Employer's name ▶ Very Public Corporation

4a Employer's U.S. address ▶ 90 Fifth Avenue, New York, NY 10011

b Employer's foreign address ▶ 11 Rue de Nanettes / 5e' Etage, 75011 Paris France

5 Employer is (check any that apply): a ☐ A foreign entity b ☒ A U.S. company c ☐ Self d ☐ A foreign affiliate of a U.S. company e ☐ Other (specify) ▶

6a If, after 1981, you filed Form 2555 to claim either of the exclusions or Form 2555-EZ to claim the foreign earned income exclusion, enter the last year you filed the form. ▶ 1995

b If you did not file Form 2555 or 2555-EZ after 1981 to claim either of the exclusions, check here ▶ ☐ and go to line 7 now.

c Have you ever revoked either of the exclusions? ☐ Yes ☒ No

d If you answered "Yes," enter the type of exclusion and the tax year for which the revocation was effective. ▶

7 Of what country are you a citizen/national? ▶ United States

8a Did you maintain a separate foreign residence for your family because of adverse living conditions at your tax home? See **Second foreign household** on page 3 of the instructions ☐ Yes ☒ No

b If "Yes," enter city and country of the separate foreign residence. Also, enter the number of days during your tax year that you maintained a second household at that address. ▶ N/A

9 List your tax home(s) during your tax year and date(s) established. ▶ 123 Rue de Harve, 75011 Paris France. July 10, 1990

Next, complete either Part II or Part III. If an item does not apply, write "NA." If you do not give the information asked for, any exclusion or deduction you claim may be disallowed.

Part II Taxpayers Qualifying Under Bona Fide Residence Test (See page 2 of the instructions.)

10 Date bona fide residence began ▶ July 10, 1990, and ended ▶ Presently a resident

11 Kind of living quarters in foreign country ▶ a ☐ Purchased house b ☒ Rented house or apartment c ☐ Rented room d ☐ Quarters furnished by employer

12a Did any of your family live with you abroad during any part of the tax year? ☒ Yes ☐ No

b If "Yes," who and for what period? ▶ Wife and two children for entire year

13a Have you submitted a statement to the authorities of the foreign country where you claim bona fide residence that you are not a resident of that country? (See instructions.) ☐ Yes ☒ No

b Are you required to pay income tax to the country where you claim bona fide residence? (See instructions.) ☒ Yes ☐ No

If you answered "Yes" to 13a and "No" to 13b, you do not qualify as a bona fide resident. Do not complete the rest of this part.

14 If you were present in the United States or its possessions during the tax year, complete columns **(a)–(d)** below. **Do not** include the income from column **(d)** in Part IV, but report it on Form 1040.

(a) Date arrived in U.S.	(b) Date left U.S.	(c) Number of days in U.S. on business	(d) Income earned in U.S. on business (attach computation)	(a) Date arrived in U.S.	(b) Date left U.S.	(c) Number of days in U.S. on business	(d) Income earned in U.S. on business (attach computation)
2-16-96	2-21-96	5	1200 00				
			(see attached				
			schedule)				

15a List any contractual terms or other conditions relating to the length of your employment abroad. ▶ Indefinite time period

b Enter the type of visa under which you entered the foreign country. ▶ Resident

c Did your visa limit the length of your stay or employment in a foreign country? If "Yes," attach explanation ☐ Yes ☒ No

d Did you maintain a home in the United States while living abroad? ☒ Yes ☐ No

e If "Yes," enter address of your home, whether it was rented, the names of the occupants, and their relationship to you. ▶ 4710 N.W. 68th Terrace, Gainesville, FL 32601 (rented to unrelated party)

Form 2555 (1996) Page **2**

Part III **Taxpayers Qualifying Under Physical Presence Test** (See page 2 of the instructions.)

16 The physical presence test is based on the 12-month period from ▶ .... through ▶ ....

17 Enter your principal country of employment during your tax year. ▶ ....

18 If you traveled abroad during the 12-month period entered on line 16, complete columns **(a)–(f)** below. Exclude travel between foreign countries that did not involve travel on or over international waters, or in or over the United States, for 24 hours or more. If you have no travel to report during the period, enter "Physically present in a foreign country or countries for the entire 12-month period." **Do not** include the income from column **(f)** below in Part IV, but report it on Form 1040.

(a) Name of country (including U.S.)	**(b)** Date arrived	**(c)** Date left	**(d)** Full days present in country	**(e)** Number of days in U.S. on business	**(f)** Income earned in U.S. on business (attach computation)

Part IV **All Taxpayers**

Note: *Enter on lines 19 through 23 all income, including noncash income, you earned and actually or constructively received during your 1996 tax year for services you performed in a foreign country. If any of the foreign earned income received this tax year was earned in a prior tax year, or will be earned in a later tax year (such as a bonus), see the instructions.* ***Do not*** *include income from line 14, column* ***(d)****, or line 18, column* ***(f)****. Report amounts in U.S. dollars, using the exchange rates in effect when you actually or constructively received the income.*

If you are a cash basis taxpayer, report on Form 1040 all income you received in 1996, no matter when you performed the service.

1996 Foreign Earned Income				**Amount (in U.S. dollars)**
19 Total wages, salaries, bonuses, commissions, etc.			**19**	60,000
20 Allowable share of income for personal services performed (see instructions):				
a In a business (including farming) or profession			**20a**	
b In a partnership. List partnership's name and address and type of income. ▶			**20b**	
21 Noncash income (market value of property or facilities furnished by employer—attach statement showing how it was determined):				
a Home (lodging)			**21a**	
b Meals			**21b**	
c Car			**21c**	
d Other property or facilities. List type and amount. ▶			**21d**	
22 Allowances, reimbursements, or expenses paid on your behalf for services you performed:				
a Cost of living and overseas differential	**22a**	27,000		
b Family	**22b**			
c Education	**22c**	8,000		
d Home leave	**22d**	6,400		
e Quarters	**22e**	21,300		
f For any other purpose. List type and amount. ▶ Less: US source income	**22f**	<1,200>		
g Add lines 22a through 22f			**22g**	61,500
23 Other foreign earned income. List type and amount. ▶			**23**	
24 Add lines 19 through 21d, line 22g, and line 23			**24**	121,500
25 Total amount of meals and lodging included on line 24 that is excludable (see instructions)			**25**	
26 Subtract line 25 from line 24. Enter the result here and on line 27 on page 3. This is your **foreign earned income** ▶			**26**	121,500

Form 2555 (1996) Page **3**

Part V **All Taxpayers**

27	Enter the amount from line 26	27	121,500
	Are you claiming the housing exclusion or housing deduction? **Yes.** Complete Part VI. **No.** Go to Part VII.		

Part VI **For Taxpayers Claiming the Housing Exclusion AND/OR Deduction**

28	Qualified housing expenses for the tax year (see instructions)	28	21,300
29	Number of days in your qualifying period that fall within your 1996 tax year (see instructions) — 29: 366		
30	Multiply $25.25 by the number of days on line 29. If 366 entered on line 29, enter $9,242.00 here	30	9,242
31	Subtract line 30 from line 28. If zero or less, do not complete the rest of this part or any of Part IX	31	12,058
32	Enter employer-provided amounts (see instructions) — 32: 121,500		
33	Divide line 32 by line 27. Enter the result as a decimal (to two places), but do not enter more than "1.00"	33	× 1.00
34	**Housing exclusion.** Multiply line 31 by line 33. Enter the result but do not enter more than the amount on line 32. Also, complete Part VIII ▶	34	12,058

Note: *The housing deduction is figured in Part IX. If you choose to claim the foreign earned income exclusion, complete Parts VII and VIII before Part IX.*

Part VII **For Taxpayers Claiming the Foreign Earned Income Exclusion**

35	Maximum foreign earned income exclusion	35	$70,000 00
36	• If you completed Part VI, enter the number from line 29. • All others, enter the number of days in your qualifying period that fall within your 1996 tax year (see the instructions for line 29). — 36: 366		
37	• If line 36 and the number of days in your 1996 tax year (usually 366) are the same, enter "1.00." • Otherwise, divide line 36 by the number of days in your 1996 tax year and enter the result as a decimal (to two places).	37	× 1.00
38	Multiply line 35 by line 37	38	70,000
39	Subtract line 34 from line 27	39	109,260
40	**Foreign earned income exclusion.** Enter the **smaller** of line 38 or line 39. Also, complete Part VIII ▶	40	70,000

Part VIII **For Taxpayers Claiming the Housing Exclusion, Foreign Earned Income Exclusion, or Both**

41	Add lines 34 and 40	41	82,058
42	Deductions allowed in figuring your adjusted gross income (Form 1040, line 31) that are allocable to the excluded income. See instructions and attach computation	42	
43	Subtract line 42 from line 41. Enter the result here and in parentheses on **Form 1040, line 21.** Next to the amount write "Form 2555." On Form 1040, subtract this amount from your income to arrive at total income on Form 1040, line 22 ▶	43	82,058

Part IX **For Taxpayers Claiming the Housing Deduction**—Complete this part only if **(a)** line 31 is more than line 34 and **(b)** line 27 is more than line 41.

44	Subtract line 34 from line 31	44	
45	Subtract line 41 from line 27	45	
46	Enter the **smaller** of line 44 or line 45	46	
	Note: *If line 45 is **more than** line 46 and you could not deduct all of your 1995 housing deduction because of the 1995 limit, use the worksheet on page 4 of the instructions to figure the amount to enter on line 47. Otherwise, go to line 48.*		
47	Housing deduction carryover from 1995 (from worksheet on page 4 of the instructions)	47	
48	**Housing deduction.** Add lines 46 and 47. Enter the total here and on Form 1040 to the left of line 30. Next to the amount on Form 1040, write "Form 2555." Add it to the total adjustments reported on that line ▶	48	N/A

APPENDIX C

MACRS AND ACRS TABLES

ACRS, MACRS and ADS Depreciation Methods Summary

System	Characteristics	Depreciation Method: MACRS	Depreciation Method: ADS	Table No.[a]: MACRS	Table No.[a]: ADS
MACRS & ADS	Personal Property:				
	1. Accounting Convention	Half-year or mid-quarter	Half-year or mid-quarter[b]		
	2. Life and Method				
	a. 3-year, 5-year, 7-year, 10-year	200% DB or elect straight-line	150% DB or elect straight-line	1, 2, 3, 4, 5, 8	9, 10[c]
	b. 15-year, 20-year	150% DB or elect straight-line	150% DB or elect straight-line[d]	1, 2, 3, 4, 5, 8	
	Real Property:				
	1. Accounting Convention	Mid-month	Mid-month		
	2. Life and Method				
	a. Residential rental property	27.5 years, straight-line	40 years straight-line	6	11
	b. Nonresidential real property	39 years, straight-line[e]	40 years straight-line	8A	11

System	Characteristics	ACRS	Table No.[a]: ACRS
ACRS	Personal Property		
	1. Accounting Convention	Half-year	
	2. Life and Method		
	a. 3-year, 5-year, 10-year, 15-year	150% DB or elect straight-line[f]	12
	Real Property		
	1. Accounting Convention	First of month or Mid-month[g]	
	2. Life		
	a. 15-year property	Placed in service after 12/31/80 and before 3/16/84	16
	b. 18-year property	Placed in service after 3/15/84 and before 5/9/85	14, 15
	c. 19-year property	Placed in service after 5/8/85 and before 1/1/87	13
	3. Method		
	a. All but low-income housing	175% DB or elect straight-line	
	b. Low-income housing property	200% DB or elect straight-line	

	Table No.[a]
LUXURY AUTOMOBILE LIMITATIONS	17

[a] All depreciation tables in this appendix are based upon tables contained in Rev. Proc. 87-57.

[b] General and ADS tables are available for property lives from 2.5-50.0 years using the straight-line method. These tables are contained in Rev. Proc. 87-57 and are only partially reproduced here.

[c] The mid-quarter tables are available in Rev. Proc. 87-57, but are not reproduced here.

[d] Special recovery periods are assigned certain MACRS properties under the alternative depreciation system.

[e] A 31.5-year recovery period applied to nonresidential real property placed in service under the MACRS rules prior to May 13, 1993. (See Table 7)

[f] Special recovery periods are required or able to be elected for personalty and realty for which a straight-line ACRS election is made. These recovery periods can be as long as 45 years.

[g] The first-of-the-month convention is used with 15-year property and 18-year real property placed in service before June 23, 1984. The mid-month convention is used with 18-year real property placed in service after June 22, 1984 and 19-year real property.

▼ **TABLE 1**

General Depreciation System—MACRS
Personal Property Placed in Service after 12/31/86
Applicable Convention: Half-year
Applicable Depreciation Method: 200 or 150 Percent Declining Balance Switching to Straight Line

If the Recovery Year Is:	And the Recovery Period Is: 3-Year	5-Year	7-Year	10-Year	15-Year	20-Year
	The Depreciation Rate Is:					
1	33.33	20.00	14.29	10.00	5.00	3.750
2	44.45	32.00	24.49	18.00	9.50	7.219
3	14.81	19.20	17.49	14.40	8.55	6.677
4	7.41	11.52	12.49	11.52	7.70	6.177
5		11.52	8.93	9.22	6.93	5.713
6		5.76	8.92	7.37	6.23	5.285
7			8.93	6.55	5.90	4.888
8			4.46	6.55	5.90	4.522
9				6.56	5.91	4.462
10				6.55	5.90	4.461
11				3.28	5.91	4.462
12					5.90	4.461
13					5.91	4.462
14					5.90	4.461
15					5.91	4.462
16					2.95	4.461
17						4.462
18						4.461
19						4.462
20						4.461
21						2.231

▼ **TABLE 2**

General Depreciation System—MACRS
Personal Property Placed in Service after 12/31/86
Applicable Convention: Mid-quarter (Property Placed in Service in First Quarter)
Applicable Depreciation Method: 200 or 150 Percent Declining Balance Switching to Straight Line

If the Recovery Year Is:	And the Recovery Period Is: 3-Year	5-Year	7-Year	10-Year	15-Year	20-Year
	The Depreciation Rate Is:					
1	58.33	35.00	25.00	17.50	8.75	6.563
2	27.78	26.00	21.43	16.50	9.13	7.000
3	12.35	15.60	15.31	13.20	8.21	6.482
4	1.54	11.01	10.93	10.56	7.39	5.996
5		11.01	8.74	8.45	6.65	5.546
6		1.38	8.74	6.76	5.99	5.130
7			8.75	6.55	5.90	4.746
8			1.09	6.55	5.91	4.459
9				6.56	5.90	4.459
10				6.55	5.91	4.459
11				0.82	5.90	4.459
12					5.91	4.460
13					5.90	4.459
14					5.91	4.460
15					5.90	4.459
16					0.74	4.460
17						4.459
18						4.460
19						4.459
20						4.460
21						0.557

▼ TABLE 3

General Depreciation System—MACRS
Personal Property Placed in Service after 12/31/86
Applicable Convention: Mid-quarter (Property Placed in Service in Second Quarter)
Applicable Depreciation Method: 200 or 150 Percent Declining Balance Switching to Straight Line

If the Recovery Year Is:	And the Recovery Period Is: 3-Year	5-Year	7-Year	10-Year	15-Year	20-Year
	The Depreciation Rate Is:					
1	41.67	25.00	17.85	12.50	6.25	4.688
2	38.89	30.00	23.47	17.50	9.38	7.148
3	14.14	18.00	16.76	14.00	8.44	6.612
4	5.30	11.37	11.97	11.20	7.59	6.116
5		11.37	8.87	8.96	6.83	5.658
6		4.26	8.87	7.17	6.15	5.233
7			8.87	6.55	5.91	4.841
8			3.33	6.55	5.90	4.478
9				6.56	5.91	4.463
10				6.55	5.90	4.463
11				2.46	5.91	4.463
12					5.90	4.463
13					5.91	4.463
14					5.90	4.463
15					5.91	4.462
16					2.21	4.463
17						4.462
18						4.463
19						4.462
20						4.463
21						1.673

▼ TABLE 4

General Depreciation System—MACRS
Personal Property Placed in Service after 12/31/86
Applicable Convention: Mid-quarter (Property Placed in Service in Third Quarter)
Applicable Depreciation Method: 200 or 150 Percent Declining Balance Switching to Straight Line

If the Recovery Year Is:	And the Recovery Period Is: 3-Year	5-Year	7-Year	10-Year	15-Year	20-Year
	The Depreciation Rate Is:					
1	25.00	15.00	10.71	7.50	3.75	2.813
2	50.00	34.00	25.51	18.50	9.63	7.289
3	16.67	20.40	18.22	14.80	8.66	6.742
4	8.33	12.24	13.02	11.84	7.80	6.237
5		11.30	9.30	9.47	7.02	5.769
6		7.06	8.85	7.58	6.31	5.336
7			8.86	6.55	5.90	4.936
8			5.53	6.55	5.90	4.566
9				6.56	5.91	4.460
10				6.55	5.90	4.460
11				4.10	5.91	4.460
12					5.90	4.460
13					5.91	4.461
14					5.90	4.460
15					5.91	4.461
16					3.69	4.460
17						4.461
18						4.460
19						4.461
20						4.460
21						2.788

▼ TABLE 5

General Depreciation System—MACRS
Personal Property Placed in Service after 12/31/86
Applicable Convention: Mid-quarter (Property Placed in Service in Fourth Quarter)
Applicable Depreciation Method: 200 or 150 Percent Declining Balance Switching to Straight Line

If the Recovery Year Is:	And the Recovery Period Is: 3-Year	5-Year	7-Year	10-Year	15-Year	20-Year
	The Depreciation Rate Is:					
1	8.33	5.00	3.57	2.50	1.25	0.938
2	61.11	38.00	27.55	19.50	9.88	7.430
3	20.37	22.80	19.68	15.60	8.89	6.872
4	10.19	13.68	14.06	12.48	8.00	6.357
5		10.94	10.04	9.98	7.20	5.880
6		9.58	8.73	7.99	6.48	5.439
7			8.73	6.55	5.90	5.031
8			7.64	6.55	5.90	4.654
9				6.56	5.90	4.458
10				6.55	5.91	4.458
11				5.74	5.90	4.458
12					5.91	4.458
13					5.90	4.458
14					5.91	4.458
15					5.90	4.458
16					5.17	4.458
17						4.458
18						4.459
19						4.458
20						4.459
21						3.901

▼ **TABLE 6**

General Depreciation System—MACRS
Residential Rental Real Property Placed in Service after 12/31/86
Applicable Recovery Period: 27.5 Years
Applicable Convention: Mid-month
Applicable Depreciation Method: Straight Line

If the Recovery Year Is:	**And the Month in the First Recovery Year the Property Is Placed in Service Is:**											
	1	**2**	**3**	**4**	**5**	**6**	**7**	**8**	**9**	**10**	**11**	**12**
	The Depreciation Rate Is:											
1	3.485	3.182	2.879	2.576	2.273	1.970	1.667	1.364	1.061	0.758	0.455	0.152
2	3.636	3.636	3.636	3.636	3.636	3.636	3.636	3.636	3.636	3.636	3.636	3.636
3	3.636	3.636	3.636	3.636	3.636	3.636	3.636	3.636	3.636	3.636	3.636	3.636
4	3.636	3.636	3.636	3.636	3.636	3.636	3.636	3.636	3.636	3.636	3.636	3.636
5	3.636	3.636	3.636	3.636	3.636	3.636	3.636	3.636	3.636	3.636	3.636	3.636
6	3.636	3.636	3.636	3.636	3.636	3.636	3.636	3.636	3.636	3.636	3.636	3.636
7	3.636	3.636	3.636	3.636	3.636	3.636	3.636	3.636	3.636	3.636	3.636	3.636
8	3.636	3.636	3.636	3.636	3.636	3.636	3.636	3.636	3.636	3.636	3.636	3.636
9	3.636	3.636	3.636	3.636	3.636	3.636	3.636	3.636	3.636	3.636	3.636	3.636
10	3.637	3.637	3.637	3.637	3.637	3.637	3.636	3.636	3.636	3.636	3.636	3.636
11	3.636	3.636	3.636	3.636	3.636	3.636	3.637	3.637	3.637	3.637	3.637	3.637
12	3.637	3.637	3.637	3.637	3.637	3.637	3.636	3.636	3.636	3.636	3.636	3.636
13	3.636	3.636	3.636	3.636	3.636	3.636	3.637	3.637	3.637	3.637	3.637	3.637
14	3.637	3.637	3.637	3.637	3.637	3.637	3.636	3.636	3.636	3.636	3.636	3.636
15	3.636	3.636	3.636	3.636	3.636	3.636	3.637	3.637	3.637	3.637	3.637	3.637
16	3.637	3.637	3.637	3.637	3.637	3.637	3.636	3.636	3.636	3.636	3.636	3.636
17	3.636	3.636	3.636	3.636	3.636	3.636	3.637	3.637	3.637	3.637	3.637	3.637
18	3.637	3.637	3.637	3.637	3.637	3.637	3.636	3.636	3.636	3.636	3.636	3.636
19	3.636	3.636	3.636	3.636	3.636	3.636	3.637	3.637	3.637	3.637	3.637	3.637
20	3.637	3.637	3.637	3.637	3.637	3.637	3.636	3.636	3.636	3.636	3.636	3.636
21	3.636	3.636	3.636	3.636	3.636	3.636	3.637	3.637	3.637	3.637	3.637	3.637
22	3.637	3.637	3.637	3.637	3.637	3.637	3.636	3.636	3.636	3.636	3.636	3.636
23	3.636	3.636	3.636	3.636	3.636	3.636	3.637	3.637	3.637	3.637	3.637	3.637
24	3.637	3.637	3.637	3.637	3.637	3.637	3.636	3.636	3.636	3.636	3.636	3.636
25	3.636	3.636	3.636	3.636	3.636	3.636	3.637	3.637	3.637	3.637	3.637	3.637
26	3.637	3.637	3.637	3.637	3.637	3.637	3.636	3.636	3.636	3.636	3.636	3.636
27	3.636	3.636	3.636	3.636	3.636	3.636	3.637	3.637	3.637	3.637	3.637	3.637
28	1.970	2.273	2.576	2.879	3.182	3.485	3.636	3.636	3.636	3.636	3.636	3.636
29	0.000	0.000	0.000	0.000	0.000	0.000	0.152	0.455	0.758	1.061	1.364	1.667

▼ TABLE 7

General Depreciation System—MACRS
Nonresidential Rental Real Property Placed in Service after 12/31/86 and before 5/13/93
Applicable Recovery Period: 31.5 Years
Applicable Convention: Mid-month
Applicable Depreciation Method: Straight Line

If the Recovery Year Is:	And the Month in the First Recovery Year the Property Is Placed in Service Is: 1	2	3	4	5	6	7	8	9	10	11	12
	The Depreciation Rate Is:											
1	3.042	2.778	2.513	2.249	1.984	1.720	1.455	1.190	0.926	0.661	0.397	0.132
2	3.175	3.175	3.175	3.175	3.175	3.175	3.175	3.175	3.175	3.175	3.175	3.175
3	3.175	3.175	3.175	3.175	3.175	3.175	3.175	3.175	3.175	3.175	3.175	3.175
4	3.175	3.175	3.175	3.175	3.175	3.175	3.175	3.175	3.175	3.175	3.175	3.175
5	3.175	3.175	3.175	3.175	3.175	3.175	3.175	3.175	3.175	3.175	3.175	3.175
6	3.175	3.175	3.175	3.175	3.175	3.175	3.175	3.175	3.175	3.175	3.175	3.175
7	3.175	3.175	3.175	3.175	3.175	3.175	3.175	3.175	3.175	3.175	3.175	3.175
8	3.175	3.174	3.175	3.174	3.175	3.174	3.175	3.175	3.175	3.175	3.175	3.175
9	3.174	3.175	3.174	3.175	3.174	3.175	3.174	3.175	3.174	3.175	3.174	3.175
10	3.175	3.174	3.175	3.174	3.175	3.174	3.175	3.174	3.175	3.174	3.175	3.174
11	3.174	3.175	3.174	3.175	3.174	3.175	3.174	3.175	3.174	3.175	3.174	3.175
12	3.175	3.174	3.175	3.174	3.175	3.174	3.175	3.174	3.175	3.174	3.175	3.174
13	3.174	3.175	3.174	3.175	3.174	3.175	3.174	3.175	3.174	3.175	3.174	3.175
14	3.175	3.174	3.175	3.174	3.175	3.174	3.175	3.174	3.175	3.174	3.175	3.174
15	3.174	3.175	3.174	3.175	3.174	3.175	3.174	3.175	3.174	3.175	3.174	3.175
16	3.175	3.174	3.175	3.174	3.175	3.174	3.175	3.174	3.175	3.174	3.175	3.174
17	3.174	3.175	3.174	3.175	3.174	3.175	3.174	3.175	3.174	3.175	3.174	3.175
18	3.175	3.174	3.175	3.174	3.175	3.174	3.175	3.174	3.175	3.174	3.175	3.174
19	3.174	3.175	3.174	3.175	3.174	3.175	3.174	3.175	3.174	3.175	3.174	3.175
20	3.175	3.174	3.175	3.174	3.175	3.174	3.175	3.174	3.175	3.174	3.175	3.174
21	3.174	3.175	3.174	3.175	3.174	3.175	3.174	3.175	3.174	3.175	3.174	3.175
22	3.175	3.174	3.175	3.174	3.175	3.174	3.175	3.174	3.175	3.174	3.175	3.174
23	3.174	3.175	3.174	3.175	3.174	3.175	3.174	3.175	3.174	3.175	3.174	3.175
24	3.175	3.174	3.175	3.174	3.175	3.174	3.175	3.174	3.175	3.174	3.175	3.174
25	3.174	3.175	3.174	3.175	3.174	3.175	3.174	3.175	3.174	3.175	3.174	3.175
26	3.175	3.174	3.175	3.174	3.175	3.174	3.175	3.174	3.175	3.174	3.175	3.174
27	3.174	3.175	3.174	3.175	3.174	3.175	3.174	3.175	3.174	3.175	3.174	3.175
28	3.175	3.174	3.175	3.174	3.175	3.174	3.175	3.174	3.175	3.174	3.175	3.174
29	3.174	3.175	3.174	3.175	3.174	3.175	3.174	3.175	3.174	3.175	3.174	3.175
30	3.175	3.174	3.175	3.174	3.175	3.174	3.175	3.174	3.175	3.174	3.175	3.174
31	3.174	3.175	3.174	3.175	3.174	3.175	3.174	3.175	3.174	3.175	3.174	3.175
32	1.720	1.984	2.249	2.513	2.778	3.042	3.175	3.174	3.175	3.174	3.175	3.174
33	0.000	0.000	0.000	0.000	0.000	0.000	0.132	0.397	0.661	0.926	1.190	1.455

▼ TABLE 8

General Depreciation System—MACRS
Nonresidential Rental Real Property Placed in Service after 5/12/93
Applicable Recovery Period: 39 years
Applicable Depreciation Method: Straight Line

If the Recovery Year Is:	And the Month in the First Recovery Year the Property Is Placed in Service Is: 1	2	3	4	5	6	7	8	9	10	11	12
	The Depreciation Rate Is:											
1	2.461	2.247	2.033	1.819	1.605	1.391	1.177	0.963	0.749	0.535	0.321	0.107
2-39	2.564	2.564	2.564	2.564	2.564	2.564	2.564	2.564	2.564	2.564	2.564	2.564
40	0.107	0.321	0.535	0.749	0.963	1.177	1.391	1.605	1.819	2.033	2.247	2.461

Source: IRS Publication No. 534 [Depreciation]

▼ TABLE 9

Alternative Depreciation System—MACRS (Partial Table)
Property Placed in Service after 12/31/86
Applicable Convention: Half-year
Applicable Depreciation Method: 150 Percent Declining Balance Switching to Straight Line

If the Recovery Year Is:	And the Recovery Period Is: 3	4	5	7	10	12
	The Depreciation Rate Is:					
1	25.00	18.75	15.00	10.71	7.50	6.25
2	37.50	30.47	25.50	19.13	13.88	11.72
3	25.00	20.31	17.85	15.03	11.79	10.25
4	12.50	20.31	16.66	12.25	10.02	8.97
5		10.16	16.66	12.25	8.74	7.85
6			8.33	12.25	8.74	7.33
7				12.25	8.74	7.33
8				6.13	8.74	7.33
9					8.74	7.33
10					8.74	7.33
11					4.37	7.32
12						7.33
13						3.66

▼ TABLE 10

Alternative Depreciation System—MACRS (Partial Table)
Property Placed in Service after 12/31/86
Applicable Convention: Half-year
Applicable Depreciation Method: Straight Line

If the Recovery Year Is:	And the Recovery Period Is: 3	4	5	7	10	12
	The Depreciation Rate Is:					
1	16.67	12.50	10.00	7.14	5.00	4.17
2	33.33	25.00	20.00	14.29	10.00	8.33
3	33.33	25.00	20.00	14.29	10.00	8.33
4	16.67	25.00	20.00	14.28	10.00	8.33
5		12.50	20.00	14.29	10.00	8.33
6			10.00	14.28	10.00	8.33
7				14.29	10.00	8.34
8				7.14	10.00	8.33
9					10.00	8.34
10					10.00	8.33
11					5.00	8.34
12						8.33
13						4.17

▼ TABLE 11

Alternative Depreciation System—MACRS
Real Property Placed into Service after 12/31/86
Applicable Recovery Period: 40 years
Applicable Convention: Mid-month
Applicable Depreciation Method: Straight Line

If the Recovery Year Is:	And the Month in the First Recovery Year the Property Is Placed in Service Is: 1	2	3	4	5	6	7	8	9	10	11	12
	The Depreciation Rate Is:											
1	2.396	2.188	1.979	1.771	1.563	1.354	1.146	0.938	0.729	0.521	0.313	0.104
2 to 40	2.500	2.500	2.500	2.500	2.500	2.500	2.500	2.500	2.500	2.500	2.500	2.500
41	0.104	0.312	0.521	0.729	0.937	1.146	1.354	1.562	1.771	1.979	2.187	2.396

▼ TABLE 12

Depreciation System—ACRS Cost-Recovery Rates for Tangible Personal Property
Property Placed in Service after 12/31/80 and before 1/1/87

Recovery Year	Recovery Classes[a] 3-Year	5-Year
1	25%	15%
2	38	22
3	37	21
4	—	21
5	—	21
Totals	100%	100%

[a] The percentages that are applicable to each year for 10-year property are year 1, 8%; year 2, 14%; year 3, 12%; years 4 through 6, 10%; and years 7 through 10, 9%. The percentages that apply to 15-year property are year 1, 5%; year 2, 10%; year 3, 9%; year 4, 8%; years 5 and 6, 7%; and years 7 through 15, 6%.

▼ TABLE 13

Depreciation System—ACRS
19-Year Real Property (19-Year 175% Declining Balance)
Mid-Month Convention
Property Placed in Service after 5/8/85 and before 1/1/87

If the Recovery Year Is:	And the Month in the First Recovery Year the Property Is Placed in Service Is: 1	2	3	4	5	6	7	8	9	10	11	12
	The Depreciation Rate Is:											
1	8.8	8.1	7.3	6.5	5.8	5.0	4.2	3.5	2.7	1.9	1.1	0.4
2	8.4	8.5	8.5	8.6	8.7	8.8	8.8	8.9	9.0	9.0	9.1	9.2
3	7.6	7.7	7.7	7.8	7.9	7.9	8.0	8.1	8.1	8.2	8.3	8.3
4	6.9	7.0	7.0	7.1	7.1	7.2	7.3	7.3	7.4	7.4	7.5	7.6
5	6.3	6.3	6.4	6.4	6.5	6.5	6.6	6.6	6.7	6.8	6.8	6.9
6	5.7	5.7	5.8	5.9	5.9	5.9	6.0	6.0	6.1	6.1	6.2	6.2
7	5.2	5.2	5.3	5.3	5.3	5.4	5.4	5.5	5.5	5.6	5.6	5.6
8	4.7	4.7	4.8	4.8	4.8	4.9	4.9	5.0	5.0	5.1	5.1	5.1
9	4.2	4.3	4.3	4.4	4.4	4.5	4.5	4.5	4.5	4.6	4.6	4.7
10	4.2	4.2	4.2	4.2	4.2	4.2	4.2	4.2	4.2	4.2	4.2	4.2
11	4.2	4.2	4.2	4.2	4.2	4.2	4.2	4.2	4.2	4.2	4.2	4.2
12	4.2	4.2	4.2	4.2	4.2	4.2	4.2	4.2	4.2	4.2	4.2	4.2
13	4.2	4.2	4.2	4.2	4.2	4.2	4.2	4.2	4.2	4.2	4.2	4.2
14	4.2	4.2	4.2	4.2	4.2	4.2	4.2	4.2	4.2	4.2	4.2	4.2
15	4.2	4.2	4.2	4.2	4.2	4.2	4.2	4.2	4.2	4.2	4.2	4.2
16	4.2	4.2	4.2	4.2	4.2	4.2	4.2	4.2	4.2	4.2	4.2	4.2
17	4.2	4.2	4.2	4.2	4.2	4.2	4.2	4.2	4.2	4.2	4.2	4.2
18	4.2	4.2	4.2	4.2	4.2	4.2	4.2	4.2	4.2	4.2	4.2	4.2
19	4.2	4.2	4.2	4.2	4.2	4.2	4.2	4.2	4.2	4.2	4.2	4.2
20	0.2	0.5	0.9	1.2	1.6	1.9	2.3	2.6	3.0	3.3	3.7	4.0

▼ TABLE 14

Depreciation System—ACRS
18-Year Real Property (18-Year 175% Declining Balance)
Mid-Month Convention
Property Placed in Service after 6/22/84 and before 5/9/85

If the Recovery Year Is:	And the Month in the First Recovery Year the Property Is Placed in Service Is: 1	2	3	4	5	6	7	8	9	10	11	12
	The Applicable Percentage Is:											
1	9	9	8	7	6	5	4	4	3	2	1	0.4
2	9	9	9	9	9	9	9	9	9	10	10	10.0
3	8	8	8	8	8	8	8	8	9	9	9	9.0
4	7	7	7	7	7	8	8	8	8	8	8	8.0
5	7	7	7	7	7	7	7	7	7	7	7	7.0
6	6	6	6	6	6	6	6	6	6	6	6	6.0
7	5	5	5	5	6	6	6	6	6	6	6	6.0
8	5	5	5	5	5	5	5	5	5	5	5	5.0
9	5	5	5	5	5	5	5	5	5	5	5	5.0
10	5	5	5	5	5	5	5	5	5	5	5	5.0
11	5	5	5	5	5	5	5	5	5	5	5	5.0
12	5	5	5	5	5	5	5	5	5	5	5	5.0
13	4	4	4	5	4	4	5	4	4	4	5	5.0
14	4	4	4	4	4	4	4	4	4	4	4	4.0
15	4	4	4	4	4	4	4	4	4	4	4	4.0
16	4	4	4	4	4	4	4	4	4	4	4	4.0
17	4	4	4	4	4	4	4	4	4	4	4	4.0
18	4	3	4	4	4	4	4	4	4	4	4	4.0
19		1	1	1	2	2	2	3	3	3	3	3.6

▼ TABLE 15

Depreciation System—ACRS
18-Year Real Property (18-Year 175% Declining Balance)
Full-Month Convention
Property Placed in Service after 3/15/84 and before 6/23/84

If the Recovery Year Is:	And the Month in the First Recovery Year the Property Is Placed in Service Is: 1	2	3	4	5	6	7	8	9	10	11	12
	The Applicable Percentage Is:											
1	10	9	8	7	6	6	5	4	3	2	2	1
2	9	9	9	9	9	9	9	9	9	10	10	10
3	8	8	8	8	8	8	8	8	9	9	9	9
4	7	7	7	7	7	7	8	8	8	8	8	8
5	6	7	7	7	7	7	7	7	7	7	7	7
6	6	6	6	6	6	6	6	6	6	6	6	6
7	5	5	5	5	6	6	6	6	6	6	6	6
8	5	5	5	5	5	5	5	5	5	5	5	5
9	5	5	5	5	5	5	5	5	5	5	5	5
10	5	5	5	5	5	5	5	5	5	5	5	5
11	5	5	5	5	5	5	5	5	5	5	5	5
12	5	5	5	5	5	5	5	5	5	5	5	5
13	4	4	4	5	5	4	4	5	4	4	4	4
14	4	4	4	4	4	4	4	4	4	4	4	4
15	4	4	4	4	4	4	4	4	4	4	4	4
16	4	4	4	4	4	4	4	4	4	4	4	4
17	4	4	4	4	4	4	4	4	4	4	4	4
18	4	4	4	4	4	4	4	4	4	4	4	4
19			1	1	1	2	2	2	3	3	3	4

▼ TABLE 16

Depreciation System—ACRS
Full Month Convention
1. All 15-Year Real Estate (Except Low-Income Housing)
Property Placed in Service after 12/31/80 and before 3/16/84

If the Recovery Year Is:	And the Month in the First Year the Property Is Placed in Service Is: 1	2	3	4	5	6	7	8	9	10	11	12
	The Applicable Percentage Is:											
1	12	11	10	9	8	7	6	5	4	3	2	1
2	10	10	11	11	11	11	11	11	11	11	11	12
3	9	9	9	9	10	10	10	10	10	10	10	10
4	8	8	8	8	8	8	9	9	9	9	9	9
5	7	7	7	7	7	7	8	8	8	8	8	8
6	6	6	6	6	7	7	7	7	7	7	7	7
7	6	6	6	6	6	6	6	6	6	6	6	6
8	6	6	6	6	6	6	5	6	6	6	6	6
9	6	6	6	6	5	6	5	5	5	6	6	6
10	5	6	5	6	5	5	5	5	5	5	6	5
11	5	5	5	5	5	5	5	5	5	5	5	5
12	5	5	5	5	5	5	5	5	5	5	5	5
13	5	5	5	5	5	5	5	5	5	5	5	5
14	5	5	5	5	5	5	5	5	5	5	5	5
15	5	5	5	5	5	5	5	5	5	5	5	5
16	—	—	1	1	2	2	3	3	4	4	4	5

2. Low-Income Housing
Property Placed in Service after 12/31/80 and before 5/9/85[a]

If the Recovery Year Is:	And the Month in the First Year the Property Is Placed in Service Is: 1	2	3	4	5	6	7	8	9	10	11	12
	The Applicable Percentage Is:											
1	13	12	11	10	9	8	7	6	4	3	2	1
2	12	12	12	12	12	12	12	13	13	13	13	13
3	10	10	10	10	11	11	11	11	11	11	11	11
4	9	9	9	9	9	9	9	9	10	10	10	10
5	8	8	8	8	8	8	8	8	8	8	8	8
6	7	7	7	7	7	7	7	7	7	7	7	7
7	6	6	6	6	6	6	6	6	6	6	6	6
8	5	5	5	5	5	5	5	5	5	5	6	6
9	5	5	5	5	5	5	5	5	5	5	5	5
10	5	5	5	5	5	5	5	5	5	5	5	5
11	4	5	5	5	5	5	5	5	5	5	5	5
12	4	4	4	5	4	5	5	5	5	5	5	5
13	4	4	4	4	4	4	5	4	5	5	5	5
14	4	4	4	4	4	4	4	4	4	5	4	4
15	4	4	4	4	4	4	4	4	4	4	4	4
16	—	—	1	1	2	2	2	3	3	3	4	4

[a]For the period after 5/8/85, see special IRS tables (not reproduced here).

▼ TABLE 17
Luxury Automobile Limitations

	Year Automobile is Placed in Service[a]:						
	1997	**1996**	**1995**	**1994**	**1993**	**1992**	**1991**
Year 1		3,060	3,060	2,960	2,860	2,760	2,660
Year 2		4,900	4,900	4,700	4,600	4,400	4,300
Year 3		2,950	2,950	2,850	2,750	2,650	2,550
Year 4 and Each Succeeding Year		1,775	1,775	1,675	1,675	1,575	1,575

[a]For years prior to 1991, see Revenue Procedure for appropriate year.

APPENDIX D

GLOSSARY

Abusive tax shelter Investment whose principal purpose is the avoidance or evasion of federal income taxes.

Accounting method The rules used to determine the tax year in which income and expenses are reported for tax purposes. Generally, the same accounting method must be used for tax purposes as is used for keeping books and records. The accounting treatment used for any item of income or expense and for specific items (e.g., installment sales and contracts) is included in this term.

Accounting period See Tax year.

Accumulated Adjustments Account (AAA) Account that must be kept by S corporations. The cumulative total of the ordinary income or loss and separately stated items for the most recent S corporation election period.

Accumulated earnings and profits The sum of the undistributed current earnings and profits balances (and deficits) from previous years reduced by any distributions that have been made out of accumulated earnings and profits.

Accumulated earnings credit Deduction that reduces the accumulated taxable income amount. It does not offset the accumulated earnings tax on a dollar-for-dollar basis. Different rules apply for operating companies, service companies, and holding or investment companies.

Accumulated earnings tax Penalty tax on corporations other than those subject to the personal holding company tax among others. It is levied on a corporation's current year addition to its accumulated earnings balance in excess of the amount needed for reasonable business purposes and not distributed to the shareholders. This tax is intended to discourage companies from retaining excessive amounts of earnings if the funds are invested in activities that are unrelated to business needs. The tax is 39.6% of accumulated taxable income.

Accumulated taxable income The tax base for the accumulated earnings tax which is determined by taking the corporation's taxable income and increasing (decreasing) it by positive (negative) adjustments and decreasing it by the accumulated earnings credit and available dividends-paid deductions.

Accumulation distribution rules (throwback rules) Exception to the general rule that distributable net income (DNI) serves as a ceiling on the amount taxable to a beneficiary. Under the general rule, the beneficiary excludes the portion of any distribution in excess of DNI from his gross income. Accumulation distributions made by a trust are taxable to the beneficiaries in the year received.

ACE See adjusted current earnings.

Acquiescence policy IRS policy of announcing whether it agrees or disagrees with a Tax Court regular decision decided in favor of the taxpayer. Such statements are not issued for every case.

Acquisitive reorganization A transaction in which the acquiring corporation obtains all or part of the stock or assets of a target corporation.

Adjusted current earnings (ACE) Alternative minimum taxable income for the tax year plus or minus a series of special adjusted current earnings adjustments specified in Sec. 56(g)(4) (e.g., special depreciation calculation, special E&P rules, etc.).

Adjusted current earnings adjustment 75% of the excess (if any) of the adjusted current earnings of the corporation over the preadjustment AMTI. A downward adjustment is provided for 75% of the excess (if any) of preadjustment AMTI over the adjusted current earnings of the corporation.

Adjusted grossed-up basis For Sec. 338 purposes, the sum of (1) the basis of a purchasing corporation's stock interest in a target corporation plus (2) an adjustment for the target corporation's liabilities on the day following the acquisition date plus or minus (3) other relevant items.

Adjusted income from rents (AIR) This amount is equal to the corporation's gross income from rents reduced by the deductions claimed for amortization or depreciation, property taxes, interest, and rent.

Adjusted ordinary gross income (AOGI) A corporation's adjusted ordinary gross income is its ordinary gross income reduced by (1) certain expenses incurred in connection with gross income from rents, mineral, oil and gas royalties, and working interests in oil or gas wells, (2) interest received by dealers on certain U.S. obligations, (3) interest received from condemnation awards, judgments, or tax refunds, and (4) rents from certain tangible personal property manufactured or produced by the corporation.

Adjusted taxable gift Taxable gifts made after 1976 that are valued at their date-of-gift value. These gifts affect the size of the transfer tax base at death.

Administrative interpretation Treasury Department interpretation of a provision of the Code. Such interpretations may be in the form of Treasury Regulations, revenue rulings, or revenue procedures.

Advance ruling See letter ruling.

Affiliated group A group consisting of a parent corporation and at least one subsidiary corporation.

AIR See Adjusted income from rents.

Alien Individuals who are not U.S. citizens.

Alternate valuation date The alternate valuation date is the earlier of six months after the date of death or the date the property is sold, exchanged, distributed,etc. by the estate. Unless this option is elected, the gross estate is valued at its FMV on the date of the decedent's death.

Alternative minimum tax (AMT) Tax which applies to individuals, corporations, and estates and trusts if it exceeds the taxpayer's regular tax. Most taxpayers are not subject to this tax. This tax equals the amount by which the tentative minimum tax exceeds the regular tax.

Alternative minimum taxable income (AMTI) The taxpayer's taxable income (1) increased by tax preference items and (2) adjusted for income, gain, deduction, and loss items that have to be recomputed under the AMT system.

AMT See Alternative minimum tax.

AMTI See Alternative minimum taxable income.

Announcement Information release issued by the IRS to provide a technical explanation of a current tax issue. Announcements are aimed at tax practitioners rather than the general public.

Annual exclusion An exemption that is intended to relieve a donor from keeping an account of and reporting the numerous small gifts (e.g., wedding and Christmas gifts) made throughout the year. This exclusion is currently $10,000 per donee.

AOGI See Adjusted ordinary gross income.

Appeals coordinated issue Issue over which the appeals officer must obtain a concurrence of guidance from the regional director of appeals in order to render a decision.

Assignment of income doctrine A judicial requirement that income be taxed to the person that earns it.

Association A business trust, partnership, or other unincorporated entity that is made up of associates and has a joint profit motive is taxed as a corporation because it has continuity of life, centralized management, limited liability, or free transferability of interests.

At-risk basis Essentially the same amount as the regular partnership basis with the exception that liabilities increase the at-risk basis only if the partner is at-risk for such an amount.

At-risk rules These rules limit the partner's loss deductions to his at-risk basis.

Bardahl formula Mathematical formula for determining the amount of working capital that a business reasonably needs for accumulated earnings tax purposes. For a manufacturing company, the formula is based on the business's operating cycle.

Boot Property that may not be received tax-free in certain tax-free transactions (i.e., any money, debt obligations, and so on).

Bootstrap acquisition An acquisition where an investor purchases part of a corporation's stock and then has the corporation redeem the remainder of the seller's stock.

Branch profits tax Special tax levied by the U.S. government on the branch activities of a foreign corporation doing business in the United States.

Brother-sister controlled group This type of controlled group exists if (1) five or fewer individuals, estates, or trusts own at least 80% of the voting stock or 80% of the value of each corporation and (2) there is common ownership of more than 50% of the voting power or 50% of the value of all classes of stock.

Built-in deduction A deduction that accrues in a separate return limitation year but which is recognized for tax purposes in a consolidated return year.

Built-in gain A gain that accrued prior to the conversion of a C corporation to an S corporation.

Built-in gains (Sec. 1374) tax Tax on built-in gains that are recognized by the S corporation during the ten-year period commencing on the date that the S corporation election took effect.

Built-in loss A loss that accrued prior to the conversion of a C corporation to an S corporation.

Business purpose doctrine A judicial doctrine established by the U.S. Supreme Court that a transaction cannot be solely motivated by a tax avoidance purpose. Transactions which serve no business purpose are usually ignored by the IRS and the courts.

Capital gain property For charitable contribution deduction purposes, property upon which a long-term capital gain would be recognized if that property was sold at its FMV.

Capital interest An interest in the assets owned by a partnership.

C corporation Form of business entity that is taxed as a separate taxpaying entity. Its income is subject to an initial tax at the corporate level. Its shareholders are subject to a second tax if dividends are paid from the corporation's earnings and profits. This type of corporation is sometimes referred to as a regular corporation.

Certiorari An appeal from a lower court (i.e., a federal court of appeals) which the U.S. Supreme Court agrees to hear. Such appeals, which are made as a writ of certiorari, are generally not granted unless (1) a constitutional issue needs to be decided or (2) there is a conflict among the lower court decisions that must be clarified.

CFC See Controlled foreign corporation.

Charitable contribution deduction Contributions of money or property made to qualified organizations (i.e., public charities and private nonoperating foundations). For income tax purposes, the amount of the deduction depends upon (1) the type of charity receiving the contribution, (2) the type of property contributed, and (3) other limitations mandated by the tax law. Charitable contributions are also deductible under the unified transfer tax (i.e., gift tax and estate tax rules).

Charitable remainder annuity trust This type of trust makes distributions to individuals for a certain time period or for life. The annual distributions are a uniform percentage (5% or higher) of the value of the trust property as valued on the date of transfer.

Charitable remainder unitrust This type of trust makes annual distributions for either a specified time period or for life. The distributions are a uniform percentage (5% or higher) of the value of the property as revalued annually.

Check-the-box-regulations Treasury regulations which permit certain entities (e.g., partnerships and limited liability companies) to select an income tax status that is different from their basic classification.

Clifford trust A trust that is normally held for a 10-year period after which the principal reverts to the grantor. The trust accounting income is not generally taxed to the grantor.

Closed-fact situation Situation or transaction that has already occurred.

Closed transaction Situation where the property in question (e.g., property distributed in a corporate liquidation) can be valued with reasonable certainty. The gain or loss reported on the transaction is determinable at the time the transaction occurs. See open transaction doctrine.

Closely held corporation A corporation that is owned by either a single individual or a small group of individuals who may or may not be family members.

Closely held C corporation For purposes of the at-risk rules, a C corporation in which more than 50% of the stock is owned by five or fewer individuals at any time during the last half of the corporation's tax year.

Combined controlled group A group of three or more corporations which are members of a parent-subsidiary or brother-sister controlled group. In addition, at least one of the corporations must be the parent corporation of the parent-subsidiary controlled group and a member of a brother-sister controlled group.

Combined taxable income The total amount of the separate taxable incomes of the individual group members of an affiliated group that is filing a consolidated tax return.

Common law state All states other than the community property states are common law states. In such states, all assets acquired during the marriage are the property of the acquiring spouse.

Community property law Law in community property states mandating that all property acquired after marriage is generally community property unless acquired by gift or inheritance. Each spouse owns a one-half interest in community property.

Community property state The eight traditional community property states (Louisiana, Texas, New Mexico, Arizona, California, Washington, Idaho, and Nevada) and Wisconsin (which adopted a similar law). These states do not follow the common law concept of property ownership.

Complex trust Trust that is not required to distribute all of its income currently.

Consent dividend Hypothetical dividend generally deemed paid to a personal holding company's shareholders on the last day of the corporation's tax year. May also be paid so as to avoid the personal holding company tax or accumulated earnings tax.

Consolidated return change of ownership (CRCO) rules These rules affect affiliated groups who have (1) incurred net operating losses and (2) had a major change in the parent corporation's stock ownership and (3) acquired a profitable corporation. They restrict the affiliated group's ability to use its net operating loss carryforwards to the extent its old members contribute to consolidated taxable income. Under proposed regulations, the CRCO rules will be replaced by the consolidated Sec. 382 rules.

Consolidated return year A tax year for which a consolidated return is filed or is required to be filed by an affiliated group.

Consolidated taxable income The taxable income amount reported on a consolidated return filed by a group of affiliated corporations. The calculation of this amount is determined by establishing each member's separate taxable income and then following a series of steps that result in a consolidated amount.

Consolidated tax return A single tax return filed by a group of related corporations (i.e., affiliated group).

Consolidation A form of tax-free reorganization involving two or more corporations whose assets are acquired by a new corporation. The stock, securities, and other consideration transferred by the acquiring corporation is then distributed by each target corporation to its shareholders and security holders in exchange for their stock and securities.

Constructive dividend An indirect payment, or undeclared dividend, made to a shareholder without the benefit of a formal declaration usually resulting from a reclassification of a transaction by the IRS. Transactions that can produce constructive dividends include the payment of unreasonable compensation or the making of loans to shareholders.

Continuity of interest doctrine The judicial requirement that shareholders who transfer property to a transferee corporation continue their ownership in the property through holding the transferee corporation's stock in order to defer recognition of their gains.

Controlled foreign corporation (CFC) Foreign corporation that is (1) directly or indirectly controlled by U.S. shareholders at any time during the taxable year provided that (2) such U.S. shareholders control more than 50% of its voting power or more than 50% of the value of the outstanding stock.

Controlled group A controlled group is two or more separately incorporated businesses owned by a related group of individuals or entities. Such groups include parent-subsidiary groups, brother-sister groups, or combined groups.

Corporation A separate taxpaying entity (such as an association, joint stock company, or insurance company) that must file a tax return every year, even when it had no income or loss for the year.

Corresponding item The buyer's income, gain, deduction, or loss from an intercompany transaction, or from property acquired in an intercompany transaction. Corresponding items cause intercompany items to be recognized. See intercompany item.

Crummey trust Technique that allows a donor to set up a discretionary trust and obtain an annual exclusion. Such a trust arrangement allows the beneficiary to demand an annual distribution of the lesser of $10,000 or the amount transferred to the trust that year.

C short year That portion of an S termination year that commences on the day on which the termination is effective and continues through to the last day of the corporation's tax year.

Current distribution See Nonliquidating distribution.

Current earnings and profits Earnings and profits calculated annually by (1) adjusting the corporation's taxable income (or net operating loss) for items that must be recomputed, (2) adding back any excluded income items, income deferrals, and deductions not allowed in computing earnings and profits, and (3) subtracting any expenses and losses not deductible in computing the corporation's taxable income.

Curtesy A widower's interest in his deceased wife's property.

Deductions in respect of a decedent (DRD) Deduction accrued prior to death but not includible on decedent's final tax return because of the decedent's method of accounting.

Deemed liquidation election Election under Sec. 338 permitting an acquiring corporation that acquires a controlling interest in a target corporation's stock to step-up or step-down the basis of the target corporation's assets to their adjusted grossed-up basis by having the target corporation be liquidated for tax purposes only.

Deemed paid foreign tax credit An indirect foreign tax credit that is available to a domestic corporation owning at least 10% of the voting stock of a foreign corporation when the foreign corporation pays or accrues creditable foreign taxes.

Deferral privilege A tax exemption provided U.S. taxpayers who own stock of a foreign corporation. The foreign corporation's earnings are generally not taxed in the United States until repatriated unless an exception such as the Subpart F rules applies.

Deficiency dividend This type of dividend substitutes an income tax levy on the dividend payment at the shareholder level for the payment of the personal holding company tax.

DIF See Discriminant Function Program.

Discriminant Function Program Program used by the IRS to select individual returns for audit. This system is intended to identify those tax returns which are most likely to contain errors.

Dissolution A legal term implying that a corporation has surrendered the charter that it originally received from the state.

Distributable net income (DNI) Maximum amount of distributions taxed to the beneficiaries and deducted by a trust or estate.

Distributive share The portion of partnership taxable and nontaxable income, losses, credits, and so on that the partner must report for tax purposes.

Dividend A distribution of property made by a corporation out of its earnings and profits.

Dividends-paid deduction Distributions made out of a corporation's earnings and profits are eligible for this deduction for personal holding company tax and accumulated earnings tax purposes. The deduction is equal to the amount of money plus the adjusted basis of the nonmoney property distributed.

Dividends-received deduction This deduction attempts to mitigate the triple taxation that would occur if one corporation paid dividends to a corporate shareholder who, in turn, distributed such amounts to its individual shareholders. Certain restrictions and limitations apply to this deduction.

Divisive reorganization Transaction in which part of a transferor corporation's assets are transferred to a second, newly created corporation that is controlled by either the transferee or its shareholders.

DISC See Domestic International Sales Corporation.

DNI See Distributable net income.

Domestic corporation Corporation that is incorporated in one of the 50 states or under federal law.

Domestic International Sales Corporation (DISC) A domestic corporation that earns most of its income from exports.

Dower A widow's interest in her deceased husband's property.

DRD See Deductions in respect of a decedent.

E&P See Earnings and profits.

Earnings and profits A measure of the corporation's ability to pay a dividend from its current and accumulated earnings without an impairment of capital.

Estate A legal entity which comes into being only upon the death of the person whose assets are being administered. The estate continues in existence until the duties of the executor have been completed.

Excess loss account A negative investment account of a member of an affiliated group that files a consolidated tax return which attaches to an investment in a lower-tier subsidiary corporation.

Excess net passive income An amount equal to the S corporation's net passive income multiplied by the fraction consisting of its passive investment income less 25% of its gross receipts divided by its passive investment income. It is limited to the corporation's taxable income.

Excess net passive income (Sec. 1375) tax Tax levied when (1) an S corporation has passive investment income for the taxable year that exceeds 25% of its gross receipts and (2) at the close of the tax year the S corporation has earnings and profits from C corporation tax years.

Exemption equivalent That portion of the tax base that is completely free of transfer taxes as a result of the unified credit.

Failure-to-file-penalty Penalty imposed for the failure to file a timely return. The penalty is assessed in the amount of 5% per month (or fraction thereof) on the amount of the net tax due. The maximum penalty for failing to file is 25%.

Failure-to-pay penalty Penalty imposed at the rate of 0.5% per month (or fraction thereof) on the amount of tax shown on the return less any tax payments made before the beginning of the month for which the penalty is being calculated. The maximum penalty is 25%.

Fair market value (FMV) The amount that would be realized from the sale of a property at a price that is agreeable to both the buyer and the seller when neither party is obligated to participate in the transaction.

Fiduciary A person or other entity (e.g., a guardian, executor, trustee, or administrator) who holds and manages property for someone else.

Fiduciary accounting income The excess of accounting income over expenses for a fiduciary (i.e., an estate or trust). Excluded are any items credited to or charged against capital.

Fiduciary taxation The special tax rules that apply to fiduciaries (e.g., trusts and estates).

FMV See Fair market value.

Foreign branch An office or other establishment of a domestic entity that operates in a foreign country.

Foreign corporation A corporation that is incorporated under the laws of a country other than the United States.

Foreign personal holding company (FPHC) A foreign corporation that (1) is more than 50% owned by no more than five U.S. citizens or residents at any time during the taxable year and (2) earns at least 50% of its gross income from foreign personal holding company income. The gross income amount increases to 60% if the company did not have foreign personal holding company status in the previous taxable year.

Foreign Sales Corporation (FSC) Corporation that is created or organized under the laws of certain foreign countries or U.S. possessions (other than Puerto Rico) and that earns most of its income from export activities.

Foreign tax credit Tax credit given to mitigate the possibility of double taxation faced by U.S. citizens, residents, and corporations earning foreign income.

Foreign trade income Income earned by a foreign sales corporation that is attributable to foreign trading gross receipts.

Forum shopping The ability to consider differing precedents in choosing the forum for litigation.

FPHC See Foreign Personal Holding Company.

FSC See Foreign sales corporation.

Future interest Such interests include reversions, remainders, and other interests that may not be used, owned, or enjoyed until some future date.

General partner Partner or partners with (1) the authority to make management decisions and commitments for the partnership and (2) unlimited liability for all partnership debts.

General partnership A partnership with two or more partners where no partner is a limited partner.

General power of appointment Power of appointment under which the holder can appoint the property to himself, his estate, his creditors, or the creditors of his estate. Such power may be exercisable during the decedent's life, by his will, or both.

Generation-skipping transfer A disposition that (1) provides interests for more than one generation of beneficiaries who are in a younger generation than the transferor or (2) provides an interest solely for a person two or more generations younger than the transferor.

Gift tax A wealth transfer tax that applies if the property transfer occurs during a person's lifetime.

Grantor The transferor who creates a trust.

Grantor trust Trust governed by Secs. 671 through 679. The income from such trusts is taxed to the grantor even if some or all of the income has been distributed.

Gross estate The gross estate includes items to which the decedent held title at death as well as certain incomplete transfers made by the decedent prior to death.

Guaranteed minimum Minimum amount of payment guaranteed to a partner. This amount is important if the partner's distributive share is less than his guaranteed minimum. See also Guaranteed payment.

Guaranteed payment Minimum amount of payment guaranteed to a partner in the form of a salary-like payment made for services provided to the partnership and interest-like payments for the use of invested capital. Guaranteed payments, which may be in the form of a guaranteed minimum amount or a set amount, are taxed as ordinary income. See also Guaranteed minimum.

Hedge agreement This is an obligation on the part of a shareholder-employee to repay to the corporation any portion of salary that is disallowed by the IRS as a deduction. It is also used in connection with other corporate payments to shareholder-employees (e.g., travel and entertainment expenses).

Housing cost amount A special deduction or exclusion equal to the housing expenses incurred by a taxpayer eligible for the Sec. 911 earned income exclusion minus the base housing amount.

Income beneficiary Entity or individual that receives the income from a trust.

Income in respect of a decedent (IRD) Amount to which the decedent was entitled as gross income but which were not properly includible in computing his taxable income for the tax year ending with his date of death or for a previous tax year under the method of accounting employed by the decedent.

Information release An administrative pronouncement concerning an issue that the IRS thinks the general public will be interested in. Such releases are issued in lay terms and widely published.

Innocent spouse provision This provision exempts a spouse from penalty and liability for tax if such spouse had no knowledge of nor reason to know about an item of taxable income that is in dispute.

Intercompany item The seller's income, gain, deduction, or loss from an intercompany transaction. Intercompany items are recognized when a corresponding item is incurred. See corresponding item.

Intercompany transaction Transaction that takes place during a consolidated return year between corporations that are members of the same group immediately after the transaction.

Interpretative Regulations Treasury Regulations that serve to interpret the provisions of the Internal Revenue Code.

Inter vivos trust Transfer to a trust that is made during the grantor's lifetime.

IRD See Income in respect of a decedent.

Irrevocable trust Trust under which the grantor cannot require the trustee to return the trust's assets.

Joint tenancy A popular form of property ownership that serves as a substitute for a will. Each joint tenant is deemed to have an equal interest in the property.

Judicial decisions Decision rendered by a court deciding the case that is presented to it by a plaintiff and defendant. These decisions are important sources of the tax law and can come from trial courts and appellate courts.

Legislative reenactment doctrine Rule holding that Congress's failure to change the wording in the Code over an extended period signifies that Congress has approved the treatment provided in the regulations.

Letter ruling Letter rulings originate from the IRS at the taxpayer's request. They describe how the IRS will treat a proposed transaction. It is only binding on the person requesting the ruling provided the transaction is completed as proposed in the ruling. Letter rulings that are of general interest are published as Revenue rulings.

Life estate A property transfer in trust that results in the transferor reserving the right to income for life. Another individual is named to receive the property upon the transferor's death.

LIFO recapture tax A tax imposed on a C corporation that uses the LIFO inventory method and which elects S corporation treatment. The tax is imposed in the final C corporation tax year and paid over a four-year period.

Limited liability company A business entity that combines the legal and tax benefits of partnerships and S corporations. Generally these entities are taxed as partnerships for federal tax purposes since they do not have three or four of the "nonneutral" corporate characteristics present.

Limited liability partnership (LLP) Similar to a limited liability company, but formed under a separate state statute that generally applies to service companies.

Limited partner Partner who has no right to be active in the management of the partnership and whose liability is limited to his original investment plus any additional amounts that he is obligated to contribute.

Limited partnership A partnership where one or more of the partners is designated as a limited partner.

Liquidating distribution A distribution that (1) liquidates a partner's entire partnership interest due to retirement, death, or other business reason or (2) partially or totally liquidates a shareholder's stock interest in a corporation following the adoption of a plan at liquidation.

Loss corporation A corporation entitled to use a net operating loss carryover or having a net operating loss for the taxable year in which an ownership change occurs.

Majority partners The one or more partners in a partnership who have an aggregate interest in partnership profits and capital in excess of 50%.

Marital deduction Deduction allowed for tax-free inter-spousal transfers other than those for gifts of certain terminable interests.

Memorandum (memo) decision Decision issued by the Tax Court dealing with a factual variation on a matter where the law has already been decided in an earlier case.

Merger A tax-free reorganization one form of which has the acquiring corporation transfer its stock, securities, and other consideration to the target corporation in exchange for its assets and liabilities. The target corporation then distributes the consideration that it receives to its shareholders and security holders in exchange for their stock and securities.

Minimum tax credit (MTC) A tax credit allowed for the amount of alternative minimum tax that arose because of deferral and permanent adjustments and preference items. This credit may be carried over and used to offset regular tax liabilities in subsequent years.

MTC See Minimum tax credit.

Negligence The Code defines negligence as (1) any failure to reasonably attempt to comply with the Code and (2) "careless, reckless, or intentional disregard" of the rules and regulations.

Negligence penalty Penalty assessed if the IRS finds that the taxpayer has filed an incorrect return because of negligence. Generally this penalty is 20% of the underpayment attributable to negligence.

Net gift A gift upon which the donee pays the gift tax as a condition to receiving the gift.

Net operating loss (NOL) A net operating loss occurs when business expenses exceed business income for any taxable year. Such losses may be carried back 3 years or carried forward 15 years to a year in which the taxpayer has taxable income. The loss is carried back first and must be deducted from years in chronological order unless a special election is made to forgo the carryback.

New loss corporation Any corporation permitted to use a net operating loss carryover after an ownership change occurs.

Ninety-day letter Officially called a Statutory Notice of Deficiency, this letter is sent when (1) the taxpayer does not file a protest letter within 30 days of receipt of the 30-day letter or (2) the taxpayer has met with an appeals officer but no agreement was reached. The letter notifies the taxpayer of the amount of the deficiency, how that amount was determined, and that a deficiency will be assessed if a petition is not filed with the Tax Court within 90 days. The taxpayer is also advised of the alternatives available to him.

NOL See Net operating loss.

Nonliquidating (current) distribution Distribution that (1) reduces, but does not eliminate, a partner's partnership interest or (2) is made with respect to a shareholder's stock interest in a corporation at a time when no plan of liquidation has been adopted and may or may not reduce the shareholder's interest in the corporation.

Nonrecourse loan Loan for which the borrower has no liability.

Nonresident alien Individual whose residence is not the United States and who is not a U.S. citizen.

Notice An interpretation by the IRS that provides quidance concerning how to interpret a statute, perhaps one recently enacted.

OGI See Ordinary gross income.

Old loss corporation Any corporation that is allowed to use a net operating loss carryover, or which has a net operating loss for the tax year in which an ownership change occurs, and which undergoes the requisite stock ownership change.

Open-fact or tax-planning situation A situation that is pending but has not yet occurred. That is, the facts and events surrounding the transaction are still controllable.

Open transaction doctrine Valuation technique for property that can only be valued on the basis of uncertain future payments. This doctrine determines the shareholder's gain or loss when the asset is sold, collected, or able to be valued. Assets that cannot be valued are assigned a value of zero.

Optional basis adjustment An elective technique that adjusts the basis for the partnership interest and the underlying assets up or down as a result of (1) distributions from the partnership to its partners, (2) sales of partnership interests by existing partners, or (3) transfers of the interest following the death of a partner.

Ordinary gross income (OGI) A corporation's ordinary gross income is its gross income reduced by (1) capital gains and (2) Sec. 1231 gains.

Ordinary income property For charitable contribution deduction purposes, any property that would result in the recognition of ordinary income if it was sold. Such property includes inventory, works of art or manuscripts created by the taxpayer, capital assets that have been held for one year or less, and Sec. 1231 property that results in ordinary income due to depreciation recapture.

Other intercompany transactions An intercompany transaction that is not a deferred intercompany transaction. See deferred intercompany transaction.

Parent-subsidiary controlled group To qualify as such, a common parent must own at least 80% of the voting stock or at least 80% of the value of at least one subsidiary corporation and at least 80% of each other component member of the controlled group must be owned by other members of the controlled group.

Partial liquidation This occurs when a corporation discontinues one line of business, distributes the assets related to that business to its shareholders, and continues in at least one other line of business.

Partner A member of a partnership. The member may be an individual, trust, estate, or corporation. See also general partner and limited partner.

Partnership Syndicate, group, pool, joint venture, or other unincorporated organization which carries on a business or financial operation or venture and which has at least two partners.

Partnership agreement Agreement that governs the relationship between the partners and the partnership.

Partnership item Virtually all items reported by the partnership for the taxable year, including tax preference items, credit recapture items, guaranteed payments, and at-risk amounts.

Partnership ordinary income The positive sum of all partnership items of income, gain, loss, or deduction that do not have to be separately stated.

Partnership ordinary loss The negative sum of all partnership items of income, gain, loss, or deduction that do not have to be separately stated.

Partnership taxable income The sum of all taxable items among the separately stated items plus the partnership ordinary income or ordinary loss.

Party to a reorganization Such parties include (1) corporations that result from a reorganization and (2) the corporations involved in a reorganization where one corporation acquires the stock or assets of the other corporation.

Passive activity limitation Separate limitation on the amount of losses and credits that can be claimed with respect to a passive activity.

Passive foreign investment company (PFIC) A foreign corporation having passive income as 75% or more of its gross income for the tax year, or at least 50% of the average value of its assets during the tax year producing or held for producing passive income.

Passive income Income from an activity that does not require the taxpayer's material involvement or participation. Thus, income from tax shelters and rental activities generally fall into this category.

Passive loss Loss generated from a passive activity. Such losses are computed separately. They may be used to offset income from other passive activities, but may not be used to offset either active income or portfolio income.

Permanent difference Items that are reported in taxable income but not book income or vice versa. Such differences include book income items that are nontaxable in the current year and will never be taxable and book expense items that are nondeductible in computing taxable income for the current year and will never be deductible.

Personal holding company (PHC) A closely held corporation (1) that is owned by five or fewer shareholders who own more than 50% of the corporation's outstanding stock at any time during the last half of its tax year and (2) whose PHC income equals at least 60% of the corporation's adjusted ordinary gross income for the tax year. Certain corporations (e.g., S corporations) are exempt from this definition.

Personal holding company income (PHCI) Twelve categories of income including the following: dividends; interest; annuities; royalties (other than minerals, oil and gas, computer software, and copyright royalties); adjusted income from rents; adjusted income from mineral, oil and gas royalties or working interests in oil and gas wells; computer software royalties; copyright royalties; produced film rents; income from personal service contracts involving a 25% or more shareholder; rental income from corporate property used by a 25% or more shareholder; and distributions from estates and trusts.

Personal holding company penalty tax This tax is equal to 39.6% of the undistributed personal holding company income. It is intended to prevent closely held companies from converting an operating company into a nonoperating company. Thus, it is assessed in addition to the regular corporate income tax and AMT.

Personal service corporation Corporation whose principal activity is the performance of personal services.

PHC See Personal holding company.

PHCI See Personal holding company income.

Plan of liquidation. A written document detailing the steps to be undertaken while carrying out the complete liquidation of a corporation.

Plan of reorganization A consummated transaction that is specifically defined as a reorganization.

Pooled income fund A fund in which individuals receive an income interest for life and a charitable contribution deduction equal to the remainder interest for amounts contributed to the fund. The various individual beneficiaries receive annual distributions of income based upon their proportionate share of the fund's earnings.

Post-termination transition period The period of time following the termination of the S corporation election during which (1) loss and deduction carryovers can be deducted or (2) distributions of S corporation previously taxed earnings can be made tax-free.

Power of appointment The power to designate the eventual owner of a property. Such appointments may be general or specific. See also General power of appointment.

Pre-adjustment AMTI Alternative minimum taxable income determined without the adjusted current earnings adjustment and the alternative tax NOL deduction.

Pre-adjustment year For purposes of the innocent spouse provisions, the most recent tax year of the spouse ending before the date the deficiency is mailed.

Preferential dividend Dividends are preferential if (1) the amount distributed to a shareholder exceeds his ratable share of the distribution as determined by the number of shares that are owned or (2) the distribution amount for a class of stock is more or less than its rightful amount.

Preferred stock bailout A tax treatment mandated by Sec. 306 which prevents shareholders who receive nontaxable preferred stock dividends from receiving capital gain treatment upon the sale or redemption of the preferred stock.

Present interest An unrestricted right to the immediate use, possession, or enjoyment of property or the income from property (e.g., a life estate or term certain).

Previously taxed income (PTI) Income earned in a pre-1983 S corporation tax year and which was taxed to the shareholder. A money distribution of PTI can be distributed tax-free once all of a corporation's AAA balance has been distributed. See Accumulated Adjustment Account.

Primary cite The highest level official reporter which reports a particular case is called the primary cite.

Principal partner Partner who owns at least a 5% interest in the partnership's capital or profits.

Private Letter Ruling See Letter Ruling.

Probate estate Those properties that (1) pass subject to the will or under an intestacy statute and (2) are subject to court administration are part of the probate estate.

Profits interest Interest in the partnership's future earnings.

Property Cash, tangible property (e.g., buildings and land) and intangible property (e.g., franchise rights, trademarks, and leases).

Protest letter If the additional tax in question is more than $10,000 and the IRS audit was a field audit, the taxpayer must file a protest letter within 30 days. If no such letter is sent, then the IRS will follow-up with a 90-day letter. See also Ninety-day letter.

Publicly traded partnership A partnership that is actively traded on an established securities exchange or is traded in a secondary market or the equivalent thereof. Such partnerships which are formed after December 17, 1987 are taxed as corporations unless they earn predominantly passive income; publicly traded partnerships that existed before that date will be treated as partnerships until their first tax year beginning after 1997 except when they add a new line of business.

QTIP See Qualified terminable interest property.

Qualified disclaimer Disclaimer made by a person named to receive property under a decedent's will who wishes to renounce the property and any of its benefits. Such a disclaimer must be in written form and be irrevocable. In addition, it must be made no later than 9 months after the later of the day the transfer is made or the day the recipient becomes 21 years old. The property must pass to either the decedent's spouse or another person not named by the person making the disclaimer.

Qualified joint interest If spouses are the only joint owners of a property, that property is classified as a qualified joint interest.

Qualified Subchapter S Subsidiary (QSSS) An S corporation that is 100%-owned by another S corporation. The income earned by a QSSS is treated and reported as if earned by its parent corporation.

Qualified Subchapter S trusts (QSSTs) A domestic trust that owns stock in one or more S corporations and distributes (or is required to distribute) all of its income to its sole income beneficiary. The beneficiary must make an irrevocable election to be treated as the owner of the trust consisting of the S corporation stock. A separate QSST election must be made for each corporation's stock that is owned by the trust.

Qualified terminable interest property (QTIP) QTIP property is property for which a special election has been made that makes it eligible for the marital deduction. Such property must be transferred by the donor-spouse to a donee-spouse who has a qualifying interest for life. In other words, the donor does not have to grant full control over the property to his spouse.

Reasonable business needs For accumulated earnings tax purposes, the amount that a prudent businessman would consider appropriate for the business's bona fide present and future needs, Sec. 303 (death tax) redemption needs, and excess business holding redemption needs.

Recapitalization A tax-free change in the capital structure of an existing corporation for a bona fide business purpose.

Recourse loan Loan for which the borrower remains liable until repayment is complete. If the loan is secured, the lender can be repaid by selling the security. Any difference in the sale amount and the loan amount must be paid by the borrower.

Regular corporation See C corporation.

Regular decision Tax Court decision that is issued on a particular issue for the first time.

Regular tax A corporation's tax liability for income tax purposes reduced by foreign tax credits allowable for income tax purposes.

Remainder interest The portion of an interest in the property retained by a transferor who is not transferring his entire interest in a property.

Remainderman The person entitled to the remainder interest.

Resident alien An individual whose residence is the United States, but who is not a U.S. citizen.

Revenue procedure Issued by the national office of the IRS and reflects the IRS's position on procedural aspects of tax practice issues. Revenue procedures are published in the Cumulative Bulletin.

Revenue ruling Issued by the national office of the IRS and reflects the IRS's interpretation of a narrow tax issue. Revenue rulings, which are published in the Cumulative Bulletin, have less weight than the Treasury Regulations.

Reverse triangular merger Type of tax-free transaction in which a subsidiary corporation is merged into a target corporation and the target corporation stays alive as a subsidiary of the parent corporation.

Reversionary interest The interest in a property that might revert back to the transferor under the terms of the transfer. If the amount of reversionary interest is 5% or less, it is not included in the gross estate.

Revocable trust Trust under which the grantor may demand that the assets be returned.

Rule against perpetuities The requirement that no property interet vest more than 21 years, plus the gestation period, after some life or lives in being at the time the interest is created.

S corporation Election that can be made by small business corporations that allows them to be taxed like partnerships rather than like C corporations. Small business corporations are those that meet the 35-shareholder limitation, the type of shareholder restrictions, and the one class of stock restriction.

Secondary cite Citation to a secondary source (i.e., an unofficial reporter) for a particular case.

Section 306 stock Preferred stock that is received as a stock dividend or a part of a tax-free reorganization. Section 306 stock is subject to the special preferred stock bailout rules when sold or redeemed. See preferred stock bailouts.

Section 382 loss limitation rules Limitation which principally prevents trafficking in NOLs. Applies to corporate acquisitions, stock redemptions, and reorganizations when a more than 50 percentage point change in ownership occurs. The NOL that can be used in a tax year is limited to the value of the loss corporation's stock times a long-term tax exempt federal rate.

Sec. 444 election Personal service corporations, partnerships, and S corporations that are unable to otherwise elect a fiscal year, instead of their required tax year, can under Sec. 444 elect a fiscal year as their taxable year.

Sec. 482 rules The IRS has the power under Sec. 482 to distribute, apportion, or allocate income, deductions, credits, or allowances between or among controlled entities to prevent tax evasion and to clearly reflect the income of the entities.

Section 2503(c) trust Trust created for children under age 21 that need not distribute all of its income annually. The undistributed interest passes to the beneficiary when age 21 is attained or his estate should he die before age 21.

Security A security includes (1) shares of stock in a corporation; (2) a right to subscribe for, or the right to receive, a share of stock in a corporation; and (3) a bond, debenture, note, or other evidence of indebtedness issued by a corporation with interest coupons or in registered form.

Separate return limitation year Any separate return year except (1) a separate return year of the group member that is designated as the parent corporation for the consolidated return year to which the tax attribute is carried or (2) a separate return year of any corporation that was a group member for every day of the loss year.

Separate return limitation year (SRLY) rules Limitation on the amount of net operating loss and other deduction and loss amounts from a separate return year that can be used by an affiliated group in a consolidated return year to the member's contribution to consolidated taxable income.

Separate return year A tax year for which a corporation (1) files a separate return or (2) joins in the filing of a consolidated return with a different affiliated group.

Separate share rule Rule permitting a trust with several beneficiaries to treat each beneficiary as having a separate trust interest for purposes of determining (1) the amount of the distribution deduction and (2) the beneficiary's gross income.

Separate taxable income The taxable income of an individual corporate member of an affiliated group filing a consolidated tax return. This amount is used to calculate the group's combined taxable income.

Short-period tax return A tax return covering a period of less than 12 months. Short period returns are commonly filed in the first or final tax year or when a change in tax year is made.

Short-term trust Trust whose period is long enough for the grantor to escape being taxed on the trust's accounting income. A *Clifford* trust is a short-term trust.

Simple trust Trust that must distribute all of its income currently and is not empowered to make a charitable contribution.

Small business trust A type of trust that can own stock in a small business corporation that has made an S election to be taxed as an S corporation.

Small cases procedure When $10,000 or less is in question for a particular year, a taxpayer may opt to have the case heard by a special commissioner rather than a Tax Court judge. The commissioner's opinion cannot be appealed and has no precedential value.

Sole proprietorship Form of business entity owned by an individual who reports all items of income and expense on Schedule C (or Schedule C-EZ) of his individual return.

Special agents The IRS agents responsible for criminal fraud investigations.

Spinoff A tax-free distribution in which a parent corporation distributes the stock and securities of a subsidiary to its shareholders without receiving anything in exchange.

Split-interest transfer A transfer made for both private (i.e., an individual) and public (i.e., a charitable organization) purposes.

Splitoff Tax-free distribution in which a parent corporation distributes a subsidiary's stock and securities to some or all of its shareholders in exchange for part or all of their stock and securities in the parent corporation.

Split-up Tax-free distribution in which a parent corporation distributes the stock or securities of two or more subsidiaries to its shareholders in exchange for all of their stock and securities in the parent corporation. The parent corporation then goes out of existence.

Sprinkling trust A discretionary trust with several beneficiaries.

SRTP See Statements on Responsibilities in Tax Practice.

S short year That portion of an S termination year that commences on the first day of the tax year and ends on the day preceding the day on which the termination is effective.

Statements on Responsibilities in Tax Practice (SRTP) Ethical standards of practice and compliance set by the Tax Division of the American Institute of Certified Public Accountants. These statements, which are not legally binding, have a great deal of influence over ethics in tax practice.

Statutory (or legislative) regulations Treasury Regulations that are treated as law. Such regulations may be over-turned by the courts on the grounds that they (1) exceed the scope of the delegated authority or (2) are unreasonable.

Step transaction doctrine A judicial doctrine which the IRS can use to collapse a multistep transaction into a single transaction (either taxable or tax-free) in order to prevent the taxpayers from arranging a series of business transactions to obtain a tax result that is not available if only a single transaction is used.

S termination year A tax year in which a termination event occurs on any day other than the first day of the tax year. It is divided into an S short year and a C short year.

Stock dividend A dividend paid in the form of stock in the corporation issuing the dividend.

Stock redemption The acquisition by a corporation of its own stock in exchange for property. Such stock may be cancelled, retired, or held as treasury stock.

Stock rights Rights issued by a corporation to its shareholders or creditors which permits the purchase of an additional share(s) of stock at a designated exercise price with the surrender of one or more of the stock rights.

Subpart F income A series of income categories that are deemed distributed to the U.S. shareholders of a controlled foreign corporation on the last day of its tax year. Subpart F income includes: income from insurance of U.S. and foreign risks, foreign base company income, boycott-related income, bribes, and income from countries where for political reasons, etc. the deferral privilege is denied.

Substantially appreciated inventory This type of inventory includes (1) items held for sale in the normal course of partnership business, (2) other property which would not be considered a capital asset or Sec. 1231 property if it was sold by the partnership, and (3) any other property held by the partnership which would fall into the above classification if it was held by the selling or distributee partner.

Superfund environmental tax A tax enacted to assist in the environmental clean-up. The tax base is a corporation's modified AMTI minus a $2 million statutory exemption. The tax rate is 0.0012.

Target corporation The corporation that transfers its assets as part of a taxable or tax-free acquisition transaction. May also be known as the acquired or transferor company.

Tax attributes Corporations have various tax items, such as earnings and profits, deduction and credit carryovers, and depreciation recapture potential, that are called tax attributes. The tax attributes of a target or liquidating corporation are assumed by the acquiring or parent corporation, respectively, in acquisitive reorganizations and tax-free liquidations.

Tax matters partner (1) Partner who is designated by the partnership or (2) the gerneral partner having the largest profits interests at the close of the partnership's tax year.

Taxpayer Compliance Measurement Program (TCMP) A stratified random sample used to select tax returns for audit. The program is intended to test the extent to which taxpayers are in compliance with the law.

Tax preference items Designated items, such as accelerated depreciation claimed on pre-1987 realty, that increase taxable income to arrive at AMTI. Unlike AMT adjustments, tax preference items do not reverse in later years and reduce AMTI.

Tax research The process of solving a specific tax-related question on the basis of both tax law sources and the specific circumstances surrounding the particular situation.

Tax services Multivolume commentaries on the tax law. Generally these commentaries contain copies of the Internal Revenue Code and the Treasury Regulations. Also included are editorial comments prepared by the publisher of the tax service, current matters, and a cross-reference to various government promulgations and judicial decisions.

Tax treaty A bilateral agreement entered into between two nations which addresses tax and other matters. Treaties provide for modifications to the basic tax laws involving residents of the two countries (e.g., reductions in the withholding rates).

Tax year The period of time (usually 12 months) selected by a taxpayer to compute their taxable income. The tax year may be a calendar year or a fiscal year. The election is made on the taxpayer's first return and cannot be changed without IRS approval. The tax year may be less than 12 months if it is the taxpayer's first or final return or if the taxpayer is changing accounting periods.

TCMP See Taxpayer Compliance Measurement Program.

Technical advice memorandum Such memoranda are administrative interpretations issued by the national office of the IRS in the form of a letter ruling. Taxpayers may request them if they need guidance about the tax treatment of complicated technical matters which are being audited.

Temporary differences Items which are included in book income in the current year but which were included in taxable income in the past or will be included in the future. Book income items that are nontaxable in the current year even though they were taxed in the past or will be taxed in the future and book expenses that are not currently deductible even though that status was different in the past or will be different in the future are categorized as temporary differences.

Temporary Regulations Regulations issued to provide guidance for taxpayers pending the issuance of the final regulations. Temporary Regulations are binding upon taxpayers.

Tentative minimum tax (TMT) Tax calculated by (1) multiplying 20% times the corporation's alternative minimum taxable income less a statutory exemption amount and (2) deducting allowable foreign tax credits.

Term certain interest A person holding such an interest has a right to receive income from property for a specified term, but does not own or hold title to such property. The property reverts to the grantor at the end of the term.

Terminable interest A property interest that ends when (1) some event occurs (or fails to occur) or (2) a specified amount of time passes.

Testamentary Of, pertaining to, or of the nature of a testament or will.

Testamentary transfers A transferor's control or enjoyment of a property ceases at death.

Testamentary trust Trust created under the direction of a decedent's will and funded by the decedent's estate.

Thirty-day letter A report sent to the taxpayer if the taxpayer does not sign Form 870 (Waiver of Statutory Notice) concerning any additional taxes assessed. The letter details the proposed changes and advises the taxpayer of his right to pursue the matter with the Appeals Office. The taxpayer then has 30 days in which to request a conference.

Throwback dividends For accumulated earnings tax and personal holding company tax purposes, these are distributions made out of current or accumulated earnings and profits in the first two and one-half months after the close of the tax year.

Tier-1 beneficiary Beneficiary to whom a distribution must be made.

Tier-2 beneficiary Beneficiary who receives a discretionary distribution.

TMT See Tentative minimum tax.

Transferor corporation The corporation that transfers its assets as part of a reorganization. May also be known as acquired or target corporation.

Triangular merger A type of merger transaction where the parent corporation uses a subsidiary corporation to serve as the acquiring corporation.

Triangular reorganization A type of reorganization (i.e., Type A, B, or C) where the parent corporation uses a subsidiary corporation to serve as the acquiring corporation. See triangular merger.

Trust An arrangement created either by will or by an inter vivos declaration whereby trustees take title to property for the purpose of protecting it or conserving it for the beneficiaries.

Trustee An individual or institution which administers a trust for the benefit of a beneficiary.

Trustor The grantor or transferor of a trust.

Type A reorganization Type of corporate reorganization that meets the requirements of state or federal law, may take the form of a consolidation, a merger, a triangular merger, or a reverse triangular merger.

Type B reorganization Reorganization characterized by a stock-for-stock exchange. The target corporation remains in existence as a subsidiary of the acquiring corporation.

Type C reorganization A transaction that requires the acquiring corporation to obtain substantially all of the target corporation's assets in exchange for its voting stock and a limited amount of other consideration. The target corporation is generally liquidated.

Type D reorganization This type of reorganization may be either acquisitive or divisive. In the former, substantially all of the transferor corporation's assets (and possibly some or all of its liabilities) are acquired by a controlled corporation. The target corporation is liquidated. The latter involves the acquisition of the part or all of the transferor corporation's assets (and liabilities) by a controlled subsidiary corporation(s). The transferor corporation may either remain in existence or be liquidated.

Type E reorganization This type of reorganization changes the capital structure of a corporation. The corporation remains in existence.

Type F reorganization The old corporation's assets or stock are transferred to a single newly formed corporation in this type of transaction. The "old" corporation is liquidated.

Type G reorganization This type of reorganization may be either acquisitive or divisive. In either case, part or all of the target or transferor corporation's assets (and possibly some or all of its liabilities) are transferred to another corporation as part of a bankruptcy proceeding. The target or transferor corporation may either remain in existence or be liquidated.

Unified credit The unified credit enables a tax base of a certain size (i.e., the exemption equivalent) to be completely free of transfer taxes. This credit is phased out for tax bases in excess of $10,500,000 if the decedent dies after 1987. It may only be subtracted once against all of a person's transfers—throughout one's lifetime and at death. See exemption equivalent.

Unified rate schedule Progressive rate schedule for estate and gift taxes. These rates are effective for gifts made after 1976 and deaths occurring after 1976.

Unrealized receivable Right to payment for goods and services that has not been included in the owner's income because of its method of accounting.

Unreported decisions District court decisions that are not reported in official reporters. Such decisions may be reported in secondary reporters that report only tax-related cases.

U.S. shareholder For controlled foreign corporation purposes, a U.S. person who owns at least 10% of the foreign corporation's voting stock.

Voting trust An arrangement whereby the stock owned by a number of shareholders is placed under the control of a trustee for purposes of exercising the voting rights possessed by the stock. This practice increases the voting power of the minority shareholders.

Wealth transfer taxes Estate taxes (i.e., the tax on dispositions of property that occur as a result of the transferor's death) and gift taxes (i.e., the tax on lifetime transfers) are wealth transfer taxes.

Writ of certiorari See Certiorari.

APPENDIX E

AICPA STATEMENTS ON RESPONSIBILITIES IN TAX PRACTICE NOS. 1–8 (1991 REVISION)

STATEMENT NO. 1
TAX RETURN POSITIONS

INTRODUCTION

.01 This statement sets forth the standards a CPA should follow in recommending tax return positions and in preparing or signing tax returns including claims for refunds. For this purpose, a "tax return position" is (1) a position reflected on the tax return as to which the client has been specifically advised by the CPA or (2) a position as to which the CPA has knowledge of all material facts and, on the basis of those facts, has concluded that the position is appropriate.

STATEMENT

.02 With respect to tax return positions, a CPA should comply with the following standards:

a. A CPA should not recommend to a client that a position be taken with respect to the tax treatment of any item on a return unless the CPA has a good faith belief that the position has a realistic possibility of being sustained administratively or judicially on its merits if challenged.

b. A CPA should not prepare or sign a return as an income tax return preparer if the CPA knows that the return takes a position that the CPA could not recommend under the standard expressed in paragraph .02*a*.

c. Notwithstanding paragraphs .02*a* and .02*b*, a CPA may recommend a position that the CPA concludes is not frivolous so long as the position is adequately disclosed on the return or claim for refund.

d. In recommending certain tax return positions and in signing a return on which a tax return position is taken, a CPA should, where relevant, advise the client as to the potential penalty consequences of the recommended tax return position and the opportunity, if any, to avoid such penalties through disclosure.

.03 The CPA should not recommend a tax return position that—

a. Exploits the Internal Revenue Service (IRS) audit selection process; or

b. Serves as a mere "arguing" position advanced solely to obtain leverage in the bargaining process of settlement negotiation with the Internal Revenue Service.

.04 A CPA has both the right and responsibility to be an advocate for the client with respect to any positions satisfying the aforementioned standards.

EXPLANATION

.05 Our self-assessment tax system can only function effectively if taxpayers report their income on a tax return that is true, correct, and complete. A tax return is primarily a taxpayer's representation of facts, and the taxpayer has the final responsibility for positions taken on the return.

.06 CPAs have a duty to the tax system as well as to their clients. However, it is well-established that the taxpayer has no obligation to pay more taxes than are legally owed, and the CPA has a duty to the client to assist in achieving that result. The aforementioned standards will guide the CPA in meeting responsibilities to the tax system and to clients.

.07 The standards suggested herein require that a CPA in good faith believe that the position is warranted in existing law or can be supported by a good faith argument for an extension, modification, or reversal of existing law. For example, the CPA may reach such a conclusion on the basis of well-reasoned articles, treatises, IRS General Counsel Memoranda, a General Explanation of a Revenue Act prepared by the staff of the Joint Committee on Taxation and Internal Revenue Service written determinations (for example, private letter rulings), whether or not such sources are treated as "authority" under section 6661. A position would meet these standards even though, for example, it is later abandoned due to practical or procedural aspects of an IRS administrative hearing or in the litigation process.

.08 Where the CPA has a good faith belief that more than one position meets the standards suggested herein, the CPA's advice concerning alternative acceptable positions may include a discussion of the likelihood that each such position might or might not cause the client's tax return to be examined and whether the position would be challenged in an examination.

.09 In some cases, a CPA may conclude that a position is not warranted under the standard set forth in the preceding paragraph, .02*a*. A client may, however, still wish to take such a tax return position. Under such circumstances, the client should have the opportunity to make such an assertion, and the CPA should be able to prepare and sign the return provided the the position is adequately disclosed on the return or claim for refund and the position is not frivolous. A "frivolous" position is one which is knowingly advanced in bad faith and is patently improper.

.10 The CPA's determination of whether information is adequately disclosed by the client is based on the facts and circumstances of the particular case. No detailed rules have been formulated, for purposes of this statement, to prescribe the manner in which information should be disclosed.

.11 Where the particular facts and circumstances lead the CPA to believe that a taxpayer penalty might be asserted, the CPA should so advise the client and should discuss with the client issues related to disclosure on the tax return. Although disclosure is not required if the position meets the standard in paragraph .02*a*, the CPA may nevertheless recommend that a client disclose a position. Disclosure should be considered when the CPA believes it would mitigate the likelihood of claims of taxpayer penalties under the Internal Revenue Code or would avoid the possible application of the six-year statutory period for assessment under section 6501(e). Although the CPA should advise the client with respect to disclosure, it is the client's responsibility to decide whether and how to disclose.

TAX RETURN POSITIONS: TAX PRACTICE INTERPRETATION OF STATEMENT NO. 1

1. REALISTIC POSSIBILITY STANDARD BACKGROUND

.01 The AICPA Tax Division issues Statements on Responsibilities in Tax Practice (SRTPs). The primary purpose of these advisory statements on appropriate standards of tax practice is educational. This interpretation does not have the force of authority, in contrast, for example, to the regulations contained in Treasury Department Circular 230 or the preparer penalty provisions of the Internal Revenue Code.

.02 SRTP No. 1, *Tax Return Positions,* contains the standards a CPA should follow in recommending tax return positions and in preparing or signing tax returns and claims for refunds. In general, a CPA should have "a good-faith belief that the [tax return] position [being recommended] has a realistic possibility of being sustained administratively or judicially on its merits if challenged" (see SRTP No. 1, paragraph .02*a*). This is referred to here as the "realistic possibility standard." If a CPA concludes that a tax return position does not meet the realistic possibility standard, the CPA may still recommend the position to the client or, if the position is not frivolous and is adequately disclosed on the tax return or claim for refund, the CPA may prepare and sign a return containing the position.

.03 A "frivolous" position is one which is knowingly advanced in bad faith and is patently improper (see SRTP No. 1, paragraph .09). The CPA's determination of whether information is adequately disclosed on the client's tax return or claim for refund is based on the facts and circumstances of the particular case (see SRTP No. 1, paragraph .10).

.04 If the CPA believes there is a possibility that a tax return position might result in penalties being asserted against the client, the CPA should so advise the client and should discuss with the client the opportunity, if any, of avoiding such penalties through disclosure (see SRTP No. 1, paragraph .11).

GENERAL INTERPRETATION

.05 To meet the realistic possibility standard, a CPA should have a good-faith belief that the position is warranted in existing law or can be supported by a good faith argument for an extension, modification, or reversal of existing law through the administrative or judicial process. The CPA should have an honest belief that the position meets the realistic possibility standard. Such a belief must be based on sound interpretations of the tax law. A CPA should not take into account the likelihood of audit or detection in determining whether this standard is met (see SRTP No. 1, paragraph .03a).

.06 The realistic possibility standard cannot be expressed in terms of percentage odds. The realistic possibility standard is less stringent than the "substantial authority" and the "more likely than not" standards that apply under the Internal Revenue Code to substantial understatements of liability by taxpayers. It is more strict than the "reasonable basis" standard under regulations issued prior to the Revenue Reconciliation Act of 1989.

.07 In determining whether a tax return position meets the realistic possibility standard, a CPA may rely on authorities in addition to those evaluated when determining whether substantial authority exists. Accordingly, CPAs may rely on well-reasoned treatises, articles in recognized professional tax publications, and other reference tools and sources of tax analysis commonly used by tax advisors and preparers of returns.

.08 In determining whether a realistic possibility exists, the CPA should do all of the following.[1]

1. Establish relevant background facts.
2. Distill the appropriate questions from those facts.
3. Search for authoritative answers to those questions.
4. Resolve the questions by weighing the authorities uncovered by that search.
5. Arrive at a conclusion supported by the authorities.

.09 The CPA should consider the weight of each authority in order to conclude whether a position meets the realistic possibility standard. In determining the weight of an authority, the CPA should consider its persuasiveness, relevance, and source. Thus, the type of authority is a significant factor. Other important factors include whether the facts stated by the authority are distinguishable from those of the client and whether the authority contains an analysis of the issue or merely states a conclusion.

.10 The realistic possibility standard may be met despite the absence of certain types of authority. For example, a CPA may conclude that the realistic possibility standard is met when the position is supported only by a well-reasoned construction of the applicable statutory provision.

.11 In determining whether the realistic possibility standard has been met, the extent of research required is left to the judgment of the CPA with respect to all the facts and circumstances known to the CPA. The CPA may conclude that more than one position meets the realistic possibility standard.

SPECIFIC ILLUSTRATIONS

.12 The following illustrations deal with general fact patterns. Accordingly, the application of the guidance discussed above to variances in such general facts or to particular facts or circumstances may lead to different conclusions. In each illustration there is no authority other than that indicated.

Illustration 1. The CPA's client has engaged in a transaction that is adversely affected by a new statutory provision. Prior law supports a position favorable to the client. The client believes, and the CPA concurs, that the new statute is inequitable as applied to the client's situation. The statute is clearly drafted and unambiguous. The committee reports discussing the new statute contain general comments that do not specifically address the client's situation.

The CPA should recommend the return position supported by the new statute. A position contrary to a clear, unambiguous statute would ordinarily be considered a frivolous position.

Illustration 2. The facts are the same as in illustration 1 except that the committee reports discussing the new statute specifically address the client's situation and take a position favorable to the client.

In a case where the statute is clearly and unambiguously against the taxpayer's position but a contrary position exists based on committee reports specifically addressing the client's situation, a return position based on either the statutory language or the legislative history satisfies the realistic possibility standard.

Illustration 3. The facts are the same as in illustration 1 except that the committee reports can be interpreted to provide some evidence or authority in support of the taxpayer's position; however, the legislative history does not specifically address the situation.

In a case where the statute is clear and unambiguous, a contrary position based on an interpretation of committee reports that do not explicitly address the client's situation does not meet the realistic possibility standard. However, since the committee reports provide some support or evidence for the taxpayer's position, such a return position is not frivolous. The CPA may recommend the position to the client if it is adequately disclosed on the tax return.

Illustration 4. A client is faced with an issue involving the interpretation of a new statute. Following its passage, the statute was widely recognized to contain a drafting error, and a technical correction proposal has been introduced. The IRS issues an announcement indicating how it will administer the provision. The IRS pronouncement interprets the statute in accordance with the proposed technical correction.

Return positions based on either the existing statutory language or the IRS pronouncement satisfy the realistic possibility standard.

Illustration 5. The facts are the same as in illustration 4 except that no IRS pronouncement has been issued.

In the absence of an IRS pronouncement interpreting the statute in accordance with the technical correction, only a return position based on the existing statutory language will meet the realistic possibility standard. A return position based on the proposed technical correction may be recommended if it is adequately disclosed, since it is not frivolous.

Illustration 6. A client is seeking advice from a CPA regarding a recently amended Internal Revenue Code (Code) section. The CPA has reviewed the Code section, committee reports that specifically address the issue, and a recently published IRS

[1] See Ray M. Sommerfeld, et al., *Tax Research Techniques,* 3d rev. ed. (New York: AICPA, 1989), for a discussion of this process.

Notice. The CPA has concluded in good faith that, based on the Code section and the committee reports, the IRS's position as stated in the Notice does not reflect congressional intent.

The CPA may recommend the position supported by the Internal Revenue Code section and the committee reports since it meets the realistic possibility standard.

Illustration 7. The facts are the same as in illustration 6 except that the IRS pronouncement is a temporary regulation.

In determining whether the position meets the realistic possibility standard, the CPA should determine the weight to be given the regulation by analyzing factors such as whether the regulation is legislative, interpretative, or inconsistent with the statute. If the CPA concludes the position does not meet the realistic possibility standard, the position may nevertheless be recommended if it is adequately disclosed, since it is not frivolous.

Illustration 8. A tax form published by the IRS is incorrect, but completion of the form as published provides a benefit to the client. The CPA knows that the IRS has published an announcement acknowledging the error.

In these circumstances, a return position in accordance with the published form is a frivolous position.

Illustration 9. The client wants to take a position that the CPA has concluded is frivolous. The client maintains that even if the return is examined by the IRS, the issue will not be raised.

The CPA should not consider the likelihood of audit or detection when determining whether the realistic possibility standard has been met. The CPA should not prepare or sign a return that contains a frivolous position even if it is disclosed.

Illustration 10. Congress passes a statute requiring the capitalization of certain expenditures. The client believes, and the CPA concurs, that in order to comply fully, the client will need to acquire new computer hardware and software and implement a number of new accounting procedures. The client and the CPA agree that the costs of full compliance will be significantly greater than the resulting increase in tax due under the new provision. Because of these cost considerations, the client makes no effort to comply. The client wants the CPA to prepare and sign a return on which the new requirement is simply ignored.

The return position desired by the client is frivolous, and the CPA should neither prepare nor sign the return.

Illustration 11. The facts are the same as in illustration 10 except that the client has made a good-faith effort to comply with the law by calculating an estimate of expenditures to be capitalized under the new provision.

In this situation, the realistic possibility standard has been met. When using estimates in the preparation of a return, the CPA should refer to SRTP No. 4, *Use of Estimates.*

Illustration 12. On a given issue, the CPA has located and weighed two authorities. The IRS has published its clearly enunciated position in a Revenue Ruling. A court opinion is favorable to the client. The CPA has considered the source of both authorities and has concluded that both are persuasive and relevant.

The realistic possibility standard is met by either position.

Illustration 13. A tax statute is silent on the treatment of an item under the statute. However, the committee reports explaining the statute direct the IRS to issue regulations that will require specified treatment of this item. No regulations have been issued at the time the CPA must recommend a position on the tax treatment of the item.

The CPA may recommend the position supported by the committee reports, since it meets the realistic possibility standard.

Illustration 14. The client wants to take a position that the CPA concludes meets the realistic possibility standard based on an assumption regarding an underlying nontax legal issue. The CPA recommends that the client seek advice from its legal counsel, and the client's attorney gives an opinion on the nontax legal issue.

A legal opinion on a nontax legal issue may, in general, be relied upon by a CPA. The CPA must, however, use professional judgment when relying on a legal opinion. If, on its face, the opinion of the client's attorney appears to be unreasonable, unsubstantiated, or unwarranted, the CPA should consult his or her attorney before relying on the opinion.

Illustration 15. The client has obtained from its attorney an opinion on the tax treatment of an item and requests that the CPA rely on the opinion.

The authorities on which a CPA may rely include well-reasoned sources of tax analysis. If the CPA is satisfied as to the source, relevance, and persuasiveness of the legal opinion, the CPA may rely on that opinion when determining whether the realistic possibility standard has been met.

STATEMENT NO. 2 ANSWERS TO QUESTIONS ON RETURNS

INTRODUCTION

.01 This statement considers whether a CPA may sign the preparer's declaration on a tax return where one or more questions on the return have not been answered. The term "questions" includes requests for information on the return, in the instructions, or in the regulations, whether or not stated in the form of a question.

STATEMENT

.02 A CPA should make a reasonable effort to obtain from the client, and provide, appropriate answers to all questions on a tax return before signing as pre-parer.

EXPLANATION

.03 It is recognized that the questions on tax returns are not of uniform importance, and often they are not applicable to the particular taxpayer. Nevertheless, aside from administrative convenience to the Internal Revenue Service, there are at least two considerations which dictate that a CPA should be satisfied that a reasonable effort has been made to provide appropriate answers to the questions on the return which are applicable to the taxpayer:

a. A question may be of importance in determining taxable income or loss, or the tax liability shown on the return, in which circumstance the omission tends to detract from the quality of the return.

b. The CPA must sign the preparer's declaration stating that the return is true, correct, and complete.

.04 While an effort should be made to provide an answer to each question on the return that is applicable to the taxpayer, reasonable grounds may exist for omitting an answer. For example, reasonable grounds may include the following:

a. The information is not readily available and the answer is not significant in terms of taxable income or loss, or the tax liability shown on the return.

b. Genuine uncertainty exists regarding the meaning of the question in relation to the particular return.

c. The answer to the question is voluminous; in such cases, assurance should be given on the return that the data will be supplied upon examination.

.05 The fact that an answer to a question might prove disadvantageous to the client does not justify omitting an answer.

.06 Where reasonable grounds exist for omission of an answer to an applicable question, a CPA is not required to provide on the return an explanation of the reason for the omission. In this connection, the CPA should consider whether the omission of an answer to a question may cause the return to be deemed incomplete.

STATEMENT NO. 3 CERTAIN PROCEDURAL ASPECTS OF PREPARING RETURNS

INTRODUCTION

.01 This statement considers the responsibility of the CPA to examine or verify certain supporting data or to consider information related to another client when preparing a client's tax return.

STATEMENT

.02 In preparing or signing a return, the CPA may in good faith rely without verification upon information furnished by the client or by third parties. However, the CPA should not ignore the implications of information furnished and should make reasonable inquiries if the information furnished appears to be incorrect, incomplete, or inconsistent either on its face or on the basis of other facts known to the CPA. In this connection, the CPA should refer to the client's returns for prior years whenever feasible.

.03 Where the Internal Revenue Code or income tax regulations impose a condition to deductibility or other tax treatment of an item (such as taxpayer maintenance of books and records or substantiating documentation to support the reported deduction or tax treatment), the CPA should make appropriate inquiries to determine to his or her satisfaction whether such condition has been met.

.04 The individual CPA who is required to sign the return should consider information actually known to that CPA from the tax return of another client when preparing a tax return if the information is relevant to that tax return, its consideration is necessary to properly prepare that tax return, and use of such information does not violate any law or rule relating to confidentiality.

EXPLANATION

.05 The preparer's declaration on the income tax return states that the information contained therein is true, correct, and complete to the best of the preparer's knowledge and belief "based on all information of which preparer has any knowledge." This reference should be understood to relate to information furnished by the client or by third parties to the CPA in connection with the preparation of the return.

.06 The preparer's declaration does not require the CPA to examine or verify supporting data. However, a distinction should be made between (1) the need to either determine by inquiry that a specifically required condition (such as maintaining books and records or substantiating documentation) has been satisfied, or to obtain information when the material furnished appears to be incorrect or incomplete, and (2) the need for the CPA to examine underlying information. In fulfilling his or her obligation to exercise due diligence in preparing a return, the CPA ordinarily may rely on information furnished by the client unless it appears to be incorrect, incomplete, or inconsistent. Although the CPA has certain responsibilities in exercising due diligence in preparing a return, the client has ultimate responsibility for the contents of the return. Thus, where the client presents unsupported data in the form of lists of tax information, such as dividends and interest received, charitable contributions, and medical expenses, such information may be used in the preparation of a tax return without verification unless it appears to be incorrect, incomplete, or inconsistent either on its face or on the basis of other facts known to the CPA.

.07 Even though there is no requirement to examine underlying documentation, the CPA should encourage the client to provide supporting data where appropriate. For example, the CPA should encourage the client to submit underlying documents for use in tax return preparation to permit full consider-ation of income and deductions arising from security transactions and from pass-through entities such as estates, trusts, partnerships, and S corporations. This should reduce the possibility of misunderstanding, inadvertent errors, and administrative problems in the examination of returns by the Internal Revenue Service.

.08 The source of information provided to the CPA by a client for use in preparing the return is often a pass-through entity, such as a limited partnership, in which the client has an interest but is not involved in management. In some instances, it may be appropriate for the CPA to advise the client to ascertain the nature and amount of possible exposures to tax deficiencies, interest, and penalties, by contact with management of the pass-through entity. However, the CPA need not require the client to do so and may accept the information provided by the pass-through entity without further inquiry, unless there is reason to believe it is incorrect, incomplete, or inconsistent either on its face or on the basis of other facts known to the CPA.

.09 The CPA should make use of the client's prior years' returns in preparing the current return whenever feasible. Reference to prior returns and discussion with the client of prior year tax determinations should provide information as to the client's general tax status, avoid the omission or duplication of items, and afford a basis for the treatment of similar or related transactions. As with the examination of information supplied for the current year's return, the extent of comparison of the details of income and deduction between years depends upon the particular circumstances.

STATEMENT NO. 4 USE OF ESTIMATES

INTRODUCTION

.01 This statement considers the CPA's responsibility in connection with the CPA's use of the taxpayer's estimates in the preparation of a tax return. The CPA may advise on estimates used in the preparation of a tax return, but responsibility for estimated data is that of the client, who should provide the estimated data. Appraisals or valuations are not considered estimates for purposes of this statement.

STATEMENT

.02 A CPA may prepare tax returns involving the use of the taxpayer's estimates if it is impracticable to obtain exact data and the estimated amounts are reasonable under the facts and circumstances known to the CPA. When the taxpayer's estimates are used, they should be presented in such a manner as to avoid the implication of greater accuracy than exists.

EXPLANATION

.03 Accounting requires the exercise of judgment and in many instances the use of approximations based on judgment. The application of such accounting judgments, as long as not in conflict with methods set forth in the Internal Revenue Code, is acceptable and expected. These judgments are not estimates within the purview of this statement. For example, the income tax regulations provide that if all other conditions for accrual are met, the exact amount of income or expense need not be known or ascertained at year end if the amount can be determined with reasonable accuracy.

.04 In the case of transactions involving small expenditures, accuracy in recording some data may be difficult to achieve. Therefore, the use of estimates by the taxpayer in determining the amount to be deducted for such items may be appropriate.

.05 In other cases where all of the facts relating to a transaction are not accurately known, either because records are missing or because precise information is not available at the time the return must be filed, estimates of the missing data may be made by the taxpayer.

.06 Estimated amounts should not be presented in a manner which provides a misleading impression as to the degree of factual accuracy.

.07 Although specific disclosure that an estimate is used for an item in the return is not required in most instances, there are unusual circumstances where such disclosure is needed to avoid misleading the Internal Revenue Service regarding the degree of accuracy of the return. Some examples of unusual circumstances include the following:

a. The taxpayer has died or is ill at the time the return must be filed.
b. The taxpayer has not received a K-1 for a flow-through entity at the time the tax return is to be filed.
c. There is litigation pending (for example, a bankruptcy proceeding) which bears on the return.
d. Fire or computer failure destroyed the relevant records.

STATEMENT NO. 5 DEPARTURE FROM A POSITION PREVIOUSLY CONCLUDED IN AN ADMINISTRATIVE PROCEEDING OR COURT DECISION

INTRODUCTION

.01 This statement discusses whether a CPA may recommend a tax return position that departs from the treatment of an item as concluded in an administrative proceeding or a court decision with respect to a prior return of the taxpayer. For this purpose, a "tax return position" is (1) a position reflected on the tax return as to which the client has been specifically advised by the CPA, or (2) a position about which the CPA has knowledge of all material facts and, on the basis of those facts, has concluded that the position is appropriate.

.02 For purposes of this statement, "administrative proceeding" includes an examination by the Internal Revenue Service or an appeals conference relating to a return or a claim for refund.

.03 For purposes of this statement, "court decision" means a decision by any federal court having jurisdiction over tax matters.

STATEMENT

.04 The recommendation of a position to be taken concerning the tax treatment of an item in the preparation or signing of a tax return should be based upon the facts and the law as they are evaluated at the time the return is prepared or signed by the CPA. Unless the taxpayer is bound to a specified treatment in the later year, such as by a formal closing agreement, the treatment of an item as part of concluding an administrative proceeding or as part of a court decision does not restrict the CPA from recommending a different tax treatment in a later year's return. Therefore, if the CPA follows the standards in SRTP No. 1, the CPA may recommend a tax return position, prepare, or sign a tax return that departs from the treatment of an item as concluded in an administrative proceeding or a court decision with respect to a prior return of the taxpayer.

EXPLANATION

.05 A CPA usually will recommend a position with respect to the tax treatment of an item that is the same as was consented to by the taxpayer for a similar item as a result of an administrative proceeding or that was subject to a court decision concerning a prior year's return of the taxpayer. The question is whether the CPA is required to do so. Considerations include the following:

a. The Internal Revenue Service tends to act consistently with the manner in which an item was disposed of in a prior administrative proceeding, but is not bound to do so. Similarly, a taxpayer is not bound to follow the tax treatment of an item as consented to in an earlier administrative proceeding.
b. An unfavorable court decision does not prevent a taxpayer from taking a position contrary to the earlier court decision in a subsequent year.
c. The consent in an earlier administrative proceeding and the existence of an unfavorable court decision are factors that the CPA should consider in evaluating whether the standards in SRTP No. 1 are met.
d. The taxpayer's consent to the treatment in the administrative proceeding or the court's decision may have been caused by a lack of documentation, whereas supporting data for the later year is adequate.
e. The taxpayer may have yielded in the administrative proceeding for settlement purposes or not appealed the court decision even though the position met the standards in SRTP No. 1.
f. Court decisions, rulings, or other authorities that are more favorable to the taxpayer's current position may have developed since the prior administrative proceeding was concluded or the prior court decision was rendered.

STATEMENT NO. 6 KNOWLEDGE OF ERROR: RETURN PREPARATION

INTRODUCTION

.01 This statement considers the responsibility of a CPA who becomes aware of an error in a client's previously filed tax return or of the client's failure to file a required tax return. As used herein, the term "error" includes any position, omission, or method of accounting that, at the time the return is filed, fails to meet the standards set out in SRTP No. 1. The term "error" also includes a position taken on a prior year's return that no longer meets these standards due to legislation, judicial decisions, or administrative pronouncements having retroactive effect. However, an error does not include an item that has an insignificant effect on the client's tax liability.

.02 This statement applies whether or not the CPA prepared or signed the return that contains the error.

STATEMENT

.03 The CPA should inform the client promptly upon becoming aware of an error in a previously filed return or upon becoming aware of a client's failure to file a required return. The CPA should recommend the measures to be taken. Such recommendation may be given orally. The CPA is not obligated to inform the Internal Revenue Service, and the CPA may not do so without the client's permission, except where required by law.

.04 If the CPA is requested to prepare the current year's return and the client has not taken appropriate action to correct an error in a prior year's return, the CPA should consider whether to withdraw from preparing the return and whether to continue a professional relationship with the client. If the CPA does prepare such current year's return, the CPA should take reasonable steps to ensure that the error is not repeated.

EXPLANATION

.05 While performing services for a client, a CPA may become aware of an error in a previously filed return or may become aware that the client failed to file a required return. The CPA should advise the client of the error (as required by Treasury Department Circular 230) and the measures to be taken. It is the client's responsibility to decide whether to correct the error. In appropriate cases, particularly where it appears that the Internal Revenue Service might assert the charge of fraud or other criminal misconduct, the client should be advised to consult legal counsel before taking any action. In the event that the client does not correct an error, or agree to take the necessary steps to change from an erroneous method of accounting, the CPA should consider whether to continue a professional relationship with the client.[2]

.06 If the CPA decides to continue a professional relationship with the client and is requested to prepare a tax return for a year subsequent to that in which the error occurred, then the CPA should take reasonable steps to ensure that the error is not repeated. If a CPA learns the client is using an erroneous method of accounting, when it is past the due date to request IRS permission to change to a method meeting the standards of SRTP No. 1, the CPA may sign a return for the current year, providing the return includes appropriate disclosure of the use of the erroneous method.

.07 Whether an error has no more than an insignificant effect on the client's tax liability is left to the judgment of the individual CPA based on all the facts and circumstances known to the CPA. In judging whether an erroneous method of accounting has more than an insignificant effect, the CPA should consider the method's cumulative effect and its effect on the current year's return.

.08 Where the CPA becomes aware of the error during an engagement which does not involve tax return preparation, the responsibility of the CPA is to advise the client of the existence of the error and to recommend that the error be discussed with the client's tax return preparer.

STATEMENT NO. 7 KNOWLEDGE OF ERROR: ADMINISTRATIVE PROCEEDINGS

INTRODUCTION

.01 This statement considers the responsibility of a CPA who becomes aware of an error in a return that is the subject of an administrative proceeding, such as an examination by the IRS or an appeals conference relating to a return or a claim for refund. As used herein, the term "error" includes any position, omission, or method of accounting, which, at the time the return is filed, fails to meet the standards set out in SRTP No. 1. The term "error" also includes a position taken on a prior year's return that no longer meets these standards due to legislation, judicial decisions, or administrative pronouncements having retroactive effect. However, an error does not include an item that has an insignificant effect on the client's tax liability.

.02 This statement applies whether or not the CPA prepared or signed the return that contains the error; it does not apply where a CPA has been engaged by legal counsel to provide assistance in a matter relating to the counsel's client.

STATEMENT

.03 When the CPA is representing a client in an administrative proceeding with respect to a return which contains an error of which the CPA is aware, the CPA should inform the client promptly upon becoming aware of the error. The CPA should recommend the measures to be taken. Such recommendation may be given orally. The CPA is neither obligated to inform the Internal Revenue Service nor may the CPA do so without the client's permission, except where required by law.

---

[2] The CPA should consider consulting his or her own legal counsel before deciding upon recommendations to the client and whether to continue a professional relationship with the client. The potential for violating AICPA Rule of Conduct 301 (relating to the CPA's confidential client relationship), the Internal Revenue Code and income tax regulations, or state laws on privileged communications and other considerations may create a conflict between the CPA's interests and those of the client.

.04 The CPA should request the client's agreement to disclose the error to the Internal Revenue Service. Lacking such agreement, the CPA should consider whether to withdraw from representing the client in the administrative proceeding and whether to continue a professional relationship with the client.

EXPLANATION

.05 When the CPA is engaged to represent the client before the Internal Revenue Service in an administrative proceeding with respect to a return containing an error of which the CPA is aware, the CPA should advise the client to disclose the error to the Internal Revenue Service. It is the client's responsibility to decide whether to disclose the error. In appropriate cases, particularly where it appears that the Internal Revenue Service might assert the charge of fraud or other criminal misconduct, the client should be advised to consult legal counsel before taking any action. If the client refuses to disclose or permit disclosure of an error, the CPA should consider whether to withdraw from representing the client in the administrative proceeding and whether to continue a professional relationship with the client.[3]

.06 Once disclosure is agreed upon, it should not be delayed to such a degree that the client or CPA might be considered to have failed to act in good faith or to have, in effect, provided misleading information. In any event, disclosure should be made before the conclusion of the administrative proceeding.

.07 Whether an error has an insignificant effect on the client's tax liability should be left to the judgment of the individual CPA based on all the facts and circumstances known to the CPA. In judging whether an erroneous method of accounting has more than an insignificant effect, the CPA should consider the method's cumulative effect and its effect on the return which is the subject of the administrative proceeding.

STATEMENT NO. 8 FORM AND CONTENT OF ADVICE TO CLIENTS

INTRODUCTION

.01 This statement discusses certain aspects of providing tax advice to a client and considers the circumstances in which the CPA has a responsibility to communicate with the client when subsequent developments affect advice previously provided. The statement does not, however, cover the CPA's responsibilities when it is expected that the advice rendered is likely to be relied upon by parties other than the CPA's client.[4]

STATEMENT

.02 In providing tax advice to a client, the CPA should use judgment to ensure that the advice given reflects professional competence and appropriately serves the client's needs. The CPA is not required to follow a standard format or guidelines in communicating written or oral advice to a client.

.03 In advising or consulting with a client on tax matters, the CPA should assume that the advice will affect the manner in which the matters or transactions considered ultimately will be reported on the client's tax returns. Thus, for all tax advice the CPA gives to a client, the CPA should follow the standards in SRTP No. 1 relating to tax return positions.

.04 The CPA may choose to communicate with a client when subsequent developments affect advice previously provided with respect to significant matters. However, the CPA cannot be expected to have assumed responsibility for initiating such communication except while assisting a client in implementing procedures or plans associated with the advice provided or when the CPA undertakes this obligation by specific agreement with the client.

EXPLANATION

.05 Tax advice is recognized as a valuable service provided by CPAs. The form of advice may be oral or written and the subject matter may range from routine to complex. Because the range of advice is so extensive and because advice should meet specific needs of a client, neither standard format nor guidelines for communicating advice to the client can be established to cover all situations.

.06 Although oral advice may serve a client's needs appropriately in routine matters or in well-defined areas, written communications are recommended in important, unusual, or complicated transactions. In the judgment of the CPA, oral advice may be followed by a written confirmation to the client.

.07 In deciding on the form of advice provided to a client, the CPA should exercise professional judgment and should consider such factors as the following:

a. The importance of the transaction and amounts involved

b. The specific or general nature of the client's inquiry

c. The time available for development and submission of the advice

d. The technical complications presented

[3] The CPA should consider consulting his or her own legal counsel before deciding upon recommendations to the client and whether to continue a professional relationship with the client. The potential of violating Rule of Conduct 301 (relating to the CPA's confidential client relationship), the Internal Revenue Code and income tax regulations, or state laws on privileged communications and other considerations may create a conflict between the CPA's interests and those of the client.

[4] The CPA's responsibilities when providing advice that will be relied upon by third parties will be addressed in a future statement.

e. The existence of authorities and precedents
f. The tax sophistication of the client and the client's staff
g. The need to seek legal advice

.08 The CPA may assist a client in implementing procedures or plans associated with the advice offered. During this active participation, the CPA continues to advise and should review and revise such advice as warranted by new developments and factors affecting the transaction.

.09 Sometimes the CPA is requested to provide tax advice but does not assist in implementing the plans adopted. While developments such as legislative or administrative changes or further judicial interpretations may affect the advice previously provided, the CPA cannot be expected to communicate later developments that affect such advice unless the CPA undertakes this obligation by specific agreement with the client. Thus, the communication of significant developments affecting previous advice should be considered an additional service rather than an implied obligation in the normal CPA-client relationship.

.10 The client should be informed that advice reflects professional judgment based on an existing situation and that subsequent developments could affect previous professional advice. CPAs should use precautionary language to the effect that their advice is based on facts as stated and authorities that are subject to change.

APPENDIX F

COMPARISON OF TAX ATTRIBUTES FOR C CORPORATIONS, PARTNERSHIPS, AND S CORPORATIONS

APPENDIX F: COMPARISON OF TAX ATTRIBUTES FOR C CORPORATIONS, PARTNERSHIPS, AND S CORPORATIONS

Tax Attribute	C Corporation	Partnership	S Corporation
		I. General Characteristics	
Application of the separate entity versus conduit (flow through) concept.	*Entity:* The corporation is treated as a separate taxpaying entity. If income is distributed to shareholders in the form of dividends, the shareholders are subject to a second tax levy on such amounts.	*Modified conduit:* The partners report their distributive share of partnership ordinary income and separately stated items on their tax returns. Most elections, such as depreciation methods, accounting period and methods, are made at the partnership level.	*Modified conduit:* Similar to the partnership form of organization. However, the S Corporation may be subject to tax at the corporate level on excess net passive income, or built-in gains under special circumstances.
Period of Existence.	Continues until dissolution; not effected by sales of stock by shareholders.	Termination can occur by agreement, or by death, retirement, or disaffiliation of a partner.	Same as for C Corporation.
Transferability of Interest.	Stock can be easily transferred; corporation may retain right to buy back shares.	Addition of new partner or transfer of partner's interest generally requires approval of other partners.	Same as for C Corporation.
Liability Exposure.	Shareholders generally only liable for capital contributions.	General partners are personally, jointly, and severally liable for partnership obligations. Limited partner usually liable only for capital contributions.	Same as for C Corporation.
Management Responsibility.	Shareholders may be part of management or may hire outside management.	All general partners participate in management. Limited partners generally do not participate.	Because of limited number of shareholders, shareholders are usually part of management.
		II. Election and Restrictions	
1. Restrictions on:			
a. Type of owners.	No restriction.	No restriction.	Limited to individuals, estates, charitable organizations, and certain kinds of trusts.
b. Number of owners.	No restriction.	No restriction.	Limited to 75 shareholders.
c. Type of entity.	Includes domestic or foreign corporations, unincorporated entities known as associations, and certain kinds of trusts. A publicly traded partnership is taxed as a corporation unless more than 90% of its income is qualifying income. Partnerships, LLCs, and proprietorships can elect to be taxed as a corporation under the check-the-box regulations.	Includes a variety of unincorporated entities including limited liability company and limited liability partnership forms. Certain joint undertakings are excluded from partnership status.	Domestic corporations and unincorporated entities (e.g., associations) are eligible. Partnerships, LLCs, and proprietorships can elect to be taxed as a corporation under the check-the-box regulations.
d. Special tax classifications.	No restriction.	No restriction.	Domestic corporation cannot be a Domestic International Sales Corporation, or have elected the special Puerto Rico and U.S. Possessions tax credit. Certain financial institutions and insurance companies are also ineligible.

Tax Attribute	C Corporation	Partnership	S Corporation
e. Investments made by entity.	No restriction.	No restriction.	S Corporation can own 80% or more of a C corporation, but cannot file a consolidated tax return with the C corporation.
f. Capital structure.	No restriction.	No restriction.	Limited to a single class of stock that is outstanding. Differences in voting rights are disregarded. Special "safe harbor" rules are available for debt issues.
g. Passive interest income.	No restriction.	No restriction.	Passive investment income cannot exceed 25% of gross receipts for three consecutive tax years when the corporation also has Subchapter C E&P at the end of the year.
2. Election and shareholder consent.	No election required.	No election required.	Election can be made during the preceding tax year or first 2½ months of the tax year. Shareholders must consent to the election.
3. Termination of election.	Not applicable.	The partnership can terminate if it does not carry on any business, financial operation, or venture or if a sale or exchange of at least 50% of the profits and capital interests occurs within a 12-month period.	Occurs if one of the requirements is failed after the election is first effective or if the passive investment income test is failed for three consecutive tax years. IRS has permission to waive invalid elections and to permit inadvertent terminations not to break the S election.
4. Revocation of election.	Not applicable.	Not applicable.	Election may be revoked only by shareholders owning more than one-half of the stock. Must be made in first 2½ months of tax year or on a prospective basis.
5. New election.	Not applicable.	Not applicable.	Not permitted for five-year period without IRS consent to early reelection.
		III. Accounting Periods and Elections	
1. Taxable year.	Calendar year or fiscal year is permitted. Personal service corporations are restricted to using a calendar year unless approval is obtained to use a fiscal year. A special election is available to use a fiscal year resulting in a three-month or less income deferral if a series of minimum distribution requirements are met.	Generally use tax year of majority or principal partners. Otherwise use of the least aggregate deferral year is required. Can use a fiscal year that has a business purpose for which IRS approval is obtained. An electing partnership may use a fiscal year resulting in a three-month or less income deferral if an additional required payment is made.	Can use a fiscal year that has a business purpose for which IRS approval is obtained. An S corporation may use a fiscal year resulting in a three-month or less income deferral if an additional required payment is made. If neither of the above applies, a calendar year must be used.

APPENDIX F: COMPARISON OF TAX ATTRIBUTES FOR C CORPORATIONS, PARTNERSHIPS, AND S CORPORATIONS

Tax Attribute	C Corporation	Partnership	S Corporation
2. Accounting methods.	Elected by the corporation. Use of cash method of accounting is restricted for certain personal service corporations and C Corporations having $5,000,000 or more annual gross receipts.	Elected by the partnership. Restrictions on the use of the cash method of accounting apply to partnerships having a C Corporation as a partner or that are tax shelters.	Elected by the S Corporation. Restrictions on the use of the cash method of accounting apply to S corporations that are tax shelters.
		IV. Taxability of Profits	
1. Taxability of profits.	Ordinary income and capital gains are taxed to the corporation. Profits are taxed a second time when distributed.	Ordinary income and separately stated income and gain items are passed through to the partners at the end of the partnership's tax year whether or not distributed.	Same as partnership.
2. Allocation of profits.	Not applicable.	Based on partnership agreement. Special allocations are permitted.	Based on stock ownership on each day of the tax year. Special allocations are not permitted.
3. Character of income.	Profits that are distributed (including tax-exempt income) are dividends to extent of earnings and profits (E&P).	Items receiving special treatment (e.g., capital gains or tax-exempt income) are passed through separately to the partner and retain same character as when earned by the partnership.	Same as partnership.
4. Maximum tax rate for earnings.	15% on the first $50,000; 25% from $50,000 to $75,000; 34% from $75,000 to $10 million. The rate is 35% for taxable income above $10 million. A 5 percentage point surcharge applies to taxable income from $100,000 to $335,000 and a 3 percentage point surcharge applies to taxable income between $15 and $18.333 million. Special rules apply to controlled groups. Personal service corporations are taxed at a flat 35% rate.	Rates of tax applicable to noncorporate partners from 15% through 39.6% are levied on the income from the partnership. C Corporation rates apply to corporate partners.	Same as partnership except for certain special situations where a special corporate tax applies to the S Corporation.
5. Special tax levies.	Can be subject to accumulated earnings tax, personal holding company tax, and corporate alternative minimum tax.	Not applicable.	Can be subject to built-in gains tax, excess net passive income tax, LIFO recapture tax, and investment tax credit recapture.
6. Income splitting between family members.	Only possible when earnings are distributed to shareholder. Dividends received by shareholder under age 14 are taxed at parents' marginal tax rate.	Transfer of partnership interest by gift will permit income splitting. Subject to special rules for transactions involving family members requiring payment of reasonable compensation for capital and services. Income received by partner under age 14 is taxed at parents' marginal tax rate.	Transfer of S Corporation interest by gift will permit income splitting. Special rules apply to transactions involving family members requiring payment of reasonable compensation for capital and services. Income received by shareholder under age 14 is taxed at parents' marginal tax rate.

Tax Attribute	C Corporation	Partnership	S Corporation
7. Sale of ownership interest.	Gain is taxed as capital gain; 50% of gain may be excluded under qualified small business stock rules. Loss is eligible for Sec. 1244 treatment.	Gain may be either ordinary income or capital gain. Losses are usually capital.	Gain is capital in nature, but not eligible for special small business stock rules. Loss is eligible for Sec. 1244 treatment.
V. Treatment of Special Income, Gain, Loss, Deduction and Credit Items			
1. Capital gains and losses.	Long-term capital gains are taxed at regular tax rates. Capital losses offset capital gains; excess losses carried back three years and forward five years.	Passed through to partners (according to partnership agreement).	Passed through to shareholders (on a daily basis according to stock ownership).
2. Section 1231 gains and losses.	Eligible for long-term capital gain or ordinary loss treatment. Loss recapture occurs at the corporate level.	Passed through to partners. Loss recapture occurs at the partner level.	Same as partnership.
3. Dividends received from domestic corporation.	Eligible for 70%, 80%, or 100% dividends-received deduction.	Passed through to partners.	Same as partnership.
4. Organizational expenditures.	Amortize over 60 or more months.	Same as C Corporation.	Same as partnership.
5. Charitable contributions.	Limited to 10% of taxable income.	Passed through to partners. Limitations apply at partner level.	Same as partnership.
6. Expensing of asset acquisition costs.	Limited to $18,000 in 1997.	Limited to $18,000 in 1997 for the partnership and for each partner.	Same as partnership.
7. Expenses owed to related parties.	Regular Sec. 267 rules apply to payments and sales or exchanges made to or by the corporation and certain other related parties (e.g., controlling shareholder and corporation or members of a controlled group).	Regular Sec. 267 rules can apply. Special Sec. 267 rules for passthrough entities apply to payments made by the partnership to a partner.	Same as partnership.
8. Employment-related tax considerations.	An owner-employee may be treated as an employee for Social Security tax and corporate fringe benefit purposes. The corporate qualified pension and profit-sharing benefits available to owner-employees are comparable to the plan benefits for self-employed individuals (partners and sole proprietors).	A partner is not considered an employee of the business. Therefore, the partner must pay self-employment tax on the net self-employment income from the business. Corporate fringe benefit exclusions such as group term life insurance are not available (i.e., the premiums are not deductible by the business and are not excludable from the partner's income). Fringe benefits may be provided as nontaxable distribution or as taxable compensation.	Corporate fringe benefit exclusions are not generally available to S Corporation shareholders. Fringe benefits are generally provided as nontaxable distribution or taxable compensation. S Corporation shareholders may be treated as employees, however, for Social Security tax payments and qualified pension and profit sharing plan rules.

Tax Attribute	C Corporation	Partnership	S Corporation
9. Tax preference items.	Subject to the corporate alternative minimum tax at the corporate level.	Passed through to partners and taxed under the alternative minimum tax rules applicable to the partner.	Same as partnership.
		VI. Deductibility of Losses and Special Items	
1. Deductibility of losses.	Losses create net operating loss (NOL) which can be carried back three years or forward 15 years or capital loss which can be carried back three years or forward five years.	Ordinary losses and separately stated loss and deduction items are passed through to the partners at the end of the partnership tax year. May create a personal NOL.	Same as partnership.
2. Allocation of losses.	Not applicable.	Based on partnership agreement. Special allocations are permitted.	Based on stock ownership on each day of the tax year. Special allocations are not permitted.
3. Shareholder and entity loss limitations.	Passive losses may be restricted under the passive activity limitation if the C Corporation is closely-held.	Limited to partner's basis for the partnership interest. Ratable share of all partnership liabilities is included in basis of partnership interest. Excess losses are carried over indefinitely until partnership interest again has a basis. Subject to at risk, passive activity, and hobby loss restrictions.	Limited to shareholder's basis for the stock interest plus basis of S Corporation debts to the shareholder. Excess losses are carried over indefinitely until shareholder again has basis for stock or debt. Subject to the at risk, passive activity, and hobby loss restrictions.
4. Basis adjustments for debt and equity interests.	Not applicable.	Basis in partnership interest reduced by loss and deduction passthrough. Subsequent profits will increase basis of partnership interest.	Basis in S Corporation stock reduced by loss and deduction passthrough. Once basis of stock has been reduced to zero, any other losses and deductions reduce basis of debt (but not below zero). Subsequent profits will restore basis reductions to debt before increasing basis of stock.
5. Investment interest deduction limitation.	Not applicable.	Investment interest expenses and income are passed through to the partners. Limitation applies at partner level.	Same as partnership.
		VII. Distributions	
1. Taxability of nonliquidating distributions to shareholder.	Taxable as dividends if made from current or accumulated E&P. Additional distributions reduce shareholder's basis for stock, or cause capital gain to be recognized.	Tax-free unless the money, money equivalents or marketable securities that are received by the partner exceeds his basis for the partnership interest.	Tax-free if made from the Accumulated Adjustment Account, PTI, or shareholder's basis for his stock. Taxable if made out of accumulated E&P or after stock basis has been reduced to zero.

Tax Attribute	C Corporation	Partnership	S Corporation
2. Taxability of nonliquidating distributions to distributing entity.	Gain (but not loss) recognized as if the property had been sold for its FMV immediately before the distribution.	No gain or loss recognized by the partnership except when a disproportionate distribution of Sec. 751 property occurs.	Gain (but not loss) recognized and passed through to the shareholders as if the property had been sold for its FMV immediately before the distribution. Gain may be taxed to the S Corporation under one of the special tax levies.
3. Basis adjustment to owner's investment for distribution.	None unless the distribution is in excess of E&P.	Amount of money or adjusted basis of distributed property reduces basis in partnership interest.	Amount of money or FMV of distributed property reduces basis of stock except when distribution is made out of accumulated E&P.
		VIII. Other Items	
1. Tax return.	Form 1120 or 1120-A	Form 1065 (Information Return).	Form 1120S (Information Return).
2. Due date.	March 15 for calendar-year C Corporation.	April 15 for calendar-year partnership.	March 15 for calendar-year S Corporation.
3. Extensions of time permitted.	Six months.	Four months.	Six months.
4. Estimated tax payments required.	Yes—April 15, June 15, September 15, and December 15 for calendar-year C Corporation.	No—estimated taxes are required of the partners for passed through income, etc.	Yes—Applies only to built-in gains tax, excess net passive income tax, and investment tax credit recapture amount.
5. Audit rules.	Corporation is audited independently of its shareholders.	Special audit rules apply requiring audit of partnership and requiring partners to take a position consistent with the partnership tax return.	Special rules require consistent tax treatment for Subchapter S items on the corporations and shareholder returns.

APPENDIX G

CREDIT FOR STATE DEATH TAXES

IF THE ADJUSTED TAXABLE ESTATE[a] IS:	THE MAXIMUM TAX CREDIT SHALL BE:
Not over $90,000	8/10ths of 1% of the amount by which the adjusted taxable estate exceeds $40,000.
Over $90,000 but not over $140,000	$400 plus 1.6% of the excess over $90,000.
Over $140,000 but not over $240,000	$1,200 plus 2.4% of the excess over $140,000.
Over $240,000 but not over $440,000	$3,600 plus 3.2% of the excess over $240,000.
Over $440,000 but not over $640,000	$10,000 plus 4% of the excess over $440,000.
Over $640,000 but not over $840,000	$18,000 plus 4.8% of the excess over $640,000.
Over $840,000 but not over $1,040,000	$27,600 plus 5.6% of the excess over $840,000.
Over $1,040,000 but not over $1,540,000	$38,800 plus 6.4% of the excess over $1,040,000.
Over $1,540,000 but not over $2,040,000	$70,800 plus 7.2% of the excess over $1,540,000.
Over $2,040,000 but not over $2,540,000	$106,800 plus 8% of the excess over $2,040,000.
Over $2,540,000 but not over $3,040,000	$146,800 plus 8.8% of the excess over $2,540,000.
Over $3,040,000 but not over $3,540,000	$190,800 plus 9.6% of the excess over $3,040,000.
Over $3,540,000 but not over $4,040,000	$238,800 plus 10.4% of the excess over $3,540,000.
Over $4,040,000 but not over $5,040,000	$290,800 plus 11.2% of the excess over $4,040,000.
Over $5,040,000 but not over $6,040,000	$402,800 plus 12% of the excess over $5,040,000.
Over $6,040,000 but not over $7,040,000	$522,800 plus 12.8% of the excess over $6,040,000.
Over $7,040,000 but not over $8,040,000	$650,800 plus 13.6% of the excess over $7,040,000.
Over $8,040,000 but not over $9,040,000	$786,800 plus 14.4% of the excess over $8,040,000.
Over $9,040,000 but not over $10,040,000	$930,800 plus 15.2% of the excess over $9,040,000.
Over $10,040,000	$1,082,800 plus 16% of the excess over $10,040,000.

[a]Taxable estate minus $60,000.
Source: IRC, Sec. 2011(b).

APPENDIX H

ACTUARIAL TABLES

TRANSFERS MADE AFTER APRIL 30, 1989
EXCERPT FROM TABLE S
SINGLE LIFE REMAINDER FACTORS

	INTEREST RATE								
AGE	7%	8%	9%	10%	AGE	7%	8%	9%	10%
25	.05861	.04438	.03465	.02784	58	.29621	.25962	.22956	.20464
26	.06142	.04662	.03644	.02928	59	.30859	.27155	.24097	.21551
27	.06446	.04906	.03841	.03088	60	.32124	.28379	.25272	.22674
28	.06772	.05170	.04056	.03264	61	.33414	.29633	.26480	.23831
29	.07120	.05456	.04291	.03458	62	.34726	.30912	.27717	.25020
30	.07492	.05763	.04546	.03671	63	.36060	.32217	.28982	.26240
31	.07891	.06095	.04824	.03905	64	.37415	.33548	.30278	.27493
32	.08315	.06451	.05124	.04160	65	.38798	.34912	.31610	.28787
33	.08767	.06834	.05449	.04438	66	.40211	.36312	.32983	.30124
34	.09246	.07243	.05799	.04738	67	.41655	.37749	.34398	.31508
35	.09754	.07679	.06174	.05063	68	.43129	.39221	.35854	.32937
36	.10288	.08140	.06573	.05411	69	.44625	.40722	.37344	.34405
37	.10850	.08628	.06999	.05783	70	.46140	.42248	.38864	.35907
38	.11441	.09145	.07451	.06180	71	.47666	.43790	.40405	.37436
39	.12061	.09690	.07931	.06604	72	.49203	.45349	.41969	.38991
40	.12712	.10266	.08440	.07055	73	.50751	.46926	.43556	.40575
41	.13393	.10871	.08978	.07535	74	.52317	.48527	.45173	.42195
42	.14103	.11505	.09544	.08041	75	.53904	.50156	.46826	.43856
43	.14842	.12169	.10140	.08576	76	.55515	.51817	.48517	.45563
44	.15613	.12864	.10766	.09141	77	.57144	.53504	.50243	.47311
45	.16414	.13591	.11423	.09736	78	.58787	.55212	.51996	.49094
46	.17247	.14350	.12113	.10363	79	.60428	.56925	.53762	.50897
47	.18112	.15141	.12835	.11022	80	.62058	.58632	.55527	.52705
48	.19007	.15964	.13589	.11713	81	.63659	.60316	.57274	.54499
49	.19930	.16816	.14373	.12433	82	.65226	.61968	.58993	.56270
50	.20881	.17697	.15186	.13182	83	.66749	.63579	.60675	.58007
51	.21861	.18609	.16030	.13963	84	.68233	.65153	.62321	.59713
52	.22874	.19556	.16911	.14780	85	.69681	.66693	.63938	.61392
53	.23919	.20537	.17828	.15635	86	.71081	.68188	.65511	.63030
54	.24995	.21552	.18779	.16524	87	.72417	.69616	.67018	.64602
55	.26103	.22601	.19767	.17450	88	.73695	.70986	.68466	.66117
56	.27242	.23685	.20791	.18414	89	.74938	.72323	.69882	.67601
57	.28415	.24805	.21854	.19419					

Source: Reg. Sec. 20.7520-1(a)(2).

EXCERPT FROM TABLE B
TERM CERTAIN REMAINDER FACTORS

	INTEREST RATE			
YEARS	7.0%	8.0%	9.0%	10.0%
1	.934579	.925926	.917431	.909091
2	.873439	.857339	.841680	.826446
3	.816298	.793832	.772183	.751315
4	.762895	.735030	.708425	.683013
5	.712986	.680583	.649931	.620921
6	.666342	.630170	.596267	.564474
7	.622750	.583490	.547034	.513158
8	.582009	.540269	.501866	.466507
9	.543934	.500249	.460428	.424098
10	.508349	.463193	.422411	.385543
11	.475093	.428883	.387533	.350494
12	.444012	.397114	.355535	.318631
13	.414964	.367698	.326179	.289664
14	.387817	.340461	.299246	.263331
15	.362446	.315242	.274538	.239392
16	.338735	.291890	.251870	.217629
17	.316574	.270269	.231073	.197845
18	.295864	.250249	.211994	.179859
19	.276508	.231712	.194490	.163508
20	.258419	.214548	.178431	.148644
21	.241513	.198656	.163698	.135131
22	.225713	.183941	.150182	.122846
23	.210947	.170315	.137781	.111678
24	.197147	.157699	.126405	.101526
25	.184249	.146018	.115968	.092296

Source: Reg. Sec. 20.7520-1(a)(2).

APPENDIX

INDEX OF CODE SECTIONS

APPENDIX J

INDEX OF TREASURY REGULATIONS

Proposed Regulations

APPENDIX K

INDEX OF GOVERNMENT PROMULGATIONS

APPENDIX L

Index of Court Cases

APPENDIX M

SUBJECT INDEX

1997
TAX RATE SCHEDULES

ESTATES AND TRUSTS

If Taxable Income Is: Over—	But Not Over—	The Tax Is:	Of the Amount Over—
$0	$1,650	15%	$0
1,650	3,900	$247.50 + 28%	1,650
3,900	5,950	877.50 + 31%	3,900
5,950	8,100	1,513.00 + 36%	5,950
8,100		2,287.00 + 39.6%	8,100

CORPORATIONS

If Taxable Income Is: Over—	But Not Over—	The Tax Is:	Of the Amount Over—
$ 0	$ 50,000	15%	$ 0
50,000	75,000	$ 7,500 + 25%	50,000
75,000	100,000	13,750 + 34%	75,000
100,000	335,000	22,250 + 39%	100,000
335,000	10,000,000	113,900 + 34%	335,000
10,000,000	15,000,000	3,400,000 + 35%	10,000,000
15,000,000	18,333,333	5,150,000 + 38%	15,000,000
18,333,333		6,416,667 + 35%	18,333,333

UNIFIED CREDIT AMOUNT FOR ESTATE AND GIFT TAX

Year of Gift/ Year of Death	Amount of Credit	Exemption Equivalent
January through June, 1977	$ 6,000	$ 30,000
July through December, 1977	30,000	120,666
1978	34,000	134,000
1979	38,000	147,333
1980	42,500	161,563
1981	47,000	175,625
1982	62,800	225,000
1983	79,300	275,000
1984	96,300	325,000
1985	121,800	400,000
1986	155,800	500,000
1987 and later years	192,800	600,000